# Handbook of Positive Behavior Support

## Issues in Clinical Child Psychology

*Series Editor:* **Michael C. Roberts,** University of Kansas – Lawrence, Kansas

CHILDREN AND DISASTERS
Edited by Conway F. Saylor

HANDBOOK OF ADOLESCENT HEALTH RISH BEHAVIOR
Edited by Ralph J. DiClemente, William B. Hansen, and Lynn E. Ponton

HANDBOOK OF BEHAVIORAL AND EMOTIONAL PROBLEMS IN GIRLS
Edited by Debora Bell, Sharon L. Foster, and Eric J. Mash

HANDBOOK OF CHILD ABUSE RESEARCH AND TREATMENT
Edited by T. Steuart Watson and Frank M. Gresham

HANDBOOK OF CHILDREN'S COPING: Linking Theory and Intervention
Edited by Sharlene A. Wolchik and Irwin N. Sandler

HANDBOOK OF DEPRESSION IN CHILDREN AND ADOLESCENTS
Edited by William M. Reynolds and Hugh F. Johnson

HANDBOOK OF EVIDENCE-BASED THERAPIES FOR CHILDREN AND ADOLESCENTS: Bridging Science and Practice
Edited by Ric G. Steele, T. David Elkin, and Michael C. Roberts

HANDBOOK OF INTELLECTUAL AND DEVELOPMENTAL DISABILITIES
Edited by John W. Jacobson,† James A. Mulick, and Johannes Rojahn

HANDBOOK OF MENTAL HEALTH SERVICES FOR CHILDREN, ADOLESCENTS, AND FAMILIES
Edited by Ric G. Steele and Michael C. Roberts

HANDBOOK OF PSYCHOTHERPAIES WITH CHILDREN AND FAMILIES
Edited by Sandra W. Russ and Thomas H. Ollendick

HANDBOOK OF RESEARCH IN PEDIATRIC AND CLINICAL CHILD PSYCHOLOGY
Edited by Dennis Drotar

HANDBOOK OF SCHOOL MENTAL HEALTH: Advancing Practice and Research
Edited by Mark D. Weist, Steven W. Evans, and Nancy A. Lever

INTERNATIONAL HANDBOOK OF PHOBIC AND ANXIETY DISORDERS IN CHILDREN AND ADOLESCENTS
Edited by Thomas H. Ollendick, Neville J. King, and William Yule

MENTAL HEALTH INTERVENTIONS WITH PRESCHOOL CHILDREN
Edited by Robert D. Lyman and Toni L. Hembree-Kigin

SCHOOL CONSULTATION: Conceptual and Empirical Bases of Practice
William P. Erchul and Brian K. Martens

SUCCESSFUL PREVENTION PROGRAMS FOR CHILDREN AND ADOLESCENTS
Joseph A. Durlak

A continuation Order Plan is available for this series. A continuation order will bring delivery of each new volume immediately upon publication. Volumes are billed only upon actual shipment. For further information please contact the publisher.

# Handbook of Positive Behavior Support

Edited by

Wayne Sailor

*University of Kansas, Lawrence, USA*

Glen Dunlap

*University of South Florida, Tampa, USA*

George Sugai

*University of Connecticut, Storrs, USA*

Rob Horner

*University of Oregon, Eugene, USA*

Springer

*Editors*
Wayne Sailor
University of Kansas
Dept. Special Education
1000 Sunnyside Ave.
Lawrence KS 66045-7534
Dole Hall
USA
wsailor@ku.edu

George Sugai
University of Connecticut
Neag School of Education
249 Glenbrook Road
Storrs CT 06269-2064
Unit 2064
USA
george.sugai@uconn.edu

Glen Dunlap
University of South Florida
Florida Mental Health Institute
Div. Applied Research &
2778 Mayberry Drive
Reno NV 89509
USA
glendunlap@sbcglobal.net

Rob Horner
University of Oregon
Dept. Special Education
1235 University of Oregon
Eugene OR 97403-1235
USA
robh@oregon.uoregon.edu

ISBN: 978-0-387-09631-5 e-ISBN: 978-0-387-09632-2
DOI: 10.1007/978-0-387-09632-2

Library of Congress Control Number: 2008931176



Printed on acid-free paper

springer.com

# Foreword

In 1998, the Office of Special Education Programs (OSEP) of the U.S. Department of Education awarded a cooperative agreement to the University of Oregon to establish a national technical assistance Center on Positive Behavior Interventions and Support (PBIS). This center competition came on the heels of 15 years of intensive research and development by three cycles of the Rehabilitation Research and Training Center on Positive Behavior Support (PBS) funded by the National Institute on Disability and Rehabilitation Research and numerous research and demonstration projects funded by the OSEP. The editors and many of the authors of this volume were key researchers and developers involved in the history of investments in this area.

The technical assistance (TA) center on PBIS was funded based in part on the recognition of the large and growing base of evidence from controlled studies employing a variety of methodologies that PBIS (also referenced similarly as PBS) provides an effective, positive, strength-based, relevant, and efficient technology to assist persons requiring specialized behavioral support and services.

OSEP recognized in the late 1990s that the research agenda and funding for PBS was expanding rapidly from an increasing number of federal and state agencies. With interest in PBS expanding across the country, a mechanism was needed so states could move this growing research base into practice in schools and other programs serving children and to influence the preparation of personnel to implement this growing knowledge base. Since its inception in 1997, the National TA Center on PBIS has helped fulfill this initial goal by establishing school leadership teams in more than 7,700 schools in more than 35 states; publishing numerous papers in scholarly journals; developing needed technical assistance guides and implementation and evaluation tools; and documenting more than 7 million hits on its Web site (www.pbis.org).

This volume is a product of the National TA Center on PBIS and has been designed to acquaint clinical child psychologists and other human services professionals, including educators, with an overview and summary of the current knowledge base that is subsumed under the term PBS. This volume represents the first attempt to produce a single scholarly summation of PBS professional practices, research, and examples.

With conceptual and empirical underpinnings in applied behavior analysis, PBS emerged during the 1980s as a comprehensive approach for organizing and providing community supports and resources for persons with disabilities who engage in challenging behavior. As a field, PBS has experienced phenomenal growth over a span of 25 years and is now an integral component of public education in many schools in practically every state in the United States, improving not only the behavior of those children with the most challenging behaviors but also the behavior of all children.

As an applied science of human behavior, PBS unites the precision of a careful, analytical examination of the functions of problem behavior, a broader framework of person-centered values and processes, and an emphasis on teaching alternative skill repertoires. PBS involves a conceptual shift in our approach to addressing difficult behavior associated with disabilities away from a simple reduction of the occurrence of such behavior (e.g., punishment) to a comprehensive strengths-based teaching approach that considers the person and his or her total life span or ecology.

Currently, the PBS field offers a significant and expanding scientific basis for the functional analysis of problem behavior and positive and preventive strategies that emphasizes maximum quality of life. Thus, PBS is conceptualized as a risk prevention system applicable to three levels of intervention:

- Primary-tier interventions, which are directed to all members across all settings and contexts of a specialized social ecology (e.g., a school).
- Secondary-tier interventions, which are directed to individuals of a specific group or aspect of the total ecology (e.g., a classroom) because their behaviors have been unresponsive to primary-tier interventions.
- Tertiary-tier interventions, which are directed in more individualized and intensive forms to individuals whose behaviors are unresponsive to secondary- and primary-tier interventions.

This continuum generally consists of three tiers that provide the basis for a framework of supports that begins with a systematic examination of the total context in which the behavior of interest occurs. Based on information from this examination, interventions are selected and adapted to maximize consideration of each individual's well-being and overall quality of life rather than making individual's "fit in" to existing systems. As problem behavior becomes more challenging, the process emphasizes a systematic examination of the total context in which problem behavior occurs, including "setting events," biological factors, antecedent occurrences, environmental arrangements, learning styles and histories, and immediate as well as long-range consequences for problem behavior. The science of delineating functions of behavior is called functional behavioral assessment (FBA).

Results of FBA are then directed to a set of teaching interventions (PBS plan) that consider each of the contextual features: (a) strategies to neutralize or minimize the impact of setting events; (b) antecedent manipulations that remove triggers of problem behavior and add prompts that occasion desirable behavior; (c) lessons for teaching and practicing more acceptable behaviors that are more effective, efficient, and relevant than the problem behavior; and (d) manipulations that remove consequence events that maintain problem behavior and add contingent events that encourage acceptable behavior. The technology of this function-based support is complimented by a person-centered system focus that considers the student and his or her social support system (e.g., friends, siblings, relatives, parents); the multiple settings through which the student moves (e.g., home, afterschool activities, neighborhood "hangouts"); and the stated needs and priorities of the student and family. Progress on implementation of the plan is carefully monitored and resultant data periodically reviewed for progress or any needed modifications.

A three-tier system of PBS affords a comprehensive approach to preventing emergence of life-restricting behavior through increasing degrees of positive individualized supports across social systems. As such, PBS represents a scientifically validated, applied body of knowledge that spans all ages from early childhood through adulthood. Thus, educational and other service providers are able to fully integrate a technology of sociobehavioral development with other pedagogical efforts to enhance the quality of life of recipients. A framework of expressed values emphasizes positive interactions directed to sustained lifestyle changes that enable recipients to participate fully in day-to-day life.

This volume is divided into four sections. Section 1 provides an overview of the field of PBS, including origins and history, contemporary definitions, empirical research, and ethics-based framework of values. The first chapter, authored by three of the editors, presents a historical overview of the origins and scope of the field of PBS. The second chapter, by Singer and Wang, examines the development of PBS within a philosophical and moral framework, coming to the conclusion that PBS can best be understood as "ethically grounded contextualism."

Section 2 examines the rapidly developing body of research, training, and application within early childhood service systems, with a particular focus on families. The section includes chapters by PBS scholars in the field of early childhood who examine applications in a variety of settings, including Head Start programs and treatment programs for children with autism. Summaries of PBS research on the topics of foster care, urban (inner-city) applications, and mental health settings can be found in this section as well as issues and evaluation in parenting.

Section 3 is devoted to the research, training, and application of PBS within the nation's schools as a major component of compulsory education. Schoolwide applications of PBS are examined in this section, including recent extensions into urban inner-city schools wherein a sociobehavioral pedagogy is of major concern, as one significant enhancement for schools, to counter effects of poverty and neighborhood blight. Framed as school-wide positive behavior support (SW-PBS), chapters in this section include definitions, issues of sustainability in application, and research and development activities within each of the three tiers of SW-PBS in a variety of educational settings. Research and development in extension of SW-PBS to juvenile justice and community mental health settings and nonclassroom settings also are summarized. In addition, personnel training issues, high school applications, and recent efforts to examine the relationship of SW-PBS to enhanced academic achievement for all students are examined.

The handbook concludes with a section on new directions in the field of PBS, including recent efforts to align schoolwide applications within comprehensive and structural models of school reform. Chapters in section 4 examine the relationship of SW-PBS to school-based mental health "wraparound" systems of support and to an emerging reconceptualization of ways to identify students in educational settings for more extensive and specialized systems of support. This process, response to intervention (RTI), a problem-solving logic model with its origins in special education, affords a potential for further integration of evidence-based supports directed to sociobehavioral aspects of the teaching-learning process with academic supports designed to prevent student's academic as well as behavioral failure.

The contributors to this volume hope that this collection of chapters further guides research and practice associated with the growing field of PBS.

Renée Bradley

# Contents

# Contributors


Sarah L. Adolphson
University of Utah

Robert F. Algozzine
University of North Carolina at Charlotte

Kate M. Algozzine
University of North Carolina at Charlotte

Peter Alter
University of Louisville

Cynthia M. Anderson
University of Oregon

Lauren Binnendyk
University of British Columbia

Hank Bohanon
Loyola University of Chicago

Chris Borgmeier
Portland State University

Cheryl Anne Boyce
National Institute of Mental Health

Renée Bradley
US Office of Special Education Programs

Kimberli Breen
Illinois PBS Network

Christy Cheremshynski
University of British Columbia

Jeong Hoon Choi
University of Kansas

Hewitt B. Clark
University of South Florida

Shelley Clarke
University of South Florida Tanpa

Geoff Colvin
Behavior Associates – Eugene, Oregon

Kimberly Crosland
University of South Florida

Lou Danielson
US Office of Special Education Programs

Jennifer Doolittle
US Office of Special Education Programs

Albert J. Duchnowski
University of South Florida

Glen Dunlap
University of South Florida

V. Mark Durand
University of South Florida St. Petersburg

Lucille Eber
Illinois PBS Network

Lauren Elkinson
University of Medicine and Dentistry of New Jersey

Pamela Fenning
Loyola University of Chicago

Jolenea Ferro
PBISAZ Project Coordinator

K. Brigid Flannery
University of Oregon

Brenda Fossett
University of British Columbia

Lise Fox
Univeristy of South Florida

Rachel Freeman
University of Fansas

Andy Frey
University of Louisville

Heather Peshak George
University of South Florida

Peter Griggs
University of Kansas

Leanne S. Hawken
University of Utah

Mary Louise Hemmeter
Vanderbitt University

Meme Hieneman
University of South Florida St. Petersburg

Robert H. Horner
University of Oregon

Kelly Hyde
Illinois PBS Network

Larry K. Irvin
Lawrence, KS

Kristine Jolivette
Georgia State University

Don Kincaid
University of South Florida

Lynn Kern Koegel
University of California, Santa Barbara

Robert L. Koegel
University of California, Santa Barbara

Krista Kutash
University of South Florida

Holly Lewandowski
Illinois PBS Network

Timothy J. Lewis
University of Missouri-Columbia

Sharon Lohrmann
University of Medicine & Dentistry of New Jersey

Joseph M. Lucyshyn
University of British Columbia

K. Sandra MacLeod
University of Utah

JoAnne Malloy
University of New Hampshire

Richmond Mancil
University of Central Florida

D. J. Markey
Pyramid Parent Training Community Parent Resource Center

Ursula Markey
Pyramid Parent Training Community Parent Resource Center

Amy McCart
University of Kansas

Diane McDonald
Illinois PBS Network

Kent McIntosh
University of British Columbia

Lynn Miller
University of British Columbia

Bryon Neff
University of South Florida

C. Michael Nelson
University of Louisville

Lori Newcomer
University of Missouri – St. Louis

J. Stephen Newton
University of Oregon

Jenna Pollard-Sage
University of South Florida

Robert Putnam
May Institute

Suzanne Robinson
University of California, Santa Barbara

Blair Roger
Oakland, CA

Jennifer Rose
Illinois PBS Network

Wayne Sailor
University of Kansas

Joan Schumann
University of Utah

Ilene Schwartz
University of Washington

Terrance M. Scott
University of Louisville

George H.S. Singer
University of California Santa Barbara

Carl R. Smith
Iowa State University

Jeffrey R. Sprague
University of Oregan

Phillip S. Strain
University of Colorado at Denver Health Sciences Center

George Sugai
University of Connecticut

Holly M. Sweeney
University of Kansas

Louisa Banks Tarullo
Mathematica Policy Research, Inc.

Tary J. Tobin
University of Oregon

Anne W. Todd
University of Oregon

Victoria Vossler
Topeka Public School, Topeka, Kansas

Mian Wang
University of California Santa Barbara

Nikki Wolf
University of Kansas

Melissa Zona
University of Albany-Suny

# Section I
# Introduction

# 1

# Overview and History of Positive Behavior Support

## GLEN DUNLAP, WAYNE SAILOR, ROBERT H. HORNER, and GEORGE SUGAI

In this chapter, we examine the core features of what has come to be described as positive behavior support, or PBS. We examine milestones in the development of PBS following its inception in the 1980s. We conclude with a glimpse of the emergence of new lines of PBS research and application as reflected in the chapters to follow in this summative volume of a work in progress. PBS is a broad approach for organizing the physical, social, educational, biomedical, and logistical supports needed to achieve basic lifestyle goals while reducing problem behaviors that pose barriers to these goals (Dunlap & Carr, 2007; Koegel, Koegel, & Dunlap, 1996). PBS emerged as a distinctive approach to behavior support because of a strong commitment to values and technology. The PBS values emphasize a commitment to helping individuals (and their advocates) achieve a quality of life that is defined by their personal choices. How people behave affects how they live and how they receive support guided by their preferences. For example, what you do, where you do it, how competently you do it, and when you choose to do it affects your ability to build and retain relationships, acquire new skills, establish and sustain employment, and achieve personal leisure goals. Problem behaviors such as aggression, self-injury, disruption, pica, noncompliance, withdrawal, and disruption are more than a nuisance for parents and teachers. Problem behaviors are a major barrier to the social, vocational, and physical success of each individual. The basic foundation of PBS presupposes that the valued elements of personal life, those things each of us hold as truly important, depend at some level on our ability to behave competently. Defining the technology

---

**GLEN DUNLAP** • University of South Florida
**WAYNE SAILOR** • University of Kansas
**ROBERT H. HORNER** • University of Oregon
**GEORGE SUGAI** • University of Connecticut

that allows people to more closely achieve the lifestyle they value is at the heart of PBS.

The technology of PBS is based on the scientific assumption that human behavior, while affected by a complex mix of biological, societal, and learning factors, can change as a function of certain actions performed by others in a supportive, caregiving role for people from all cultures, ages, and levels of competence. PBS is about using our understanding of human behavioral science to organize supports that result in more productive, preferred, and healthy lives. Our goal in this chapter is to provide a context for PBS that is discussed in more detail throughout this book. We focus on (a) the defining features that make PBS distinct and (b) the historical roots that led to the emergence of PBS. Subsequent chapters examine applications of PBS with families; with young children with social, emotional, and behavioral difficulties; to kindergarten through Grade 12 education in the United States; and, by extension, within communities of practice that are working for broad systems change.

## CORE FEATURES OF POSITIVE BEHAVIOR SUPPORT

Positive behavior support is a technology with four core, defining features: (a) application of research-validated behavioral science; (b) integration of multiple intervention elements to provide ecologically valid, practical support; (c) commitment to substantive, durable lifestyle outcomes; and (d) implementation of support within organizational systems that facilitate sustained effects (Carr et al., 1994, 2002; Durand, 1990; Horner et al., 1990; Sugai et al., 2000). Together, these features comprise a commitment to empirically validated practices that are guided by the values, perspectives, and preferences of those receiving support and embedded in the organizational systems needed to make support comprehensive, durable, and effective.

### *Application of Behavioral Science*

PBS combines behavioral, cognitive, biophysical, social, developmental, and environmental psychology. PBS is focused on the design of environments that promote desired behaviors and minimize the development and support of problem behaviors. Applied behavior analysis (ABA) (Baer, Wolf, & Risley, 1968) is the conceptual foundation for these empirically proven intervention practices. ABA is grounded in the assumption that human behavior can change and provides a conceptually powerful operant model for validating support to address the unique needs of individuals with problem behavior. Within this commitment to applying behavioral science, PBS emphasizes the (a) use of functional behavioral assessment (FBA) to enhance the match between individual needs and specific supports (Dunlap, Kern-Dunlap, Clarke, & Robbins, 1991); (b) prevention of problem behavior through environmental redesign (Luiselli, 2006; Luiselli & Cameron, 1998); (c) active instruction of desired behaviors, especially desired behaviors that may serve the same behavioral function as problem behaviors (Carr, 1977; Carr & Durand, 1985); and (d) the organization of consequences that promote desired behavior, minimize rewards for problem behavior, and if appropriate, provide consequences for problem behavior (Koegel et al., 1996).

### Practical, Multicomponent Interventions

PBS focuses on supports that can be delivered in natural contexts by families, teachers, and typical support personnel. The emphasis is on behavior change that spans the full spectrum of activities, locations, time of day, and social context that an individual typically encounters. To achieve this breadth of effect, support is assumed to include multiple intervention components that are linked to a common FBA. Dunlap and Carr (2007) pointed out that PBS draws from multiple theoretical perspectives, leading to diverse interventions that are measurably practical and effective for the contexts in which they are implemented. The breadth of PBS interventions includes a strong emphasis on the collection and use of data. Assessment data (a) guide the design of effective and efficient support plans, (b) validate the implementation of support with fidelity, and (c) allow assessment of the impact that support has on valued outcomes. Through the collection and use of data, the support a person receives can be assessed and adapted to new challenges and opportunities.

### Lifestyle Outcomes

The third central feature of PBS as an intervention technology is the commitment to lifestyle change guided by the values of individuals receiving support and their advocates. Behavior support that meets this criterion is longitudinal in scope; is comprehensive in attention to change that occurs across time, context, and activity; is ecologically valid given the setting where support is provided; and produces change that is durable (Carr et al., 2002). The central message is that the application of PBS should result not only in reduction in problem behavior, but also include the development of positive behaviors that have substantive lifestyle impact for the individual. In the end, the quality of life a person experiences determines the success of support.

### Systems Change

An important contribution of PBS is an emphasis on the sociology of behavior that emphasizes organizational and cultural “systems” within which support is provided. The emphasis on person-centered planning and team-based decision making extends behavior support beyond manipulation of events in the immediate life space of the individual to recognition that schedules, staffing patterns, cultural expectations, physical conditions, budgeting, and organizational policy are also likely to affect the success of support. Decisions made by administrators are as important to successful behavior support as decisions made by those in immediate contact with an individual. This comprehensive emphasis on the systems needed to nurture and sustain effective interventions distinguishes PBS from many other intervention approaches.

## THE ORIGINS AND EMERGENCE OF PBS

The technology of PBS emerged from gradual shifts in expectations and intervention practices over the past 30 years. The decade of the 1980s was a period of significant advancement in conceptualizing how services should be organized and provided to persons with disabilities. The dominant theme was *emancipation*, with the American civil rights movement as a driver and an increasing national discontent with large, congregate settings such as state institutions for the "mentally retarded." The *deinstitutionalization* movement began in earnest during this period with publications of Blatt and Kaplan's *Christmas in Purgatory* (1966), about conditions in New York's Willowbrook institution, and the Gannett News Service exposé, *Oklahoma Shame* (Dubill, 1982), revealing conditions in Hissom and other large institutions in Oklahoma.

At the same time, significant strides were made in scientifically verified methods of treating severe behavior disorders. Described as "behavior modification," researchers in the expanding field of ABA reported remarkable successes in a wide range of very debilitating manifestations of disability, including aggression, self-injurious behavior, sexually deviant behavior, and other problems that had been considered sufficient grounds to cause a person to be institutionalized or to remain a resident in an institution if such behaviors emerged in that context. Many of the published successes of behavior modification with institutionalized persons involved systematic applications of contingent punishers (later called "aversives"). The technology of punishment extended to the use of contingent electric shock in many published examples and even to the use of powerful electronic stimulation in a negative reinforcement paradigm (Lovaas, Schaeffer, & Simmons, 1965).

These two areas of development, *movements* in a sense—deinstitutionalization/civil rights on one hand and behavior modification/use of aversives on the other—began to form a conceptual paradox that put these movements on a collision course. The result was controversy, both in the scientific community of behavioral researchers and in the professional community of practice (cf., Repp & Singh, 1990); that is, how could the very procedures (aversives) that freed individuals from the debilitating behaviors that kept them confined to institutions possibly be transferred to community-based settings, where the community at large would regard the treatments as immoral and abusive (Freagon, 1990)? Scientifically validated uses of electric shock could be carried out in the sheltered circumstances of an institution free of public reaction as long as those "in the know" were accepting of the moral position that inflicting physical or psychological pain on an individual was justified if the result was successful treatment of a debilitating behavioral condition. No such moral position could be found in community settings. Public schools, for example, during the 1980s were in the last throes of imposing state-legislated bans on corporal punishment. Use of painful aversives on students with disabilities was not likely to be tolerated, and indeed, a number of federal lawsuits (cf., *Beard v. Hissom* in Oklahoma) confirmed this public reaction.

## VALUES AND AVERSIVES

A number of researchers during this period (early 1980s) attempted to delineate frameworks under which punishers (aversives) could be understood in a broad context of school and community settings. Renzaglia and Bates (1983), for example, in a methods textbook for special education teacher trainees, proposed a conceptual framework for addressing behavior problems in schools that would place the degree of intrusiveness of interventions on a continuum from least (or most natural) to most intrusive (least natural) by evaluating

> a) the extent to which a procedure can be applied in the natural environment without interfering with learning; b) the necessity for involving artificial or prosthetic devices, c) the amount of staff time required, d) the potential for abuse of the technique, e) the potential for increasing behavior, and f) the degree to which the people required to carry out the program feel comfortable with the techniques selected. (p. 327)

The authors provided a substantive review of evidence-based punishment procedures that had appeared in the literature to date. Much of this body of work had addressed problems of stereotypic behavior (i.e., Forehand & Baumeister, 1970); self-injurious behavior (i.e., Horner & Barton, 1980); aggression (i.e., Repp & Deitz, 1974); and problems of food and liquid ingestion (i.e., Davis & Cuvo, 1980).

Renzaglia and Bates (1983) listed extinction, time-out, verbal reprimands, restraint, overcorrection, and response cost as "more intrusive" (but acceptable in schools) in application to such problems as vomiting and pica. Further along the intrusiveness continuum of their conceptual model, however, they listed "aversive consequences" such as application of Tabasco sauce to the tongue and electric shock as potentially justifiable when behavior problems are of a life-threatening nature.

The chapter by Renzaglia and Bates (1983) captured concisely the dilemma confronting community- and school-based professionals in the early 1980s in seeking to establish a technology for developing social skills in a population of students with severe behavioral disabilities with procedures applicable to school settings but necessarily having to rely on methods developed through research on institutionalized populations. The relatively "quick fix" of contingent aversives, such as shock, could suppress aberrant responses in a short time so that alternative, more socially desirable responses that achieved the same function could be taught (Axelrod, 1990; Birnbauer, 1990). Such techniques, however, were abhorrent to most school professional communities, a circumstance that led to an immediate need for research and development on new technologies that (a) could address the same population of students (or adults in the case of community-based facilities), (b) would be socially appropriate and acceptable to laypeople and others in the community of practice, and (c) would be durable, efficient, and effective.

Meanwhile, the values clash over the legitimacy of the use of aversives widened in the literature of the 1980s and in some cases became quite acrimonious. Guess, Helmstetter, Turnbull, and Knowlton (1987) characterized the debate and resultant controversy that erupted in the mid-1980s as nothing less than "a major paradigm crisis in an applied science" (p. 224).

Special educators (Donnellan, Mirenda, Mesaros & Fassbender, 1984) and behavioral psychologists (Carr, 1977; Iwata, Dorsey, Slifer, Bauman, & Richman, 1982) contributed immensely during this period by publishing research and conceptual perspectives focusing on why aberrant behavior was occurring and under what circumstances rather than simply asking how to most expediently eliminate the behavior. This early work led directly to the technologies of functional analysis (Dunlap et al., 1993; Iwata et al., 1982; Repp & Horner, 1999) and functional assessment (Foster-Johnson & Dunlap, 1993; O'Neill et al., 1997), which have now formed an essential foundation of PBS.

The emergence of functional analysis allowed community-oriented investigators to concentrate on the development of new technologies for the management of aberrant behavior that would be socially acceptable as well as efficient and durable in application (cf., Snell & Zirpoli, 1987). At about the same time, new research into the effects of punishment (aversives) cast further doubt on the use of highly intrusive consequence-based strategies in schools and other community settings. Newsom, Favell, and Rincover (1983), for example, provided an examination of "secondary effects of the punisher," such as concomitant suppression of socially desirable behavior, emotional outbursts, avoidance behaviors, and escape behaviors and heightened emotional states, such as anxiety, that interfered with new learning. By 1987, educators were calling for formal examination by review boards of any proposal to engage "more instrusive practices" to treat aberrant behaviors in school settings (Snell & Zirpoli, 1987).

Singh, Lloyd, and Kendall (1990) suggested that the real issue for analysis and debate came down to "being able to provide treatments that are effective, rapid, and socially acceptable [italics added]" (p. 8). Clearly, the need was high during this decade of sweeping changes in services to people with disabilities for a scientifically grounded technology of nonaversive behavioral intervention. PBS became the name associated with research and practice dedicated to development of this technology.

## EARLY DEVELOPMENT OF FUNCTION-BASED INTERVENTIONS

One of the first significant position papers to appear on the topic was that of Gaylord-Ross (1980). The paper described a structured decision model that could extend applied behavior analytic treatments to remediation of aberrant behavior in public settings. The decision model provided a sequence of decision steps for dealing with deviant behavior that could be "justified on empirical and ethical grounds" (p. 137). Punishment, in the model, could be used as a last step and "only after a number of 'positive' approaches have been tried and evaluated" (p. 132). The Gaylord-Ross paper was particularly significant for its focus on *behavior ecology*, the interplay of behaviors and their host's environment as determiners of successful living as well as development of problem behavior (cf., Rogers-Warren & Warren, 1977).

This early focus on ecological contributions to development of a behavioral alternative later became a major theme in the work of Todd Risley, one of the principal founders of the field of ABA. Risley (1996) stated:

Getting a life for people and coaching them into it should be considered obligatory features of modern behavioral interventions. Fortunately, just as daily contingency management programming requires less-technical precision and specialty training than micromomentary behavior analysis programming, so do life arrangement and life coaching require less than either. Most people with some experience in caring for others need only a little training to help another person design a good life and help him or her to implement it (professionals may actually need "detraining").

In general, there is a negative correlation between the flexibility of life arrangements available and the technical precision of the behavior programming needed. The wider the latitude available for modifying the life arrangements for a person with challenging behaviors, the less precise and technical the behavior programming needs to be. The opposite is also true in that the less flexible a person's life arrangements are, the more technical and precise the behavior programming must be (p. 429).

One of the first comprehensive manuals for practitioners to promote this functional theme was *Nonaversive Interventions for Behavior Problems: A Manual for Home and Community* (Meyer & Evans, 1989). This work was strongly influenced by research in the 1980s reporting successes in the treatment of severe behavior disorders through communicative replacement repertoires (Carr & Durand, 1985; Donnellan et al., 1984; Horner & Budd, 1985).

The contributions of Luana Meyer and Ian Evans were timely and significant (Evans & Meyer, 1985; Meyer & Evans, 1986, 1989, 1993, 2004). While standard ABA applications tended to be focused on solving problems through consequence-based strategies, Meyer and Evans made a case for "function-based" interventions that would be more focused on analyses of why aberrant behavior occurs, and what replacement behaviors might be taught to a person that would serve the same function and that would be socially acceptable in everyday, community settings. Meyer and Evans (1986, 1989) thus laid the groundwork for a pedagogical approach to the treatment of aberrant behavior. By shifting the focus to the ecology of behavior and examining the role of antecedent events to a larger degree, the two authors developed what would later come to be called *functional behavioral assessment* as a part of, or alternative to, *functional analysis*, the applied behavior-analytic, hypothesis-testing procedure used to reveal the exact circumstances controlling discrete behavioral events.

Carr (1988) and Favell and Reid (1988) further set the stage for the emergence of FBA by delineating the concept of *functional equivalence*. Carr defined functional equivalence as a circumstance in which various classes of responses are maintained by the same reinforcers even through the features ("topographies") of the response may be quite different. Carr and his colleagues conducted experiments to show that establishment of functional equivalence was key to enhancing response generalization (i.e., Kemp & Carr, 1995).

Favell and Reid (1988) developed the concept of functional equivalence as a potential extension of the concept of *functional incompatibility*. Two behaviors, one unacceptable and the other socially desirable, are maintained by the same reinforcer (i.e., are functionally equivalent and members of the same response class). Rendering them functionally incompatible by differentially reinforcing one over the other potentially achieves both elimination of the undesirable alternative and improved likelihood of generalization and maintenance of the desirable alternative. These analyses of functional equivalent response classes contributed immensely to the emergence of FBA and PBS, particularly by guiding researchers and practitioners to investigations of functionally equivalent response classes prior to selecting an intervention.

## ESTABLISHMENT OF POSITIVE BEHAVIOR SUPPORT AS A DISTINCT APPROACH

By the latter half of the 1980s, promoting (a) community and educational inclusion for people with disabilities and (b) functional, nonaversive interventions for behavior problems led to significant advocacy and policy initiatives on the part of some national organizations as well as various state and federal agencies. In 1987, the U.S. Department of Education provided funding for a national research and training center on the topic of nonaversive behavior management. The faculty of the new center published an article describing the emergence of a "technology of nonaversive behavioral support" and introduced a new, preferable term, "positive behavioral support" (Horner et al., 1990). These authors also presented a list of features that characterized the new technology.

This first formal iteration of PBS focused on individuals with severe disabilities whose characteristics were associated with histories of aversive interventions. The PBS technology consisted of FBA and the assessment-based selection of antecedent manipulations, teaching strategies, and a rearrangement of reinforcement contingencies to emphasize the use of positive events and the reduction or removal of aversive consequences. These elements were based on ABA research conducted in the 1970s and 1980s but assembled in a manner that emphasized ecological and social validity, lifestyle outcomes, and a pervasive respect for individual dignity. The approach was defined in a training curriculum that was disseminated through a system of state training teams (Anderson, Albin, Mesaros, Dunlap, & Morelli-Robbins, 1993).

Clearly, the PBS approach had applications for many populations in addition to the group of individuals referred to as "severely disabled." As a result, the approach was extended through controlled research with students with emotional and behavioral disorders (EBDs) and severe emotional disturbance (SED) (e.g., Dunlap et al., 1991, 1993), young children with disabilities (e.g., Dunlap & Fox, 1999; Gettinger & Stoiber, 2006; Reeve & Carr, 2000), as well as with numerous other populations of individuals with behavioral challenges (cf., Bambara & Kern, 2005; Lucyshyn, Dunlap, & Albin, 2002; Repp & Horner, 1999).

Within the past decade, PBS has become increasingly recognized as a distinctive approach with a widespread base of practitioners, proponents, and constituencies and as a means of improving the general public's access to the ABA technology (Sugai et al., 2002). An international organization, the Association for PBS, was established in 2003, and a professional periodical, the *Journal of Positive Behavior Interventions,* began operations in 1999. Meta analyses and syntheses of PBS research have been published (e.g., Carr et al., 1999; Conroy, Dunlap, Clarke, & Alter, 2005; Dunlap & Carr, 2007), and definitions have been refined and explained (e.g., Carr et al., 2002; Dunlap, Carr, Horner, Zarcone, & Schwartz, in press). Dozens of textbooks and practitioner manuals and hundreds of research reports have been published since 2000, and the rate of expansion continues to accelerate.

Along with a substantial increase in the proponents, beneficiaries, and practitioners of PBS, various implementation aspects have been expanded. In particular, PBS is now defined as being applied at different levels or tiers of application, and integrated into a growing number of practitioner communities. We turn now to a brief consideration of these important developments.

## A MULTITIERED MODEL OF PBS

As the technology of PBS developed in its applications with individuals, it became increasingly evident that the success of these efforts was dependent to a large extent on the context in which the support plans were implemented. In schools, for example, individual programs were generally ineffective if they were implemented in the context of chaotic classrooms and schools, where teachers were constantly addressing behavior problems of multiple students and where schoolwide or classroomwide discipline was clearly absent. Similarly, in these situations the resources needed to design and implement individual support plans could not be replicated on a scale sufficient to address the needs of the large numbers of students with significant behavioral difficulties. In other words, a great need clearly existed for strategies to be implemented at larger units of analysis (e.g., classrooms, schools) to promote improved behavior among greater populations of students, thereby reducing the number of students in need of more intensive and individualized behavior support.

Fortunately, useful precedents existed. First, important conceptual work in the realm of large-scale prevention efforts demonstrated that a multitiered strategy for a continuum of procedures needed to be implemented with a narrowing proportion of the overall population. At the beginning or primary tier, low-intensity strategies could be provided for the entire population of interest (e.g., all of the students, all of the staff, in all settings of a school). Such "universal" strategies would be expected to prevent the development of problem behaviors for a substantial number of the population. For those individuals in need of additional (moderate-intensity) procedures, the next level of procedures would be implemented. These secondary tier strategies would be intended to redirect individuals from potential behavior problems to more compliant patterns of appropriate and prosocial behavior. Then, those individuals who continued to exhibit patterns of problem behavior (nonresponders to primary or secondary tier interventions) would be provided tertiary tier procedures comprised of more intensive and individualized interventions. Ordinarily, these third tier strategies are the assessment-based PBS interventions we discussed. This multitiered framework had been described as a prevention framework in the context of public health but was also evident in early intervention and other fields (e.g., Simeonsson, 1991) and subsequently has been described in various applications within public education (Lewis & Sugai, 1999; Sugai et al., 2000; Walker et al., 1996; Weisz, Sandler, Durlak, & Anton, 2005).

A second vital precedent was formative behavioral research that focused on entire schools as the units of analysis. In the early 1990s, for example, a series of studies was conducted with the intent of developing procedures for improving the overall discipline of schools (e.g., Colvin, Kame'enui, & Sugai, 1993; Colvin, Sugai, & Kame'enui, 1994). Based on the principles of ABA, these investigatgions were among the first to establish the importance of explicitly teaching and positively reinforcing behavioral expectations for all students in a school. As these approaches were fully consistent with the definitions and critical features that had been established for PBS, the process became straightforward for adding these strategies that were pertinent to larger units of analysis. In this manner, by the late 1990s and early 2000s, the multitiered framework of schoolwide PBS (SW-PBS) became a vital element of the PBS approach (Sugai et al., 2000). These contributions are extensively summarized and updated in section III of this volume.

## EXTENSIONS TO ADDITIONAL COMMUNITIES OF PRACTICE

Another important development with the potential for substantial impact involves the incorporation of PBS perspectives and practices into existing systems and communities of practice. Such processes are gradual and rarely marked by specific milestones, policy mandates, or publications. Nevertheless, evidence suggests that PBS is influencing communities of practice as diverse as children's mental health, juvenile justice, Head Start, family therapy and support, and child welfare. A number of chapters in the current volume are indicative of this trend. For example, Frey, Boyce, and Tarullo (chapter 6) describe the integration of PBS into a large Head Start program, a development that already has some noteworthy precedents (cf., Fox, Jack, & Broyles, 2005). Duchnowski and Kutash (chapter 9) address the integration of PBS in family-centered mental health services for children. In some respects, the incorporation of PBS into systems of mental health service delivery can be seen as indicative of a growing paradigmatic flexibility, and such transformations are increasingly evident in the mental health arena (cf., Kutash, Duchnowski, & Lynn, 2006). Similarly,

Crosland, Dunlap, Clark, and Neff (chapter 12) present evidence of PBS being incorporated into systems of child welfare and, more specifically, into the systems of preparing foster parents to interact more effectively with their foster children. Other chapters provide additional descriptions of communities of practice being influenced by the PBS features and strategies (e.g., Fox & Hemmeter, chapter 8; Lucyshyn et al., chapter 4).

## SUMMARY

Since its emergence in the mid-1980s, PBS has developed rapidly as a broad and multifaceted approach for addressing difficulties in behavioral adaptation and for encompassing interventions addressed not only to enhancing individual as well as collective lifestyles. From its inception in the disability rights movement and ABA foundations, PBS has amassed a large number of practitioners, advocates, innovators, researchers, and beneficiaries. The essential goal associated with PBS is to improve the quality of the lives of people who are the recipients of its supports and interventions. The crucial determinant of its future will be the extent to which this goal is achieved and validated through scientific research, sustained accurate implementation, scaled applications, and continuous regenerations of its adaptations. The chapters in this volume represent current thinking, research, and practice in PBS. This collection was conceived and developed by some of the most conspicuous and productive contributors in the field; represents the diversity of topics and populations impacted by PBS; and offers a glimpse of future developments in the topical areas surveyed by the volume.

The intent of this brief chapter has been to provide a description of the essential elements of PBS as well as a glimpse of the historical context within which they emerged. In the remainder of this volume, the editors have assembled a broad sweep of the various strands of PBS research and development leading directly to application in professional practice by a wide spectrum of social service providers, educators, and child clinical psychologists. Our hope is that members of this broad community of professional practice as well as those primarily engaged in research find this volume scholarly and useful as a momentary summation of the current status of relatively new and emerging technologies of support within the field of positive behavior support.

## REFERENCES

Anderson, J., Albin, R., Mesaros, R., Dunlap, G., & Morelli-Robbins, M. (1993). Objectives and processes of comprehensive training in community-referenced behavior management. In J. Reichle & D. Wacker (Eds.), *Communicative approaches to the management of challenging behavior* (pp. 363–406). Baltimore: Brookes.

Axelrod, S. (1990). Myths that (mis)guide our profession. In A. C. Repp & N. N. Singh (Eds.), *Perspectives on the use of nonaversive and aversive interventions for persons with developmental disabilities*. Pacific Grove, CA: Brooks/Cole, 57–72.

Baer, D. M., Wolf, M. M., & Risley, T. R. (1968). Some current dimensions of applied behavior analysis. *Journal of Applied Behavior Analysis*, 1, 91–97.

Bambara, L., & Kern, L. (Eds.). (2005). *Individualized supports for students with problem behaviors: Designing positive behavior plans.* New York: Guilford Press.

Birnbauer, J. S. (1990). Responsibility and quality of life. In A. C. Repp & N. N. Singh (Eds.), *Perspectives on the use of nonaversive and aversive interventions for persons with developmental disabilities* (pp. 231–236). Sycamore, IL: Sycamore.

Blatt, B., & Kaplan, F. (1966). *Christmas in purgatory.* Newton, MA: Allyn & Bacon.

Carr, E. G. (1977). The motivation of self-injurious behavior: A review of some hypotheses. *Psychological Bulletin,* 84, 800–816.

Carr, E. G. (1988). Functional equivalence as a mechanism of response generalization. In R. H. Horner, G. Dunlap, & R. L. (Eds.), *Generalization and maintenance: Lifestyle changes in applied settings* (pp. 221–241). Baltimore: Brookes.

Carr, E. G., Dunlap, G., Horner, R. H., Koegel, R. L., Turnbull, A. P., Sailor, W., et al. (2002). Positive behavior support: Evolution of an applied science. Journal of Positive *Behavior Interventions,* 4(1), 4–16.

Carr, E. G., & Durand, V.M. (1985). Reducing behavior problems through functional communication training. *Journal of Applied Behavior Analysis,* 18, 111–126.

Carr, E. G., Horner, R. H., Turnbull, A. P., Marquis, J., Magito-McLaughlin, D., McAtee, M. L., et al. (1999). *Positive behavior support for people with developmental disabilities: A research synthesis.* Washington, DC: American Association on Mental Retardation.

Carr, E. G., Levin, L., McConnachie, G., Carlson, J. I., Kemp, D. C., & Smith, C. E. (1994). *Communication-based interventions for problem behavior: A user's guide for producing behavior change.* Baltimore: Brookes.

Colvin, G., Kame'enui, E. J., & Sugai, G. (1993). School-wide and classroom management: Reconceptualizing the integration and management of students with behavior problems in general education. *Education and Treatment of Children, 16,* 361–381.

Colvin, G., Sugai, G., & Kame'enui, E. (1994). *Curriculum for establishing a proactive school-wide discipline plan.* Project Prepare. Behavioral Research and Teaching. Eugene: College of Education, University of Oregon.

Conroy, M. A., Dunlap, G., Clarke, S., & Alter, P. J. (2005). A descriptive analysis of positive behavioral intervention research with young children with challenging behavior. *Topics in Early Childhood Special Education,* 25, 157–166.

Davis, P. K., & Cuvo, A. J. (1980). Chronic vomiting and rumination in intellectually normal and retarded individuals: Review and evaluation of behavior research. *Behavior Research of Severe Developmental Disabilities,* 1, 31–59.

Donnellan, A., Mirenda, P., Mesaros, R., & Fassbender, L. (1984). Analyzing the communicative functions of aberrant behavior. *Journal of the Association for Persons With Severe Handicaps, 9,* 201–212.

Dubill, R. A. (Ed.). (1982, November). *Oklahoma shame* [Special report]. Gannett News Service.

Dunlap, G., & Carr, E. G. (2007). Positive behavior support and developmental disabilities: A summary and analysis of research. In S. L. Odom, R. H. Horner, M. Snell, & J. Blacher (Eds.), *Handbook of developmental disabilities* (pp. 469–482). New York: Guilford.

Dunlap, G., Carr, E.G., Horner, R.H., Zarcone, J., & Schwartz, I. (2008). Positive behavior support and applied behavior analysis: A familial alliance. *Behavior Modification, 32,* 682–698.

Dunlap, G., & Fox, L. (1999). A demonstration of behavioral support for young children with autism. *Journal of Positive Behavior Interventions,* 1(2), 77–87.

Dunlap, G., Kern, L., dePerczel, M., Clarke, S., Wilson, D., Childs, K. E., et al. (1993). Functional analysis of classroom variables for students with emotional and behavioral challenges. *Behavioral Disorders,* 18, 275–291.

Dunlap, G., Kern-Dunlap, L., Clarke, S., & Robbins, F. R. (1991). Functional assessment, curricular revision, and severe problems. *Journal of Applied Behavior Analysis, 24,* 387–397.

Durand, V. M. (1990). *Functional communication training: An intervention program for severe behavior problems.* New York: Guilford.

Evans, I. M., & Meyer, L. H. (1985). *An educative approach to behavior problems: A practical decision model for interventions with severely handicapped learners.* Baltimore: Brookes.

Favell, J. E., & Reid, D. H. (1988). Generalizing and maintaining improvement in problem behavior. In R. H. Horner, G. Dunlap, & R. L. Koegel (Eds.), *Generalization and maintenance* (pp. 171–196). Baltimore: Brookes.

Forehand, R., & Baumeister, A.A. (1970). The effect of auditory and visual stimulation on sterotyped rocking behavior and general activity of severe retardates. *Journal of Clinical Psychology*, 26, 426–429.

Foster-Johnson, L., & Dunlap, G. (1993). Using functional assessment to develop effective, individualized interventions. *Teaching Exceptional Children, 25*, 44–50.

Fox, L., Jack, S., & Broyles, L. (2005). *Program-wide positive behavior support: Supporting young children's social-emotional development and addressing challenging behavior.* Tampa: University of South Florida, Louis de la Parte Florida Mental Health Institute.

Freagon, S. (1990). One educator's perspective on the use of punishment or aversives: Advocating for supportive and protective systems. In A. C. Repp & N. N. Singh (Eds.), *Perspectives on the use of nonaversive and aversive interventions for persons with developmental disabilities* (pp. 145–155). Pacific Grove, CA: Brooks/Cole.

Gaylord-Ross, R. (1980). A decision model for the treatment of aberrant behavior in applied settings. In W. Sailor, B. Wilcox, & L. Brown (Eds.) *Methods of instruction for severely handicapped students* (135–158). Baltimore: Brookes.

Gettinger, M., & Stoiber, K. C. (2006). Functional assessment, collaboration, and evidence-based treatment: Analysis of a team approach for addressing challenging behaviors in young children. *Journal of School Psychology*, 44, 231–252.

Guess, D., Helmstetter, E., Turnbull, H. R., & Knowlton, S. (1987). *Use of aversive procedures with persons who are disabled: An historical review and critical analysis.* Seattle: Association for Persons With Severe Handicaps.

Horner, R. D., & Barton, E. S. (1980). Operant techniques in the analysis and modification of self-injurious behavior: A review. *Behavior Research of Severe Developmental Disabilities, 1*, 61–91.

Horner, R. H., & Budd, C. M. (1985). Acquisition of manual sign use: Collateral reduction of maladaptive behavior, and factors limiting generalization. *Education and Training of the Mentally Retarded, 20*, 39–47.

Horner, R. H., Dunlap, G., Koegel, R. L., Carr, E. G., Sailor, W., Anderson, J., et al. (1990). Toward a technology of "nonaversive" behavioral support. *Journal of the Association for Persons With Severe Handicaps*, 15, 125–132.

Iwata, B., Dorsey, M., Slifer, K., Bauman, K., & Richman, G. (1982). Toward a functional analysis of self-injury. *Analysis and Intervention in Developmental Disabilities, 2*, 3–20, 1982. (Reprinted in Journal of Applied Behavior Analysis, 27, 197–209)

Kemp, D. C., & Carr, E. G. (1995). Reduction of severe problem behavior in community employment using an hypothesis-driven multicomponent intervention approach. *Journal of the Association for Persons With Severe Handicaps*, 20, 229–247.

Koegel, L. K., Koegel, R. L., & Dunlap, G. (Eds.) (1996). *Positive behavioral support: Including people with difficult behavior in the community*. Baltimore: Brookes.

Kutash, K., Duchnowski, A. J., & Lynn, N. (2006). *School-based mental health: An empirical guide for decision-makers.* Tampa: University of South Florida, Louis de la Parte Florida Mental Health Institute, Department of Child and Family Studies, Research and Training Center for Children's Mental Health.

Lewis, T. J., & Sugai, G. (1999). Effective behavior support: A systems approach to proactive school-wide management. *Focus on Exceptional Children*, 31, 1–24.

Lovaas, O.I., Schaeffer, B., & Simmons, J.Q. (1965). Building social behavior in autistic children by use of electric shock. *Journal of Experimental Research in Personality, 1*, 99–65.

Lucyshyn, J., Dunlap, G., & Albin, R. W. (Eds.). (2002). *Families and positive behavior support: Addressing problem behaviors in family contexts.* Baltimore: Brookes.

Luiselli, J. K. (Ed.). (2006). *Antecedent intervention: Recent developments in community focused behavior support.* Baltimore: Brookes.

Luiselli, J. K., & Cameron, M. J. (Eds.). (1998). *Antecedent control: Innovative approaches to behavioral support.* Baltimore: Brookes.

Meyer, L. H., & Evans, I. M. (1986). Modification of excess behavior: An adaptive and functional approach for educational and community contexts. In. R. H. Horner, L. H. Meyer, & H. D. B. Fredericks (Eds.), *Education of learners with severe handicaps: Exemplary service strategies* (pp. 315–350). Baltimore: Brookes.

Meyer, L. H., & Evans, I. M. (1989). *Nonaversive interventions for problem behaviors: A manual for home and community.* Baltimore: Brookes.

Meyer, L. H., & Evans, I. (1993). Science and practice in behavioral intervention: Meaningful outcomes, research validity and usable knowledge. *Journal of the Association for Persons With severe Handicaps*, 18, 224–234.

Meyer, L. H., & Evans, I. M. (2004). Science and practice in behavioral interventions: Meaningful outcomes, research validity, and usable knowledge. In L. M. Bambara, G. Dunlap, & I. S. Schwartz, *Positive behavior support: Critical articles for individuals with severe disabilities* (pp. 11–21). Pro-Ed and TASH, Austin, TX.

Newsom, C., Favell, J. E., & Rincover, A. (1983). The side effects of punishment. In S. Axelrod & J. Apsche (Eds.), *The effects of punishment on human behavior* (pp. 285–316). New York: Academic Press.

O'Neill, R. E., Horner, R. H., Albin, R. W., Storey, K., Sprague, J. R., & Newton, J. S. (1997). *Functional assessment of problem behavior: A practical assessment guide.* Pacific Grove, CA: Brooks/Cole.

Reeve, C. E., & Carr, E. G. (2000). Prevention of severe behavior problems in children with developmental disorders. *Journal of Positive Behavior Interventions, 2*, 144–160.

Renzaglia, A., & Bates, P. (1983). Socially appropriate behavior. In M. E. Snell (Ed.), *Systematic instruction of the moderately and severely handicapped* (2nd ed., pp. 314–356). Columbus, OH: Merrill.

Repp, A., & Deitz, S. M. (1974). Reducing aggressive and self-injurious behavior of institutionalized retarded children through reinforcement of other behavior. *Journal of Applied Behavior Analysis*, 7, 554–558.

Repp, A. C., & Horner, R. H. (Eds.) (1999). *Functional analysis of problem behavior: From effective assessment to effective support.* Belmont, CA: Wadsworth.

Repp, A. C., & Singh, N. N. (Eds.). (1990). *Current perspectives in the use of non-aversive and aversive interventions with developmentally disabled persons. Sycamore*, IL: Sycamore Press.

Risley, T. R. (1996). Get a life! In L. K. Koegel, R. L. Koegel, & G. Dunlap (Eds.), *Positive behavioral support* (pp. 425–437). Baltimore: Brookes.

Rogers-Warren, A., & Warren, S. (Eds.). (1977). *Ecological perspectives in behavior analysis.* Baltimore: University Park Press.

Simeonsson, R. J. (1991). Primary, secondary, and tertiary prevention in early intervention. *Journal of Early Intervention*, 15, 124–134.

Singh, N. N., Lloyd, J. W., & Kendall, K. A. (1990). Nonaversive and aversive interventions: Introduction. In A. C. Repp & N. N. Singh (Eds.), *Perspectives on the use of nonaversive and aversive interventions for persons with developmental disabilities* (pp. 3–16). Pacific Grove, CA: Brooks/Cole.

Snell, M. E., & Zirpoli, T. J. (1987). Intervention strategies. In M. E. Snell (Ed.), *Systematic instruction of persons with severe handicaps* (pp. 110–149). Columbus, OH: Merrill.

Sugai, G., Horner, R. H., Dunlap, G., Hieneman, M., Lewis, T. J., Nelson, C. M., et al. (2000). Applying positive behavior support and functional behavioral assessment in schools. *Journal of Positive Behavior Interventions*, 2(3), 131–143.

Walker, H. M., Horner, R. H., Sugai, G., Bullis, M., Sprague, J. R., Bricker, D., et al. (1996). Integrated approaches to preventing antisocial behavior patterns among school-age children and youth. *Journal of Emotional and Behavioral Disorders, 4*, 194–209.

Weisz, J., Sandler, I., Durlak, J., & Anton, B. (2005). Promoting and protecting youth mental health through evidence-based prevention and treatment. *American Psychologist, 60*, 628–648.

# 2

# The Intellectual Roots of Positive Behavior Support and Their Implications for Its Development

GEORGE H. S. SINGER and MIAN WANG

## WHAT IS POSITIVE BEHAVIOR SUPPORT?

The purpose of this chapter is twofold. Positive Behavior support (PBS) has emerged as an endeavor by researchers and practitioners, and it is in the process of defining its identity as a distinctive approach to studying and addressing important social problems. It is not clear if it is best understood as a new applied science (Carr et al., 1999), as a branch of the field of applied behavior analysis (ABA) emphasizing Positive Behavior technologies (Horner et al., 1990), or as an approach to delivering social services (Wacker & Berg, 2002). In this chapter, we examine some key ideas underlying the development of PBS in the hope of helping to inform the ongoing process of defining PBS and demarcating its boundaries. We review the roots of PBS in the field of ABA and Skinnerian radical behaviorism (Skinner, 1957) and provide an account for the ethical imperative, which initially caused ABA practitioners and researchers to develop a new professional identity as practitioners of PBS. This ethical dimension is described in terms of a contemporary philosophical analysis of moral prohibitions and moral ideals (Gert, 2005). We link the emergence of new treatment components in PBS with both the historical context in which they were developed and the implicit moral rules and ideals that make them compelling. Further, we

**GEORGE H. S. SINGER and MAIN WANG** • University of California Santa Barbara

analyze a key question about the future of PBS, which centers on whether it will preserve or jettison the core components of behavioral theory (Lakatos, 1970) as PBS embraces a broader contextualism and pragmatism (Biglan & Hayes, 1995; Pepper, 1942).

## RADICAL BEHAVIORISM

Although it is in its early stages of development, PBS grows out of a research and applied social science tradition, ABA, spanning four decades (Baer, Wolf, & Risley, 1968, 1987; Cooper, Heron, & Heward, 2007). Much of what we describe as components of PBS are also elements of ABA. The distinctions between the two fields are drawn in terms of ideal models that necessarily simplify the actual historical condition in which the two overlap considerably. Further, we maintain that presently ABA and PBS share the same core theory (Lakatos, 1970) based on operant conditioning (Skinner, 1957), and that it is an open question whether this will continue to be so as PBS evolves toward a more eclectic pragmatic contextualism (Biglan & Hayes, 1995; Pepper, 1942).

The history of PBS reveals foundational ideas that are still central to its definition and purpose. PBS originally was a breakaway movement from the field of ABA based on moral revulsion at aversive treatments developed and promoted by prominent behavior analysts. Originally, it differed from ABA in two major respects: (a) the foundational belief that there are effective positive alternatives to aversive treatments and so it is immoral to use harsher methods (Singer, Gert, & Koegel, 1999; Turnbull, Wilcox, Turnbull, Sailor, & Wickham, 2001); and (b) a commitment to use behavioral interventions not only to change discrete target behaviors but also to have a broader impact by improving the quality of life of the recipients of PBS interventions. Evolving descriptions of PBS have included other prominent ideas, such as normalization, self-determination, comprehensive service design, contextual fit, and parent professional partnerships (Carr, et al., 2002). These additions naturally emerged from the history of efforts to make changes in larger social units in addition to microsocial interactions.

## IN THE BEGINNING: APPLIED BEHAVIOR ANALYSIS

The initial researchers and practitioners of PBS were steeped in the theory and practice of ABA and its application to people who have been vulnerable to societal mistreatment, primarily individuals with developmental disabilities in preschool, K–12 school, home, and work settings (Dunlap, 2006). Others had years of experience with behavioral parent training (BPT) to treat a variety of childhood problems by teaching parents new ways to interact with their children. Similarly, the initial researchers and practitioners of the field were all well versed in the use of ABA techniques to manage individual and classroomwide behaviors of students in public schools. A brief overview of ABA helps to explain the choice of treatment and research methods that continue to characterize

PBS as represented in the articles published in the *Journal of Positive Behavior Interventions*.

ABA is a methodology for carefully studying and changing behavior to address serious social problems. It is based on research on operant learning that provides the basic structure of radical behavioral theory (Skinner, 1957). The core terms of the theory of ABA pertain to the relationship between the proximate antecedents and consequences of behavior. Radical behaviorism, the form of behavior analysis that has been most prominent in education and treatment of individuals with developmental disabilities, in BPT, and in school interventions, focuses directly on observable behavior. Changes in the environment are tested experimentally using direct observation of operationalized target behaviors so that what is measured requires very low levels of inference. ABA assumes that all durable behavior is ultimately caused and maintained by the environment rather than intrapsychological variables. It is centered on the assumption that there are identifiable recurrent patterns of environmental variables and of the temporally determined functional relationships within any stream of behavior. Usually, but not always, the environment of concern is the social environment made up of microsocial interactions between the person whose behavior must change and the change agent. ABA assumes that these relationships can be structured according to the basic features of operant learning, and that once a functional relationship between behaviors and their antecedents and consequences is demonstrated, it is possible to predict and control many behaviors of concern. Setting events, establishing operations, discriminative stimuli, positive and negative reinforcement, and punishment are some of the core terms in this theory.

In terms of recent discussions of the philosophy of social science, ABA is firmly rooted in the tradition of objectivist epistemology and realist ontology (Skritic, 1991). That is, it is taken for granted that direct observation of the visible features of behavior is sufficient to create a shared understanding in a community of researchers and practitioners to organize meaningful action to change behavior. The meanings of behavior are not of major concern as they are in fields like cultural anthropology, which focus not only on descriptions of behavior but also what its semantic and symbolic dimensions are in the context of different ways of life and ways of explaining actions (Striker, 1997). Further, ABA takes for granted that there is a real world outside our senses and our language, and that it is knowable at least to the extent that meaningful action can be taken to address important problems.

ABA is a far cry from most forms of postmodernism; to the contrary, it is a quintessential modernist system of thought implemented via technical /rational forms of action and organization for the purpose of predicting and controlling human behavior in the same way that physics and chemistry aim to predict and control the natural world (Graham, 2007; Habermas, 1988). The practice of ABA is replete with the social apparatus of modernism. Those who use it are members of professions with licensures and credentials. Social agreements are written in terms of objectives determined by professionals and validated with quantitative measures of social validity. Efficiency is highly valued and interventions are described as technologies

(Willems, 1974). Behavior analysis hews to a very stringent form of empiricism to determine if there are functional relationships between the characteristics of environmental interventions and their outcomes (Barlow, Hayes, Nelson, 1984). It only counts directly observable, Newtonian properties of behavior as scientific evidence. These characteristics include rate, latency, frequency, duration, and intensity of directly observable behavior. The social construction of the meanings of behavior is not part of a behavioral analysis.

Some of the philosophical roots of ABA can be found in some elements of logical positivism and in earlier forms of empiricism. Its family resemblance to logical positivism can be seen in the requirement in ABA experimental methodology that all variables must be operationalized, and that inferences beyond what is immediately observable are generally distrusted and kept to a bare minimum. Functional relationships between behavior and its consequences are held to be self-evidently true as a result of their definition and are thus privileged and constitute a core theory, operant conditioning. That is, if an event that follows a behavior increases the probability that the organism will enact the behavior again, the event functions as positive reinforcement. Similarly, the core terms of punishment and negative reinforcement are defined in ways that are logically self-evident. Behaviorists assume that these relationships, which make up the core of operant learning theory, are self-evidently true. Radical behaviorism deems these relationships to be so central that they assert that all behaviors are caused by their relationships with environmental conditions functioning as one of the three forms of consequences. Further, these relationships are a part of nature and constitute a kind of natural law in the same way that Newton's theories are held to be natural laws. That is, a basic feature of the behavior of higher organisms is that their behavior exhibits the core relationships between behavior and consequent conditions. Lakatos (1970) maintained that scientific programs have a core theory that remains impervious to most challenges to hypotheses derived from it. The functional relationship of behavior with its consequences is the hard-core theory at the heart of behaviorism. At present, it is also at the core of PBS.

ABA sets the bar high for demonstrating that there is a functional relationship between a specific intervention and desired behavior change (internal validity). It does so by utilizing single-subject research designs with repeated direct observations of behavior and carefully controlled introduction of intervention techniques (Hersen & Barlow, 1976). A successful behavioral intervention requires readily demonstrable behavior change as evaluated with visual analysis of graphed data without recourse to statistical analysis. An important tenet of ABA is that the targets for change are discrete behaviors rather than larger patterns of complex behaviors such as social roles or ways of life.

The philosopher Jurgen Habermas, who has devoted a great deal of his work to revealing the problems of modernism, also argued that we must give modernity its due (Habermas, 1988). Technical/rational social organization and scientific knowledge have worked wonders as well as given rise to horrors. ABA also must be given its due. In some fields, such as special education, it has been so important, and in some cases so effective, that the discipline is almost inconceivable without it. ABA's hard-nosed demand that interventions be clearly specified, microsocial interactions carefully planned and delivered precisely, and the proof of an intervention's effectiveness must be directly observable and countable has given it a pragmatic approach to problems that has sometimes served it and its recipients well. Because of ABA, children with autism can often be taught to talk for the first time in human history (Koegel, Koegel, Shoshan, & McNerny, 1999 (National Research Council, 2001)). Children who were considered unteachable and kept out of public view merely 30 years ago are routinely educated in public schools (Winzer, 1994). Individuals whose aberrant behavior would have caused them to be institutionalized 20 years ago live in their home communities and enjoy access to many of the same benefits of community life as other citizens (Singer, 1986). These are only a few of ABA's achievements.

While behaviorism has had many notable successes, it has also generated its critics. After 40 years, contemporary behaviorism has arguably been largely marginalized in the fields of psychology and general education in many universities, although it has held its own in the fields of special education and early intervention. Objections to behaviorism have focused on concerns about power and its allocation in the behavior change process and on its rejection of mental phenomena as possible causes of behavior. Further objections have been the reduction of complex human phenomena to only a few basic functional relationships, and on ABA's demand for minimal inference in measurement of dependent and independent variables so that many variables commonly believed to be important in psychology do not count as evidence in this tradition: constructs such as self-esteem, self-efficacy, and depression, which all require self-report to measure. It must be said that ABA researchers and practitioners have often remained aloof from other neighboring areas in the social sciences; consequently, the field has been unnecessarily insular. The belief that other fields are based on a delusional understanding of human behavior, mentalism, has led many to reject or simply ignore ways of thought and action from other neighboring disciplines that may have much to offer. Further, the rejection of mental phenomena as possible causes of behavior is difficult to reconcile with a cultural context that emphasizes a strong sense of personal identity and self-determination based on individualized beliefs and feeling.

## PBS AS A BREAKAWAY MOVEMENT FROM ABA BASED ON MORAL OBJECTIONS

One aspect of ABA was divisive to such an extent that a group of prominent behaviorists launched its own academic journal and professional organization. The triggering events that occasioned the break involved behavior analysts promoting and vigorously defending a device that administers automatic electric shock to developmentally disabled individuals (Linscheid, Iwata, Ricketts, Williams, & Griffin, 1990) and helmets, which emit white noise and spray water in the face to punish serious problem behavior of people with autism (Butterfield, 1985). ABA's legitimatization of certain forms of punishment was a cause for moral revulsion for many of the initial researchers and practitioners of PBS. Thus, commonly understood morality was at the center of the formation of PBS. At the same time that prominent behavior analysts were defending and even promoting aversive treatments in segregated institutions, a major social movement was under way aiming to create ways of life that were not barren, overly regimented, and isolating for people with intellectual disabilities. Many of the people who established PBS were active in creating these alternatives and in efforts to close state institutions—again, on the moral grounds that institutionalization denied people the benefits of a normal life and restricted both liberty and access to normal pleasures. The theory of normalization (Nirje, 1994) provided a rationale for bringing people out of large segregated institutions into home communities. It is based on the idea that individuals with intellectual disabilities who have been devalued in society should be allowed to assume socially valued roles in typical community environments. Proponents of normalization developed a whole range of practices aimed at allowing people with developmental disabilities access to more of the pleasures and societal goods available to citizens who are not disadvantaged.

Most of the social innovators who worked to establish early models of normalization were trained in ABA and used its methods in establishing new ways of life for formerly excluded people, particularly individuals with intellectual disabilities who were resettled from institutions to community homes. However, as the normalization effort led to the creation of new ways of supporting people with disabilities in the community, a significant group of researchers and practitioners became disenchanted with ABA. *Supported work* (Wehman, Inge, Revell, & Brooke, 2006) was developed to allow people with intellectual disabilities to work in normal places of employment rather than in centers, which amounted to little more than day care for adults, or in segregated sheltered workshops. New work options have been established, including self-owned businesses and microenterprises. *Supported living* was created for people with developmental disabilities who would otherwise live until middle age in their parent's homes or in institutions. It provides a way to help individuals from this population live in apartments and group homes and, more recently, in owning their own homes. *Family support* was created to help families of children with developmental disabilities succeed in parenting and in creating a desirable quality of life for all family members in their home communities (Singer & Irvin, 1989). Public school inclusion in regular education classrooms was also developed out of a commitment to normalization. It should be acknowledged that ABA methods were often used to test microsocial practices that were essential to creating these support systems. At the same time, these support practices required interventions on larger social units—classrooms, vocational agencies, public schools and districts, neighborhoods, and towns. They also required interventionists to use multiple methods simultaneously. Expansion from microsocial to larger units of analysis also pushed the boundaries of ABA. Both moral and pragmatic considerations led to the establishment of PBS.

Another essentially moral grievance that drove the founding of PBS was the fact that some prominent ABA researchers remained aloof from the normalization movement, instead focusing on the microsocial level of analysis without much concern for the bigger picture. By contrast, many of the researchers who later identified with PBS viewed segregation of children and adults with developmental disabilities as a violation of the moral rule regarding restricting another person's liberty, and they asserted that research should be conducted in community environments rather than in institutions.

The process of moving people with severe developmental disabilities into the community also brought to light some of the limitations of ABA. One of the lessons learned was that institutionalized residents who had severe problem behaviors in the institution behaved much more normally when they were given access to a richer quality of life in the community. It was the access to the community and its complex and rewarding activities, in addition to planned behavior interventions, that contributed greatly to the success of the deinstitutionalization of people with severe cognitive disabilities and severe behavior problems. The standard for measuring success with deinstitutionalization came to be understood in terms of global quality of life.

The people who were the original recipients of PBS interventions were individuals who historically have been denied the common goods and pleasures of community life and who have been the objects of official and unofficial mistreatment. Consequently, in addition to the emphasis on alternatives to aversive treatments in the formation of PBS, the second foundational belief was a commitment to improve the global quality of life of vulnerable people by giving them access to and supporting them in valued social roles.

In summary, PBS was created out of moral concerns as well as an appreciation of the complexity of addressing the context in which microsocial behavior occurred. These two influences have two different philosophical roots.

Two major lines of thought provide useful intellectual tools for connecting the moral imperative in PBS and its concern with quality of life: a justification of the moral rules (Gert, 2005) and pragmatic contextualism (Biglan & Hayes, 1995; Pepper, 1948). One unifying base of PBS is its rejection of practices involving deliberate infliction of pain, restriction of freedom, or deprivation of pleasure carried out on people with aberrant behavior (Horner et al., 1990). Singer et al. (1999) applied Gert's theory of morality to the controversy over aversive procedures. Here, we briefly revisit some of the key features of Gert's (2005) analysis of the moral rules before moving into a discussion of pragmatism and contextualism.

## GERT'S ANALYSIS OF MORALITY

Gert's (2005) explication of common morality remains relevant and can provide important insights into the process of redefining the field of positive behavior support. Gert has devoted his professional life as a philosopher at Dartmouth to explaining common morality in rigorous but plain language accessible to educated people and tightly reasoned so that it holds up to critical scrutiny from other philosophers. Gert's book, *Morality: Its Nature and Justification*, has been in print since 1970 with periodic revisions, a remarkable shelf life for the work of a contemporary living philosopher, a fact that attests its usefulness for understanding morality and for clarifying issues in applied ethics. There are several points in Gert's justification of the moral rules that pertain to the evolution of PBS. Gert (2005) defined morality in this way: "Morality is an informal public system applying to all rational persons and governing behavior that affects others, and includes what are commonly known as the moral rules, ideals, and virtues and has the lessening of evil or harm as its goal" (p. 27).

There is no external foundation to morality as Gert (2005) conceives of it, no grand ethical principle, evolutionary justification, religious belief, or ultimate good. Rather, it is based on the simple precept that anyone who inflicts the acts proscribed by the common moral rules on themselves or others without a good reason is, prima facie, irrational. Conversely, it is always rational to follow these rules. In an era when postmodern philosophers have called into question all forms of foundationalism, Gert's elegant and spare point of origin for explaining the moral rules fits with the tenor of the times. It is also an alternative to ethics based on religion at a time when morality has been distorted in the name of religious fundamentalisms. The first five rules are as follows: do not kill, do not cause pain, do not disable, do not deprive of freedom, and do not deprive of pleasure. These are all acts that one would not want committed on oneself or cherished others and that would be irrational to commit for no good reason. When the concern for others in addition to oneself is taken into consideration, another set of five moral rules necessarily come to light: do not deceive, keep your promises, do not cheat, obey the law, and do your duty. These are unremarkable, as they should be, because they are common to all and are inculcated in most people during childhood and thus taken for granted. One way to test the relationship between the moral rules and rationality is to ask if it would be rational for a person to wake up one morning and announce that for no reason whatsoever he or she was going to break one of the rules. "This morning I will cut off my arm," or "Tonight I will kill a person just because I feel like it."

Adequate reasons to violate a moral rule can transform an act from irrational to rational. In the first case, the same woman might consent to having her arm amputated to prevent the spread of a fatal illness, and in a dire emergency a person might kill a terrorist to prevent innocent people from being killed. The center of major moral controversies is whether there is sufficient justification to warrant violating the moral rules. Gert (2005) provided a set of key questions to help people guide their decision making when they are trying to determine whether there is a good enough reason to violate a moral rule. Gert's system of thought cannot resolve any major moral conflict, but it can offer guidance about the questions that should be asked to determine whether breaking one of the moral rules is justified. Table 2.1 presents the set of questions he recommended.

Singer et al. (1999) applied Gert's (2005) questions to the controversy over the use of aversive procedures. We revisit two points from this analysis. The

**Table 2.1.** Morally Relevant Features of Moral Rule Violations

1. Which moral rule is being violated?
2. A. Which harms are being caused by the violation?
   B. Which harms are being avoided (not being caused) by violating the rules?
   C. What harms are being prevented by the violation?
3. A. What are the relevant desires and beliefs of the person toward whom the rule is being violated?
   B. What are the relevant beliefs of the person toward whom the rule is being violated?
4. Is the relationship between the person violating the rule and the persons toward whom the rule is being violated such that the former sometimes has a duty to violate moral rules with regard to the later independent of their consent?
5. What goods (including kind, degree, probability, duration, and distribution) are being promoted by the violation?
6. Is the rule being violated toward a person in order to prevent her from violating a moral rule when the violation would be (1) unjustified or (2) weakly justified?
7. Is the rule being violated toward a person because he has violated a moral rule unjustifiably or with a weak justification?
8. Are there any alternative actions or policies that would be preferable?
9. Is the violation done intentionally or only knowingly?
10. Is the situation an emergency such that people are not likely to plan to be in that kind of situation?

Note. From B. Gert, 2004, Morality: Its *Nature and Justification*, Oxford, England: Oxford University Press (pp. 59–72).

first concerned the distinction between moral agency and who deserves protection of the moral rules. Punishment for violation of the moral rules is deserved by anyone who understands that breaking these rules causes harm and whose volition is not impaired. People in this category are rightly subject to praise and blame for their behavior. They are deemed to be subject to obeying the law and to be sanctioned for not doing so. Children and some people with severe intellectual disabilities are generally not considered to be moral agents because they may not understand the harm caused by breaking a moral rule, or they may not have sufficient volitional control to be able to stop breaking a moral rule. Most people believe that a moral society should not subject children and people with mental impairments to judicially sanctioned punishment such as a jail sentence. The question of whether people with mental retardation are subject to the death penalty was recently taken up by the Supreme Court, which decided capital punishment for this group constitutes cruel and unusual punishment (*Atkins v. Virginia*, 2002).

People do not have to be moral agents to be protected by the moral rules. Children, people with intellectual disabilities, and people with mental illness are not moral agents, but they are protected by the moral rules. We commonly hold it to be a sign of a civilized society that such individuals are fully protected from normal punishment for breaking the moral rules and are protected from harm by the moral rules. People who are not moral agents but who deserve the protection of the moral rules historically have been highly vulnerable to mistreatment. Their protection from the moral rules is fragile and needs to be carefully safeguarded. We argued that extra vigilance was needed to protect people with severe disabilities, and that the use of aversive procedures risked dehumanizing them, a fate they have suffered many times in the history of Western civilization (Winzer, 1994).

A second key question was whether there were alternatives available to inflicting pain and restricting liberty, particularly in regard to people with developmental disabilities. Proponents of aversive methods asserted that these were necessary to prevent greater harm and were the most effective option available for treating some people with developmental disabilities (Gerhardt, Holmes, Alessandri, & Goodman, 1991). Those who subsequently became disenchanted with ABA maintained that many years of research on positive alternatives to aversive treatments had yielded effective treatments that did not necessitate the breaking of the moral rules regarding infliction of pain and deprivation of freedom (Carr et al., 1999). In addition, these researchers had also worked out new ways to enhance positive interventions through functional assessment procedures (O'Neill et al., 1997) and new ways to prevent or replace problem behavior with communication skills (Carr & Durand, 1985); choice making (Dyer, Dunlap, & Winterling, 1990); and teaching of key social skills (Koegel & Frea, 1993). Further, new ways were validated for preventing problem behavior with antecedent interventions (Horner, Vaughn, Day, & Ard, 2002; Singer, Singer, & Horner, 1987). These researchers and practitioners believed there were no good reasons for using aversive treatments given the availability of effective positive alternatives (Guess, Helmstetter, Turnbull, & Knowlton, 1986; Meyer & Evans, 1985). The center of the controversy then was the claim that there were effective positive procedures, which accomplished the same ends as aversive procedures but without inflicting pain or deprivation of freedom and pleasure (Evans & Meyer, 1985; Koegel, Koegel, & Dunlap, 2002). This was an empirical argument; for social scientists, a key feature of Gert's (2005) thought is his assertion that data are always relevant in moral decision making. Evidence about the consequences of one's actions, while not the only relevant feature, is always relevant in making ethical decisions, and this evidence is never trumped by reference to any absolutist position concerning morality, rights, or values. Thus, actual moral disagreements will often be a matter of differential weighing of evidence, but never one in which the evidence about consequences of one's moral decisions are irrelevant.

## PROTECTION OF THE MORAL RULES: FUNCTIONAL ANALYSIS AND ABERRANT BEHAVIOR

Individuals with developmental disabilities are at high risk of developing serious problem behavior. Serious problem behavior involves some of the key harms, which the moral rules are meant to prohibit and prevent. Normally, when moral agents harm other people without justifiable reasons, they are subject to legal punishment, and they are considered deserving of blame and censure. They often make other people angry, and they place themselves at risk by violating the moral rules. Anger and the desire for retribution at moral agents who violate the moral rules is a common reaction that is often considered understandable (Vidmar, 2002). When people who are not moral agents commit harms, the societal response is more complicated. A person who does not understand that it is wrong to harm oneself or others without justification should rightfully not be subject to the same kind of blame and punishment. This point, unfortunately, is often misunderstood, and people with mental retardation and severe mental illness are still arrested, jailed, and not provided with treatment. The root of the misunderstanding is the mistaken idea that the same harmful behavior deserves the same punishment whether or not the person who committed the harm has volitional control and understands that others do not want to be harmed. This misunderstanding can arise with strong feelings of anger and a desire to exact retribution. Violent children, aggressive individuals with intellectual disabilities, and people with severe mental illness are often subjected to others' anger and are vulnerable to acts of retribution or revenge. The protection of the moral rules is fragile, and people with these conditions have often been dehumanized (Mostert, 2002; Winzer & O'Connor, 1982).

People who commit harmful behaviors that seem bizarre and inexplicable are frightening. It is difficult for many people to empathize with them. One of the important contributions to more humane treatment of people with intellectual disabilities with serious problem behavior is the practice of functional behavioral assessment (FBA). Working out the details of FBA and promoting its use was central to the development of PBS (Horner & Carr, 1997). FBA centers on establishing a clear understanding of how aberrant behaviors function for the person who enacts them. Here, the basic operant relationships between a behavior and its consequences are indispensable to understanding the reason for otherwise inexplicable harmful acts. Careful observation, interviews with those who know the offending person well, and when feasible, conversations with the offender lead to a hypothesis about how otherwise inexplicable behavior is elicited and maintained. From the point of view of the observer, understanding the functional relationship between problem behavior and its consequences does not make the agent moral or render his or her behavior rational, but it does make it understandable. With a measure of understanding, the possibility of empathy and recognition of fellow humanity of people who otherwise seem threateningly strange is more likely. Functional assessments often lead to understanding the potential of teaching communication skills, which can let the person with aberrant behavior obtain the same result without harm (Reichle & Johnston, 1993). An important feature of PBS functional assessment, which may differentiate it from its ABA roots, is the clear recognition of the importance of understanding the cultural context and meanings associated with problem behavior as well as its functional relationships with antecedent and subsequent conditions (Wang, McCart, & Turnbull, 2007).

PBS provides practices and a professional culture that may be particularly well suited to providing help to vulnerable groups of people who are the victims of mistreatment or at risk of it. PBS cut its teeth by providing positive alternatives for the treatment of people who may not be moral agents but who are all the more vulnerable to mistreatment in the name of social control. The urge to punish such people appears to be a strong one as can be seen in the histories of mistreatment of people with intellectual disabilities, children of color who violate the moral rules in the United States, and people with severe mental illness who are jailed rather than provided treatment.

## PREVENTION AND THE MORAL IDEALS

Recent reformulations of PBS emphasize that reducing and replacing problem behavior is now a secondary concern, and improving quality of life is primary. Gert's (2005) analysis of the moral rules and ideals can be useful in providing a rationale for this larger goal. The justification for focusing PBS on quality of life comes out of the fact that a good quality of life is currently not available to many vulnerable people in our society. These groups are obstructed in living normal lives and enjoying the common benefits of our society. Thus, PBS is, in part, a system of empirically validated strategies for assisting vulnerable people who have been the victims of unjustified violations of the moral rules to obtain the benefits of society available to most people. The relationship between a desirable quality of life and the history of denial of access to it is important in explaining why PBS centers on the ambitious goal of improving major elements of quality of life for the people it serves.

Gert's (2005) discussion of the moral ideals offers a useful tool for thinking through the rationale for PBS to aim at actively improving lives. The moral rules involve injunctions against various forms of harm. They are mostly concerned with not committing certain acts. But a good life for most people consists of more than just not being immoral. It includes active efforts to do what is good in addition to doing no harm. The moral ideals that are intended to guide positive efforts to do what is good are aimed not only at ceasing or refraining from unjustified violations of the moral rules but also at preventing these harms from happening. A physician not only treats a child for a broken arm but also inoculates the child against tetanus to prevent future harms. A practitioner of PBS not only stops a child's aggressive acts but also teaches the child skills that will make these harms unnecessary in the future. One way to do so is by identifying what communicative intent can accurately be attributed to a problem behavior. By determining the function of problem behaviors, it is often possible to replace them with communication. Part of what provided PBS practitioners with the confidence that they can deal with severe problem behaviors without recourse to inflicting pain on vulnerable individuals was the working out of new antecedent treatment procedures, such as functional communication training (FCT).

PBS researchers and practitioners have been open to finding antecedents that have previously been obscured by the conceptual restrictions of radical behaviorism. McLaughlin & Carr (2005) documented the power of the quality of the rapport between staff members and individuals with intellectual disabilities as a predictor of problem behavior. Their research also provides relatively simple and straightforward procedures for creating positive rapport. Park, Singer, and Gibson (2005) demonstrated that special education teachers' affective expression when giving instruction influenced students' responding, and that they responded differentially so that enthusiastic expression and voice tones were helpful in improving some students' performance but served as antecedents to problem behaviors of another.

PBS includes other antecedent interventions, including offering choice of tasks and rewards to individuals with disabilities as ways to prevent problem behavior. These involve ways to arrange the environment and microsocial interactions to elicit communication from individuals who otherwise do not initiate speech acts. When taken together, the antecedent assessment and intervention methods of PBS practices amount to a major effort to prevent the occurrence of problem behavior and thereby render punishment and other weakly justified violations of the moral rules unnecessary.

## GROUNDING SUPPORT IN THE MORAL IDEALS

PBS has increasingly come to focus on promoting quality of life in its various dimensions. A question that arises in promoting an enhanced quality of life for people who have been, or are vulnerable to, unnecessary suffering is how far one should go in trying to enhance others' lives. A focus on the moral ideals is informative in thinking about the boundaries of enhancing others' lives. Should every person with an intellectual disability and that person's family live like a king, or is it sufficient to give them access to Burger King? This kind of question arises in cash benefit programs for families of children with developmental disabilities. A real example may help to clarify this point. The question of what constitutes a legitimate use of public funds under conditions of economic scarcity is ever present, particularly as agencies try to break out of the mold of offering only traditional therapeutic services. In the early 1990s, a new family support program in a city in the Pacific Northwest used a form of person-centered planning and flexible funding for providing family support to families of children with developmental disabilities. In keeping with the philosophy of encouraging self-determination, the government-funded agency providing the services agreed to a parent's request to pay for the cost of installing padding in the family's small fishing boat so that their child with cerebral palsy could be positioned comfortably and be able to participate in fishing with his father.

Word of this decision found its way onto the front page of the city's main newspaper and provoked complaints about what was assumed to be wasteful use of public funds. The incident was presented in the paper without a clear explanation of the fact that the child had been excluded from leisure activities the family valued, and that the family's leisure life had been unusually restricted because of caregiving demands. The family support program did not try to present its case and folded under public pressure perhaps, in part, because the people who ran the program were not clear in their own minds about what was and was not a legitimate cost. They might have been better able to defend their decision if it was explicitly linked to prevention of deprivation of access to normal pleasant family activities and deprivation of normal freedom. Purchasing boat padding to prevent isolation and give access to participation in family life would be readily understandable (DeBord, 2005).

## WHAT MORAL IDEALS SHOULD CHARACTERIZE PBS?

What are reasonable ideals for the field of PBS? What should the boundaries be? It is easy to imagine a self-definition that would be too narrow, such as a sole focus on preventing the use of electric shock as a treatment, or one that is too broad, such as improving the quality of life for all worldwide. One way to think about this question is to imagine writing a code of professional ethics for the Association for Positive Behavior Support. Gert (2005) provided an analysis of codes of ethics for the helping professions. He pointed out that they inevitably include proscribing the harms that are covered by the moral rules. Again, this is to be expected given that the moral rules address common beliefs shared by all rational people. Many professional ethics begin with a statement like, "First do no harm." They then include directions to avoid inflicting harms that are particularly relevant to a given profession. In addition to these negative prohibitions, professional codes of ethics also enjoin members of the profession to act on certain moral ideals. For example, the professional ethics of the Council for Exceptional Children (CEC; 1993) includes the following proscription against breaking the moral rules: "Special education professionals do not condone or participate in unethical or illegal acts, nor violate professional standards adopted by the Delegate Assembly of CEC" (p. 4).

After dispensing with violations of the moral rules with this statement, the code expresses positive ideals in the form of seven statements of benefits to be actively promoted by special educators. One of these ideals, for example, reads: "Special education professionals are committed to developing the highest educational and quality of life potential of individuals with exceptionalities" (CEC, 1993, p. 4). It will be necessary to identify which moral ideals are most relevant for practitioners of PBS and to link them to statements of the aspirations that characterize the field.

PBS necessarily will need to delineate the limits of what it does and to what it aspires. For example, a member is unlikely to attend a future APBS conference to learn about the slow-cooking movement for improving the cuisine in middle-class families. But, one might expect to attend a presentation of a new method for teaching and updating cooking skills for people with developmental disabilities living on their own or acquiring the skills so they can live independently. The distinction is the relationship between the ideal of improving quality of life and the harms that are either now being inflicted on vulnerable people or that could be if attitudes and social norms do not change. Middle-class people are usually not required to live in places where they have no choice about what they eat or how it is cooked, but many people with disabilities are living lives with such restrictions on freedom of choice and access to normal pleasure (Wehmeyer & Metzler, 1994).

## PREVENTING RESTRICTIONS OF FREEDOM BY TEACHING SELF-DETERMINATION

One of the major ways that individuals with disabilities suffer from restriction of liberty derives from the ways social service systems operate. Most human services in the United States, including public schools, offer a highly restricted range of services for people with disabilities. Although the planning and delivery of services is meant to be individualized and stated in the form of individualized educational or service plans, in fact the choices are often severely limited. For adults, these professional-dominated planning meetings, which offer a highly restricted menu of options, makes a mockery of the idea that a person is freely designing the support they require to live as they prefer.

Developmentally disabled children, for example, are provided with individualized educational plans (IEPs) by federal law. The choice of full inclusion with special education services provided in the general education classroom is not a real option in many districts because of the weight of tradition, entrenched routines, restricted expectations, and a lack of knowledge about how to accomplish it (Cook, Semmel, & Gerber, 1999). Similarly, many adults with disabilities depend on the restricted range of choices available from a specific social service. For example, personal assistance services may only be available for a few hours a day at times that are determined by the service agency's scheduling rather than the recipient's needs and preferences. Adults with physical disabilities have complained of not being able to take a bath or eat a meal until 3:00 in the afternoon, the only time a personal assistant is available (Doty, Kasper, & Litvak, 1996).

Because of their dependence on highly constrained public and private social service agencies for many necessities, individuals with developmental disabilities are often provided with very limited choices about where they work, what they eat, who they recreate with, and where they can travel. In the last two decades, special educators have been sensitized to the possibility that they teach students with disabilities in ways that prepare them for a life in which personal choice is largely unavailable. Often, students with disabilities have not been encouraged to set their own goals, negotiate their own plans, and experience the consequences of their own decisions. The self-determination movement aims to right these historic wrongs. The list of practices that are meant to be part of PBS includes self-determination. This is a prime example of aiming to undo historic wrongs and prevent future ones by educating individuals so they have the skills to pursue their own goals. A key component of such prevention requires a change in the typical power relationships between professionals and the recipients of their services.

## PBS AND ABUSES OF PROFESSIONAL POWER

In addition to rejecting certain forms of treatment and aiming to promote moral ideals in helping people at risk of exclusion from the protection of the moral rules, PBS has also demonstrated a movement toward a different model of relationships between professionals and its recipients. Professions gain their power in society by laying claim to technical knowledge and then establishing the social apparatus of the professions, including credentialing, professional associations, peer-reviewed journals, delineation of what counts as relevant knowledge, the creation of domain-specific vocabularies inaccessible to the uninitiated, and an objectivist knowledge base. Professions are a key feature of late modernism with its faith in objectivism, bureaucratic forms of organization, and allocation of high status to experts. Medicine and engineering are fields that exemplify modernist professionalism. Critics of this model of professionalism have long decried the way power accrues to the professions and to the bureaucracies housing them (Foucault, 1977).

Foucault (1977) analyzed the way that power both permeated professional-client relationships and was hidden. Power is often implicit rather than explicit. Clients do not bow to dentists, psychologists, or behaviorists and kiss their feet, but they do readily go along with editing what they say to these professionals to speak in the language that is allowable in each professional domain. Mishler (1984) documented the way that physicians effectively edited and silenced their patients through the ways in which they conduct interviews with patients to produce a diagnosis. By studying transcripts of physician-patient interactions in doctors' offices, he found that much of what patients say to physicians is ignored. Patients' stories of how they got ill and the impact of the sickness on their emotions and life circumstances was of much less interest than descriptions of the symptoms that might be clues to the kind of illness the patient experienced. Rather than respond to the narrative elements of patients' stories in the way that people in friendly informal contexts talk to each other, the physician reveals nothing about himself or herself and closes down discussion of material that he or she deems irrelevant to making a diagnosis. This editing is accomplished by responding to patients' statements with closed-ended questions designed to steer the patients' talk in the direction of describing bodily signs of illness. A problem with this approach is that it is often critical information that would help the physician with the diagnosis or help the physician to promote compliance with a treatment regimen.

Professional dominance often characterizes an IEP meeting. Professional "power over" is manifested in the way the parent is outnumbered by several professionals and their apparent united front in responding to parental requests and criticisms (Harry, Allen, & McLaughlin, 1995). Studies of IEP meetings showed that professionals do most of the talking, and the topics under discussion are determined by them (Turnbull & Turnbull, 2001). In these direct observation studies, parents were mostly silent, passive, and urged to ratify educational plans that were usually written prior to the meeting, thus making a mockery of the mandate in the Individuals With Disabilities Education Act (IDEA) that parents are equal members of the IEP teams in planning their children's education. The language of goals and objectives as well as discipline-specific jargon further disadvantage parents who are not informed about its meanings. According to Harry et al., school professionals simultaneously behaved with unusual politeness and expressions of concern while unanimously rejecting parents' observations, criticisms, and requests. They characterized this kind of interaction as the parent-professional power differential masked as kindness.

Given that interactions between professionals and their clients are often marked by inequity in power, is there any reason to believe that this problem will be lessened in PBS practices? Recent formulations of PBS include an emphasis on establishing partnerships between professionals and the people who are the recipients of their services and, whenever possible, having the individuals with problematic behavior participate in the planning of their treatment. The most recent account of PBS (Carr et al., 2002) lists professional-client partnerships as one of its distinguishing characteristics. Blue-Banning, Summers, Frankland, Nelson, and Beegle (2004), using focus groups, identified the attitudes and behaviors that parents report as most conducive to establishing trusting partnerships with human service professionals. These include being nonjudgmental, listening to, being courteous, being honest, being open, communicating positively, being reliable, being willing to explore all options, fostering harmony among partners, being flexible, being easily accessible, being consistent, and being sensitive to the family's needs and emotions. When professionals act in these ways, the relationship is much less hierarchical than in the traditional expert-client model.

These partnerships also need to be established with the recipients of PBS whenever possible. In ABA, the views of the participant are often collected after the intervention in the form of social validity measures (Risley, 2005; Wolf, 1978) to elicit clients' evaluation of treatment acceptability and effectiveness. PBS has expanded its approach to social validity. Recent discourse within the emerging field of PBS concerns the lack of voice and participation of stakeholders in the process of planning and implementing behavioral interventions. PBS uses humanistic values to inform empiricism and suggests that certain behaviors are worth changing from the viewpoint of the "consumer" of professional practice rather than exclusively from the viewpoint of the service providers (Sailor & James, 2004).

## FUNCTIONAL CONTEXTUALISM

The philosopher Steven Pepper (1948) described major meta-theories in philosophy and what counted as evidence in each of them. These included mysticism, organicism, mechanism, and contextualism. He believed that each worldview has a different set of truth criteria—ways of warranting claims. In contextualism, the primary truth criterion is *successful working.* Pepper was strongly influenced by American pragmatists, who held that the value of an idea or endeavor should be evaluated based upon the degree to which it effectively helps to solve specific problems. For the pragmatist

John Dewey (1916/1997), an idea was valid to the extent that it was practically useful for addressing the public problems of a democracy.

When contextualism is used as the root metaphor for social science and social action, it directs attention to those variables in the environment that function as the most proximate causes of the social phenomena of interest. PBS and ABA are paradigmatic examples of functional contextualism. In accounting for individual behavior, the behavior analyst as a functional contextualist aims to identify those aspects of the surrounding ecology that, if manipulated, can be used to change it for the good of society (Dunlap, 2006). PBS shares this orientation with other applied social science disciplines, including public health, applied anthropology, microeconomics, public administration, social work, ecological psychology, community psychology, and special education, to name a few. PBS differs from these other disciplines to the extent that it adheres to the behaviorist's premise that the flow of ongoing behavior can be segmented and organized into functional relationships derived from the study of operant learning. It inevitably focuses on the rewards and sanctions at each ecological level when these concepts apply. Setting events, establishing operations, and discriminative stimuli—those segments of the flow of behavior that precede it—are defined according to their relationship with consequent events. These functional relationship are a sine qua non of ABA and are assumed as fundamental in PBS. A key question for the future of PBS is the extent to which it will continue to adhere to the basic operant template as a core theory.

One of the dominant contextual theories in the field of developmental psychology and one that is widely cited in special education is Bronfenbrenner's (1986) social-ecological model. His theory is often presented in a graphic that looks like a target—a series of concentric circles, which progress from a small inner circle to progressively larger circles. The innermost circle, the microsystem, is where key face-to-face interactions take place. In homes, the microsystem of concern is usually parent-child interactions. In schools, it is the way teachers and students interact during instruction and in enforcing school rules. In residential programs, it is often the interactions of people served by supported living programs and their staff members. One of the great strengths of the behavioral tradition is its insistence on working out very carefully a description of what a change agent needs to do to effectively teach new behaviors and maintain them. A great deal of the research in ABA and PBS is devoted to determining whether specific microsocial routines are effective in creating desirable behavior change.

In regard to the microsystem, PBS has wisely adhered to the ways of thinking and methods derived from ABA, which give it a methodology and theoretical framework for working out the details of ways to improve key interactions. In clinical and highly controlled model demonstration settings or under the "hothouse" conditions of a graduate student's doctoral research, it is relatively easy to achieve desired behavior change by implementing highly specified procedures. When behavioral methods have been injected into complex organizations, including schools, families, and places of employment, it has often been necessary to work out ways to intervene at the organizational level to support the acquisition and maintenance of the intervention procedures (Sugai et al., 2000). In turn, complex human service organizations also exist in an ecology that, among other key variables, includes operative social policy and law, funding, availability of personnel and necessary expertise, community values, and broad historical events such as immigration patterns.

In its short history, PBS has targeted several of these organizational and surrounding ecological variables to facilitate implementation of PBS in public schools (Crone & Horner, 2003). To change the behavior of students, PBS interventionists provide training to teachers in how to implement the procedures and to administrators who are responsible for creating and maintaining schoolwide intervention teams and for setting up and consistently using outcomes-based feedback (Horner et al., 2004). Horner and colleagues recognized the necessity of measuring changes at the whole school level in indicators that are broader than the microsocial level, and their schoolwide PBS model includes a data system for monitoring office referrals and special education placements as outcome indicators. These are organizational-level indices of student behavior change. Further, they have developed a formative evaluation measure that measures the extent to which key schoolwide PBS model components are established within a school and a district. This measure tops organizational variables such as leadership and personnel training as well as the school districts' practices in regard to the target school. In moving from direct observation of individuals' behaviors to measuring indices of organizational change, they have adopted evaluation methodologies from the psychometric tradition. The schoolwide developers recognized that different targets of intervention require different units of analysis larger than individual behaviors, and measurement of these larger units requires resorting to a different approach to measurement. PBS practitioners further moved into the policy and legal ecology of public schools by influencing Congress to change the federal special education law, the IDEA, so that school systems are legally required to adopt and implement PBS procedures to meet the needs of students served in special education who have behavior problems. When analyzing this level of intervention, PBS advocates have drawn from the fields of legal and policy analysis (Turnbull, Wilcox, Stowe, & Turnbull, 2001.

Behaviorists and PBS practitioners have necessarily moved into the larger social contexts surrounding the microsystems of concern. This move into increasingly larger social entities has brought to light some key issues about the limitations of traditional ABA and raised questions of whether PBS should adhere to its core theory and methods when it moves into working with larger social units such as whole schools, neighborhoods, communities, states, and the nation. It would be unwise to dismiss the considerable knowledge that has been built up over decades in social sciences that specifically study these entities.

The logic of moving into the context surrounding microsocial interventions can be readily seen in the development of parent training over the past three decades. BPT is one of the most thoroughly studied approaches to helping parents with the problematic behaviors and skill deficits of their children with and without disabilities. Reviews of the literature have consistently attested to its effectiveness, but only when parents participate in learning the procedures, implement them correctly, and maintain the implementation over sufficient time (Singer, Goldberg-Hamblin, Peckham-Hardin, Barry, & Santarelli, 2002). BPT is a contextual intervention in that it addresses parent-child interactions and parental structuring of home environments as the proximal cause of children's problem behavior. The techniques taught in BPT have each been thoroughly evaluated in well-designed research over a 40-year period (Kazdin, 1997). It has proven to be effective with children without disabilities with a variety of behavior problems, including anxiety and aggressive behavior associated with conduct disorder. It has been similarly effective in helping parents improve the misbehavior and skill deficits of children with intellectual disabilities and autism. Its impressive evidentiary base suggests that it should be the treatment of choice for many very common developmental problems. However, the caveat that parents must participate in training, implement the BPT procedures with fidelity, and maintain the use of the procedures over time is momentous.

Research clearly indicates that a large percentage of parents who could benefit from BPT do not respond to invitations and advertisements to undergo training. When parents do enter into training, rates of attrition are substantial. Further, of parents who do attend BPT training programs, only a minority learn the positive parenting skills to the level of competence required for implementation with fidelity. Researchers have identified subgroups of parents who are dealing with contextual factors that impede acquisition and implementation of BPT. These include maternal depression, parental physical illness, marital discord, poverty, and social isolation. Further, BPT in the absence of cultural accommodations can be ineffective for parents from minority cultures in the United States (Singer et al., 2002).

In response to these concerns, several researchers have developed cultural accommodations and adjunctive treatments designed to overcome the barriers to acquisition and implementation of BPT. These include treatment for depression, stress management training, marriage counseling or therapy, and instruction in problem-solving skills. When combined with traditional BPT, these additions have boosted its uptake and application significantly. There have also been some notable successes in serving low-income parents who live in impoverished neighborhoods. Webster-Stratton, Reid, and Hammond (2001) reported on ways to greatly enhance the effectiveness of a behavioral/developmental parent training package for low-income and ethnic minority parents of young children with externalizing behavior problems. They attended carefully to several contextual variables to expand the numbers of parents who availed themselves of the training, learned the skills, and implemented them effectively. The parent training was carried out in the neighborhoods close to parents' places of residence by trained parents of the same ethnicity as the participants. In a paradigmatic example of contextualism, they argued that parent training for people under the stresses of poverty and discrimination needs to include community building. Thus, ABA practitioners have moved into work on increasingly larger social units.

## PBS AND CONTEXTUAL FIT

A way in which PBS is moving past its ABA origins in moving into the larger context surrounding microsocial interventions is its growing emphasis on contextual fit. Lucyshyn, Dunlap, and Albin (2002), in their work on parent training, emphasized the need to adapt to parents' values, schedules, and routines to be successful in teaching them how to implement PBS interventions. A study by Moes and Frea (2002) demonstrated the importance of establishing contextual fit and specified how it was achieved. They worked in home environments with the families of three young children with autism. After conducting a FBA, they taught parents how to teach the children communication skills to replace problem behaviors. FCT was first taught in the context of one family caregiving routine, and generalization probes were collected in other caregiving interactions. Once the FCT practices were in place, they interviewed parents about their daily routines, family interactions during them, and the meanings the parents assigned to these routines. Parents in one family reported that they were not using the same disciplinary procedures with siblings, and this was a source of stress. Moes and Frea then worked with the parents to come to an agreement about how they would deal with the brothers and sisters. One family's parents stressed the importance they placed on family togetherness during dinner and their frustration at needing to attend to the child with autism to the exclusion of the other children and each other. To help with this problem, a trained respite care provider began to care for the child with autism during dinner. In each of the families, the therapists prompted spouses to provide encouragement and emotional support to their partners. When these and other contextual interventions were added to FCT, problem behaviors were reduced to zero, and mothers rated the interventions as more sustainable than FCT alone. Qualitative interviews were used to identify and address contextual problems and to record the social support goals parents chose in collaboration with the therapists. It will be important to replicate this study with families from diverse ethnic groups in an increasingly multicultural United States.

## CONTEXTUAL FIT AND CULTURAL DIFFERENCES

It is impossible to address the needs of families in the contemporary United States without taking into account demographic changes in the ethnic makeup in the nation. From a functional contextualist point of view, ABA and PBS involve the assumption that behavior is defined and understood in a context. Culture, as an indispensable ecological context of human development, has a profound impact on human behavior (Kalyanpur & Harry, 1999; Lynch & Hanson, 2004). In a society like the United States, composed of people who have different cultural heritages and live in diverse cultures defined by shared ethnicity, language, and religion or by any other specific social identity, people determine a particular behavior as appropriate or inappropriate or even problematic on the basis of specific cultural values and beliefs as well as certain circumstances in which the behavior occurs. Therefore, some behaviors viewed by most professionals from the mainstream culture as unconventional or problematic might not be unacceptable or troublesome to individuals and families of diverse cultures and vice versa.

However, there is a long history and tradition of behaviorism prior to PBS in negating cultural context as a necessary component of behavior definition and behavioral analysis in conformity to the objectivist rules of inquiry. In defining a particular behavior, behaviorism requires an operational definition of behavior, which entails a clear typography of behavior as well as other behavioral dimensions such as frequency and duration to make it as observable and measurable. It is believed that such a definition of behavior is objective by nature and can provide a good basis for empirical inquiry as well as a measurable target for behavioral interventions toward the change of behavior.

Maybe to the surprise of those people who believe this is the only scientific way of defining and understanding a behavior, this "culture-blind" description of behavior is often not adequate for effective intervention. A behavior with the same topography acted out by people from different cultures may be viewed the same visually but interpreted differently in the specific cultural context for different cultures assign different meanings to it. For instance, nodding is a common gesture used on many occasions by people in the United States to indicate "Yes." Interestingly, it turns out to indicate an opposite meaning of "No" in other cultures/countries like Bulgaria and Greece.

The issue of defining a behavior without taking into account its existing cultural context becomes even more problematic when educators come to determine a student's behavior as deviant and maladaptive for the purpose of identifying emotional and behavioral disorder. The fact that there is a disproportionate representation of African and Hispanic students in special education, especially under the category of emotional and behavioral disorders, well illustrates the matter. According to the U.S. Department of Education (2003), African American, Hispanic, and Native American students tend to be overrepresented in programs for students with emotional disturbance. In particular, African American children and youth, who represent 17% of the school-age population, account for 27.3% of students in programs for emotional/behavioral disorders (McCray, Webb-Johnson, & Neal, 2003).

In part, disproportionate placement of African American teenagers in special education may be based on a culturally biased diagnostic system developed and used by professionals with their culturally bound norms that are not appropriate and sensitive to the population being assessed. A classification system centered on symptom-based diagnostic criteria under the assumption of scientific rigor from a positivist point of view can be maladaptive for it does not address the cultural context of individuals being assessed.

Determining the exact nature of an emotional or behavioral disorder is inherently a subjective judgment, influenced by people's perceptions of human behavior in the context of acceptable social-cultural norms and values (Meyen & Bui, 2006). The multitude of factors affecting people's judgments about the existence of emotional or behavioral disorder further complicates the identification process. Coleman and Webber (2002) pointed out that, along with the sociological parameters of behavior, people's tolerance for problem behavior to some extent reflects their cultural understanding of behavior.

FBA is mandated by law to be used in the process of identification of problem behaviors (Individuals With Disabilities Education Act Amendments, 1997). FBA derives from the assessment approach of ABA, which attempts to discover functional relationships between behavior and its existing environments. PBS has expanded this form of assessment to become a more comprehensive approach that includes not only multiple sources of data but also multiple perspectives of individuals who are regularly involved in the life of a person of concern for his or her behavior issues. Such a shift in the focus of method of assessment may reflect a move toward philosophical pragmatism by PBS founders. Researchers and practitioners involved in PBS may come to understand that there are limitations to the use of FBA tools for individuals and families from diverse cultural backgrounds. Most of the FBA assessment tools designed to assess child behavior quantitatively were developed, standardized, and applied primarily by using data from children of middle- to upper-class European American families

Many of the PBS features reflect values and beliefs embedded in the American mainstream culture that differ from beliefs found in some other cultures. For instance, the feature of FBA-based multicomponent interventions reflect American mainstream cultural values in the following aspects: individualism (e.g., focus on personal choice and needs); change and progress for the future (e.g., predict the occurrence of problem behavior, control and redesign the environment of behavior, and manipulate antecedents and consequences for the change of behavior); time (e.g., efficiency of behavior change and future-oriented prevention); and action and achievement (e.g., reduce or eliminate problem behavior to achieve desirable goals). The feature of PBS centered on promoting richer lifestyle outcomes also represents key American cultural values, such as individualism (e.g., person-centered planning and individualized support systems for better life outcome); change and progress for the future (e.g., focus on the long-term life goals); and work and achievement (e.g., supported employment and independent living) (Wang et al., 2007).

Individuals and families may define comprehensive lifestyle outcomes differently depending on their own cultural values and beliefs. This is also true for contrasting cultural values for viewing other PBS features. It is important for researchers and practitioners in PBS to come to realize the existence of contrasting cultural values and their impact on understanding human behavior and behavioral intervention practices. Especially for those who represent the American mainstream culture, they can easily lose sight of the fact that social behavior norms defined as criteria to help identify maladaptive and problem behaviors are not defined in a cultural vacuum. The reason for the difficulty of understanding may be due to a lack of awareness of people's own cultural values and beliefs as well as a lack of understanding of other cultures. In addressing such a challenge in the process of planning and implementing PBS, researchers have recommended culturally responsive PBS practice (Chen, Downing, & Peckham-Hardin, 2002; Lucyshyn et al., 2002). While implementing culturally responsive PBS practices, professionals need clear awareness of the embedded cultural values of PBS as well as cultural-specific knowledge about the recipients of PBS services. Acknowledgment of the variation of cultural values of families within the same culture will be necessary given the great variability within cultural groups. In addition, professionals must be motivated to engage in a constant process of applying their knowledge and skills as well as engaging simultaneously in new learning (Wang et al., 2007).

The endeavor of building a support system to help an individual overcome his or her problem behavior for better life outcomes is arduous and requires professionals' consistent commitment to inquiry, application, and reflection. The elements recommended for the success of culturally responsive PBS practices reflect a shift of philosophical thinking regarding behavioral interventions.

## PRAGMATISM AND CONTEXTUALISM

The contextualism criterion for warranting claims, the truth criterion, is successful working. We have emphasized the important of making sure that part of what is meant by successful working includes adherence to the moral ideals in choosing problems to address and in the means of dealing with them.

Researchers and practitioners who take seriously the need to establish a contextual fit between their assessment and intervention methods and the ecology of a family or school increasingly encounter the need for new ways of understanding complex environments, particularly in a multicultural context. It has become apparent that some of the strictures imposed by ABA's radical behaviorism need to be loosened to make sense of and operate effectively in increasingly complex environments. Pragmatism offers some guidance in this process of expansion. Often, it is the case that different ways of collecting data and different schools of thought about interventions can be reconciled by concentrating on what is done rather than what is believed. There are incommensurable beliefs and practices, but we believe there are not as many as it seems from the ABA viewpoint.

Sailor and James (2004) discussed the need for the field of PBS to be more open to the input of the people it serves as well as to other ways of understanding the social world. They suggested that a pragmatic stance will not prematurely shut down discussion of other research and practice methodologies. Their notion of pragmatism is heavily influenced by Dewey (1916/1997), with his central concern of using ideas and education to promote key values inherent in a healthy democracy. In our view of pragmatism, we place Gert's (2005) ideas about the common moral rules and ideals as central values rather than democratic virtues. We agree with much that Sailor and James (2004) have to say about opening to a larger discourse. They argued that PBS, whether as an "applied science" (Carr et al., 2002) or a "service delivery system" (Wacker & Berg, 2002), includes the value that researchers and practitioners work collaboratively with their beneficiaries to build up a community of critical inquiry where the democratic ideas of voice, participation, and inclusion are fulfilled and "experts" and "consumers" value and learn from each other in the process of planning and implementing PBS practices. These changes reflect the philosophical perspective of "neopragmatism" or critical pragmatism, which can offer a framework for the continuous improvement of professional practice in which it enables, through the process of critical discourse, professionals and researchers, together with their beneficiaries, to continually evaluate and examine the practical consequences of what they do in terms of desirable social values (Sailor & James, 2004, p. 39).

It will be necessary to enlarge the scope of what is considered meaningful empirical data if PBS is to remain an applied science and take seriously the need to be pragmatic in investigating what works in solving societal problems in ways consistent with the moral ideals. Simply put, it is necessary to understand what anthropologists refer as the "emic" dimension of culture—the subjective dimension in which what behaviors mean is the main focus. These meanings cannot be determined without careful observation and without asking people directly to talk about them. It is no accident that anthropology and sociology developed qualitative methods for gathering empirical evidence in these subjective dimensions. We believe that it will be important for PBS to embrace other methodologies for gaining data and other forms of warranting claims of efficacy in addition to low-inference coding of behaviors and single-subject designs to demonstrate functional relationships. These methods have been well worked out in neighboring social sciences, and increasingly researchers in education have begun to use both quantitative and qualitative data to understand which interventions are needed and their intended and unintended effects.

The PBS research and practitioner community will need to come to some rough consensus about which research methods and data are appropriate to different kinds of questions. ABA has been too restrictive in what counts as data and as sufficient evidence for warranting claims of efficacy. Its distrust of psychometrics and of group comparison research is surely too rigid and will have to be resolved in order to ask questions involving larger units of analysis and cultural differences. Toulmin (2001) argued the need for our sense of what constitutes reason to be broadened and recommended the ways that cases are made in jurisprudential reasoning. The law usually deals with problems after they have occurred, and lawyers and judges need to do the best they can to understand what has happened. As in all legitimate social science disciplines, there are strict rules of evidence. In jurisprudential reasoning, multiple sources of data are combined to build a layered understanding of contested phenomena. Interestingly, this way of establishing the facts of the matter has long been used in social science research in the field of program evaluation (Patton, 1986). Evaluations use multiple methods and multiple sources of data to try to establish both which interventions were implemented and what changed as a consequence. Even when strict experimental control is possible, a much richer understanding of the independent and dependent variables is achieved when layers of different kinds of evidence are used.

Singer, Singer, Hamblin, Denney, and Barry (2007) used this multimethod, multiple perspective approach to evaluate a model for improving family-centered practices in newborn intensive care units (NICUs). They embedded a traditional single-subject design study demonstrating that when nurses learned new ways of caring for premature infants, the infants showed demonstrably fewer signs of stress (Goldberg-Hamblin, 2007). In addition, a nurse trained in qualitative methods made visits to the NICU at 6-month intervals and described the care processes and nurse-family interactions. These data showed changes in nursing practices that went beyond the independent variables. More important, the model demonstration project used ways of creating change that bore little resemblance to ABA interventions. These included interviewing nurses and doctors up front to determine who would be likely allies in a system change project, the creation of a cross-disciplinary steering committee, demonstrations of new care procedures, and training of nurses who had high informal prestige in the unit to model new ways of caring for infants. The intervention included periodic meetings with the lead neonatologist and efforts to change the negative talk about families that characterized morning rounds led by physicians. Interagency coordination was facilitated to more closely link early intervention services to the NICU. Education sessions were established on a regular schedule for parents. In addition, the physicians advocated for changes in hospital policies to expand the visiting hours for parents and to allow siblings to enter the NICU. This kind of multiple-component project had several different targeted outcomes and required different kinds of dependent measures with varying degrees of precision.

The microsocial interactions between nurses and infants were amenable to traditional ABA research methods and did show evidence of a functional relationship between changes in nurses' caregiving practices and behavioral indicators of distress in the premature infants. Many of the changes that were needed in the surrounding context were not amenable to this kind of analysis. These were measured through interviews, researcher-developed questionnaires, and qualitative observations. In its last year, the project began to deal with differences in cultural understandings of practices in the NICU from recent Spanish-speaking immigrant parents. Interview and questionnaire-based measurement methods were used to reveal how these parents made sense of an unfamiliar highly technological environment. A traditional set of beliefs around heat and cold came to light, and it became clear for the first time that some of the practices in the hospital, such as giving mothers ice cubes after the birthing of their infants, were perceived as potentially dangerous. Without using qualitative methods, the researchers would have missed some of the key problems facing the NICU that served many Spanish-speaking parents but had no bilingual nurses on staff.

In sum, we believe that the emerging field of PBS research and practice can best be understood as ethically grounded contextualism. Some of the sacred cows of ABA may need to be sacrificed to answer certain kinds of questions. So long as "what works" is consistent with the moral rules and ideals, we believe that the field will need to further diverge from some of its beginnings in ABA. At the same time, we believe that ABA's strict requirements for determining the efficacy of new microsocial interventions before they are embedded in larger social units should be honored. It will matter a great deal to understand what kinds of questions are best answered with certain kinds of data and of evaluation designs. The need for rigor and for openness to other research traditions will require continuing discussion to arrive at effective approaches to address important social problems while maintaining a commitment to rigorous empiricism.

## REFERENCES

Atkins v. Virginia, 536 U.S. 304 (2002).

Baer, D. M., Wolf, M. M., & Risley, T. R. (1968). Some current dimensions of applied behavior analysis. *Journal of Applied Behavior Analysis, 1*, 91–97.

Baer, D. M., Wolf, M. M., & Risley, T. R. (1987). Some still current dimensions of applied behavior analysis. *Journal of Applied Behavior Analysis, 20*, 313–327.

Barlow, D. H., Hayes, S. C., & Nelson, R. M. (1984). *The scientist practitioner: Research and accountability in clinical and educational settings*. New York: Pergamon.

Biglan, A., & Hayes, S. (1995). Should the behavioral sciences become more pragmatic? The case for functional contextualism in research on human behavior. *Applied and Preventive Psychology, 5*, 47–57.

Blue-Banning M., Summers, J. A., Frankland, H. C., Nelson, L. L., & Beegle, G. (2004). Dimensions of family and professional partnerships: Constructive guidelines for collaboration. *Exceptional Children, 70*, 167–184.

Bronfenbrenner, U. (1986). Ecology of the family as a context for human development: Research perspectives. *Developmental Psychology, 22*, 723–742.

Butterfield, F. (1985, November 19). School's use of physical punishment and therapy is challenged. *New York Times*, p. A20.

Carr, E. G., Dunlap, G., Horner, R. H., Koegel, R. L., Turnbull, A. P., Sailor, W., et al. (2002). Positive behavior support: Evolution of an applied science. *Journal of Positive Behavior Interventions, 4*, 4–16.

Carr, E. G., & Durand, V. M. (1985). Reducing behavior problems through functional communication training. *Journal of Applied Behavior Analysis, 18*, 111–126.

Carr, E. G., Horner, R., Turnbull, A. P., Marquis, J. G., McLaughlin, D. M., McAtee, M. L., et al. (Eds.). (1999). *Positive behavioral support in people with developmental disabilities: A research synthesis*. Washington, DC: American Association on Mental Retardation.

Chen, D., Downing, J. E., & Peckham-Hardin, K. D. (2002). Working with families of diverse cultural and linguistic backgrounds: Considerations for culturally responsive positive behavior support. In J. M. Lucyshyn, G. Dunlap, & R. W. Albin (Eds.), *Family and positive behavioral support: Addressing problem behavior in family contexts* (pp. 133–152). Baltimore: Brookes.

Coleman, M. C., & Webber, J. (2002). *Emotional and behavioral disorders: Theory and practice*. Boston: Allyn & Bacon.

Cook, B. G., Semmel, M. I., & Gerber, M. M.(1999). Attitudes of principals and special education teachers toward the inclusion of students with mild disabilities: Critical differences of opinion. *Remedial and Special Education, 20*, 199–207.

Cooper, J. O., Heron, T. E., & Heward, W. L. (2007). Applied behavior analysis (2nd ed.). Upper Saddle River, NJ: Pearson.

Council for Exceptional Children. (1993). *CEC code of ethics for educators of persons with exceptionalities. CEC policy manual.* Reston, VA: Council for Exceptional Children. Retrieved November 2, 2006, from http://www.cec.sped.org/Content/NavigationMenu/Professional Standards/EthicsPracticeStandards/default.htm

Crone, D. A., & Horner, R. H. (2003). *Building positive behavior support systems in schools: Functional behavioral assessment.* New York: Guildford Press.

Dewey, J. (1997). *Democracy and education: An introduction to the philosophy of education.* New York: Free Press. (Original work published in 1916)

Doty, P., Kasper, J., & Litvak, S. (1996). Consumer-directed models of personal care: Lessons from Medicaid. *Milbank Memorial Fund Quarterly, 74*, 377–409.

Dunlap, G. (2006). The applied behavior analytic heritage of PBS: A dynamic model of action-oriented research. *Journal of Positive Behavior Interventions.* 8(1), 58-60.

Dyer, K., Dunlap, G., & Winterling, V. (1990). Effects of choice making on the serious problem behaviors of students with severe handicaps. *Journal of Applied Behavior Analysis*, 23, 515–524.

Evans, I. M., & Meyer, L. H. (1985). *An educative approach to behavior problems.* Baltimore: Brookes.

Foucault. (1977). *Discipline and punish: The birth of the prison* (A. Sheridan, Trans.). New York: Vintage Books

Gerhardt, P., Holmes, D. L., Alessandri, M., & Goodman, M. (1991). Social policy on the use of aversive interventions: Empirical, ethical, and legal considerations. *Journal of Autism and Developmental Disorders, 21*, 265–277.

Gert, B. (2004). *Common morality: Deciding what to do. New York:* Oxford University Press.

Gert, B. (2005). *Morality: Its nature and justification.* Oxford, England: Oxford University Press.

Goldberg-Hamblin, S., Singer, J., Singer, G.H.S., & Denney, M.K. (2007). Early intervention in neonatal nurseries: The promising practice of developmental care. *Infants & Young Children*, 20(2).

Graham, G. (2007). Behaviorism. In E. N. Zalta (Ed.), *The Stanford encyclopedia of philosophy* (Fall 2007 ed.). Retrieved October 4, 2007, from http://plato.stanford.edu/archives/fall2007/entries/behaviorism/

Guess, D., Helmstetter, E., Turnbull, H. R., & Knowlton, S. (1986). *Use of aversive procedures with persons who are disabled: A historical review and critical analysis.* Seattle, WA: Association for Persons With Severe Handicaps.

Habermas, J. (1988). *On the logic of the social sciences.* Cambridge, MA: MIT Press.

Harry, B., Allen, N., & McLaughlin, M. (1995). Communication versus compliance: African American parents' involvement in special education. *Exceptional Children, 61*, 364–377.

Hersen, M., & Barlow, D. (1976). *Single-case experimental designs: Strategies for studying behavior change.* Oxford, England: Pergamon Press.

Horner, R. H., & Carr, E. G. (1997). Behavioral support for students with severe disabilities: Functional assessment and comprehensive intervention. *Journal of Special Education, 31*, 84–104.

Horner, R. H., Dunlap, G., Koegel, R. L., Carr, E. G., Sailor, W., Anderson, J., et al. (1990). Toward a technology of "nonaversive" behavioral support. *The Journal of the Association for Persons with Severe Handicaps, 15*, 125–132.

Horner, R. H., Todd, A. W., Lewis-Palmer, T., Irvin, L. K., Sugai, G., & Boland, J. B. (2004). The School-Wide Evaluation Tool (SET): A research instrument for assessing school-wide positive behavior support. *Journal of Positive Behavior Interventions, 6*, 3–13.

Horner, R. H., Vaughn, B. J., Day, H. M., & Ard, W. R. (2002). The relationship between setting events and problem behavior: Expanding our understanding of behavioral support. In L. K. Koegel, R. L. Koegel, & G. Dunlap (Eds.), *Positive behavioral support: Including people with difficult behavior in the community* (pp. 381–402). Baltimore: Brookes.

Individuals With Disabilities Education Act Amendments of 1997. 20 U.S.C. 1400.

Kalyanpur, M., & Harry, B. (1999). *Culture in special education: Building reciprocal family-professional relationships.* Baltimore: Brookes.

Kazdin, A. E. (1997). Parent management training: Evidence, outcomes, and issues. *Journal of the American Academy of Child and Adolescent Psychiatry. 36*, 1349–1356.

Koegel, R. L., & Frea, W. D. (1993). Treatment of social behavior in autism through the modification of pivotal social skills. *Journal of Applied Behavior Analysis, 26*, 369–377.

Koegel, L. K., Koegel, R. L., & Dunlap, G. (2002). *Positive behavioral support: Including people with difficult behavior in the community*. Baltimore: Brookes.

Koegel, L. K., Koegel, R. L., Shoshan, Y., & McNerney, E. (1999). Pivotal response intervention II: Preliminary long-term outcomes data. *Journal of the Association for Persons with Severe Handicaps, 24*, 186–198.

Lakatos, 1. (1970). Falsification and the methodology of scientific research programs. In I. Lakatos & A. Musgrave (Eds.), *Criticism and the growth of knowledge* (pp. 91–196), Cambridge, England: Cambridge University Press.

Linscheid, T. R., Iwata, B. A., Ricketts, R. W., Williams, D. E., & Griffin, J. C. (1990). Clinical evaluation of the self-injurious behavior inhibiting system (SIBIS). *Journal of Applied Behavior Analysis, 23*, 53–78.

Lucyshyn, J. M., Dunlap, G., & Albin, R. W. (Eds.). (2002). *Families and positive behavior support: Addressing problem behavior in family contexts*. Baltimore: Brookes.

Lynch, E. W., & Hanson, M. J. (2004). *Developing cross-cultural competence: A guide for working with children and their families* (3rd ed.). Baltimore: Brookes.

McCray, A. D., Webb-Johnson, G., & Neal, L. I. (2003). The disproportionality of African Americans in special education: An enduring threat to equality and opportunity. In C. C. Yeakey & R. D. Henderson (Eds.), *Surmounting all odds: Education, opportunity and society in the new millennium* (pp. 455–485). Greenwich, CT: Information Age.

McLaughlin, D.M. & Carr, E. (2005). Quality of rapport as a setting event for problem behavior: Assessment and intervention. Journal of Positive Behavior Interventions. 7(2), 68-91.

Meyen, E., & Bui, Y. (2006). *Exceptional children in today's schools. What teachers need to know* (4th ed.). Denver: Love.

Meyer, L. H., & Evans, I. M. (1985). *Nonaversive intervention for behavior problems*. Baltimore: Brookes.

Mishler, E. (1984). *The discourse of medicine: The dialectics of medical interviews*. Norwood, NJ: Ablex.

Moes, W. R., & Frea, W. D. (2002). Contextualized behavioral support in early intervention for children with autism and their families. *Journal of Autism and Developmental Disorders, 32*, 519–533.

Mostert, M. (2002). Useless eaters: Disability as a genocidal marker in Nazi Germany. *The Journal of Special Education, 36*, 155–168.

National Research Council, Division of Behavioral and Social Sciences. (2001). *Educating children with autism*. Washington, DC: National Academy Press.

Nirje, B. (1994). The principle of normalization and its human management implications. *SRV-VRS Journal*, 1, 19–23.

O'Neill, R. E., Horner, R. H., Albin, R. W., Sprague, J. R., Storey, K., & Newton, J. S. (1997). *Functional assessment and program development for problem behavior: A practical handbook* (2nd ed.). Pacific Grove, CA: Brooks/Cole.

Park, S., Singer, G. H. S., & Gibson, M. (2005). The functional effect of teacher positive and neutral affect on task performance of students with significant disabilities. *The Journal of Positive Behavior Interventions, 7*, 237–246.

Patton, M. Q. (1986). *Utilization focused evaluation* (2nd ed.). Thousand Oaks, CA: Sage.

Pepper, S. C. (1942). *World hypotheses: A study in evidence*. Berkeley: University of California Press.

Reichle, J., & Johnston, S. S. (1993). Replacing challenging behavior: The role of communication intervention. *Topics in Language Disorders*, 13, 61–76.

Risley, T. (2005). Montrose M. Wolf (1935–2004). *Journal of Applied Behavior Analysis, 38*, 279–287.

Sailor, W., & James, L. P. (2004). Framing positive behavior support in the ongoing discourse concerning the politics of knowledge. *Journal of Positive Behavior Interventions*, 6, 37–49.

Singer, G. H. S. (1986). *Community living: A training home model for young people who experience severely handicapping conditions*. Portland, OR: Ednick Communications.

Singer, G. H. S., Gert, B., & Koegel, R. (1999). A moral framework for analyzing the controversy over aversive behavioral interventions for people with severe mental retardation. *Journal of Positive Behavioral Interventions*, 1, 88–100.

Singer, G. H. S., & Irvin, L. K. (1989). *Support for caregiving families: Enabling positive adaptation to disability*. Baltimore: Brookes.

Singer, G. H. S., Goldberg-Hamblin, S., Peckham-Hardin, K., D., Barry, L., & Santarelli, G. (2002). In J. M. Lucyshyn, G. Dunlap, & R. Albin (Eds.), *Families and positive behavioral support: Addressing problem behavior in family contexts* (pp. 155–183). Baltimore: Brookes.

Singer, G. H., Singer, J., & Horner, R. H. (1987). Using pretest requests to increase the probability of compliance for students with severe with severe disabilities. *Journal of the Association for Persons With Severe Handicaps*. 12, 287–291.

Singer, G. H. S., Singer, J., Hamblin, S., Denney, M., & Barry, L. (2007). Systems change and positive behavior support in the Neonatal Intensive Care Nursery. University of California, Santa Barbara: Manuscript in preparation.

Skinner, B. F. (1957). *Verbal behavior*. New York: Appleton-Century-Crofts.

Skritic, T. (1991). *Behind special education: A critical analysis of professional culture and school organization*. Denver: Love.

Striker, H. (1997), *A history of disability* (W. Sayers, Trans.), Ann Arbor: University of Michigan Press.

Sugai, G., Horner, R. H., Dunlap, G., Hieneman, M., Lewis, T., Neslon, C. M., et al. (2000). Applying positive behavior support and functional behavioral assessment in schools. *Journal of Positive Behavior Interventions*, 2, 131–143.

Toulmin, S. (2001). *Return to reason*, Cambridge MA: Harvard University Press.

Turnbull, A. P., & Turnbull, R. (2001). *Families, professionals, and exceptionality* (4th ed.). Upper Saddle River, NJ: Merrill.

Turnbull, H. R., Wilcox, B. L., Stowe, M., & Turnbull, A P. (2001). IDEA requirements for use of PBS: Guidelines for responsible agencies. *Journal of Positive Behavior Interventions, 3*, 11–18.

Turnbull, H. R., Wilcox, B. L., Turnbull, A. P., Sailor, W., & Wickham, D. (2001). IDEA, Positive behavioral supports, and school safety. *Journal of Law and Education, 30*, 445–503.

U.S. Department of Education. (2003). *To assure the free appropriate public education of all children with disabilities: Twenty-fifth annual report to Congress on the implementation of the Individuals With Disabilities Education Act*. Washington, DC: Author.

Vidmar, N. (2002). Retribution and revenge. In J. Sanders & V. L. Hamilton (Eds.), *Handbook of justice research in law* (pp. 31–63). New York: Springer.

Wacker, D. P., & Berg, W. K. (2002). PBS as a service delivery system. *Journal of Positive Behavior Interventions, 4.1*, 25.

Wang, M., McCart, A., & Turnbull, A. (2007). Implementing positive behavior support with Chinese American families: Enhancing cultural competence. *Journal of Positive Behavioral Interventions, 9*, 38–51.

Webster-Stratton, C., Reid, M.J., & Hammond, M. (2001). Preventing conduct problems, promoting social competence: A parent and teacher training partnership in Head Start. *Journal of Clinical Child Psychology, 30*, 283–302.

Wehman, P., Inge, K. J., Revell, W. G., & Brooke, V. A. (Eds.). (2006). *Real work for real pay: Inclusive employment for people with disabilities*. Baltimore: Brookes.

Wehmeyer, M. L., & Metzler, C. A. (1994). How self-determined are people with mental retardation? The national consumer survey. *Mental Retardation, 33*, 111–119.

Willems, E. P. (1974). Behavioral technology and behavioral ecology. *Journal of Applied Behavior Analysis, 7*, 151–165.

Winzer, M. (1994). *The history of special education: From isolation to integration*. Washington, DC: Gallaudet University Press.

Winzer, M., & O'Connor, A. (1982). Eugenics: The threat of the feeble minded. *Journal of Special Education, 6*, 217–229.

Wolf, M. M. (1978). Social validity: The case for subjective measurement or how applied behavior analysis is finding its heart. *Journal of Applied Behavior Analysis, 11*, 203–214.

# Section II

## Early Childhood, Family, and Community

# 3

# Positive Behavior Support and Early Intervention

## GLEN DUNLAP and LISE FOX

Challenging behaviors of toddlers and preschoolers have begun to occupy a position of conspicuous concern among professionals in the fields of child development, early education, and children's mental health. While this was not the case as recently as one decade ago, it is now understood that concerns regarding challenging behavior are well grounded. For instance, it is abundantly clear that challenging behaviors can interfere with optimal social-emotional and intellectual development, that challenging behaviors that persist beyond early childhood can be increasingly resistant to subsequent intervention, and that the unfavorable sequelae of challenging behaviors can last for long periods of time, even into adulthood. Therefore, recent years have brought considerable attention to efforts to understand challenging behaviors in young children and, especially, to improve efforts of prevention and intervention.

*Challenging behavior* has been defined by Smith and Fox (2003) as "any repeated pattern of behavior, or perception of behavior, that interferes with or is at risk of interfering with optimal learning or engagement in pro-social interactions with peers and adults" (p. 5). This definition positions challenging behavior as a phenomenon that is noteworthy because of the effects it produces on the child's interaction with the environment and, especially, the social environment. Smith and Fox continued by listing some of the behavioral topographies that are commonly categorized as challenging. These include externalizing behaviors such as prolonged tantrums, physical and verbal aggression, property destruction, self-injury, and disruptive motor and vocal responding (such as screaming and persistent echolalia). They may also include internalizing behaviors such as

**GLEN DUNLAP** • University of South Florida
**LISE FOX** • Univeristy of South Florida

noncompliance and severe withdrawal. It should be pointed out that the term *challenging behaviors* is used commonly in the field of early childhood (and in other contexts) and is directly analogous to the term *problem behaviors*, which is more typically adopted when referring to difficulties with older populations.

One reason for the increased attention being paid to young children's challenging behaviors is that research is beginning to reveal the alarming prevalence of such behaviors. For instance, in a frequently cited review of prevalence studies, Campbell (1995) observed that approximately 10–15% of young children have noteworthy behavior problems. Other studies have found that roughly the same rates of children entering kindergarten present with challenging behavior (e.g., West, Denton, & Germino-Hausken, 2000). Using somewhat broader criteria, Lavigne and colleagues (1996) reported that 21% of preschool children were considered to have a diagnosable psychiatric disorder, with 9% having a "severe" disorder of social-emotional development. These prevalence figures are expected to be considerably higher for children with risk factors such as developmental disabilities (Baker, Blacher, Crnic, & Edelbrock, 2002), prenatal exposure to toxic substances (Sood, Delaney-Black, Covington, & Nordstrom, 2001), and exposure to violence (Shahinfar, Fox, & Leavitt, 2000). For instance, Qi and Kaiser (2003) reported increased rates of challenging behaviors with children living in poverty.

Another reason for elevated attention to challenging behaviors is an increased appreciation that the challenging behaviors of young children do not simply fade away but, in many cases, continue to deleteriously impact the child's development and social competence for many years (Arnold et al., 1999; Peth-Pierce, 2000). In addition to data testifying to the stability of challenging behavior over extended periods of time (Kazdin, 1987), there are considerable data indicating that early behavior problems are highly associated with teenage delinquency, gang membership, school dropout, and contact with the adult criminal justice system as adults (Loeber & Farrrington, 1998; Reid, 1993). In a summation of knowledge related to the impact of early-occurring challenging behaviors, Dunlap, Strain et al. (2006) indicated that the costs of persistent challenging behaviors could also include patterns of early and persistent peer rejection, mostly punitive contacts with teachers, unpleasant family interactions, school failure, and an absence of fulfilling community integration (Coie & Dodge, 1998; Kazdin, 1985; Patterson, 1986; Tremblay, 2000; Wehby, Symons, Canale, & Go, 1998).

As a result of this increased awareness, there have been numerous public calls for a greater programmatic emphasis on the social-emotional development of young children as well as concerted efforts to prevent the development of challenging behaviors and to intervene when challenging behaviors already occur (e.g., Knitzer, 2002; Raver, 2002; Shonkoff & Phillips, 2000; U.S. Public Health Service, 2000). For instance, within the past decade, the U.S. Departments of Education and Health and Human Services have funded the first national research and training and technical assistance centers to explicitly address these concerns (e.g., Dunlap, Fox, Smith, & Strain, 2002; Hemmeter & Strain, 2001), and the Administration on Children, Youth, and Families and the National Institute of Mental

Health instituted a new young children's mental health research initiative. These initiatives, along with the work of numerous other advocates and researchers, have led to new conceptual frameworks and practical strategies for addressing challenging behaviors. An important element of much of these recent efforts is positive behavior support.

The purpose of this chapter is to describe the use of positive behavior support (PBS) to address the challenging behaviors of young children. We begin with a discussion of the relevance of PBS to early childhood and the extent to which the recognized features of PBS are congruent with current expectations related to service and support for young children and their families. We then provide a brief overview of the tiered prevention model that serves as a conceptual framework for identifying and developing service and support strategies. This leads to a discussion of PBS approaches for children with severe challenging behavior; the discussion has a principal focus of a model for building PBS capacity within the context of the family system. We then consider more situation-specific behavior problems and a consultant model for implementing PBS within child care and preschool settings. A final section briefly addresses recent extensions of PBS, incorporation of PBS in existing service systems, and enabling the application of PBS at a larger unit of analysis (program-wide PBS, PW-PBS).

Positive Behavior Support: Relevance to Challenging Behaviors and Young Children

Positive behavior support first emerged as an alternative to the prevailing behavior management strategies being used with individuals with severe disabilities in the mid-1980s. At that time, there were growing concerns about the use of aversive and stigmatizing punishment procedures that were commonly implemented with the intention of suppressing serious problem behaviors, such as aggression and self-injury (Guess, Helmstetter, Turnbull, & Knowlton, 1987). The use of aversive stimuli as punishing consequences was associated with the field's overreliance on contingency management as the dominating approach to behavior management. Without alternatives, a lack of satisfactory effects from using normative contingencies (e.g., praise for desired behavior; correction or extinction for problem behavior) led to an escalation in the intensity of the stimuli used as consequences (e.g., candy or other tangible items for desired behavior; physical punishers for problem behavior). Inevitably, the overdependence on contingency management meant that the intensification needed to modify highly resistant behaviors was manifested in the form of aversive consequences, including hand slaps, applications of noxious tastes and odors, and even electric shock (Linsheid & Reichenbach, 2002; Repp & Singh, 1990). Such aversive strategies became popular in many settings serving individuals with severe disabilities; however, they were met with a crescendo of protests from advocates who noted that such procedures were inconsistent with standards of human rights and with the growing movements of deinstitutionalization and community inclusion. By the early 1980s, it had become clear that a great need existed for effective alternatives to aversive interventions and to the strict reliance on contingency management from which the use of aversives was derived.

The treatment of problem behaviors exhibited by individuals with severe disabilities is the context in which PBS was first established. It emerged from several sources: (a) the insistence that alternatives to the use of aversive stimuli needed to be developed; (b) the need to identify effective strategies to support individuals with problem behaviors in inclusive (public) settings; and of essential importance (c) the formulation of broader, functional conceptualizations of problem behavior (e.g., Carr, 1977). Functional conceptualizations of problem behavior indicated that problem behaviors have a purpose, that the purposes could be understood, that they were often equivalent to acts of communication, and that interventions could be devised that focused on teaching individuals new skills (e.g., Carr & Durand, 1985), rearranging the antecedent environment (e.g., Dunlap, Kern-Dunlap, Clarke, & Robbins, 1991), and developing and implementing multicomponent intervention strategies (Carr et al., 1994). While contingency management remains a core element in the armamentarium of PBS, the PBS approach has been broadened and supplemented to the extent that powerful and artificial consequences are no longer the major consideration in achieving effective behavior support (Bambara & Kern, 2005).

As PBS was defined and demonstrated in the context of severe disabilities, it quickly became apparent that the approach was applicable for many other populations. One of the earliest extensions was to the population of young children with autism, for whom it was evident that an emphasis on developing communicative skills and preventing challenging behaviors was an urgent priority (Dunlap & Fox, 1996; Dunlap, Johnson, & Robbins, 1990; Fox, Dunlap, & Philbrick, 1997). In short order, the compatibility of the PBS approach to the needs of *all* young children with challenging behavior was soon recognized. This recognition occurred because of the increasing appreciation for the prevalence and urgency of challenging behaviors in young children and because it was apparent that a number of the key features of PBS were highly congruent with perspectives and priorities in the early childhood professional community. This congruence is clear when one considers some of the most conspicuous of the features of PBS (cf. Carr et al., 2002; Dunlap, 2004).

One of the prominent features of PBS is that principal stakeholders, such as parents, should function as collaborators and partners in the development and implementation of interventions. The PBS approach is explicitly committed to a collaborative, rather than the traditional “expert,” model of support. This collaborative approach is fully consistent with that of early childhood education and intervention, in which the full participation of parents (and other family members, etc.) is widely embraced as an inviolable tenet of practice. Indeed, parent involvement and collaboration is even specified in the Individuals With Disabilities Education Act (IDEA), particularly Part C of the IDEA, which mandates that services for every eligible child between the ages of 0 and 3 be described in an individualized family support plan (IFSP).

A second major feature of PBS is that interventions and support plans should have “ecological validity,” meaning that they should be relevant to and implemented in the natural environments in which the focus person regularly interacts. In other words, PBS endorses procedures designed for use in the actual settings in which the child's problems occur rather than in artificial clinical contexts that may be irrelevant to the circumstances responsible for the challenging behaviors in the first place. Providing services and supports in natural environments is similarly a central principle of early intervention. Early interventionists regard the active participation of children within natural settings in their community as operationalizing the value of inclusion and view their role as the provider of interventions and supports that facilitate the child and family's ability to be actively engaged in those settings (Division for Early Childhood [DEC], 1996; IDEA Infant and Toddlers Coordinators Association, 2000). This value is also mandated within the IDEA of 2004 that requires that the delivery of interventions and supports to infants and toddlers "to the maximum extent appropriate, are provided in natural environments, including the home, and community settings in which children without disabilities participate," and that services to preschool children should be provided in the least-restrictive environment (PL 108–446).

A third feature of PBS that pertains clearly to early intervention is its emphasis on prevention. Authors in the area of PBS have noted that PBS support plans should be structured with a comprehensive focus on prevention and an acknowledgment that the most effective intervention occurs when challenging behaviors are not present. This emphasis is congruent with the early childhood perspectives that optimal social-emotional growth is a function of attention being paid to nurturing relationships and instructional guidance that directs the young child toward prosocial competence and away from challenging behaviors (e.g., Fox, Dunlap, Hemmeter, Joseph, & Strain, 2003)

These three PBS features are notably consistent with early intervention perspectives and priorities; however, other features described in the PBS literature are also agreeable to many professionals in the field of early childhood. For instance, the openness of PBS to multiple theoretical and methodological orientations (Carr et al., 2002) indicates a willingness to consider practices and conceptual frameworks that might be rejected out of hand by other disciplinary approaches to behavior management. Similarly, PBS's emphasis on evaluating outcomes from a comprehensive, holistic, and longitudinal perspective is consistent with the overall aims of many early interventionists, who view their roles as preparing a child for optimal success in *all* developmental domains so that the child is best equipped to address the coming challenges of childhood and adolescence. Finally, the commitment of PBS to evidence-based practices and empirical accountability is perfectly compatible with the increased emphasis in early intervention on documenting progress and justifying the use of selected intervention procedures.

## A TIERED MODEL OF PREVENTION AND INTERVENTION

Positive behavior support in the context of early intervention, like PBS in other contexts, is conceptualized best in the larger framework of prevention. The general framework of prevention that has been adopted by many authors in PBS, as is illustrated in chapters throughout the current volume, is the tiered model derived from the field of public health (Simeonsson, 1991; Sugai et al., 2000; Walker et al., 1996). Ordinarily, this model is constructed of three tiers or levels. The *universal* level is relevant for all members of a population who might conceivably contract the problem (e.g., challenging behavior) and consists of primary prevention strategies intended to reduce the probability of the problem occurring. The next level targets segments of the population that are deemed to be especially at risk for the problem and is comprised of secondary prevention strategies involving greater intensity and focus. The highest level is directed at those members of the population who have already been affected by the problem and are in need of tertiary interventions that are generally individualized and intensive. In essence, the tiered model of prevention offers a hierarchy of prevention and intervention strategies with the intensity of the strategies geared to the level of perceived need.

Fox and her colleagues (2003) described an application of a tiered prevention framework for young children. They presented the "teaching pyramid" as a continuum of supports and services designed to build social competence and prevent challenging behaviors for young children. The pyramid consists of four levels, with the first two being primary (universal) strategies applicable for all young children. The third level addresses the needs of children who are demonstrably at risk for disturbances in social-emotional development, and the fourth level is concerned with children who display persistent, serious challenging behaviors. The teaching pyramid has been elaborated on in several articles and book chapters (e.g., Fox & Dunlap, 2007; Powell, Dunlap, & Fox, 2006). It is also described in some detail in chapter 8 by Fox and Hemmeter in the current volume. Therefore, for the present purposes, we simply provide a very brief overview of the primary and secondary levels of the hierarchy. We do so because these levels constitute the foundations of effective prevention practices, and it is assumed that the efficacy of focused efforts of PBS for children with serious challenging behaviors is dependent, to some extent, on the quality of services and supports delivered at these levels.

As described, the universal level of primary prevention consists of two major categories on the teaching pyramid. The first and, arguably, the most fundamental category concerns the quality of positive relationships developed between the child and the child's parents, teachers, child care professionals, other caring adults, and eventually, peers. It is well understood that a child's healthy social-emotional development is a function of the stability, security, and consistency of trusting, affectionate relationships that are developed during the child's years as an infant and toddler. These relationships provide the context and the mold from which the child's future relationships and interactions will emerge, and they serve as the basis for the early guidance and instruction that adults offer for the child. The stronger the positive relationship an adult has with a child, the more effective the adult will be in helping the child acquire social competencies.

Also warranting consideration as primary prevention practices are basic levels of adult-child interactions, guidance, and modeling with respect to empathy for others, assistance with problem solving, and the provision of comprehensible, predictable, and stimulating environments. These practices are manifested as fundamental guidelines for positive parenting and the physical arrangements associated with safety and orderliness in home, child care, and classroom settings. It is understood that adherence to such guidelines for all children will help promote healthy social-emotional development and reduce the incidence of serious challenging behavior.

Secondary prevention practices are geared for children who experience circumstances known to increase the risk of social-emotional disorders and the development of challenging behaviors. Such risk factors may include poverty; exposure to abusive, neglectful, or violent home situations; delays or disabilities in learning or communication; maternal depression; and other variables (see research summaries in Campbell, 1995; Huffman, Mehlinger, & Kerivan, 2000; Qi & Kaiser, 2003). A variety of parent training, social skills and social-emotional curricula, and multicomponent intervention programs have been developed to provide assistance for these children. Joseph and Strain (2003) reported evaluation data for a number of social-emotional curriculum packages and found a high level of evidence for two of the programs (Walker et al., 1998; Webster-Stratton, 1990), with several others showing some promising, albeit limited, data.

The top level of the teaching pyramid refers to those relatively few young children who already demonstrate patterns of persistent challenging behavior and who require more concerted and individualized intervention efforts. The challenging behaviors of these children may accompany a developmental delay or disability (due to increased risk factors), although a diagnosis or identified disability is not necessarily present.

PBS is an approach that is well suited for addressing the needs of children who are identified as having serious challenging behaviors. It incorporates the strengths of several disciplines, including applied behavior analysis; it has been demonstrated to be effective (Carr et al., 1999; Conroy, Dunlap, Clarke, & Alter, 2005); and as discussed, it has substantial congruence with the field of early intervention. In the following sections of this chapter, we describe some PBS strategies for addressing the needs of young children with severe challenging behavior. We begin by detailing a family-centered model of PBS and continue by describing the application of PBS in child care and classroom settings. We conclude with brief discussions of PBS applications in more circumscribed circumstances and in a variety of systems in which young children with challenging behavior are commonly seen.

## FAMILY-CENTERED POSITIVE BEHAVIOR SUPPORT

Families have an immense impact in the course of children's development, especially when children are young and without access to regular peer and school influences. The prominence of the family role is emphasized even further, and for extended durations, when children experience disabilities or challenging behaviors that inhibit and impede participation in community activities with friends and classmates. Recognition of the importance of the family for children with developmental and behavioral challenges has swayed many professionals toward an appreciation of family systems theory (Minuchin, 1974) and the need to involve and empower families as much as possible in programs of support and intervention (Dunlap, Newton, Fox, Benito, & Vaughn, 2001; Dunst & Dempsey, 2007; Turnbull & Turnbull, 2001). The notion of family support has been adopted as an approach for helping families, in multiple ways, to build on family strengths and acquire new skills needed to facilitate the child's development while enhancing family cohesion and family quality of life (Lucyshyn, Dunlap, & Albin, 2002; Turnbull & Turnbull, 2000). Numerous authors have indicated that family support is particularly important when children have challenging behaviors (Dunlap & Fox, 2007; Dunlap et al., 2001; Lucyshyn, Dunlap et al., 2002).

Family-centered PBS refers to PBS conducted within a family environment in which the family not only partners with professionals to design and implement behavior support for a child with challenging behavior, but also in which the family unit is viewed as the primary beneficiaries and as the primary decision makers. Professionals provide the technical knowledge and experience in PBS, while families provide knowledge of the child, the child's behavior, the family, and everything about the contexts in which PBS is to be implemented. Because families are destined to be the principal intervention agents, perhaps for many years, it is vital that families be the ultimate judges regarding the appropriateness of PBS plans (Albin, Lucyshyn, Horner, & Flannery, 1996). Professionals may provide the technical guidance regarding evidence-based practices and the process of PBS, but it is families who must live with the procedures and outcomes.

In our work over the past two decades with children who have serious challenging behaviors, we have developed and refined a process of family-centered PBS that has been applied for young children and families affected by autism (e.g., Dunlap & Fox, 1999a; Fox et al., 1997) as well as for the broader population of children who have challenging behavior irrespective of a label of disability (Dunlap & Fox; 1996; Fox, Dunlap, & Powell, 2002). The process is similar to most models of PBS (e.g., Bambara & Kern, 2005; Janney & Snell, 2000), but it is tailored to emphasize the principles of family centeredness and the contexts of early intervention (Fox et al., 1997). The process is facilitated by a professional, or team of professionals, with expertise and experience in (a) assessment and intervention strategies of PBS; (b) early childhood development and early intervention; and (c) family functioning, family systems, and cultural differences.

The process can be described as consisting of five major steps. These are described next.

### *Step 1: Teaming and Goal Setting*

The first step in family-centered PBS is establishing a trusting relationship between the professional and the pertinent family members. Building a strong rapport with the family is key to a successful PBS process because a relationship characterized by trust and candor can greatly facilitate the assessment and intervention process. The professional must listen and be responsive to the family members' concerns and priorities and interact with respect and honesty (Keen, 2007). The relationship should strengthen over time, but often the initial few meetings set the tone and determine the course that future interactions will take. Many families, even those with young children, have experienced disappointing interactions with service agencies and professionals, so trust and openness cannot be assumed. The desired relationship of mutual respect and partnership has to be developed.

A second priority is the development of a team who will work with the family to develop and implement the PBS plan. The team should consist of those individuals who are connected to the child and family and who are involved and invested in the child's healthy development. Teams always include the child's parents (or those filling parenting roles) and often include extended family members, close friends, teachers, therapists, consultants (including the PBS professional), and administrators. Well-functioning teams bring numerous advantages to the PBS process. They offer multiple sources of knowledge, multiple perspectives on the child's development and behavior, and resources that may be useful in implementing PBS.

When a team is established, it is important to set short- and long-term goals for the child's future. A purpose is to create a shared vision so that all team members agree on the desired outcomes for the coming few months as well as for longer periods of time (such as 1 year, 2 years, or entry into kindergarten). We have found that an excellent method for establishing team unity and for setting goals is the process of person-centered planning (Kincaid & Fox, 2002; Mount & Zwernick, 1988). In our early intervention programs for children with serious problem behaviors and significant disabilities, we conduct a first person-centered planning meeting shortly after a team has been identified, and then we conduct a second meeting after about 4–5 months, at the time that PBS has been implemented for several weeks and clear behavioral changes have been observed. While the first meeting serves to build the team through a process of developing goals for the child and family, the second meeting usually includes some celebration regarding progress that has occurred, a reconsideration of goals, possible revisions to the plan, and a renewal of the team's commitment to the child and family. Subsequent planning meetings are then scheduled on a periodic (e.g., annual) and as-needed basis to revisit the supports needed by the child and family, to establish new goals, and to add new team members.

### Step 2: Functional Behavioral Assessment

When a team is assembled and goals have been established, the next step is to conduct a thorough functional assessment of the child's challenging behaviors (Dunlap & Kincaid, 2001; O'Neill et al., 1997). The functional assessment typically involves interviews with key observers (parents, teachers) and some direct observation. The purpose is to operationally define the challenging behaviors in all of the contexts in which they occur, identify the function or purpose of the behavior from the child's perspective, and specify the specific antecedent conditions associated with high and low probabilities of the behavior occurring. Confident answers to these assessment questions are tantamount to developing a functional understanding of the behavior and how it is related to and governed by the child's environment. In some cases, completing a valid functional assessment can require many hours over several days or even weeks. However, with young children, who have not been exposed to many interventions and whose challenging behavior has not been demonstrated in many different settings, the functional assessment process is usually straightforward and can be completed in a fairly short period of time.

A primary outcome of the functional assessment process is a set of hypothesis statements that summarize the assessment results for each relevant behavior and each distinctive routine. A hypothesis statement specifies the context, the behavior, and the behavior's function. For instance, one statement might read: "When asked or prompted to come to the dinner table, Jenny will fuss and occasionally scream or throw objects to escape the request and remain in her ongoing activity." Another example might be: "When Terrell is left alone for 15 minutes or more, he is likely to hit one of his classmates or disrupt their play activities to obtain attention from one of the adults in the classroom." Hypothesis statements are very useful because they suggest intervention components that address the antecedent conditions under which challenging behaviors occur, and they suggest instructional objectives to serve as alternatives to the behavior challenges.

### *Step 3: Developing the PBS Plan*

The PBS plan is developed as a collaborative process by the core members of the team, including those who will be responsible for its implementation. The plan components are based on information provided by (a) the functional assessment; (b) the goals established during the initial planning process; (c) all other available information about the child; and (d) team members' opinions regarding the feasibility of consistent implementation (Albin et al., 1996). In our experience, plans are most effective if they include, for each targeted routine, at least one intervention strategy for each of the three main plan components: prevention techniques based on arrangements of the antecedent environment; teaching strategies aligned with the function of the challenging behavior; and reinforcement strategies involving adults' responses to challenging and desirable behaviors.

The "prevention" component involves manipulations of setting events (Friman & Hawkins, 2006) or antecedent stimuli (Dunlap & Kern, 1996; Luiselli, 2006). A *setting event* is an occasion or circumstance that increases the likelihood that challenging behavior will occur. For instance, for one young boy, the absence of a comfort item (a blanket) produced stress that increased the likelihood that a subsequent request (to get ready for school) would be followed by a tantrum. A prevention intervention was to consistently place the blanket in a predictable location where the boy could find it. *Antecedent events* are any actions that evoke challenging behavior or, alternatively, desirable behavior. In a previous example, being called to dinner was an antecedent event that produced Jenny's fussing. Antecedent stimuli can be requests or demands, materials, the presence of particular people, and even odors, sounds, and tactile events. In school settings, antecedent events are often part of the instruction and curriculum (Dunlap & Kern, 1996; Dunlap et al., 1991). Interventions involve removing or ameliorating antecedent stimuli associated with challenging behavior and adding antecedent events associated with desirable behavior. Additional prevention strategies include picture schedules, social stories, pretask requesting, and similar techniques designed to make the environment more predictable and comprehensible (Crimmins, Farrell, Smith, & Bailey, 2007; Kern & Clarke, 2005; Westling & Fox, 2004).

The "teaching" component involves identifying an instructional objective and making arrangements to provide instruction on the new target behavior during pertinent times of the day. A major purpose is to develop an alternative to the challenging behaviors so that the child no longer needs to engage in challenging behavior to achieve the purpose (function) of the behavior. The term for this type of assessment-based instruction is functional communication training (FCT), which was originated by Carr and Durand (1985). In the past 20 years, FCT has been replicated and extended numerous times, and its efficacy has been demonstrated with various populations, including toddlers with behavioral challenges (Dunlap, Ester, Langhans, & Fox, 2006). In addition to function-based communication, there are numerous other skills that can be taught to an important behavioral advantage. Self-regulation and self-management, social skills, independence, cooperative play, and emotional literacy are all worthwhile objectives that can yield gains in behavioral adaptation and that can be fruitful elements of the PBS repertoire.

The "reinforcement" component simply means using the principles of contingency management and positive reinforcement to their best advantage. Challenging behaviors often arise because the child obtains inadequate reinforcement in the course of unplanned daily interactions. Therefore, it is important in any PBS plan to provide for some alteration in the way in which reinforcers are delivered. This may involve a systematic preference assessment, enhancement of noncontingent reinforcement (and environmental enrichment) and care to see that challenging behaviors are not inadvertently rewarded.

In addition to the three main components just described, team members often recommend structural changes in a child's daily routine that can have salutary effects. For instance, it may be advisable to change a child's preschool classroom to one that provides more consistent encouragement of social interaction and communication, or it may be useful to add structured play groups or to remove unnecessary or unproductive therapies from an already overcrowded schedule. Family support is also a consideration. For instance, respite might be an important service for parents, as might counseling, financial planning, or additional advice on medical care. Although in this chapter we are not focusing our attention on parents' or families' needs for supports, we do not want to overlook the importance of family functioning in the overall promotion of healthy social-emotional development of the child, and we encourage consideration of appropriate supports in PBS plans (e.g., Dunlap & Fox, 1999b; Singer, Goldberg-Hamblin, Peckham-Hardin, Barry, & Santarelli, 2002)

### *Step 4: Implementation*

Implementation of the PBS plan often requires explicit assignments and supports. Training in the form of coaching and support within the target routine or setting may be required for personnel, including parents, to effectively use some techniques indicated in the plan. In addition, it is often useful to provide for written scripts of how to conduct routines and prompts (such as schedules, cue cards, and checklists) to help remind teachers and parents to deliver instruction and reinforcers on schedule. It is important always to remember that even the most thoughtful and precise plan will be ineffective if it is not implemented with adequate consistency and integrity.

### *Step 5: Evaluation, Refinement, and Follow-Up*

Evaluation is an essential element in the implementation of PBS. The team should identify the highest-priority behaviors, settings, and outcomes and formulate efficient methods of data collection to determine if sufficient progress is occurring. In most cases, ongoing direct data collection is not feasible, so we frequently recommend the use of 5- or 6-point rating scales with clear anchors. For instance, if one of Missy's most challenging routines is the transition from snack to center activities and her PBS plan focuses on intervention during that time, a 5-point scale could be devised in which a score of 1 might represent "loud screaming, strenuous resistance, and at least a 10-minute delay before calming down," and a score of 5 might mean "very cooperative with no resistance or complaints and a positive affect throughout transition." Similarly specific intermediate descriptors would be assigned to scores 2, 3, and 4. The teacher would complete the scale soon after the transition was completed. By recording such data on a daily basis, a time series evaluation of the effects of the plan could be accomplished in a feasible and reliable manner. In addition to child performance, evaluations can also be conducted on the implementation of the plan. Checklists of the key components can be developed and completed to determine if the plan is being implemented as intended.

The purpose of the evaluations of child performance and implementation fidelity is to determine if changes and refinements need to be made to the plan. It is common for this to be the case. If behavior is not changing as rapidly as expected, adjustments can be made. Occasionally, it is found that certain components are not being implemented. If so, it is necessary to learn the reason and either add prompts or other cues to increase fidelity or make adjustments to the components to make it more likely that they would be implemented.

Finally, the importance of planning and conducting follow-up evaluations and assessments cannot be overstated. If a child has serious challenging behaviors at a young age, it is very likely that some manifestations of these behaviors will reoccur, especially as new settings and new challenges arise along with the child's maturation. Transitions to new programs and to kindergarten are often challenging and can precipitate escalations of difficult behaviors. Thus, the team should explicitly and carefully plan for the transition and provide the new setting with information on the child (e.g., preferences, communication skills, interests, potential triggers for challenging behavior) and instruction on the behavior support strategies that are currently being implemented.

### *Summary of Family-Centered PBS Model*

The model of family-centered PBS described has been demonstrated, replicated in whole and in part, and fashioned for application for various populations, including children with challenging behaviors served by Part C and toddlers and preschoolers with autism. The program model designed for children and families affected by autism is referred to as the Individualized Support Project (ISP) (Fox et al., 1997). While following the five-step model, the ISP is based on three primary programmatic emphases: (a) development of functional skills, especially functional communication; (b) development of active participation in socially inclusive environments; and (c) family support with the objective of enhancing family competence and confidence (Dunlap & Fox, 1996). The ISP was recognized and described by the National Research Council as 1 of 10 comprehensive model programs (National Research Council, 2001).

The ISP model has been evaluated largely via interrupted time series designs and, occasionally, with experimental replication. For instance, Dunlap and Fox (1999a) provided a program description along with data on the first 6 children who participated in a demonstration of ISP in the Tampa Bay region of Florida. Improvements were evident for all children on the Autism Behavior Checklist (ABC) (Krug, Arick, & Almond, 1980) as well as the Battelle Developmental Inventory (Newborg, Stock, & Wnek, 1984). More important, time series data illustrated clear reductions in challenging behaviors (e.g., tantrums, aggression, self-injury, intensive stereotypy) for all 6 children.

An example is the case of Tom (a pseudonym; all individual participant names in this chapter are pseudonyms) who was one of the first ISP participants (Dunlap & Fox, 1999a; Fox, Benito, & Dunlap, 2002). Tom was 29 months when he and his family enrolled in the program. Tom lived with both parents and an older brother, who would also be diagnosed with autism. His score on the ABC was 90, which was the highest (most indicative of autism) of all children in the sample. Tom was nonverbal, and his chief challenging behavior was described as frequent, prolonged, and intense tantrums. At the time of enrollment, he was coming close to being expelled from his child care setting because his tantrums were considered uncontrollable.

Teams were assembled around the child care and home environments, and person-centered planning (Kincaid & Fox, 2002) was used to build a clear consensus around Tom's strengths and challenges and goals for the coming months and years. Functional assessments were conducted in the priority settings. The assessments indicated that Tom's tantrums were governed by multiple functions. In some circumstances, tantrums occurred in order to escape nonpreferred events or stimuli or to postpone transitions. In other circumstances, tantrums occurred to solicit an adult's attention or assistance in obtaining a desired object (e.g., cracker, blanket). Therefore, with the full involvement of Tom's parents and child care providers, multicomponent support plans were developed.

The plans consisted of (a) environmental arrangements (e.g., establishing more consistency in the placement of preferred objects; promoting peer interactions and friendships); (b) specific antecedent manipulations (e.g., use of visual schedules, choice making); (c) teaching replacement skills (e.g., verbal and gestural expressions of "no"); and (d) changes in the use of consequences (e.g., redirection to use replacement skills, prevention of escape behavior via escape extinction). Implementation of the support plan was engineered first in the child care environment in hopes of salvaging Tom's placement. The ISP early interventionist facilitated implementation by modeling the components of the support plan, coaching the child care staff to use the components, and then observing and evaluating the staff's implementation. As the plan gained success in the child care setting, the plan was implemented by Tom's parents at home. Within a month, it was clear that the plan was producing important reductions in the number of severe tantrums in both environments. Tom's placement status was preserved, and much more harmony was evident at home. The data on Tom's tantrums are reproduced in Fig. 3.1. More detail regarding this case is available in the work of Fox, Benito, & Dunlap (2002).

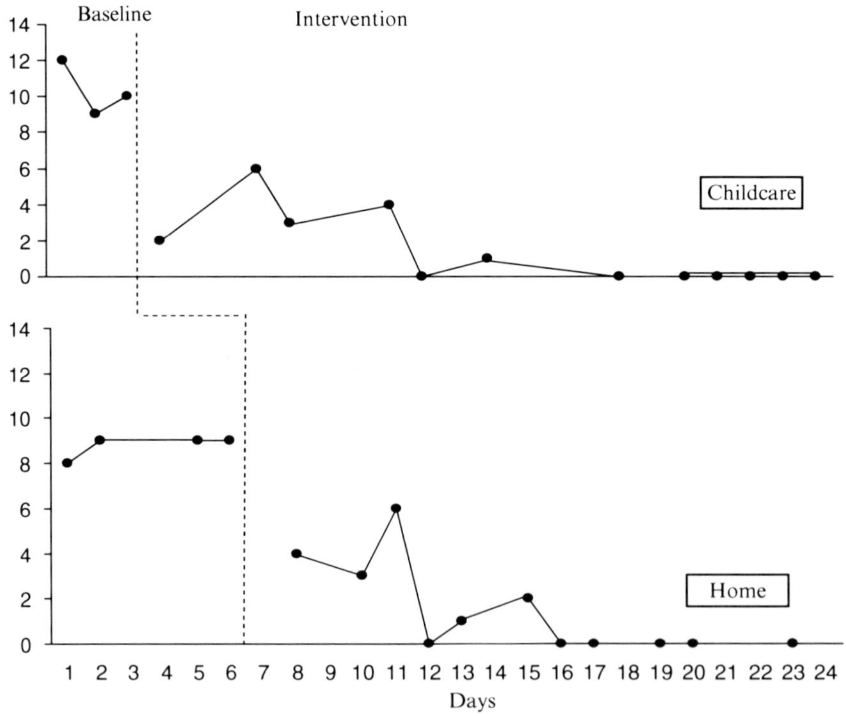


**Fig. 3.1.** Number of tantrums displayed by Tom in child care and home settings. Reprinted with permission from "A Demonstration of Behavioral Support for Young Children With Autism, by G. Dunlap & L. Fox, 1999, *Journal of Positive Behavior Interventions*, 1, 77–87.

## APPLICATIONS OF PBS IN CHILD CARE AND PRE-K CLASSROOMS

As the case of Tom illustrates, young children's challenging behavior in child care and preschool settings can have very serious consequences if not resolved quickly and efficiently. Indeed, programs providing early child care and education are often the settings where serious challenging behaviors are first observed. It is common for challenging behaviors to be more pronounced, and to have greater impact, in these group settings than in the child's home, where accommodations are more easily implemented and where perceived demands and restrictions may be less conspicuous.

The application of PBS in child care and preschool settings generally follows the same general process as the family-centered model we have just described. That is, the process begins with the assembling of a team and the establishment of a consensus regarding goals. Functional assessment of the challenging behaviors in all relevant contexts comes next, and the results of the functional assessment are used to construct a behavior support plan. The plan is then implemented, evaluated, and as necessary, refined and redeployed. The process is generally facilitated by an experienced and knowledgeable consultant, but the assessments and the behavior support plan are constructed through a collaborative process. The process typically requires less time than the family-centered model because the plan is limited to a particular setting that tends to be more structured than the home environment and because the complexities of family functioning are not on the agenda (Dunlap & Fox, 1999b; Lucyshyn, Dunlap et al., 2002). Still, serious challenging behaviors identified in a setting such as preschool are often indicative of problems that might be manifested in other settings, so it is prudent for school-based teams to be alert to the need for even more comprehensive support plans that would transcend the initial situation-specific concern.

The empirical literature documenting effects of PBS in child care and preschool settings is growing rapidly. For instance, Gettinger and Stoiber (2006) published a study in which they compared classrooms where PBS was implemented by school-based teams (referred to as the "FACET" program) with control classrooms that did not implement the PBS process. The PBS classrooms, with functional assessments, collaborative processes, and evidence-based intervention components, proved superior to the control classrooms in terms of ratios of positive to negative child behaviors. These authors also reported that behavioral improvements were positively correlated with the level of fidelity of the school teams in implementing the PBS model.

The consultant model of providing PBS in preschool classrooms is described by Fox and Clarke (2006), who included a case illustration. Cooper was a 2½-year-old boy who displayed intense aggression, including biting, hitting, pinching, and head butting. Understandably, these behaviors caused tremendous concern among parents of the children in the community preschool program and among the program staff. Because all efforts to reduce the aggression were unsuccessful, the school's director was on the verge of asking Cooper's parents to withdraw him from the program. A PBS consultant was recruited, and she facilitated the development of a team that included Cooper's parents, the preschool director, the speech therapist, and two teachers. After a thorough functional assessment, it was determined that a number of factors provoked and maintained Cooper's aggression, and a multicomponent support plan was developed and implemented. The plan was based on the assessment information indicating that aggression was motivated by (a) escape from nonpreferred, unpredictable, difficult, or confusing school activities; and, in some circumstances, (b) attention from a teacher or peer. A synopsis of Cooper's support plan is shown in Table 3.1, with more detail regarding targeted replacement skills in Table 3.2. Implementation of the support plan, facilitated by the PBS consultant, produced rapid reductions in Copper's aggressive behaviors (Fox & Clarke, 2006).

**Table 3.1.** Cooper's Behavior Support Plan

| Prevention Strategies | Replacement Skills | Adult Responses |
|---|---|---|
| Visual cues/photo schedule/stop signs | Teach how to initiate/terminate interactions | Clear instructions |
| Social stories | Teach how to initiate appropriate physical affection | Redirect and ignore |
| First/then boards | Teach how to appropriately ask for "break" or "help" | Specific praise |
| Choice | Teach how to respond to environmental sensitivities | Provide choice |
| Preferred items | Teach how to make and express choice | Materials ready |
| Manipulatives | | Consistent verbal cues |
| Add quiet area | | "All done," countdowns |
| Add breaks | | Model |
| Peer buddy | | Encourage verbal interactions |
| Remove distractions | | Monitor and anticipate difficult activities |

*Note:* From "Aggression? Using Positive Behavior Support to Address Challenging Behavior," by L. Fox & S. Clarke, 2006, *Young Exceptional Children Monograph Series No. 8*, 42–56; reprinted with permission.

**Table 3.2.** Replacement Skills Taught to Cooper

| Skills Taught to Replace Aggressive Behavior | Attention | Escape |
|---|---|---|
| Verbal | "I want to share" | "Go away" |
| | "I need help" | "I want a break" |
| | "I want a hug/kiss" | "All done" |
| Nonverbal | Gesture with toy to share | Gesture with STOP sign to end routine/request break |
| | Gesture for hug/kiss | Point to picture or leave area |

*Note:* From "Aggression? Using Positive Behavior Support to Address Challenging Behavior," by L. Fox & S. Clarke, 2006, *Young Exceptional Children Monograph Series No. 8*, 42–56; reprinted with permission.

Another example of PBS consultation in a typical preschool setting was reported by Duda and her colleagues (Duda, Dunlap, Fox, Lentini, & Clarke, 2004). Two 3-year-old girls (Vanessa and Layla) participated in the study. Vanessa had Down syndrome, and Layla was described as having a variety of (undiagnosed) developmental, speech, and physical concerns. The girls displayed a variety of challenging behaviors. For instance, Vanessa engaged in aggression, running away, mouthing objects, and disrupting peers' play activities. The PBS consultant worked with the school team to carry out functional assessments and develop and implement support plans. The plans were evaluated for both girls within the context of ABAB experimental designs replicated across two daily routines, opening circle and planning time. The routines were videotaped, and data collectors coded the tapes for the percentage of intervals with challenging behavior as well as appropriate engagement with the ongoing activities. The results for both girls indicated considerable improvement, as is illustrated by the data for Vanessa in Fig. 3.2.

The escalating spread of PBS applications in preschool and child care settings is exemplified also by a study carried out in South Korea (Blair, Umbreit, Dunlap, & Jung, 2007). Minsu, a 6-year-old boy with autism and intellectual disabilities, exhibited severe challenging behavior in his inclusive kindergarten placement. A thorough implementation of the PBS process, including experimental validation of the functional assessment hypotheses, resulted in significant reductions in challenging behavior, increases in appropriate behavior, and increases in positive interactions with a designated classroom peer. This study helps to document the feasibility of the PBS approach (the teacher led all of the interventions) as well as the benefits of PBS not only in reducing behavioral challenges but also in increasing vital patterns of behavior, such as social interaction.

## SUMMARY, EXTENSIONS, AND CONCLUSIONS

In this chapter, we described a PBS approach to challenging behaviors exhibited by young children. We discussed the rationale for such early intervention and presented the familiar tiered framework of prevention as it applies to infants, toddlers, and preschoolers. We then devoted considerable attention to the family-centered model of PBS, as well as PBS applications in child care and preschool settings. It is important to note that these last two sections presented strategies that apply to the most serious and intense of challenging behaviors, the circumstances that call for the most individualized and concerted efforts of home and school-based teams. However, it is important to acknowledge that these intensive processes are pertinent for only the most severe cases. The majority of challenging behaviors can (and should) be resolved with less-intensive and less-comprehensive approaches. In keeping with the logic of the tiered framework of prevention (and the teaching pyramid), there should be a balance between the intensity and severity of the challenging behaviors (and the circumstances under which the behaviors occur) and the intensity of the prevention and intervention strategies that are used to address them. In the majority of cases, high-quality implementation of primary

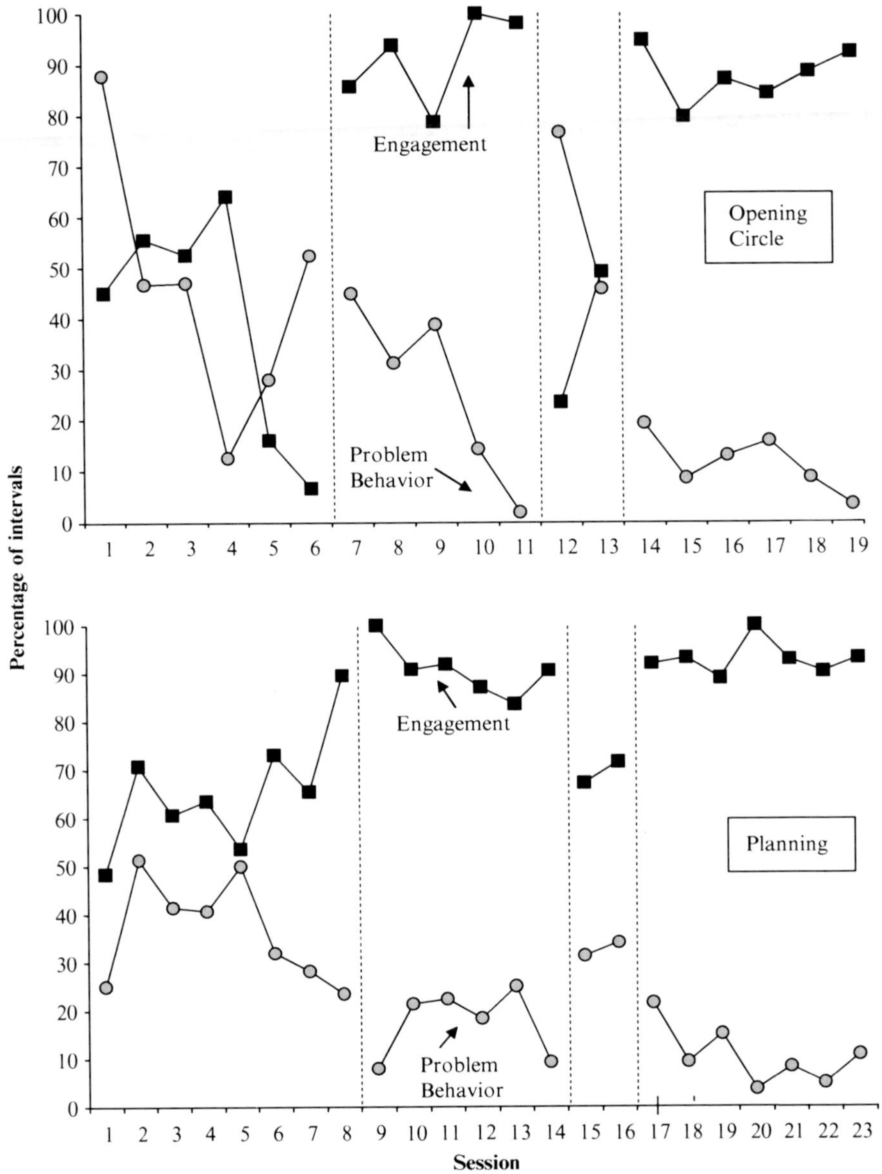


**Fig. 3.2.** Percentage of continuous 10-s intervals of engagement and challenging behaviors for Vanessa during opening circle and planning. The first and third phases are baseline (business as usual), and the second and fourth phases are positive behavior support (PBS) implementation. Reprinted with permission from "An Experimental Evaluation of Positive Behavior Support in a Community Preschool Program," by M. A. Duda, G. Dunlap, L. Fox, R. Lentini, & S. Clarke, 2004, *Topics in Early Childhood Special Education, 24*, 143–155.

and secondary supports is sufficient to guide children toward more prosocial patterns of behavior. When these supports are inadequate, the individualized and intensive (tertiary) interventions are appropriate, but these also should be modulated to fit the needs of the child, the family, and the entire caregiving context.

While PBS in early intervention began with specialized programs and case-by-case demonstrations, it is rapidly being extended to larger-scale applications. Some of the more exciting directions that are being pursued include the integration of PBS into existing systems of child care and education. For instance, there have been efforts to apply PBS approaches to the support of infants and toddlers and their families (Powell et al., 2006). There have also been extensions of PBS into the realms of mental health consultation and Head Start. In illustration, chapter 6 in this volume by Frey, Boyce, and Tarullo provides a detailed description of a community's progress in building PBS into the entire mental health service system of a large Head Start program in Louisville, Kentucky.

Another vital extension involves the application of PBS for young children at a larger unit of analysis. While PBS in early intervention has been developed with the individual child and family as the principal unit of analysis, efforts have now been undertaken to establish and evaluate PBS at the level of the classroom and multiclassroom program. The development of programwide positive behavior support (PW-PBS) has followed from the lead of schoolwide PBS (Sugai et al., 2000), although some important differences are considered (Hemmeter, Fox, Jack, & Broyles, 2007; Stormont, Lewis, & Beckner, 2005). This important development is described in detail in chapter 8 by Fox and Hemmeter in this volume.

In summary, PBS has demonstrated important relevance in the field of early intervention, and its applications and contributions are expanding rapidly. Given the trends over the past two decades, it is reasonable to project further expansion and much broader adoption of PBS in early childhood service programs as well as refinement of the PBS approach so that it is increasingly effective, efficient, and feasible for use in all the contexts inhabited by young children and their families.

## ACKNOWLEDGMENT

Preparation of this chapter was facilitated by support from several sources: funding from the U.S. Department of Education, Office of Special Education Programs, grant no. H324Z010001, the Center for Evidence-Based Practice: Young Children With Challenging Behavior; and from the Administration on Developmental Disabilities, grant no. 90DD0592, the University of South Florida University Center for Excellence in Developmental Disabilities.

## REFERENCES

Albin, R. W., Lucyshyn, J. M., Horner, R. H., & Flannery, K. B. (1996). Contextual fit for behavior support plans: A model for a "goodness of fit." In L. K. Koegel, R. L. Koegel, & G. Dunlap (Eds.), *Positive behavioral support: Including people with difficult behavior in the community* (pp. 81–98). Baltimore: Brookes.

Arnold, D. H., Ortiz, C., Curry, J. C., Stowe, R. M., Goldstein, N. E., Fisher, P. H., et al. (1999). Promoting academic success and preventing disruptive behavior disorders through community partnership. *Journal of Community Psychology, 27*, 589–598.

Baker, B. L., Blacher, J., Crnic, K., & Edelbrock, C. (2002). Behavior problems and parenting stress in families of three-year old children with and without developmental disabilities. *American Journal on Mental Retardation, 107*, 433–444.

Bambara, L., & Kern, L. (Eds.). (2005). *Individualized supports for students with problem behaviors: Designing positive behavior plans.* New York: Guilford Press.

Blair, K.C., Umbreit, J., Dunlap, G., & Jung, G. (2007). Promoting inclusion and peer participation through assessment-based intervention. *Topics in Early Childhood Special Education*, 27, 134–147.

Campbell, S. B. (1995). Behavior problems in preschool children: A review of recent research. *Journal of Child Psychology and Psychiatry, 36*, 113–149.

Carr, E. G. (1977). The motivation of self-injurious behavior: A review of some hypotheses. *Psychological Bulletin*, 84, 800–816.

Carr, E. G., & Durand, V. M. (1985). Reducing behavior problems through functional communication training. *Journal of Applied Behavior Analysis, 18*, 111–126.

Carr, E. G., Levin, L., McConnachie, G., Carlson, J. I., Kemp, D. C., & Smith, C. E. (1994). *Communication-based interventions for problem behavior: A user's guide for producing behavior change.* Baltimore: Brookes.

Carr, E. G., Dunlap, G., Horner, R. H., Koegel, R. L., Turnbull, A. P., Sailor, W., et al. (2002). Positive behavior support. Evolution of an applied science. *Journal of Positive Behavior Interventions, 4*, 4–16.

Carr, E. G., Horner, R. H., Turnbull, A. P., Marquis, J., Magito-Mclaughlin, D., McAtee, M. L., Smith, C. E., Anderson-Ryan, K., Ruef, M. B., & Doolabh, A. (1999). *Positive behavior support for people with developmental disabilities: A research synthesis.* Washington, DC: American Association on Mental Retardation.

Coie, J. D., & Dodge, K. A. (1998). Aggression and antisocial behavior. In W. Damon (Editor-in-Chief) & N. Eisenberg (Vol. Ed.), *Handbook of child psychology. Vol. 3. Social, emotional, and personality development* (5th ed., pp. 103–145). New York: Wiley.

Conroy, M. A., Dunlap, G., Clarke, S., & Alter, P. J. (2005). A descriptive analysis of positive behavioral intervention research with young children with challenging behavior. *Topics in Early Childhood Special Education, 25*, 157–166.

Crimmins, D., Farrell, A. F., Smith, P. W., & Bailey, A. (2007). *Positive strategies for students with behavior problems.* Baltimore: Brookes.

Division for Early Childhood of the Council for Exceptional Children. (1996). *DEC position statement on inclusion.* Retrieved from www.dec-sped.org, November 30, 2007

Duda, M. A., Dunlap, G., Fox, L., Lentini, R., & Clarke, S. (2004). An experimental evaluation of positive behavior support in a community preschool program. *Topics in Early Childhood Special Education, 24*, 143–155.

Dunlap, G. (2004). Critical features of positive behavior support. *APBS Newsletter, 1*, 1–3.

Dunlap, G., Ester, T., Langhans, S., & Fox, L. (2006). Functional communication training with toddlers in home environments. *Journal of Early Intervention, 28*, 81–96.

Dunlap, G., & Fox, L. (1996). Early intervention and serious problem behaviors: A comprehensive approach. In L. K. Koegel, R. L. Koegel, & G. Dunlap (Eds.), *Positive behavioral support: Including people with difficult behavior in the community* (pp. 31–50). Baltimore: Brookes.

Dunlap, G., & Fox, L. (1999a). A demonstration of behavioral support for young children with autism. *Journal of Positive Behavior Interventions, 1*, 77–87.

Dunlap, G., & Fox, L. (1999b). Supporting families of young children with autism. *Infants and Young Children, 12*, 48–54.

Dunlap, G., & Fox, L. (2007). Parent-professional partnerships: A valuable context for addressing challenging behaviors. *International Journal of Development, Disability and Education, 54*, 273–285.

Dunlap, G., Fox, L., Smith, B. & Strain, P. (2002). *Center for Evidence-based Practice: Young Children with Challenging Behaviors.* Grant # H324Z010001 funded by the Office of Special Education Programs, US Department of Education.

Dunlap, G., Johnson, L. F., & Robbins, F. R. (1990). Preventing serious behavior problems through skill development and early intervention. In A. C. Repp & N. N. Singh (Eds.), *Current perspectives in the use of non-aversive and aversive interventions with developmentally disabled persons* (pp. 273–286). Sycamore, IL: Sycamore Press.

Dunlap, G., & Kern, L. (1996). Modifying instructional activities to promote desirable behavior: A conceptual and practical framework. *School Psychology Quarterly, 11*, 297–312.
Dunlap, G., Kern-Dunlap, L., Clarke, S., & Robbins, F. R. (1991). Functional assessment, curriculum revision, and severe behavior problems. *Journal of Applied Behavior Analysis, 24*, 387–397.
Dunlap, G., & Kincaid, D. (2001). The widening world of functional assessment: Comments on four manuals and beyond. *Journal of Applied Behavior Analysis, 34*, 365–377.
Dunlap, G., Newton, J. S., Fox, L., Benito, N., & Vaughn, B. (2001). Family involvement in functional assessment and positive behavior support. *Focus on Autism and Other Developmental Disabilities, 16*, 215–221.
Dunlap, G., Strain, P. S., Fox, L., Carta, J. J., Conroy, M., Smith, B., et al. (2006). Prevention and intervention with young children's challenging behavior: A summary and perspective regarding current knowledge. *Behavioral Disorders, 32*, 29–45.
Dunst, C. J., & Dempsey, I. (2007). Family-professional partnerships and parenting competence, confidence, and enjoyment. *International Journal of Development, Disability and Education, 54*, 305–318.
Fox, L., Benito, N., & Dunlap, G. (2002). Early intervention with families of young children with autism and problem behaviors. In J. Lucyshyn, G. Dunlap, & R. W. Albin (Eds.), *Families and positive behavior support: Addressing problem behaviors in family contexts* (pp. 251–269). Baltimore: Brookes.
Fox, L., & Clarke, S. (2006). Aggression? Using positive behavior support to address challenging behavior. *Young Exceptional Children Monograph Series No. 8*, 42–56.
Fox, L., & Dunlap, G. (2007). Evidence-based practices for young children with and at risk for social-emotional or behavior problems. In D. F. Perry, R. K. Kaufmann, & J. Knitzer (Eds.), *Social and emotional health in early childhood: Building bridges between services and systems* (pp. 313–334). Baltimore: Brookes.
Fox, L., Dunlap, G., Hemmeter, M. L., Joseph, G. E., & Strain, P. S. (2003, July). The teaching pyramid: A model for supporting social competence and preventing challenging behavior in young children. *Young Children*, 48–52.
Fox. L., Dunlap, G., & Philbrick, L. A. (1997). Providing individual supports to young children with autism and their families. *Journal of Early Intervention, 21*, 1–14.
Fox, L., Dunlap, G., & Powell, D. (2002). Young children and challenging behavior: Issues and considerations for behavior support. *Journal of Positive Behavior Interventions, 4*, 208–217.
Friman, P. C., & Hawkins, R. O. (2006). Contribution of establishing operations to antecedent intervention: Clinical implications of motivating events. In J. K. Luiselli (Ed.), *Antecedent intervention: Recent developments in community focused behavior support* (pp. 31–52). Baltimore: Brookes.
Gettinger, M., & Stoiber, K. C. (2006). Functional assessment, collaboration, and evidence-based treatment: Analysis of a team approach for addressing challenging behaviors in young children. *Journal of School Psychology, 44*, 231–252.
Guess, D., Helmstetter, E., Turnbull, R. H., & Knowlton, S. (1987). *Use of aversive procedures with persons who are disabled: An historical review and critical analysis.* Seattle, WA: Association for Persons With Severe Handicaps.
Hemmeter, M.L., & Strain, P. (2001). Center on the Social and Emotional Foundations for Early Learning. Grant #PHS 90YD0119 funded by the US Department of Health and Human Services.
Hemmeter, M. L., Fox, L., Jack, S., & Broyles, L. (2007). A program-wide model of positive behavior support in early childhood settings. *Journal of Early Intervention, 29*, 337–355.
Huffman, L. C., Mehlinger, S. L., & Kerivan, A. S. (2000). *Risk factors for academic and behavioral problems at the beginning of school.* Bethesda, MD: National Institute of Mental Health.
Individuals With Disabilities Education Improvement Act (IDEA) of 2004, PL 108–446 20 U.S.C. §§ 1400 *et seq.*
IDEA Infant and Toddlers Coordinators Association. (2000). *Position paper on the provision of early intervention services in accordance with federal requirements on natural environments.* Retrieved from www.nectac.org/~pdfs/topics/inclusion/InfntTdlrNE.pdf; November 1, 2007.

Janney, R., & Snell, M. E. (2000). *Behavioral support.* Baltimore: Brookes.

Joseph, G. E., & Strain, P. S. (2003). Comprehensive evidence-based social-emotional curricula for young children: An analysis of efficacious adoption potential. *Topics in Early Childhood Special Education, 23*, 65–76.

Kazdin, A. (1985). *Treatment of antisocial behavior.* Homewood, IL: Dorsey.

Kazdin, A. (1987). *Conduct disorders in childhood.* Newbury Park, CA: Sage.

Keen, D. (2007). Parents, families, and partnerships: Issues and considerations. *International Journal of Development, Disability and Education, 54*, 339–349.

Kern, L., & Clarke, S. (2005). Antecedent and setting event interventions. In L. M. Bambara and L. Kern (Eds.), *Individualized supports for students with problem behaviors: Designing positive behavior plans* (pp. 201–236). New York: Guilford Press.

Kincaid, D., & Fox, L. (2002). Person-centered planning and positive behavior support. In S. Holburn & P. M. Vietze (Eds.), *Person-centered planning. Research, practice, and future directions* (pp. 29–50). Baltimore: Brookes.

Knitzer, J. (2002). *Building services and systems to support the healthy emotional development of young children: An action guide for policymakers.* New York: National Center for Children in Poverty, Columbia University, Mailman School of Public Health.

Krug, D. A., Arick, J. R., & Almond, P. J. (1980). *Autism behavior checklist.* Austin, TX: Pro-Ed.

Lavigne, J. V., Gibbons, R. D., Christoffel, K. K., Arend, R., Rosenbaum, D., Binns, H., et al. (1996). Prevalence rates and correlates of psychiatric disorders among preschool children. *Journal of the American Academy of Child and Adolescent Psychiatry, 35*, 204–214.

Linsheid, T. R., & Reichenbach, H. (2002). Multiple factors in the long-term effectiveness of contingent electric shock treatment for self-injurious behavior: A case example. *Research in Developmental Disabilities, 23*, 161–177.

Loeber, R., & Farrington, D. P. (1998). *Serious and violent juvenile offenders: Risk factors and successful intervention.* Thousand Oaks, CA: Sage.

Lucyshyn, J., Dunlap, G., & Albin, R.W. (Eds.) (2002). *Families and positive behavior support: Addressing problem behaviors in family contexts.* Baltimore: Brookes.

Lucyshyn, J., Horner, R. H., Dunlap, G., & Albin, R. W., & Ben, K. R. (2002). Positive behavior support with families. In J. Lucyshyn, G. Dunlap, & R. W. Albin (Eds.), *Families and positive behavior support: Addressing problem behaviors in family contexts* (pp. 3–43). Baltimore: Brookes.

Luiselli, J. K. (Ed.). (2006). *Antecedent intervention: Recent developments in community focused behavior support.* Baltimore: Brookes.

Minuchin, S. (1974). *Families and family therapy.* Cambridge, MA: Harvard University Press.

Mount, B., & Zwernick, K. (1988). *It's never too early, it's never too late* [booklet about personal futures planning]. St. Paul, MN: Metropolitan Council.

National Research Council. (2001). *Educating children with autism.* Committee on Educational Interventions for Children with Autism. C. Lord & J. McGee, Eds. Division of Behavioral and Social Sciences and Education. Washington, DC: National Academy Press.

Newborg, J., Stock, J. R., & Wnek, L. (1984). *Battelle Developmental Inventory.* Allen, TX: DLM Teaching Resources.

O'Neill, R. E., Horner, R. H., Albin, R. W., Sprague, Storey, K., &. Newton, J.S. (1997). *Functional assessment and program development for problem behavior.* Pacific Grove, CA: Brooks/Cole.

Patterson, G. R. (1986). Performance models for antisocial boys. *American Psychologist, 41*, 432–444.

Peth-Pierce, R. (2000). *A good beginning: Sending America's children to school with the social and emotional competence they need to succeed.* Bethesda, MD: National Institute of Mental Health.

Powell, D., Dunlap, G., & Fox, L. (2006). Prevention and intervention for the challenging behaviors of toddlers and preschoolers. *Infants and Young Children, 19*, 25–35.

Qi, C. H., & Kaiser, A. P. (2003). Behavior problems of preschool children from low-income families: Review of the literature. *Topics in Early Childhood Special Education, 23*, 188–216.

Raver, C. C. (2002). Emotions matter: Making the case for the role of young children's emotional development for early school readiness. *Social Policy Report, 16*, 1–20.

Reid, J. (1993). Prevention of conduct disorder before and after school entry: Relating interventions to developmental findings. *Development and Psychopathology, 5*, 243–262.

Repp, A.C., & Singh, N.N. (Eds.). (1990). *Current perspectives in the use of non-aversive and aversive interventions with developmentally disabled persons*. Sycamore, IL: Sycamore Press.

Shahinfar, A., Fox, N. A., & Leavitt, L. A. (2000). Preschool children's exposure to violence: Relation of behavior problems to parent and child reports. *American Journal of Orthopsychiatry, 70*, 115–125.

Shonkoff, J. P., & Phillips, D. A. (Eds.) (2000). *From neurons to neighborhoods: The science of early development*. Washington, DC: National Academy Press.

Simeonsson, R. J. (1991). Primary, secondary, and tertiary prevention in early intervention. *Journal of Early Intervention, 15*, 124–134.

Singer, G. H. S., Goldberg-Hamblin, S. E., Peckham-Hardin, K. D., Barry, L., & Santarelli, G. E. (2002). Toward a synthesis of family support practices and positive behavior support. In J. Lucyshyn, G. Dunlap, & R. W. Albin (Eds.), *Families and positive behavior support: Addressing problem behaviors in family contexts* (pp. 155–183). Baltimore: Brookes.

Smith, B., & Fox, L. (2003). *Systems of service delivery: A synthesis of evidence relevant to young children at risk of or who have challenging behavior*. Tampa, FL: University of South Florida, Center for Evidence-Based Practice: Young Children with Challenging Behavior. Retrieved September 4, 2007, from www.challengingbehavior.org

Sood, B., Delaney-Black, V., Covington, C., & Nordstrom, B. (2001). Prenatal alcohol exposure and childhood behavior at age 6 to 7 years: I. Dose-response effect. *Pediatrics, 108*(2), e34.

Stormont, M., Lewis, T. J., & Beckner, R. (2005). Positive behavior support systems: Applying key features in preschool settings. *Teaching Exceptional Children, 37*, 42–49.

Sugai, G., Horner, R. H., Dunlap, G., Hieneman, M., Lewis, T. J., Nelson, C. M., et al. (2000). Applying positive behavior support and functional behavioral assessment in schools. *Journal of Positive Behavior Interventions, 2*, 131–143.

Tremblay, R. E. (2000). The development of aggressive behavior during childhood: What have we learned in the past century? *International Journal of Behavioral Development, 24*, 129–141.

Turnbull, A. P., & Turnbull, H. R. (2000). Achieving "rich" lifestyles. *Journal of Positive Behavior Interventions, 2*, 190–192.

Turnbull, A. P., & Turnbull, H. R. (2001). *Families, professionals, and exceptionality: Collaborating for empowerment*. Upper Saddle River, NJ: Prentice-Hall.

U.S. Public Health Service. (2000). *Report of the surgeon general's conference on children's mental health: A national action agenda*. Washington, DC: Department of Health and Human Services.

Walker, H. M., Horner, R. H., Sugai, G., Bullis, M., Sprague, J., Bricker, D., et al. (1996). Integrated approaches to preventing antisocial behavior patterns among school age children and youth. *Journal of Emotional and Behavioral Disorders, 4*, 194–209.

Walker, H. M., Kavanagh, K., Stiller, B., Golly, A., Severson, H. H., & Feil, E. G. (1998). First step to success: An early intervention approach for preventing school antisocial behavior. *Journal of Emotional and Behavioral Disorders, 6*(2), 66–80.

Webster-Stratton, C. (1990). *Dina dinosaur's social skills and problem-solving curriculum*. Seattle, WA: Incredible Years.

Wehby, J. H., Symons, F. M., Canale, J., & Go, F. (1998). Teaching practices in classrooms for students with emotional and behavioral disorders: Discrepancies between recommendations and observations. *Behavioral Disorders, 24*, 52–57.

West, J., Denton, K., & Germino-Hausken, E. (2000). *America's Kindergartener: Findings from the early childhood longitudinal study, kindergarten class of 1998-99, fall 1998*. Washington DC: US Department of Education, National Center for Educational Statistics.

Westling, D. L., & Fox, L. (2004). *Teaching students with severe disabilities* (3rd ed.). Upper Saddle River, NJ: Pearson Education.

# 4

# Toward an Ecological Unit of Analysis in Behavioral Assessment and Intervention With Families of Children With Developmental Disabilities

**LAUREN BINNENDYK, BRENDA FOSSETT, CHRISTY CHEREMSHYNSKI, SHARON LOHRMANN, LAUREN ELKINSON, and LYNN MILLER**

The purpose of this chapter is to present our work and that of colleagues in the field of positive behavior support (PBS) (Carr et al., 2002; Koegel, Koegel, Dunlap, 1996) on the development of an empirically grounded ecological unit of analysis for behavioral assessment and intervention with families of children with developmental disabilities and severe problem behavior. Our aim is to provide practitioners and families with an empirical foundation for the design of comprehensive PBS plans in family contexts that are likely to be acceptable to family members, implemented by

**LAUREN BINNENDYK** • University of British Columbia
**BRENDA FOSSETT** • University of British Columbia
**CHRISTY CHEREMSHYNSKI** • University of British Columbia
**SHARON LOHRMANN** • University of Medicine & Dentistry of New Jersey
**LAUREN ELKINSON** • University of Medicine and Dentistry of New Jersey
**LYNN MILLER** • University of British Columbia

family members with fidelity, effective at improving the behavior and quality of life of the child and family, sustainable within the family ecology, and durable across a long period of time.

This work has been guided by one central question: What are the necessary and sufficient conditions for the design of *survivable* positive behavior interventions in family contexts? In collaboration with parents of children with developmental disabilities and severe problem behavior, we have empirically investigated a unit of analysis—coercive processes in family routines—that has served as the organizing center of our research and practice with families. In the first half of the chapter, we define the problem and need; describe an ecological unit of analysis that integrates child behavior, parent-child interaction, and family activity settings (routines); and summarize assessment and intervention research that validates key components of the ecological model. In the second half of the chapter, we briefly summarize our current longitudinal research with families of children with developmental disabilities in which we have been investigating the validity of the ecological unit of analysis for transforming coercive processes in family routines. Following this summary, we discuss five implications of our research for assessment and intervention in natural family contexts in collaboration with family members.

## PROBLEM AND NEED

As a result of changes in law and public policy in the United States and Canada over the past 35 years, children with developmental disabilities such as autism and mental retardation are being raised by their families at home and attending neighborhood schools (Turnbull, Turnbull, Erwin and Soodak, 2006). These advances in social policy, as important as they are, also have placed significant caregiving challenges on families. Foremost among these challenges is the presence of child problem behavior. In a study of 3-year-old children with and without developmental delays, Baker, Blacher, Crnic, and Edelbrock (2002) reported that the children with disabilities were three times more likely to be in the clinical range for problem behavior compared to typically developing children (26% vs. 3% of children). Among children with mental retardation 5 to 17 years old, Jacobson (1990) found that problem behavior was present in 40%. Problem behaviors are a major source of stress for families and are associated with significant social costs, including parental health problems, maternal depression, social isolation, marital strain, divorce, out-of-home placement, and institutionalization (Bromley & Blacher, 1991; Risdal & Singer, 2004). Consequently, many families of children with developmental disabilities have a significant need for behavior support services (Floyd & Gallagher, 1997; Lucyshyn, Dunlap, & Albin, 2002).

Although models of service delivery to families of children with developmental disabilities and problem behavior have improved (Feldman, Condillac, Tough, Hunt, & Griffiths, 2002; Roberts, Mazzucchelli, Studman, & Sanders, 2006), families continue to report difficulty in obtaining effective behavior support services (Rocco, Metzger, Zangerele, & Skouge, 2002). Families and practitioners report the need for: (a) assessments that are strength based and help families understand problem behavior; (b) behavior support services that address all of the family contexts in which problem behaviors occur; (c) behavior support procedures that are positive, practical, and culturally sensitive; and (d) outcomes that are sustainable within the natural contexts of family life (Carr, 2007; Turnbull & Ruef, 1996).

## GAPS IN THE EMPIRICAL FOUNDATION FOR BEHAVIORAL FAMILY INTERVENTION

Behavioral scientists (Baer, 1986; Baer, Wolf, & Risley, 1987) speak directly to these consumer needs when they argue that the ultimate criterion for the value of behavioral interventions is their "survivability" in natural settings. For families of children with disabilities and problem behavior, survivable interventions are those that remain acceptable, effective, and sustainable across a long period of time, best measured in years *after* formal behavior support services have been terminated. Although there has been much progress in the development of empirically validated behavioral interventions (Kazdin & Weisz, 2003; Scotti & Meyer, 1999), little of this knowledge has been developed in the lives of families raising children with developmental disabilities (Bristol et al., 1996; Helm & Kozloff, 1986).

Three gaps in the literature exist. First, there are very few studies of parent-child interaction in natural family contexts. Consequently, our understanding of the etiology of problem behavior in family life is not well developed (Crnic et al., 2002). Second, only a relatively small number of empirical analyses have documented the effectiveness of positive behavior interventions used by parents of children with developmental disabilities in family contexts (Buschbacher, Fox, & Clarke, 2004; Clarke, Dunlap, & Vaughn, 1999; Koegel, Steibel, & Koegel, 1998; Lucyshyn, Albin, et al., 2007; Lucyshyn, Albin, & Nixon, 1997; Moes & Frea, 2002; Vaughn, Clarke, & Dunlap, 1997). Third, very few studies have documented the long-term maintenance of behavioral intervention in home and community settings (Kern, Gallagher, Starosta, Hickman, & George, 2006). Carr et al. (1999), in a review of functional assessment-based intervention studies from 1985 to 1996 that emphasized the use of positive behavior supports, found that only 5% of the studies documented the maintenance of behavior change at 13 to 24 months, and no studies gathered follow-up data beyond 2 years.

## INTEGRATED ECOLOGICAL UNIT OF ANALYSIS

We believe the design of PBS plans that meet the criterion of survivability (i.e., acceptable, effective, sustainable, and durable) across a diversity of families requires an ecological unit of analysis that more thoroughly addresses the sources of variability that affect child and parent behavior during a PBS process. The ecological unit of analysis that we propose is comprised of three theoretical frameworks that are well established, respectively, in the fields of applied behavior analysis, clinical and community psychology, and cross-cultural anthropology. The three theoretical frameworks, described next, are behavioral theory (Bijou & Baer, 1961; Skinner, 1953), coercion theory (Patterson, 1982; Reid, Patterson, & Snyder, 2002), and ecocultural theory and the construct of the activity setting (Gallimore, Weisner, Kaufman, & Bernheimer, 1989; O'Donnell, Tharp, & Wilson, 1993).

### *Behavioral Theory*

Behavioral theory offers a comprehensive set of empirically validated principles or laws of behavior for understanding how individual behavior changes over time in interaction with one's environment. These principles include motivational operations, stimulus control, positive reinforcement, negative reinforcement, extinction, and punishment (Cooper, Heron, & Heward, 2007). Based on this science of behavior, the field of applied behavior analysis over the past 40 years has developed a technology of assessment and intervention aimed at understanding problem behavior in children, adolescents, and adults and designing behavioral interventions that promote socially valid and durable behavioral change (Baer, Wolf, & Risley, 1968; 1987). Over the past 15 years, the emerging discipline of PBS, closely allied to applied behavior analysis, has continued to expand this assessment and intervention technology with an emphasis on improving the focus individual's quality of life, on the proactive prevention of problem behavior, and on ecological validity (Carr et al., 2002). Central to applied behavior analysis and positive behavior support is the technology of functional assessment, which is based on the four-part contingency, comprised of (a) motivational operations (also referred to as establishing operations or setting events), (b) immediate antecedent events, (c) target behaviors, and (d) maintaining consequences (Repp & Horner, 1999).

Functional assessment or analysis is a process that involves gathering information to understand the function or purpose of a person's problem behavior (O'Neill et al., 1997). Assessment procedures (e.g., interviews, direction observations, experimental manipulations) are used to identify the environmental variables that set the stage for, occasion, and maintain problem behavior. This information is then used to design a behavior support plan. A meta-analysis by Carr et al. (1999) of 109 behavior intervention studies showed that behavior interventions based on a functional assessment were more likely to be effective compared to behavior interventions that were selected arbitrarily, with no regard to the function of behavior.

A large body of research demonstrates that children with developmental disabilities engage in problem behaviors for specific functions (Carr & Durand, 1985; Derby et al., 1994; Iwata, Dorsey, Sliter, Bauman, and Richman, 1982). These functions fall into four broad categories: (a) getting social attention; (b) avoiding or escaping nonpreferred or aversive demands, tasks, or people; (c) getting access to a preferred item, activity, or situation; and (d) getting sensory or automatic reinforcement (O'Neill et al., 1997).

Recent behavioral intervention research with families of children with developmental disabilities suggests how typical family settings lend themselves to the development of problem behaviors with particular functions. Werle, Murphy, and Budd (1993) described the way in which young children with limited food preferences refuse food during mealtimes at home and consequently receive negative or positive reinforcement through parental withdrawal of nonpreferred foods or delivery of preferred foods. In a community-based study with a child with autism and a severe intellectual disability, Vaughn, Wilson, and Dunlap, (2002) showed how specific subroutines within a fast food restaurant activity were associated with different functions of problem behavior. During arrival at the restaurant, problem behavior served an escape function, while during departure it served a tangible function (i.e., maintain a preferred activity). In each of these studies, knowledge of the functions of child problem behaviors guided the design of individualized interventions that proved to be effective at decreasing problem behavior and improving child adaptive behavior. Given this research, we believe that understanding the functions of problem behavior and designing interventions linked to these functions and the specific environmental events that set the stage for, occasion, and maintain problem behavior are the first necessary conditions for the development of survivable interventions in family contexts.

## *Coercion Theory*

Observational and intervention research with aggressive children (Patterson, 1982; Reid et al., 2002) offers longitudinal evidence for a theory of coercion in which problem behaviors in young children have their etiology in the cumulative moment-by-moment (micro-) actions and reactions that occur between parents and children. The core of coercion theory involves an aversive, four-step, escape-conditioning sequence: (a) parent makes a demand, (b) child engages in problem behavior; (c) parent withdraws the demand, and (d) child terminates problem behavior. The parent's effect on the child occurs when he or she withdraws the demand, thus negatively reinforcing child problem behavior. The child's effect on the parent occurs when he or she terminates problem behavior, thus negatively reinforcing parental submission. Over time, this well-rehearsed sequence of exchanges can become automatic or reflexive (Dumas, 2005). Both the parent and child are unaware of the consequences of their own behavior and thus become trapped in a relationship that reciprocally maintains child problem behavior and ineffective parenting practices. Contextual variables that affect the development of coercive family processes include difficult infant temperament, poor parenting skills, maternal depression, family stress (i.e., life events and daily hassles), marital conflict, and divorce (Capaldi, DeGarmo, Patterson, & Forgatch, 2002). Without early and intensive intervention, coercive parent-child interactions set children on a trajectory toward antisocial behavior, academic failure, affiliation with deviant peer groups, and juvenile delinquency (Patterson, Forgatch, Yoerger, & Stoolmiller, 1998).

To date, very little research has examined the presence of coercive processes in families raising children with developmental disabilities. Floyd and Phillippe (1993) conducted the first comparative observational study of coercive parent-child interactions in families of children with and without mental retardation. Across two 50-min videotaped sessions during typical family activities in the home (e.g., preparing dinner, eating dinner, baking cookies), they documented the presence of two-step coercive exchanges in which a parent directive was followed by child problem behavior. Carr, Taylor, and Robinson (1991), in a single-subject analysis with children with developmental disabilities, provided the first empirical documentation of child effects on the behavior of adults in teaching contexts. Their analysis showed that, in response to an instructional demand, child problem behavior over time decreased the number of instructional requests made by adults.

Lucyshyn et al. (2004) conducted the first comprehensive study of the construct of coercion in the daily routines of families raising young children with developmental disabilities and problem behavior. Following Messick's model of construct validation (Messick, 1988), the observational study investigated the *evidential validity* and *social validity* of the construct. Research questions included the following: (a) Do stable coercive family processes exist in family routines in the home, as measured by statistically significant conditional probabilities; and (b) Do families view the construct as important and acceptable? Ten families participated in videotaped observations in valued but problematic home routines across a 9-month period.

Results indicated the presence of two stable coercive processes. In routines in which the parents were busy and unable to fully attend to their child with a disability (e.g., preparing dinner, doing household chores, talking with older daughter), attention-driven coercive processes were observed. The steps in this process were (a) parent is occupied, (b) child engages in problem behavior, (c) parent provides negative or positive attention, and (d) child terminates or reduces problem behavior. Results offered modest support for the presence of stable escape-driven coercive processes in routines in which parent demands were common (e.g., dinner, homework, reading to child). The steps in this moderated coercive exchange were (a) parent makes demand, (b) child engages in problem behavior, (c) parent reduces demand (i.e., delivers positive or negative attention or provides physical assistance), and (d) child terminates or reduces problem behavior. During postobservation interviews focused on the social validity of the construct of coercion in family routines, 9 of 10 families viewed the construct as accurate, important, and potentially useful. Parents also reported two perceived effects of coercive exchanges on family life. First, parents reported that to avoid problem behavior they altered family routines in ways that made them less normative and acceptable. For example, one parent reported that she regularly served her son with autism preferred but less healthy foods during dinner. Second, parents reported that they avoided, altogether, valued routines in which coercive exchanges were common. For example, another parent reported that she no longer read to her young son with autism due to his problem behavior. Finally, parents reported that until they received professional assistance that improved parent-child interaction, they had little choice but to submit to their child's problem behavior. They perceived that doing so had the short-term benefit of reducing stress levels and preserving the family unit. Based on these studies of coercive processes among children with and without developmental disabilities, we believe that the assessment of coercive processes and the design of interventions directly aimed at ameliorating coercive parent-child interactions constitute the second necessary condition for the survivability of positive behavior interventions in family contexts.

### *Ecocultural Theory and the Activity Setting*

Family theorists and interventionists have long recognized the importance of the ecology that surrounds the child and family (Bronfenbrenner, 1986; Peters & McMahon, 1989). Failure to attend to ecological variables can result in lack of treatment adherence, negative side effects, or a loss of maintenance (Griest & Forehand, 1982). Ecocultural theory provides an empirically grounded theoretical framework for understanding the ecology of child development in the family (Gallimore et al., 1989; Gallimore, Coots, Weisner, Garnier, & Guthrie, 1996). Ecocultural theory supposes that ecological (e.g., income, neighborhood, available services) and cultural influences (e.g., parental goals, parental beliefs, scripts of interaction) are mediated through the activity settings of daily routines with family members. Activity settings are the routines of everyday life (e.g., dinner, bedtime, visiting grandparents, attending religious services) in which parent-child interactions are embedded. The specific activities a child participates in during the day and the quality of interactions with family members are believed to have a profound impact on the child's cognitive and adaptive skill development.

Over the past decade, researchers conducting PBS research with families of children with developmental disabilities have used the activity settings of daily routines as a unit of analysis. The results of their research offer priliminary evidence of the activity setting's value for the design of acceptable, effective, and durable interventions in family contexts (Buschbacher et al., 2004; Clarke et al., 1999; Lucyshyn et al., 1997; Lucyshyn, Albin et al., 2007; Moes & Frea, 2002; Vaughn et al., 1997).

Vaughn et al. (1997) conducted a behavioral intervention study in collaboration with the family of an 8-year-old boy with a severe intellectual disability and severe problem behavior. Two family routines were selected for intervention: a bathroom routine at home and a restaurant routine in the community. An experimental, multiple-baseline design across routines documented the effectiveness of a functional assessment-based PBS plan for decreasing problem behavior and improving the boy's successful engagement in each routine.

In collaboration with the parents of an adolescent girl with multiple disabilities and severe problem behavior, Lucyshyn et al. (1997) developed a PBS plan that the youth's parents implemented sequentially in four routines in the home and community across a 26-month period. The routines selected were dinner at home, going to a restaurant, free time at home while parents were busy, and grocery shopping. A multiple-baseline design across routines indicated that the intervention effected an 88% reduction in problem behavior, and that these improvements were maintained, with further gains at 3 and 9 months postintervention. Parent social validity evaluations indicated that the family perceived intervention goals, procedures, and outcomes to be important and acceptable. Goodness-of-fit evaluations indicated that the PBS plan was perceived by the youth's parents as possessing a good contextual fit with each routine.

Buschbacher et al. (2004) conducted an experimental and descriptive analysis of the acceptability, effectiveness, and durability of a PBS approach with a family of a 7-year-old boy with autistic like characteristics and Landau-Kleffner syndrome who engaged in severe problem behavior. The family selected three problematic routines for intervention: dinner, family television watching, and bedtime. Following functional assessment procedures, an individualized behavior support plan was designed for each routine. A multiple-baseline design across routines documented substantial decreases in problem behavior and increases in task engagement at the point of intervention for each routine. Follow-up data at 2, 4, and 12 months postintervention showed that these gains were maintained, and further improvement was evidenced.

Lucyshyn et al. (2007) conducted a longitudinal experimental and descriptive analysis of family implementation of PBS with a child with autism. The study was conducted across a 10-year period beginning when the child was 5 years old and concluding when the child was 15. A multiple baseline across four routines evaluated the efficacy of the approach. The routines selected were dinner, bedtime, eating at a fast food restaurant, and grocery shopping. Results documented a 94% decrease in problem behavior from baseline to intervention and an improvement in successful routine participation from 0% of routines during baseline to 75% during intervention. Follow-up data at 6 months, 18 months, 3 years, and 7 years postintervention showed that these gains were maintained and showed further improvement. Social validity and goodness-of-fit evaluations indicated that the child's parents perceived the support process to be acceptable and important and the behavior support plan to be contextually appropriate. Based on the research evidence described, we believe that a third necessary condition for the design of survivable behavioral interventions in family contexts is the analysis of valued but problematic family routines and the design of behavior supports that are both technically sound and contextually appropriate within natural family contexts.

## SYNTHESIS: COERCIVE PROCESSES IN FAMILY ROUTINES

The three theoretical frameworks and the empirical support for each level of analysis offer an opportunity to integrate child behavior, parent-child interaction, and the activity setting of daily routines into a highly useful ecological unit of analysis: coercive processes in family routines. First, because child behavior and parent-child interaction occur in family activity settings, the functional assessment of problem behavior and the assessment of coercive processes can easily be integrated with an assessment of activity settings (Lucyshyn et al., 2004). Second, activity settings include both objective (e.g., persons present, tasks, resources) and subjective (e.g., goals, values, beliefs about parenting and disability) elements and therefore provide a useful context for designing contextually appropriate or culturally sensitive interventions in collaboration with families (Chen, Downing, & Peckman-Hardin, 2002; Galimore, Goldenberg, & Weisner, 2003). Given the growing diversity of families in the United States and Canada, the development of cultural competence in assessment and intervention planning is becoming an essential requirement of service delivery systems (Lynch & Hanson, 2004). Third, the activity settings of daily life offer the interventionist an opportunity to embed interventions within the key elements of specific routines such as getting ready for school in the morning, having dinner with family members, or accompanying a parent on a shopping trip. Ensuring that positive behavior interventions possess a good contextual fit with the time and place of the routine, the people who participate in the routine, the tasks of the routine, and the goals and values of participants may (a) increase the acceptability of interventions to family members, (b) improve the effectiveness of behavioral parent training, and (c) enhance the ability of family members to implement interventions with fidelity. Fourth, because the ecological unit of analysis offers an expanded view of potential sources of variability that may affect child or parent behavior (e.g., function of child behavior, coercive patterns of interaction, elements of activity settings), the long-term maintenance of treatment outcomes may be enhanced by directly addressing these sources of variability while teaching parents to build successful activity settings (Gallimore, 2005; Lucyshyn et al., 2007). Fifth, because family activity settings represent instantiations of the broader ecology that surrounds the child and family, they offer a window into contextual influences that may need to be taken into account when working with families. Contextual influences such as sibling problem behavior, marital strain, and extended family relationships may need to be addressed beyond the focus on PBS with the child with a disability if target family routines are to be successful. Figure 4.1 presents a conceptual model of the integrated ecological unit of analysis. The model represents an adaptation of the conceptual model presented by Patterson, Reid, and Dishion (1992).

## Transforming Coercive Relationships in Family Routines

For the past 3½ years, we have been investigating the construct of coercive processes in family routines and its contribution to improving the behavior and quality of life of children with developmental disabilities and severe problem behavior and their families (Lucyshyn, Lohrmann, et al., 2007). Funded by a 5-year public health services grant from the National Institute of Child Health and Human Development (NICHD) of the National Institutes of Health (NIH), the goal of the research project has been to evaluate the internal, external, and social validity of the construct for designing PBS plans that *transform* coercive patterns of parent-child interaction into constructive patterns of interaction in the context of valued but problematic family activity settings. The project represents the second stage in Messick's (1988) model of construct validation. In the first stage, Lucyshyn et al. (2004) documented the *evidential validity* of the construct of coercion in family routines. In this second stage, our aim has

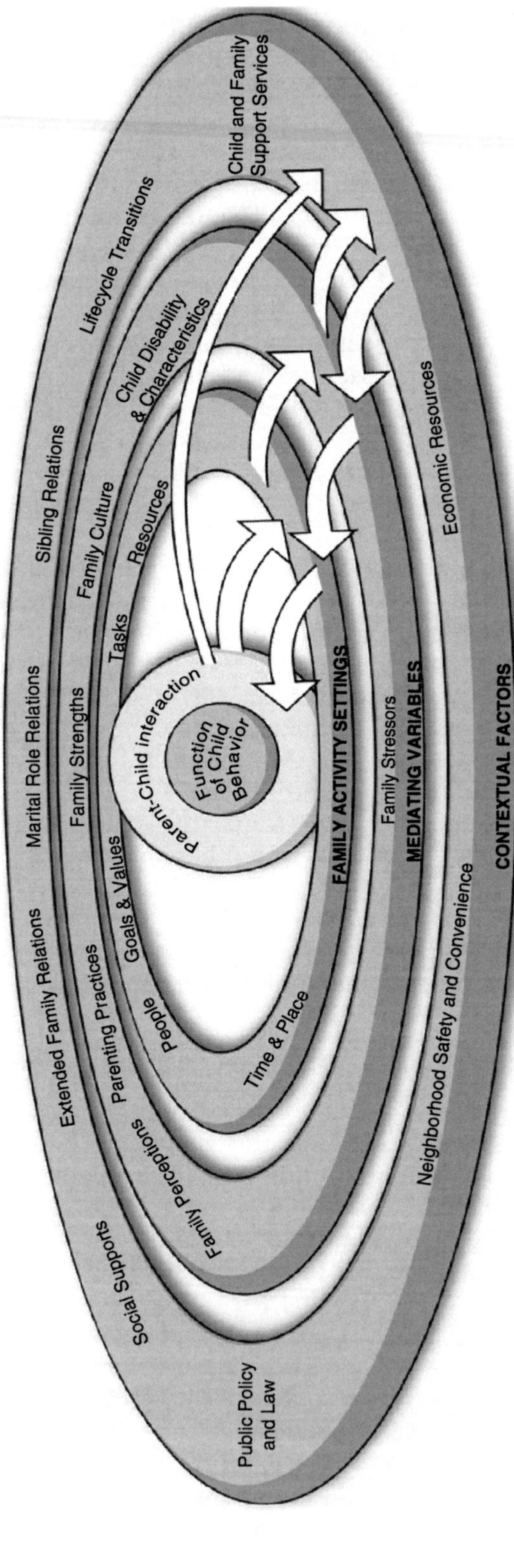


**Fig. 4.1.** Conceptual model of ecological influences on parent-child interaction in family routines. Adapted with permission from *Antisocial Boys*, by G. R. Patterson, J. B. Reid, & T. J. Dishion, 1992, Eugene, OR: Castalia.

been to evaluate the *consequential validity* of the construct; that is, the extent to which the ecological unit of analysis promotes the design of family-centered PBS plans that, when implemented, prove to be acceptable, effective, sustainable, and durable (i.e., survivable) in natural family contexts. A brief summary of the project and its preliminary results are presented. This is followed by an in-depth discussion of the implications of our preliminary findings for assessment and intervention aimed at designing and implementing survivable PBS plans in natural family contexts.

## Participants and Settings

Twelve families of children with developmental disabilities and severe problem behavior have participated in the study. Participating children were between 3 and 8 years old at the start of the project. Diagnosed developmental disabilities include autism, Asperger syndrome, moderate intellectual disability, and CHARGE syndrome. CHARGE syndrome is a rare genetic disorder in children that affects multiple organ systems. Common features include cranial nerve abnormalities, heart defects, blocked nasal passages, mental retardation, genital abnormalities, and ear abnormalities (Davenport, Hefner, & Mitchell, 1986).

Eleven of 12 families included a mother and father, while 1 family was composed of a mother and two children living in Canada while her husband lived abroad. Children's problem behaviors have included noncompliance; elopement (i.e., leaving assigned area); defiance; negative vocalizations (e.g., whining, crying, screaming); food refusal; verbal and physical aggression; disruptive behavior; destructive behavior; vomiting; and feces smearing. Eleven of 12 families included one or more siblings. The study has included six Caucasian families of European heritage; four families of Asian heritage (Chinese, Taiwanese, and Japanese); one African American family; and one Iranian family. The study has been conducted across two consortium sites, with nine families in British Columbia and three families in New Jersey.

Three to four valued but problematic routines in the home and community were selected and defined in collaboration with each family. Across the 12 families, a total of 45 routines were selected for assessment and intervention, including 31 home routines (e.g., morning routine, dinner routine, going-to-bed routine) and 14 community routines (e.g., going to grocery store, eating at a restaurant, attending church services). Across 3 years of assessment and intervention, the retention rate has been 83% (10 of 12 families).

## Methods

Several dependent measures have been gathered to evaluate the extent to which the expanded ecological approach to PBS with families has transformed coercive patterns of parent-child interaction in problematic family routines into constructive patterns of interaction in successful routines. Dependent measures have included (a) percentage of intervals of child problem behavior; (b) percentage of routine steps successfully completed;

(c) conditional probability of a coercive pattern of parent-child interaction; (d) conditional probability of a constructive pattern of parent-child interaction; (e) parent social validity ratings; and (f) parent goodness-of-fit indexes.

The independent variable has been a family-centered PBS approach that has included the following key components: (a) building and sustaining a collaborative partnership with the family; (b) conducting a comprehensive assessment, including functional, coercive process, and family ecology assessments; (c) designing routine-specific PBS plans and implementation plans that are technically sound and contextually appropriate; (d) identifying family-centered adjunctive supports; (e) providing initial training and support in one routine at a time using behavioral parent training strategies (e.g., written plan, modeling, coaching, self-monitoring and self-management, behavioral rehearsal; Briesmeister & Schaefer, 1998); (f) providing or coordinating the provision of family-centered adjunctive supports as needed; (g) providing maintenance support, including relapse prevention training (Goldstein & Martens, 2000) and parent self-monitoring of coercive processes. PBS plans have been based on a functional assessment and have included the following components: (a) setting event strategies; (b) antecedent preventive strategies; (c) teaching strategies; and (d) consequence strategies. An example of a routine-based behavior support plan for one family is presented in Table 4.1. For a detailed description of the family-centered PBS approach, refer to the works of Lucyshyn, Kayser, Irvin, & Blumberg, (2002); Koegel, Koegel, Boettcher, and Brookman-Frazee (2005); and Hieneman, Childs, and Sergay (2006).

A multiple-baseline design across routines for each family (i.e., one multiple baseline consisting of three to four routines for each family) using a multiple-probe measurement strategy (R. D. Horner & Baer, 1978; Kennedy, 2005) was employed to evaluate the functional relationship between the intervention approach and improvements in child behavior and routine participation. The design has three phases: (a) baseline; (b) intervention, consisting of initial training and support and maintenance support; and (c) follow-up. Sequential analyses were used to evaluate the transformation of coercive processes into constructive processes of parent-child interaction in routines. Videotaped observation probes of parent and child behavior were coded in real time using the Parent and Child Coding System (PACCS; Lucyshyn et al., 2004) and the Observer 5.0 software program (Noldus, Trienes, Hendriksen, Jansen, & Jansen, 2000). These interaction data were then submitted to a sequential analysis using the General Sequential Querier software program (GSEQ; Bakeman & Quera, 1995). For one family to date, conditional probabilities of coercive and constructive patterns of parent-child interaction were computed for a random sample of 10 baseline phase observation sessions and 10 intervention phase observation sessions across four family routines. The presence of statistically significant coercive processes in the baseline phase but not in the intervention phase and statistically significant constructive processes in the intervention phase but not in the baseline phase were viewed as preliminary evidence of the transformation of coercive processes into constructive processes in family routines.

**Table 4.1.** Positive Behavior Support Plan for a Dinner Routine

*Introduction.* This is a behavior support plan for Nathan (pseudonym), an affectionate and charming 4-year-old boy with the diagnosis of autism. The plan is necessary because Nathan engages in severe food refusal behavior that threatens his health and development.

*Summary Hypothesis Statement:* When requested to come to the dinner table, eat, or use a utensil, Nathan will physically resist, engage in food refusal (push food away, throw food on floor), cry, run from table, fall to floor, or tantrum to escape eating the food and using his utensil. Setting events that set the stage for or exaggerate the occurrence of problem behavior include a long history of food refusal (since 7 months old), snacks available within 2 hr of dinner, and lack of predictability about expectations at the dinner table.

*Setting Event Strategies*

1. Use a visual schedule to increase predictability regarding the steps in the routine (sit, eat, wipe hands/face, say "finished," put dish in sink).
2. Use a visually mediated positive contingency that shows the steps that need to be completed and the reward that Nathan will receive for doing so.
3. Restrict access to snacks to at least 2 hr before dinner.

*Preventive Strategies*

1. Use stimulus-fading strategy, moving from pea-size amounts of food and gradually increasing food to normal size.
2. Use positive contingency (first-then) statements to motivate using utensil and eating food served (e.g., first eat this, then play with toy; first use utensil, then get juice).

*Teaching Strategies*

1. Teach Nathan to ask for a break using a BigMack® voice output device.
2. Teach Nathan to use fork to stab food.

*Consequence Strategies*

1. Provide praise, tickles, and preferred items contingent on complying with requests, eating foods served, and using utensils.
2. Provide praise and preferred dessert item contingent on successfully completing meal.
3. Provide break contingent on using BigMack to request a break.
4. Use escape extinction contingent on problem behavior: (a) physical redirection when he leaves table; (b) physical guidance when he refuses to use (safe, plastic) utensil; (c) non-removal of spoon when he refuse to eat food.

*Evaluation Procedures*

Use implementation checklist to self-monitor and self-evaluate (a) implementation fidelity; (b) problem behavior; and (c) social validity.

## *Preliminary Results*

To date, multiple-baseline data across 11 families and 40 routines have evidenced a decrease in total percentage of child problem behavior from a baseline phase average of 51% of intervals observed (range 22–90%) to an initial training and support subphase average of 16% of intervals (range 1.5–37%). The maintenance support subphase has evidenced further improvement to an average of 7% of intervals (range 0–10%). Steps successfully completed have shown an increase from an average of 27% (range 0–65%) during baseline to an average of 71% (range 55–91%) during initial training and support. Maintenance support has evidenced further improvement to an average of 93% of steps completed (range 80–100%). Overall, preliminary results showed that, in comparison to baseline, child problem behavior decreased by 69% during initial training and support and by 86% during maintenance support. Child steps completed increased by 62% during initial training and 71% during maintenance support. The average social validity rating (1 = low; 5 = high) across two to three measures for each family was 4.8 (range 3.4–5.0), suggesting that behavior support plan goals, procedures, and outcomes have been perceived by parents as important and acceptable. The average goodness-of-fit index was 4.4 (range 3.7–5.0), suggesting that parents perceived behavior support plans to be contextually appropriate.

Preliminary sequential analysis results are presented in Tables 4.2 and 4.3 for one family. Coercive process and constructive process results are presented across baseline and intervention phases for four routines in which parental demands were common (i.e., going to bed, drinking milk from a cup, dinner, and eating at a restaurant) (see Tables 4.2 and 4.3). Table 4.2 shows that during baseline, after a parent demand followed by child problem behavior, for the next one to three parent-child interactions (i.e., Lags 1–3), the parent persisted with the demand and the child persisted with problem behavior. The conditional probabilities of this pattern of interaction ranged from .31 to .57, with statistical significance ranging from <.05 to <.001. During intervention, however, this stable (i.e., statistically significant) relationship was no longer observed. The conditional probabilities of a parent demand and child problem behavior followed by another parent demand and child problem behavior was 0 across Lags 1 to 3. Conditional probabilities were nonsignificant.

Table 4.3 shows the results of our examination of a four-step escape-driven coercive process (i.e., parent demand → child problem behavior → parent withdraw or reduce demand → child terminate or reduce problem behavior) and a four-step constructive process (i.e., parent demand → child compliance → parent positive attention → child positive or neutral behavior). With respect to the coercive process, during baseline after a parent demand followed by child problem behavior, by the fourth or fifth interaction (Lags 4 and 5), the parent withdrew or reduced the demand,

**Table 4.2.** Relative Frequency and Conditional Probability of Parent Demand and Child Problem Behavior Followed by Parent Demand and Child Problem Behavior

| Steps in Parent-Child Interaction | Baseline | | | | Intervention | | | |
|---|---|---|---|---|---|---|---|---|
| | Lag: | 1 | 2 | 3 | Lag: | 1 | 2 | 3 |
| Coercive process: | | | | | | | | |
| 1. Parent request/ demand | JNTF: | 102 | 70 | 43 | JNTF: | 0 | 0 | 0 |
| 2. Child problem behavior | ConP: | .57* | .59* | .24* | ConP: | .00 | .00 | .00 |
| 3. Parent request/ demand | ADJR: | 11.61* | 5.29* | 2.38* | ADJR: | −.18 | −.18[a] | −.16 |
| 4. Child problem behavior | PVal: | <.001 | <.001 | <.001 | PVal: | ns | ns | ns |

*Note.* JNTF, relative frequency; ConP, conditional probability; ADJR, adjusted residual (binomial z-score equivalent); PVal, probability value; *, statistically significant probability value; ns, statistically nonsignificant probability value. [a]adjusted residuals do not meet conditions for normal distribution.

**Table 4.3.** Relative Frequency and Conditional Probability of Coercive and Constructive Processes in Baseline and Intervention Phases

| | Baseline | | | Intervention | | |
|---|---|---|---|---|---|---|
| Steps in Parent-Child Interaction | Lag: | 4 | 5 | Lag: | 4 | 5 |
| Coercive process: | | | | | | |
| 1. Parent request/demand | JNTF: | 38 | 40 | JNTF: | 2 | 1 |
| 2. Child problem behavior | ConP: | .22* | .24* | ConP: | .50 | .25 |
| 3. Parent withdraw or reduce demand | ADJR: | 2.01+ | 2.93+ | ADJR: | +.95[a] | −.18[a] |
| 4. Child terminate or reduce problem behavior | PVal: | <.05 | <.01 | PVal: | ns | ns |
| | Lag: | 1 | | Lag | 1 | |
| Constructive process: | | | | | | |
| 1. Parent request/demand | JNTF: | 0 | | JNTF: | 27 | |
| 2. Child compliance | ConP: | .00 | | ConP: | .40* | |
| 3. Parent positive attention | ADJR: | −.78[a] | | ADJR: | +3.71 | |
| 4. Child positive or neutral behavior | PVal: | ns | | PVal: | <.001 | |

*Note.* JNTF, relative frequency; ConP, conditional probability; ADJR, adjusted residual (binomial z-score equivalent); PVal, probability value; *, statistically significant probability value; ns, statistically nonsignificant probability value. [a]Adjusted residuals do not meet conditions for normal distribution.

and the child terminated or reduced problem behavior. The conditional probabilities of this coercive process were .22 and .24, respectively, with statistical significance at < .05 and < .01. During intervention, however, this stable escape-driven coercive process was not observed. At Lags 4 and 5, although conditional probabilities were .50 and .25, respectively, they were nonsignificant.

With respect to the constructive process, during baseline across four family routines, a constructive pattern of parent interaction was not observed. At Lag 1, the conditional probability that a parent demand would lead to child compliance followed by parent positive attention and child positive or neutral behavior was zero, which was nonsignificant. During intervention, however, a stable constructive process was evidenced. At Lag 1, the conditional probability of parent demand and child compliance followed by parent positive attention and child positive or neutral behavior was .40. This was statistically significant at $p < .001$. Taken together, these results provide preliminary evidence for one family of the transformation of escape-driven coercive processes into constructive patterns of parent-child interaction in valued family routines.

## IMPLICATIONS FOR ASSESSMENT AND INTERVENTION

The preliminary results of our research with families offer five implications for assessment and intervention aimed at building survivable PBS plans in natural family contexts: (a) assessing and intervening on coercive patterns of parent-child interaction; (b) using the family routine as a unit of analysis; (c) assessing the broader ecology of the family and providing family-centered adjunctive supports as needed; (d) ensuring clinical supervision during implementation support; and (e) adopting a life-span perspective for promoting the sustainability of behavior support plans and the durability of behavior and quality-of-life improvements. These implications are discussed next.

## Assessing Coercive Patterns of Parent-Child Interaction

During a functional assessment with families, interview items and observation procedures should include an assessment of the coercive processes that may be operating between the child with a disability and his or her parents. Functional assessment procedures help us understand the behavioral mechanisms that maintain child problem behavior, such as negative reinforcement or positive reinforcement. These procedures define the first three steps in a coercive exchange. For example, in a routine in which the child engages in problem behavior to escape parental demands, the first three steps in the coercive exchange are: (a) parent makes demand; (b) child engages in problem behavior; and (c) parent withdraws or reduces demand (i.e., delivers negative reinforcement). In a routine in which the child engages in problem behavior to gain parental attention, the first three steps are (a) parent is occupied in a task or unresponsive to child social bids for attention; (b) child engages in problem behavior; and (c) parent gives positive or negative attention (i.e., delivers positive reinforcement). These functional assessment results are then used to design interventions that are logically linked to the purpose of the child's problem behavior and the events that set up or trigger problem behavior.

An assessment of coercive parent-child interaction helps us understand the *reciprocal effect* of the parent on the child and the child on the parent. In addition to understanding the behavioral mechanisms that maintain child problem behavior, we also gain insight into the behavioral mechanism that maintains ineffective parenting practices. Of particular importance is examination of the fourth step in the coercive exchange, a step in the sequence of parent-child interaction that largely has gone unexamined in the empirical literature. This step involves the child negatively reinforcing parent submission (i.e., withdrawing a demand, giving attention) by terminating or reducing problem behavior. The parent's experience of negative reinforcement increases the likelihood that in the future he or she will again engage in actions that serve to terminate or reduce child problem behavior. Over time, with much practice, such parent-child coercive exchanges can become automatic and highly resistant to change (Dumas, 2005). Without an assessment of the effects of the child on parent behavior, the survivability of a PBS plan within a targeted family routine may be compromised. Due to the parent's past history of negative reinforcement for submission to the child, one cannot assume that the parent will implement all of the components (i.e., antecedent, teaching, and consequence strategies) of a behavior support plan with fidelity or maintain plan use over a long period of time.

Assessing coercive processes in family routines involve three questions. The first two questions are already part of a functional assessment, while the third one easily can be added:

1. After a parent antecedent triggering behavior (e.g., demand, no attention, deny item or activity), does the child engage in problem behavior?
2. After the child engages in problem behavior, does the parent deliver the function of the child's problem behavior (e.g., escape from demand, get social attention, obtain preferred item or activity)?
3. After the parent delivers the functional reinforcer (e.g., withdraws the demand, provides positive or negative attention, gives child preferred item or activity), does the child terminate or reduce problem behavior?

If the answer to all three questions, based on interview and observation results, is yes, then a coercive process has been confirmed. In our research with families, this finding is far from trivial. By the time a functional assessment has been conducted with a family, the coercive processes identified most likely have been operating in the family for years. The number of times that the parent and child have reciprocally reinforced each other, respectively, for problem behavior and ineffective parenting practices is likely in the hundreds if not thousands. Because the parent has been negatively reinforced for submission so many times and for so long, changing this pattern of interaction may prove daunting for both the parent and the interventionist. In our experience, even though a parent is fully apprised of the coercive dance and is sincerely committed to changing it, his or her history of negative reinforcement for submitting to the child (and thus terminating problem behavior) can make the change process an arduous one.

Coercive processes also teach parents to wholly *avoid* demands, circumstances, and routines in which child problem behavior is likely to occur. For example, parents may avoid altogether asking the child with a disability to get dressed in the morning, leaving the child alone for more than 30 s, or taking the child to the grocery store. Helping parents reintroduce such normative expectations and routines into their lives also can be difficult because at the start of the change process it also means reintroducing the entire four-step coercive dance, a dance that the parents may be understandably weary and fearful of reengaging.

In addition to the powerful effect of negative reinforcement on parents, we have found that psychological and contextual factors also play a role in the fourth step. These factors appear to overshadow or block the parent's use of behavior support plan strategies (Mackintosh, 1975) and thus maintain the likelihood of the parent submitting to the child following problem behavior. With respect to psychological factors, parent beliefs and emotions can play a part in the parent submitting to the child. For example, during a going-to-bed routine, a mother of an 8-year-old daughter with CHARGE syndrome may fear that failure to submit to attention-motivated crying behavior will cause the child irreparable emotional harm. Giving the child attention contingent on crying, in addition to terminating problem behavior, also assuages the mother's fear and anxiety. With respect to contextual factors, changes in key elements of an activity setting (e.g., time, people present, parental goals) can increase the likelihood of parent submission. For example, a father may be able to effectively administer a graduated extinction procedure in the middle of the night when his daughter engages in attention-motivated problem behavior but is unable to do so when his work life is particularly stressful and he needs a good night's rest.

For these families, a functional assessment-based PBS plan and an implementation plan based on standard behavioral parent training practices may not be sufficient to ameliorate coercive processes in these routines. Additional interventions and adaptations that address parent beliefs and emotions or contextual obstacles may need to be developed and implemented in collaboration with the family before sustainable change is observed. For example, a cognitive restructuring intervention may be necessary to help a mother overcome her belief that submitting to her 8-year-old daughter's attention-motivated crying behavior prevents emotional harm. The interventionist informs the mother of an alternative view that delivering comforting attention every time the child cries at night prevents her daughter from learning to self-sooth, an important developmental task for children; that submitting to the child may actually interfere with the child's emotional development. During a debriefing session after parent training in the bedtime routine, the interventionist also reminds the mother that her use of a graduated extinction procedure resulted in her daughter, rather than becoming more anxious, becoming calmer and eventually falling asleep. For the father who understandably is unwilling on some nights to get out of bed to implement the graduated extinction procedure with his daughter, the interventionist and the family negotiate two enhancements to the plan that strengthen its sustainability. First, the father and mother agree to a weekly schedule of overnight responsibility that ensures that neither parent has to implement behavior support plan procedures in the middle of the night 2 days in a row. Second, the child's maternal grandparents agree to provide 2 days per week of overnight respite care at their own home so that both parents get adequate sleep at least 2 days a week until their daughter learns to sleep through the night in her bedroom. The message here is that an assessment of coercive processes in family routines increases the interventionist's understanding of sources of variability that affect parent implementation fidelity and the sustainability of behavior support plan procedures. This knowledge can help the interventionist improve the quality of support to the family so that interventions are more likely to survive within the natural complexity of family life.

A final point about assessing and intervening directly on coercive processes in family routines is the singular importance of the collaborative partnership or therapeutic alliance between the interventionist and family. In our experience, a strong, trusting, collaborative partnership is essential if parents are to marshal the faith, courage, and energy that often are necessary to change patterns of interaction with their child that have been going on for years, that have led to reciprocal forms of reinforcement for parent and child, and that may have altered the architecture of family life in ways that, although less desirable to the family, may have become at least familiar and comfortable (Lucyshyn et al., 2004). The importance of the relationship between parents and interventionists is well recognized in the behavioral parent training literature (Forehand & Kotchick, 2002; Webster-Stratton & Herbert, 1993). As noted by Forehand and Kotchick, "The quality of the relationship between parents and the therapist has been identified as a critical factor in parental compliance or resistance ... accounting for up to 45% of the variance in predicting treatment outcomes" (p. 382). In addition to the teaching skills necessary to promote positive child and family outcomes, research on behavioral parent training has shown that interventionists also need to possess personal skills such as genuineness, empathy, warmth, and humor to achieve meaningful outcomes (Forehand & Kotchick, 2002; Forgatch & Patterson, 1985).

## Assessing and Intervening Within Family Activity Settings

In our research with families, the family activity setting appears to be a particularly potent unit of analysis for understanding family contexts and for designing interventions that are acceptable, effective, sustainable, and durable. First, assessing and intervening in family routines ensures that family values are taken into account because the family's selection of routines for intervention directly influences the focus and direction of the interventionist's effort to produce meaningful change in a family's life (Carr, 2007). For example, a family of a 4-year-old son with autism who engages in severe food refusal behavior chooses to work on snack and dinner routines. The family of an 8-year-old daughter who continues to sleep with her parents in their bed at night chooses a bedtime routine that is more normative for a daughter in middle childhood. The routine as a unit of analysis facilitates the selection of child and family goals that match the family's values about what is most important in their lives. When families then generate a vision of a realistic but successful routine based on the elements of an activity setting (e.g., time and place, people, resources, tasks, goals and values, scripts of interaction), they experience a family-centered process in which their hopes for a better life with their child with a disability are instantiated in a meaningful and practical way.

Second, the activity setting as a unit of analysis facilitates the design of a contextually or culturally appropriate behavior support plan (Albin, Lucyshyn, Horner, & Flannery, 1996). When families define the elements of a successful routine, they inform the interventionist of important contextual information, such as the time and place that the routine will occur, the people who will participate in the routine beyond the child and one parent, the tasks and expectations for the child as well as for other participants, the material resources that are available and that will be used during the routine, and the goals and values that are to be achieved during the routine. For example, a family of European ancestry envisions a dinner routine that begins at 6:00 pm and includes the nuclear family members of father, mother, and two sons. Foods served include chicken, beef, potatoes, gravy, corn, carrots, broccoli, and breads. In addition to eating foods served, a culturally informed goal is for the child with a disability to participate in conversation at the dinner table with other family members. In contrast, a family of Chinese ancestry envisions a dinner routine that also begins at 6:00 pm but includes mother, father, son with a disability, and grandmother. Foods served include chicken, pork, tofu, bok choy, Chinese cabbage, and white rice. A culturally informed goal for this family is that the child eats quietly, and that there is no conversation at the table.

The activity setting as a unit of analysis also lends itself to the identification of natural variations in routine elements across the span of a week or month. For example, a going-to-bed routine may vary by who assists the child to get ready for bed (e.g., mother or father). A grocery store routine may vary by the presence of a younger sibling who also needs attention and support. Since naturally occurring variations may affect the focus child's ability to participate or the parent's ability to sustain the use of PBS strategies, it is important to identify and address these variations during plan design and implementation. A thorough understanding of the structural elements of family routines and their natural variation can inform the design of contextually or culturally appropriate behavior support plans in which positive behavior supports are effectively embedded in the routine, implemented with fidelity by family members, and adapted to common changes in routine structure. Such an understanding also enhances the *ecological validity* of the support effort because it requires the interventionist to help the family improve child behavior within the natural, complex, and changing conditions of family life as defined by the family.

Third, family activity settings provide a well-defined and practical context in which coercive family processes can be assessed and ameliorated. Preliminary research has shown that coercive patterns of parent-child interaction are at the core of problematic family routines (Lucyshyn et al., 2004; Lucyshyn, Lohrmann, et al., 2007). Given that the amelioration of coercive processes may be daunting, intervention on these patterns of interaction in family routines may simplify the change process and thus make it more feasible for families. Transforming coercive processes into constructive processes of parent-child interaction one routine at a time decreases the amount of time that parents have to commit to promoting change in the family in the midst of other roles and responsibilities. Doing so also may facilitate parent mastery of a behavior support plan that includes several components by moderating the amount of change that parents need to make in their own behavior and by reducing the number of contextual variables that may interfere with the parent's initial success. A parent's sense of self-efficacy also can be strengthened during initial work on one or two routines, allowing the parent to approach subsequent targeted routines with greater confidence and resolve.

Fourth, the ecological nature of the activity setting as a unit of analysis allows the interventionist and family to collaborate at a more strategic level when planning for change in the context of family life. After selecting and defining target routines, the sequence by which the interventionist and family prioritize routines for intervention can define a *critical path* toward meaningful change in family life. For families who perceive the process of change to be daunting, either because of the severity of child

**Table 4.4.** Question Guide to Help in the Selection and Prioritization of Family Routines for Intervention

1. How much change is required for this routine to be successful?
2. How may people are involved in the routine, and how many of these people will have to make changes in their behavior for the routine to be successful?
3. Should both parents be involved in the change process from the start, or should one parent start the change process and the other enter the process later?
4. How much time and effort will be required?
5. How much knowledge and skill will be needed?
6. Is there a potential for reasonably quick success with minimal training and support to the family?
7. Will intervention and success in the routine potentially have a positive impact on other areas of the child's or family's life?
8. Is the routine similar in structure to other family routines, such that improvement in the routine may lead to (a) generalized improvement in other nontrained routines or (b) a more efficient change process when similar routines receive intervention?
9. Are there potential obstacles that may arise over the next few months or year that could impede family progress in the routine?

problem behavior or due to other family stressors, a *path of least resistance* may represent the critical path toward meaningful change. This path involves prioritizing routines by those perceived to be the easiest to change and then progressing toward routines perceived to be more difficult. An alternative critical path is to select *pivotal routines* that may be quite challenging but once successful predict generalized changes in child behavior at other times of the day or more efficient change in related target routines that are even more challenging (Binnendyk & Lucyshyn, 2008). Table 4.4 presents a set of questions that can help to guide the strategic selection of routines in collaboration with family members.

## Assessing Family Ecology and Providing Adjunctive Family-Centered Supports

In addition to an assessment of family routines, a broader assessment of family ecology also can be helpful in the development of PBS plans that are survivable in family contexts. Relevant features of the broader ecology of families include family and child strengths, family resources and social supports, family stressors, and family goals for the child with a disability and for the family as a whole (see Lucyshyn, Kayser, et al., 2002). Such an assessment, conducted in a collegial and collaborative fashion with family members (Turnbull & Turnbull, 1991), can serve three important purposes. First, a discussion of child and family strengths can contribute to the rekindling of hope in the family and the development of trust and a collaborative partnership or therapeutic alliance (Kanfer & Grimm, 1980; Lucyshyn & Albin, 1993). Second, knowledge of family strengths, community resources, social supports, and child and family goals can contribute further to the design of a contextually appropriate behavior support plan. Such a plan would build on family strengths, utilize community resources and natural social supports available to the family, and address the family's priority goals. Third, a discussion of family stressors, including the effect of the child's problem behavior on the family and other stressors within the family system, can contribute to the identification of adjunctive family-centered supports (Singer, Goldberg-Hamblin, Peckham-Hardin, Barry, & Santarelli, 2002) that may be necessary to ensure parent success in the use of positive behavior supports and improvement in family quality of life. Stressors within the family system may involve parent health or psychological problems, sibling difficulties, marital conflict, extended family issues, or employment-related stressors. For example, parental exhaustion due to chronic caregiving of the child with a disability informs the identification and use of respite care opportunities in the family's community. A mother's anxiety disorder may require adjunctive cognitive behavior therapy with a clinical or counseling psychologist. Marital conflict may be addressed by the interventionist under the guidance of a counseling psychologist who supervises the implementation of marital supports such as a behavior exchange contract on positive and respectful communication (Patterson, 1978). Alternatively, the parents may choose to receive marital counseling directly from a psychologist.

We have found that attention to stressors within the family system that extend beyond the focus child's problem behavior is essential if we are to succeed in ameliorating coercive processes in family routines. If there are other problems occurring within the family system beyond the coercive dance between the parents and child with a disability, these problems will manifest within the routine and act to further disrupt it. For example, during the dinner routine of one family, the mother and father share responsibility for implementing a behavior support plan with their 8-year-old son with a moderate intellectual disability. However, the parents have a history of marital discord that manifests in the routine:

> The mother criticizes one of the father's parenting actions. The father tersely replies that it would be better if she paid attention to her own behavior. The mother rolls her eyes and whispers, "I can't see how things can get better unless you do the things I am learning to do." Meanwhile, the child with a disability, having received little to no parental attention or support in the past 15 to 20 s shouts "I've had it!" and flees the dinner table.

As this example suggests, unless the parents' marital conflict is addressed, there is little chance of durably improving child behavior and participation in the dinner routine as well as other valued routines in the family's life.

If parents report family systems issues that may need to be addressed, it behooves the interventionist to determine whether he or she or someone in his or her work group or agency possesses the necessary expertise. If not, the interventionist can alternatively determine whether there is a professional in the community to whom the family can be referred for appropriate treatment. Prior to the provision or pursuit of adjunctive family-centered supports, the family would need to be informed, the rationale for the additional support would need to be explained, and the family would need to provide their assent.

One caution in the use of a family ecology assessment that is designed to be collegial and collaborative is that a discussion of family stressors with parents may not reveal all of the family systems issues that confront a family and that may serve as obstacles to improvement in child behavior and family quality of life. First, although such an assessment protocol is designed to build trust with the family, it may be too early in the parent-professional relationship for parents to disclose information that is of a deeply personal nature. Second, parents may not be aware of a particular family systems-level problem or recognize its relevance to a process of PBS. In these cases, the identification of family systems-level problems may not occur until after the interventionist and family have developed a behavior support plan and begun to implement it. For example, the mother of a 6-year-old son with autism was not aware of a psychological tendency toward pessimism and so did not report this during the family ecology assessment. This only came to light when this tendency interfered with the mother's use of positive behavior supports in a dinner routine. Given this obstacle to progress, the interventionist broached this concern with the mother, gained her assent to address her pessimism during implementation support, and received guidance from a counseling psychologist on the use of an adjunctive treatment for pessimism, a form of optimism training (Hieneman & Durand, 2008).

A final caution during a process of family ecology assessment is the importance of evaluating the severity of family systems problems and determining whether PBS services focused on the child are appropriate. For example, if the ecology assessment reveals that a parent is suicidal or divorce is imminent, it may be better for the parents first to receive psychological counseling focused on these acute problems before attempting to collaborate with an interventionist to improve child behavior and participation in family life (Forehand & Kotchick, 2002). In this event, the interventionist would refer the family to an appropriate mental health professional and initiate PBS services after the family had begun to address and make progress on these more pressing concerns.

## Receiving Clinical Supervision During Implementation Support

Practitioners of PBS working with families of children with developmental disabilities and severe problem behavior will benefit from receiving clinical supervision and support from a licensed psychologist or clinical social worker with expertise in science-informed theory and practice in family systems-level interventions with families (Falender & Shafranske, 2004; Stoltenberg & Delworth, 1987). There are two primary reasons for this recommendation. First, many professionals who work with families of children with developmental disabilities and severe problem behavior receive their professional training at the master's or doctoral level in the allied fields of applied behavior analysis or special education. Few of these professionals receive formal training in family systems-level interventions such as psychological counseling or marital therapy. Although there are clinical psychology programs at the master's or doctoral level that prepare professionals to work with families of children with developmental disabilities and provide graduate students with science-informed knowledge and skills in applied behavior analysis, behavioral parent training, and more recently PBS, due to the specialized focus of these programs, graduating professionals may still lack expertise in family systems-level interventions. Through clinical supervision by a psychologist or clinical social worker with requisite expertise, interventionists supporting parents in the implementation of PBS plans in the home can receive continuing education that expands their technical competence in theory and science-informed clinical practice, allowing them to effectively serve a greater diversity of families and a wider range of problems (Falender & Shafranske, 2004). Knowledge and skills that can be imparted by the clinical supervisor and implemented by interventionists under clinical supervision include: (a) family systems analysis based on Minuchin's (1974) structural family theory; (b) therapeutic interaction skills that facilitate the change process, such as cognitive restructuring, reframing, prophesizing, and the therapeutic use of metaphor and self-disclosure (Hayes, 2004; Webster-Stratton & Herbert, 1993); (c) behavioral marital therapy methods such as contracting for behavior exchanges and improving communication skills (Gottman & Silver, 1999; Patterson, Miller, Carnes, & Wilson, 2004); (d) problem-solving methods that teach parents how to reduce life stressors (Kazdin & Whitley, 2003); and (e) positive psychology methods for increasing mindfulness and optimism (Seligman, Steen, Park, & Peterson, 2005; Singh et al., 2006).

A second reason that clinical supervision is important is the phenomenon of parent resistance or nonadherence to treatment (Allen & Warzak, 2000; Forehand & Kotchick, 2002). If left unresolved, resistance or nonadherence can affect the behavior of the interventionist, reducing his or her effectiveness. Although in our experience the development of a collaborative partnership with parents and the design of a contextually appropriate behavior support plan can prevent or minimize parental resistance or nonadherence, this is not the case for all families. A fundamental aim of PBS is the design of effective environments in which problem behavior is irrelevant and ineffective at achieving the child's purpose. PBS plans define changes in adult behavior and enhancements in the focus child's environment, and it is these changes that lead to improvement in child behavior and quality of life. In family contexts, this means that child behavior only changes when parents and other family members change their behavior and improve family systems so that these systems support positive behavior.

There are several reasons why parents who have agreed to participate in a process of family-centered PBS might resist or not adhere to the implementation of PBS plan procedures. Parental beliefs and attitudes that only come to light during plan implementation may occasion resistance. For example, a father may hold a negative attitude toward the use of extrinsic rewards as reinforcers for desired behavior. When, during plan implementation, it is time to deliver a tangible reinforcer to the child, the father balks, arguing that his parents never rewarded him for the same behavior as a child. Cultural values or interaction patterns also may inform treatment nonadherence. For example, a Chinese mother of a young boy with autism has difficulty using an escape extinction procedure with her son because her culture has taught her that a mother should never allow a son to cry. Last, parents who experience psychological problems also are likely to be nonadherent to behavior support plan procedures. For example, mothers who experience chronic worry or maternal depression have difficulty using proactive behavior support strategies that reliably prevent problem behavior, such as giving advanced warning prior to transitions or offering choices to promote cooperation.

In our experience, overcoming such sources of treatment resistance or nonadherence requires patience, cultural sensitivity, therapeutic interaction skills, and a strong collaborative partnership with the family. To the extent that an interventionist is in the process of developing these qualities, he or she may experience feelings of frustration, exhaustion, or powerlessness. Clinical supervision by a psychologist or clinical social worker familiar with treatment resistance can validate and normalize these feelings, help interventionists maintain their energy and commitment to the family, and guide problem-solving discussions in which sources of resistance are assessed, and appropriate, respectful, and effective solutions are generated. Overall, clinical supervision can ensure that high standards of professional and ethical conduct with families are maintained by members of an intervention team or agency and that the best possible clinical outcomes for children and families are achieved (Falender & Shafranske, 2004).

## Adopting a Life-Span Perspective

A final consideration for the design and implementation of survivable interventions in family contexts is the value of adopting a life-span perspective (Carr et al., 2002). Interventionists who operate from a life-span perspective understand that no matter how successful a family has been in implementing a PBS plan when provided with implementation support, the true test of success is whether the parents' effective use of positive behavior supports and improvements in child behavior can survive across the family life cycle (Cusinato, 1994) as the child matures from childhood to adolescence to early adulthood. A life-span perspective also alerts the interventionist to the setting events (Wahler & Fox, 1981) that naturally occur across months and years that may function to provoke a regression in child behavior or make it difficult for parents to sustain the use of positive behavior supports. Setting events that have, in our experience, negatively affected the ability of parents to sustain behavior support plans and maintain child and family outcomes include child or parent illness or injury, yearly holiday transitions from school to home or from home back to school (e.g., Christmas, summer vacation), extended visits by relatives, seasonal increases in a parent's employment workload, yearly work-related trips away from home by a parent, and a child having a stressful day at school.

Unless such obstacles to survivability are addressed during a process of behavior support with families, the likelihood of child and family outcomes maintaining across the family life cycle is small. A life-span perspective offers two implications for practice: (a) the design and implementation of maintenance/relapse prevention plans; and (b) the provision of on-going maintenance support aimed at strengthening family resilience. These implications are discussed below. After a parent has succeeded in improving child behavior and participation in a target routine, interventionists should develop a maintenance/relapse prevention plan (Goldstein & Martens, 2000). The goals of this plan are to ensure that: (a) parents continue to use core PBS strategies in targeted routines; (b) obstacles to maintenance are identified and prevented from interfering with long-term success; and (c) coercive patterns of interaction do not regain a foothold in the routines. Given these goals, a maintenance/relapse prevention plan may be comprised of three parts. The first part involves collaborating with the family to reduce the child's behavior support plan to only those strategies that are necessary and sufficient to maintain improvements in child behavior and routine participation. In our experience, the number of behavior support strategies necessary to *attain* initial success in target routines typically is more than what is required to *maintain* success in routines. For example, a bedtime routine PBS plan for an 8-year-old girl with CHARGE syndrome included a social story about going to bed and a visual timer to help her predict when she could get out of bed in the early morning. After the parents had succeeded in teaching their daughter to go to sleep in her bed and stay in bed until 6:00 a.m., these strategies were no longer necessary and thus not included in an abridged maintenance checklist of strategies for the routine.

The second part of a maintenance/relapse prevention plan addresses family systems-level problems that have interfered with child and family progress as well as other events in the family's life that have been disruptive or are anticipated to be so. For example, obstacles addressed in a snack routine maintenance plan for the mother of the 4-year-old boy with severe food refusal behavior included (a) child or parent illness or tiredness/fatigue and (b) parent stress and anxiety. The strategies used by the parent to address these obstacles are presented in Table 4.5.

**Table 4.5.** Maintenance/Relapse Prevention Plan for Dinner Routine of Family With 4-Year-Old Son With Autism

1. *Child Illness or Tiredness/Fatigue*: (a) Provide additional assistance and require less independence from child; (b) provide more preferred foods instead of nonpreferred foods; and (c) if Nathan is experiencing an intestinal-related illness (e.g., flu, diarrhea), discontinue snack until he is well.
2. *Parent Illness or Tiredness/Fatigue*: (a) Provide more preferred foods instead of nonpreferred foods so that Nathan will be more cooperative (because when you are ill or tired, you will be less able to respond effectively to problem behavior); (b) do not introduce new foods (for same reason as above); and/or (c) ask dad to do the routine for you.
3. *Parent Stress and Anxiety*: (a) Increase contact with friends and engage in leisure activities with friends (away from children) to allow you to rest from caregiving responsibilities and receive emotional support from friends; (b) develop a relaxation strategy with Dr. Miller (counseling psychologist) to use when you are experiencing a heightened state of stress or anxiety; in particular, this strategy should be used just before engaging in the dinner routine so that you are more able to implement the strategies effectively.

The final part of a maintenance/relapse prevention plan is a brief assessment tool customized to the family that allows parents to self-monitor the reoccurrence of coercive patterns of interaction in target routines. After parents succeed in transforming a problematic routine into a successful one, we encourage them to use the assessment tool at least once a week to self-monitor parent-child interaction. If parent self-assessment indicates that the coercive process has reasserted itself in the routine, parents are encouraged to reapply behavior support plan procedures or contact us for further assistance. We also use the tool to guide discussions with parents about the occurrence or nonoccurrence of coercive processes for the purpose of strengthening the family's awareness and conceptual understanding of coercive processes and how to prevent or recover from them. An example of a coercive process assessment tool for one family and routine is presented in Table 4.6.

The second implication of a life-span perspective is the importance of offering parents ongoing maintenance support, knowing that all possible threats to maintenance are unlikely to be addressed in even the most well-considered maintenance/relapse prevention plan. During maintenance support across several months or a year, disruptive setting events that could not have been predicted can be identified, and a plan to minimize their impact can be made. For example, a mother falls and suffers a severe elbow injury, rendering her unable to implement behavior supports effectively with her son with autism for approximately 4 weeks in a bedtime routine that she has successfully maintained for several months. The family experiences a setback in the bedtime routine, so the mother contacts the interventionist to request assistance. The interventionist provides maintenance support by helping the parents analyze the impact of the setting event and develop an adjunctive plan to eliminate or minimize further disruption. The plan includes: (a) increasing reinforcement

**Table 4.6.** *Parent Self-Assessment of Coercive Processes in a Dinner Routine*

Once a week, you should consider the following questions after completing a family dinner and record your answers on this form. If you experience a difficult dinner, you also should fill out this form. This will help you to recognize when problems begin to reemerge and assist you in addressing minor problems before they become major problems.

1. Did Nathan engage in problem behavior during the dinner routine: (a) physical aggression; (b) throwing items/knocking items on floor; (c) leaving table; (d) physical resistance; (e) food refusal (turn away from food, push away food); and/or (f) cry/scream/yell? YES or NO
2. If Nathan engaged in problem behavior, did you do any of the following: (a) remove the food; (b) offer a different food; and/or (c) offer a treat to motivate Nathan to eat the non-preferred food? YES or NO
3. If you did any of the things in Question 2, did Nathan do any of the following: (a) stop engaging in problem behavior; or (b) decrease the level of problem behavior? YES or NO

If you answered yes to all three questions, please review the dinner routine PBS plan implementation checklist and implement all of the strategies in the plan during the next dinner routine. If a disruptive event was present during dinner (e.g., child or parent illness), then review the maintenance/relapse prevention plan and implement the strategies that are relevant from that plan. If you need additional assistance, please call Brenda.

for child positive behavior at home; (b) setting smaller, more manageable expectations during the going-to-bed routine; and (c) adding extra support by teaching the father to implement the behavior support plan during the routine. The parents implement the adjunctive plan and succeed in recovering their previous success in the routine. As this example suggests, each disruptive event identified and overcome provides parents with an opportunity to fortify their knowledge and skills in supporting their child with a disability. Adopting a life-span perspective encourages the interventionist and family to view setbacks as not merely unfortunate regressions in progress but also as valuable opportunities that can contribute to the family's resilience in the face of future challenges.

## SUMMARY

In this chapter, we described an ecological unit of analysis—coercive processes in family routines—that holds promise for the design of PBS plans that are acceptable, effective, sustainable, and durable in family contexts when implemented by parents of children with developmental disabilities and severe problem behavior. The unit of analysis integrates three levels of ecology that can be observed in family contexts: (a) functions of child problem behavior; (b) coercive patterns of parent-child interaction; and (c) family activity settings. Theoretical foundations for the unit of analysis are found in behavioral theory, coercion theory, and ecocultural theory. Empirical support is found in recent observational and intervention research with families of children with developmental disabilities that documented: (a) the functions of problem behavior in family routines; (b) the presence of coercive patterns of parent-child interaction in routines; and (c) the acceptability and effectiveness of a family-centered PBS approach for improving child behavior and participation in family routines. The potency of the construct lies in its ability to more fully reveal sources of variability that influence child behavior and parenting practices during a persence of behavioral support in family contexts.

The construct of coercion in family routines offers five implications for behavioral assessment and intervention with families of children with developmental disabilities and severe problem behavior. First, in addition to a functional assessment of child problem behavior, an assessment of coercive patterns of parent-child interaction also should be conducted during a PBS process with families. Second, the activity setting of daily and weekly routines in the home and community provides a practical context for collaborating with families to design PBS plans that are effective and contextually appropriate and for promoting meaningful and durable improvements in child and parent behavior. Third, a broad assessment of family ecology, in the form of a collegial and collaborative dialogue with the child's parents, can serve to build trust, enhance contextual fit, and inform the selection of adjunctive family-centered supports that may be necessary. Fourth, clinical supervision can help interventionists working with families to more effectively address family systems-level issues and treatment adherence problems that may be encountered during a process of family-centered PBS. Fifth, a life-span perspective encourages interventionists to directly plan for the long-term maintenance of parent use of positive behavior supports by developing, in collaboration with families, maintenance/relapse prevention plans and by providing less-frequent but ongoing maintenance support to strengthen family resilience in the face of common obstacles to the long-term maintenance of child and family outcomes.

## ACKNOWLEDGMENTS

The chapter was supported by grant 5R01HD041671 from the National Institute of Child Health and Human Development (NICHD) of the National Institutes of Health (NIH) to the University of British Columbia (UBC). The opinions expressed within do not necessarily reflect the position or policy of NICHD, NIH, or UBC, and no official endorsement should be inferred.

We would like to thank the following individuals for their invaluable assistance in preparing the grant proposal and in conducting the family intervention study of which preliminary results are presented in the chapter. Drs. Larry Irvin, Robert Horner, Michael Stoolmiller, Robert Bakeman, and Paul Yovanoff. We also would like to thank the following current and former members of the data collection, coding, or analysis team: Sophia Khan, David Nordstokke, Stephen Chinn, Samantha Kwon, Ashleigh Toulson, Jacqui Boonstra, and Silvia Liu.

Finally, we would like to thank current and former parent consultants to our research with families: Clair Shuman, Kathy Roberson, and Laurie and Carr Steubing.

## REFERENCES

Albin, R. W., Lucyshyn, J. M., Horner, R. H., & Flannery, K. B. (1996). Contextual-fit for behavioral support plans: A model for "goodness-of-fit." In L. K. Koegel, R. L. Koegel, & G. Dunlap (Eds.), *Positive behavioral support: Including people with difficult behavior in the community* (pp. 81–98). Baltimore: Brookes.

Allen, K. D., & Warzak, W. J. (2000). The problem of parental nonadherence in clinical behavior analysis: Effective treatment is not enough. *Journal of Applied Behavior Analysis, 33*, 373–391.

Baer, D. M. (1986). "Exemplary services to what outcome?" Review of education of learners with severe handicaps: Exemplary service strategies. *The Journal of the Association for the Severely Handicapped, 11*, 145–147.

Baer, D. M., Wolf, M. M., & Risley, T. R. (1968). Some current dimensions of applied behavior analysis. *Journal of Applied Behavior Analysis, 1*, 91–97.

Baer, D. M., Wolf, M. M., & Risley, T. R. (1987). Some still current dimensions of applied behavior analysis. *Journal of Applied Behavior Analysis, 20*, 313–327.

Bakeman, R., & Quera, V. (1995). *Analyzing interaction: Sequential analysis with SDIS and GSEQ*. New York: Cambridge University Press.

Baker, B. L., Blacher, J., Crnic, K., & Edelbrock, C. (2002). Behavior problems and parenting stress in families of 3-year old children with and without developmental disabilities. *American Journal on Mental Retardation, 107*, 433–444.

Bijou, S. W., & Baer, D. M. (1961). *Child development: Vol. 1. A systematic and empirical theory*. New York: Appleton-Century-Crofts.

Binnendyk, L., & Lucyshyn, J. M. (2008). A family-centered positive behavior support approach to the amelioration of food refusal behavior: A case study analysis. *Journal of Positive Behavior Interventions.*

Briesmeister, J. M., & Schaefer, C. E. (1998). *Handbook of parent training: Parents as co-therapists for children's problem behavior.* New York: Wiley.

Bristol, M. M., Cohen, D. J., Costello, E. J., Denckla, M., Eckberg, T. J., Kallen, R., et al. (1996). State of the science in autism: Report to the National Institute of Health. *Journal of Autism and Developmental Disorders, 26,* 121–154.

Bromley, B. E., & Blacher, J. (1991). Parental reasons for out-of-home placement of children with severe handicaps, *Mental Retardation, 29,* 275–280.

Bronfenbrenner, U. (1986). Ecology of the family as a context for human development: Research perspectives, *Developmental Psychology, 22,* 723–742.

Buschbacher, P., Fox, L., Clarke, S. (2004). Capturing desired family routines: A parent-professional behavioral collaboration. *Research and Practice for Persons With Severe Disabilities, 29,* 25–39.

Capaldi, D. M., DeGarmo, D. S., Patterson, G. R., & Forgatch, M. S. (2002). Contextual risk across the early life span and association with antisocial behavior. In J. B. Reid, G. R. Patterson, & J. Snyder (Eds.), *Antisocial behavior in children and adolescents: A developmental analysis and model for intervention* (pp. 123–145). Washington, DC: American Psychological Association.

Carr, E. G. (2007). The expanding vision of positive behavior support: Research perspectives on happiness, helpfulness, and hopefulness. *Journal of Positive Behavior Interventions, 9,* 3–14.

Carr, E. G., Dunlap, G., Horner, R. H., Koegel, R. L., Turnbull, A., Sailor, W., et al. (2002). Positive behavior support: Evolution of an applied science. *Journal of Positive Behavior Interventions, 4,* 4–16.

Carr, E. G., & Durand, V. M. (1985). Reducing of severe behavior problems in the community through a multicomponent intervention approach. *Journal of Applied Behavior Analysis, 26,* 157–172.

Carr, E. G., Horner, R. H., Turnbull, A. Marquis, J., Magito-McLaughlin, D., McAtee, M., et al. (1999). *Positive behavior support for people with developmental disabilities: A research synthesis.* Washington, DC: American Association on Mental Retardation.

Carr, E. G., Taylor, J. C., & Robinson, S. (1991). The effects of severe problem behaviors in children on the teaching behavior of adults. *Journal of Applied Behavior Analysis, 24,* 523–535.

Chen, D., Downing, J. E., & Peckman-Hardin, K. D. (2002). Working with families of diverse cultural and linguistic backgrounds: Considerations for culturally responsive positive behavior support. In J. M. Lucyshyn, G. Dunlap, & R. W. Albin, (Eds.), *Families and positive behavior support: Addressing problem behavior in family contexts* (pp. 133–154). Baltimore: Brookes.

Clarke, S., Dunlap, G., & Vaughn, B. (1999). Family-centered, assessment-based intervention to improve behavior during an early morning routine. *Journal of Positive Behavior Interventions, 1,* 235–241.

Cooper, J. O., Heron, T. E., & Heward, W. L. (2007). *Applied behavior analysis* (2nd ed.). Upper Saddle River, NJ: Pearson.

Cusinato, M. (1994). Parenting over the family lifecycle. In L. L'Abate (Ed.), *Handbook of developmental family psychology and psychopathology* (pp. 83–115). New York: Wiley.

Davenport, S. L., Hefner, M. A., & Mitchell, J. A. (1986). The spectrum of clinical features in CHARGE syndrome. *Clinical Genetics, 29,* 298–310

Derby, K. M., Wacker, D. P., Peck, S., Sasso, G., DeRaad, A., Berg, W., et al. (1994). Functional analysis of separate topographies of aberrant behavior. *Journal of Applied Behavior Analysis, 27,* 267–278.

Durand, V. M., & Hieneman, M. (2008). *Helping parents with challenging children: Positive family intervention.* New York: Oxford University Press.

Dumas, J. E. (2005). Mindfulness-based parent training: Strategies to lessen the grip of automaticity in families with disruptive children. *Journal of Clinical Child and Adolescent Psychology, 34,* 779–791.

Falender, C. A., & Shafranske, E. P. (2004). *Clinical supervision: A competency-based approach.* Washington, DC: American Psychological Association.

Feldman, M. A., Condillac, R. A., Tough, S., Hunt, S., & Griffiths, D. (2002). Effectiveness of community positive behavioral intervention for persons with developmental disabilities and severe behavioral challenges. *Behavior Therapy, 33,* 377–398.

Floyd, F. J., & Gallagher, E. M. (1997). Parental stress, care demands, and use of support services for school-aged children with disabilities and problem behavior. *Family Relations, 40,* 359–371.

Floyd, F. J., & Phillippe, K. A. (1993). Parental interactions with children with and without mental retardation: Behavior management, coerciveness, and positive exchanges. *American Journal on Mental Retardation, 97,* 673–684.

Forehand, R., & Kotchick, B. A., (2002). Behavioral parent training: Current challenges and potential solutions. *Journal of Child and Family Studies, 11,* 377–384.

Gallimore, R. (2005). Behavior change in the natural environment: Everyday activity settings as a workshop of change. In C. R. O'Donnell & L. A. Yamauchi (Eds.), *Culture and context in human behavior change: Theory, research, and applications,* New york, Peter Lang, 207–231.

Gallimore, R., Goldenberg, C. N., & Weisner, T. S. (1993). The social construction and subjective reality of activity settings: Implications for community psychology. *American Journal of Community Psychology, 21,* 537–559.

Gallimore, R., Coots, J., Weisner, T., Garnier, H., & Guthrie, D. (1996). Family responses to children with early developmental delays II: Accommodation intensity and activity in early and middle childhood. *American Journal of Mental Retardation, 101,* 215–232.

Gallimore, R., Weisner, T. S., Kaufman, S. Z. & Bernheimer, L. P. (1989). The social construction of ecocultural niches: Family accommodation of developmentally delayed children. *American Journal of Mental Retardation, 94,* 216–230.

Goldstein, A. P., & Martens, B. K. (2000) *Lasting change.* Champaign, IL: Research Press.

Gottman, J. M., & Silver, N. (1999). *The seven principles for making marriage work.* New York: Crown.

Griest, D. L., & Forehand, K. C. (1982). How can I get any parent training done with all these other problems going on? The role of family variables in child behavior therapy. *Child and Behavior Therapy, 14,* 37–53.

Hayes, S. C. (2004). Acceptance and commitment therapy, relational frame theory, and the third wave of behavior therapy. *Behavior Therapy, 35,* 639–665.

Helm, D. T., & Kozloff, M. A. (1986). Research on parent training: Shortcomings and remedies. *Journal of Autism and Developmental Disorders, 16,* 1–22.

Hieneman, M., Childs, K., & Sergay, J. (2006). *Parenting and positive behavior support: A practical guide to resolving your child's difficult behavior.* Baltimore: Brookes.

Horner, R. D., & Baer, D. M. (1978). Multiple-probe technique: A variation of the multiple baseline. *Journal of Applied Behavior Analysis, 11,* 186–196.

Iwata, B. A., Dorsey, M. F., Slifer, K. J., Bauman, K. E., & Richman, G. S. (1982). Toward a functional analysis of self-injury. *Analysis and Intervention in Developmental Disabilities, 2,* 3–20.

Jacobson, J. (1990). Do some mental disorders occur less frequently among persons with mental retardation? *American Journal on Mental Retardation, 94,* 596–602.

Kanfer, F. H., & Grimm, L. G. (1980). Managing clinical change. *Behavior Modification, 4,* 419–444.

Kazdin, A. E., & Weisz, M. K. (2003). Treatment of parental stress to enhance therapeutic change among children referred for aggressive and antisocial behavior. *Journal of Consulting and Clinical Psychology, 71,* 504–514.

Kennedy, C. H. (2005). *Single-case designs for educational research.* Boston: Allyn & Bacon.

Kern, L., Gallagher, P., Starosta, K., Hickman, W., & George, M. (2006). Longitudinal outcomes of functional assessment-based intervention. *Journal of Positive Behavior Interventions, 8,* 67–78.

Koegel, L. K., Koegel, R. L., Boettcher, M., & Brookman-Frazee, L. (2005). Extending behavior support in home and community settings. In L. M. Bambara & L. Kern

(Eds.), *Individualized supports for students with problem behaviors: Designing positive behavior support plans* (pp. 334–358). New York: Guilford.

Koegel, L. K., Koegel, R. L., & Dunlap, G. (Eds.). (1996). *Positive behavioral support: Including people with difficult behavior in the community*. Baltimore: Brookes.

Koegel, L. K., Steibel, D., & Koegel, R. L. (1998). Reducing aggression in children with autism toward infant or toddler siblings. *The Journal of the Association for Persons With Severe Handicaps, 23*, 111–118.

Lucyshyn, J. M., & Albin, R. W. (1993). Comprehensive support to families of children with disabilities and problem behaviors: Keeping it "friendly." In G. H. S. Singer & L. E. Powers (Eds.), *Families, disability, and empowerment: Active coping skills and strategies for family interventions* (pp. 365–407). Baltimore: Brookes.

Lucyshyn, J. M., Albin, R. W., Horner, R., Mann, J., Mann, J., & Wadsworth, G. (2007). Family implementation of positive behavior support with a child with autism: A longitudinal, single case experimental and descriptive replication and extension. *Journal of Positive Behavior Interventions, 9*, 131–150.

Lucyshyn, J. M., Albin, R. W., & Nixon, C. D. (1997). Embedding comprehensive behavioral support in family ecology: An experimental, single-case analysis. *Journal of Consulting and Clinical Psychology, 65*, 241–251.

Lucyshyn, J. M., Dunlap, G., & Albin, R. W. (Eds.). (2002). *Families, and positive behavioral support: Addressing problem behaviors in family contexts*. Baltimore: Brookes.

Lucyshyn, J. M., Horner, R. H., Dunlap, G., Albin, R. W., & Ben, K. R. (2002). Positive behavioral support with families. In J. M. Lucyshyn, G. Dunlap, & R. W. Albin (Eds.), *Families, and positive behavioral support: Addressing problem behaviors in family contexts* (pp. 3–43). Baltimore: Brookes.

Lucyshyn, J. M., Irvin, L. K., Blumberg, E. R., Laverty, R., Horner, R. H., & Sprague, J. R. (2004). Validating the construct of coercion in family routines: Expanding the unit of analysis in behavioral assessment with families of children with developmental disabilities. *Research and Practice for Persons With Severe Handicaps, 29*, 104–121.

Lucyshyn, J. M., Kayser, A. T., Irvin, L. R., & Blumberg, E. R. (2002). Functional assessment and positive behavior support plan development at home with families: Defining effective and contextually-appropriate plans. In J. M. Lucyshyn, G. Dunlap, & R. W. Albin (Eds.), *Families, and positive behavioral support: Addressing problem behaviors in family contexts* (pp. 97–132). Baltimore: Brookes.

Lucyshyn, J. M., Lohrmann, S., Binnendyk, L., Fossett, B., Cheremshynski, C., Elkinson, L., et al. (2007, March). *Transforming coercive processes in family routines: Preliminary results and lessons learned*. Paper presented at the annual International Conference on Positive Behavior Support, Boston.

Lynch, E. W., & Hanson, M. J. (2004). *Developing cross-cultural competence: A guide for working with children and their families* (3rd ed.). Baltimore: Brookes.

Mackintosh, N. J. (1975). A theory of attention: Variations in the associability of stimulus and reinforcement. *Psychological Review, 82*, 276–298.

Messick, S. (1988). The once and future issues of validity: Assessing the meaning and consequences of measurement. In H. Wainer & H. I. Braun (Eds.), *Test validity* (pp. 33–45). Hillsdale, NJ: Erlbaum.

Minuchin, S. (1974). *Families and family therapy*. Cambridge, MA: Harvard University Press.

Moes, D. R., & Frea, W.D. (2002). Contextualized behavioral support in early intervention for children with autism and their families. *Journal of Autism and Developmental Disabilities, 23*, 521–534.

Noldus, L. P. J. J., Trienes, R. J. H., Hendriksen, A. H. M., Jansen, H., & Jansen, R. G., (2000). The Observer Video Pro: New software for the collection, management, and presentation of time-structured data from videotapes and digital media files. *Behavior Research Methods, Instruments, and Computers, 32*, 197–206.

O'Donnell, C. R., Tharp, R. G., & Wilson, K. (1993). Activity settings as the unit of analysis: a theoretical basis for community intervention and development. *American Journal of Community Psychology, 21*, 501–520.

O'Neill, R. E., Horner, R. H., Albin, R. W., Sprague, J. R., Storey, K., & Newton, J. S. (1997). *Functional assessment and program development for problem behavior: A practical handbook*. Pacific Grove, CA: Brooks/Cole.

Patterson, G. R. (1978). *Families: Applications of social learning to family life.* Champaign, IL: Research Press.

Patterson, G. R. (1982). *Coercive family processes.* Eugene, OR: Castalia.

Patterson, G. R., & Forgatch, M. S. (1985). Therapist behavior as a determinant for client non-compliance: A paradox for the behavior modifier. *Journal of Consulting and Clinical Psychology, 6,* 846–851.

Patterson, G. R., Forgatch, M. S., Yoerger, K., & Stoolmiller, M. (1998). Variables that initiate and maintain an early-onset trajectory for juvenile offending. *Development and Psychopathology, 10,* 531–547.

Patterson, J. E., Miller, R. B., Carnes, S., & Wilson, S. (2004). Evidence-based practice for marriage and family therapists. *Journal of Marital and Family Therapy, 30,* 183–195.

Patterson, G. R., Reid, J. B., & Dishion, T. J. (1992). *Antisocial boys.* Eugene, OR: Castalia.

Peters, R. D., & McMahon, R. J. (1989). *Social learning and systems approaches to marriage and the family.* New York: Brunner/Mazel.

Reid, J. B., Patterson, G. R., & Snyder, J. J. (2002). *Antisocial behavior in children and adolescents: A developmental analysis and the Oregon model for intervention.* Washington, DC: American Psychological Association.

Repp, A., & Horner, R. H. (Eds.). (1999). *Functional analysis of problem behavior: From effective assessment to effective support.* Belmont, CA: Wadsworth.

Risdal, & Singer, G. H. S. (2004). Marital adjustment in parents of children with disabilities: A historical review and meta-analysis. *Research and Practice for Persons With Severe Disabilities, 29,* 95–103.

Roberts, C., Mazzucchelli, T., Studman, L., & Sanders, M. R. (2006). Behavioral family intervention for children with developmental disabilities and behavioral problems. *Journal of Clinical Child and Adolescent Psychology, 35,* 180–193.

Rocco, S., Metzger, J., Zangerele, A., & Skouge, J. R. (2002). Three families' perspectives on assessment, intervention, and parent-professional partnerships. In J. M. Lucyshyn, G. Dunlap, & R. W. Albin (Eds.), *Families, and positive behavioral support: Addressing problem behaviors in family contexts* (pp. 75–91). Baltimore: Brookes

Scotti, J. R., & Meyer, L. H. (Eds.). (1999) *Behavioral intervention: Principals, models, and practices.* Baltimore: Brookes.

Seligman, M. E. P., Steen, T. A., Park, N., & Peterson, C. (2005). Positive psychology progress: Empirical validation of interventions. *American Psychologist, 60,* 410–421.

Singer, G. H., Goldberg-Hamblin, S. E., Peckham-Hardin, K. D., Barry, L., & Santarelli, G. E. (2002). Toward a synthesis of family support practices and positive behavior support. In J. M. Lucyshyn, G. Dunlap, & R. W. Albin (Eds.), *Families and positive behavior support: Addressing problem behavior in family contexts* (pp. 155–183). Baltimore: Brookes.

Singh, N. N., Lancioni, G. E., Winton, A. S. W., Fisher, B. C., Wahler, R. G., McAleavey, K., et al. (2006). Mindful parenting decreases aggression, noncompliance and self-injury in children with autism. *Journal of Emotional and Behavioral Disorders, 14,* 169–177.

Skinner, B. F. (1953). *Science and human behavior.* New York: Macmillan.

Stoltenberg, C. D., & Delworth, U. (1987) *Supervising counselors and therapists.* San Francisco: Jossey-Bass.

Turnbull, A. P., & Turnbull, H. R. (1991). Family assessment and family empowerment: An ethical analysis. In L. H. Meyer, C. A. Peck, & L. Brown (Eds.), *Critical issues in the lives of people with severe disabilities* (pp. 485–488). Baltimore: Brookes.

Turnbull, A. P., & Ruef, M. B. (1996). Family perspectives on problem behavior. *Mental Retardation, 34,* 280–293.

Turnbull, A. P., Turnbull, H. R., Erwin, E., & Soodak, L. (2006). *Families, professionals, and exceptionality: Positive outcomes through partnerships and trust.* Columbus, OH, and Upper Saddle River, NJ. Pearson/Merrill-Prentice Hall.

Vaughn, B. J., Clarke, S., & Dunlap, G. (1997). Assessment-based intervention for severe behavior problems in a natural family context. *Journal of Applied Behavior Analysis, 30,* 713–716.

Vaughn, B. J., Wilson, D., & Dunlap, G. (2002). Family-centered intervention to resolve problem behaviors in a fast-food restaurant. *Journal of Positive Behavior Interventions, 4,* 38–45.

Wahler, R. G., & Fox, J. J. (1981). Setting events in social networks: Ally or enemy in child behavior therapy? Behavior *Therapy, 14,* 19–36.

Webster-Stratton, C., & Herbert, M. (1993). What really happens in parent training? *Behavior Modification, 17,* 407–456.

Werle, M. A., Murphy, T. B., & Budd, K. S. (1993). Treating chronic food refusal in young children: Home-based parent training. *Journal of Applied Behavior Analysis, 26,* 421–433.

# 5

# Positive Behavior Support and Early Intervention for Young Children With Autism: Case Studies on the Efficacy of Proactive Treatment of Problem Behavior

**PHILLIP S. STRAIN and ILENE SCHWARTZ**

The number of children with autism is increasing dramatically and having a tremendous impact on the resources attached to every type of service and support that include young children (e.g., health, child care, school). The most recent numbers released by the Centers for Disease Control and Prevention in 2007 reports that the prevalence of autism is 1 in 150 live births. Autism is a spectrum disorder, which means that children who receive this diagnosis differ dramatically in their abilities, preferences, needs, and area of delay. There is no "typical" child with autism; there is no one right way of educating a child with autism; and every child with autism and the child's family brings a unique story to the early intervention process, and that story must be woven into the fabric of intervention and support for the process to be successful. Positive behavior support (PBS) offers early intervention providers with a set of tools and a process that can serve as the centerpiece of an effective intervention program for young children with autism and their families.

**PHILLIP S. STRAIN** • University of Colorado at Denver Health Sciences Center
**ILENE SCHWARTZ** • University of Washington

The purpose of this chapter is to provide a description of how PBS and early intervention for children with autism converge philosophically and procedurally. Then, we provide two examples of comprehensive evidence-based intervention programs for young children with autism and describe how these programs have used PBS to facilitate positive outcomes for young children with autism across developmental domains. Finally, we provide case study examples from these comprehensive programs that highlight the merger of PBS with early intervention for young children with autism.

First, how are we defining PBS in this context? In a recent article describing the familial alliance between PBS and applied behavior analysis (ABA), Dunlap and his colleagues (Dunlap, Carr, Horner, Zarcone, & Schwartz, in press) proposed 10 defining features of PBS. Given the centrality of ABA in high-quality programs for children with autism, it seems like this would be a good place to begin the description. Intervention programs that could be described as providing PBS, according to Dunlap et al., include a view of global intervention goals such as comprehensive lifestyle change and improved quality of life; life-span perspective; high ecological validity; principal stakeholders as collaborators and partners; high ratings of social validity; an emphasis on ensuring the fidelity of intervention by examining how interventions affect systems variables; an emphasis on prevention; intervention and support plans based on solid assessment data, evidence-based practices, and data-based decision making; the use of evidence from a variety of methodological practices; and an appreciation of the contribution of multiple theoretical perspectives.

Like PBS, early intervention for children with autism has its historical roots in ABA. Therefore, the philosophical convergence between PBS and early intervention for children with autism is strong and gathering more strength as we collect more information on the long-term outcomes of children with autism who have participated in high-quality early intervention programs. The primary points of convergence that we want to highlight and promote are the attention to global outcomes such as quality of life (rather than IQ scores), attention to ecological validity (rather than receiving treatment in a small clinic room), and the use of evidence from a variety of methodological practices (rather than a belief that a board-certified behavior analyst is the only professional qualified to work with a child with autism). These three points of convergence between PBS and early intervention for students with autism emphasize the importance of looking beyond what a practice might be called (e.g., discrete trial, teaching loop, intentional teaching) to focusing on the outcome the practice achieves for children and their families, that is, looking beyond labels and attempting to understand the function or utility of an intervention. The goal of both PBS and early intervention for children with autism is to increase the confidence and competence of the recipients of the intervention, the children, their families, and the communities that support them.

In addition to philosophical similarities, there are many points of procedural convergence between PBS and early intervention for children with autism. The primary point of convergence is the reliance on data to determine the effectiveness of the intervention. Early intervention and early childhood special education (ECSE) are often said to be "value driven and data determined."

Researchers and practitioners implementing early intervention for young children with autism rely on data to determine the types of skills to be taught, to evaluate the effectiveness of the intervention at the level of individual children and lessons, and to make programmatic decisions about the necessary intensity of programming for individual children. Like PBS, early intervention for children with autism will incorporate interventions from different theoretical perspectives (e.g., social stories, activity schedules, self-monitoring techniques) but rely on clear, objective data and data analysis techniques from ABA to evaluate the effectiveness of the specific interventions for individual children.

## THE SPECIFIC CASE FOR CONVERGENCE WITH CHILDREN WITH AUTISM: LEAP AND PROJECT DATA

Providing effective, developmentally appropriate, socially valid, and sustainable early intervention programs for young children with autism and their families is a challenge that is confronting early intervention providers and educators around the world. Not only has the dramatic increase in numbers of children with autism taxed current providers, but the earlier identification of children with this diagnosis is requiring some practitioners (e.g., early intervention providers serving children under age 3) to begin serving this population. In addition, the recommended standards for early intervention for children with disabilities in general and those for children with autism differ on many dimensions. For example, looking at the number of hours of week of service, a metric often used to indicate the intensity of the intervention, highlights these differences. The results of the National Early Intervention Longitudinal Study (Hebbeler et al., 2007) reported that on average children and families receiving early intervention in the United States receive 1.5 hr a week of service. Compare this to the 25 hr a week of services recommended by the National Research Council (2001) as the minimum number of hours a week young children with autism should receive. This makes it clear that early intervention providers looking for guidance about how to serve children with autism and their families are not going to find the answers among traditional early intervention providers. The answers for how to provide services for children with autism can be found in programs that blend the approaches of ABA and PBS. In the next section, we present two examples of effective programs for young children with autism that are sustainable LEAP [Learning Experience in An Alternative Program for Preschoolers and Parents] has been in existence for 26 years and Project DATA [Developmentally Appropriate Treatment for Autism] for 11) and replicable. Both also blend approaches from ABA, PBS, and ECSE to meet the needs of individual children and their families.

### LEAP

Brief History of LEAP. LEAP Preschool began in 1981 as a model demonstration program funded by the Handicapped Children's Early Education Program, U.S. Department of Education. The original LEAP effort was developed in collaboration with the Pittsburgh, Pennsylvania, city schools. Four years later, the program moved to the Fox Chapel public schools, Fox Chapel, Pennsylvania. In 1998, the Douglas County, Colorado, public schools became the prime demonstration and training site for LEAP. LEAP model classrooms continue to operate in the Pittsburgh area.

In the 25-year history of LEAP, the program has been the site for extensive research and training activities. LEAP research initiatives have focused on demonstrating the unique contributions of specific program components to child and family behavior change. Over 30 peer-reviewed studies have demonstrated the efficacy of LEAP strategies for teaching peer-related social skills, communication skills, and cognitive and preacademic skills. Other studies have demonstrated parents' skill acquisition and subsequent changes in child behavior in home settings that are attributable to LEAP's family skill training. In 1984, LEAP began to establish replication sites and provide general skill training for school districts throughout the United States and numerous foreign countries. Currently, there are over 80 LEAP preschool replications. Funding has been acquired to conduct a randomized clinical trial of LEAP's 2-year consultative model of replication training.

### *LEAP Program Overview*

LEAP classrooms include 3 to 4 young children with autism and 8 to 10 typically developing preschoolers. At least three adults are always present in LEAP classrooms each day. Speech and language specialists, occupational therapists, and classroom assistants are typically involved as team members. In the service of promoting child skill generalization, LEAP professionals practice a transdisciplinary model of service delivery. That is, all staff engage in role exchange on a planned, daily basis. Staff responsible for delivering the in-home skill training for families often include experienced family members. One full-time equivalent staff person is capable of serving approximately 12 families.

LEAP preschools typically operate 15 hr per week (staff are responsible for daily double sessions). Family skill training begins with staff delivering the nine modules of behavior teaching strategies, resulting in families delivering intervention throughout the day in home and community settings. Families determine the contexts in which training occurs by nominating routines that are of particular difficulty.

### *Special Features*

The LEAP model has a number of special features:

1. Inclusion begins full time from day 1. Children with autism are provided with the necessary level of adult prompting and support to participate in all classroom activities.
2. The design of LEAP classrooms begins with establishing a setting of high quality for typically developing children. Sites often use the Creative Curriculum for Preschool (Dodge, Colker, Heroman, and Bickart, 2002) or the Storybook Journey: Pathways to Literacy Through Story and Play (McCord, 1995) curricula for this purpose.

LEAP has also been implemented effectively in classrooms utilizing a variety of other preschool models and curricula including High Scope and Head Start programs. These sites represent replications in which the "typically developing" children come from backgrounds that put them at risk for developmental problems and in which these children come from ethnic, racial, and language minorities. In the context of this programming, systematic intervention for children with autism is embedded in typical preschool routines (e.g., circle time, free play/centers, snack, small groups, etc.).

3. Typically developing children play a major intervention role in LEAP. These children are provided with comprehensive training such that they can facilitate the social and communicative behaviors of peers with autism. This teaching method for typically developing peers is available in the work of Strain (2002).
4. Learning objectives are written in such a fashion that teaching continues until generalized behavior change is achieved. Learning objectives are further described according to relevant prompting hierarchies. Thus, program data are collected on children's behavioral movement toward independent performance, not in terms of percent correct, trial accomplished, or similar indices.
5. Skill training for families focuses on providing adult family members with the behavioral teaching strategies sufficient for them to experience less stress and more pleasure in daily routines such as meals, bedtime, dressing, and community outings.
6. Intensity in the LEAP model is not defined by hours per week that individuals are paid to deliver service. We believe that the algorithm defining intensity is complex and includes, for each developmental domain of concern, the following factors: (a) number of opportunities to respond; (b) the functionality of objectives chosen; (c) the selection of an instructional method that maximizes children's engagement and minimizes errors; (d) the competence of staff to deliver with fidelity the chosen intervention; and (e) the use of data systems and decision-making rules that minimize children's exposure to less-than-optimal interventions.
7. LEAP utilizes a variety of science-based intervention approaches, including (a) peer-mediated interventions; (b) errorless learning; (c) time delay; (d) incidental teaching; (e) pivotal response training; (f) Picture Exchange Communication System (PECS) (Frost & Bondy, 1994); and (g) PBS.
8. Behavior management strategies used at LEAP Preschool support the use of preventive and positive approaches for managing challenging behavior of young children with autism. A variety of classroomwide preventive strategies are used to support children's engagement in positive prosocial behaviors. Such strategies include the effective use of classroom rules, daily schedules, activities, instructional materials, and staff arrangements (Strain & Hemmeter, 1999). In addition, curricular activities are designed to provide children with autism numerous opportunities to make choices and exercise control over their environment, as well as teach important skills in the areas of

play, social development, and communication. Instructional planning teams that include the teachers and classroom assistants, the family service coordinator, speech therapist, parents, program supervisor, and other primary caregivers meet as needed to discuss concerns related to individual children's behavior in school, home, and community environments. When a specific behavior is identified as a concern, the conditions and circumstances that may predict when the behavior will or will not occur are identified, as well as hypotheses regarding the possible functions of the behavior and the adult consequences that may be maintaining the behavior. Individualized preventive strategies for teaching these behaviors are identified, as well as intervention strategies to be used when the child engages in the undesirable behavior. Procedures are identified for promoting generalization and maintenance of desired behaviors across environments, activities, and persons and for evaluating the effectiveness of intervention strategies. In practice, preventive strategies are successful in over 80% of the situations in which children present challenging behaviors in the classroom, community, or at home.

## Project DATA Program Overview

In 1997, at the University of Washington Project DATA began with the help of a Department of Education, Office of Special Education Model Demonstration Grant. Project DATA has been running continually since and is now funded by a combination of school district tuition and private contributions. Project DATA was designed to meet a need of the community: How could school districts meet the needs of young children with autism and their families in a manner that was effective, acceptable to all parties, and sustainable? The project was developed to combine the best practices from ABA and ECSE into a program for children that recognized the unique learning characteristics and support needs of children with autism and that children with autism are children first.

Project DATA consists of five components that are illustrated in Fig. 5.1. The core component of the program is an integrated early childhood program. A primary goal of the Project DATA model is to ensure that every child with autism will have opportunities to interact successfully with typically developing children every day. To make the interactions successful, they need to be planned and supported systematically. This component is not just about being with typically developing children; it is about interacting with and developing relationships with typically developing children. To achieve this, preschoolers in Project DATA attend an integrated preschool classroom for about 12 hr a week.

### *High-Quality Early Intervention Program*

To provide opportunities for the children with autism to interact successfully with their typically developing peers, the preschool environments pay special attention to:

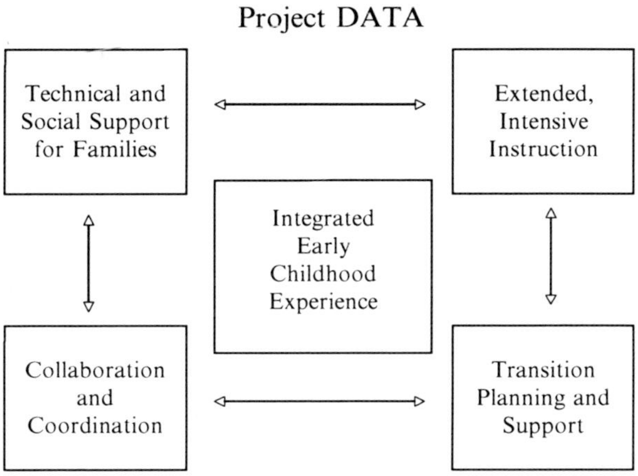


**Fig. 5.1.** The five program components of Project DATA (Developmentally Appropriate Treatment for Autism).

- Structuring the classroom environment to promote independence, participation, and successful interactions with typically developing peers
- Developing a consistent schedule and using it
- Creating the need to communicate with adults and peers
- Using preferred materials and activities to promote engagement
- Providing embedded and explicit instruction on valued skills
- Providing frequent reinforcement and developing effective motivation systems

One of the primary considerations of an effective program for young children with autism is an environment designed to prevent problem behaviors, promote engagement and participation, and facilitate successful interactions with typically developing peers. Because children with autism are children first, the first step in structuring a high-quality environment for children with autism is to ensure attention to the overall classroom environment for all children (Strain, 2001). Recommended practices for early childhood environments highlight the importance of the physical aspects of a learning environment, including the availability of developmentally and age appropriate materials, the use of a consistent schedule of routines, and the availability of responsive adults and peers (Bredekamp & Copple, 1997; DEC Recommended Practices, Sandall, McLean, & Smith, 2000). Because children with autism are children first, it follows that the components that comprise a high-quality early childhood environment for all young children are necessary but may not be sufficient for children with autism. It is important, however, to begin with a high-quality environment as defined by early childhood professional groups (e.g., National Association for the Education of Young Children and the Division of Early Childhood of the Council for Exceptional Children).

Many classrooms or intervention settings have schedules that outline the different activities children will participate in each day. To provide a child with autism a comprehensible environment, a schedule of daily activities should be available in a format that is understandable to the child. Using pictures and symbols in addition to words may increase a child's understanding. Showing a younger child an object that he or she associates with a common activity or routine can facilitate comprehension of what is coming next. A schedule alone may not be meaningful to a child with autism if the child is not taught to use it. Teachers need to refer to the schedule frequently and consistently and use the schedule to teach the classroom routine, cue transitions, and teach children to understand changes to the routine. A variety of strategies are useful for cueing a child that a change is about to occur (i.e., timers, counting, singing songs, etc.). Again, whatever strategy is utilized will only be effective if the child is taught the purpose and meaning of the transition cue. It is important to remember that schedules are not panaceas, and that used incorrectly a schedule could end up making a child with autism more rigid. Schedules need to be used to help children navigate the environment and be independent. Children need to learn that changes to the schedule will occur and how to handle them. A teacher can use a schedule to help children with autism understand that specific activities will not be occurring that day (e.g., mark those activities with the international "no" symbol of a circle with a line through it) or that activities will be occurring in a different order. Schedules are instructional tools; they are as useful as the instruction that accompanies them.

The classroom environment can promote children's opportunities and motivation to communicate. The number of opportunities a child with autism has to learn how to ask for things he or she wants, reject something not wanted, or initiate or respond to others is dependent on how the environment supports, and perhaps demands, those communicative behaviors. All children who participate in Project DATA have a functional communication system. Our goal, of course, is to help all children develop functional speech, but those children who are not yet verbal are taught to use the PECS across all school, home, and community settings. In Project DATA, we view every classroom activity as a language-learning and -using opportunity. For instance, snack time provides an excellent opportunity for a child to learn how to ask for something he or she wants (i.e., favorite food), reject something not wanted (i.e., food he or she dislikes), and respond to the request of a peer. Children with autism are also put in charge of snack items, a wonderful opportunity to work on receptive language when the child with autism must respond to classmates who are asking for orange slices or other snack items. Finally, across all activities students are required to use communicative behavior to request preferred materials and activities and to control their environment. These communicative opportunities add up across the day to provide multiple opportunities to respond, which is essential in language acquisition (Hart & Risley, 1995).

Systematically teaching children with autism to engage in play or learning activities independently is an important goal of the preschool portion of Project DATA. To achieve this outcome, teachers identify materials and activities that children find interesting and make them available to the child as part of the classroom activities (McGee, Daly, Izeman, Mann, & Risley, 1991). Within the classroom, staff ensure that there are preferred items for every child, and that within every activity center there is a range of materials that will engage the child with the most severe disabilities and that will challenge the most capable child.

Recommended practices for young children with autism emphasize the importance of systematic instruction on core areas of need related to autism (National Research Council, 2001). To promote the most optimal and generalized outcomes, this instruction needs to take place across settings, activities, people, and materials. It also requires that teachers and interventionists have knowledge of different techniques to teach specific skills and to be able to assess whether the child is making adequate progress using the selected technique so that changes can be made if progress is not sufficient.

Teachers in the preschool must plan what is going to be taught, where and how the instruction will occur, and how child progress will be assessed to determine if the child can demonstrate the targeted skill or behavior in a fluent and generalized manner. To achieve this high frequency of instruction and data collection, teachers in the Project DATA classrooms develop an activity matrix that outlines the instructional needs for all the students in their classroom (Sandall & Schwartz, 2002). The purpose of an activity matrix is to use a grid to plan when specially designed instruction will be provided in the classroom and when data collection on specific targeted skills and behaviors will occur.

A common characteristic of children with autism is that they fail to take advantage of the social rewards that are available to others for behaving in certain ways (Smith Myles, 2005). They often fail to "pick up" important information that is communicated by adults and peers through a variety of unstated social cues or rules and even if aware of the social rules are often not motivated by the social contingencies present to follow the rules. Children with autism do, however, respond extremely well to positive reinforcement. Therefore, the systematic selection of reinforcers (i.e., reinforcer assessment) and the contingent application of reinforcement to change behavior or teach new skills are necessary (Durand, Crimmins, Caulfield, & Taylor, 1989).

When starting out in a preschool classroom, a child may have a limited set of items or activities that function as reinforcers. (Remember, if an item or activity does not increase the probability of the behavior happening again it is not a reinforcer, even if teachers think it is a preferred item.) Therefore, early in a child's preschool career we may be more likely to use more artificial (e.g., items that are unrelated to the task) reinforcers. These may include a favorite toy, stickers, bubbles, or food. As children learn to participate in more activities and be reinforced by more items and social praise from the teacher, we attempt to use more natural reinforcers. Natural reinforcers are those that are logically related to the task at hand. For example, if a child wants to go outside and is standing at a closed door and says "Open," opening the door and letting the child go outside is a natural reinforcer. Natural reinforcers are often the most powerful type of reinforcer because the child's motivation is high at that moment to achieve that specific outcome. Although natural reinforcers may be more acceptable in preschool classrooms, the rule in the Project DATA classroom is that whatever type and amount of reinforcement is needed to promote skill development and appropriate behavior is the type and amount of reinforcement that we use.

Project DATA has been extremely successful. Over 50% of the children leave our program and are placed in inclusive kindergarten programs (Schwartz, Sandall, McBride, & Boulware, 2004). Parents and school officials have been extremely satisfied with the program, and many school districts in our state are now implementing their local version of Project DATA. Our program is only one example of what effective early intervention services can look like for children with autism. The important thing to remember is that there is no one right way to educate children with autism, and a program is only successful if a child is making progress.

## CASE STUDIES ON THE CONVERGENCE OF PBA AND EARLY AUTISM TREATMENT

Next, we present four case studies in which a wide variety of problem behaviorsand skill deficits was addressed successfully using an assortment of intervention tactics. For example, two of the case studies demonstrate the power of promoting general engagement with toys, materials, and routines as a sufficient intervention. The final two cases show a more traditional implementation of function-based treatment for problem behavior.

### LEAP Case Study on Engagement Intervention

Child. Eric began his 3-year stay in LEAP at 32 months of age. On program entry, he was not toilet trained; he had an intelligible three-word vocabulary (Momma, dog, Wally); he repetitively flapped his arms; and he whimpered when approached by peers or strangers. Eric's major presenting problem behavior at school and home consisted of his mouthing, throwing, and banging of objects, including toys and eating utensils.

#### *Decision-Making Process Leading to Engagement Intervention*

LEAP staff conducted per incident observations of Eric's mouthing, throwing, and banging behaviors for 3 days in all school and home routines using a simple antecedent-behavior-consequence chart. Results showed that these problem behaviors occurred in all settings, with and without response demands, with and without correction consequences, and with and without social reinforcement for appropriate object use. In addition, staff informally observed that Eric used one object (toy truck) appropriately for a matter of seconds across the 3 days. Based on these data, staff hypothesized that Eric's problem behaviors were, in fact, his best attempts at object manipulation and that directly teaching appropriate object use was the best intervention approach.

### *Components of the Appropriate Engagement Intervention*

Staff and family members initially created a priority ranking of routines and objects within routines that were of greatest concern because of safety reasons. Based on rankings, family members decided to concentrate their initial efforts on feeding routines in which utensils were present and bath time, during which his behavior with soap and toys had caused injury to others. Preschool staff targeted a 45-min child choice time during which several small rubber toys had been removed from his mouth. In both home and preschool settings, a two-fold intervention approach was implemented. First, if Eric engaged in any identified problem behavior with objects, adults immediately interrupted the behavior in a physical manner (e.g., stopping him with hand-over-hand prompting as he directed the rubber toys toward his mouth). Next, adults immediately labeled the object (e.g., "It's soap") and then gave a simultaneous full-physical and verbal prompt (e.g., "Scrub with soap" and use hand-over-hand prompting to get Eric to use the soap on his body). Adults immediately gave Eric descriptive praise (e.g., "Eric, you're scrubbing with soap!") and a hug (his preferred social reinforcer). After 3 days of this routine, a 2-s time delay was instituted between the verbal prompt (e.g., "Scrub with soap") and the physical prompt to do so. Several additional sequential steps were made in the increasing time-delay strategy such that Eric was responding immediately after verbal prompting in all three settings after 3 weeks.

The second component to this intervention involved teaching appropriate object use for very brief (less than 2 min/day) periods of time in settings other than the criteria ones. So, for example, parents would prompt Eric to use soap appropriately with a toy wash basin and doll shortly before his bath time. Similarly, teachers had peers model appropriate toy use behaviors at a circle time that occurred immediately before choice time. After peers modeled play, Eric always had a turn at circle with the toy. At these instructional times, adults used response prompting and social reinforcement strategies identical to those employed in criteria settings.

### *Appropriate Engagement and Problem Behavior Data*

For all three initial intervention settings, adults were asked to complete two 5-point rating scales immediately after the session. The first scale measured problem behaviors, with anchor Point 1 labeled as "totally acceptable," anchor Point 3 labeled "somewhat acceptable," and anchor Point 5 labeled "totally unacceptable." The second scale measured appropriate engagement with objects. Anchor Point 5 was labeled "appropriate with all objects all of the time." Anchor Point 3 was labeled "appropriate some of the time with some objects." Anchor Point 1 was "appropriate with no objects at any time."

Figure 5.2 presents the intervention agent's ratings of Eric's problem behavior and appropriate object use during bath time. Prior to intervention, Eric's problem behavior was rated as totally unacceptable for three consecutive baseline sessions. Similarly, his appropriate object use was rated as appropriate with no objects at any time during this same period. With

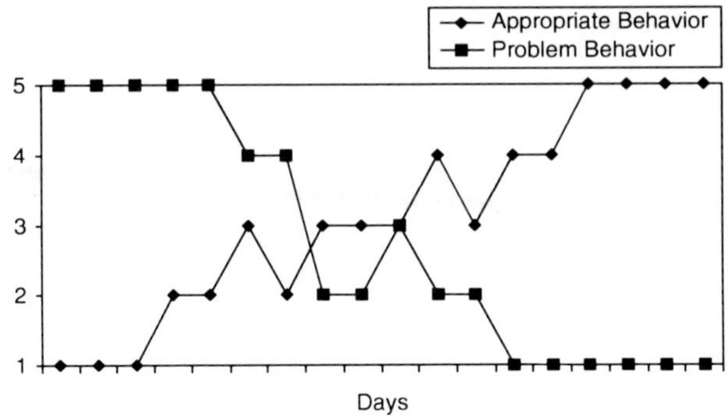


**Fig. 5.2.** Intervention agents' ratings of problem behavior and appropriate object use during bath time based on a 5-point rating scale.

the onset of the intervention procedures, rapid improvement in both problem behavior and object use was seen. In 2 weeks, his problem behavior was maintained at totally acceptable levels, and his object use was maintained at the appropriate with all objects all the time level. This type of data path was replicated in the home mealtime and the preschool choice time settings.

## Project DATA Case Study on Engagement

### *Child*

Brian enrolled in Project DATA when he was 3 years old. He was nonverbal, although he had a high rate of vocalizations. He lived with his parents and an older sister, who were all bilingual (English and Mandarin). His grandmother also lived with them and provided child care to Brian during the day. His grandmother was a monolingual Mandarin speaker. Brian had no intentional play skills, did not imitate peers or adults, and responded to most instructions by hitting the adult who provided the instruction or himself.

### *Decision-Making Process Leading to Engagement Intervention*

Child data are collected daily on all instructional programs addressed in the extended day program and weekly for all individualized educational plan (IEP) objectives addressed in the integrated preschool classroom. For Brian, appropriate engagement with materials was a priority across settings. In addition to taking data on the amount of time that Brian interacted with materials appropriately, program staff kept track of the materials with which he interacted. These data were used to conduct a naturalistic preference assessment. That is, when left alone to pick materials in the classroom, what did he select and how did he spend his time? The assumption is that if teachers can identify toys, materials, or activities that were already preferred, they could build these into a program to increase engagement as natural reinforcers. In Brian's case, there were no preferred activities or materials. He interacted with all the materials in the classroom with about the same frequency (low) and for the same duration (short). The team, including a teacher, speech-language pathologist, and occupational therapist met to interpret the data and make a plan. The intervention they developed is described next.

### *Components of the Appropriate Engagement Intervention*

The team members agreed on three conclusions based on the data and their own observations. Brian engaged in a hand-flapping behavior when left alone; there were no clearly preferred activities or materials; and any intervention needed to use a minimum of physical prompting. The team members also noted that when they gave Brian markers and lead him to a paper-covered table, he would engage in a behavior that looked like his self-stimulatory behavior but resulted in making marks on the paper. The team developed an intervention for Brian in which they introduced a simple activity schedule that initially consisted of three steps: art, another choice such as a tabletop manipulative toy, and "Brian's choice." Using Brian's "drawing" as a choice provided the teachers with an opportunity to reinforce him for engaging in an independent and appropriate behavior. After he drew for a while, a teacher would prompt him to look at his schedule and then give him an opportunity to make his own choice. The result was that Brian quickly learned to engage appropriately in a variety of classroom activities. It is interesting to note that, for reasons still not entirely clear or reflected in any data the program collected, art and specifically drawing have remained Brian's favorite activities. Brian is now in fifth grade, and his artwork is displayed regularly at his elementary school and other district venues.

## LEAP Function-Based Case Study

### *Child*

Mark was enrolled in LEAP at 36 months of age. At that time, he had a five-word vocabulary, he engaged in tantrums for periods up to 1 hr, and he spent most of his time playing repetitively with miniature "action figures." Mark's overall developmental functioning placed him at about 12 months of age.

### *Decision Making Leading to Function-Based Intervention*

Preschool staff and family members agreed that reducing the number and length of his tantrums was a major priority. During Mark's first week at LEAP he tantrumed, on average, six times per day. These episodes averaged 12 min. An analysis of the antecedent-behavior-consequence data collected for each episode revealed the following: (a) 90% of his tantrums were preceded by an adult request (e.g., "Come here, Mark"); (b) when adults gave a request, Mark would first fall to the floor, then he would begin to flair about, throw objects, and cry; and (c) consequences for tantrum behavior varied widely. On 40% of the occasions, adults physically directed him to comply, on 36% of the occasions adults ignored him, and on 24% of the occasions adults briefly interrupted his tantruming to protect other children or property. Finally, team members consulted with each other and the family in reaching the conclusion that some 80% of the requests made to Mark were clearly within his range of competence. That is, he could understand the requests from a language comprehension standpoint, and he had complied with identical requests in the past or contemporaneously. Based on all these factors, staff hypothesized that Mark's tantrums were primarily attempts to avoid complying with the requests.

### *Components of Function-Based (Avoidance) Intervention Plan*

The intervention plan was designed to accomplish three procedural goals: (a) to ensure that Mark only received directions that he understood and could perform independently; (b) to prevent the escalation in his behavior from falling on the floor, to screaming and crying, to throwing objects; and (c) to eliminate any reinforcement for his avoidance repertoire by always prompting and reinforcing compliance. To accomplish, the first point staff and family members generated a list of 20 directions that they all agreed were readily understood and doable for Mark. Then, staff examined their preschool routines and decided in which contexts (e.g., group time, transitions, snack) each direction would be delivered in a functional, meaningful way each day. To accomplish the second point, staff created a daily chart by which personal assignments were made regarding who was going to deliver each directive in each context. For the time period immediately surrounding delivery of specific directions, it was understood that staff delivering the direction had instructional responsibility for Mark only. This allowed staff to achieve close physical proximity to Mark prior to the delivery of a direction. To achieve the third point, staff elected to implement a number of strategies. First, directions to Mark were followed immediately by a response prompting hierarchy of least-to-most prompts (see Wolery et al., 1988 for a through description). The response system ensured that Mark responded to directions within less than 30 s. Second, if Mark would begin to tantrum, adults simply continued with the response prompting strategy. Finally, Mark received verbal praise and a brief (1-min) period of time to play with his favorite toys following completion of each direction. Over the course of 2 months, the play time reinforcer was systematically withdrawn.

### *Data on Mark's Tantrums and Level of Prompting*

Staff used a stopwatch to keep a cumulative daily total of the time Mark spent engaged in tantrum behavior. Also, staff completed a 5-point daily rating to provide an indication of the "typical" level of prompting needed to achieve compliance to directions. Point 5 on the scale was designated as "full physical prompting"; Point 4 was "partial physical prompting"; Point 3 was "pointing to pictorial representation of desired behavior"; Point 2 was "repeated verbal cue"; and Point 1 was "single, initial direction."

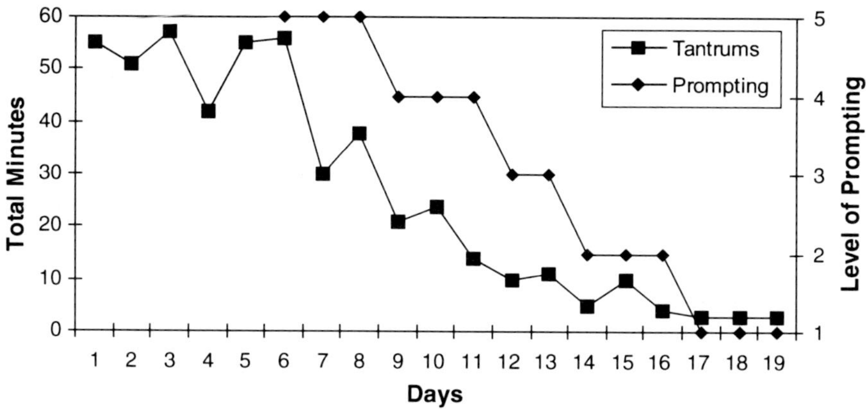


**Fig. 5.3.** Duration of tantrum behavior and rated level of adult prompting of appropriate behavior.

Figure 5.3 depicts Mark's total duration of tantrum behavior and adult prompting levels across baseline and intervention time periods.

## Project DATA Function-Based Case Study

### *Child*

Antonio was 28 months old and recently diagnosed with autism when he started Project DATA. He was verbal; loved looking at, sorting, and collecting cards of all types; and was rigid in his adherence to previously learned schedules and routines. When he was 40 months old, he began to engage in self-injurious behavior (e.g., head banging) when presented with demands or unexpected changes in routines.

### *Decision Making Leading to Function-Based Intervention*

The team, including the parents, met to determine how and where data would be collected to determine the function of the self-injurious behavior. Observations were conducted at home, in the integrated preschool classroom, and in the extended day component of Project DATA. The results of the observations, which identified the antecedent and consequences of the head banging, were consistent across time and settings. It appeared that Antonio engaged in head banging when presented with nonpreferred tasks or if a work session had gone on for a long time.

### *Components of Function-Based (Avoidance) Intervention Plan*

The complexity of this behavior required a multicomponent intervention. First, Antonio was taught how to ask for a break from work, and staff provided him with a picture symbol so that he did not have to rely on memory to ask for a break during nonpreferred or stressful activities. A token system was implemented so that Antonio had a visual representation of how many more tokens (i.e., how much more work) had to be earned before the session ended. He also was provided with choices about which activities he wanted to do first within any session. All tasks had to be completed during any work session, but they were implemented in the order chosen by Antonio. In addition to all of these preventive measures, there was also a plan in place of which consequence would be implemented if the behavior occurred. Because the function was so clearly identified as avoidance, the team decided to ignore the behavior and continue with the task if the behavior occurred. The team members wanted to ensure that there was a plan in place to keep Antonio safe while the consequence of ignoring was being implemented. To ensure his safety, a soft-sided martial arts helmet was purchased with the plan that it would be put on contingent on head banging and left on until he went for 5 min with no head banging. Within 1 month, this behavior was completely extinguished. Antonio went on to be fully included in general education and was elected to be a student council representative in his elementary school.

## CONCLUDING COMMENTS

In this chapter, we argued and demonstrated with global program descriptions and case study examples the convergence of PBS and early intervention for young children with autism. As the program developers, we see both the LEAP and Project DATA models of early autism treatment as indistinguishable from PBS at the philosophical and procedural levels. The benefit that both models derive from a PBS tradition (perhaps even pre-dating PBS as a "named" entity) is the flexibility to respond to children with widely discrepant needs. As the case studies hopefully demonstrate, there is nothing uniform or a priori about the specific interventions utilized in LEAP and Project DATA. In the best tradition, and perhaps the most groundbreaking tradition of PBS, we build specific interventions for the individual case.

## REFERENCES

Bredekamp, S., & Copple, C.(1997). Appropriate practice in early childhood programs (Rev. ed.). Washington, DC: National Association for the Education of Young Children.

Dodge, D. T., Colker, L. J., Heroman, C., & Bickart, T. S. (2002). Creative curriculum for preschool (4th ed.). Albany, NY: Delmar Thompson Learning.

Dunlap, G., Carr, E. G., Horner, R. H., Zarcone, J. R., & Schwartz, I. S. (in press). Positive behavior support and applied behavior analysis: A familial alliance. Behavior Modification.

Durand, V. M., Crimmins, D. B., Caulfield, M., & Taylor, J. (1989). Reinforcer assessment I: Using problem behavior to select reinforcers. Journal of the Association for Persons With Severe Handicaps, 14, 113–126.

Frost, I., & Bondy, A. (1994). The Picture Exchange Communication System training manual. Cherry Hill, NJ: PECS.

Hart, B. M., & Risley, T. R. (1995). Meaningful differences in the lives of American children. Baltimore: Brookes.

Hebbeler, K., Spiker, D., Bailey, D. B., Scarborough, A., Mallik, S., Simeonsson, R., et al. (2007). Early intervention for infants and toddlers with disabilities and their families: Participants, services, and outcomes. Menlo Park, CA: SRI International.

McCord, S. (1995). Storybook journey: Pathways to literacy through story and play. New York: Macmillan.

McGee, G. G., Daly, T., Izeman, S. G., Mann, L., & Risley, T. R. (1991). Use of classroom materials to promote preschool engagement. Teaching Exceptional Children, 23, 44–47.

National Research Council. (2001). Educating children with autism. Committee on Educational Interventions for Children with Autism. C. Lord and J. P. McGee, Eds. Division of Behavioral and Social Sciences and Education. Washington, DC: National Academy Press.

Sandall, S. R., McLean, M. E., & Smith, B. J. (2000). DEC recommended practices in early intervention/early childhood special education. Longmont, CO: Sopris West.

Sandall, S. R., & Schwartz, I. S. (2002). Building blocks for teaching preschoolers with special needs. Baltimore: Brookes.

Schwartz, I. S., Sandall, S. R., McBride, B. J., & Boulware, G. L. (2004). Project DATA (Developmentally Appropriate Treatment for Autism): An inclusive, school-based approach to educating children with autism. Topics in Early Childhood Special Education, 24, 156–168.

Smith Myles, B. (2005). Children and youth with Asperger syndrome: Strategies for success in inclusive settings. Thousand Oaks, CA: Corwin Press.

Strain, P. S. (2001). Empirically-based social skill intervention. Behavioral Disorders, 27, 30–36.

Strain, P. S. (2002). Quality inclusion curriculum. Portland, OR: Teacher's Toolbox.

Strain, P. S., & Hemmeter, M. L. (1999). Keys to being successful when confronted with challenging behaviors. Young Exceptional Children, Monograph Series 1, 17–27.

Wolery, M., Bailey, D. B., Sugai, G. M. (1988). Effective teaching: Principles and Procedures of Applied behavior analysis with exceptional students. Boston: Allyn & Bacon.

# 6

# Integrating a Positive Behavior Support Approach Within Head Start

**ANDY J. FREY, CHERYL ANNE BOYCE, and LOUISA BANKS TARULLO**

Head Start is the largest federally funded primary prevention program in the United States and represents an important component of the early childhood service delivery system. The purpose of this chapter is to discuss the compatibility of the positive behavior support (PBS) approach and the Head Start program. Specifically, this chapter (a) gives an overview of Head Start and Early Head Start's (EHS's) role in child development; (b) examines the features of Head Start that are compatible with the PBS approach; (c) identifies the potential challenges for implementing a PBS approach in Head Start settings; and (d) provides an example of a Head Start program's journey integrating a PBS approach into the existing program structure.

## HEAD START AND EARLY HEAD START'S ROLE IN CHILDHOOD DEVELOPMENT

Launched in 1965 as a part of President Johnson's War on Poverty, Head Start was conceptualized as a social service program to provide comprehensive developmental interventions, mostly for children at risk due to their family's economic, social, health, or mental health status, with a goal of improving the social competence of children prior to entering the formal schooling process (Zigler & Styfco 1997). *Social competence* is

**ANDY J. FREY** • University of Louisville
**CHERYL A. BOYCE** • National Institute of Mental Health
**LOUISA BANKS TARULLO** • Mathematica Policy Research, Inc.

defined comprehensively and includes cognitive, intellectual, and social development as well as physical and mental health (U.S. Department of Health and Human Services [USDHHS], 1996). In the years since its inception, Head Start has undergone many changes, but it has always served as a laboratory for a variety of prevention, early intervention, and program evaluation research (Love, Tarullo, Raikes, & Chazen-Cohen, 2006). As new knowledge on child development and behavior has increased, Head Start has notably integrated new models for research and practice. A decade ago, in *Lessons From the Field*, Yoshikawa and Knitzer (1997) advocat for increased attention to mental health needs of Head Start children. Since that time mental health efforts within Head Start have increased with specific federal agency and university research partnerships to promote mental health (e.g., Boyce, Hoagwood, Lopez, & Tarullo, 2000; Lopez, Tarullo, Forness & Boyce, 2000). This targeted research agenda helps explore how program experiences affect child development, as well as examines the effectiveness of a variety of interventions for children from culturally diverse low-income families for the prevention of social-emotional and behavioral problems. EHS was launched in 1995 to expand Head Start services to pregnant women and to children during the birth-to-3-year period, thereby providing earlier opportunities for preventive interventions. Emerging evidence from a national evaluation of the EHS program suggests that both child and parent mental health benefits are related to program participation (e.g., Love et al., 2005; Vogel et al., 2007).

Influenced by the national education agenda, later formulations of Head Start have incorporated initiatives including the National Education Goals Panel's view of the "whole child," comprising cognitive, language, social-emotional, and physical/motor development (Kagen, Moore, & Bredekamp, 1995). A revision of the Head Start Program Performance Measures unified the linkage between process and outcome measures and defined this multifaceted conceptualization of school readiness as the primary goal of Head Start (Administration for Children and Families [ACF], 2003a). Notably, Head Start's funding structure, performance standards, and eligibility criteria are the primary features that distinguish it from other early childhood programs. All of these factors influence the selection and delivery of services. Unlike other early childhood programs and most social service programs, local Head Start grantees receive federal funds directly rather than though states. Although all programs must meet minimum standards, they are locally designed and administrated by a large network of public and private nonprofit agencies, strengthening the community-based approach. Federal appropriations for Head Start tripled during the 1900s, both to increase the number of children served and to improve the quality of programs. However, funding has remained level since the early 2000s. Head Start and EHS served 909,201 children in the 2006 fiscal year in more than 50,000 classrooms located in over 18,800 centers funded through 1,600 grantees (ACF, 2007). With an overall federal budget of $6.7 billion, the average cost per child is currently calculated as $7,209 annually (ACF, 2007). Eligibility for Head Start services is largely income based. Children from diverse families who are at 100% of the federal poverty level qualify. In addition, each locally operated program can impose additional eligibility criteria as long as the enrollment of over-income families in any program does not exceed 10%. Head Start grantees are also mandated to serve children with disabilities as at least 10% of their program enrollment.

Perhaps the single most important distinguishing feature of Head Start is the detailed educational standards, or Head Start Program Performance Standards (HSPPS), which provide a blueprint and accountability structure for all Head Start grantees (USDHHS, 1996). The principles that drive HSPPS include providing comprehensive services (i.e., education, health, mental health, nutrition, and social services); empowering parents to promote their child's development; encouraging parent advocacy in policy and programmatic decisions; and establishing partnerships with community agencies. The federal Office of Head Start (OHS) emphasizes quality through these standards and places a premium on monitoring compliance (Love et al., 2006). These performance standards have become the benchmark by which high-quality preschool education programs are judged nationally and can be important indicators for outcomes for program development and preventive interventions.

## FEATURES OF HEAD START COMPATIBLE WITH THE PBS APPROACH

According to Sugai and Horner (2002), PBS can be viewed as a broad range of systemic and individualized strategies for achieving important social and learning outcomes while preventing problem behavior. In this respect, a number of articles have provided descriptive analyses or syntheses of PBS strategies to address young children's challenging behavior in preschool (e.g., Conroy, Dunlap, Clarke, & Alter, 2005; Dunlap, Strain, et al., 2006; Powell, Dunlap, & Fox, 2006). However, the majority of these intervention efforts have consisted of secondary- or tertiary-level interventions, responding to challenging behavior at the group or individual level once challenging behaviors have emerged (see Dunlap, Lewis, & McCart, 2006; Fox, Dunlap, & Cushing, 2002; Joseph & Strain, 2003; Powell et al., 2006). In response, a number of efforts have begun to conceptualize and implement systemic, proactive approaches, referred to as programwide positive behavior support (PW-PBS), that seek to prevent challenging behavior from developing and address the needs of children whose challenging behaviors require more intensive supports (e.g., Fox & Little, 2001; Hemmeter, Fox, Jack, & Broyles, 2007; Stormont, Lewis, & Beckner, 2005). These efforts have largely adapted the process of schoolwide positive behavior support (SW-PBS; see Sugai & Horner, 2002), which refers to a more general approach to assist organizations to adopt and effectively implement proven and promising practices to obtain their goals. SW-PBS and PW-PBS comprise a process that integrates user (e.g., teachers, parents, consultants, or other staff) preferences and data-based decision making. In addition, within the context of this approach, individuals (e.g., children within Head Start or EHS) receiving support and their advocates (e.g., teachers, parents, consultants, or other professionals) are the key decision makers in defining the goals and the support necessary to obtain them. This process should occur in an appropriate cultural and linguistic context (Chen, Downing, & Peckham-Hardin, 2005). As shown in Fig. 6.1, SW-PBS and PW-PBS approaches combine four key elements: (a) outcomes; (b) practices validated by behavioral science to support children's behavior; (c) procedures and systems to support staff behavior; and (d) data to support decision making. In addition, they are guided by a systems perspective and conceptualize behavioral support on a traditional public health prevention continuum (i.e., primary, secondary, and tertiary) that integrates preventive intervention characteristics (i.e., universal, selected, and indicated (Gordon, 1987; Walker & Shinn, 2002; see Fig. 6.2). Although there are differences between PBS, SW-PBS, and PW-PBS, the terms are often used interchangeably. The more general PBS approach (e.g., SW-PBS and PW-PBS) is the focus of this chapter.

The PBS approach includes aspects of evidence-based frameworks for successful organizational change in other child service systems (Glisson & Hemmelgarn, 1998; Hemmelgarn, Glisson, & James, 2006). For example, the process should be led by a leadership team that represents key stakeholders, with 80% of staff and administration who pledge a 3- to 5-year commitment prior to engaging in PBS efforts. In addition, PBS includes a data-based implementation plan to monitor implementation fidelity and to make data-based decisions to determine when, and with which children, more intensive interventions (e.g., selected and indicated preventive interventions) are needed. Further, monitering extent to which the implementation plan is executed with fidelity is part of the PBS process. Using these implementation components, PBS has been a popular and increasingly effective approach for increasing children's social competency and reducing challenging behavior in education over the past decade.

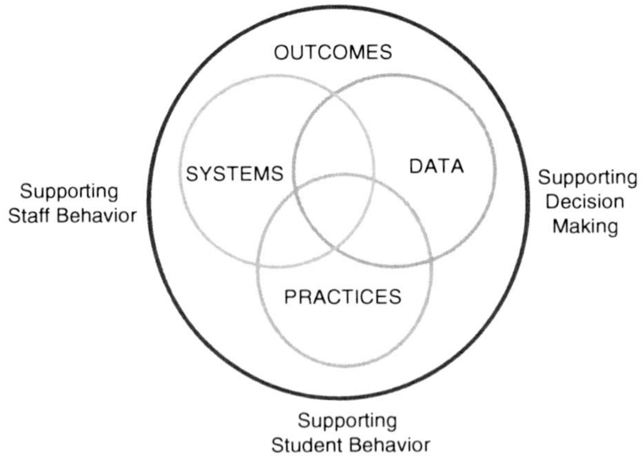


**Fig. 6.1.** The four key elements of positive behavior support. Reprinted with permission from "Schoolwide PBS: Core Features, Behavioral Outcomes, and Impact on Academic Gains," by R. H. Horner & G. Sugai, 2005, paper presented at Annual Positive Behavior Support Conference, Reno, NV.

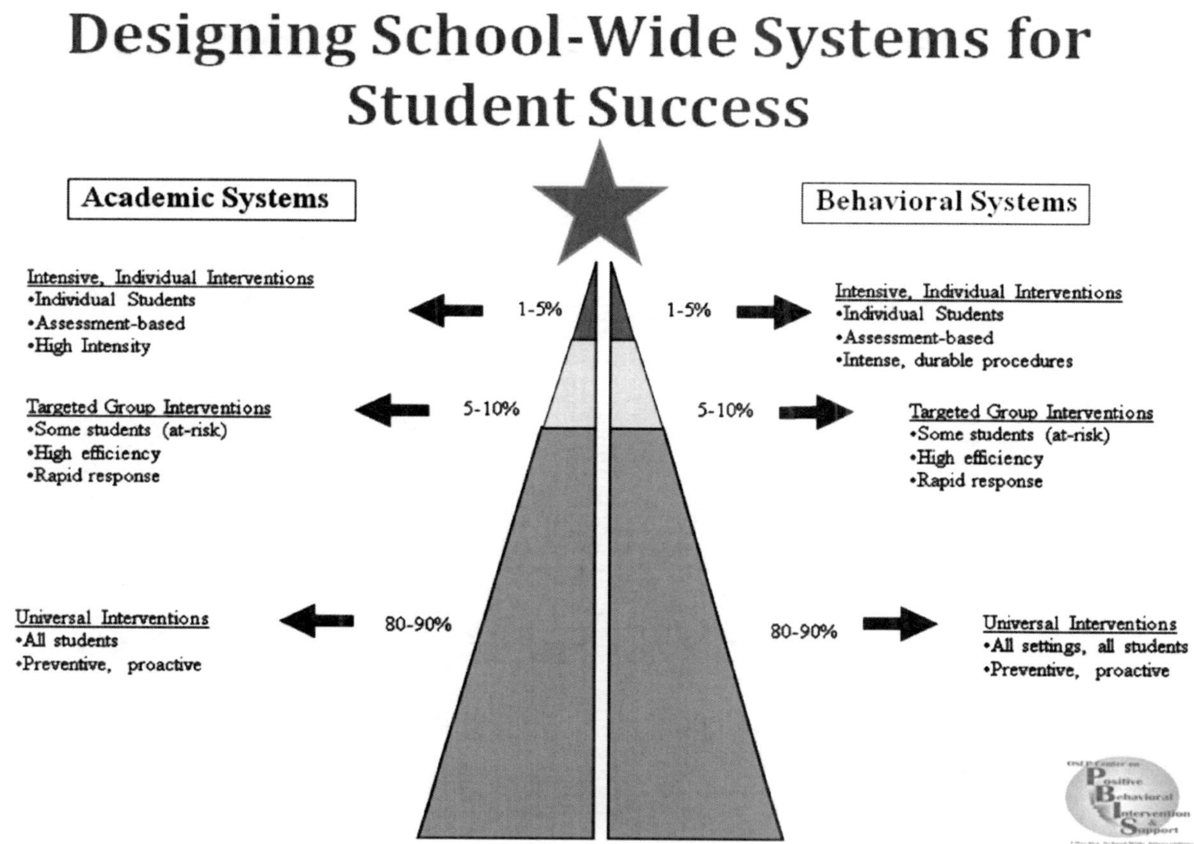


**Fig. 6.2.** Three-tiered model of support. Reprinted with permission from "SW-PBS and RtI: Lessons Being Learned," R. Sugai & R. Horner, 2007, retrieved October 2, 2007, from OSEP Center on Positive Behavior Interventions and Supports Web site, http://www.pbis.org/main.htm

Although there have been some initial attempts to apply a PBS approach in early childhood settings (see Frey, Faith, Elliott, & Royer, 2006; Hemmeter et al., 2005, 2007), the compatibility of this approach and the Head Start program has not yet been thoroughly examined. In this section, the features of the program that make the PBS approach appropriate and appealing in Head Start settings are considered. These features include (a) the risk status of participating children and families; (b) an emphasis on improving child social-emotional/behavioral competence; (c) systemic integration of behavioral interventions or mental health services into program planning; (d) commitment to an ecological approach; and (e) emphasis on positive approaches.

### *The Risk Status of Participating Children and Families*

Children enrolled in Head Start often have family characteristics that place them at risk. An analysis of Head Start Program Information Report (PIR) data by the Center for Law and Social Policy (Hart & Schumacher, 2004) and reports of data from the Family and Child Experiences Survey (FACES; ACF 2003a, 2006), indicate that children enrolled in Head Start have family characteristics that place them at considerable risk. For example, Hart and Schumacher reported that 74% of families enrolled in Head Start had incomes at or below the federal poverty level (i.e., $18,400 for a family of four in 2003), and 21% were receiving public assistance (i.e., Temporary Assistance for Needy Families) at the time of enrollment. Hart and Schumacher also noted that 56% of families were headed by a single parent, of which over half were currently employed. In addition, approximately only 25% of families had a parent with more than a high school diploma. Data from the nationally representative sample of Head Start families in FACES 2003 generally confirm these social and economic risk factors. FACES (ACF, 2006) described that more than two thirds of mothers with preschool-aged children had a high school diploma or equivalent, while only 4% had a college degree or higher. More than half of the fathers of Head Start children reportedly did not reside with their child, and nearly one third of nonhousehold fathers saw their children very infrequently (ACF, 2006).

Not surprisingly given these risk factors, many children enter Head Start at age 3 or 4 with preacademic school readiness skills below national norms, as evidenced by almost a full standard deviation lower scores for vocabulary, math, and early writing and a third of a standard deviation lower scores for early reading (ACF, 2006). However, during their first year in Head Start, children showed significant gains in the first three areas. Since FACES began in 1997, annual gains in letter identification and early reading (although not in vocabulary) have increased. In the social-emotional domain, both 3- and 4-year-olds showed significant growth in social skills and cooperative classroom behavior according to teacher reports (ACF, 2006).

While the demographic characteristics and academic performance of Head Start children and their families are well documented, much less is known about the prevalence, severity, and classification of social-emotional school readiness needs of enrolled children. Nonetheless, it is clear that the risk for mental health-related problems is high among all preschoolers and even higher for preschoolers from low-income families. Of the 10 preschool samples included in Roberts, Atkinson, and Rosenblat's (1998) review of epidemiological studies of children's mental health, the mean prevalence of psychopathology was 10.2%. In contrast, Qi and Kaiser (2003) reviewed 30 recent studies on problem behavior in young children from low-income families and found a mean prevalence of approximately 30%. The range of prevalence across the 40 studies in these reviews was from 3.6% to 57%. Feil et al. (2005) examined multisite data from the Head Start Mental Health Research Consortium and suggested the differences in these estimates are at least partially explained by the generally higher risk for mental health problems in diverse children from low-income families. Together, both large longitudinal national research data surveys (ACF 2003a, 2006) and smaller research studies (e.g., Feil et al., 2005) document considerable risk for emotional and behavioral problems among Head Start families as well as potential targets for preventive intervention approaches such as PBS. The eligibility criteria for Head Start make a PBS approach, or any approach that holds promise for targeting risk factors, extremely appealing.

### *Emphasis on Improving Child Social-Emotional and Behavioral Competence*

The Head Start Child Outcomes Framework (ACF, 2003b) provides evidence of the importance the Head Start program places on improving social-emotional and behavioral competence. The outcomes framework is composed of 8 general domains, 27 domain elements, and 100 examples of indicators of children's skills, abilities, knowledge, and behaviors. This framework is designed to guide agencies in selecting, developing, or adapting instruments to assess children's progress and program effectiveness at the local level and to report on children's progress at the national level. Two of the eight domains—social and emotional development and approaches to learning—are particularly relevant to improving social-emotional and behavioral competence. Within the social and emotional development domain, five elements are recognized: (a) self-concept, (b) self-control, (c) cooperation, (d) social relationships, and (e) knowledge of families and communities. Within the approaches to learning domain, three elements are identified: (a) initiative and curiosity, (b) engagement and persistence, and (c) reasoning and problem solving. This framework serves as the conceptual model for Head Start's Program Performance Measures (Administration on Children, Youth, and Families and the Head Start Bureau, 1997) and demonstrates the appropriateness of embedding a PBS approach within the context of Head Start programs.

### *Systematic Integration of Behavioral/Mental Health Services Into Program Planning*

Another feature of the Head Start program since its inception is the stated goal of infusing mental health services into all program components (D. J. Cohen, Solnit, & Wohlford, 1997; Yoshikawa & Knitzer, 1997; Zigler & Styfco, 1997). Several authorities in early childhood mental health have promoted principles or models of mental health services in Head Start that encourage the integration of mental health services and other program components. For example, many experts have endorsed an integrated, holistic approach to mental health services in Head Start (E. Cohen & Kaufmann, 2000; Forness et al., 2000; Green, Simpson, Everhart, Vale, & Gettman, 2004; Knitzer, 1996; Piotrkowski, Collins, Knitzer, & Robinson, 1994; Yoshikawa & Knitzer, 1997; Yoshikawa & Zigler, 2000). Green et al. suggest that the HSPPS that were approved in 1996 and took effect in 1998 "began to shape this new approach by requiring a comprehensive, family-focused approach to delivering mental health services" (p. 36).

In addition, E. Cohen and Kaufmann (2000) put forward two mental health consultation models: child centered and program centered. Child-centered services involve specialists treating specific children who have been identified with mental health needs. In contrast, program-centered services involve consultative work with program managers and staff to improve the overall quality of the mental health support offered by all program staff to all children. Finally, Green et al. (2004) and Yoshikawa and Knitzer (1997) recommended that mental health services should be integrated with other program services, and that mental health consultants should play an active role in program delivery by participating in management team meetings and assisting with program planning. The recognition that this level of integration is needed for optimal service delivery is another feature that makes a PBS approach highly compatible within the context of Head Start. PBS offers principles and processes for achieving the integration consistent with the HSPPS and implementing the models and services advocated by experts in early childhood mental health.

## *Commitment to an Ecological Approach*

The primary concept of ecology stems from the study of environmental factors and their effects on human behavior. *Behavioral ecology* refers to the study of the influence of interpersonal factors (e.g., friendship patterns, teacher-student interactions, parent-child relationships, social contingencies, and social support networks) as well as environmental arrangements (e.g., seating charts, classroom organization, rules governing behavioral and academic expectations, etc.) on both student and teacher behavior (Bronfenbrenner, 1979). Applying behavioral ecology to child service programs emphasizes development in context. Head Start embraces a behavioral ecological perspective, forwarding the notion that it is through improvements to the surrounding care and educational environment contexts that Head Start children can reach their optimal development. Examples of this orientation can be seen in the Education and Early Childhood Development (1304.21) and Child Mental Health (1304.24) sections of the HSPPS (ACF, 2003b), which focus largely on interpersonal factors (i.e., building positive relationships among children, families, staff, and mental health professions) and environmental arrangements (i.e., consistent and clear rules, daily schedule, and regular routings). In addition, the Child Health and Developmental Services (1304.20) section emphasizes both interpersonal factors (i.e., building positive relationships with parents) and consultation with parents (ACF, 2003b). Notably, the conceptual model for the Head Start FACES 2006 study also offers a classic ecological model. In the model, the child is placed at the center of a series of concentric circles leading out in the environment: first to parent and family, then to the Head Start classroom, the Head Start program, and finally community, state, and national policies (West et al., 2007).

Comparably, PBS embodies a behavioral ecological perspective in its approach. Dunlap, Carr, Horner, Zarcone, and Schwartz (2008) described PBS as an approach in which intervention practices are selected to "fit" the social context in which they are applied and to focus on organizational variables that affect fidelity and sustainability of intervention implementation and effects. The focus of PBS interventions at primary, secondary, and tertiary levels of support is to change child behavior indirectly by promoting change in the environmental arrangements (i.e., physical environment, daily schedule, the timing of interactions with certain individuals) or the behaviors of adults or peers. The emphasis on ecology distinguishes PBS from many other intervention frameworks, which include only one level of approach for children, and makes PBS well matched for Head Start programs.

### *Emphasis on Positive Approaches*

The HSPPS emphasize a positive approach to supporting child development. For example, the Child Mental Health (1304.24) section of the HSPPS highlights the importance of discussing and identifying with parents appropriate responses to their child's behavior (USDHHS, 1996). The guidelines in this section focus on the environment and other positive techniques, such as providing choices, redirecting, and implementing natural consequences. Also in this section, it is clear that Head Start staff are not to support the use of negative strategies such as corporal punishment, lecturing, and criticism. Horner and Sugai (2005) suggested that the PBS approach offers an alternative to negative approaches such as "get tough" methods (see Skiba, 2002). Specifically, the PBS approach:

> Emphasizes prevention of problem behavior, active instruction of adaptive skills, a continuum of consequences for problem behavior, function-based interventions for children with the most intractable problem behaviors, the implementation of organizational systems to support effective behavioral practices, and the use of information to guide decision-making. (Horner and Sugai, 2005 p. 2)

In addition, the PBS approach requires consideration of cultural influences, including the family's perspective on discipline and child-rearing practices (Chen et al., 2002).

While the features of Head Start programs highlighted suggest the program is highly compatible with the PBS approach, there are a number of challenges that may be encountered when implementing this approach within the context of Head Start that are important to consider.

## POTENTIAL CHALLENGES FOR IMPLEMENTING A POSITIVE BEHAVIOR SUPPORT APPROACH WITHIN HEAD START

The infancy of PW-PBS in early childhood settings, the reality of mental health services in Head Start programs, and the characteristics of those who support social-emotional and behavioral services are issues that may make implementing a PW-PBS approach in Head Start settings difficult. In addition, the Head Start program's approach to both data-based decision making and accountability may constitute differences in perspective that could make implementing the PW-PBS approach in the context of Head Start complicated.

### *The Infancy of the PBS Approach in Early Childhood Settings*

At present, the PW-PBS approach is in its infancy in early childhood settings. This constitutes a challenge to some adopting PW-PBS in Head Start settings. Some initial work has been done to conceptualize the distinctions that make the PW-PBS approach more functional in early intervention contexts and to define the practices that support student behavior (Hemmeter et al., 2007; Stormont, Lewis & Beckner, 2005). However, it is unlikely that programs with mental health consultants who lack extensive knowledge of the PW-PBS approach would be able to successfully adopt it with the existing resources and without training. For example, few specific professional development materials, guidelines, tools to guide the PW-PBS implementation process, and measures to evaluate the fidelity of implementation are currently available at the preschool level. It is likely that these resources will need to be developed through intervention development research projects. It is also critical to increase the understanding of factors that serve as barriers and facilitators of successful implementation of PW-PBS in early childhood settings. While a good deal of research has examined barriers and facilitators of SW-PBS implementation in high- and low-fidelity schools in K through 12 settings (e.g., Kincaid, Childs, Blase, & Wallace, 2007), similar research in early childhood settings is critical before PBS efforts are likely to become widely adopted in Head Start programs.

### *The Reality of Mental Health Services in Head Start*

Despite the intent of Head Start policy to integrate mental health services by making them a core part of the delivery system, many experts have suggested that the mental health services in the majority of Head Start programs are narrowly focused, and that mental health consultants are often used in limited ways (see D. J. Cohen et al., 1997; E. Cohen & Kaufmann, 2000; Forness et al., 2000; Green et al., 2004; Knitzer, 1993, 1996; Yoshikawa & Knitzer, 1997; Yoshikawa & Zigler, 2000). Plus, Forness et al. (2000) and Knitzer (1996) also observed that traditional mental health services in Head Start do not reflect current promising practices.

After reviewing 1,500 Head Start programs' mental health services, Yoshikawa and Knitzer (1997) characterized traditional mental health services in Head Start as relying on a contracted consultant who provides a global assessment of the classroom environment and identifies children who may be in need of additional assessment. These authors reported that only occasionally does the consultant also provide the additional assessment and services recommended or offer recommendations to program staff so they can follow up. Yoshikawa and Knitzer also concluded that integrated (child-centered and program-centered) or prevention-oriented mental health service delivery models were rare (of the 1,500 programs reviewed, 14 were identified as model programs) and urged mental health consultants to expand their role. Similarly, Piotrkowski et al. (1994) noted that child-centered models were far more common than program-centered models. More recently, Forness et al. (2000) found that many programs have not shifted from the traditional child-centered approach.

While the amount and quality of mental services have increased overall in Head Start since these reviews, several barriers remain to the adoption of holistic, integrated mental health service delivery models. D. J. Cohen et al. (1997) posited that many programs have failed to integrate a mental health perspective into all program components as a result of (a) unsatisfactory consulting relationships, which are influenced by the lack of qualified staff, limited resources, and complex organizational issues; (b) value conflicts between program staff and external consultants; and (c) lack of a consistent program vision for mental health services. They further asserted that mental health is the least viable, adequately funded, or valued of the Head Start components (i.e., physical well-being and motor development; social and emotional development, including mental health; approaches to learning; language development; and cognition and general knowledge). In fact, in 1994 a Task Force on Head Start and Mental Health report concluded that mental health issues were a low priority, locally and nationally, in the staffing, administrative structure, budgeting, and training and technical assistance efforts of Head Start (American Orthopsychiatry Association, 1994). Whatever the reason, it appears that the PBS approach, with its emphasis on prevention, could represent a departure from existing mental health services within many Head Start programs.

### *The Characteristics of Staff Providing Social-Emotional/ Behavioral Services*

It is important to note that the roles and qualifications of staff or consultants who provide mental health services in Head Start programs are distinct from those who provide other behavior-related services, including social-emotional support. These roles and qualifications are clearly addressed in the Child Mental Health (1304.24a) and Family Partnerships (1304.40) sections of the HSPPS (USDHHS, 1996). The objective of the Child Mental Health section is to build collaborative relationships among children, families, staff, mental health professionals, and the larger community to enhance awareness and understanding of mental wellness and the contribution that mental health information and services can make to the wellness of all children and families. This involves working collaboratively with parents, securing the services of other professionals, and developing a regular schedule of on-site consultations involving mental health professionals, program staff, and parents. The HSPPS are not prescriptive regarding the role or activities of the professionals supporting mental health services, thus respecting the individual needs of local programs. Indeed, the role of staff or consultants supporting mental health services needs to vary depending several factors, including but not limited to the number of Head Start staff who are certified or licensed mental health professionals, the size of the program, the percentage of the program's overall budget that is devoted specifically to mental health services, and the needs of the children and families the program serves.

Although the role of the mental health professionals that support mental health services is not restrictive, the qualifications of these individuals are. The Management Systems and Procedures (1304.51) section requires that mental health services be supported by staff or consultants who are licensed or certified mental health professionals with experience and expertise serving young children and their families (USDHHS, 1996). The HSPPS guidelines recommend staff or consultants have the following characteristics: (a) be knowledgeable of treatment strategies in the area of child behavior management and family crisis intervention; (b) have the ability to work with families in a supportive manner throughout the diagnostic and referral processes; (c) have the ability to work with staff to improve their own health as they in turn provide supportive services to families; and (d) have the ability to broker the services or to provide counseling and treatment for children and families with diagnosed problems (USDHHS, 1996). The HSPPS suggest that mental health professionals represent a variety of behavioral science and clinical disciplines, including, but not limited to, psychiatry, psychology, psychiatric nursing, marriage and family therapy, clinical social work, behavioral and developmental pediatrics, and mental health counseling (USDHHS, 1996).

Within the PW-PBS approach, the leadership team is charged with organizing the delivery of services across the continuum of support. Whenever possible, a single schoolwide leadership role should be established regarding all behavior-related initiatives, actions, and decisions; this would be an ideal role for a mental health consultant within a Head Start program. However, the characteristics of mental health consultants in the HSPPS promote a different vision. Specifically, although the HSPPS suggest mental health consultants be knowledgeable about intervention strategies for young children and their families, it does not require expertise in prevention strategies, which is a hallmark of the PBS approach. A prevention framework is a consistent theme among current promising practices and a characteristic of mental health services advocated consistently in the literature. For behavior supports to be well integrated, service providers should be involved in and knowledgeable about interventions at all levels. One caution is that if professionals are involved at only one level, it may be tempting for educators to refer children with challenging behavior to the next level to remedy the behavioral issues. The individualized and isolated services that may characterize Head Start programs' mental health services can pose a challenge to adopting an integrated, prevention-focused, PBS approach.

### *Approach to Data-Based Decision Making*

While the Head Start program and PW-PBS both advocate data-based decision making, they approach it from different perspectives. Specifically, the types of data that are collected, how they are used, and who determines their meaning, differ substantially. In Head Start, the Child Health and Developmental Services (1304.20) section of the HSPPS requires the use of standardized assessments to screen children for developmental, sensory, and behavioral concerns within 45 days after starting school (USDHHS, 1996). Within the PW-PBS approach, the use of standardized instruments is not always indicated because the PW-PBS approach uses a response to intervention. Framework using response to intervention, one provides effective instruction and interventions that match students' needs, monitoring progress regularly to inform decision making about changes in instruction or goals and using child response data to guide these decisions (Batsche et al., 2005). Response to intervention can provide a decision-making framework for identifying students who need more intensive levels of academic or behavioral support. Children move through the continuum of support only after they have been unresponsive to empirically validated practices. Within both frameworks, data are used to determine which children may require more intensive supports. By contrast, the PW-PBS approach assumes that one cannot identify deficits until a child has been exposed to high-quality universal interventions, while the Head Start approach assumes reliable and valid information regarding the child's developmental status is needed before determining which validated practice would be appropriate.

### *The Accountability Structure*

A final potential challenge to implementing a PW-PBS approach in the context of Head Start is the different accountability structures. This contrast is evident in the different ways interventions are monitored, systems are structured, and data are collected. The Head Start Program Review Instrument for Systems Monitoring (PRISM) review, conducted every 3 years with each grantee, ensures that programs are adequately meeting requirements across all of their systems, including health and mental health services (USDHHS, 1996). In addition, the programs annually report the average total hours per operating month that a mental health professional spends on site and the number of children served, and the number of enrolled children about whom the mental health professional consulted with program staff regarding the child's behavior/mental health. The following indicators are recorded:

- children for whom the professional provided three or more consultations with program staff

- children for whom the professional consulted with the parents about their child's behavior
- children for whom he or she provided an individual mental health assessment
- children for whom he or she facilitated a referral for mental health services
- children referred for mental health services outside of the program
- children who received mental health services

In contrast, within a PBS approach, accountability relates to the accuracy, or fidelity, with which implementation plans are enacted as well as the extent to which the key stakeholders perceive the process and interventions as usable, productive, and effective. Head Start research programs are similarly oriented toward studying fidelity of implementation and the required context for mounting program enhancements. The PW-PBS approach emphasizes that interventions be of high quality and implemented with high levels of fidelity.

## ONE HEAD START PROGRAM'S PBS JOURNEY

The following case study conveys well some of the features of a local Head Start program that make the PW-PBS approach desirable, particularly given its scope and potential influence. In addition, this case study describes some of the challenges associated with implementing a PW-PBS approach in the context of Head Start. The Jefferson County Public Schools' (JCPS), Kentucky, Early Childhood Program, which includes Head Start and EHS programs, has adopted a PBS approach. Integrating PW-PBS practices and perspectives into this program has been facilitated by thier mental health consultanty. In this section, the term *mental health* is used to refer to all services to promote mental wellness, social and emotional development, and social competency or to prevent or reduce challenging behavior. The JCPS early childhood program's approach to mental health services has evolved considerably over the past 6 years. The major phases have included evidence-based interventions at the secondary and tertiary levels, a three-tiered model of support, and most recently, a PW-PBS approach.

### *Evidence-Based Interventions at the Secondary and Tertiary Levels*

In 2001, the current mental health consultant assumed leadership over the mental health consultation contract between JCPS Head Start/EHS and the University of Louisville. At this time, the mental health services approach was child and family centered only. Mental health consultants provided family therapy to address parenting skills for children who were referred by teachers. This is a model the Head Start administration embraced after the former contractual arrangement primarily provided wraparound services after diagnosing referred children with a mental illness, which was a prerequisite to bill for services. As the mental health consultant and the Head Start leadership became more systematic in their efforts, they employed evidence-based interventions, both selected (i.e., "First Step to Success" early intervention; Walker et al., 1998) and indicated (i.e., behavior intervention planning; Scott, 2004; Scott, Liaupin, & Nelson, 2002; Scott, Liaupsin, Nelson, & Conroy, 2004; as well as wraparound planning; Eber & Nelson, 1997; Eber, Sugai, Smith, & Scott, 2002; Scott & Eber, 2003) for children who were referred for mental health services.

The behavior intervention planning process, which can stand alone as an indicated intensive intervention or be part of a multitiered support system such as PW-PBS, is to determine the function served by a child's challenging behavior so that alternative, acceptable behaviors can be identified and taught or other changes in the environment can be made (Gable, Quinn, Rutherford Jr., & Howell, 1998; Scott & Nelson, 1998). Wraparound planning is a valuable addition to the orchestration of intervention systems within school (Eber & Nelson, 1997; Eber, et al. 2002) and community settings (Burns & Hoagwood, 2002) for children with the most challenging behavior problems. The elements embrace strength-based approaches, respect the needs and preferences of children and families, and promote strong community collaboration. These services were supported by the mental health consultant, supervised by a certified mental health professional, and implemented by social work graduate students completing their practicum, hereafter referred to as prevention specialists. In addition to distinguishing between the master's level students providing services from our certified mental health consultants within the program, this title reduces the stigmatization that may be associated with the use of the terms *mental health* or *mental health services*.

After implementing the targeted and intensive interventions, the mental health consultant and the Head Start leadership noticed large variations in the extent to which the program's classrooms had universal strategies in place. When these universal prevention practices were not strong, it was very difficult to successfully change the behavior of a few students with challenging behaviors. The mental health consultant, in collaboration with the Head Start administration and several support staff, enhanced the mental health services model to include all three tiers of behavior support: primary, secondary, and tertiary.

### *A Three-Tiered Model of Support*

To transition to a three-tiered model, the mental health consultants supported the prevention specialists in facilitating a team-based process that resulted in the creation and implementation of a "supportive classroom environment plan" in classrooms where a referral for mental health services was made. Prevention specialists, resource teachers, and disability liaisons attended 2 days of training, which emphasized the five key features for primary prevention supports (Scott & Nelson, 1998; Sugai & Horner, 2002) as well as four topics identified by Hemmeter and Ostrosky (2003) as critical to early childhood classrooms. The five key features for primary prevention are (a) clear definition of three to five primary prevention behavioral expectations in simple, succinct, and positive terms; (b) explicit teaching of expectations so that all students know exactly what is expected of them; (c) extensive communication of the primary prevention expectations (e.g., reviewing expectations frequently and rewarding and acknowledging children by "catching them being good"); (d) implementation of a positive reinforcement system; and (e) evaluation of progress followed by adaptations through a team process (Scott & Nelson, 1998; Sugai & Horner, 2002). The four early childhood issues related to supportive classroom environments are (a) classroom arrangement, (b) transition planning, (c) schedules and routines, and (d) classroom rules and expectations (Hemmeter & Ostrosky, 2003).

After teachers who referred children for mental health services implemented a supportive classroom environment plan, the prevention specialist began to implement child-centered services at the secondary and tertiary levels. At this point, the major intervention strategy at the secondary level consisted of behavior intervention planning (Turnbull et al., 2002). Mental health consultants utilized the Center on the Social and Emotional Foundations for Learning (CSEFEL) free, online training modules (i.e., Modules 3a and 3b) to train Head Start disability liaisons, resource teachers, and prevention specialists to conduct functional assessments and implement the behavior intervention planning process with referred children (CSEFEL, 2006). Wraparound planning, the indicated intervention, was provided to two types of children: (a) those who did not respond to secondary prevention interventions and (b) those who were already receiving services from multiple service sectors (e.g., mental health, child welfare, special education, and medical) when they were identified as needing secondary prevention interventions. The latter group included almost all of the children referred for mental health services.

While the mental health consultants and the Head Start leadership team were able to demonstrate that the efforts at the primary and tertiary levels were somewhat effective (Frey, Faith, Elliott, & Royer, 2006; Stauble, Lingo, Frey, Alter, & Daniel, 2007), they were still unsatisfied with the model. Specifically, the primary prevention efforts failed to reach the majority of the classrooms in the program and were not implemented regularly in program activities outside the context of a mental health referral; although often perceived to be effective by prevention specialists and staff, they reached a very small portion of the total number of children who would be predicted to need these types of interventions based on prevalence statistics. In addition, an informal evaluation of the social validity of the intervention indicated that some teachers became resentful when they referred a child for mental health services and their classroom environment became the initial focus of an intervention. Perhaps the most discouraging result was that these services were still perceived as additional and not integrated as part of the routine Head Start program structure. These efforts did little to build capacity within Head Start staff or to implement a mental health services approach that would be sustainable without the mental health consultant's involvement. These observations led to the adoption of the PBS approach to improve mental health services.

## *Programwide Positive Behavior Support*

In 2005, the mental health consultant attended the Association for Positive Behavior Support annual conference and was inspired by several recent PW-PBS initiatives that had been launched in Head Start programs or programs that include Head Start. For example, the New Hampshire Center for Effective Behavioral Interventions and Supports had provided technical support and consultation for PW-PBS efforts in 39 sites, including 5 of the 6 Head Start programs in the state (Muscott, Mann, Lapointe, & Lane, 2005). Additionally, the Southeast Kansas Community Action Head Start program in Kansas, reported successful implementation of PW-PBS through two projects funded by the Department of Education, Office of Special Education Programs (i.e., Center on the Social and Emotional Foundations for Early Learning and Center on Evidence-Based Practices: Young Children With Challenging Behavior; Dunlap & Fox, 2005; Hemmeter et al., 2005; Quesenberry & Hemmeter, 2005). Emboldened by these efforts, the mental health consultant proposed another reconceptualization to the JCPS early childhood administration. This conceptualization involved a strict adherence to the PW-PBS elements, operational features, and implementation considerations as well as the unique features associated with PW-PBS applications in early childhood settings (see Stormont, Lewis & Beckner, 2005). Although selected and indicated interventions continue to be employed with individual children and their families who are referred for mental health services, the PW-PBS approach has renewed the mental health consultant and the Head Start leadership team's focus on primary prevention, family supports, and staff development. Thus, those involved in the delivery of mental health services strive for capacity building and systems change that support staff behavior, practices (at all three levels) that support child behavior, and data-based decision making that informs all aspects of the mental health services.

Due to some of the barriers to adopting the PW-PBS approach noted, the size and complexity of the Head Start program, and the simultaneous merger of four additional preschool programs in fall 2006, implementation has been slow but constant. During the 2005–2006 school year, the PW-PBS model was presented to several early childhood administrators to secure administrative buy-in. In the spring of 2006, all Head Start staff were provided an overview of the PW-PBS approach and asked to indicate whether they were in favor of adopting this model to guide the mental health services for a 3- to 5-year period. When over 90% of the staff were in support, the mental health consultant and the Head Start leadership team ascertained that the readiness requirements highlighted in the PW-PBS literature had been met. Simultaneously, financial support was garnered, additional expertise in early childhood practices solicited, and state and county support for the PW-PBS effort obtained by collaborating with the Kentucky Department of Education (Division of Secondary and Virtual Learning and Division of Early Childhood and Child Development), the Kentucky Center for Instructional Discipline, and the Anderson County Regional Training Center.

The mental health consultant and the Head Start leadership team anticipated that it would take the entire 2006–2007 school year to train an initial cohort in universal practices, convene a leadership team with the goal of developing a 2007–2008 implementation plan, and collect pilot data. During the 2006–2007 school year planning phase, 100 representatives of the JCPS early childhood program participated in 3 days of professional development, provided by representatives of the Anderson County Early Childhood Regional Training Center, in universal practices to promote social skills and emotional development. This training was provided to all JCPS early childhood leadership personnel, representatives of the Head Start mental health consultation contract, and 12 randomly assigned classroom teams. After the trainings, the PW-PBS leadership team, cochaired by the mental health consultant, Head Start disability coordinator, and special education resource teacher coordinator, began meeting monthly to develop and obtain systematic feedback of a 2007–2008 implementation plan. The implementation committee consisted of 20 individuals representing every aspect of the program.

The implementation plan that was developed out of this process is based on the teaching pyramid (Fig. 6.3) developed by Fox, Dunlap, Hemmeter, Joseph, and Strain (2003) and the key elements of PBS ("Early Childhood Stars," 2007). The JCPS early childhood program branded their PBS effort as "Early Childhood Stars: Bright Minds ... Bright Futures." The implementation plan for the first year recommends programwide strategies for building positive relationships among children, staff, and parents and for creating supportive environments (e.g., schedules, routines, transitions, organization of the physical environment). In addition, the program adopted three programwide behavioral expectations: "Be safe, be responsible, and be respectful." Furthermore, several resource teachers within the program created uniform lesson plans for explicitly teaching these expectations in a variety of settings, including the classroom, hallways, cafeteria, bathroom, and playground, and parents were provided strategies for teaching these expectations in the home setting. The implementation plan also articulates programwide procedures for acknowledging behavioral expectations and for acknowledging and encouraging staff who are model implementers. Finally, this initial plan provides recommended procedures for responding to challenging behaviors. During the planning year, a research team field tested the Pre-School Evaluation Tool (Horner, Benedict, & Todd, 2005) in over 40 classrooms and collected pretest data using the Work Sampling System (Meisels, Liaw, Dorfman, & Nelson, 1995) instrument. During the 2007–2008 school year, researchers continued to collect data using these measures and convened multiple focus groups to assess the social validity of the PW-PBS approach in early childhood settings. The classroom observations and child outcome data will be helpful to document if the critical features of PW-PBS are affected by this process, and

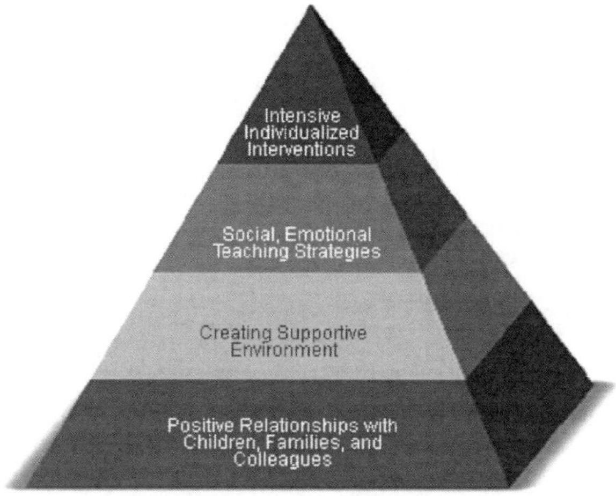


**Fig. 6.3.** The teaching pyramid. Reprinted with permission from "The Teaching Pyramid: A Model Supporting Social Competence and Preventing Challenging Behavior in Young Children," by L. Fox, G. Dunlap, M. L. Hemmeter, G. Joseph, & P. Strain, 2003, *Young Children, 58*, 48–52.

if so, if there is any correlation between the presence of these features in classrooms and classroom quality and child outcomes. Also during the 2007–2008 school year, the Early Childhood Stars leadership team focused on expanding the plan for next year by (a) examining and refining the program's policies and procedures to reflect the values of the PBS approach; (b) developing a plan for data-based decision making; (c) expanding the services provided to families; (d) increasing parent involvement in the leadership team; and (e) building an Early Childhood Stars Web site.

## CONCLUSION

Head Start represents one of the most innovative and potentially important education programs for at-risk children from birth through age 5. While research advancements and interventions have targeted multiple problems faced by children in Head Start, behavioral problems remain a key area of concern. Meeting the requirements of the HSPPS may be necessary but not sufficient to generate the positive child outcomes desired by the Head Start program. Given that PW-PBS and Head Start are philosophically compatible, PW-PBS is a viable and promising approach for Head Start programs to implement mental health services through empirically proven interventions and programs. The lessons of PW-PBS can thereby strengthen Head Start's ability to improve social-emotional development among children from low-income families and again demonstrate its role as a national laboratory for preschool care and education.

## ACKNOWLEDGMENTS

The views expressed are solely those of the authors and do not necessarily represent the views or policy of the U.S. Department of Health and Human Services.

The case study project was supported by funds from the Kentucky Department of Education, Division of Community and Family Supports, and Division of Early Childhood Development. However, the opinions and positions are those of the authors, and no endorsement by the Kentucky Department of Education should be inferred.

## REFERENCES

Administration for Children and Families. (2003a). *Head Start FACES 2000: A whole-child perspective on program performance*. Washington, DC: U.S. Department of Health and Human Services.

Administration for Children and Families. (2003b). *The Head Start leaders guide to positive child outcomes: Strategies to support positive child outcomes*. Washington, DC: U.S. Department of Health and Human Services.

Administration for Children and Families. (2006). *FACES 2003 research brief: Children's outcomes and program quality in Head Start*. Washington, DC: U.S. Department of Health and Human Services.

Administration for Children and Families. (2007). *Head Start fact sheet*. Washington, DC: U.S. Department of Health and Human Services. Retrieved may 12, 2008, from http://www.acf.hhs.gov/programs/hsb/research/factsheets.htm

Administration on Children, Youth, and Families and the Head Start Bureau. (1997). *First progress report on the Head Start program performance measures. Head Start research*. Washington, DC: U.S. Department of Health and Human Services.

American Orthopsychiatry Association. (1994). *Strengthening mental health in Head Start: Pathways to quality improvement*. New York: Report of the Task Force on Head Start and Mental Health.

Batsche, G. M., Elliot, J., Gradon, J.L., Grimes, J., Kovaleski, J.F., & Prassse, D. (2005). Response to intervention: Policy Considerations and Implementation Alexandria, VA: National Association of State Directors of Special Education.

Boyce, C. A., Hoagwood, K., Lopez, M., & Tarullo, L. B. (2000). The Head Start Mental Health Research Consortium: New directions for research partnerships. *Behavioral Disorders, 26*, 7–12.

Bronfenbrenner, U. (1979). *The ecology of human development: Experiments by design and nature*. Cambridge, MA: Harvard University Press.

Burns, B. J., & Hoagwood, K. (2002). *Community treatment for youth: Evidence-based interventions for severe emotional and behavioral disorders*. New York: Oxford University Press.

Center for evidence-based practice: Young children with challenging behavior. (2006). Retrieved May 12, 2006, from http://challengingbehavior.fmhi.usf.edu/index.html

Center on the Social and Emotional Foundations for Early Learning. (2006). Retrieved September 27, 2007, from http://www.vanderbilt.ude/csefel/.

Chen, D., Downing, J. E., & Peckham-Hardin, K.D. (2002). Working with families of diverse cultural and linguistic backgrounds: Considerations for culturally responsive positive behavior support. In J. M. Lucyshyn, G. Dunlap, & R. W. Albin (Eds.), *Families and positive behavior support: Addressing problem behaviors in family contexts* (pp. 133–154). Baltimore: Brookes.

Cohen, D. J., Solnit, A. J., & Wohlford, P. (1997). Mental health services in Head Start. In E. Zigler & J. Valentine (Eds.), *Project Head Start: A legacy of the War on Poverty* (2nd ed., pp. 259–282). Alexandria, VA: National Head Start Association.

Cohen, E., & Kauffman, R. (2000). *Early childhood mental health consultation*. Washington, DC: Center for Mental Health Services, SAMHSA, U.S. Department of Health and Human Services.

Conroy, M. A., Dunlap, G., Clarke, S. & Alter, P. J. (2005). A descriptive analysis of positive behavioral interventions research with young children with challenging behavior. Topics in Early Childhood Special Education, 25, 157–166.

Dunlap, G., Carr, E. G., Horner, R. H., Zarcone, J., & Schwartz, I. (2008). Positive behavior support and applied behavior analysis: *Behavior Modification* 32, 682–698.

Dunlap, G., & Fox, L. (2005, March 10–13). *Early intervention for children with serious challenging behaviors: Strategies and recent research*. Paper presented at the second annual International Conference on Positive Behavior Support, Tampa, FL.

Dunlap, G., Lewis, T. J., & McCart, A. (2006). *Program-wide Positive Behavior Support for Young Children* (Vol. 2007). Positive Bihavioral Interventions and Supports, 3.

Dunlap, G., Strain, P., Fox, L., Carta, J. J., Conroy, J., Smith, B. J., et al. (2006). Prevention and intervention with young children's challenging behavior: Perspectives regarding current knowledge. *Behavioral Disorders, 32*, 29–45.

*Early childhood stars: Bright minds ... bright futures*. (2007). Retrieved October 2, 2007, from http://louisville.edu/kent/jcps/

Eber, L., & Nelson, C. M. (1997). School-based wraparound for students with emotional and behavioral challenges. *Exceptional Children, 63*, 539–555.

Eber, L., Sugai, G., Smith, C., & Scott, T. (2002). Wraparound and positive behavioral interventions and supports in the schools. *Journal of Emotional and Behavioral Disorders, 10*, 171–181.

Feil, E. G., Small, J. W., Forness, S. R., Serna, L. A., Kaiser, A. P., Hancock, T. B., et al. (2005). Using different measures, informants, and clinical cut-off points to estimate prevalence of emotional or behavioral disorders in preschoolers: Effects on age, gender, and ethnicity. *Behavioral Disorders, 40*, 375–391.

Forness, S. R., Serna, L. A., Nielsen, E., Lambros, K., Hale, M. J., & Kavale, K. A. (2000). A model for early detection and primary prevention of emotional or behavioral disorders. *Education and Treatment of Children, 23*, 325–345.

Fox, L., Dunlap, G., & Cushing, L. S. (2002). Early intervention, positive behavior support, and transition to school. *Journal of Emotional and Behavioral Disorders, 10*, 149–157.

Fox, L., Dunlap, G., Hemmeter, M. L., Joseph, G., & Strain, P. (2003). The teaching pyramid: A model supporting social competence and preventing challenging behavior in young children. *Young Children, 58*, 48–52.

Fox, L., & Little, N. (2001). Starting early: Developing school-wide behavior support in a community preschool. *Journal of Positive Behavior Interventions, 3*, 251–254.

Frey, A. J., Faith, T., Elliott, A., & Royer, B. (2006). A pilot study examining the social validity and effectiveness of a positive behavior support model in Head Start. *School Social Work Journal, 30*, 22–44.

Gable, R. A., Quinn, M. M., Rutherford, R. B., Jr., & Howell, K. (1998). Addressing problem behaviors in schools: Use of functional assessments and behavior intervention plans. *Preventing School Failure, 42*, 106–119.

Glisson, C., & Hemmelgarn, A. (1998). The effects of organizational climate and interorganizational coordination on the quality and outcomes of children's service systems. *Child Abuse and Neglect*, 22, 401–421.

Green, B. L., Simpson, J., Everhart, M. C., Vale, E., & Gettman, M. G. (2004). Understanding integrated mental health services in Head Start: Staff perceptions on mental health consultation. *National Head Start Association Dialog, 7*, 35–60.

Gordon, R. (1987). An operational classification of disease prevention. In J. A. Steinberg & M. M. Silverman (Eds.), *Preventing mental disorders*. Rockville, MD: U.S. Department of Health and Human Services.

Hart, K., & Schumacher, R. (2004, June). *Moving forward: Head Start children, families, and programs in 2003* (Center for Law and Social Policy [CLASP], Policy Brief No. 5). Washington, DC: CLASP.

*Head Start child outcomes framework*. Retrieved may 3, 2008, from http://www.hsnrc.org/CDI/pdfs/UGCOF.pdf

Hemmelgarn, A. L., Glisson, C., & James, L. R. (2006). Organizational culture and climate: Implications for services and interventions research. *Clinical Psychology: Science and Practice, 13*, 73–89.

Hemmeter, M. L., Fox, L., Broyles, L., Burke, J., Jack, S., & Doubet, S. (2005, March 10–13). *Program wide approaches for addressing children's challenging behavior.* Paper presented at the second annual International Conference on Positive Behavior Support, Tampa, FL.

Hemmeter, M. L., Fox, L., Jack, S., Broyles (2007). A program-wide model of positive behavior support in early childhood settings. *Journal of Early Intervention, 29*, 337–355.

Hemmeter, M. L., & Ostrosky, M. (2003). *Classroom prevention practices.* Retrieved April 26, 2004, from http://challengingbehavior.fmhi.usf.edu/text.pdf

Horner, R. H., Benedict, E. A., & Todd, A. (2005). Preschool-wide evaluation tool. Eugene, OR: Educational and Community Supports.

Horner, R.H., & Sugai, G. (2005). *School wide PBS: Core features, behavioral outcomes, and impact on academic gains.* Paper presented at annual Positive Behavior Support Conference, Reno, NV.

Horner, R. H., Sugai, G. (2005). School wide positive behavior support: An alternative approach to discipline in schools. In L. Bambara & L. Kern (Eds.), *Positive behavior support.* (pp. 359–390) New York: Guilford Press.

Horner, R. H., & Todd, A. W. (2005). *School wide information system.* Retrieved June 10, 2005, from http://www.swis.org/

Jellinek, M. S., Bishop-Josef, S. J., Michael Murphy, M., & Zigler, E. F. (2005). Mental health in Head Start: Leave no child behind. *National Head Start Association Dialog, 8*, 25–35.

Joseph, G. E., & Strain, P. S. (2003). Comprehensive evidence-based social-emotional curricula for young children: An analysis of efficacious adoption potential. *Topics in Early Childhood Special Education, 23*, 65–76.

Kagen, S. L., Moore, E., & Bredekamp, S. (1995). *Reconsidering children's early development and learning: Toward common views and vocabulary.* Washington, DC: National Education Goals Panel.

Kincaid, D., Childs, K., Blase, K. A., & Wallace, F. (2007). Identifying barriers and facilitators in implementing schoolwide positive behavior support. *Journal of Positive Behavior Interventions, 9*, 174–184.

Knitzer, J. (1993). Children's mental health policy: Challenging the future. *Journal of Emotional and Behavioral Disorders, 1*, 8–16.

Knitzer, J. (1996). Meeting the mental health needs of young children and their families. In B. A. Stroul (Ed.), *Children's mental health: Creating systems of care in a changing society.* (pp. 553–572) Baltimore: Brookes.

Lopez, M., Tarullo, L. B., Forness, S., & Boyce, C. A. (2000). Early identification and intervention: Head Start's response to mental health challenges. *Early Education and Development: Mental Health in Low-Income Preschool Youngsters, 11*, 265–282.

Love, J. M., Kisker, E. E., Ross, C., Raikes, H., Constantine, J., Boller, K., et al. (2005). The effectiveness of Early Head Start for 3-year-old children and their parents: Lessons for policy and programs. *Developmental Psychology, 41*, 885–901.

Love, J. M., Tarullo, L. B., Raikes, H., & Chazen-Cohen, R. (2006). Head Start: What do we know about its effectiveness? What do we need to know? In K. McCartney & D. Phillips (Eds.), *Blackwell handbook on early childhood development.* (pp. 550–575) Malden, MA: Blackwell.

Meisels, S. J., Liaw, R., Dorfman, A., & Nelson, R. F. (1995). The Work Sampling System: Reliability and validity of a performance assessment for young children. *Early Childhood Research Quarterly, 10*, 277–296.

Muscott, H. S., Mann, E., Lapointe, T., & Lane, P. (2005, March 10–13). *Catch them early! PBIS in early childhood education programs.* Paper presented at the second annual International Conference on Positive Behavior Support, Tampa, FL.

Piotrkowski, C. S., Collins, R. C., Knitzer, J., & Robinson, R. (1994). Strengthening mental health services in Head Start: A challenge for the 1990s. *American Psychologist, 49*, 133–139.

Powell, D., Dunlap, G., & Fox, L. (2006). Prevention and intervention for the challenging behaviors of toddlers and preschoolers. *Infants and Young Children, 19*, 25–35.

Qi, C. H., & Kaiser, A. P. (2003). Behavior problems of preschool children from low-income families: Review of the literature. *Teaching Early Childhood Special Education, 23*, 188–216.

Quesenberry, A., & Hemmeter, M. L. (2005, March 10–13). *Implementing a program-wide model of behavior support in early childhood settings: Current practices, challenges and barriers.* Paper presented at the second annual International Conference on Positive Behavior Support, Tampa, FL.

Roberts, R. E., Atkinson, C. C., & Rosenblat, A. (1998). Prevalence of psychopathology among children and adolescents. *American Journal of Psychiatry, 155*, 715–725.

Scott, T. M. (2004). Making behavior intervention planning decisions in a schoolwide system of positive behavior support. *Focus on Exceptional Children, 36*, 1–18.

Scott, T. M., & Eber, L. (2003). Functional assessment and wraparound as systemic school processes: Primary, secondary, and tertiary systems examples. *Journal of Positive Behavior Interventions, 5*, 131–143.

Scott, T. M., Liaupin, C. J., & Nelson, C. M. (2002). *Behavior intervention planning: Using the functional assessment data.* Longmont, CO: Sopris West.

Scott, T. M., Liaupsin, C., Nelson, C. M., & Conroy, M. (2004). An examination of team-based functional behavior assessment in public school settings: Collaborative teams, experts, and technology. *Behavior Disorders, 29*, 384–395.

Scott, T. M., & Nelson, C. M. (1998). Confusion and failure in facilitating generalized social responding in the school setting: Sometimes 2 + 2 = 5. *Behavioral Disorders, 23*, 264–275.

Skiba, R. J. (2002). Special education and school discipline: A precarious balance. *Behavioral Disorders, 27*, 81–97.

Stauble, K. Lingo, A., Frey, A., Alter, P. and Daniel, A. (2007, April). *The feasibility and impact of early childhood intervention planning.* Paper presented at the Council for Exceptional Children conference, Louisville, KY.

Stormont, M., Lewis, T. J., & Beckner, R. (2005). Positive behavior support systems: Applying key features in preschool settings. *Teaching Exceptional Children, 37*, 42–49.

Stormont, M., Lewis, T. J., & Covington Smith, S. (2005). Behavior support strategies in early childhood settings: Teachers' importance and feasibility ratings. *Journal of Positive Behavior Interventions, 7*, 131–139.

Sugai, G., & Horner, R. H. (2002). The evolution of discipline practices: School-wide positive behavior supports. In J. K. Luiselli & C. Diament (Eds.), *Behavior psychology in the schools: Innovations in evaluation, support, and consultation* (pp. 23–50). Hawthorne, NJ: Hawthorne Press.

Sugai, R., & Horner, R. (2007). SW-PBS and RtI: Lessons being learned. OSEP Center on Positive Behavior Interventions and Supports. Retrieved October 2, 2007, from http://www.pbis.org/main.htm

Turnbull, A., Edmonson, P. G., Sailor, R. F., Guess, D., Lassen, S., McCart, A., et al. (2002). A blueprint for schoolwide positive behavioral support: Implementation of three components. *Exceptional Children, 68*, 377–402.

U.S. Department of Health and Human Services: Administration for Children and Families. (1996). Head Start Performance Standards, *Federal Register*, 61(215) 57186–57227.

Vogel, C., Love, J. M., Raikes, H., Chazan-Cohen, R., Kisker, E. E., Constantine, J., et al.., & (2007, March). *Impacts of Early Head Start at the end of the program and 2 years later.* Paper presented at biennial meeting of the Society for Research in Child Development, Boston.

Walker, H. M., Kavanagh, K., Stiller, B., Golly, A., Severson, H. H., & Feil, E. G. (1998). First Step to Success: An early intervention approach for preventing antisocial behavior. *Journal of Emotional & Behavioral Disorders, 6*, 66–80.

Walker, H. M., Kavenagh, K., Stiller, B., Golly, A., Severson, H. H., & Feil, E. G. (2001). First Step to Success: An early intervention approach for preventing antisocial behavior. In H. M. Walker & C. E. Epstein (Eds.), *Making schools safer and violence free: Critical issues, solutions, and recommended practices* (pp. 73–87). Austin, TX: Pro-ed.

Walker, H., & Shinn, M. R. (2002). Structuring school-based interventions to achieve integrated primary, secondary, and tertiary prevention goals for safe and effective schools. In M. R. Shinn, H. M. Walker, & G. Stoner (Eds.), *Interventions for academic and behavior problems II: Preventative and remedial approaches* (pp. 1–25). Bethesda, MD: NASP.

West, J., Tarullo, L. B., Aikens, N., Sprachman, S., Ross, C., & Carlson, B. L. (2007). *FACES 2006 study design*. Washington, DC: U.S. Department of Health and Human Services. Retrieved may 3 2008, 25 from http://www.acf.hhs.gov/programs/opre/hs/faces/reports/faces_studydesign/faces_studydesign.pdf

Yoshikawa, H., & Knitzer, J. (1997). *Lessons from the field: Head Start mental health strategies to meet changing needs*. New York: National Center for Children in Poverty.

Yoshikawa, H., & Zigler, E. (2000). Mental health in Head Start: New directions for the twenty-first century. *Early Education and Development, 11*, 247–264.

Zigler, E., & Styfco, S. J. (1997). Preface. In E. Zigler & J. Valentine (Eds.), *Project Head Start: A legacy of the War on Poverty* (2nd ed., pp. ix–xxxix). Alexandria, VA: National Head Start Association.

# 7

# Empirically Supported Intervention Practices for Autism Spectrum Disorders in School and Community Settings: Issues and Practices

**LYNN KERN KOEGEL, SUZANNE ROBINSON, and ROBERT L. KOEGEL**

With the increasing numbers of children who qualify for a diagnosis of autism spectrum disorders (ASDs), researchers have also seen a contemporaneous increase in the number of interventions available to families of children with autism. Unfortunately, many interventions lack a sound research foundation and are minimally effective or ineffective altogether. Furthermore, research suggests that an eclectic approach to intervention for children with autism is less effective than a single, intensive, scientifically sound intervention in terms of improving cognition, language, and adaptive behavior (Howard, Sparkman, Cohen, Green, & Stanislaw, 2005). Because the earlier that intervention starts the higher the likelihood of more positive outcomes (L. K. Koegel, 2000), ineffective and inefficient interventions can be damaging to the development of a child with autism. In short, if we are to accelerate the habilitation process during the early years, efficacious, effective, and efficient individualized interventions are critical.

**LYNN KERN KOEGEL** • University of California, Santa Barbara
**SUZANNE ROBINSON** • University of California, Santa Barbara
**ROBERT L. KOEGEL** • University of California, Santa Barbara

Despite the strong and immediate need for effective and comprehensive programs, many children are not receiving adequate programs. In fact, lawsuits relating to the appropriateness of school programs for children with autism represent the fastest-growing and most expensive area of litigation in special education (Etscheidt, 2003). The analysis of administrative and judicial hearings provides information on the areas of dispute between school districts and parents of children with autism. Analyzing the rulings on these lawsuits can help us to understand shortcomings of educational programs. Three primary areas of litigation emerge from the legal rulings that relate to (a) the matching of individualized education program (IEP) goals to evaluation data; (2) the qualifications of the school personnel; and (3) the adequacy of the selected intervention in helping children make progress toward meeting the IEP goals (Etscheidt, 2003).

While these three areas are interrelated, each has been ruled on in separate cases. In regard to matching the evaluation data to IEP goals, schools need to conduct a valid evaluation and, consequently, use that evaluation to develop appropriate educational goals that will result in educational benefit for the child with autism. This necessitates having trained and competent assessors who implement comprehensive evaluations and to consider any independent evaluations (Etscheidt, 2003). In regard to the qualifications of the school personnel, the IEP teams must be able to competently evaluate the child (knowing the child *and* appropriate evaluation procedures) as well as provide placement options. Generally, the schools have lost cases in which school staff did not have an expert or expertise in the area of autism. To determine whether an IEP constitutes a free and appropriate education, the school district must have a methodology for teaching so that the child will benefit. If a child is indeed benefiting from the intervention, the courts are unlikely to intervene in deciding which particular methodology a child should receive, such as an applied behavior analysis (ABA) versus a TEACCH (Treatment and Education of Autistic and Related Communication Handicapped Children) program (National Research Council, 2001). However, if a child is not making adequate gains toward the IEP goals because the school did not use an appropriate methodology, the schools may have to incur any private expenses the family paid to specialists, provide compensatory education, and revise the child's program (Etscheidt, 2003). Again, evaluating and understanding these cases can help professionals avoid stressful, expensive, and time-consuming litigation by understanding the courts' decisions in determining how best to educate children with autism. In brief, families of children with autism want programs that are scientifically sound, with measurable gains, and well-trained staff supervising and implementing the programs.

In this light, the purpose of this chapter is to provide scientifically sound techniques of positive behavior support (PBS) that are effective for children with autism in school and community settings. We also discuss this in the context of important themes that need to be considered with children with autism. That is, effective intervention programs are only successful if specific underlying procedures are in place. These include attention to tracking the child's progress, the settings in which intervention is implemented, attention to the child's affect, coordination across environments, the specific goals that are selected, and the competency of the staff. All of these areas should be considered when developing maximally effective interventions within the context of positive behavior programs and are discussed in detail in this chapter. Lack of attention to these issues may result in ineffective programs and increases in the child's problem behaviors.

## EMPIRICALLY VALIDATED INTERVENTION PROCEDURES AND RESPONSE TO INTERVENTION MONITORING ARE CRITICAL

As stated, a number of different interventions are available for children with autism, some of which are empirically validated as effective; others have been shown to be ineffective or even, in some cases, harmful. Simpson (2005) evaluated over 100 various types of programs, including interpersonal relationship interventions and treatments, skill-based interventions, cognitive interventions, psychological/biological/neurological interventions, and other related interventions. These interventions were rated in regard to the research findings that support the methodology. Four programs emerged as having undergone a substantial amount of research, with evidence repeatedly and consistently showing that individuals with autism display significant improvements as a result of the intervention. These four programs are ABA (Lovaas, 1987), discrete trial teaching (DTT), pivotal response teaching (PRT) (Koegel, R.L. & Koegel, 2006), and Learning Experiences, an Alternative Program for Preschoolers and Parents (LEAP) (Strain & Hoyson, 2000). These four techniques are supported by a plethora of scientifically sound research studies showing the effectiveness of the interventions in a wide variety of areas. Again, school and community-based programs have the highest likelihood of positive change as well as decreased litigation if effective empirically validated strategies are implemented by competent staff.

The child's response to intervention (RTI) is also important. Regardless of setting, some type of measurement system needs to be intact that will track the child's progress. This necessitates taking data prior to the start of implementing an intervention. Ideally, at least two representative data points, without an increasing trend, help confirm that changes are not a result of maturation. While there are a number of interventions available for children with autism, there is also considerable diversity within the diagnosis itself. Thus, programs that are effective with one child may not necessarily be effective with all children labeled as having autism. To be assured that a child is responding and improving when an intervention is implemented, careful, systematic, and ongoing monitoring needs to be in place (Reschly, 2004)

## NATURALISTIC INTERVENTIONS ARE MOST EFFECTIVE

Children with autism often have difficulties with generalization and spontaneity. A number of research studies have shown that naturalistic interventions result in greater generalization. For example, McGee, Krantz, and McClannahan (1985) showed that incidental teaching resulted in greater generalization and more spontaneity than nonnaturalistic approaches.

R. L. Koegel, O'Dell, and Koegel (1987) also showed that children learned faster and exhibited great generalization when naturalistic interventions were used rather than a more structured setting that used arbitrary materials and rewards. Miranda-Linne and Melin (1992) showed that naturalistic strategies resulted in greater generalization and equal or more spontaneity than a more structured format. Such settings usually include intervention in natural environments, the use of actual items rather than flash cards or other types of unnatural stimuli that are not found in the student's natural environment, rewards that are intrinsically related to the task, and incorporating meaningful activities.

## INCLUSIVE EDUCATIONAL SETTINGS ARE PREFERABLE

One major goal of inclusion is to facilitate the social development of children with disabilities (Harrower, 1999; Harrower & Dunlap, 2001). In general, research investigating inclusion as an educational intervention has been quite positive (Harrower & Dunlap, 2001; Odom, 2000). Specifically looking into social outcomes, inclusion has been effective for children with autism and other severe disabilities by increasing social interactions, social contacts, friendship networks, reciprocal social support, durable relationships, and importance ratings of peers as nominated by the focal students with disabilities (Fryxell & Kennedy, 1995; Kennedy, Cushing, & Itkonen, 1997; Kennedy & Itkonen, 1994; Kraemer, Blacher, & Marshal, 1997). Investigations comparing the outcomes of children with severe disabilities in inclusive and noninclusive settings have shown that the integrated classroom is *at least* comparable, if not more conducive to developmental progress (Bricker, 2000; Cross, Traub, Hutter-Pishgahi, & Shelton, 2004; Gelzheiser, McLane, Meyers, & Pruzek, 1998; Holahan & Costenbader, 2000; Odom, 2000). As a case in point, consider a study by Holahan and Costenbader (2000) that assessed the outcomes of 15 children with disabilities placed in inclusive classrooms compared with another 15 placed in self-contained classrooms. While initially matched at preassessment, results of a postassessment measuring social-emotional development indicated that children with disabilities educated in the inclusive environment often outperformed their counterparts (Holahan & Costenbader, 2000). Further, Fisher and Meyer (2002) conducted a longitudinal study that followed children with severe disabilities over a 2-year period in the context of a group design. The students were matched on chronological age and scales of behavior, including motor, social, language, and daily living. Results showed that children with disabilities who were included made significantly more progress on social competence and a variety of areas of developmental domains than the children who were placed in segregated classes. Thus, as a whole, the data support the inclusion of students with autism and other significant disabilities in regular education classes for both social and academic development.

Other researchers have compared inclusive and segregated programs by examining developed IEPs of children with severe disabilities served within each setting. Surprisingly, regardless of placement, the majority of

IEPs for children with autism do not involve social objectives despite the obvious need for such goals (Brown, Odom, & Conroy, 2001). However, IEPs written for students with severe disabilities in integrated classrooms include more social goals and are of higher quality, in contrast to IEPs written for students placed in segregated environments (Espin, Deno, & Albayrak-Kaymak, 1998). Given that children with autism have such severe deficits in social skills, some researchers have argued that educating these students in autism-only settings is inappropriate (Strain, 2001).

In addition to looking at outcomes of children with autism in included classrooms, researchers have importantly investigated the academic and social effects on the typical children. Odom, Deklyen, and Jenkins (1984) assessed the cognitive, language, and social performance of typical children in integrated and nonintegrated classrooms and found no negative effects of inclusion. Similarly, Salend and Duhaney (1999) found no negative effects on the instructional engagement time or academic performance of typical children as a result of having children with disabilities included in the classroom. Moreover, the authors presented findings that typical children who participated in cooperative learning groups with children with disabilities outperformed other typical children in a traditional classroom in the areas of reading and math. In terms of social outcomes, it has been shown that typical children benefit in meaningful ways as a result of their experiences in inclusive classrooms. Specifically, peers have expressed increased acceptance, understanding, and self-concept as well as friendships with and positive views of the included students with disabilities (Salend & Duhaney, 1999). Corroborating these findings, Kamps, Kravits, and Gonalez-Lopez (1998) interviewed 203 typical children (across a 5-year span) who participated in social activities with children with disabilities. Findings indicated that the majority of the children expressed that they enjoyed participating in the programs and perceived academic and social benefits as a result. Thus, as a whole, inclusion appears to be beneficial not only for the child with autism, but also for typically developing children.

Again, as the database accumulates, it is becoming generally agreed that a foundation consisting of an individualized plan for targeting social competency and opportunities for interaction with socially competent peers needs to be established to provide students with autism a socially beneficial education. To accomplish this, physical inclusion with same-aged typical peers, while necessary, is not sufficient in addressing the comprehensive social needs of students with autism (Hemmeter, 2000; Wolery & Gast, 2000). Rather, *supported inclusion*, a term that implies physical integration along with the use of effective instruction and embedded learning opportunities, appears to be necessary to achieve positive outcomes (Hemmeter, 2000; Horn, Lieber, Li, Sandall, & Schwartz, 2000; Janney & Snell, 1997; Wolery & Gast, 2000). In other words, inclusion should be considered a "reallocation of specialized educational services" and not a lone intervention (Harrower & Dunlap, 2001, p. 764). In summary, while there have been improvements in accepting inclusion in philosophical terms, the successes of inclusive programming only occur when careful and systematic programming of goals and effective intervention are in place.

## MOTIVATION IS CRITICAL FOR LEARNING AND REDUCING BEHAVIOR PROBLEMS

It is now well documented that most behavior problems have a communicative function (Carr, 1997; Iwata, Smith, & Michael, 2000; R. L. Koegel, Koegel, & Dunlap, 1996). To reduce behavior problems, many researchers have focused on antecedent manipulation and proactive strategies. Koegel, Koegel, and Surratt (1992) showed that specific motivational strategies (described in this section below) incorporated into the intervention greatly reduces disruptive behaviors while simultaneously improving learning. In general, the motivational teaching techniques (also called *milieu teaching* and PRT) are defined as "a family of procedures that are designed to capitalize on children's desires and interests in their natural environments to embed teaching opportunities" (Goldstein, 2002, p. 387). Again, these are generally more efficient than traditional analogue therapies in that the techniques promote generalization from the onset (Delprato, 2001; Gillum, Camarata, Nelson, & Camarata, 2003; R. L. Koegel et al., 1987). For example, PRT is a systematic approach that is implemented within the child's daily routines via parents, teachers, clinicians, and peers (L. K. Koegel, Koegel, Harrower, & Carter, 1999; Pierce & Schreibman, 1995). The intervention efficiently focuses on key, researched, "pivotal" areas (i.e., a group of behaviors from a single response class), which result in collateral improvements across untargeted skills, leading to the improvements in the overall quality of social-communicative interactions (R. L. Koegel & Frea, 1993; R. L. Koegel & Koegel, 1995).

Similarly, incidental teaching (Hart & Risley, 1968; McGee, Almeida, Sulzer-Azaroff, & Feldman, 1992; McGee, Morrier, & Daly, 1999) utilizes "teachable moments" within the child's natural environment to provide instruction based on the child's interests and routines. The Walden Early Childhood Program is a university-based center where teachers and, uniquely, typical peers implement the incidental teaching techniques within the inclusion classrooms. In a study by McGee et al. (1999), 82% of the children exiting the preschool program exhibited functional verbal language, and all but one participant improved in peer proximity levels. Similarly, studies of PRT suggest that at least 85–90% of children exhibited functional verbal language if intervention started before the age of 5 (L. K. Koegel, 2000).

Important motivational procedures include the following:

1. Allowing the child to choose the stimulus materials and activities within the context of the intervention.
2. Task variation rather than repetitively drilling the child.
3. Interspersing maintenance tasks so that the child experiences success and behavioral momentum.
4. Using natural reinforcers, inherently connected to the activity, rather than arbitrary rewards, to emphasize the response-reinforcer contingency.
5. Rewarding attempts rather than using a stricter shaping paradigm.

These components, as a package, result in higher levels of correct responding (R. L. Koegel et al., 1987), improved affect (R. L. Koegel, Bimbela, & Schreibman, 1996), and lower levels of disruptive behavior (Koegel, Koegel, & Surratt, 1994). Again, these procedures result in lower levels of problem behaviors and thus can be viewed as a PBS package in the context of an antecedent intervention.

## COLLABORATION AND COORDINATION RESULTS IN MORE RAPID AND GENERALIZED LEARNING

It is believed by many that family-school collaboration is essential in developing appropriate, effective educational plans for individuals with disabilities, and that the successful inclusion of these students can only be achieved via family support (Duhaney & Salend, 2000; Soodak & Erwin, 2000). Given that children develop, learn, and behave within the context of multiple systems (e.g., family, school, community), it appears to be important that schools operate within the ecological or systems framework as they attempt to meet the needs of students with disabilities and other challenges (Bernheimer & Keogh, 1995; Bronfenbrenner, 1986; Ho, 2002; Lucyshyn & Albin, 1993; Ruble & Dalrymple, 2002; Santarelli, Koegel, Casas, & Koegel, 2001; Turnbull, Blue-Banning, Turbiville, & Park, 1999). One critical component of this framework is the family-school partnership.

Research has shown that family-school partnerships are positively associated with educational outcomes for children with challenges (Albin, Lucyshyn, Horner, & Flannery, 1996; Bronfenbrenner, 1986; Christenson, 2004; Dunlap & Fox, 1996; Ho, 2002; Lucyshyn & Albin, 1993; Minke & Anderson, 2005; Osher & Osher, 2002; Peterson, Derby, Berg, & Horner, 2002; Ruble & Dalrymple, 2002; Turnbull & Turnbull, 1996; Wacker, Peck, Derby, Berg, & Harding, 1996). Furthermore, the active involvement of family members in the assessment-planning-intervention process increases the generalization, maintenance, and social significance of the targeted goals (Lucyshyn, Albin, & Nixon, 1997; Moes & Frea, 2000; Peterson et al., 2002; Ruble & Dalrymple, 2002; Stiebel, 1999). In other words, when parents are positively and effectively included as active team members, the benefits of educational treatments for children are more fully realized.

Researchers have outlined a host of recommended practices as a means to guide the development and maintenance of successful partnerships (e.g., Brookman-Frazee, 2004; Christensen, 2004). First, it is suggested that schools adopt a family-driven approach (instead of a provider- or resource-driven approach) that focuses on strengths and solutions, ecological variables, social validity, and the family's quality of life (Christenson, 2004; Dinnebeil, Hale, & Rule, 1999; Lucyshyn & Albin, 1993). Second, it appears to be important that all team members experience shared responsibility and shared decision making and have a strong commitment (Minke & Anderson, 2005; Osher & Osher, 2002). Third, relationship-building opportunities to enhance mutual trust, respect, and ongoing communication appear to be critical, as is administrative support in the allocation of training and resources (K. S. Adams & Christenson, 2000; Dinnebeil et al., 1999; Lucyshyn & Albin, 1993; Minke & Anderson, 2005; Osher & Osher, 2002). Finally, personality variables such as enthusiasm, friendliness, and cooperativeness have also been found to positively affect the relationship (Dinnebeil et al., 1999). In short, schools have the power to influence parent participation by their responsiveness, their attitudes, and the opportunities they create for interaction and communication (Ho, 2002). That is, schools that collaborate with parents not only may improve their ability to affect positive changes in the lives of their students, but also may reduce unfavorable situations, like litigation (Ruble & Dalrymple, 2002).

Because the literature shows that parents play a key role in the overall educational success of their children (Duhaney & Salend, 2000; Soodak & Erwin, 2000), it is important to know how they feel about topics such as inclusion. In regard to inclusion, parent perceptions have been mixed and multidimensional (Duhaney & Salend, 2000; Gibb, Young, Allred, Dyches, Egan, & Ingram, 1997; Palmer, Fuller, Arora, & Nelson, 2001). For the most part, however, parents of children with and without disabilities have positive views toward inclusion and express many perceived benefits (e.g., learned prosocial behaviors) (Duhaney & Salend, 2000; Giangreco, Edelman, Cloninger, & Dennis, 1993; Seery, Davis, & Johnson, 2000).

Parents who are hesitant or resistant to placing their child in regular classrooms tend to attribute their unfavorable view of inclusion to teacher qualities (e.g., uncaring, incompetent) and classroom qualities (e.g., insufficient support, hostile, inappropriate given child's disability), as opposed to child qualities alone, although parents of children with severe disabilities are less likely to favor educational inclusion than parents of children with mild disabilities (Palmer et al., 2001). Results from a regression analysis by Kraemer et al. (1997) indicated that adolescent-specific variables (over family characteristics) predicted level of educational inclusion despite the fact that the Individuals With Disabilities Education Act (IDEA) mandates that placement not be determined by a child's functioning level. Parents in the study actively included their adolescents with severe disabilities, regardless of age or functioning level, in social and community outings. However, integration in typical school settings for this same group was minimal, with only 4% fully included (Kraemer et al., 1997). While there are a number of different reasons why this might be the case, the general discrepancy between the levels of inclusion at home and school is concerning. The authors wondered if the level of inclusion at school would have been improved had parents played a more active role in the decision-making process and understood the possible benefits of inclusive school settings.

However, as a whole, researchers have made numerous recommendations for increasing the likelihood that inclusion will continue to expand for children with autism. Indeed, several intricate components need to be in place at the state, district, building, and classroom levels (Mamlin, 1999). To begin, strong leadership from the top down and a universal design consisting of positive behavioral supports and established best practices are highly recommended (Mamlin, 1999; Renzaglia, Karvonen, Drasgow, & Stoxen, 2003). Best practices for inclusion include the principle of normalization, developmentally appropriate practices (DAPs), individualization, and collaboration (Cross et al., 2004). Second, assessment and planning within the inclusive program should be person and family centered and strength based and involve ecological analyses (Mamlin, 1999; Renzaglia et al., 2003). Third, as a means of maintaining a well-devised plan, school personnel should have positive attitudes, a belief in shared responsibility, and necessary training and support; parents should be involved and satisfied with their child's progress, and parent-teacher communication and collaboration must be intact (Cross et al., 2004). Finally, evaluations must indicate that the children are attaining their individualized goals, actively engaged, interacting with typical peers, and acquiring skills in the general education curriculum (Cross et al., 2004). As stated by Odom and Strain (2002), "Programs, not children, have to be 'ready' for inclusion" (p. 156).

## Most commonly used discipline systems, including many schoolwide support systems, are ineffective with children with autism

Many school administrators and teachers use the same type of discipline systems for children with autism as are being used for their typically developing students. Because children with autism are not generally as socially motivated as their peers, many of the reward systems (e.g., praise) and punishment procedures (time-out, sending to principal's office, sending home from school, and so on) are frequently ineffective. In an effort to review the literature on evidence-based interventions available to schools, the next section presents schoolwide, classroomwide, and individualized techniques that are designed to effectively address the needs of students with autism within the school setting.

Literally hundreds of programs have been developed to address behavioral, social, and academic needs at the schoolwide level (Borman, Hewes, Overman, & Brown, 2003). In a meta-analysis of over 230 studies, Borman et al. identified three models as having demonstrated the "strongest evidence for effectiveness:" Direct instruction (G. Adams & Carnine, 2003; Carnine & Engelmann, 1984), Comer's School Development Program (Cook, Murphy, & Hunt, 2000; Haynes, Comer, & Hamilton-Lee, 1988), and Success for All (Borman et al., 2005). Each of these programs has been data driven, successfully "scaled up" (Elias, Zins, Graczyk, Weissberg, 2003; Hanley, 2003), replicated (Borman et al., 2003, 2005), and deservedly received much attention for producing positive outcomes for students considered academically and, to a lesser extent, behaviorally at risk.

An empirically validated, school wide intervention that seems particularly relevant for the behavioral needs of children with mild-to-severe disabilities is PBS (Bagnell & Bostic, 2004; Ervin et al., 2001; Fisher-Polites, 2004; R. L. Koegel, Koegel, et al., 1996; Lewis, Powers, Kelk, & Newcomer, 2002; McCurdy, Mannella, & Eldridge, 2003; Netzel & Eber, 2003; Smith & Heflin, 2001; Snell, Voorhees, & Chen, 2005; Turnbull, Wilcox, & Stowe, 2002).

PBS is an approach that evolved from traditional ABA, which focused on experimental control, internal validity, and the microanalysis of the child. In addition, PBS focuses on practicality, feasibility, and meaningful outcomes as perceived by the consumer, external validity, and the macroanalysis of systems (Carr, 1997). Given that schools are complex, multidimensional environments within which children are socialized among their peers, it is important that effective and efficient practices, structures, and routines be in place (Sugai et al., 2000). PBS is an approach that offers to link these environments to empirically validated strategies to achieve sustained, meaningful, positive behavior change (Sugai et al., 2000).

The developers and proponents of PBS (and other universal interventions) propose a three-tiered systems model (borrowed from public health services; see Asarnow & Koegel, 1994) to prevent the occurrence of problem behavior as well as to reduce the frequency and intensity of chronic problems (Gresham, 2004; Lucyshyn, Dunlap, & Albin, 2002). At the primary level, universal interventions (i.e., schoolwide) target 80–90% of the students and work to reduce the number of new cases. For the 5–15% of students at risk for behavior problems, the secondary level offers specialized, small-group interventions that work to reduce the number of current cases. For the remaining 1–7% with serious (i.e., severe, chronic, or intense) negative behaviors, the tertiary level includes individualized interventions that target the reduction in the intensity and complexity of current problem behavior (Walker et al., 1996). Within each of these levels, functional behavioral assessments are used to evaluate student behavior within the context of specific school environments (e.g., classroom, playground). As Reschly (2004) discussed, this model moves us away from the insufficient "refer-test-place" approach, toward an RTI model by which intervention intensity is matched to problem severity, as determined by data-based evaluations and subsequent treatment adjustments (when necessary).

As mentioned, although students diagnosed with ASDs may benefit from universal interventions and having systematic PBS programs in place in schools may benefit the child with autism indirectly; the disability presents complex challenges requiring intensive, comprehensive programming. Furthermore, given the legal and social push for inclusive educational placements, the composition of the regular classroom is diversifying rapidly (Hemmeter, 2000). Thus, within the context of individual classrooms, the need for effective and efficient secondary (i.e., classwide) and tertiary (i.e., highly individualized) intervention components is greater than ever before.

Currently, it seems that most educational programs available for children with autism are limited in that they provide either participation in integrated activities or effective systematic instruction (Bricker, 2000; Hemmeter, 2000). Less common are programs that offer both simultaneously. However, to maximize educational (e.g., social, instructional) benefits for students with autism, it is recommended that secondary and tertiary interventions consist of effective instruction *embedded within* integrated activities and routines (Hemmeter, 2000; Wolery & Gast, 2000).

Brown et al. (2001) suggested that practitioners utilize a decision-making hierarchy as a guide to identifying effective, efficient, functional, and normalized interventions. The proposed hierarchy begins with three classwide approaches: DAPs and effective interventions built into inclusive early childhood education programs. This level of intervention aims at creating an inclusive, socially conducive environment by incorporating socially responsive typical peers, age-appropriate engaging activities, structured learning centers, and techniques designed to promote positive attitudes about individuals with disabilities (Brown et al., 2001).

Next, the hierarchy moves toward a smaller unit of analysis: child-peer interactions. This level includes incidental teaching, friendship activities, and social integration activities. Examples of these activities entail mutually reinforcing activities, environmental arrangements, peer mediation, "buddies," and so on. Finally, provided that additional instruction is required, the hierarchy delineates explicit socialization training, including extensive work with peers and the target child. While Brown et al.'s (2001) hierarchy is aimed at early education; it can be modified for older children. For example, the secondary and tertiary levels may include interventions such as buddy systems, peer tutoring, cooperative learning groups, peer networks, group contingencies, initiation training, priming, and self-management.

## SOCIALIZATION IS EQUALLY IMPORTANT AS ACADEMIC DEVELOPMENT

Children with autism have far fewer play dates and spend less time interacting with peers than do typical children (L. K. Koegel, Koegel, Frea, & Fredeen, 2001). Often, the children socially isolate themselves at recess, lunch, and free time and engage in fewer afterschool peer-related activities. Social isolation in childhood can lead to difficulties with later employment, leisure activities, and mental health. Thus, it is extremely important that children with autism have comprehensive social programs implemented at both school and home. A number of effective techniques and comprehensive programs exist to improve socialization in children with ASD; however, issues concerning meaningful and generalized global social improvement that lead to reciprocal friendships in the lives of children with autism have yet to be fully understood (Hurley-Geffner, 1995). For example, children with Asperger's and high-functioning autism (HFA), as compared to their typical peers, are more likely to experience unilateral friendships (Guralnick, Gottman, & Hammond, 1996); poorer quality friendships (Bauminger, Shulman, & Agam, 2004); friendships with younger children; and friendships only with children with disabilities (Bauminger & Shulman, 2003). Further, they often experience loneliness (Bauminger & Kasari, 2000). Hurley-Geffner (1995) suggests that a prerequisite step to helping these children to develop meaningful friendships may be to establish methods of defining and measuring *friendship* as a variable and then subsequently examining ways to facilitate its development.

Researchers have acknowledged that children with ASD also need adequate opportunities to use newly learned skills to develop meaningful relationships with same-aged peers (Bauminger & Shulman, 2003). District and state-level administrators play a key role in the selection of programs designed to facilitate socialization in schools. Odom (2000) explained that policy and the subsequent allocation of funding drive practice, and that the interpretation of the policy by significant administrators has a major impact on the implementation of the inclusive program. At the building level, research indicates that school principals play an important role in the attitudes and practices of inclusion given that their leadership and values influence teachers and help shape the culture of the school at large (Bricker, 2000; Mamlin, 1999; Praisner, 2003). As suggested by Praisner (2003), principals' positive views of inclusion are often associated with a higher likelihood of students being placed in inclusive classrooms. Moreover, positive experiences with students with disabilities are associated with more positive views of inclusion. While some principals view inclusion in a positive light, studies (Barnett & Monda-Amaya, 1998; Praisner, 2003) have shown that most believe that it is more appropriate for those with mild disabilities. In addition, most are uncertain about how to make inclusion "work" and feel that their teachers are not prepared to successfully include students with disabilities, particularly those with moderate-to-severe disabilities like autism (Barnett & Monda-Amaya, 1998; Praisner, 2003).

Similarly, teachers have mixed feelings about inclusion in general (Bricker, 2000; Soodak, Podell, & Lehman, 1998). However, unlike the data that show no relationship between principals' attitudes on inclusion and years of experience (Barnett & Monda-Amaya, 1998), there is a positive correlation between teachers' hostility toward inclusion and years of teaching experience (O'Conner & French, 1998; Soodak et al., 1998). One possible explanation for the decline in teacher attitude over the years may be negative experiences due to inadequate support. Researchers have repeatedly documented teachers' concerns over the lack of training and support (Kavale & Forness, 2000; Salend & Duhaney, 1999; Scruggs & Mastropieri, 1996). In fact, studies have reported a positive relationship between levels of support and training and teachers' "comfort" level with inclusion (Sadler, 2005; Seery et al., 2000). Furthermore, there is some evidence that less assistance and less social support are associated with teacher burnout, particularly when more than 20% of the students in the classroom have a disability (Talmor, Reiter, & Feigin, 2005). In contrast, it has been shown that initial hesitation can evolve into positive attitudes when supports are in place (Janney & Snell, 1997).

If children with disabilities require support and training and those two resources are inadequately available (at least as perceived by teachers), then it is not surprising that teachers, along with principals, are less willing to include these students. Successful inclusion (e.g., children's satisfaction, amount of time included, teacher and child receptivity, positive behavior change) is predicted by teachers' positive attitudes (Cross et al., 2004; Kavale & Forness, 2000) and the interactions or relationship the teacher has with the included student (Pianta & Stuhlman, 2004; Robertson, Chamberlain, & Kasari, 2003; Wigle & Wilcox, 1996). Further, teachers' attitudes are predicted by adequate training and support as well as teacher efficacy (Cross et al., 2004; Salend & Duhaney, 1999; Soodak et al., 1998). Thus, a beginning step in fostering successful inclusive practices schoolwide may be providing adequate training and support to classroom teachers, even at the level of preservice teacher education programs (Eichinger & Downing, 2000; Rainforth, 2000), as a means of reducing anxiety and burnout and increasing teacher efficacy, attitudes, and comfort levels (Seery et al., 2000).

## STAFF TRAINING IS ESSENTIAL

As discussed, staff training and support are critical for successful inclusive settings. One of the most commonly used supports for children with autism (and other severe disabilities) educated in the inclusive classroom is the assignment of paraprofessionals (Downing, Ryndak, & Clark, 2000; Giangreco, Broer, & Edelman, 1999; Marks, Schrader, & Levine, 1999). The number of paraprofessionals currently working in special education across the country has increased substantially over the past decade (Giangreco, Edelman, Broer, & Doyle, 2001; Katsiyannis, Hodge, & Lanford, 2000; Pickett, Likins, & Wallace, 2003). The use of paraprofessionals began primarily in response to teacher shortages, parent advocacy efforts, and increases in the number of included students (Pickett et al., 2003). In addition, districts have recognized the financial benefits of hiring "pseudoprofessionals" as well as the advantages of having cultural and linguistic liaisons (French, 2004; Pickett et al., 2003).

Although support for children with disabilities and other challenges is generally welcomed and considered beneficial to both the child and the classroom teacher, paraprofessionals fundamentally are underprepared, underpaid, and underappreciated (Hilton & Gerlach, 1997; Katsiyannis et al., 2000). Consequently, some question the apparent reliance on these individuals. Several researchers have raised specific concerns regarding paraprofessionals' roles, responsibilities, behavior, and impact (French, 2004; Giangreco et al., 2001; Marks et al., 1999; Pickett et al., 2003). In looking at roles and responsibilities, Marks et al. (1999), along with others (e.g., Downing et al., 2000; Giangreco et al., 2001), have found that paraprofessionals assume the majority of the responsibility over the instructional (e.g., planning, delivering, accommodating) and behavioral (e.g., management) needs of an included student, despite the fact that IDEA mandates that certified teachers maintain primary responsibility (Etscheidt, 2005; Katsiyannis et al., 2000). In looking at the behaviors and subsequent impact of paraprofessional support, researchers have found that untrained paraprofessionals are generally either over- or underuninvolved. Studies have shown that paraprofessionals tend to exhibit "hovering" behaviors that limit student interaction with peers and teachers and increase adult dependency (Giangreco, Edelman, Luiselli, & MacFarland, 1997; Giangreco, Broer, & Edelman, 2001; Harper & McCluskey, 2003). Other studies (Young, Simpson, Myles, & Kamps, 1997) have found that paraprofessionals fail to initiate any interactions toward the student with autism. In either case, it seems that paraprofessionals need specific training to positively impact the educational progress of the children they serve (Fox, 1999).

Giangreco and colleagues (Giangreco et al., 1999, 2001) noted the increasing reliance on paraprofessionals and cautioned against having the least-qualified people responsible for the most challenging students. This reliance is problematic on multiple levels (e.g., educational, occupational, and legal). Thus, the authors called for guidelines in determining the need for an assigned paraprofessional, clear role descriptions, training and support in the service they provide, and systematic data on their impact. Furthermore, while acknowledging and appreciating the efforts that paraprofessionals put forth and the benefits that many children have experienced as a result, the authors suggested that the current service delivery model be more closely examined as there are limited data on student outcomes related to the direct and indirect support of paraprofessionals (Giangreco et al., 2001).

## RESEARCH TO PRACTICE: UNDERSTANDING "THE GAP"

Researchers and practitioners alike have recognized the significant gap that exists between that which is published in the literature and that which schools actually carry out (Brown et al., 2001; King-Sears, 2001; Snell, 2003). A variety of barriers contributing to this phenomenon have been identified, including inadequate preservice preparation and training, a lack of ongoing support, time constraints, teacher efficacy, and teachers' perceived importance and feasibility ratings of techniques (Morin, 2001; Reinoehl & Halle, 1994). Although researchers have discussed this gap at length and offer explanations for why and how it occurs, there are no simple or definite answers regarding what to do about it. Key themes of school-related issues and challenges that contribute to the research-to-practice gap related to delivering a successful education program for students with autism within the inclusive classroom include staff training (as described here), goodness of fit, and the replication of research-based inclusion programs.

Current research on instruction in general shows that teachers and paraprofessionals implement both research-based and non-researched-based instructional strategies (Hemmeter, 2000; Howard, Sparkman, Cohen, Green & Stanislaw, 2005; Kohler, Ezell, & Paluselli, 1999; Stahmer, Collings, & Palinkas, 2005) but rarely provide social intervention, particularly peer-mediated social instruction (Brown et al., 2001; Gelzheiser et al., 1998; Kohler et al., 1999). With respect to autism, Lerman, Vorndarn, Addison, and Kohn (2004) pointed out that few teachers are given any formal instruction in empirically based techniques specific to educating children with autism either academically or socially. This is in spite of the rapid increase in incidence rates and the growing requests by parents, professionals, and advocates that such techniques be employed. As a result of this paucity of training, parents and other team members often find themselves in a dilemma when making placement decisions. That is, parents may have to choose between various components of successfully documented models (e.g., participation in inclusive activities vs. effective instruction via trained staff) rather than implementing a complete and comprehensive package (Bricker, 2000; Kohler & Strain, 1999; Schwartz, Sandall, McBride, Boulware, 2004).

Eichinger and Downing (2000) contended that current teacher certification programs are outdated and inappropriate as they continue to prepare educators for segregated environments instead of inclusive classrooms. Furthermore, attitudes favoring segregated education have been found among preservice teachers, perhaps indicating that university preparation programs are failing to teach proinclusion pedagogy (Rainforth, 2000). To address these problems, Eichinger and Downing (2000) recommended restructuring the certification process by aligning the preparation programs of general and special education preservice teachers, providing collaboration training, and offering advanced specialization within special education. Other recommendations include offering university-based professional development summer programs (Lerman et al., 2004); increasing field experiences in quality inclusive classrooms (Wigle & Wilcox, 1996); modeling team teaching in university courses (Eichinger & Downing, 2000); emphasizing creative thinking, innovation, empowerment, and motivation (Rainforth, 2000); and establishing university-district partnership programs as a model for teacher education (Sindelar, Daunic, & Rennells, 2004).

In addition to reevaluating current certification programs, researchers have investigated ways to effectively and efficiently train teachers already in the classroom. For example, Kohler and colleagues (Kohler, Anthony, Steighner, & Hoyson, 2001; Kohler et al., 1999; Kohler & Strain, 1999; Kohler, Strain, Hoyson, & Jamieson, 1997) impressively produced changes in the teaching behaviors of kindergarten general education teachers, early childhood teachers, and paraprofessionals via training techniques such as peer coaching (i.e., teacher to teacher), daily and weekly feedback, and technical assistance. These techniques, particularly the technical assistance (e.g., on-the-spot suggestions) strategies, were successful in improving teachers' skills in social facilitation, activity adaptation, and the implementation of peer-based instruction of IEP goals. Subsequently, their students with disabilities experienced increases in social interaction, greater engagement in teaching episodes, and progress toward IEP goals. Similarly, Schepis and colleagues (Schepis, Ownbey, Parsons, & Reid, 2000; Schepis, Reid, Ownbey, & Clary, 2003) successfully trained preschool staff to teach adaptive and cooperative participation skills by way of on-the-job feedback, verbal/written/video instructions, and role-playing techniques. Moreover, the training was conducted in approximately 7 hr, demonstrating the plausibility of brief, yet effective, training programs.

Although numerous teacher training tools are available for use, in vivo performance feedback appears to be a highly effective training, and most likely essential, component (Kohler et al., 2001; Schepis et al., 2000). Unfortunately, traditional teacher training methods primarily include didactic instruction and in-service workshops despite the evidence that these training methods are insufficient by themselves. Instead, it is recommended that training programs take place in the natural environment (i.e., in vivo feedback within classroom routines); consist of feasible, embedded strategies; and include teacher collaboration and problem solving as well as adequate social and administrative support to ensure sustainability (Snell & Janney, 2000).

In addition to teacher and preschool staff training, researchers have also examined paraprofessional training. Katsiyannis et al. (2000) noted that most paraprofessionals begin their jobs with no formal training and continue to work with limited knowledge, skill, and support. Subsequently, parents, teachers, researchers, policy makers, and the paraprofessionals themselves have called for a working training model (Giangreco et al., 2001; Katsiyannis et al., 2000; Marks et al., 1999; Pickett et al., 2003; Riggs & Mueller, 2001). Given that families and school systems appear to be relying on paraprofessionals to provide students with disabilities a socially beneficial inclusive education, it is ever more critical that these team members be successfully trained to implement empirically based strategies that foster development.

Clearly, there is a need for general and special education teachers to have preservice training on training others (such as paraprofessionals) to implement social and inclusion programs, among other skills pertaining to the education of students with autism (Etscheidt, 2005; French, 1998, 2001; Katsiyannis et al., 2000; Pickett, et al., 2003). Hilton and Gerlach (1997) outlined recommendations for the employment of paraprofessionals, as presented in position statements by the Teacher Education Division of the Council for Exceptional Children (CEC) and the Board of Directors of the Division on Mental Retardation and Developmental Disabilities (MRDD). These recommendations include clear role distinctions and job descriptions; effective, systematic strategies for training and supervision; guidelines for legal and ethical responsibilities; professional development and career advancement opportunities; and the preparation of teachers as supervisors (Hilton & Gerlach, 1997).

## GOODNESS OF FIT

Variables other than teachers' training, preparation, and ability level also can affect the delivery of effective treatments within the classroom. In fact, researchers have documented a wide variety of contextual factors that can contribute to the lack of consistent implementation of intervention, including time constraints, acceptability and feasibility ratings of techniques, teacher efficacy, and transactional variables related to child and teacher characteristics and contextual variables such as structure, values, and resources (Odom, McConnell, & Chandler, 1994). As a result, the field has acknowledged the importance of good contextual fit. Contextual fit indicates the match or compatibility between the interventions itself and the implementers or related environments (Albin et al., 1996; Snell, 2003). For the implementation to be delivered consistently and with a high degree of fidelity, the intervention agents must perceive the plan to be important, useful, acceptable, and feasible (Odom et al., 1994; Snell, 2003; Stormont, Lewis, & Smith, 2005). Odom et al. (1994) found that teachers' use of classroom-based social intervention procedures were more associated with perceived feasibility than acceptability.

Likewise, Stormont et al. (2005) found that teachers rated the same behavioral support strategies as significantly more "important" than "feasible." Given that effectiveness may be sacrificed when interventions are implemented inconsistently or with poor precision, these findings emphasize the value of providing schools with strategies that are not only effective but also practical. For that reason, Detrich (1999) recommended that proposed interventions, in addition to being appropriate and effective for the child, match the values and skills of the implementers, maintain some overlap with current practices and previous training experience, and be supported within the available resources to the greatest extent possible.

## TRAINING: REPLICATING SUCCESSFUL PROGRAMS

It appears that concerns over maintenance and generalization present in treatments for children are also present in treatments for systems. The majority of researched inclusion programs, and many intervention procedures, have been university-based models with highly trained personnel, relatively low student-teacher ratios, and a high percentage of students with disabilities per class (Brown, Odom, Li, & Zercher, 1999; Horn et al., 2000). In contrast, most inclusive community-based and public school programs across the country are comprised of high student-to-teacher ratios, few children with disabilities per class, untrained staff, and limited resources (Brown et al., 1999; Wolery & Gast, 2000). Consequently, even though valuable techniques for improving the social deficits of children with autism in the inclusive setting are outlined in the literature, further research is needed to demonstrate successful implementation within community-based and public school inclusive classrooms (i.e., external validity) and subsequent long-term outcomes. Moreover, success needs to be demonstrated across grade levels and functioning levels using existing teaching staff and available resources.

One large-scale community replication approach that easily could be replicated in educational settings involves a "train-the-trainers" model. Bryson, Koegel, Koegel, Openden, Smith, and Nefdt (2007) disseminated PRT in the context of parent education throughout the province of Nova Scotia. Groups of professionals and parents of children with autism participated in several week-long workshops. During these workshops, participants were provided with classroom work along with feedback on tapes they brought to the daily sessions of themselves working with a child with autism each previous afternoon or evening. Following the week-long workshops, participants mailed a series of videotapes to the United States for additional feedback. Trainers were also given instruction and feedback on their feedback to parents as well as their training of community-based clinicians. The project was successful in training trainers to implement in-home programs on a large-scale basis with a relatively short amount of training time. Results demonstrated improvements in the implementation of intervention by trainers and their trainees. As well, improvements were evidenced in child behaviors following the training. Further, there was very high consumer satisfaction with the training courses. Such programs provide immediate dissemination of the latest university-researched interventions to geographically remote areas and serve as possible models for other school and community-based programs.

Further, focusing on the system as the unit of analysis, King-Sears (2001) pointed out the difficulties in institutionalizing effective interventions within schools and suggested that researchers collaborate with practitioners, receive feedback from staff, and conduct investigations within the natural, "realistic" environment. In agreement, White (2002) suggested that the value of research outcomes should be determined by those to whom the research is directed. Participatory action research (PAR) is a method of research that attempts to accomplish this end (Meline & Paradiso, 2003). More specifically, PAR offers a framework involving the collaboration between researchers and consumers that provides an avenue for researchers to gain a first-hand understanding of the existing issues, including training and support, goodness of fit, as well as variables related to both internal and external validity. The goal of this process is to empower consumers and, ultimately, to produce effective, acceptable, and sustainable changes (i.e., solutions) (Balcazar, Keys, Kaplan, & Suarez-Balcazar, 1998; Ho, 2002; Hughes, 2003; Rogers & Palmer-Erbs, 1994; Ward & Trigler, 2001). Overall, PAR appears to be a promising approach in the efforts toward closing the research-to-practice gap.

Specific to the student population with ASD, several models and demonstration programs have achieved successful outcomes and have consequently been presented in the National Research Council's (2001) report on comprehensive programs for children with autism. These demonstrations include UCLA's Young Autism Project (Lovaas, 1987; McEachin, Smith, & Lovass, 1993); LEAP (Kohler, Strain, & Shearer, 1996; Strain, 1987; Strain & Hoyson, 2000), the Walden Preschool (McGee, Morrier, & Daly, 2001); the Denver model (Rogers, Hall, Osaki, Reaven, & Herbison, 2001); the Douglas Developmental Disabilities Center (Harris, Handleman, Arnold, & Gordon, 2001); pivotal response training (Koegel & Koegel, 2006); the Children's Unit at the State University of New York at Binghamton (Romanczyk, Lockshin, & Matey, 2000); developmental intervention model at the George Washington University School of Medicine (Greenspan & Wieder, 1999); TEACCH (Scholpler, Mesibov, & Hearsey, 1995); and individualized support program (Dunlap & Fox, 1996).

Various other new and promising models also have attempted to provide children with autism a comprehensive university-based model for intervention. For example, a school-based, inclusive education model is Project DATA (Developmentally Appropriate Treatment for Autism; Schwartz et al., 2004). This model, aiming to provide effective, acceptable, and sustainable services, consists of high-quality inclusive best practices; extended, intensive instruction; family and transition support; and collaborative services (Schwartz et al., 2004). The data on child outcomes and consumer satisfaction are convincing; further, the developers have provided training in over 35 school districts (Schwartz et al., 2004), suggesting a high likelihood that the model will prove to be replicable in scientific research.

Overall, however, it appears that there is a continued need for effective dissemination (i.e., the distribution of knowledge, buy-in, and support and the assistance for replication and sustained use; Paine, Bellamy, & Wilcox, 1984). Specific to children with autism, some programs have met the criteria to be considered a model; however, some models either do not address the social deficits or do not have documented effective, wide-scale dissemination. This is important as effective dissemination to close the gaps in serving children with autism within school and community settings is critical.

## CONCLUSIONS

Children with ASD require effective, intensive, comprehensive positive programming, and it is the responsibility of the school system, community, families, and the research community to ensure that these children receive the socially beneficial and meaningful education they need and deserve. Developing a comprehensive intervention package requires accurate evaluations. Because children with autism often have behavior problems that interfere with accurate measurement on standardized testing (L. K. Koegel, Koegel, & Smith, 1997), a variety of observations as well as coordinating with parents and other individuals who have interacted with the child in natural settings is important. Once goals are developed based on accurate evaluations, well-researched, scientifically sound intervention procedures can be implemented. We have stressed the importance of RTI and constant monitoring once an intervention program is in place. There is considerable heterogeneity in the diagnosis of autism, and procedures need to be adapted or changed if a child is not responding to an intervention. Often, children need a variety of programs, implemented simultaneously, to be effective (Carr, 2007). This chapter also discussed the importance of well-trained staff. Inexperienced or untrained staff and paraprofessionals often inadvertently are overinvolved or uninvolved. Lack of staff training can interfere with important interventions. Finally, the importance of coordinating goals and working as a team cannot be underemphasized. Although exasperated parents often resort to lawsuits, such actions are stressful for all involved. Comprehensive, multicomponent, scientifically sound interventions conducted in a coordinated fashion across home, school, and community settings, with well-trained staff offer the child with autism the best possible outcome.

## ACKNOWLEDGMENTS

We would like to thank the Eli and Edythe L. Broad Foundation, the Kelly Family Foundation, and the National Institute of Mental Health (grant MH28210) for their support of this work. Their generosity has allowed us to work toward creating better lives for individuals with autism and Asperger's disorder.

## REFERENCES

Adams, G., & Carnine, D. (2003). Direct Instruction. In S. L. Swanson, K. R. Harris, & S. Graham (Eds.), *Handbook of learning disabilities* (pp. 403–416). New York: Guilford Press.

Adams, K. S., & Christenson, S. L. (2000). Trust and the family-school relationship examination of parent-teacher differences on elementary and secondary grades. *Journal of School Psychology, 38*, 477–497.

Albin, R. W, Lucyshyn, J. M., Horner, R. H., & Flannery, K. B. (1996). Contextual fit for behavioral support plan: A model for "goodness of fit." In L. K. Koegel, R. L. Koegel, & G. Dunlap (Eds.), *Positive behavioral support: Including people with difficult behavior in the community* (pp. 81–98). Baltimore: Brookes.

Asarnow, J., & Koegel, R. L. (1994). Prevention of mental disorders in children. In P. J. Mrazek & R. J. Haggerty (Eds.), *Background materials for reducing risks for mental disorders*. Washington, DC: National Academy Press, 315–332.

Bagnell, A., & Bostic, J. Q. (2004). Assessment and behavior psychology in the schools. *Journal of the American Academy of Child and Adolescent Psychiatry, 43*, 1179–1181.

Balcazar, F. E., Keys, C. B., Kaplan, D. L., & Suarez-Balcazar, Y. (1998). Participatory action research and people with disabilities: Principles and challenges. *Canadian Journal of Rehabilitation, 12*, 105–112.

Bauminger, N., & Kasari, C. (2000). Loneliness and friendship in high-functioning children with autism. *Child development*, 71(2), 447-456.

Barnett, C., & Monda-Amaya, L.E. (1998). Principals' knowledge of and attitudes toward inclusion. *Remedial and Special Education, 19*, 181–192.

Bauminger, N., & Shulman, C. (2003). The development and maintenance of friendship in high-functioning children with autism: Maternal perceptions. *Autism*, 7(1), 81-97.

Bauminger, N., Shulman, C., & Agam, G. (2004). The link between perceptions of self and of social relationships in high-functioning children with autism. *Journal of Developmental and Physical Disabilities, 16*, 193–214.

Bernheimer, L. P., & Keogh, B. K. (1995). Weaving interventions into the fabric of everyday life: An approach to family assessment. *Topics in Early Childhood Special Education, 15*, 415–433.

Borman, G. D., Hewes, G. M., Overman, L. T., & Brown, S. (2003). Comprehensive school reform and achievement: A meta-analysis. *Review of Educational Research, 73*, 125–230.

Borman, G. D., Slavin, R. E., Cheung, A., Chamberlain, A. M., Madden, N. A., & Chambers, B. (2005). Success for all: First-year results from the national randomized field trial. *Educational Evaluation and Policy Analysis, 27*, 1–22.

Bricker, D. (2000). Inclusion: How the scene has changed. *Topics of Early Childhood Special Education, 20*, 14–19.

Bronfenbrenner, U. (1986). Ecology of the family as a context for human development: Research perspectives. *Developmental Psychology, 22*, 723–742.

Brookman-Frazee, L. (2004). Using parent/clinician partnerships in parent education programs for children with autism. *Journal of Positive Behavior Interventions, 6*, 195–213.

Brown, W. H., Odom, S. L., & Conroy, M. A. (2001). An intervention hierarchy for promoting young children's peer interactions in natural environments. *Topics in Early Childhood Special Education, 21*, 162–175.

Brown, W. H, Odom, S. L., Li, S., & Zercher, C. (1999). Ecobehavioral assessment in early childhood programs: A portrait of preschool inclusion. *Journal of Special Education, 33*, 138–153.

Bryson, S.E., Koegel, L.K., Koegel, R.L., Openden, D., Smith, I.M., & Nefdt, N. (2007). Large scale dissemination and community implementation of pivotal response treatment: Program description and preliminary data. *Research and Practice for Persons with Severe Disabilities*, 32(2), 142-153.

Carr, E. G. (1997). Invited commentary: The evolution of applied behavior analysis into positive behavior support. *Journal of the Association for Persons with Severe Handicaps, 22*, 208–209.

Carr, E. G. (2007). The expanding vision of positive behavior support: Research perspectives on happiness, helpfulness, hopefulness. *Journal of Positive Behavior Interventions, 9*, 3–14.

Carnine, D., & Engelmann, S. (1984). The direct instruction model. In S. C. Paine, G. T. Bellamy, & B. Wilcox (Eds.), *Human services that work: From innovation to standard practice* (pp. 133–148). Baltimore: Brookes Co.

Christenson, S. L. (2004). The family-school partnership: An opportunity to promote the learning competence of all students. *School Psychology Review, 33*, 83–104.

Cook, T. D., Murphy, R. F., & Hunt, H. D. (2000). Comer's school development program in Chicago: A theory-based evaluation. *American Educational Research Journal, 37*, 535–597.

Cross, A. F., Traub, E. K., Hutter-Pishgahi, L., & Shelton, G. (2004). Elements of successful inclusion for children with significant disabilities. *Topics in Early Childhood Special Edition, 24*, 169–183.

Delprato, D. J. (2001). Comparisons of discrete-trial and normalized behavioral intervention for young children with autism. *Journal of Autism and Developmental Disorders, 31*, 315–325.

Detrich, R. (1999). Increasing treatment fidelity by matching interventions to contextual variables within the educational setting. *School Psychology Review, 28*, 608–620.

Dinnebeil, L. A., Hale, L., & Rule, S. (1999). Early intervention program practices that support collaboration. *Topics in Early Childhood Special Education, 19*, 225–235.

Downing, J. E., Ryndak, D. L., & Clark, D. (2000). Paraeducators in inclusive classrooms: Their own perceptions. *Remedial and Special Education, 21*, 171–181.

Duhaney, L. M., & Salend, S. J. (2000). Parental perceptions of inclusive educational placements. *Remedial and Special Education, 21*, 121–128.

Dunlap, G., & Fox, L. (1996). Early intervention and serious problem behaviors: A comprehensive approach. In L. K. Koegel, R. L. Koegel, & G. Dunlap (Eds.), *Positive behavioral support: Including people with difficult behavior in the community* (pp. 31–50). Baltimore: Brookes Co.

Eichinger, J., & Downing, J. (2000). Restructuring special education certification: What should be done? *The Journal of the Association for Persons With Severe Handicaps, 25*, 109–112.

Elias, M. J., Zins, J. E., Graczyk, P. A., & Weissberg, R. P. (2003). Implementation, sustainability, and scaling up of social-emotional and academic innovations in public schools. *School Psychology Review, 32*, 303–319.

Ervin, R. A., Radford, P. M., Bertsch, K., Piper, A. L., Ehrhardt, K. E., & Poling, A. (2001). A descriptive analysis and critique of the empirical literature on school-based functional assessment. *School Psychology Review, 30*, 193–210.

Espin, C. A., Deno, S. L., & Albayrak-Kaymak, D. (1998). Individualized education programs in resource and inclusive settings: How "individualized" are they? *Journal of Special Education, 32*, 164–174.

Etscheidt, S. (2003). An analysis of legal hearings and cases related to individualized education programs for children with autism. *Research and Practice for Persons With Severe Disabilities, 28*, 51–69.

Etscheidt, S. (2005). Paraprofessional services for students with disabilities: A legal analysis of issues. *Research and Practice for Persons With Severe Disabilities, 30*, 60–80.

Fisher, M., & Meyer, L. H. (2002). Development and social competence after two years for students enrolled in inclusive and self-contained educational programs. *Research and Practice for Persons With Severe Disabilities, 27*, 165–174.

Fisher-Polites, C. (2004). We all fit in: A program designed to promote understanding among typical children for children with disabilities. *Journal of Positive Behavior Interventions, 6*, 181–187.

Fox, J. (1999). *Failing grade: The trouble with teacher's aide*. New Republic, 16.

French, N. K. (1998). Working together: Resource teachers and paraeducators. *Remedial and Special Education, 19*, 357–368.

French, N. K. (2001). Supervising paraprofessionals: A survey of teacher practices. *Journal of Special Education, 35*, 41–53.

French, N. K. (2004). Introduction to the special series. *Remedial and Special Education, 25*, 203–204.

Fryxell, D., & Kennedy, C. H. (1995). Placement along the continuum of services and its impact on students' social relationships. *Journal of the Association for Persons With Severe Handicaps, 20*, 259–269.

Gelzheiser, L. M., McLane, M., Meyers, J., & Pruzek, R. M. (1998). IEP-specified peer interaction needs: Accurate but ignored. *Exceptional Children, 65*, 51–65.

Giangreco, M. F., Broer, S. M., & Edelman, S. W. (1999). The tip of the iceberg: Determining whether paraprofessional support is needed for students with disabilities in general education settings. *Journal of the Association for Persons With Severe Handicaps, 24*, 281–291.

Giangreco, M.F., Broer, S.F., & Edelman, S. (2001). Teacher engagement with students with disabilities: Differences between paraprofessional service delivery models. *Journal of the Association for the Severely Handicapped*, 26(2), 75-86.

Giangreco, M. F., Edelman, S. W., Broer, S. M., & Doyle, M. B. (2001). Paraprofessional support of students with disabilities: Literature from the past decade. *Exceptional Children, 68*, 45–63.

Giangreco, M. F., Edelman, S., Cloninger, C., & Dennis, R. E. (1993). My child has a classmate with severe disabilities: What parents of nondisabled children think about full inclusion. *Developmental Disabilities Bulletin, 21*, 77–91.

Giangreco, M. F., Edelman, S. W., Luiselli, T. E., & MacFarland, S. (1997). Helping or hovering? Effects of instructional assistant proximity on students with disabilities. *Exceptional Children, 64*, 7–18.

Gibb, G. S., Young, J. R., Allred, K. W., Dyches, T. T., Egan, & Ingram, C. F. (1997). A team-based junior high inclusion program: Parent perceptions and feedback. *Remedial and Special Education, 18*, 243–249, 256.

Gillum, H., Camarata, S., Nelson, K. E., & Camarata, M. N. (2003). A comparison of naturalistic and analog treatment effects in children with expressive language disorder and poor preintervention imitation. *Journal of Positive Behavior Interventions, 5*, 171–178.

Goldstein, H. (2002). Communication intervention for children with autism: A review of treatment efficiency. *Journal of Autism and Developmental Disorders*, 32, 373–396.

Greenspan, S. I., & Wieder, S. (1999). A functional developmental approach to autism spectrum disorders. *The Journal of the Association for Persons With Severe Handicaps, 24*, 147–161.

Gresham, F. M. (2004). Current status and future directions of school-based behavioral interventions. *School Psychology Review, 33*, 326–343.

Guralnick, M. J., Gottman, J. M., & Hammond, M. (1996). Effects of social setting on the friendship formation of young children differing in developmental status. *Journal of Applied Developmental Psychology, 17*, 645–651.

Hanley, T. V. (2003). Commentary: Scaling up social-emotional and academic supports for all students, including students with disabilities. *School Psychology Review, 32*, 327–330.

Harper, L. V., & McCluskey, K. S. (2003). Teacher-child and child-child interactions in inclusive preschool settings: Do adults inhibit peer interactions? *Early Childhood Research Quarterly, 18*, 163–184.

Harris, S. L., Handleman, J. S., Arnold, M., & Gordon, R. (2001). The Douglass Developmental Disabilities Center: Two models of service delivery. In J. S. Handleman & S. L. Harris (Eds.), *Preschool Education Programs for Children With Autism* (2nd ed., pp. 233–260). Austin, Texas: Pro-ed.

Harrower, J. K. (1999). Educational inclusion of children with severe disabilities. *Journal of Positive Behavior Interventions, 1*, 215–230.

Harrower, J. K., & Dunlap, G. (2001). Including children with autism in general education classrooms: A review of effective strategies. *Behavior Modification, 25*, 762–784.

Hart, B. M., & Risley, T. R. (1968). Establishing use of descriptive adjectives in the spontaneous speech of disadvantaged preschool children. *Journal of Applied Behavioral Analysis, 1*, 109–120.

Haynes, N. M., Comer, J. P., & Hamilton-Lee, M.(1988). The school development problem: A model for school improvement. *Journal for Negro Education, 57*, 11–21.

Hemmeter, M. L. (2000). Classroom-based interventions: Evaluating the past and looking toward the future. *Topics in Early Childhood Special Education, 20*, 56–61.

Hilton, A., & Gerlach, K. (1997). Employment, preparation and management of paraeducators: Challenges to appropriate service for students with developmental disabilities. *Education and Training in Mental Retardation and Developmental Disabilities, 32*, 71–76.

Ho, B. (2002). Application of participatory action research to family-school intervention. *School Psychology Review, 31*, 106–121.

Holahan, A., & Costenbader, V. (2000). A comparison of developmental gains for preschool children with disabilities in inclusive and self-contained classrooms. *Topics in Early Childhood Special Education, 20*, 224–235.

Horn, E., Lieber, J., Li, S., Sandall, S., & Schwartz, I. (2000). Supporting young children's IEP goals in inclusive settings through embedded learning opportunities. *Topics in Early Childhood Special Education, 20*, 208–223.

Howard, J. S., Sparkman, C. R., Cohen, H. G., Green, G., & Stanislaw, H. (2005). A comparison of intensive behavior analytic and eclectic treatments for young children with autism. *Research in Developmental Disabilities, 26*, 359–383.

Hughes, J. N. (2003). Commentary: Participatory action research leads to sustainable school and community improvement. *School Psychology Review, 32*, 38–43.

Hurley-Geffner, C. M. (1995). Friendships between children with and without developmental disabilities. In R. L. Koegel & L. K. Koegel (Eds.), *Teaching children with autism: Strategies for initiating positive interactions and improving learning opportunities* (pp. 105–125). Baltimore: Brookes.

Janney, R. E., & Snell, M. E. (1997). How teachers include students with moderate and severe disabilities in elementary classes: The means and meaning of inclusion. *Journal of the Association for Persons With Severe Handicaps, 22*, 159–169.

Kamps, D. M., Kravits, T., Gonzalez-Lopez, A. (1998). What do the peers think? Social validity of peer-mediated programs. *Education and Treatment of Children, 21*, 107–134.

Katsiyannis, A., Hodge, J., & Lanford, A. (2000). Paraeducators: Legal and practice considerations. *Remedial and Special Education, 21*, 297–304.

Kavale, K. A., & Forness, S. R. (2000). History, rhetoric, and reality: Analysis of the inclusion debate. *Remedial and Special Education, 21*, 279–292.

Kennedy, C. H., Cushing, L. S., & Itkonen, T. (1997). General education participation improves the social contacts and friendship networks of students with severe disabilities. *Journal of Behavioral Education, 7*, 167–189.

Kennedy, C. H., & Itkonen, T. (1994). Some effects of regular class participation on the social contacts and social networks of high school students with severe disabilities. *Journal of the Association for Persons With Severe Handicaps, 19*, 1–10.

King-Sears, M. E. (2001). Institutionalizing peer-mediated instruction and intervention in schools: Beyond "train and hope". *Remedial and Special Education, 22*, 89–101.

Koegel, L. K. (2000). Communication in autism. *Journal of Autism and Developmental Disorders*, B30, 383–392.

Koegel, R.L., & Koegel, L.K. (1995) *Teaching children with autism: Strategies for initiating positive interactions and improving learning opportunities*. Baltimore, MD: Paul H. Brookes Publishing

Koegel, R.L., & Koegel, L.K. (2006). *Pivotal Response Treatments for autism: Communication, social, & academic development*. Baltimore, MD: Paul H Brookes Publishing.

Koegel, L. K., Koegel, R. L., Frea, W. D., & Fredeen, R. M. (2001). Identifying early intervention targets for children with autism in inclusive school settings. *Behavior Modification, 25*, 745–761.

Koegel, L. K., Koegel, R. L., Harrower, J. K., & Carter, C. M. (1999). Pivotal response intervention I: Overview of approach. *Journal of the Association for Persons With Severe Handicaps, 24*, 174–185.

Koegel, L. K., Koegel, R. L., & Smith, A. (1997). Variables related to differences in standardized test outcomes for children with autism. *Journal of Autism and Developmental Disorders, 27*, 233–243.
Koegel, R. L., Bimbela, A., & Schreibman, L. (1996). Collateral effects of parent training on family interactions. *Journal of Autism and Developmental Disorders, 26*, 347–359.
Koegel, R. L., & Frea, W.D. (1993). Treatment of social behavior in autism through the modification of pivotal social skills. *Journal of Applied Behavior Analysis 26*, 369–377.
Koegel, R. L., & Koegel, L. K. (Eds.). (1995). Teaching children with autism: Strategies for initiating positive interactions and improving learning opportunities. Baltimore: Brookes.
Koegel, R. L., Koegel, L. K., & Dunlap, G. (Eds.). (1996). *Positive behavioral support: Including people with difficult behavior in the community*. Baltimore: Brookes.
Koegel, R.L., & Koegel, L.K. (2006). *Pivotal Response Treatments for autism: Communication, social, & academic development*. Baltimore, MD: Paul H Brookes Publishing.
Koegel, R.L., Koegel, L.K., & Surratt, A. (1992). Language intervention and disruptive behavior in preschool children with autism. *Journal of Autism and Developmental Disorders, 22* (2), 141-153.
Koegel, R. L., O'Dell, M. C., & Koegel, L. K. (1987). A natural language teaching paradigm for nonverbal autistic children. *Journal of Autism and Developmental Disorders, 17*, 187–200.
Kohler, F. W., Anthony, L. J., Steighner, S. A., & Hoyson, M. (2001). Teaching social interaction skills in the integrated preschool: An examination of naturalistic tactics. *Topics in Early Childhood Special Education, 21*, 93–103.
Kohler, F. W., Ezell, H. K., & Paluselli, M. (1999). Promoting changes in teachers' conduct of student pair activities: An examination of reciprocal peer coaching. *Journal of Special Education, 33*, 154–165.
Kohler, F. W., & Strain, P. S. (1999). Maximizing peer-mediated resources in integrated preschool classrooms. *Topics in Early Childhood Special Education, 19*, 92–102.
Kohler, F. W., Strain, P. S., Hoyson, M., & Jamieson, B. (1997). Merging naturalistic teaching and peer-based strategies to address the IEP objectives of preschoolers with autism: An examination of structural and child behavior outcomes. *Focus on Autism and Other Developmental Disabilities, 12*, 196–206.
Kohler, F. W., Strain, P. S., & Shearer, D. D. (1996). Examining levels of social inclusion within an integrated preschool for children with autism. In L. K. Koegel, R. L. Koegel, & G. Dunlap (Eds.), *Positive behavioral support: Including people with difficult behavior in the community* (pp. 305–332). Baltimore: Brookes.
Kraemer, B. R., Blacher, J., & Marshal, M. P. (1997). Adolescents with severe disabilities: Family, school, and community integration. *Journal of the Association for Persons With Severe Handicaps, 22*, 224–234.
Lerman, D. C., Vorndarn, C. M., Addison, L., & Kohn, S. C. (2004). Preparing teachers in evidence-based practices for young children with autism. *School Psychology Review, 33*. 510–526.
Lewis, T. J., Powers, L. J., Kelk, M. J., & Newcomer, L. L. (2002). Reducing problem behaviors on the playground: An investigation of the application of the schoolwide positive behavior supports. *Psychology in the Schools, 39*, 181–190.
Lovaas, I. O. (1987). Behavioral treatment and normal educational and intellectual functioning in young autistic children. *Journal of Consulting and Clinical Psychology, 55*, 3–9.
Lucyshyn, J. M., & Albin, R. W. (1993). Comprehensive support of families with children with disabilities and behavior problems: Keeping it "friendly." In G. H. S. Singer & L. E. Powers (Eds.), *Families, disability, and empowerment: Active coping skills and strategies for family interventions* (pp. 365–407). Baltimore: Brookes.
Lucyshyn, J. M., Albin, R. W., & Nixon, C. D. (1997). Embedding comprehensive behavioral support in family ecology: An experimental, single case analysis. *Journal of Consulting and Clinical Psychology, 65*, 241–251.
Lucyshyn, J.M., Dunlap, G.M., & Albin, R. (2002). Families and positive behavior support: Addressing problem behavior in family contexts. In J.M. Lucyshyn, G.M. Dunlap, &

R.W. Albin (eds.), *Family, Community, & Disability* (pp.391-416). Baltimore, MD, US: Paul H Brookes Publishing.

Mamlin, N. (1999). Despite best intentions: When inclusion fails. *Journal of Special Education, 33*, 36–49.

Marks, S. U., Schrader, C., & Levine, M. (1999). Paraeducator experiences in inclusive settings: Helping, hovering, or holding their own? *Exceptional Children, 65*, 315–328.

McCurdy, B. L., Mannella, M. C., & Eldridge, N. (2003). Positive behavior support in urban schools: Can we prevent the escalation of antisocial behavior? *Journal of Positive Behavior Interventions, 5*, 158–170.

McEachin, J. J., Smith, T., & Lovaas, O. I. (1993). Long-term outcome for children with autism who received early intensive behavioral treatment. *American Journal of Mental Retardation, 97*, 359–372.

McGee, G. G., Almeida, M. C., Sulzer-Azaroff, B., & Feldman, R. S. (1992). Promoting reciprocal interactions via peer incidental teaching. *Journal of Applied Behavior Analysis, 25*, 117–126.

McGee, G. G., Krantz, P. J., & McClannahan, L. E. (1985). The facilitative effects of incidental teaching on preposition use by autistic children. *Journal of Applied Behavioral Analysis, 18*, 17–31.

McGee, G. G., Morrier, M. J., & Daly, T. (1999). An incidental teaching approach to early intervention for toddlers with autism. *Journal of the Association for Persons With Severe Handicaps, 24*, 133–146.

McGee, G. G., Morrier, M. J., & Daly, T. (2001). The Walden Early Childhood Programs. In J. S. Handleman & S. L. Harris (Eds.), *Preschool education programs for children with autism* (2nd ed.). Austin, Texas: Pro-ed, 157–190.

Meline, T., & Paradiso, T. (2003). Evidence-based practice in schools: Evaluating research and reducing barriers. *Language, Speech, and Hearing Services in Schools, 34*, 273–283.

Minke, K. M., & Anderson, K. J. (2005). Family-school collaboration and positive behavior support. *Journal of Positive Behavior Interventions, 7*, 181–185.

Miranda-Linne, F., & Melin, L. (1992). Acquisition, generalization, and spontaneous use of color adjectives: A comparison of incidental teaching and traditional discrete-trial procedures for children with autism. *Research in Developmental Disabilities, 13*, 191–210.

Moes, D. R., & Frea, W. D. (2000). Using family context to inform intervention planning for the treatment of a child with autism. *Journal of Positive Behavior Interventions, 2*, 40–46.

Morin, J. E. (2001). Winning over the resistant teacher. *Journal of Positive Behavior Interventions, 3*, 62–64.

National Research Council. (2001). *Educating Children with Autism*. Committee on educational interventions for children with autism. Division of behavioral and social sciences and education. Washington, DC: National Academy Press.

Netzel, D. M., & Eber, L. (2003). Shifting from reactive to proactive discipline in an urban school district: A change of focus through the PBIS implementation. *Journal of Positive Behavior Interventions, 5*, 71–79.

O'Conner, J., & French, R. (1998). Paraprofessionals' attitudes toward inclusion of students with disabilities in physical education. *Perceptual and Motor Skills, 86*, 98.

Odom, S. L. (2000). Preschool inclusion: What we know and where we go from here. *Topics in Early Childhood Special Education, 20, 20–27*.

Odom, S. L., Deklyen, M., & Jenkins, J. R. (1984). Integrating handicapped and nonhandicapped preschoolers: Developmental impact on the nonhandicapped children. *Exceptional Children, 51*, 41–48.

Odom, S. L., McConnell, S. R., & Chandler, L. K. (1994). Acceptability and feasibility of classroom-based social interactions interventions for young children with disabilities. *Exceptional Children, 60*, 226–236.

Odom, S. L., & Strain, P. S. (2002). Evidence-based practice in early intervention/early childhood special education: Single-subject design research. *Journal of Early Intervention, 25*, 151–160.

Osher, T. W., & Osher, D. M. (2002). The paradigm shift to true collaboration with families. *Journal of Child and Family Studies, 11*, 47–60.

Paine, S. C., Bellamy, G. T., & Wilcox, B. (Eds.). (1984). *Human services that work: From innovation to standard practice.* Baltimore: Brookes.

Palmer, D. S., Fuller, K., Arora, T., & Nelson, M. (2001). Taking sides: Parent views on inclusion for their children with severe disabilities. *Exceptional Children, 67*, 467–484.

Peterson, S. M., Derby, K. M., Berg, W. K., & Horner, R. H. (2002). Collaboration with families in the functional behavior assessment of and intervention for severe behavior problems. *Education and Treatment of Children, 25*, 5–25.

Pianta, RC, & Stuhlman, MC. (2004). Teacher-child relationships and children's success in the first years of school. *School Psychology Review*, 33(3), 444-458.

Pickett, A. L., Likins, M., & Wallace, T. (2003). *The employment and preparation of paraeducators: The state of the art.* National Resource Center for Paraprofessionals. Utah State University, Logan, UT.

Pierce, K., & Schreibman, L. (1995). Increasing complex social behaviors in children with autism: A review. *Journal of Applied Behavior Analysis, 28*, 285–295.

Praisner, C. L. (2003). Attitudes of elementary school principals toward the inclusion of students with disabilities. *Exceptional Children, 69*, 135–145.

Rainforth, B. (2000). Preparing teachers to educate students with severe disabilities in inclusive settings despite contextual constraints. *Journal of the Association for Persons With Severe Handicaps, 25*, 83–91.

Reinoehl, B. R., & Halle, J. W. (1994). Increasing the assessment probe performance of teacher aides through written prompts. *Journal of the Association for Persons With Severe Handicaps, 19*, 32–42.

Renzaglia, A., Karvonen, M., Drasgow, E., & Stoxen, C. C. (2003). Promoting a lifetime of inclusion. *Focus on Autism and Other Developmental Disabilities, 18*, 140–149.

Reschly, D. (2004). Commentary: Paradigm shift, outcomes criteria, and behavioral interventions: Foundations for the future of school psychology. *School Psychology Review, 33*, 408–416.

Riggs, C. G., & Mueller, P. H. (2001). Employment and utilization of paraeducators in inclusive settings. *Journal of Special Education, 35*, 54–62.

Robertson, K., Chamberlain, B., & Kasari, C. (2003). General education teachers' relationships with included students with autism. *Journal of Autism and Developmental Disorders*, 33(2), 123-130.

Rogers, S. J., Hall, T., Osaki, D., Reavon, J., & Herbison, J. (2001). The Denver Model: A comprehensive integrated educational approach to young children with autism and their families. In J. S. Handleman & S. L. Harris (Eds.), *Preschool education programs for children with autism* (pp. 95–133). Austin, TX: Pro-ed.

Rogers, E. S., & Palmer-Erbs, V. (1994). Participatory action research: Implications for research and evaluation in psychiatric rehabilitation. *Psychosocial Rehabilitation Journal, 18*, 3–12.

Romanczyk, R. G., Lockshin, S. B., & Matey, L. (2000). The children's unit for treatment and evaluation. In J. S. Handleman & S. L. Harris (Eds.), *Preschool education programs for children with autism* (2nd ed., pp. 49–94). Austin, TX: Pro-ed.

Ruble, L. A., & Dalrymple, N. J. (2002). COMPASS: A parent-teacher collaborative model for students with autism. *Focus on Autism and Other Developmental Disabilities, 17*, 76–83.

Sadler, J. (2005). Knowledge, attitudes, and beliefs of the mainstream teachers of children with a preschool diagnosis of speech/language impairment. *Child Language Teaching and Therapy, 21*, 147–163.

Salend, S. J., & Duhaney, L. M. G. (1999). The impact of inclusion on students with and without disabilities and their educators. *Remedial and Special Education, 20*, 114–126.

Santarelli, G., Koegel, R. L., Casas, M. J., & Koegel, L. K. (2001). Culturally diverse families participating in behavior therapy parent education programs for children with developmental disabilities. *Journal of Positive Behavior Interventions, 3*, 120–123.

Schepis, M. M., Ownbey, J. B., Parsons, M., & Reid, D. H. (2000). Training support staff for teaching young children with disabilities in an inclusive preschool setting. *Journal of Positive Behavior Interventions, 2*, 170–178.

Schepis, M. M., Reid, D. H., Ownbey, D. H., & Clary, J. (2003). Training preschool staff to promote cooperative participation among young children with severe disabilities and their classmates. *Research and Practice for Persons With Severe Disabilities, 28*, 37–42.

Scholpler, E., Mesibov, G. B., & Hearsey, K. (1995). Structured teaching in the TEACCH system. In E. Shopler & G. B. Mesibov (Eds.), *Learning and cognition in autism* (pp. 243–268). New York: Plenum Press.

Schwartz, I. S., Sandall, S. R., McBride, B. J., & Boulware, G. L. (2004). Project DATA (developmentally appropriate treatment for autism): An inclusive school-based approach to educating young children with autism. *Topics in Early Childhood Special Education, 24*, 156–168.

Scruggs, T. E., & Mastropieri, M. A. (1996). Teacher perceptions of mainstreaming/inclusion, 1958–1995: A research synthesis. *Exceptional Children, 63*, 59–74.

Seery, M. E., Davis, P. M., & Johnson, L. J. (2000). Seeing eye-to-eye: Are parents and professionals in agreement about the benefits of preschool inclusion? *Remedial and Special Education, 21*, 268–278.

Simpson, R. (2005). Evidence-based practices and students with autism spectrum disorders. *Focus on Autism and Other Developmental Disabilities, 20*, 140–149.

Sindelar, P. T., Daunic, A., & Rennells, M. S. (2004). Comparisons of traditionally and alternatively trained teachers. *Exceptionality, 12*, 209–223.

Smith, M. L., & Heflin, L. J. (2001). Supporting positive behavior in public schools: An intervention program in Georgia. *Journal of Positive Behavior Interventions, 3*, 39–47.

Snell, M. E. (2003). Applying research to practice: The more pervasive problem? *Research and Practice for Persons With Severe Disabilities, 28*, 143–147.

Snell, M. E., & Janney, R. E. (2000). Teachers' problem-solving about children with moderate and severe disabilities in elementary classrooms. *Exceptional Children, 66*, 472–490.

Snell, M. E., Voorhees, M. D., & Chen, L. (2005). Team involvement in assessment-based interventions with problem behavior: 1997–2002. *Journal of Positive Behavior Interventions, 7*, 140–152.

Soodak, L. C., & Erwin, E. J. (2000). Valued member or tolerated participant: Parents' experiences in inclusive early childhood settings. *Journal of the Association for Persons With Severe Handicaps, 25*, 29–41.

Soodak, L. C., Podell, D. M., & Lehman, L. R. (1998). Teacher, student, and school attributes as predictors of teachers' responses to inclusion. *Journal of Special Education, 31*, 480–497.

Stahmer, A. C., Collings, N. M., & Palinkas, L. A. (2005). Early intervention practices for children with autism: Descriptions from community providers. *Focus on Autism and Other Developmental Disabilities, 20*, 66–79.

Stiebel, D. (1999). Promoting augmentative communication during daily routines: A parent problem-solving intervention. *Journal of Positive Behavior Interventions, 1*, 159–169.

Stormont, M., Lewis, T. J., Smith, S. C. (2005). Behavior support strategies in early childhood settings: Teachers' importance and feasibility ratings. *Journal of Positive Behavior Interventions, 7*, 131–139.

Strain, P. S. (1987). Parent training with young autistic children: A report on the LEAP model. *Zero to Three, 7*, 7–12.

Strain, P. S. (2001). Empirically based social skill intervention: A case for quality-of-life improvement. *Behavioral Disorders, 27*, 30–36.

Strain, P. S., & Hoyson, M. (2000). The need for longitudinal, intensive social skill intervention: LEAP follow-up outcomes for children with autism. *Topics in Early Childhood Special Education, 20*, 116–122.

Sugai, G., Horner, R. H., Dunlap, G., Hieneman, M., Lewis, T. J., Nelson, M. C., et al. (2000). Applying positive behavior support and functional behavioral assessment in schools. *Journal of Positive Behavior Interventions, 2*, 131–143.

Talmor, R., Reiter, S., & Feigin, N. (2005). Factors relating to regular education teacher burnout in inclusive education. *European Journal of Special Needs Education, 20*, 215–229.

Turnbull, A. P., Blue-Banning, M., Turbiville, V., & Park, J. (1999). From parent education to partnership education: A call for a transformed focus. *Topics in Early Childhood Special Education, 19*, 164–172.

Turnbull, A. P., & Turnbull, H. R. (1996). Group action planning as a strategy for providing comprehensive family support. In L. K. Koegel, R. L. Koegel, & G. Dunlap (Eds.), *Positive behavioral support: Including people with difficult behavior in the community* (pp. 99–114). Baltimore: Brookes.

Turnbull, H. R., Wilcox, B. L., & Stowe, M. J. (2002). A brief overview of special education law with focus on autism. *Journal of Autism and Developmental Disorders, 32*, 479–493.

Wacker, D. P., Peck, S., Derby, M. K., Berg, W., & Harding, J. (1996). Developing long-term reciprocal interactions between parents and their young children with problematic behavior. In L. K. Koegel, R. L. Koegel, & G. Dunlap (Eds.), *Positive behavioral support: Including people with difficult behavior in the community* (pp. 99–114). Baltimore: Brookes.

Walker, H. M., Horner, R. H., Sugai, G., Bullis, M., Sprague, J., Bricker, D., et al. (1996). Integrated approaches to preventing antisocial behavior patterns among school-age children and youth. *Journal of Emotional and Behavioral Disorders, 4*, 194–209.

Ward, K., & Trigler, J. S. (2001). Reflections on participatory action research with people who have developmental disabilities. *Mental Retardation, 39*, 57–59.

White, G. W. (2002). Consumer participation in disability research: The golden rule as a guide for ethical practice. *Rehabilitation Psychology, 47*, 438–446.

Wigle, S. E., & Wilcox, D. J. (1996). Inclusion: Criteria for the preparation of education personnel. *Remedial and Special Education, 17*, 323–328.

Wolery, M., & Gast, D. L. (2000). Classroom research for young children with disabilities: Assumptions that guided the conduct of research. *Topics in Early Childhood Special Education, 20*, 49–55.

Young, B., Simpson, R. L., Myles, B. S., & Kamps, D. M. (1997). An examination of paraprofessional involvement in supporting inclusion of students with autism. *Focus on Autism and Other Developmental Disabilities, 12*, 31–38.

# 8

# A Programwide Model for Supporting Social Emotional Development and Addressing Challenging Behavior in Early Childhood Settings

**LISE FOX and MARY LOUISE HEMMETER**

In 2005, popular press headlines reported that expulsion rates for preschool children due to behavioral concerns exceeded those of elementary and secondary school students. This report put a national spotlight on an issue that has been quietly hidden within private and public preschool programs; challenging behavior is an issue for many children in the early childhood years. The national survey indicated that expulsion rates were higher for older children, boys, and African American children and were higher within private and faith-based settings (Gilliam, 2005). Programs that had access to mental health or behavioral consultation were less likely to expel children than programs without access to those resources.

While the headlines may have been surprising to the general public, they were not surprising to early childhood researchers, who have become increasingly concerned about the need to identify effective interventions for promoting very young children's social emotional competence and addressing challenging behavior. Research on the developmental trajectory of young children who have challenging behavior presents a disturbing forecast; young children who have persistent challenging behaviors are highly likely to

**LISE FOX** • Univeristy of South Florida
**MARY LOUISE HEMMETER** • Vanderbitt University

continue to have problems with socialization and school success and mental health concerns into adolescence and adulthood (Dunlap et al., 2006).

The significant rates at which emotional and behavior problems occur in young children are well established, with estimates of prevalence rates varying depending on the sample and criteria used. Campbell (1995) reviewed prevalence studies and estimated that 10–15% of young children have mild-to-moderate behavior problems. Lavigne et al. (1996) conducted a 5-year longitudinal study of about 500 children 2–5 years old from pediatric practices in Chicago and determined that 21% of the children met criteria for a diagnosable disorder, with 9% classified as severe. Data from the Early Childhood Longitudinal Study revealed that 10% of kindergarteners arrive at school with problematic behavior (West, Denton, & Germino-Hausken, 2000). Children living in poverty appear to be especially vulnerable, exhibiting rates that are higher than the general population (Qi & Kaiser, 2003). Data from a Head Start sample estimated prevalence rates between 10% and 23% for externalizing behaviors (Kupersmidt, Bryant, & Willoughby, 2000). The presence of social emotional problems can also be found in very young children, with a report of 4.5% of 1-year-olds in a large community sample having extreme scores on the difficult child index of the Parenting Stress Index (Briggs-Gowan, Carter, Skuban, & Horwitz, 2001).

In addition to concerns about the numbers of children with emotional and behavioral problems, research has demonstrated that early problems often persist well beyond early childhood. A review of longitudinal studies revealed that approximately 50% of preschool children with externalizing problems continued to show problems during their school years, with disruptive behavior showing the highest rates of persistence (Campbell, 1995). There appears to be remarkable stability both within the early years, with 88% of boys identified as aggressive at age 2 continuing to show clinical symptomology at age 5 and 58% remaining in the clinical range at age 6 (Shaw, Gilliom, & Giovannelli, 2000) and into adolescence (Egeland, Kalkoske, Gottesman, & Erickson, 1990; Pierce, Ewing, & Campbell, 1999). The diagnosis of oppositional defiance disorder (ODD) in the preschool years is predictive of subsequent diagnoses of ODD and attention deficit/hyperactivity disorder (ADHD) in grade school, with 50% of children who are diagnosed with ODD in preschool continuing to have difficulties in second and third grade (Lavigne et al., 2001). When children enter school with problem behavior and poor social skills, those problems are likely to persist (National Institute of Child Health and Human Development, 2003).

The prevalence and stability of severe problem behavior has resulted in a national interest in providing early intervention to children in the toddler and preschool years and prior to school entry (Shonkoff & Phillips, 2000; Simpson, Jivanjee, Koroloff, Doerfler, & Garcia, 2001; U.S. Public Health Service, 2000). The primary settings in which this effort is likely to occur are community-based early childhood programs, including public preschool programs, head start programs, and community child care. Tragically, many early childhood programs feel unequipped to meet the needs of children who are emotionally delayed or have problem behavior (Kaufmann & Wischmann, 1999). Teachers report that disruptive behavior is one of the single greatest challenges they face in providing a quality program, and that there seem to be an increasing number of children who present with these problems (Arnold, McWilliams, & Arnold, 1998).

In this chapter, we describe a tiered model of prevention and promotion practices as a framework for the implementation of supports and interventions for young children within early childhood classrooms and programs (Fox, Dunlap, Hemmeter, Joseph, & Strain, 2003). The model that we describe is used in a similar fashion to schoolwide positive behavior support (SW-PBS) as a programwide effort to create systems of support for all children, including those with the most challenging behavior, and contributes to recent efforts to adapt the SW-PBS adoption process for early education programs (Benedict, Horner, & Squires, 2007; Frey, Boyce, & Tarullo, chapter 6, this volume; Stormont, Lewis, & Beckner, 2005; Stormont, Smith, & Lewis, 2007). The chapter provides an overview of the model and the practices affiliated with each tier and then discusses the issues related to programwide adoption with early childhood systems of care. The discussion of programwide adoption includes information on the steps to programwide adoption and illustrations of the process and outcomes in a range of early childhood programs. The chapter ends with a discussion of future directions for this promising model.

## THE TEACHING PYRAMID MODEL

The inspiration for the teaching pyramid model came from public health models of promotion, prevention, and intervention frameworks (Gordon, 1983; Simeonsson, 1991) and the SW-PBS three-tiered triangle (Horner, Sugai, Todd, & Lewis-Palmer, 2005; Walker et al., 1996). Thus, similar to the public health model, we describe the need for universal, secondary, and tertiary interventions to ensure the social-emotional development of all children, the provision of targeted supports to children at risk, and the inclusion of interventions for children with persistent challenges (Fox et al., 2003; Hemmeter, Ostrosky, & Fox, 2006; Powell, Dunlap, & Fox, 2006). In addition, the teaching pyramid model includes a detailed description of the research-based teaching practices that should be included at each level of the model within early childhood programs. These practices are drawn from the research on the classroom and teaching variables that promote children's social emotional development or are effective in addressing challenging behavior (Hemmeter, et al., 2006).

### *Universal Promotion Practices*

The universal level of the teaching pyramid model describes practices that have been shown to promote the social development of children in early childhood programs. These practices include the development of responsive and positive relationships with children and the provision of high-quality environments (Howes, Phillips, & Whitebrook, 1992; Peisner-Feinberg & Burchinal, 1997; Peisner-Feinberg et al., 2000; Phillips, McCartney, & Scarr, 1987).

In the teaching pyramid model (see Fig. 8.1), we place building positive relationships with children, families, and colleagues as the foundation for all other practices and the universal conditions that are necessary for social competence promotion and behavior guidance. The focus on relationships puts primary importance on the teacher engaging in responsive and positive interactions with children and the development of partnerships with families. Moreover, it includes the critical importance of collaboration and teaming that is essential to the provision of a high-quality classroom environment and early childhood program.

The relationships level of the pyramid model includes teaching practices that are linked to positive child outcomes in behavior and social skills (Birch & Ladd, 1998; Bodrova & Leong, 1998; Cox, 2005; Howes & Hamilton, 1992; Howes & Smith, 1995; Kontos, 1999; Mill & Romano-White, 1999; National Research Council, 2001; Pianta, Steinberg, & Rollins, 1995). These practices include actively supporting children's play; responding to children's conversations; promoting the communicative attempts of children with language delays and disabilities; providing specific praise to encourage appropriate behavior; developing positive relationships with children and families; and collaborative teaming with colleagues and other professionals.

The second category of universal practice that is linked to promoting the social competence of all children is the provision of supportive environments and teaching interactions that support children's appropriate engagement in classroom activities and routines (DeKlyen & Odom, 1998; Frede, Austin, & Lindauer, 1993; Holloway & Reichart-Erickson, 1988; Jolivette, Wehby, Canale, & Massey, 2001; National Research Council, 2001; Peisner-Feinberg et al., 2000). This level of the pyramid includes the following practices: providing adequate materials; defining play centers; offering a developmentally appropriate and balanced schedule of activities; structuring transitions; providing individualized instructions for children who need support; teaching and promoting a small number of rules; providing clear directions; and providing engaging activities. These are all practices that are recognized by early educators as fundamental to a high-quality learning environment that fosters children's skill development and learning.

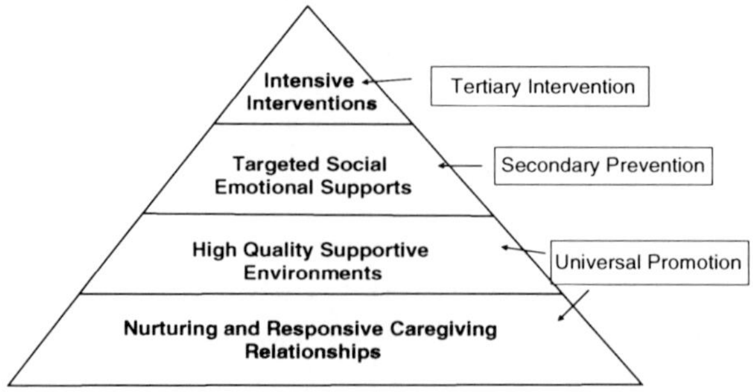


**Fig. 8.1.** The teaching pyramid model.

### *Social Emotional Teaching Strategies*

In the teaching pyramid model, the provision of explicit instruction in social skills and emotional regulation comprises the secondary practices tier (Coie & Koeppl, 1990; Denham & Burton, 1996; Mize & Ladd, 1990; National Research Council, 2001; Schneider, 1974; Serna, Nielsen, Lambros, & Forness, 2000; Shure & Spivack, 1980; Vaughn & Ridley, 1983; Webster-Stratton, Reid, & Hammond, 2001). In early childhood programs, all young children will require adult guidance and instruction to learn how to express their emotions appropriately, play cooperatively with peers, and use social problem-solving strategies. However, for some children it will be necessary to provide systematic and focused instruction to teach children discrete social emotional skills.

In this tier of the model, teachers are guided to provide instruction on the following skills: identifying and expressing emotions; self-regulation; social problem solving; initiating and maintaining interactions; cooperative responding; strategies for handling disappointment and anger; and friendship skills (e.g., being helpful, taking turns, giving compliments). In addition, teachers should develop strategies for partnering with families in the instruction of these skills in both the home and preschool settings. Many teachers use commercially developed curricula to support their instruction of these skills, and several curricula have empirical support for their effectiveness (Joseph & Strain, 2003).

Some early educators believed that the instruction of social skills occurs naturally within preschool programs as children are developmentally moving from solitary play skills to playing with others. However, the teaching pyramid model requires that teachers become intentional about how to teach social skills in a manner that moves beyond the provision of well-planned environments and supportive interactions. The instruction of social and emotional skills requires a systematic and comprehensive approach using embedded instruction within planned and routine activities. Effective teaching strategies include teaching the concept, modeling, rehearsing, role-playing, prompting children in context, and providing feedback when the behavior occurs (Grisham-Brown, Hemmeter, Pretti-Frontczak, 2005; Landy, 2002).

The objective of a secondary tier of practices is to provide instruction to children who are at risk of developing problem behavior but for whom an individualized behavior support plan may not be necessary. The precise distinction of that level of risk is often difficult to discern among young children, who are all developmentally expected to engage in minor levels of challenging behavior. For example, early educators expected to guide the behavior of preschool children who tantrum to express their frustration or who grab toys from peers when they want a turn. Thus, the teaching pyramid model includes the instruction of social emotional skills for all children and the need to provide targeted skill instruction that is individualized and systematic to children who may have challenges in social interaction or emotional regulation and are at risk of developing challenging behavior.

## *Intensive, Individualized Interventions*

The teaching pyramid model includes the implementation of comprehensive, assessment-based behavior support plans for children with persistent challenging behavior (Chandler, Dahlquist, Repp, & Feltz, 1999; Fox & Clarke, 2006; Fox, Dunlap, & Cushing, 2002; Reichle et al., 1996). When a child has persistent challenging behavior that is unresponsive to classroom guidance procedures and the instruction of social and emotional skills, a collaborative team is formed with the family to engage in the process of individualized positive behavior support (I-PBS). This process is guided by a trained behavior specialist who is on staff or by a consultant (e.g., school psychologist, behavior specialist, mental health consultant) who provides consultation and support to the program.

The I-PBS process begins with a team meeting to discuss the child's challenging behavior and to develop strategies to gather information through a functional assessment. The classroom teacher and family contribute to the functional assessment process by providing observation data and participating in interviews. Once functional assessment data have been gathered, the collaborative team meets again to affirm behavior hypotheses and brainstorm behavior support strategies. The behavior support plan includes antecedent prevention strategies to address the triggers of challenging behavior; replacement skills that are alternatives to the challenging behavior; and consequence strategies that ensure challenging behavior is not reinforced or maintained. The behavior support plan is designed to address both home and preschool routines where challenging behavior is occurring. In this process, the team also considers supports to the families and strategies to address broader ecological factors that affect the family and their support of the child (e.g., housing, transportation, mental health supports) and issues that may affect the developmental status of the child (e.g., trauma counseling, medical treatment).

Once the behavior support plan is designed, it is implemented by classroom staff and the family. The behavior specialist or consultant provides the teacher with coaching during the initial days of implementation and is available to the family as they implement the behavior support strategies at home and in the community. The teacher and family collect ongoing data, usually in the form of a behavior rating scale, to provide information on the effectiveness of the plan in reducing behavior incidents. The collaborative team meets on a regular basis to review plan implementation and child outcomes.

## *The Teaching Pyramid in Action*

The teaching pyramid defines the classroom practices needed to support the social emotional development of young children. Thus, there is a focus on the strategies that teachers will use in their relationships with individual children and families. This focus on individual children and their families is considered an essential practice in early education, and the use of whole class behavior management systems without regard for a child's developmental level or individual needs would violate how the field defines appropriate practice (Bredekamp & Copple, 1997). However, when you enter into a classroom where the teaching pyramid model is in place, there is a palpable difference in comparison to classrooms where there is less focus on promoting social emotional competence.

We have developed and are field testing the Teaching Pyramid Observation Tool (TPOT) (Hemmeter & Fox, 2006), which is an implementation fidelity tool that reliably assesses the implementation of the teaching pyramid practices in preschool classrooms. In classrooms with high implementation fidelity, the adoption of these practices is immediately observable (Hemmeter, Fox, & Doubet, 2006; Hemmeter, Fox, Jack, Broyles, & Doubet, 2007). Classrooms that have adopted the teaching pyramid have visual displays of behavior expectations and classroom rules that are used in the instruction of children to review expectations or discuss the importance of rules. Teaching staff remind children of expected behavior and reference the behavior expectations within the ongoing activities of the day. In the high-implementation classrooms, we see well-planned transitions; carefully designed learning activities or centers and classroom schedules that promote child engagement; and the intentional teaching of social skills within all activities (e.g., group time, centers, outdoor play, bathroom, and snack). Classroom staff are constantly interacting with children, guiding their play, promoting their communication, and providing specific instruction, encouragement, and praise for appropriate behavior and the use of social skills.

In classrooms with implementation fidelity, there may still be behavior incidents, but the teacher's response to those incidents is different. Teachers confidently intervene with child disagreements and guide children to use problem solving or conflict resolution procedures. When children express frustration or anger, teachers validate the emotion and support children to use more appropriate forms of expression. If a child has severe behavior challenges, teachers calmly intervene or use program-adopted procedures to gain assistance with the child. In our observations of classrooms with implementation fidelity, we see children who are highly engaged and teachers who are guiding children's engagement and learning with confidence.

## IMPLEMENTING THE TEACHING PYRAMID IN EARLY CHILDHOOD PROGRAMS

Since 2000, we have worked with a variety of early childhood programs to implement programwide positive behavior support (PBS) (Fox & Little, 2001; Hemmeter, Fox, et al., 2006; Hemmeter et al., 2007). These programs have included a small faith-based child care program, large Head Start programs, public school early childhood programs, and state-level implementation across multiple early childhood service delivery systems. Through this work, we have found that the implementation of programwide PBS in early childhood settings requires a different approach than theimplementation of SW-PBS because of the range of early childhood service delivery systems, the developmental needs of very young children, and the availability of (or lack thereof) systems and resources to support programwide implementation. Unlike public school education for school-aged children, preschool children are served in a variety of early childhood systems, including Head Start, child care, and public preschool. These systems vary in the education level and qualifications of their teachers, access to resources and behavior support expertise, administrative staff to support the process, and implementation of data collection systems.

### *Head Start*

Head Start is a federally funded child development program that serves children from birth through age 5 in center and home-based programs. Children are eligible for Head Start if their families' income is below the federal poverty level, and 10% of enrollment slots are reserved for children with special needs regardless of the income level of their family. Head Start is a federal-to-local program, meaning that money flows directly from the federal program to local grantees. A local grantee agency may have multiple programs housed in multiple sites. All Head Start programs must adhere to federal program performance standards.

As a result of the federal program and mandates, Head Start has a variety of supports and resources in place that could provide support for programwide implementation. Head Start programs have performance standards for mental health and behavior support services and as a result must have written policies and procedures in place related to these issues. They have resources for mental health consultants, management staff responsible for training and coaching teachers, and an ongoing program improvement process in place.

Data from the most recent FACES (National Head Start Families and Child Experiences Survey) study (Zill et al., 2006) found the quality of programs to range from minimal to excellent, with over 60% of the study programs falling in the good-to-excellent range. This represents an ongoing trend toward quality improvement in Head Start. Traditionally, teachers have not been required to have a college degree or required to have a teaching license. While there are regulations in place to increase the number of teachers with credentials that include college degrees, associate degrees, and or Child Development Associate (CDA) credentials, the regulations give programs several years to meet these regulations and only require that a certain percentage of staff meet the credentialing requirements. Another issue in Head Start programs is the tendency for national initiatives to drive what happens in local programs. The most recent example of this is the implementation of the National Reporting System, which requires all programs to assess all children multiple times during the school year (Hill, 2003). These initiatives have demanded the program's attention and resources, making it difficult to be proactive about more locally determined needs such as behavior support. Finally, while Head Start programs have resources, policies, and procedures related to behavior support in place as described, the effective implementation of these practices varies a great deal. Written policies and procedures related to behavior do not always translate into the consistent or effective implementation of those practices in programs (Quesenberry, 2007).

### *Public School Preschool*

Public school preschool programs vary in type, funding, and location of programs. For over 20 years, states have been providing services to preschool children with disabilities in a variety of settings. Over the last 15 years, states have become involved in providing programs for preschool children who are at risk; most recently, many states have begun looking toward universal pre-K for all 4-year-old children. In 2006, 38 states were working on some type of pre-K initiative for at-risk children (Barnett, Hustedt, Hawkinson, & Robin, 2006). States have different service delivery models, with some states housing pre-K programs primarily in schools, and other states choosing to house pre-K programs in a variety of community-based settings, including Head Start and child care.

It is difficult to describe the resources available to publicly funded pre-K programs because of the variability of funding and models of implementation across states. When the pre-K programs are housed in public school settings such as elementary schools, programs may have resources available to implement programwide PBS, including hiring licensed teachers, behavior support personnel, and administrative staff responsible for professional development. However, when pre-K programs are housed in public schools or community-based settings such as Head Start or child care centers, access to resources may be determined by the setting in which they are housed. Even when pre-K programs are housed in public schools, there may be limitations to the resources that are available. For example, there may be a schoolwide PBS initiative, but the pre-K program may not be included in the initiative, or there may be behavior support personnel but they do not have experience working with very young children.

There are some limited national data available on the quality of state pre-K programs. Of those states that have pre-K initiatives, just over half require teachers to have a bachelor's degree, while others require a credential such as a CDA. The quality of state-funded pre-K programs is difficult to summarize as evaluations are typically state funded and implemented. Recent data available across states describe the extent to which state pre-K programs are meeting 10 benchmarks of quality. Of the programs that were reviewed, there was a wide range of quality, with 11 programs scoring below 5, 18 meeting 5–7 of the benchmarks, 16 meeting 8–9, and 2 meeting all 10 of the benchmarks (Barnett et al., 2006). Sixteen states raised their quality standards enough to meet benchmarks they had not met in previous years.

### *Child Care*

Child care is a complex service delivery system that includes a variety of different program models, none of which is funded fully by federal or state resources. Child care includes center-based programs, family day care homes, and family, friends, and neighbor care. There are federal subsidies that can be used to assist needy families in accessing child care. These monies are administered through state block grants. The federal government also provides monies to states to work toward quality improvements in child care and funds a national network of child care resource and referral agencies. Child care is, in many cases, the system least likely to have access to the resources needed to implement programwide behavior support. Probably the most compelling difference in child care is the lack of financial resources. Many child care programs depend almost entirely on paid tuition and state subsidies, neither of which is typically adequate for running a high-quality child care program. Many child care centers have no administrative staff other than the director, and in some small child care centers, the director also serves as a teacher. Many child care centers have relatively few training and degree requirements for teachers and require minimal ongoing professional development experiences. These characteristics can seriously affect the quality of care. The Cost, Quality, and Outcomes study, a national evaluation of child care programs, found that the quality of care in the settings in their study was frequently below average, with only 25% of the programs scoring in the good range or higher (Peisner-Feinberg et al., 2000).

One resource that is available to child care programs is the Resource and Referral Network. This network is designed to support families by providing information about child care in their community. In addition, they support local child care programs by providing training and technical assistance, but typically they cannot provide the level of support that is needed for programs to be able to implement a programwide PBS model. Finally, many states have started implementing quality rating systems for child care programs. These systems often provide incentives for programs to improve their quality rating and some professional development support to address quality improvement. Regardless of these potential resources, child care programs generally have the fewest resources for implementing a programwide model.

The descriptions of these systems provide a framework for understanding the complexity of developing a programwide model of behavior support in early childhood settings. Within and across these settings, there is a great deal of variability in program quality, training and qualifications of staff, and resources available to support a programwide model. An early childhood programwide model must be adapted to address the diverse needs of all early childhood settings.

In addition to the issues described, there are a number of other issues that should be addressed in the design and implementation of a programwide model for early childhood settings. The cognitive abilities of young children and the developmental nature of problem behavior in young children have significant implications for the practices that are implemented within a programwide model. For example, a token system that works with older children to support prosocial behaviors may be less effective for young children given their cognitive and social development levels and might not be consistent with recommended practice. Finally, the application of a programwide PBS model in early childhood programs should be focused on the classroom adoption of prevention and intervention strategies that are effective in promoting young children's social and emotional development and addressing challenging behavior (Fox et al., 2003). As described, the teaching pyramid includes primary promotion practices of building positive adult-child relationships and the development of supportive classroom environments (e.g., routines, transitions, engaging activities, clear expectations); secondary practices of providing intentional and systematic instruction of social skills and emotional competencies (e.g., friendship skills, problem solving, communicating emotions, anger management); and at the tertiary level the provision of individualized interventions for children with persistent challenging behavior. Within an early childhood setting, the implementation of all levels of practice concurrently will be necessary for addressing the social emotional needs of all children in a preschool classroom.

## PROGRAMWIDE ADOPTION OF THE TEACHING PYRAMID

The implementation of programwide PBS follows many of the essential elements of SW-PBS, but has been tailored to address the unique configuration, services, and resources of early childhood programs and the developmental needs of young children. An essential component of programwide PBS in early childhood settings is family involvement. Families should be involved in the development, implementation, and evaluation of the programwide PBS plan. Many of the strategies associated with the teaching pyramid involve families, with the assumption that outcomes for children will be better if there is consistency between home and school. In addition, the early childhood years provide the context for supporting families in taking an active role in their child's education, which sets the foundation for their involvement throughout the child's schooling. Second, the teaching pyramid model provides the system of practices that should be implemented in early childhood classrooms at the universal, secondary, and tertiary levels. Rather then phasing in universal, secondary, and tertiary interventions, teachers are trained and supported in using practices at all levels of the pyramid from the beginning.

In our work, we have identified several "readiness indicators" that need to be in place for a program to be successful. First, programs have to have a "champion." An administrator within the program who understands the model, can articulate the benefits to staff, is willing to commit necessary resources, and who is trusted by the staff has to be willing to lead the initiative. Second, programs must have or find resources for providing ongoing training and support to those staff who work directly with children and families. Programwide implementation will simply not work if teachers do not have the competence and supports necessary to implement the model. Third, the program has to identify a leadership team that includes administrators, staff, families, and personnel with expertise in behavior support. It is the responsibility of the team to meet regularly; collect data; monitor progress, fidelity, and outcomes; and use the data to modify the plan. The team has to commit to a longitudinal process.

The leadership team begins the process by developing an implementation plan that includes the steps described on pages 188-190. These steps are designed to increase the likelihood that programwide adoption and implementation will occur by ensuring that staff are committed to the process, have the training needed to implement the teaching pyramid practices, and that there are systems within the program that are supportive of teachers and are effective in addressing problem behavior.

### *Determine Staff Commitment*

In schoolwide behavior support, commitment from at least 80% of program staff is required (Horner & Sugai, 2000). This is also essential to programwide implementation of the teaching pyramid model. Leadership teams can design strategies to establish buy-in and develop a process for obtaining commitment from program staff, including classroom staff, administrators, and other support staff (e.g., secretaries, custodians, kitchen staff). Programs with which we have worked have used a video on the teaching pyramid to provide an overview of the model to staff and then have staff complete a survey indicating the extent to which they can be committed to the model. Showing video is an effective strategy for describing the approach, including the importance of providing support systems for staff to implement the model.

### *Develop a Plan for Family Involvement*

As we described, family involvement should be a key component of programwide implementation in early childhood programs. The leadership team should plan strategies for (a) providing information to families, (b) creating opportunities for training and supporting families, (c) developing a team-based process that includes family members when addressing an individual child's problem behavior, and (d) providing opportunities for families to give feedback and input to the program about the programwide initiative.

### *Identify Programwide Expectations*

A primary component of universal practices in the schoolwide model is the identification of schoolwide expectations for children's behavior that create a focus on teaching positive, prosocial behaviors and preventing problem behaviors (Horner & Sugai, 2000; Lohrmann-O'Rourke et al., 2000; Taylor-Greene & Kartub, 2000). The implementation of programwide expectations by all staff increases the frequency with which children get feedback on their social behaviors across multiple settings in a school or program. The adoption of programwide expectations provides staff, families, and children with a positive way to talk about behavior. We guide early childhood programs to generate a list of developmentally appropriate expectations they have for children and to categorize those into a small number of expectations that are written in terms that young children can learn to use (Benedict et al., 2007). Programs then define what the expectations look like in different settings in the school or program. In the classroom, the expectation, "be respectful," might be translated into classroom rules that include use quiet voices, use soft touches, pick up your toys, and help your friend.

### *Develop Strategies for Teaching and Acknowledging the Expectations*

Once expectations are identified, a systematic plan for teaching and acknowledging the expectations should be developed. For young children to learn what the expectations mean and what they look like (e.g., rules), it will be important to teach the expectations within meaningful contexts across multiple program environments (e.g., classroom, bathroom, hallway, bus, playground). Programs should develop strategies, activities, and schedules for teaching the expectations. A range of strategies should be used, including role-playing, modeling, discussion, practice, feedback in context, and reflection. Early childhood programs often use social emotional curricula that can be linked to the expectations identified by the program. In addition, a variety of materials, including books, puppets, social stories, and games, can be used to teach the expectations. Programs should also be intentional about developing strategies for acknowledging the expectations. Our experience with programs is that they have chosen acknowledgment strategies that can be embedded naturally into ongoing interactions with children (e.g., positive descriptive feedback, discussion during group times).

### *Develop Processes for Addressing Problem Behavior*

Through our work with programs (Hemmeter, Fox, et al., 2006; Hemmeter et al., 2007), interviews with program staff (Quesenberry & Hemmeter, 2005), and review of program policies and procedures (Quesenberry, Ostrosky, & Hemmeter, 2007), we have found that many early childhood programs do not have systems in place for addressing the needs of children with persistent problem behavior, or there are systems in place that are either not effective or not consistent. We also know that children with persistent challenging behavior are at risk for being expelled from preschool programs (Gilliam, 2005). To ensure that teachers remain committed to the programwide plan and children are not expelled from the program, there must be processes in place for addressing the needs of those children with the most challenging behaviors, including a process for responding to short-term crisis situations (e.g., a child is "out of control" in a classroom) as well as addressing the needs of individual children with ongoing, persistent problem behavior. The process should specify (a) what teachers do in each situation in terms of documentation that is needed, (b) the staff responsible for responding to teacher requests, and (c) strategies for addressing the situation.

### *Develop a Professional Development Plan*

The programwide implementation plan should include strategies for ensuring that all staff have the training needed to effectively implement the teaching pyramid practices. In addition, staff need training in the processes that will be used for addressing persistently challenging behavior. Finally, training related to teaching the expectations will be necessary to ensure all staff (e.g., teachers, teaching assistants, administrators, custodians, kitchen staff, bus drivers) are supporting children around the expectations. The plan should also provide professional development opportunities that are individualized, provided in the teachers' classroom, and ongoing. The TPOT (Hemmeter & Fox, 2006) can be used as a tool for determining what practices teachers are implementing and in what areas they might need additional training and support.

### *Develop a Data Collection Plan That Addresses Implementation Fidelity and Outcomes*

An important activity of the leadership team will be to use data for planning and decision making (Horner, Sugai, & Todd, 2001). In schoolwide models, "office discipline referrals" are used as a primary measure of the effectiveness of the schoolwide plan for reducing discipline problems. Sending children to the office is not a typical practice in early childhood programs. We have developed a tool called the Behavior Incident Report (BIR) that some early childhood programs have adopted to track the frequency and type of challenging behavior. The BIR provides information on the specific behaviors that occur as well as the settings, activities, and times when problem behavior is most likely to occur. These data can be used to document the change in behavior incidents over time, and information on variables that predict problem behavior can be used to develop professional development activities and other strategies. For example, if behavior incidents occur most frequently during large groups, the program might provide professional development opportunities on designing and implementing large-group activities. The BIR data might also provide the team with information that would lead to other changes. For example, if there is a significant number of behaviors that occur on the playground, observations might be conducted and strategies developed to decrease the likelihood that challenging behavior will occur in that setting (e.g., increase supervision, add more activities or toys, decrease number of children on the playground at the same time). The leadership team also should gather data on the progress of the program and individual teachers in the adoption of the programwide model and the teaching pyramid practices. We have developed a checklist for leadership teams to use to assess the implementation of the essential elements of the programwide model (i.e., Early Childhood Benchmarks of Quality, available from the authors). In addition, as described, the team may decide to use the TPOT to track individual teacher's progress toward implementation of the pyramid practices.

## EXAMPLES OF PROGRAMWIDE IMPLEMENTATION

In this section, we provide an overview of programwide implementation in a child care program and a public school program as well as an example of statewide implementation that includes multiple early childhood service delivery systems. The three programs have approached programwide implementation somewhat differently but include many of the key features we described.

### *Palma Ceia Presbyterian Preschool*

Palma Ceia Presbyterian Preschool is a faith-based preschool program that has been operating for over 25 years. It was started as a program to provide early education experiences to young children with disabilities and also enrolled typically developing children to serve as playmates. As models for providing inclusive early childhood special education were refined over time, the program evolved into its current status of a high-quality early childhood program that serves primarily typically developing children with a natural proportion of children with disabilities.

The program is highly regarded within the community and typically has a substantial waiting list for admissions. The founding director still operates the preschool and is recognized as a leader in early childhood education and the provision of high-quality programs for young children with and without disabilities. The preschool was one of the first early childhood programs in its community to receive accreditation from the National Association for the Education of Young Children (NAEYC), and staff have served as trainers and validators for other programs that pursue accreditation.

The preschool is small and enrolls about 60 children from ages 12 months to 5 years who attend a half-day program. The inclusion of children with disabilities is at the heart of the program, and the preschool is committed to the support of children with physical, medical, and mental challenges. The program became interested in the adoption of a model for supporting the enrollment of children with challenging behavior when they were confronted with children whose behavior was not responsive to their typical child guidance procedures. While problem behavior was rare in the program, staff felt unequipped to deal with the most extreme challenges that were exhibited by some children in their program who had disabilities and autism.

In 1997, the program director sought the assistance of a university consultant to implement a model that would be developmentally appropriate, have contextual fit with their educational approach and program values, and could be implemented by program staff within the context of classroom routines (Fox & Little, 2001). Prior to the initiation of this effort, the program had consulted several outside experts for advice about individual children but did not feel that their recommendations were feasible for implementation within the program or a match to the school's values and instructional philosophy.

Palma Ceia Preschool had many of the elements of the teaching pyramid model in place. Teachers within the program were highly skilled and received ongoing professional development and supervision. The small size and stable leadership of the program allowed for the development of intimate and strong relationships between families and preschool staff. In the structure of classroom environments and teaching interactions, there was very little need of improvement. However, the program was concerned that they were completely unprepared to effectively and appropriately respond to some of the challenging behaviors of their children.

The adoption of the programwide initiative at Palma Ceia Preschool occurred during the time reports were first being published on the concept of SW-PBS. The effort at Palma Ceia initially included only some of the elements that are now more common to a schoolwide or programwide effort. At Palma Ceia Preschool, the focus was on the development of tertiary supports for children with the most severe challenging behavior. It was the explicit desire of the preschool to have a zero-reject policy in the program and ensure that they had the capacity to support all children who chose to enroll in the school.

The university consultant assisted the program by teaching program staff the process of I-PBS (see chapter 3, this volume). This effort was launched with a training workshop for all program staff on PBS and the implementation of comprehensive behavior support plans. The preschool included information on PBS within the parent handbook and stated clearly what steps would be taken to collaboratively develop a plan with the family when there were concerns about challenging behavior.

In the first year of the effort, four children received a functional assessment and behavior support plan. The I-PBS process was conducted by a collaborative team (director or assistant director, teacher, parent) with guidance from the university consultant. The explicit goal of the effort was to ensure that effective support was provided to children and to build the capacity of the program to be able to implement I-PBS without reliance on outside consultation. In the next 2 years of adoption, the consultant was available to assist with training of staff and refining the model. During this period, an additional four behavior support plans were developed and implemented.

In the last decade, Palma Ceia has continued to rely on I-PBS as their process for addressing the needs of children with persistent behavior challenges. Each year, they typically have one or two children who need that level of individualized, intensive support. In addition, the preschool has added elements from the teaching pyramid model and now has adopted programwide expectations that are promoted in classrooms and with their families.

### *Valeska-Hinton Early Childhood Education Center*

Valeska Hinton Early Childhood Education Center (VHECEC) is a NAEYC-accredited public school program in Peoria, Illinois, that serves over 400 children in preschool through first grade. In addition, the center houses a variety of other programs. Highly qualified staff, family involvement, and ongoing professional development are key components of the program.

At the time that they began thinking about a programwide approach, VHECEC had ongoing concerns about challenging behavior. In the spring of 2002, the existing administrative team (i.e., principal, professional development coordinator, lead teacher, family liaison) discussed the need to focus on supporting children, teachers, and families in the area of social and emotional development and challenging behavior. The May 2002 Professional Development Goals Survey gathered from the staff identified challenging behavior as the most requested training need. Staff members felt unsupported, frustrated, and overwhelmed. The administrative team and staff members wanted to develop a plan for addressing social and emotional development and challenging behavior that would increase time for instruction, encourage more positive interactions with children, provide ongoing training and support for staff, and involve families.

After considering different approaches, the team decided that a programwide system of PBS would include all of the components they were looking for, including instruction and promotion of positive social behavior, prevention of challenging behavior, and individual supports for children with persistent challenging behavior as well as supports for teachers and staff. The principal and other administrators were instrumental in the development of PBS at Valeska Hinton. This was critical because it took a great deal of time and resources to develop the plan. The administrative team contacted staff from the Center on the Social and Emotional Foundations for Early Learning (CSEFEL) to assist with the development of the plan. A CSEFEL staff person facilitated the development of the plan. A PBS leadership team was formed and included the administrative team members as well as staff representing the variety of programs, ages of children, and staff positions in their school. The team met at least monthly to develop the plan. Families were kept informed throughout the process and were invited to participate in the development the PBS plan. Updates and opportunities were provided at monthly parent meetings. One set of parent-teacher conferences focused on sharing programwide expectations with families.

The leadership team identified Together We Can as the name for their initiative and began work on developing programwide expectations. Staff members said that the process of identifying developmentally appropriate expectations gave them the opportunity to explore their own beliefs and philosophies about how young children develop and learn. After many hours of engaging debates, the group chose three programwide behavior expectations: Children and adults at VHECEC are expected to be respectful, be safe, and be team players. An important lesson the staff learned through this process was the need to establish expectations for both children and adults. Thus, their programwide expectations meant a commitment to holding themselves accountable for the expectations not only in their interactions with the children but in their interactions with their colleagues and with families.

The team decided to develop a time line for teaching the expectations but did not expect all teachers to teach and acknowledge the expectations in the same way. This was important in terms of addressing the unique developmental needs of children in preschool to first grade. Strategies for teaching the expectations were generated, including integrating the expectations into their use of the SECOND STEP CURRICULUM, modeling and role-playing expectations, and taking and discussing photos of students demonstrating the expectations. A variety of strategies were developed to recognize positive, prosocial behavior, including verbal descriptive feedback (e.g., "Thank you for being safe on the playground today when you walked around the swing"), photos of the children engaged in the expectations displayed on a bulletin board in the center court of the building, and a book developed by a class that included pictures and descriptions of children engaging in the expectations.

Next, the team focused on developing the program's capacity to develop plans for supporting children with the most significant problem behaviors.

The team developed a plan for what teachers would do when they needed immediate help (e.g., when behavior was immediately dangerous or overly disruptive) as well as a process for developing individualized support plans. For immediate help, classroom staff could call the office to request that a support person come to the classroom right away to help with the situation. The support person was supposed to help with the classroom while the teacher dealt with the individual child. A form was developed that teachers were to complete to indicate how useful the assistance was. The goal was to decrease crisis situations. In addition, a process was developed for addressing the needs of children with ongoing challenging behavior. Staff were trained in conducting observations, gathering information (including family and staff), developing behavior hypotheses, and writing a behavior support plan for a child.

VHECEC had a commitment to effective approaches to professional development, including having a professional development staff member to coordinate all professional development activities. A variety of professional development activities were planned and implemented related to the PBS initiative. A series of in-service workshops was conducted for all staff members (i.e., support staff, associate teachers, teachers, student teachers, administration) on the topics of (a) positive relationships with children, families, and colleagues; (b) classroom preventive practices; (c) social and emotional skills strategies; and (d) intensive individualized interventions. This series followed the components of the teaching pyramid described here (Fox et al., 2003). Second, the team developed a plan for how they would orient new staff to the model as they were hired. Finally, the professional development coordinator and lead teacher made themselves available to support teachers as they implemented these strategies in their classroom.

Once the plan was developed, the work group took more of an advisory role. They met regularly to review the plan; arrange professional development activities for staff, students, and families; and advise the administrative team. Some of the outcomes of the PBS approach at Valeska Hinton include schoolwide agreement and focus on PBS, an increased feeling of unity among staff members, shared common language surrounding children's behaviors, and a reduction in children being "sent (taken) to the office."

While the initiative at VHECEC produced some important outcomes, they did not develop a comprehensive data collection system for use in monitoring implementation and outcomes. The team conducted staff surveys and kept records on calls to the office for crisis help, the development of plans for individual children, and staff satisfaction. However, data were not collected or summarized on a regular basis, and data were not used for decision making in a systematic way.

### *Iowa Initiative for Programwide PBS*

In 2006, state education officials became interested in the application of programwide PBS to early childhood programs following the states' extensive and successful engagement in schoolwide applications of PBS. Since 2002, schools in Iowa have been systematically expanding their implementation of SW-PBS within elementary and secondary schools with the support of Department of Education technical assistance providers and national consultants. Iowa was excited about the outcomes they had experienced with implementing SW-PBS and was interested in bringing this approach to their preschool classrooms within public schools, community child care, and Head Start programs.

The early childhood programwide effort began in the fall of 2006 with the training of leadership teams from 14 Head Start programs in a variety of communities across the state. Each leadership team included an Area Education Agency (AEA) technical assistance provider who was familiar with SW-PBS and charged with providing training, consultation, and other educational services to local programs. The structure of program leadership teams mirrored the requirements of SW-PBS initiatives with the requirement of administrative support, teacher representation, the use of data-based decision making, and a commitment to a multiple-year systems change process. The leadership teams were provided with a 3-day workshop on the essential features of programwide PBS and the activities involved in adoption and implementation. Teams returned to their programs and worked with AEA personnel in the adoption of the model. Teams were provided with an evaluation package to collect ongoing data on their implementation progress and program outcomes. The evaluation package included the use of an Early Childhood Benchmarks of Quality to track programwide implementation and the TPOT to track classroom implementation of the teaching pyramid model. Teams were provided with a mechanism to track program incidents (e.g., calls to families, behavior consultations) and behavior incidents. Behavior incident tracking involved a data system that provided teams with a visual analysis of the incidents over time and by other factors (e.g., location, teacher, type of behavior) that could be used by leadership teams for data-based decision making. Teachers also completed the Social Skills Rating System (SSRS; Gresham & Elliot, 1990) to identify children who were at risk or had significant concerns. The SSRS also provided a measure that could be used to track child outcomes.

The assistance provided to Iowa teams was locally determined. Consultants provided the initial 3-day team training and several team implementation workshops during the year. Workshops during the year focused on implementing the evaluation plan and the use of the I-PBS process for children with persistent challenges. Each team was provided with training materials on the teaching pyramid and was instructed to develop individualized professional development plans on implementation of the teaching pyramid and to provide general training on the teaching pyramid model. Leadership teams were instructed to meet monthly to guide implementation efforts and review data.

In the initial year of implementation, programs were encouraged to ensure that teachers were making progress in implementing the teaching pyramid model and that the program was developing the universal elements that provide a programwide focus on promoting expectations and implementing systems for supporting children with behavioral challenges. Data from the first year indicated that classroom teachers improved in the implementation of the teaching pyramid model as measured by the TPOT, and that program teams made progress in the implementation of the model as measured by the Early Childhood Benchmarks of Quality. Programs reported that they found the TPOT to be helpful in identifying where teachers needed support to improve practice and the identification of individual and programwide professional development activities.

Data collection was a challenge for the Iowa programs as Head Start has many reporting requirements, and practitioners in the program have limited training and experience in the use of data for making decisions and tracking outcomes. The programs began using the BIR to track children's challenging behavior and to gather analytic information that could assist in problem solving the factors related to incidents of challenging behavior. In the first year of implementation, half of the programs were able to use the BIR productively, and half the programs were inconsistent in their use of the system. All of the programs collected child assessment information on social skills and problem behavior using the SSRS (Gresham & Elliot, 1990). The programs used the SSRS information to identify children in need of targeted and tertiary interventions. One of the programs was able to gather pre- and postmeasures using the SSRS to document child growth in the first year. That program showed evidence of growth in implementation on the benchmarks and TPOT and documented a statistically significant change in the overall average standard score in children's social skills and a meaningful decrease in the average standard score for problem behavior.

In 2007, a second cohort of programs applied to participate and have received training on implementation and evaluation procedures. This cohort includes Head Start programs, private community child care programs, and public school classrooms. As the state expands its efforts in programwide adoption, it is also building statewide capacity to offer training in the teaching pyramid model. State leaders from the various early childhood programs and initiatives (e.g., Head Start, child care, special education, child care resource and referral, higher education, etc.) have formed a state leadership team to work in partnership with the CSEFEL to develop a cadre of trainers who can provide training and technical assistance in the implementation of the teaching pyramid model.

## SUMMARY AND FUTURE DIRECTIONS

Over the last 5 years, we have made substantial progress in articulating and implementing a model for programwide PBS in early childhood settings (Fox & Little, 2001; Hemmeter, Fox, et al., 2006; Hemmeter et al., 2007) and have engaged in national efforts with numerous colleagues to facilitate the adoption of the teaching pyramid model as a framework for promoting young children's social-emotional development and addressing challenging behavior through two federally funded national centers (CESEFEL, www.vanderbilt.edu/csefel; Center for Evidence-Based Practice: Young Children with Challenging Behavior, www.challengingbehavior.org). These efforts have built on the current database of effective early childhood intervention practices and a careful translation of the pioneering work of the SW-PBS model (Hemmeter, Fox, et al., 2006). As we have worked within early childhood programs, there have been several lessons learned and challenges associated with the model. These are described next.

Schoolwide and districtwide PBS involves core features, approaches to intervention, processes for adoption, and the measurement of outcomes that overlays on a fairly uniform setting: a school or school district. In early childhood applications, the settings may be quite varied and do not involve standard features. For example, we have worked with small child care programs, large programs with multiple centers and services (including home consultation), public school classrooms, and public schools. Within these settings, there may or may not be resource personnel, data collection systems, professional development resources, and behavior consultation expertise. The diversity of these programs translates into model adoption efforts that are often idiosyncratic to the setting. In addition, we have yet to work in an early childhood program that uses a standard process for noting when a child has problem behavior and needs support or intervention. The lack of the office discipline referral as a measure that is common to the program or a similar measure that can be used as an analytic tool or to gauge a program's progress has been a challenge for implementation.

In SW-PBS, the assessment of whether universal interventions are in place considers whether a team has been established, expectations have been taught and are monitored, problem behaviors are being prevented and discouraged, and data are used for decision making (Horner et al., 2005). In early childhood implementation, while there is an emphasis on programwide expectations and systems for data-based decision making and team implementation, the prevention power of the pyramid model is predicated on the implementation of the practices associated with the model by individual teachers within their classrooms. In our efforts toward programwide implementation, we have focused on ensuring that the teaching pyramid model is being implemented with fidelity within every classroom. The teaching pyramid model describes the practices and processes that teachers should use to support the social development of all children and to address the social and behavioral needs of individual children. It is the consistent delivery of these research-based strategies that leads to improved outcomes for all children.

We have also found it necessary to support programs in implementing all tiers of the model simultaneously to ensure that children with persistent challenges can continue to be enrolled in the program and receive services. Without the safety net of an entitlement to education, young children who pose behavior challenges are at significant risk of being expelled from their current placement. To ensure that an assessment-based process for developing behavior support plans is a part of the programwide effort, we have guided leadership teams to identify internal resources for making this a systematic part of the program or to partner with a consultant (e.g., behavior specialist, mental health consultant) to offer these supports. We have also provided training in the individualized behavior support process to all program staff, with more targeted training to staff members who will serve as behavior support facilitators.

As the teaching pyramid model has increased in its national visibility as a framework for supporting social emotional development and addressing the challenging behavior of young children, there have been numerous inquiries about its fit for preschool classrooms within schools that are implementing SW-PBS. It is our hope that the teaching pyramid model framework nests neatly within a schoolwide effort and can be recognized as the approach to instruction and behavior intervention that should be used within preschool classrooms.

In our programwide implementation work, we have identified some challenges that will inevitably lead to refinements in the model. We have found that early childhood programs have very limited experience with teaming at a program level and developing systems for innovation sustainability. While the notion that teachers work together at a committee level to implement an innovation or initiative in schools is common, this opportunity is rare within early childhood programs. This has important implications for the training and support of a program leadership team. Another challenge that must be noted is the adoption of data collection systems that are meaningful for use with young children and yield data that can guide the refinement of the model. While we have experienced some success in developing data systems that programs are using, many programs have a difficult time integrating simple data collection measures into their ongoing procedures.

Despite these challenges, we have been encouraged by the enthusiastic interest in programwide PBS by early childhood educators, programs, and policy makers. We have received an overwhelming response from state systems that wish to build the capacity of their professional development systems to ensure that training and coaching in the teaching pyramid model is available within their early care and education programs. Since 2000, there has been a crescendo of activity in states focused on the development of models for addressing young children's behavioral challenges and mental health concerns. Programwide adoption of the teaching pyramid has been welcomed as an approach that can be implemented by early educators within their daily nurturance of young children. We are confident that over the next few years data from programs that are implementing this model will demonstrate its value.

## ACKNOWLEDGMENT

The preparation of this chapter was supported by the Center for Evidence-Based Practice: Young Children With Challenging Behaviors, Office of Special Education Programs, U.S. Department of Education (H324Z010001); the Center on the Social and Emotional Foundations for Early Learning, U.S. Department of Health and Human Services (90YD0215/01); and the Institute of Education Sciences (R324A07212).

## REFERENCES

Arnold, D. H., McWilliams, L., & Arnold, E. H. (1998). Teacher discipline and child misbehavior in day care: Untangling causality with correlational data. *Developmental Psychology, 34*, 276–287.

Barnett, W. S., Hustedt, J. T., Hawkinson, M. P. A., & Robin, K. B. (2006). *The state of preschool: 2006 state preschool yearbook*. Rutgers: National Institute for Early Education Research, State University of New Jersey.

Benedict, E. A., Horner, R. H., & Squires, J. (2007). Assessment and implementation of positive behavior support in preschools. *Topics in Early Childhood Special Education, 27*, 174–192.

Birch, S. H., & Ladd, G. W. (1998). Children's interpersonal behaviors and the teacher-child relationship. *Developmental Psychology, 34*, 934–946.

Bodrova, E., & Leong, D. J. (1998). Development of dramatic play in young children and its effects on self-regulation: The Vygotskian approach. *Journal of Early Childhood Teacher Education, 19*, 115–124.

Bredekamp, S., & Copple, C. (Eds.). (1997). *Developmentally appropriate practices in early childhood programs* (Rev. ed.). Washington, DC: National Association for the Education of Young Children.

Briggs-Gowan, M. J., Carter, A. S., Skuban, E. M., & Horwitz, S. M. (2001). Prevalence of social emotional and behavioral problems in a community sample of 1- and 2-year-old children. *Journal of the American Academy of Child and Adolescent Psychiatry, 40*, 811–819.

Campbell, S. B. (1995). Behavior problems in preschool children: A review of recent research. *Journal of Child Psychology and Psychiatry, 36*, 113–149.

Chandler, L. K., Dahlquist, C. M., Repp, A. C., & Feltz, C. (1999). The effects of team-based functional assessment on the behavior of students in classroom settings. *Exceptional Children, 66*, 101–122.

Coie, J. D., & Koeppl, G. K. (1990). Adapting intervention to the problems of aggressive and disruptive rejected children. In S. R. Asher & J. D. Coie (Eds.), *Peer rejection in childhood* (pp. 309–337). New York: Cambridge University Press.

Cox, D. D. (2005). Evidence-based interventions using home-school collaboration. *School Psychology Quarterly, 20*, 473–497.

Denham, S. A., & Burton, R. (1996). A social-emotional intervention for at-risk 4-year olds. *Journal of School Psychology, 34*, 225–245.

DeKlyen, M., & Odom, S. L. (1989). Activity structure and social interactions with peers in developmentally integrated play groups. *Journal of Early Intervention, 13*, 342–352.

Dunlap, G., Strain, P. S., Fox, L., Carta, J., Conroy, M., Smith, B., et al. (2006). Prevention and intervention with young children's challenging behavior: A summary of current knowledge. *Behavioral Disorders, 32*, 29–45.

Egeland, B., Kalkoske, M., Gottesman, N., & Erickson, M. F. (1990). Preschool behavior problems: Stability and factors accounting for change. *Journal of Child Psychology and Psychiatry, 31*, 891–909.

Fox, L., & Clarke, S. (2006). Aggression? Using positive behavior support to address challenging behavior. *Young Exceptional Children Monograph Series, 8*, 42–56.

Fox, L., Dunlap, G., & Cushing, L. (2002). Early intervention, positive behavior support, and transition to school. *Journal of Emotional and Behavior Disorders, 10*, 149–157.

Fox, L., Dunlap, G., Hemmeter, M. L., Joseph, G. E., & Strain, P. S. (2003). The teaching pyramid: A model for supporting social competence and preventing challenging behavior in young children. *Young Children, 58*, 48–52.

Fox, L., & Little, N. (2001). Starting early: School-wide behavior support in a community preschool. *Journal of Positive Behavior Interventions, 3*, 251–254.

Frede, E. C., Austin, A. B., & Lindauer, S. K. (1993). The relationship of specific developmentally appropriate teaching practices to children's skills in first grade. *Advances in Early Education and Child Care, 5*, 95–111

Gilliam, W. S. (2005). *Prekindergarteners left behind: Expulsion rates in state prekindergarten systems*. Retrieved July 20, 2005, from http://www.fcd-us.org/PDFs/NationalPreKExpulsionPaper03.02_new.pdf

Gordon, R. (1983). An operational classification of disease prevention. *Public Health Reports, 98*, 107–109.

Gresham, F. M., & Elliott, S. N. (1990). *Social Skills Rating System.* Bloomington, MN: Pearson Assessments.

Grisham-Brown, J., Hemmeter, M. L., & Pretti-Frontczak, K. (2005). *Blended practices for teaching young children in inclusive settings.* Baltimore: Brookes.

Hemmeter, M. L., & Fox, L. (2006). *Teaching Pyramid Observation Tool.* Unpublished assessment instrument.

Hemmeter, M. L., Fox, L., & Doubet, S. (2006). Together we can: An early childhood center's program wide approach to addressing challenging behavior. *Young Exceptional Children Monograph Series, 8*, 1–14.

Hemmeter, M. L., Fox, L., Jack, S., Broyles, L., & Doubet, S. (2007). A program-wide model of positive behavior support in early childhood settings. *Journal of Early Intervention, 29*, 337–355.

Hemmeter, M.L., Ostrosky, M., & Fox, L. (2006). Social and emotional foundations for early learning: A conceptual model for intervention. *School Psychology Review, 35*, 583–601.

Hill, W. (2003). *The National Reporting System: What is it and how will it work? Head Start child outcomes—setting the context for the National Reporting System* (Head Start Bulletin 76). Washington, DC: Department of Health and Human Services, Administration for Children and Families, Head Start Bureau.

Holloway, S. D., & Reichart-Erickson, M. (1988). The relationship of day care quality to children's free play behavior and social problem-solving skills. *Early Childhood Research Quarterly, 3*, 39–53.

Horner, R. H., & Sugai, G. (2000). School-wide behavior support: An emerging initiative. *Journal of Positive Behavior Interventions, 2*, 231–232.

Horner, R. H., Sugai, G., & Todd, A.W. (2001). "Data" need not be a four letter word: Using data to improve school wide discipline. *Beyond Behavior, 11*, 20–22.

Horner, R. H., Sugai, G., Todd, A. W., & Lewis-Palmer, T. (2005). Schoolwide positive behavior support. In L. M. Bambara & L. Kern (Eds.), *Individualized supports for students with problem behaviors: Designing positive behavior plans.* (pp. 359–390). New York: Guilford Press.

Howes, C., & Hamilton, C. E. (1992). Children's relationships with child care teachers: Stability and concordance with parental attachments. *Child Development, 63*, 867–878.

Howes, C., Phillips, D., & Whitebrook, M. (1992). Thresholds of quality: Implications for the social development of children in center-based child care. *Child Development, 63*, 449–460.

Howes, C., & Smith, E. (1995). Relations among child care quality, teacher behavior, children's play activities, emotional security, and cognitive activity in child care. *Early Childhood Research Quarterly, 10*, 381–404.

Jolivette, K., Wehby, J. H., Canale, J., & Massey, N.G. (2001). Effects of choice making opportunities on the behaviors of students with emotional and behavioral disorders. *Behavioral Disorders, 26*, 131–145.

Joseph, G. E., & Strain, P. S. (2003). Comprehensive evidence-based social emotional curricula for young children: An analysis of efficacious adoption potential. *Topics in Early Childhood Special Education, 23*, 65–76.

Kaufmann, R., & Wischmann, A. L. (1999). Communities supporting the mental health of young children and their families. In R. N. Roberts & R. R. Magrab (Eds.), *Where children live: Solutions for serving young children and their families* (pp. 175–210). Stamford, CT: Ablex.

Kontos, S. (1999). Preschool teachers' talk, roles, and activity settings during free play. *Early Childhood Research Quarterly, 14*, 363–383.

Kupersmidt, J. B., Bryant, D., & Willoughby, M. T. (2000). Prevalence of aggressive behaviors among preschoolers in Head Start and community child care programs. *Behavioral Disorders, 26*, 42–52.

Landy, S. (2002). Pathways to competence: Encouraging healthy social and emotional development in young children. Baltimore: Brookes.

Lavigne, J. V., Gibbons, R. D., Christoffel, K. K., Arend, R., Rosenbaum, D., Binns, H., et al. (1996). Prevalence rates and correlates of psychiatric disorders among preschool children. *Journal of the American Academy of Child and Adolescent Psychiatry, 35*, 204–214.

Lavigne, J. V., Cicchetti, C., Gibbons, R. D., Binns, H. J., Larsen, L., & DeVito, C. (2001). Oppositional defiant disorder with onset in preschool years: Longitudinal stability and pathways to other disorders. Journal of the Academy of Child and Adolescent Psychiatry, 40, 1393-1400.

Lohrmann-O'Rourke, S., Knoster, T., Sabatine, K., Smith, D., Horvath, B., & Llewellyn, G. (2000). School-wide application of PBS in the Bangor Area School District. *Journal of Positive Behavior Interventions, 2*, 238–240.

Mill, D., & Romano-White, D. (1999). Correlates of affectionate and angry behavior in child care educators of preschool-aged children. *Early Childhood Research Quarterly, 14*, 155–178.

Mize, J., & Ladd, G. W. (1990). Toward the development of successful social skills training for pre-school children. In S. R. Asher & J. D. Coie (Eds.), *Peer rejection in childhood* (pp. 338–361). New York: Cambridge University Press.

National Institute of Child Health and Human Development Early Child Care Research Network. (2003). Social functioning in first grade: Associations with earlier home and child care predictors and with current classroom experiences. *Child Development, 74*, 1639–1662.

National Research Council. (2001). *Eager to learn: Educating our preschoolers*. Committee on Early Childhood Pedagogy, Commission on Behavioral and Social Sciences and Education, B. T. Bowman, M. S. Donovan, & M. S. Burns (Eds.). Washington, DC: National Academy Press.

Peisner-Feinberg, E., & Burchinal, M. (1997). Concurrent relations between child care quality and child outcomes: The study of cost, quality, and outcomes in child care centers. *Merrill-Palmer Quarterly, 43*, 451–477.

Peisner-Feinberg, E. S., Burchinal, M. R., Clifford, R. M., Culkin, M. L., Howes, C., Kagan, S. L., et al. (2000). *The children of the cost, quality, and outcomes study go to school: Technical report*. Chapel Hill: University of North Carolina at Chapel Hill, Frank Porter Graham Child Development Center.

Phillips, D. A., McCartney, K., & Scarr, S. (1987). Child-care quality and children's social development. *Developmental Psychology, 23*, 537–544.

Pianta, R. C., Steinberg, M., & Rollins, K. (1995). The first two years of school: Teacher child relationships and deflections in children's classroom adjustment. *Developmental and Psychopathology, 7*, 295–312.

Pierce, E. W., Ewing, L. J., & Campbell, S. B. (1999). Diagnostic status and symptomatic behavior of hard-to-manage preschool children in middle childhood and early adolescence. *Journal of Clinical Child Psychology, 28*, 44–57.

Powell, D., Dunlap, G., & Fox, L. (2006). Prevention and intervention for the challenging behaviors of toddlers and preschoolers. *Infants and Young Children, 19*, 25–35.

Qi, C. H., & Kaiser, A. P. (2003). Behavior problems of preschool children from low-income families: Review of the literature. *Topics in Early Childhood Special Education, 23*, 188–216.

Quesenberry, A (2007). *Examining the relationships between behavior policies and procedures, teachers' perceptions of efficacy and job satisfaction, and children's social skills and challenging behaviors in head start settings*. Unpublished doctoral dissertation, University of Illinois, Champaign.

Quesenberry, A., & Hemmeter, M. L. (2005, March). *Implementing a program-wide model of positive behavior supports in early childhood settings: Current practices, challenges and barriers*. Paper presented at the Association for Positive Behavior Supports Conference, Tampa, FL.

Quesenberry, A., Ostrosky, M. M., & Hemmeter, M. L. (2007, October). *Recommended practices in behavior policy and procedure development and implementation*. Paper presented at the Division of Early Childhood of the Council for Exceptional Children International Conference, Niagara Falls, Ontario, Canada.

Reichle, J., McEvoy, M., Davis, C., Rogers, E., Feeley, K., Johnston, S., et al. (1996). Coordinating preservice and in-service training of early interventionists to serve preschoolers who engage in challenging behavior. In L. K. Koegel, R. L. Koegel, & G. Dunlap (Eds.), *Positive behavioral support: Including people with difficult behavior in the community* (pp. 227–264). Baltimore: Brookes.

Schneider, J. (1974). Turtle technique in the classroom. *Teaching Exceptional Children, 7*, 21–24.

Serna, L., Nielsen, E., Lambros, K., & Forness, S. (2000). Primary prevention with children at risk for emotional or behavioral disorders: Data on a universal intervention for Head Start classrooms. *Behavioral Disorders, 26*, 70–84.

Shaw, D., Gilliom, M., & Giovannelli, J. (2000). Aggressive behavior disorders. In C. H. Zeanah (Ed.), *Handbook of infant mental health* (pp. 397–411). New York: Guilford Press.

Shonkoff, J. P., & Phillips, D.A. (Eds.) (2000). *From neurons to neighborhoods: The science of early childhood development.* Washington, DC: National Academy Press.

Shure, M. B., & Spivack, G. (1980). Interpersonal problem solving as a mediator of behavioral adjustment in preschool and kindergarten children. *Journal of Applied Developmental Psychology, 1*, 29–44.

Simeonsson, R. J. (1991). Primary, secondary, and tertiary prevention in early intervention. *Journal of Early Intervention, 15*, 124–134.

Simpson, J. S., Jivanjee, P., Koroloff, N., Doerfler, A., & Garcia, M. (2001). *Promising practices in early childhood mental health.* Systems of care: Promising practices in children's mental health, 2001 series, Vol. 3. Washington, DC: Center for Effective Collaboration and Practice, American Institutes for Research.

Stormont, M., Lewis, T. J., & Beckner, R. (2005). Positive behavior support systems: Applying key features in preschool settings. *Teaching Exceptional Children, 37*, 42–49.

Stormont, M. A., Smith, S. C. & Lewis, T. J. (2007). Teacher implementation of precorrection and praise statements in head start classrooms as a component of a program-wide system of positive behavior support. *Journal of Behavioral Education, 16*, 280–290.

Taylor-Greene, S. J., & Kartub, D. T., (2000). Durable implementation of school-wide behavior support: The high five program. *Journal of Positive Behavior Interventions, 2*, 231–232.

U.S. Public Health Service. (2000). *Report of the surgeon general's conference on children's mental health: A national action agenda.* Washington, DC: Department of Health and Human Services.

Vaughn, S. R., & Ridley, C. R. (1983). A preschool interpersonal problem solving program: Does it affect behavior in the classroom? *Child Study Journal, 13*, 1–11.

Walker, H. M., Horner, R. H., Sugai, G., Bullis, M., Sprague, J. R., Bricker, D., et al. (1996). Integrated approaches to preventing antisocial behavior patterns among school-age children and youth. *Journal of Emotional and Behavioral Disorders, 4*, 194–209.

Webster-Stratton, C., Reid, M. J., & Hammond, M. (2001). Preventing conduct problems, promoting social competence: A parent and teacher training partnership in Head Start. *Journal of Clinical Child Psychology, 30*, 283–302.

West, J., Denton, K., & Germino-Hausken, E. (2000). *America's kindergartener: Findings from the early childhood longitudinal study, kindergarten class of 1998–99, fall 1998.* Washington, D.C.: U.S. Department of Education, National Center for Educational Statistics.

Zill, N., Resnick, G., Kwang, K., O'Donnell, K., Sorongon, A., Ziv, Y., et al. (2006). *Head Start Performance Measures Center Family and Child Experiences Survey (FACES 2000)* (Technical Report). Washington, DC: Administration for Children and Families, U.S. Department of Health and Human Services.

# 9

# Integrating PBS, Mental Health Services, and Family-Driven Care

**ALBERT J. DUCHNOWSKI and KRISTA KUTASH**

The purpose of this chapter is to provide information on and a framework for the necessary and ongoing merger and collaboration between the positive behavior support (PBS) and mental health communities to provide effective services for families and their children who have challenging behaviors. While both communities have recognized the need to collaborate with families as equal decision-making partners, the process has evolved to another level with the recent promotion of family-driven care as a necessary characteristic of effective services. The findings and recommendations from the president's New Freedom Commission on Mental Health (2003) are serving as a catalyst to advance a transformation of mental health care in this country to a system that is family and consumer driven.

The integration of the PBS and mental health communities with families has the potential to achieve significant improvement in access to services and the outcomes of the receipt of services for children and youth who have emotional and behavioral disturbances. This is a time of great opportunity for advancement in achieving this goal, and this chapter presents information aimed at contributing to this effort.

We present a mental health perspective on treating children and youth who have emotional and behavioral disturbances and highlight the fit with PBS. In addition, we present details on the emerging concept of family-driven care and how the integration of PBS and mental health can accommodate this evolving model of service delivery. The chapter incorporates the common themes emphasized in the other chapters in this text if feasible and closes

**ALBERT J. DUCHNOWSKI** • University of South Florida
**KRISTA KUTASH** • University of South Florida

with a discussion of the public health model as a potential framework to guide the future integration of PBS, mental health, and families.

While PBS and mental health services for children can be implemented in a variety of settings that include the home, schools, mental health center offices, and other community settings, there is a major focus in this chapter on school-based services. We have chosen this focus because there are approximately 100,000 school buildings in the United States with about 53 million students and 6 million adults working in these schools. This is about one fifth of the population of the country. Add to this the parents and caregivers of these children and the professionals who work for mental health agencies and other social services agencies that visit schools and provide related services to children, and the portion of the population that interfaces in some way with schools is substantial. Consequently, by targeting schools as a focal point, there is tremendous potential to realize the promise of federal, state, and local policies and reforms, and the benefits of interventions developed from the broad research community that are aimed at improving the lives of children who exhibit challenging behaviors. We examine the theoretical and empirical contributions of the discipline of mental health and emphasize the expanded scope of influence of these contributions when implementation in schools is emphasized. Another factor in adopting a school focus is the finding that fewer than one third of children who need mental health service receive it (Farmer, Mustillo, Burns, & Costello, 2005), and of those children who receive any mental health service at all, the majority receive it from their school (Burns et al., 1995).

## SYSTEM REFORM: IMPETUS FOR CHANGE AND IMPROVEMENT

Children who have emotional and behavioral disorders (EBDs) and their families interact with many agencies in the search for effective services to improve the functioning of their children. Among the array of social service providers that have some responsibility for and expertise in implementing programs for children who have EBD, the education and the mental health systems typically are the major sources of resources. The laws, policies, and reform initiatives of the education and mental health agencies establish a milieu within which current services and practices are developed and made available to children and families in need. While an in-depth examination of the education and special education systems is provided in other chapters of this text, we start with a summary of those policies and reforms to provide context for the analysis of the mental health system that will follow.

### Education and Special Education Policy and Reform

Arguably, the Individuals With Disabilities Education Act (IDEA), originally passed in 1976 as the Education of All Handicapped Children's Act, is the most comprehensive piece of federal legislation to affect children who have disabilities and their families, including children who have emotional disturbances. In the case of children who have emotional disabilities, however, IDEA is narrowly focused on students who have an identifiable disability that may affect various life domains but *must also interfere with the student's educational achievement.* The variability in interpretation of eligibility criteria at the local level has resulted in the continuous underidentification of this disability group. There has never been more than 1% of the school-aged population identified as having EBDs and served in special education programs despite prevalence estimates closer to 5% (Kutash, Duchnowski, & Friedman, 2005).

On the positive side, under the IDEA regulations the related services needed to ensure an appropriate education are prescribed as an entitlement of the act. Related services may include psychological counseling, the implementation of behavioral plans based on functional behavioral assessments, and the inclusion of positive behavioral interventions and supports. While there is room to improve the amount of related services provided to children who have EBDs (Wagner et al., 2006), the requirements of IDEA provide the only "entitlement" at present that children have to receive mental health services.

The other major piece of legislation in the education system is the No Child Left Behind (NCLB) Act, signed into law in 2002. It provides a detailed description of goals set forth for the educational system. The primary purpose of the act is to improve achievement of students by (a) increasing accountability for student performance; (b) focusing on what works (research-based programs and practices); (c) reducing bureaucracy and increasing flexibility (increasing flexible funding at the local level); and (d) empowering parents.

In addition, NCLB addresses the emotional functioning of all children, and a specific section of the act (Title V) outlines initiatives aimed at ensuring the emotional well-being of America's youth. With 53 million children in school and an estimated 20% of all children meeting criteria, at a point in time, for a diagnosable mental illness at a level of impairment that requires some type of intervention (Kutash et al., 2005), there is the potential that over 10 million children need some type of help to meet the goals relating to emotional well-being in NCLB. These numbers reveal the scope of the challenge for the nation to ensure the emotional development of America's school-aged children and youth and the need for effective interagency collaboration.

While NCLB has been the major impetus for reform in the general education system, a report from a commission appointed by President Bush specifically addressed the special education system and needed reforms and improvements. *A New Era: Revitalizing Special Education for Children and Their Families* (2002) is the report of the President's Commission on Excellence in Special Education. Like NCLB, this report called for an emphasis on results as opposed to an overemphasis on documenting compliance in the implementation of IDEA. Evidence-based practices and rigorous research to evaluate the practices are major activities promoted in the report. Increased family involvement was presented as one of the major goals of the report. As in NCLB, parents are taken to a level of empowerment at which they may choose a different school for their child if the child's progress is considered to be unsatisfactory over a period of time. This is a very powerful mechanism aimed at self-determination of parents in designing the education program for their child and very consistent with the policy of "family-driven care," discussed in this chapter as a major part of reform in the mental health system.

## Transforming the Mental Health System

A significant set of sentinel public health findings were summarized in the surgeon general's report on the mental health of the nation (U.S. Department of Health and Human Services [USDHHS], 1999) and documented the extent of unmet mental health needs for both adults and children and the burden to the nation in terms of lost and ruined lives as well as devastatingly high financial costs (Rice & Miller, 1996). In chapter 3 of the surgeon general's report, issues specific to children were presented, including evidence of a strengthening of the knowledge base over the past decade on efficacious treatments and services for children who have serious emotional disturbances. For example, there have been advances in the treatment of specific disorders such as depression in children (e.g., Kaslow & Thomson, 1998) and attention deficit disorder with hyperactivity (e.g., MTA Cooperative Group, 1998). Home-based services such as multisystemic therapy and therapeutic foster care have been demonstrated to have a positive impact on child and family outcomes (Burns & Hoagwood, 2002). Unfortunately, these efficacious services present many challenges to the provider network when they attempt to transfer these interventions and programs to community-based settings. The net result is that unmet needs have continued into the new millennium, prompting a call for a transformation of the mental health system in this country into one that is more responsive and has the capacity to better meet the mental health needs of its citizens.

In April 2002, President Bush appointed the New Freedom Commission on Mental Health, charging the commission to "study the mental health service delivery system, and to make recommendations that would enable adults with serious mental illnesses and children with serious emotional disturbance to live, work, learn, and participate fully in their communities" (2003, p. 1). The commission adopted two broad principles to guide its work. These were (a) services and treatments must be consumer and family centered, with a real commitment to giving choices and options, and (b) a focus on recovery and resilience, increasing consumers' ability to cope with challenges, not just reduce symptoms.

The commission utilized the action word *transform* as the hallmark characteristic of the reform activities it would promote. The mental health system needed to undergo a fundamental *transformation* into a consumer- and family-driven approach that that would facilitate recovery and build resilience to face life's challenges at all developmental stages. The commission identified six goals as the foundation for transforming mental health care in America. These goals are listed in Table 9.1.

While all six goals are important, Goals 2 and 4 are specifically related to the subject of this chapter and are more fully discussed. In proposing

**Table 9.1.** Goals of the New Freedom Commission on Mental Health (2003)

1. Americans will understand that mental health is essential to overall health;
2. Mental health care is consumer and family driven;
3. Disparities in mental health care are eliminated;
4. Early mental health screening, assessment, and referral to services are common practice;
5. Excellent mental health care is delivered and research is accelerated; and
6. Technology is used to access mental health care and information.

*Note.* From President's New Freedom Commission on Mental Health (2003). *Achieving the Promise: Transforming mental health care use in America.* Final Report (DHHS Publication No. SMA 03-3832). Rockville MD: US Dept of Helth and Human Services.

Goal 2, the commission envisioned a mental health system in which every consumer would have an individualized treatment plan, and consumers and families of children would be fully involved in directing the system toward providing interventions and programs that would lead toward recovery and full participation in life.

Goal 4 promotes the mental health of children and recommends the improvement and expansion of school mental health programs. While the commission agreed that the mission of schools is to educate students, it also noted that children who have EBDs have the highest rates of school failure. The commission further noted that school is where children spend most of their day and echoed the surgeon general in identifying school as the ideal location for implementing the whole range of mental health services from prevention to treatment. To this, we would add that there is a growing body of research (e.g., Greenberg et al., 2003; Zins, Weissberg, Wang, & Wahlberg, 2004) examining the reciprocal nature of academic and emotional functioning, and early findings support the conclusion that learning strategies for children who have EBDs should include both academic and emotional/behavioral components.

## Reform and Family Impact

Families of children who have EBDs seek and hope for help from a variety of agencies in the community, with education and mental health probably the major participants in the process. The goals and mission of these agencies define the nature of the assistance they will provide, and the current reform initiatives that are being implemented in each will further delineate the kind of services that are available. While the agencies do have their differences, there are many areas of overlap. In education, there is the individualized educational plan (IEP), which is mandated, and the mental health system has set a goal to require an individual treatment plan for all consumers. Both systems are oriented toward empowering families in the development of services for their children, and both systems seek a focus on results through making services available that are supported by research. While the degree to which these reforms are present in local communities varies, the more families become informed, the faster the scaling up process will occur, leading to more effective services.

## THE MENTAL HEALTH MODEL

Both the education and mental health systems play an important role in providing services to children who have EBDs. However, the two systems have not produced a record of effective collaboration, contributing to the disappointing outcomes for this group of children. While there are areas of commonality in the two systems, as pointed out, there are some fundamental differences between the systems that affect their perspective in serving children who have EBDs. Table 9.2 contains a list of some key factors that shape the perspectives of the two systems and also can serve as barriers to more effective collaboration.

As Table 9.2 illustrates, there are more areas in which the differing perspectives can impede collaboration compared to facilitating the implementation of effective services. For example, the emergence of distinct conceptual frameworks describing the target behavior for each system has resulted in different terminology that goes beyond simple semantic differences. Services and programs from the perspective of the education system are likely to be described as meeting the needs of children who have "behavior disorders or challenging behaviors" or preventing such behaviors. The number of discipline referrals to the principal's office is a major outcome measure along with improved academic achievement, especially in math and reading. Programs and interventions implemented by the mental health system target children who are mentally ill or emotionally disturbed and who meet the criteria for a diagnosis in the current edition of the *Diagnostic and Statistical Manual of Mental Disorders* (American Psychiatric Association, 1994) or those that may be at risk for mental illness. The emphasis is on diagnosing and treating to improve functioning and reduce relapse and reoccurrence. Functioning in school is one domain of interest, along with home and community. One consequence of

**Table 9.2.** Contrasting Perspectives in the Education and Mental Health Systems

| | Education System | Mental Health System |
|---|---|---|
| Overarching influence | Individuals with Disabilities Education Act (IDEA) | *Diagnostic and Statistical Manual (DSM)* |
| Conceptual framework, language | Behavior disorders, challenging behavior, academic deficits | Psychopathology, abnormal behavior, impaired functioning |
| Important theoretical influences | Behaviorism, social learning theory | Psychoanalytic approaches, behavior theory, cognitive psychology, developmental psychology, biological/genetic perspectives, psychopharmacology |
| Focus of intervention | Behavior management, skill development, academic improvement | Insight, awareness, improved emotional functioning |
| Common focus | Improving social and adaptive functioning<br>Importance of and need to increase availability, access, and range of services | |

the difference in vocabulary used in each system is the observation that reports of research from the different perspectives are frequently published in journals and texts that are not read by all the disciplines concerned with children who have EBDs. This results in a failure to understand the different approaches to intervention across disciplines and impedes the implementation of comprehensive, effective programs at a level of scale needed for significant improvement in outcomes for the millions of children affected by EBD.

In addition, researchers and practitioners are shaped and guided by the theoretical context in which they have been trained or have developed after their formal training. Clearly, these perspectives filter how they view the world, human behavior, and specific processes such as how they conceive of services for children who have EBDs. Researchers and practitioners trained in the college of education are more likely to be influenced by behavioral and social learning approaches. On the other hand, those trained in a psychology department in the college of arts and sciences are more likely to have been exposed to a broad array of theories that include psychodynamic, behavioral, cognitive-behavioral, and neurological and biochemical premises, among others. These theoretical perspectives guide thinking about the nature and goals of interventions as well as indicators of success. As a result, programs for children who have or are at risk for EBDs can be found that range from schoolwide approaches to promote prosocial behavior as an alternative to aggression at recess (Todd, Haugen, Anderson, & Spriggs, 2002) to the coping with stress course (Clarke et al., 1995), which uses cognitive-behavioral interventions to help students cope with irrational thoughts associated with depression.

In general, PBS can be considered to be an educational program or intervention. Its theoretical roots in applied behavior analysis and its relationship to special education are extensively discussed in other chapters of this text. In this section, we examine more fully the mental health model, emphasizing its application to services in schools and potential areas of collaboration and merger with PBS.

## The Mental Health Spectrum

Mrazek and Haggerty (1994) conceptualized the array of services and interventions designed for children who are considered to be mentally ill or emotionally disturbed or at risk as a continuum that they called the *mental health spectrum*. They originally developed the spectrum as a framework for prevention research in the broad mental health field, and its effectiveness as a guiding framework in the field is evidenced by continued reference to it and adaptations by more recent mental health services researchers. An example is the recent adaptation by Weisz, Sandler, Durlak, and Anton (2005) presented in Fig. 9.1. In their updated framework, they linked evidence-based prevention and treatment and include health promotion/ positive development strategies to the mental health spectrum as a component that precedes universal prevention strategies. They emphasized the "permeable" separation between indicated prevention strategies and

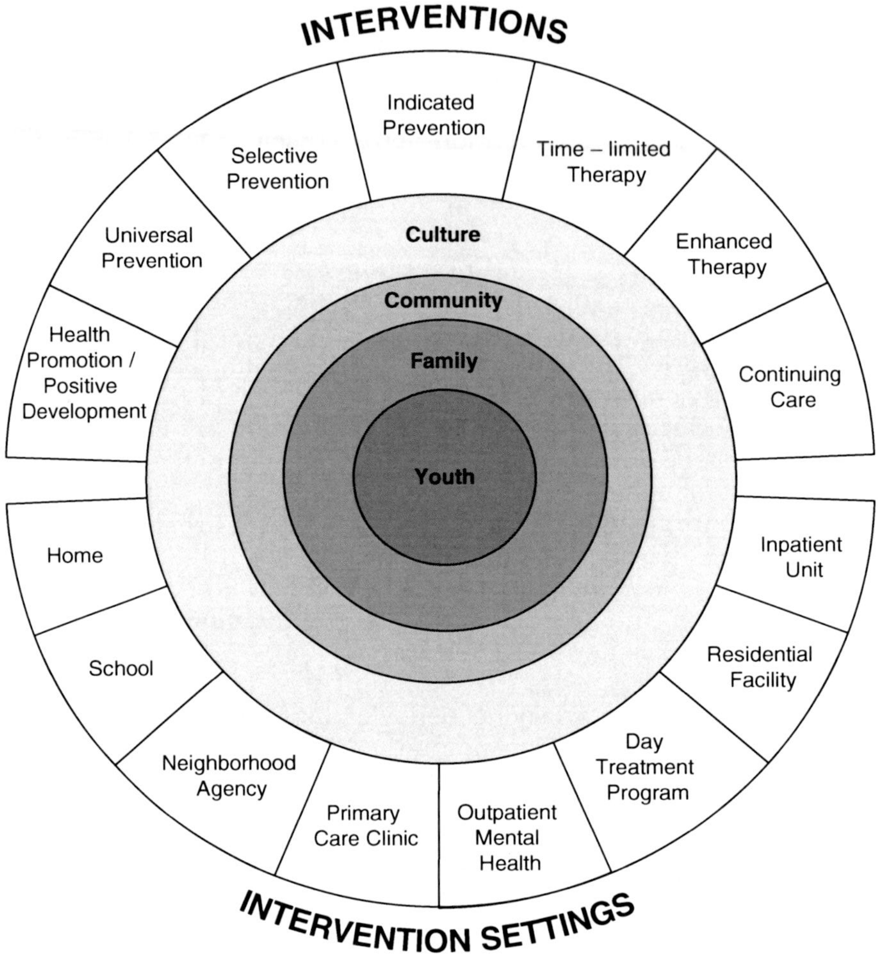


**Fig. 9.1.** The continuum of mental health services and interventions. From "Promoting and Protecting Youth Mental Health Through Evidence-Based Prevention and Treatment," by J. Weisz, I. Sandler, J. Durlak, & B. Anton, 2005, *American Psychologist, 60*, p. 633. Copyright 2005 by American Psychological Association.

treatment and promote a focus on evidence-based practice as a unifying construct throughout the entire spectrum. The framework proposes that strengths reside in youth, families, communities, and culture depicted in the center of the illustration. Interventions that offer support are arrayed in the upper semicircle and setting locations in the lower semicircle.

While the role of the mental health system in the schools has not always been readily accepted or effectively implemented, Weisz and his colleagues have brought attention to the need for school-mental health collaboration by clearly identifying "school" as a setting for many mental health interventions in the spectrum of services. This fits well with the growing movement to expand school-based mental health services that are provided by community mental health centers (Weist, Lowie, Flaherty, & Pruitt, 2001). The framework developed by Weisz and colleagues is the result of an extended period of research, analysis of findings, advocacy, and rethinking the process of providing mental health service to children by the broad mental health community.

## The Multidisciplinary, Multiagency Imperative

Office-based individual or group therapy and residential treatment were the mainstays of mental health service to children for decades. Growing dissatisfaction with the outcomes of this service array and the relatively low number of children in need of service who could actually access these services prompted a call for reform and improvement. In the early 1980s, the Children's Defense Fund commissioned Jane Knitzer to study the mental health system in America and how children in need received services. The results of her study were published in the landmark book *Unclaimed Children* (Knitzer, 1982), in which the multifaceted problems of children in need of mental health services were described, and the failure of the multiple agencies responsible for providing care was documented. Knitzer described the frustrating journey of families from schools, to the mental health center, the child welfare agency, and ultimately the juvenile justice agency as a revolving door from office to office and the passing on of responsibility for providing adequate care.

Responding to Knitzer's findings and those from other researchers, the National Institute of Mental Health (NIMH) initiated the Child and Adolescent Service System Program (CASSP) in 1984 (Day & Roberts, 1991), a modestly funded program to provide seed money at the state level to coordinate the agencies that are involved with children who have mental health problems. The CASSP program stimulated research that further examined the multiple problems of children who were called seriously emotionally disturbed and the multiple agencies and disciplines that attempted to provide care (e.g., Greenbaum et al., 1998; Silver et al., 1992). In addition, the guiding principles and framework of interagency collaboration promoted by CASSP prompted Stroul and Friedman (1986) to produce the monograph *A System of Care*, which has come to serve as the blueprint for children's mental health services in this country (Kutash, Duchnowski, & Lynn, 2006).

## The System of Care

The System of Care (SOC) was developed for children with severe problems, persisting for at least a year, resulting in impairment in multiple domains of functioning (see Fig. 9.2). Children who are served by the SOC will most likely (although not always) be in special education programs in school. Their families may be clients of the child welfare system, and some children may be involved with the juvenile justice system. The children have more health problems than peers with other types of disability, and as they get older co-occurring substance abuse problems increase (Greenbaum et al., 1998).

The SOC can provide crisis intervention, long-term therapy, and hospitalization if necessary. Out-of-home placements such as foster care, detention, and residential treatment may be provided, but intensive family

**Fig. 9.2.** System of care. 'From *A System of Care for Children and Youth With Severe Emotional Disturbances* (p. 30), by B. A. Stroul and R. M. Friedman, 1986, Washington, DC: Georgetown University Child Development Center, CASSP Technical Assistance Center.

preservation services are also available. At this intensive level of service, the "wraparound" approach may be used in a community. Essential to wraparound is the notion that the child and the family are central; services are individually tailored to the strengths and needs of the family and are "wrapped around" them rather than the child being placed into a program because of his or her diagnosis or pattern of behavior (Eber, Sugai, Smith, & Scott, 2002; Robbins & Armstrong, 2005; VanDenBerg & Grealish, 1996). Policy makers and practitioners need to understand that the SOC and wraparound are more of a philosophy of support for children and families rather than a specific intervention. They are heavily value laden and promote strengths-based assessment, families being accepted as equal decision-making partners, culturally competent services, and a commitment to least-restrictive, community-based treatment.

The SOC and wraparound are designed for children exhibiting the most severe level of impairment, and in the ideal, there will be a community team of professionals joined by the family and their advocates engaged in developing an individualized treatment or service plan. There should be a level of collaboration to ensure that the plan will be compatible with an existing IEP if the child is in a special education program. Because of the complexity of the problems and the services array, a case manager is available to support the family and assist the agencies to better coordinate service delivery. While a community may designate a lead agency to implement the SOC, it must be recognized that all agency representatives and the family are equal decision-making partners.

The SOC is over 20 years old now, with wraparound slightly more recent. Funded by the Children's Community Mental Health Services Act of 1992, over 140 communities and tribal nations have implemented SOCs, affecting several thousand children. In general, the engagement of schools in this initiative has been weak, and the overall effectiveness of the SOC has been mixed but promising (Kutash et al., 2005). In addition, there are very few examples of the implementation of PBS as part of the service array in the SOC communities.

## Interconnected Systems

Given the barriers facing the traditional mental health system in its attempts to implement services that are more integrated, accessible, and effective, a model that is guided by a public health strategy and based on collaboration between systems has emerged as an alternative approach for implementing mental health services for children. This model, which we call interconnected systems (see Fig. 9.3), is composed of a continuum of services that aims to balance efforts at mental health promotion, prevention programs, early detection and treatment, and intensive intervention, maintenance, and recovery programs (National Institute for Health Care Management, 2005). The model is a series of three interconnected ovals representing systems of prevention, systems of early intervention, and systems of care. The model has been most clearly articulated and promoted by the Center for Mental Health in Schools at the University of California at Los Angeles (Adelman & Taylor, 2006) and the Center for School Mental Health Assistance at the University of Maryland (Weist, Goldstein, Morris, & Bryant, 2003). In this model, resources from the school and the community are pooled to produce integrated programs at the three levels of service need.

## The Collaboration of PBS and SOC

The lack of widespread implementation of PBS as a component of services provided in communities utilizing the SOC is puzzling. There are examples in Kentucky (Robbins & Armstrong, 2005) and Illinois (Eber et al., 2002) demonstrating its feasibility and positive results. In addition, PBS and the SOC share fundamental values and principles. In their monograph on the SOC, Stroul and Friedman (1986) identified three core values for the SOC: child

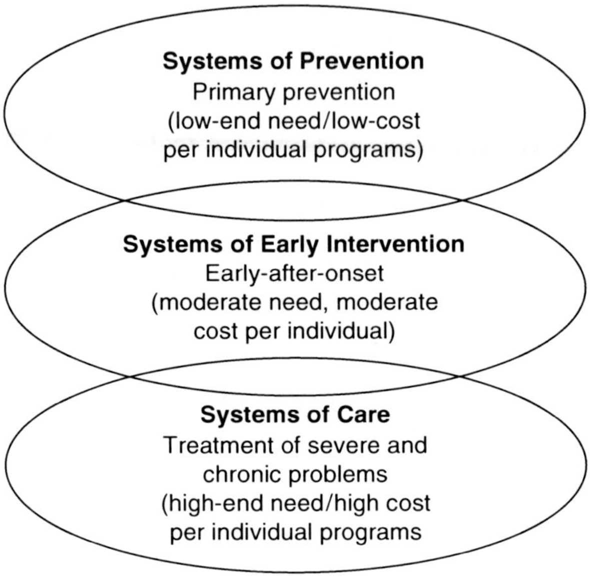


**Fig. 9.3.** The mental health (MH) model of interconnected systems. Adapted from *The School Leader's Guide to Student Learning Supports: New Directions for Addressing Barriers to Learning* (p. 32), by H. S. Adelman and L. Taylor, 2006, Thousand Oaks, CA: Corwin Press.

**Table 9.3.** Guiding Principles of the System of Care

| |
|---|
| 1 Access to an array of comprehensive services |
| 2. Individualized services guided by an individual plan |
| 3. The least restrictive normative environment possible |
| 4. Families should be equal decision-making partners |
| 5. Services should be linked and integrated across agencies |
| 6. Case management should be available to ensure coordination of services |
| 7. Early identification and intervention should be promoted |
| 8. Transition services to adulthood should be available |
| 9. The rights of children with EBD should be protected through advocacy |
| 10. Services should be provided without regard to race, religion, national origin, sex, or any other characteristic in a culturally responsive manner. |

*Note*. From *A System of Care for Children and Youth With Severe Emotional Disturbances* (Rev. ed.), by B. A. Stroul & R. M. Friedman R. M., 1986, Washington, DC: Georgetown University Child Development Center, CASSP Technical Assistance Center.

centered and family focused; community based; and culturally competent. They also developed 10 guiding principles, presented in Table 9.3.

The core values and principles of PBS are fully discussed in several other chapters in this text. For example, see Chapter 1 and 2 in this text.

Clearly, there is a great deal of compatibility in these two processes that would have predicted a greater degree of cooperation and collaboration between them. The barriers summarized in Table 9.1 may be more formidable than we would like to admit. Fortunately, the network of researchers and practitioners who are becoming literate with the multidisciplinary literature on children's mental health issues is increasing. Another source of optimism is the potential for the widespread influence of family-driven care to contribute to producing more effective SOCs with a substantial presence of PBS. The following section examines this possibility.

## FAMILY-DRIVEN CARE

As noted, there is growing support across the country to transform the mental health system into one that is more responsive to consumers and families and accessible. In the case of services for children, the term *family-driven care* is used to describe the process of transformation. While the concept of family-driven care is new and evolving, there are emerging definitions in the field. A definition has been proposed in a working draft of a training guide developed through collaboration between the national office of the Federation of Families for Children's Mental Health and the federal Substance Abuse and Mental Health Services Administration (SAMHSA) (Osher, Osher, & Blau, 2006); see Table 9.4 for the definition.

The concept of family-driven care is new for most of us, although it has roots in both the education and mental health systems. For many years now, IDEA has called for family- and student-directed IEPs, admittedly with little success. Practitioners of PBS have promoted person-centered planning and engaging families in the treatment of children. In the mental health field, the SOC model and wraparound services have promoted a planning process for treatment that is family focused. Today, under the transformation initiative, both the ED and mental health systems are beginning to use "family-driven" language. Transformation that is effective will require attitudinal change, new skills, redeployment of resources, and time for all of this to occur. Transformation to family-driven care is complex and multidimensional and in

**Table 9.4.** Definition of Family-Driven Care

Family-driven means families have a primary decision-making role in the care of their own children as well as the policies and procedures governing care for all children in their community, state, tribe, territory, and nation. This includes

- choosing supports, services, and providers
- setting goals
- designing and implementing programs
- monitoring outcomes
- participating in funding decisions
- determining the effectiveness of all efforts to promote the mental health and well being of children and youth

*Note.* From *Shifting Gears to Family-Driven Care: Ambassadors Tool Kit*, by T. W. Osher, D. Osher, & G. Blau, 2006, Rockville, MD: Federation of Families for Children's Mental Health.

some cases will be revolutionary. Osher and colleagues (2006) listed 10 principles (see Table 9.5) that guide the development of family-driven care, and these principles illustrate the multifaceted nature of the task. For many practitioners, the adoption of these principles is visionary and definitely revolutionary, but for parents and their children, it is viewed as obligatory.

## Changing the Culture

Many education and mental health professionals, during their training, have been presented with faulty information about the causal relationship between parent characteristics and the emotional and behavioral characteristics of their children. Concepts such as "icebox mother," "schizophrenegenic mother," parents who put their children in double-bind situations in which they must fail, and so on do not have supporting evidence, and the results of rigorous studies disprove their validity. Unfortunately, the influence of these rejected theories continues to affect how many professionals perceive families. Professionals need to incorporate into their understanding of families the concept that the roles of families have changed over time and continue to evolve at present. These roles have changed due to new research, federal initiatives, and new interventions for children who have emotional and behavioral disturbances. This evolution encompasses the last six decades, is an ongoing process, and is summarized in Table 9.6.

**Table 9.5.** Principles of Family-Driven Care

- Families and youth are given accurate, understandable, and complete information necessary to set goals and to make choices for improved planning for individual children and their families.
- Families and youth, providers, and administrators embrace the concept of sharing decision making and responsibility for outcomes.
- Families and youth are organized to collectively use their knowledge and skills as a force for systems transformation.
- Families and family-run organizations engage in peer support activities to reduce isolation, gather and disseminate accurate information, and strengthen the family voice.
- Families and family-run organizations provide direction for decisions that have an impact on funding for services, treatments, and supports.
- Providers take the initiative to change practice from provider driven to family driven.
- Administrators allocate staff, training, support, and resources to make family-driven practice work at the point at which services and supports are delivered to children, youth, and families.
- Community attitude change efforts focus on removing barriers and discrimination created by stigma.
- Communities embrace, value, and celebrate the diverse cultures of their children, youth, and families.
- Everyone who connects with children, youth, and families continually advances their own cultural and linguistic responsiveness as the population served changes.

*Note.* From *Shifting Gears to Family-Driven Care: Ambassadors Tool Kit*, by T. W. Osher, D. Osher, & G. Blau, 2006, Rockville, MD: Federation of Families for Children's Mental Health.

**Table 9.6.** Evolution of the Role of Families

| | |
|---|---|
| Mid-1900s | Family members not involved in child's treatment. |
| 1950–1960s | Mental health professionals began to question the absence of families from their child's care. "Family therapy" as treatment became increasingly popular. |
| 1960–1970s | Families of children with developmental disabilities began advocating for increased family participation in children's health services. |
| 1980s | Mental health professionals questioned beliefs that family members were responsible for their child's mental health problems. Parents and supportive professionals continue to advocate for increased family participation in services. |
| 1990s | Systems of care offer services based on child and family strengths. Collaboration increasingly a goal of participants in system of care. |
| 2000s | Emergence of family-driven care. |

The early beliefs that families caused mental illness in their children or that they all required therapy themselves were challenged by data from new research. This does not deny the possibility that a family may abuse their children or neglect their children because of substance abuse, for example. Some parents may experience stress that is related to their child's disability and may benefit from therapy. The research literature does indicate that there are many causes of impaired functioning in children, and we must not engage in unproven stereotypical thinking.

In the 1980s and 1890s, the SOC movement, wraparound programs, and PBS emerged to help children who have emotional and behavioral disturbances. At this time, families began to be accepted as partners in planning effective treatment for their children. More recently, families have been trained and given the role of evaluators of programs that are intended to help their children. This has evolved into the current role of families as policy makers through the development of family-driven care.

The basic foundation of family-driven care is the partnership between families and the professionals who provide services for their children. This partnership can serve as the impetus and support to change the culture that currently exists in many communities. From the perspective of families, the current culture promoted by the professional community is too often characterized by blame, suspicion, mistrust, condescension, frustration, and litigation. A shift is needed to a culture that values each partner, focuses on strengths, shares a common vision, pools resources, shows respect and understanding of each other, and advocates to strengthen families and the systems that serve them.

Strategies need to be implemented through schools, PBS programs, and mental health centers that will support families in the transformation process and increase the degree to which families are engaged with professionals. In this way, family involvement in the education and treatment of their child who has an EBD will increase with an ultimate positive impact on the child's functioning and outcomes.

## Families Need Information

Families will play a critical role in the transformation to a family-driven system of care. While they cannot be expected to master the service delivery system at the level of a professional, they will need to become familiar with basic components of the major models of service currently available. Both the education system and the mental health system have produced interventions aimed at skill training to promote the social and adaptive functioning of children as well as academic improvement. Three important processes, PBS, wraparound, and response to intervention (RtI) offer frameworks that are congruent and can serve to help unify the efforts of education staff, mental health practitioners, and families to provide evidence-based practices to improve the functioning of children who have EBDs. There are specific chapters in this text on the three frameworks (PBS, wraparound, and RtI), and families are encouraged to read the information in these chapters and use the knowledge they gain to further the progress of family-driven care.

To some degree, the implementation of a synthesis of PBS, wraparound, and RtI will require a restructuring of how services are provided, what kinds of services are provided, and a mutual understanding of the language, theories, and perspectives by members of each system. These three processes require a team approach (that includes families), an emphasis on problem solving, a need to ensure continuous progress, and the use of interventions that are empirically supported and aimed at the development of skills to improve functioning. The goals of the national transformation initiative are consistent with the development and implementation of these types of services.

Essentially, what is needed for the community, made up of children and families, schools, and service providers, is to become an organized team that has three basic features:

1. Common vision: The mission, goal, and purpose of the team that provides support and service to children who have emotional disturbances is shared by all the stakeholders and serves as the basis for decision making and action planning.
2. Common language: Communication is informative, efficient, effective, and relevant to all the members of the team, especially families.
3. Common experience: The actions, procedures, and operations are experienced by all the members of the team.

As in most reform movements, there are small steps and large steps that can be taken to achieve desired change in how care is provided. Osher and colleagues (2006) proposed some examples of methods and procedures to increase family voice and choice. These include (a) ensuring that meetings occur at times that are realistic for families to attend; (b) conducting meetings in culturally and linguistically competent environments; (c) ensuring that family and youth voices are heard and valued; (d) ensuring that families and youth have access to useful, usable, and understandable information and data; (e) providing sound professional expertise to help families make decisions; (f) sharing power, authority, resources, and responsibility;

and (g) constructing funding mechanisms to allow families and youth to have a choice. One of the most important choices facing families seeking treatment for children who have EBDs is to decide which intervention to request for their child. Today, the practice community has produced an impressive list of interventions that have been tested with rigorous evaluation techniques and are considered to be evidence-based practices. The next section explores these practices.

## EVIDENCE-BASED MENTAL HEALTH INTERVENTIONS

Nationally, there are numerous attempts to increase the amount and types of mental health services in schools, with state policy makers and school boards demanding more and better mental health services for all students (Adelman & Taylor, 2000). Recent studies indicated that virtually all schools have some type of mental health services available (Foster et al., 2005), and on average, schools offer 14 different programs aimed at improving the social emotional learning of students (Zins et al., 2004). These efforts, however, are frequently not empirically based interventions. The challenge, therefore, is to better coordinate and implement an array of evidence-based mental health interventions targeting specific behaviors across a heterogeneous population of students. To accomplish this task, a better understanding by mental health, school staff, and families of the universal, selective, and indicated evidence-based mental health interventions that can be implemented in schools is necessary. This section summarizes some of the current evidence-based programs that can be implemented in schools and complement PBS efforts.

In 2006, Kutash and her colleagues summarized the evidence-based mental health interventions for children. Information on the interventions was complied by five national organizations: the National Registry of Evidence-Based Programs and Practices (NREPP) operated by SAMHSA (Schinke, Brounstein, & Gardner, 2002); a report issued by the Collaborative for Academic, Social, and Emotional Learning (CASEL, 2003); a review of programs by the Prevention Research Center for the Promotion of Human Development at Penn State (Greenberg, Domitrovich, & Bumbarger, 2000); a review by the Center for the Study and Prevention of Violence (CSPV; Elliott & Mihalic, 2004); and the U.S. Department of Education report on behalf of the Office of Educational Research and Improvement (OERI; U.S. Department of Education [USDOE], 2001). These five sources generated a list of 92 interventions, with 23% of the programs appearing on more than one of the five sources.

Overall, within this listing of evidence-based programs, approximately one third of the programs are designated as targeting substance abuse, trauma, or health problems; the remaining two thirds address the regulation of emotions or social functioning in children and adolescents. The approaches focus equally on universal levels of prevention (53%) and selective/indicated levels of prevention (47%). The majority of the programs listed across these five sources are to be implemented in schools (58%); 26% are to be implemented in community settings, and 16% are to be implemented simultaneously in schools and in community settings. This finding clearly supports the notion that for evidence-based programs to be implemented, schools must be involved. The next sections describe a sample of universal, selective, and indicated evidence-based programs that can be implemented in schools.

## Universal Interventions

According to Weisz and colleagues (2005), universal strategies are "approaches designed to address risk factors in entire populations of youth—for example, all youngsters in a classroom, all in a school, or all in multiple schools—without attempting to discern which youths are at elevated risk" (p. 632). Some examples of universal interventions are presented in Table 9.7. Perhaps the two most common universal interventions include Promoting Alternative Thinking Strategies (PATHS; Kusche & Greenberg, 1994) and the Life Skills Training (Botvin, Eng, & Williams, 1980). The PATHS curriculum has six sections that cover emotional literacy, self-control, social competence, positive peer relations, and interpersonal problem-solving skills. The program targets children between 5 and 12 years of age and can continue across five grade levels. The Life Skills Training program includes 15 sessions of 45 minutes for middle school students and 24 sessions at 30 to 45 minutes for elementary students. Within each session, lessons on drug resistance skills, self-management skills, and general social skills are presented. Generally, approaches at the universal level of prevention include curriculums to be delivered

**Table 9.7.** A Sample of Evidence-Based Universal Programs

| | Name | Source List | School Based | Age Range | Length of Program | Family Component? | Teacher Component? |
|---|---|---|---|---|---|---|---|
| 1 | Promoting Alternative Thinking Strategies (PATHS) | A, B, C, E | Yes | 5–12 | 5 years | Yes | Yes |
| 2 | Linking the Interest of Family and Teachers (LIFT) | B | Yes | 6–11 | 10 weeks | Yes | Yes |
| 3 | Second Step: A violence prevention program | A, B, E | Yes | 4–14 | 15–30 weeks | Yes | Yes |
| 4 | Life Skills Training | A, C, D, E | Yes | 11–16 | 3 years | No | Yes |
| 5 | I can problem solve | B, E | Yes | 4–12 | School year | Yes | Yes |

*Note.* A, Substance Abuse and Mental Health Services Administration (SAMHSA): http://www.modelprograms.samhsa.gov; B, Penn State: http://www.prevention.psu.edu/pubs/docs/CMHS.pdf; C, Center for the Study and Prevention of Violence (CSPV): http://www.colorado.edu/cspv/blueprints/; D, U.S. Department of Education (USDOE): http://www.ed.gov/admins/lead/safety/exemplary01/exemplary01.pdf; E, Collaborative for Academic, Social, and Emotional Learning (CASEL): http://www.casel.org/projects_products/safeandsound.php. From *School-Based Mental Health: An Empirical Guide for Decision-Makers*, by K. Kutash, A. J. Duchnowski, & N. Lynn, 2006, Tampa: University of South Florida, Louis de la Parte Florida Mental Health Institute, Department of Child and Family Studies.

within the classroom to teach specific behaviors and opportunities for the students to practice the newly acquired skills. The key strategies for effective school-based prevention programming according to Greenberg and his colleagues (2003) include teaching and reinforcing skills in students; fostering supportive relationships among students, school staff, and parents; implementing systemic school and community approaches; starting programs before risky behaviors begin; and continuing multicomponent programs across multiple years (see Table 9.8).

## Selective Interventions

According to Weisz and colleagues (2005), selective interventions target "groups of youth identified because they share a significant risk factor and mount interventions designed to counter that risk" (p. 632). Selective strategies are used with students who require more than universal strategies but less than intensive individualized interventions. The purpose of selective or targeted interventions is to support students who are at risk for or are beginning to exhibit signs of more serious problem behaviors. Such interventions can be offered in small-group settings for students exhibiting similar behaviors or to individual students. A sample of selective interventions is listed in Table 9.9. For older youth, the Coping With Stress Course (Clarke et al., 1995) has been used as a selective intervention and promotes adaptive coping skills for adolescents with depressive symptomatology through 15 group sessions, such as progressive relaxation, cue-controlled relaxation, and cognitive restructuring. For younger youth, First Step to Success (Walker et al., 1997) is implemented in the classroom with behavioral criteria set each day; in the home portion of the program, parents are taught to reward appropriate behaviors. There are also selective programs that are community based and may augment school programs. These include Big Brothers/Big Sisters (Grossman & Tierney, 1998), a mentoring program for youth; and functional family ther-

**Table 9.8.** Key Strategies for Effective School-Based Prevention Programming Involve the Following Student Focused, Relationship-Oriented, and Classroom and School-Level Organizational Changes

1. Teach children to apply social and emotional learning (SEL) skills with ethical values in daily life through interactive classroom instruction and provide frequent opportunities for student self-direction, participation, and school and community service.
2. Foster respectful supportive relationships among students, school staff, and parents.
3. Support and reward positive social, health, and academic behavior through systematic school-family-community approaches.
4. Multiyear, multicomponent interventions are more effective than single-component short-term programs.
5. Competence and health promotion efforts are best begun before signs of risky behaviors emerge and should continue through adolescence.

*Note.* From "Enhancing School-Based Prevention and Youth Development Through Coordinated Social, Emotional, and Academic Learning," M. T. Greenberg, R. P. Weissberg, M. E. O'Brien, J. E. Zins, L. Fredericks, H. Resnik, et al., 2003, *American Psychologist, 58*, p. 470.

**Table 9.9.** A Sample of Evidence-Based Selective Programs

| | Name | Source List | School Based | Age Range | Length of Program | Family Component? | Teacher Component? |
|---|---|---|---|---|---|---|---|
| 1 | First Step to Success | B | Yes | 4–5 | 3 months | Y | Y |
| 2 | Functional Family Therapy | C | No | 11–18 | 8–26 years | Y | N |
| 3 | Big Brothers/Big Sisters | B, C | No | 5–18 | 1 year | N | N |
| 4 | Coping With Stress Course | B | Yes | 13–18 | 15 sessions | N | N |
| 5 | Olweus Bullying Prevention Program | A, C | Yes | 6–18 | School year | N | Y |

*Note.* A, Substance Abuse and Mental Health Services Administration (SAMHSA): http://www.modelprograms.samhsa.gov; B, Penn State: http://www.prevention.psu.edu/pubs/docs/CMHS.pdf; C, Center for the Study and Prevention of Violence (CSPV): http://www.colorado.edu/cspv/blueprints/; D, U.S. Department of Education (USDOE): http://www.ed.gov/admins/lead/safety/exemplary01/exemplary01.pdf; E, Collaborative for Academic, Social, and Emotional Learning (CASEL): http://www.casel.org/projects_products/safeandsound.php. From *School-Based Mental Health: An Empirical Guide for Decision-Makers*, by K. Kutash, A. J. Duchnowski, & N. Lynn, 2006, Tampa: University of South Florida, Louis de la Parte Florida Mental Health Institute, Department of Child and Family Studies.

apy (Alexander & Parsons, 1982), which includes 8 to 26 hours of direct service time with youth and family and consists of five phases: engagement, motivation, assessment, behavior change, and generalization.

## Indicated Interventions

According to Weisz and colleagues (2005), indicated prevention strategies are "aimed at youth who have significant symptoms of a disorder ... but do not currently meet diagnostic criteria for the disorder" (p. 623). As stated earlier, there is very little difference between indicated prevention strategies and those interventions focused on treatment of a diagnostic condition. For examples of indicated programs see Table 9.10. For young children, between 8 and 12 years of age, *Incredible Years* (Webster-Stratton, 1992) can be implemented in schools and is used as both a selective and indicated prevention program. The program uses four formats: 18 to 22 two-hours weekly Dina Dinosaur group therapy sessions for children; 60 Dina Dinosaur lesson plans for the classroom; 12 to 14 two hour weekly parenting groups; and 14, two-hour teacher classroom management sessions. The *Earlscourt Social Skills Group Program* (Pepler, King, Craig, Byrd, & Bream, 1995) is aimed at reducing aggression in elementary school students through twice weekly, 75-minute group sessions for 12 to 15 weeks. Sessions teach eight basic skills in program modules, classroom activities, and homework. Training sessions are also offered to parents.

There are several indicated programs that are community-based and may augment school programs. Two of these are *Multisystemic Therapy* (MST; Henggeler et al., 1986) and *Brief Strategic Therapy* (Szapocznik,

**Table 9.10.** A Sample of Evidence-Based Indicated Programs

| | Name | Source List | School Based | Age Range | Length of program | Family Component? | Teacher Component? |
|---|---|---|---|---|---|---|---|
| 1 | Incredible years | A, C | Yes | 2–8 | Up to 22 weeks | Yes | Yes |
| 2 | Multisystemic therapy | A, C | No | 12–17 | 4 months | Yes | No |
| 3 | Brief strategic family therapy | A | No | 6–17 | 8–12 weeks | Yes | No |
| 4 | Peer coping skills training | B | Yes | 6–12 | 22 weeks | No | Yes |
| 5 | Earlscourt Social Skills Group Program | B | Yes | 6–12 | 12–15 weeks | Yes | Yes |

A, Substance Abuse and Mental Health Services Administration (SAMHSA): http://www.modelprograms.samhsa.gov; B, Penn State: http://www.prevention.psu.edu/pubs/docs/CMHS.pdf; C, Center for the Study and Prevention of Violence (CSPV): http://www.colorado.edu/cspv/blueprints/; D, U.S. Department of Education (USDOE): http://www.ed.gov/admins/lead/safety/exemplary01/exemplary01.pdf; E, Collaborative for Academic, Social, and Emotional Learning (CASEL): http://www.casel.org/projects_products/safeandsound.php. From *School-Based Mental Health: An Empirical Guide for Decision-Makers*, by K. Kutash, A. J. Duchnowski, & N. Lynn, 2006, Tampa: University of South Florida, Louis de la Parte Florida Mental Health Institute, Department of Child and Family Studies.

Hervis, & Schwartz, 2003). MST targets older adolescents and has an average duration of 60 contact hours over 4 months. Intervention strategies are integrated into social ecological contexts (including the school system) and include strategic family therapy, structural family therapy, behavioral parent training, and cognitive behavior therapy. *Brief Strategic Therapy* can be used with students between the ages of 6 and 17 and is delivered in sixty to ninety minute sessions over the course of eight to twelve weeks. A counselor meets with the family and develops a therapeutic alliance, diagnosis family strengths and problem relations, develops a change strategy and helps implement those strategies.

In summary, there are many evidence-based mental health programs aimed at strengthening the emotional and behavioral competences of children and youth that can be implemented in school and complement PBS. The challenge is to implement these efforts in schools in an integrative manner so that teachers, school staff, and parents each understand their role in the implementation and the expected outcomes. In an integrative team based model of supporting positive emotional and behavioral functioning, see Fig. 9.4, there is a common vision for families, mental health and ED staff. Additionally, there are programs implemented at the universal, selective, and indicated levels that integrate PBS, mental health programs and RtI in an organizational environment that supports and facilitates collaborative, integrated systems of service.

## Achieving Integration: A Blueprint for the Future

Among the many barriers that impede the fruition of the promise of integrating PBS, mental health, and family driven care, financing issues play a major role. It may be surprising to readers that over $12 billion is

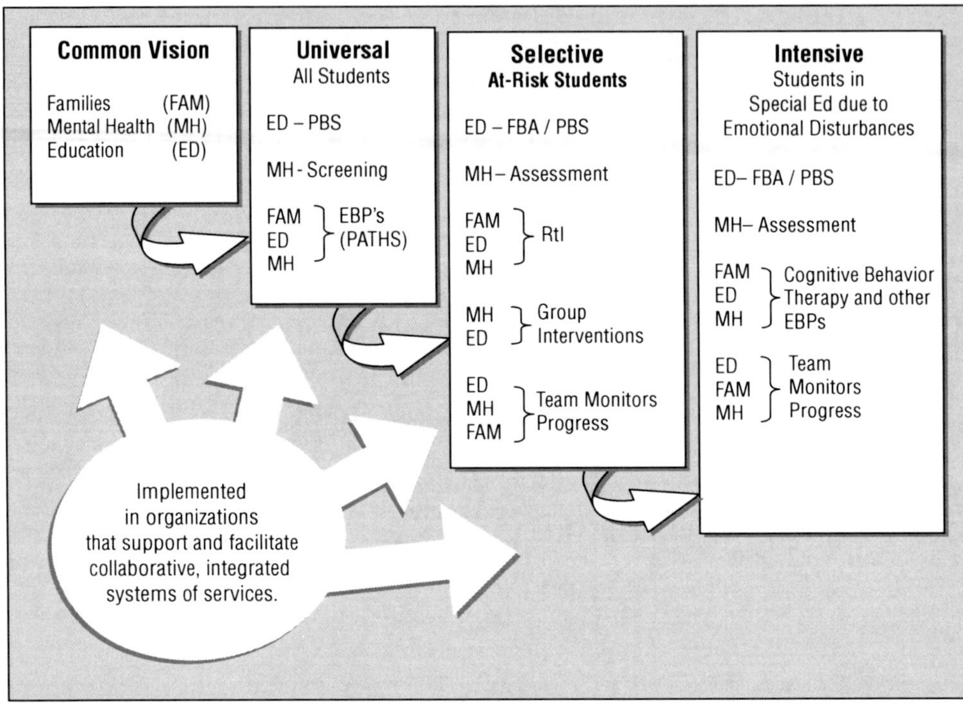


**Fig. 9.4.** An integrative team-based model of positive emotional and behavioral functioning in children and youth. Note: FBA=Functional Behavior Assessment; EBP=Evidence Based Practice.

spent annually on children's mental health services in this country (Kutash et al., 2006). Unfortunately, there is a paucity of research on financing children's mental health services in general leaving many important questions unanswered concerning how these billions are spent. We know that the majority of children who receive any mental health service at all, receive it in their school. We also know that two-thirds of all schools use some IDEA funds to pay for mental health services and Medicaid funds support over half of all mental health services received by children. Finally, the few studies that have been conducted reveal great disparity between states in terms of the numbers of children who receive services that are funded by Medicaid as well as in the level of funding offered by the states. Many schools have developed home-grown strategies to blend federal, state, and local funds with collaborating community agencies in order to leverage the pool of available funds to achieve maximum support for programs that address the needs of children who have EBD.

While the knowledge base describing the funding of mental health service may be sparse, we noted in the first section of this chapter the many policies bearing on children who have EBD. Most federal agencies that have some responsibility for the welfare of children, have some policy initiative related to improving services by capitalizing on the potential advantages afforded by locating services in the schools and coordinating efforts with such programs as PBS and Wraparound. These federal policies are passed down to the states and ultimately local level bureaucracies. An analysis of these policies reveals a common thread not previously mentioned, i.e., the need to implement the "public health model" more fully. This view can be found in the reports of the President's Commission on Excellence in Special Education (2002), the Surgeon General's Report (USDHHS, 1999), NCLB, and the report of the President's New Freedom Commission on Mental Health (2003). This as an encouraging prospect and provides support for the use of the public health model as a framework for integrating PBS, the mental health system and family driven care.

In spite of the wide-spread reference to the public health model, however, there are very few citations in which this model is fully elaborated. In many reports in the literature, the discussion of the public health model does not go beyond the emphasis on the development of strategies for prevention through the implementation of universal, selective, and indicated interventions. While prevention certainly is a fundamental principle, the model is richer and more encompassing. The public health model has its focus on populations rather than individuals, i.e., society is the client (Strein, Hoagwood, & Cohn, 2003). The interaction of risk and protective factors in individuals are examined at the community level. Decisions are data-based and the goal of public health research is to develop specific interventions that are targeted toward enhancing protective factors and reducing the risk factors that lead to undesirable outcomes.

The public health model may be conceived of as having four components or steps (see Fig. 9.5). The first component is a focus on the population as opposed to individuals. Surveillance, which entails defining a specific problem through systematic information collection at the population level, is the major mechanism used in this component. The goal is to be able to describe the scope, characteristics, and the consequences of a

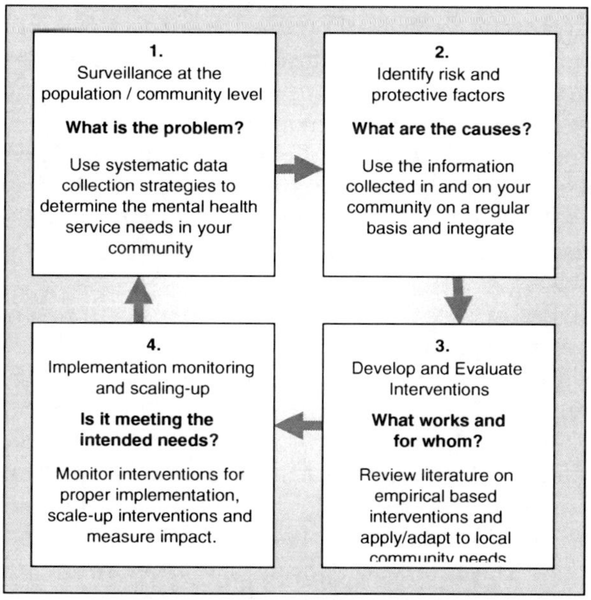


**Fig. 9.5.** The four phases in implementing the public health model.

problem facing the community. In the second step the causes are identified through an analysis of the risk and protective factors, their correlates, and how these factors could be modified to decrease the risk. In the third step interventions are developed and evaluated. The interventions are on a continuum that includes health promotion/positive individual development, universal prevention interventions, selective interventions, and indicated interventions. The fourth step consists of activities to scale up implementation at a level that will have significant positive impact on the population. In this step effective practices are implemented and monitored and their cost effectiveness is evaluated.

This is a comprehensive approach aimed at reducing the negative consequences of a condition or behavior. However, it is also practical, makes use of multi-disciplinary involvement, and monitors costs and benefit. In Fig. 9.6, we have illustrated an example of how a community may implement the public health model with the goal of producing an integrated service system for meeting the mental health needs of its children. As this example illustrates, the PBS and mental health communities can provide the leadership necessary to achieve the goal of implementing more effective and family driven system of care for children who have EBDs. Practitioners of PBS have already developed software programs to collect extensive school-wide data on the daily behavior of students. Schools produce annual report cards that describe risk factors, student achievement, attendance, and graduation information. Mental health and social services agencies compile reports on numbers of referrals, in-patient episodes, foster care placements, and other indicators of risk in the community. While the coordination and organization of these data sources and the analysis and selection of the best interventions to meet the community's needs is formidable, it is not impossible. At this point in time one of the best examples of galvanizing families and professionals in order to improve outcomes for children who have EBD comes from the state of Hawaii (Daleiden & Chorpita, 2005). Family organizations, individual family members, researchers, and administrators from the child serving agencies conducted community assessments, reviewed compendia of evidence based practices, assessed the fit with local needs and contexts, and produced an integrated set of interventions to improve outcomes for their children. Family voice and the best available evidence were the key components of this endeavor and its feasibility for action in other communities across the country was demonstrated.

The integration of PBS, the mental health system, and family driven care presents a challenge at the federal, state, and local level, in the 100,000 schools in the nation, and in the approximately three million homes in which a child with EBD resides. For 30 years, the research literature has described children who have EBD as a complex group of youths who have multiple problems that cut across the domains of multiple agencies and require the expertise of the multiple disciplines involved in providing care to the children and their families. We know the problem is complex and requires a multi-disciplinary response and the inclusion of families as partners. Will we see a response at a scale that will make a difference in a reasonable time period? This handbook on PBS, of which this is one chapter,

Assess the boundaries of the problem

**What is the problem?**

Use systematic data collection strategies to determine the specific educational and mental health challenges in your community relating to aggression in youth.

**Steps to Identify Priority Problems**

- Establish a task force comprised of school advisory councils and mental health planning team members that has resources and authority for engaging in decision-making for service planning.
- Use existing data to create a composite picture of the amount of violence committed by youth in the community.
- Existing data should be examined for indicators of aggressive and violent behavior in youth in your community to help direct actions.
- Examples:
  - What is the rate of juvenile arrests for violent crimes in your community?
  - What are the rates of suspensions and dropping out of school in your community?
  - What are some indicators of substance abuse problems among
  - the youth in your community?
  - What are the rates of behavior referrals in schools due to fighting?
- Prioritize the problems to be addressed.

Identify risk and protective factors

**What are the causes?**

Use the information collected on your community to identify the individual and social constraints relating to aggression in youth.

**Steps to Identify Risk & Protective Factors**

- Identify individual and social risk and protective factors for each prioritized problem. Risk factors are those conditions that increase the likelihood of a negative outcome for children. Protective factors are conditions that reduce the probability of the negative outcome.
- Examine the empirical literature and condense the information to identify the risk and protective factors associated with the priority problem.
- Examples:
  - A common risk factor associated with the problems of aggression and substance use is negative peer influence. What is the capacity of the community and each school for providing clubs, extra curricular activities, supervised after school programs?
  - A common risk factor for aggression in youth is school failure. What programs exists for the early identification and remediation of at risk learners?
  - What is the capacity to provide parents with positive parenting skills?
  - To what extent are teachers effective in working with diverse populations of students and families?
- Integrate the community data with the research literature to identify and prioritize risk and protective factors needing to be addressed in your community.

Develop and evaluate interventions

**What works and for whom?**

Review literature on empirically based interventions and apply/adapt to local community needs.

**Steps to Implement Evidence-Based Programs and Practices**

- Use the research literature to identify evidence-based programs and practices that are appropriate for addressing the prioritized risk and protective factors in your community.
- Communities need to be aware of the need to integrate and balance the implementation of universal, selective, and indicated interventions. After universal interventions have been established, the effectiveness of implementing selective and indicated interventions will be facilitated.
- The Task Force must also investigate the feasibility of implementing the selected evidence-based program for issues such as cost of the program, staff training necessary for implementation, and cultural relevance. Additionally, Task Force members should outline the resources needed to support the implementation of the selected intervention over the life of the program.
- A Task Force that prioritizes aggression and substance abuse for possible action, for example, could examine the feasibility of implementing the following programs:
  - For aggression – the PATHS Program (Promoting Alternative Thinking Strategies) is a universal prevention program that teaches skills such as self-control, social competence, and interpersonal problem-solving skills. An example of an indicated intervention is the Anger Coping Program, which uses a group setting to reduce antisocial behavior.
  - For substance use – the Midwestern Prevention Project focuses on drug abuse prevention with classroom-based sessions and parent involvement.

Implementation monitoring & scaling-up

**Is it meeting intended needs?**

Monitor interventions for proper implementation, scale-up interventions, and measure impact.

**Steps for Implementation, Monitoring, and Scaling-Up**

- Create infrastructure to examine and monitor youth and community outcomes to determine the effectiveness of efforts.
- Create quality assurance standards and training opportunities to support the dissemination and widespread adoption of successful efforts.

**Fig. 9.6.** Example of the components of implementing a public health model.

is a very positive sign. The great number of chapters and the even greater number of authors is an indication of a knowledge base that is mature and ready to inform the transformation of the system. The authors of the chapters represent virtually every discipline and theoretical orientation in the professional community, indicating a presence of the collaborative process necessary for meaningful change. In addition, the chapters in this book contain good science that can inform effective advocacy. These are critical ingredients for change.

In Fig. 9.4, we produced a complicated graphic representation of an integrated team-based model for action. While we admit to its complexity, we hope that readers will examine it carefully and see the distinct components of the model that are being implemented in many places across the country and are described in many chapters in this handbook. Our vision is a professional workforce that has the values and skills necessary to put this model into practice in all of the schools in the nation and families that have the information necessary to take their place at the table and direct services for their children to achieve recovery and resilience.

## REFERENCES

Adelman, H. S., & Taylor, L. (2000). Looking at school health and school reform policy through the lens of addressing barriers to learning. *Children's services: Social policy, research, and practice, 3* (2), 117–132.

Adelman, H. S., & Taylor, L. (2006). *The school leader's guide to student learning supports: New directions for addressing barriers to learning.* Thousand Oaks, CA: Corwin Press.

Alexander, J. F., & Parsons, B. V. (1982). *Functional family therapy: Principles and procedures.* Carmel, CA: Brooks/Cole.

American Psychiatric Association. (1994). *Diagnostic and statistical manual of mental disorders* (4th ed.). Washington, DC: Author.

Botvin, G. J., Eng, A., & Williams, C. L. (1980). Preventing the onset of cigarette smoking through Life Skills Training. *Preventive Medicine, 9,* 135–143.

Burns, B. J., Costello, E. J., Angold, A., Tweed, D., Stangle, D., Farmer, E. M. Z., et al. (1995). Children's mental health service use across service sectors. *Health Affairs, 14,* 148–159.

Burns, B., & Hoagwood, K. (Eds.). (2002). *Community treatment for youth: Evidence-based interventions for severe emotional and behavioral disorders.* New York: Oxford University Press.

Clarke, G., Hawkins, W., Murphy, M., Sheeber, L., Lewinsohn, P., & Seeley, J. (1995). Targeted prevention of unipolar depressive disorder in an at-risk sample of high school adolescents: A randomized trial of a group cognitive intervention. *Journal of the American Academy of Child and Adolescent Psychiatry, 34,* 312–321.

Collaborative for Academic, Social, and Emotional Learning (CASEL). (2003). *Safe and sound: An education leader's guide to evidence-based social and emotional learning (SEL) programs.* Chicago: Author.

Daleiden, E. L., & Chorpita B. F. (2005). From data to wisdom: Quality improvements strategies supporting large-scale implementation of evidence based services. In B. J. Burns & K. E. Hoagwood (Eds.), *Evidence-Based Practice, Part II: Effecting change, Child and Adolescent Psychiatric Clinic of North America, 14,* 329–349.

Day, C., & Roberts, M. (1991). Activities of the child and adolescent service system program for improving mental health services for children and families. *Journal of Clinical Child Psychology, 20,* 340–350.

Eber, L., Sugai, G., Smith, C. R., & Scott, T. M. (2002). Wraparound and positive behavioral intervention and supports in the schools. *Journal of Emotional and Behavioral Disorders, 10*(3), 171–180.

Elliott, D. S., & Mihalic, S. (2004). Issues in disseminating and replicating effective prevention programs. *Prevention Science, 5*(1), 47–52.

Farmer, E. M. Z., Mustillo, S., Burns, B. J., & Costello, E. J. (2005). The epidemiology of mental health problems and service use in youth. In M. H. Epstein, K. Kutash & A. Duchnowski (Eds.), *Outcomes for children and youth with emotional and behavioral disorders and their families: programs and evaluation best practices* (2nd ed., pp. 23–44). Austin, TX: Pro-Ed.

Foster, S., Rollefson, M., Doksum, T., Noonan, D., Robinson, G., & Teich, J. (2005). *School mental health services in the United States, 2002–2003* (DHHS Publication No. SMA 05–4068). Rockville, MD: Center for Mental Health Services, Substance Abuse and Mental Health Services Administration.

Greenbaum, P. E., Dedrick, R. F., Friedman, R. M., Kutash, K., Brown, E. C., Lardieri, S. P., et al. (1998). National Adolescent and Child Treatment Study (NACTS): Outcomes for children with serious emotional and behavioral disturbance. In M. H. Epstein, K. Kutash, & A. J. Duchnowski (Eds.), *Outcomes for children and youth with emotional and behavioral disorders and their families: Programs and evaluation best practices* (pp. 21–54). Austin, TX: Pro-Ed.

Greenberg, M. T., Domitrovich, C., & Bumbarger, B. (2000). *Preventing mental disorders in school-age children: A review of the effectiveness of prevention programs.* Prevention Research Center for the Promotion of Human Development, College of Health and Human Development, Pennsylvania State University. Retrieved July 30, 2007, from http://www.prevention.psu.edu/pubs/docs/CMHS.pdf

Greenberg, M. T., Weissberg, R. P., O'Brien, M. E., Zins, J. E., Fredericks, L., Resnik, H., et al. (2003). Enhancing school-based prevention and youth development through coordinated social, emotional, and academic learning. *American Psychologist, 58*, 466–474.

Grossman, J. B., & Tierney, J. P. (1998). Does mentoring work? An impact study of the Big Brothers Big Sisters. *Evaluation Review, 22*, 403–426.

Henggeler, S. W., Rodick, J. D., Borduin, C. M., Hanson, C. L., Watson, S. M., & Urey, J. R. (1986). Multisystemic treatment of juvenile offenders: Effects on adolescent behavior and family interactions. *Developmental Psychology, 22*, 132–141.

Kaslow, N. J., & Thomson, M. P. (1998). Applying the criteria for empirically supported treatments to studies of psychosocial interventions for child and adolescent depression. *Journal of Clinical Child Psychology, 27*, 146–155.

Knitzer, J. (1982). *Unclaimed children: The failure of public responsibility to children and adolescents in need of mental health services.* Washington, DC: Children's Defense Fund.

Kusche, C., & Greenberg, M. (1994). PATHS: *Promoting alternative thinking strategies.* South Deerfield, MA: Developmental Research Programs Inc.

Kutash, K., Duchnowski, A. J., & Friedman, R. M. (2005). The system of care twenty years later. In M. H. Epstein, K. Kutash, & A. J. Duchnowski (Eds.), *Outcomes for children with emotional and behavioral disorders and their families: Program and evaluation best practices* (2nd ed., pp.3–22). Austin, TX: Pro-Ed.

Kutash, K., Duchnowski, A. J., & Lynn, N. (2006). *School-based mental health: An empirical guide for decision-makers.* Tampa: University of South Florida, Louis de la Parte Florida Mental Health Institute, Department of Child and Family Studies.

Mrazek, P. J., & Haggerty, R. J. (Eds.). (1994). *Reducing risks for mental disorders: Frontiers for preventive intervention research.* Washington, DC: National Academy Press.

MTA Cooperative Group. (1998, October). *A 14-month randomized clinical trial of treatment strategies for attention deficit hyperactivity disorder.* Paper presented at the annual meeting of the American Academy of Child and Adolescent Psychiatry, Anaheim, CA.

National Institute for Health Care Management. (2005). *Children's mental health: An overview and key considerations for health system stakeholders.* Washington, DC: Author.

Osher, T. W., Osher, D., & Blau, G. (2006). *Shifting gears to family-driven care: Ambassadors tool kit.* Rockville, MD: Federation of Families for Children's Mental Health.

Pepler, D. J., King, G., Craig, W., Byrd, B., & Bream, L. (1995). The development and evaluation of a multisystem social skills group training programs for aggressive children. *Child & Youth Care Forum, 24*, 297–313.

President's Commission on Excellence in Special Education. (2002). *A new era: Revitalizing special education and their families*. Retrieved July 30, 2007, from http://www.ed.gov/inits/commissionsboards/whspecialeducation/index.html

President's New Freedom Commission on Mental Health. (2003). *Achieving the promise: Transforming mental health care in America. Final report* (DHHS Publication No. SMA-03–3832). Rockville, MD: U.S. Department of Health and Human Services.

Rice, D. P., & Miller, L. S. (1996). The economic burden of schizophrenia: Conceptual and methodological issues, and cost estimates. In M. Moscarelli, A. Rupp, & N. Sartorious (Eds.), *Handbook of mental health economics and health policy. Vol. 1: Schizophrenia* (pp. 321–324). New York: John Wiley and Sons.

Robbins, V., & Armstrong, B. J. (2005). The Bridges Project: Description and evaluation of a school-based mental health program in eastern Kentucky. In M. H. Epstein, K. Kutash, & A. J. Duchnowski (Eds.), *Outcomes for children and youth with emotional disorders and their families: Programs and evaluation best practices* (2nd ed.; pp. 355–373). Austin, TX: Pro-Ed.

Schinke, S., Brounstein, P., & Gardner, S. E. (2002). *Science-based prevention programs and principles, 2002* (DHHS Publication No. SMA 03–3764). Rockville, MD: Center for Substance Abuse Prevention, Substance Abuse and Mental Health Services Administration.

Silver, S. E., Duchnowski, A. J., Kutash, K., Friedman, R. M., Eisen, M., Prange, M. E., et al. (1992). A comparison of children with serious emotional disturbance served in residential and school settings. *Journal of Child and Family Studies, 1*, 43–59.

Strein, W., Hoagwood, K., & Cohn, A. (2003). School psychology: A public health perspective I. Prevention, populations, and systems change. *Journal of School Psychology, 41(1), 23–38.*

Stroul, B. A., & Friedman, R. M. (1986). *A system of care for children and youth with severe emotional disturbances*. (Rev. ed.). Washington, DC: Georgetown University Child Development Center, CASSP Technical Assistance Center.

Szapocznik, J., Hervis, O. E., & Schwartz, S. (2003). *Brief strategic family therapy for adolescent drug abuse* (NIH Publication No. 03–4751). Rockville, MD: National Institute on Drug Abuse.

Todd, A., Haugen, L., Anderson, K., & Spriggs, M. (2002). Teaching recess: Low-cost efforts producing effective results. *Journal of Positive Behavior Interventions, 4*(1), 46–52.

U.S. Department of Education. (2001). *Exemplary and promising safe, disciplined, and drug-free schools programs, 2001*. Washington DC: Author.

U.S. Department of Health and Human Services (USDHHS). (1999). *Mental health: A report of the Surgeon General*. Rockville, MD: Author, Substance Abuse and Mental Health Services Administration, Center for Mental Health Services, National Institutes of Health, National Institute of Mental Health.

VanDenBerg, J. E., & Grealish, E. M. (1996). Individualized services and supports through the wraparound process: Philosophy and procedures. *Journal of Child and Family Studies, 5* (1), 1–15.

Wagner, M., Friend, M., Bursuck, W., Kutash, K., Duchnowski, A. J. Sumi, W. C., et al. (2006). Educating students with emotional disturbances: A national perspective on programs and services. *Journal of Emotional and Behavioral Disorders, 14*, 12–30.

Walker, H. M., Kavanagh, K., Golly, A. M., Stiller, B., Severson, H. H., & Feil, E. G. (1997). *First Step to Success*. Longmont, CO: Sopris West.

Webster-Stratton, C. (1992). *The Incredible Years: A trouble-shooting guide for parents of children ages 3–8 years*. Toronto, Canada: Umbrella Press

Weist, M. D., Goldstein, A., Morris, L., & Bryant, T. (2003). Integrating expanded school mental health programs and school-based health centers. *Psychology in the Schools, 40*(3)297–308.

Weist, M. D., Lowie, J. A., Flaherty, L. T., & Pruitt, D. (2001). Collaboration among the education, mental health, and public health systems to promote youth mental health. *Psychiatric Services, 52*(10), 1348–1351.

Weisz, J., Sandler, I., Durlak, J., & Anton, B. (2005). Promoting and protecting youth mental health through evidence-based prevention and treatment. *American Psychologist, 60*(6), 628–648.

Zins, J. E., Weissberg, R. P., Wang, M. C., & Walberg, H. J. (Eds.). (2004). *Building academic success on social and emotional learning: What does the research say?* New York: Teachers College Press.

# 10

# Optimistic Parenting: Hope and Help for Parents With Challenging Children

**V. MARK DURAND, MEME HIENEMAN, SHELLEY CLARKE, and MELISSA ZONA**

Challenging behaviors—including aggressive, disruptive, and socially inappropriate behaviors—are highly prevalent among children with disabilities. Research suggests that problem behavior in general is three to four times more frequent in this population than among children without disabilities, and that between 10% and 40% of children with disabilities display frequent and severe challenging behaviors (Einfeld & Tonge, 1996; Lowe et al., 2007). In addition to frequency, the stability of these behaviors is also of serious concern. Several studies document that, even with efforts to treat these behaviors, they may still be problematic a decade later (Einfeld & Tonge, 1996; Einfeld, Tonge, & Rees, 2001; Emerson et al., 2001; Green, O'Reilly, Itchon, & Sigafoos, 2005; Jones, 1999).

Challenging behaviors often represent a major obstacle for students with disabilities in their efforts to fully participate in meaningful educational and community activities. These behaviors are among the most frequently cited obstacles in attempting to place students in community settings (Eyman & Call, 1977; Jacobson, 1982), and they increase recidivism significantly for those individuals referred to crisis intervention programs from community placements (Shoham-Vardi et al., 1996). Challenging behavior interferes with such essential activities as family life (Cole & Meyer, 1989), educational activities (R. L. Koegel & Covert, 1972), and employment (Hayes, 1987). For

**V. MARK DURAND** • University of South Florida St. Petersburg
**MEME HIENEMAN** • University of South Florida St. Petersburg
**SHELLEY CLARKE** • University of South Florida Tanpa
**MELISSA ZONA** • University of Albany-Suny

example, in one of the largest studies of its kind, researchers examining almost 10,000 children found that the single best predictor of early school failure was the presence of behavior problems (Byrd & Weitzman, 1994). The presence of behavior problems was a better predictor of school difficulties than factors such as poverty, speech and hearing impairments, and low birth weight. One study found that almost 40% of preschool teachers reported expelling a child each year due to behavior problems (Gilliam & Shahar, 2006). In addition, such behaviors can pose a physical threat to these individuals and those who work with them. As a result, improving problem behavior in children with disabilities is one of the major priorities in the effort to improve academic and social achievement among these students.

Although there is a growing body of literature documenting the effectiveness of behavioral parent training (BPT; including the use of positive behavior supports [PBS]) to assist families with these challenges, obstacles to implementation are apparent. For a variety of reasons, some families are not able to carry out the plans designed for their children, and this limits the effectiveness of these intervention strategies. After a review of the relevant literature, we describe a new intervention approach for families who experience difficulties implementing these plans. This approach, called positive family intervention (PFI), combines PBS with an added cognitive behavioral intervention designed to assist families in completing treatment. Our prior research suggested that many families are at risk for dropping out of treatment due to attitudinal barriers; we developed a unique treatment program that appears to significantly improve participation.

## BEHAVIORAL PARENT TRAINING

Helping families intervene with their child's behavior problems is a theme that goes back to the earliest efforts of the pioneering behavioral scientists (e.g., Hawkins, Peterson, Schweid, & Bijou, 1966). BPT employs the principles of applied behavior analysis (ABA; Baer, Wolf, & Risley, 1968) to help families develop the skills they need to support and manage their children's behavior (Dangel, Yu, Slot, & Fashinger, 1994; Gimpel & Collett, 2002; Kazdin, 1997). In general, BPT has been demonstrated to be effective (Maughan, Christiansen, & Jensen, 2005, Serketich & Dumas, 1996); however, that effectiveness may vary with the stressors experienced by the family, the specific features of the intervention protocols, and the adjunctive supports provided to the family (Assemany & McIntosh, 2002; Forehand & Kotchick, 2002; MacKenzie, Fite, & Bates, 2004; McCart, Priester, & Hobart, 2006). The purpose of this section is to describe briefly the key features that contribute to the effectiveness of BPT, and behavioral intervention in general, and to introduce PBS as an approach for integrating those elements into a comprehensive, community-based approach.

Generally, effective behavioral intervention includes (a) consequence-based strategies that employ reinforcement (and punishment), (b) systematic instructional procedures to promote skill development, (c) assessment-based interventions that target the functions of behavior, and (d) preventive strategies involving modification of antecedent events and conditions.

### *Consequence-Based Strategies That Employ Reinforcement (and Punishment)*

One of the most basic features of behavioral intervention is the ability to control access to reinforcement and deliver consequences that produce observable and predictable changes in behavior. Early behavioral methods focused almost exclusively on arranging contingencies to increase or decrease behavior, including delivery of social and tangible reinforcement, token systems, and time-out from positive reinforcement, and these methods were key components of BPT programs. Consequence-based interventions, specifically differential reinforcement and firm and consistent disciplinary practices, have been defined as components of BPT (Dumas, 1989; Eyberg & Boggs, 1989; Forehand & McMahon, 1981); however, the field is expanding to use consequences more effectively and broaden intervention approaches.

### *Systematic Instructional Procedures to Promote Skill Development*

Another important feature of behavioral intervention is the use of specific procedures to teach desirable behaviors. These procedures—shaping, task analysis, prompting, fading, and chaining—are essential elements of any effective instructional program. One example of how systematic instruction has been used to promote skill development is discrete trial training (Lovaas, 1993). In this approach, the principles of behavior modification are embedded in systematic instruction using repetitive trials to build language and social skills of young children with autism and related disabilities. Discrete trial training has been demonstrated to produce rapid development of skill repertoires and long-term gains in adaptive functioning; however, concerns have been raised about the acceptability of this approach when used as the only teaching approach as well as its ability to produce generalized behavior change (Steege, Mace, Perry, & Longenecker, 2007).

Alternatively, efforts have been made to embed teaching trials within natural settings and circumstances, especially play and social interaction. Approaches such as incidental or milieu teaching (Alpert & Kaiser, 1992: Charlop-Christy & Carpenter, 2000; McGee, Morrier, & Daly, 1999) and pivotal response training (R. L. Koegel & Frea, 1993) have been investigated and found not only as effective, but also preferred by families and care providers (Delprato, 2001). Systematic instruction methods allow parents to teach their children the generalized skills they need to be successful in integrated settings.

### *Assessment-Based Interventions That Target the Functions of Behavior*

A third essential foundation of behavioral intervention is functional assessment or analysis (FA) and the strategies derived from this process. Functional assessment (and more precisely functional analysis) involves identification of the consequences maintaining the problem behavior (Day, Horner, & O'Neill, 1994; Durand & Crimmins, 1988; Iwata, Dorsey, & Slifer, 1994). Functions can include obtaining some social or tangible reward, escaping or avoiding an undesirable event, or gaining some type of sensory stimulation. Behavior interventions based on FA involve providing access to these specific reinforcers contingent on positive behavior, but not problematic behavior. It has been reported that treatments based on FA increase intervention effectiveness by as much as 50% (Carr et al., 1999), although other reviews suggest the influence may be more limited (Machalicek, O'Reilly, Beretvas, Sigafoos, & Lancioni, 2007).

The approach to intervention based on FA that has received considerable empirical support is functional communication training (FCT). FCT involves assessing the variables maintaining behavior and then teaching functionally equivalent responses such as communication, which serve the same purpose as a child's problem behavior (Durand, 1990, 1999). For example, if a child is having tantrums to escape a difficult task, that child might be taught to sign or say "stop" to obtain breaks. As a result of this instructional intervention, problem behavior is no longer necessary to access reinforcers, and the problem behavior is diminished. FCT has been demonstrated to be both effective as compared to other strategies and acceptable to direct support providers (Durand, 1999; Durand & Carr, 1992; Hanley, Piazza, Fisher, Contrucci, & Maglieri, 1997).

FA and FCT have increasingly been integrated into BPT, as evidenced by single-subject research and intervention conducted in partnership with families, and have demonstrated the efficacy of a range of BPT approaches to reduce challenging behavior (Clarke, Dunlap, & Vaughn, 1999; Dunlap & Fox, 1999; L. K. Koegel, Steibel, Koegel, 1998; Lucyshyn, Albin, & Nixon, 1997; Moes & Frea, 2000, 2002; Vaughn, Clarke, & Dunlap, 1997; Vaughn, Wilson, & Dunlap, 2002). Lucyshyn and colleagues, for example, reported on a 10-year follow-up of their work with the family of one young girl and found maintenance of treatment gains (Lucyshyn et al., 2007). By including parents in the process and teaching them to use ABA principles and to implement simple FAs, they can more effectively manage their children's behavior and resolve problems on an ongoing basis (Dunlap, Newton, Fox, Benito, & Vaughn, 2001; Frea & Hepburn, 1999; James & Scotti, 2000; S. M. Peterson, Derby, Berg, & Horner, 2002).

### *Preventive Strategies Involving Modification of Antecedents and Setting Events*

A final feature of effective behavioral intervention that has been the focus of empirical investigation is the manipulation of antecedents (Horner, Vaughn, Day, & Ard, 1996; Luiselli & Cameron, 1998). Antecedent-based interventions are based on the recognition that behavior is influenced not only by consequences, but also by the contexts in which it occurs. By modifying features of the social or physical environment, problem behavior may be prevented or ameliorated. Demonstrations of the effectiveness of antecedent-based interventions have included curricular modifications

(Dunlap, Kern-Dunlap, Clarke, & Robbins, 1991), incorporation of choice or preference (Blair, Umbreit, & Bos, 1999), and introduction of "neutralizing" routines to diminish problem behavior (Horner, Day, & Day, 1997).

Although antecedent-based interventions have not yet been explored to the extent that consequence-based strategies have (Conroy & Stichter, 2003), they offer important directions for the field and BPT. Modifying the family structure or routines and social interactions to prevent behavior may be more feasible and acceptable and therefore more readily implemented than teaching and consequence-based strategies for parents as they begin addressing children's behavioral difficulties. Several studies demonstrated the positive impact of prevention strategies (Boettcher, Koegel, McNerney, & Koegel, 2003; Buschbacher, Fox, & Clarke, 2004). Experts working in the area of parent support recommend adopting this ecological perspective to provide comprehensive and proactive supports, such as wraparound services, to families (Moes & Frea, 2000; Singer, Goldberg-Hamblin, Peckham-Hardin, Barry, & Santarelli, 2002).

### *Integration and Contextualization of Intervention Through PBS*

Whereas each of the components described in the preceding sections are sometimes effective in and of themselves, multicomponent interventions that combine these features may be even more powerful in producing long-standing behavior change. PBS is an effort to integrate and package these features to be successfully implemented in complex community environments (Carr et al., 2002; Dunlap, Hieneman, & Knoster, 2000; Horner et al, 1990; L. K. Koegel, Koegel, & Dunlap, 1996; Sugai et al., 2000). PBS shifts the focus from modifying single behaviors through individual interventions to treatment packages geared toward broader lifestyle improvement. In addition to incorporating FA and comprehensive interventions, PBS explicitly focuses attention on improving broader quality of life, collaborative teaming, and ensuring contextual fit for support plans. The process is facilitated, but not directed, by an individual with expertise in PBS and focuses on producing improvements in not only the problem behavior but also the children's and families' lives in general.

PBS integrates the traditions of BPT and family support because of its comprehensive orientation, individualized approach, and underlying values of inclusion and respect. As a result, it has become the foundation of many intervention and parent support practices (Hieneman, Childs, & Sergay, 2006; Lucyshyn, Dunlap, & Albin, 2002); however, actual implementation of PBS with families in integrated, real-life situations is complicated and requires attention to a variety of factors to be successful.

## CLINICAL EFFICACY AND CLINICAL UTILITY

As we study the components of our interventions to assess the "active ingredients" of treatment (i.e., those essential aspects that contribute to success), it is also important to examine those factors that serve as barriers to widespread implementation. These issues are being discussed extensively outside the field of developmental disabilities and are characterized as considerations of clinical efficacy and clinical utility (American Psychological Association, 2002). *Clinical efficacy* refers to the scientific evidence that collectively determines if a particular intervention is effective. The American Psychological Association review suggests growing evidence for the clinical efficacy of behavioral interventions for reducing challenging behaviors and improving adaptive functioning. In contrast, clinical utility is concerned with the effectiveness of the intervention in typical settings and under typical circumstances (Durand & Barlow, 2006). For example, it is important to demonstrate that our interventions are successful in unpredictable settings such as shopping malls, and that they do not require more controlled and therefore artificial situations to reduce problem behavior.

One aspect of clinical utility that is of current interest to us involves the populations with whom we are successful (Durand & Rost, 2005). Are our treatments effective with all families who have children with severe behavior problems, or are there subgroups with whom we are more or less successful? For example, how many families give up on efforts to assist their children (Munro, 2007)? Our clinical experience and research from other areas of study outside the disabilities field suggest that up to 50% of families fail to complete parent training for a variety of reasons (e.g., Irvine, Biglan, Smolkowski, Metzler, & Ary, 1999). For example, between 40% and 60% of families who begin treatment related to child mental health issues terminate services prematurely (Kazdin, 1996). It is unclear, however, how many families of children with more severe cognitive and developmental disorders who begin BPT drop out or otherwise do not complete intervention.

To begin to answer this question, we recently conducted a review of the behavioral intervention literature to more accurately gauge these rates and made a surprising discovery (Durand & Rost, 2005). Reviewing 149 research articles published in the *Journal of Applied Behavior Analysis* from 1968 to 2001 revealed that fewer than 3% of these studies noted if participants dropped out from their research. In other words, no mention was made of any participants who did not finish treatment. In addition, none of the handful of studies that did mention dropout analyzed the characteristics of those not completing the research, and no studies indicated whether any participants or their guardians refused to participate (Durand & Rost, 2005). The relative lack of information on attrition leaves open questions about the generalizability of this research to the population of persons exhibiting challenging behavior. In other words, are behavioral interventions only successful with highly motivated families and educators? We as yet do not know the answer to this question.

The research culture in single-subject design research rarely addresses population issues, an essential concern for issues of clinical efficacy and utility. Interestingly, one handbook on single-subject research methods recommended that researchers select only those participants who will reliably show up for sessions (Bailey & Burch, 2002, pp. 30–31). Although this is a practical suggestion, its consequences—studying only highly motivated and reliable people—leave us wondering if our interventions work with the larger population of people who request our help. A report from the meeting sponsored by the National Institutes of Health (NIH) on methodological challenges in psychosocial interventions in autism spectrum disorders (Lord et al., 2005) addressed this issue and listed the need for additional randomized clinical trials in this area as the highest priority. The work outlined in this chapter addresses the need to answer questions about the clinical utility of our effective interventions.

## BARRIERS TO TREATMENT

A variety of potential reasons have been cited as contributing to the lack of success of behavioral interventions in homes, schools, and the community. For example, research on factors that influence attrition rates in child-related therapy frequently note the role of socioeconomic status (SES) and minority status (Armbruster & Fallon, 1994; Armbruster & Kazdin, 1994). The correlation between SES and minority status with dropout, however, can be proxies for numerous other variables, making it difficult to pinpoint the factors that are directly related to attrition.

Three related concepts—"social validity" (Wolf, 1978), "treatment acceptability" (Kazdin, 1981; Reimers, Wacker, & Koeppl, 1987), and "contextual fit" (Albin, Lucyshyn, & Horner, 1996)—are among the concepts used to explain why behavior plans may or may not be implemented as designed. *Social validity* refers to the appropriateness of the behaviors targeted for change, the methods used for this change, and the outcomes of these processes; *treatment acceptability* relates to "buy-in" by those instituting the interventions; and *contextual fit* describes various factors associated with individuals, settings, and the support plan that may influence a person's commitment and capacity to use behavior plans as designed. Although there are subtle nuances in the definitions of these terms, the ongoing attention to these concepts reflects the importance of exploring variables affecting the acceptance and follow-through with behavioral interventions.

Research by Kazdin and colleagues in the field of clinical child therapy (Kazdin, 2000; Kazdin, Holland, & Crowley, 1997; Kazdin, Holland, Crowley, & Breton, 1997; Kazdin, Marciano, & Whitley, 2005; Kazdin & Wassell, 1999; Nock & Kazdin, 2001) has resulted in a model to explain the factors that influence parents who drop out of treatment, the barriers-to-treatment model. The model proposes that there are four factors that relate to dropping out of treatment: (a) stressors and obstacles that compete with treatment, (b) treatment demands and issues, (c) perceived relevance of treatment, and (d) relationship with the therapist.

Research on the barriers-to-treatment model has found that, when tested on a large sample of children and parents participating in treatment for conduct disorder, these barriers did significantly contribute to attrition from therapy, even when family, parent, and child characteristics that also predicted dropping out were taken into consideration (Kazdin, Holland, & Crowley, 1997). In addition, among families who were at high risk of dropping out based on risk factor assessed prior to treatment, the perception of low barriers to treatment served as a protective factor.

A related study found that, in addition to higher attrition rates, increased barriers to treatment also predicted fewer weeks in treatment and higher rates of not showing up and canceling sessions (Kazdin, Holland, Crowley, & Breton, 1997). Another study (Kazdin & Wassell, 1999), examining the relationship between perceived barriers to treatment and outcome of treatment, found that as the perceived barriers to treatment increased, the therapeutic change decreased, and the reverse was also true; lower perceived barriers to treatment were correlated with a better treatment outcome. Accordingly, there appears to be strong support that perceived barriers to treatment relate to attrition rates, adherence to treatment, and therapeutic outcome.

Research on the obstacles faced by families of children with disabilities is emerging. For example, two studies by Hieneman and Dunlap (2000, 2001), involving national surveys of parents and professionals with expertise in PBS, produced a range of factors perceived as key to effective behavioral intervention and ratings of their relative importance. Various factors were identified (supporting previous literature); however, a most interesting finding was that parent or service provider buy-in and capacity were actually rated as more important than the other variables (e.g., administrative support, material resources, plan design) in determining the outcomes of intervention.

A related factor found to influence treatment drop-out is a high level of parental stress. Parental stress can also be related to a number of variables, however, and several models explore these factors (i.e., Beresford, 1994; McCubbin & Patterson, 1983). One such model that has been used frequently in the developmental disabilities literature is the "double ABCX" (McCubbin & Patterson, 1983). According to this model, parental stress is influenced by (a) child characteristics, (b) the amount of resources available, and (c) the family's perception of the child.

Studies that have used the double ABCX model as a guide for research on parental stress demonstrated that perhaps the most important factor relating to stress is family perception (Hassall & Rose, 2005). For example, one study found that the single most important predictor of stress in parents of a child with an intellectual disability was a negative perception of the disability (Saloviita, Italinna, & Leinonen, 2003). In another study, *hardiness*, or characteristics that allow an individual to remain healthy after stressful situations, and social support predicted successful adaptation to stress in mothers of children with autism (Weiss, 2002). Hardiness includes perceived control of circumstances, commitment to a purpose and values, and willingness to accept challenges. Other studies have found similar results in which a "positive perspective" relates to better outcomes (Baker, Blacher, & Olsson, 2005).

An additional related model with significant empirical support has been outlined by Konstantareas (1991) and includes four factors: child-related stress, resource-related stress, parental perception, and family adaptation. *Child-related stress* refers to the difficulties families face as a result of their child's medical and behavioral challenges. In fact, this is one of the rationales for providing families with the skills to help improve their child's behaviors and in turn hopefully reduce this type of stress.

*Resource-related stress* is related to the provision of adequate resources and supports, both financial and emotional. Respite, for example, is often offered as a way to help reduce this stress. *Parental perception* refers to an individual parent's view of the nature of their child's disability. For example, a study by Bristol (1987) found that mothers adapted poorly to their child's disability if they defined it as "a family catastrophe." As we describe, this corresponds to measures of parental pessimism. Finally, the fourth factor, *family adaptation*, is viewed as the combined contribution of the other three factors.

In BPT as well as other approaches, practitioners are making efforts to overcome some of these barriers. Embedded within PBS training manuals one may find suggestions to address logistical (e.g., scheduling) issues, obtain administrative support, arrange for incentives, and maximize the effectiveness of the training itself (Dunlap, Hieneman, & Knoster, 2000; Reid & Parsons, 2004; Reid et al., 2003). It is common to offer financial assistance, respite care, or support in the form of family groups in conjunction with parent education efforts. Whereas these supports may be helpful in engaging and retaining participants, they are not always sufficient or long lasting, possibly because other factors—such as parental perceptions—interfere with implementation. Again, much of our attention in providing services to families of children with disabilities in general and those with challenging behavior specifically has focused on child-related and resource-related stress. Teaching behavior management skills and assisting with social support and respite activities are examples of this focus. However, little research is focused on parental attitudes and how they may have an impact on the ability to intervene with a child as well as efforts to assist families overcome this barrier.

## ATTITUDINAL BARRIERS

Research suggests that an individual's optimistic or pessimistic outlook on the world affects numerous outcomes, such as their health (Aspinwall & Brunhart, 2000) and motivation to achieve goals (Carver & Scheier, 1990). Indeed, the influence of parental characteristics on treatment may be greater than previously noted; in a review of the literature on child and adolescent treatment, Morrissey-Kane and Prinz (1999) noted that parental cognitions and attributions were found to influence three aspects of treatment: help seeking, treatment engagement and retention, and treatment outcome.

This research on the impact of attitudes in treatment participation and outcomes points to an important consideration that has not been adequately addressed in BPT. In fact, there is reason to believe that interventions may only be effective with the portion of our population that has the ability and motivation to complete all aspects of the intervention (Durand, 2001). If so, it only makes sense that interventions be developed to overcome such barriers. Interventions based on the principles of ABA follow a consistent logic (Baer et al., 1968). If they do not result in improvements in behavior, we do not attribute the failure to the recipient of the intervention;

instead, we reevaluate and modify our approach to be effective. However, we have a tendency to attribute failure to fully implement interventions by parents and teachers to their lack of motivation (calling them uncooperative or noncompliant). Viewing the behavior of these families from a functional perspective—asking what it is about our intervention that may be contributing to attrition and resistance—could result in an important reconceptualization of our intervention process.

Some preliminary research on the development of challenging behavior among young children suggests that the attitudes of family members may play an important role in treatment outcome. Fortunately, this research also may open up a new avenue for understanding the obstacles to successful intervention. We conducted a 3-year longitudinal prospective study to examine factors that might contribute to later behavior problems in young children (Durand, 2001). We identified 140 children who were 3 years of age and who had a cognitive or developmental disability and displayed behavior problems; the children were followed for up to 3 years. A number of factors were measured to assess their role in predicting which children would later display more severe behavior problems. These included measures of IQ; *Diagnostic and Statistical Manual of Mental Disorders, Fourth Edition* (*DSM-IV*; American Psychiatric Association, 1994) diagnosis; child behavior problems; child adaptive skills (communication and social skills); and a variety of family indicators (e.g., stress, attitudes, etc.).

Surprisingly, the most significant factor in predicting later behavior problems was not the severity of child's problems at age 3 or the extent of cognitive or adaptive behavior deficits initially displayed by the children. Rather, the best predictor of which children would have more severe problems 3 years later was a measure of parental optimism/pessimism. In other words, parents who had limited confidence in their ability to influence their child's behaviors by the time the child was 3 years of age were most likely to have children with more difficult behaviors later in life. For example, if parents resisted placing demands on their child for fear of escalating behavior problems, then children were more likely to develop severe behavior problems as they became older. This finding was true despite the fact that some of the children with more optimistic parents initially had more severe deficits and behavior problems. It appeared that parental optimism may have served as a protective factor for these children, and parental pessimism may put a child more at risk for developing severe behavior problems.

To return to the issue of clinical efficacy and utility, our data on parental pessimism suggest that we may be overestimating our success rates if we report data only on those families who complete our interventions. A more conservative view of our outcomes is that behavioral interventions are effective with that portion of the population who have the ability or the motivation to complete all aspects of our intervention.

Our research on problems surrounding sleep may provide another example. Studies of behavioral intervention for sleep-related behavior problems indicated that although we are able to design minimally invasive home-based interventions and can assist with bedtime support, some of these efforts still fail. Despite these efforts, many families who experience extreme stress report that they cannot carry out the plan (e.g., sending a child back to her room) and postpone or drop out of treatment (Durand, 1998). Again, many families view their situations as quite negative and have little confidence in their ability to successfully intervene with their child. This is consistent with the research on pessimism, which suggests that individuals who score high on this factor are less likely to persist in difficult situations than individuals who score higher on measures of optimism (C. Peterson, 2000).

As mentioned, there is a long history of recommending support for families in the form of financial assistance, respite services, and parent support groups to help reduce some of the obstacles to successful intervention. Although these are important considerations, our experience is that these efforts are less effective with families who are highly pessimistic (Durand, 2007). Respite, for example, is used as a temporary reprieve for these families rather than an opportunity to learn new skills or prepare them to become reinvolved with their children. Parent support groups are often viewed as negative experiences. For family members who already feel guilty about their performance as parents, being in the company of parents perceived as more successful—for example, those who seem unmoved by people in the supermarket who comment on their misbehaving child—results in even more negative self-talk and pessimism. Pessimistic families need very specific intervention to assist them with becoming engaged in BPT.

## OPTIMISTIC PARENTING

If an important obstacle to successful BPT is the pessimistic attitudes of some family members, the logical next question is, Can we intervene with these families in a way that will help them feel more optimistic about their abilities to work with their children? In turn, if we can successfully intervene with these families to assist them with this attitudinal barrier, will it help them continue and complete BPT, and will this lead to improvements in child behavior? The answers to these questions have been tested in a pilot study of children with behavior problems and their families.

The Positive Family Intervention Project is a multisite study designed to develop and assess the effectiveness of a treatment package that integrates cognitive-behavioral intervention with function-based BPT (i.e., PBS); this approach is referred to as *positive family intervention* (PFI). Families from throughout the Tampa Bay region in Florida (through the University of South Florida St. Petersburg) and the capitol region in New York (through the University at Albany, State University of New York) participated in this project. Our experience to date is that over 80% of the families referred to our project meet criterion for pessimism. This number is higher than expected and may, in part, represent an ascertainment issue (families may be more likely to be referred to this project if they express reservations about their ability to intervene with their child).

At-risk families with high scores on our measure of pessimism were assigned to one of two groups: (a) family members who received training in PBS for their child and (b) individuals who received PBS along with a cognitive-behavioral component (PFI). We evaluated if PFI would (a) increase family participation in training, and (b) if it would successfully prevent child behavior problems from escalating into more severe problems. Follow-up of the children is being conducted up to 2 years following initial intervention both at home and in school.

PFI is a clinically based approach to provide family members with the skills they need to cope with the stressors associated with everyday life along with the added stress of having a child with significant challenges. More specifically, we adapt cognitive-behavioral intervention techniques to meet the specific needs of these families and combine this approach with the components of PBS. Fortunately, there is work under way addressing pessimism—through "learned optimism"—and the need for some people to address feelings of being out of control, and this research appears to be an invaluable addition to our traditional approaches for helping these families. Seligman (1998), for example, outlined a treatment protocol that focuses on the way people view events and attempted to provide them with more adaptive styles. Research on this cognitive-behavioral therapy approach suggests that significant improvements can be observed in persons with pessimistic styles, which in turn results in improvements in such areas as depression.

PFI is an adaptation of PBS integrating Seligman's work for use with families of children with disabilities and challenging behavior. For example, in our preliminary work, we found that parents who score high on a measure of pessimism might describe a child's difficult trip to the supermarket this way: "Shopping with my child is a disaster." On the other hand, parents scoring high on optimism might describe it this way: "My child is not ready yet for long shopping trips." The former pessimistic description suggests that the problem is pervasive (all shopping is a problem) and permanent (shopping may never get better), while the latter optimistic view is local (it is just long shopping trips that are a problem) and temporary (someday, the child will be ready). Presenting families with their styles of describing situations and having them practice more adaptive optimistic styles—referred to as PFI—is proving to be quite successful.

Eight weekly individual sessions, lasting 90 min each, were provided to families in each group. All families received PBS (Durand, 1990; Hieneman et al., 2006). For those families receiving PFI, the cognitive-behavioral intervention component was integrated into the same sessions. Through this project, we developed standard protocols for both PBS alone and PFI.

The PBS process begins with an assessment that involves identification of goals and specific behaviors of concern and the collection and analysis of information through interviews and observations to determine the purposes problem behaviors serve. Based on the assessment, a team (including parents, teachers, and other support providers under guidance of someone trained in PBS) designs a behavior support plan for the child. The multicomponent intervention includes strategies designed to:

**Table 10.1.** Outline of Treatment Protocol

| | Positive Behavior Support | Cognitive-Behavioral Integration |
|---|---|---|
| Session 1 | Introduction and goal setting | Identify situations and associated self-talk |
| Session 2 | Gathering information | Determine the consequences of beliefs on behavior |
| Session 3 | Analysis and plan design | Dispute current thinking (accuracy and impact) |
| Session 4 | Preventing problems | Use a distraction to interrupt negative thinking |
| Session 5 | Managing consequences | Substitute with more positive, productive thoughts |
| Session 6 | Replacing behavior | Practice skills developed for recognizing and modifying pessimistic self-talk |
| Session 7 | Putting plan in place | Practice skills developed for recognizing and modifying pessimistic self-talk |
| Session 8 | Monitoring results and wrap-up | Help identify strategies to maintain positive changes in self-talk |

1. Prevent problems through modifications to the physical and social environment.
2. Manage consequences to maximize reinforcement for positive behavior rather than problem behavior.
3. Develop skills to replace problem behavior (e.g., via FCT).

The optimism training component is integrated into the sessions for the parents assigned to that condition. The sessions vary by parent but typically begin with a discussion of the recent successes and challenges with the child with a disability. Parents are encouraged to speak freely (which is why these sessions occur individually and not in groups), and the therapist's role is to be supportive but also to note how the parent describes situations. For example, if a parent makes a statement such as, "Shopping with my child is a disaster" or "I will never have my own life," these are brought up later in the session for discussion. The overall goal is to reduce pessimistic beliefs by learning to (a) identify them when they occur and (b) develop coping skills (Seligman, 1998). So, for example, the previous statements will be mentioned along with a discussion of how to dispute them. Pointing out that not all shopping has been problematic and that there are times when the parent may have opportunities just for personal activities begins the discussion. Parents are asked to identify such self-statements over the next week and to practice disputing them. The content of the sessions for each of the two conditions is summarized in Table 10.1. The intervention with one family is presented next to illustrate the PFI process.

## CASE EXAMPLE

Sylvia was referred to the PFI Project by a local program that provides support to families and direct service personnel of individuals with autism. Sylvia was a single parent in her early 30s who had completed her general equivalency diploma (GED) after she dropped out of high school. She lived in a low-income urban neighborhood and supported her family via government assistance.

Sylvia had two children with autism and significant behavioral challenges, one of whom (Lashawn) met the age criteria for inclusion into our program. Despite extensive efforts of the referring agency, schools, and other professionals working with Sylvia, she was unable to adopt effective behavioral intervention methods for either of her children. Sylvia was extremely pleasant and appreciative, but she frequently forgot appointments, disregarded suggestions, or simply failed to follow through. Although initially Sylvia was quite resistant to becoming involved in our program (i.e., she had to be coaxed by the referring agency and contacted multiple times), she eventually relented because she was concerned that her children's escalating behavior problems were putting them at risk for more restrictive educational placements. She was worried that she might ultimately "lose them" if she could not manage their behavior more effectively.

Sylvia's 5-year-old daughter Lashawn was the focus of the intervention sessions. Lashawn was a large, energetic girl. Although Lashawn was able to produce a few words, she communicated primarily through gestures and her problem behavior. She was able to assist in her basic self-care skills, but it was unclear how much she could actually do for herself since her mother typically did everything. Lashawn was being educated in a self-contained classroom for children with autism and receiving biweekly occupational and speech therapies. Her behaviors of concern included tantrums that involved screaming, crying, throwing or destroying property, and aggression (e.g., hitting, biting, kicking, head butting). She also tried to exit the car when it was moving or she ran out of the house. Tantrums occurred one or two times per day and often lasted in excess of an hour. In addition to the tantrums, Lashawn would jump up and down, run in circles, and laugh directly in her mother's face when she was not receiving attention. Her behavior was interfering with her social and educational progress (e.g., therapy sessions often had to be cut short) and isolating Lashawn and her family from community life.

Sylvia felt that Lashawn's behaviors occurred for essentially "no reason" except that Lashawn was plagued with autism. Because of this perspective, Sylvia's efforts to manage Lashawn's behavior consisted primarily of praying for her, seeking assistance from physicians and therapy providers (e.g., she was prescribed escalating dosages of medications for behavioral control), and trying to soothe Lashawn during her tantrums by providing massages, favorite snacks, and other pleasant activities. Syvia's attitudes and reactions to Lashawn's behavior were clearly barriers to effective intervention.

Our intervention process followed the protocol described in this chapter. The therapist introduced the basic principles of PBS and provided a variety of case examples to illustrate. She then began guiding Sylvia to identify members of Lashawn's support team. This included the variety of professionals working with the family as well as her ex-husband, older son, and friends through her church. Part of her homework each week was to communicate with this team about what she was learning and to facilitate their input and involvement. The therapist asked Sylvia to identify goals for Lashawn and her family as a whole. She identified improving Lashawn's ability to communicate, accept limits, and participate in social activities as important targets. She also stated that she wanted to be able to attend church as a family and have some time to herself (e.g., to go back to school). The therapist also helped Sylvia define Lashawn's problem behavior objectively and asked her to collect simple frequency data on her tantrums for baseline.

The therapist taught Sylvia to obtain input from the other members of the team through a structured interview tool and to observe Lashawn's behavior and the events surrounding her behavior without interpretation. Although writing was quite difficult for Sylvia (i.e., due to her educational background), she agreed to record these observations using ABC (antecedent-behavior-consequence) recording. Surprisingly, Sylvia took to this with great enthusiasm and continued to collect data in this way throughout the eight sessions. Using input from the interviews and observational data, the therapist helped Sylvia develop "hypotheses" to summarize the patterns. Lashawn's behavior served a variety of functions, depending on the context; these included (a) obtaining attention when her mother was engaged in another activity or interaction, (b) gaining access to food or other items (including physical contact) after initially being told no, and (c) avoiding or delaying participation in demanding activities, such as therapy and social play.

Using the summary statements, the therapist assisted Sylvia to identify and design intervention strategies to prevent, teach, and manage Lashawn's behavior. Although the space constraints of this chapter prohibit sharing all the details of this plan, some of the key features were to

- Communicate expectations clearly to Lashawn (e.g., "I need to make a phone call. While I am talking, you may play quietly with toys.").
- Provide snacks and toys during particularly challenging routines, especially when Lashawn has to wait or during transitions.
- Attend to behaviors that typically lead to tantrums (e.g., humming noises, rolling eyes, increased movement) and prompt appropriate ways for Lashawn to ask for what she needs or change the activity.
- Teach verbal and nonverbal methods for Lashawn to communicate her needs (e.g., bring Mom a book or touch her arm to obtain attention, sign or say "stop" to terminate an activity, request items by saying "I want ___" or pointing).
- Gradually build Lashawn's tolerance for nonpreferred activities (e.g., therapy, waiting) by increasing the time required in those activities before escape.
- Provide praise, treats, and opportunities to escape unpleasant activities contingent on communication or appropriate behavior.
- Withhold or delay these consequences for a period of time (5 min) following problem behavior.

For three consecutive weeks, Sylvia was given homework assignments to implement particular methods during daily activities and routines.

Once the interventions were identified, they were compiled into a comprehensive behavior support plan. The therapist asked Sylvia to identify specific steps for putting the plan in place (including enlisting support from the other team members) and to devise a plan for monitoring her use of the plan and its impact on Lashawn's behavior over time. (She chose to continue recording ABC data so she could analyze patterns and adjust the plan as needed.)

Importantly, interspersed throughout this typical PBS parent education process the therapist embedded an examination of and intervention with Sylvia's impeding attitudes or "self-talk." As mentioned, Sylvia believed that Lashawn's behavior was arbitrary, permanent, and beyond her control. These views were clearly barriers to intervention and cropped up frequently throughout the sessions. Through the optimism training protocol, the therapist guided Sylvia to clearly articulate her beliefs about Lashawn's behavior and her capacity to address it as well as the consequences those beliefs had in terns of her reactions to Lashawn and ultimately long-term outcomes. Using this information, the therapist guided Sylvia to dispute the beliefs to determine whether the way she was thinking was accurate and helpful and, when her beliefs were unproductive, to replace them with other thoughts. Sylvia's self-talk and process facilitated by the therapist are summarized in Table 10.2.

During the optimism training component of the intervention, the therapist had to help Sylvia recognize that Lashawn's behavior varied in relation to environmental events, including reactions from Sylvia, that the behavior was in fact predictable. This was a critical first step because without this recognition, Sylvia would be unable to adopt any intervention. She also helped Sylvia realize that she could make a difference and was not completely reliant on professionals (or even God) to "fix" Lashawn. The therapist continually prompted her to consider who she was expecting to resolve problems and to affirm that Sylvia herself was competent. Sylvia came to believe that she was powerful and could produce changes on her own. As she began implementing interventions and seeing the outcomes, Sylvia was surprised to find that Lashawn was capable of doing much more than she originally realized and could be taught skills (e.g., communication) that would make her problem behavior unnecessary.

Probably the most important and difficult lesson the therapist addressed was that Sylvia could sustain her beliefs and practices even in the face of hardships and mistakes. This occurred during a particularly difficult week when Lashawn's behavior escalated, and Sylvia felt overwhelmed. Sylvia promptly abandoned the behavior plan and sought an increase in her daughter's medications. The therapist confronted Sylvia with this situation and guided her through the self-talk process, helping her to recognize that—while it might be necessary to seek medical assistance—abandoning the plan was not helpful, and that she needed to be committed to it to make a long-term difference.

As a result of the PBS process combined with optimism training, Sylvia now has a behavior plan for Lashawn for which she has a sense of ownership. During the 8-week training sessions, Lashawn's tantrums continued to occur but decreased in both their length and severity (e.g., she would

**Table 10.2.** Sylvia's Self-Talk Journal.

| Situation: What happened (success or difficulty)? | Beliefs: What did you think or feel (self-talk)? | Consequences: What happened as a result (actions)? | Disputation: Was this a useful or accurate belief? | Substitution: What is a more positive belief (affirmation)? |
|---|---|---|---|---|
| Lashawn has "fighting spells" at different times throughout the day (laughs sometimes) | Lashawn's behavior is "out of the blue"—there is no reason for it<br>Lashawn is bad or evil<br>Lashawn can't help her behavior (due to disability | Waits for problems and reacts to them by soothing (e.g., with food, activities, massage)<br>Prays to God/uses holy oil to heal her | There are patterns to Lashawn's behavior; we can relate it to certain situations and reactions<br>Soothing makes the behavior worse | If I look for the W's, I can find out why Lashawn is misbehaving<br>My behavior affects Lashawn's behavior |
| Lashawn does not take care of her needs or communicate in a traditional sense | Lashawn is not capable of behaving (because she has a disability or is bad/evil) | Does not hold Lashawn accountable for her behavior or have expectations that are reasonable | Lashawn understands—her behavior is working and she can learn | Lashawn is capable of learning and should be held responsible for her actions |
| Efforts to support Lashawn are not resulting in improvement<br>Fails to implement strategies and Lashawn's behavior escalates | I don't know what to do to help Lashawn. I am not capable. I can't handle this.<br>I screwed up, and this is not fair to Lashawn (I need to make it better). | Does not develop consistent plan<br>Fails to attend or is late for meetings; pretends she does not understand<br>Looks to others to fix the problem<br>Gives in; placates Lashawn | When I respond consistently, I see improvements<br>There is no quick fix for Lashawn's behavior<br>I have to do this<br>It's okay to make mistakes<br>Giving in or giving up makes it worse | I am capable of helping Lashawn to behave better—"I am powerful" |
| Begins to make progress and see improvements | This is temporary and things will get worse (maybe I don't deserve for things to improve) | Gives up and goes back to status quo<br>Sabotages plan | Improvements have occurred over time and relate to what I am doing | Lashawn and I deserve to have better lives |

yell and smack at her mother and promptly stop when her communication was acknowledged). The standardized instruments (Scales of Independent Behavior–Revised, SIB-R) used in the postassessment at the end of the sessions showed change in Lashawn's maladaptive behavior as well as a much more pronounced change in adaptive behavior as her mother prompted new skills. More important, the mother has developed some new perspectives that may help her sustain the intervention. She even referred to her therapist as a "gift from God."

## PFI PRELIMINARY OUTCOMES

Results from the 18 families participating in the project provide support for this approach to helping parents at risk for dropping out of BPT. First, all families that completed the eight therapy sessions—regardless of the condition—experienced improvements in their reported pessimism as well as child problem behavior (using both observational data and scores from the SIB-R; Bruininks, Woodcock, Weatherman, & Hill, 1996). These findings suggest that PBS (whether or not the cognitive-behavioral component is included) is effective for improving child behavior if families complete all sessions. The fact that pessimism scores improve as well—again, even among families who did not receive the added cognitive-behavioral intervention—may mean that families feel more empowered just through experiencing success with their children.

A major finding from the study so far is that significantly more families drop out of intervention in the PBS condition. Almost half of these "pessimistic" families dropped out of PBS compared to only 11% of families who were in the PFI condition. Adding the cognitive-behavioral intervention appeared to help these at-risk families persist through the full 8-week therapy period, thus improving the odds of observing improvements in child behavior. To reiterate, our behavior interventions can be highly successful with children who have challenging behavior if families will persist in parent training. Adding "optimism training," a cognitive-behavioral approach to addressing the self-talk, seems to be a good adjunctive treatment for highly pessimistic parents.

## CONCLUSIONS

Our research to date points to the value of exploring the perceptions of family members prior to implementing BPT. Parental attitudinal barriers variously labeled pessimism, lack of self-efficacy, or lack of self-confidence may be significant obstacles to successful intervention for reducing child challenging behavior. The treatment approach just outlined (PFI) appears to be an effective approach for helping families overcome these attitudinal obstacles.

It is time to rethink how we view families who struggle with our interventions. First, we need to identify those families who are not being successful with our assessments and intervention plans and consider how our approaches must change. Less than full participation by parents should be a signal for the interventionist to change strategies rather than simply assigning blame. Second, just as we analyze the functions of the child behaviors we wish to change, we must begin to analyze the functions of parental behaviors that may interfere with successful outcomes. In our research, we are exploring attitudinal "themes" that run through the self-talk of family members and will use these concepts to direct our future intervention efforts. More information about why parents have difficulties with PBS should lead to intervention strategies designed to better assist these families.

## ACKNOWLEDGMENT

Portions of this chapter are based on "Positive Family Intervention: Hope and Help for Parents With Challenging Children," by V. M. Durand, 2007, *Psychology in Mental Retardation and Developmental Disabilities, 32*, 9–13.

## REFERENCES

Albin, R. W., Lucyshyn, J. M., & Horner, R. H. (1996). Contextual fit for behavioral support plan: A model for "goodness of fit." In L. K. Koegel, R. L. Koegel, & G. Dunlap (Eds.), *Positive behavioral support: Including people with difficult behavior in the community* (pp. 81–98). Baltimore: Brookes.

Alpert, C. L., & Kaiser, A. P. (1992). Training parents as milieu language teachers. *Journal of Early Intervention. 16*, 31–52.

American Psychiatric Association. (1994). *Diagnostic and statistical manual of mental disorders* (4th ed.). Washington, DC: Author.

American Psychological Association. (2002). Criteria for practice guideline development and evaluation. *American Psychologist, 57*, 1048–1059.

Armbruster, P., & Fallon, T. (1994). Clinical, sociodemographic, and systems risk factors for attrition in a children's mental health clinic. *American Journal of Orthopsychiatry, 64*, 677–585.

Armbruster, P., & Kazdin, A. E. (1994). Attrition in child psychotherapy. In T. H. Ollendick & R. J. Prinz (Eds.), *Advances in clinical child psychology* (Vol. 16, pp. 18–108). New York: Plenum.

Aspinwall, L. G., & Brunhart, S. M. (2000). What I do know won't hurt me: Optimism, attention to negative information, coping, and health. In J. E. Gillham (Ed.), *The science of optimism and hope: Research essays in honor of Martin E. P. Seligman* (pp. 163–200). Philadelphia: Templeton Foundation Press.

Assemany, A. E., & McIntosh, D. E., 2002). Negative treatment outcomes of behavioral parent training programs. *Psychology in the Schools, 39*, 209–219.

Baer, D. M., Wolf, M., & Risley, T. R. (1968). Some current dimensions of applied behavior analysis. *Journal of Applied Behavior Analysis, 1*, 91–97.

Bailey, J. S., & Burch, M. R. (2002). *Research methods in applied behavior analysis.* Thousand Oaks, CA: Sage.

Baker, B. L., Blacher, J., & Olsson M. B. (2005). Preschool children with and without developmental delay: Behaviour problems, parents' optimism and well-being. *Journal of Intellectual Disability Research, 49*, 575–590.

Beresford, B. A. (1994). Resources and strategies: How parents cope with the care of a disabled child. *Journal of Child Psychology and Psychiatry, 35*, 171–209.

Blair, K., Umbreit, J., & Bos, C. (1999). Using functional assessment and children's preferences to improve the behavior of your children with behavior disorders. *Behavior Disorders, 24*, 151–166.

Boettcher, M., Koegel, R. L., McNerney, E. K., & Koegel, L. K. (2003). A family-centered prevention approach to positive behavior support in a time of crisis. *Journal of Positive Behavior Interventions, 5*, 55–59.

Bristol, M. M. (1987). Mothers of children with autism or communication disorders: Successful adaptation and the double ABCX model. *Journal of Autism and Developmental Disorders, 17*, 469–486.

Bruininks, R. H., Woodcock, R. W., Weatherman, R. F., & Hill, B. K. (1996). *Scales of independent behavior- revised.* Chicago: Riverside.

Buschbacher, P., Fox, L., & Clarke, S. (2004). Recapturing a desired family routine: A parent-professional behavioral collaboration. *Research and Practice for Persons With Severe Disabilities, 29*, 25–39.

Byrd, R. S., & Weitzman, M. L. (1994). Predictors of early grade retention among children in the United States. *Pediatrics, 93*, 481–487.

Carr, E. G., Dunlap, G., Horner, R. H., Koegel, R. L., Turnbull, A. P., Sailor, W., et al. (2002). Positive behavior support: Evolution of an applied science. *Journal of Positive Behavior Interventions, 4*, 4–16.

Carr, E. G., Horner, R. H., Turnbull, A. P., Marquis, J, Magito-Mclaughlin, D., McAtee, M. I., et al. (1999). *Positive behavior support for people with developmental disabilities: A research synthesis.* Washington, DC: American Association on Mental Retardation.

Carver, C. S., & Scheier, M. F. (1990). Origins and functions of positive and negative affect: A control process view. *Psychological Review, 97*, 19–35.

Charlop-Christy, M. H., & Carpenter, M. H. (2000). Modified incidental teaching sessions: A procedure for parents to increase spontaneous speech in their children with autism. *Journal of Positive Behavior Interventions, 2*, 98–112.

Clarke, S., Dunlap, G., & Vaughn, B. (1999). Family-centered assessment-based intervention to improve an early morning routine. *Journal of Positive Behavior Interventions, 1*, 235–241.

Cole, D. A., & Meyer, L. H. (1989). Impact of needs and resources on family plans to seek out-of-home placement. *American Journal on Mental Retardation, 93*, 380–387.

Conroy, M. A., & Stichter, J. P. (2003). The application of antecedents in the functional assessment process: Existing research, issues, and recommendations. *Journal of Special Education, 37*, 15–25.

Dangel, R. F., Yu, M., Slot, N. W., & Fashinger, G. (1994). Behavioral parent training. In D. Granold (Ed.), *Cognitive and behavioral treatment: Methods and applications* (pp. 108–122). Belmont, CA: Thompson Brooks/Cole.

Day, H. M., Horner, R. H., & O'Neill, R. E. (1994). Multiple functions of problem behaviors: Assessment and intervention. *Journal of Applied Behavior Analysis, 27*, 279–289.

Delprato, D. (2001). Comparisons of discrete trial and normalized behavior intervention for young children with autism. *Journal of Autism and Developmental Disabilities, 31*, 315–325.

Dumas, J. E. (1989). Treating antisocial behavior in children: Child and family approaches. *Clinical Psychology Review, 9*, 197–222.

Dunlap, G., & Fox, L. (1999). A demonstration of behavioral support for young children with autism. *Journal of Positive Behavior Interventions, 1*, 77–88.

Dunlap, G., Hieneman, M., & Knoster, T. (2000). Essential elements of inservice training in positive behavior support. *Journal of Positive Behavior Interventions, 2*, 22–32.

Dunlap, G., Kern-Dunlap, L., Clarke, S., & Robbins, F. R. (1991). Functional assessment, curricular revision, and severe behavior problems. *Journal of Applied Behavior Analysis, 24*, 387–397.

Dunlap, G., Newton, S., Fox, L., Benito, N., & Vaughn, B. (2001). Family involvement in functional assessment and positive behavior support. *Focus on Autism and Other Developmental Disabilities, 16*, 215–221.

Durand, V. M. (1990). *Severe behavior problems: A functional communication training approach.* New York: Guilford Press.

Durand, V. M. (1998). *Sleep better! A guide to improving sleep for children with special needs.* Baltimore: Brookes.

Durand, V. M. (1999). Functional communication training using assistive devices: Recruiting natural communities of reinforcement. *Journal of Applied Behavior Analysis, 32*, 247–267.

Durand, V. M. (2001). Future directions for children and adolescents with mental retardation. *Behavior Therapy, 32*, 633–650.

Durand, V. M. (2007). Positive family intervention: Hope and help for parents with challenging children. *Psychology in Mental Retardation and Developmental Disabilities, 32*(3), 9–13.

Durand, V. M., & Barlow, D. H. (2006). *Essentials of abnormal psychology* (4th ed.). Belmont, CA: Wadsworth/Thomson Learning.

Durand, V. M., & Carr, E. G. (1992). An analysis of maintenance following functional communication training. *Journal of Applied Behavior Analysis, 25*, 777–794.

Durand, V. M., & Crimmins, D. B. (1988). Identifying the variables maintaining self-injurious behavior. *Journal of Autism and Developmental Disorders, 18*, 99–117.

Durand, V. M., & Rost, N. (2005). Does it matter who participates in our studies? A caution when interpreting the research on positive behavioral support. *Journal of Positive Behavior Interventions, 7*, 186–188.

Einfeld, S. E., & Tonge, B. J. (1996). Population prevalence of psychopathology in children and adolescents with mental retardation: II. Epidemiological findings, *Journal of Intellectual Disability Research, 40*, 99–109.

Einfeld, S. E., Tonge, B. J., & Rees, V. W. (2001). Longitudinal course of behavioral and emotional problems in Williams syndrome. *American Journal on Mental Retardation, 106*, 73–81.

Emerson, E., Kiernan, C., Alborz, A., Reeves, D., Mason, H., Swarbrick, R., et al. (2001). Predicting the persistence of severe self-injurious behavior, *Research in Developmental Disabilities 22*, 67–75.

Eyberg, S. M., & Boggs, S. R. (1989). Parent training for oppositional defiant preschoolers. In C. E. Schaefer & J. M. Briesmeister (Eds.), *Handbook of parent training* (pp. 105–132). New York: Wiley.

Eyman, R. K., & Call, T. (1977). Maladaptive behavior and community placement of mentally retarded persons. *American Journal of Mental Deficiency, 82*, 137–144.

Forehand, R., & Kotchick, B. (2002). Behavioral parent training: Current challenges and potential solutions. *Journal of Child and Family Studies, 11*, 377–384.

Forehand, R., & McMahon, R. J. (1981). *Helping the noncompliant child: A clinician's guide to parent training.* New York: Guilford Press.

Frea, W. D., & Hepburn, S. L. (1999). Teaching parents of children with autism to perform functional assessments to plan interventions for extremely disruptive behaviors. *Journal of Positive Behavior Interventions, 1*, 112–116.

Gilliam, W. S., & Shahar, G. (2006). Preschool and child care expulsion and suspension: Rates and predictors in one state. *Infants and Young Children, 19*, 228–245.

Gimpel, G. A., & Collett, B. R. (2002). Best practices in behavioral parent training. In A. Thomas & J. Grimes (Eds.), *Best practices in school psychology* (Vol. 1, pp. 451–465). Washington, DC: National Association for School Psychologists.

Green, V. A., O'Reilly, M., Itchon, J., & Sigafoos, J. (2005). Persistence of early emerging aberrant behavior in children with developmental disabilities. *Research in Developmental Disabilities, 26*, 47–55.

Hanley, G. P., Piazza, C. C., Fisher, W. W., Contrucci, S. A., & Maglieri, K. A. (1997). Evaluation of client preference for function-based treatment packages. *Journal of Applied Behavior Analysis, 30*, 459–473.

Hassall, R., & Rose, J. (2005). Parental cognitions and adaptation to the demands of caring for a child with an intellectual disability: A review of the literature and implication for clinical interventions. *Behavioural and Cognitive Psychotherapy, 33*, 71–88.

Hawkins, R. P., Peterson, R. F., Schweid, E., & Bijou, S. W. (1966). Behavior therapy in the home: Amelioration of problem parent-child relations with the parent in a therapeutic role. *Journal of Experimental Child Psychology, 4*, 99–107.

Hayes, R. P. (1987). Training for work. In D. C. Cohen & A. M. Donellan (Eds.), *Handbook of autism and pervasive developmental disorders* (pp. 360–370). New York: Wiley.

Hieneman, M., Childs, K., & Sergay, J (2006). *Parenting with positive behavior support: A practical guide to resolving your child's difficult behavior.* Baltimore: Brookes.

Hieneman, M., & Dunlap, G. (2000). Factors affecting the outcomes of community-based behavioral support: I. Factor category importance. *Journal of Positive Behavior Interventions, 3*, 67–74.

Hieneman, M., & Dunlap, G. (2001). Factors affecting the outcomes of community-based behavioral support: II. Identification and description of factor categories. *Journal of Positive Behavior Interventions, 2*, 161–169.

Horner, R. H., Day, H. M., & Day, J. R. (1997). Using neutralizing routines to reduce problem behavior. *Journal of Applied Behavior Analysis, 30*, 601–614.

Horner, R. H., Dunlap, G., Koegel, R. L., Carr, E. G., Sailor, W., Anderson, J., et al. (1990). Toward a technology of "nonaversive" behavioral support. *Journal of the Association for Persons With Severe Handicaps, 3*, 125–132.

Horner, R. H., Vaughn, B. J., Day, H. M., & Ard, W. R. (1996). The relationship between setting events and problem behavior: Expanding our understanding of behavioral support. In L. K. Koegel, R. L. Koegel, & G. Dunlap (Eds.), *Positive behavioral support: Including people with difficult behavior in the community* (pp. 381–402). Baltimore: Brookes.

Irvine, A. B., Biglan, A., Smolkowski, K., Metzler, C. W., & Ary, D. V. (1999). The effectiveness of a parenting skills program for parents of middle school students in small communities. *Journal of Consulting and Clinical Psychology, 67*, 811–825.

Iwata, B. A., Dorsey, M. F., & Slifer, K. J. (1994). Toward a functional analysis of self-injury. *Journal of Applied Behavior Analysis, 27*, 197–209.

Jacobson, J. W. (1982). Problem behavior and psychiatric impairment within a developmentally disabled population I: Behavior frequency. *Applied Research in Mental Retardation, 3*, 121–139.

James, K. M., & Scotti, J. R. (2000). The educative approach to intervention with child excess behavior: Toward an application to parent education packages. *Child and Family Behavior Therapy, 22*(3), 1–37.

Jones, R. S. P. (1999). A 10 year follow-up of stereotypic behavior with eight participants. *Behavioral Intervention, 14*, 45–54.

Kazdin, A. E. (1981). Assessment techniques for childhood depression: A critical appraisal. *Journal of the American Academy of Child Psychiatry, 20*, 358–375.

Kazdin, A. E. (1996). Dropping out of child therapy: Issues for research and implications for practice. *Clinical Child Psychology and Psychiatry, 1*, 133–156.

Kazdin, A. E. (1997). Parent management training: Evidence, outcomes, and issues. *Journal of the American Academy of Child and Adolescent Psychiatry, 36*, 1349–1356.

Kazdin, A. E. (2000). Perceived barriers to treatment participation and treatment acceptability among antisocial children and their families. *Journal of Child and Family Studies, 9*, 157–174.

Kazdin, A. E., Holland, L., & Crowley, M. (1997). Family experience of barriers to treatment and premature termination from child therapy. *Journal of Consulting and Clinical Psychology, 65*, 453–463.

Kazdin, A. E., Holland, L., Crowley, M., & Breton. (1997). Barriers to treatment participation scale: Evaluation and validation in the context of child outpatient treatment. *Journal of Child Psychology and Psychiatry, 38*, 1051–1062.

Kazdin, A. E., Marciano, P. L., & Whitley, M. K. (2005). The therapeutic alliance in cognitive-behavioral treatment of children referred for oppositional, aggressive, and antisocial behavior. *Journal of Consulting and Clinical Psychology, 73*, 726–730.

Kazdin, A. E., & Wassell, G. (1999).Barriers to treatment participation and therapeutic change among children referred for conduct disorder. *Journal of Clinical Child Psychology, 28*, 160–172.

Koegel, L. K., Koegel, R. L., & Dunlap, G. (1996). *Positive behavioral support: Including people with difficult behavior in the community.* Baltimore: Brookes.

Koegel, L. K., Steibel, D., & Koegel, R. L. (1998). Reducing aggression in children with autism toward infant or toddler siblings. *Journal of the Association for Persons With Severe Handicaps, 23*, 111–118.

Koegel, R. L., & Covert, A. (1972). The relationship of self-stimulation to learning in autistic children. *Journal of Applied Behavior Analysis, 5*, 381–387.

Koegel, R. L., & Frea, W. D. (1993). Treatment of social behavior in autism through the modification of pivotal social skills. *Journal of Applied Behavior Analysis, 26*, 369–377.

Konstantareas, M. M. (1991). Dysfunctional children's impact on their parents. *Canadian Journal of Behavioural Science, 23*, 358–375.

Lord, C., Wagner, A., Rogers, S., Szatmari, P., Aman, M., Charman, T., et al. (2005). Challenges in evaluating psychosocial interventions for autistic spectrum disorders. *Journal of Autism and Developmental Disorders, 35*, 695–708.

Lovaas, O. I. (1993). The development of a treatment-research project for developmentally disabled and autistic children. *Journal of Applied Behavior Analysis, 26*, 617–630.

Lowe, K., Allen, D., Jones, E., Brophy, S., Moore, K., & James, W. (2007). Challenging behaviours: Prevalence and topographies. *Journal of Intellectual Disability Research, 51*, 625–636.

Luiselli, J. K., & Cameron, M. J. (1998). *Antecedent control: Innovative approaches to behavioral support.* Baltimore: Brookes.

Lucyshyn, J. M., Albin, R. W., Horner, R. H., Mann, J. C., Mann, J. A., & Wadsworth, G. (2007). Family implementation of positive behavior support for a child with autism. *Journal of Positive Behavior Interventions, 9*(3), 131–150.

Lucyshyn, J. M., Albin, R. W., & Nixon, C. D. (1997). Embedding comprehensive behavior support in family ecology: A single case analysis. *Journal of Consulting and Clinical Psychology, 65*, 241–251.

Lucyshyn, J. M., Dunlap, G., & Albin, R. W. (2002). *Families and positive behavior support: Addressing problem behavior in family contexts.* Baltimore: Brookes.

Machalicek, W., O'Reilly, M. F., Beretvas, N., Sigafoos, J., & Lancioni, G. E. (2007). A review of interventions to reduce challenging behavior in school settings for students with autism spectrum disorders. *Research in Autism Spectrum Disorders, 1*, 229–246.

MacKenzie, E. P., Fite, P. J., & Bates, J. E. (2004). Predicting outcomes in behavioral parent training: Expected and unexpected results. *Child and Family Behavior Therapy, 26*, 37–53.

Maughan, D. R., Christiansen, E., & Jensen, W. R. (2005). Behavioral parent training as a treatment for externalizing behavior and disruptive behavior disorders: A meta-analysis. *School Psychology Review, 34*, 267–286

McCart, M. R., Priester, P. E., & Hobart, W. (2006). Differential effectiveness of behavioral parent training and cognitive-behavioral treatment for antisocial youth: A meta-analysis. *Journal of Abnormal Child Psychology, 34*, 527–543.

McCubbin, H. I., & Patterson, J. M. (1983). The family stress process: The double ABCX model of adjustment and adaptation. *Marriage and Family Review, 6*(1–2), 7–37.

McGee, G. G., Morrier, M. J., & Daly, T. (1999). An incidental teaching approach to early intervention for toddlers with autism. *Journal of the Association for Persons With Severe Handicaps, 24*, 133–146.

Moes, D. R., & Frea, W. D. (2000). Using family context to inform intervention planning for the treatment of a child with autism. *Journal of Positive Behavior Interventions, 2*, 40–46.

Moes, D. R., & Frea, W. D. (2002). Contextualized behavioral support in early intervention for children with autism and their families. *Journal of Autism and Developmental Disorders, 32*, 519–533.

Morrissey-Kane, E., & Prinz, R. J. (1999). Engagement in child and adolescent treatment: The role of parental cognitions and attributions. *Clinical Child and Family Psychology Review, 2*, 183–198.

Munro, J. D. (2007). A positive intervention model for understanding, helping, and coping with "challenging" families. In I. Brown & M. Percy (Eds.), *A comprehensive guide to intellectual and developmental disabilities* (pp. 373–382). Baltimore: Brookes.

Nock, M. K., & Kazdin, A. E. (2001). Parent expectancies for child therapy: Assessment and relation to participation in treatment. *Journal of Child and Family Studies, 10*, 155–180.

Peterson, C. (2000). The future of optimism. *American Psychologist, 55*, 44–55.

Peterson, S. M., Derby, K. M., Berg, W. K., & Horner, R. H. (2002). Collaboration with families in the functional behavior assessment of and intervention for severe behavior problems. *Education and Treatment of Children, 25*, 5–25.

Reid, D. H., & Parsons, M. B. (2004). *Positive behavior support training curriculum.* Washington, DC: American Association on Mental Retardation.

Reid, D. H., Rothholz, D. A., Parsons, M. B., Morris, L., Braswell, B. A., Green, C. W., et al., (2003). Training human service supervisors in aspects of PBS: Evaluation of a statewide, performance-based program. *Journal of Positive Behavior Interventions, 5*, 35–46.

Reimers, T. M., Wacker, D. P., & Koeppl, G. (1987). Acceptability of behavioral interventions: A review of the literature. *School Psychology Review, 16*, 212–217.

Saloviita, T., Italinna, M., and Leinonen, E. (2003). Explaining the parental stress of fathers and mothers caring for a child with intellectual disability: A Double ABCX model. *Journal of Intellectual Disability Research, 47*, 300–312.

Seligman, M. E. P. (1998). *Learned optimism: How to change your mind and your life.* New York: Pocket Books.

Serketich, W. J., & Dumas, J. E. (1996). The effectiveness of behavioral parent training to modify antisocial behavior in children: A meta-analysis. *Behavior Therapy, 27*, 171–186.

Shoham-Vardi, I., Davidson, P. W., Cain, N. N., Sloane-Reeves, J. E., Giesow, V. E., Quijano, L. E., et al. (1996). Factors predicting re-referral following crisis intervention for community-based persons with developmental disabilities and behavioral and psychiatric disorders. *American Journal on Mental Retardation, 101*, 109–117.

Singer, G. H. S., Goldberg-Hamblin, S. E., Peckham-Hardin, K. D., Barry, L., & Santarelli, G. E. (2002). Toward a synthesis of family support practices and positive behavior support. In J. Lucyshyn, G. Dunlap, & R. Albin (Eds.), *Families and positive behavior support: Addressing problem behavior in family contexts* (pp. 155–183). Baltimore: Brookes.

Steege, M. W., Mace, F. C., Perry, L., & Longenecker, H. (2007). Applied behavior analysis: Beyond discrete trial teaching. *Journal of Applied Behavior Analysis, 44*, 91–99.

Sugai, G., Horner, R. H., Dunlap, G., Hieneman, M., Lewis, T. J., Nelsen, C. M., et al. (2000). Applying positive behavior support and functional behavioral assessment in schools. *Journal of Positive Behavior Interventions, 2*, 131–143.

Vaughn, B. J., Clarke, S., & Dunlap, G. (1997). Assessment-based intervention for severe behavior problems in a natural family context. *Journal of Applied Behavior Analysis, 30*, 713–716.

Vaughn, B. J., Wilson, D., & Dunlap, G. (2002). Family-centered intervention to resolve problem behaviors in a fast-food restaurant. *Journal of Positive Behavior Interventions, 4*, 38–45.

Weiss, M. J. (2002). Hardiness and social support as predictors of stress in mothers of typical children, children with autism, and children with mental retardation. *Autism, 6*, 115–130.

Wolf, M. M. (1978). Social validity: The case for subjective measurement or how applied behavior analysis is finding its heart. *Journal of Applied Behavior Analysis, 11*, 203–214.

# 11

# Families Facing Extraordinary Challenges in Urban Communities: Systems-Level Application of Positive Behavior Support

**AMY McCART, NIKKI WOLF, HOLLY M. SWEENEY, URSULA MARKEY, and D. J. MARKEY**

As the parents of two children with disabilities living in the urban core, Ursula and D. J. Markey of New Orleans understand the challenges that families face in urban communities. Fueled by their own experiences with their sons and the encouragement of friends and neighbors, they started a support and advocacy group called Pyramid Parent Training Community Parent Resource Center. Their goals were to share with other families living in urban communities what research and experience taught them about supporting children with challenges. As the Markeys learned more about positive behavior support (PBS), they began a project to teach and support parents in the principles and practical applications of PBS strategies. The aim of the program is to bring best research-based practices in PBS to families in traditionally underserved, poverty-stricken communities in crisis. Here, they share their perspectives on the definition of a community in crisis and the role of PBS for families facing challenges in these communities:

**AMY McCART** • University of Kansas
**NIKKI WOLF** • University of Kansas
**HOLLY M. SWEENEY** • University of Kansas
**URSULA MARKEY** • Pyramid Parent Training Community Parent Resource Center
**D. J. MARKEY** • Pyramid Parent Training Community Parent Resource Center

> In the United States, urban communities are in distress. First and foremost a community in crisis is an underserved community. Getting to this point of crisis does not happen in a vacuum. How do you determine when a community is in crisis? A community is in crisis when conditions such as extreme poverty and educational disparity become the norm rather than the exception. PBS offers communities in crisis a frame of reference where families can create venues for their children to excel. There is clear evidence that PBS helps parents work more positively and successfully with schools to improve services for their children. Pre-civil rights, underserved parents in poverty created opportunities for their children to shine; they gave us the strength of knowing there were many things that could be done. These parents showed support, and most importantly they created expectations for those of us who now continue efforts towards positive change. PBS has revolutionary potential as it considers historical successes such as these for families and communities, it creates expectations again. If we can show families something that works well, they will demand it when it is not present in their schools and communities. In a community, PBS raises the bar for everyone. There is a commonality that professionals, community members, families and schools work towards—common positive expectations and language. PBS is a different way of being in the world; it offers and reinforces support rather than control. In an urban community, especially one in crisis, teaching parents and families the skills to become leaders in addition to PBS strategies is critical so that they can help the communities' efforts to move forward more successfully. Teach families and those that support them and they can be the voice. Families will support those who support them. This reciprocal support will hopefully grow and result in lasting systems change. Leadership is about empowering others to lead. This is what PBS is about for families and communities in crisis. (D. J. & U. Markey, personal communication, September 2007)

Currently, PBS is an effective model of multitier intervention used in schools across the nation (Lewis, Sugai, & Colvin, 1998; Luiselli, Putnam, & Sunderland, 2002; Sugai et al., 2000; Taylor-Greene & Kartub, 2000; Turnbull et al., 2002). This evidence-based approach demonstrates solid effects on student behavior and school climate (Horner & Sugai, 2004). Walker and colleagues (1996) indicated the need for schools to reconceptualize how they provide support to students who have antisocial or challenging behavior. This reconstructive thought process leads to the use of a preventive model of behavior support originating in the health industry and resulting in a new framework for schools. This model of support culminated with a large number of schools rethinking and revising how they approach discipline for their students from a systems perspective. These outcomes are a result of giving all students the behavioral and academic supports they need. In the past, resources in school settings were often directed to the children with the most significant needs, while those with fewer needs waited for support. A systems approach of multitier intervention promotes behavioral support for all students in the school (primary), students at risk for academic failure or behavioral needs (secondary), and students who are currently experiencing school failure (tertiary). Yet, ensuring the safety and security of our children reaches far beyond the school itself into the families, business partners, community leaders, and the community as a whole (Dwyer, Osher, & Hoffman, 2000).

For families living in poverty in urban communities and, more specifically, communities in crisis, consideration of how the PBS multitier approach may be applied to an entire community organization supporting families, or family support agency, has merit for researchers and practitioners. For the purposes of this chapter, a *family support agency* is an organization that (a) offers services and assistance in areas such as social-emotional, physiological, and economic support for families with children who are experiencing challenges socially that may or may not be related to a disability; (b) helps families learn to better access and coordinate school and community supports; and (c) provides families with new skills with which to improve the outcomes or quality of life for their children and themselves. A *community in crisis* includes individuals living in close proximity to one another facing: (a) widespread poverty; (b) elevated crime rates; (c) mobility and transient populations; (d) deteriorated or ineffective community infrastructure (i.e., schools, hospitals, transportation systems); or (e) pervasive discrepancy of available supports and services based on community/family needs. Singer and colleagues (Singer, Goldberg-Hamblin, Peckham-Hardin, Barry, & Santarelli, 2002) indicated the importance of the family support movement in obtaining resources for children with multiple needs. They noted that PBS is closely aligned with the family support core features indicated by Dunst, Trivette, Gordon, and Starnes (1993), in which family support services (a) enhance a sense of community; (b) mobilize resources and supports; (c) are consumer driven, so responsibility is shared by the family and the family support program; (d) protect family integrity; (e) strengthen family functioning; and (f) are proactive and preventive. PBS as a family support mechanism is a system of support with the ability to enhance the efforts of agencies working with families to meet their goals of sustainable change.

Applying a multitier prevention framework to family support agencies involves understanding not only the unique features of that agency, but also the unique features of the families they support, each clearly distinct. The purposes of this chapter are to (a) identify the circumstances affecting communities and their families in crisis; (b) propose a systems-level PBS approach as a model for family support agencies; (c) describe a systems-level PBS implementation exemplar in a family support agency; and (d) discuss implications and future directions.

Offering support to families and youth who face extraordinary challenges in urban environments requires effective use of resources and services (Markey, Markey, Quant, Santelli, & Turnbull, 2002; Utley, Kozleski, Smith, & Draper 2002). Schorr (1997) indicated that agencies and programs supporting families with multiple needs must "take on an extended role in the lives of the children and families they work with" (p. 6). Given that, how can agencies meet the magnitude of need of these families while facing limited financial and human resources? Through the use of a PBS prevention and problem-solving model, family support agencies can more effectively and efficiently meet the diverse and complex needs of families who are in crisis. Exploring the application of PBS as an evidence-based multitier system of support in urban communities and drawing from the lessons learned in those settings offers promising outcomes for family support agencies and their families.

## CIRCUMSTANCES AFFECTING COMMUNITIES AND THEIR FAMILIES IN CRISIS

Clearly, efforts of family support agencies must include an understanding of the circumstances families face. Services should be guided with a full awareness of the context. Building optimal community support is reliant on the (a) establishment of effective partnerships, (b) creation of school and community connections, (c) enlistment of broad family and support, (d) understanding of the implications of poverty, and (e) acknowledgment of the role of crisis within a family.

### Effective Partnerships

Just as it is not appropriate to simply add PBS as a school reform model to the complex mix of practices in schools (Tyack & Cuban, 1995), likewise it is inappropriate to do so when considering implementation of PBS within family support agencies. To have an impact on change at the community level through the use of PBS, an effective community or family support agency partnership with schools must be formed.

Lessons can be learned from the research on the challenges schools face when establishing partnerships with families. Ineffective communication between parents and school settings, along with lack of child care and lack of transportation have been noted as significant barriers for parents (particularly African Americans) interested in participating in parent-school events (Reglin, King, Losike-Sedimo, & Ketterer, 2003). Some of these same barriers exist for families when attempting to participate in agency-supported events. Fostering the engagement of parents and their children with family support agencies is important given children in urban settings are often more likely to have chronic, intense challenging behavior (Eber, Sugai, Smith, & Scott, 2002; Frankland, Edmonson, & Turnbull, 2001; Minke & Anderson, 2005; Warren et al., 2003).

### School and Community Connection

The need for a strong, interdependent connection between school and community is obvious; yet, the practice of school community interconnectedness has not yet been effectively realized (Lawson & Sailor, 2000). Schools can facilitate the strengthening of a community; likewise, schools can be the beneficiary of a strong community. The importance of moving from the implementation of solely school-based intervention to a culturally and contextually responsive intervention that is directly linked with school and community is imperative (Santarelli, Koegel, Casas, & Koegel, 2001).

Community support and school support have common qualities; most important are the need for a systematic application of prevention and data-based interventions as well as local problem solving and involvement. Schorr (1997) shared the critically important role the community plays in making meaningful changes for students through school reform, including sending children to school prepared to deal with the various academic and social requirements of a school setting as well as stronger support and participation from community members. Taylor (2002) stated the connection between school and community is so strong that, "Any school reform movement that is not linked to the transformation and redevelopment of distressed, underdeveloped neighborhoods is doomed to failure" (p. 7). Further, Cuban (2001) pointed out that schools alone are not able to "save" poor children; poverty is a community issue, not just a school issue.

Establishing effective community partnership in urban settings is often challenging. Yet, the rationale for family support in urban communities is necessary due to the fact that there are limited educational opportunities and access to research-based practices; the environmental circumstances are compound and complex, and the schools are implementing punitive, directive practices with little parent involvement (Markey et al., 2002). Cultural considerations for supporting diverse families are paramount as community partnerships are formed. Families from varying cultural perspectives and those supporting families must be engaged in the process of contextual and cultural understanding (Fox, Dunlap, & Powell, 2002; Santarelli et al., 2001). A strong interdependent connection between a family support agency and the community, in which the culture is considered in developing contextually responsive interventions, may result in a stronger community, which in turn strengthens the abilities of the family support agency.

## Family Support

The cornerstones of effective family support are detailed in the literature as Table 11.1 indicates (Lucyshyn, Horner, Dunlap, Albin, & Ben, 2002). These features provide a foundation for family support implementation; yet, the application of these features in communities facing multiple challenges is difficult. When family support agencies apply a systemwide approach to service provision, the implementation of these core features is attainable. For example, not all families who have children with challenging behavior need a functional assessment; this feature is utilized for families with tertiary-level need. Yet, the application of collaborative partnerships and relationship development is important for all families. Turnbull and her colleagues (Turnbull, Blue-Banning, Turbiville, & Park, 1999) cautioned that, "If we truly are a field of professionals, families, and community members working in partnerships, we must transform the whole process of how issues such as a new conceptualization of partnership education are discussed to make sure that we do not have a predominantly professional dialogue" (p. 170). This dialogue within urban community environments can support the investment of the family in community growth and invest the community in the family growth. Family "buy-in" or engagement in the process of intervention is also critical to the ultimate success of the child, family, school, and community partnership (Hieneman & Dunlap, 2001).

**Table 11.1.** Elements of Effective Family Support

- Collaborative partnerships and effective relationship development
- Family-centered principles and practices
- Meaningful lifestyle outcomes
- Functional assessment
- Problem behaviors as problems of learning
- Communication as the foundation of positive behavior
- Multicomponent support plans
- Contextual fit with family life
- Family setting as a unit of analysis and intervention
- Implementation support
- Continuous evaluation
- Support with sincerity and humility

## Community Research

Sanders (1997) reminded us that successful and long-standing community partnerships require (a) a shared vision and responsibility with community partners, (b) time to develop and sustain the community relationships, (c) willingness to systematically progress with long-term (over several years) planning, (d) centering and focusing on child-family-student relationships, and (e) a strategic and persistent identification process for those with significant needs in the school and community. In addition to the above recommended community components, Riley (1997) shared a review of local research efforts for communities, families, and children with interesting implications for practice: (a) Communities are more likely to have confidence in research conducted locally; (b) local research leads to a greater sense of community (working together on an effort brings people closer together); (c) local communities want to help others in ways that are meaningful; and (d) local collaboration with core community members expands the scope and impact of community work.

Riley (1997) also indicated several forms of community-focused research that are effective at promoting successful outcomes for community citizens and children, including action-oriented research (Lewin, 1946), participatory research (Gaventa, 1988; Turnbull, Friesen, & Ramirez, 1998), and empowerment research (Cochran, 1995; Markey, Santelli, & Turnbull, 1998; Perkins & Zimmerman, 1995; Rappaport, Swift, & Hess, 1984). These avenues of research provide an active voice for the community in the transformation or intervention efforts.

To adequately address the family or community support, it is necessary to be aware of and to utilize the knowledge and capacity of existing community organizations. Locally established professionals are best situated to understand the challenges in context as well as the resources available. Locally based community research is consistent with the recommendations of Sarason (1974) in that a solidification of common community interests can emerge when community members are engaged together in action. In sum, work done in the community and for the community must simply involve the community.

## Urban/Poverty Impact

The implications of poverty on urban communities cannot be underestimated, as Turner and Kaye (2006) noted: "The incidences of undesirable outcomes rise with neighborhood poverty rate for almost every indicator of adult and child well-being" (p. 7). A study by Kotchick, Dorsey, and Heller (2005) of African American mothers living in urban settings found that when persistent stressors were consistently faced, fewer positive parenting practices resulted. Park, Turnbull, and Turnbull (2002) pointed out the impact of poverty on quality of life for families, particularly those with children with disabilities, can be staggering. Issues such as health care, productivity, physical environment, emotional well-being, and family interactions are all impacted. The quality of life for families in poverty is directly tied to the impact of stress on the family unit. Family stressors evolve from both internal (health and physical challenges) and external factors (lack of resources, poor living conditions).

Effectively supporting the improvement of urban communities is a shared national goal to decrease violence, crime rates, and poverty. Fortunately, improvements in some urban communities are being made (Lerman & McKernan, 2007). When low-income communities coalesce around common themes or directives such as job placement support for parents, quality child care, and the promotion of social/emotional child development, safety nets of support are created (Golden, Winston, Acs, & Chaudry, 2007). In 2000, Wynn examined effective programs that offer benefit to urban children and their families impacted by poverty. Findings indicated that community-based programs encourage child well-being and focus on teaching new skills, learning about and participating in new opportunities, and a commitment/obligation of those involved for social responsibility and the learning of life skills (adulthood preparation).

When Hieneman and Dunlap (2001) discussed the factors that have an impact on outcomes for families, they indicated the complexity and importance of attending to the context, the individual child, and the systems that support the child and family. The impact of urban environments on family stress and childhood outcomes is significant and has the resultant outcome of heightened parental distress, parenting difficulties, and child social/emotional concerns (Kotchick et al., 2005).

## The Impact of Crisis

When families in urban communities face crisis, it can take shape in multiple ways: (a) crisis brought on by natural disasters (i.e., hurricane, tornado, or earthquake); (b) familial crisis (i.e., death of a family member, severe illness of a child, or crime committed within a family); and (c) the crisis of poverty (i.e., crisis brought on the daily circumstances of poverty such as lack of food, housing, medical care). National and local media cover natural disasters and the tragedy of familial crisis, yet the crisis of poverty is consistently ignored. The pervasive nature of poverty rather than incidental circumstances surrounding episodic crises such as natural disasters is the likely rationale for the lack of attention. This sporadic attention to crisis is most notably signified by the fact that the New Orleans community was in crisis years before Hurricane Katrina struck in August 2005. The education system, extent of poverty, and crime were devastating the community long before the hurricane.

Families facing the day-to-day crisis of poverty or les-frequent intensity of familial or natural crisis still have the common interest of improving the quality of life for their children. It is clear that families are passionate about advocating for their children, and that advocacy enhances parents' abilities to cope with life's challenges while simultaneously causing family stress and struggle (Wang, Mannan, Poston, Turnbull, & Summers, 2004). This dichotomous circumstance it not uncommon in a family's support of their children, and the role stress plays in the family unit cannot be underestimated in its impact on the ability of families to function in a way that promote family cohesion and adaptability as opposed to ongoing familial and contextual chaos (McCubbin & Patterson, 1983).

Families facing circumstances such as poverty, lack of school and community partnerships, and crisis have multiple and differing needs. So, how can urban community change (addressing familial need, child need, and societal need) blanketed in context of crisis (natural, familial, and pervasive) have an impact? The application of a systemic PBS approach offers support for agencies trying to meet the multiple needs of multiple families.

## SYSTEMS-LEVEL PBS APPROACH AS A MODEL FOR FAMILY SUPPORT AGENCIES

Systems-level application of PBS for family support agencies includes several key tenets that include (a) the core PBS features; (b) schoolwide literature as a guiding framework; (c) the shift from proactive rather than reactive support; (d) primary-, secondary-, and tertiary-level support (multitier prevention framework); (e) general implementation of the model and parental leadership and advocacy in the process.

Adaptation of the PBS core features as illustrated in Fig. 11.1 (Horner & Sugai, 2004, p. 12) for use with family support agencies in urban communities requires a conceptual application shift of the schoolwide PBS model. In the school setting, the primary point of intervention is the school system and school personnel, while the desired outcome of PBS is directed at the student population. In a family support agency, the primary focus of intervention is the family support staff, with the desired outcomes directed at the parents and their children. While engaging in systematic implementation of PBS multitier support, family support agencies must also consider the additional challenges posed by poor, urban communities in crisis.

There are six core features of PBS implementation relevant to implementation within a family support agency in an urban setting: (a) understanding and respecting the local community, with an awareness of strengths, resources, and needs; (b) accessing PBS services for all families and only those who need more intensive support receive it (prevention logic beginning with needs assessment for all families; however, not all families receive all available supports);

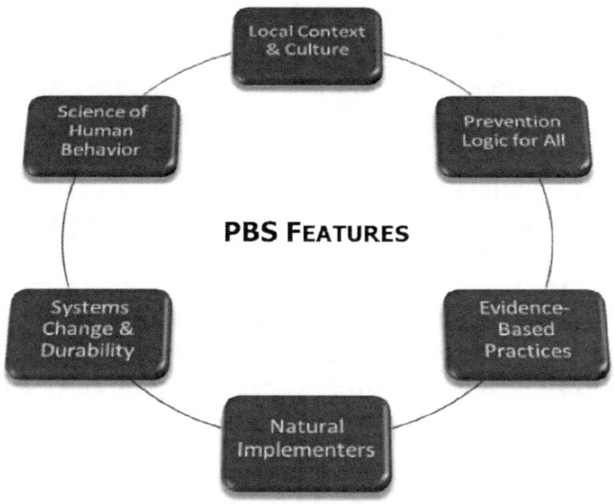


**Fig. 11.1.** Six core features of positive behavior support.

(c) focusing on teaching families evidence-based interventions for their children and supporting them in the prevention of problem behavior rather than punishment; (d) implementing interventions with and through family support staff and subsequently parents and caregivers (natural implementers); (e) sustaining the system and the outcomes with ongoing implementation with families and effectively utilizing data to make decisions at both an agency and family level; and (f) the assurance of PBS grounding in the behavioral sciences.

When examining the application of PBS systems to family support agencies, exploring the literature on schoolwide PBS provides a pathway of conceptualizing this shift (Carr et al., 2002; Koegel, Koegel, & Dunlap, 1996; Turnbull et al., 2002; Wacker & Berg, 2002). Horner and Sugai (2004) prompted schools to determine their unit of analysis as the point or place of action or need. In addition, Horner (2003) noted: "Systems are needed to support the collective use of best practices by individuals within the organization" (p. 14). As with schoolwide PBS, the primary point of intervention is the school and the staff within it. The primary point of intervention in the proposed application of PBS is the family support agency and the staff within it.

When schools implement PBS, it is their hope and intent that individual students have better social/emotional and academic outcomes. To achieve these outcomes, the schoolwide system must effectively be established to respond to the behavioral and academic needs of those students. Likewise, within a family support agency, the multitier system of PBS and structure for the agency must effectively be established to result in better outcomes for families with multiple needs. Just as it is clear with school systems that addressing the behavioral needs of students one by one is an inefficient use of resources and support, the same is true of agencies meeting the needs of families and their children.

Families who access supports from these community agencies pose a wide variety of needs requiring various levels of support. These supports largely depend on the particular mission of the agency. Generally, family support is coordinated by agency staff and focused on child development, education, financial, vocational, health, housing, and emotional resources. The role of these agencies is often to respond or react to the needs posed by families. As family support agencies adopt PBS practices, core elements of multitier systems emerge, which shifts agency practice. For example, in the process of stabilizing a family and meeting immediate, critical needs, the agency may consider specific assessments of family need (gathering additional data). Implementation of the data collection process with families shifts practice, resulting in proactive rather than reactive systems. This prevention framework utilizes key aspects of PBS (data, practices, and systems) and facilitates a family service agency that anticipates family need proactively, efficiently, and effectively. The application of intervention is based on family/child need; it is not a one-size-fits-all approach; support is matched to need. Each family has differing skills and abilities to handle stress, poor quality-of-life variables, and crisis events; therefore, family support agencies must be prepared with a menu of support specifically targeted to the unique needs of their families.

Thus far, when addressing the needs of families with multiple issues, it is difficult to shift the thinking from a response model (reacting to day-to-day crisis) to a prevention model (proactively addressing needs before they arise). This is particularly true given the scope and scale of challenges that may be present due to varying issues (i.e., parenting skill deficits, cognitive issues, underlying mental health disorders, behavioral histories and patterns, poverty, and associated community risk factors; Lutzker & Bigelow, 2002). Senge (1990) reminded us that focusing on small aspects of a larger system may result in the failure to understand and be effective as a system of support (Senge, 1990; Senge, Kleiner, Roberts, Ross, & Smith, 1994).

Consider the multitier system of PBS applied to a family support agency. Figure 11.2 graphically depicts a comparison of the multitier systems of support for schoolwide PBS and family agency PBS. *Primary-level support* includes strategies for *all* families aimed at general parenting information. This information may include basic parenting skills all families benefit from, such as positive interactions with children, basics of positive reinforcement, general home safety tips, health information, and basic child development. This information may be shared with all families in large-group training sessions. These sessions not only convey information in an efficient manner, but also the contacts made with other families can facilitate relationships and support networks among the families themselves. *Secondary-level support* for *some* families includes targeted training and support based on common needs of groups of families. In addition to the primary level of training content that all families receive, this smaller group of families may also benefit from more specific training, such as those for bedtime routines, toilet training, or schedules and routines for their children. This information offers additional information in small groups for parents who specifically request more information or have expressed an interest in these topics. As demonstrated in schoolwide PBS, secondary support strategies reduce the likelihood that families

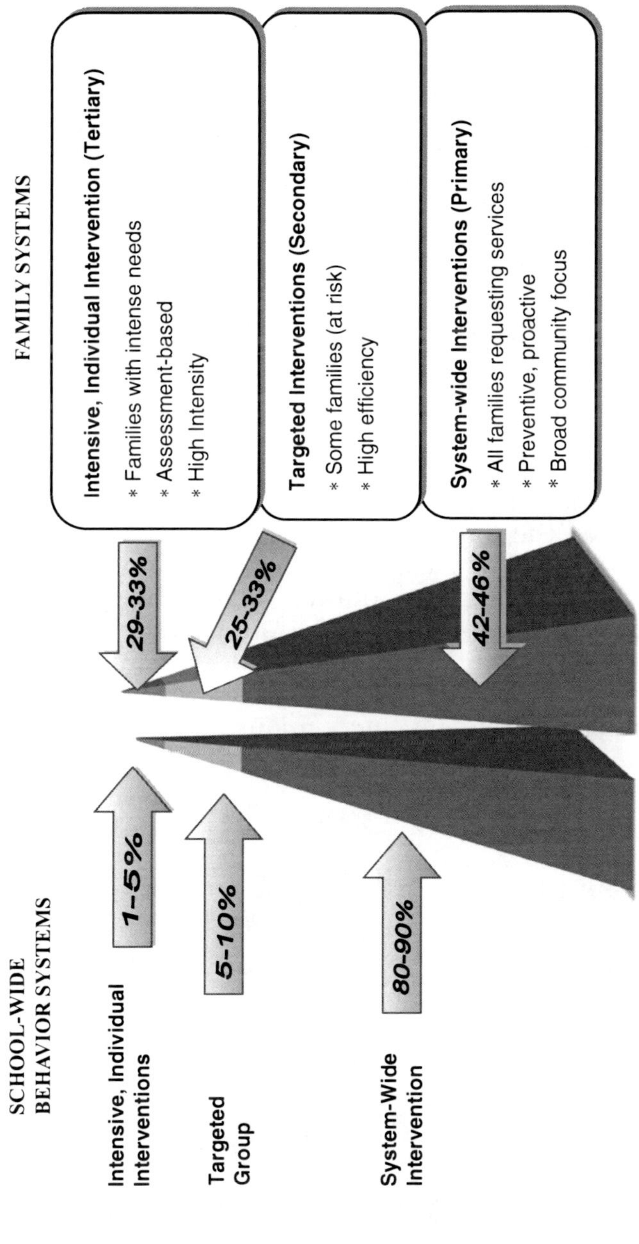


**Fig. 11.2.** Comparative model of schoolwide versus family systems application of positive behavior support in a sample family support agency.

will need more intensive or tertiary-level support. *Tertiary-level support* includes individualized training and support for a *few* families within an agency. These services and supports meet the needs of a few identified families who are experiencing either serious or chronic severe problems. This level of support typically calls for in-home attention, which may include an individualized behavior support plan for a child or immediate attention for physical or mental health needs. With implementation of tertiary-level support for families who are accessing services within a family support agency, it is imperative that the agency has a mechanism by which to determine the families' needs, values, and characteristics. When systems-level application of tertiary-level support includes goals that are clearly matched to the family needs the likelihood of consistent, long-term implementation is improved (Santarelli et al., 2001).

In Fig. 11.3, Sugai and Dickey (2005) detailed the general implementation process for PBS in the school setting. This process is also appropriate for application in a family support agency, which includes (a) systems change team, (b) agreements of participation and support, (c) agency data-based action plan, (d) implementation of the process, and (e) ongoing evaluation. For a family support agency, a *systems change team* consists of representatives from key service areas. Typically, family service agencies have an existing leadership team that could take on this role For example, the core management team or site leadership team that oversees the day-to-day operation of the agency might be a likely match for the role of the systems change team. That team has the primary goal of efficient implementation of an action plan, which starts with obtaining clear agreements of the supports offered and provided for and with families.

*Agreements and supports* within the agency and services offered to families need to be clearly delineated among agency personnel to ensure

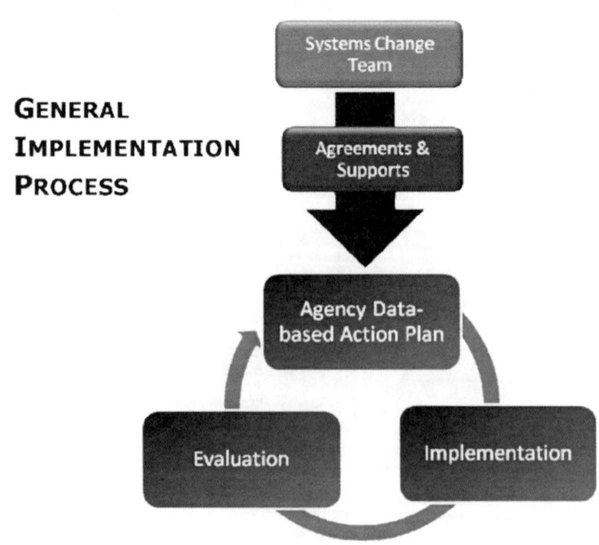


**Fig. 11.3.** General implementation of the positive behavior support (PBS) process.

mission implementation and a vision of the multitier intervention framework. Support for families should be responsive and timely, as it should for staff directly interacting with families. The agency data-based action plan provides clearly identified and staff agreed-on steps toward implementing multitier interventions. In addition, the agency action plan has delineated methods and processes for data collection and review. This plan guides implementation and allows for consistent examination of data addressing both feasibility and effectiveness. Many agencies have an existing format for such action planning that could be adapted to include multitier service provision. For example, an annual board report or monthly service reports could easily be modified to support the framework.

*Implementation* of PBS includes execution of all goals and objectives or tasks noted in the action plan. Some of these include staff development supporting appropriate implementation, initial screening for families determining level of need, and a process intended to match level of support to family need.

Last, *evaluation* of the PBS process in a family support agency consists of regular reviews of selected data and information (both qualitative and quantitative). Depending on the specific nature of the agency, these data may include progress on parental skill level, successful housing, job attainment, or child skill acquisition. Due to the funding structure of agencies receiving state or federal monies, existing agency data are reviewed as a function of licensing or continued fiscal support, some of which may be appropriate for the evaluation component of this model.

The implementation process in a family support agency must also address building effective partnerships with parents. Not only does the agency provide support for families, but also it must actively work in partnership with parents to support long-term success in the family unit and the community as a whole. Building a partnership with parents establishes much-needed ties and helps to better meet the needs of the child (Forness et al., 2000; Walker, Stiller, & Golly, 1998). Supporting parents through a collaborative relationship that provides education, communication, and services for the child and family is needed for positive, productive partnerships (Huaqing Qi & Kaiser, 2003). Parent and community involvement improves child outcomes. To reach their potential, children need their parents and the community to take an active role in their education. Family-professional collaboration is a core value in supporting children at risk for problems (Turnbull & Turnbull, 2001). Families and professionals both have expertise in areas that may be mutually beneficial (Turnbull et al., 1999). Professionals must rely on parental input. Families working as equals with professionals to support their children are critical, yet parents facing crisis may not have all the skills to successfully share information and advocate for their children. Parent leadership and advocacy for their child, albeit stressful, is often most successful in achieving better supports and services (Wang et al., 2004). Knowing that, then how can we best support families in their advocacy efforts while utilizing the multitier prevention framework?

One local community project follows as an example of implementation of multitier supports in a family service agency with a strong emphasis on parental involvement. This project is based in a community deeply impacted by the effects of poverty, long-standing issues with violence and crime rates, and the struggle to support their children in attaining successful social and academic outcomes. This project is representative of successful support of families and lies in the application of PBS utilizing a community-based systems-wide approach.

## SYSTEMS-LEVEL IMPLEMENTATION EXEMPLAR: NEW ORLEANS, LOUISIANA

The Pyramid Parent Training Community Parent Resource Center in New Orleans, Louisiana, exemplifies the application of multitier levels of intervention within a family support agency. The mission of Pyramid is to empower families facing the many challenges of disability, racism, and poverty. It is important to note at this point, as with much of the community in New Orleans, the physical structure and many of the families of Pyramid were devastated when the levees broke during the aftermath of Hurricane Katrina in 2005, resulting in widespread flooding, loss of life, displacement, and community devastation. Of the 450,000 residents of New Orleans, 80% of the residents were required to leave their city, and 228,000 homes and apartments were flooded (De Vita, 2007).

In 1991, Ursula and D. J. Markey founded Pyramid Parent Training Community Parent Resource Center in New Orleans, a city with a disproportionably large percentage of people who are vulnerable (Zedlewski, 2006) and a community in which a significant number of residents live in poverty. Pyramid offers support to families who desperately need research-based information to support their children with disabilities. In 2005, Louisiana ranked 49th of all 50 states on a composite index of 10 key indicators of child well-being, including poverty (Annie E. Casey Foundation, 2007). "In one year alone (1998–1999) in New Orleans, out of 174 families served by Pyramid, 90% were African American, 54% had incomes of less than $15,000 annually, and 81% were single parents and all of the families had one or more children with disabilities" (Markey et al., 2002, p. 220). Family support through Pyramid addresses the compelling and often-desperate needs of underserved New Orleans parents and children. Pyramid families deal with not only disability issues but also racism, poverty, abuse, unemployment, poor-performing public schools, and limited access to medical care.

With the help of funding from the Institute of Mental Hygiene of New Orleans, Pyramid created Operation Positive Change, a number of training and support opportunities for families in their community. Operation Positive Change was designed as a series of workshops to educate parents about PBS. In addition to the PBS workshops, Pyramid offered roundtables, support groups, best practices luncheons, leadership development, one-to-one assistance, and training of trainers as indicated in Table 11.2 (Markey et al., 2002).

The training opportunities conceptualized and implemented for families who had children with disabilities in the New Orleans community

**Table 11.2.** Multitier Implementation Components of Pyramid Community Parent Resource Center in New Orleans, Louisiana

| Tier Level | Components |
|---|---|
| *Primary Support:* Offered to all families seeking from family support agency (less-intensive services, broad-scale implementation) | *Operation Positive Change Workshops:* A regular schedule of workshops to educate parents about positive behavior support<br>*Best Practice Luncheons:* An avenue to connect parents and researchers; researchers would present information important to the parents |
| *Secondary Support:* Offered to groups of families with common needs or challenges from family support agency (moderate intensity of services, targeted implementation) | *Roundtables:* Informal gatherings at an actual round table at the resource center; 10–12 people (parents and Pyramid staff) work together to problem solve concerns<br>*Support Groups:* Discussions and resources specific to common issues for Pyramid families<br>*Leadership Academy:* Sessions focused on leadership development of the parents to better prepare them for advocacy activities |
| *Tertiary Support:* Offered to fewer families with the most intensive needs from family support agency (significant, intensive implementation to individual families with persistent needs) | *One-to-One Assistance:* Based on presenting needs of the family; assistance included individualized educational plan meetings and suspension hearings with school personnel |

are a good example of a multitier intervention model in a family support agency. Education and support offered included interventions at the primary, secondary, and tertiary levels.

## Primary Support

The primary level of intervention or support in schoolwide PBS offers a whole-school focus for all students. Family support agencies can function in a like manner with a focus to meet the needs of all parents who are served by the organization. The primary level of support provided by Pyramid consisted of Operation Positive Change, a regular schedule of PBS workshops open to all parents. In addition to the PBS workshops, best practice luncheons were also offered to all families. These luncheons were designed to bridge the gap between researchers and families. Researchers presented relevant information to approximately 25 families who regularly attended the luncheons. There were five or six luncheons offered each year, topics included early childhood behavioral intervention; smooth transition from school to work; juvenile justice; inclusion of students in the general education classroom; adapting materials for children with special needs; medications; and social services. Many of these topics went beyond special education issues. Satisfaction data were gathered from the workshop and best practice luncheons to allow the Pyramid staff to gauge the usefulness of the information presented. These satisfaction evaluations were designed to be simple and meaningful.

For example, one survey was a visual representation of stairsteps; the parents indicated how confident they were with the particular skill being reviewed by circling the step they were on prior to the training; at the end of each session, they rated how confident they were by circling the step they were now at—all families felt more confident and typically circled four to five steps up. This type of evaluation was best suited for underserved families with multiple needs.

## Secondary Support

The secondary level of support in schoolwide PBS focuses on groups of students who may need extra support; similarly, family support at the secondary level may be fashioned to meet the needs of a group of parents or families who share a common function or challenge. At Pyramid, there were several secondary levels of support for families: roundtable discus sions, support groups, and the leadership academy. Roundtable discussions were held for families who needed to solve specific problems. The families came to the roundtable discussions, and Pyramid staff as well as other families gathered to help. As the family described their problem, the staff was ready to teach them the needed skills and next appropriate steps, such as letter writing or phone calls. From the roundtables, families were directed to workshops and relevant support groups. Support groups were based on common areas of interest or need such as autism, attention deficit/hyperactivity disorder (ADHD), or accessing services.

The leadership academy, a third example of secondary support, was offered to parents who were interested in learning more about self-advocacy. This training was done in conjunction with the Louisiana State Improvement Grant, with approximately 25 parents participating across five sessions. The primary focus was on leadership development along with the Individuals With Disabilities Education Act (IDEA) and inclusion. Other topics included all aspects of IDEA from its history to the intent of the law and how inclusion was incorporated; listening and communication skills; team building; anger management; and problem solving. After completing the leadership academy, parents positioned themselves to serve on boards and committees around town. Prior to Hurricane Katrina, eight of these parents were on boards and committees in town.

These secondary interventions not only provided useful information and modeled problem-solving strategies, but also created lasting connections and a sense of community. Parents began to share information about doctors and resources they were using along with suggestions about who they would recommend and who they would not; as a result, this still continues. This connection has continued even through and after Hurricane Katrina; these families sought each other out after the storm. Due to these discussions, families were able to be more discerning about services for their children.

## Tertiary Support

Tertiary-level support within PBS provides targeted, function-based support to individuals. Pyramid also designed a tertiary level of support in much the same way by offering one-on-one training and assistance to individual families (i.e., attendance at individualized educational plan [IEP] meetings with school personnel, individual advocacy, due process manifestation meetings, and functional assessment). As with tertiary-level support in school settings, the needs of the individual child are identified, and all relevant parties participate in an intervention. The one-on-one assistance that Pyramid offered its families provided technical assistance and training to parents and school personnel for children receiving services. Between 75 and 100 families per year received this tertiary level of support from Pyramid.

Post-Katrina, the Markeys are committed to rebuilding the family support Pyramid once provided. Many of the Pyramid families lost their homes and are scattered throughout the United States. Ursula, D. J., and the Pyramid staff have continued to help families long distance by participating in IEP meetings via telephone; in addition, a Pyramid social worker continues to address the trauma and grief among the families. The use of a multitier support framework to the Pyramid family support agency enabled the provision of services targeted to family need. Not all Pyramid families needed all available supports; by understanding which families needed primary-, secondary-, and tertiary-level support, Pyramid was better able to meet the diverse and sweeping needs.

## IMPLICATIONS AND FUTURE DIRECTIONS

As family implementation support evolves, Senge (1990) reminded us that:

> From a very early age, we are taught to break apart problems, to fragment the world. This apparently makes complex task[s] and subjects more manageable, but we pay a hidden, enormous price. We can no longer see the consequences of our actions; we lose our intrinsic sense of connection to a larger whole. (p. 3)

Systems-level application of PBS directs the focus of intervention on a planned, proactive effective system of support rather than a reactive, intermittent application of support.

The application of the multitier system of PBS as it applies to families in urban communities, in particular New Orleans, offers new direction for supporting community agencies, their families, and children. PBS, originating in the field of applied behavior analysis and focusing on individual students with challenging behavior, has evolved into a systemswide prevention model that offers structure and guidance to family support agencies with stretched resources.

Future applications of this model of support offer interesting implications for families and community agencies. Consideration of how systemwide PBS application might be applied to rural family support agencies might also yield efficiency in resource allocation. In addition, this dialogue gives way to Lucyshyn et al.'s (Lucyshyn, Kayser, Irvin, & Blumberg, 2002) work on cultural influences and intervention effectiveness as it applies to families. The intervention implications for both family support agencies and their individual families are influenced by these variables. The role of the contextualization of interventions for individual families, although addressed in the literature (see Bernheimer & Keough, 1995; Lucyshyn, Kayser, et al., 2002, Wang, McCart, & Turnbull, 2007) needs much further exploration. If family support agencies are to effectively utilize PBS as a multitier process of intervention, intervention contextualization must be at the forefront of research, particularly for families facing multiple challenges together with pervasive and episodic crisis.

As noted, there is clear and convincing evidence of PBS effectiveness in urban schools (McCurdy, Manella, & Eldridge, 2003; Netzel & Eber, 2003; Utley et al., 2002; Warren et al., 2003). There is also solid evidence of promising PBS outcomes for individual family members (Vaughn, Wilson, & Dunlap, 2002; Vaughn, White, Johnston, & Dunlap, Koegel, 2005). However, examples, let alone evidence of effective implementation of PBS for families in poverty, using a systemwide application are rare. Replication of systems-level PBS at family support agencies, particularly those impacted by poverty and crisis, provides a framework to meet many needs with few resources. Further examining this preventive multitier PBS effort moves families and their children in crisis closer to much-needed resources and supports.

## REFERENCES


Annie E. Casey Foundation. (2007). *The Annie E. Casey Foundation 2007 kids count data book: State profiles of child well-being.* Retrieved August 28, 2007, from http://www.kidscount.org/sld/databook.jsp

Bernheimer, L. P., & Keough, B. K. (1995). Weaving interventions into the fabric of everyday life. *Topics in Early Childhood Special Education, 3,* 28–38.

Carr, E. G., Dunlap, G., Horner, R. H., Koegel, R. L., Turnbull, A. P., Sailor, W., et al. (2002). Positive behavior support: Evolution of an applied science. *Journal of Positive Behavior Interventions, 4,* 4–16, 20.

Cochran, M. (1995). *Empowerment and family support.* Ithaca, NY: Cornell Media Services.

Cuban, L. (2001, September). *Leadership for student learning: Urban school leadership—different in kind and degree.* Retrieved July 26, 2007, from http://www.iel.org/programs/21st/reports/urbanlead.pdf

De Vita, C. J. (2007, March). *After Katrina: Shared challenges for rebuilding communities.* Retrieved November 11, 2007, from http://www.urban.org/url.cfm ID=311440

Dunst, C. J., Trivette, C.M., Gordon, N.J., and Starnes, A. L. (1993). Family-centered case management practices: Characteristics and Consequences, in H. Singer and L. E. Powers (eds.). Families, disability and empowerment: active coping Skills and Strategies for family interventions (pp. 88–118). Baltimore: Brookes.

Dwyer, K. P., Osher, D. & Hoffman, C., C. (2000). Creating responsive schools: Contextualizing early warning, timely response. *Exceptional Children, 66,* 347–365.

Eber, L., Sugai, G., Smith, C. R., & Scott, T. M. (2002). Wraparound and positive behavioral interventions and supports in the schools. *Journal of Emotional and Behavioral Disorders, 10,* 171–180.

Forness, S. R., Serna, L. A., Nielsen, E., Lambros, K., Hale, M. J., & Kavale, L. A. (2000). A model for early detection and primary prevention of emotional or behavioral disorders. *Education and Treatment of Children, 23,* 325–345.

Fox, L., Dunlap, G., & Powell, D. (2002). Young children with challenging behavior: Issues and considerations for behavior support. *Journal of Positive Behavioral Interventions, 4*, 208–217.

Frankland, C., Edmonson, H., & Turnbull, A. P. (2001, fall). Positive behavioral support: Family, school and community partnerships. *Beyond Behavior, pp.* 7–9.

Gaventa, J. (1988). Participatory research in North America. *Convergence, 24*, 19–28.

Golden, O., Winston, P., Acs, G., & Chaudry, A. (2007, June). *Framework for a new safety net for low-income working families.* Retrieved July 31, 2007, from http://www.urban.org/publications/411475.html

Hieneman, M., & Dunlap, G. (2001). Factors affecting the outcomes of community-based behavioral support: II. Factor category importance. *Journal of Positive Behavior Interventions, 3*(2), 67–74.

Horner, R. H. (2003, June). *Extending positive behavior support to whole schools: Sustainable implementation.* Keynote address presented at the First International Conference on Positive Behavior Support, Orlando, FL.

Horner, R. H., & Sugai, G. (2004). *School-wide positive behavior support: Implementers' blueprint and self-assessment.* OSEP Technical Assistance Center on Positive Behavioral Interventions and Supports Web site. Retrieved July 31, 2007, from http://www.pbis.org/tools.htm

Huaqing Qi, C., & Kaiser, A. P. (2003). Behavior problems of preschool children from low income families: Review of the literature. *Topics in Early Childhood Special Education, 23*, 188–216.

Koegel, L. K., Koegel, R. L., & Dunlap, G. (Eds.). (1996). *Positive behavioral support. Including people with difficult behavior in the community.* Boston: Brookes.

Kotchick, B. A., Dorsey, S., & Heller, L. (2005). Predictors of parenting among African American single mothers: Personal and contextual factors. *Journal of Marriage and Family, 67*, 448–460.

Lawson, H. A., & Sailor, W. (2000). Integrating services, collaborating, and developing connections with schools. *Focus on Exceptional Children, 33*(2), 1–22.

Lerman, R. I., & McKernan, S. M. (2007, May). *Promoting neighborhood improvement while protecting low-income families.* Retrieved July 31, 2007, from http://www.urban.org/publications/311457.html

Lewin, K. (1946). Action research and minority problems. *Journal of Social Issues, 2*, 34–36.

Lewis, T. J., Sugai, G., & Colvin, G. (1998). Reducing problem behavior through a school-wide system of effective behavioral support: Investigation of a school-wide social skills training program and contextual interventions. *School Psychology Review, 27*, 446–459.

Lucyshyn, J. M., Horner, R. H., Dunlap, G., Albin, R. W., & Ben, K. R. (2002). Positive behavior support with families. In J. M. Lucyshyn, G. Dunlap, & R. W. Albin (Eds.), *Families and positive behavior support: Addressing problem behavior in family contexts* (pp. 3–43). Baltimore: Brookes.

Lucyshyn, J. M., Kayser, A. T., Irvin, L. K., & Blumberg E. R. (2002). Functional assessment and positive behavior support at home with families. In J. M. Lucyshyn, G. Dunlap, & R. W. Albin (Eds.), *Families and positive behavior support: Addressing problem behavior in family contexts* (pp. 97–132). Baltimore: Brookes.

Luiselli, J. K., Putnam, B., & Sunderland, M. (2002). Longitudinal evaluation of a behavior support intervention in a public middle school. *Journal of Positive Behavior Interventions, 4*, 182–188.

Lutzker, J. R., & Bigelow, K. M. (2002). *Reducing child maltreatment. A guidebook for parent services.* New York: Guilford Press.

Markey, U., Markey, D. J., Quant, B., Santelli, B., & Turnbull, A. (2002). Operation positive Change: PBS in an urban context. *Journal for Positive Behavior Interventions, 4*, 218–230.

Markey, U., Santelli, B., & Turnbull, A. P. (1998). Participatory action research involving families from underserved communities and researchers: Respecting cultural and linguistic diversity. In V. A. Ford (Ed.), *Compendium: Writing on effective practice for culturally and linguistically diverse exceptional learners.* Reston, VA: Council for Exceptional Children, Division of Culturally and Linguistically and Diverse Exceptional Learners. pp. 20–32.

McCubbin, H. I., & Patterson, J. M. (1983). The family stress process: The double ABCX model of adjustment and adaptation. In H. McCubbin, M. Sussman, & J. Patterson (Eds.), *Advances and development in family stress theory and research* (pp. 7–37). Binghamton, NY: Hayworth Press.

McCurdy, B. L., Manella, M. C., & Eldridge, N. (2003). Positive behavior support in urban schools: Can we prevent the escalation of antisocial behavior? *Journal of Positive Behavior Interventions, 5*, 158–170.

Minke, K. M., & Anderson, K. J. (2005). Family-school collaboration and positive behavior support. *Journal of Positive Behavior Interventions, 7*, 181–185.

Netzel, D. M., & Eber, L. (2003). Shifting from reactive to proactive discipline in an urban school district: A change of focus through PBIS implementation. *Journal of Positive Behavior Interventions, 5*(2), 71–79.

Park, J., Turnbull, A., & Turnbull R. (2002). Impacts of poverty on quality of life in families of children with disabilities. *Exceptional Children, 68*, 151–170.

Perkins, D. D., & Zimmerman, M. A. (1995). Empowerment theory, research, and application. *American Journal of Community Psychology, 23*, 569–579.

Rappaport, J., Swift, C., & Hess, R. (1984). *Studies in empowerment*. New York: Haworth Press.

Reglin, G. L., King, S., Losike-Sedimo, N., & Ketterer, A. (2003). Barriers to school involvement and strategies to enhance involvement from parents at low-performing urban schools. *Journal of At-Risk Issues, 9*(2), 1–7.

Riley, D. A. (1997). Using local research to change 100 communities for children and families. *American Psychologist, 52*, 424–433.

Sanders, M. G, (1997). *Building effective school—family—community partnerships in a large urban school district*. Center for Research on the Education of Students Placed at Risk. (ERIC Document Reproduction Service No. ED408403) Washington DC.

Santarelli, G., Koegel, R. L., Casas, J. M., & Koegel, L. K. (2001).Culturally diverse families participating in behavior therapy parent education programs for children with developmental disabilities. *Journal of Positive Behavior Interventions, 3*, 120–123.

Sarason, S. (1974). *The psychological sense of community: Prospects for a community psychology*. San Francisco: Jossey-Bass.

Schorr, L. B. (1997). *Common purpose: Strengthening families and neighborhoods to rebuild America*. New York: Anchor Books, Doubleday.

Senge, P. M. (1990). *The fifth discipline*. New York: Currency Doubleday.

Senge, P. M., Kleiner, A., Roberts, C., Ross, R. B., & Smith, B. J. (1994). *The fifth discipline fieldbook: Strategies and tools for building a learning organization*. New York: Currency Doubleday.

Singer, G. H., Goldberg-Hamblin, S. E., Peckham-Hardin, K. D., Barry, L. & Santarelli, G. E. (2002). Functional assessment and positive behavior support at home with families. In J. M. Lucyshyn, G. Dunlap, & R. W. Albin (Eds.), *Families and positive behavior support: Addressing problem behavior in family contexts* (pp. 155–184). Baltimore: Brookes.

Sugai, G., & Dickey, C. (2005, January). *School-wide positive behavior support: Getting started*. Powerpoint presentation at the DC-SIG Team Meeting, Washington, DC. Retrieved August 17, 2007, from http://www.pbis.org/Archived%20Presentations.htm

Sugai, G., Horner, R. H., Dunlap, G., Hieneman, M., Lewis, T. J., Nelson, C. M., et al. (2000). Applying positive behavior support and functional behavioral assessment in schools. *Journal of Positive Behavior Interventions, 2*, 131–143.

Taylor, H. L. (2002, March). *Linking school reform to the revitalization neighborhood movement*. Keynote at the Leave No Child Behind: Improving Under-Performing Urban Schools, University at Albany, State University of New York.

Taylor-Greene, S. J., & Kartub, D. T. (2000). Durable implementation of school-wide behavior support: The high five program. *Journal of Positive Behavior Interventions, 2*, 233–235.

Turnbull, A. P., Blue-Banning, M., Turbiville, V., & Park, J. (1999). From parent education to partnership education: A call for a transformed focus. *Topics in Early Childhood Special Education, 19*, 164–171.

Turnbull, A. P., Edmonson, H., Griggs, P., Wickham, D., Sailor, W., Freeman, R., et al. (2002). A blueprint for school-wide positive behavior support: Implementation of three components. *Council for Exceptional Children, 68*, 377–402.

Turnbull, A. P., Friesen, B. J., & Ramirez, C. (1998). Participatory action research as a model for conducting family research. *Research and Practice for Persons With Disabilities, 23*, 178–188.

Turnbull, A. P., & Turnbull, H. R. (2001). *Families, professional, and exceptionality: Collaborating for empowerment* (4th ed.). Upper Saddle River, NJ: Merrill/Prentice Hall.

Turner, M. A., & Kaye, D. R. (2006, April). *How does family well-being vary across different types of neighborhoods?* Retrieved July 24, 2007, from http://www.urban.org/publications/311322.html

Tyack, D., & Cuban, L. (1995). *Tinkering toward utopia: A century of public school reform.* Cambridge, MA: Harvard University Press.

Utley, C. A., Kozleski, E., Smith, A., & Draper, I. L. (2002). Positive behavior support: A proactive strategy for minimizing behavior problems in urban multicultural youth. *Journal of Positive Behavior Interventions, 4*, 196–207.

Vaughn, B. J., White, R., Johnston, S., Dunlap, & G., Koeqel, R. L. (2005). Positive behavior support as a family-centered endeavor. *Journal of Positive Behavior Interventions, 7*, 55–58.

Vaughn, B. J., Wilson, D., & Dunlap, G. (2002). Family-centered intervention to resolve problem behaviors in a fast food restaurant. *Journal of Positive Behavior Interventions, 4*, 38–45.

Wacker, D. P., & Berg, W. K. (2002). PBS as a service delivery system. *Journal of Positive Behavior Interventions, 4*(3), 25–28.

Walker, H. M., Horner, R. H., Sugai, G., Bullis, M., Sprague, J. R., Bricker, D., et al. (1996). Integrated approaches to preventing antisocial behavior patterns among school-age children and youth. *Journal of Emotional and Behavioral Disorders, 4*, 194–209.

Walker, H., Stiller, B., & Golly, A. (1998). First step to success: A collaborative home-school intervention for preventing antisocial behavior at the point of school entry. *Young Exceptional Children, 1*(2), 2–6.

Wang, M., Mannan, H., Poston, D., Turnbull, A. P., & Summers J. A. (2004). Parents' perceptions of advocacy activities and their impact on family quality of life. *Research and Practice for Persons With Severe Disabilities, 29*, 144–145.

Wang, M., McCart, A., & Turnbull, A. P. (2007). Implementing positive behavioral support with Chinese American families: Enhancing cultural competence. *Journal of Positive Behavioral Interventions, 9*, 38–51.

Warren, J. S., Edmonson H. M., Griggs, P., Lassen, S. R., McCart, A., Turnbull, A., et al. (2003). Urban applications of school-wide PBS: Critical issues and lessons learned. *Journal of Positive Behavior Interventions, 5*, 80–91.

Wynn, J. (2000). *The role of local intermediary organizations in the youth development field.* Chicago: Chapin Hall Center for Children at the University of Chicago.

Zedlewski, S. R. (2006, February). *After Katrina: Rebuilding opportunity and equity into the new New Orleans.* The Urban Institute. Retrieved July 24, 2007, from http://www.urban.org/publications

# 12

# Delivering Behavior Support in the Foster Care System

**KIMBERLY CROSLAND, GLEN DUNLAP, HEWITT B. CLARK, and BRYON NEFF**

## PREFACE

*Positive behavior support (PBS) emerged in the mid-1980s with a focus on the behavior support needs of individuals with severe intellectual disabilities and problem behavior (Carr et al., 2002; Dunlap & Carr, 2007; Dunlap & Hieneman, 2005). Since then, PBS has been demonstrated with many additional populations in schools, homes, and other community settings. As is evident in chapters throughout the current volume, PBS has been used effectively in an increasing number of human service systems, including early intervention (e.g., Head Start), public schools, and mental health.*

*One system that has received little attention with respect to systematic behavior support (including PBS) is child welfare. The child welfare system provides care for the many thousands of children who are without a biological family home within the context of an array of settings, such as foster care, therapeutic foster care, group shelters, group homes, and specialized adoptions. Principal reasons for children being placed in the child welfare system are abuse, neglect, and parental incarceration. Such children, of course, are extremely vulnerable to serious problems in social-emotional development and the emergence of problem behaviors.*

---

**KIMBERLY CROSLAND** • University of South Florida
**GLEN DUNLAP** • University of South Florida
**HEWITT B. CLARK** • University of South Florida
**BRYON NEFF** • University of South Florida

*There is a significant need for programs of effective behavior support in the child welfare system. First, it is widely known that, nationally, the child welfare system has been in disarray, and there have been frequent, horrific stories in the media about children being lost and mistreated. In 2000, Time magazine described foster care as "a quagmire that is spawning a generation of forgotten and forsaken children" (November 13, 2000, p. 5). Second, the children who comprise the population of the system typically have a considerable accumulation of risk factors that are known to contribute to social, emotional, and behavioral difficulties. Such risk factors include poverty, inconsistent parenting, exposure to violence in the home, exposure to violence in the community, and in general, an absence of stable, secure, and nurturing relationships with parents or parental figures. It is not unusual for children in child welfare to experience many of these risk factors, making them one of the most vulnerable of any population of children.*

*Although to our knowledge there have been no published accounts of programs identified as PBS serving children or caregivers in the child welfare system, there have been a handful of documented efforts using behavioral procedures to train caregivers and provide technical assistance to improve child functioning and well-being (Barth et al., 2005; Lutzker, Tymchuk, & Bigelow, 2001; Smagner & Sullivan, 2005). The program described in this chapter comes from this tradition. The Behavior Analysis Services Program (BASP) was established as a statewide initiative in the state of Florida in 2001 to improve the delivery of foster care by (a) providing training to foster parents; (b) conducting functional assessments; (c) delivering technical assistance in foster homes and other facilities in the child welfare system; and (d) assisting in special, high-profile circumstances, such as analyzing and intervening with the challenge of "runaways."*

*The BASP was founded on the principles of applied behavior analysis and continues to operate as a behavior analytic enterprise. Professional employees within the BASP are board-certified behavior analysts. At the same time, BASP conducts its program in a manner that is fully consistent with the features and tenets of PBS (cf. Carr et al., 2002). This is understandable because BASP operates within the context of real-world circumstances and therefore must maintain a high level of ecological validity to be effective. BASP also emphasizes prevention of problem behaviors through skills development and environmental arrangements; seeks to build capacities of children, youth, and caregivers; and focuses on the accomplishment of positive outcomes. In other words, BASP is an example of a program that shares alliance with applied behavior analysis as well as PBS. As several authors have pointed out (Anderson & Freeman, 2000; Dunlap, 2006; Dunlap, Carr, Horner, Zarcone, & Schwartz, 2008), this congruence is not surprising since PBS emerged from the strong conceptual and procedural foundations of applied behavior analysis, and a good deal of community-based behavior analysis (though not all) is indistinguishable from contemporary applications of PBS.*

*This chapter presents an overview of the BASP and some empirical examples of data collection that illustrate some of its functions. We are all centrally involved in the design, development, and implementation of the BASP.*

## DELIVERING BEHAVIOR SUPPORT IN THE FOSTER CARE SYSTEM

Over 3 million children are reported as abused or neglected each year in the United States, approximately 900,000 of these are confirmed cases, and over 500,000 children are removed from their homes by child protective services (U.S. Department of Health and Human Services, 2006). The child welfare system was designed to ensure the safety of these children by providing essential services, including substitute care. Since the passing of federal laws and regulations such as the Adoption Assistance and Child Welfare Act of 1980, there has been a renewed effort to preserve children's placements with their biological families (Adoption Assistance and Child Welfare, P.L. 96–272, 1980). Despite this effort, the numbers of children in out-of-home placements have continued to increase each year. The news headlines of tragic cases in which children have died, have been severely injured at the hands of a parent or caregiver, or have gone missing also continue to plague the child welfare system.

There is a growing consensus that the child welfare system needs to be reformed. The monetary costs alone for child maltreatment are immense. In the year 2000, it was estimated that $20 billion was spent on child welfare services (Bess, 2002). Other additional costs such as mental health treatment, law enforcement, special education services, and criminal conduct have been estimated at $80 billion, bringing the total cost of child maltreatment to approximately $100 billion a year (Prevent Child Abuse America, 2001). The human costs to children in foster care cannot be adequately calculated. Children in foster care often face unimaginable emotional trauma, social insecurity, inadequate services, and sometimes even further abuse and neglect. The needs of these children are not being met with the current system. Although there are dedicated caseworkers and administrators, the child welfare system itself is hampered by high turnover, poor training, low pay, unmanageable caseloads, and a lack of resources (Center for the Study of Social Policy, 2003).

The purposes of this chapter are to (a) describe the population of children in foster care; (b) discuss some of the challenges associated with supports for children in foster care; (c) describe a statewide initiative, the BASP; and (d) illustrate the impact of BASP practices through a description of some preliminary research findings. The BASP was designed to improve the quality of care and outcomes for children and youth in the child welfare system by providing training and technical assistance for caregivers and child welfare employees. Behavior analytic assessments and intervention strategies hold some strong implications for improving the quality and effectiveness of the child welfare field; these implications are discussed.

## POPULATION AND CHALLENGES ASSOCIATED WITH FOSTER CARE

Children end up in the foster care system for a variety of reasons. A child can enter the system when a parent has died or is no longer able to provide adequate care, either physically or financially. Children may also end up in foster care because they have been abused or neglected by their parents. Their parents may also be addicted to drugs or alcohol. Experts have suggested that as much as 75–90% of foster care placements in some areas can be traced to substance abuse (U.S. General Accounting Office, 1997). On average, children stay in foster care for approximately 3 years before being either reunited with their family or adopted. Almost 20% remain in foster care for 5 years (U.S. Department of Health and Human Services, 2006). Around 20,000 children each year never leave the system and instead remain in foster care until they "age out." The average age of a child in foster care is 10 years old, with half of the children in care 10 years old or younger (U.S. Department of Health and Human Services, 2006).

A variety of placement options exist within foster care. Emergency placements are used when an urgent placement is needed for children, typically when they first enter the welfare system, or when children are too challenging, or for other reasons are required to leave their foster homes or alternative out-of-home placements. Temporary or short-term placements are utilized for children whose case plan emphasizes reunification with biological parents within 6 months. If reunification does not appear to be feasible or parental rights are terminated, children are placed in either long-term foster care or a preadoptive placement with the goal of adoption. In terms of the actual setting for each of these placements, there are several types: in a home with foster parents (e.g., family foster care, therapeutic foster care), in a home with relatives (also referred to as "kinship care"), or in a group setting. Group settings can include small group homes, shelters, residential treatment facilities, and other mental health facilities. Family foster care remains the most prevalent type of placement for children in care and is also considered the least restrictive and most preferred type of placement (Buehler, Orme, Post, & Patterson, 2000).

Children in foster care are among the most vulnerable for developing social, emotional, and behavioral problems. The American Academy of Children and Adolescent Psychiatry (2005) reported that approximately 30% of children in foster care have severe emotional, behavioral, or developmental problems. Burns et al. (2004) conducted a national study of the child welfare system and found that almost half of the youth in care aged 2–14 years old had clinically significant emotional or behavioral problems. The incidence of behavioral, emotional, academic, and developmental problems appears to have a negative effect on life skill acquisition as well as placement stability and length of time in care (Cooper, Peterson, & Meier, 1987; Klee & Halfon, 1987; Proch & Taber, 1985). Newton, Litrownik, and Landsverk (2000) found that some children who came into foster care developed behavior problems in response to placement instability. The foster care system itself, with its reliance on the use of group shelters and frequent placement changes, may contribute greatly to the emotional trauma many youth experience. According to several studies, youth residing in group home facilities may exhibit higher levels of social, emotional, and behavioral needs (Burns et al., 2004; Landsverk, Garland, & Leslie, 2002; Litronwnik, Taussig, Landsverk, & Garland, 1999). Type of placement may also be associated with better outcomes as foster families may offer more individualized attention and support compared to group home and residential settings.

Placement stability within family foster care and long-term group placements is a leading concern among professionals, caregivers, and researchers in the field of child welfare. The definition of what constitutes a placement disruption varies in the literature since placement changes can occur for various reasons, both acceptable and problematic. An *acceptable* placement disruption could be when a child is moved to rejoin siblings, is moved to a less-restrictive setting, or moves back with a biological family member. A *negative* or *problematic* placement disruption could include when a child is moved due to the inability of a foster parent to manage the child's behavioral difficulties or when the foster parent requests that the child be removed from the home, which interrupts stabilization or treatment efforts.

Research on risk factors associated with placement disruptions have shown that increased age at the time of entering foster care, length of time in care, and the presence of behavioral and emotional problems are correlated with an increased risk for placement instability (Pardeck, 1984; Pardeck, Murphy, & Fitzwater, 1985; Walsh & Walsh, 1990; Widom, 1991). Webster, Barth, and Needell (2000) reported in their sample that children entering care as toddlers were almost twice as likely as those entering care as infants to experience placement instability. Other researchers have found similar associations between age and increased risk of disruptions (Berridge & Cleaver, 1987; Rowe, Hundleby, & Garnett, 1989). Studies have also demonstrated an association between race and placement stability. Several studies have suggested that Caucasian children are more likely to experience placement instability (Pardeck, 1984; Webster et al., 2000). Webster et al. (2000) indicated that African American children were 25% less likely than Caucasian children to experience instability. This study only included children who entered care under the age of 6. It is not clear if race would continue to remain a factor for older children entering care.

System-level contextual factors, such as high level of contact, positive foster parent relationship with agency, and caseworker continuity have been associated with increased placement stability (Pardeck, 1984; Stone & Stone, 1983). Unfortunately, in most communities and states, children and foster parents are stuck in a system with little continuity or support. Systemwide challenges include unwieldy organization structure, unreliable tracking methods, massive caseloads, high turnover of caseworkers, insufficient numbers of foster parents, and inadequate training and assistance for foster parents. Caseworkers leave the profession in very high numbers, with the annual turnover rate in the child welfare workforce more than 20% (U.S. Department of Health and Human Services, 2006).

## BEHAVIOR ANALYSIS SERVICES PROGRAM IN FLORIDA

Historically, in the state of Florida behavioral analytic services were almost exclusively recommended and provided for children with developmental disabilities (Florida Statues, Section 393.17, 2001). Even though behavior analytic services were well established within the developmental disabilities system, such services were rarely offered to children without developmental disabilities within the foster care system, even for children who were displaying challenging behaviors. The reason for the lack of these services is not entirely clear, although it may be related to philosophical differences between traditional mental health services and behavioral orientations. Children receiving mental health services were often provided with psychological testing and some form of psychoanalytic therapy as treatment for emotional and behavioral problems. The overall effectiveness and outcomes of these treatments have not been adequately studied, especially with children in foster care (Weisz, Donenberg, Han, & Kauneckis, 1995).

The discrepancy in the needs of the children and youth in the foster care system and the availability of behavior analytical services is further complicated by system funding issues. Behavior analytic services do not have a separate funding stream under the current Medicaid waiver; therefore, a behavior analyst must be supervised by a licensed health care provider. Licensed health care providers in the state of Florida rarely employ behavior analysts due to philosophical differences, and board-certified behavior analysts typically warrant higher salaries than other health care professionals.

The positive effects associated with behavior analysis in the area of developmental disabilities led other agencies in Florida to explore the possibility of using behavior analysis with additional populations. As a result, behavior analytic services were soon extended to include children and families within the Family Safety division. Family Safety is the division that provides an array of services, including out-of-home placements, for children who have been abused, neglected, or both. In 1994, a small project in family safety, which became the pilot of the BASP (Stoutimore, Neff, Williams, & Foster, 2008), was funded to provide behavior analysis services and supports to families and children living in the Tampa Bay area. The purpose of the pilot project was to provide protection and services, similar in concept to the services within developmental disabilities, to improve caregiver competence and confidence, to increase stability of placements for children, and to reduce the need for highly restrictive placements for children, thereby producing short- and long-term cost savings.

The overriding assumption of the BASP was, and still ascertains, that the most effective way of treating child problem behavior is to teach caregivers (e.g., foster parents and staff members) basic behavioral parenting methods for increasing appropriate child repertoires and replacing inappropriate child behaviors with "replacement" behaviors that will benefit the child. Caregivers are also instructed on ways to alter environmental arrangements to increase appropriate behavior and decrease inappropriate behavior. To manage this in an efficient manner, behavior analysts and colleagues within Florida's Department of Children and Families (DCF) developed a comprehensive training curriculum that could be presented in a group format. In addition to the training program, the pilot program offered in-home services to caregivers. Intensive behavioral treatment interventions were also developed for seven foster children residing in highly restrictive placements. The success of these interventions resulted in all of these children moving to less-restrictive placements in a relatively short period of time. The cost savings for these seven children was over $300,000 over the course of 15 months, which was enough to fund the entire behavior analytic program at that time (C. Williams, History of the behavior analysis services program, personal communication received by K. A. Crosland, 2003).

Due to the success of the pilot program, the Florida legislature approved funds for a statewide expansion in 2000. Contracts were established with the University of Florida and the University of South Florida to provide the hiring, oversight, and supervision of behavior analysts across the state. The University of Florida oversees services in the eight northern districts, while the University of South Florida oversees the seven remaining districts in the southern part of the state. The principal investigators, program coordinators, and additional research personnel are housed at each university and share responsibility in program development, management, and evaluation. Each individual district employs one senior behavior analyst and three behavior analysts. All behavior analysts must be board certified either at the time of employment or within 15 months of hire.

Currently, a range of services are provided by the BASP, including performance-based group caregiver training, in-home caregiver training and services, individualized child assessment and treatments, 24-hr on call emergency services, and other consultative services. The BASP is often requested to assist with special projects, usually district specific, such as providing support services to runaways and adapting the training curriculum for other populations. The parent training curriculum, Tools for Positive Behavior Change, that is taught throughout the state emphasizes positive proactive behavior management techniques that are based on behavior analysis principles and procedures. The curriculum is typically taught in a group classroom format, although if necessary, it can be taught individually for those caregivers who are unable to attend a group class. Teaching methods include a combination of didactic instruction, group discussions, activities, practice, role-playing scenarios, and corrective feedback. During all classes there is an emphasis on the demonstration of parenting skills that are taught through role-playing in which a behavior analyst plays the role of the child while the class participant demonstrates his or her ability to use a new tool. Parenting skills are assessed via role-playing scenarios both prior to training and at the end of training. The basic curriculum content includes training in the use of nine behavioral intervention techniques, referred to as "tools," to increase desirable child behaviors and decrease undesirable behaviors. The curriculum is based on basic behavior analytic principles and was developed primarily from the book *The Power of Positive Parenting* (Latham, 1990).

**Table 12.1.** Description of Tools in Curriculum

| Tool Name | Behavioral Procedure/Rationale |
|---|---|
| Stay close | Noncontingent attention/Used to make the caregiver's approval and disapproval important to the child, thus establishing the child's attention as a reinforcer |
| Use reinforcement | Positive reinforcement in the form of praise or access to desired items and activities/Used to strengthen desirable behavior and weaken undesirable behaviors |
| Redirect-use reinforcement | Extinction of attention maintained behavior and reinforcement for desired behavior/Used to reduce minor, nonharmful problem behavior and increase appropriate behavior |
| Pivot | Extinction of attention maintained behavior and reinforcement for desired behavior/Used to reduce problem behavior and increase appropriate behavior |
| Set expectations | Reinforcement for meeting expectations set by caregiver and child/ Used to strengthen desired behaviors |
| Use a contract | Reinforcement for meeting contractual agreement between caregiver and child (formal written form of set expectations)/Used to strengthen desired behaviors |

This text is used during class and recommended reading for all class participants. Table 12.1 describes each tool and the behavioral procedure and rationale associated with that tool. In the curriculum, each of the tools is task analyzed with a list of steps to provide caregivers with a structured way to learn each tool and provide a concrete way to measure caregiver competence.

All caregivers who attend the training are offered weekly in-home visits by a behavior analyst both during and after the completion of classroom training. During in-home visits, the tools taught in class are reviewed, feedback is provided regarding the implementation of the tools taught in class, and if needed, individualized treatment recommendations for specific child behavior problems are addressed. Behavioral services may also be provided to other caregivers of a foster child, such as a teacher, day care provider, or any other individual in contact with the child.

## RESEARCH

Since its inception, the BASP has collected data on numerous aspects of service delivery to determine the effectiveness and efficacy of different aspects of the program. Systematic observation, including data collection, is an essential part of behavior analytic assessment and intervention. Specific research studies have been conducted to determine if BASP caregiver training and individual consultation have an impact on various dependent variables. In this section, three specific studies are presented to illustrate the kinds of services and the range of behaviors targeted by the BASP. These studies, along with several others, are reported in a special issue of the journal *Research on Social Work Practice*.

## Use of Invasive or Aversive Procedures

### *The Problem*

Regarding the problem (Crosland et al., in press), there has been an emerging consensus within the field of mental health that reducing and possibly eliminating the use of restrictive procedures in various treatment settings should be a major priority (Honberg & Miller, 2003). Within the child protection system, there are both short- and long-term restrictive facilities for children with severe emotional and behavioral problems for whom alternative placement options are not available. The national law (Children's Health Act of 2000) requires that seclusion and restraint only be used in emergency situations for physical safety purposes and also includes stipulations regarding who is authorized to order and implement restraint procedures (i.e., physician, certified individuals, supervisors). This law was a product of strenuous advocacy aided by a series of published articles revealing 142 deaths connected to the use of physical restraints in health care facilities (Weiss, 1998). Although the new law exists and although there has been wide discussion among professionals to reduce restrictive and invasive procedures, there appears to be a reluctance to change, and many facilities continue to have a high rate of implementing such procedures (Day, 2002).

Children and adolescents in foster care are particularly vulnerable due to the fact that many of these children have already experienced significant abuse, trauma, and loss. It has been argued that the use of seclusion and restraint procedures should be reduced to as minimal as possible with children, particularly because these experiences could cause additional trauma and an increase in behavior problems (Goren, Singh, & Best, 1993; Irwin, 1987). Many of the facilities in which children in foster care reside have large staffs that are usually poorly trained, and the majority of their training focuses on how to handle "crisis" situations by using various forms of restrictive procedures (e.g., restraint, seclusion, time-out).

### *BASP Approach*

Professionals employed by the BASP were interested in evaluating the specific effects of a behavioral staff training program designed to promote positive staff-child interactions and reduce negative and punitive interactions. By utilizing a proactive behavioral approach to train staff how to interact with children in positive ways, the BASP hypothesized that the need for restrictive procedures might decrease.

Due to high levels of the use of restrictive and invasive procedures at two facilities, the BASP was asked by DCF to provide training to staff members. The BASP was somewhat surprised but pleased with this training opportunity since in the past it was highly unusual for facility training to be requested and provided on positive and preventive strategies. The two facilities were a children's shelter and a locked residential facility. Training for staff members at both facilities consisted of 15 hr of classroom-based instruction on the Tools for Positive Behavior Change Curriculum. Table 12.1 lists the name of each tool taught in the curriculum along with the associated behavioral rationale. A total of 19 employees were trained at the children's shelter, and 25 were trained at the locked residential facility. Trained employees included direct care staff, supervisors, nurses, teachers, therapists, and psychologists. In addition to the classroom training, staff at the locked residential facility also received on-site coaching in which a behavior analyst observed and prompted staff to use specific tools with children.

The primary dependent measure at both facilities was the number of restrictive procedures performed prior to and after training. As an ongoing facility requirement, staff were required to record on either an emergency procedure form (locked residential treatment facility) or an incident report form (children's shelter) when a restrictive procedure was implemented. At the locked residential facility, the four different types of procedures recorded were physical holds, mechanical restraints, seclusion, and chemical restraint. The categories of restrictive procedures used at the children's shelter included: physical takedowns, time-out, elbow control, and an "other hands-on intervention" category. In addition, the children's shelter staff recorded on the incident report forms the specific antecedents and child behaviors that led to the use of restrictive procedures. For example, a record might indicate that a child was noncompliant with a staff request (antecedent), the staff member then approached the child, the child then became aggressive (behavior), and this led to the implementation of a restrictive procedure (e.g., time-out). In this way, both the antecedents and the child behaviors that led to the use of restrictive procedures were recorded.

A nonconcurrent multiple baseline across facilities was implemented to assess the effects of the training on the frequency of restrictive procedures. The baseline was staggered by 1 month. Therefore, pretraining data were collected for 3 months at the children's shelter and for 4 months at the locked residential facility prior to the implementation of training.

## *Results*

The results showed decreases in the reported use of restrictive procedures at both facilities following BASP training. Figure 12.1 displays the total frequency of restrictive procedures reported to have been implemented for each month at both facilities during pretraining and posttraining. The locked residential treatment facility showed a 70% reduction in reported restrictive procedures, while the children's shelter showed a 47% reduction in reported restrictive procedures. Figure 12.2 shows a breakdown of the frequency of each specific type of restrictive procedure that was reported to be implemented during each month of the pretraining and posttraining periods. At the locked residential facility, all types of restrictive procedures decreased, although the frequency of seclusion only decreased during Month 6 of the posttraining period. At the children's shelter, three of five restrictive procedures decreased. Figure 12.3 shows the reported child antecedents and child behaviors that led to the use of restrictive procedures at the children's shelter. The child antecedent and behavior, respectively, with the highest frequency in both pretraining and posttraining were

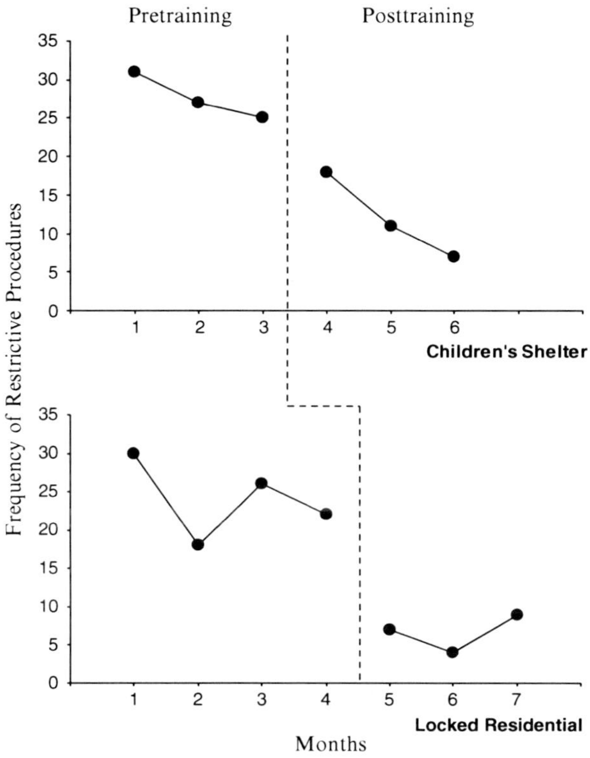


**Fig. 12.1.** Total frequency of restrictive procedures implemented per month at the locked residential treatment facility and a children's shelter. Reprinted with permission from "Using Staff Training to Decrease the Use of Restrictive Procedures at Two Facilities for Foster Care Children," by K. A. Crosland, M. Cigales, G. Dunlap, B. Neff, H. B. Clark, T. Giddings, & A. Blanco, 2008, *Research on Social Work Practice, 18*, 401–409.

noncompliance and aggression. The reported use of a restrictive procedure after a child engaged in "verbal junk/nonharmful" behavior (i.e., defined as any age-typical behavior that may be annoying but is not physically harmful to self, others, property, or animals) appeared to decrease substantially from 24 times pretraining to 7 times posttraining.

These results suggest that utilizing a proactive behavioral approach to train staff how to interact with children in positive ways may help to decrease the need for restrictive procedures. The greatest reductions were observed in those procedures that might be considered more restrictive than others, including mechanical restraint (82% decrease) at the locked residential treatment facility and takedowns (95% decrease) at the children's shelter. A reduction in time-out was not observed at the children's shelter; however, this might be considered one of the least-restrictive procedures since it does not involve any physical holding of a child. A 50% decrease in staff injuries at the children's shelter was also noted. These findings highlight the importance of providing behavioral parent training, both in proactive strategies and in appropriate ways to manage problem behavior, to staff at group facilities for children.

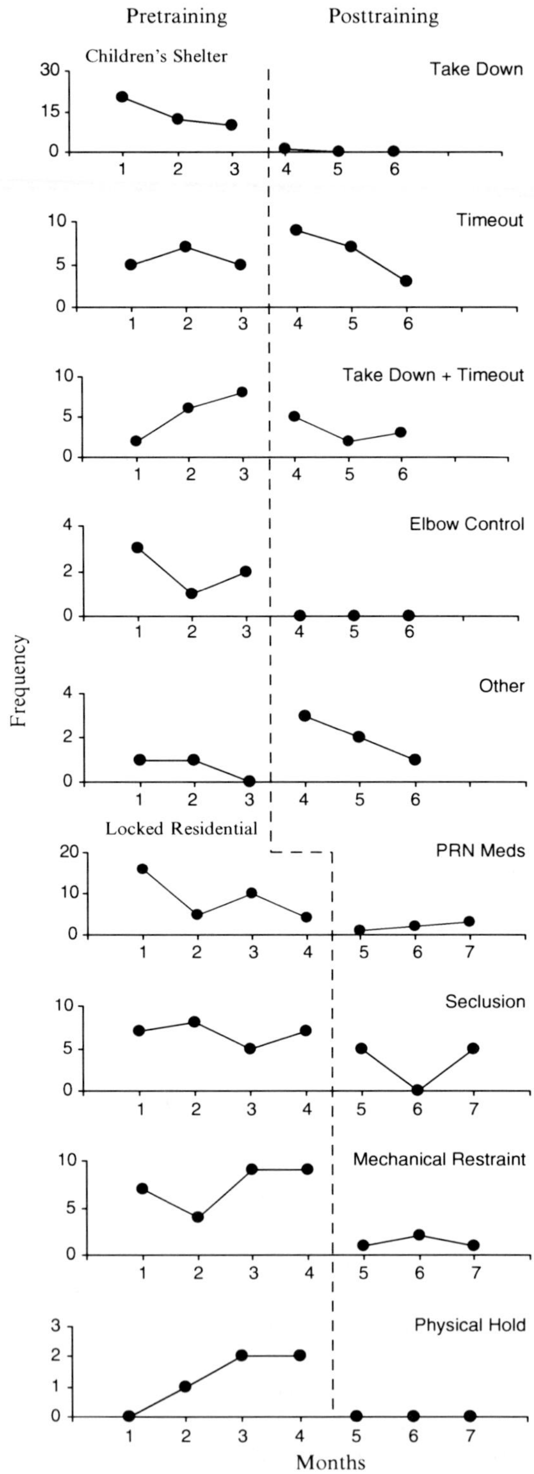


**Fig. 12.2.** Frequency of each specific type of restrictive procedure implemented per month at the locked residential treatment facility and the children's shelter. PRN, as needed. Reprinted with permission from "Using Staff Training to Decrease the Use of Restrictive Procedures at Two Facilities for Foster Care Children," by K. A. Crosland, M. Cigales, G. Dunlap, B. Neff, H. B. Clark, T. Giddings, & A. Blanco, 2008, *Research on Social Work Practice, 18, 401–409.*

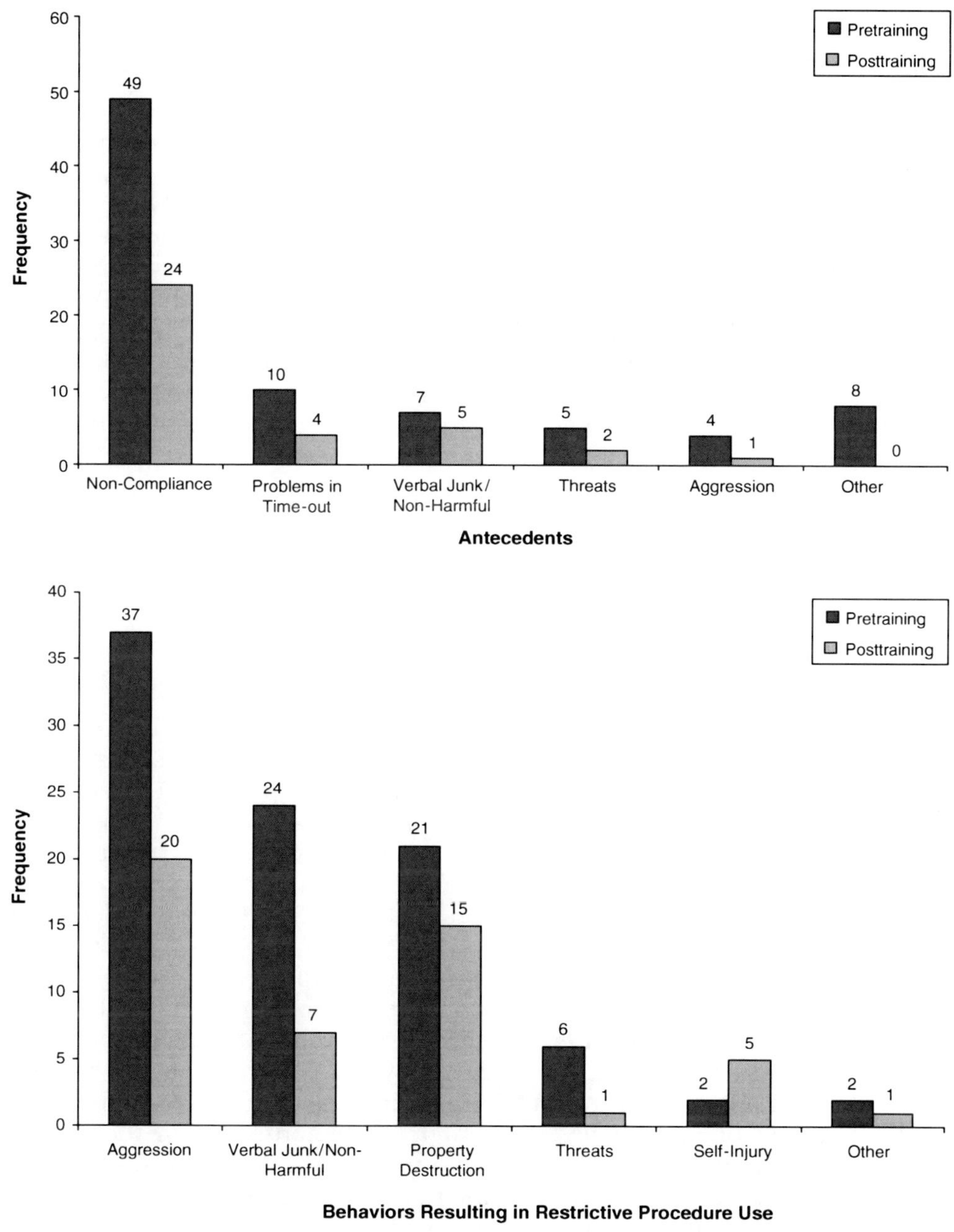


**Fig. 12.3.** Total frequency of specific antecedents (top) and behaviors (bottom) resulting in restrictive procedure use recorded during pretraining and posttraining at the children's shelter. Reprinted with permission from "Using Staff Training to Decrease the Use of Restrictive Procedures at Two Facilities for Foster Care Children," by K. A. Crosland, M. Cigales, G. Dunlap, B. Neff, H. B. Clark, T. Giddings, & A. Blanco, 2008, *Research on Social Work Practice, 18, 401–409.*

## Nocturnal Enuresis

### *The Problem*

Nocturnal enuresis (Stover, Dunlap, & Neff, in press), or bed-wetting, is a fairly common problem, affecting as many as 5 to 7 million children in the United States, with the prevalence decreasing with age (Ullom-Minnich, 1996). It is estimated that nocturnal enuresis is seen in 15–20% of 5-year-old children, with the percentages decreasing to approximately 5% by the age of 10 and to less than 3% between the ages of 12 and 14 (American Psychiatric Association, 1994; Fletcher, 2000; Ullom-Minnich, 1996). The occurrence of bed-wetting for children in foster care is probably higher, but no hard data are available. Children in foster care are considered more likely than other children to experience myriad emotional and behavioral problems (Leathers, 2002), and it has also been noted that persistent bed-wetting can be associated with increased conduct problems, anxiety, and withdrawal in early adolescence (Fergusson & Horwood, 1994). Also, bed-wetting along with other behavioral problems can be associated with an increased risk for placement disruptions. Therefore, early and effective treatment of nocturnal enuresis is important and, arguably, even more important for children who have been placed in the child protection system.

### *BASP Approach*

With the exception of studies of bed alarm systems (e.g., Azrin et al., 1974), there is a conspicuous dearth of experimental investigations of behavioral interventions for the relatively common problem of nocturnal enuresis. Bed alarm systems have the disadvantages of being relatively intrusive, potentially cumbersome, and expensive. Researchers with BASP wanted to evaluate a treatment package that did not require the use of a bed alarm and was primarily based on positive reinforcement procedures to reduce bed-wetting.

Three children, aged 5 to 12 (Jimmy, Paul, and Susie) were referred to BASP because each had recurring bed-wetting problems along with other behavioral concerns, and their caregivers had indicated that nocturnal enuresis was the primary concern that they did not know how to resolve. Two of the children (Jimmy and Paul) were living in foster homes and were at risk of being removed from their placements due to their problem behaviors. Jimmy was 12 years old with multiple diagnoses, including attention deficit/hyperactivity disorder, disruptive behavior disorder, oppositional defiant disorder, and mild mental retardation, receiving a full-scale IQ score of 50 on the Wechsler Intelligence Scale for Children—Third Edition (Wechsler, 1991). Paul was 6 years old, had been a victim of abuse, was living in his second foster home placement, and was at risk of losing this placement due to behavior problems. The third participant was Susie, a 5-year-old biological child of a foster care case manager who was suspected of having a developmental disorder that had not yet been diagnosed. Prior to enrolling in this study, all participants received an evaluation to rule out any medically related problems associated with nocturnal enuresis.

During baseline, all of the children wore Pull-Ups, and there were no systematic consequences in place for bed-wetting. The intervention package consisted of a contingency contract, removal of Pull-Ups, and a cleanup procedure (e.g., removing wet sheets from bed and placing them in the washer). The primary component of the intervention package was the contingency contract, which was a written contract between the caregiver and child clearly defining the expectations of the child and the consequences to be earned when the expectations were met (Cooper, Heron, & Heward, 1987). Individual contracts were developed for each child based on stimulus preference assessments. All three of the caregivers received training in the design and implementation of contracts through their participation in the BASP training curriculum. Throughout the duration of the study, data were recorded by the children and caregivers during the daily review of the contract. A nonconcurrent multiple baseline across children design was used to evaluate the effects of the intervention. The baselines were staggered in periods of 1, 3, and 5 weeks.

### *Results*

Results showed that the contingency contracting program was effective in eliminating nocturnal enuresis for all three participants. Figure 12.4 shows the number of dry nights per week (7 days) for all participants throughout the duration of the study. Baseline and intervention data were recorded for 16–18 weeks, with an additional 3-month follow-up probe. The data indicate steady improvements for all participants following the introduction of the contingency contracting program, such that each child achieved full weeks without bed-wetting within 7 weeks of treatment. Most encouraging were the data from the 3-month probes, which showed no bed-wetting for any of the children. From a clinical perspective, the successful resolution of the bed-wetting problems for the three participants was highly gratifying for the children and for their care providers. It is noteworthy to also mention that the children's placements were maintained, and that informal follow-up checks 1 year following the data collection indicated that nocturnal enuresis was no longer a behavior of concern for any of the three children.

## The Challenge of Runaways

### *The Problem*

A significant problem in the field of child protection is that of teenagers running away from foster placements (Clark et al., in press). In the foster care system, runaway escapes can hold serious consequences for young people. They may be exposed to the risk of abusing alcohol and drugs and criminal and sexual victimization, or they may commit crimes themselves while on a run (Courtney et al., 2005). Running away from foster care settings not only places young people in harm's way, but frequently jeopardizes their current placement, resulting in a more restrictive placement, and interrupting their learning opportunities at school. These

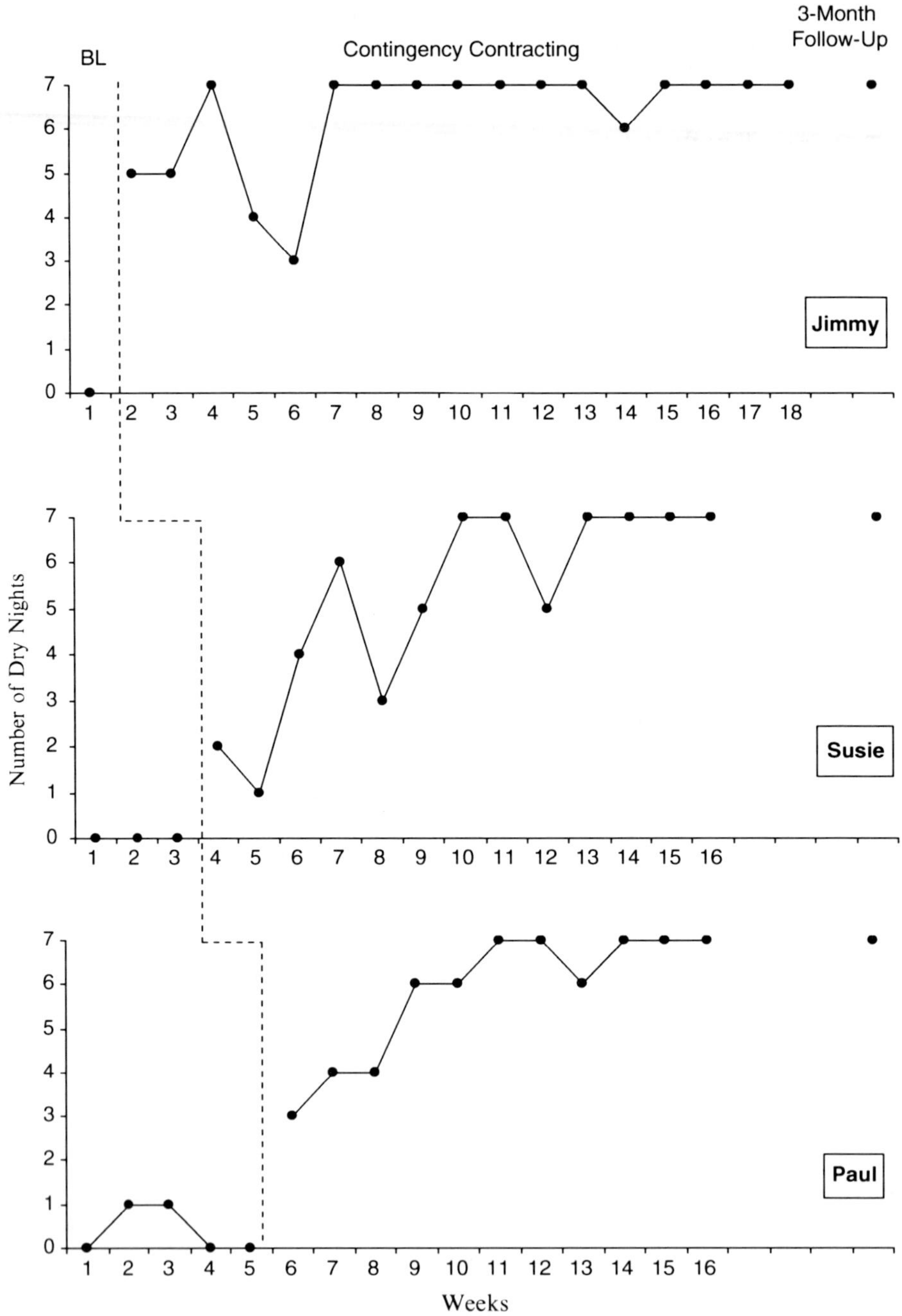


**Fig. 12.4.** Number of dry nights for each week of the study for each of the three participants, depicted in accordance with the multiple-baseline framework. Reprinted with permission from "The Effects of a Contingency Contracting Program on the Nocturnal Enuresis of Three Children," by A. C. Stover, G. Dunlap, & B. Neff, 2008, *Research on Social Work Practice, 18*, 421–428.

types of interruptions hinder youths' abilities to build the life skills needed for greater self-sufficiency and to form the social support network essential for resilience and quality of life (Choca et al., 2004; Christenson, 2002; Clark & Crosland, in press; Iglehart, 1994).

A large-scale study of children running away from out-of-home placements in Illinois provided factors that may be predictive of youth and situations associated with running away from placements (Courtney et al., 2005). Girls were more likely to run than were boys. Ninety percent of runners were 12–18 years of age, most of these being 14 years old or older. Other factors associated with higher likelihoods of running were histories of placement instability, the presence of mental health diagnoses or substance abuse problems, placements in residential facilities, and prior runaway episodes. Some of the factors that were associated with a lower likelihood of running were living with a relative or living in a setting with a sibling. The reasons for children running away from placements are numerous. When interviewed, some adolescents reported that they were running to family or friends, while others reported that they were running away from unfavorable caregivers or settings (Courtney et al., 2005).

### *BASP Approach*

There is literature suggesting that runaway behavior, like other behaviors, is maintained by specific functions such as "escape/avoidance" or "positive reinforcement" factors (Piazza et al., 1997; Tarbox, Wallace, & Williams, 2003). BASP researchers were interested in utilizing a functional approach for the assessment and treatment of runway behavior. A functional approach to the issue of runaways in foster care would consist of information gathering via multiple methods, including focused interviews with caregivers, friends, family, and the youth themselves (Kern & Dunlap, 1999). The functional assessment process in this study involved an attempt to determine (a) the motivations for the adolescent's running (e.g., what the youth was seeking to obtain by running or what the youth was attempting to avoid by leaving the foster care placement); as well as (b) the specific circumstances or situations that might have motivated the running episode. This information was then used to devise an individualized, multicomponent intervention plan focused on reducing each youth's reasons for running away. This approach is different from typical child welfare services for youth who run away. Typical services usually include a Comprehensive Behavioral Health Assessment for every child entering into dependent care (conducted by a licensed mental health provider), minimum monthly face-to-face visits by a caseworker, staffing to address specific needs and recommendations for therapy/placements, and judicial reviews, typically two or three times per year. The development of individualized behavior plans focused on the motivation (or "function") for youth running away are rare within typical services. Two case studies are presented first, followed by a group analysis of 13 habitual runners receiving BASP services.

*Case of Katrina.* Katrina, a Hispanic female, was removed from her home at the age of 14 due to confirmed physical and sexual abuse. During her first 2.5 years in the foster care system, Katrina experienced some 20 plus placement changes and at least 16 runaways, some of which were for extended periods. Altogether, she was missing from the foster care system (having run away) for over 160 days. Also, during this period she had numerous different caseworkers. It was at this time, when Katrina was on a run, that the BASP was asked to assist with her. As soon as Katrina returned from her run, an informal functional assessment was conducted by a BASP professional to assess the reasons why she was running and what type of setting she would find more to her liking. She indicated that she was running to escape the group home, where she did not feel as though staff cared for her; to show the group home staff "who is in charge"; and to see her brother and friends. Katrina indicated that she wanted a place where she would feel like she is part of a family. Based on this "runaway assessment" conversation, the behavior analyst and caseworker told Katrina that they would (a) talk with the group home staff to help mediate a resolution to some of her complaints (e.g., allow her to have visits to see her brother, ask that staff not yell at her, provide her with a lunch that includes some preferred foods to take to the day treatment program); (b) arrange for someone to listen to her each day and help her deal with things that "bug her"; (c) assist her in finding a job; and (d) find a family-type home with people who would care about her.

The behavior analyst and the caseworker were successful in arranging for Katrina to meet a foster family, and based on her interest, she moved in with the family. This foster parent had experience with older youth and had been trained and certified by the BASP as a competency trained home in the Tools for Positive Behavior Change Curriculum. Over time, Katrina reported that she really felt a part of this family and that they cared about her. She stayed in this home consistently for almost a year (310 days), with the foster family and funding agency allowing her to continue living with them beyond her 18th birthday, when she was emancipated.

Figure 12.5 depicts the placement and runaway pattern from Katrina's first out-of-home placement through to her achieving independent living at age 18 years 4 months; she remained in the placement to the time of this writing.

*Case of Jamal.* Jamal, a biracial male, was removed from his home due to alleged physical abuse and placed in foster care at the age of 11. Jamal was initially placed in a Florida group emergency shelter. After about 4 months, Jamal was placed in several different foster homes over a 4½ month period. Shortly thereafter, he began running away from placements. After approximately 1¾ years in the foster care system, with most of Jamal's time being in a group emergency shelter facility and with his running becoming more frequent and of longer duration, his caseworker sought assistance from the BASP. Thus, on his return from a run, the behavior analyst conducted a functional assessment to determine the reasons why he was running and what type of setting he would prefer. He told the behavior analyst that he was running to get away from the shelter

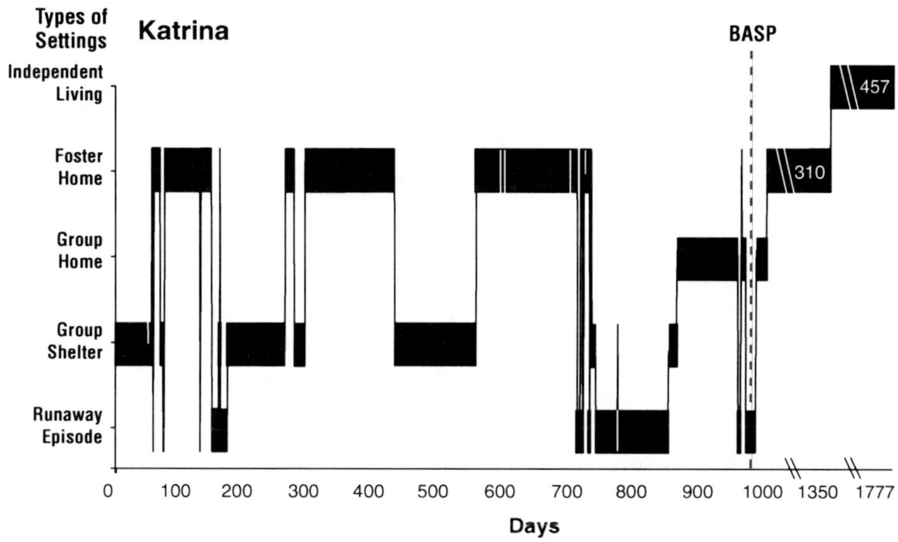


**Fig. 12.5.** Katrina's placement and run history from her entry into the foster care system at about 14 years 9 months old to her first run at about 14 years 11 months, through to the Behavior Analysis Services Program (BASP) intervention starting at about 17 years 5 months (vertical broken line) and ending with her independent living experience, shown through to her age of about 19 years 6 months. Reprinted with permission from "A Functional Approach to Reducing Runaway Behavior and Stabilizing Placements for Adolescents in Foster Care," H. B. Clark, K. Crosland, D. Geller, M. Cripe, T. Kenney, B. Neff, et al., 2008, *Research in Social Work Practice, 18*, 429–441.

and would stay at a friend's home. He also said that he had spent one night on the streets, and that it was really fun, but then got very scary. The behavior analyst asked Jamal what types of things he would like to earn if he met some simple behavioral expectations. His first choice was money. This seemed appropriate because he could gain access to several other reinforcers (e.g., music CDs, candy, comic books) by earning money. It was specified that he would also have to follow house rules in order to go shopping and use the money.

The behavior analyst and caseworker worked with Jamal to set up a simple behavioral contract plan for remaining at his placement and attending school. On implementation of the contract, Jamal's running away ceased, and his school behaviors remained within an appropriate range. The behavior analyst called to check in on Jamal about every other day. In these conversations, the behavior analyst praised Jamal's efforts and provided him with suggestions and encouragement as relevant. After about 2 months of involvement with the behavior analyst and caseworker, Jamal was moved to a preferred placement with a distant relative. The behavior analyst, with help from the caseworker, implemented a simple and effective intervention that was correlated with an immediate cessation of Jamal's running away and severe school disruptive behaviors. The period of stability that followed the BASP's involvement had a positive influence on the relative caregiver's decision to take Jamal into her home.

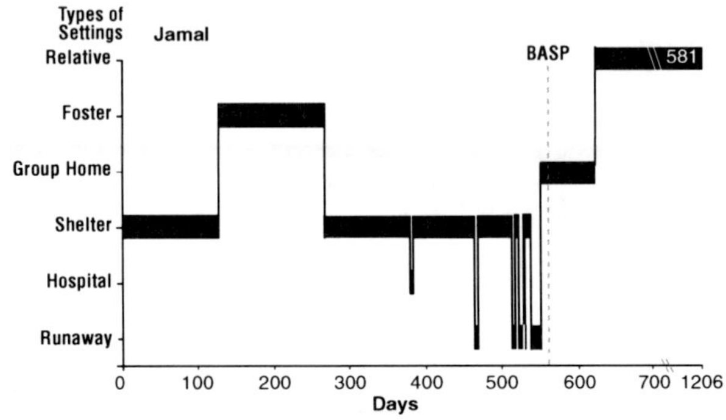


**Fig. 12.6.** Jamal's placement and run history from his entry into the foster care system at about 11 years old to his first run at about the age of 12 years 3 months, through to the Behavior Analysis Services Program (BASP) intervention starting at about 13 years of age (vertical broken line) and ending with his placement with a relative shown at his age of about 15 years 9 months.

Figure 12.6 depicts the placement and runaway pattern from Jamal's first out-of-home placement through his current placement.

## *Group Analysis of Habitual Runners*

Habitual runners, those with three or more runs, have recently gained high priority for Florida's DCF. Participants in this analysis were the first 13 habitual runners located in one district in Florida that received BASP services. These youths ranged in age from 12 to 17 years at the time of intervention. Of the 13 BASP participants, 11 were female, 9 were Caucasian, 2 were African American, 1 was Hispanic, and 1 was biracial. The intervention for the BASP participants included individualized functional assessments, which included record reviews and an interview with each youth, to determine the function of the runaway behavior. The intervention was then based on the results of the functional assessments and included one or more of the following: contingency contracts, change in living arrangements, training and consultation for caregivers, enriched activities.

From the Florida State foster care data set, a pool of possible comparison youth from this same time period and geographic area was established. These comparison youth met the definition of a habitual runner, and neither they, nor their parents or foster parents, had been served previously, or during this study period, by the BASP. For a youth to qualify as a match to a BASP youth, the following set of criteria were applied to have a "best fit": (a) gender; (b) age of first run; (c) ethnicity; (d) having data covering the period of pre- and postconditions that match the BASP youth; and (e) no extended periods of incarceration during the comparison pre- and postconditions. To strengthen the power of a statistical comparison between the BASP group and the comparison group, three youth from the comparison pool were matched to each of the BASP participants. Due to the multiple match criteria and the relatively small pool of youth who were

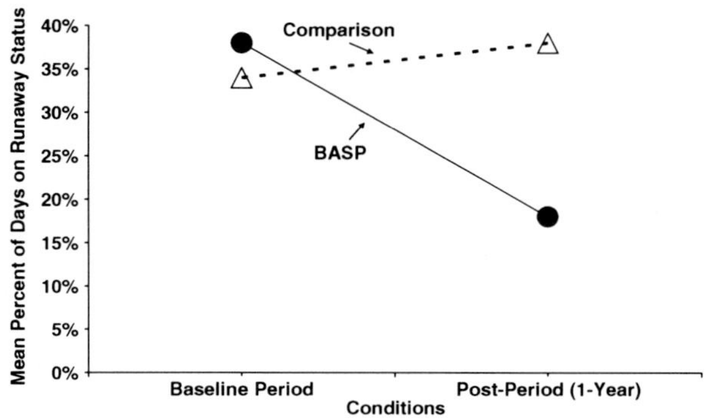


**Fig. 12.7.** The mean percent of days on runaway status shown for the BASP group (solid dots) and the matched comparison group (open triangles) across the baselines and the postperiods. Reprinted with permission from "A Functional Approach to Reducing Runaway Behavior and Stabilizing Placements for Adolescents in Foster Care," H. B. Clark, K. Crosland, D. Geller, M. Cripe, T. Kenney, B. Neff, et al., in press, *Research in Social Work Practice.*

habitual runners, six comparison youth served as matches to two different BASP participants. Thus, 33 comparison youth met the best-fit criteria in the matched sample from this same geographic area.

The principal dependent variable of interest was the percentage of days on the run for each group illustrated in Fig. 12.7. The BASP group was on runaway 38% of the time during baseline, decreasing to 18% after the intervention. The baseline for the comparison group was 34% of days on runaway status, and the postcondition was slightly higher at 38%. A two-sample Wilcoxon rank-sum test (two-sample test), a nonparametric equivalent of independent sample $t$ test, showed that the baseline levels between the two groups were not significantly different. The change from baseline to the postperiod was significantly larger for the BASP group than for the comparison group ($p \leq .05$), and the direction of change for the BASP group showed a reduction in the percent of days on runaway status. Using a functional assessment framework for interviewing and developing treatment plans for these youth resulted in decreased running and a related increase in placement stability.

## CONCLUSIONS AND IMPLICATIONS FOR CHILD WELFARE

The child welfare system has been crippled for years by mismanagement and poor practice standards (Kessler & Greene, 1999; Stein, Gambrill, & Wiltse, 1978). The BASP is the first recognized statewide initiative designed to provide empirically tested behavioral services and supports to caregivers and children within the child welfare system. The primary goal of the BASP is to scientifically address child problem behavior by improving caregiver and caseworker competence and confidence to prevent and address the challenging behaviors presented by children and youth through a behaviorally based curriculum and in-home supports. Research to date has shown a positive impact on reducing the use of restrictive procedures by caregivers, decreasing child runaway behavior, and increasing appropriate child behaviors (e.g., staying dry at night).

Caregiver training programs that specifically teach behavioral principles and skills have shown more positive changes in caregiver behavior when compared to those that do not (Lundahl, Nimer, & Parsons, 2006). Therefore, the theoretical orientation of training programs can influence the degree to which parents learn and successfully implement new practices. The child welfare system would require a paradigm shift from typical psychotherapy treatments prescribed for children to behavior analytic approaches aimed at caregivers, such as those implemented by the BASP. Currently, the only required training in the state of Florida, and at least 10 other states, for new foster parents is the Model Approach to Partnerships in Parenting (MAPP). The goal of MAPP is for foster parents to develop the knowledge, attitudes, and skills needed to be effective as parents (*Model Approach*, 1987). Despite the widespread adoption of this program, no states have collected data or reported on any outcome measures related to the training. One pilot study, conducted by Lee and Holland (1991), reported no significant differences between MAPP-trained foster parents and their untrained counterparts in the areas targeted by the training (e.g., developmental expectations of children, value placed on physical punishment, understanding of appropriate parent-child roles, and empathy toward children's needs). Enhancing the effectiveness of foster parent training seems crucial for retaining foster parents and increasing the placement stability of children. Foster parents play the essential role in the child welfare system, and the demands on foster parents continue to increase without any subsequent increase in adequate training or competent consultative support (Runyan & Fullerton, 1981). Due to the increased stressors and lack of support, there continues to be a shortage of new foster parents, and increasing numbers of foster parents are deciding to discontinue their services (Pasztor, 1989).

Group training, in general, has both advantages and disadvantages. It can be cost-effective and time efficient, and caregivers can engage in mutual sharing during and even outside class times. Some caregivers may not benefit from group training and instead may require individualized instruction. Eyberg and Matarazzo (1980) and Hampson et al. (1983) found both types of training resulted in improvements, but individual in-home training showed greater differences in child behavior and parent satisfaction when compared to group training. Kaiser at al. (1995) found that in-home coaching and feedback were necessary for parents to reach criterion levels after attending a group training. The BASP has always provided in-home coaching and support during and after caregivers have attended group training. Although this service is strongly suggested for all caregivers who attend group classes, it is optional, and some caregivers choose not to receive home-based services. Studies have recently been initiated within BASP to evaluate the impact of receiving home-based support to determine if this component is an integral part for improvement in caregiver and child behaviors. It is hypothesized that in-home services would enhance the class training caregivers receive and may be essential for the generalization and maintenance of parenting skills.

The BASP strives to decrease the stress levels of both caregivers and children by creating a positive enriched environment. Caregivers are taught to seize opportunities to have positive productive interactions and to establish reasonable expectations for their children. Research within BASP will continue to examine the effects of the caregiver training curriculum and in-home services on both caregiver and child outcomes. Specifically, stress levels, skill acquisition, generalization and maintenance of skills, and retention rates will be examined for caregivers. Placement stability, frequency and severity of behavior problems, medication use, and stress levels will be investigated for children.

The BASP and the field of behavior analysis and PBS in general have a great deal to offer in improving the lives of children in the child welfare system. The BASP remains committed to providing high-quality services that make a socially significant difference to children and families. It is hypothesized that teaching caregivers effective behavioral parenting methods to enhance parent interactions with children will decrease child problem behavior and ultimately result in greater placement stability and more positive outcomes for children. It is with great anticipation that a shift in services will eventually occur in the child welfare system to increase the use of empirically validated behavioral intervention strategies.

## REFERENCES

Adoption Assistance and Child Welfare Act, P.L. 96–272, (1980).

American Academy of Child and Adolescent Psychiatry. (2005). *Facts for families: Foster care*. Washington, DC: Author.

American Psychiatric Association (1994). Diagnostic and statistical manual of mental disorders (4th Ed., Revised). Washington DC: Author.

Anderson, C. M., & Freeman, K. A. (2000). Positive behavior support: Expanding the application of applied behavior analysis. *The Behavior Analyst, 23*, 85–94.

Azrin, N.H., Sneed, T.J., & Foxx, R.M. (1974). Dry bed: Rapid elimination of childhood enuresis. *Behaviour Research and Therapy, 12*, 147–156.

Barth, R. P., Landsverk, J., Chamberlain, P., Reid, J. B., Rolls, J. A., Hurlburt, M. S., et al. (2005). Parent-training programs in child welfare services: Planning for a more evidence-based approach to serving biological parents. *Research on Social Work Practice, 15*, 353–371.

Berridge, D., & Cleaver, H. (1987). *Foster home breakdown*. Oxford, England: Blackwell.

Bess, R. (2002). *The cost of protecting vulnerable children III: What factors affect states' fiscal decisions?* Washington, DC: Urban Institute.

Buehler, C., Orme, J. G., Post, J., & Patterson, D. A. (2000). The long-term correlates of family foster care. *Children and Youth Services Review, 22*, 595–625.

Burns, B. J., Phillips, S. D., Wagner, H. R., Barth, R. P., Kolko, D. J., Campbell, Y., et al. (2004). Mental health need and access to mental health services by youth involved with child welfare: A national survey. *Journal of the American Academy of Child and Adolescent Psychiatry, 43*, 960–970.

Carr, E. G., Dunlap, G., Horner, R. H., Koegel, R. L., Turnbull, A. P., Sailor, W., et al. (2002). Positive behavior support. Evolution of an applied science. *Journal of Positive Behavior Interventions, 4*, 4–16.

Center for the Study of Social Policy and Its Center for the Study of Social Policy and Its Center for Community Partnerships in Child Welfare. (2003). *Child Welfare Summit: Looking to the future. An examination of the state of child welfare and recommendations for action*. Washington, DC.

Chapin Hall Center for Children. (2005). *Youth who run away from out-of-home care* (Issue Brief 103). Chicago.

Children's Health Act of 2000 (Public Law 106–310 Section 1004).

Choca, M. J., Minoff, J., Angene, L., Byrnes, M., Kenneally, L., Norris, D., et al. (2004). Can't do it alone: Housing collaborations to improve foster youth outcomes. *Child Welfare, 83*, 469–492.

Christenson, S. L. (2002, November). *Families, educators, and the family-school partnership: Issues or opportunities for promoting children's learning competence?* Paper presented at the 2002 Invitational Conference: The Future of School Psychology, Indianapolis, IN.

Clark, H. B., & Crosland, K. (in press). Social and life skills development: Preparing and facilitating youth for transition into young adult roles. In B. Kerman, A. Maluccio, & M. Freundlich (Eds.), *Achieving permanence for older children and youth in foster care*. New York: Columbia University Press.

Clark, H. B., Crosland, K., Geller, D., Cripe, M., Kenney, T., Neff, B., et al. (2008). A functional approach to reducing runaway behavior and stabilizing placements for adolescents in foster care. *Research in Social Work Practice, 18*, 429–441.

Cooper, J.O., Heron, T.E., & Heward, W.L. (1987). *Applied behavior analysis*. Upper Saddle River, NJ: Merrill.

Cooper, C. S., Peterson, N. L., & Meier, J. H. (1987). Variables associated with disrupted placement in a select sample of abused and neglected children. *Child Abuse and Neglect, 11*, 75–86.

Courtney, M. E., Skyles, A., Miranda, G., Zinn, A., Howard, E., & Goerge, R. M. (2005). *Youth who run away from substitute care* (Issue Brief No. 103). Chicago, IL: Chapin Hall Center for Children, University of Chicago.

Crosland, K. A., Cigales, M., Dunlap, G., Neff, B., Clark, H. B., Giddings, T., & Blanco, A. (2008). Using staff training to decrease the use of restrictive procedures at two facilities for foster care children. *Research on Social Work Practice, 18*, 401–409.

Day, D. M. (2002). Examining the therapeutic utility of restraints and seclusion with children and youth: The role of theory and research in practice. *American Journal of Orthopsychiatry, 72*, 266–278.

Dunlap, G. (2006). The applied behavior analytic heritage of PBS: A dynamic model of action-oriented research. *Journal of Positive Behavior Interventions, 8*, 58–60.

Dunlap, G., & Carr, E. G. (2007). Positive behavior support and developmental disabilities: A summary and analysis of research. In S. L. Odom, R. H. Horner, M. Snell, & J. Blacher (Eds.), *Handbook of developmental disabilities* (pp. 469–482). New York: Guilford.

Dunlap, G., Carr, E.G., Horner, R.H., Zarcone, J., & Schwartz, I. (2008). Positive behavior support and applied behavior analysis: A familial alliance. *Behavior Modification, 32*, 682–698.

Dunlap, G., & Hieneman, M. (2005). Positive behavior support. In G. Sugai & R. Horner (Eds.), *Encyclopedia of behavior modification and cognitive behavior therapy. Vol. 3: Educational applications* (pp. 1421–1428). Thousand Oaks, CA: Sage.

Eyberg, S.M. & Matarazzo, R.G. (1980). Training parents as therapists: A comparison between individual parent-child interaction training and parent group didactic training. *Journal of Clinical Psychology, 36*, 492–499.

Fergusson, D.M, & Horwood, L.J. (1994). Nocturnal enuresis and behavioral problems in adolescence: A 15-year longitudinal study. *Pediatrics, 94*, 662–668.

Fletcher, T.B. (2000). Primary nocturnal enuresis: A structural and strategic family systems approach. *Journal of Mental Health Counseling, 22*, 32–44.

Florida Statues, Section 393.17 (2001).

Goren, S., Singh, N. N., & Best, A. M. (1993). The aggression-coercion cycle: Use of seclusion and restraint in a child psychiatric hospital. *Journal of Child and Family Studies, 2*, 61–73.

Hampson, R. B., Schulte, M. A., & Ricks, C. C. (1983). Individual vs. group training for foster parents: Efficiency/effectiveness evaluations. *Family Relations, 32*, 191–201.

Honberg, R., & Miller, J. (2003). *Seclusion and restraints*. The Nation's Voice on Mental Illness (NAMI) Task Force Report. Arlington, VA: Policy Research Institute.

Iglehart, A. (1994). Kinship foster care: Placement services and outcome issues. *Children and Youth Services Review, 16,* 107–127.

Irwin, M. (1987). Are seclusion rooms needed on child psychiatric units? *American Journal of Orthopsychiatry, 57,* 125–126.

Keiser, A.P., Hemmeter, M.L., Ostrosky, M.M., Alpert, C.L., & Hancock, T.B. (1995). The effects of group training and individual feedback on parent use of Milieu teaching. *Journal of Childhood Communication Disorders, 16,* 39–48.

Kern, L., & Dunlap, G. (1999). Assessment-based interventions for children with emotional and behavioral disorders. In A. C. Repp & R. H. Horner (Eds.), *Functional analysis of problem behavior: From effective assessment to effective support* (pp. 197–218). Belmont, CA: Wadsworth.

Kessler, M. L., & Greene, B. F. (1999). Behavior analysis in child welfare: Competency training caseworkers to manage visits between parents and their children in foster care. *Research on Social Work Practice, 9,* 148–170.

Klee, L., & Halfon, N. (1987). Communicating health information in the California Foster Care System: Problems and recommendations. *Children and Youth Services Review, 9,* 171–185.

Landsverk, J., Garland, A. F., & Leslie, L. K. (2002). Mental health services for children reported to child protective services. In J. E. B. Meyers, L. Berliner, J. Briere, C. T. Hendrix, C. Jenny, & T. A. Reid (Eds.), *The APSAC handbook on child maltreatment* (2nd ed., pp. 487–507). Thousand Oaks, CA: Sage.

Latham, G. I. (1990). *The power of positive parenting.* North Logan, UT: P & I Ink.

Leathers, S. J. (2002). Foster children's behavioral disturbance and detachment from caregivers and community institutions. *Children and Youth Services Review, 24,* 239–268.

Lee, J. H., & Holland, T. P. (1991). Evaluating the effectiveness of foster parent training. *Research on Social Work Practice, 1,* 162–174.

Litronwnik, A. J., Taussig, H. N., Landsverk, J. A., & Garland, A. F. (1999). Youth entering an emergency shelter care facility: Prior involvement in juvenile justice and mental health systems. *Journal of Social Service Review, 25,* 5–19.

Lundahl, B. W., Nimer, J., & Parsons, B. (2006). Preventing child abuse: A meta-analysis of parent training programs. *Research on Social Work Practice, 16,* 251–262.

Lutzker, J. R., Tymchuk, A. J., & Bigelow, K. M. (2001). Applied research in child maltreatment: Practicalities and pitfalls. *Children's Services: Social Policy, Research, and Practice, 4,* 141–156.

*Model approach to partnerships in parenting: Group preparation and selection of foster and/or adoptive families.* (1987). (Available from the Child Welfare Institute, 1430 West Peachtree Street, Suite 570, Atlanta, GA 30309)

Newton, R. R., Litrownik, A. J., & Landsverk, J. A. (2000). Children and youth in foster care: Distangling the relationship between problem behaviors and number of placements. *Child Abuse and Neglect, 24,* 1363–1374.

Pardeck, J. T. (1984). Multiple placement of children in foster family care: An empirical analysis. *Social Work, 29,* 506–509.

Pardeck, J. T., Murphy, J. W., & Fitzwater, L. (1985). Profile of the foster child likely to experience unstable care: A re-examination. *Early Child Development and Care, 22,* 137–146.

Pasztor, E. M. (1989). *The influence of foster parent ownership of permanency planning tasks on role retention and permanent placements.* Unpublished doctoral dissertation, Catholic University, Washington, DC.

Piazza, C. C., Hanley, G. P., Bowman, L. G., Ruyter, J. M., Lindauer, S. E., & Saiontz, D. M. (1997). Functional analysis and treatment of elopement. *Journal of Applied Behavior Analysis, 30,* 653–672.

Prevent Child Abuse America. (2001). *Total estimated cost of child abuse and neglect in the United States.* Retrieved December 15, 2007, from http://member.preventchildabuse.org/site/DocServer/cost_analysis.pdf?docID=144 (PDF-44 KB) - *NOTE: must register to view document.*

Proch, K., & Taber, M. (1985). Placement disruption: A review of research. *Children and Youth Services Review, 7,* 309–320.

Rowe, J., Hundleby, M., & Garnett, L. (1989). *Child care now: A survey of placement patterns*. London: British Agencies for Fostering and Adoption.

Runyan, A., & Fullerton, S. (1981). Foster care provider training: A preventative program. *Children and Youth Services Review, 3*, 127–141.

Smagner, J. P., & Sullivan, M. H. (2005). Investigating the effectiveness of behavioral parent training with involuntary clients in child welfare settings. *Research on Social Work Practice, 15*, 431–439.

Stein, T. J., Gambrill, E. D., & Wiltse, K. T. (1978). *Children in foster homes: Achieving continuity of care*. New York: Praeger.

Stone, N. M., & Stone, S. F. (1983). The prediction of successful foster placement. *The Journal of Contemporary Social Work, 1*, 11–17.

Stoutimore, M.R., Williams, C.E., Neff, B., Foster, M. (2008). The Florida child welfare Behavior Analysis Services Program. *Research on Social Work Practice, 18*, 367–376.

Stover, A. C., Dunlap, G., & Neff, B. (2008). The effects of a contingency contracting program on the nocturnal enuresis of three children. *Research on Social Work Practice, 18*, 421–428.

Tarbox, R. S. F., Wallace, M. D., & Williams, L. (2003). Assessment and treatment of elopement: A replication and extension. *Journal of Applied Behavior Analysis, 36*, 239–244.

Timothy Roche (2000, November 13). The crisis of foster care. *Time Magazine, 156*, 5.

Ullom-Minnich, M.R. (1996). Diagnosis and management of nocturnal enuresis, *American Family Physician, 54*, 2259–2266.

U.S. Department of Health and Human Services. (2006). *The Adoption and Foster Care Analysis and Reporting System report*. Washington, DC: U.S. Department of Health and Human Services. Retrieved from http://www.acf.hhs.gov/programs/cb/stats_research/afcars/tar/report13.htm, Nov. 21st, 2007.

U.S. General Accounting Office. (1997). *Parental substance abuse: Implications for children, the child welfare system, and foster care outcomes*. Washington, DC.

Walsh, J. A., & Walsh, R. A. (1990). *Quality care for tough kids*. Washington, DC: Child Welfare League of America.

Webster, D., Barth, R. P., & Needell, B. (2000). Placement stability for children in out-of-home care: A longitudinal analysis. *Child Welfare, 79*, 614–632.

Wechsler, D. (1991). Wechsler Intelligence Scale for Children – Third Edition. San Antonio, TX; The Psychological Corporation.

Weiss, E. (1998, October 11–15). Deadly restraint: A nationwide pattern. *The Hartford Courant*. pp. A1 and A12.

Weisz, J. R., Donenberg, G. R., Han, S. S., & Kauneckis, D. (1995). Child and adolescent psychotherapy outcomes in experiments versus clinics: Why the disparity? *Journal of Abnormal Child Psychology, 23*, 83–106.

Widom, C. S. (1991). The role of placement experiences in mediating the criminal consequences of early childhood victimization. *American Journal of Orthopsychiatry, 61*, 195–209.

Williams, C. (2003). History of the behavior analysis services program. Personal communication received by Crosland, K.A.

# Section III

## Schoolwide

# 13

# Defining and Describing Schoolwide Positive Behavior Support

GEORGE SUGAI and ROBERT H. HORNER

Schools have two important goals: maximize the academic achievement and social competence of all learners. To achieve these goals, schools must focus on the specific skills of individual students, but increasingly we are learning that they must also focus on the overall social culture of a school. The social culture of a school can vary from highly controlled and rule governed to loosely structured and spontaneous. However, successful learning environments most often are characterized as preventive, predictable, positive, instructional, safe, and responsive for all students and staff across all school settings and activities.

The purpose of this chapter is to describe those characteristics of schoolwide positive behavior support (SW-PBS) practices and systems that establish and maintain an effective, efficient, and relevant social culture in which teaching and learning are maximized. This chapter leads this section of the handbook because SW-PBS serves as the foundation or basis for successful implementation of a full continuum of academic and social behavior supports occurring school- and classroomwide, for example, individual behavior supports (e.g., function-based supports, wraparound), academic programming, data-based decision making and evaluation, discipline, family and community participation, and early intervention.

The SW-PBS content of this chapter is organized into three main sections: (a) historical influences and theoretical foundations, (b) defining practices, and (c) implementation processes and guidelines.

**GEORGE SUGAI** • University of Connecticut
**ROBERT H. HORNER** • University of Oregon

## HISTORICAL INFLUENCES AND THEORETICAL FOUNDATIONS

Maximizing academic achievement and preparing a skilled and knowledgeable citizenry have been primary education goals since the beginning of the first American public school system. However, as families, communities, and cultures have matured and become more complex over generations, the curricular responsibilities of schools have become boarder, larger, and more sophisticated (National Center on Education and the Economy, 2007). One area of increased recent attention has been the school's role in affecting the social development of children and youth. Over the years, this attention has manifested itself in the form of different school social initiatives, for example, values and character education, safe and drug-free schools, citizenship and civil responsibility, and sex and family education.

### Need for SW-PBS

Classroom behavior management and schoolwide discipline in particular have sustained high levels of concern, controversy, and discussion. To illustrate, both the general public and educators have rated behavior related issues in the top three concerns facing the public schools over the last 35 years in the "36th Annual Phi Delta Kappa/Gallup Poll of the Public's Attitude Toward the Public Schools" (Rose & Gallup, 2007). Attention to the behavior and social development of all students has become a priority in recent major national legislative acts (e.g., Individuals With Disabilities Act [IDEA], No Child Left Behind).

Despite this long-time concern and increased attention, a curriculum for the social development of children and youth in schools has not been formally and widely embraced (Sugai, Horner, & McIntosh, 2008). First, debate about whether the social development of children should be the primary responsibility of the family, community, or school remains unresolved. Second, as rates and kinds of problem behaviors worsen, the tendency has been to move toward tougher consequence systems to "teach" students that their rule-violating behavior is unacceptable. Third, behavior and classroom management and schoolwide disciplinary practices have not been implemented in a systemic or integrated fashion but instead introduced reactively to individualized problem events or situations. Fourth, the preservice and in-service professional development structures have not formalized or emphasized their behavior-related curricula, instead giving preference and priority to academic curricula and instruction. Fifth, a cohesive continuum of evidence-based behavior support practices has not been established to guide educators to the most appropriate and effective interventions. Finally, attention has focused on adoption of a given behavior practice and not on the accurate and sustained implementation of that practice.

Schoolwide discipline has been of particular interest. When educators experience increased rates and intensities of rule-violating behavior, attention shifts to regaining classroom order, eliminating disruptive and disturbing behaviors, and increasing compliance to school expectations. These programs share a focus on establishing teaching and environments in which prosocial behaviors are promoted, problem behaviors are treated consistently and effectively, schoolwide implementation includes all students and staff members across all school settings, and priority is given to school safety and academic achievement (Lewis & Sugai, 1999; Mayer, 1998; Safran & Oswald, 2003; Walker et al., 1996).

## Schoolwide Positive Behavior Supports Defined

Schoolwide positive behavior support (SW-PBS) is a systems approach for establishing the social culture and individualized behavior supports needed for a school to be a safe and effective learning environment for all students. SW-PBS was initiated in the late 1980s and early 1990s in response to renewed interest in improving student social behavior development and implementing effective behavior management practices (Kame'enui, Colvin, & Sugai, 1996; Lewis & Sugai, 1999; Sprick, Sprick, & Garrison, 1992; Walker et al., 1996). This effort was influenced positively by initiatives related, for example, to school violence study and prevention (Gottfredson, Gottfredson, & Hyble, 1993; Mayer, 1995); social and emotional development (Greenwood, Delquadri, & Bulgren, 1993); safe and drug-free schools; school-based mental health (Biglan, 1995; Kutash, Duchnowski, & Lynne, 2006); special education (IDEA); character education; social skills instruction (Gresham, Sugai, & Horner, 2001); and alternative and afterschool programming (Nelson, 1996; Nelson, Johnson, & Marchand-Martella, 1996).

SW-PBS is not a curriculum, intervention, or program. However, it is an approach designed to improve the adoption, accurate implementation, and sustained use of evidence-based practices related to behavior and classroom management and school discipline systems. SW-PBS gives equal emphasis to the integration of contextually defined and valued outcomes, behavioral and biomedical science, and systems change (Horner, Sugai, Todd, & Lewis-Palmer, 2005; Sugai et al., 2000). Operationally, SW-PBS is the systematic and formal consideration of (a) measurable academic and social behavior outcomes, (b) information or data to guide decision making and selection of effective behavioral interventions, (c) evidence-based interventions that support student academic and social behavior success, and (d) systems supports designed to increase the accuracy and durability of practice implementation (Sugai & Horner, 2002; Sugai et al., 2008.

## Theoretical and Conceptual Characteristics of SW-PBS

The theoretical and conceptual foundations of SWPB are firmly linked to *behavioral theory and applied behavior analysis* (Carr et al., 2002; Filter, 2007; Simonsen & Sugai, in press). This perspective emphasizes that observable behavior is an important indicator of what individuals have learned and how they operate in their environment, behavior is learned and rule governed, environmental factors (antecedent and consequence events) are influential in determining whether a behavior is likely to occur, and new and alternative prosocial behaviors can be taught (see Sugai & Horner, 2002; Sugai et al., 2008, for a complete overview of the historical and conceptual foundations of SW-PBS).

In addition to having behavioral roots, SW-PBS has a number of other defining characteristics. For example, *prevention* emphasizes the establishment of a continuum of behavior support interventions and systems designed specifically to prevent the (a) development of new problem behaviors, (b) triggering of occurrences of problem behavior, and (c) increase in intensity of existing problem behaviors. This continuum is often organized within a three-tier prevention logic borrowed from community health and disease prevention: (a) primary tier, with behavioral support for all students across all school settings; (b) secondary tier, with more intensive behavioral supports for students whose behaviors are not responsive to primary-tier interventions; and (c) tertiary tier, with highly individualized and intensive behavioral supports for students whose behaviors are not responsive to primary- or secondary-tier interventions (Kutash et al., 2006; Walker et al., 1996).

An *instructional focus* is a third defining characteristic of SW-PBS. Whether considering individual students or all students in a school, priority is given to directly teaching social behaviors that increase social and academic success at school. At the schoolwide (primary-tier) level, a small number of schoolwide behavioral expectations are taught directly to all student to establish a common language and experience for students and family and staff members. At the small-group (secondary-tier) level, the emphasis is on building skill fluency through more direct and frequent social skill-learning opportunities. At the individual student (tertiary-tier) level, information about what triggers and maintains problem behavior (function) is used to carefully select individual social skills that can compete (be more efficient, more effective, more relevant) with factors that occasion problem behavior (Horner, 1994; O'Neill et al., 1997).

A fourth defining characteristic of SW-PBS is high priority for the selection, adoption, and use of *evidence-* or *research-based behavioral practices*. Although any intervention or practice must be contextualized for the individuals who will implement it and the students who will experience it, SW-PBS emphasizes that the search begin with practices that have been tested, replicated, and applied through experimental and quasi-experimental research designs. These practices include an array of specific interventions and a host of strategies for (a) acknowledging, or rewarding, appropriate behavior and (b) establishing consequences for problem behavior (Alberto & Troutman, 2006; Cooper, Heron & Heward, 2007).

A fifth defining characteristic of SW-PBS is the adoption of a *systems perspective* when selecting and implementing a behavioral intervention. Rather than disseminating a new practice through a typical professional development model consisting of a series of group training events, a SW-PBS systems perspective gives priority to establishing local capacity and expertise, majority agreements and commitments, high levels of implementation readiness, high fidelity of implementation, continuous implementation and outcome evaluation, and more (PBIS Blueprint, 2004).

A final characteristic defining the core of SW-PBS is the *collection and use of data* for active decision making (Horner & Sugai, 2001; Irvin et al., 2006; Lewis-Palmer, Sugai, & Larson, 1999; Wright & Dusek, 1998). The systems that support SW-PBS practices revolve around continual collection of data to determine (a) if defined practices are being implemented with fidelity and (b) if those practices are having a positive impact on student outcomes. These data are used by school teams, administrators, and individual faculty to improve the behavior supports available within the school.

### Summary

Concern for formally addressing the social behavior and discipline needs of schools has consistently been high in public education, especially in relation to supporting safe and effective teaching and learning environments. Responses, however, have not been organized and formal; in fact, most schools develop an overreliance on reactive schoolwide discipline codes that rely on reprimands and punishers to inhibit rule-violating behaviors and actually hinder the establishment of a positive school social culture (Skiba & Peterson, 1999, 2000).

SW-PBS was established as an approach to support social behavior development and teaching and learning environments of the school for all students by emphasizing prevention, an instructional perspective, evidence-based interventions, behavioral theory and behavior analysis, and a systems perspective. In the next section, we elaborate on the practices and systems that characterize a SW-PBS approach at the school level.

## DEFINING PRACTICES OF SW-PBS

To reiterate, the two main goals of SW-PBS are to positively support teaching and learning environments so that the academic outcomes are maximized and to formalize the school and classroom organization and operation so that a positive social culture is established. If successful in achieving these goals, schools and classrooms experience a social culture in which a common positive language and means of communication are established across students and members of staff and community.

In general, the practices of SW-PBS can be organized within the three-tier schoolwide continuum of behavior support described: primary, secondary, and tertiary. In this section, we describe the interventions and practices that characterize SW-PBS. Systems and implementation features are described in the next section.

### Primary-Tier SW-PBS Interventions

Primary-tier interventions of SW-PBS are not individual strategies or practices but a set of interventions that are optimized to foster a comprehensive and positive social culture for all students and staff and community members across all school settings (Colvin, Kame'enui, & Sugai, 1993).

This set of interventions is designed around the needs and characteristics of the larger school culture and is meant to successfully "influence" or support most students in the school (Walker et al., 1996). If primary-tier interventions are done well, a relatively smaller percentage of students will be quickly identified for more intensive interventions (secondary/tertiary) because their behaviors have not been responsive (Fairbanks, Sugai, Guardino, & Lathrop, 2007; Gresham, 1995).

Schoolwide discipline procedures are universal prevention interventions that are *presented to all students* to (a) foster prosocial behavior, (b) maximize opportunities for teaching and academic achievement, and (c) inhibit occurrences of problem behavior. A relatively small proportion of students (1–15%) have learning histories that cause general schoolwide interventions to be ineffective for them, and these students require additional specialized and individualized interventions (Horner et al., 2005; Walker et al., 1996). Thus, schoolwide discipline systems should not be abandoned because these students are unresponsive. Instead, schools should think of schoolwide discipline systems as important foundations for (a) supporting the majority of students, (b) preventing the development of chronic problem behavior for students with high-risk backgrounds and learning histories, and (c) identifying and providing more specialized and individualized behavior supports for students with high-intensity problem behaviors (Sugai et al., 2000).

## Primary-Tier SW-PBS Interventions

Generally, six major intervention features characterize primary-tier SW-PBS interventions (Colvin, Sugai, & Kame'enui, 1993; Lewis & Sugai, 1999). First, a majority of the staff agrees to embrace a common approach to discipline that is positive, comprehensive, formal, and ongoing. In the case of SW-PBS, this approach is behaviorally oriented, research based, culturally/contextually appropriate, and instructionally based. This common approach is presented in the form of a schoolwide purpose statement, for example, "Manzanita School is a community of learners. We are here to learn, grow, and become good citizens."

Second, students and staff and community members identify a set of schoolwide expectations that (a) are few in number (i.e., three to five); (b) are stated positively and succinctly; (c) focus on all staff, all students, and all settings; (d) emphasize support for academic and behavioral outcomes; and (e) are contextually/culturally appropriate. Schools select expectations that are relevant to who they are, but examples of common expectations are as follows:

- Respect for self, others, and environment
- Safe, respectful, and responsible
- Achievement, respect, responsibility
- Respect, responsibility, relationships

Third, these schoolwide expectations are taught directly and continuously in the same manner as academic skills, that is, they are (a) defined, (b) modeled, (c) practiced, (d) given corrective and positive feedback, and (e) encouraged in the natural and applied setting. More important, positive expectations are taught using local and real behavioral examples in real contexts or settings of the school. These examples are observable, relevant, and doable. Behavioral expectations are rules that enable consistent communications and support an efficient verbal community in which all members have clear understandings of what is expected of themselves and others. A useful and efficient format for teaching schoolwide examples is illustrated in Fig. 13.1.

Fourth, primary-tier SW-PBS interventions provide a continuum of procedures for regular acknowledgments or rewards of student displays of these behavioral expectations. If newly taught and acquired behaviors are to be strengthened, occur more often in the future, and maintained over time, students must receive positive feedback/acknowledgments for their displays of those behaviors. In general, the following guidelines are used when developing and implementing primary-tier acknowledgment interventions:

1. Move from other to self-delivered, frequent to infrequent, predictable to unpredictable, and tangible to social reinforcers.
2. Individualize and contextualize as much as possible to accommodate student and community characteristics.
3. Build on positive person-to-person relationships.
4. Strive for giving acknowledgments and rewards at rates higher than consequences for rule violations (e.g., four to eight positive for each negative).
5. Emphasize and label the behavior being displayed and for which the positive acknowledgment is intended.

Fifth, although teaching and acknowledging positive behavioral expectations are paramount, developing a continuum of consequences for responding to rule violations is also important. Procedures for responding to problem behaviors are designed to communicate to and teach students and staff and family members which behaviors represent violations of schoolwide behavioral expectations. Severity, consequences, and behavioral supports are indicated. The following guidelines are considered when developing this continuum:

1. Define rule violations in observable terms and teach directly and explicitly with a contextually relevant and representative set of behavior examples.
2. Develop clear distinctions between problem behaviors that are managed by staff/classroom teacher and by office/administrative staff and establish agreed-on strategies for handling problem behaviors across classroom and administrative settings.
3. Develop an office discipline referral (ODR), behavior incident record ing sheet, or tracking system that provides minimum information about (a) who violated rule (name, grade); (b) who observed and responded to the rule violation; (c) when (day, time) the rule violation occurred; (d) where the rule violation occurred; (e) who else was involved in the problem situation; (f) what was the possible motivation or purpose of the problem behavior; and (g) which schoolwide behavioral expectation was violated.

| | SETTING | | | | | | |
|---|---|---|---|---|---|---|---|
| EXPECTATION | All Settings | Hallways | Playgrounds | Cafeteria | Library/ Computer Lab | Assembly | Bus |
| Respect Ourselves | Be on task. Give your best effort. Be prepared. | Walk. | Have a plan. | Eat all your food. Select healthy foods. | Study, read, compute. | Sit in one spot. | Watch for your stop. |
| Respect Others | Be kind. Hands/feet to self. Help/share with others. | Use normal voice volume. Walk to right. | Play safe. Include others. Share equipment. | Practice good table manners | Whisper. Return books. | Listen/watch. Use appropriate applause. | Use a quiet voice. Stay in your seat. |
| Respect Property | Recycle. Clean up after self. | Pick up litter. Maintain physical space. | Use equipment properly. Put litter in garbage can. | Replace trays & utensils. Clean up eating area. | Push in chairs. Treat books carefully. | Pick up. Treat chairs appropriately. | Wipe your feet. Sit appropriately. |

**Fig. 13.1.** Example of teaching matrix.

4. Establish procedures for preventing and responding to students with repeated rule violations that include (a) prereferral intervention or behavior support team; (b) data-decision rule for initiating positive behavior support (e.g., three ODRs for major rule-violating infraction); (c) precorrection intervention to prevent future occurrences of problem behavior; (d) formal procedures for teaching, practicing, and reinforcing positively prosocial behaviors to replace problem behavior; and (e) adult mentor/advocate.
5. Assign corrective consequences based on the purpose/motivation (function) of the problem behavior, that is, access/get (attention, activities, objects, etc.) or escape/avoid (attention, activities, tasks, etc.).
6. Establish secondary and tertiary practices and systems for students who are not responsive to schoolwide discipline system.

Two of the most important requirements of a successful and effective schoolwide continuum of consequences are having an equally formal and accurately implemented system of teaching and acknowledging prosocial or appropriate behaviors and having a structured and ongoing process for responding differently for students whose behaviors do not respond to this schoolwide continuum. The goal is for all students to have at least equal, but preferably more, opportunities and experiences with the prosocial aspects of SW-PBS. This priority increases the saliency of the procedures for handling rule violations and teaches students the importance and utility of engaging in rule-following behaviors. The goal of having more intensive interventions for students who do not respond is to prevent the tendency to "get tough" or overly repeat ineffective consequences and to move more quickly to more supportive and constructive specialized interventions that consider the function or factors that maintain problem behavior and actively teach effective and efficient alternative behaviors.

Finally, to support the implementation of a SW-PBS system, information must be accurate, timely, and easily available to guide decision making. In general, a record-keeping and decision-making system must have (a) structures and routines for data collection; (b) mechanisms for data entry, storage, and manipulation; and (c) procedures and routines for review and analysis of data. The following guidelines summarize how record-keeping and data decision-making systems can be effective, efficient, and relevant:

1. Develop data collection procedures that are integrated into typical routines (e.g., ODRs, attendance rolls, behavior incident reports).
2. Regularly assess the accuracy of data collection procedures.
3. Limit data collection to information that answers important student, classroom, and school questions.
4. Establish specific structures and routines for staff members to receive weekly/monthly data reports about the status of schoolwide discipline.
5. Precede all decision-making efforts with, "What do data suggest/indicate?"
6. Use teams to review data and develop data-based action plans.
7. Establish specific data-decision rules to guide review of data.

8. Develop data storage and management procedures that (a) can be managed accurately by two or three staff members at any time; (b) consume no more than 1% of the time available in a school day; and (c) can summarize data in an efficient, timely, and graphically informative manner.

Once an accurate, dependable, and efficient data management system is in place, important questions about interventions and practices can be addressed. For example, the following questions are considered on a regular basis:

1. What practice should we adopt to address our needs?
2. What evidence supports the effectiveness of a practice?
3. What evidence suggests that a practice is appropriate for our school?
4. Can a practice be modified for the unique features of our school?
5. What can we learn from other schools that have used a practice?
6. How would we track progress with a practice?
7. How do we know if adequate progress is being made with a practice?
8. Are current practices being implemented with high fidelity or accuracy?
9. Are supports in place to support sustained implementation of a practice?
10. What elements of a practice can be eliminated and still maintain the same level of progress?
11. What practices should be modified to improve progress with a practice?
12. Do students, staff members, parents, or community members support the use of current practices and their impact?

## Secondary-Tier SW-PBS Interventions

Estimates range from 15% to 30% of students having behaviors that are unresponsive to effective and accurately implemented primary-tier SW-PBS interventions (Gottfredson & Gottfredson, 1996; Walker, Ramsey, & Gresham, 2005). That is, the rule-violating behavior of these students needs more than typically available in a schoolwide system of support. Secondary-tier SW-PBS interventions are characterized as (a) more intensive in terms of effort, resources, and frequency of implementation activity; (b) applied to a subset of a larger population of students; (c) comprised of research/evidence-based practices; and (d) involve a team of staff members who have more frequent and ongoing interaction with the student. Staff members with more specialized behavioral skills and capacity are involved in supporting these students (e.g., school psychologists, counselors, special educators, physical/occupational therapists, speech-language specialists).

A variety of secondary-tier intervention demonstrations have been documented in the literature. For example, the Behavior Education Program (Crone, Hawken, & Horner, 2004) has been effective with elementary and middle school age students. Check In/Check Out (Fairbanks et al., 2007) has been applied successfully with elementary students. Check and Connect (Anderson, Christenson, Sinclair, & Lehr, 2004; Lehr, Sinclair, & Christenson, 2004) has been demonstrated with high school students.

A number of evidence-based practices are found consistently across the variety of secondary-tier interventions, for example, self-management strategies (i.e., self-recording, self-assessment, self-delivery of reinforcement); token economies (e.g., points given for displays of appropriate social behavior); targeted or direct social skills instruction of behaviors that are aligned directly with the schoolwide positive behavioral expectations; and peer-based contingency management strategies.

Although some implementation differences exist, secondary-tier interventions are implemented as an integrated component of a comprehensive SW-PBS approach, especially in connection with primary-tier interventions. In addition, most secondary-tier interventions have five common implementation features. First, the implementation process is guided by a schoolwide intervention team whose members coordinate who, when, where, and how secondary-tier interventions might be implemented. This team has a leader or coordinator who manages the operational features of the implementation (e.g., team meetings, schedules, data summaries, and reports). Although regular members include behavior specialists (e.g., school psychologists, special educators, counselors), other team members might vary depending on which students are participating in secondary-tier interventions.

The second implementation is a regular and frequent (e.g., monthly) screening for and identification of students whose behaviors have been unresponsive to primary-tier interventions and might benefit for a more intensive intervention approach. This team also reviews implementation fidelity and progress of students who are receiving secondary-tier interventions.

Third, secondary-tier intervention students stay connected with the schoolwide positive expectations, which serve as the focus of behavior feedback, social skills instruction, positive reinforcement, and data-based decision making. This connection maintains the link with the rest of the student body and school, increases implementation efficiency, and continues the emphasis on prevention and positive expectations.

Fourth, a regular (daily, weekly, quarterly) system of communication is established with students, parents, faculty, and administration. Students are scheduled one or more times each day to evaluate their individual behaviors against the schoolwide expectations. This evaluation can be teacher provided, self-assessed, or some combination of teacher and student determined. The goal is to increase the opportunities for the student to receive feedback on their school behavior. Parental commitments and involvement include (a) an agreement to support a preventive intervention approach, (b) daily and weekly feedback on the progress of their child's behavior, and (c) suggestions on how to encourage their child's participation. Faculty members and school administrators receive information on a regular basis on the overall impact and progress of the secondary-tier intervention program through faculty meetings, program evaluation reports, and the like.

Fifth, secondary-tier interventions emphasize the use of a range of positive reinforcement procedures. Students receive daily feedback on their behaviors through progress-monitoring tools (e.g., cards, posters), which usually include token economies, social praise, activity and tangible rewards, and access to positive peer time and activities. When students are successful in meeting the daily, weekly, or programmatic goals, they also receive acknowledgments from other school faculty and from their parents.

Last, data-based decisions are made on a regular basis to make adjustments for individual students. These adjustments might include, for example, adjusting the difficulty for daily/weekly performance success (e.g., 75% to 85% of daily points); frequency of daily assessments (e.g., every hour to morning and afternoon); or nature of the positive reinforcement (e.g., tangible to social) or nature of the feedback (e.g., teacher to peer interactions). An adjustment also might involve moving to a tertiary-tier intervention level because a student's behavior is unresponsive to adjustments in secondary-tier interventions.

## Tertiary-Tier SW-PBS Interventions

If a student's behavior is unresponsive to best efforts to provide primary- and secondary-tier interventions, a shift to more specialized and individualized interventions is considered (Gresham, 1995). Tertiary-tier interventions are less connected to the schoolwide primary-tier intervention than secondary-tier interventions, in part because they are more individualized to the specific conditions that are associated with the problem behavior.

Within a SW-PBS approach, tertiary-tier interventions are characterized as function based and team driven (Crone & Horner, 2003; O'Neill et al., 1997; Sugai, Lewis-Palmer, & Hagen-Burke, 1999–2000). *Function based* refers to a careful and specific consideration of the environmental conditions (function) that occasion (antecedent) and maintain (consequence) occurrences of problem behavior when developing individualized behavior intervention plans. In particular, priority is given to the selection and teaching/strengthening of replacement behaviors that are more effective, efficient, and relevant than the problem behaviors. *Effective* refers to occurrences of the replacement behavior being more likely to result in reinforcing consequences than occurrences of the problem behavior. *Efficiency* refers to the extent that replacement behaviors require less effort to emit than problem behaviors, and *relevance* is related to the extent to which antecedent events that previously occasioned problem behaviors are more likely to occasion replacement behaviors.

A function-based approach is dependent on having a team that has (a) high levels of behavioral competence and fluency; (b) an efficient, data-based, and outcome-based approach to problem solving and behavior intervention planning; (c) a collaborative and participatory approach to conducting business; and (d) participation by key individuals who know, relate to, and interact with the student. Depending on the size of the school and district/region, this team may require specialized supports from an external source (e.g., district team, school psychologist, behavior specialists) to have access to the level of specialized expertise needed to implement tertiary-tier interventions.

In situations with the most challenging behavior disorders, tertiary-tier interventions include school-based mental health supports, in which case community and family involvement might be increased. For example, systems of care and wraparound processes represent excellent examples of how resources and supports can be organized across disciplines and agencies (Eber, Sugai, smith, & Scott, 2005; Kutash et al., 2006). In these approaches, family and student strengths, goals, and resources are emphasized as a means of addressing student behavior challenges and limitations. As such, efficient collaboration and interaction are emphasized among staff and resources associated with, for example, schools, mental and community health, juvenile justice, child and family welfare, and so on.

### Summary

SW-PBS is characterized by a continuum of practices and supports that are organized logically and efficiently within three-tier interventions. The features and criteria between these tiers are not set in stone but instead serve as decision-making points for evaluating student responsiveness to implementation of prevailing interventions and supports. The real key is timely data review and decision making so that adjustments are made to improve student responsiveness and outcomes. The intervention features and structural organization of the SW-PBS continuum, however, requires an infrastructure that maximizes accurate and sustained implementation and regular review to maximize efficiency and impact. In the next section, processes and guidelines for implementation of the SW-PBS continuum are reviewed.

## IMPLEMENTATION PROCESSES AND GUIDELINES

Having evidence-based interventions (e.g., targeted social skills instruction, positive reinforcement) organized in a common and comprehensive schoolwide discipline system is necessary but not sufficient to ensure that these interventions will be adopted by a majority of the staff, implemented with fidelity, and sustained over time. The SW-PBS approach also requires a formal and systematic implementation process. In this section, implementation steps and guidelines are described at the systems and school levels.

### Systems-Level Implementation

To maximize the adoption and accurate and sustained implementation of SW-PBS at the school level, systems and supports also must be formally organized and managed at the state, regional, or district levels. Traditionally, systems-level initiatives are considered and adopted at the superintendent and school board levels, with the initiatives then communicated to the schools through building or school administrators. A series of district- or school-level events is conducted to increase the knowledge and implementation skills of school staff. Although this approach is effective for general policies and information dissemination, it is not effective or efficient in terms of increasing fluency of actual teaching practices or interventions, especially for comprehensive continua, like SW-PBS.

Systems-level implementation of SW-PBS emphasizes establishment of capacity for (a) local team-based leadership and coordination, (b) facilitation or coaching assistance, (c) local training fluency, (d) on-going and meaningful evaluation, (e) long-term funding, (f) formalized political support and visibility, and (g) exemplar demonstrations of school-level implementation (McIntosh, Horner, & Sugai, Chapter 14 in this handbook; Center on PBIS, 2004; Sugai, Horner, & McIntosh, in press). A brief description of each of these elements is provided in Fig. 13.2.

## School-Level Implementation

Implementation of SW-PBS at the school level is focused on creating a social culture in which a continuum of effective academic and social behavior practices and interventions can be implemented schoolwide, that is, for all students, staff, and community members across all classroom and nonclassroom settings. The goal is to ensure that adoption is widespread, implementation is accurate and sustainable, and adaptations are made based on local data and culture/context.

| Element | Description |
|---|---|
| Leadership Team | • Group of key stakeholders and implementers works together to collectively develop data-based action plans for systems level implementation of SWPBS interventions and practices.<br>• Action plan is based on data from careful self-assessments, determination of measurable outcomes, links to research-based interventions, and support for implementers.<br>• Activities of the group are managed by a coordinator who has dedicated FTE and resources. |
| Coaching Capacity | • State or district resources and structures are dedicated for monitoring and guiding SWPBS implementation by school teams.<br>• Coaching responsibilities include, for example, giving program and task reminders, providing positive acknowledgements, and assisting in data management and fidelity of implementation. |
| Training Capacity | • State or district personnel are trained to high fluency on the background, features, evidence-based practices, implementation, and evaluation of SWPBS implementation. |
| Evaluation Capacity | • Formative and summative information are collected to answers evaluation questions related to student outcomes, fidelity of implementation, program enhancements, and future action planning. |
| Funding | • SWPBS implementation is linked to sufficient, recurring, and stable funding for 2-3 years. |
| Political Support & Visibility | • Linkages, endorsements, and supports by policymakers and systems leaders are in place and formalized.<br>• Outcomes and processes from successful demonstrations, exemplars, and implementations are presented regularly to the larger community. |
| Demonstrations | • Self-sustaining, effective, relevant, and efficient implementation examples are in documented to showcase outcomes and processes. |

**Fig. 13.2.** Elements of systems implementation of schoolwide positive behavior support (SW-PBS).

In general, the process of SW-PBS implementation at the school level is comprised of five basic components (PBIS Blueprint, 2004): (a) schoolwide leadership team, (b) schoolwide agreements and resource management, (c) data-based action plan, (d) implementation supports, and (e) ongoing evaluation.

### *Schoolwide Leadership Team*

Systems-level implementation of SW-PBS is lead by a team that assumes responsibility and authority to organize, integrate, and coordinate implementation of effective behavioral interventions and practices. Team membership includes administrator; general and special education representatives; instructional support staff (e.g., school psychologists, nurse, counselor); noncertified staff (e.g., custodian, resource officer, bus driver); family member; student; and special instructors (e.g., art, music, physical education). The goal is to establish membership and routines so that communications and representation are efficient and maximized. Administrators' participation must be active and consistent because they have control and access to school implementation resources (e.g., budget, schedule, personnel).

### *Schoolwide Agreements and Resource Management*

After the team is formed, an important first step is to secure agreements about the purpose and activities of this team within the team and across the faculty and staff. The following statements are considered: (a) establish behavior improvement as one of the school's top three priories for 3–4 years to achieve sustained implementation; (b) organize behavioral practices and interventions within the three-tier continuum of support; (c) give priority to an instructional and preventive approach to behavior management and discipline; (d) emphasize the selection and adoption of evidence-based behavioral interventions; (e) integrate behavioral and academic programming; (f) make adaptations to consider cultural and contextual characteristics of community and school members; and (g) establish data system to guide planning and evaluation of implementation impact.

After agreements have been finalized, attention shifts to resource management and operation logistics. The team establishes a meeting schedule (at least monthly) and procedures for conducting meetings, communicating with school staff, and arranging professional development opportunities that are embedded in the typical routines and activities of the school. These decisions are shaped by the implementation efforts and activities that are guided by district, regional, or state leadership teams.

### *Data-Based Action Planning*

Although the basic features of practices and behavioral interventions are generally similar across schools and contexts, their specific appearance and implementation might vary according to the unique cultural, contextual, and experiential histories of each school, for example, enrollment, social economic status, racial/ethnic makeup, teacher characteristics, and so on.

To increase the likelihood that action planning considers these factors, leadership teams give priority to collecting information about their students and staff and community members. A variety of data are considered: (a) extant or historical data (e.g., records); (b) discipline data (e.g., attendance, ODRs, in- and out-of-school suspensions); (c) student and staff/community member perceptions (e.g., surveys, focus groups); (d) referrals for specialized assistance (e.g., special education, mental health, counseling); and (e) observation data (e.g., academic engagement, tardies, behavioral incidents).

These data are used to direct action planning to areas of concern and to contextualize intervention and implementation features. ODR data are collected by most schools to monitor the social climate of classrooms and nonclassroom settings. Since ODRs reflect an interaction involving student behavior, staff implementation, and office procedures, they can be a useful indicator of school climate and social climate. For example, five useful summaries are (a) how many ODRs occur per day in a given month, (b) how many of each problem behavior have occurred each month, (c) where problem behaviors occur most and least often, (d) when during the day rule violations are most and least likely to occur, and (e) what proportion of the students have zero or one, two to five, and six or more (http://www.swis.org/).

If data types are carefully defined to be comprehensive and mutually exclusive and systems are arranged to ensure accurate, efficient, and consistent data collection, teams can develop intervention action plans that are important, relevant, and doable for their school. For example, a school might identify three positive schoolwide expectations (Be Safe, Be Respectful, Be Responsible) that are reflective of their discipline data for the past 2 years and translate them into Spanish to represent the relatively high proportion of families from Central American backgrounds (e.g., "*Sea Seguro, Sea Resputuoso, Sea Responsable*"). Teaching of these expectations begins in the nonclassroom settings (e.g., lunchroom, hallway, and assemblies) because of high rates of problem behaviors in those contexts. Since peer-to-peer influences are high, peer-led teaching activities are guided by staff members.

Data collection procedures are likely to reveal students whose behaviors have not been responsive to primary-tier interventions, and action planning might include efforts to provide behavior supports that meet the behavioral needs of these students at the secondary- or tertiary-tier levels. For example, a leadership team might form a subgroup to build an action plan for reconfiguring specialized resources and supports available through special education, school psychology, and counseling. The action plan would include activities that build from efforts to establish primary-tier SW-PBS, specialized behavioral expertise inside the school, function-based support and intervention planning, and wraparound processes that increase family and community participation.

### *Implementation*

After leadership team and staff develop their action plan, a vote or assessment is made to determine if a majority of the staff (e.g., >80%) agree to the features of the plan and to make a good faith effort to support implementation. If a majority of staff do not agree, then leadership teams reevaluate their data and modify their plan to consider local concerns and increase acceptability.

After agreements are achieved, action plan implementation is initiated, and attention is focused on high fidelity of implementation, sustained implementation, and continuous improvement. These outcomes are maximized by ensuring that staff members are trained to fluency, resources are available to support implementation, activities are culturally and contextually relevant/appropriate, data are collected continuously to enable timely adaptations, and reinforcers and acknowledgments are proved for staff members who are implementing accurately and consistently.

### *Evaluation*

An important component of SW-PBS implementation at the school level is continuous evaluation. Leadership teams collect and review data to answer a range of evaluation questions, for example: (a) Are action plan activities being implemented? (b) Are SW-PBS interventions and practices being implemented accurately? (c) Are a majority of staff implementing accurately? (d) Are the majority of students responding to the intervention? (e) Is implementation by staff being sustained with accuracy? (f) Are student outcomes being maintained at appropriate levels? (g) Are students and staff and community members satisfied with implementation efforts and outcomes?

In general, evaluation efforts start with a relevant and measurable evaluation question, then follow with the specification of behavioral indicators that permit answering of the question, development of data collection instruments and procedures that are efficient and doable, production of data summaries that are easy to interpret, and means for leadership team and staff to review and make recommendations for modifications and enhancements to the action plan.

### Summary

The impact and outcomes of the best evidence-based practices are linked to the systems in place for supporting the full adoption, accurate implementation, sustained use, and continuous improvement. Important systems-level considerations include a representative leadership team, team and staff agreement for a behavior priority, data-based action plan, support for accurate and sustained implementation, and continuous evaluation for effectiveness, efficiency, and relevance.

## CONCLUSION

Clearly, behavior is an ongoing concern for schools, families, and communities, and indirect, reactive, and punishing approaches to controlling behavior are ineffective in supporting the educational mission of schools. The purpose of this chapter was to define and describe a schoolwide approach to improving the social culture or climate of schools that also supports efforts to maximize academic achievement. This approach, SW-PBS, focuses on the adoption of the best interventions and practices that match the data-based and contextualized needs and goals of a school. Equal, if not more, emphasis is directed toward the systems and organizational supports that are needed to ensure accurate and sustained implementation and continuous data-based enhancements. In sum, the continuous interaction of measurable outcomes, evidence-based practices, data-based decision making, and systems supports define SW-PBS.

## REFERENCES

Alberto, P. A., & Troutman, A. C. (2006). *Applied behavior analysis for teachers* (7th edition). Upper Saddle River, NJ: Pearson.

Anderson, A. R., Christenson, S. L., Sinclair, M. F., & Lehr, C. A. (2004). Check and Connect: The importance of relationships for promoting engagement with school. *Journal of School Psychology, 42*, 95–113.

Biglan, A. (1995). Translating what we know about the context of antisocial behavior in to a lower prevalence of such behavior. *Journal of Applied Behavior Analysis, 28*, 479–492.

Carr, E. G., Dunlap, G., Horner, R. H., Koegel, R. L., Turnbull, A. P., & Sailor, W. (2002). Positive behavior support: Evolution of an applied science. *Journal of Positive Behavior Interventions, 4*, 4–16.

Center on Positive Behavioral Interventions and Supports. (2004). *School-Wide Positive Behavior Support: Implementers' blueprint and self-assessment.* Washington, DC: Office of Special Education Programs, U.S. Department of Education.

Colvin, G., Kameenui, E. J., & Sugai, G. (1993). School-wide and classroom management: Reconceptualizing the integration and management of students with behavior problems in general education. *Education and Treatment of Children, 16*, 361–381.

Cooper, J. O., Heron, T. E., & Heward, W. L. (2007). *Applied behavior analysis* (2nd ed.). Upper Saddle River, NJ: Pearson.

Crone, D. A., & Horner, R. H. (2003). *Building positive behavior support systems in schools: Functional behavioral assessment.* Guildford Press, NY.

Crone, D., Horner, R.H., & Hawken, L. (2004). *Responding to problem behavior in schools: The behavior education plan.* New York: Guilford.

Eber, L., Sugai, G., Smith, C., & Scott, T. (2002). Blending process and practice to maximize outcomes: Wraparound and positive behavioral interventions and supports in the schools. *Journal of Emotional and Behavioral Disorders, 10*, 171–181.

Fairbanks, S., Sugai, G., Guardino, D., & Lathrop, M. (2007). Response to intervention: Examining classroom behavior support in second grade. *Exceptional Children, 73*, 288–310.

Filter, K. J. (2007). Positive behavior support: Considerations for the future of a model. *Behavior Analyst, 30*(1). 87–90.

Gottfredson, D. C., Gottfredson, G. D., & Hybl, L. G. (1993). Managing adolescent behavior: A multiyear, multischool study. *American Educational Research Journal, 30*, 179–215.

Gottfredson, G. D., & Gottfredson, D. C. (1996). *A national study of delinquency prevention in schools: Rationale for a study to describe the extensiveness and implementation of programs to prevent adolescent problem behavior in schools.* Ellicott City, MD: Gottfredson Associates, Inc.

Greenwood, C. R., Delquadri, J., & Bulgren, J. (1993). Current challenges to behavioral technology in the reform of schooling: Large-scale, high-quality implementation and sustained use of effective educational practices. *Education and Treatment of Children, 16*(4), 401–404.

Gresham, F. M., Sugai, G., & Horner, R. H. (2001). Social competence of students with high-incidence disabilities: Conceptual and methodological issues in interpreting outcomes of social skills training. *Exceptional Children, 67,* 311.

Gresham, R. M. (2005). Response to intervention: An alternative means of identifying students as emotionally disturbed. *Education and Treatment of Children, 28,* 328–344.

Horner, R. H. (1994). Functional assessment: Contributions and future directions. *Journal of Applied Behavior Analysis, 27,* 401–404.

Horner, R. H., Sugai, G., & Todd, A. W. (2001). "Data" need not be a four-letter word: Using data to improve schoolwide discipline. *Beyond Behavior, 11*(1), 20–26.

Horner, R. H., Sugai, G., Todd, A. W., & Lewis-Palmer, T. (2005). School-wide positive behavior support: An alternative approach to discipline in schools. In L. Bambara & L. Kern (Eds.), *Individualized supports for students with problem behaviors: Designing positive behavior plans* (pp. 359–390). New York: Guilford Press.

Irvin, L. K., Horner, R. H., Ingram, K., Todd, A. W., Sugai, G., Sampson, N. K., & Boland, J. B. (2006). Using office discipline referral data for decision making about student behavior in elementary and middle schools: An empirical evaluation of validity. *Journal of Positive Behavior Interventions, 8,* 10–23.

Kutash, K., Duchnowski, A., & Lynn, N. (2006). *School-based Mental Health: An Empirical Guild for Decision-makers.* The Research and Training Center for Children's Mental Health, Florida Mental Health Institute, University of South Florida

Lehr, C. A., Sinclair, M. F., & Christenson, S. L. (2004). Addressing student engagement and truancy prevention during the elementary years: A replication study of the Check and Connect model. *Journal of Education for Students Placed At Risk, 9,* 279–301.

Lewis-Palmer, T., Sugai, G., & Larson, S. (1999). Using data to guide decisions about program implementation and effectiveness. *Effective School Practices, 17*(4), 47–53.

Lewis, T. J., & Sugai, G. (1999). Effective behavior support: A systems approach to proactive school-wide management. *Focus on Exceptional Children, 31*(6), 1–24.

Mayer, G. (1995). Preventing antisocial behavior in the schools. *Journal of Applied Behavior Analysis, 28,* 467–478.

Mayer, R. G. (1998). Constructive discipline for school personnel. *Education and Treatment of Children, 22,* 36–54.

National Center on Education and the Economy. (2007). *Tough choices or tough times.* Hoboken, NJ: Jossey–Bass.

Nelson, J. R. (1996). Designing schools to meet the needs of students who exhibit disruptive behavior. *Journal of Emotional and Behavioral Disorders, 4,* 147–161.

Nelson, J. R., Johnson, A., & Marchand-Martella, N. (1996). Effects of direct instruction, cooperative learning, and independent learning practices on the classroom behavior of students with behavioral disorders: A comparative analysis. *Journal of Emotional and Behavioral Disorders, 4,* 53–62.

O'Neill, R. E., Horner, R. H., Albin, R. W., Sprague, J. R., Storey, K., & Newton, J. S. (1997). *Functional assessment and program development for problem behavior: A practical handbook*(2nd ed.). Pacific Grove, CA: Brooks/Cole.

Rose, L. C., & Gallup, A. M. (2007, September). 39th annual Phi Delta Kappa/Gallup poll of the public's attitude toward the public schools. *Kappan,* 33–48.

Safran, S. P., & Oswald, K. (2003). Positive behavior supports: Can schools reshape disciplinary practices? *Exceptional Children, 69,* 361–373.

Simonsen, B., & Sugai, G. (2007). School-wide positive behavior support: A systems level application of behavioral principles. In S. W. Evans, Mark D. Weist, & Z. N. Serpell (Eds.), *Advances in school-based mental health interventions: Best practices and program models* (pp. 8-2 – 8-17). Kingston, NJ: Civic Research Institute.

Skiba, R. J., & Peterson, R. L. (1999). The dark side of zero tolerance: Can punishment lead to safe schools? *Phi Delta Kappan, 80,* 372–382.

Skiba, R. J., & Peterson, R. L. (2000). School discipline at a crossroads: From zero tolerance to early response. *Exceptional Children, 66,* 335–347.

Sprick, R., Sprick, M., & Garrison, M. (1992). *Foundations: Developing positive schoolwide discipline polices.* Longmont, CO: Sopris West.

Sugai, G., Lewis-Palmer, T., & Hagan-Burke, S. (1999–2000). Overview of the functional behavioral assessment process. *Exceptionality, 8,* 149–160.

Sugai, G., Horner, R. H., Dunlap, G. Hieneman, M., Lewis, T. J., Nelson, C. M., Scott, T., Liaupsin, C., Sailor, W., Turnbull, A. P., Turnbull, H. R., III, Wickham, D. Reuf, M., & Wilcox, B. (2000). Applying positive behavioral support and functional behavioral assessment in schools. *Journal of Positive Behavioral Interventions, 2, 131–143.*

Sugai, G., & Horner, R.H. (2002). The evolution of discipline practices: School-wide positive behavior supports. *Child and Family Behavior Therapy, 24,* 23–50.

Sugai, G., Horner, R. H., & McIntosh, K. (2008). Best practices in developing a broad-scale system of support for school-wide positive behavior support. In A. Thomas & J. P. Grimes (Eds.), *Best practices in school psychology V* (Vol. 3, pp. 765–780). Bethesda, MD: National Association of School Psychologists.

Walker, H. M., Horner, R. H., Sugai, G., Bullis, M., Sprague, J. R., Bricker, D., et al. (1996). Integrated approaches to preventing antisocial behavior patterns among school-age children and youth. *Journal of Emotional and Behavioral Disorders, 4,* 194–209.

Walker, H. M., Ramsey, E., & Gresham, F. M. (2005). *Antisocial behavior in school: Evidence-based practices* (2nd ed.). Belmont, CA: Wadsworth/Thomson Learning.

Wright, J. A., & Dusek, J. B. (1998). Compiling school base rates for disruptive behaviors from student disciplinary referral data. *School Psychology Review, 27,* 138–147.

# 14

# Sustainability of Systems-Level Evidence-Based Practices in Schools: Current Knowledge and Future Directions

**KENT MCINTOSH, ROBERT H. HORNER, and GEORGE SUGAI**

## INTRODUCTION

Recent research advances have focused on the use of evidence-based practices to improve academic and behavior support in schools (Hoagwood, 2004; Walker, 2004). Simultaneously, education policy has advocated for strategies that will allow implementation of these practices on a meaningful scale (Adelman & Taylor, 2003; Elias, Zins, Graczyk, & Weissburg, 2003; Mihalic & Irwin, 2003). These complementary efforts are shaping an agenda for transforming research to practice by training typical school personnel to provide efficient and effective interventions. The effectiveness of these practices is measured in part not only by immediate effects but also by sustained effects (Adelman & Taylor, 2003), and some have argued that the widespread use of practices is only significant to the extent that these practices are sustained (Coburn, 2003; McLaughlin & Mitra, 2001). Therefore, if comprehensive school reform is to occur, researchers must make efforts to ensure that implemented practices are both effective and sustainable.

---

**KENT MCINTOSH** • University of British Columbia
**ROBERT H. HORNER** • University of Oregon
**GEORGE SUGAI** • University of Connecticut

Sustainability may be defined as durable, long-term implementation of a practice at a level of fidelity that continues to produce valued outcomes (Han & Weiss, 2005). In practical, school-level terms, sustainability is the creation of a social norm, the point at which a practice ceases to be a project or initiative and becomes institutionalized. Descriptions of certain practices by personnel as "what we've always done" or "the way we do business" are an indication that these practices are being sustained (Rogers, 2003), at least at the present moment. Such comments may also indicate that the process becomes easier to continue than it was to initiate.

As a behavioral principle, sustainability is different from maintenance. For the sake of clarity, we draw a distinction between maintenance of effects and sustainability of practices designed to produce those effects. At the student level, maintenance describes the continued benefit in individual student outcomes from a practice that was implemented and is no longer is in place. After a successful intervention is discontinued, students who initially received and benefited from the intervention may not necessarily continue to benefit (August, Lee, Bloomquist, Realmuto, & Hektner, 2004; Hinshaw, Klein, & Abikoff, 2002); further, incoming students who did not receive the intervention are highly unlikely to benefit. At the systems level (e.g., school, district, or state), maintenance describes the continued use of a practice by school personnel once initially trained. What distinguishes sustainability from maintenance are the continual reexamination and *changes* in regular adult behavior that continue a practice. The regular turnover of the student population in schools ensures a dynamic, changing environment that makes a static practice obsolete. And, mirroring the continual replenishment of students, the regular, predictable turnover of personnel in schools provides a challenge to maintenance that may be addressed through sustainable practices, in which new hires are introduced to the practice as a regular, integral part of the workplace. Clearly, the best way for school personnel to improve student outcomes is to implement and sustain effective practices.

Sustainability is often perceived by researchers and implementers as a desirable, yet elusive phenomenon in which continued use is controlled by unknown variables (Vaughn, Klingner, & Hughes, 2000). This mystery occasions many questions. How can a research community predict if an effective, evidence-based practice will be implemented for 5, 10, or even 25 years? Which variables make practices more likely to sustain? Are there critical features of the practices themselves, or the implementation contexts, that increase the probability of sustained use? These questions have been raised regularly in the literature, but what little current research is available is primarily anecdotal (Gersten, Chard, & Baker, 2000). Because of its importance, a consistent, focused research agenda is needed to understand the principle of sustainability and increased durability of evidence-based practices. We provide here a conceptual model of sustainability, an example of how this model applies to one educational innovative (schoolwide positive behavior support, SW-PBS), and the initial elements of a research agenda addressing sustainability in education.

## Understanding the Importance of Sustainability

In general terms, the sustained use of evidence-based practices clearly may be viewed as an important goal for researchers and one that benefits key stakeholders—any practice that results in short-term benefits could potentially result in benefits from continued use. Logically, continuing with an effective intervention to address an area of concern is a better use of resources than changing interventions every few years, as is evident by the volumes of program manuals gathering dust in school supply closets across the world. Cycles of repeated implementation without significant durable change have distinct costs, not only in terms of money, effort, direct intervention time, and school in-service programming, but also in terms of increased resistance to new implementation efforts, regardless of need or demonstrated efficacy. This may perpetuate a cynical view that any new programs will soon be replaced with a new program within the year. All in all, the expenses of continual reimplementation may far exceed the costs associated with sustainability efforts. If so, implementing a practice without taking specific actions to sustain it may be irresponsible or even unethical (Coburn, 2003; McLaughlin & Mitra, 2001).

Yet, universally adopting a goal of sustaining every intervention implemented in schools may overlook a critical variable in sustainability. Sustainability is difficult to achieve in large part because the importance of sustaining a practice may be directly associated with the importance of the outcome the practice delivers. If the outcome is important, attention to sustained use of effective practices becomes relevant. If the outcome is no longer viewed as important or relevant (e.g., a shift in priorities takes place), the practice is likely to be reevaluated and abandoned. One message is that first identifying an important, valued outcome and then identifying a practice that can produce the outcome may lead to more sustainability than identifying a practice and then determining how it can be sustained. The outcome must be valued by the school-level implementers, not just researchers assisting with adoption and initial implementation (Bernfield, Blase, & Fixsen, 1990; Greenberg, Weissburg, & O'Brien, 2003). Without outcomes that are valued by school-level personnel, sustainability is unlikely and perhaps undesirable.

## Barriers to Sustainability

Implementation of any systems-level practice can be difficult to achieve in schools, but sustainability is a challenge on a higher level of magnitude. Sustainability is the exception rather than the rule, and we should take immediate notice when it occurs by carefully examining any conditions that allow it to occur (Vaughn et al., 2000). We would also do well to take notice when it does not occur and analyze the variables at work in those circumstances. The literature points to a number of commonly identified threats and barriers to sustained implementation of a practice that has already been implemented to criterion. From a behavior analytic view of this research, they fall into three categories that align with the traditional

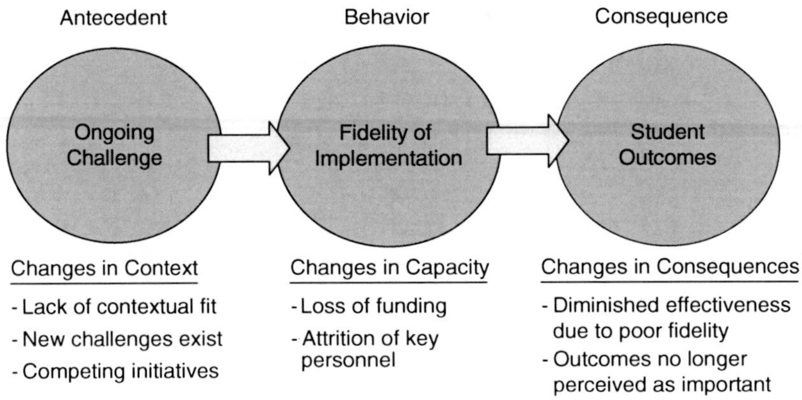


**Fig. 14.1.** Competing variables that prevent sustainability.

three-term contingency of behavior (see Fig. 14.1): change in context, change in capacity, and change in contingencies.

### *Change in Context*

Initial implementers may adapt a practice to the needs of the school based on contextual fit, an assessment of the match among the identified need (outcome), the practice, and the beliefs, skills, resources, and values of school personnel (Albin, Lucyshyn, Horner, & Flannery, 1996; Elias et al., 2003; Fixsen, Naoom, Blase, Friedman, & Wallace, 2005; Wolf, 1978). The results of this assessment are used to improve the alignment between the practice and the presenting problem and desired outcomes. If the school context should change, as often occurs, the new and previous antecedent variables may no longer occasion use of the practice or may occasion use of another practice entirely, resulting in discontinuation of the previous practice (Han & Weiss, 2005; McLaughlin & Mitra, 2001). In other words, the nature of the problems change, rendering the practice irrelevant and necessitating a different solution.

Another context change is the introduction of competing initiatives or priorities that occasion adoption of different and frequently competing practices. Schools today face a constant barrage of new initiatives at the district, state, and national levels. When these new initiatives are associated with powerful contingencies (e.g., legislative mandates, funding reductions, and publication of failure in local newspapers), school administrators may dilute existing efforts by, for example, adding new practices, redirecting limited resources, and reducing time investments. Even when competing initiatives are striving toward similar outcomes, differences in programmatic and implementation features inhibit integration and collaboration. The result can be constant addition of new initiatives, none of which are implemented with adequate fidelity or produce effects (Furney, Hasazi, Clark-Keefe, & Hartnett, 2003; Sindelar, Shearer, Yendol-Hoppey, & Liebert, 2006).

## Change in Capacity

*Change in capacity* refers to adjustments made to the personnel, systems, or resources supporting the implementation of the intervention. To maximize effects or outcomes, an intervention must be implemented with fidelity or accuracy. Any reduction in fidelity risks loss of effects. Clearly, funding plays a role in many failures to sustain. For example, states and districts frequently use external funding to "seed" or pilot a practice or initiative, which often has a lifespan of 1 to 3 years. When this funding stream comes to an end, school personnel must continue with their additional responsibilities but without the funding that may have provided additional personnel or release time (Adelman & Taylor, 2003; Coburn, 2003; Han & Weiss, 2005). If the state or district has not used the external funding strategically to build capacity that can be sustained under existing budget and resource conditions, the fidelity of practice or initiative implementation is likely to decrease because of competition for a limited and static general fund, creating a strain in existing personnel and material resources (Waterhouse & Chapman, 2006). If the funding allocated to implement a new initiative is not accompanied by the resources needed for continued operation, the new practice may cease to be implemented, even if initial implementation produced desired effects (Latham, 1988).

A reduction in local implementation capacity can affect fidelity of implementation in two phases. First, if implementation leadership and coordination are not established at the local level, the withdrawal of researchers or outside implementers creates a deficit in which sites no longer have the skills to continue the practice. Second, fidelity of implementation is decreased when key personnel (particularly administrators), who have experience with the practice through initial implementation and training, move to other positions (Mihalic & Irwin, 2003; Sindelar et al., 2006). The impact is especially damaging when these individuals have championed the program and held pivotal roles in essential implementation tasks and responsibilities (Elliott, Kratochwill, & Roach, 2003; Hanley, 2003). In this case, a strength during initial implementation becomes a liability for sustainability.

## Change in Contingencies

In a well-run system, outcomes drive the process, and a reduction in desired outcomes can be disastrous. If using the practice no longer leads to desired outcomes, the practice is no longer useful to personnel. Outcomes can be affected negatively by a number of mechanisms, although the most obvious is poor fidelity of implementation. As noted, when fidelity suffers (as a result of change in capacity or context), outcomes are likely to suffer as well, in turn reducing interest in implementation.

Another mechanism for change in consequences occurs when the outcomes that the practice produces are no longer valued by school personnel or stakeholders, even if still effective (Wolf, 1978). This situation could occur if the school context changes or if the outcome is experienced differently. A pertinent metaphor is the pharmacological wellness myth—individuals experience negative symptoms, take medications that eliminate those symptoms, and then stop their course of medication, assuming that it is no longer needed. For example, school personnel who implement an intervention to reduce bullying behavior may stop implementing the intervention because bullying events are reduced, not knowing that ending the intervention could lead to an upswing in future bullying behavior.

It is likely that these competing variables have an additive risk effect in that school personnel may sustain a practice when one or a few of these variables are present, but sustainability becomes far more difficult as the number of risks increase (Sindelar et al., 2006). Although this may be the case, these barriers need not be viewed as death knells for a particular practice. It is a distinct possibility that practices do not sustain because (a) sustainability is not a stated goal; (b) when stated, sustainability efforts are not enacted directly and formally; or (c) sustainability efforts themselves are not implemented with fidelity over time. For instance, just as the "train-and-hope" strategy is ineffective for implementing a program, an "intervene-and-hope" strategy is unlikely to promote sustainability (Newton, 2008). Rather, formal sustainability efforts should be part of the plan at initial implementation (Adelman & Taylor, 2003).

## A PROPOSED MODEL OF SUSTAINABILITY

To better understand the factors that contribute to or compete with sustainability, we reviewed the literature base. The results of this review indicated that most efforts to identify factors that affect sustainability have been theoretical or descriptive analyses. In this section, we propose a model of sustainable implementation for any school-based systems-level practices, including academic, social-emotional, or behavioral programs, based on this literature and our experiences implementing SW-PBS (Horner, Sugai, Todd, & Lewis-Palmer, 2005). Much of this model is based on the work of many pioneers in the field, whom we cite regularly in the following sections and to whom we are indebted. To present this model, we detail (a) the principles under which the model operates, (b) the features and process of the model itself, and (c) descriptions of the sustained implementation variables.

### Principles

The model is based on the science and principles of behavior that have been documented with individuals and applied to groups of individuals (e.g., school-level personnel) over the past 60 years. The principles emphasize observable behavior, reinforcement, maintenance, competing schedules of reinforcement, and generalization. The behaviors of interest in the model include tasks involved in implementing the program as well as the skills needed to implement them correctly. Reinforcement is related to the impact of valued outcomes achieved by implementing the practice. Maintenance describes conditions in which personnel continue to implement the practice because they have the needed skills and regular opportunities to use them and perceive that this use leads to beneficial outcomes. The principle of competing schedules of reinforcement explains how personnel make decisions about continuing the practice, abandoning it, or adopting a new practice. Generalization describes how personnel might adapt the practice or use it in different contexts.

## Features and Process

The process of the model is comprised of three mechanisms by which the variables, situated within the context of the particular school, affect sustainability (see Fig. 14.2). First, school personnel identify valued outcomes as targets for the change process. Second, practices that may produce those outcomes are identified and adopted. Third, school personnel implement the critical features of the practices with fidelity. Fidelity (i.e., accurate and consistent change in adult behavior) is a key component of the model because it is the mechanism by which valued outcomes (change in student performance) are achieved (see a review by Mihalic & Irwin, 2003). If fidelity is high, an effective practice is more likely to produce the desired outcomes. If fidelity is low, outcomes are less likely to be reached. If the valued outcomes are produced, momentum to maintain implementation increases, but if outcomes do not improve, maintenance is threatened. As school personnel gain experience through continued implementation, the

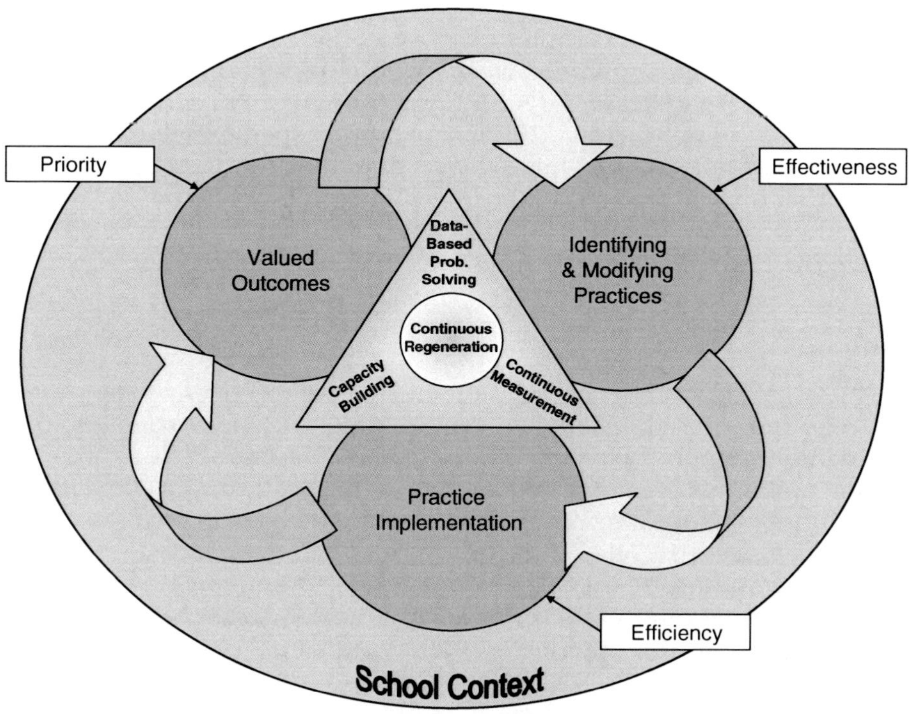


**Fig. 14.2.** A proposed model of sustainable implementation of school-based practices.

steps to achieve fidelity may become more efficient, and the practice may be modified to improve its effectiveness within the context. A continuous cycle, or feedback loop, develops in which each iteration may change the relation among the variables. This iterative process is known as *continuous regeneration*, a central element of the model.

## Sustained Implementation Variables

### *Effectiveness*

The effectiveness of a practice is the extent to which implementation results in desired outcomes; this is directly related to its fidelity of implementation and potential impact. Before change in outcomes should be expected, practices should be implemented initially to a criterion degree of fidelity and stability (August et al., 2004). Practices that are excessively difficult to implement or do not improve outcomes without perfect fidelity are unlikely candidates for sustained implementation. As noted, a practice is deemed effective to the extent that outcomes are experienced by large numbers of students and are valued and perceptible by school personnel (Adelman & Taylor, 2003; Datnow & Castellano, 2000; Kealey, Peterson, Gaul, & Dinh, 2000; Merrell & Buchanan, 2006). Accordingly, selection of ineffective, non-evidence-based practices is a critical error that would make meeting valued outcomes, and hence sustaining those practices, highly unlikely.

The principle of *reinforcement* is central to considerations of effectiveness. That is, school personnel must experience the effects of their practice implementation through improved outcomes, including improved student performance, improved work climate, reduction in work effort, or reduction of aversive teaching situations (Klingner, Arguelles, Hughes, & Vaughn, 2001; Vaughn et al., 2000). In addition, personnel may only view the practice as effective if they believe that their implementation of the practice was directly related to improved outcomes. If personnel attribute improved outcomes to other events or factors, they may be less likely to perceive the practice as worthwhile (Han & Weiss, 2005).

### *Efficiency*

Efficiency describes the relationship between effectiveness and the effort required to produce effects, that is, weighing the costs of continued implementation with the benefits of outcomes (Vaughn et al., 2000). If the potential outcomes are perceived as more valuable than the effort required to sustain the practice, use of the practice is more likely to continue (Rogers, 2003). Efficiency also relates to the overall costs associated with continued implementation. If the resources needed to sustain the practice are so large that they interfere with other practices or exceed the capacity of the school system, the practice cannot be efficient, even if the outcomes are immensely valuable. For example, providing all students with daily one-on-one instruction could significantly increase academic skills, but the cost of continuing it would be prohibitive. As such, resource-heavy programs implemented with the support of substantial grant money have little chance of sustained implementation once that support is removed (Elias et al., 2003).

In terms of sustainability, the critical features of efficient practices include efficiency in relation to other practices and differences in effort between initial and sustained implementation. First, practices are more likely to be sustained if they are the most cost-effective or the only viable method of obtaining desired outcomes. If more efficient alternative practices exist for obtaining the same outcome, school personnel are more likely to select those practices than to continue with a more expensive option (Rogers, 2003). Second, an important planning objective during initial implementation is to decrease the effort required to sustain a practice after initial implementation. In essence, the process should become more efficient over time in terms of personnel (i.e., the experience of using the practice should make continued use easier) and money (e.g., fewer release days for staff training and visits by external consultants).

*Maintenance* is the principle related to efficiency of practice implementation. Use of the practice continues because the practice is already in place, and school personnel are fluent in its use (i.e., its procedures become familiar to personnel with use), regular opportunities exist to use it, and valued outcomes are being achieved (Sindelar et al., 2006). If these conditions exist and it is viewed as a low-cost alternative to other approaches, the practice is more likely to be sustained.

### *Priority*

Priority describes the relative visibility and importance of a practice in comparison to other practices. Priority is essential to retain the support initially offered by stakeholders, including administrators, school personnel, and families. Sustained implementation may take place if a practice has visibility as an effective, efficient, and essential part of the school system (Gager & Elias, 1997). This visibility can be affected by connecting the practice to the core values of individual school personnel who are implementing the practice (Han & Weiss, 2005) or with the vision and mission of larger entities, such as school boards or state departments of education (Benz, Lindstrom, Unruh, & Waintrup, 2004; Center for Mental Health in Schools, 2001; Coburn, 2003; Greenwood, Tapia, Abbott, & Walton, 2003). Such visibility is essential for securing access to ongoing resources, particularly when projects move from grants to regular funding (Coburn, 2003; Sadler, 2004).

Priority is not a vague, ethereal concept but rather the result of careful planning. Implementers can take a number of specific actions to increase the priority of a practice, including advocacy, policy, and blending with new initiatives. An important advocacy activity is presenting to important groups who control funding for the practice or otherwise exert influence on its priority and value. Effective presentations include sharing successful outcomes, such as data showing large-scale benefits or case studies illustrating individual benefits, and describing the continued need for the practice, possibly explaining the costs associated with abandoning the practice (Adelman & Taylor, 2003). Policy actions include incorporating the practice into existing written policy (Vaughn et al., 2000). Such policies may include mission, vision, or goal statements; long-term school or district improvement plans; or statements of practices used or supported by the school system as core components.

Blending or "braiding" the practice into new initiatives may be an especially potent method of ensuring high priority for a practice (Adelman & Taylor, 2003; McLaughlin & Mitra, 2001). These terms describe a process in which the practice is regularly incorporated into new initiatives in the school system. If implementers can explain how the practice can be a vital part of new projects, they are more likely to be able to keep the practice on the list of important, worthwhile programs (Waterhouse & Chapman, 2006). If the practice cannot be reshaped as important to new projects, it may be abandoned in favor of practices that are aligned with new critical objectives (Sindelar et al., 2006). Local administrators can play a key role in this area by acting as a buffer between new initiatives and their personnel. Principals can continue to support the existing practice and reframe new initiatives as new phases of the current practice (Cherniss, 2006; Huberman, 1983). These minor changes in language allow school personnel to continue implementing the practice without receiving conflicting information about district or state priorities that might signal a lack of priority (Waterhouse & Chapman, 2006). In the current climate of school reform, new initiatives are inevitable, and the extent to which practices can be regarded as components of future initiatives may ensure their continued priority and hence their survival.

The principle involved in the priority variable is *competing schedules of reinforcement*. This principle influences both groups with funding capabilities and individual school personnel. Just as students are faced with choices in responding to antecedent events (i.e., engaging in problem behaviors or desired behaviors), funding agencies and school personnel are faced with similar choices, such as continuing to implement a practice or discarding it and adopting a new practice. Given the limited resources of most school systems, administrators and personnel must regularly choose among a sea of competing initiatives, all with different purposes, outcomes, and competing contingencies (schedules of reinforcement). When implementation tasks are viewed as a high priority by staff and contingencies are in place for completion, these behaviors may be seen as more viable than other tasks. The actions described may result in increased priority for certain practices, thereby increasing the probability that they are selected over tasks for implementing other practices.

### *Continuous Regeneration*

Continuous regeneration is the process of (a) iterative monitoring of both fidelity and outcomes, (b) adaptation and readaptation of a practice over time while keeping its critical features intact, and (c) ongoing investment in implementation and reimplementation (Han & Weiss, 2005; McLaughlin & Mitra, 2001). Adaptation of a practice is crucial because it allows the practice to be spread to new areas, modified to meet changing features of the context, and adjusted to become more efficient or effective. A practice that can evolve in this way is eminently valuable and is ultimately more likely to remain relevant to the school, particularly after significant changes in the implementation context over time (Elias et al., 2003; Rogers, 2003).

Continuous regeneration may take place in two ways. First, the practice may be regenerated through application to new areas (Coburn, 2003). A practice may be expanded to new settings (e.g., from classrooms to common areas), new stakeholders (e.g., from students to parents), or new levels of support (e.g., from all students to individual student support). Such an expansion could broaden the practice, making it more effective, visible, and valuable, and preserve the practice's novelty to staff, thereby avoiding stagnation.

Another form of continuous regeneration is responsiveness to change, which is needed for problem solving when environments and needs change or greater implementation effectiveness and efficiency are indicated. If the practice can be regenerated in response to changes in context, its worth to a school can be maximized (Han & Weiss, 2005; McLaughlin & Mitra, 2001; Newton, 2008). Yet, this process is more difficult in practice than in theory. For example, although they provide potential for high fidelity of implementation, the use of manualized treatment protocols may be too strictly interpreted by school personnel and run the risk of failing when the context and needs change (Elias et al., 2003; Carter & Horner, 2007). Practices that do not evolve to meet these demands may cease to be effective or be viewed as incompatible with new initiatives (McLaughlin & Mitra, 2001). As such, school personnel may need explicit instruction in how to adapt the practice to address contextual challenges while still maintaining the integrity of the practice (Coburn, 2003; Han & Weiss, 2005).

One method of promoting continuous regeneration is to connect a specific implementer to a larger community of practice implementers. Such a community could be accessed through Web-based listserves or conferences, particularly if the community is focused on the specific practice being implemented. Such connections allow school personnel to learn and share new approaches, receive encouragement and inspiration from each other, and use their collective strengths to respond to common challenges (Coburn, 2003; McLaughlin & Mitra, 2001; Sadler, 2004; Waterhouse & Chapman, 2006). Too often, schools and school districts enact reform and adopt practices in isolation from each other, which is less advantageous than connecting with other schools implementing similar programs (Togneri & Anderson, 2003).

Continuous regeneration is most related to the principle of *generalization*. Although an ambitious goal, generalization is important to sustainability in many ways. A practice becomes more valuable when used in a variety of contexts rather than limited to the original area of implementation (known as *stimulus generalization*). The result is increased effectiveness and efficiency, as well as continued behavioral momentum. In addition, a practice that is flexible can be adapted to changing situations to produce similar outcomes (known as *response generalization*). To allow for generalization to take place, continuous regeneration has three core components: capacity building, continuous measurement, and data-based problem solving.

### *Capacity Building*

Capacity building describes the ongoing and systematic process of cultivating local expertise, which is the extent to which school or district-level personnel have the skills needed to continue the practice when trainers and external startup supports fade and are discontinued. In contrast, external expertise is provided by those outside of the school system, such as practice developers, implementers, or researchers at the university or regional level. After initial implementation, these external individuals or groups often transition out of active, regular consultation with the school system, leaving the active implementation of the practice to internal personnel. If these internal personnel do not have the knowledge and fluency to implement and use the practice, fidelity of implementation may drop to levels that render the practice ineffective, preventing access to reinforcement through achieving valued outcomes (Adelman & Taylor, 2003; Coburn, 2003; Han & Weiss, 2005; Stokes, Sato, McLaughlin, & Talbert, 1997). As such, the cultivation of local expertise, and thus capacity, is a critical concern for sustainability.

Local expertise is unlikely to develop as a result of initial implementation alone (Blase & Fixsen, 2004; Sarason, 2004). Rather, capacity building should be considered as one of the primary initial goals in an implementation plan (Lucyshyn et al., 2007). The central task in such a plan includes creating a structured system for developing and maintaining such expertise (Greenwood et al., 2003). Such a system can provide existing personnel with needed skills in initial implementation and show incoming personnel that the practice is an integral part of the school staff culture (McLaughlin & Mitra, 2001). Training may occur through multiday trainings or summer institutes or a schedule of half- and full-day training throughout the school year. These trainings focus on the day-to-day skills typical personnel need to use the practice effectively. Eventually, individual schools may discontinue implementation trainings and instead send new staff to a district or regional practice orientation training. A strategic, long-term vision of sustainability assumes that schools will lose personnel every year, and this system of training is targeted to ensure that each school maintains a basic level of skill in using the practice (Elias et al., 2003; Hatch, 2000).

This basic level of knowledge about a practice is necessary but not sufficient to sustain its complex, systems-level use. Core personnel with key skills are also needed to ensure sustainability at the district, regional, and state levels (Adelman & Taylor, 1997). These personnel should have not only a familiarity with the daily activities associated with the practice but also a deep understanding of its theory and critical features (Han & Weiss, 2005; McLaughlin & Mitra, 2001). Such an understanding allows school personnel to customize some aspects while maintaining the integrity of the practice (Elias et al., 2003). Without this knowledge, personnel may preserve irrelevant features and discard the effective components, leading to what McLaughlin and Mitra described as "lethal mutations" (2001). For example, school personnel may continue to provide schoolwide reinforcement tickets to students but cease to acknowledge the expectations that students followed to earn them. Experienced core personnel can take on a number of important roles in sustaining the practice, including coordinating the capacity-building and training system described, presenting to stakeholders and funding agencies, measuring fidelity of implementation, evaluating outcomes, and providing ongoing consultation and performance feedback (Ikeda et al., 2002; Noell et al., 2005).

Although individuals certainly play vital parts in motivating staff to adopt and fully implement practices (Rogers, 2003), the practice is likely to suffer when these powerful advocates leave without a plan for replacement (Elliott et al., 2003; Han & Weiss, 2005). As such, there is a distinct advantage to creating ongoing positions rather than relying on specific individuals to fill these roles. In fact, establishing ongoing district-level positions can play a critical role in sustaining practices when key school-level personnel, such as building administrators, turn over. Hence, we recommend that school systems create ongoing positions with duties pertaining to the practice written into the job descriptions (e.g., Comer, Ben-Avie, Haynes, & Joyner, 1999).

### *Continuous Measurement*

Ongoing measurement and evaluation of the practice is not simply best practice, but rather a critical element of sustainability. Indeed, the sole act of measurement itself may make a difference, even without data-based decision making (Mihalic & Irwin, 2003). Scheduling regular cycles of measurement as an integral part of the practice signals two important messages: The practice and its outcomes are valued, and personnel will hold themselves accountable for its implementation. Measurement on a regular, scheduled cycle should be built into the practice itself (Elliott et al., 2003). If measurement does not play a role in initial implementation, adding it as a later component or measuring only sporadically may not improve prospects for sustained implementation.

A valuable plan for continuous measurement consists of two sets of variables: valued outcomes and fidelity of implementation (Elias et al., 2003). Outcomes to be measured include the direct effects of the practice as well as indirect effects as they apply to other initiatives. Practices that have such complementary, or crossover, effects may have even greater value to schools than those that affect only one area (Kellam, Mayer, Rebok, & Hawkins, 1998). For example, a schoolwide behavior intervention might result in improved outcomes in student behavior and school safety (direct effects) as well as improved academic performance (indirect effects). Documenting both direct and indirect effects would be likely to increase the practice's value, particularly in terms of its value to academic achievement initiatives. In addition, fidelity of implementation, as a key mechanism in the model, plays a vital role in sustainability (NIMH Intervention Workgroup, 2001). Any loss in fidelity could lead to a loss in effectiveness, setting into motion a downward spiral that could end in abandonment of the practice (Hanley, 2003). With regular measurement, such a reduction in fidelity could be detected and remediated. As such, measuring fidelity of implementation is as important as measuring outcomes.

### *Data-Based Problem Solving*

Data-based problem solving is the process of systematically and regularly assessing the measurement data described and converting it into action planning. When action plans are based on the results of measurement, problem solving is a powerful method of continuous regeneration through systematically altering components of the practice to improve its effectiveness, efficiency, and relevance (Deno, 1995; Gray, 1963; Riley, 1997). These changes are made to counter threats to sustainability (i.e., changes in context, capacity, and consequences) outlined in the first section. The effectiveness of the program can be enhanced by monitoring and improving fidelity of implementation. The efficiency of the process can be improved by assessing the steps of the process and allocating resources based on the severity of the problem. The relevance of the practice can be assessed by considering the school context and determining if the practice should be modified based on the changing needs of the school and key stakeholders (e.g., parents, community members). Such alterations of the practice, if completed systematically and based on available data, would not only improve its relevance but also could improve effectiveness and efficiency (Fullan, 2005; Greenwood, Delquadri, & Bulgren, 1993). These actions are completed not simultaneously but rather in a targeted manner, based on careful analysis of data, through a process in which measurement information is used to diagnose and find solutions to problems that would interfere with sustainability.

## DEMONSTRATION OF SUSTAINABILITY: SCHOOLWIDE PBS

Schoolwide positive behavior support offers an example of one educational reform approach that formally considers and plans for sustainability (Lewis & Sugai, 1999; Sugai & Horner, 2005). SW-PBS has emerged over the past 20 years from (a) application of behavior analysis (Sulzer-Azaroff & Mayer, 1994; Walker, Ramsey, & Gresham, 2005), (b) implementation of effective practices at larger units of analysis (e.g., whole schools and communities; Biglan, 1995; Mayer, 1995), and (c) integration of social skills instruction, academic instruction, environmental redesign, and systems-level interventions (Greenberg et al., 2003; Greenwood et al., 1993; Gresham, Sugai, & Horner, 2001; Sugai & Horner, 2005, 2006). SW-PBS is a multitier approach to establishing the schoolwide social culture needed to improve social competence and academic achievement for all students. Attention to the social culture of a school is achieved by defining, teaching, monitoring, and regularly acknowledging the positive social behaviors expected for all students in a school. In addition, school personnel employ a continuum of corrective consequences for inappropriate behavior and collect data on social behavior and academic performance to assess the effectiveness of the school's efforts.

According to the logic of the SW-PBS approach, these initial efforts to establish a positive social culture can result in behavioral success for approximately 80% of students. Students who do not respond to this primary intervention will require additional support (secondary or tertiary tiers). These additional tiers of support become increasingly more individualized and intensive to meet the needs of individual students.

## Core Features of Sustainable SW-PBS Systems

The SW-PBS approach has been adopted by over 5,300 schools over the past 15 years, with large-scale evaluation reports documenting (a) high fidelity of implementation, (b) improved social behavior, (c) improved academic performance, and (d) sustained effects (Mass-Galloway, Barrett, Bradshaw, & Lewis-Palmer, 2008; Doolittle, 2006; Eber, 2006; Mass-Galloway Panyon, Smith, & Wessendorf, 2008; Horner et al., in press; Muscott, Mann, & LeBrun, 2008). Based on its effectiveness and large-scale adoption, we use SW-PBS as an example to demonstrate how a school-based practice can be applied with a deliberate goal of sustained implementation. The following are critical features for implementing SW-PBS systems that can sustain (Center on Positive Behavioral Interventions and Supports, 2004):

### *Implementation Is Coordinated by a Leadership Team*

Implementation of SW-PBS typically is coordinated by a state, regional, or district leadership team with the responsibility for providing the funding, political support, and coordination of the implementation effort, especially related to developing coaching, training, and evaluation capacity. This team also is responsible for evaluating the effects of implementation and reporting on the extent to which school teams not only receive training, but also actually implement SW-PBS with fidelity.

Educational reforms are seldom simple efforts. The coordination, adaptation, monitoring, and support for large-scale educational reform start with establishing the political, administrative, and financial foundation that will allow initial implementation to occur with high fidelity. If practices are not initially implemented with high fidelity, their chances of taking root are severely diminished.

### *Social Behavior Is Defined as a High Priority*

School teams adopting SW-PBS practices agree to establish the social behavior of students as one of the top three improvement goals for their school. In addition, a school moving to adopt SW-PBS is expected to demonstrate formal administrative support, an 80% commitment from the full faculty, and an agreement to invest in improving behavioral capacity for at least a 3-year period.

### *Specific Practices Are Effective and Efficient*

SW-PBS systems have been adopted and adapted from a wide range of research and demonstration efforts over the past 50 years (Biglan, 1995; Colvin, Kame'enui, & Sugai, 1993; Lewis & Sugai, 1999; Nelson, 1996; Nelson, Martella, & Marchand-Martella, 2002; Sugai,

Horner, et al., 2000; Walker et al., 2005). A key feature, however, has been a commitment to adopting practices that are both evidence based (Kratochwill & Shernoff, 2004) and consistent with principles of human behavior (Sugai, Horner, et al., 2000).

The practices that typically compose SW-PBS systems are drawn from research literature, but the practices are not implemented without attention to contextual features. To achieve efficiency, SWPBS implementation efforts emphasize that school teams should (a) self-assess what they already do well, (b) never stop doing things that already work, (c) always look to implement the smallest changes that will have the largest effects on student outcomes, and (d) adapt practices and systems to fit the culture and context of the school and community.

### *Collection and Use of Data for Decision Making*

Among the major contributions of SW-PBS to the discussion of sustainable educational reform is the commitment to use evaluation data for ongoing problem solving and decision making. Educators have long been involved in measuring the academic achievement of students, but seldom have schools (a) included ongoing measures of social behavior, (b) adopted the expectation that student outcomes should be reported frequently within an academic year, and (c) measured the fidelity of implementation as well as impact of implementation on student outcomes. Yet, these three features of measurement are core tools in promoting data-based decision making, a component necessary for continuous regeneration.

Leadership teams coordinating implementation of SW-PBS are expected to develop an evaluation plan that specifies measurement of both implementation fidelity and impact on student behavior. Two measures of implementation fidelity have been most common:

1. The Team Implementation Checklist (TIC; Sugai, Horner, & Lewis-Palmer, 2001) is a brief, 17-item, self-assessment used by a school implementation team to assess their status/progress on implementation of core SW-PBS features. The team builds a single "team summary" and can enter these data on a Web site (www.pbssurveys.org), where the results are instantly transformed into a visual display and compared with previous scores. The summary of the TIC is used by the school team for action planning.
2. The School-wide Evaluation Tool (SET; Sugai, Lewis-Palmer, Todd, & Horner, 2001) is a research-validated instrument that employs external observation of school practices to document if a school is implementing the core features of SW-PBS (Horner et al., 2004). The SET is used annually to validate TIC self-assessment scores.

In addition to regular monitoring of implementation fidelity, schools adopting SW-PBS are expected to establish formal systems for assessing student behavior. Ideally, a measure of student social behavior would focus on the social and emotional strengths of students. At present, however, direct observation of appropriate behavior and standardized assessment of social and emotional well-being remain prohibitively expensive (McIntosh, Reinke, & Herman, in press). The most common option for school teams to monitor student social behavior is to assess levels of problem behavior. The pattern of office discipline referrals serves as one functional metric (Irvin et al., 2006; Irvin, Tobin, Sprague, Sugai, & Vincent, 2004; Sugai, Sprague, Horner, & Walker, 2000; Tobin, Sugai, & Colvin, 1996). The School-wide Information System (SWIS; May et al., 2006) is a Web-based information system used by over 3,000 schools to monitor ongoing patterns of office discipline referrals. The key feature of this process is that data about the type, frequency, location, and time of problem behavior is easily available to teachers, school psychologists/counselors, administrators, and the whole faculty for both ongoing action planning and evaluation of social behavior support efforts.

The use of data within SW-PBS efforts moves beyond the traditional summative (end-of-year) evaluation of academic achievement. Measures of social behavior and regular assessment of implementation fidelity both become sources of information that are readily available to the whole school and can be used for ongoing problem solving.

### *Capacity Building and Continuous Regeneration*

The process of SW-PBS implementation addresses directly the expectation that building capacity of school systems is as important as building the skills of individual faculty and staff. School teams, teachers, and staff receive direct training and support in implementation of SW-PBS procedures. In addition, initial training typically also includes support from a district coach, who is present in the school at least monthly for ongoing problem solving. The coach is available to help a team when school personnel, administration, or local policies change. An explicit role of the coach is to help build the knowledge of the school teams, thereby cultivating local expertise.

The team also has a regular, annual process for planning, implementing, assessing, and adapting SW-PBS practices. Once the practices and procedures are implemented with fidelity, the amount of effort decreases, but because schools are dynamic environments, a modest investment is reserved for (a) orientation of new teachers, (b) orientation of substitute teachers, (c) annual teaching of behavioral expectations to students, and (d) annual review of data for adjustments and adaptation of more intense behavior support practices. The basic assumption is that as the context changes (e.g., new students, school personnel, and administrators join the school; district and state policies shift; community of families changes), the school team will need to adapt SW-PBS practices to ensure that the core features and outcomes are sustained.

## Current Results

Two examples suggest that sustained implementation of schoolwide behavior support is feasible. A school-level example comes from Fern Ridge Middle School (FRMS) in Lane County, Oregon. The rural middle school of approximately 500 students (Grades 6–8) has been cited as an exemplar of SW-PBS in earlier publications (Taylor-Greene et al., 1997; Taylor-Greene & Kartoub, 2000). During the 1994–1995 academic year, FRMS was in a state of significant social behavior unrest. Students were sent to the office for unacceptable behavior over 2,500 times in a 9-month period, and faculty identified the social behavior of students as a major barrier to effective instruction. In 1995–1996, the faculty began implementation of SW-PBS and were among the first schools to demonstrate high fidelity of implementation using the TIC and SET. The school's implementation of SW-PBS was associated with a dramatic reduction in the level of problem behaviors that resulted in office discipline referrals (47% reduction in the first year). The annual number of major office discipline referrals from FRMS from 1994–1995 to 2005–2006 is provided in Fig. 14.3. This school has retained high-fidelity implementation even with transitions in administrators and school personnel and fading of external expertise and funding provided by the University of Oregon. Ongoing use of data and annual adaptations to the practices in the school have retained core SW-PBS features and been associated with a sustained low level of office discipline referrals.

A national-level study of sustained SW-PBS implementation was conducted by Doolittle (2006), who examined 285 schools adopting SW-PBS over a 3-year period. Doolittle used SET total and subscale scores to examine if schools were actually implementing SW-PBS with fidelity (i.e., at the 80% criterion recommended by Sugai, Lewis-Palmer et al., 2001), and which core features of SWPBS were sustained over time. Doolittle found that 214 of the 285 schools (75%) met the implementation criterion within a 2-year period, and 140 of these 214 schools (65%) sustained criterion levels for at least 2 years.

Doolittle (2006) used logistic regression analysis to examine which features best predicted sustained implementation. The factors in her model that accounted for the largest effect sizes were (a) the presence of an ongoing

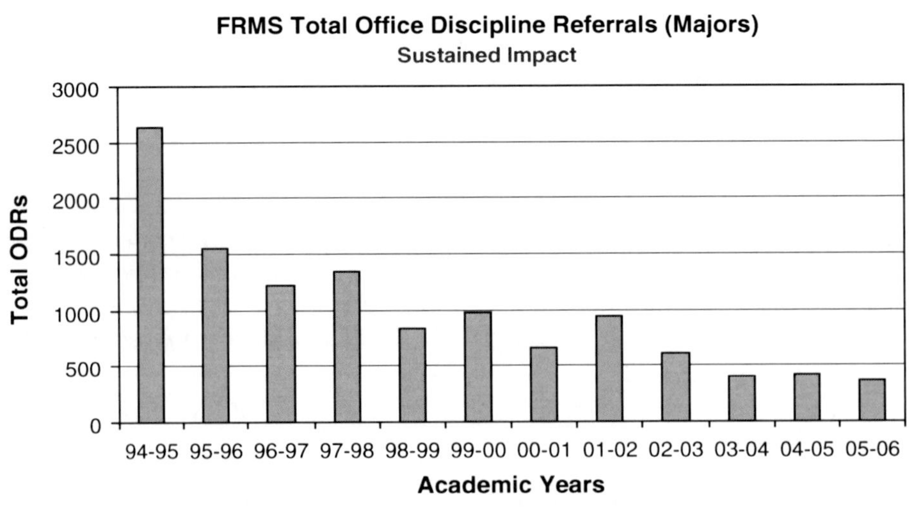


**Fig. 14.3.** The total number of major office discipline referrals per year from 1994–1995 to 2005–2006 for Fern Ridge Middle School (FRMS). ODR, office discipline referral.

system for acknowledging student appropriate behavior and (b) consistent administrative support in the form of active leadership, ongoing use of schoolwide action planning, and coordination of regular team meetings. Implementing effective strategies for encouraging prosocial behavior and retaining administrative support and coordination were the variables that distinguished schools with sustained implementation. These data are consistent with conceptual models that predict the need for an administrative infrastructure that monitors and supports implementation of educational practices that are sustained (Adelman & Taylor, 2003).

## ESTABLISHING A RESEARCH AGENDA TO ADDRESS SUSTAINABILITY

The descriptive data given are both encouraging and provocative. Demonstrations of schools adopting and sustaining educational reforms suggest that meaningful school reform is possible. However, these results remain only suggestive without the causal links between model features, adoption fidelity, implementation protocol, and sustainability. Our conceptual thinking about sustainability exceeds our empirical demonstrations. We need to move our understanding of sustainability beyond theory and into effective and relevant practice. Effective policy on large-scale application of educational reform will require clear information about the variables that affect sustained use of effective practices. The absence of a research foundation addressing sustainability is a major barrier to large-scale dissemination of effective educational reform.

Conducting research on sustainability, however, presents a number of logistical challenges. First, the current models for funding national research lack the scale and length to conduct empirical tests of sustainability (Adelman & Taylor, 2003). Traditional funding cycles of 3 and 5 years allow the study of practice implementation but will not allow a functional test of sustainability, which can only be measured *after* controlled implementation (Elliott et al., 2003). Second, conducting studies on questions related to sustainability requires using a school or school district as the unit of analysis. When applied to the current "gold standard" of randomized control trails, the number of schools needed for a rigorous analysis stretches the study of sustainability beyond current levels of educational research funding and support. Finally, sophisticated statistical tests are needed to analyze results that are associated with schools as the unit of analysis; such approaches involve multiclass, nested, multitier subject and data clustering, and increased sources of error variance (Hedges, 2007).

These challenges notwithstanding, a research agenda on sustainability is possible (Han & Weiss, 2005). An effective sustainability research agenda will include formal systems for assessing and exploring failure, assessing fidelity, and documenting outcomes after external support is removed (Coburn, 2003). The methods needed for this research agenda will include multiple repeated measures that range from direct observation and indirect data sources (e.g., ratings, surveys, archival review) to large-scale assessment results (e.g., standardized statewide assessments).

To be convincing, the research will need to be conducted by multiple collaborating research centers. In general, sustainability research is likely to look more like the research programs conducted by other large social change disciplines, such as pharmacology, public health, medicine, and disease control (Brass, Nunez-Neto, & Williams, 2006).

In addition, careful consideration of the types of acceptable research designs will be needed. Many kinds of designs, ranging from quasi-experimental to experimental, possibly within the same program of research, will be needed (Kratochwill, 2002). The research community must define the value and role of single-subject research designs, requirements for conducting large-scale longitudinal studies, and statistical and design rules and guidelines for confirming and validating functional or causal relationships between molecular and molar variables. The value, trustworthiness, and meaningfulness and role of basic and applied research will need to be discussed, especially as research efforts move toward replication, effectiveness, and adaptation.

As our research methodologies improve in sophistication, scope, sensitivity, and trustworthiness, we will be able to launch credible programs of research addressing sustainability. Organizing to support these endeavors will benefit from attention to the following: conceptual models, investment in measures, innovative designs, integration of research methods, and analysis procedures.

### *Conceptual Models*

Large-scale analysis of sustainability will require clearly defined conceptual models that define valued outcomes, the practices needed to achieve those outcomes, and the variables needed to sustain implementation of effective practices. Although the outcomes and specific practices of the model may vary by domain (e.g., reading improvement model), the principles of sustainability would remain constant in these models.

### *Investment in Measures*

The conceptual models will be useful in defining the measures that will be essential for conducting the descriptive, correlational, and experimental research base for understanding sustainability. It will be necessary to measure a broad range of variables beyond immediate student outcomes and fidelity of implementation. Effective designs will include precise measurement of the process and context of implementation, such as dosage (i.e., intensity, quality, and duration) of training and technical assistance provided to school teams, and features of school and community environments that enhance and inhibit sustainability.

### *Innovative Designs*

A functional research program addressing sustainability of educational practices will require application of all currently available research designs and additional innovations. It will be essential to document both the strategies and practices needed to transform a school from ineffective to effective *and* the strategies and practices needed to sustain this achievement. Historically, education has operated as if initial implementation is sufficient to achieve sustainability. Emerging conceptual models of sustainability rely more on assumptions that ongoing procedures (e.g., continuous regeneration) will be needed for sustained implementation. This conceptual shift will require design adaptations and poses new challenges for isolating nested effects.

### *Integration of Research Methods*

Any substantive study of sustainability will likely include systematic measurement and analysis of the efficiency and costs associated with educational reforms. Researcher precision will be needed to separate the efforts needed to achieve initial effects from those needed to sustain the effects.

### *Analysis Procedures*

Interpreting sustainability research for scholars, policy makers, practitioners, decision makers, and the public will require multiple modes of analysis. Measurement and documentation of direct effects will fit within traditional models. Challenges will remain, including complex documentation of interaction effects, mediator/moderator variables, and the effects of variables that may be insignificant early in implementation and of large importance later in implementation.

Taken together, it seems likely that a substantive research agenda addressing sustainability of education reform will require a larger scope and duration than traditionally has guided federal funding. Useful investment in a research agenda focused on sustainability is likely to require (a) documentation of conceptual models with predictive validity; (b) measures that assess outcomes, practices, and implementation protocols and contextual variables; (c) designs that allow assessment of initial and delayed effects; and (d) analysis protocols that allow both a systematic testing of the conceptual model and definition of effects that can guide future policy making.

## CONCLUSION

The evolution of efforts and knowledge to improve the social climate of school classrooms, hallways, cafeterias, and other common school settings is growing exponentially. In this chapter, we suggested that attention must be given to research and practice related to the sustained and adapted use of effective educational practices and approaches. Focusing this attention is not without challenges, especially with respect to designing and conducting sustainability research in real, applied settings.

However, we believe that this shift in attention and focus is critical given our current focus in education reform and evidence-based practices.

We believe that such investments will be highly valuable in all areas of education (e.g., behavior support, early literacy, response-to-intervention models). An inherent tension exists between "exciting and new" (constant innovation) and "the way we do business" (institutionalization); however, the ultimate goal is to bring the two together to maximize student outcomes over the long term.

## ACKNOWLEDGMENT

This research was supported in part by Educational and Community Supports, University of Oregon, and U.S. Department of Education grant H326S980003. Opinions expressed herein do not necessarily reflect the policy of the Department of Education, and no official endorsement by the department should be inferred. We would like to acknowledge Susan Barrett and Jennifer Doolittle for their thoughtful contributions.

## REFERENCES

Adelman, H. S., & Taylor, L. (1997). Addressing barriers to learning: Beyond school-linked services and full service schools. *American Journal of Orthopsychiatry, 67*, 408–421.

Adelman, H. S., & Taylor, L. (2003). On sustainability of project innovations as systemic change. *Journal of Educational and Psychological Consultation, 14*, 1–25.

Albin, R. W., Lucyshyn, J. M., Horner, R. H., & Flannery, K. B. (1996). Contextual fit for behavioral support plans: A model for "goodness of fit." In L. K. Koegel, R. L. Koegel, & G. Dunlap (Eds.), *Positive behavioral support: Including people with difficult behavior in the community* (pp. 81–98). Baltimore: Brookes.

August, G. J., Lee, S. S., Bloomquist, M. L., Realmuto, G. M., & Hektner, J. M. (2004). Maintenance effects of an evidence-based prevention innovation for aggressive children living in culturally diverse urban neighborhoods: The Early Risers effectiveness study. *Journal of Emotional and Behavioral Disorders, 12*, 194–205.

Barrett, S. B., Bradshaw, C., & Lewis-Palmer, T. L. (2008). Maryland statewide Positive Behavior Interventions and Supports Initiative: Systems, evaluation, and next steps. *Journal of Positive Behavior Interventions, 10*, 105–114.

Benz, M. R., Lindstrom, L., Unruh, D., & Waintrup, M. (2004). Sustaining secondary transition programs in local schools. *Remedial and Special Education, 25*, 39–50.

Bernfield, G. A., Blase, K. A., & Fixsen, D. L. (1990). Toward a unified perspective on human service delivery systems: Application of the teaching-family model. In R. J. McMahon & R. D. Peters (Eds.), *Behavior disorders of adolescence: Research, intervention, and policy in clinical and school settings* (pp. 191–205). New York: Plenum Press.

Biglan, A. (1995). Translating what we know about the context of antisocial behavior into a lower prevalence of such behavior. *Journal of Applied Behavior Analysis, 28*, 479–492.

Blase, K. A., & Fixsen, D. L. (2004). *Infrastructure for implementing and sustaining evidence-based programs with fidelity*. Tampa, FL: National Implementation Research Network.

Brass, C. T., Nunez-Neto, B., & Williams, E. D. (2006). *Congress and program evaluation: An overview of randomized controlled trials (RCTs) and related issues*. Washington, DC: Congressional Research Service, Library of Congress. Congressional Research Service Order Code RL 33301.

Carter, D. R., & Horner, R. H. (2007). Adding functional behavioral assessment to First Step to Success: A case study. *Journal of Positive Behavior Interventions*. 9, 229–238.

Center for Mental Health in Schools. (2001). *Sustaining school-community partnerships to enhance outcomes for children and youth: A guidebook and tool kit*. Los Angeles: Center for Mental Health in Schools at UCLA.

Center on Positive Behavioral Interventions and Supports. (2004). *School-wide positive behavior support implementers' blueprint and self-assessment*. Eugene: University of Oregon. Available at http://www.pbis.org/tools.htm

Cherniss, C. (2006). *School change and the microsociety program*. Thousand Oaks, CA: Corwin Press.

Coburn, C. E. (2003). Rethinking scale: Moving beyond numbers to deep and lasting change. *Educational Researcher, 32*(6), 3–12.

Colvin, G., Kame'enui, E. J., & Sugai, G. (1993). Reconceptualizing behavior management and school-wide discipline in general education, *Education and Treatment of Children, 16*, 361–381.

Comer, J. P., Ben-Avie, M., Haynes, N. M., & Joyner, E. T. (Eds.). (1999). *Child by child: The Comer process for change in education*. New York: Teachers College Press.

Datnow, A., & Castellano, M. (2000). Teachers' responses to Success for All: How beliefs, experiences, and adaptations shape implementation. *American Educational Research Journal, 37*, 775–799.

Deno, S. L. (1995). School psychologist as problem solver. In A. Thomas & J. P. Grimes (Eds.), *Best practices in school psychology III* (pp. 471–484). Bethesda, MD: National Association of School Psychologists.

Doolittle, J. H. (2006). *Sustainability of positive behavior supports in schools*. Unpublished doctoral dissertation, University of Oregon.

Eber, L. (2006). *Illinois PBIS evaluation report*. LaGrange Park, IL: Illinois State Board of Education, PBIS/EBD Network.

Elias, M. J., Zins, J. E., Graczyk, P. A., & Weissburg, R. P. (2003). Implementation, sustainability, and scaling up of social-emotional and academic innovations in public schools. *School Psychology Review, 32*, 303–319.

Elliott, S. N., Kratochwill, T. R., & Roach, A. T. (2003). Commentary: Implementing social-emotional and academic innovations: Reflections, reactions, and research. *School Psychology Review, 32*, 320–326.

Fixsen, D. L., Naoom, S. F., Blase, K. A., Friedman, R. M., & Wallace, F. (2005). *Implementation research: Synthesis of the literature*. Tampa, FL: National Implementation Research Network.

Fullan, M. (2005). *Leadership and sustainability*. Thousand Oaks, CA: Corwin Press.

Furney, K. S., Hasazi, S. B., Clark-Keefe, K., & Hartnett, J. (2003). A longitudinal analysis of shifting policy landscapes in special and general education reform. *Exceptional Children, 70*(1), 81–94.

Gager, P. J., & Elias, M. J. (1997). Implementing prevention programs in high-risk environments: Application of the resiliency paradigm. *American Journal of Orthopsychiatry, 67*, 363–373.

Gersten, R., Chard, D. J., & Baker, S. (2000). Factors enhancing sustained use of research-based instructional practices. *Journal of Learning Disabilities, 33*, 445–457.

Gray, S. W. (1963). *The psychologist in the schools*. New York: Holt, Rhinehart, & Wilson.

Greenberg, M. T., Weissburg, R. P., & O'Brien, M. E. (2003). Enhancing school-based prevention and youth development through coordinated social, emotional, and academic learning. *American Psychologist, 58*, 466–474.

Greenwood, C. R., Delquadri, J., & Bulgren, J. (1993). Current challenges to behavioral technology in the reform of schooling: Large-scale, high-quality implementation and sustained use of effective educational practices. *Education and Treatment of Children, 16*, 401–404.

Greenwood, C. R., Tapia, Y., Abbott, M., & Walton, C. (2003). A building-based case study of evidence-based literacy practices: Implementation, reading behavior, and growth in reading fluency, K–4. *Journal of Special Education, 37*, 95–110.

Gresham, F. M., Sugai, G., & Horner, R. H. (2001). Interpreting outcomes of social skills training for students with high-incidence disabilities. *Exceptional Children, 67*, 331–344.

Han, S. S., & Weiss, B. (2005). Sustainability of teacher implementation of school-based mental health programs. *Journal of Abnormal Child Psychology, 33*, 665–679.

Hanley, T. V. (2003). Commentary: Scaling up social-emotional and academic supports for all students, including students with disabilities. *School Psychology Review, 32*, 327–330.

Hatch, T. (2000). What does it take to break the mold? Rhetoric and reality in new American schools. *Teachers College Record, 102*, 561–589.

Hedges, L. V. (2007). Meta-analysis. In C. R. Rao & S. Sinbaray (Eds.), *The handbook of statistics* (Vol. 26, pp. 919–953). New York: Elsevier Scientific.

Hinshaw, S. P., Klein, R. G., & Abikoff, H. B. (2002). Childhood attention-deficit hyperactivity disorder: Nonpharmalogical treatments and their combination with medication. In P. E. Nathan & J. M. Gorman (Eds.), *A guide to treatments that work* (2nd ed., pp. 3–23). New York: Oxford University Press.

Hoagwood, K. (2004). Evidence-based practice in child and adolescent mental health: Its meaning, application and limitations. *Emotional and Behavioral Disorders in Youth, 4*, 7–8.

Horner, R. H., Sugai, G., Smolkowski, K., Eber, L., Nakasato, J., Todd, A. W., et al. (in press). A randomized, controlled trial assessing school-wide positive behavior support in elementary schools. *Journal of Positive Behavior Interventions.*

Horner, R. H., Sugai, G., Todd, A. W., & Lewis-Palmer, T. (2005). School-wide positive behavior support. In L. Bambara & L. Kern (Eds.), *Individualized supports for students with problem behaviors: Designing positive behavior plans* (pp. 359–390). New York: Guilford Press.

Horner, R. H., Todd, A. W., Lewis-Palmer, T., Irvin, L. K., Sugai, G., & Boland, J. B. (2004). The School-wide Evaluation Tool (SET): A research instrument for assessing school-wide positive behavior support. *Journal of Positive Behavior Interventions, 6*, 3–12.

Huberman, A. M. (1983). School improvement strategies that work: Some scenarios. *Educational Leadership, 43*, 23–27.

Ikeda, M. J., Grimes, J. P., Tilly, W. D., Allison, S., Kurns, S., & Stumme, J. (2002). Implementing an intervention-based approach to service delivery: A case example. In M. R. Shinn, H. M. Walker, & G. Stoner (Eds.), *Interventions for academic and behavioral problems II: Preventive and remedial approaches* (pp. 53–69). Bethesda, MD: National Association of School Psychologists.

Irvin, L. K., Horner, R. H., Ingram, K., Todd, A. W., Sugai, G., Sampson, N. K., et al. (2006). Using office discipline referral data for decision making about student behavior in elementary and middle schools: An empirical evaluation of validity. *Journal of Positive Behavior Interventions, 8*, 10–23.

Irvin, L. K., Tobin, T. J., Sprague, J. R., Sugai, G., & Vincent, C. G. (2004). Validity of office discipline referral measures as indices of school-wide behavioral status and effects of school-wide behavioral interventions. *Journal of Positive Behavior Interventions, 6*, 131–147.

Kealey, K. A., Peterson, A. V., Gaul, M. A., & Dinh, K. T. (2000). Teacher training as a behavior change process: Principles and results from a longitudinal study. *Health Education and Behavior, 27*, 64–81.

Kellam, S. G., Mayer, L. S., Rebok, G. W., & Hawkins, W. E. (1998). Effects of improving achievement on aggressive behavior and of improving aggressive behavior on achievement through two preventive interventions: An investigation of causal paths. In B. P. Dohrenwend (Ed.), *Adversity, stress, and psychopathology* (pp. 486–505). London: Oxford University Press.

Klingner, J. K., Arguelles, M. E., Hughes, M. T., & Vaughn, S. (2001). Examining the school-wide "spread" of research-based practices. *Learning Disability Quarterly, 24*, 221–234.

Kratochwill, T. R. (2002). Evidence-based interventions in school psychology: Thoughts on thoughtful commentary. *School Psychology Quarterly, 17*, 518–532.

Kratochwill, T. R., & Shernoff, E. S. (2004). Evidence-based practice: Promoting evidence-based interventions in school psychology. *School Psychology Review, 33*, 34–48.

Latham, G. (1988). The birth and death cycles of educational innovations. *Principal, 68*, 41–43.

Lewis, T. J., & Sugai, G. (1999). Effective behavior support: A systems approach to proactive schoolwide management. *Focus on Exceptional Children, 31*, 1–24.

Lucyshyn, J. M., Albin, R. A., Horner, R. H., Mann, J. C., Mann, J. A., & Wadsworth, G. (2007). Family implementation of positive behavior support with a child with Autism: A longitudinal, single case experimental and descriptive replication and extension. *Journal of Positive Behavior Interventions, 9*, 131–150.

Mass-Galloway, R. L., Panyon, M. V., Smith, C. R., & Wessendord, S. (2008). Systems change with school-wide positive behavior support: Iowa's work in progress. *Journal of Positive Behavior Interventions. 10*, 129–135.

May, S., Ard, W. I., Todd, A. W., Horner, R. H., Glasgow, A., Sugai, G., et al. (2006). *School-wide information system*. Eugene: Educational and Community Supports, University of Oregon.

Mayer, G. R. (1995). Preventing antisocial behavior in the schools. *Journal of Applied Behavior Analysis, 28*, 467–478.

McIntosh, K., Reinke, W. M., & Herman, K. E. (in press). School-wide analysis of data for social behavior problems: Assessing outcomes, selecting targets for intervention, and indentifying need for support. In R. A. Ervin, G. Peacock, E. J. Daly & K. W. Merrell (Eds.), *The practical handbook of school psychology*, New York: Guilford.

McLaughlin, M. W., & Mitra, D. (2001). Theory-based change and change-based theory: Going deeper, going broader. *Journal of Educational Change, 2*, 301–323.

Merrell, K. W., & Buchanan, R. S. (2006). Intervention selection in school-based practice: Using public health models to enhance systems capacity of schools. *School Psychology Review, 35*, 167–180.

Mihalic, S. F., & Irwin, K. (2003). Blueprints for violence prevention: From research to real-world settings—Factors influencing the successful replication of model programs. *Youth Violence and Juvenile Justice, 1*, 307–329.

Muscott, H., Mann, E.L. & LeBrun, M. (2008). Positive Behavioral Interventions and Supports in New Hampshire: Effects of large-scale implementation of Schoolwide Positive Behavior Support on student discipline and academic achievement. *Journal of Positive Behavior Interventions, 10*, 190–205.

Nelson, J. R. (1996). Designing schools to meet the needs of students who exhibit disruptive behavior. *Journal of Emotional and Behavioral Disorders, 4*, 147–161.

Nelson, J. R., Martella, R. M., & Marchand-Martella, N. (2002). Maximizing student learning: The effects of a comprehensive school-based program for preventing problem behaviors. *Journal of Emotional and Behavioral Disorders, 10*, 136–148.

Newton, J. S. (2008). *Toward a technology of sustainable positive behavior support*. Manuscript in preparation.

NIMH Intervention Workgroup. (2001, November). *An integrated framework for preventive and treatment interventions*. Paper presented at the National Institute of Mental Health workgroup meeting, Washington, DC.

Noell, G. H., Witt, J. C., Slider, N. J., Connell, J. E., Gatti, S. L., Williams, K. L., et al. (2005). Treatment implementation following behavioral consultation in schools: A comparison of three follow-up strategies. *School Psychology Review, 34*, 87–106.

Riley, D. A. (1997). Using local research to change 100 communities for children and families. *American Psychologist, 52*, 424–433.

Rogers, E. (2003). *Diffusion of innovations* (5th ed.). New York: Free Press.

Sadler, C. (2004, March). *Sustaining PBS*. Paper presented at the Second Annual Oregon Statewide Positive Behavior Support Conference, Corvallis.

Sarason, S. B. (2004). What we need to know about intervention and interventionists. *American Journal of Community Psychology, 33*, 275–277.

Sindelar, P. T., Shearer, D. K., Yendol-Hoppey, D., & Liebert, T. W. (2006). The sustainability of inclusive school reform. *Exceptional Children, 72*, 317–331.

Stokes, L. M., Sato, N. E., McLaughlin, M. W., & Talbert, J. E. (1997). *Theory-based reform and problems of change: Contexts that matter for teachers' learning and community*. Palo Alto, CA: Stanford University.

Sugai, G., & Horner, R. H. (2005). School-wide positive behavior supports: Achieving and sustaining effective learning environments for all students. In W. H. Heward

(Ed.), *Focus on behavior analysis in education: Achievements, challenges, and opportunities* (pp. 90–102). Upper Saddle River, NJ: Pearson Prentice-Hall.

Sugai, G., & Horner, R. H. (2006). A promising approach for expanding and sustaining the implementation of school-wide positive behavior support. *School Psychology Review, 35*, 245–259.

Sugai, G., Horner, R. H., Dunlap, G., Hieneman, M., Lewis, T. J., Nelson, C. M., et al. (2000). Applying positive behavior support and functional behavioral assessment in schools. *Journal of Positive Behavior Interventions, 2*, 131–143.

Sugai, G., Horner, R. H., & Lewis-Palmer, T. L. (2001). *Team Implementation Checklist (TIC)*. Eugene, OR: Educational and Community Supports. Available at http://www.pbis.org

Sugai, G., Lewis-Palmer, T. L., Todd, A. W., & Horner, R. H. (2001). *School-wide Evaluation Tool (SET)*. Eugene, OR: Educational and Community Supports. Available at http://www.pbis.org

Sugai, G., Sprague, J. R., Horner, R. H., & Walker, H. M. (2000). Preventing school violence: The use of office discipline referrals to assess and monitor school-wide discipline interventions. *Journal of Emotional and Behavioral Disorders, 8*, 94–101.

Sulzer-Azaroff, B., & Mayer, G. R. (1994). *Achieving educational excellence: Behavior analysis for achieving classroom and schoolwide behavior change*. San Marcos, CA: Western Image.

Taylor-Greene, S., Brown, D., Nelson, L., Longton, J., Gassman, T., Cohen, J., et al. (1997). School-wide behavioral support: Starting the year off right *Journal of Behavioral Education, 7*, 99–112.

Taylor-Greene, S., & Kartoub, D. T. (2000). Durable implementation of school-wide behavior support: The High Five Program. *Journal of Positive Behavior Interventions, 2*, 233–235.

Tobin, T. J., Sugai, G., & Colvin, G. (1996). Patterns in middle school discipline records. *Journal of Emotional and Behavioral Disorders, 4*, 82–94.

Togneri, W., & Anderson, S. E. (2003). *Beyond islands of excellence: What districts can do to improve instruction and achievement in all schools*. Washington, DC: Learning First Alliance.

Vaughn, S., Klingner, J., & Hughes, M. (2000). Sustainability of research-based practices. *Exceptional Children, 66*, 163–171.

Walker, H. M. (2004). Commentary: Use of evidence-based intervention in schools: Where we've been, where we are, and where we need to go. *School Psychology Review, 33*, 398–407.

Walker, H. M., Ramsey, E., & Gresham, F. M. (2005). *Antisocial behavior in school: Strategies and best practices* (2nd ed.). Pacific Grove, CA: Brooks/Cole.

Waterhouse, T., & Chapman, D. (2006). *Effective behavior support and school-wide discipline: A review of implementation and sustainability in BC schools*. Abbotsford, BC: Institute for Safe Schools of British Columbia.

Wolf, M. M. (1978). Social validity: The case for subjective measurement, or how behavior analysis is finding its heart. *Journal of Applied Behavior Analysis, 11*, 203–214.

# 15

# Increasing Family Participation Through Schoolwide Positive Behavior Supports

**TIMOTHY J. LEWIS**

Involving, informing, and supporting families of children and youth with disabilities has been a topic that has received a fair amount of attention since the passage of the Education for All Handicapped Children Act (P.L. 94-142, 1975). Since the first iteration of the act, parents and guardians were invited and encouraged to participate in the development of educational plans for their children. An expansion of simple participation is also evident with the extension of the act to include infants and toddlers. The onus was placed on educators not only to address the individual child but also to create plans that address family needs as they attempt to provide for their child with significant disabilities through the creation of individual family service plans (P.L. 99-457, the Infants and Toddlers With Disabilities Act, 1986). Given this federal mandate, the field has responded and provided several guides focusing on the intersection between school-based positive behavior supports (PBS) and family support (e.g., Lucyshyn, Dunlap, & Albin, 2002). While the field has provided excellent work toward involving families in the PBS process at the individual student level, less is known about how to involve families across the continuum of supports promoted through a schoolwide PBS (SW-PBS) process (Lucyshyn, Dunlap, & Albin, 2002). The purpose of this chapter is to provide a suggested heuristic, building on the foundation of family supports at the individual student level, to increase family awareness, involvement, and supports across the three tiers of SW-PBS support. Unfortunately, there is a paucity of research exploring the impact of

**TIMOTHY J. LEWIS** • University of Missouri-Columbia

SW-PBS on family participation. The information provided in this chapter is based on work conducted at the individual student level (Lucyshyn, Horner, Dunlap, Albin, & Ben, 2002), descriptive work to date within SW-PBS, and using the basic logic of PBS.

Throughout this chapter, the fundamental logic of SW-PBS is emphasized. During the establishment of systems of SW-PBS, school teams engage in several key steps (Sugai et al., 2000). First, school teams identify and focus on "prosocial replacement" behaviors versus creating lists of offenses and consequences. Second, teams clearly define expected prosocial behaviors in response to local problems and guided by acceptable norms. Third, school teams develop clear and explicit instructional steps and practice activities to teach students how to meet expectations. Finally, school teams develop a mechanism to provide feedback to students and to acknowledge and celebrate mastery of key expectations.

The extension of SW-PBS to include families should follow the same basic steps. First, teams should focus on replacement behaviors versus problems. In other words, teams should identify outcomes for family participation versus lamenting the fact that parent/guardians are not involved. Second, school teams should clearly define what participation looks like across the continuum. Third, school teams should identify and implement strategies to actively engage families in the process; fourth, schools should acknowledge incremental increases toward meeting their set goals.

In addition to using the basic logic of SW-PBS, school teams should also follow the same problem-solving logic of gathering and using data to identify which practices should be in place to support students and paying equal attention to the systemic supports the adults within the school will need to successfully implement each practice (Lewis & Sugai, 1999; Sugai et al., 2000). In relation to family participation, data should be gathered on the present level and appropriateness of family participation and on outcomes as a result of specific school team activities related to family participation. Practices are those activities educators engage in to promote family participation, with systems focusing both on supporting educator implementation and interconnecting families with school and related agencies.

The remainder of this chapter is organized around preferred and promising strategies to increase family participation, with emphasis on connections to the schoolwide system. Similar to the SW-PBS process of developing specific behavioral expectations based on local issues, each school team must clearly define what "participation" means relative to issues they are currently experiencing along with defining clear outcomes that are observable and measurable.

## CONSIDERATIONS IN DEFINING FAMILY PARTICIPATION

Several considerations should be made prior to school teams setting specific goals related to family participation. First, *family* should be broadly defined to include any and all caregivers in the home, not limiting the definition to the traditional two parents and siblings. Second, there is no universal definition of *family participation*. Similar to developing behavioral expectations for students based on current problems, school teams must define family participation relative to presenting issues. Issues can range from little to no family presence in the school to the other extreme, too much parent presence to the point of disrupting the school day. Within working definitions, schools should strive toward building a system that is open and accessible to families. Third, family participation should vary along the continuum of supports from primary to tertiary parallel to which supports their child requires. Fourth, educators should ensure that targeted practices and related outcomes relative to family participation are sensitive to language, cultural, and other norms found across their community. Fifth, school teams should build their SW-PBS systems independent of present levels of family participation. In other words, school system success should not be contingent on increased levels or altered patterns of family participation given that schools cannot mandate family participation within school activities or mandate which practices are, or are not, in the home. Finally, SW-PBS teams should ensure all personnel within their school have an awareness of family ecology and likewise inform parents/guardians of the limitations and realities of the school day and existing educational resources.

With respect to school personnel understanding the ecology of the family, SW-PBS teams should provide training and information relative to both typically developing student family ecology and the impact a child with a disability or those at high risk pose within the dynamics of the family. General information such as developing partnerships and interacting in a respectful and culturally sensitive manner as well as specific information such as understanding how at-risk children or children with disabilities create unique family stressors should be provided (Boettcher, Koegel, McNerney, & Koegel, 2003; Fox, Vaughn, Wyatte, & Dunlap, 2002; Frea & Kasari, 2004; Koegel, Koegel, Boettcher, Brookman-Frazee, 2005; Lucyshyn & Albin, 1993; Smith-Bird, Turnbull, & Koegel, 2005). Across all information, similar to the basic logic of SW-PBS focusing on replacement behaviors, an emphasis should be placed on the "strengths" of the family and not just problems or needs (Vaughn, White, Johnston, & Dunlap, 2005).

Once schools clearly establish a definition of family participation across the continuum of student supports and target outcomes, school personnel should share with parents/guardians the realities of the school day, which involves issues such as the central purpose of school is to educate children and youth; while schools are open to family participation, a protocol to visit or observe may be established; creating an understanding that their child is just as important to the school as it is to the parents/guardians but also communicating there are often hundreds of children in the school who also warrant and deserve attention; and while school personnel often extend themselves to connect families with other agencies, school personnel themselves typically cannot provide that service (e.g., teachers are not trained counselors). Having delineated these school realities, in no way should this list be interpreted as creating limitations for services and supports provided or excuses for not involving and supporting families. The list is offered simply as a set of suggestions to create a dialogue with parents in understanding what a typical school day encompasses and working toward an understanding of how best to support children and youth across school and home. This caveat is especially salient when addressing the needs of individual students with disabilities. The multidisciplinary team developing the individualized educational plan or accommodations per section 504, 29 U.S.C. 794(a) of the Vocational Rehabilitation Act (1973) should determine what supports should be in place independent of all other general school factors.

A final consideration in increasing family participation is underscoring the importance of creating supportive "host environments" within school and home settings (Zins & Ponti, 1990). Within the SW-PBS logic, all aspects of support are built on clear and consistent primary preventive support practices. The behavioral assumption is that in the absence of consistent practice and opportunities to earn reinforcement, key behaviors that may be learned within unique settings, such as the classroom or through specialists, will not generalize and thereby will fail to be maintained over time. By linking secondary and tertiary supports to the primary system, students who receive those supports will be exposed to repeated practice opportunities and access consistent positive reinforcement for engaging in appropriate behavior through the primary practices. Educators should also strive to the degree they can in assisting families in creating functional host environments in the home. As stated by Singer and colleagues (Singer, Goldberg-Hamblin, Peckham-Hardin, Barry, & Santarelli, 2002):

> Research on parents of children with and without disabilities repeatedly shows that parents who benefit the least from parent training… struggle with one or more of the following issues: Poverty, low SES [socioeconomic status], social isolation, single parenthood, marital discord, and depression or mental illness. (p. 159)

While educators do not have the power to change any of the above-listed risk factors, awareness and efforts to lessen the impact of any or all can assist families in creating supportive host environments that will then be more receptive to inclusion of effective strategies and fostering partnerships between school and home (Lucyshyn & Albin, 1993; Lucyshyn, Horner, Dunlap, Albin, & Ben, 2002; Smith-Bird et al., 2005; Vaughn et al., 2005).

## A WORKING DEFINITION OF FAMILY PARTICIPATION

As stated, a universally accepted definition of family participation across the continuum of SW-PBS does not appear in the professional literature (Horner & Koegel, 2005). Building on the basic logic of SW-PBS, a working definition is offered to guide school teams in their formulation of supports across the continuum (Lewis, 2007). Three key outcomes are offered for consideration; each should be addressed across the three levels of SW-PBS support and measured in terms of both family and educator participation.

The first is awareness. *Awareness* is defined as information about SW-PBS flowing between school and home. Awareness can be measured by parent demonstration of familiarity with key school expectations or related school social and academic goals. Likewise, awareness can be measured as the degree to which educators are familiar with current and needed strategies to promote family participation. The second key outcome is involvement.

*Involvement* is defined as family members of students within a given school actively participating in school functions. Involvement may be measured by the percentage of families participating in general school functions or specific activities relative to their child. Educator involvement can be measured by teacher presence and interaction with families across school functions. The third is support. *Support* is defined as the school taking an active role in providing, coordinating, or arranging from a third party the strategies for use by parents/guardians in tandem with school social and academic behavioral expectations or services for family members to assist their at-risk child or child with a disability. Support outcomes can be measured through the number of families with students on tertiary levels of support actively engaged in the school plan or external support agencies.

Educator outcomes could include teacher knowledge of the tertiary process and their role in implementation across school and home environments. For example, understanding how a functional assessment is conducted or what services external agencies provide. School teams are encouraged to consider each of the three key participation components across the continuum of supports for students but shift emphasis contingent on the level of the continuum of "primary/universal," "secondary/targeted," or "tertiary/intensive" supports along with targeted measurable outcomes (see Table 15.1 for sample outcomes across the continuum of SW-PBS).

The next section of this chapter provides additional information and examples of each participation component organized by level of SW-PBS support. Across the continuum, increased levels or appropriate participation (i.e., awareness, involvement, support) should serve as the outcome of SW-PBS efforts. Strategies outlined within the three tiers are those educators undertake to reach defined targeted outcomes.

## Primary/Universal Supports

Primary supports within SW-PBS include practices and systems of support that focus on all students, all settings, and all school staff (Sugai et al., 2000). The emphasis within the school is on teaching and practicing the identified expectations to both prevent problem behavior from occurring and supporting those at risk (see chapter 14 for a comprehensive discussion of key features of each level of the continuum). At the primary level, schools should focus mainly on awareness relative to family participation, but also consider involvement and support within their working definition.

### *Awareness*

At the primary level, a two-way exchange of information should be the main focus. Information, including the schoolwide expectations; strategies to teach and supporting activities; targeted acknowledgment of mastery, including the range of reinforcement used, should be shared with parents/guardians through concise written materials, general meetings involving parents/guardians, and individual teacher contacts with parents/guardians. Information should be presented in "user-friendly" formats such as brochures or short bulleted overviews. The goal is to increase understanding of

**Table 15.1.** Sample Family and Educator Participation Targeted Outcomes Across the Continuum of Schoolwide Positive Behavior Support (SW-PBS)

| | | Prevention Tiers | | |
|---|---|---|---|---|
| | | Primary | Secondary | Tertiary |
| Awareness | Family outcome | Family members can identify school expectations and continuum of supports | Family members understand how to access supports for their child | Family members understand the range of supports available to them and their rights to services when disabilities are involved |
| | Educator outcome | Educators make frequent connections to families to discuss primary supports | Educators understand the range of secondary supports used in school, their role in follow-along activities, and strategies family members can use in the home | Educators demonstrate understanding of and show a sensitivity to the impact a child with a disability, or one who is at risk, may have on family dynamics |
| Involvement | Family outcome | Increase in family presence at school functions | Family members participate in intervention selection and implementation | Family members are active partners in assessment, plan development, and intervention |
| | Educator outcome | Educators make connections with families during school-based functions | Educators are open and respectful of family participation in secondary supports | Educators are active partners in the assessment, plan development, and intervention |
| Support | Family outcome | Family members aware of within-school supports and related community agencies | Family members participate in follow-along activities at home to support in-school interventions | Family members are active participants in a coordinated set of interventions across school and, if needed, community agencies |
| | Educator outcome | Educators available to answer family questions/concerns about primary supports | Educators share strategies for use in home that compliment secondary supports and acknowledge family suggestions and strategies | Educators actively seek out within-district and community supports for families in need |

the SW-PBS process and targeted student outcomes. Language and readability level should reflect the local community. If meetings are scheduled to share information with parents/guardians, consider three factors that are likely to increase attendance when most school meetings are poorly attended: (a) offer transportation to the meeting, (b) provide food at the meeting, and (c) provide child care at the meeting.

An example that has been used by many school teams to promote awareness is inclusion of a "SW-PBS quiz" with general information that is sent home. The quiz is accompanied by information relative to the schoolwide expectations and support strategies. A fill-in-the-blank format is used with parent/guardian instructions to sit down with their child and complete the quiz by writing in the school expectations or generating an example of one of the schoolwide rules. Extending the logic of PBS, many schools also add an incentive to increase return rates, such as all those returned are entered into a drawing to win a gift certificate. The purpose of the awareness information and quiz is threefold. First, families receive information relative to what the school is attempting to accomplish with SW-PBS. Second, it creates an opportunity for families to discuss school expectations at home. Finally, it provides a follow-up opportunity to contact families who do not return the quiz. The purpose of the follow-up contact is not to chastise families who failed to return the quiz; rather, it is to ask first if the information made it home, second if there are any questions or concerns about what the school is attempting to accomplish, and third to provide encouragement to contact the school if they do have questions or comments. Experience, as well as research (Singer et al., 2002), indicates families of students who are at high risk often are experiencing stress or dysfunction, lessening the likelihood of active participation in their child's school. The follow-up contact sets a different tone that many high-risk families have not experienced: the school calling home to discuss positives about their child versus the traditional contact when problems arise.

Equally important, schools should solicit information from parents/guardians relative to the SW-PBS system and their perceptions of access across the continuum. It is important that schools determine the most efficient and effective manner to gather these data. The typical format is a survey sent home. However, plan for the possibility that surveys may not be returned and consider other formats to gather the information (e.g., phone calls home, home visits, visits with parents at athletic events).

### *Involvement*

Involvement at the primary level of supports should follow the main focus of awareness with an eye toward expanding beyond simple one-way communication to the home. Here, the goal is to seek active participation on the part of families within the SW-PBS process to promote a two-way understanding of what the school is attempting to accomplish and develop partnerships in the effort. Two strategies should be considered. The first is the inclusion of a family member on the SW-PBS team. The role of the family member is to lend a different voice to the planning and discussion of SW-PBS within the team and to advocate the school's use of SW-PBS among other families. Simply put, a family SW-PBS team member can challenge other families to support and become active in school activities in a manner employees of the school district cannot.

Within the state of Michigan, the inclusion of parents on SW-PBS teams to promote involvement was extended a step further through the involvement of family members within new school team training (Ballard-Krishan et al., 2003). As identified by the authors, the purposes and outcomes of including family members on training teams included (a) demonstrating respect for each other's knowledge about children, (b) recognizing strengths among each trainer, (c) providing financial assistance to family members who participated as trainers, and (d) creating an opportunity to provide ongoing mentoring to family members through the collaborative training process.

The second consideration to increase family involvement at the primary level of support is to extend invitations to all families to participate in school activities. The outcome of participation should continue to be focused on promoting awareness and extending the two-way dialogue about student outcomes. Within schools where levels of family volunteering or participation are often low, consider the following suggestions: First, clearly delineate timelines and expectation of the event. Open calls for family members to volunteer may be met with apprehension based on the impression that it will require a lot of time or a unique set of skills (e.g., reading tutors or open calls to "volunteer" without provided specifics). Second, across all events, provide training or ensure a school staff member will be on hand to assist. Finally, keep the primary focus of the event in mind: to open or continue the dialogue with parents/guardians about supporting their children.

Benton Elementary School, like many, noted the low level of family participation across school events (Lewis & Lewis, 2006). Benton Elementary exemplifies many of the risk factors schools with similar low rates of parent/guardian involvement possess, including Title 1 status denoting significant rates of poverty, large percentages of children from ethnic minority groups, and a highly transient population. In an effort to increase family involvement at the primary level of support, the SW-PBS team developed a "Family Buzz Passport." The passport contained both activities to become involved in school and follow-up activities to put in place in the home to increase the impact of their SW-PBS efforts (see Table 15.2). At all school events, staff were on hand to visit with parents/guardians about their SW-PBS efforts, support them in the activity, and "stamp" their passport to acknowledge participation (see Fig. 15.1). As an added incentive, completed passports earned the family a pizza dinner. Each trimester across the school year, the involvement level within the school increased. Reported outcomes included over one third of families earning completed passports and marked increases in family participation in school events such as parent-teacher association (PTA) meetings, back-to-school night, parent-teacher conferences, and family volunteers to chaperone during school outings and events (Lewis & Lewis, 2006).

### *Support*

Support at the primary level continues to follow the main focus of awareness through information dissemination. Information should be shared that (a) outlines the steps parents/guardians must take to refer their child for services, (b) indicates how to access community agencies, and (c) lists the range of options available for support across the school district and related community agencies. A second focus within supports should also include building connect points between internal and external family supports and the larger schoolwide systems. For example, the state of New York PBS initiative created a sample matrix of connect points across

**Table 15.2.** Activity Options Within the "Benton Family Buzz Passport" to Promote Family Participation at School and Family Prosocial Interactions at Home, at the Primary/Universal Level of Support

| | Activities to Increase Awareness Through Family Participation in School Events | Activities to Increase Involvement of Family Members in the School | Activities to Support Family Interactions |
|---|---|---|---|
| First trimester | • Attend back-to-school night<br>• Attend parent-teacher conference<br>• Prearrange with your child's teacher a time to visit the classroom<br>• Attend parent-teacher association (PTA) meeting | • Have breakfast or lunch with your child at school<br>• Provide a family photo for the "Benton Family Bulletin Board" at school | • Have a "no TV" night at home<br>• Have your child(ren) read a story to the family<br>• Eat dinner together as a family and discuss each person's day<br>• Play a board game together<br>• Go for a walk together in your neighborhood or park<br>• Go on your choice of a family outing |
| Second trimester | • Attend Family Dinner Night<br>• Attend "Benton Family Night" at the library<br>• Volunteer to help PTA at the Sock Hop<br>• Attend a PTA meeting | • Have breakfast or lunch with your child at school<br>• Contribute treats to your child's classroom winter party<br>• Provide a family photo for the "Benton Family Bulletin Board" at school | • Go on your choice of a family outing<br>• Eat dinner together as a family and discuss each person's day<br>• Play a card or board game together<br>• Work on a homework assignment together |
| Third trimester | • Attend McTeacher's Night (fundraiser with McDonalds)<br>• Attend Math Night<br>• Volunteer or contribute food for the Festival of the Arts<br>• Attend Honors Day assembly<br>• Be a parent helper on Field Day | • \Have breakfast or lunch with your child at school<br>• Attend Benton Family night at CiCi's Pizza<br>• Go to the library and check out a book together<br>• Provide a family photo for the "Benton Family Bulletin Board" at school | • Open ended: requires family to generate an activity to do together outside the school day |

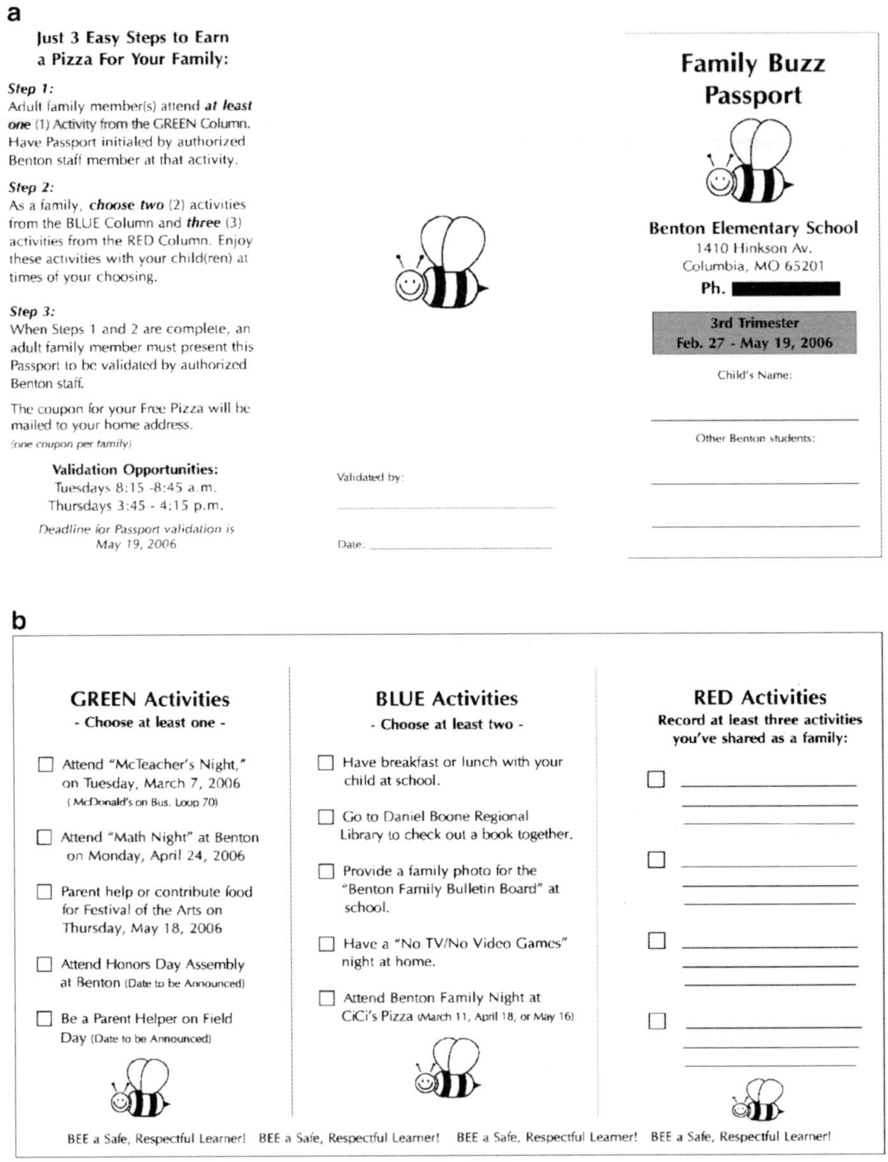

a

**Just 3 Easy Steps to Earn a Pizza For Your Family:**

*Step 1:*
Adult family member(s) attend ***at least one*** (1) Activity from the GREEN Column. Have Passport initialed by authorized Benton staff member at that activity.

*Step 2:*
As a family, ***choose two*** (2) activities from the BLUE Column and ***three*** (3) activities from the RED Column. Enjoy these activities with your child(ren) at times of your choosing.

*Step 3:*
When Steps 1 and 2 are complete, an adult family member must present this Passport to be validated by authorized Benton staff.

The coupon for your Free Pizza will be mailed to your home address.
*(one coupon per family)*

**Validation Opportunities:**
Tuesdays 8:15 -8:45 a.m.
Thursdays 3:45 - 4:15 p.m.

*Deadline for Passport validation is May 19, 2006*

Validated by:

Date:

**Family Buzz Passport**

**Benton Elementary School**
1410 Hinkson Av.
Columbia, MO 65201
**Ph.**

**3rd Trimester**
**Feb. 27 - May 19, 2006**

Child's Name:

Other Benton students:

b

**GREEN Activities**
**- Choose at least one -**

- ☐ Attend "McTeacher's Night," on Tuesday, March 7, 2006 (McDonald's on Bus. Loop 70)
- ☐ Attend "Math Night" at Benton on Monday, April 24, 2006
- ☐ Parent help or contribute food for Festival of the Arts on Thursday, May 18, 2006
- ☐ Attend Honors Day Assembly at Benton (Date to be Announced)
- ☐ Be a Parent Helper on Field Day (Date to be Announced)

**BLUE Activities**
**- Choose at least two -**

- ☐ Have breakfast or lunch with your child at school.
- ☐ Go to Daniel Boone Regional Library to check out a book together.
- ☐ Provide a family photo for the "Benton Family Bulletin Board" at school.
- ☐ Have a "No TV/No Video Games" night at home.
- ☐ Attend Benton Family Night at CiCi's Pizza (March 11, April 18, or May 16)

**RED Activities**
**Record at least three activities you've shared as a family:**

- ☐
- ☐
- ☐
- ☐

BEE a Safe, Respectful Learner! BEE a Safe, Respectful Learner! BEE a Safe, Respectful Learner! BEE a Safe, Respectful Learner!

**Fig. 15.1.** Benton Elementary Family Passport, Trimester 3.

the continuum relative to family supports to serve as a guide for increasing levels of interaction between schools and families along the three-tier continuum (see Fig. 15.2). The matrix delineates key outcomes across the continuum relative to family support as well as targets for educator implementation to reach family participation outcomes. Similarly developed local matrices should be developed by SW-PBS teams with family input and disseminated across the school staff to illustrate the connect points to family supports, foster awareness, and identify needed strategies to reach desired outcomes.

Matrix for Family Involvement: Family Resource Developers (FRD) and Parents/Caregivers*

| | Phase I | Phase II | Phase III |
|---|---|---|---|
| Primary/ Universal | **FRD:**<br>- FRD attends 75% of team meetings<br>- FRD participates in the development of the schoolwide expectations and strategies<br>- FRD provides in-service training for LSC, parents, and other community groups<br>- FRD becomes familiar with baseline data<br>**Parents/Caregivers:**<br>- Attend in-service presented by FRD on System of Care – Chicago PBIS model<br>- Participate in a focused discussion to establish congruence between parent/ caregiver expectations and schoolwide expectations<br>- Discuss schoolwide expectations with their children and their support for these behaviors | **FRD:**<br>- Reviews data trends with team and assists with identification of appropriate strategies<br>- FRD develops periodic updates/ progress reports for LSC, parents and caregivers<br>- FRD, in conjunction with parents/ caregivers, assists the team to support parent-led initiatives<br>- FRD recruits parents to implement the strategies within the school<br>**Parents/ Caregivers:**<br>- Implement strategies developed by the team<br>- Develop parent initiatives<br>- Participate on the Universal Team<br>- Parents/caregivers begin to establish ongoing linkages and supports with each other<br>- Parents/caregivers, in conjunction with the MHP, begin to develop linkages to community resources | **FRD:**<br>- FRD reviews Time 1 and Time 2 data with team and participates in priority setting (based upon parent/caregiver input) and decision making<br>- FRD supports parents/caregivers to work with targeted and intensive teams<br>- FRD seeks out community-based supports and resources aligned with the school's efforts<br>- FRD provides updates and information to parents/caregivers and parent organizations<br>**Parents/ Caregivers:**<br>- Provide information for FRD on priorities and issues<br>- Provide necessary information regarding the community's cultural values, beliefs, and practices<br>- Join the work with the targeted and intensive teams<br>- Actively engage community and faith-based supports for the school's efforts |

**Fig. 15.2**. (continued)

**Fig. 15.2**. (continued)

| | Phase I | Phase II | Phase III |
|---|---|---|---|
| Secondary/ Targeted | **FRD:**<br>- Participates in targeted team meetings<br>- Participates in plans for targeted students and provides input based on the family perspective<br>- Informs the development of targeted strategies based on their personal experiences with a child with behavioral challenges<br>- Helps provide supports for the target teachers<br>**Parents/Caregivers:**<br>- Develop a working understanding of what a targeted team is and does<br>- Support targeted team efforts with their children | **FRD:**<br>- FRD participates in the team and helps refine the utility of the behavior plans<br>- FRD continues to update the LSC, parents/caregivers, and parent groups<br>- FRD identifies community resources in support of the targeted plans<br>**Parents/Caregivers:**<br>- Begin to attend targeted team meetings<br>- Share suggestions on effective behavior management techniques<br>- Reinforce desired behaviors in the home setting where appropriate<br>- Provide support and training for other parents whose children might be experiencing similar challenges<br>- Develop a respect for and an understanding of the importance of confidentiality including policies and procedures the agency and school utilize | **FRD:**<br>- Agency works with the FRD to identify resources and supports for parents/caregivers whose children are targeted for intervention<br>- Agency and school work with FRD to refine their parent involvement plans based on the experiences of parents/ caregivers and their children<br>- FRD reports to agency board and LSC on progress of targeted teams to aid in policy development and the identification of possible funding sources to develop needed resources<br>- FRD shares their school experiences with agency staff to inform their work with other schools in the community<br>**Parents/Caregivers:**<br>- Participate in the development and implementation of targeted interventions<br>- Provide necessary information regarding the family's cultural values, beliefs, and practices<br>- Provide ongoing support for other parents whose children are receiving targeted interventions<br>- Encourage other parents/ caregivers to become involved in the targeted team process |

| | | |
|---|---|---|
| - participates, at the request of parents or caregivers, on some child and family wraparound teams<br>- provides education for parents on the wraparound process<br>- works to engage families identified for the wraparound planning process<br>- supports the parent's or caregiver's self/family/child advocacy efforts | - participates on all wraparound teams<br>- provides crisis support as determined by the wraparound plan<br>- plans and implements strategies as determined by the wraparound<br>- reviews data at each team meeting to determine the efficacy of strategies and suggests additional interventions as necessary<br>- provides education for parent organizations, LSC, and PTO (parent-teacher organization) on the wraparound process | - convenes wraparounds and facilitates the planning process for identified youth and their families<br>- provides support to parents who are beginning to facilitate their own wraparound team<br>- collects outcome data used to review the efficacy of the wraparound plan<br>- surveys families at the intensive level regarding the level of family voice evident during the wraparound planning process |
| **Parents/Caregivers**<br>- participates on their child's wraparound team<br>- identifies key members for the wraparound team<br>- identifies strengths and needs in order to develop the wraparound plan<br>- offers suggestions to the team based on their unique perspective and knowledge of their child | **Parents/Caregivers**<br>- collects and reviews outcome data to determine the effectiveness of strategies implemented by the wraparound plan<br>- educates the team regarding strategies or interventions that are most acceptable to family members<br>- advocates for the child's needs with other team members | **Parents/Caregivers**<br>- facilitates a wraparound team on behalf of their child and family<br>- facilitates a wraparound team on behalf of an identified child and family<br>- collects outcome data used to review the efficacy of the wraparound plan<br>- participates on the wraparound planning teams of other identified children<br>- encourages other families to become involved with the wraparound planning process |

Eber, L. (2005) for the New York School-wide Positive Behavior Support Initiative, available at pbis.org
LSC = Local School Council
PBIS = Positive Behavior Interventions and Supports
MHP= Mental Health Professional

**Fig. 15.2.** New York State positive behavior support (PBS) family involvement matrix available at pbis.org.

Extending the process of SW-PBS to family participation, school teams should continually self-assess their efforts to promote awareness as well as involvement and support. The appendix provides the *Family Engagement Checklist* (Muscott & Mann, 2004) as an exemplar that addresses awareness, involvement, and support. Using a similar format as other SW-PBS school-based tools such as the Effective Behavior Support (pbis.org), educators can use the tool to determine what is currently in place and, equally important, what is not consistently in place for purposes of action planning. The assignment of priority per individual items can also be used by school teams to identify critical components deemed necessary across the school to reach outcomes. The tool can be used as a self-assessment or completed by an external SW-PBS facilitator to provide an independent measure of meeting family participation goals.

## Secondary/Targeted Supports

The focus at the secondary/targeted level of the continuum is on supporting students whose needs require intervention beyond primary supports to be successful and those who are at risk. Secondary-level strategies are targeted in response to student need beyond primary supports but not highly individualized. Secondary strategies are grounded and linked to primary supports and may include practices such as small-group social skills, academic support, self-management, peer tutoring, or working with an adult mentor (Lewis, Newcomer, Trussell, & Richter, 2006). At the secondary support level, the emphasis in family participation shifts from awareness to "involvement" and indirect supports.

### *Awareness*

The focus of awareness activities should include three considerations. The first is information regarding which practices the school typically puts in place to support students at this level of the continuum. Second, referral points and data decision rules to identify students who may benefit from secondary supports should be explained. Finally, information should be shared regarding the family members' role in development and implementation of secondary supports.

### *Involvement*

Involvement of family members within secondary supports should be the primary focal point of SW-PBS team activities. School teams should develop policy and practices to include the following three steps: First, schools should establish a consent process to inform families that their child has been identified to receive additional supports. While secondary strategies typically advocated within SW-PBS systems are those that are commonly used in educational environments, parents/guardians should be informed of the school efforts. School teams should (a) consult their district policy regarding parent/guardian consent and (b) clearly differentiate supporting students at the secondary SW-PBS level from starting the process for possible referral to special education if a disability is suspected.

Within the consent form, school teams should extend an invitation to parents/guardians to participate in the initial information-gathering problem-solving meeting (Dunlap, Newton, Fox, Benito, & Vaughn, 2001; Koegel et al., 2005). During the planning meeting to determine which supports are appropriate for the child, encourage the family members also to share strengths of the child beyond the concerns that brought the child to the attention of the PBS team (Lucyshyn, Horner, et al., 2002).

The final target for increasing involvement is scheduling follow-up meetings and outcome sharing. The latter point is especially relevant in that educators often involve family members when there is a problem but are remiss to share outcomes when improvements occur.

### *Support*

Regardless of the level of family involvement in the planning and implementation of secondary supports, strategies to develop home-school partnerships focusing on improved outcomes should be explored. At this level of the continuum, the focus should be on providing the family with easy generalization strategies to provide additional practice opportunities at home. For example, the school team could enlist family members to sign self-monitoring sheets in which the student self-reports use of key social skills. The team may offer suggested family activities to increase their involvement with their child (see Table 15.2 for example activities from the Family Passport). Similar to the basic strategy of providing secondary supports for students, the foci of supports for families are matched to need but not highly individualized. In other words, follow-along strategies to support families within the home can follow general case strategies mapped back to the school-based strategy without individualized specificity.

## Tertiary/Intensive Supports

Tertiary/intensive supports are provided for those students who continue to display high rates of academic and social problems while primary and secondary supports are in place or those whose problem behaviors are severe and chronic. Students who need an intensive level of supports within the school also may need additional supports beyond the educational setting, such as mental health services; however, school teams should continue to work within their expertise and continue to stress an instructional focus. Individual PBS plans should be guided by a functional behavioral assessment. Once a hypothesis is developed about what occasions or maintains problem behavior, replacement behaviors that both connect with the larger schoolwide set of expectations and can serve as functional equivalents for the student should be taught (Newcomer & Lewis, 2004). The critical next step in developing and implementing successful function-based interventions is altering the environment to prevent the problem behavior from accessing the previous outcome while simultaneously providing high rates of reinforcement for the replacement behavior. For schools that have primary supports firmly in place, including classroom-level supports, the environmental modifications necessary for the success of individual plans simply become an extension of the primary system (i.e., clear expectations, consistent feedback, and high rates of reinforcement).

For schools that do not have primary supports in place, the impact of the individual plan will be minimized due to the lack of consistent control across the school environment. In other words, if the school or classroom environment is inconsistent, nonresponsive to demonstrated prosocial behavior on the student's part, and primarily relying on reactive and negative strategies in an attempt to control behavior, an individualized function-based PBS plan has little chance of successfully changing student behavior. The same can be said for the home environment (Singer et al., 2002). Therefore, the primary focus of family participation in the SW-PBS process now shifts to "support," while continuing to feature awareness and involvement. Similar to adopting an instructional approach to address intensive behavioral challenges, educators should continue to keep an instructional focus as they attempt to support families through strategies such as parent training, extensions of school function-based interventions, and educating parents/guardians to access and utilize related services that may benefit their child.

As stated in the introduction to this chapter, numerous publications (e.g., Lucyshyn & Albin, 1993; Lucyshyn, Dunlap, et al., 2002; Lucyshyn & Albin, 1993) and resources exist relative to working with families at the individual student level (e.g., state and regional parent training and information [PTI] centers and community parent resource centers [CPRCs; http://taalliance.org]; Center for Effective Collaboration and Practice [CECP; http://cecp.air.org]; National Alliance on Mental Illness [NAMI; http://nami.org]). Interested readers are encouraged to consult these and other resources in their planning. The focus in the remainder of this section is on best practices found within the literature that have demonstrated outcomes within tertiary supports as well as making connections to the larger SW-PBS system and following the basic instructional logic of SW-PBS.

### *Awareness*

Awareness activities include disseminating information about family rights and service entitlement (e.g., Individuals With Disabilities Education Act [IDEA], Americans With Disabilities Act, mental health services) and steps families can take to access services or express concerns. School teams should also conduct awareness trainings for school staff relative to the impact of risk factors on family functioning and understanding disabi-lities relative to family interactions. Information dissemination and awareness training sessions should be linked to the larger SW-PBS system. For example, in reviewing risk factors with school personnel, show how facets along the continuum can serve as protective factors that buffer risk. Likewise, underscore the importance of consistently using primary support strategies for students who are receiving individual supports. Similarly, inform parents/guardians of the continuum of supports in place within the school to increase the likelihood of success of all individual strategies.

An additional awareness activity at the individual level is targeting related agencies and service providers. The goal should be to reach understanding of school and agency foci, connect points along the continuum, and provide a common language to use when working with families.

### *Involvement*

Involvement should focus on building partnerships with families to assist them in supporting their child and assist school personnel in deepening the understanding of the child's needs from the family's perspective (Boettcher et al., 2003; Dunlap et al., 2001; Frea & Kasari, 2004; Marshall & Mirenda, 2002; Minke & Anderson, 2005; Vaughn et al., 2005). Further considerations are offered next relative to supports. An additional involvement outcome at the individual student level is to increase representation of families with children who require individual/intensive supports on school teams or through related ad hoc committees. For example, including a parent or guardian of a child with a disability or an advocate for children and youth with disabilities on the school or district team should be considered.

### *Support*

The primary focus of family participation at the individual level should be on supports. The desired outcome is to engage in collaborative planning and intervention implementation with the family to address their child's social and academic challenges. As underscored throughout this chapter, education's role should continue to emphasize connect points to instructional supports and work toward educating families. Educators should not assume roles in which they have not been trained, such as counselor, social worker, or legal advocate. Rather, educators should assume the role as family advocate and educate families about their options, facilitate access to external service, and foster connections between external service agencies, the family, and school (Lucyshyn, Dunlap, et al., 2002).

The first level of support offered should focus on the development and implementation of individual behavioral support plans. Parents/ guardians should be invited to be active participants in the planning process. The invitation should be shaped to express the school's desire to assist their child to be successful in school versus a threat that things must change for their child to remain in school. Within the process, a strength-based problem-solving logic should be emphasized (Frea & Kasari, 2004; Koegel et al., 2005; Marshall & Mirenda, 2002; Minke & Anderson, 2005; Vaughn et al., 2006). Focus on which social skills the child currently possesses and which additional skills are needed, along with the instructional and environmental supports that will be necessary to achieve the improvements. In addition, develop simple strategies that can be used in the home to promote generalization of the school-based targeted skills.

The next level of support should focus on fostering interagency collaborations. Ideally, the SW-PBS core set of expectations serves as the nexus for each service provider to provide a common language and key behavioral outcomes. The final level of support educators should consider

Essential Features of Foster School-Family Partnerships at the Tertiary/ Individual Student Level

1. Build collaborative partnerships with families and other professionals who serve the child or youth with a disability.
2. Adhere to family-centered principles and practices throughout assessment, support plan development, and implementation of support activities.
3. Help families identify and achieve meaningful lifestyle outcomes for their child with a disability and the family as a whole.
4. Recognize that problem behaviors are primarily problems of learning.
5. Understand that communication is the foundation of positive behavior.
6. Conduct functional assessments to understand the functions of problem behavior and the variables that influence behavior and to improve the effectiveness and efficiency of behavior support plans.
7. Develop individualized, multicomponent support plans that help families create effective family contexts in which problem behaviors are irrelevant, ineffective, and inefficient at achieving their purpose.
8. Ensure that positive behavior support (PBS) plans are a good contextual fit with family life.
9. Utilize the family activity setting as a unit of analysis and intervention that can help families embed interventions into family life.
10. Provide implementation support that is tailored to family needs and preferences.
11. Engage in a process of continuous evaluation of child and family outcomes.
12. Offer support to families, professionals, and other members of a support team in a spirit of sincerity and humility.

**Fig. 15.3.** Essential features to foster school/family partnerships at the individual student level. Adapted from "Positive Behavior Support With Families," by J. M. Lucyshyn, R. H. Horner, G. Dunlap, R. W. Albin, &K. Ben, 2002, in J. M. Lucyshyn, G. Dunlap, & R. W. Albin (Eds.), Families and Positive Behavior Support, Baltimore: Brookes, p. 13.

is to provide training or technical assistance to families. Support at this level takes the shape of providing families with strategies to manage behavior in the home or promoting academic achievement. Support at this level can include formal training, fostering parent support groups, as well as providing informal assistance through suggestions or sending home support materials.

Across the secondary and tertiary levels of family participation, the emphasis shifts from keeping families informed to increasing their involvement with the school in an effort to increase the success of behavioral and academic interventions. While "involvement" and "support" will require educators to expand their focus beyond the school, educators are strongly encouraged to retain an instructional focus in their approach to working with families. Lucyshyn, Horner et al. (2002) summarized this expanded instructional focus through 12 key considerations to build connections with families (Fig. 15.3).

## CONCLUSION

The purpose of this chapter was to propose a framework for increasing beneficial family participation across the continuum of SW-PBS. Building on PBS work conducted at the individual level and general SW-PBS strategies, a call was made for school teams to develop their own definition of family participation using three outcomes at each level of the continuum. First, schools should target family awareness of student outcomes and supports provided at the primary, secondary, and tertiary levels of support. Likewise, schools should target awareness on the part of school personnel relative to the impacts children and youth with disabilities and those at risk have on family function. Second, schools should strive to increase family involvement within the educational process across school and home environments. At the primary level of support, the emphasis is on increasing family presence in the school environment. At the secondary and tertiary levels, the emphasis shifts to increasing family participation in the planning and implementation of behavioral and academic supports. Third, schools should strive to increase supports to all families, from information dissemination and awareness activities at the primary level to active partnering at the secondary and tertiary levels.

The theme throughout this chapter has been the fostering of active participation on behalf of educators and families to increase academic and social success among all children and youth. While much work remains on empirically validating strategies to increase family participation at each level, schools can use the well-established literature base on supporting individual students as well as recent descriptive work. In addition to referring to the professional literature and looking toward advocacy groups and technical assistance centers, the field should put equal stock in the voices of parents. In a recent series of articles focusing on families and PBS, several recommendations were offered from parents of children with disabilities who have been actively advocating PBS within their children's schools. The following list paraphrases some of their recommendations and is offered in support of educators' current efforts to establish SW-PBS (Fisher, 2000; Johnson, 2000):

- All educators who work with children should also strive to equally support the family.
- To provide more timely service and supports, education should divorce "early intervention" from "early diagnosis."
- Given the lag and their quickly growing children, service providers should work toward shortening the gap between research and practice.
- Researchers and policy makers should work toward ensuring all educators understand PBS.

As emphasized within SW- PBS, a set of ready-made steps to address academic and social behavior challenges does not exist. However, a process of using data to drive decisions and evaluate outcomes, carefully matching research-based practices to identified needs, and creating systemic support to assist school personnel in implementation efforts significantly increases the likelihood of improved student outcomes. This same "process" shows promise in increasing family participation in schools, educator supports in the home, or the achievement of partnerships to support children and youth and their families. At the same time, school teams should proceed with caution given the limited empirical work to date. Researchers should also heed this caution and begin to extend their work from the individual student, family, school connect point to the larger schoolwide system of supports, including the preventive effect the primary level of supports may have on both children and youth and their families.

## REFERENCES


Ballard-Krishan, S. A., McClure, L., Schmatz, B., Travnikar, B., Friedrich, G., & Nolan, M. (2003). The Michigan PBS initiative: Advancing the spirit of collaboration by including parents in the delivery of personnel development opportunities. *Journal of Positive Behavior Interventions, 5,* 122–126.

Boettcher, M., Koegel, R. L., McNerney, E. K., & Koegel, L. K. (2003). A family-centered prevention approach to PBS in a time of crisis. *Journal of Positive Behavior Interventions, 5,* 55–59.

Dunlap, G., Newton, J. S., Fox, L., Benito, N., & Vaughn, B. (2001). Family involvement in functional assessment and positive behavior support. *Focus on Autism and Other Developmental Disabilities, 16,* 215–221.

Fisher, C. (2000). Ripple or tidal wave: What can make a difference? *Journal of Positive Behavior Interventions, 2,* 120–122.

Fox, L., Vaughn, B. J., Wyatte, M. L., & Dunlap, G. (2002). "We can't expect other people to understand": Family perspectives on problem behavior. *Exceptional Children, 68,* 437–450.

Frea, W. D., & Kasari, C. (2004). Families and positive behavior support: Addressing problem behaviors in family context. *American Journal on Mental Retardation, 109,* 264–265.

Johnson, C. (2000). What do families need? *Journal of Positive Behavior Interventions, 2,* 115–117.

Koegel, L. K., Koegel, R. L., Boettcher, M., & Brookman-Frazee, L. (2005). Extending behavior support in home and community settings. In L. M. Bambara & L. Kern (Eds.), *Individualized supports for students with problem behaviors: Designing positive behavior support plans* (pp. 334–358). New York: Guilford Press.

Lewis, T. J. (2007, March). *Increasing family participation in school activities through school-wide positive behavior support.* Invited presentation at the Fourth International Conference on Positive Behavior Support, Association of Positive Behavior Support, Boston.

Lewis, T. J., & Lewis, L. (2006, October). *Essential features of individual systems of support: Data, practices, and systems.* Presentation at the Third Annual School-wide PBS Implementation Forum, Chicago.

Lewis, T. J., Newcomer, L., Trussell, R., & Richter, M. (2006). School-wide positive behavior support: Building systems to develop and maintain appropriate social behavior. In C. S. Everston & C. M. Weinstein (Eds.), *Handbook of classroom Management: Research, practice and contemporary issues* (pp. 833–854). New York: Erlbaum.

Lewis, T. J., & Sugai, G. (1999). Effective behavior support: A systems approach to proactive school-wide management. *Focus on Exceptional Children, 31*(6), 1–24.

Lucyshyn, J. M., & Albin, R. W. (1993). Comprehensive support to families of children with disabilities and behavior problems: Keeping it "friendly." In G. H. S. Singer & L. E. Powers (Eds.), *Families, disability, and empowerment: Active coping skills and strategies for family interventions* (pp. 365–407). Baltimore: Brookes.

Lucyshyn, J. M., Dunlap, G., & Albin, R. W. (Eds.). (2002). *Families and positive behavior support.* Baltimore: Brookes.

Lucyshyn, J. M., Horner, R. H., Dunlap, G., Albin, R. W., & Ben, K. (2002). Positive behavior support with families. In J. M. Lucyshyn, G. Dunlap, & R. W. Albin (Eds.), *Families and positive behavior support* (pp. 3–44). Baltimore: Brookes.

Marshall, J. K., & Mirenda, P. (2002). Parent-professional collaboration for positive behavior support in the home. *Focus on Autism and Other Developmental Disabilities, 17,* 216–228.

Minke, K. M., & Anderson, K. (2005). Family-school collaboration and positive behavior support. *Journal of Positive Behavior Interventions, 7*, 181–185.

Muscott, H. S., & Mann, E. (2004). *Family Engagement Checklist.* Bedford: New Hampshire Center for Effective Behavioral Interventions and Supports.

Newcomer, L. L. & Lewis, T. J. (2004). Functional behavioral assessment: An investigation of assessment reliability and effectiveness of function-based interventions. *Journal of Emotional and Behavioral Disorders, 12*, 168–181.

Singer, G. H. S., Goldberg-Hamblin, S. E., Peckham-Hardin, K. D., Barry, L., & Santarelli, G. E. (2002). In J. M. Lucyshyn, G. Dunlap, & R. W. Albin (Eds.), *Families and positive behavior support* (pp. 155–183). Baltimore: Brookes.

Smith-Bird, E., Turnbull, A. P., & Koegel, R. L. (2005). Linking positive behavior support to family quality-of-life outcomes. *Journal of Positive Behavior Interventions, 7*, 174–180.

Sugai, G., Horner, R. H., Dunlap, G., Hieneman, M., Lewis, T. J., Nelson, C. M., et al. (2000). Applying positive behavior support and functional behavioral assessment in schools. *Journal of Positive Behavior Interventions, 2*, 131–143.

Vaughn, B. J., White, R., Johnston, S., & Dunlap, G. (2005). Positive behavior support as a family-centered endeavor. *Journal of Positive Behavior Interventions, 27*, 55–58.

Zins, J. E., & Ponti, C. R. (1990). Best practices in school-based consultation. In A. Thomas and J. Grimes (Eds.), *Best practices in school psychology—II* (pp. 673–694). Washington, DC: National Association of School Psychologists.

# 16

# Primary-Tier Interventions and Supports

**HEATHER PESHAK GEORGE, DON KINCAID, and JENNA POLLARD-SAGE**

## INTRODUCTION AND RATIONALE

Recent media attention has focused on a number of violent acts that have threatened the safety of students on school campuses across the United States (Institute of Education Sciences, 2007). Focus on such violent incidences on school campuses has led to an increased use of security cameras, metal detectors, and locked and barred windows and doors, thus creating a false sense of security (Dufresne & Dorn, 2005; M. J. Mayer & Leone, 1999). In addition, education systems have a long and ineffective history with the use of punitive measures, compulsory attendance, corporal punishment, and reactionary procedures to address student problem behavior (Aucoin, Frick, & Bodin, 2006; Yell, Rogers, & Lodge-Rodgers, 1998). This state of education has also led to an increased use of zero tolerance and "one strike, you're out" policies that have not increased safety on school campuses by students or staff (Anderson & Kincaid, 2005; M. J. Mayer & Leone, 1999).

Understanding that these policies and procedures are not ameliorating the issue of violence in schools, national school reform and federal legislation have moved toward the promotion of prevention models. The Individuals With Disabilities Education Act (IDEA; 2004) and No Child Left Behind (NCLB; 2001) legislation advocate for the use of research-based preventive models. IDEA legislation recognizes whole-school approaches and early intervention as keys to making the education of children with disabilities more effective. IDEA also focuses on developing positive

**HEATHER PESHAK GEORGE** • University of South Florida
**DON KINCAID** • University of South Florida
**JENNA POLLARD-SAGE** • University of South Florida

programming that leads to meaningful improvements in students' lives. This whole-school approach also supports standards of NCLB legislation by focusing on the success of every child and making appropriate accommodations. As a result, schools continue to search for approaches to assist in creating whole-school systems change and supporting students across settings, behaviors, and skill levels.

Positive behavior support (PBS) is one such collaborative, assessment-based approach to developing effective interventions for problem behavior. PBS emphasizes the use of preventive, teaching, and reinforcement-based strategies to achieve meaningful and durable behavior and lifestyle outcomes (Lewis & Sugai, 1999; Sugai & Horner, 2002; Sugai et al., 2005). Schoolwide PBS (SW-PBS) is the application of evidence-based strategies and systems to assist schools to increase academic performance, increase safety, decrease problem behavior, and establish positive school cultures (Florida's Positive Behavior Support Project, 2007). The core elements of PBS reinforce legislation focused on prevention-based strategies that support all students within a school. The foundation of PBS utilizes strategies that ameliorate the need for extensive reactionary measures that result in the overuse of ineffective policies such as those described (Anderson & Kincaid, 2005; Sailor et al., 2006). PBS is a system of processes and procedures that aims to build effective environments in which positive behavior is more effective than problem behavior.

PBS promotes a three-tier model of prevention, derived from over 50 years of research in applied behavior analysis as well as research from the public health domain (Carr et al., 2002; Sugai & Horner, 2002; Sugai et al., 2000). The foundational tier of PBS, the universal/primary tier, is designed to have an impact on 80–90% of the students and staff across settings on a school campus, with supports and interventions designed to create successful and safe environments. With a whole-school approach and universal/primary-level interventions, there is a foundation for a majority of students to engage in an effective system, thereby creating more meaningful and lasting change. Implementation of the primary tier of PBS within a school is one effective method to prevent problem behavior and academic failure at all academic levels, preschool through high school. This prevention level of PBS may be referred to as primary, universal, tier 1, or even SW-PBS. For purposes of this chapter, the term *primary tier* refers to this foundational level of PBS intended to have an impact on the behavior of all students in all settings.

This primary tier is of critical importance in that it establishes the safe and efficient environment in which effective teaching and learning can occur. The primary tier can best be considered as the "core curriculum" for teaching behavior, just as a school may have a core curriculum for reading, math, and so on. An effective PBS core curriculum at the primary tier has the potential to prevent the development of more serious problem behaviors in both typical and "at-risk" students and ensure continued academic growth in students. In addition to these academic and behavioral outcomes, the primary tier has an added resource and fiscal impact. A preventive approach that effectively impacts the behavior of 80–90% of students can decrease the use of more expensive and time-consuming interventions at the secondary and tertiary tiers of SW-PBS. Without first establishing implementation fidelity at the primary tier, interventions introduced at the secondary or tertiary tiers may have a higher likelihood of failure due to a poor foundation on which they are implemented (Carr, 2006). Behaviors are often setting specific and often do not generalize across settings (i.e., from classroom instruction to cafeteria behavior) (Ferro & Dunlap, 1993; Dunlap, 1993). For example, comprehensive and functional behavior intervention plans (BIPs) that are created based on functional behavior assessments (FBAs) only address those issues specific to the setting in which they occur (i.e., the classroom). The difficulty persists when the student interacts with multiple teachers and noninstructional staff across multiple settings on a school campus. If systems are not arranged to support individual BIPs as well as the teaching of expected behaviors for all students across multiple staff and in multiple settings, the comprehensive plan is thereby ineffective and does not create a positive environment for that student, the student's peers, and school staff. A whole-school systems approach must be present for a large percentage of the students and staff at a school to be successful in academics and behavior.

This chapter describes the implementation process and the practice components of the primary tier of PBS that are applied within any school. The core elements of SW-PBS serve as the "blueprint" for the primary tier of the implementation process (Sugai et al., 2005). These elements are designed for organizing structures and supports for the adults (i.e., practitioners, educators, school psychologists, administrators, etc.) to implement the primary tier with fidelity, consistency, and sustainability and to successfully expand SW-PBS throughout the three-tier continuum. The elements include (a) development of a leadership team, (b) coordination of efforts, (c) funding issues and opportunities, (d) visibility and public relations, (e) political support, (f) training capacity, (g) coaching capacity, (h) demonstration sites, and (i) evaluation. Following a discussion of this implementation process, the chapter focuses on the primary-tier practice components. The chapter concludes with future directions for SW-PBS and how to proceed with new initiatives and policies, including the integration of response to intervention (RTI).

## PRIMARY-TIER IMPLEMENTATION PROCESS

The goal for a school undergoing change at the primary-tier level is to create a cohesive and efficient system of behavioral support. The nine core elements of SW-PBS provide structure to this section of the chapter; emphasis is placed on the implementation process of the primary tier at the school level and focus on the structures and supports needed for the adults as agents of systems change.

### Leadership Team

Establishing a PBS leadership team on campus provides the vision, leadership, and resources necessary for initiating and sustaining primary-tier interventions in a school. Research indicates the three most critical variables to the success of the primary tier are administrator commitment, staff buy-in, and leadership team functioning, with team functioning the most critical (Cohen, 2005). That said, the success of the primary-tier plan will be a result of the leadership team's commitment to the process. Therefore, the individuals who are selected to actively participate on the leadership team must be carefully chosen, dedicated to long-term systems change, well-respected among colleagues, and involved in the development, implementation, and monitoring of the primary-tier plan.

The leadership team should consider representatives from administration, general and special education, guidance, specials areas, parents, and student support services (i.e., school psychologist, behavior specialist, social worker, etc.). To build continuity and enhance cohesiveness across initiatives, some school advisory council or school improvement team members should also actively serve on the PBS leadership team. It is best to keep the team to no more than six to eight members, thus enhancing a higher likelihood of follow-through on action plan items. If the school has a large number of faculty (i.e., a high school), the PBS leadership team may want to consider forming two teams: a core and a peripheral team. The goal of the core team is to complete established activities, whereas the peripheral team works to gain buy-in, provides feedback, and provides additional resources (when necessary). The ongoing, overall tasks of the PBS leadership team at the primary-tier level include

1. Developing an action plan.
2. Monitoring and analyzing existing behavior data.
3. Holding regular team meetings (at least monthly).
4. Maintaining communication with staff and PBS coach/facilitator.
5. Evaluating progress.
6. Reporting outcomes to staff, students, parents, PBS coach/facilitator, and PBS district coordinator.

Teams must have clearly identified roles and responsibilities to function effectively and efficiently. For the team to adequately address these tasks, individual members are selected or volunteer to assume roles that may include team leader, recorder, timekeeper, data specialist, behavior specialist, administrator, communications specialist, PBS coach, and snack master.

## Establishing a Foundation for Collaboration, Operations, and Faculty Buy-In

After establishing a PBS leadership team and prior to implementing the primary tier, the team must first determine the following: (a) Is there a problem that we need to address? (b) What is the nature of this problem? (c) Do we want to do anything about it? and (d) What are we going to do about it? By establishing a foundation for collaboration and operations (i.e., forming a PBS leadership team, developing a schoolwide communication system, and revising procedures on campus), the team is initiating long-term change and enhancing sustainability. In addressing the first question, the team investigates current programs and identifies the procedures and policies in place; examines existing committees that address behavioral concerns (e.g., discipline, safety, social skills, anger management, peer mediation/mentoring, etc.); reviews any existing data (office referrals, suspensions, expulsions, etc.) that may indicate a significant problem exists; and surveys the faculty, parents, and students for areas of discontent and suggestions for improvement on campus. It is essential that the team develops a solid understanding of the issues and determines the level of interest across faculty to address those issues. This can be established through staff surveys, which can promote effective change if the PBS leadership team takes steps to modify the primary-tier system/plan based on staff feedback.

Since the faculty and staff are critical stakeholders in the success of the primary-tier plan, it is essential that they are committed to decreasing problem behaviors and increasing academics across campus. Teams face challenges with systemic change when any of the following occurs: The reasons for change are not perceived as compelling enough; faculty and staff feel a lack of ownership in the process; insufficient modeling occurs from the leadership team or administration; faculty and staff lack a clear vision of how the changes will have an impact on them personally; and an insufficient system of support exists. Addressing or preventing these issues assists the team in moving forward and implementing a schoolwide system of support. Possible solutions to prevent resistance include

1. Develop a common understanding across all faculty and staff.
2. Enlist leaders with integrity, authority, resources, and willingness to assist.
3. Expect, respect, and respond to resistance (i.e., encourage questions and open discussion).
4. Clarify how changes will align with other initiatives.
5. Emphasize clear and imminent consequences for not changing.
6. Emphasize the benefits (conservation of time and efforts, greater professional accountability).
7. Stay in touch with peer leaders during the change process.

There are several strategies the leadership team can use to obtain the needed staff input and begin to increase staff interest. One strategy is to complete the Working Smarter Activity (University of Oregon, 2004). This activity allows the PBS team to assess which committees/work groups already exist at the school and combine efforts of those groups to increase efficiency and accountability. Another strategy is to complete a team-planning process such as Planning Alternative Tomorrows With Hope (Pearpoint, O'Brien, & Forest, 1993) to begin to solicit faculty input and build buy-in. A third strategy to solicit information and build faculty and staff buy-in is to arrange a schoolwide meeting (include all teachers, aides, administrators, office and cafeteria workers, custodians, counselors, bus drivers, etc.) to discuss the four questions mentioned. This is an efficient method to establish consensus and allows staff to respond either verbally or in writing to the questions pertaining to staff satisfaction. Conducting a staff survey is a fourth strategy for gathering staff input and commitment. When working to achieve consensus, the goal is to identify whether 80% of the school's staff members are committed to initiating the first steps in a systems change process. It is critical that all faculty and staff in the school have input to generate new ideas and to agree on which strategies will be implemented to build a sense of faculty ownership (OSEP Technical Assistance Center, 2007). For additional examples of these and other activities to establish and maintain buy-in, refer to Florida's PBS Project Web site (http://flpbs.fmhi.usf.edu).

These suggestions are not exhaustive, and additional strategies may be utilized (e.g., present school's discipline data in graphic form, a comments bulletin board/box for feedback, a faculty/staff retreat, etc.). It is important to note that all of these strategies not only will assist the PBS leadership team in collecting information and getting faculty and staff buy-in, but also will assist in maintaining buy-in and communication across campus and throughout the process of implementation. The PBS leadership team should consider establishing a process for informing the staff of changes that are being made based on feedback and comments. These strategies are critical for teams to utilize across the school year and subsequent years to sustain the established supports and continue to expand the continuum of supports available on campus.

## Coordination

The coordination of activities involved in changing the behaviors of adults and students are significant and can appear overwhelming to the PBS leadership team. The team is responsible for addressing the key elements of the implementation process and for establishing the PBS practice components with fidelity. Initially, however, the team addresses some critical coordination efforts that include establishing a data-based decision-making system, developing appropriate definitions for problem behavior, creating behavior tracking forms, developing a coherent discipline referral process, and creating effective consequences and interventions. As the process continues throughout the year, the PBS leadership team assesses the current status of behavior management practice, examines patterns of behavior, develops a primary-tier plan, obtains staff commitment, obtains parental participation and input, and oversees, monitors, and evaluates all planned objectives and activities developed.

## Funding

The PBS leadership team needs to address the issue of funding their SW-PBS initiative for both sustaining and expanding efforts within the school. Funding is for (a) primary-tier activities (e.g., posters, forms, stocking a school store, incentives, transportation for families to participate, duplication costs for tickets/tokens/dollars, etc.); (b) the salary of a data entry clerk; (c) the time provided to team members for planning; and (d) substitute teachers for team members attending local, state, and national conferences on PBS. The team investigates fund-raising activities to support primary-tier activities, expands the type of activities/incentives provided that does not incur an expense, and recruits the district and local parent-teacher association (PTA) for further assistance in this area.

Schools should address discipline, behavior, climate, safety, and so on in the school improvement plan, which may allow for access to additional monies to support primary-tier activities. Schools may also apply for "minigrants" from community partners, local universities, their state Department of Education, and their local education agency (LEA). Although these external funds can provide a boost for "startup" monies, they should be used to "boost" efforts, not create them (i.e., a school cannot become completely reliant on those funds to develop the infrastructure). When external funds disappear, the infrastructure that was once supported by them may also disappear. Therefore, it is important to utilize the funds in such a way to create systems change within the school and work to embed or reduce costs as the school becomes more proficient in delivering a system of support at the primary tier (George & Kincaid, 2008).

## Visibility

Building visibility is critical to increase awareness of the primary-tier activities, maintain communication across key stakeholders, and solicit increased interest in expanding PBS efforts throughout the school, district, and community. Dissemination efforts may include newsletters, Web sites (school, district, and state); announcements; and various media (e.g., television, newspaper, radio, fliers, etc.). The PBS leadership team develops dissemination strategies to maintain communication and participation particularly with staff, but also with students, parents, and community partners.

## Political Support

*Political support* refers to the written or verbal commitment to the primary tier that is communicated to and by school administrators, personnel, parents, and students. This may occur via faculty meetings, public board meetings, school open houses, written policies, and redistribution of resources (George & Kincaid, 2008). The administrator is a key stakeholder in the success of the primary-tier plan. Administrators can enhance team success by identifying how to free staff time for participation on the PBS leadership team, maintaining active participation, and reminding staff of the purpose, significant impact, and ultimate success that they are working to achieve on their campus. If an administrator is not committed to the change process, it is recommended that the school-based PBS leadership team not proceed until buy-in can be secured (George & Martinez, 2007).

## Training Capacity

*Training capacity* refers to establishing systems to support staff and student training. Ongoing staff training is essential in building fluency in implementing the primary-tier components. The more that implementers practice and are reminded of the primary-tier established procedures, the more likely the interventions will be delivered. Staff are trained on changes related to a data-based decision-making system (new referral forms and processes, the behaviors that are addressed at the classroom level and those referred to the office, etc.) as well as specific changes in interaction with students (how to reward or precorrect a student, classroom intervention strategies, how to teach general expectations and specific rules to students, etc.). Students are also trained on expectations, rules, the school's reward system, and the consequences of problem behaviors.

The challenge for the PBS leadership team is to plan and implement initial training and booster/retraining throughout the year for staff and students. In addition, the team plans strategies for orienting and training new staff and students throughout the year. Just as students learn academic skills through different teaching methods, the PBS leadership team utilizes a variety of teaching techniques (videos, role-playing, lecture, verbal and visual prompts, practice, etc.) as well as forums (assemblies, direct instruction, posted rules/expectations, curriculum infusion, etc.) to present the initial and ongoing training on processes and procedures at the primary tier.

## Coaching Capacity

Coaches are often school personnel who are released from some of their prior responsibilities to facilitate the participating school-based PBS Team through implementation of primary-tier activities (George & Kincaid, 2008). Coaches are selected based on their function (what they can do and what is required of them to do), not by their titles. The characteristics and responsibilities of the PBS coach include being (a) the main contact person for the school-based team and the district support; (b) familiar with the primary-tier process; (c) a facilitator to the team throughout the process (ensuring critical elements are in place); (d) an active participant and attendant at all trainings/meetings with their school-based teams; (e) available for additional training; and (f) accessible to the PBS district coordinator (if available). The PBS coach's primary function is to maintain fidelity of implementation following PBS training. Coaches must have a wide array of team facilitation and interpersonal skills in addition to understanding how the primary-tier process works on a school campus (George & Kincaid, 2008).

## Demonstrations

Leadership teams and school staff want to see examples of school products, student outcomes, and sites that are implementing with fidelity and that share common demographics with their own school (i.e., size, grade levels, socioeconomic status, and location). These demonstrations occur during initial training of the team but are often more effective after training has occurred. Teams may visit other schools implementing the primary tier or may access additional information from the Web or via phone contact.

In addition to demonstrations of similar schools, the leadership team may also seek demonstrations of the impact of a PBS process on one targeted issue or setting in the school. A demonstration of the impact of

PBS in decreasing bullying on the playground, noise in the lunchroom, or classroom tardies may provide an example to faculty about the possible impact of the primary-tier interventions if applied across all settings, staff, and students. Such demonstrations may gain the necessary staff buy-in and support for expanding the primary-tier approach within the school.

## Evaluation

PBS leadership teams need to know whether they are implementing the primary-tier process with fidelity (Are we really doing the process the way it should be done?). Then, they need to know whether they are being effective (Is what we are doing working?). Finally, the PBS leadership team needs to identify areas of strength and weakness in their plans and process (Let's celebrate our success! or In what areas do we need to improve?). Although many types of data can be used to answer these evaluation questions, the most common types of data are related to team functioning, implementation, and student/school outcomes.

Tools such as the Team Process Evaluation (http://flpbs.fmhi.usf.edu/coachescorner.asp) and the Leadership Checklist (Sugai et al., 2005) can be useful for assessing the commitment and functioning of the leadership team at the school level. Tools such as the Team Implementation Checklist (www.pbssurveys.org), the School-wide Evaluation Tool (Horner et al., 2003), the Benchmarks of Quality (Kincaid, Childs, & George, 2005), and an action plan provide important information for the team about the fidelity of their implementation efforts and the areas of success and need. An action-planning process is essential to managing the multitude of activities that must be addressed in establishing the primary-tier system. An evaluation process is necessary for determining the implementation of the primary-tier system at a given point in time, generally once each year.

Standard outcomes assessed in most primary-tier systems include behavioral data, academic performance data, and perceptual data. Behavioral data include office discipline referrals (ODRs), suspension, expulsions, referrals to special education or alternative settings, as well as attendance data. Academic performance data may include direct measures such as Dynamic Indicators of Basic Early Literacy Skills (DIBELS; 2007), curriculum-based measures, or performance on state or standardized tests of academic achievement. Indirect measures such as grade point averages, graduation rates, and dropout rates may also be measured. Finally, perceptions of staff, students, parents, and community members can be measured via school climate surveys. School climate surveys can be developed specific to the primary-tier process or may contain only a few (two to four) questions about the process embedded into an existing school survey. The results of these surveys allow the PBS leadership team to see whether all of the target groups perceive that the changes undertaken in the primary-tier process have indeed had a positive impact on the school. All of these sources of data (team process, implementation, and outcomes) provide feedback to the leadership team and serve to get and maintain buy-in and reinforce the behaviors of school personnel, students, parents, and the community.

## PRIMARY-TIER PRACTICE COMPONENTS

By establishing processes and procedures intended for *all* students, staff, and settings (i.e., schoolwide, classroom, and nonclassroom settings such as the cafeteria, hallway, and restroom), schools become proficient and proactive in preventing new cases of problem behavior from occurring. For example, many students lose instructional time when the expectations for their performance (i.e., what is expected of them behaviorally) are not defined, modeled, or practiced. By lacking a behavioral repertoire, students are more likely to create errors within their environment, whether intentional or accidental. They may be more likely to engage in problem behavior, break the rules, and so on, thus resulting in a major discipline incident (i.e., ODR).

The main practice components of primary-tier implementation include the following:

1. A committed team leading all PBS efforts (as described).
2. A method for identifying current problems through accurate data or establishing a data-based decision-making system (i.e., developing appropriate definitions for problem behavior, behavior-tracking forms, and establishing a coherent discipline referral process).
3. Procedures for discouraging violations of schoolwide expectations and rules (i.e., developing effective consequences and interventions).
4. Positively stated behavior expectations and rules.
5. Procedures for encouraging expected behaviors (i.e., establishing a reward system).
6. Lesson plans to teach the expectations and rules.
7. A plan for monitoring implementation and effectiveness.

### Establishing a Data-Based Decision-Making System

Prior to making changes within the school environment, it is important to know what needs to be changed. Information about what is happening on campus must be accurate and useful in identifying problems and strategizing the appropriate interventions to address those problems. Creating an efficient and durable data-based decision-making system is essential to develop accurate solutions and conveys professional accountability. By making decisions from accurate data, interventions are more likely to be implemented and effective. Not only is it important to collect data for accuracy in decision making, but also the data collected must be meaningful or functional and available on an ongoing basis throughout the school year to monitor student behavior change across campus.

A school must first determine the types of data that are necessary to collect. Just because data are collected does not mean that they are useful for school-based decision making. The school-based team should evaluate the information the school may already have (or to which the district has access): ODRs, suspensions, expulsions, referrals by student behavior, climate surveys, attendance, referrals to special education programs

**Table 16.1.** Identify Problems: Self-Check Form for Evaluating the Data System

| Data Entry | Data Analysis | Decision Making |
|---|---|---|
| • The data (referral forms) are easy to complete and collect.<br>• The data can be entered into the database quickly.<br>• The data are accurate and valid.<br>• There is a plan for how data are to be entered into the system. | • If necessary, data are analyzed more than once a month.<br>• Some data are analyzed more frequently to see if specific interventions are working.<br>• Student information is reviewed frequently for counseling and parent contacts.<br>• Specific behavior incidents are reviewed frequently regarding effective interventions. | • The information collected allow the team to understand the when, where, who, why, and what of problem behaviors.<br>• Data are gathered continuously.<br>• Data are an embedded part of the school cycle, not something "extra."<br>• Data are used for decision making.<br>• Data are accurate and valid.<br>• Data are easy to collect (1% of staff time).<br>• Data are summarized prior to meetings of decision makers.<br>• Data are available when decisions need to be made.<br>• Different data needs are identified at a school building versus a school district. |

Identify areas with potential for enhancement

(more restrictive environments), and the like. When analyzing these data, it is important to ask some critical questions, such as those regarding how many referrals there are per day each month, based on location, based on the type of behavior, by student, by time of day, originating from Special Education and general education and what the range of consequences provided is based on the type of behavior exhibited.

Evaluating the current data system provides the PBS leadership team at the school with direction regarding how to best gather the data and retrieve it from their current system. Table 16.1 provides a checklist to guide teams in evaluating their current discipline data system and to determine the areas that are needed for improving data-based decision making at the school level. A PBS leadership team may want to utilize SWIS™ (see http://www.swis.org for more information; May et al., 2002) to begin making effective data-based decisions at their school until a comprehensive district data-based system is well established.

### *Appropriate Definitions for Problem Behavior*

Once a system is developed that allows for accurate and reliable data-based decision making, it is essential that the data entered into the system are accurate. One method to ensure that the data are accurate is to develop appropriate definitions for problem behaviors. What one teacher may consider disrespect may not be considered disrespect to another teacher or staff member. For that reason, behaviors must be operationally defined so that referrals to the office are appropriate, and that the behavior indicated on the referral form matches the consequence or intervention to be delivered. The PBS leadership team may refer to SWIS (May et al., 2002) for a complete list of operationally defined categories of behavior that are mutually exclusive.

### *Behavior-Tracking Forms*

Once behaviors are defined, the next steps in the process are to implement a behavior-tracking system and to develop forms to assist in the process. There are two types of behavior-tracking forms to consider: classroom and office. Classroom tracking forms are for minor discipline incidents (i.e., behaviors that do not warrant ceasing instruction) that are teacher managed; these forms may also be referred to as classroom infraction forms. Minor behaviors may include tardiness to class, lack of classroom material, gum chewing, dress code violations, and the like. ODRs are for major discipline incidents that warrant a referral to the office for administrative action. These are the severe or intense incidents that must be handled by administration and may include physical fights, property damage, drugs, weapons, and other incidents.

It is important to track the minor behaviors as a history or accumulation of these behaviors can lead to a major incident as well as the discovery of patterns of behavior. Collecting these data assists in identifying effective interventions for changing the problem behavior before it results or escalates into an ODR. The minor tracking form is intended to be utilized by classroom teachers to track one specific recurring behavior, document "what is working," and gain insight regarding "why the behavior is occurring." By identifying the patterns of the minor behavior (i.e., conducting a "mini" FBA) the teacher can work to prevent the behavior from occurring, teach a replacement or more appropriate behavior and encourage the desired behavior by utilizing the schoolwide reward system developed.

Just as it is important to track the minor behaviors to prevent future problems from occurring, it is just as important to track the major behaviors to provide appropriate interventions, initiate a possible functional assessment, and work to prevent a more restrictive placement. It is important that the major referral forms address the following: who, what, where, when, and why. A form that captures the information derived from these assists the administrator in determining the consequence that "matches" the behavior (effective consequences and interventions are also discussed in this section) and in delivering an effective intervention to prevent the behavior from occurring in the future. In addition, a coherent form that is easy to complete will increase the likelihood that the information entered onto the form and into a database are accurate. The PBS leadership team may refer to Florida's Positive Behavior Support Project Web site (http://flpbs.fmhi.usf.edu) or SWIS (May et al., 2002; http://www.swis.org) for examples of behavior-tracking forms.

### *Coherent Discipline Referral Process*

After problem behaviors are defined and minor and major behavior-tracking forms have been developed, the PBS leadership team will need to examine the current discipline process and procedures to determine if they are effective and efficient. This process needs to be defined and the steps or stages of the discipline process clearly outlined (either in graphic or narrative format), taught, and agreed on by all staff so that an efficient and effective discipline process is established. Once the PBS leadership team has developed this discipline procedural flowchart, it is essential that faculty members are trained in the process, and that it is disseminated across all faculty, including new staff, and families and posted in each classroom for reference. Refer to Florida's Positive Behavior Support Project for examples of coherent discipline process flowcharts (http://flpbs.fmhi.usf.edu).

## Effective Consequences and Interventions

Once a coherent discipline flowchart or process is developed, the leadership team develops a hierarchy of consequences to assist administrators in delivering the appropriate consequence and build communication across teachers, families, and students so that everyone knows what to expect following a particular behavioral incident. There is a tendency to think of all consequences as negative or punishment. For the purposes of this chapter, we refer to *consequences* as those actions that are taken after a behavior, that are related to the function of that behavior, and that change that behavior. Thus, consequences may also include prevention, teaching, and reinforcement approaches. The absence of a primary-tier plan incorporating a hierarchy of consequences and possible interventions to address problem behaviors may lead to (a) inconsistent administration of consequences; (b) exclusionary practices that encourage further misbehavior through escape; (c) disproportionate amounts of staff time and attention to inappropriate behaviors; (d) miscommunication among staff, administration, students, and parents; and (5) an overreliance on punishment for problem behaviors (Florida PBS Project, 2006).

Many schools are adapting primary-tier approaches because traditional consequences for student misbehavior have not been effective in that most consequences are not related to the function of the behavior. If a student tries to avoid a task by disrupting the class and the teacher sends the student to the office, the behavior has served its function (i.e., the task has been avoided), and neither the student nor the teacher will have any reason to change. When determining patterns of behavior and reviewing the referral process, the team is cognizant of the effects of negative reinforcement for both student and teacher and creates interventions and plans that assist both in creating lasting change. In addition, since there is a range of behavioral intensities (e.g., fighting, tardies, dress code violations, etc.), the team establishes a range of consequences/interventions for those misbehaviors. The level of the consequence should match the level of the behavior while still addressing the function of the behavior.

Therefore, a continuum of discipline procedures should be outlined by the leadership team that allows for an array of responses to student problem behaviors.

When developing consequences, the leadership team also develops a system for notifying staff involved, the student's caregivers, and the involved students to remind them of their responsibilities in regard to the consequences. The PBS leadership team at the school level determines reentry procedures for staff and students to follow when a student returns to class, which is important for follow-through with interventions and consequences. Regardless of the level of the behavior (whether the behavior warrants a referral to the office or not), following the problem behavior, staff must be trained to immediately (a) name the problem behavior observed, (b) state the schoolwide expected behavior, (c) model the expected behavior for the student, (d) ask the student to demonstrate the expected behavior, and (e) provide acknowledgment to the student for demonstrating the behavior.

An effective strategy to assist in establishing a list of effective classroom interventions is to solicit examples of interventions during a faculty meeting. The leadership team can then provide formal or informal training on the most effective strategies to teachers who need additional support. Examples of interventions at the classroom level include reteaching the expectations and rules, changing seating arrangements, conferencing with parent or student, peer mediation, student contracts, providing choices, removing tempting items from the classroom, using humor, letting the student "save face," redirection, failure to earn a privilege in that moment, restitution/apology, prompting and cueing both verbally and nonverbally as warnings, rewarding alternate positive behavior, and more (Florida's PBS Project, 2006).

## Identifying Expectations and Rules

Another critical practice component of the primary-tier plan is the identification and dissemination of behavioral expectations and rules. Expectations are a list of broad, positively stated behaviors aligned with the school's mission statement that are desired of all students, faculty, and parents in all settings (G. R. Mayer, 1995, 1999). Expectations are specific to a school as they are based on the school's discipline data and the values of the faculty and community. For example, if many students have been referred for disrespect, tardies, fighting, and experience low achievement scores, a school may want their students to strive to be respectful, prepared, self-controlled, and active learners. Posters of the expectations throughout the school campus serve as reminders to students, staff, faculty, parents, and visitors of the desired behaviors and assist in building visibility, increasing buy-in, and maintaining support.

Once expectations are defined, rules for how these expectations look in particular settings need to be developed. How a student is respectful in the classroom may differ from how they are respectful in the cafeteria, restroom, or hallway. Therefore, rules are specific, observable behaviors that will assist

Expectations and Rules by Setting Matrix

| Expectations and Rules Matrix | Hallway/ Breezeway | Cafeteria | Restroom | Bus Loading Zone | Media Center |
|---|---|---|---|---|---|
| Be Respectful | Walk Facing Forward<br><br>Place Books Neatly in Locker | Listen to the Adult in Charge<br><br>Use a Quiet Voice<br><br>Throw Trash Away Before Leaving | Throw Trash in Garbage Can<br><br>Give Others Privacy | Listen to the Adult in Charge | Use a Quiet Voice |
| Be Prepared | Walk Straight to your Destination | Know your Lunch ID Number | Stand in Line | for your Bus | Bring ID with you to Media Center |
| Show Self Control | Keep Hands, Feet, and all other Objects to Self | Keep Hands, Feet, and all other Objects to Self | Keep Hands, Feet, and all other Objects to Self | Keep Hands, Feet, and all other Objects to Self | Keep Hands, Feet, and all other Objects to Self |

**Fig. 16.1.** Expectations and rules by setting matrix.

the leadership team in teaching the expectations across different settings (see Fig. 16.1). Establishing behavioral procedures for specific settings allows for uniform instruction across multiple programs; builds communication across faculty, staff, and parents; promotes curriculum design; and assists in professional accountability. By stating the rules positively, students can be easily taught what they are supposed to do rather than what they are not to do (Colvin, Kameenui, & Sugai, 1993; G. R. Mayer, 1995, 1999).

## Reward System

Once behavioral expectations and rules are developed, the leadership team creates rewards or incentives not only for the students but also for the faculty and staff to encourage the expected adult and student behaviors on campus. Developing a reward system is a critical component in that it increases the likelihood that desired behaviors will be repeated, focuses staff and student attention on the desired behaviors, fosters a positive school climate, and reduces the need for engaging in time-consuming disciplinary measures (Florida's PBS Project, 2006). The team should vary the types of rewards to maintain interest (e.g., social, activity, sensory, escape, tangible items such as edibles, materials, and tokens). When developing a reward system, the leadership team considers the following guidelines: (a) keep it simple; (b) target all students; (c) reward frequently in the beginning; (d) reward students contingent on desired behavior; (e) use age-appropriate rewards; (f) refrain from taking or threatening to take earned items or activities from a student once they have been earned;

(g) provide rewards throughout the day; (h) clearly define the criteria for earning rewards; (i) ensure portability for use in multiple settings; (j) provide flexibility to meet the needs of diverse students; (k) vary rewards to maintain student interest; (l) plan for encouraging and monitoring staff use of reward system; (m) provide staff with opportunities to recognize students in common areas who are not in their classes; (n) ensure that rewards are hierarchical (small increments of success are recognized with small rewards); and (o) promote opportunities for naturally occurring reinforcement in multiple settings (Florida's PBS Project, 2006).

The development of a reward system contingent on desired behavior is not without its challenges, especially when it is new to a school. It may be difficult for the leadership team and entire school to remain focused on the positive, provide meaningful rewards, maintain consistency, and track the rewards distributed. Therefore, it is important that the PBS leadership team and school staff strive to keep the ratio of reinforcement to correction high, involve students on the PBS leadership team to assist in identifying rewards (especially rewards that are inexpensive), and provide ongoing training to staff and students. The team should keep in mind that the reward system is only one component of the primary-tier plan and should not drive the PBS process but rather assist in efforts by increasing awareness of positive behaviors and providing a reason for motivating students to use new skills (i.e., the expected behaviors taught to them). Without developing a solid foundation (i.e., data-based decision-making system) and teaching the expected behaviors, a reward system may not be able to produce and sustain long-term systems change on campus.

## Lesson Plans for Teaching the Expected Behaviors

Once expectations and rules have been developed, it is not enough just to post them on the walls throughout the school. These behavioral skills must be taught. Appropriate behaviors are prerequisites for academics, procedures and routines create structure, and repetition is a factor in learning new skills. The leadership team behavior can chose to teach appropriate behavior through a variety of activities, including introductory kickoff events, ongoing direct instruction, embedding into other curriculum, and booster/retrainings. The more that desired behaviors are modeled by adults/staff on campus, students are provided with written and graphic cues in the setting where the behaviors are expected, efforts are acknowledged, plans to reteach and restructure teaching are developed, students are allowed to participate in the development process, and "teachable" moments are used in core subject areas and during nonacademic times, the more successfully the new skills will be acquired and maintained. The leadership team may select a variety of methods to teach the expectations and rules, including rotating classes through stations across campus to learn about rules in particular settings, principals/administrators and teachers coleading an event to creatively introduce to students in an assembly format (e.g., teacher role-playing examples and nonexamples, asking for volunteers, etc.), and students performing skits on the morning news to be broadcast daily.

### Evaluation

As discussed, there are a number of sources of data to assist the leadership team in assessing their own ability to work effectively, evaluating whether their school is implementing the primary-tier strategies with fidelity and measuring outcomes for students. The leadership team plans how to gather and access the data necessary to evaluate each of these areas, who will analyze and report on the data, how the data will be reported, and when will the data be discussed and shared. These data should direct the future steps of the leadership team as they make decisions based on the data that may include restructuring their team, examining why primary-tier strategies did or did not work, revising their primary-tier processes, or moving on to secondary and tertiary tiers.

## CONCLUSIONS AND FUTURE DIRECTIONS

This chapter described the primary tier of PBS as the foundation of a three-tier model of systems change. Although all three levels are essential to providing comprehensive behavioral supports to all students, the primary tier provides a critical prevention component that must be implemented with fidelity for secondary and tertiary intervention to be most effective. As a result, the primary tier of PBS is indeed primary to the accomplishment of effective and efficient systems change. The systems change process involves not just changing the behavior of students, but more importantly the changing of policies, procedures, and processes that have an impact on the behavior of adults (i.e., teachers, school administrators, PBS coaches, and a variety of district personnel) throughout the school system. Thus, primary-tier PBS is about developing multiple levels of support for students, teachers, schools, districts, and states. While the primary-tier practice components described in this chapter are essential for changing the behavior of students, the core elements of the primary-tier implementation process create the foundation and support for staff behavior that can ultimately result in sustainable systems change.

This sustainable systems change has resulted in the adoption of primary-tier SW-PBS across many districts and states and may at first glance appear remarkable. However, it is important to remember that SW-PBS is currently implemented in fewer than 10% of all U.S. schools and in even fewer schools with maintained fidelity. A significant issue impacting the further expansion of an evidence-based support system like PBS is the "competition" from other behavioral initiatives. Many districts utilize behavioral programs and practices that do not have significant research and outcomes demonstrating their effectiveness. Other districts utilize evidence-based practices but do not develop the systems supports to implement any approach with fidelity. There are literally hundreds of behavioral initiatives that schools and districts currently employ, own, or encourage. One Florida school district alone had access to over 5 primary, 90 secondary, and 9 tertiary interventions within its district implementation capacity. While these initiatives could be seen as competing with PBS for time, resources, and support, it is understood that most research-based initiatives are a good match within a PBS system. The primary-tier "process" can be adapted to fit many of the effective and attractive aspects of related "programs." The key for the PBS field is to support school, district, and state personnel to identify evidence-based practices and to learn to blend the elements of primary-tier SW-PBS with existing evidence-based practices.

This adaptation is especially pertinent as schools, districts, and states move toward an RTI model and begin to understand how all of their initiatives, curriculums, and interventions fit within a three-tier model of supports. RTI is a framework for incorporating a problem-solving and data-based decision-making system across the three tiers of prevention and support. The primary tier of SW-PBS is a Tier 1 intervention within an RTI framework. PBS and RTI primary-tier interventions are the foundation on which all other behavioral and academic initiatives can produce more effective outcomes (i.e., secondary- and tertiary-level interventions and supports). While SW-PBS includes primary, secondary (targeted group and classroom), and tertiary (individual) levels of support, the PBS process is still developing a means of systematically moving students through the tiers in a way that is consistent with an academic model of RTI. Most academic RTI processes utilize systematic screenings and assessments to determine the academic RTI or engage in a structured problem-solving process. There may not be one definitive behavioral measure of response to behavioral intervention at all three levels. ODRs may not identify all the students who would benefit from secondary and tertiary levels of supports (i.e., referral data do not capture the unique needs of students with internalizing behaviors) (Sandomierski, Kincaid, & Algozzine, 2007). There is, so far, no systematic and agreed-on way to progress monitor the behavior of students engaged in a particular secondary- or tertiary-level intervention. There are also few validated methods with which to evaluate the effectiveness and fidelity of implementation of interventions at the secondary and tertiary levels. It is likely that additional teacher nomination processes, screenings, rating scales, and other assessment approaches will need to be developed to assist with data-based decision making across all three levels of SW-PBS.

As SW-PBS continues to collaborate with related initiatives or expand into underserved areas, there will be additional challenges to systems change. The application of primary-tier processes and practices may need to be adapted to address urban, low-poverty, academic-underachieving settings and schools that are reluctant to engage in a systems change process such as SW-PBS. It is also likely that the critical elements of SW-PBS may need to be adapted to meet differing contexts (early childhood, transportation, mental health, juvenile justice systems, etc.).

In addition to evaluating outcomes and implementation of primary-tier interventions, it is also important for future research to evaluate the specific elements and components of primary-tier SW-PBS within standard contexts. For instance, while primary-tier training is a necessary element, additional research may be necessary to define the most effective and efficient training processes to prepare school-based PBS leadership teams to understand and implement systems change activities. While we know that SW-PBS implementation at the primary-tier/universal level requires attention to multiple components (establishing a data-based decision-making system, identifying expectations and rules, teaching expectations and rules, implementing a reward system, etc.), we do not know the relative impact of each component on the outcomes achieved for students. If any component is missing from the process, does it not result in the anticipated systems change? Does more emphasis need to be placed on one component or another because it produces more significant change in the behaviors of staff and students? For all schools to adapt a primary-tier process, future research activities will need to emphasize making the training and implementation of SW-PBS at the primary tier even more effective and efficient.

## REFERENCES

Anderson, C. M., & Kincaid, D. (2005). Applying behavior analysis to school violence and discipline problems: Schoolwide positive behavior support. *The Behavior Analyst, 28*, 49–63.

Aucoin, K. J., Frick, P. J., & Bodin, S. D. (2006). Corporal punishment and child adjustment. *Journal of Applied Developmental Psychology, 27*, 527–541.

Carr, E. G. (2006). SWPBS: The greatest good for the greatest number, or the needs of the majority trump the needs of the minority? *Research and Practice for Persons With Severe Disabilities, 31*, 54–56.

Carr, E. G., Dunlap, G., Horner, R. H., Koegel, R. L., Turnbull, L. K., Sailor, W., et al. (2002). Positive behavior support: Evolution of an applied science. *Journal of Positive Behavior Interventions, 4*, 4–16.

Cohen, R. (2006). Implementing school-wide positive behavior support: Exploring the influence of socio-cultural, academic, behavioral, and implementation process variables. Unpublished doctoral dissertation, University of South Florida, Tampa.

Colvin, G., Kameenui, E. J., & Sugai, G. (1993). Reconceptualizing behavior management and school-wide discipline in general education. *Education and Treatment of Children, 16*, 361–381.

Dufresne, J., & Dorn, M. (2005) Keeping students and schools safe. *Reclaiming Children and Youth, 14*, 93–96.

Dunlap, G. (1993). Promoting generalization: Current status and functional considerations. In R. VanHouten & S. Axelrod (Eds.), *Behavior analysis and treatment* (pp. 269–296). New York: Plenum Press.

Dynamic indicators of basic early literacy skills. Deno & Fuchs (1987), Retrieved August 25, 2008, from http://dibels.uoregon.edu/

Ferro, J., & Dunlap, G. (1993). Generalization and maintenance. In M. Smith (Ed.), *Behavior modification for exceptional children and youth* (pp. 190–211). Boston: Andover Medical.

Florida's Positive Behavior Support Project. Retrieved July 31, 2007, from http://flpbs.fmhi.usf.edu/

George, H. P., & Kincaid, D. (2008). Building district-wide capacity for positive behavior support. *Journal of Positive Behavioral Interventions, 10*, 20–32.

George, H. P. & Martinez, S. A. (2007). How to get PBS in my school (Vol. 4). OSEP Technical Assistance Center on Positive Behavioral Interventions and Supports Web site. Retrieved August 25, 2008, from http://www.pbis.org/news/New/Newsletters/Newsletter5.aspx

Horner, R. H., Todd, A. W., Lewis-Palmer, T., Irvin, L. K., Sugai, G., & Boland, J. B. (2003). The School-wide Evaluation Tool (SET): A research instrument for assessing school-wide positive behavior support. *Journal of Positive Behavior Interventions, 6*, 3–12.

Individuals With Disabilities Education Improvement Act 2004, 20 USC § 1400 et seq. (2004).

Institute of Education Sciences, U.S. Department of Education (2004) *Indicators of school crime and safety:* Executive summary. Retrieved August 25, 2008 from the National Center for Education Statistics: http://nces.ed.gov/pubs2005/crime_safe04/

Kincaid, D., Childs, K., & George, H. (2005). *School-wide benchmarks of quality*. Unpublished instrument. University of South Florida, Tampa.

Lewis, T. J., & Sugai, G. (1999). Effective behavior support: A systems approach to proactive school-wide management. *Focus on Exceptional Children, 31*, 1–24.

May, S., Ard, W., III, Todd, A. W., Horner, R. H., Glasgow, A., Sugai, G., et al. (2002). *School-wide information system.* Eugene: Educational and Community Supports, University of Oregon. Available at http://www.swis.org

Mayer, G. R. (1995). Preventing antisocial behavior in schools. *Journal of Applied Behavior Analysis, 28*, 467–478.

Mayer, G. R. (1999). Constructive discipline for school personnel. *Education and Treatment of Children, 22*, 36–54.

Mayer, M. J., & Leone, P. E. (1999). A structural analysis of school violence and disruption: Implications for creating safer schools. *Education and Treatment of Children, 22*, 333–356.

No Child Left Behind Act of 2001, 20 USC § 6311 et seq. (2002).

OSEP Technical Assistance Center on Positive Behavioral Interventions and Supports. *School-wide PBS: Primary prevention* Retrieved July 31, 2007, from http://www.pbis.org

Pearpoint, J., O'Brien, J., & Forest, M. (1993). *PATH (Planning Alternative Tomorrows With Hope): A workbook for planning positive futures.* Toronto: Inclusion Press.

Sandomierski, T., Kincaid, D., & Algozzine, B. (2007). *Response to intervention and positive behavior support: Brothers from different mothers or sisters from different misters.* OSEP Technical Assistance Center on Positive Behavioral Interventions and Supports Web site. Retrieved August 25, 2008, from http://www.pbis.org/news/New/Newsletters/Newsletter4-2.aspx

Sailor, W., Zuna, N., Choi, J.-H., C., Thomas, J., McCart, A., & Blair, R. (2006). Anchoring schoolwide positive behavior support in structural school reform. *Research and Practice for Persons With Severe Disabilities, 31*, 18–30.

Scott, T. M., & Eber, L. (2003). Functional assessment and wraparound as systemic school processes: Primary, secondary, and tertiary systems examples. *Journal of Positive Behavior Interventions, 5*, 131–143.

Sugai, G., & Horner, R. H. (2002). The evolution of discipline practices: School-wide positive behavior supports. *Child and Family Behavior Therapy, 24*, 23–50.

Sugai, G., Horner, R. H., Dunlap, G., Heineman, M., Lewis, T. J., Nelson, C. M., et al. (2000). Applying positive behavioral support and functional behavioral assessment in schools. *Journal of Positive Behavioral Interventions, 2*, 131–143.

Sugai, G., Horner, R., Sailor, W., Dunlap, G., Eber, L., Lewis, T., et al. (2005). *School-wide positive behavior support: Implementers' blueprint and self-assessment.* Technical Assistance Center on Positive Behavioral Interventions and Supports. University of Oregon: Eugene, OR.

University of Oregon, College of Education. *School-wide positive behavior support team training manual: School-wide application of positive behavior support building primary systems and practices.* PowerPoint presentation. Retrieved September 27, 2007, from http://pbismanual.uoecs.org/manual.htm

Yell, M. L., Rogers, D., & Lodge-Rogers, E. (1998). The legal history of special education. *Remedial and Special Education, 19*, 219–229.

# 17

# Secondary-Tier Interventions and Supports

**LEANNE S. HAWKEN, SARAH L. ADOLPHSON, K. SANDRA MACLEOD, and JOAN SCHUMANN**

Implementing a continuum of schoolwide positive behavior support (SW-PBS) from least to most intensive is recommended to prevent and respond to problem behavior in school settings (Walker et al., 1996). This continuum of support includes three main prevention tiers: (a) primary, which involves schoolwide interventions for all students and staff across all school settings; (b) secondary, which targets the 10–15% of students at risk of social behavior failure; and (c) tertiary, which focuses on approximately 5% of the student population who need significant intervention strategies and supports (Sugai & Horner, 2002). For additional information on SW-PBS, see chapter 14.

Students who do not respond to primary-tier prevention programs may benefit from efficient secondary-tier (ST) interventions, also referred to as "selected" or "targeted" interventions. The group of students who benefit from ST interventions includes approximately 10–15% of the student population who are at risk for developing severe problem behavior due to their (a) poor peer relations, (b) low academic achievement, or (c) chaotic home environments (Lewis & Sugai, 1999). The behaviors of these students are unresponsive to interventions provided at the primary tier (Fairbanks, Sugai, Guardino, & Lathrop, 2007; Kincaid 2007), and these students typically require more practice in learning behavioral expectations and may need academic modifications to ensure learning success (Lee, Sugai, & Horner, 1999).

**LEANNE S. HAWKEN** • University of Utah
**SARAH L. ADOLPHSON** • University of Utah
**K. SANDRA MACLEOD** • University of Utah
**JOAN SCHUMANN** • University of Utah

In recent years, many schools have been implementing extensive prevention activities, especially related to problems such as substance abuse and violence prevention. Gottfredson and Gottfredson (2002) conducted a national survey among a sample of public, private, and Catholic schools stratified by location (i.e., urban, suburban, and rural), representing all grades (kindergarten to 12th grade) and all states. These researchers found that schools responding to the survey had a median number of 14 prevention programs operating at one time. Most schools would not be able to effectively support this many programs simultaneously. Schools need effective and efficient mechanisms for selecting the most appropriate ST prevention and intervention programs to meet their needs. The purposes of this chapter are to provide an overview of (a) the critical features of ST interventions, (b) issues related to implementation and evaluation of ST interventions, (c) examples of evidenced-based ST interventions, and (d) suggestions for research and practice.

## KEY FEATURES OF SECONDARY-TIER INTERVENTIONS

Secondary-tier interventions play a key role in supporting students at risk of academic and social problems and may prevent the need for more intensive interventions (Hawken, O'Neill, & MacLeod, 2008; Hawken, MacLeod, & Rawlings, 2007; OSEP, 2005; Sinclair, Christenson, Evelo, & Hurley, 1998). ST interventions contain features that differentiate them from primary and tertiary tiers of behavior support, including (a) similar implementation across students (i.e., low effort by teachers); (b) continuous availability and quick access to the intervention; (c) training of all staff on how to make a referral and, if appropriate, how to implement the intervention; (d) consistency with schoolwide expectations; (e) continuous data-based progress monitoring; and (f) flexible intervention based on functional assessment (Hawken & Horner, 2003; MacLeod, Hawken, & O'Neill, 2008; March & Horner, 2002; OSEP, 2005). Each of these features is discussed in further detail here.

The goal of ST interventions is to support the 10–15% of the student population at risk of but not currently engaging in severe problem behavior (Walker et al., 1996). In a school of 1,000 students, for example, 100–150 students would need support beyond the schoolwide discipline plan and proactive classroom management strategies. For this reason, ST interventions need to be efficient in terms of time and resources. ST interventions involve using a similar set of procedures across a group of students. For example, if social skills training is required for students who have problems with anger management, a similar curriculum is used across a group of students. If several students are having difficulty with tardiness and attendance, ST procedures are designed to target those problem behaviors.

To be effective in preventing problem behavior, students must be able to access ST interventions quickly. Unlike more intensive and individualized interventions, which may take weeks of assessment, ST interventions should be accessed relatively quickly—usually within a week (Crone, Horner,

& Hawken, 2004; OSEP, 2005). Students are identified quickly and proactively, either by frequently assessing risk factors such as the number of office discipline referrals (ODRs), absences, and tardies or by teacher nomination or referral (Cheney, Blum, & Walker, 2004; Crone et al., 2004; Walker, Stiller, Severson, Golly, & Feil, 1998). Although not all school staff are directly involved in the implementation of ST interventions, each staff member should be trained on who the intervention is appropriate for, how and when to make a referral, and how to support the intervention once a student is referred. More information on how and when ST interventions are implemented is presented in the next section.

The ST interventions should be consistent with schoolwide expectations (OSEP, 2005). For example if a middle school has these schoolwide rules: Be safe, be respectful, be responsible, and hands and feet to self the ST intervention should provide more practice and feedback on how to meet the following expectations. Often, ST interventions are implemented with the support of a school psychologist, counselor, or paraprofessionals so that the burden of the intervention is not solely on the student's teacher (Crone et al., 2004; Hawken, 2006; Lane et al., 2003). Usually, consultation from experts outside the school is not necessary or is minimized because the intervention procedures are systematic and follow standardized treatment protocols (OSEP, 2005).

The ST interventions should have systems in place to monitor student progress, make modifications, and gradually decrease support as student behavior improves. One component of this system is a team, which may already exist, such as a student study team or a more individualized team consisting of teachers, counselors, parents, and students (Christenson, Sinclair, Lehr, & Hurley, 2000). Teams should meet regularly and have systematic procedures for monitoring, troubleshooting, and adding or removing students to or from the intervention (Crone et al., 2004). Team decisions and monitoring of student progress are based on data from a number of different sources depending on the type of program. More detailed information on monitoring student progress is presented in this chapter.

Interventions should be flexible so that they can be modified or intensified based on the function of student problem behavior. For example, after implementing the Behavior Education Program/Check-In, Check-Out (BEP/CICO) for 12 weeks, a school behavior team noticed that Jalen, a middle school student, was not making progress. Based on teacher observations and an interview with Jalen, it became apparent that most of his problem behavior (e.g., talking with peers, making clicking noises with his tongue, throwing paper airplanes across the room) was related to trying to gain attention from his peers. Based on this information, the team modified Jalen's reinforcers so that when he met his daily point goal he could earn time with peers in a preferred activity (i.e., extra gym time with three friends).

Teams should also consider the function of the student's problem behavior prior to selecting the most appropriate ST intervention (Newcomer, 2004). For example, if the student is acting out to gain adult attention, ST interventions that increase adult attention, such as mentoring, may be good starting points. In contrast, if the student is acting out to escape difficult work, afterschool tutoring or other academic interventions may be more appropriate. ST interventions such as First Steps to Success (FSS) have been more effective for some students if the function of student problem behavior is identified (Carter & Horner, 2007). However, it should be noted that some ST interventions have also been effective across functions of student behavior (Hawken et al., 2008; MacLeod, O'Neill, & Hawken, 2008; March & Horner, 2002).

Although many of the ST interventions described in this chapter include some of the features outlines, none of the interventions meet all of the recommended features as implementation will vary depending on individual school and student needs. (OSEP) Office Of Special Education-Procedures for identifying students requiring ST interventions and selecting evidence-based interventions are provided in the following sections.

## TARGET POPULATIONS AND IDENTIFICATION METHODS FOR ST INTERVENTIONS

Students who fail to respond to primary-tier interventions are self-selected candidates for more systematic and intensive support. These students are identified for ST interventions in a number of ways, including (a) as a response to screening, (b) as a preventive intervention, and (c) as a response to intervention (White, 2007).

### Secondary-Tier Interventions as a Response to Screening

Frequently, students are selected for ST interventions based on universal screening procedures to detect students at risk. Regularly, screening all students (two or three times per academic year) is important to ensure that this population of students is not overlooked. When primary tier interventions are carried out with fidelity, schools can then target students who are in need of more frequent monitoring and more intensive levels of support. In some cases, ODR data provide sufficient information to identify students who are unresponsive to primary-tier interventions. Sugai, Sprague, Horner, and Walker (2000) have recommended a guideline for using ODRs to make data-based decisions regarding necessary levels of support, including (a) students who receive zero to one ODRs per year are likely adequately supported by primary-tier interventions, (b) students receiving two to five ODRs potentially require ST interventions, and (c) students who receive six or more ODRs may require tertiary-tier interventions.

Although not a perfect metric, ODRs are easily collected and summarized by schools—particularly with Web-based systems such as the School-wide Information System (SWIS; May et al., 2000). Because the use of ODRs as a screening tool for identifying students who are at risk has been debated (Nelson, Benner, Reid, Epstein, & Currin, 2002), additional research is needed to provide more reliable and valid screening tools for students nonresponsive to primary-level supports, which are also gathered & summarized as effeciently as ODR data. Examples of reliable and valid screening tools follow; however, these screening mechanisms may extend beyond what schools typically employ to assess for problem behavior.

While some students are easily identified as at risk by teachers and other school personnel based on their engagement in acting out or externalizing behaviors, other students engage in internalizing behaviors (i.e., depression, anxiety, withdrawal), requiring more comprehensive assessment for identification. For students who engage in internalizing behaviors or present less-intensive externalizing behaviors, ODRs may not provide adequate information, and other effective screening tools are necessary to proactively identify at-risk students.

The Systematic Screening for Behavior Disorders (SSBD; Walker & Severson, 1992) is one such screening measure used during the elementary grades to assist school personnel to identify students likely to be negatively impacted by externalizing or internalizing behaviors (Walker, Cheney, Stage, & Blum, 2005). The SSBD utilizes a three-stage process to identify students potentially at risk. The first stage involves teacher nomination of students with behavioral characteristics predictive of school failure. Students identified in the first stage are then further screened using a series of rating items to determine behavioral severity and the content of the problem behavior. In the final stage, students are systematically observed in the classroom and on the playground to determine their performance in social and classroom situations.

A second screening measure that can be used to identify a student for ST interventions is the Social Skills Rating System (SSRS; Gresham & Elliot, 1990). The SSRS is a set of three norm-referenced rating scales that allow educators to combine teacher, parent, and student reports to gain a more complete understanding of a student's social behavior. The SSRS, in combination with the *Social Skills Intervention Guide: Practical Strategies for Social Skills Training* (Elliot & Gresham, 1991) can be useful in helping educators identify specific social skill deficits in students and coordinate appropriate interventions that are founded on the principles of applied behavior analysis.

All of the mentioned screening measures provide valuable guidelines for teachers in making objective decisions about students who may require support beyond the primary tier level. However, if systematic screening procedures are not in place, teacher nomination is the main way students are identified for ST behavioral interventions (Hawken & Horner, 2003; Hawken et al., 2007). Recent research indicates that screening tools such as the SSBD and other teacher nomination strategies are more accurate mechanisms in identifying students who are at risk, particularly students who display internalizing (i.e., anxiety, depression) behaviors (Blum, 2006; Kincaid, 2007).

## Secondary-Tier Support as a Preventive Intervention

Prior to entering school, many children are exposed to various family and community-based risk factors in their formative years, which increase the likelihood of behavioral problems. These risk factors include, but are not limited to, large families headed by a single parent, poverty, abusive conditions, exposure to drug and alcohol abuse, crime, violence, gang activity, and poor academic preparation (McCrudy, Mannella, & Eldridge, 2003; Warren et al., 2003). Risk factors for school failure are multifaceted and involve both academic and social or emotional factors. Students who enter school with social risk factors typically display poor problem-solving skills, may engage in attention-seeking behaviors that cause classroom disruptions, and may attempt to escape social interactions (McIntosh, Horner, Chard, Boland, & Good, 2006). Other students may enter school with academic deficits but do not engage in routine problem behavior. If these students do not respond to academic interventions, the academic deficits are likely to become contributing factors to problem behavior. Failure to recognize and respond to these risk factors early on increases the challenges that these students will present to teachers and administrators.

Research emphasizes the need to implement preventive interventions early on in the educational process (Fox, Dunlap, & Powell, 2002; Lane & Menzies, 2003). The forms of problem behavior more common to elementary school settings (e.g., bullying, classroom disruptions, failure to complete assignments) are triggers of more severe forms of misconduct (e.g., aggression toward others, school dropout, substance abuse, criminal activity) occurring as students reach adolescence (Fox et al., 2002; McCurdy, Kunsch, & Reibstein, 2007; H. M. Walker et al., 1998). While some environmental factors in family and community environments occur outside of the school context, when schools are aware of these risk factors, ST interventions can be implemented proactively, prior to the student engaging in problem behavior. It should be noted that although ST interventions are designed to address many of the risk factors mentioned, they are not comprehensive interventions and therefore do not address all of the factors that influence problem behavior.

## Secondary-Tier Interventions as a Response to Intervention

Primary-tier intervention involves implementing a schoolwide behavior support plan along with a proactive classroom management plan (Sugai, Horner, & Gresham, 2002). Once these are implemented with fidelity and students are not responding to these interventions, teachers may choose to provide additional interventions in the classroom setting, such as behavioral contracting or a home note system to further meet the needs of a student (or students). If the student fails to respond to these interventions, this lack of response to intervention may signal the need for an ST intervention.

Schools use different systems to track problem behavior and, as mentioned, increasing numbers of ODRs may be a sign that a student needs additional behavior support. Schools may use other data such as lack of work completion, grades, frequency of tardiness, or attendance to provide evidence that the primary-tier intervention procedures have been ineffective. Often, younger students (i.e., kindergarten or first grade) will not engage in problem behavior that is considered extreme enough to warrant an ODR, but data should be gathered on the low-level, chronic problem behavior via a mechanism such as behavior logs (i.e., student must sign a behavior log for not following behavioral expectations). Many schools implement procedures like interclass time-outs, also called "think time," in which a student who has engaged in problem behavior spends time in a cooperating teacher's classroom, completes a debriefing form, and reenters the classroom once the form has been completed (Nelson, 1997). In schools that use these procedures, data should be gathered on when (i.e., which times of the day) and for how long students are in think time. If students are repeatedly sent to a cooperating teacher's classroom, this may signal the need for more intensive support that can be provided by an ST intervention.

## EXAMPLES OF SECONDARY-TIER INTERVENTIONS

Much research has been conducted examining the effects of implementing primary-tier intervention strategies (e.g., Colvin, Kameenui, & Sugai, 1993; Lewis & Sugai, 1999; Lewis, Sugai, & Colvin, 1998; Taylor-Greene et al., 1997). Further, since the reauthorization of the Individuals With Disabilities Education Act (IDEA), there is increased evidence of the effectiveness of using functional assessment strategies and behavior support interventions for students needing tertiary-tier support (for a review, see Heckaman, Conroy, Fox, & Chait, 2000). In contrast, little research has been reported on ST interventions implemented as part of a continuum of behavior support; the purpose of this section is to provide some examples of promising, evidenced-based ST interventions. As Osher, Dwyer, and Jackson (2004) suggested, schools need to first identify effective interventions, then select an intervention that meets the specific needs of the school community. For this reason, a quick reference summary of empirical support has been provided for each of the following ST interventions. These tables provide summaries of the participants involved, key features of the study, and the primary outcomes of the intervention. Finally, this discussion concludes with a summary table of critical features across ST programs and interventions.

### Check and Connect

The Check and Connect intervention involves connecting a student with a school-based monitor to improve student engagement, decrease absences, and ultimately prevent school dropout (Sinclair et al., 1998). Students are identified as candidates for Check and Connect by assessing risk factors such as attendance, presence of learning disabilities, tardiness, skipping class, suspensions, and academic performance. A full-time monitor acts as a liaison between the student, the school, the student's parents, and the community. This person works individually with each student ensuring that he or she is attending school, participating in school activities, and maintaining academic progress. Student progress is tracked using information such as attendance, end-of-year enrollment, academic performance, number of credits, number of ODRs, and whether the student is expected to graduate (Christenson et al., 2000).

**Table 17.1.** Summary of Empirical Support: Check and Connect

| Reference | Participants | Key Features of Investigation | Intervention Outcomes |
|---|---|---|---|
| Lehr, Sinclair, & Christenson, 2004 | Elementary | • Prevented later truancy behavior in elementary students<br>• Evaluated teacher perceptions of program effectiveness | • Results suggest Check and Connect worked to improve student engagement while reducing high-risk behaviors<br>• Teacher perceptions indicated program effectiveness |
| Sinclair, Christenson, & Thurlow, 2005 | 70 urban high school students with emotional and behavioral disorders | • Compared a group of students participating in Check and Connect program to a similar group of students who served as the control group to observe effects over a 4- to 5-year period | • When compared to control group, students participating in Check and Connect were significantly less likely to drop out of school<br>• Participating students were more likely to be enrolled in an educational program |
| Sinclair et al., 1998 | Seventh- and eighth-grade students | • Three-year study<br>• Sought to evaluate overall program effectiveness as an ongoing dropout prevention program | • Check and Connect participants were more likely to stay enrolled in school, had more graduation credits, and had a higher completion of class assignments versus control<br>• Participants also had a reduction in severity of behavior problems |

Check and Connect has two levels of program delivery: basic and intensive. At the basic level, the monitor meets with students at least monthly to discuss school-related problems, apply problem-solving techniques, and emphasize the importance of staying in school. The monitor uses strategies such as behavioral contracting, tutoring, or community and school-based recreation activities (Sinclair et al., 1998). The second level is a more intensive intervention for students who are considered to be high risk for dropping out of school. This level provides more frequent contact and individualized interventions by the monitor as well as additional skill development and practice opportunities Table 17.1 provides a summary of the studies evaluating checked connect.

## Behavior Education Program

Another example of an ST intervention is the Behavior Education Program (BEP), also known as Check-In, Check-Out (CICO; Crone et al., 2004; Fairbanks et al., 2007; Hawken, 2006; Hawken & Horner, 2003; Hawken et al., in press; March & Horner, 2002) (Table 17.2). The BEP is a highly efficient

**Table 17.2.** Summary of Empirical Support: Behavior Education Program

| Reference | Participants | Key Features of Investigation | Intervention Outcomes |
|---|---|---|---|
| Fairbanks, Sugai, Guardino, & Lathrop, 2007 | 10 elementary schools | • Examined BEP/CICO application to students who displayed problem behavior after general classroom management procedures were implemented; provided more individualized intervention to students unresponsive to BEP/CICO | • BEP/CICO was an effective targeted intervention for four students who did not respond to general classroom management procedures<br>• Four students who were unresponsive to CICO responded to individualized function-based interventions |
| Filter et al., 2007 | Elementary school | • Examined effects of the BEP on ODRs | • 67% of students on BEP had reductions in ODRs<br>• Statistically significant difference in pre- and post-measures of ODRs<br>• District personnel found the program to be highly effective and efficient |
| Hawken, 2006 | Middle school | • Examined effects of the BEP on ODRs | • 70% of students on BEP had reductions in ODRs |
| Hawken & Horner, 2003 | Middle school | • Examined effects of BEP on direct observation of problem behavior and academic engagement | • Significant reduction in problem behavior<br>• Increase of academic engagement<br>• BEP implemented with high fidelity<br>• High social validity ratings from parents, teachers, and students |
| Hawken, MacLeod, & O'Neill, 2007 | Elementary school | • Examined the effects of BEP on ODRs<br>• Examined role of function of problem behavior on BEP effectiveness | • 71% and 80% of students on BEP had reductions in ODRs across School 1 and School 2, respectively<br>• Statistically significant difference in pre- and post-measures of ODRs<br>• BEP was effective across behavioral functions |
| Hawken, o'neill, & macles, 2008 | Elementary school | • Examined effects of the BEP on ODRs using multiple-baseline design across groups of students | • 75% of students on BEP had reductions in ODRs<br>• Statistically significant difference in pre- and post-measures of ODRs |
| March & Horner, 2002 | Middle school | • Examined effects of the BEP on ODRs | • 50% of students on BEP had reductions in ODRs |
| McCurdy, Kunsch, & Reibstein, 2007 | Elementary school | • Examined effects of BEP in urban school setting using a case study format | • Results indicated increases in appropriate behavior in majority of students<br>• Students and teachers rated BEP as highly acceptable |
| Todd, Kaufman, Meyer, & Horner (in press) | Elementary school | • Examined effects of BEP/CICO on direct observation of problem behavior | • Reductions in problem behavior<br>• High social validity ratings |

BEP/CICO, Behavior Education Program/Check-In Check-Out; ODR, office discipline referral.

program that, depending on school size and resources, may support 15–30 students at one time in an elementary or middle school setting. The BEP builds on schoolwide expectations by providing students with frequent feedback and reinforcement for demonstrating appropriate behavior.

Similar to the Check and Connect program, the BEP is structured around a regular checking-in system; however, unlike Check and Connect, the BEP is designed to have students check in a daily basis. Students check in with the BEP coordinator once in the morning and again at the end of the school day. The BEP coordinator is usually a paraprofessional who spends 10–15 hrs a week implementing the BEP. During check in, the BEP coordinator asks whether students have their materials (e.g., pencils, paper, and homework) and provides them with a daily progress report (DPR). The DPR lists the schoolwide behavioral expectations for students to follow and provides a place for teachers to rank how well the students followed the expectations for a specified period of time. Following check in, the students take the DPR to their teachers and receive feedback and evaluation on their social behavior at the end of each class period in middle or high school or during natural transitions in elementary school. At the end of the school day, the students check out with the BEP coordinator, who totals the daily points and provides praise, encouragement, and a tangible reward to the student based on his or her performance. Again, the BEP is similar to the Check and Connect program in that students are receiving positive feedback, praise, and encouragement on a regular basis for their improvements in both academic and social behavior.

Functioning as a home component of the BEP, the student takes a copy of the DPR home for parent signature. In addition, parents are provided with monthly updates on student progress. Behavior support team meetings (weekly or biweekly) include a discussion of the BEP to determine whether students are making progress, if the program needs to be modified, or if the students are ready to transition off the BEP (Crone et al., 2004).

## First Steps to Success

First Steps to Success (FSS) is a ST intervention intended for kindergarten students who show indications of developing antisocial behaviors (Walker, 1998; Walker, Stiller, et al., 1998) (Table 17.3). The program consists of three components: (a) a universal, schoolwide screening to identify students who may be at risk for developing more severe problem behavior; (b) instructional intervention of prosocial behaviors for students who are identified through the screening process; and (c) a parent training referred to as Home-Base, which supports parents of students who qualify for this ST intervention (Golly, Stiller, & Walker, 1998).

FSS is implemented in the school by a consultant (e.g., counselor, behavior specialist, or school psychologist), who develops and coordinates the home and school program components (Golly et al., 1998). Once a student is identified for the program, the school component involves providing additional feedback to the target student using a red card/green card system. In this system, the student is able to earn

**Table 17.3.** Summary of Empirical Support: First Steps to Success (FSS)

| Reference | Participants | Key Features of Investigation | Intervention Outcomes |
|---|---|---|---|
| H. M. Walker, 1998; Epstein & Walker, 2002; Golly, Stiller, & Walker, 1998 | 46 kindergarten students and families | • Participants randomly assigned to treatment and wait list cohorts | • Increased appropriate and adaptive behavior<br>• Decreased aggressive behavior<br>• Positive outcomes maintained for 2 years after intervention<br>• High acceptability ratings by students, parents, and teachers |
| Golly et al., 1998 | 20 kindergarten students across 10 different schools | • Study sought to replicate previous findings with the exception of random assignment | • Increased academic engaged time<br>• Decreased problem behavior |
| Golly et al., 1998 | 141 general educators (Grades K–1), teacher assistants, school counselors, parent volunteers | • Trained on intervention components through a series of 1-day workshops<br>• Follow-up survey sent | • 58% of returned surveys indicated current use of First Steps program<br>• Most reported training was worthwhile use of time |
| Golly, Sprague, Walker, Beard, & Gorham, 2000 | 2 sets of 5-year-old twins who met screening criteria | • Multiple-baseline design<br>• Brief daily sessions with consultant for a minimum of 5 days<br>• Follow-up implementation by classroom teacher<br>• Parent training conducted by consultant | • Significant improvement in academic engagement<br>• Significant reduction in problem behaviors<br>• Improved teacher-child interaction in the classroom |
| Diken & Rutherford, 2005 | 4 Native American students, their teachers, and families | • Implemented classwide and individual interventions using FSS in early intervention setting | • Immediately following FSS implementation, student prosocial behavior increased while problem behavior decreased |

rewards for his or her class on meeting daily predetermined point goals. Initially, the consultant is in the classroom providing direct feedback to the student consistently (consultant phase). As the intervention progresses, the feedback card is transitioned to the teacher (teacher phase), and the length of time between point earning opportunities is expanded (Golly et al., 1998).

Once the school program is established, the consultant meets once a week with the parents for 6 weeks in the home for approximately 45–60 min. During these six sessions, the following topics are addressed: (a) communication and sharing, (b) cooperation, (c) limit setting, (d) problem solving, (e) making friends, and (f) developing confidence.

Walker and colleagues (1998) estimated that the consultant invests 50–60 hr of time in the program over a 3-month period. The consultant has four primary responsibilities throughout the duration of the program: (a) coordinating child screening procedures in cooperation with the classroom teachers, (b) contacting and encouraging parent participation, (c) modeling FSS at the school so classroom teachers may continue with the intervention, and (d) providing parent training in the home environment on how to effectively intervene with problem behavior (Golly et al., 1998).

## Social Skills Club/Social Skill Training

Social skills training (SST) interventions involve directly teaching prosocial skills to enhance a student's ability to interact with peers and adults (Table 17.4). While some schools implement SST as part of their primary-tier efforts, SST has also been found to be effective as an ST intervention (Lane et al., 2003; Powers, 2003). When used as an ST intervention, SST efforts are applied to a subgroup of students who require additional practice and feedback on their behavior. This type of targeted instruction

**Table 17.4.** Summary of Empirical Support: Social Skills Training (SST)

| Reference | Participants | Key Features of Investigation | Intervention Outcomes |
|---|---|---|---|
| Lane et al., 2003 | 17 first- through sixth-grade students identified as nonresponsive to the school's primary-tier intervention | • Sought to evaluate effectiveness of SST as secondary tier intervention<br>• Provided additional practice to subgroup of students with problem behavior | • Reductions in disruptive classroom behavior<br>• Reductions in inappropriate social interactions on playground<br>• Increase in academic engaged time in classroom |
| Powers, 2003 | 19 elementary students at risk for school failure | • Compared intervention across two different settings<br>• Taught seven social skills through daily scripted instruction for 16 weeks | • Improved classroom behavior<br>• Reduction of problem behavior on playground<br>• Year follow-up study showed positive results maintained<br>• Students who attended school using schoolwide discipline plan showed greater reductions in problem behavior as well as higher levels of long-term maintained behavior |
| Gresham, Sugai, & Horner, 2001 | | • Meta-analysis of social skills studies | • SST may be effective in teaching new social skills<br>• SST appears to be more effective when skill deficits are targeted for instruction versus a set curriculum |

occurs most frequently in a small-group versus in a whole-class setting (i.e., Powers, 2003). Some key features of SST interventions include (a) targeting specific social skill deficits, (b) providing modeling and feedback, and (c) providing additional opportunities to practice the newly learned skills (Gresham, Sugai, & Horner, 2001).

## Mentoring

As an ST intervention, mentoring interventions involve pairing the target student with another successful student or community mentor, who serves as a "coach" or "mentor" by establishing a supportive relationship with the student at-risk while modeling appropriate social and academic behaviors. Mentoring programs have been used for many years, both formally and informally, to assist in reducing antisocial behaviors in children and youth (DuBois & Karcher, 2005; Roberts, Liabo, Lucas, DuBois, & Sheldon, 2004). Formalized mentoring programs are designed to fill in the roles previously carried out by relatives, teachers, and community members (Rhodes, Bogat, Roffman, Edelman, & Galasso, 2002). These programs typically address the needs of students who are considered to be at risk due to their home environments, academic challenges, or low socioeconomic status. Moreover, mentoring-based interventions have been cited by positive behavior support researchers as efficient interventions that can be included as part of a school's ST behavior support system (Hawken, 2006; Newcomer, 2004) (Table 17.5).

The largest formal youth mentoring program is Big Brothers Big Sisters (BBBS), which is found in more than 5,000 communities. Furthermore,

**Table 17.5.** Summary of Empirical Support: Mentoring Programs

| Reference | Participants | Key Features of Investigation | Intervention Outcomes |
|---|---|---|---|
| Big Brothers Big Sisters (BBBS), 2006 | 500 children; ages 10–16 | • Evaluate the effectiveness of BBBS mentoring programs through self-report<br>• Control group consisted of children who did not have a BBBS mentor | • Children who had a BBBS mentor had fewer incidents of hitting others, felt more competent about schoolwork, and had better attendance than control group |
| Rollin, Kaiser-Ulrey, & Potts, 2003 | At-risk eighth-grade students in three different schools | • Matched intervention students to community-based mentors in a career setting for 1:1 mentoring<br>• Compared to control group of students who did not have mentors | • Students who received mentoring program showed significant reductions in number of days suspended and number of infractions of school property compared to control |
| DuBois, Holloway, Valentine, & Cooper, 2002 | | • Meta-analysis of 55 mentoring studies | • Factors that seemed to improve mentoring effectiveness included mentor training as well as parent involvement components |

**Table 17.6.** Summary of Critical Features Across Secondary-Tier Programs/Interventions

| | Similar Implementation Across Students | Quick Access to the Intervention | Implemented by All School Staff/Faculty | Consistent With Schoolwide Expectations | Flexible Intervention Based on FBA | Data Are Used Continuously to Monitor Progress |
|---|---|---|---|---|---|---|
| Check and Connect | Yes | Unclear | No | Unclear | Intervention intensified not based on FBA | Yes |
| Behavior Education Program/ Check-In Check-Out (BEP/CICO) | Yes | Yes | All staff trained, implemented only by teachers with students at risk | Yes | FBA-based data can be used to modify intervention | Yes |
| First Steps to Success | Yes | Somewhat lengthy screening and assessment | No | Individualized goals vs. schoolwide goals | No | Yes |
| Social Skills Training | Yes | Possibly: depends on screening criteria and availability of intervention groups | No: usually pull out or small group for ST intervention | Depends on focus of training | Some programs focus skills based on FBA | In some cases |
| Mentoring | Yes | Usually requires screening and perhaps waiting period | No | Depends on if school or agency is implementing the intervention | Intervention can be tailored to student; usually not FBA based | Unclear |

FBA, functional behavioral assessment.
ST, Secondarytier

over 4,000 additional mentoring organizations operate throughout the United States (DuBois & Karcher, 2005). These youth mentoring programs are sponsored by corporations, nonprofits, and foundations as well as government programs, such as the National Mentoring Center funding the Juvenile Mentoring Program (JUMP) through the Office of Juvenile Justice and Delinquency Prevention Center (DuBois & Karcher, 2005; National Mentoring Center, 2003).

The primary objective of youth mentoring programs is to connect a child with a more experienced adult who can serve as a role model and provide guidance to a student or child at risk (DuBois & Karcher, 2005). Key features of mentoring programs vary depending on which agency or school offers the program but should include elements such as (a) screening and matching of mentors to students, (b) training on the purpose and goals of mentoring, and (c) an expectation of long-term student involvement (Roberts et al., 2004). In addition, a recent meta-analytic research review of youth mentoring programs identified several key features linked to improved outcomes for students receiving mentoring. These critical features include (a) ongoing mentor training, (b) structured training activities, (c) mentor expectations of how often they will meet with the child, and (d) some mechanism of including parents in the mentoring process such as communication of mentor/student goals (DuBois, Holloway, Valentine, & Cooper, 2002). Mentoring programs frequently incorporate standardized procedures (i.e., similar implementation across students), involve low effort by teacher/staff, and monitor student progress throughout the program, which are some of the essential features of ST interventions (DuBois et al., 2002; National Mentoring Center, 2003).

Table 17.6 provides a list of all of the aforementioned ST interventions and the extent to which each intervention includes the critical features of ST supports.

## MEASURING RESPONSE TO SECONDARY-TIER INTERVENTIONS

Determining how to measure response to ST interventions is not an easy task. Unlike academic performance, social behavior performance is locally and contextually defined by the values of the school's stakeholders, tolerance levels of school personnel, and overall school culture (Gresham, 2004; Jones, Caravaca, Cizek, Horner, & Vincent, 2006). For example, in relation to reading, the standard to be met can be stated as "student reads 100 words correct per minute during oral reading," and students who obtain the target score on an oral reading fluency measure will be successful readers. In addition, the metric for which reading progress is measured formatively (i.e., along the way vs. at the end of the school year) tends to be the same or similar across primary, secondary, and tertiary intervention levels, and data are gathered relatively quickly (i.e., 1–3 min). For example, schools interested in screening all students for reading difficulties typically use Dynamic Indicators of Basic Early Literacy Skills (DIBELS; Good & Kaminski, 2001) or some other type of

Curriculum-Based Measurement system (Batsche et al., 2005; Vaughn, Linan-Thompson, & Hickman-Davis, 2003). DIBELS are 1-min, fluency-based measures that are not designed to be comprehensive measures of reading but rather provide an indicator of a student's overall early literacy health (Good & Kaminski, 2001). Once students have been identified as at risk, an ST intervention can be implemented, and progress is monitored formatively using the same measure. If the student is not making progress, a tertiary-level intervention may be warranted, and progress is monitored once again using the academic indicator of reading success (Batsche et al., 2005; Vaughn et al., 2003).

In relation to social behavior, there is not an established reliable and valid "indicator" of a student's overall behavioral health that can be used across primary-, secondary-, and tertiary-tier interventions. In addition, response to behavioral interventions is measured differently across interventions. For example, percentage of points on a daily progress report is one way progress is monitored for the BEP/CICO intervention (Crone et al., 2004), whereas absences, tardies, and dropout rates are used to monitor progress for Check and Connect (Sinclair et al., 1998). For some ST interventions, unless researchers are involved in the implementation and evaluation, data are not systematically gathered to determine the success of the intervention; this is particularly true for interventions such as SST and mentoring. The final issue/question when measuring social behavior is the extent to which we allow for cultural differences when we compare a student to his or her peers (Kincaid, 2007) as cultural norms can have a significant impact on which behaviors are considered acceptable or problematic (Crijnen, Achenbach, & Verhuist, 1999).

Although direct observation of problem behavior would be a preferred metric to evaluate response to intervention (Gresham 2005), it is not efficient or cost-effective to conduct direct observations on the estimated 20% of the student population who are at risk for poor behavioral outcomes. Direct observation is more likely to be used with tertiary-tier interventions or when researchers are trying to establish a functional relation between the implementation of an intervention and the reduction in problem behavior (e.g., Fairbanks et al., 2007).

Kincaid (2007) argued for an integrated data system that can be used across ST interventions and stated that the data system should include the following features: (a) assesses specific, targeted behavioral skills, (b) is sensitive to small changes in behavior over time, (c) can be administered quickly and easily, (d) can be administered repeatedly, (e) can be easily summarized, and (f) can be used to make comparisons across students. He proposed that a DPR could be modified to be used across ST interventions; an example of a generic DPR can be seen in Fig. 17.1.

In the DPR included in Fig. 17.1, the schoolwide behavioral expectations are listed along the left column, and each student problem behavior could be further defined under the "List Behavior" section. In addition, in its current form the periods of the day are listed across the top, but this can be changed depending on the needs of the specific interventions. A pull-out social skills intervention may need the time periods broken down

Adapted from Crone, Horner & Hawken (2004)

**Daily Progress Report**

| Points Possible: ____ |
|---|
| Points Received: ____ |
| % of Points: ____ |

**Name:** ______________________ **Date:** ____________

**Rating Scale: 3=Good day 2= Mixed day 1=Will try harder tomorrow**

**GOALS:**

| | HR | 1st | 2nd | 3rd | 4th | L | 5th | 6th |
|---|---|---|---|---|---|---|---|---|
| **BE RESPECTFUL** List Behavior: | 1 2 3 | 1 2 3 | 1 2 3 | 1 2 3 | 1 2 3 | 1 2 3 | 1 2 3 | 1 2 3 |
| **BE RESPONSIBLE** List Behavior: | 1 2 3 | 1 2 3 | 1 2 3 | 1 2 3 | 1 2 3 | 1 2 3 | 1 2 3 | 1 2 3 |
| **BE PREPARED** List Behavior: | 1 2 3 | 1 2 3 | 1 2 3 | 1 2 3 | 1 2 3 | 1 2 3 | 1 2 3 | 1 2 3 |

**Teacher Comments: I really like how...**

______________________________________________

______________________________________________

**Parent Signature(s) and Comments:** ______________________________

**Fig. 17.1.** Generic daily progress report. Adapted from *Responding to Problem Behavior in Schools*, by D. A. Crone, R.H. Horner, & L. S. Hawken, 2004. New York: Guilford Press.

into 5-min increments. If a student is participating in a 1-hr afterschool mentoring program, the time periods could broken down into 10- or 15-min increments. The key benefit to using the DPR across ST interventions is that percentage of points could be used as a common metric and allow for comparison of effectiveness across interventions. In fact, preliminary research indicated that points earned on DPRS can serve as indicators of the effectiveness of behavior interventions (Chafouleas, Christ, Riley-Tillman, Briesch, & Chanese, 2007; Chafouleas, Riley-Tillman, Sassu, LaFrance, & Patwa, 2007; Cheney, Flower, & Templeton, 2007; Stage, Cheney, Flower, Templeton, Waugh, 2008). It should be noted that no research-based guideline or cutoff score (e.g., 80% of points) has been established regarding what constitutes adequate response to intervention.

Data from DPRs can be easily summarized using SWIS (May et al., 2000) or graphed using Excel (e.g., see http://www.ed.utah.edu/~ hawken_l/BEPresources.htm for a graphing template program). Other indicators besides DPRs and direct observation that can be used to assess response to intervention include (a) teacher rating on norm-referenced behavior ratings scales, (b) number of ODRs, (c) number of absences or tardies, (d) reduction in students needing tertiary-tier support, (e) academic performance data, and (f) reduction in referrals to special education for behavior problems. A list of these measures and the extent to which these measures have the key elements described by Kinkaid (2007) is provided in Table 17.7.

**Table 17.7.** Measuring Response to Secondary-Tier Interventions

| Methods | Assesses Specific Behavioral Targets | Sensitive to Small Changes | Administered Quickly and Easily | Can Be Administered Repeatedly | Easily Summarized | Used to Make Comparison Across Students |
|---|---|---|---|---|---|---|
| Teacher rating and percentage of points on daily or weekly reports | X | X | X | X | X | X |
| Direct observation | X | X | | X | X | X |
| Teacher rating on norm-referenced behavior rating scales | | | X | X | X | X |
| Office discipline referrals (ODRs) | | | X | X | X | X |
| Absences and/or tardies | | | X | X | X | X |
| Grades, assignment completion, performance on standardized tests | | | X | X | X | X |
| Reduced need for tertiary level of support | | | X | X | X | X |
| Referrals to special education for behavior problems (suspected ED) | | | X | X | X | X |

ED: Emotional Disturbance

## SYSTEMS AND SUPPORT FOR SECONDARY-TIER INTERVENTIONS

### Schoolwide Discipline Plan in Place

Before considering the use of ST interventions, a primary-tier, schoolwide discipline system must be well established. The School-wide Evaluation Tool (SET; Horner et al., 2004) is used to determine the extent to which a school has reliably implemented a behavior support plan (see chapter 14 for a more detailed explanation of the SET). By clearly outlining behavioral expectations that foster a respectful school climate, primary-tier interventions effectively prevent the majority of disciplinary problems. Without these systems in place, ST interventions would be unmanageable due to the numbers of students who would require support. In addition, research indicates that schools that have an established schoolwide discipline plan are better equipped to implement ST interventions (Hawken et al., 2007; Powers, 2003).

### Leadership Team

Schools need to determine which team is going to be in charge of processing referrals along with examining data on effectiveness of ST interventions. Some schools have established a schoolwide behavior support leadership team that meets bimonthly to evaluate schoolwide discipline plan implementation; this team also oversees ST intervention implementation. In other schools, an interdisciplinary team meets to discuss students with academic and behavioral difficulties, and this team is in charge of evaluating the effectiveness of ST interventions. No matter which team is involved in overseeing implementation, the team should meet at least every other week to make sure progress is monitored formatively and so that intervention modifications can be made proactively (Crone et al., 2004; Hawken, 2006). The team for ST interventions is responsible for making programmatic decisions and should include members from general and special education, the principal or vice principal, school psychologists and counselors, as well as parents and, when appropriate, students (Sugai & Horner, 2006; Todd, Horner, Sugai, & Colvin, 1999). At least one member should have expertise in the area of functional behavioral assessment so that the procedures can be included in ST support when necessary.

## Resources

For ST interventions to succeed, administrators and staff must agree that the benefits of creating a positive school climate will merit the resources required for implementation. While ST interventions are designed to support a broader group of students while minimizing resources required, schools must commit a portion of total resources for planning and implementation. ST support requires initial training for all members of the behavior support team, monies allocated for staff training, paid time for regular team meetings (2–4 hr per month), materials for interventions and student rewards, and sometimes an outside expert who serves as a coach for the behavior support team such as a district PBS coach (Nersesian, Todd, Lehmann, & Watson, 2000; Scott & Martinek, 2006). Many schools use educational assistants (i.e., paraprofessionals), who are typically supervised by school psychologists or school counselors to help support implementation of ST interventions.

Staff training for implementing ST interventions can vary depending on the intervention but typically involves an initial 2- to 3-day professional development training provided by a coach, an individual with experience developing, implementing, and overseeing interventions (Scott & Martinek, 2006). The coach will play a more integral role in sustaining a ST intervention during the initial years of implementation. The role of the coach is to help the team problem solve and troubleshoot, building confidence and capacity within the members of the team.

Specific costs for implementing ST supports are not consistent from school to school. To assist administrators in creating an accurate budget, Crone et al. (2004) categorized financial needs into three areas: (a) personnel, including the coach, a team coordinator, training, and paid meeting time for all members of the team; (b) materials, including software, written materials of secondary support policies, and all required forms for students receiving support; and (c) rewards for students receiving ST support. Annual costs of sustaining ST supports vary based on school size, the number of students receiving intervention, and the amount of required support from the PBS coach.

## FUTURE DIRECTIONS FOR RESEARCH AND PRACTICE

### Empirical Data Supporting Critical Features

As detailed in this chapter, ST interventions have been shown to be effective in reducing problem behavior, increasing academic engagement, and decreasing the need for more intensive levels of behavior support. Certain future research should provide empirical data on the critical features of ST interventions as detailed in Table 17.6. For example, although parental participation is a component of several ST interventions (i.e., FSS, BEP/CICO, Check and Connect), the extent to which this component is a necessary element has not been empirically validated. In fact, multiple studies on BEP/CICO indicated that students demonstrate reductions in problem behavior following implementation even if parents are unable to participate (Hawken, 2006; Hawken & Horner, 2003, Hawken et al., 2007).

Additional key elements of ST interventions that appear to cut across those described in this chapter but were not included in the OSEP (2005) website are teacher/adult feedback and reinforcement along with building a connection with a key adult in the school. The prevention literature is clear; students who are connected to at least one adult are less likely to engage in criminal activity or severe problem behavior, drop out of school, or use drugs or alcohol (Bernard, 1995; Biglan, 1995; Cheney et al., 2007; Furlong & Morrison, 2000; Masten, Best, & Garmezy, 1990; Metzler et al., 1998). In addition, contingent praise and feedback have been shown to be important components across prevention programs (Wilson, Gottfredson, & Najaka, 2001). Future research should examine the extent to which each of these critical features contributes to the effectiveness of ST interventions.

### Issues Related to Implementation

As mentioned, schools reported implementing a median of 14 prevention programs (Gottfredson & Gottfredson, 2002). This number of interventions is not easily sustainable, and fidelity of implementation is likely compromised given the distribution of time and resources across interventions. Future research should document the time, resources, and training needed to implement each ST intervention.

In addition to evaluating the costs associated with implementing ST interventions, future research should compare which interventions are more readily implemented by school staff with fidelity and have good social validity. For example, although FSS (Walker, 1998) has been shown to be successful in reducing antisocial behavior, the intervention is implemented with one student at a time and requires a consultant to implement the intervention. In addition, SST should be provided by someone skilled in behavioral principles and in managing the behavior of small groups, such as a school psychologist or prevention specialist. In contrast, programs like Check and Connect (Sinclair & Christianson, 1998) and BEP/CICO (Crone et al., 2004) support many students (for BEP/CICO, up to 30 depending on school size and resources) with the support of one paraprofessional or mentor to implement the intervention. Research should be conducted to develop guidelines for helping schools choose the most effective prevention programs to fit the needs and culture of their school.

### Combining Academic and Behavioral Supports

Although there is not exact agreement in the field about when to increase academic support, there are research-based guidelines that allow schools to determine students' level of risk for reading failure depending on goals at different times of the year (Good & Kaminski, 2001). In contrast, as mentioned, there are no standardized progress-monitoring tools for social behavior, and research-based goals have not been established. For schools to successfully implement the ST interventions, future research should help define the decision rules for increasing or decreasing behavioral support.

Although some evidence exists that schools can successfully implement both academic and behavioral support following a three-tier model (e.g., Lewis-Palmer, Bounds, & Sugai, 2004; McIntosh et al., 2006; Sadler & Sugai, in press), developing a comprehensive service delivery model is challenging. Future research should address the extent to which school teams have the capacity and knowledge to respond to academic and social behavior data to design interventions and efficiently evaluate progress of those interventions. For example, although formative assessment of academic performance has been well established in the research literature as an effective way to prevent reading failure (e.g., Deno, 1985; Shinn, 1989), it is only recently with the passing of No Child Left Behind and the push for schools to make adequate yearly progress that many schools have started to monitor the progress of all students at least three times a year. Many schools are just becoming fluent with collecting these types of data and still struggle with how to use the data for decision making (Chard & Harn, in press; Simmons et al., 2002). In addition, schools often use different systems for managing behavior and academic data. For example, over 12,000 schools across the country use the DIBELS data system (http://dibels.uoregon.edu/) or some other Web-based system to summarize reading performance data. In terms of social behavior, over 4,000 schools across the country use SWIS (May et al., 2000; http://www.swis.org/) to organize and summarize ODR data. In terms of teams managing data, future research should address whether a single data system can be used to monitor both academic and social behavior data or the most efficient way to combine data from multiple systems for use by team members. In addition, the DIBELS data system and SWIS primarily summarize screening and progress-monitoring types of data, and teams will also need efficient ways to organize both academic and behavioral diagnostic data.

## CONCLUSION

To meet the challenge of providing safe and effective schools, educators must use resources that are efficient in meeting the behavioral and academic needs of all students. ST interventions are essential in schools because they have features that permit early identification of the problematic behaviors and, when implemented with fidelity, prevent more serious problem behaviors from occurring. Without intervention, students with challenging behaviors risk continued school failure and discipline problems. ST interventions interrupt this progression and have a strong influence on students staying in school and being connected with peers and adults and in the academic environment. Such prevention efforts are implemented at relatively little cost and use of school resources but have a considerable impact on the outcomes of each of these students.

## REFERENCES


Batsche, G., Elliot, J., Graden, J. L., Grimes, J., Kovaleski, J. F., Prasse, D., et al. (2005). *Response to intervention: Policy considerations and implementation.* Alexandria, VA: National Association of State Directors of Special Education.

Bernard, B. (1995). *Fostering resilience in children* (Report No. EDO-PS-95-9). Washington, DC: Department of Education. (ERIC Document Reproduction Service No. 386327)

Big Brothers Big Sisters International. Retrieved January 14, 2006, from http://www.colorado.edu/cspv/blueprints/model/programs/details/BBBSdetails.html

Biglan, A. (1995). Translating what we know about the context of antisocial behavior into a lower prevalence of such behavior. *Journal of Applied Behavior Analysis, 28,* 479–492.

Blum, C. (2006). *Staff development and the validity of measures for schoolwide positive behavior supports.* Paper presentation at the International Positive Behavior Support Conference, Reno, NV.

Carter, D. R., & Horner, R. H. (2007). Adding functional behavioral assessment to First Step to Success: A case study. *Journal of Positive Behavior Interventions, 9,* 229–238.

Chafouleas, S. M., Christ, T. J., Riley-Tillman, T. C., Briesch, A. M., & Chanese, J. M. (2007). Generalizability and dependability of daily behavior report cards to measure social behavior of preschoolers. *School Psychology Review 36,* 63–79.

Chafouleas, S. M., Riley-Tillman, T. C., Sassu, K. A., LaFrance, M. J., & Patwa, S. S. (2007). Daily behavior report cards (DBRCs): An investigation of consistency of on-task data across raters and method. *Journal of Positive Behavior Interventions, 9,* 30–37.

Chard, D., & Harn, B. (in press). Project CIRCUITS: Center for improving reading competence using intensive treatments schoolwide. In C. Greenwood, I. Oxall, G. Sugai, & R. Horner (Eds.), *Summaries and findings from three-tiered approaches to behavior and reading supports.* New York: Guilford Press.

Cheney, D., Blum, C., & Walker, B. (2004). An analysis of leadership teams' perceptions of positive behavior support and the outcomes of typically developing and at-risk students in their schools. *Assessment for Effective Intervention, 30,* 7–24.

Cheney, D., Flower, A., & Templeton, T. (2008). *Applying response to intervention metrics in the social domain for students at risk of developing emotional or behavioral disorders. Journal of special education, 42,* 108–126.

Christenson, S. L., Sinclair, M. F., Lehr, M. F., & Hurley, C. M. (2000). Promoting successful school completion. In K. M. Minke & G. C. Bear (Eds.), *Preventing school problems—Promoting school success: Strategies and programs that work* (pp. 211–257).

Colvin, G., Kameenui, E. J., & Sugai, G. (1993). Reconceptualizing behavior management and school-wide discipline in general education. *Education and Treatment of Children, 14,* 361–381.

Crijnen, A. M., Achenbach, T. M., & Verhuist, F. C. (1999). Problems reported by parents of children from multiple cultures: The Child Behavior Checklist syndrome constructs. *American Journal of Psychiatry, 156,* 569–574.

Crone, D. A., Horner, R. H., & Hawken, L. S. (2004). *Responding to problem behavior in schools.* New York: Guilford Press.

Deno, S. L. (1985). Curriculum-based measurement: The emerging alternative. *Exceptional Children, 52*, 219–232.

Diken, I. H., & Rutherford, R. B. (2005). First Steps early intervention program: A study of effectiveness with Native-American children. *Education and Treatment of Young Children, 28*, 444–465.

DuBois, D. L., & Karcher, M. J. (2005). Youth mentoring: Theory, research and practice. In D. L. DuBois & M. J. Karcher (Eds.), *Handbook of youth mentoring* (pp. 2–11), Thousand Oaks, CA: Sage.

DuBois, D. L., Holloway, B. E., Valentine, J. C., & Cooper, H. (2002). Effectiveness of mentoring programs for youth: A meta-analytic review. *American Journal of Community Psychology, 30*, 157–197.

Elliot, S. N., & Gresham, F. M. (1991). *Social skills intervention guide: Practical strategies for social skills training.* Circle Pines, MN: American Guidance Service.

Fairbanks, S., Sugai, G., Guardino, D., & Lathrop, M (2007). Response to intervention: Examining classroom behavior support in second grade. *Exceptional Children, 73*, 288–310.

Filter, K. J.,. McKenna, M. K., Benedict, E. A., Horner, R. H., Todd, A. W., & Watson, J. (2007). Check in/Check out: A post-hoc evaluation of an efficient, secondary-level targeted intervention for reducing problem behaviors in schools. *Education and Treatment of Children, 30*, 69–84.

Fox, L., Dunlap, G., & Powell, D. (2002). Young children with challenging behavior: Issues and considerations for behavior support. *Journal of Positive Behavior Interventions, 4*, 208–217.

Golly, A., Sprague, J., Walker, H., Beard, K., & Gorham, G. (2000). The First Step to Success program: An analysis of outcomes with identical twins across multiple baselines. *Behavioral Disorders, 25*, 170–182.

Golly, A., Stiller, B., & Walker, H. M. (1998). First Step to Success: Replication and social validation of an early intervention program. *Journal of Emotional and Behavioral Disorders, 6*, 243–250.

Good, R. H., & Kaminski, R. A. (Eds.). 2001. *Dynamic indicators of basic early literacy skills* (6th ed.). Eugene, OR: Institute for the Development of Educational Achievement.

Gottfredson, D. C., & Gottfredson, G. D. (2002). Quality of school-based prevention program: Results from a national survey. *Journal of Research in Crime and Delinquency, 39*, 3–35.

Gresham, F. M. (2004). Current status and future directions of school-based behavioral interventions. *School Psychology Review, 33*, 326–343.

Gresham, F. M. (2005). Response to intervention: An alternative means of identifying students as emotionally disturbed. *Education and Treatment of Children 28*, 328–344.

Gresham, F. M., & Elliot, S. N. (1990). *Social skills rating system.* Circle Pines, MN: American Guidance Service.

Gresham, F. M., Sugai, G., & Horner, R. H. (2001). Interpreting outcomes of social skills training for students with high-incidence disabilities. *Exceptional Children, 67*, 331–334.

Hawken, L. S. (2006). School psychologists as leaders in the implementation of a targeted intervention. *School Psychology Quarterly, 21*, 91–111.

Hawken, L. S., & Horner, R. H. (2003). Evaluation of a targeted intervention within a school-wide system of behavior support. *Journal of Behavioral Education, 12*, 225–240.

Hawken, L. S., O'Neill, R. E., & MacLeod, K. S. (2008). *Effects of function of problem behavior on the responsiveness to the Behavior Education Program.* Manuscript submitted for publication.

Hawken, L. S., MacLeod, K.S., & Rawlings, L. (2007). Effects of the Behavior Education Program (BEP) on problem behavior with elementary school students. *Journal of Positive Behavior Interventions, 9*, 94–101.

Heckaman, K., Conroy, M., Fox, J., & Chait, A. (2000). Functional assessment-based intervention research on students with or at risk for emotional and behavioral disorders in school settings. *Journal of Emotional and Behavioral Disorders in School Settings, 25*, 196–210.

Horner, R. H., Todd, A. W., Lewis-Palmer, T., Irvin, L. K., Sugai, G., & Boland, J. B. (2004). The School-wide Evaluation Tool (SET): A research instrument for assessing school-wide positive behavior support. *Journal of Positive Behavior Interventions, 6*, 3–12.

Jones, C., Caravaca, L., Cizek, S., Horner, R. H., & Vincent, C. G. (2006). Culturally responsive schoolwide positive behavior support: A case study in one school with a high proportion of Native American students. *Multiple Voices, 9*, 108–119.

Kincaid, D. (2007). *Response to intervention and PBS*. Paper presented at the International Positive Behavior Support Conference, Boston. March

Lane, K. L., & Menzies, H. M. (2003). A school-wide intervention with primary and secondary tiers of support for elementary students: Outcomes and considerations. *Education and Treatment of Children, 26*, 431–451.

Lane, K. L., Wehby, J., Menzies, H. M., Doukas, G. L., Munton, S. M., & Gregg, R. M. (2003). Social skills instruction for students at risk for antisocial behavior: The effects of small-group instruction. *Behavioral Disorders, 28*, 229–248.

Lee, Y., Sugai, G., & Horner, R. H. (1999). Effect of component skill instruction on math performance and on-task, problem, and off-task behavior of students with emotional and behavioral disorders. *Journal of Positive Behavioral Interventions, 1*, 195–204.

Lehr, C. A., Sinclair, M. F., & Christenson, S. L. (2004). Addressing student engagement and truancy prevention during elementary school years: A replication study of the check and connect model. *Journal of Education for Students Placed At-Risk, 9*, 279–301.

Lewis, T. J., & Sugai, G. (1999). Effective behavior support: A systems approach to proactive school-wide management. *Effective School Practices, 17*, 47–53.

Lewis, T. J., Sugai, G., & Colvin, G. (1998). Reducing problem behavior through a school-wide system of behavior support: Investigation of a school-wide social skills training program and contextual interventions. *School Psychology Review, 27*, 446–459.

Lewis-Palmer, T., Bounds, M., & Sugai, G. (2004). District-wide system for providing individual student support [invited special issue]. *Assessment for Effective Instruction, 30*, 53–66.

MacLeod, K. S., Hawken, L. S., & O'Neill, R. E. (2008). *Secondary tier interventions: Efficient and effective supports for students at risk*. Manuscript submitted for publication.

MacLeod, K. S., O'Neill, R. E., & Hawken, L. S. (2008). *Examining the combined effects of secondary tier interventions and individualized function-based support strategies*. Manuscript in preparation.

March, R. E., & Horner, R. H. (2002). Feasibility and contributions of functional behavioral Assessments in schools. *Journal of Emotional and Behavioral Disorders, 10*, 158–170.

Masten, A. S., Best, K. M., & Garmezy, N. (1990). Resilience and development: Contributions from the study of children who overcome adversity. *Development and Psychopathology, 2*, 425–444.

May, S., Ard, W., III., Todd, A. W., Horner, R. H., Glasgow, A., Sugai, G., et al. (2000). *School-wide Information System*. Eugene: Educational and Community Supports, University of Oregon. Available at http://www.swis.org

McCurdy, B. L., Kunsch, C., & Reibstein, S. (2007). Secondary prevention in the urban school: Implementing the Behavior Education Program. *Preventing School Failure, 51*, 12–19.

McIntosh, K., Horner, R. H., Chard, D. J., Boland, J. B., & Good, R. H., III. (2006). The use of reading and behavior screening measures to predict nonresponse to school-wide positive behavior support: A longitudinal analysis. *School Psychology Review, 35*, 275–291.

Metzler, C. W., Taylor, T. K., Gunn, B., Fowler, R. C., Biglan, A., & Ary, D. (1998). A comprehensive approach to the prevention of behavior problems: Integrating family and community-based approaches to strengthen behavior management programs in schools. *Effective School Practices, 17*, 8–24.

National Mentoring Center. (2003). *Foundations of successful youth mentoring: A guidebook for program development*. Office of Juvenile Justice and Delinquency Prevention, Northwest Regional Laboratory. Oregon, Poztons

Nelson, J. R. (1996). Designing schools to meet the needs of students who exhibit disruptive behavior. *Journal of Emotional and Behavioral Disorders, 4*, 147–161.

Nelson, J. R., Benner, G. J., Reid, R. C., Epstein, M. H., & Currin, D. (2002). The convergent validity of office discipline referrals with the CBCL-TRF. *Journal of Emotional and Behavior Disorders, 10*, 181–189.

Nersesian, M., Todd, A. W., Lehmann, J., & Watson, J. (2000). School-wide behavior support through district-level system change. *Journal of Positive Behavior Interventions, 2*, 244–247.

Newcomer, L. (2004). *Establishing a targeted group intervention process.* Paper presented at the meeting of the Trainers of School-wide PBS, Naperville, IL. October.

OSEP Technical Assistance Center on Positive Behavioral Interventions and Supports. (n.d.) *School-wide PBS: Secondary prevention.* Retrieved February 18, 2005, from http://www.pbis.org/secondaryprevention.htm.PB

Osher, D., Dwyer, K., & Jackson, S. (2004). *Safe, supportive and successful schools step by step.* Longmont, CO: Sopris West.

Powers, L. J. (2003). *Examining the effects of targeted group social skills intervention in schools with and without school-wide systems of positive behavior support.* Unpublished doctoral dissertation, University of Missouri, Columbia.

Rhodes, J. E., Bogat, G. A., Roffman, J., Edelman, P., & Galasso, L. (2002). Youth mentoring in perspective: Introduction to the special issue. *American Journal of Community Psychology, 30*, 149–155.

Roberts, H., Liabo, K., Lucas, P., DuBois, D., & Sheldon, T. A. (2004). Mentoring to reduce antisocial behavior in childhood. *British Medical Journal, 328*, 512–514.

Sadler, C., & Sugai, G. (in press). *Effective behavior and instructional support: A district model for early identification and prevention of reading and behavior disabilities.* Journal of Postive Bettause Interventions.

Scott, T. M., & Martinek, G. (2006). Coaching positive behavior support in school settings: Tactics and data-based decision making. *Journal of Positive Behavior Interventions, 8*, 165–173.

Shinn, M. R. (1989). *Curriculum-based measurement: Assessing special children.* New York: Guilford Press.

Simmons, D. C., Kame'enui, E. J., Good, R. H., Harn, B. A., Cole, C., & Braun, D. (2001).

Sinclair, M. F., Christenson, S. L., Evelo, D. L., & Hurley, C. M. (1998). Dropout prevention for youth with disabilities: Efficacy of a sustained school engagement procedure. *Exceptional Children, 65*, 7–21.

Stage, S. A., Cheney, D., Flower, A., Templeton, T., & Waugh, M. (2007). *A concurrent validity study for a targeted group intervention using an Internet-based daily performance report and chart review process using four student behavior constructs: Externalizing problem behavior, internalizing problem behavior, social skills, and academic skills.* Manuscript submitted for publication.

Sugai, G., & Horner, R. H. (2002). The evolution of discipline practices: School-wide positive behavior supports. *Child and Family Behavior Therapy, 24*, 23–50.

Sugai, G., & Horner, R. R. (2006). A promising approach for expanding and sustaining school-wide positive behavior support. *School Psychology Review, 35*, 245–259.

Sugai, G., Horner, R. H., & Gresham, F. M. (2002). Behaviorally effective school environments. In M. R. Shinn, H. M. Walker, & G. Stoner (Eds.), *Interventions for academic and behavior problems II: Preventive and remedial approaches.* Bethesda, MD: NASP. *315*–350

Sugai, G., Sprague, J., Horner, R. R., & Walker, H. (2000). Preventing school violence: The use of office referral to assess and monitor school-wide discipline interventions. *Journal of Emotional and Behavioral Disorders, 8*, 94–101.

Taylor-Greene, S., Brown, D., Nelson, L. Longton, J., Gassman, T., Cohen, J., et al. (1997). School-wide behavior support: Starting the year off right. *Journal of Behavioral Education, 7*, 99–112.

Todd, A. W., Horner, R. H., Sugai, G., & Colvin, G. (1999). Individualizing school-wide discipline for students with chronic problem behaviors: A team approach. *Effective School Practices, 17*, 72–82.

Walker, B., Cheney, D., Stage, S., & Blum, C. (2005). Schoolwide screening and positive behavior supports: Identifying and supporting students as risk for school failure. *Journal of Positive Behavior Interventions, 7*, 194–204.

Walker, H. M. (1998). First steps to prevent antisocial behavior. *Teaching Exceptional Children, 30*, 16–19.

Walker, H. M., Horner, R. H., Sugai, G., Bullis, M., Sprague, J. R., Bricker, D., et al. (1996). Integrated approaches to preventing antisocial behavior patterns among school-age children and youth. *Journal of Emotional Behavior Disorders, 4*, 194–209.

Walker, H. M., Kavanagh, K., Stiller, B., Golly, A., Severson, H. H., & Feil, E. G. (1998). First Step to Success: An early intervention approach for preventing school failure. *Journal of Emotional Behavior Disorders, 4*, 66–80.

Walker, H. M., Stiller, B., Severson, H. H., Golly, A., & Feil, E. G. (1998). First step to success: Intervening at the point of school entry to prevent antisocial behavior patterns. *Psychology in the Schools, 35*, 259–269.

Warren, J. S., Edmonson, H. M., Griggs, P., Lassen, S. R., McCart, A., Turnbull, A., et al. (2003). Urban applications of school-wide positive behavior support: Critical issues and lessons learned. *Journal of Positive Behavior Interventions, 5*, 80–91.

White, R. (2007). *Positive behavior support team decisions regarding secondary tier interventions*. Paper presented at the International Positive Behavior Support Conference, Boston. March

Wilson, D. B., Gottfredson, D. C., & Najaka, S. S. (2001). School-based prevention of problem behaviors: A meta-analysis. *Journal of Quantitative Criminology, 17*, 247–272.

Vaughn, S., Linan-Thompson, S., & Hickman-Davis, P. (2003). Response to treatment as a means of identifying students with reading/learning disabilities. *Exceptional Children, 69*, 391–409.

# 18

# Function-Based Supports for Individual Students in School Settings

**TERRANCE M. SCOTT, CYNTHIA ANDERSON, RICHMOND MANCIL, and PETER ALTER**

When considering behavior supports for students whose behaviors have not responded to primary- or secondary-tier interventions, the need to align interventions with assessment information becomes crucially important. If effective interventions are not developed, these students are likely to experience a range of negative outcomes, including academic failure, school dropout (Rylance, 1997; Tremblay, Mass, Pagani, & Vitaro, 1996), chronic unemployment, criminal involvement, and poor family adjustment (Duncan, Forness, & Hartsough, 1995; Jay & Padilla, 1987). Successful outcomes for these students are dependent on our ability to intervene as early as possible with appropriate, evidence-based interventions. Fortunately, efforts to intervene early and effectively have been bolstered in recent years by function-based approaches to behavior intervention support.

A function-based approach to prevention is an essential feature of positive behavior support (PBS). At the primary tier, consideration of predictability of failure is a fundamental component of the development of school rules. While such efforts do not constitute what would typically be defined as functional behavior assessment (FBA), the practice is similar to what is more commonly considered effective assessment at the secondary or tertiary tiers. That is, understanding who, what, when, and where student

**TERRANCE M. SCOTT** • University of Louisville
**CYNTHIA ANDERSON** • University of Oregon
**RICHMOND MANCIL** • University of Central Florida
**PETER ALTER** • University of Louisville

failures occur is helpful in understanding why they occur and thus provides a direction for intervention (e.g., effective rules, routines, and arrangements to maximize the probability of student success). Still, the term FBA is typically applied to students for whom primary- and secondary-tier interventions have proven insufficient to facilitate student success.

As a process, FBA can be considered in two phases: assessment and hypothesis development and intervention planning. While the term FBA is sometimes used to refer to both the assessment and intervention components, FBA more appropriately refers only to the assessment and hypothesis development phase, and the term *behavior intervention plan* (BIP) more appropriately describes the resulting function-based intervention plan.

This chapter begins by defining the key features of FBA as both a process and practice at the tertiary tier. This includes a component description of the steps involved in both the FBA and BIP processes. Next, the connection between FBA and BIP is discussed, making the case for the two to be thought of as parts of a single process. Finally, a critical review and discussion of assessment methodology is presented, highlighting the limitations of FBA in school settings, connecting assessment to the development of functional hypotheses, and providing recommendations for practice and future research.

## PHASE 1: CONDUCTING AN FBA IN SCHOOL SETTINGS

The FBA process is prescriptive in that there are key steps that guide component practices. Structured protocols have been developed and studied as tools for facilitating the fidelity of the process (e.g., Functional Assessment and Intervention Team Meeting Record, Scott, Liaupsin, & Nelson, 2005; Functional Assessment and Program Development for Problem Behavior: A Practical Handbook, O'Neill et al., 1997). In addition to enhancing the rigor and fidelity of the process, these instruments can also provide efficiency by keeping the process focused on the key steps and avoiding tangential or irrelevant issues. The steps described next are summarized in Table 18.1.

### *Define the Problem*

The first step in the process of completing an FBA is to develop an operational definition of the behavior so that everyone agrees on the behavior of concern. An operational definition is best obtained via discussion with those who know and have observed the student. Operational definitions describe the behavior in observable and objective terms—the focus is on the problematic actions of a student. Consider Destiny, a seventh grader who often is defiant in biology and history classes. Before moving forward, her teachers need to come to consensus regarding the problem—simply targeting "defiance" is not sufficient as this may mean different things to different people. Destiny's teachers defined defiance as failure to begin working on a task within 20 s of a request and used saying "No" or swearing at a teacher when asked to do something as examples.

**Table 18.1.** Key Steps in the Functional Behavioral Assessment (FBA) Process

| | |
|---|---|
| Step 1: Define behavior of concern | • Create an operational definition of behavior<br>• Describe why it is a problem<br>• Determine whether the student can engage in appropriate behavior<br>• List what you have already tried |
| Step 2: Identify relationships between the behavior and surrounding environment | Determine what times, locations, contexts, conditions, etc., tend to predict or precede:<br>• Problem behavior<br>• Appropriate behavior<br>Determine what types of events tend to follow behavior:<br>• Peers, instruction, consequences, etc.<br>• After problem behavior<br>• After appropriate behavior |
| Step 3: Hypothesize function of behavior | • Make a guess at the function: Why do you think he or she is doing this?<br>• Access to ... (persons, objects, attention, etc.)<br>• Escape or avoid ... (persons, activities, attention, etc.) |
| Step 4: Verify hypothesis | Manipulate environment and observe predictable changes in behavior:<br>• Functional analysis: Manipulate consequences and observe any resulting changes in behavior<br>• Structural analysis: Manipulate antecedents and observe any resulting changes in behavior<br>Verify hypothesis and develop intervention or deny and collect more information to revise hypothesis |

### *Identify Functional Relationships Between Behavior and the Environment*

Once a definition is developed, the next step is to identify environmental events or circumstances that predictably occur both prior to and immediately following behavior. When considering antecedents and consequences, it is important to remember that the environment consists of all actions, items, and events. The teacher, peers, tasks, instruction, and other subtle conditions are part of the environment and must be considered. Identification of these variables may be accomplished succinctly by first identifying routines that are often problematic. For example, it may be prudent to ask whether noncompliance occurs during all structured activities or just during math or whether teasing peers occurs during activities in all less-structured settings or only at recess. Identifying problematic contexts and conditions in the environment allows the focus of assessment to be narrowed. Importantly, if problem behavior occurs across routines, such as academic tasks *and* during recess, it will be important to conduct separate assessments as problem behavior may very well be affected by very different variables in these different settings. To illustrate, consider a child Joan who hits peers in math class and in the cafeteria. Observations and interviews revealed that, in math class, hitting most often occurs when Joan is asked to write on the board and predictably results in removal from the class. In contrast, hitting in the cafeteria occurs most often when other students ignore Joan and results in attention and laughter from students nearby. In math class, it seems likely that the function is to escape math work at the board, while in the cafeteria the function of the same hitting behavior is to access peer attention. This distinction will be important in determining the most appropriate intervention in each setting.

When developing a statement of the function of behavior, the proper sequence is first to focus on predictable patterns. That is, the first step is to focus on what happens in sequence when observing the behavior in its natural context. Preconceptions of what should or should not be functional should be at least temporarily abandoned in favor of a logical analysis of how the environment actually affects behavior. For example, if a student is regularly admonished by the teacher for forgetting homework, it may be tempting to assume that such reprimands are aversive. However, even though public admonishment may be aversive for most, some may actually find it reinforcing (e.g., 1:1 teacher attention with others observing). Thus, it is critical that function be determined solely by predictable patterns.

Identification of predictable antecedents and consequences provides information leading to a hypothesis of function. As noted, a hypothesis statement describes the events that evoke and maintain the problem behavior and identifies the likely function. For example, if inappropriate noise making is generally preceded by situations in which the teacher's attention is directed elsewhere and is almost always followed by a reprimand from the teacher, it is logical to hypothesize that, when teacher attention is not directly available, noise making serves a function of accessing teacher attention (positively reinforced). Similarly, if inappropriate noises generally occur when the teacher makes a request of the student and results in peers and the teacher moving away, it would be logical to hypothesize that, given a teacher request, noise making serves a function of escaping that request (negatively reinforced). In both cases, the noise making is reinforced and is functional, but the function itself is different and indicates different intervention strategies. Obviously, time-out as a consequence for the student who is attempting to escape will provide further escape and thus will not be effective.

### *Verify Functional Hypothesis*

Hypotheses of function are simply guesses based on information gathered. Once a hypothesis is derived, the next step is either to move forward with intervention development or to attempt to verify the hypothesis prior to intervention development. When there are strong data in support of the hypothesis, consensus among those participating, or the need for expediency supersedes the need for formal hypothesis testing, intervention is implemented and monitored. The results of a logical function-based intervention would then be used as a means of hypothesis verification. For example, if inappropriate noises are evoked by the absence of teacher attention and maintained by attention, an intervention might consist of ignoring noises and instead providing attention when the student's hand was raised. After collecting data on rates of inappropriate noises prior to intervention for several days, the intervention is implemented. If problem behavior is reduced, the next step is to briefly remove the intervention to see whether problem behavior increases (i.e., if rates of problem behavior are a function of the presence or absence of the intervention).

However, when data are not strong, there is no clear consensus among those participating, or the consequences of intervention based on an incorrectly identified function are too dire, hypothesis verification may be accomplished via an experimental functional analysis in which identified consequences are experimentally manipulated or, to a lesser extent, a structural analysis in which antecedents are manipulated (see Stichter & Conroy, 2005; Stichter, Sasso, & Jolivette, 2004). For example, take a case in which observational data are not conclusive regarding whether the function of a behavior is to access peer attention. Two clearly identified conditions may exist in which peer attention is and is not provided on student behavior. The two conditions could be systematically manipulated, and if behavior were more likely when attention was provided, the function would be identified as access to peer attention. However, if there were no differences in behavior, then peer attention would be discarded and more data collected in an attempt to identify a more valid hypothesis.

In summary, regardless of the methods used, an FBA involves several steps: operationally defining the behavior, gathering information about events that reliably precede and follow problem behavior, using that information to develop a hypothesis statement, verifying the hypothesis, and then intervening. This manner of FBA process has been used extensively in empirical studies and has been documented as useful for developing interventions (Dunlap et al., 1993). Unfortunately, although the utility of FBA is well supported by the literature, more demonstrations of school-based FBA are needed. The vast majority of studies on FBA have been conducted in atypical settings (e.g., clinics) with individuals with significant disabilities (Ervin, Ehrhardt, & Poling, 2001; Nelson, Roberts, Mathur, & Rutherford, 1999). Second and more troubling, of those studies conducted in educational settings, very few focused on "typical" school-based FBA. Most school-based studies have focused on FBAs conducted entirely by researchers and interventions either implemented by researchers or implemented by teachers with extensive support from researchers (Scott, Bucalos et al., 2004). Despite these inadequacies and the clearly defined issues for future research, FBA represents a logical and effective practice for assessing students and prescribing the development of intervention (Ingram, Lewis-Palmer, & Sugai, 2005; Newcomer & Lewis, 2004; Payne, Scott, & Conroy, 2007). The next section presents the development of function-based intervention plans.

## PHASE 2: BEHAVIOR INTERVENTION PLANNING

The process of developing a function-based intervention plan is dependent on the identification of function. As such, the FBA is not complete until a function-sufficient consensus or experimental verification has been identified. Intervention planning also is fairly prescriptive in that some key steps can guide the process. These steps are summarized in Table 18.2.

**Table 18.2.** Key Steps in the Function-Based Support Process

| | |
|---|---|
| Step 1: Develop an appropriate replacement behavior | Determine what times, locations, contexts, conditions, etc. tend to predict or precede:<br>• Fair pair: Incompatible with problem (cannot do at same time)<br>• Functional: Meets the same function as problem behavior |
| Step 2: Determine how the replacement behavior will be taught | Determine how the replacement behavior and intervention plan will be taught:<br>• Rules (what it is and when, where, how, and why to use behavior)<br>• Examples (modeling and use of naturally occurring examples)<br>• Practice (opportunities to practice with teacher feedback) |
| Step 3: Create routines and arrangements to facilitate success | Consider realistic routines and physical arrangements that could be implemented to facilitate student success (avoid predictable failure and create success opportunities)<br>• Prompts and reminders<br>• Supervise<br>• Avoid spoilers |
| Step 4: Determine appropriate consequences for replacement and problem behaviors | Determine appropriate consequences for replacement and problem behaviors – and consider what is realistic for you to do<br>• Reinforcement (matches function)<br>• Correction (how might this happen?)<br>• Negative consequences (matches function)<br>• Natural (try to keep it as realistic as possible) |
| Step 5: Monitor and evaluate the plan | Consider realistic strategies for measuring behavior:<br>• Keep it simple<br>• Consider times and conditions where measurement would be particularly meaningful and realistic<br>• Consider what your measure will look like when the behavior is no longer a problem<br>• Measurable behavior<br>• By what time should this happen? |

### *Identify an Appropriate Replacement Behavior*

If we continue to assume that behavior is purposeful, attempting to decrease behavior solely by means of punishing its occurrence will likely be ineffective, if not counterproductive (Sulzer-Azaroff & Mayer, 1991). That is, when a functional behavior is made inefficient, the individual likely will develop a new behavior to continue meeting the desired function. However, the new behavior may be even less desired and more resistant to intervention. Problem behaviors are best reduced by replacing them with other similarly functional but more appropriate alternatives. Appropriate replacement behaviors are both functional for the student (i.e., meet desired function) and represent what is widely considered to be acceptable in the culture and context in which it occurs. For example, hand raising is an appropriate replacement behavior for noise making as it is both appropriate for the teacher and environment and can serve the same function of accessing teacher attention. Replacement behaviors may be selected by creating two lists, one with all the behaviors that the teacher would accept as appropriate and another with all the behaviors that the student is capable of performing. The overlap on these two lists represents appropriate replacement behaviors for the context. As a general rule, the most appropriate of these possibilities is the one that the other students also use and that represents the best chance of student success. As a general rule, students will only adopt replacement behaviors when they are at least as effective (work as well), efficient (work as easily), and relevant (look like what others do) as the problem behavior.

### *Determine How the Replacement Behavior Will Be Taught*

Instruction is perhaps the most important step in the behavior intervention planning process (Walker & Shinn, 2002). Of important consideration at this stage is the type of instruction that will be necessary. Some students will require instruction of what a behavior is and how to do it (acquisition). Other students already have familiarity with the skill but engage in other behaviors that are either more effective or efficient. For many of these students, instruction will be more focused on using the behavior with more ease to make it efficient or at the right time to make it more effective (fluency). For other students, instruction may focus on providing prompts and cues to help them remember when, where, and how it is best used in a functional manner. In all cases, instruction of replacement behaviors involves teaching the student not just what to do but also when and why that behavior will be the most functional. In fact, the teaching component of the intervention involves teaching all the components of the plan: what is expected, when, how, and what will happen when it does and does not happen as directed. Effective instruction involves presentation of key rules (what behavior is and when, where, how, and why to use behavior); effective examples (modeling and use of naturally occurring examples); and opportunities for practice (with teacher feedback). As with any instructional sequence, instruction is completed when the student demonstrates mastery. Only after mastery of instruction should the full plan be implemented.

### *Create Routines and Arrangements to Facilitate Success*

While planning for instruction involves determining what it is that the student should do, when it should be done, and why (consequences), routines and physical arrangements are things that adults do to increase the likelihood of success. Recall that the environment is made up of all the things that occur both before and after behavior. Considering this array of antecedent and consequence variables, the instructional environment, and any environment in which behavior is to be expected, should be modified so that prompts and cues that trigger desirable behavior are present and those that occasion problem behavior are removed. Similarly, consequence events that maintain problem behavior should be eliminated, and reinforcers that maintain replacement behavior should be increased. For example, having taught a student to raise her hand to get the teacher's attention during independent work times, a verbal prompt may be provided immediately prior to this time: "Remember during independent work time that if you need anything all you have to do is raise your hand, and I'll come over as soon as I can." In addition, the teacher may attempt to find a position in the classroom to better see the student, move the student to a more visible location, place a reminder sticker on the student's desk, and put the directions for work on the board so that the student can see them.

All instruction requires performance feedback to achieve acquisition. That is, a student will not understand when a skill is performed correctly unless there is specific feedback on performance. When behavior is performed correctly, it must be acknowledged so that the student is reinforced. Likewise, when behavior is performed incorrectly, it must also be acknowledged so that the student understands what represents an incorrect behavior. When the student does raise her hand, the teacher must immediately and consistently provide the attention that is functional for that behavior. Conversely, when the student makes noises, the teacher must find a way to respond in a way that is not functional for the student (e.g., ignore, time-out). All strategies considered here must involve thought of what is realistic for school personnel to implement in a consistent manner.

The presentation of a stimulus immediately following a behavior, resulting in an increase of the future probability of that behavior is known as a *positive reinforcement*. The action of acknowledging behavior is intended as positive reinforcement. Reinforcers include all consequence stimuli that have the effect of increasing responding when presented contingently on behavior. Thus, we reinforce appropriate behavior because we want it to happen again. Reinforcement may be as simple as a nod, a "thank you," or a token. An understanding of function allows for the identification of natural reinforcement. For example, understanding that a behavior serves to access teacher attention means using teacher attention as a consequence for appropriate behavior will be effective. The goal is to maintain use of natural (functional) reinforcers and to use the least amount of reinforcement necessary to facilitate student success. In general, simple acknowledgment of success should fade as students recognize their own success and are reinforced naturally.

Actions taken contingent on and immediately following a behavior, resulting in a decreased future probability of that behavior are known as a *punishment*. Providing consequences for problem behavior is intended to decrease the occurrence of that behavior. Effective punishments include both the removal of reinforcing stimuli and the introduction of aversive stimuli contingent on behavior. Thus, the purpose of providing punishment for behavior is to decrease the likelihood of its reoccurrence. Effective punishment may be as simple as a ignoring a behavior that functions to get attention or having a student engage in an overcorrection procedure (return all the way to the start and walk for running in the hall). Both instances make the problem behavior less effective and efficient. An understanding of function allows for the identification of natural consequences for problem behavior. For example, understanding that a problem behavior serves to access teacher attention means that using ignoring as a consequence for noise-making behavior will not allow the student's behavior to access the intended functional reinforcer. The goal is to maintain use of natural (functional) consequences and to use the least amount necessary to facilitate student success.

### *Monitor and Evaluate Plan*

While a complete discussion of methods of monitoring student behavior is beyond the scope of this chapter, some simple considerations for developing realistic strategies for measuring behavior are offered. First, determine the context of problem behavior and measure only during those times and conditions. For example, if the problem is noises during independent work time, measure only during that time and do not attempt to implement measurement all day. Second, use methods that are realistic given other teaching activities. For example, do not attempt to measure the precise beginning and ending of recurrent behaviors if the classroom context requires a great deal of movement and individual attention to a variety of students. Third, find a measure that provides you with the best index of the behavior where you want it to be in the end. For example, if the goal is to have the student call out no more than five times, be sure to begin monitoring call outs and not time engaged in instruction. Last, consider a reasonable timeline for success and use that as a measure of progress. That is, a line between current performance and desired performance at a certain date provides a line of minimal progress by which the success of the plan can be evaluated on a daily basis.

## PROBLEMS WITH TRADITIONAL FBA IN SCHOOL SETTINGS

### Complicated and Time-Consuming Methods of FBA

As alluded to here and documented in the literature (e.g., McKerchar & Thompson, 2004; Sasso, Conroy, Peck Stichter, & Fox, 2001), there exists a significant research-to-practice gap on FBA. More specifically, for schools attempting to implement FBA, the research literature often is of little assistance as the FBA methods considered to be the most reliable and valid also require extensive time and expertise in FBA—two resources most schools have precious little to spare.

The vast majority of empirical studies on FBA incorporated complex manipulations of environmental events and generally were conducted by researchers. In the few studies in which teachers conducted all or part of the FBA, extensive training and coaching was used. For example, Kamps, Wendland, and Culpepper (2006) worked with the teacher of two students with behavior problems. They initially conducted a functional assessment interview and then direct observations. Next, the teacher conducted a functional analysis with extensive coaching from the researchers. Although this FBA process resulted in an effective intervention, it is unlikely that any school would have access to individuals trained to conduct such complex FBAs or who could train and supervise teachers in the conduct of the FBA.

Even if a school has access to individuals with expertise in advanced methods of FBA, it is unlikely that teachers will be able or willing to participate in extensive and complex FBAs. Further, if the chosen method of FBA involves removing the student from the classroom (e.g., to complete a functional analysis) teachers may be unwilling to allow the student to participate as so doing would result in a loss of instructional minutes. This is somewhat disconcerting as many individuals advocate for extensive direct observations and experimental confirmation of hypotheses prior to development of an intervention (see Sasso et al., 2001).

To illustrate more clearly, consider what is involved in conducting a functional analysis—the most research-validated method of FBA—in a school setting. Functional analysis involves extensive data collection during tightly controlled and repeated analog sessions. From the examples in the available literature, this process has been considered a multiperson job. Even if teachers conduct the analog, time (and individuals) are needed to train them in the process prior to conducting the analysis. If the teacher does not conduct the analysis, then one or more trained individuals is needed to do so. Further, trained observers must count and record the occurrences of the targeted behavior, and someone with expertise is needed to coordinate the entire process. In the absence of trained data coders, sessions would have to be videotaped and teachers trained to count and record behaviors in post hoc observation sessions. This, of course, requires even more time and expertise—all heaped on top of the long list of other demands placed on educators. Even conducting significantly less-complex methods of FBA such as antecedent-behavior-consequence (ABC) observations requires one or more individuals with expertise in the process to coordinate the FBA (e.g., determine when to observe, develop a data collection device, identify how many observations to conduct, and analyze the resulting data) and collect data.

A second issue is that aspects of functional analysis and direct descriptive observation may seem counterintuitive to many practitioners or may be impossible to implement due to safety or ethical reasons. In the case of functional analysis, manipulating the environment in an effort to evoke, as opposed to reduce, certain challenging behaviors may be highly problematic for teachers. For example, consider the teacher of 26 second-grade students, one of whom occasionally engages in prolonged episodes of screaming. When told that the FBA will involve repeatedly setting up situations that you have found often evoke screaming and then leaving those events in place for several minutes—often 10 min or more—the teacher likely will not be motivated to participate. In the case of direct observations, teachers trying to collect data on their own may find it difficult to objectively observe students' behavior and resist intervening collect data, especially with students who create havoc in the classrooms. Further, if these behaviors are dangerous to the student or others or are detrimental to the classroom milieu, then ethical issues may also make delaying intervention to conduct observations questionable.

Third, in regard to functional analysis and structural analysis, control of the environment is the distinguishing characteristic separating descriptive observations from functional analysis (Sasso et al., 1992). However, classrooms, compared to clinics, are free operant environments (Scott, Bucalos et al., 2004), meaning that many things typically are happening at once. For example, during independent work, a specific task has been assigned, other students are close by and engaging in a variety of behavior, the teacher often is moving about the room, and there may be noise in the hallway or outside the classroom—any one of these events might evoke problem behavior. As a result, classrooms often are not conducive to controlled experimentation for a single student during typical classroom contexts. Similarly, in the case of teacher-conducted direct observations, it would be difficult to assess the accuracy with which a busy teacher was able to capture all of the antecedents and consequences that surround a target behavior, thus resulting in a higher probability of inaccurate results.

Due to problems such as these, researchers increasingly are arguing for development and evaluation of more feasible methodologies such as team-based processes and the use of interviews, questionnaires, and checklists that, while necessarily less formalized and direct, might offer a more realistic methodology for public school settings and set the occasion for valid teacher implementation of FBA (Scott, Bucalos et al., 2004). This is not to say that rigorous research using complex methods of FBA in schools is not important or necessary. Indeed, there is a significant need for rigorous studies documenting the validity of FBA with general education students in school settings, and conducting such research will need to involve methods such as those used by Kamps et al. (2006) and others. There is, however an equally great need for research documenting FBA procedures that can be implemented in schools by typical school personnel.

## Lack of Trained Personnel

Closely related to the preceding problem is that schools lack personnel trained in FBA. Schools attempting to implement function-based interventions often rely on one person to both conduct all FBAs and develop the interventions. As noted by Scott, Anderson, and Spaulding (2008), this presents three critical problems. First, there generally are more students who need an intervention than can adequately or realistically be addressed by a single person. Second, if the individual does not possess adequate skills or training, the integrity of the FBA will likely be compromised and be of little use in developing an effective intervention. Third, if the individual takes a position in another school or takes on new responsibilities in the current school, there may be no one to step in and conduct FBAs, thus leaving a void in the services to those with challenging behavior.

Although a single person in charge of all FBA processes and procedures is logically unrealistic, training all school personnel to be fluent in the conceptual basis and methodology of FBA is similarly unrealistic (Benazzi, Horner, & Good, 2006). First, teachers already have a vast array of demands on their time, including instruction, assessment, grading, faculty meetings, parent-teacher conferences, lesson planning, and the like. There simply is not enough additional time for all teachers to attend sufficient training to learn about the conceptual basis of FBA and to become fluent in the various methods of FBA that might be applicable for a given student.

As described next (and in more depth in chapter 28), the most sustainable process for completing a school-based FBA will be team based, involving a cadre of persons to facilitate FBA at various levels.

## FUNCTION-BASED SUPPORT AND EFFICIENCY

As described, procedures for conducting FBA may be considered on a continuum of simplest to most complex. The purpose of this section is to describe promising structures and processes that fall on the simpler and more efficient end of this continuum. Schools will need additional resources and expertise to conduct more advanced methods of FBA (see chapter 28 for a description of a districtwide system of implementation). The key features of more simple processes include three critical features. First, the process must be efficient in that the time and effort involved must be realistic in the context of what school personnel are already required to do in an average day. More time or effort will not be realistic and therefore will not be sustained (Fullan, 1993, 2001). Second, application must occur within the multitier intervention model such that FBA is not solely used with those students with the most chronic problem behaviors. Effective use of FBA is more proactive, with students exhibiting less-chronic and frequent problems but who have been identified as nonresponsive to more general procedures. Third, simplified FBA processes must make use of existing knowledge and information prior to engaging more complex processes. As mentioned, efficiency is dependent on the extent to which those engaged in the process see it as realistic within the context of their everyday tasks. Because the team-based FBA represents a unique structure within the school, sustainability of the team-based process itself must be considered (Benazzi et al., 2006). Chapter 28 provides an extended discussion of how schools can develop and maintain systems to support the effective use of simplified FBA processes and procedures. This section provides an overview of key features and considerations involved in establishing team-based FBA and function-based support.

### Team-Based FBA and Support

A team-based approach to function-based support relies on the knowledge and expertise of typical classroom teachers and personnel. The team-based approach incorporates both efficient and formal methods of FBA. As a foundation, a "behavior support team" is formed at the school level to make initial decisions as part of a multitier approach and to refer students to the most appropriate level and type of intervention. As students are deemed unresponsive to the interventions implemented by the behavior support team, student-level teams will be developed to address student needs more directly via FBA and function-based intervention planning (See Chapter 28).

The function-based support team is developed for individual students and consists of (a) persons who are familiar with the student (teachers, staff, and parents) and (b) at least one person who is knowledgeable of FBA and function-based support to serve as the team facilitator. Procedures used by this team are described next. Referrals to these teams generally are initiated by teachers or other school personnel, who report students who have not responded positively to typical school- or classwide procedures.

Although a team-based FBA is developed for efficiency of the process, some school personnel may see such meetings as outside their charge and resist involvement. As such, the meeting process must be established as a school routine and part of the school's system of care for students experiencing failure (Benazzi et al., 2006). When set up from the beginning as an integral part of the schoolwide student support system, a better understanding of the rationale behind and need for such meetings can be established (Eber, Smith, Sugai, & Scott, 2002). Further, when invited to attend a meeting, faculty and staff should be reminded that this is a meeting to discuss how to make the student more successful and to share experiences—both positive and negative—that each has had with the student. Expertise in understanding and analyzing behavior is not an expectation—only that all staff at the meeting be familiar with the student and provide their important observations to the discussion.

Involving those who know the student creates the foundation for teaming that can be applied more broadly across students and behaviors (Carr et al., 2002; Sugai, Lewis-Palmer, & Hagan, 1998). Team-based problem solving, in which members contribute to the process of assessment and intervention planning, has been suggested as a cost-effective method of meeting the needs of individual students as well as increasing interaction and cooperation among faculty and parents (Chalfant & Pysh, 1989; Jolivette, Barton-Arwood, & Scott, 2000; Kling, 1997). Teaming as a strategy for conducting an FBA, and developing a function-based support plan warrants further consideration of the key steps for each. This process has been described by Benazzi et al. (2006) and detailed as a training package by Scott, Liaupsin, and Nelson (2005).

## Team-Based FBA Process

Definition of the problem behavior in the team-based process consists of those who know the student providing post hoc observations of behavior, which are summarized into a statement of the problem that is agreeable to all. Team members then describe the contexts in which the problem occurs. The facilitator may prompt specific responses with such questions as "Under what types of conditions would you be most likely to see this behavior?" or "What do the other students do when the student engages in this behavior?" In addition, more indirect methods of data collection are often used as a source of information. Once the facilitator has helped team members share observations, he or she offers a possible hypothesis of function for discussion. For example, the facilitator might say:

> What I am hearing from all of you is that Jerome has a lot of problems during group work situations. When he is asked to work cooperatively, he pushes, shoves, and takes materials from those in his group and sometimes calls group members mean names. When Jerome does these things, peers respond negatively, and he is often removed from the group and told that he will have to complete the assignment alone, which he does without problems. It sounds to me like our hypothesis statement is, "When Jeremy is asked to work in a group, he engages in problem behavior, which results in removal from the group but not

the assignment. Therefore, the function of the problem behavior is to escape from group interaction.

Generally, team consensus is the criterion for determining the most logical hypothesis of the function of student behavior, so the facilitator asks for feedback and works with team members to develop a hypothesis statement that team members agree is logical. When data are unclear or the team cannot reach consensus regarding a possible hypothesis of function, the team must make plans to make more formal observations and then reconvene the team to continue discussions. In general, as a team is unable to generate an agreeable hypothesis, further assessment will involve an increasing number of people, become increasingly complex, and require more time and effort in both assessment and analysis.

A key feature of team-based and other simple methods of FBA is the lack of experimental verification procedures (Snell, Voorhees, & Chen, 2005). Verification in the team-based process is generally focused on a combination of (a) team consensus given their shared data and (b) naturalistic observations as confirmation of the validity of the team's decision. Certainly, the team process does not preclude a team from developing a more complex and rigorous verification process, but the standard for keeping it simple generally prompts more efficient processes. As mentioned, experimental verification is indicated when data are not strong, there is no clear consensus among those participating, or the consequences of intervention based on an incorrectly identified function are too dire. Research on team-based processing for FBA indicated that trained teams are able to generate logical hypotheses given a process by which to complete the process (Benazzi et al., 2006). However, in the absence of a structured protocol and facilitator to lead the process, these teams often spent inordinate amounts of time with relatively simple tasks such as defining behavior (Scott, McIntyre, Liaupsin, Nelson, & Conroy, 2004), effectively defeating the efficiency of the process.

## Team-Based, Function-Based Support Planning

The team-based plan involves development of a replacement behavior, design of instructional processes, facilitation of success via routines and arrangements, development of appropriate positive and negative consequences, and plans for monitoring and evaluation. The key difference (Chalfant & Pysh, 1989) from a more expert-driven model is in the consensus of the group at each key step in planning. The resulting function-based support plan is agreed on and implemented by all. In addition, all are responsible for monitoring student performance and will be involved in any follow-up discussions regarding the plan. Research on team-based processing for function-based support indicated that trained teams are able to generate comprehensive behavior plans. However, research also indicated that, in the absence of a structured protocol to lead the team, these efforts often degenerated into protracted discussions of more punitive procedures that resulted in plans that were far more reactive and negative (Scott, McIntyre, et al., 2004, 2005).

## BEST PRACTICE IN FBA

Much of this chapter has focused on describing FBA in the context of efficiency and effectiveness given the unique challenges and issues involved in school-based application. While direct methods are supported by a long and rich research base, indirect methods (including interviews, rating scales, and a review of school records) provide a more efficient method of assessing behavior patterns. This section presents a more in-depth analysis of indirect methods and the supporting research base.

### Review of Indirect Methods

A variety of indirect methods exist; however, little is available about their relative use. To provide samples of the range of available instruments, a variety of databases were searched (e.g., PsycINFO, Academic Search Premier, Google), and queries were made to individuals who have published research on FBA in schools. A total of 10 FBA instruments (summarized in Table 18.3) met the following criteria: (a) used for an FBA, (b) available to teachers, (c) require no direct observation. Each of these instruments was then analyzed with regard to its format, content, and complexity.

#### *Format*

Identified indirect assessment instruments generally fell into three format categories: (a) checklists, (b) questionnaires, and (c) interviews. Checklists typically contain items that require a practitioner to respond by circling yes/no or on a Likert scale ranging from 1 to 5, which typically represents a range from always to never, respectively. The practitioner must then score the instrument in a manner described by the authors, leading to a hypothesis of function.

Questionnaires involve similar content, but many are comprised of open-ended questions, for example, "When does the child engage in the behavior?" Additional follow-up questions (e.g., "Does the child engage in the behavior during an academic task or mostly during transitions?") may be asked to narrow the answer. However, questionnaires generally limit opportunities for follow-up questions. In contrast, interviews generally begin with broad questions that permit the interviewer to probe for more detail with specific follow-up questions. For example, the interviewer may ask, "What behavior occurs?" or "How often does the behavior occur?" If the respondent answers, "The child screams all morning," the interviewer may ask, "Approximately how many times does the child scream?" or "Does the child scream often or for extended periods?" Thus, the interview provides opportunities for specific assessment but also requires additional time and more advanced interviewer skill. After the questionnaire or interview is complete, the information is compiled, and a hypothesis statement is developed.

**Table 18.3.** Characteristics of Indirect Functional Behavioral Assessment (FBA) Instruments

| FBA Tool | Reference | Instrument Format | Number of People | Time to Administer | Validated With Functional Assessment? |
|---|---|---|---|---|---|
| Functional Assessment Interview (FAI) form | O'Neill et al., 1997 | Interview | Minimum of 2 | 30 min to 1 hr | No |
| Motivation Assessment Scale (MAS) | Durand & Crimmins, 1992 | Questionnaire | 1 | 10–15 min | No |
| Functional Analysis Screening Tool (FAST) | Iwata, 1996 | Checklist | 1 | 10–15 min | No |
| Brief Functional Assessment Interview Form | Crone & Horner, 2003 | Interview | Minimum of 2 | 20–40 min | No |
| Student-Guided Functional Assessment Interview | Reed, Thomas, Sprague, & Horner, 1997 | Interview | Minimum of 2 | 30 min to 1 hr | No |
| Functional Assessment Checklist for Teachers and Staff (FACTS) | Crone & Horner, 2003 | Checklist | 1 | 10–15 min | No |
| Functional Behavioral Assessment—Behavior Support Plan Protocol (F-BSP Protocol) | Crone & Horner, 2003 | Questionnaire | Minimum of 2 | 30 min to 1 hr | No |
| Problem Behavior Questionnaire (PBQ) | Lewis, Scott, & Sugai, 1994 | Questionnaire | 1 | 10–15 min | No |

### *Content*

All identified instruments request demographic information, such as age, gender, grade, school history (e.g., attended schools, academic and social records, attendance), and family background (e.g., living conditions, siblings, management practices, typical home routines). Indirect methods are designed to collect information on the behaviors in which the child engages at school. Questions typically focus on obtaining information related to ABC chains in school settings. Information is gathered on what happens before the behavior occurs, what the behavior looks like, what happens after the behavior occurs, and the typical contexts in which the behaviors occurs. In addition, some instruments include questions for special situations or student populations. For example, the Functional

Assessment Interview (FAI) form (O'Neill et al., 1997) includes several extra questions related to children with communication delays and disorders. Similarly, the authors of the Motivation Assessment Scale (MAS; Durand & Crimmins, 1992) stated that the instrument is designed to determine the function for one behavior in one setting.

### *Complexity*

Each FBA tool collects similar information leading toward a hypothesis of function. However, the process varies in complexity across procedures. For example, checklists typically use a score to determine function, while information derived from interviews requires a higher degree of interpretation. Similarly, various instrument formats require a different number of people to complete. While practitioners alone may complete checklists and questionnaires, interviews require a second party to ask the questions and record the information and are therefore more time consuming. This is important because other school activities often consume a considerable portion of a teacher's time. Thus, instruments requiring hours to complete may not be feasible. Further, less time-consuming instruments may be better used on a daily basis, while longer instruments may realistically be used only weekly. For example, the MAS instrument takes approximately 10 min to complete; thus, the teacher could feasibly complete one daily. For a more detailed weekly outlook, the teacher could complete the FAI, which takes approximately 45 min to complete, once a week. The average time required to complete each tool is presented in Table 18.1.

The complexity of an instrument often corresponds with the amount of detail provided to the practitioner. Although more work is required, the FAI provides a greater breadth and depth of information that teachers may find beneficial. For example, the FAI form requires the teacher to provide several answers regarding setting events, antecedents, behaviors, and consequences. These answers may provide information regarding preferred and nonpreferred toys, activities, food, or other items or events that may have a predictable relationship with behavior. In contrast, the MAS and Functional Analysis Screening Tool (FAST; Iwata, 1996) are shorter, but generate a hypothesis of function without the abundance of detail provided by the FAI and other interviews. In addition to structured and semistructured interviews and rating scales, indirect FBA also might include an analysis of existing student data, for example, reviewing office referrals or absenteeism data to discern a pattern. In sum, indirect methods of FBA are easy to complete, can be cond-ucted fairly quickly, and thus appear to be feasible for school-based FBA.

### *Research on Indirect FBA*

While the simplicity of indirect methods is not in question, research on indirect methods of FBA is rather paltry. Most studies have focused on specific interviews or rating scales, and no studies to date have examined the use of previously collected data as part of an FBA. Further, existing research on indirect methods has produced conflicting results (Barton-Arwood, Wehby, Gunter, & Lane, 2003; Floyd, Phaneuf, & Wilczynski, 2005; Freeman, Walker, & Kaufman, 2007; Gable, 1996; Kearney, Cook, Chapman, & Bensaheb, 2006; Paclawskyj, Matson, Rush, Smalls, & Vollmer, 2001). In sum, although some studies reported good psychometric properties, taken as a whole, findings on reliability (interrater, interitem, test-retest) and validity (internal consistency, external validity, criterion) are mixed.

It is clear that indirect methods can be efficient in developing hypotheses regarding the function of problem behavior. It is equally clear, however, that more research is needed to identify the settings and contexts in which a given indirect measure will produce a valid functional hypothesis of behavior. At this point in time, although descriptive assessments can be useful, their reliability and validity have been questioned (e.g., Lerman & Iwata, 1993), and they may be less useful if problem behavior does not occur during observations or if problem behavior occurs only at very low rates. Still, when used with persons who are familiar with and understand the conceptual and practical foundations of FBA, indirect assessments are a valuable source of information to promote both the effectiveness and efficiency of FBA.

## CONCLUSIONS: EFFECTIVE AND EFFICIENT FBA AND FUNCTION-BASED SUPPORT

In review of the literature, it seems clear that the current state of FBA in public school settings is one of balancing logical rigor with realistic simplicity. Logistical and training issues prevent the use of single-expert models of FBA as a preventive schoolwide process in systems of PBS. Therefore, it seems reasonable to conclude that the team-based methods offer the best balance of logic and reality in schools. This balance is best achieved in the team-based structure by considering three basic necessities. First, teams must be developed of persons who know, have interacted with, and can describe behaviors and issues related to the student in question. Team members with no knowledge of the student are of little help in considering typical problems. Second, schools must identify and train a cadre of two to five persons who can adequately facilitate a team-based FBA and function-based support plan. This person's role is to provide direction, summarize information, and facilitate consensus of team members throughout the process. Although only one such person is necessary on a team, the number of students referred into this process likely will warrant multiple persons to fill this role to keep the time between referral and meeting as brief as possible. Third, structured protocols to lead the process provide a simple manner of guiding the process in the most efficient and effective manner—keeping the team focused and ensuring that each step is completed. While these recommendations represent a current look at best practice in schools, research will continue to validate different methodologies that will serve to make the FBA and function-based support process simpler while preserving fidelity.

## REFERENCES

Barton-Arwood, S. M., Wehby, J. H., Gunter, P. L., & Lane, K. L. (2003). Functional behavior assessment rating scales: Intrarater reliability with students with emotional or behavioral disorders. *Behavioral Disorders, 28,* 386–400.

Benazzi, L., Horner, R. H., & Good, R. H. (2006). Effects of behavior support team composition on the technical adequacy and contextual fit of behavior support plans. *Journal of Special Education, 40,* 160–170.

Carr, E. G., Dunlap, G., Horner, R. H., Koegel, R. L., Turnbull A. P., Sailor, W., et al. (2002). Positive behavior support: Evolution of an applied science. *Journal of Positive Behavior Interventions, 4,* 4–16.

Chalfant, J. C., & Pysh, M. V. (1989). Teacher assistance teams: Five descriptive studies on 96 teams. *Remedial and Special Education, 10,* 49–58.

Crone, D., & Horner, R. (2003). *Building positive behavior support systems in schools: Functional behavioral assessment.* New York: Guilford Press.

Duncan, B., Forness, S. R., & Hartsough, C. (1995). Students identified as seriously emotionally disturbed in day treatment: Cognitive, psychiatric, and special education characteristics. *Behavioral Disorders, 20,* 238–252.

Dunlap, G., Kern, L., dePerczel, M., Clarke, S., Wilson, D., Childs, K. E., et al. (1993). Functional analysis of classroom variables for students with emotional and behavioral disorders. *Behavioral Disorders, 18,* 275–291.

Durand, V. M., & Crimmins, D. B. (1992). *The Motivation Assessment Scale (MAS) administration guide.* Topeka, KS: Monaco.

Eber, L., Smith, C., Sugai, G., & Scott, T. M. (2002). Blending process and practice to maximize outcomes: Wraparound and positive behavioral interventions and supports in the schools. *Journal of Emotional and Behavioral Disorders, 10,* 171–180.

Ervin, R. A., Ehrhardt, K. E., & Poling, A. (2001). Functional assessment: Old wine in new bottles. *School Psychology Review, 30,* 156–172.

Floyd, R. G., Phaneuf, R. L., & Wilczynski, S. M. (2005). Measurement properties of indirect assessment methods for functional behavioral assessment: A review of research. *School Psychology Review, 34,* 1–19.

Freeman, K. A., Walker, M., & Kaufman, J. (2007). Psychometric properties of the Questions About Behavioral Function Scale in a child sample. *American Journal on Mental Retardation, 112,* 122–129.

Fullan, M. (1993). *Change forces: Probing the depths of education reform.* London: Falmer Press.

Fullan, M. (2001). *The new meaning of educational change.* New York: Teachers College Press.

Gable, R. A. (1996). A critical analysis of functional assessment: Issues for researchers and practitioners. *Behavioral Disorders, 22,* 36–40.

Ingram, K., Lewis-Palmer, T., & Sugai, G. (2005). Function-based intervention planning: Comparing the effectiveness of FBA indicated and contra-indicated intervention plans. *Journal of Positive Behavior Interventions, 7,* 224–236.

Iwata, B. (1996). *Functional Analysis Screening Tool (FAST).* Gainesville: Florida Center on Self-Injury, University of Florida.

Jay, D. E., & Padilla, C. L. (1987). *Special education dropouts.* Menlo Park, CA: SRI International.

Jolivette, K., Barton-Arwood, S. & Scott, T. M. (2000). Functional behavioral assessment as a collaborative process among professionals. *Education and Treatment of Children, 23,* 298–313.

Kamps, D., Wendland, M., & Culpepper, M. (2006). Active teacher participation in functional behavior assessment for students with emotional and behavioral disorders risks in general education classrooms. *Behavioral Disorders, 31,* 128–146.

Kearney, C. A., Cook, L., Chapman, G., & Bensaheb, A. (2006). Exploratory and confirmatory factor analyses of the Motivation Assessment Scale and Resident Choice Assessment Scale. *Journal of Developmental and Physical Disabilities, 18,* 1–11.

Kling, B. (1997). Empowering teachers to use successful strategies. *Teaching Exceptional Children, 30,* 20–24.

Lerman, D. C., & Iwata, B. (1993). A *Descriptive and Experimental Analysis of Variables Maintaining Self-Injurious Behavior. Journal of Applied Behavior Analysis, 26*, 293–319.

Lerman, D. C., & Iwata, B. A. (1993). Descriptive and experimental analysis of variables maintaining self-injurious behavior. *Journal of Applied Behavior Analysis, 26*, 293–319.

Lewis, T. J., Scott, T. M., & Sugai, G. M. (1994). The problem behavior questionnaire: A teacher-based instrument to develop functional hypothesis of problem behavior in general education classrooms. *Diagnostique, 19*, 103–115.

McKerchar, P. M., & Thompson, R. H. (2004). A descriptive analysis of potential reinforcement contingencies in the preschool classroom. *Journal of Applied Behavior Analysis, 37*, 431–445.

Nelson, J. R., Roberts, M. L., Mathur, S. R., & Rutherford, R. B. (1999). Has public policy exceeded out knowledge base? A review of the functional behavioral assessment literature. *Behavioral Disorders, 24*, 169–179.

Newcomer, L. L., & Lewis, T. J. (2004). Functional behavioral assessment: An investigation of assessment reliability and effectiveness of function-based interventions. *Journal of Emotional and Behavioral Disorders, 12*, 168–181.

O'Neill, R. E., Horner, R. H., Albin, R. W., Sprague, J. R., Storey, K., & Newton, J. S. (1997). *Functional assessment and program development for problem behavior: A practical handbook*. Pacific Grove, CA: Brookes/Cole.

Paclawskyj, T., Matson, J. L., Rush, K., Smalls, Y., & Vollmer, T. (2001). Assessment of the convergent validity of the Questions About Behavioral Function scale with analogue functional analysis and the Motivation Assessment Scale. *Journal of Intellectual Disability Research, 45*, 484–494.

Payne, L. D., Scott, T. M., & Conroy, M. (2007). A school-based examination of the efficacy of function-based intervention. *Behavioral Disorders, 32*, 158–174.

Reed, H., Thomas, E., Sprague, J. R., & Horner, R. H. (1997). The Student Guided Functional Assessment Interview: An analysis of student and teacher agreement. *Journal of Behavioral Education, 7*, 33–49.

Rylance, B. J. (1997). Predictors of high school graduation or dropping out for youths with severe emotional disturbances. *Behavior Disorders, 23*, 5–17.

Sasso, G. M., Conroy, M. A., Peck Stichter, J., & Fox, J. J. (2001). Slowing down the bandwagon: The misapplication of functional assessment for students with emotional or behavioral disorders. *Behavioral Disorders, 26*, 282–296

Sasso, G. M., Reimers, T. M., Cooper, L. J. Wacker, D., Berg, W., Steege, M., et al. (1992). Use of descriptive and experimental analyses to identify the functional properties of aberrant behavior in school settings. *Journal of Applied Behavior Analysis, 25*, 809–821.

Scott, T. M., Anderson, C., & Spaulding, S. (2008). Strategies for developing and carrying out functional assessment and behavior intervention planning in the general classroom. *Preventing School Failure, 52*, 39–50.

Scott, T. M., Bucalos, A., Nelson, C. M., Liaupsin, C., Jolivette, K., & Deshea, L. (2004). Using functional assessment in general education settings: Making a case for effectiveness and efficiency. *Behavioral Disorders, 29*, 190–203.

Scott, T. M., Liaupsin, C., & Nelson, C. M. (2005). *Team-based functional assessment and intervention planning: A simplified teaming process*. Longmont, CO: Sopris West.

Scott, T. M., McIntyre, J., Liaupsin, C., Nelson, C. M., & Conroy, M. (2004). An examination of team-based functional behavior assessment in public school settings: Collaborative teams, experts, and technology. *Behavioral Disorders, 29*, 384–395.

Scott, T. M., McIntyre, J., Liaupsin, C., Nelson, C. M., Conroy, M., & Payne, L. (2005). An examination of the relation between functional behavior assessment and selected intervention strategies with school-based teams. *Journal of Positive Behavior Interventions, 7*, 205–215.

Snell, M. E., Voorhees, M. D., & Chen, L. (2005). Team involvement in assessment-based interventions with problem behavior: 1997–2002. *Journal of Positive Behavior Interventions, 7*, 140–152.

Stichter, J. P., & Conroy, M. A. (2005). Using structural analysis in natural settings: A responsive functional assessment strategy. *Journal of Behavioral Education, 14*, 19–34.

Stichter, J. P., Sasso, G. M., & Jolivette, K. (2004). Structural analysis and intervention in a school setting: Effects on problem behavior for a student with an emotional/ behavioral disorder. *Journal of Positive Behavior Interventions, 6*, 166–177.

Sugai, G., Lewis-Palmer, T. & Hagan, S. L. (1998). Using functional assessments to develop behavior support plans. *Preventing School Failure, 43*, 6–13.

Sulzer-Azaroff, B., & Mayer, G. R. (1991). *Behavior analysis for lasting change.* Fort Worth, TX: Holt, Rinehart and Winston.

Tremblay, R. E., Mass, L. C., Pagani, L., & Vitaro, F. (1996). From childhood physical aggression to adolescent maladjustment: The Montreal Prevention Experiment. In R. D. Peters & R. J. MacMahon (Eds.), *Preventing childhood disorders, substance abuse and delinquency* (pp. 268–298). Thousand Oaks, CA: Sage.

Walker H. M., & Shinn, M. R. (2002). Structuring school-based interventions to achieve integrated primary, secondary, and tertiary prevention goals for safe and effective schools. In M. R. Shinn, G. Stoner, & H. M. Walker (Eds.), *Interventions for academic and behavior problems: Preventive and remedial approaches* (pp. 1–26). Silver Springs, MD: National Association of School Psychologists.

# 19

# Implementation of Schoolwide Positive Behavior Support in Urban Settings

**ROBERT PUTNAM, AMY MCCART, PETER GRIGGS, and JEONG HOON CHOI**

In 1983, the National Commission on Excellence in Education branded our nation's children at risk for failure. Kozol (1991) documented that a "differential system" of educating our children existed, and that differentiation is often tied to socioeconomic status and race. In 1995, Tyack and Cuban considered the magnitude of demands placed on schools to be the salvation of society. They also noted that schools are typically criticized for their decline, while other public entities have not had the same level of scrutiny. Efforts to reform public education are taken to resolve a multitude of societal issues. Key questions for educators and advocates for children are whether our nation's children are still at risk for educational failure, if socioeconomic factors and race/ethnicity are still critical variables associated with educational risk, and last if it is appropriate to hold all schools to the same standards.

Students in urban districts face multiple challenges, which can become exacerbated when students are not effectively supported in their schools. Students in urban districts who exit school due to suspension, expulsion, or dropping out remain in the school's neighborhood,

**ROBERT PUTNAM** • May Institute
**AMY MCCART** • University of Kansas
**PETER GRIGGS** • University of Kansas
**JEONG HOON CHOI** • University of Kansas

experiencing chronic exposure to violence, drug and alcohol abuse, and higher mortality rates (Horner, 1990; Lane., Lanza-Kaduce, Frazier, & Bishop, 2002). The desired outcomes for students in urban schools are no different from those for their rural or suburban counterparts: improved academic and social-behavioral outcomes, effective family involvement and partnerships, and communities that are committed to their students. Undoubtedly, poverty-stricken neighborhoods are more prevalent in urban districts and pose additional considerations for students, especially academic failure (Gottlieb, Alter, Gottlieb, & Wishner, 1994).

With the advent of No Child Left Behind (NCLB, 2001), urban areas with high poverty rates have clearly been shown to struggle with academic success. McLoyd (1998) and Sonnander and Claesson (1999) found that poverty has a limiting effect on child learning outcomes. Given the importance of early intervention with young children to provide stimulating experiences from birth (Bradley et al., 1994) and the fact that families in urban settings are faced with significant life challenges, academic readiness for school is often not achieved (Smith, Brooks-Gunn, & Klebanov, 1997; Huston, 1994). This lack of readiness instigates ongoing academic and social challenges, culminating in a pattern of failure with disproportionately high dropout rates (Mayer, 1997; McLoyd, 1998).

Schonhaut and Satz (1983) observed that poor students have a greater likelihood of screening for and identification of learning disabilities. Moreover, research in this area demonstrated that certain student variables (such as poverty and English as a second language) can result in exposure to increased use of exclusionary disciplinary procedures and identification and utilization of special education services (Fusarelli, 1999; Winbinger, Katsiyannis, & Archwamety, 2000). In addition, students from diverse backgrounds, particularly African American male students, have ongoing disproportional exclusionary disciplinary practices applied to them (Lietz & Gregory, 1978; McFadden, Marsh, Price, & Hwang, 1992; Skiba, 2002), and these practices put students in urban settings back in community environments that contributed to negative outcomes.

Positive behavior support (PBS), as it applies to urban settings, includes the broad range of systemic and individualized strategies for achieving important social and learning outcomes while preventing problem behavior (Horner & Sugai, 2000). The urban application of PBS requires an intensity, persistence, and contextualization for sustained, significant student success. PBS includes the integration of (a) valued outcomes, (b) the science of human behavior, (c) validated procedures, and (d) systems change to enhance quality of life and reduce problem behavior (Horner, Albin, Sprague, & Todd, 2000; Horner & Carr, 1997; Sugai, 2000).

The purpose of this chapter is to review the current research on schoolwide positive behavior support (SW-PBS) in urban settings as well as the factors that facilitate and prevent both implementation and sustainability of SW-PBS. Current practices and implications for future research also are discussed.

## URBAN IMPLEMENTATION OF SCHOOLWIDE POSITIVE BEHAVIOR SUPPORT IN SCHOOLS

Schoolwide PBS has been implemented in over 7,000 schools across the country (Kincaid, Childs, Blasé, & Wallace, 2007; Sugai, 2008). When implemented with fidelity, SW-PBS has been associated with school improvements in classroom behavior; recovered instructional time; academic performance; school climate; staff, student, and parental satisfaction; as well as improvements in individual student behavior (Horner, Sugai, Todd & Lewis-Palmer, 2005; Lassen, Steele, & Sailor, 2006; Lewis, Sugai, & Colvin, 1998; Luiselli, Putnam, Handler, & Feinberg, 2005; Nelson, Martella, & Marchand-Martella, 2002).

The implementation of SW-PBS in urban settings, however, has been reported to be more challenging due to a number of variables (Bohanon et al., 2006; Markey, Markey, Quant, Santelli, & Turnbull, 2002; McCurdy, Kunsch, & Reibstein, 2007; Netzel & Eber, 2003; Warren et al., 2003). Urban areas, as defined by the U.S. Census Bureau (2001), have "core census block groups or blocks that have a population density of at least 1,000 people per square mile and surrounding census blocks that have an overall density of at least 500 people per square mile" (p. 1). Overall, urban districts have higher rates of poverty (Iceland, 2003) and crime rates (Brooks-Gunn, Duncan, Leventhal, & Aber, 1997; Sampson, Raudenbush, & Earls, 1997) as compared to their suburban and rural counterparts. Often, in urban districts rates of staff turnover are higher, and staff are less qualified (Cuban, 2001). A higher proportion of urban schools are considered lower performing as compared to cohorts of suburban and rural schools (Williams, 1996). Some of these urban low-performing schools have also been designated as "persistently dangerous" schools [NCLB; 20 U.S.C. § 7912 (2001)]. Bohanon et al. (2006) noted that urban contexts also have low overall quality of life in inner cities, large school enrollments, high poverty rates, limited resources, and highly diverse communities (Netzel & Eber, 2003). A higher percentage of students in urban schools are hypothesized as requiring secondary and tertiary supports (Turnbull et al., 2002; Warren et al., 2003).

The combination of these factors has contributed to making urban schools targets of school reform initiatives. However, the successful implementation of these initiatives has been challenging in terms of treatment integrity, measurable meaningful outcomes, and sustained impact. SW-PBS approaches hold promise to assist these schools in improving academic performance and school climate, as well as to address the social-emotional learning needs of individual students with challenging behavior.

### Research Focused on Schoolwide Implementation of PBS

Schoolwide PBS (Luiselli, Putnam, & Handler, 2001; Luiselli et al., 2005) was implemented in an elementary school (Grades K–5) located in the Midwest region of the United States in a low socioeconomic urban area. Over 600 students were enrolled at the school, with approximately 90% of students qualifying for free/reduced lunch. The student composition was

88% African American, 5% Caucasian, 4% Hispanic, 2% Asian/Pacific, and 1% other. The implementation of SW-PBS included (a) formulating behavioral expectations; (b) increasing classroom activity engagement; (c) reinforcing positive performance; and (d) monitoring efficacy through data-based evaluation. As compared to a preintervention phase, the intervention was associated with decreased discipline problems (i.e., office referrals and school suspensions) over the course of several academic years. Student academic performance, as measured by standardized tests of reading and math, also improved concurrently with SW-PBS intervention.

Netzel and Eber (2003) described the implementation process and outcomes associated with the development of SW-PBS in an urban elementary school in the Waukegan, Illinois, district, which also was experiencing budget cuts, pressure not to adopt new programs, high staff turnover, and weak staff morale. Year 1 implementation activities focused on teaching schoolwide rules, working on classroom management issues, recognizing and acknowledging appropriate student behavior, and utilizing more productive responses to misbehavior than suspension. Although no Schoolwide Evaluation Tool (SET; Sugai, Lewis-Palmer, Todd, & Horner, 2001) data were reported, Netzel and Eber (2003) noted that a 22% reduction in overall suspensions occurred after 1 year of implementation. The authors suggested that the following factors influenced successful implementation: (a) building-level administrative buy-in and follow-through; (b) regular SW-PBS self-evaluation; (c) fostering of a shared philosophy among staff members within the building needs; and (d) a long-term commitment from building staff, building administration, and district administration for SW-PBS.

Rey, Their, Handler, and Putnam (2007) examined participants in eight New England middle schools (Grades 6–8) and two mid-Atlantic elementary schools (K–6 and K–8) located in urban school districts. Student population characteristics were similar across the two regions with respect to race and ethnicity (approximately 90% minority populations) and socioeconomic indices (approximately 75% of students receiving free/reduced lunch). District student mobility averaged 21% across regions. The purpose of this study was to examine the active and regular teaching of schoolwide behavioral expectations to build and sustain students' mastery of school-related prosocial skills. Results suggested that meeting benchmark criterion for teaching the prevention component of the revised version of the SET (Sugai et al., 2001) was associated with improved student knowledge of expectations and improved student rule-following behaviors. Although no significant difference was seen during the first year between those schools with a higher rate of students knowing the rules, schools with the greatest proportion of sampled students knowing the majority of schoolwide rules demonstrated significantly greater reductions in the rate of out-of-school suspensions in the following school year than those with the lowest proportion of students recalling the schoolwide rules. Similarly, schools with significantly greater reductions in out-of-school suspension rates in Year 2 had achieved the highest levels of SW-PBS implementation in the previous year. Strong subscale ratings on school leadership for

SW-PBS implementation, as measured by the revised SET scale, was also associated with higher fidelity PBS implementation.

McCurdy, Mannella, and Eldridge (2003) conducted a SW-PBS implementation study in an ethically and racially diverse inner-city elementary school in a large urban area in the northeastern United States. The K–5 school served approximately 500 students; the ethnic composition of the students was 44% Asian/Pacific Islanders, 33% African Americans, 18% European Americans, and 5% Latino Americans. A high percentage of the student population received free or reduced lunch. This study involved collaboration between school-based professionals and behavioral consultants from a local, community-based behavioral health care agency. Before introducing SW-PBS, the authors noted that the school was experiencing an increasing number of problem behaviors accompanied by decreasing parental support. The school leadership team and the behavioral consultants from the local behavioral health care agency implemented schoolwide structures during Year 1 to focus on targeted group and individual support structures during Year 2. After 2 years of SW-PBS implementation, significant reductions were observed in the overall level of office disciplinary referrals (46% reduction) and student fighting/assaults (55% reduction). After only 1 year of SW-PBS implementation, the total mean SET (Sugai et al., 2001) score was 82% across all seven subscales, and the subscale score specific to teaching behavioral expectations was reported to be 80% or more. Thus, this school met the 80/80 criteria (Horner et al., 2004) at the beginning of Year 2 for implementing SW-PBS with fidelity with criterion-level treatment integrity.

Bohanon et al. (2006) reported on an SW-PBS intervention effort in an inner-city Chicago high school serving 1,800 students. Approximately 36% of the student body was African American, 36% Hispanic, 16% Asian American, 8% Caucasian, 2% Native American, and 2% other. The school's populations included students from 75 countries. Over 20% of students had limited English proficiency (LEP), and 89% met the criteria for free or reduced lunch. After the first full year of implementation of SW-PBS, average daily office discipline referrals (ODRs) were reduced by 20%. The percentage of students with zero or one ODR increased from 46% to 59% after the first year of SW-PBS. Students with two to five ODRs decreased from 32% to 25%, and students with six or more ODRS decreased from 21% to 16%.

After the first full year of implementation of SW-PBS, SET (Sugai et al., 2001) data indicated that overall implementation of universal (primary-tier) supports and interventions reached or exceeded 80% across five subscales, while two subscales (behavioral expectations taught and district-level support) averaged about 40% and 50%, respectively. Noting that the school did not meet the SET 80/80 criteria for a "fully implementing" SW-PBS school (Horner et al., 2004) (overall SET score across all subscales must be 80% or more *and* the score on the "behavioral expectations taught" subscale must also be 80% or more), the authors suggested that even partial teaching of behavioral expectations, when combined with consistent acknowledgment, may produce some treatment effect. That is, benefit was more likely attained by students who already had expected schoolwide behaviors in their repertoire and who were acknowledged for practicing them, but less likely to be attained by students with skill deficits who required additional, regular teaching of expected behaviors as well as precorrection and prompting to practice them. Bohanon et al. (2006) noted the following unique challenges to implementing SW-PBS in high schools in urban contexts: (a) establishing schoolwide acknowledgment system; (b) teaching expected behaviors in a high school setting; (c) managing implementation logistics; (d) enacting consistent policies that address behavior; and (e) modifying ODR forms to track data effectively.

Utley, Kozleski, Smith, and Draper (2002) suggested that successful SW-PBS programs for urban, multicultural students require cultural sensitivity, caring, and respectful relationships between teachers and students and a nurturing school environment to create learning communities in schools. They also noted that developing and reviewing acceptable, appropriate schoolwide behavior with families, students, teachers, and administrators was an essential first step in developing SW-PBS in urban contexts. These discussions must be "anchored by multiple segments of performance-based evidence such as video clips that show a range of student deportment not only in the classroom but also on the school grounds, in the hallways, cafeteria, and library" (p. 202). Reviewing video clips of actual student behavior with all participants was considered essential to establishing a dialogue that can then lead to a broader agreement about what constitutes "acceptable" and "unacceptable" student behavior at school in various settings.

Warren et al. (2006) reported a SW-PBS implementation case study from an urban middle school. The middle school was located in a low-income, inner-city area. School demographic data showed that more than 70% of the student population was African American (40%) and Hispanic (32%), and about 80% of students received free lunch. After SW-PBS implementation, results from the comparison of data from 2 years (i.e., Year 1 and Year 2 of the implementation) indicated that the total number of ODRs decreased by 20%, time-outs decreased by 23%, and in-school suspensions decreased by 5%. The effectiveness of SW-PBS was further documented through decreases in the frequency of severe disciplinary actions. Short-term suspensions were the second most common disciplinary action in Year 1 but dropped to the fourth most common disciplinary action in Year 2 (a 57% decrease). In the study, authors described critical challenges of SW-PBS implementation in urban school settings from the research experience. In spite of encouraging disciplinary data from Year 1 to Year 2, the SW-PBS could not be sustained well in Year 3. The major reason noted by the authors was that the school started another schoolwide intervention (i.e., school uniforms were required), which was associated with increased punishment and reduced opportunities of teaching and reinforcing appropriate behavior. A "zero tolerance" policy and introduction of a school uniform policy, for example, created considerable conflicts.

Lassen et al. (2006) examined the relationship of SW-PBS to academic achievement in an urban middle school. The school was located in a low-income, inner-city area in the Midwest and had an enrollment of 623 students. Ethnicity data showed that about 70% of students were Hispanic (30%) and African American (26%), and approximately 80% of the students were economically disadvantaged. After a 3-year period of SW-PBS implementation, the status of SW-PBS repeatedly measured by the SET (Sugai et al., 2001) increased from 24.97% at baseline to 69.64% at Year 3. One-way analysis of variance (ANOVA) results indicated that the average number of ODRs per student ($F_{3,\ 2490} = 1.98$, $p < .01$) and the average number of long-term suspensions was significantly decreased ($F_{3,\ 2490} = 1.19$, $p < .01$). Standardized math scores also significantly increased from baseline to Year 3 ($F_{3,\ 810} = 6.67$, $p < .01$). Although reading scores decreased from baseline to Year 1, reading scores in Year 3 were significantly higher than Year 1 ($F_{2,\ 1936} = 9.0$, $p < .01$). Finally, the relationship between standardized test scores and ODRs/suspensions was examined through linear regression analyses. Results showed that ODRs were significant predictors for reading ($F_{1,\ 642} = 6.78$, $p < .01$) and math scores ($F_{1,\ 812} = 17.83$, $p < .01$), and suspensions also significantly predicted reading ($F_{1,\ 642} = 9.80$, $p < .01$) and math scores ($F_{1,\ 812} = 9.04$, $p < .01$).

Sailor, Zuna, Choi, Thomas, and McCart (2006) examined the effectiveness of SW-PBS within a structured school reform process called the schoolwide applications model (SAM). Authors described SAM as a broad universal school reform initiative and an integrated service approach that contains not only all levels of SW-PBS implementation but also other critical features, such as partnerships with families and community, resource configuration for all students, democratic school culture, and data-driven problem-solving system, among others. According to the results from a 3-year application and study of the SAM in a low-income, multicultural, urban school district in northern California, academic performance of Cohort 1 schools measured by the California Standardized Test (CST) significantly increased from the 2003 to the 2004 school year. The SW-PBS component within SAM's critical features was significantly correlated with CST scores, and SW-PBS status contributed a significant proportion of the variance in CST score. These results confirmed that well-integrated application of SW-PBS at all three levels (i.e., primary/universal, secondary/targeted, and tertiary/individual) within the SAM structural reform system could positively affect student academic performance in an urban school setting.

## Research Focused on Classroom Implementation of PBS

Putnam and Rey (2003) implemented classroom PBS interventions in a public elementary school located in an urban community. The student population ($N = 592$) was composed of 53% African American, 38% Caucasian, and 6% Hispanic students. Of the students, 25% had limited English proficiency, and 66% received free and reduced lunch. This study used an single-subject design to examine the implementation of a classwide PBS plan in the class room that had the most office discipline referrals. The authors, in conjun-ction with the fifth-grade classroom teacher, developed a classroom behavior support plan that consisted of (a) engaging in active monitoring; (b) establishing positive classroom rules; (c) providing reinforcement for following the classroom rules; and (d) providing effective instructions. The number of ODRs dropped by 50% from baseline levels over a 3-month period. When combined with an individual behavior support plan for the student who had the most ODRs in the class, the overall classroom referrals were reduced by over 90% from baseline levels. The individual student had no ODRs over the last 3 months of the intervention phase. The teacher, who was 1 of 70 staff, was responsible for 18% of the total school ODRs during baseline, 9% of the total ODRs during the classroom intervention phase, but only 2% during the classroom plus individual student intervention phase. The combination of whole-class and individual-student PBS interventions was shown to be effective in reducing ODRs in this urban elementary classroom.

In their study of the effects of implementing SW-PBS over a 2-year period at the Key Elementary School, Philadelphia, Pennsylvania, McCurdy et al. (2003) reported that the project team offered some additional training to the staff on basic classroom management during both implementation years. Authors noted that classroom settings were one of the two "high-referral areas" within the school prior to the beginning of the SW-PBS project. After 2 years of SW-PBS implementation, the number of ODRs per student originating from classroom settings showed a decrease of 37%.

Using an ABAB reversal design, Lambert, Cartledge, Heward, and Lo (2006) evaluated the effects of a response card intervention during math lessons on the disruptive behavior and academic responses of students in two urban fourth-grade classrooms in a midwestern elementary school. Nine students with a history of disciplinary problems in school and disruptive behavior in the two classrooms (especially during math lessons) were nominated by teachers and selected for the study. Eight of the students were African American, and one was Caucasian. All students received free or reduced lunch. Two conditions were alternated: (a) single-student responding and (b) write-on response card responding. During single-student responding, the classroom teacher called one student at a time, who had raised his or her hand to answer the question; all the other students were expected to sit quietly and listen respectfully. In the response card condition, each student in the class had access to a white laminated board on which he or she could write the answer to every question asked by the teacher. During this condition, all students in the class displayed their responses simultaneously to a teacher-generated question or problem (Cavanaugh, Heward, & Donelson, 1996). Response cards allowed all students in the class to participate with active responding to instruction (Lambert et al., 2006). Compared to the single-student responding condition, substantial reductions in disruptive behavior and increases in academic responding during the response card condition were observed. All nine students responded more frequently and correctly during the response card conditions than during the single-student response conditions. Even the most eager students, who displayed the highest frequency of hand raising under the single-student responding condition, significantly increased their responding under the response card condition. The disruptive behavior of all nine students declined to low levels after the implementation of each response card condition and returned to substantially higher levels under the single-student responding conditions.

The authors concluded that explicit teaching and direction instruction strategies, such as using the response card approach, can produce positive effects, especially for urban learners, which is a research finding supported widely (Bullara, 1994; Delpit, 1995).

## Research Focused on Nonclassroom Implementation of PBS

Urban playgrounds in elementary school settings are most often supervised by parent/caregiver volunteers or aides with little experience and skill in behavior support strategies for groups of children. Most schoolyard recess activities consist of unplanned activities, with students running around and making physical contact with other students or monopolizing balls or inappropriately throwing balls at other students (McCurdy et al., 2003). At Key Elementary School, the playground was identified as the second of two high-referral areas prior to the implementation of SW-PBS (McCurdy et al., 2003). Targeting the playground as a setting in need of additional PBS interventions and supports, (McCurdy et al., 2003) the schoolyard was divided into areas where preplanned activities could be conducted and supervised by trained aides (see also Heck, Collins , & Peterson, 2001; Nabors, Willoughby, Leff, & McMenamin, 2001, for similar studies). Aides were taught to station themselves within their designated activity area, monitor student behavior, use "keys" (tickets) as positive acknowledgments to reward desired student behavior, and employ a brief playground time-out system to reduce negative playground behavior (McCurdy et al., 2003). The authors reported a 53.8% decrease in ODRs from the schoolyard over a 2-year implementation period, a significant decrease from pre-PBS levels.

A PBS intervention was implemented by Putnam, Handler, Ramirez-Platt, and Luiselli (2003) in an elementary school (Grades K–5) located in the Midwest region of the United States in a low-socioeconomic urban community. School personnel reported problematic bus behavior, so an intervention was designed consisting of (a) definitions of appropriate bus behaviors, which were then actively taught to the students; (b) proactive monitoring of and reinforcement for students who followed the rules; and (c) a "bus of the week" acknowledgment for the bus with the fewest office referrals and suspensions. Using an ABAB design, the authors reported dramatic drops in ODRs and suspensions attributed to problematic bus behavior during intervention phases, with increases when the intervention was removed, and gains from the intervention were maintained during the follow-up phase.

# SURVEY OF BARRIERS TO IMPLEMENTATION AND SUSTAINABILITY OF SW-PBS IMPLEMENTATION IN URBAN SCHOOL CONTEXTS

A survey to determine the potential barriers to the implementation and sustainability of SW-PBS in urban settings was developed by the first author. After review by expert researchers and revision, a survey entitled

"Barriers to Implementation and Sustainability of School-wide PBS in Urban School Systems" (see Table 19.1) was circulated to senior researchers in the PBS field and invited participants who attended a special session at the Fourth Annual Meeting of the Association for Positive Behavior Supports in Boston, Massachusetts, in 2007.

Sixteen respondents completed the survey by ranking the items in order of priority with respect to impact on the implementation and sustainability of SW-PBS. Twelve of the respondents listed their role as trainers. The other respondents listed their role as either an administrator (3) or a teacher (1). The ranks of the items on the completed surveys were averaged across respondents, and total scores were then ranked (see Fig. 19.1). Teacher turnover was the highest-rated factor and was rated as one of the top three items on 38% of the surveys. The other top factors identified on at least 30% of the surveys were inadequately prepared teaching force, high bureaucratic complexity, continuous change in district leadership and priorities, and administrator turnover and disconnect between school and district administration. Other top factors were high proportion of inexperienced short-term teachers, competing initiatives that drain resources, history of failed initiatives, and cultural difference between teachers and students. From this small sample, respondents noted three major factors that had an impact on SW-PBS implementation in urban settings: (a) teacher workforce, characterized by high turnover, which results in a high proportion of inexperienced short-term teachers who are inadequately prepared; (b) district features, such as high bureaucratic complexity, continuous change in leadership, administrative turnover, and a disconnect between school and district administrators; and (c) district initiatives that have had a history of failure and other competing initiatives that drain resources.

**Table 19.1.** Survey of Urban Implementers

| Barriers to Implementation and Sustainability | Rank Order | Percent Respondents Ranked in Top Three on Surveys |
|---|---|---|
| Teacher turnover | 1 | 38 |
| Inadequately prepared teaching force | 2 | 38 |
| High bureaucratic complexity | 3 | 38 |
| Continuous change in district leadership and priorities | 4 | 31 |
| Administrator turnover | 5 | 44 |
| Disconnect between school and district administration | 6 | 31 |
| High proportion of inexperienced, short-term teachers | 8 | 25 |
| Competing initiatives that drain resources | 8 | 25 |
| History of failed initiatives | 9 | 6 |
| Cultural difference between teacher and student | 10 | 13 |

Barriers to Implementation and Sustainability of School-wide PBS in Urban School Systems

Please indicate position:

____ Trainer _____ District administrator _____ State administrator

_____ Building administrator _____ Other

Please rank order the following barriers to implementation and sustainability of school-wide PBS in urban school systems. Place the number "1" by the barrier you feel is the most significant barrier effecting implementation, "2" by the second most important barrier, etc.

_____ High bureaucratic complexity
_____ Administrator turnover
_____ Continuous change in district leadership and priorities
_____ Disconnect between school and district admini stration
_____ Teacher turnover
_____ Inadequately prepared teaching force
_____ High proportion of inexperienced, short-term teachers
_____ Child exposure to violence
_____ Lower family involvement in school
_____ High proportion of families in poverty
_____ High rate of neighborhood violence and crime
_____ Antisocial peer networks (e.g., gangs, drugs)
_____ High parental unemployment
_____ Cultural difference between teacher-student
_____ Competing initiatives that drain resources
_____ Child mobility
_____ History of failed initiatives
_____ Poor facilities
_____ Large student populations
_____ Other please indicate ___________________________
_____ Other please indicate ___________________________
_____ Other please indicate ___________________________

**Fig. 19.1.** Survey of barriers to implementation and sustainability of urban schoolwide positive behavior support (SW-PBS).

## CHARACTERISTICS OF URBAN SETTINGS THAT ARE FACTORS IN THE IMPLEMENTATION OF SW-PBS IN URBAN SETTINGS

Based on outcomes from a behavior summit convened by the National Institute of Urban School Improvement (September 2000), Utley and Sailor (2002) hypothesized four needs that influence the utility and responsiveness of SW-PBS applications to the special circumstances affecting urban education, particularly in inner-city schools: (a) cultural responsiveness; (b) prevention focus; (c) collaboration in planned, proactive, teaching-focused interventions, team-driven action planning, and data-based decision making; and (d) active participation by district leaders.

The implementation of SW-PBS in urban schools needs to build on these factors and incorporate current research findings. As such, a number of factors in urban settings have an impact on the implementation of

SW-PBS: (a) higher rates of problem behavior in these settings and the need for preventive interventions: (b) divergent cultural and contextual community issues; (c) collaborative processes as reflected in planned, proactive, teaching-focused interventions, team-driven action planning, and data-based decision making as compared to expert-driven processes; (d) competency of the workforce; and (e) district and administrative leadership.

### *Higher Rates of Problem Behavior In Urban Settings*

Warren and his colleagues (2003) reported that urban schools differ from most schools in terms of severity and frequency of students' impeding behavior. Based on data from three inner-city middle schools, they found that 32% of all students received six or more ODRs per year. In contrast, 9% of 15,713 students in 26 middle schools had similar ODR patterns (reported by the University of Oregon and referenced in Warren et al., 2003). Thus, the authors recommended (a) effective service integration across school-home-community settings through coordinated/colocated services; (b) increased family support; (c) enhanced school-family-community partnerships; and (d) joint responsibility for community resource development.

When confronted by high rates of problem behavior, the traditional urban reactive response is to direct school resources to those students with the most persistent, intensive, or chronic academic and behavioral needs. The result is increases in suspensions and expulsions and negative school climate and student-adult relations. Results from research studies described in this chapter support a more positive and preventive approach that establishes strong preventive universal interventions that are schoolwide in scope, especially classroom and nonclassroom settings (Bohanon et al., 2006; Lassen, Steele, & Sailor, 2006; Luiselli et al., 2001, 2005; McCurdy et al., 2003; Rey et al., 2007; Warren et al., 2006).

Reductive or corrective behavioral intervention procedures are made more effective by giving equal attention and effort to the schoolwide adoption, accurate implementation of fully articulated universal (primary-tier) support systems, and complementary targeted (secondary) interventions and supports. However, McCurdy et al. (2003) cautioned that professionals must be careful when considering traditional reductive/corrective strategies because they are not effective at limiting student exposure to unsafe community circumstances. For example, urban parents, who may themselves be living in impoverished life circumstances and who may be unskilled in managing their child's behavior problems, may overreact to their child's problem behaviors at school and apply overly harsh or even abusive discipline at home (McCurdy et al., 2003).

When working in urban contexts, an effective SW-PBS intervention is to focus attention and resources on modifications and adaptations to the physical structure of inner-city buildings and in the movement patterns of students within the school's multiple settings. For example, because many urban school buildings were built in the early 20th century and have poorly designed or inadequate bathrooms, cafeterias, hallways, and gyms (McCurdy et al., 2003), adaptations or accommodations may need to be focused on removing architectural barriers, reteaching routines, increasing adult active supervision, and enhancing positive attention for prosocial behavior (Nelson, 1996; Nelson & Colvin, 1996; Turnbull et al., 2002).

Given the alarming increases in rates of significant problem behaviors in young children, who are at risk for early school failure (Gilliam, 2005; Karr-Morse & Wiley, 1997; Keenan, Shaw, Walsh, Delliquadri, & Giovannelli, 1997; Lavigne et al., 1996; Qi & Kaiser, 2003), increased attention must be focused on adapting and refining SW-PBS systems and practices for early childhood, preschool, and kindergarten children and their parents/caregivers (Fox, Dunlap, & Powell, 2002; Turnbull, Blue-Banning, Turbiville, & Park, 1999). Several authors (Lucyshyn, Dunlap, & Albin, 2002; Powell, Batsche, Ferro, Fox, & Dunlap, 1997; Turnbull et al., 1999) maintained that effective practices and durable supports are created and sustained through a collaborative model of parent-professional partnerships grounded and centered in the family's own culture, beliefs, dreams, circumstances, strengths, needs and unique priorities. In contrast, efforts that emphasize the values, beliefs, or cultural background of the behavior consultant create an ineffective and traditional expert-driven model. Thus, early childhood educators must adopt "family-friendly, culturally-competent systems of early intervention ... [in order] to activate behavior support efforts in resolving challenging behaviors of young children" (Fox et al., 2002, p. 213). This approach may be especially important when working with families of children with significant problem behaviors who are living in urban environments and face challenges in health, poverty, and service (Fox et al., 2002).

Fox et al. (2002) concluded that committed efforts must be taken to make the transition from expert-driven models of behavioral support for young children to family-centered approaches—a transition that represents a dramatic shift for many professionals and administrators. Urban school contexts in particular need to transition away from expert-driven approaches that typically rush to suspend "repeat-offending" students for whom suspension is often a reinforcing consequence (Netzel & Eber, 2003) or those exclusively that direct resources to students with the most challenging problem behaviors.

### *Divergent Cultural and Contextual Community Issues*

Markey et al. (2002) suggested that life in urban environments can offer school-aged children and their families a different experience than that of rural or suburban families, for example, poverty, racism, population density, family dysfunction, crime and violence, substance abuse, and cultural and language differences. These urban areas are often characterized by limited resources to support, for instance, adequate public transportation; community recreation (e.g., theaters, community swimming pools), or basic needs (e.g., grocery stores, medical supports) (Utley et al., 2002). These factors can affect the quality of life and social development outcomes experienced by urban school-aged children and their families (Morse, 1985; Utley et al., 2002), for example: (a) poor adult-child relationships and the need for positive and supportive relationships; (b) lack a sense of personal efficacy (power) and the need to experience and develop personal responsibility and power; (c) focus on external reasons or factors (external locus of control) for explaining one's own personal behavior and the need to learn how to accept responsibility (internal locus of control) for controlling their own learning and behavior; (d) low self-esteem, especially related to school achievement and peer friendships, and the need to develop positive self-esteem by experiencing school success and friendships through positive and supportive interactions with teachers and peers; (e) a poorly defined sense of social cognition and an inability to understand the points of views or feelings of others and the need to learn to understand others' reactions and responses and to work cooperatively with them; and (f) poor problem-solving skills and the need to develop these skills as a way of enhancing feelings of self-efficacy and self-esteem.

As Bohanon et al. (2006) noted, quoting Warren et al. (2003), "For students who face dangers walking through their own neighborhood to get to school, being 'ready to learn' as they walk into the classroom is not likely to be a high priority" (p. 82). Most teachers do not know how to interpret or understand the "problematic" behaviors of many urban students, who are going through these life-challenging experiences on a daily basis, since these behaviors differ so much from their normative expectations (Gay, 1993). Therefore, teachers tend to misinterpret these student behaviors as deviant and treat them punitively (Utley et al., 2002).

Sugai et al. (2000) observed that the use of culturally appropriate interventions is strongly emphasized in PBS approaches, that is, interventions that consider the unique and individualized learning histories of all participants (students with problem behaviors, their parents/caregivers and families, teachers, administrators, community advocates and agents, etc.) who participate in the PBS process. They further noted that data-based problem solving can help establish culturally appropriate interventions that work; however, they emphasized that individual learning histories ultimately affect how data will be analyzed and used to make decisions (Sugai et al., 2000).

Cartledge, Lee, and Feng (1995) suggested that educators must understand that (a) social behaviors are influenced by culture; (b) learning and social interactions are connected and inseparable from cognition; (c) both teacher and student are engaged in constructing knowledge through shared experiences, activities, and dialogue; (d) social (problem) behaviors should be distinguished from behavioral skill deficits; and (e) multicultural instructional strategies should be employed to help culturally diverse learners maximize their school experiences and acquire the most critical and productive interpersonal skills.

Gaining family and community member commitment and involvement in SW-PBS efforts in urban schools depends on developing rapport and listening to and communicating successfully (Bohanon et al., 2006; Sailor et al., 2006; Turnbull et al., 2002; Warren et al., 2003, 2004). The success of SW-PBS efforts may hinge on the ability of administrators and the school leadership team to relate the multiple cultural contexts of families and local community members to the values, beliefs, circumstances, and history of the school (Bohanon et al., 2006; Edmonson, 2000; Turnbull et al., 2002). Establishing and demonstrating cultural affinity constitute the foundation of the school-home-community relationship and appear to be critical factors in recruiting family and community members' buy-in and participation in SW-PBS efforts (Edmonson, 2000; Fox et al., 2002; Netzel & Eber, 2003; Sailor et al., 2006).

### *Processes Must Be Collaborative as Reflected in Planned, Preventive Teaching-Focused Interventions; Team-Driven Action Planning; and Data-Based Decision Making*

Netzel and Eber (2003) observed that SW-PBS leadership teams must be open to being collaborative and willing to learn from their collective and individual mistakes (p. 77). Effective strategies should be retained and made more efficient. Ineffective intervention should be carefully self-evaluated to improve outcomes. In sum, data-based decision making should apply to all levels of SW-PBS implementation (Netzel & Eber, 2003).

McCurdy et al. (2003) observed that urban schools offer a number of real challenges to professionals, parents, and community members concerned with providing an effective and responsive educational experience for children and youth. For example, the sheer number of students who are exposed to conditions that place them at risk for developing externalizing, disruptive behavior problems poses a significant challenge for behavioral health care organizations. In addition to providing consultation to building-level leadership teams on implementing the multiple components of SW-PBS over a multiyear period, internal and external district PBS consultants must be prepared to provide credible, experience-validated, culturally grounded, supplemental or enhanced training to urban teachers on classroom behavior management strategies (McCurdy et al., 2003).

In our experience, inner-city urban junior high or middle schools have a disproportionate number of students who experience multiple ODRs (Bohanon et al., 2006; Scott, 2001; Turnbull et al., 2002; Warren et al., 2003, 2004). The result is "administrator roulette," during which administrators are rotated through to schools with high enrollment numbers and histories of chronic discipline problems. These administrators are seen as having "solved" the discipline problems in their schools and tapped to apply a "quick fix" to resolve similar discipline problems in schools with histories of ineffective approaches, negative reform experiences, and conflicting faculty values about discipline. This approach results in district administrators and boards of education pursuing crisis-driven, expert-led, and quick-fix solutions to discipline problems that ultimately are ineffective in addressing the real prevention and support needs of students, families, and school staff.

### *Competencies of the Workforce*

The results from the urban PBS implementers' survey indicated that workforce competency was one of the top barriers in the implementation of SW-PBS, specifically ill-prepared and less-experienced teachers.

McCurdy et al. (2003) reported that working with students who come from challengingfamily and community circumstances and who display significantly disruptive behaviors can be especially daunting for first- and second-year teachers. These new teachers have less experience and less skill and strategy fluency to respond to students who are highly skilled and fluent in their uses and displays of problem behavior. Lambert et al. (2006) suggested that young urban learners are more likely to be taught by inexperienced teachers, who may unintentionally offer these students fewer chances to respond by using traditional, single-student responding strategies (e.g., "hold up your hand and wait to be called on") (Arreaga-Mayer & Greenwood, 1986). When combined with other stressors and risk factors that are typically associated with poverty, the learning environments of young students in urban elementary schools may be significantly compromised, resulting in significant declines in student learning and motivation (Lambert et al., 2006).

Effective instructional strategies and classroom behavior support interventions within the context of SW-PBS have the potential to engage urban learners and their teachers in ways that increase successful outcomes and more positive learning and teaching interactions (Lambert et al., 2006; McCurdy et al., 2003; Putnam & Rey, 2003). The research literature suggests that teaching directly and explicitly is well matched to the needs of urban, multicultural students who lack early learning skills (Bullara, 1994; Delpit, 1995; Lambert et al., 2006).

### *District and Administrative Leadership*

Results from the urban PBS implementers' survey identified district and administrative leadership as a significant factor in the implementation of SW-PBS. In particular, challenges included high bureaucratic complexity, continuous change in leadership, administrative turnover, and disconnect between school and district administrators. To address these challenges, leadership must establish a common districtwide urban vision, a common districtwide language related to a multitier system of SW-PBS, and a common set of urban experiences that can sustain systems and practices (Fullan, & Stiegelbauer, 1991; Hord, 2003). When district-level leadership and support are lacking or inadequate in urban environments, results are inequitable application of SW-PBS approaches to urban schools and the perpetuation of special "schools at risk," "probationary schools," or "alternative schools."

Confronting challenges such as shrinking populations and property tax bases and higher unemployment rates tests the commitment and active participation of district leaders in school reform efforts. Decisions tend toward the most essential and efficient. For example, Netzel and Eber (2003) reported that despite unforeseen budget restrictions and cuts at an urban elementary school, a successful initial year of SW-PBS implementation, resulted in approval for continued funding by district-level leadership for further development of SW-PBS. The authors suggested that fiscally challenging conditions actually may contribute toward in increased likelihood for funding for SW-PBS implementation efforts.

## SUMMARY AND FUTURE DIRECTIONS

To conclude, current research results suggest that SW-PBS implementation in urban schools has the potential to improve school climate and academic performance. For example, reductions in suspensions or ODRs at the schoolwide level have been reported across a number of studies (Bohanon et al., 2006; Lassen et al., 2006; Luiselli et al., 2001, 2005; McCurdy et al., 2003; Rey et al., 2007; Warren et al., 2006). Similarly, reductions in ODRs and disruptive behavior have been observed at the classroom level (Lambert et al., 2006; McCurdy et al., 2003; Putnam & Rey, 2003). Reductions in ODRs or suspensions on playgrounds (McCurdy et al., 2003) and on buses (Putnam et al., 2003) also have been demonstrated. Finally, as result of the implementation of SW-PBS, improvements were also shown in academic performance (Lassen et al., 2006; Luiselli et al., 2001, 2005; Sailor et al., 2006).

Despite these positive effects, more research is needed. First, because most existing research is descriptive or quasi-experimental in nature, more rigorous experimental designs (e.g., randomized control group) must be employed to test the interaction effects of behavior climate and academic achievement in urban settings, and these studies must be replicated to enable statements about generalizability. Second, because only a relatively small number of studies reported treatment integrity data, future research efforts must demonstrate the extent to which SW-PBS has been implemented with fidelity at all levels (i.e., whole school, classroom, and nonclassroom).

The information from the PBS implementers' survey highlighted the interrelatedness between teacher commitment to implementation of systems change and the overall implementation of schoolwide PBS components. Factors such as teacher turnover, teacher competence, and staff buy-in affect implementation of prevention-focused SW-PBS schoolwide and at the classroom level. Approximately 46% of all new teachers in the United States leave the profession within 5 years of entering the classroom. Teacher turnover rates in high-poverty schools (mostly urban) approach 20% per year (National Commission on Teaching and America's Future, 2005). In addition, almost half of all teachers who leave the profession report problems with student behavior as the source of their dissatisfaction (U.S. Department of Education, 1999–2000).

Finally, evidence suggests that when SW-PBS plans and activities are developed by the staff, parents, and students, the interventions tend to be more culturally relevant to the community than other interventions that are not developed by community participants (Bohanon et al., 2006; Edmonson, 2000; Netzel & Eber, 2003; Utley et al., 2002). The authors' experience has been that once SW-PBS has been fully implemented with treatment integrity, school environments become much less chaotic, safer, and more positive places for educators to teach and students to learn. The lives of students who reside in urban inner-city communities and who typically experience less-than-desirable living and educational environments can be greatly improved if we can create effective, safe, and caring schools. We believe that the effective implementation of SW-PBS in these urban settings shows great promise in achieving this goal.

## REFERENCES

Arreaga-Mayer, C., & Greenwood, C. R. (1986). Environmental variables affecting the school achievement of culturally and linguistically different learners: An instructional perspective. *NABE: The Journal for the National Association for Bilingual Education, 10*, 113–135.

Bohanon, H., Fenning, P., Carney, K., Minnis, M., Anderson-Harris, S., Moroz, K., et al. (2006). School-wide application of urban high school positive behavior support: A case study. *Journal of Positive Behavior Interventions and Supports, 8*, 131–145.

Bradley, R. H., Whiteside, L., Mundfrom, D. J., Casey, P. H., Kelleher, K. J., & Pope, S. K. (1994). Early indications of resilience and their relation to experiences in the home environments of low birthweight, premature children living in poverty. *Child Development, 65*, 246–260.

Brooks-Gunn, J., Duncan, G. J., Leventhal, T., & Aber, J. L. (1997). Lessons learned and future directions for research on neighborhoods in which children live. In J. Brooks-Gunn, G. J. Duncan, & J. L. Aber (Eds.), *Neighborhood poverty: Context and consequences for children* (Vol. 1, pp. 279–297). New York: Russell Sage.

Bullara, D. T. (1994). *Effects of guided notes on the academic performance and off-task/disruptive behaviors of students with severe behavior handicaps during science instruction.* Unpublished doctoral dissertation. Ohio State University, Columbus.

Cartledge, G., Lee, J. W., & Feng, H. (1995). Cultural diversity: Multicultural factors in teaching social skills. In G. Cartledge & J. F. Milburn (Eds.), *Teaching social skills to children and youth: Innovative approaches.* Needham Heights, MA: Allyn & Bacon. pp. 207–221

Cavanaugh, R. A., Heward, W. L., & Donelson, F. (1996). Effects of response cards during lesson closure on the academic performance of secondary students in an earth science course. *Journal of Applied Behavior Analysis, 29*, 403–406.

Cuban, L. (2001, July 18–20). *Improving urban schools in the 21st century: Dos and don'ts, or advice to true believers and skeptics of whole school reform.* Paper presented at the OERI Symposium on Comprehensive School Reform Research and Evaluation, Denver.

Delpit, L. (1995). *Other people's children.* New York: New Press.

Edmonson, H. (2000). *A study of the process of the implementation of school reform in an urban middle school using positive behavioral support: "Not one more thing."* Doctoral dissertation, University of Kansas, Lawrence.

Fox, L., Dunlap, G., & Powell, D. (2002). Young children with challenging behavior: Issues and considerations for behavior support. *Journal of Positive Behavior Interventions, 4*, 208–217.

Fullan, M. G., & Stiegelbauer, S. (1991). *The new meaning of educational change* (2nd ed.). New York: Teachers College Press.

Fusarelli, L. D. (1999). Reinventing urban education in Texas: Charter schools, smaller schools, and the new institutionalism. *Education and Urban Society, 31*, 214–224.

Gay, G. (1993). Ethnic minorities and educational quality. In J. Banks & C. Banks (Eds.), *Multicultural education* (pp. 182–183). Boston: Allyn & Bacon.

Gilliam, W. S. (2005). *Prekindergarteners left behind: Expulsion rates in state prekindergarten systems.* Retrieved July 29, 2007, from http://info.med.yale.edu/chldstdy/

Gottlieb, J., Alter, M., Gottlieb, B. W., & Wishner, J. (1994). Special education in urban American: It's not justifiable for many. *The Journal of Special Education, 27*, 453–465.

Heck, A., Collins, J., & Peterson, L. (2001). Decreasing children's risk taking on the playground. *Journal of Applied Behavior Analysis, 34*, 349–352.

Hord, S. (2003). *Professional learning communities: Perspectives from the field.* New York: Teachers College Press.

Horner, R. D. (1990). Cancer mortality in Native-Americans in North Carolina. *American Journal of Public Health, 80*, 940–944.

Horner, R. H., Albin, R. W., Sprague, J. R., & Todd, A. W. (2000). Positive behavior support. In M. E. Snell & F. Brown (Eds.), *Instruction of students with severe disabilities* (5th ed., pp. 207–243). Upper Saddle River, NJ: Merrill.

Horner, R. H., & Carr, E. G. (1997). Behavioral support for students with severe disabilities: Functional assessment and comprehensive intervention. *Journal of Special Education, 31*, 84–104.

Horner, R. H., & Sugai, G. (2000). School-wide behavior support: An emerging initiative (special issue). Journal of Positive Behavioral Interventions, 2, 231-233.

Horner, R. H., Sugai, G., Todd, A. W., & Lewis-Palmer, T. (2005). School-wide positive behavior support: An alternative approach to discipline in schools. In L. Bambara & L. Kern (Eds.), *Positive behavior support.* New York: Guilford Press.

Horner, R. H., Todd, A. W., Lewis-Palmer, T., Irvin, L. K., Sugai, G., & Boland, J. B. (2004). The school-wide evaluation tool (SET): A research instrument for assessing school-wide positive behaviour support. *Journal of Positive Behavior Interventions, 6*, 3–12.

Huston, A. C. (1994). Children in poverty: Designing research to affect policy. *Social Policy Report, 8*, 1–12.

Iceland, John. Dynamics of Economic Well-Being, Poverty 1996-1999. Current Population Reports, P70-91. U.S. Census Bureau, Washington, DC. 2003.

Karr-Morse, R., & Wiley, M. S. (1997). *Ghosts from the nursery: Tracing the roots of violence.* New York: Atlantic Monthly Press.

Keenan, K., Shaw, D. S., Walsh, B., Delliquadri, E., & Giovannelli, J. (1997). *DSM III-R* disorders in preschool children from low-income families. *Journal of the American Academy of Child and Adolescent Psychiatry, 36*, 620–627.

Kincaid, D., Childs, K., Blasé, K. A., & Wallace, F. (2007). Identifying barriers and facilitators in implementing schoolwide positive behavior support. *Journal of Positive Interventions, 9*, 174–184.

Kozol, J. (1991). *Savage Inequalities.* New York: Crown.

Lambert, M. C., Cartledge, G., Heward, W. L., & Lo, Y.-Y. (2006). Effects of response cards on disruptive behavior and academic responding during math lessons by fourth-grade urban students. *Journal of Positive Behavior Interventions, 8*, 88–99.

Lane, J., Lanza-Kaduce, L., Frazier, C. E., & Bishop, D. M. (2002). Adult versus juvenile sanctions: Voices of incarcerated youths. *Crime and Delinquency, 48*, 431–455.

Lassen, S. R., Steele, M. M., & Sailor, W. (2006). The relationship of school-wide positive behavior support to academic achievement in an urban middle school. *Psychology in the Schools, 43*, 701–712.

Lavigne, J. V., Gibbons, R. D., Christoffel, K. K., Arend, R., Rosenbaum, D., Binns, H. J., et al. (1996). Prevalence rates and correlates of psychiatric disorders among preschool children. *Journal of the American Academy of Child and Adolescent Psychiatry, 35*, 889–897.

Lewis, T. J., Sugai, G., & Colvin, G. (1998). Reducing problem behavior through a school-wide system of effective behavioral support: Investigation of a school-wide social skills training program and contextual interventions. *School Psychology Review, 27*, 446–459.

Lietz, J. J., & Gregory, M. K. (1978). Pupil race and sex determinants of office and exceptional education referrals. *Educational Research Quarterly, 3*, 61–66.

Lucyshyn, J., Dunlap, G., & Albin, R. W. (Eds.). (2002). *Families and positive behavior support: Addressing problem behavior in family contexts.* Baltimore: Brookes.

Luiselli, J. K., Putnam, R. F., & Handler, M. W. (2001). Improving discipline practices in public schools: Description of a whole-school and district-wide model of behavior analysis consultation. *The Behavior Analyst Today, 2*, 18–27.

Luiselli, J. K., Putnam, R. F., Handler, M. W., & Feinberg, A. (2005). Whole-school positive behavior support: Effects on student discipline problems and academic performance. *Educational Psychology, 25*, 183–198.

Markey, U., Markey, D., Quant, B., Santelli, B., & Turnbull, A. (2002). Operation positive change: PBS in an urban context. *Journal of Positive Behavior Interventions, 4*, 218–230.

Mayer, S. E. (1997). *What money can't buy.* Cambridge, MA: Harvard University Press.

McCurdy, B. L., Kunsch, C., & Reibstein, S. (2007). Secondary prevention in the urban school: Implementing the behavior education program. *Preventing School Failure, 51*, 12–19.

McCurdy, B., Mannella, M., & Eldridge, N. (2003). Positive behavior support in urban schools: Can we prevent the escalation of antisocial behavior? *Journal of Positive Behavior Interventions, 5*, 158–170.

McFadden, A., Marsh, G., Price, B. J., & Hwang, Y. (1992). A study of race and gender bias in the punishment of school children. *Education and Treatment of Children, 15*, 140–146.

McLoyd, V. C. (1998). Socioeconomic disadvantage and child development. *American Psychologist, 53*, 185–204.

Morse, W. (1985). *The education and treatment of socioemotionally disturbed children and youth.* Syracuse, NY: Syracuse University Press.

Nabors, L., Willoughby, J., Leff, S., & McMenamin, S. (2001). Promoting inclusion for young children with special needs on playgrounds. *Journal of Developmental and Physical Disabilities, 13*, 179–190.

National Commission on Excellence in Education. (1983). *A nation at risk: The imperative of educational reform.* Washington, DC: U.S. Department of Education.

National Commission on Teaching and America's Future. (2005). *Induction into learning communities.* Washington, DC.

Nelson, J. R. (1996). Designing schools to meet the needs of students who exhibit disruptive behavior. *Journal of Emotional and Behavioral Disorders, 4*, 147–161.

Nelson, J. R., & Colvin, G. (1996). Designing supportive school environments. *Special Services in the Schools, 11*, 169–186.

Nelson, J. R., Martella, R. M., & Marchand-Martella, N. (2002). Maximizing student learning: The effects of a comprehensive school-based program for preventing problem behaviors. *Journal of Emotional and Behavioral Disorders, 10*, 136–148.

Netzel, D. M., & Eber, L. (2003). Shifting from reactive to proactive discipline in an urban school district: A change of focus through PBIS implementation. *Journal of Positive Behavior Interventions, 5*, 71–79.

No Child Left Behind Act of 2001, Pub. L. No. 107-110, 107th Congress, Retrieved September 5, 2008, from http:/www.ed.gov/legislation/ESEA02/.

Powell, D. S., Batsche, C. J., Ferro, J., Fox, L., & Dunlap, G. (1997). A strengths-based approach in support of multi-risk families: Principles and issues. *Topics in Early Childhood Special Education, 17*, 1–26.

Putnam, R. F., & Rey, J. (2003, November). *Maintenance outcomes of prevention-focused whole-school behavior support.* Paper presented at the annual conference for the Association for the Advancement of Behavior Therapy, Boston.

Putnam, R. F., Handler, M. W., Ramirez-Platt, C. M., & Luiselli, J. K. (2003). Improving student bus riding behavior through a school-wide intervention. *Journal of Applied Behavior Analysis, 36*, 583–589.

Qi, C. H., & Kaiser, A. P. (2003). Behavior problems of preschool children from low-income families: Review of the literature. *Topics in Early Childhood Special Education, 23*, 188–216.

Rey, J., Their, K, Handler, H., & Putnam, R. (2007). *Primary prevention in urban schools: Are teachers "ready to teach" prevention?.*

Sailor, W., Zuna, N., Choi, J.-H., Thomas, J., & McCart, A. (2006). Anchoring school-wide positive behavior support in structural school reform. *Research and Practice for Persons With Severe Disabilities, 31*, 18–30.

Sampson, R. J., Raudenbush, S. W., & Earls, F. (1997). Neighborhoods and violent crime: A multilevel study of collective efficacy. *Science, 277*, 918–924.

Schonhaut, S., & Satz, P. (1983). Prognosis for children with learning disabilities: A review of followup studies. In M. Rutter (Ed.), *Developmental neuropsychiatry* (pp. 542–563). New York: Guilford Press.

Scott, T. M. (2001). Positive behavioral support: A school-wide example. *Journal of Positive Behavior Interventions, 3*, 88–94.

Skiba, R. J. (2002). Special education and school discipline: A precarious balance. *Behavioral Disorders, 27*, 81–97.

Smith, J., Brooks-Gunn, J., & Klebanov, P.K. (1997). The consequences of living in poverty for young children's cognitive and verbal ability and early school achievement. In G. J. Duncan & J. Brooks-Gunn (Eds.), *Consequences of growing up poor* (pp. 132–189). New York: Russell Sage Foundation Press.

Sonnander, K., & Claesson, M. (1999). Predictors of developmental delay at 18 months and later school achievement problems. *Developmental Medicine and Child Neurology, 41*, 195–202.

Sugai, G. (2000). Applying positive behavior support and functional behavior assessment in schools. *Journal of Positive Behavior Interventions, 2*, 131–143.

Sugai, G. (2008, February). *Response to intervention and school-wide positive behavior support.* Paper presented at OSEP RTI, Storus, CT.

Sugai, G., Horner, R.H., Dunlap, G., Hieneman, M., Lewis, T., Nelson, C. M., et al. (2000). Applying positive behavior support and functional behavioral assessment in schools, *Journal of Positive Behavioral Interventions, 2*, 131–143.

Sugai, G., Lewis-Palmer, T., Todd, A., & Horner, R. H. (2001). *School-wide evaluation tool.* Eugene: University of Oregon.

Turnbull, A., Edmonson, H., Griggs, P., Wickham, D., Sailor, W., Freeman, R., et al. (2002). A blueprint for schoolwide positive behavior support: Implementation of three components. *Exceptional Children, 68*, 377–402.

Turnbull, A. P., Blue-Banning, M., Turbiville, V., & Park, J. (1999). From parent education to partnership education: A call for a transformed focus. *Topics in Early Childhood Special Education, 19*, 164–172.

Tyack, D., & Cuban, L. (1995). *Tinkering toward utopia: A century of public school reform.* Cambridge, MA: Harvard University Press.

U.S. Census Bureau. (2001). *Census 2000: Urban and rural classification.* Retrieved August 6, 2007, from http://www.census.gov/geo/www/ua/ua_2k.html

U.S. Congress. (2002). No Child Left Behind Act of 2001, P.L. 107-110. Retrieved August 6, 2007, from www.ed.gov/policy/elsec/leg/esea02/index.html

Utley, C. A., Kozleski, E., Smith, A., & Draper, I. L. (2002). Positive behavior support: A proactive strategy for minimizing behavior problems in urban multicultural youth. *Journal of Positive Behavior Interventions, 4*, 196–207.

Utley, C. A., & Sailor, W. (2002). Positive behavior support and urban school improvement: A special section of the *Journal of Positive Behavior Interventions* [Guest editorial]. *Journal of Positive Behavior Interventions, 4*, 195.

Warren, J. S., Bohanon-Edmonson, H. M., Turnbull, A. P., Sailor, W., Wickham, D., Griggs, P., et al. (2006). School-wide positive behavior support: Addressing behavior problems that impede student learning. *Educational Psychology Review, 18*, 187–198.

Warren, J. S., Edmonson, H. M., Griggs, P., Lassen, S., McCart, A., Turnbull, A., et al. (2003). Urban applications of school-wide positive behavior support: Critical issues and lessons learned. *Journal of Positive Behavior Interventions, 5*, 80–91.

Warren, J. S., Edmonson, H. M., Griggs, P., Lassen, S. R., McCart, A., Turnbull, A. P., et al. (2004). Urban applications of school-wide positive behavior support: Critical issues and lessons learned. In L. M. Bambara, G. Dunlap, & I. S. Schwartz (Eds.), *Positive behavior support: Critical articles on improving practice for individuals with severe disabilities* (pp. 376–387). Pro-Ed and TASH, Austin, Texas.

Williams, B. (1996). *Closing the achievement gap: A vision for changing beliefs and practices.* Alexandria, VA: Association for Supervision and Curriculum Development.

Winbinger, B., Katsiyannis, A., & Archwamety, T. (2000). Disciplinary practices in Nebraska's public schools. *Journal of Child and Family Studies, 9*, 389–399.

# 20

# Positive Behavior Support in Alternative Education, Community-Based Mental Health, and Juvenile Justice Settings

**C. MICHAEL NELSON, JEFFREY R. SPRAGUE, KRISTINE JOLIVETTE, CARL R. SMITH, and TARY J. TOBIN**

Schoolwide positive behavior support (PBS) is implemented in more than 6,000 public schools, preschools, alternative education (AE), and juvenile justice programs across the United States (Danielson, Cobb, Sanchez, & Horner, 2007). Among the beneficial outcomes reported by these schools are dramatic reductions in office discipline referral rates, increased instructional time for students formerly removed for disciplinary reasons, and improved academic performance (including gains in academic year achievement test scores). As documented elsewhere in this volume, the success of PBS has led to the mobilization of efforts to bring this multiple-systems approach to scale at the school district and state education agency levels.

**C. MICHAEL NELSON** • University of Louisville
**JEFFREY R. SPRAGUE** • University of Oregan
**KRISTINE JOLIVETTE** • Georgia State University
**CARL R. SMITH** • Iowa State University
**TARY J. TOBIN** • University of Oregon

The positive outcomes associated with PBS in public schools means that scores of students who otherwise would be at risk of social and academic failure are achieving greater success. Even so, many thousands of children and youth who are seriously at risk receive educational and other services every day in alternative settings. The implementation figures reported include 286 AE and juvenile justice programs, which is only a small fraction of the school- and non-school-based programs that serve this population. The purpose of this chapter is to examine the application of PBS in these settings, which include AE schools and programs, day treatment and residential mental health programs, and juvenile detention and correctional facilities.

Our assumption is that the systems change strategies for PBS implementation in alternative settings are similar to those adopted by public schools. These include (a) establishing a leadership team to actively coordinate implementation efforts; (b) adequate funding, visibility, and consistent political support; (c) building a cadre of individuals who can provide training and coaching support for local implementation; (d) a system for ongoing evaluation and provision of performance-based feedback to implementers; and (e) a small group of initial implementation sites that demonstrate the viability of the approach within the fiscal, political, and social climate of the state or system.

The District Survey of Alternative Programs and Schools conducted by the National Center on Education Statistics (NCES, 2001) reported that 39% of public school districts administered at least one alternative school or program for at-risk students during the 2000–2001 school year. According to the NCES survey, 612,900 students, or 1.3% of all public school students, were enrolled in public alternative schools or programs for at-risk students. The 2006 Office of Juvenile Justice and Delinquency Prevention (OJJDP) national report (Snyder & Sickmund, 2006) indicated that 109,225 juveniles were being held in secure custody in 2003. Because no national database of community-based day treatment and residential programs exists, estimates of the number of children and youth served in such programs are not available.

Children and youth in AE, mental health, or juvenile justice programs are served by three large public systems: education, mental health, or juvenile justice. Considerable overlap exists with respect to the programs operating within each system as well as the characteristics and needs of the youth served. Compared with public schools, significantly higher rates of educational disabilities, mental health disorders, and patterns of antisocial behavior have been reported in each of these settings. An estimated 33% to 75% of students in alternative and residential programs are identified as emotionally and behaviorally disordered (EBD; Duncan, Forness, & Hartsough, 1995; NCES, 2001). The National Longitudinal Transition Study-2 (Wagner & Davis, 2006) found that more students with EBDs are educated in alternative settings than any other disability group (Wagner & Davis, 2006). Of incarcerated youth, 50–80% are reported to have educational disabilities or diagnosed mental health conditions (Cocozza & Skowyra, 2000; Quinn, Rutherford, Leone, Osher, & Poirier, 2005), and 65–70% of youth in the juvenile justice system meet the criteria for a diagnosable mental health condition (Skowyra & Cocozza, 2006).

In the following sections, we describe PBS in AE, school-based mental health, and juvenile justice settings. With respect to the implementation of PBS, three basic questions are addressed:

1. What does PBS look like in the settings operated under the auspices of AE, school-based mental health, and juvenile justice?
2. What has been the impact of PBS on key outcome variables?
3. What are the major issues affecting the implementation of PBS in these systems?

Within each major section, we address the major features of each system (including the characteristics and needs of the children and youth served and the programmatic configurations in which they are found), the implementation of PBS in these programs (including impact or outcome data, where available), and specific implementation issues within each system. Our aim is consistency of reporting across all three sections. However, significant differences in perspectives, purposes, and philosophies of the education, mental health, and juvenile justice systems as well as in data-reporting standards and procedures led to inevitable discrepancies with regard to the information we were able to obtain. Our reporting also suffers from a lack of specificity regarding the extent to which PBS has been implemented in AE, school-based mental health, and juvenile justice settings. Uniform reporting systems or data collection formats do not exist to document the number of programs that are implementing PBS and the extent to which implementation is being carried out with fidelity. For example, although data provided by the National Technical Assistance Center for Positive Behavioral Interventions and Supports (Danielson et al., 2007) indicate that PBS is being implemented in 286 AE and juvenile justice sites, we were unable to disaggregate these data to identify specific sites.

## POSITIVE BEHAVIOR SUPPORT FOR YOUTH SERVED IN ALTERNATIVE EDUCATION PROGRAMS

*Alternative education* (AE) can refer to any nontraditional educational service but is often used to indicate a program provided for at-risk children or youth (Aron, 2006). Overall, 10,900 public alternative schools and programs in the nation served at-risk students during the 2000–2001 school year (NCES, 2001). According to the NCES survey, urban districts, large districts (those with 10,000 or more students), districts in the southeast, districts with high minority student enrollments, and districts with high poverty concentrations were more likely than other districts to have alternative schools and programs for at-risk students. An agreed-on definition of AE does not exist, although a range of programmatic characteristics are often suggested as essential to or important for program success by experts, administrators, or practitioners in the field. These characteristics include (a) small class size and small student body, (b) choice to attend versus involuntary placement (although students may be placed in AE involuntarily for a variety of reasons), (c) a personalized school environment,

(d) high expectations for success, (e) students feel included in the decision-making process, (f) special teacher training, (g) flexible teaching arrangements, (h) parent involvement and collaboration, (i) effective classroom management, and (j) transition support. Whether these characteristics are functionally related to student outcomes (positive or negative) is unknown (Quinn & Poirier, 2006; Tobin & Sprague, 2000a, 2000b, 2002).

## Features of Alternative Education Programs

The features of AE are shaped to a large extent by the needs of the students served. Compared with typical public school programs, AE programs vary greatly in terms of how they are organized and in their approach to instruction and behavior support.

## Characteristics and Needs of Children and Youth Served in Alternative Programs

Just as a wide range of different types of AE programs exist, the characteristics and needs of AE students also vary widely. However, a high prevalence of students with mental health diagnoses, identified educational disabilities, ethnic minority status, and antisocial behavioral patterns tend to stand out as characteristic demographics of students served in these settings.

Gamble and Satcher (2007) studied an exemplary and innovative alternative day treatment school operated by a state mental health department for students with substance abuse diagnoses and reported that 48.4% had dual diagnoses as measured by the fourth edition of the *Diagnostic and Statistical Manual of Mental Disorders* (American Psychiatric Association, 1994). Findings from the National Longitudinal Transition Study-2 (Wagner & Davis, 2006) indicated that 7.6% of all students identified as having emotional disturbance (ED) attended "an alternative school for students who struggle in general education high schools" (p. 89), 14.3% attended a school for special education students, and 74% were in general education schools. In comparison, 1.3% of students with other disabilities attended alternative schools, 2.2% were in a school for special education students, and 94.2% were educated in general education settings. Foley and Pang (2006) found that AE school administrators in Illinois reported that on average 50% of their students were identified as having ED, 12% had learning disabilities, and 13% had attention deficit with hyperactivity (and another 12% had attention deficit disorder); 6% were identified as having a developmental disability, 5% with communication disorders, and 2% with sensory impairments.

Students from ethnic minority groups tend to be overrepresented in AE programs involving involuntary placement due to disciplinary problems, whereas they are more likely to be underrepresented in voluntary charter or magnet schools that focus on specialized themes or content areas, such as foreign language immersion schools. Foley and Pang (2006) found that, of the 50 schools that responded and reported students' ethnic backgrounds, the average percentages were 63% Caucasian, 31% African American, 15% Hispanic, 4% Native American, and

2% Asian. Denny, Clark, and Watson (2003) studied the ethnic and racial backgrounds of ninth-grade students in 115 AE schools in the United States. They found that 37% were Caucasian, 25% African American, 30% Hispanic, 2% Asian, 2% Native American, and 4% other. The AE schools in this study served students at risk for drop-out and students who had been excluded from the traditional school for disciplinary or behavioral reasons.

## Alternative Education Configurations

Variations in AE configurations are described in terms of (a) which agency is responsible for their operation, (b) whether they operate in separate facilities or as a "school within a school," and (c) specific features of programs known as "day treatment" and "interim alternative educational settings."

### *Sponsoring Agencies*

Public school districts operate several different types of AE programs, including charter or magnet schools (Clark, 2000; Davis et al., 2006; Estes, 2006) that focus on specific themes, content areas, or delivery styles; "turnaround" schools for students who have been expelled (Williams, 2002) or whose behavior problems make it difficult to serve them in traditional school settings (Tobin & Sprague, 2000a, 2000b, 2002); and innovative programs, including collaborative efforts with businesses or nonprofit charitable organizations (Government Accounting Office, 2002; Schachter, 2004; Wetzel, McNaboe, Schneidermeyer, Jones, & Nash, 1997). Mental health agencies, particularly hospitals and institutions providing residential treatment, operate AE programs for their school-age patients. Similarly, juvenile justice agencies provide AE programs for youth who are detained in a correctional facility or, sometimes, who are on probation and who may be placed in a group home or other institution where they cannot attend their neighborhood schools (Kurtz, 2002). These various agencies may serve the same student at different times, creating a need for collaboration and coordination to facilitate transitioning from AE provided by one agency to AE provided by another and sometimes to a traditional neighborhood school (Mazzotti & Higgins, 2006).

### *Program Location*

The NCES (2001) survey reported that 59% (6,400) of all public alternative schools and programs for at-risk students were housed in a separate facility (i.e., not within a regular school). Results also indicated that districts administered 4% of all public alternative schools and programs that were located in juvenile detention centers, 3% in community centers, and 1% in charter schools. Some schools provide alternative classrooms or other forms of AE programs that are located in the same building or on the same campus as the traditional school. In the latter approach, the school has an alternative classroom that students attend part of the day and when they are unable to cope with traditional classrooms. A promising model of this type is the Skills for Success program (Sprague et al., 2001), which operates as a school within a school (Gottfredson, 1999) AE program.

Typically, the agency that is operating the AE program bears the expense of providing the facility, but several types of AE programs, such as cyber or home-school charter schools and "mall schools," operate in separate facilities at no cost to the school district. Students who receive AE in cyber or home-school charter schools receive instruction via the Internet or are instructed at home by their parents, respectively (Huerta, Gonsalez, & D'Etremont, 2006). The school district may provide licensed teachers to facilitate these programs by offering advice to parents or making the technology and materials available to the family.

### *Day Treatment Programs*

The majority of AE programs that focus on mental health treatment are sponsored by mental health agencies, although some are managed by juvenile courts or other juvenile justice agencies (NCES, 2001). Day treatment programs work in conjunction with mental health, recreation, and education organizations and may even be provided by them (Substance Abuse Mental Health Services Administration [SAMSHA], 2007). While many such programs primarily offer direct child and family therapy as an alternative to residential treatment, those that operate within the context of AE programs combine full- or half-day academic instruction by general or special education teachers (if students have identified educational disabilities) with small-group or individual treatment provided by mental health personnel. Students generally are placed involuntarily because of their need for treatment for a mental health condition or substance abuse. Most of these programs are located in separate facilities, such as a mental health or juvenile detention center (SAMSHA, 2001).

### *Interim Alternative Educational Settings*

Special education students who commit serious offenses, such as carrying weapons, possessing drugs, or threatening injury to others, may have their placement changed (rather than receiving out-of-school suspension or being expelled) for 45 days to an interim alternative educational setting (IAES; Ryan, Katsiyannis, Peterson, & Chmelar, 2007). Telzrow (2001) reported that the three most common types of IAES were (a) home, with some instruction provided; (b) alternative school or program; and (c) in-school suspension. Of students sent to alternative schools or programs, 51.5% received some type of specific skills instruction; a smaller percentage of students with in-school suspension or a homebound placement received skills instruction to address the problem behavior (18.2% and 9.1%, respectively). Using home instruction as an IAES is not likely to be an effective way to implement the students' individualized educational plan (IEP) (Katsiyannis & Smith, 2003).

## Implementation of Positive Behavior Support in Alternative Education Settings

To our knowledge, no formal, data-based study of efforts to implement PBS in alternative schools has been published. A search of recent (2002–2007) peer-reviewed journals, using databases such as Academic Search Premier and PsychInfo and key words such as "positive behavior support" and "alternative education or schools," identified several articles with information on AE schools' use of *elements* similar to those found in PBS, even when the full system was not being implemented.

We expanded our search for information to include a review of our own files because we had some data from alternative schools regarding their efforts to implement PBS. We reanalyzed these data to respond to questions raised for this chapter. Some alternative schools are attempting to implement PBS in accord with the *School-wide Positive Behavior Support Implementers' Blueprint and Self-Assessment* (OSEP Center on Positive Behavioral Interventions and Supports 2005, www.pbis.org/tools.htm. Implementation varies along a continuum as schools may move from having one or a few elements in place, or partially in place, to having primary, secondary, and tertiary prevention systems all fully in place.

Reports from PBS initiatives around the country indicated that, where PBS leadership and implementation teams are in place, at least some AE schools are among the implementation sites. In Miami-Dade County in Florida, 15 schools (including 2 alternative schools) implemented PBS in 2006, and "suspension rates for these schools were significantly reduced, despite various obstacles the PBS schools encountered, including staff changes, hurricanes, and philosophical differences among staff members" (Martinez, 2006, p. 4). In Maryland, which has had a PBS initiative since 1999, currently 467 schools are participating, including 28 alternative schools. One of the AE schools was highlighted in a recent report (Spanoghe, Jones, Ourand, & Knools, 2007) because it experienced an 82% decrease in the number of days students were suspended. Implementation of schoolwide PBS had a positive impact on behavior and discipline problems in participating schools in South Carolina (Irwin & Algozzine, 2007). Although results for AE schools were not presented specifically, three alternative schools were included in the schools involved in the PBS initiative. In Colorado, 40 schools, including 2 alternative schools, were part of a PBS initiative in the 2003–2004 school year (McGough, 2007). Zweig (2003) reported a positive impact on prosocial behavior in AE settings: 24% of graduates from alternative schools participated in voting and in volunteer activities, compared to 14% of their same-age peers.

## Issues

Although AE is a viable and appropriate option for many students, several key issues require consideration to ensure that such programs are operated with high fidelity and from a perspective of prevention, rather than of reactive or failure-based placement. Two of these issues are highlighted.

### *Defining Evidence-Based Practices in Alternative Education*

The absence of clear research evidence regarding promising AE practices impedes the definition of optimal program characteristics and assessment of intervention fidelity (Tobin & Sprague, 2002). Many states prescribe administrative compliance standards for AE, and some fidelity assessments have been used in studies of these programs.

Given the relatively higher cost of providing AE services compared to regular public school supports, the relative impact of individual program characteristics on overall student outcomes should be examined, especially in AE schools using PBS. Research also should guide the development of a tool to aid in identifying the optimal alternative school placement based on individual student educational needs and the philosophy and programmatic components of alternative programs.

### *Dissemination and Staff Development*

As the use of AE increases, the dissemination of information about evidence-based best practice and to provide scientifically designed staff development must be accelerated. The National Alternative Education Association (http://the-naea.org/) holds an annual conference to bring together researchers, practitioners, families, and youth to discuss effective practices in serving youth with disabilities and other at-risk youth in AE settings, but this effort is not formally linked to the PBS research and practice community (Association for Positive Behavior Supports [APBS], www.apbs.org).

## POSITIVE BEHAVIORAL SUPPORT FOR STUDENTS WITH SIGNIFICANT MENTAL HEALTH NEEDS

Although PBS now has more than a decade of history in public schools throughout the United States, the majority of experience and research has involved practices at the primary and secondary levels. The positive and often dramatic improvements in school behavior, academic engaged time, and academic achievement resulting from PBS practices (Horner & Sugai, 2000) are especially important for the sizable portion of students in public schools who manifest significant mental health needs (Bazelon Center for Mental Health Law, 2006), yet some students with mental health conditions require additional supports, whether in the context of the general education school environment or a segregated setting. The prevalence and complexity of serious mental health conditions indicates that educators must enter into interagency relationships to design collaborative service delivery models for these students. Providing tertiary-level supports for these youth and their families also will require schools to look at nontraditional outcome measures to assess the success of interventions.

### Features of School-Based Mental Health Programs

Research investigating the use of tertiary-level interventions within a model of schoolwide PBS is just beginning. The U.S. Department of Education has funded three model demonstration projects (in Kansas, Illinois, Oregon, and Washington; see http://mdcc.sri.com/Cohort2.aspx) related to tertiary behavior interventions. These projects are establishing staff development and technical assistance strategies to support educators in addressing the needs of students who are not responsive to primary and secondary prevention efforts. The recency of these projects notwithstanding, substantial consensus indicates that students with significant mental health issues require strategies that include comprehensive and coordinated services (Eber, Nelson, & Miles, 1997; Eber, Sugai, Smith, & Scott, 2002).

## Characteristics and Needs of Children and Youth With Mental Health Conditions

One of the major difficulties in making eligibility and intervention decisions for students who exhibit challenging behavior is determining when a student's behavior is, in fact, an indicator of a mental health problem versus behavioral patterns on a continuum typical of all young people at a given age. Many conditions that previously were regarded as distinct signs of a mental health problem are better conceptualized as existing on a continuum of behaviors from "normal" to "extreme" (U.S. Department of Health and Human Services, 2001b). No "bright line" demarcates behavior that is within normal boundaries from that which indicates a state of mental illness. Thus, the distinction between students who are within a normal range of mental health status and those diagnosed (or diagnosable) as having significant mental health conditions is in a constant state of flux.

The surgeon general's report on mental health (U.S. Department of Health and Human Services, 2001b) indicated that 3–5% of school-aged children are diagnosed with attention deficit-hyperactivity disorder (ADHD) in a 6-month period; 5% of children aged 9–17 are diagnosed with major depression; and the combined prevalence of various anxiety disorders for children aged 9–17 is 13%. About one fifth of the children and adolescents in this country experience the signs and symptoms of a mental health adjustment problem in the course of a year. While these data suggest that a substantial percentage of students manifest conditions that negatively affect their mental health, many who have such needs are not identified (Hoagwood, 2001). The failure to adequately address the dynamic nature of mental health adjustment may be related to a lack of proper screening and identification practices; that is, much of our knowledge is based on discrete points in time for a child or a context for behavior, rather than taking into account the changes that occur in children's mental health status over time (Mash & Dozois, 2003).

Mental health conditions that directly interfere with students' ability to meet the academic expectations of schools certainly contribute to an increased risk of academic and social failure. Students whose mental health needs are unidentified or inadequately addressed are at increased risk of becoming clients of the juvenile justice system or of the criminal justice and mental health systems as young adults (Mash & Dozois, 2003).

Determining whether students with mental health needs also are eligible for special education services is complicated by traditional identification tools and procedures that underidentify students with internalizing behavior patterns (e.g., depression and anxiety) for special education services under the EBD label, as well as an emphasis on significant impairment of academic performance as the primary criterion for identification. Case law has established that educational performance also encompasses social, emotional, and behavioral characteristics (*Roland M and Mariam M. v. The Concord School Committee*, 1990; *CJN v. Minneapolis Public Schools*, 2003). Youth with significant mental health challenges should be eligible for special education and related services under the Individuals With Disabilities Education Act (IDEA), regardless of their academic performance. However, the tendency remains to identify only students with externalizing, or acting out, behavior problems to the exclusion of those with internalizing disorders (Kauffman, 2005).

With regard to the mental health issues of youth from diverse ethnic and cultural backgrounds, the implementation of behavioral interventions in a multicultural context presents particular challenges. Reinke, Herman, and Tucker (2006, pp. 315–316) stated that:

> Perhaps the greatest impediment facing efforts toward impacting social problems is the over-focus in prevention trials on individual contributions to risk and protection (e.g., social cognitive skill training) to the neglect of social contexts and cultural variations. Prevention research to date has taken the easier route, for the most part, changing individual coping patterns while largely ignoring the social, environmental, economic, public health, epidemiological, and biomedical factors and ideologies that maintain risk for the broader society.

A supplement to the original surgeon general's report (U.S. Department of Health and Human Services, 2001a) observed that the mental health service system is a fragmented patchwork that serves a range of functions for many persons. However, people with the most complex needs and the fewest financial resources, especially those from minority groups, often find these functions most difficult to access.

## Mental Health Program Configurations

A number of program options have been devised for offering services for students with significant mental health needs (U.S. Department of Health and Human Services, 2001a, 2001b). The efficacy of these various models has yet to be firmly established; in fact, significant questions have been raised concerning some of the most frequently used models, and the efficacy of these models is not uniformly supported, particularly for those involving out-of-home placements (National Advisory Mental Health Council Workgroup, 2001; U.S. Department of Health and Human Services, 2001b).

Traditional program configurations for serving students with mental health needs can be grouped according to several points of view. From the broadest perspective, treatment location models involve mental health delivery through outpatient treatment, day treatment or partial hospitalization, residential treatment, and inpatient care. Reinke et al. (2006) contrasted interventions across psychiatric inpatient and outpatient treatment, individual and group-based psychotherapies, parent training, psychoeducational programs, and other approaches aimed at changing the behavior of a given child. Foster et al. (2005) classified five formats for mental health services in schools: (a) school-financed student support services; (b) formal relationships with community mental health services; (c) school district mental health units or clinics; (d) classroom-based curricula; and (e) comprehensive, multifaceted, and integrated approaches.

Burns, Hoagwood, and Mrazek (1999) asserted that the strongest evidence base showing positive outcomes for children and families exists for the options of home-based services, therapeutic foster care, case management, and pharmacological and psychosocial interventions for specific symptoms. Hoagwood (2001) looked more specifically at the evidence base for mental health interventions, observing that the strength of the research base varies across the complexity and situational variables surrounding a given child. She concluded that there is a strong research base supporting interventions for discrete disorders and for children and youth who are served in specialized settings with discrete treatments. However, the research base for children and youth with severe EBD or for those served through multiple, coordinated services is less supportive. The absence of a clear evidence base supporting mental health services in schools is to some extent attributable to the absence of programs that provide them.

Farmer, Quinn, Hussey, and Holahan (2001) have suggested that differentiated services should be available in schools to meet the needs of students with a range of mild to more serious disorders. They recommended that specialized expertise to serve the most severely involved students be interwoven with other support personnel (such as prevention and behavior intervention specialists) to address the needs of a wide range of youth. Despite a lack of strong evidence supporting the effectiveness of providing mental health services in schools, this approach is both logical and necessary. Schools, after all, are where most children and youth spend a major portion of their day, and a range of service providers are located here. To the extent that mental health providers are located in or near schools, the delivery of these services also is facilitated.

## Implementation of Positive Behavior Support in School-Based Mental Health Settings

Kutash, Duchnowski, and Lynn (2006) described three major approaches to providing school-based mental health services. The *mental health spectrum approach* includes traditional strategies aimed at prevention, psychotherapy, and recovery. The *interconnected systems approach* is described as prevention, intervention, and systems of care. With regard to supporting students with mental health needs in the context of PBS, the basic definition of a *system of care*, which seems to be the gold standard in addressing children's mental health, must be understood. As defined by Stroul and Friedman (1986, p. iv), "a system of care is a comprehensive spectrum of mental health and other necessary services which are organized into a coordinated network to meet the multiple and changing needs of severely emotionally disturbed children and adolescents."

The third approach to school-based mental health service delivery is secondary- and tertiary-level PBS (Kutash et al., 2006). The basic principles of systems of care are quite similar to those of PBS. Duchnowski (1994) suggested that child mental health services should be organized around guiding principles involving organizational and programmatic dimensions. Organizational principles include state and local leadership, interagency collaboration, and appreciation of the important role of families. Programmatic principles include the specific behavioral techniques and curricular approaches used in such programs. Several of these principles are articulated in PBS, specifically, a focus on the impact of organizational strategies, such as leadership teams, state-level commitment and coordination, and schoolwide implementation practices. However, current PBS efforts to articulate and test family-centered supports and interagency collaboration are far from adequate.

As part of a larger study, the Bazelon Center for Mental Health Law (2006) identified critical components in current implementation of school-based mental health and PBS. Schools were visited across Illinois, Maryland, Montana, New Hampshire, New York, and Texas. In addition to the criterion of implementing school-based mental health services and PBS, the sites were expected to demonstrate strong commitment to the implementation of PBS across all three tiers of support. The primary components identified as critical to mental health/PBS implementation were family involvement, training and technical assistance, ongoing funding, and gathering meaningful outcome data.

## Issues

With regard to serving students with mental health disorders across clinical, medical, and education perspectives, consensus exists that competent services are needed at the local level, preferably while youngsters remain in their homes and using school settings as a hub for such services. However, to be successful, schools need to be much more competent in coordinating services with other providers, such as community mental health agencies. Accomplishing coordinated services within PBS schools represents a significant challenge. This raises two important issues: building capacity and changing public policy.

### *Building Capacity*

Behavioral intervention strategies represent a powerful and evidence-based technology for encouraging positive behavior at the schoolwide and classroom levels, yet researchers and practitioners have been unable to create and sustain a "contextual fit" between effective procedures and practices and the features of the environments (e.g., classroom, workplace, home, neighborhood, playground) in which children and youth with mental health issues are found.

The systemic solution is to create effective "host environments" that support the use of preferred and effective practices. Effective host environments have policies (e.g., proactive discipline handbooks, procedural handbooks); structures (e.g., behavioral support teams); and routines (e.g., opportunities for students to learn expected behavior, staff development, data-based decision making) that promote the identification, adoption, implementation, and monitoring of research-validated practices (U.S. Department of Education, 2000, III-9).

Thus, a primary issue regarding youth with mental health needs is improving the capacity of schools to address the full continuum of behavior across all students as these efforts also will benefit those with mental health conditions. Another important policy issue is the extent to which screening procedures are used to identify and label these students (Weist, Rubin, Moore, Adelsheim, & Wrobel, 2007). In schools where PBS is implemented, mental health services can be delivered in such a way to minimize concerns regarding the stigma of a mental health label.

### *Changing Public Policy*

Individuals who oppose the expenditure of school resources for mental health may contend that these services surpass the expertise available in school settings. For example, some critics question the ability of educators to identify children with mental health conditions, while others raise concerns regarding the limited resources available in most schools for addressing these conditions. Yet, failing to identify children who require evaluation and treatment creates a catch 22 in which the needs of such children can easily be underestimated, with potentially significant implications regarding the life course of those students who fail to receive services (Jensen, 2002b). As Foster et al. (2005) observed, the definition of mental health goes far beyond the domains governed by medical personnel, especially in the context of the types of services that parents are requesting. Parents of students with ADHD frequently seek help in dealing with behavioral challenges as well as in gaining access to counseling for their children, and many of these same parents are reluctant to move to pharmacological interventions (Jensen, 2002a).

The failure to understand the manifestations of children's mental health conditions and the underestimation of their prevalence also may lead policy makers to advocate for even fewer services. For example, in a highly influential document prepared by the Fordham Foundation and the Progressive Policy Institute addressing special education reform, Horn and Tynan (2001) asserted that those students traditionally identified as having emotional or behavioral adjustment problems should be considered for exclusion from special education eligibility and instead be served though the juvenile justice system. The dangers associated with accepting such an ill-conceived policy position are immense, both for the youth and families needing supports and for society as a whole.

Knitzer, Steinberg, and Fleisch (1991) observed that our failure to accept the need for mental health services in schools has implications extending beyond the children themselves. The systems created through a coordinated mental health network (i.e., a system of care) also should provide more support for the teachers serving such youth. Critics will always remain who suggest that general and special education services for youth in schools are distinctly separate from mental health services. However, Forness (2005) observed that the reconceptualization of interventions for children with EBD in terms of primary, secondary, and tertiary prevention is bringing special education research and practice into closer alignment with a comprehensive and potentially more effective public health model.

The success of the PBS approach is dependent on the ability to ensure that it is more closely attuned to culturally sensitive practices, more inclusive of parent and community input, more sensitive to internalized behavior challenges (e.g., withdrawal, isolation, and social neglect), and better coordinated with expanded mental health services in schools (Reinke et al., 2006). The expertise to use PBS strategies to significantly assist students with mental health needs is in place. However, the bridges to connect PBS to traditional school mental health providers still must be built.

## POSITIVE BEHAVIOR SUPPORT FOR YOUTH IN THE JUVENILE JUSTICE SYSTEM

The extension of PBS into juvenile justice settings is in its infancy. However, program administrators, frontline staff (e.g., general and special education teachers of incarcerated youth), and researchers increasingly are calling for PBS as a system to better meet the complex and diverse needs of youth in the juvenile justice system. Scott et al. (2002) argued that PBS is appropriate for adjudicated youth because (a) they have the same rights to an appropriate education as do their peers in traditional school systems, (b) adjudicated youth with disabilities must be afforded the protections and services under the law that their peers with disabilities receive in the public schools, and (c) they need access to a comprehensive curriculum that emphasizes both academic and social skill instruction.

### Features of Juvenile Justice Programs

The diverse nature of juvenile justice settings, as well as their unique features, and the diverse and complex needs of the youth make the initiation of change a daunting enterprise in this system. No less formidable are the attitudes of staff and the tradition of relying on punishment to accomplish compliance with institutional rules and routines.

### Characteristics of Adjudicated Youth

Compared with public school student populations, the prevalence of disabilities, poor social skills, problem-solving deficits, and academic deficiencies is significantly higher among adjudicated youth (Keith & McCray, 2002). As noted in this chapter, studies consistently suggest that 50–80% of incarcerated youth have educational disabilities or diagnosed mental health conditions (Cocozza & Skowyra, 2000; Quinn et al., 2005). Due to the wide array of available placement options, intake procedures, and reporting practices, determining specific proportions of youth with educational disabilities in the juvenile justice system has been problematic. Quinn et al. (2005) conducted a national survey of state departments of juvenile justice and reported that, on average, 34.4% of youth in juvenile corrections were receiving special education services. The most common disabilities identified in the juvenile justice system included emotional disturbance, learning disabilities, mental retardation, and speech and language impairment (Doren, Bullis, & Benz, 1996; Katsiyannis & Murry, 2000; Quinn et al., 2005).

Numerous studies have found that youth in juvenile justice settings (whether they have identified educational disabilities or not) have serious academic deficits and may be several years behind in the areas of reading, written and oral language, and math (Archwamety & Katsiyannis, 2000; Foley, 2001; Leone, Krezmien, Mason, & Meisel, 2005; Snowling, Adams, Bowyer-Crane, & Tobin, 2000). Specifically, Harris et al. (under review) assessed the reading achievement of 398 male youth aged 12 to 18 years with (33.2%) and without (66.8%) disabilities in three long-term male juvenile justice facilities in three states and found that, overall, the youth performed approximately one standard deviation below the mean on the word identification, word attack, and passage comprehension on the Woodcock-Johnson Test of Achievement III, and that youth with disabilities scored lower across the subtests than those with no disabilities.

Having a disability also appears to exert a negative effect on the length of incarceration. For example, Seltzer (2004) found that "juveniles with mental or emotional disorders remained in short-term detention 36% longer—an average 23.4 days, compared to 17.2 days for all detainees" (p. 1). Leone, Mayer, Malmgren, & Misel (2000) reported that youth with disabilities receive a disproportionate number of disciplinary referrals and sanctions as compared to youth without disabilities.

Seltzer (2004) observed that most often youth with mental health disorders and other educational disabilities end up in the juvenile justice system due to systemic deficiencies in public school systems. Specifically, these include (a) lack of accountability (e.g., defaulting to zero tolerance practices); (b) a bias toward law enforcement solutions (e.g., referring families directly to the police); and (c) lack of coordination among agencies (e.g., varying or contradictory referrals and services). On the other hand, the juvenile justice system may be society's last chance to provide these youth with the necessary skills to promote improved and successful outcomes (Keith & McCray, 2002; Seltzer, 2004). However, positive outcomes achieved in educational or therapeutic programs for incarcerated youth may be compromised by the influence of inappropriate youth behavior in either or both the school and housing units.

African American youth are significantly overrepresented in programs operated by the juvenile justice system. According to an OJJDP survey (Snyder & Sickmund, 2006), 39% of incarcerated juveniles were white, and 61% were members of ethnic or racial minority groups (including 38% black and 19% Hispanic). In contrast, 77.9% of all juveniles in the 2002 U.S. population were white, 16.4% were black, and 18% were Hispanic.

## Juvenile Justice Program Configurations

Contrary to popular belief, the U.S. juvenile justice system is not unified; much variability exists among states in terms of how juvenile offenders are processed in the court system, especially, adjudication (corresponding to a trial) procedures, and court dispositions (corresponding to sentencing).1 The placement options that are available to juvenile courts include AE programs, detention centers, or juvenile correctional facilities. A juvenile court judge may order a youth placed in an AE or day treatment program as a predisposition option (i.e., prior to a formal disposition on the youth's case) or as a diversion from formal disposition. A youth may be confined in a detention center prior to adjudication or "sentenced" to one for a period of time (usually short term). Youth assigned to juvenile correctional facilities are serving sentences; however, unlike sentences in the adult criminal justice system, in a number of states youth dispositions are indeterminate, meaning that they remain under supervision until authorities deem that they have been rehabilitated or reach the legal age of adulthood. AE or day treatment programs may be operated by the local public school district, a community agency (e.g., local mental health center), the juvenile court itself (i.e., court schools), or a state or local juvenile justice jurisdiction. PBS may be implemented in any of these placements, either in the education program alone or across an entire facility. The implementation of PBS in AE was described; therefore, in this section we focus on its application in secure facilities.

## Implementing Positive Behavior Support in Juvenile Justice Settings

Nelson, Sugai, and Smith (2005) argued that PBS can effectively address the educational, safety, and security needs of youth in a juvenile justice program by

> establishing and teaching expectations that are positively stated, clear and behaviorally exemplified; defining and teaching typical routines that are efficient and clearly structured and prompted; and formally, regularly and positively acknowledging and recognizing youth when they display desired behavioral expectations and engage in established routines. (p. 8)

Schoolwide PBS has been cited by the National Council on Disability (2003) as an effective means to address the needs of adjudicated youth in the juvenile justice system. Such applications also should include the implementation of PBS across the multiple systems that exist in juvenile facilities (e.g., housing, mental health, recreation, security).

Given the numbers of youth with learning and behavior problems in the juvenile justice system, it is not surprising that inappropriate classroom behavior continues to be a challenge facing educators in juvenile justice settings. For example, Houchins, Shippen, and Jolivette (2006) received survey responses from 96% of the juvenile justice teachers in the state of Georgia on the effects of recent statewide reform efforts related to job satisfaction. Although most of the teachers reported positive scores related to job satisfaction and 63% reported being more equipped to handle behavior problems, they also reported that behavior management continued to be the most challenging aspect of their job. In a related study, Houchins, Puckett-Patterson, Crosby, Shippen, and Jolivette (in press) surveyed the perceptions of 80 juvenile justice general and special education teachers in the state of Louisiana regarding the top three barriers to providing youth with an appropriate education and possible strategies for counteracting perceived barriers. The majority of the teachers reported behavior and discipline as the primary barriers to effectively teaching youth. In particular, these teachers indicated that an absence of effective school rules, disruptive classroom behaviors, and inconsistency among staff contributed to this obstacle. To address this, teachers suggested the development of effective school rules, a social skills curriculum, administrative support, and a focus on positive rather than negative behavior, all of which are common features of PBS.

Research evidence also supports the use of positive practices to improve outcomes for incarcerated youth. Lipsey, Wilson, and Cothern (2000, April) conducted a meta-analysis of published research studies to determine what interventions were most effective in reducing youth recidivism rates. Comparing effective intervention programs used with youth who were or were not institutionalized, they found that programs focusing on behavior, interpersonal skills, and individual counseling were most effective. Based on their qualitative analysis of incarcerated juvenile offenders with special needs, Keith and McCray (2002) concluded:

> A prominent feature of an educational plan for juvenile offenders who are ethnically diverse should center on providing a school climate that is inclusive and respectful, with an explicit goal of teaching academics, particularly reading skills, to mastery ... the role of the school's personnel, then, is multifaceted in meeting the needs of juvenile offenders with special needs. (p. 705)

Efforts to initiate PBS have begun in several states and jurisdictions. The National Technical Assistance Center for the Education of Children and Youth who are Neglected, Delinquent, or At-risk conducted an informal survey to identify jurisdictions where PBS is being implemented in juvenile justice facilities (Quinn, personal communication, August 23, 2007). Currently, two states (NM, NC) are in the process of implementation in all facilities, and PBS is being considered in Alabama, Idaho, and Vermont. Schoolwide PBS has been implemented in at least one facility in California, Iowa, Illinois, and Washington.

The complexity of juvenile justice facilities, including multidisciplinary staff, competing priorities (e.g., security vs. rehabilitation and treatment), and attitudes favoring the use of punishment over behavior support has influenced a trend toward implementation on a smaller scale, such as within the education program. However, some jurisdictions are attempting implementation on a facility-wide or even a systemwide level. For example, the North Carolina Department of Juvenile Justice and Delinquency Prevention is implementing PBS as part of a plan to replace existing programs with small, community-oriented facilities. Four of these facilities have implemented PBS for specific target behaviors, with positive results (C. Martin, personal communication, April 3, 2007).

To date, two reports have been published regarding the effects of a PBS program on youth behavior. Sidana (2006) summarized data reported by the Iowa Juvenile Home, which serves approximately 100 youth, primarily girls, with significant mental health needs. The Iowa Juvenile Home has been implementing PBS in the education program and some housing units for several years. A 73% reduction in the rate of restraints and seclusion occurred during a 15-month period, and a 50% decrease in behavior referrals occurred during a 4-year period. In addition, administrators from the facility indicated that many of the practices used are similar to those employed in more traditional schools. During the first 3 years of PBS implementation in the school program at the Illinois Youth Center in Harrisburg (serving approximately 400 males aged 13 through 21), Clarida (2005) reported no fights and a decrease in the number of minor and major infractions each year.

## Implementing Positive Behavior Support in Secure Facilities

While a seamless 24-hr, 7-day-a-week PBS program is ideal, full implementation on this scale may not be immediately feasible in some juvenile facilities for a number of reasons. First, the facility may be too large in terms of the number of staff from each system (e.g., school, security, housing, vocation, and recreation) and too complex, given the work shifts and layers of supervisors. Second, all system program administrators may not support PBS. Third, staff buy-in may be less than optimal (i.e., below 80%). Fourth, the discipline data across the systems may not support the need for PBS across all systems (e.g., school discipline and security data indicate a need, while the housing data do not). However, PBS may be scheduled for implementation in a variety of ways that can address these barriers to full-facility PBS implementation.

For example, Jolivette, Kennedy, Puckett-Patterson, and Houchins (2007) implemented PBS in a residential treatment program (similar to a juvenile justice facility with respect to systems and a 24-hr, 7-day-a-week model) in two phases for youth identified as EBD and having comorbid mental health needs. Based on the school discipline data, the school administration requested assistance with youth discipline. However, the housing administration was not interested in such help, even though the data suggested a need. Implementation began in the school program during the last 6 months of the school year. During this phase, the school staff ($N$ = 12) were trained as the PBS team, and they created, implemented, and evaluated their PBS program. As part of implementation, security staff (who also worked on the housing units) participated in applying the program in the school. Initial discipline data indicated that the average daily office referrals per month decreased from 4.19 to 1.95 during Phase I.

At the conclusion of the first phase and based on the positive discipline data, implementation was proposed in the housing unit. At first, housing administration and staff buy-in was not evident; however, with the school year ending, students began asking why PBS was not also a part of their daily unit routines, especially when some of the security staff on their housing units were participating in PBS implementation in the school. Based on student requests, housing discipline data, and support from the school administration, the housing supervisors and staff were trained in PBS, and Phase II began. This training involved sharing the school behavioral expectations, behavioral matrix, behavioral lesson plans, and reinforcement system. As implementation proceeded, the housing staff made changes to the PBS plan based on features unique to their system. These changes included (a) adding nonclassroom environments unique to the housing units; (b) deciding that each housing unit would have a reinforcement system, using reinforcers specific to each unit, but employing a uniform reinforcement schedule and amount; and (c) staying with the housing unit data collection system instead of using the School-wide Information System (www.swis.org; May et al., 2000). Based on initial data (May thru April), the average daily discipline referrals decreased from 2.3 per month to 0.7 per month during PBS Phase II, with an average of 1.59

Because juvenile facilities are quite varied, staff members must carefully analyze all aspects of the systems and settings involved when deciding how best to implement PBS. In the case described, expecting the housing unit system to implement PBS when both administrators and staff indicated an unwillingness to do so would have been challenging and likely unsuccessful. The demonstrated success of PBS in the school program and student demand contributed to a more inviting host environment in the housing unit.

## Issues

The extension of PBS into secure care facilities operated by the juvenile justice system requires adjustments of the four major features (systems, outcomes, practices, and data) as applied in traditional elementary, middle, and high school settings. These adjustments raise several important issues.

### *Systems*

In juvenile facilities, the education program is just one of many programs, which include housing, vocational training, various treatment programs, recreation, and, of course, security. Ideally, the implementation of PBS across all the programs in a facility will maximize positive youth outcomes as greater consistency in behavioral expectations, rules, routines, procedures for supporting expected behavior, and consistent staff disciplinary responses will be achieved throughout the facility (Nelson et al., 2005).

Although partnerships that extend beyond the school are not common in juvenile justice settings, they can be helpful in addressing the complex needs of incarcerated youth and in supporting PBS efforts (Keith & McCray, 2002). For example, school personnel from the community may work alongside juvenile justice staff to monitor a youth's academic and social progress in relation to his or her outcome goals and to arrange for appropriate transitional supports when leaving the facility. In addition, the youth's family and local social service organizations may work alongside juvenile justice staff to establish appropriate family-oriented supports for transition home. Therefore, the PBS leadership team must represent all relevant stakeholders, including those who are not part of the facility staff.

### *Outcomes*

A primary desired outcome for adjudicated youth is to reduce recidivism, future patterns of inappropriate behavior, and school failure. PBS provides a platform from which both short- and long-term academic, social, and postdetention/-incarceration goals of youth can be assessed by various stakeholders, such as juvenile justice staff and youth's families (Houchins, Jolivette, Wessendorf, McGlynn, & Nelson, 2005). Stakeholders within and outside a facility should agree on a common set of youth outcome goals (Scott et al., 2002). In addition, the transition process for youth returning to their family, home, and community systems should be evaluated. For example, Brock and Keegan (2007) reported that adjudicated youth are at high risk of dropping out of school on their release from juvenile facilities. Therefore, building relationships with and providing appropriate services across the juvenile justice, family, home, and community systems should be a priority outcome for a PBS program serving these youth.

### *Practices*

Altering practices that have become traditions across programs in a juvenile facility is a significant challenge. Many facilities have a long history of relying on punitive consequences to address youth behavior. Little attention is given to teaching youth the expected appropriate behaviors or the skills necessary to successfully complete tasks or to reinforcing them for doing so. When youth do engage in inappropriate behaviors or fail at an assigned task, consequences (e.g., isolation, restriction of activities) typically are applied (albeit inconsistently across staff) according to the particular youth involved and the circumstances. Nelson et al. (2005) emphasized the importance of moving away from reliance on inconsistent and ineffective punishment strategies and toward more proactive and effective strategies, namely, supporting desired behavior.

A related obstacle is the training and experience of the staff. Whereas public schools typically are staffed with personnel who have explicit training and licensure to teach specific grade levels and content areas, staff in juvenile justice facilities may lack the educational backgrounds and specific training needed to deliver effective instruction or other services. For example, staff within a facility may not have knowledge of evidence-based practices, may lack training in the use of such practices, may perceive they lack the ability to apply them properly, or may perceive a lack of administrative support in employing these practices to address the academic and social deficits of the youth (Houchins et al., 2006, in press; Nelson et al., 2005; Scott et al., 2002). Therefore, extra time, effort, and training may be required for the PBS team to (a) identify the specific needs of the youth they serve, (b) select evidence-based practices to meet those needs, (c) select appropriate practices for each of the three tiers, and (d) implement the practices selected. Team members may need to read literature or access resources from previously unknown or unfamiliar sources and to discriminate evidence-based practices from those that are not. The additional effort, time, and training required to perform these tasks may result in shifting back to previous ineffective practices and the use of punitive consequences.

Depending on the scope of implementation, PBS teams in juvenile justice settings will need to consider more nonclassroom environments than a traditional school when constructing their behavioral expectations matrix. To facilitate the success of youth in meeting behavioral expectations across these many and varied environments, staff consistently and effectively must apply practices that promote compliance with the behavioral expectations in all these settings (e.g., precorrections or reminders, active supervision, positive reinforcement). The specific security rules of a facility may require that the PBS team must be creative in their selection and implementation of practices. In addition, teams may need to look for models and examples outside traditional services and practices for this population (Keith & McCray, 2002). For example, appropriate reinforcers should be selected to promote and support youth compliance as the PBS team may find that some reinforcers typically used in traditional school settings are considered contraband within the facility or appropriate for some systems but not others (Houchins et al., 2005).

### *Data*

As in traditional schools, the opportunity exists in juvenile justice settings to use existing discipline or behavioral incidence data as the metric from which to make data-based decisions. Data-based decisions focus on the effectiveness of primary prevention practices and identifying youth who may need secondary and tertiary levels of support. Such data can guide teams in selecting practices and setting outcome goals.

If discipline data are collected in the context of a 24-hr, 7-day-a-week PBS plan, then the systems will need to have a common (a) set of behavioral expectations, (b) shared systemwide data entry and collection system (e.g., SWIS with the 24-hr function activated), and (c) a problem-solving, data decision-making process. As with any data metric, time must be allocated for staff (e.g., security, housing, recreation, vocation, school) to debrief on patterns and instances of problem behavior, summarize behavior data, and revise PBS procedures across systems based on the analysis of behavior data (Houchins et al., 2005; Nelson et al., 2005). Discipline data may be used across the facility systems to evaluate the overall effectiveness of PBS as well as whether short- and long-term outcome goals were achieved. Continuous assessment of the effects of interventions applied across the three tiers should be a major feature of data-based decision making (Keith & McCray, 2002).

Some tools are available to facilitate the implementation of PBS in programs and facilities operated by the juvenile justice system. For example, the Effective Behavior Support School-Wide Survey and the School-wide Evaluation Tool have been adapted for use in these settings. Draft versions of these tools are available on the On-Line Library page of the National Technical Assistance Center on Positive Behavioral Interventions and Supports (PBIS) Web site (www.pbis.org/main.htm).

The hypothesis that PBS can be effectively implemented in juvenile justice settings to meet the varied educational, social, mental health, and transition needs of adjudicated youth is appealing, and preliminary results are encouraging. However, empirical studies are needed to validate this hypothesis as well as to address common misconceptions. For example, some professionals assume that all youth in juvenile justice facilities automatically require tertiary-level interventions based on their prior behavior patterns and placement failures. Until the discipline (and other) data within facilities are carefully analyzed, determining the percentage of youth who will require PBS beyond the universal tier is not possible. No matter whether youth in a juvenile justice setting have behavioral problems, educational disabilities, or mental health needs, it is imperative that proactive and preventive services across the three tiers of the PBS approach are available.

The stage has been set for future applications of PBS in juvenile justice settings. Partnerships between juvenile justice, PBS networks, and other organizations advocating for effective and preventive interventions for adjudicated youth have been formed. For example, the National Association of State Directors of Special Education and the National Disability Rights Network have created an initiative to promote the prevention of delinquency and a reduction in the number of youth with disabilities entering the juvenile justice system through prevention efforts in schools. The Juvenile Justice and Special Education shared agenda, *Tools for Promoting Educational Success and Reducing Delinquency,* is available on the Web site of the National Center for Education, Disability, and Juvenile Justice (www.edjj.org). An informational video on PBS in juvenile corrections (Nelson & Liaupsin, 2006) also is available on this Web site.

## RECOMMENDATIONS

Our view is that *any* program serving children and youth will benefit from adopting, implementing, and maintaining evidence-based PBS practices. A focus on the outcomes of social and academic competence, the ongoing use of data to support implementation decision making, systematic methods of coaching and training to support staff behavior, and use of evidence-based practices to support student behavior certainly are indicated for alternative settings, and evidence suggests that PBS practices have been adopted in some programs. The question remains whether programs can implement PBS practices to more effectively reconnect children and youth to regular public schools or whether they function to keep students disconnected and out of the educational mainstream. An overarching goal of PBS in regular public schools is to keep more students in the educational mainstream. With that in mind, we offer recommendations for research, transdisciplinary interaction, and leadership.

### Research Agenda

Further study of PBS implementation in alternative settings is needed. These studies should include longitudinal research to determine the long-term outcomes for students placed in alternative settings in which PBS is implemented. With the exception of youth who are involved with the juvenile justice system, little is known about the short- or long-term outcomes for students in alternative placements. To the extent that these programs are more widely implemented, assessment of their efficacy and possible harmful effects is critical. Studies may assess the effects of various types of alternative settings—with and without PBS—on the social, emotional, behavioral, academic, and vocational development of students. Finally, multiple regression analyses are needed to examine how effectively alternative programs that implement PBS serve students with various types of disabilities.

Jolivette et al. (2007) proposed seven specific research questions that should be addressed regarding the extension of PBS into juvenile justice settings. These apply equally to students served in AE or mental health settings:

1. Can PBS be implemented in alternative settings as effectively as in typical elementary, middle, and high school settings?
2. What are the essential features of PBS implementation in various alternative settings?
3. Will the specific interventions and strategies that are successful across the three tiers be similar or different from those in typical school settings?
4. Will the relative proportions of behavior referrals across the three tiers and various grade levels hold true for alternative settings and across diverse youth populations?
5. Will more positive youth outcomes (e.g., lower recidivism rates) be achieved if PBS is implemented across an entire facility compared with implementation in the education unit alone?
6. Will the outcomes of PBS implementation in long-term facilities be different from those for short-term facilities?
7. Will the implementation of PBS affect both academic and social youth outcomes?

## Networking

To form more effective linkages between non-public school programs and PBS, we recommend that the annual APBS conference and the PBS Implementer's Forum develop specific strands and interest groups to facilitate the further integration of PBS into the programs and services offered by AE, mental health, and juvenile justice systems. The primary goal of such networking would be to further develop a research agenda and build a body of empirical research on effective PBS practices in alternative settings. One outcome of such collaboration may be a guide to effective practices for dissemination to various stakeholder audiences (e.g., policy makers, practitioners and administrators of alternative settings where PBS is implemented and programs, and consumers [parents and students] of services).

## Changing the Culture

PBS practices contribute to an attitudinal change within settings in which the social culture is a shared sense of responsibility. Having this shared sense should reduce the stigma on certain individuals or groups as "problems." The PBS approach recognizes that, rather than limiting services to a smaller targeted group of students, *all* children and youth need PBS. Furthermore, programs should make services available across environments that are oriented to the strengths of children and families (Bazelon Center for Mental Health Law, 2006). To provide a comprehensive range of services that are responsive to individuals, educators and other service providers must move out of their narrow disciplines and create situations in which multidisciplinary planning is enacted efficiently and effectively. A more comprehensive system of care model crosses disciplinary boundaries and includes effective instruction, behavioral supports, skilled parenting, and pharmacological and psychosocial interventions (Oswald, 2002).

## State and Local Leadership Teams

While both state and local implementation of PBS practices in programs for children and youth who receive education and other services outside traditional public school settings is limited, some inferences can be made about successful system-level features that would be indicated. The systems change strategies for local and statewide PBS implementation are similar. We suggest five components for successful PBS implementation: (a) a leadership team to actively coordinate implementation efforts; (b) an organizational umbrella composed of adequate funding, broad visibility, and consistent political support; (c) a foundation for sustained and broad-scale implementation established through a cadre of individuals who can provide coaching support for local implementation, a small group of individuals who can train teams on the practices and processes of schoolwide PBS; (d) a system for ongoing evaluation and provision of performance-based feedback to implementers; and (e) a small group of sites that demonstrate the viability of the approach within the fiscal, political, and social climate of the state or system. To enable and support the leadership team's efforts, the PBS implementation must have adequate and sustained funding support; regular, wide, and meaningful visibility; and relevant and effective political support.

Members of this team should include individuals whose roles, responsibilities, and activities are associated with the prevention of the development and occurrence of problem behavior, development and maintenance of desired behavior, and management and evaluation of resources related to the provision of behavioral supports. Leadership team membership may include representatives from each of the following constituencies: state, district, or facility administration (e.g., youth services, state mental health personnel); school administration; PBS trainers or coaches; mental or behavioral health; security staff; curriculum and instruction; special education; school psychology and counseling; student health; parents and family members; students; dropout prevention; AE staff; data or information management; multiculturalism; and affirmative action.

We believe that many of the indicated features of PBS implementation for school systems also apply to programs that serve at-risk children and youth, with some important differences. Staff members come from very different backgrounds with very different training and assumptions about the causes and solutions to problem behavior. Maintaining security and safety are much more important due to the greater likelihood of behavior problems in these programs via peer-based deviancy training (Dodge, Dishion, & Lansford, 2006). Finally, the difficulty of supporting a very high-risk population can be challenging to staff members, resulting in poor implementation quality.

With regard to training and coaching, the nature of the children and youth served by these programs underscores an even greater need to define and teach behavioral expectations across the program and make the environment predictable, consistent, safe, and positive. There also will be a high need for active instruction on appropriate behaviors, as well as a greater likelihood that support is provided around the clock, which means that staff development must be linked across day and night and often from a school residential setting. In this regard, the trainers and coaches should be representative of the varying staff roles.

In evaluating these programs and providing performance-based feedback to staff, teams will need to consider additional outcome measures beyond the office discipline referrals. It is common for these types of programs to file reports on youth behavior as well as the use of physical restraint, seclusion, and administrative segregation, and PBS team meetings that include social work, mental health, or security staff members must address data elements that are perceived as critical to their roles and to the youth outcomes established for their programs.

## CONCLUSIONS

Much remains to be learned about the implementation of PBS for children and youth who receive education and other services outside traditional public school settings. As documented throughout this chapter, the significantly higher prevalence of conditions that affect learning and adjustment among youth served in AE, school-based mental health, and juvenile justice settings places more of them at risk of academic and social failure than their public school counterparts. Fortunately, as suggested by preliminary outcomes, the basic features of PBS practices (consistent and positive expectations, teaching and rewarding compliance with rules, consistent and proactive responses to behavioral errors), analysis, and modification of environmental arrangements appear to be a good fit to the needs of these children and youth.

The types of structural and programmatic changes that are necessary to implement and sustain PBS across the variety of settings in which these youth are found are much less clear. AE, day and residential treatment, detention, and correctional programs offer a wide array of configurations, and many involve multidisciplinary programming, security considerations, as well as multifaceted line and staff relationships. The translation of PBS into these nontraditional arenas calls for a reexamination of strategies and tools designed for school-based application. The work that has been done in recent years has resulted in several lessons learned that may serve as a heuristic for potential implementers. We conclude this chapter with a brief description of these lessons.

1. *Start small.* Begin implementation in a single program within a large facility or across all programs in a small facility, such as a county juvenile detention center or a residential treatment facility. To the extent that programs or facilities resemble public schools, implementation procedures that are based on schoolwide PBS applications probably will be sufficient. However, in facilities that operate 24 hr a day, 7 days a week, and involve multidisciplinary staff, security considerations, and diverse programs, sheer size and conflicting priorities present formidable obstacles to achieving staff training and buy-in, not to mention the implementation of PBS with fidelity. Even in small facilities or programs, implementers should identify all key personnel and achieve consensus that PBS is a necessary and desirable system change before going further.
2. *Obtain endorsement and support at the state level.* Although PBS was not developed as a top-down initiative, implementation is likely to be more efficient if higher-level administrators understand and support PBS as one of their priorities. Information and training are now available in a variety of formats, which permit more efficient dissemination of information and training to state directors of mental health, juvenile justice, child welfare, and other agencies that sponsor the programs and facilities described in this chapter.
3. *Link to an ongoing statewide PBS or related initiative.* Several states (e.g., Arizona, Iowa, Illinois, New Mexico, Utah) have adopted behavioral initiatives that are based on or are closely related to PBS. Obviously, the existence of an initiative that connects state children's services agencies offers a distinct advantage in terms of getting state leaders on the same page. In states that have not adopted a vision that is shared across agencies, the state PBS leadership team may be able to engage in strategic planning with key leaders and work toward a shared agenda.
4. *Adopt a data collection and decision model.* A key strategy in promoting systems change is to point out how proposed changes promote the self-interests of the parties involved (Leone, 2006). One approach is to identify data that measure key outcomes, link these outcomes to data that are collected routinely, and demonstrate how these data can be used to facilitate ongoing decision making. For example, at the Illinois Youth Center in Harrisburg, teachers reported that, following the implementation of PBS, the reduction in behavior incidents in classrooms meant that they could spend more time teaching. Student attendance and academic performance improved, resulting in better test scores, completion of general equivalency diplomas (GEDs) and high school diplomas, and enrollment in college courses. These results have meaning because staff saw a connection between a reduction in disciplinary issues and an increase in desired student performance. Students saw a connection between

academic achievement and a chance for a better life. Ultimately, of course, such social outcomes as a reduction in rates of recidivism or out-of-home placements and an increase in positive postschool adjustment will persuade policy makers that investment in PBS for these children and youth is worthwhile.

5. *Incorporate PBS into an existing treatment or discipline model (if the model is compatible with PBS).* Implementers must take stock of the treatment or discipline systems currently in place in a program or facility. Analysis of discipline data or staff surveys should assist in determining whether the system is working. However, many programs and facilities do not routinely use discipline data to evaluate practices or to make program adjustment decisions, or staff are reluctant to make their data available because of concerns about confidentiality, negative evaluations, and so on. Efficiency and simplicity are two of the strongest selling points of PBS, especially for youth with disabilities, those with long histories of school failure, and those needing more opportunities for academic and behavioral success. In addition, staff are more likely to commit to and sustain implementation of a treatment or discipline model that is positive, accomplishable, and effective. Horner (Danielson et al., 2007) emphasized that nothing is gained by asking staff to abandon an effective skill or practice. However, if approaches like PBS allow staff to accomplish the same outcomes with less effort, implementation is likely to be self-sustaining, and positive student outcomes are more likely to be experienced.

## NOTE

1. A description of the juvenile justice system is beyond the scope of this chapter, but interested readers may consult the Web site of the Bureau of Justice Statistics Criminal Justice System Description (http://www.ojp.gov/bjs/justsys.htm).

## REFERENCES

Archwamety, T., & Katsiyannis, A. (2000). Academic remediation, parole violations, and recidivism rates among delinquent youths. *Remedial and Special Education, 21*, 161–170.

American Psychiatric Association. (1994). *Diagnostic and statistical manual of mental disorders* (4th ed.). Washington, DC: Author.

Aron, Y. (2006). *An overview of alternative education.* Washington, DC: Urban Institute.

Bazelon Center for Mental Health Law. (2006). *Way to go: School success for children with mental health care needs.* Washington, DC: Bazelon Center for Mental Health Law.

Brock, L., & Keegan, N. (2007). *Students highly at risk of dropping out: Returning to school after incarceration.* National Evaluation and Technical Assistance Center for the Education of Children and Youth Who Are Neglected, Delinquent, or At-Risk. Retrieved

June 28, 2007, from http://www.neglected-delinquent.org/nd/resources/spotlight/spotlight200701b.asp

Burns, B., Hoagwood, K., & Mrazek, P. (1999). Effective treatment for mental disorders in children and adolescents. *Clinical Child and Family Psychology Review*, 4, 199–254.

CJN v. Minneapolis Public Schools, 38 IDELR 208 (8th Cir. 2003).

Clarida, M. (2005). *Positive behavior interventions and supports at the Illinois Youth enter—Harrisburg.* Retrieved June 14, 2007, from http://www.neglected-delinquent.org/nd/docs/PBIS_Doc7_IYC_full%20article.pdf

Clark, C. (2000). Texas charter schools: New choices for Texas families. *Clearing House, 74*(2), 64–69.

Cocozza, J. J., & Skowyra, K. R. (2000). Youth with mental health disorders: Issues and emerging responses. *Juvenile Justice, 7*, 3–13.

Danielson, L., Cobb, B., Sanchez, S., & Horner, R. (2007, July). *Evidence-based practices: A technical assistance perspective.* Presentation given as part of the 2007 Office of Special Education Projects Project Directors' Conference, Washington, DC.

Davis, S. M., Fox, R., Garrison, M., Justice, B., Staperl, C., & Sachry, E. (2006). Policy. *Teachers College Record, 108*, 866–889.

Denny, S. J., Clark, T. C., & Watson, P.D. (2003). Comparison of high-risk behaviours among students in alternative high schools in New Zealand and the United States. *Journal of Paediatrics and Child Health, 39*, 33–39.

Dodge, K. A., Dishion, T. J., & Lansford, J. E. (2006). *Deviant peer influences in programs for youth.* New York. Guilford.

Doren, M., Bullis, M., & Benz, M. (1996). Predicting the arrest status of adolescents with disabilities in transition. *Journal of Special Education, 29*, 363–380.

Duchnowski, A. J. (1994). Innovative service programs. *Journal of Clinical Child Psychology, 23*, 13–18.

Duncan, B. B., Forness, S. R., & Hartsough, C. (1995). Students identified as seriously emotionally disturbed in school-based day treatment: Cognitive, psychiatric, and special education characteristics. *Behavioral Disorders, 20*, 238–252.

Eber, L., Nelson, C. M., & Miles, P. (1997). School-based wraparound for students with emotional and behavioral challenges. *Exceptional Children, 63*, 539–555.

Eber, L., Sugai, G., Smith, C., & Scott, T. (2002). Wraparound and positive behavioral interventions and supports in the schools. *Journal of Emotional & Behavioral Disorders, 10*, 171–181.

Estes, M. B. (2006). Charter schools: Do they work for troubled students? *Preventing School Failure, 51*, 55–61.

Finn, J. D., & Rock, D. A. (1997). Academic success among students at risk for school failure. *Journal of Applied Psychology, 82*(2), 221–234.

Farmer, T. W., Quinn, M., Hussey, W., & Holahan, T. (2001). The development of disruptive behavioral disorders and correlated constraints: Implications for intervention. *Behavioral Disorders, 26*, 117–130

Foley, R. M. (2001). Academic characteristics of incarcerated youth and correctional educational programs: A literature review. *Journal of Emotional and Behavioral Disorders, 9*, 248–259.

Foley, R. M., & Pang, L. (2006). Alternative programs: Program and student characteristics. *The High School Journal*, 89, 10–21.

Forness, S. R. (2005). The pursuit of evidence-based practice in special education for children with emotional or behavioral disorders. *Behavioral Disorders, 30*, 311–330.

Foster, S., Rollefson, M., Doksum, T., Noonan, D., Robinson, G., & Teich, J. (2005). *School mental health services in the United States, 2002–2003* (DHHS Pub. No. (SMA) 05–4068). Rockville, MD: Center for Mental Health Services, Substance Abuse and Mental Health Services Administration.

Gamble, D., & Satcher, J. (2007). A one-room schoolhouse. *The Journal of Correctional Education, 58*, 14–26.

Gottfredson, G. D. (1999). *The effective school battery: User's manual.* Ellicott City, MD: Gottfredson.

Government Accounting Office Report. (2002, February). *School dropout: Education could play a stronger role in identifying and disseminating promising prevention strategies* (GAO-02–240). Washington, DC: Author.

Harris, P. J., Baltodano, H. M., Bal, A., Rutherford, R. B., Jolivette, K., & MulCahy, C. (under review). Reading achievement of incarcerated youth in three regions. *Journal of Correctional Education.*

Hoagwood, K. (2001). Surgeon general's conference on children's mental health sets out a national action agenda. *Emotional and Behavioral Disorders in Youth, 1*, 2, 33–34.

Horn, W. F., & Tynan, D. (2001). Time to make special education "special" again. In C. E. Finn, A. Rotherham & C. R. Hokanson (Eds.). *Rethinking special education for a new century.* Washington, DC: Thomas B. Fordham Foundation and the Progressive Policy Institute.

Horner, R. H., & Sugai, G. (2000). School-wide behavior support: An emerging initiative. *Journal of Positive Behavioral Interventions, 2*, 231–233.

Houchins, D. E., Jolivette, K., Wessendorf, S., McGlynn, M., & Nelson, C. M. (2005). Stakeholders' view of implementing positive behavioral support in a juvenile justice setting. *Education and Treatment of Children, 28*, 380–399.

Houchins, D. E., Puckett-Patterson, D., Crosby, S., Shippen, M. E., & Jolivette, K. (in press). Barriers and facilitators to providing incarcerated youth with a quality education. *Preventing School Failure.*

Houchins, D. E., Shippen, M. E., & Jolivette, K. (2006). System reform and job satisfaction of juvenile justice teachers. *Teacher Education and Special Education, 29*, 127–136.

Huerta, L. A., Gonsalez, M., & D'Etremont, C. (2006). Cyber and home school charter schools: Adopting policy to new forms of public schooling. *Peabody Journal of Education, 81*, 103–139.

Irwin, D., & Algozzine, B. (2007). *North Carolina positive behavior support initiative evaluation report 2005–2006.* Raleigh, NC: Department of Public Instruction, Exceptional Children Division, Behavioral Support Services. Retrieved July 14, 2007, from http://www.dpi.state.nc.us/docs/positivebehavior/data/evaluation/2005–06/evaluationreport.pdf

Jensen, P. (2002a). Closing the evidence-based treatment gap for children's mental health services: What we know versus what we do. *Report on Emotional & Behavioral Disorders in Youth, 2*, 2, 43–47.

Jensen, P. (2002b). Nature versus nurture and other misleading dichotomies: Conceptualizing mental health and illness in children. *Report on Emotional and Behavioral Disorders in Youth, 2*, 4, 81–86.

Jolivette, K., Houchins, D. E., Josephs, N., Waller, K, Hall, T., & Nomvete, P. (2008). Providing educational services in secure settings. L.M. Bullock & R.A. Gable (Eds.), *Ensuring a brighter future for troubled children/youth: Challenges and solutions* (pp. 193–263). Arlington, VA: Council for Children with Behavioral.

Jolivette, K., Kennedy, C., Puckett-Patterson, D., & Houchins, D.E. (Manuscript in Preparation). *Implementing a two-phase 24/7 SW-PBS program in a residential facility for students with severe emotional and behavioral disorders and mental health needs.* Manuscript submitted for publication.

Katsiyannis, A., & Murry, F. (2000). Young offenders with disabilities: Legal requirements and reform considerations. *Journal of Child and Family Studies, 9*, 75–86.

Katsiyannis, A., & Smith, C. (2003). Disciplining students with disabilities: Legal and practical concerns for students with emotional and behavioral disorders. *Behavioral Disorders, 28*, 410–418.

Kauffman, J. M. (2005). *Characteristics of emotional and behavioral disorders of children* (8th ed). Saddle Hill, NJ: Merrill Prentice Hall.

Keith, J. M., & McCray, A. D. (2002). Juvenile offenders with special needs: Critical issues and bleak outcomes. *Qualitative Studies in Education, 15*, 691–710.

Knitzer, J., Steinberg, Z., & Fleisch, B. (1991). Schools, children's mental health, and the advocacy challenge. *Journal of Clinical Child Psychology, 20*, 102–111.

Kohn, A. (1993). *Punished by rewards.* Boston: Houghton Mifflin

Kurtz, A. (2002). What works for delinquency? The effectiveness of interventions for teenage offending behavior. *The Journal of Forensic Psychiatry, 13*, 671–692.

Kutash, K., Duchnowski, A. J., & Lynn, N. (2006). *School-based mental health: An empirical guide for decision-makers.* Tampa: University of South Florida, Louis de la Parte Florida Mental Health Institute, Department of Child and Family Studies, Research and Training Center for Children's Mental Health.

Leone, P. E. (1994). Education services for youth with disabilities in a state-operated juvenile correctional system: Case study and analysis. *Journal of Special Education, 28*, 43–58.

Leone, P. E., Krezmien, M., Mason, L., & Meisel, S. M. (2005). Organizing and delivering empirically based literacy instruction to incarcerated youth. *Exceptionality, 13*, 89–102.

Leone, P. E. (2006, May). *Doing things differently: Literacy, delinquency, and 21st century skills*. Presentation given as part of the symposium Leading Change: Rethinking Juvenile Justice. Connecticut Department for Children and Families, Bureau of Juvenile Services, Storrs, CT.

Lipsey, M. W., Wilson, D. B., & Cothern, L. (2000, April). *Effective intervention for serious juvenile offenders*. Juvenile Justice Bulletin. Washington, DC: Office of Juvenile Justice and Delinquency Prevention.

Martinez, S. (2006). Feel the heat: Miami-Dade County public schools implementation of school-wide PBS. *Big IDEAs Dropout Prevention Strategies eNewsletter, 3*(3), 4–8. Retrieved July 14, 2007, from http://www2.edc.org/ndpc-sd/vol8.htm

Mash E. J., & Dozois, D. J. A. (2003). Child psychopatholgy: A developmental-systems perspective. In E. J. Mash & R. A. Barkley (Eds.), *Child psychopathology* (2nd ed., pp. 3–74) New York: Guilford Press.

May, S., Ard, W., III, Todd, A. W., Horner, R. H., Glasgow, A., Sugai, G., et al. (2000). *School-wide Information System*. Eugene: University of Oregon, Educational and Community Supports.

Mazzotti, V. L., & Higgins, K. (2006). Public schools and the juvenile justice system: Facilitating relationships. *Intervention in School and Clinic, 41*, 295–301.

McGough, K. (2007). Data highlight ... Sustainability of PBS. Positive Connection, 2(1), 3. Retrieved August 23, 2008, from http://www.cde.state.co.us/pbs/download/pdf/PBS_NewsletterWinter2007.pdf

National Advisory Mental Health Council Workgroup on Child and Adolescent Mental Health Intervention Development and Deployment. (2001). *Blueprint for Change: Research on Child and Adolescent Mental Health*. Washington, DC: National Mental Health Advisory Council.

National Center on Education Statistics. (2001). *Public alternative schools and programs for students at risk of education failure: 2000–01*. Washington, DC: U.S. Department of Education.

National Council on Disability. (2003, May). *Addressing the needs of youth with disabilities in the juvenile justice system: The current status of evidence-based research*. Washington, DC: Author. Retrieved February 11, 2005, from http://www.ncd.goov/newsroom/publications/2003/juvenile.htm

National Governor's Association. (2003). *Reaching new heights: A governor's' guide to turning around low-performing schools*. Retrieved October 1, 2004, from http://www.nga.org/cda/files/0803REACHING.PDF

Nelson, C. M., & Liaupsin, C. J. (2006) *Positive behavior support for youth involved in juvenile corrections*. Education, Disability, and Juvenile Justice (EDJJ) Professional Development Series 6. Spokane, WA: Corrections Learning Network—a Division of Educational Service District 101.

Nelson, C. M., Sugai, G., & Smith, C. (2005, Summer). Positive behavior support offered in juvenile corrections. *Counterpoint, 1*, 6–7.

OSEP Center on Positive Behavioral Interventions and Supports (2005). Retrieved August 8, 2007 from http://www.pbis.org/tools.htm.

Oswald, D. P. (2002). The new medical model and beyond: A response to Forness and Kavale. *Behavioral Disorders, 27*, 155–157.

Quinn, M. M., & Poirier, J. M. (2006). *Study of effective alternative education programs final grant report*. Washington, DC: Office of Special Education Programs, U.S. Department of Education.

Quinn, M. M., Rutherford, R. B., Leone, P. E., Osher, D. M., & Poirier, J. M. (2005). Youth with disabilities in juvenile corrections: A national survey. *Exceptional Children, 71*, 339–345.

Reinke, W. M., Herman, K. C., & Tucker, C. M. (2006). Building and sustaining communities that prevent mental disorders: Lessons from the field of special education. *Psychology in the Schools, 3*, 313–329.

Roland M. and Miriam M. v. the Concord School Committee, 16 IDELR 1129 (1st Cir. 1990).

Ryan, J. B., Katsiyannis, A., Peterson, R., & Chmelar, R. (2007). IDEA 2004 and disciplining students with disabilities. *NASSP Bulletin, 91*, 130–140.

Schachter, R. (2004, Dec.), Mall schools District Administrator, 40(12), 27–29.

Scott, T. M., Nelson, C. M., Liaupsin, C., Jolivette, K., Christle, C. A., & Riney, M. (2002). Addressing the needs of at-risk and adjudicated youth through positive behavior support: Effective prevention practices. *Education and Treatment of Children, 25*, 532–551.

Seltzer, T. (2004, July). *Statement of Tammy Seltzer, Senate Committee on Governmental Affairs, Juvenile detention centers: Are they warehousing children with mental illness.* July 7, 2004. Retrieved May 11, 2007, from http://www.senate.gov/ gove_affairs/ index.cfm?Fuseaction=Hearings.Testimony&HearingID=186&WitnessID=332

Sidana, A. (2006, February). *PBIS in juvenile justice settings.* The National Evaluation and Technical Assistance Center for the Education of Children and Youth Who are Neglected, Delinquent, or At-Risk. Retrieved May 11, 2007, from http://www.ndtac.org/ndresources/spotlight/spotlight200601b.asp

Skowyra, K., & Cocozza, J. J. (2006). *A blueprint for change: Improving the system response to youth with mental health needs involved with the juvenile justice system.* Research and program brief. National Center for Mental Health and Juvenile Justice. Retrieved May 25, 2007, from http://www.ncmhjj.com/Blueprint.

Snowling, M. J., Adams, J. W., Bowyer-Crane, C. A., & Tobin, V. (2000). Levels of literacy among juvenile offenders: The incidence of specific reading difficulties. *Criminal Behaviour and Mental Health, 10*, 229–241.

Snyder, H. N., and Sickmund, M. (2006). *Juvenile offenders and victims: 2006 national report.* Washington, DC: U.S. Department of Justice, Office of Justice Programs, Office of Juvenile Justice and Delinquency Prevention.

Spanoghe, K., Jones, M., Ourand, K., & Kolls, N. (2007). *Secondary and tertiary interventions for alternative and special settings.* PowerPoint presentation. Retrieved July 14, 2007, from www.pbismaryland.org/Presentations/SpringForum2007Forbush-GuildandStE.ppt

Sprague, J., Walker, H., Nishioka, V., Tobin, T., Bullis, M., & Eisert, D. C. (2001). Skills for success: A violence prevention intervention for socially maladjusted middle school students. Eugene: University of Oregon, Institute on Violence and Destructive Behavior.

Stroul, B. A., & Friedman, R. (1986). *A system of care of severely emotionally disturbed children and youth.* Washington, DC: Georgetown University Child Development Center, CASSP Technical Assistance Center.

Substance Abuse Mental Health Services Administration. (2001). *Annual report to Congress on the evaluation of the comprehensive community mental health services for children and their families program.* Retrieved August 21, 2007, from http://mentalhealth.samhsa.gov/publications/allpubs/CB-E201E/

Substance Abuse Mental Health Services Administration. (2007). *Glossary of terms: Child and adolescent mental health.* Retrieved August 21, 2007, from http://mentalhealth.samhsa.gov/publications/allpubs/Ca-0005/

Telzrow, C. F. (2001). Interim Alternative Educational Settings: School district implementation of IDEA 1997 Requirements. *Education and Treatment of Children, 24*, 72–99.

Tobin, T., & Sprague, J. (2000a). Alternative education programs for at-risk youth: Issues, best practices, and recommendations. In H. Walker & M. Epstein (Eds.), *Making schools safer and violence free: Critical issues, solutions, and recommended practices.* Austin, TX: Pro-ed. pp. 150–159.

Tobin, T., & Sprague, J. (2000b). Alternative education strategies: Reducing violence in school and community programs. *Journal of Emotional and Behavioral Disorders, 8*, 177–186.

Tobin, T. J., & Sprague, J. R. (2002). Alternative educational programs: Accommodating tertiary level, at-risk students. In M. R. Shinn, G. Stoner, & H. M. Walker

(Eds.), *Interventions for academic and behavior problems II: Preventive and remedial approaches* (2nd ed., pp. 961–992). Silver Spring, MD: National Association of School Psychologists (NASP).

U.S. Department of Education. (2000). Applying positive behavioral support in schools. *22nd Annual Report to Congress on the Implementation of the Individuals with Disabilities Act*, pp. III–III–31. Washington, DC.

U.S. Department of Health and Human Services. (2001a). *Mental health: Culture, race, and ethnicity—a supplement to mental health: A report of the surgeon general.* Rockville, MD: U.S. Department of Health and Human Services, Substance Abuse and Mental Health Services Administration, Center for Mental Health Services.

U.S. Department of Health and Human Services. (2001b). *Mental health: A report of the surgeon general.* Rockville, MD: U.S. Department of Health and Human Services, Substance Abuse and Mental Health Services Administration, Center for Mental Health Services, National Institutes of Health, National Institute of Mental Health.

Wagner, M., & Davis, M. (2006). How are we preparing students with emotional disturbances for transition to young adulthood? Findings from the National Longitudinal Transition Study-2. *Journal of Emotional and Behavioral Disorders, 14*, 86–98.

Weist, M., Rubin, M., Moore, E. Adelsheim, S., & Wrobel, G. (2007) Mental health screening in schools. *Journal of School Health, 77*, 53–58.

Wetzel, M. C., McNaboe, K. A., Schneidermeyer, S. A., Jones, A. B., & Nash, P. N. (1997). Public and private partnership in an alternative middle school program. *Preventing School Failure, 41*, 179–184.

Williams, K. (2002). Determining the effectiveness of anger management training and curricular infusion at an alternative school for students expelled for weapons. *Urban Education, 37*, 59–76.

Zweig, J. M. (2003). *Vulnerable youth: Identifying their need for alternative education settings.* Washington, D.C.: The Urban Institute. Retrieved July 14, 2007, from http://www.urban.org/url.cfm?ID=410828

# 21

# Behavior Supports in Nonclassroom Settings

**LORI NEWCOMER, GEOFF COLVIN, and TIMOTHY J. LEWIS**

The focus of the three-tier approach of positive behavior support (PBS) in nonclassroom settings is to provide proactive supports that include early detection and intervention at the primary, secondary, and tertiary levels. The logic of this approach rests on putting proactive structures in place and then monitoring student response. If many students are demonstrating problems, then the universal features of the setting need to be adjusted. Yet, even when effective primary prevention systems are in place, a few students may still fail to respond appropriately and will require more intensive interventions at the secondary or tertiary level to promote behavioral competence. Thus, a continuum of interventions is implemented across nonclassroom, classroom, and individual student support systems to support students who do not respond to universal procedures. Although each of these systems has unique features, they overlap and have an impact the others (Crone & Horner, 2003; Todd, Horner, Sugai, & Colvin, 1999) as represented in Fig. 21.1.

Nonclassroom systems refer to those areas outside the classroom where students gather for a specific purpose (e.g., cafeteria, playground, school assembly, hallway, bus zone, parking lot, restroom). When conditions in specific settings are characterized by less-structured activities, ambiguous rules and routines, a focus on social interaction between students, low rates of supervision, and a high density of students, significant management challenges can emerge. Primary prevention for nonclassroom settings focuses on directly teaching and encouraging clearly defined routines and behavior expectations relevant to the specific setting. A continuum of secondary (targeted) and function-based tertiary interventions may be necessary

**LORI NEWCOMER** • University of Missouri – St. Louis
**GEOFF COLVIN** • Behavior Associates – Eugene, Oregon
**TIMOTHY J. LEWIS** • University of Missouri-Columbia

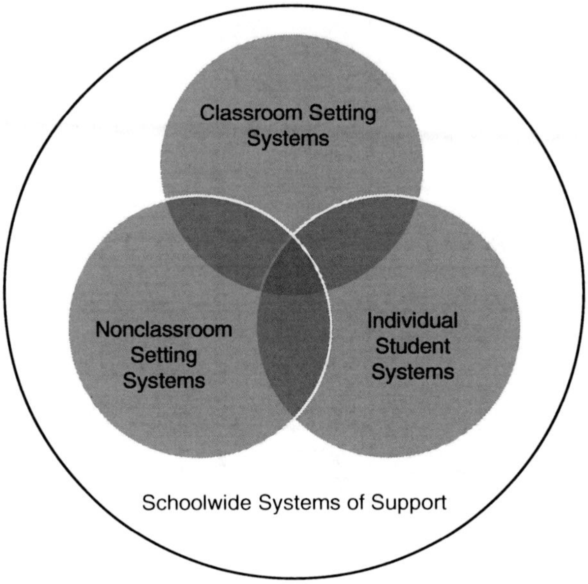


**Fig. 21.1.** Schoolwide positive behavior support practices by context.

to reduce behaviors that are not responsive to universal approaches, including (a) increased supervision and monitoring, (b) increased opportunities for positive reinforcement, (c) increased opportunities for instructional feedback, and (d) targeted social skills training.

Approximately 50% of the problem behavior reported for disciplinary action originates from nonclassroom settings (Leedy, Bates, & Safran, 2004; Nelson & Colvin, 1996; Nelson, Smith, & Colvin, 1995; Taylor-Greene et al., 1997; Todd, Haugen, Anderson, & Spriggs, 2002). Common settings in most schools include the cafeteria, bus zone, hallways, and bathrooms. Some settings are unique to a particular grade level. Preschools typically have an outdoor space or playground, a multipurpose room, and distinct activity zones (e.g., gross motor, dramatic play, arts and crafts, quiet or rest zone). At the middle school and high school grade levels, the number and nature of specific settings expand to include more diverse locations and events such as dances, afterschool organizations and meetings, sporting events, locker rooms, athletic fields, and student parking areas. This chapter extends the discussion of the larger schoolwide system by focusing on the unique challenges of nonclassroom settings. Specifically, we present an overview of (a) effective practices and considerations, (b) systems to address implementation and monitoring, and (c) current research and examples.

## EFFECTIVE PRACTICES AND CONSIDERATIONS

Common areas must be systematically managed for the area to serve its proper function and to minimize the chance of problems or serious behavior. To support appropriate behavior in nonclassroom settings, Lewis and

Sugai (1999) emphasized a focus on supervision with attention directed toward (a) features of the physical environment, (b) establishing predictable routines, (c) teaching students appropriate setting-specific behaviors, and (d) focusing staff on the effective use of active supervision strategies. The following section addresses each of these features.

## Features of the Physical Environment

The physical characteristics of the area may set the occasion for problem behaviors. These areas should be structured to remove or modify problematic features such as unsafe objects, crowded conditions, or extended wait times. Preventive practices include (a) identification and removal of unsafe objects, (b) reduction of physical space that is difficult to supervise or does not allow a clear field of visual surveillance, (c) provision of adequate space or efficient schedules to minimize lines and wait time, and (d) reduction of student density in common areas with strategic scheduling (Lewis & Sugai, 1999; Nelson & Colvin, 1996).

Hallways are frequently cited as a setting for problem behavior and excess noise. This is especially true in middle and high schools, where hallways must accommodate large numbers of students during transitions. Removal of free-standing objects and obstacles (e.g., display cases, vending machines, trash containers) that impede traffic flow will facilitate movement through the hallways and the intersections between those hallways.

Reduction of student density to promote efficient transitions, reduce long lines and wait times, and minimize congestion can be accomplished with staggered scheduling and careful consideration of entry and exit points for common areas. Allowing adequate space between groups of students in transition can prevent large groups of students from assembling in one area (e.g., lining up in cafeteria, bus zone).

Areas that are difficult to supervise or have obstacles that prevent clear visual surveillance should be made "off limits." This would include areas such as isolated stairwells or restrooms or recessed storage. Outdoors, this would include areas where visual surveillance is blocked by the building, walls, or landscaping.

Parking areas and vehicular traffic present numerous challenges, particularly at high schools where students have driving privileges. Congestion and obscured views can be minimized by establishing pedestrian and vehicular circulation routes to and from parent drop-off, bus drop-off, bicycle racks and pedestrian walks, and student parking zones. Clearly marked transitions from parking areas to pedestrian routes will help maintain a separation between pedestrian and vehicular traffic. Opportunities for high-speed driving can be reduced by placing barriers and closing unsupervised entrances and exits to student parking zones during low-use times and increasing supervision during high-use periods.

## Establish Predictable Routines

A majority of problem behaviors in nonclassroom settings are caused by lack of adequate routines. Thoughtful, carefully constructed routines establish both student and adult expectations and allow activities to take place more efficiently, thereby decreasing the likelihood of inappropriate behaviors. Common areas should be assessed to determine if (a) routines to facilitate orderly transitions have been established, (b) students have been taught the routines, and (c) staff are aware of and consistently enforcing established routines. Areas in which routines should be considered include the cafeteria (e.g., going through the lunch line, dismissal from tables, traffic flow); playground (lining up, equipment use, games); bus (arrival, dismissal, riding); or assembly (enter, exit, active listening). Some routines will be the same and can be taught similarly across multiple settings (e.g., pick up litter, use inside voice, walk on the right), whereas some behaviors and routines will be specific to the setting (e.g., returning trays in the cafeteria, listening to a speaker at an assembly, getting equipment for intramurals). Posting visual displays of routines (e.g., posters, visual cues) supports consistent implementation and compliance with routines.

## Teaching Appropriate Setting-Specific Behavior

The heart of a proactive approach to establishing discipline is the assumption that student behavioral expectations are a set of skills that need to be directly taught to the students. The same teaching principles and strategies employed to provide instruction for academic, sport, art, or music skills are used to teach behavioral expectations (Colvin, 2007). Cotton (1995), in an extensive review of research on effective practices for establishing schoolwide discipline, highlighted the critical role of teaching behavior with the finding, "Children below fourth grade require a great deal of instruction and practice in classroom rules and procedures ... effective management, especially in the early grades is more an instructional than a disciplinary enterprise" (p. 8). Similar findings were also reported for older students (Grades 4–12), showing strong positive results were obtained by using a teaching approach: "With older students, researchers have noted that the best results are obtained through vigilantly reminding students about the rules and procedures and monitoring their compliance with them" (p. 8). In addition to providing reminders and supervision, Colvin, Kame'enui, and Sugai (1995) found that including the instructional component of providing feedback also significantly assisted in teaching older students (Grades 4–12) classroom expectations.

Behavior instruction should be taught uniformly through the use of a common set of scripted lessons (Sugai & Lewis, 1996). Acquisition and generalization of the behavioral skills are enhanced when instruction is based on preferred practices:

1. Provide multiple examples and nonexamples and variations of the skill that are relevant to the specific setting.
2. Sequence positive and negative examples that are minimally different to maximize discriminations about when and where the skill should be used. Teach the skills within and across a range of contexts where they will be applied.

3. Teach directly and actively by modeling and demonstrating the skill, variations of the skill, and the conditions under which the skill should be used (i.e., critical rule). To increase the salience of the relevant features of a demonstration, teachers should describe or point out the critical features of the demonstrations as they are being presented. Descriptions can be provided during the demonstration (e.g., "See how he is moving quietly along the right side of the hallway, leaving space between the person in front of and the person behind him?").
4. Provide opportunities for students to practice or rehearse the skill with assistance (e.g., verbal prompts) and feedback and then without assistance to test their knowledge and accurate use of the skill.
5. Review skills and routines regularly. Reviews can include opportunities for students to answer questions, demonstrate the skills, or describe the context in which a skill is used.
6. Acknowledge appropriate displays of the skill frequently.
7. Make adaptations for unique demographics, taking into consideration the diversity of the student population (i.e., culture, ethnicity, disability). Using examples from the students' natural environment will ensure that lessons are culturally, age, and ability appropriate.

Examples of lesson development for young children and for older students follow.

### *Teaching Behavioral Expectations to Younger Students (K–3)*

There are two steps in developing a plan to teach the behavioral expectations for a nonclassroom setting to younger students. The first step involves identifying the specific behaviors or routines that the students are expected to follow in each of the settings. These specific behaviors should be clearly observable and understandable for the students and need to be linked to the schoolwide behavioral expectations. The second step involves developing explicit lesson plans for teaching the behavior expectations. This teaching plan would follow the same steps used to provide instruction in other content areas. A sample teaching plan is presented in Table 21.1, in which the steps for teaching hallway behavior are described.

### *Teaching Behavioral Expectations to Older Students (Grades 4–12)*

The instruction plan for teaching behavioral expectations to students in 4th through 12th grades involves three steps: (a) remind, (b) supervise, and (c) provide feedback. An illustration of this teaching plan for older students is presented in Table 21.2.

## Effective Use of Active Supervision and Precorrection

*Active supervision* is best described as the behaviors displayed by teachers and adult supervisors to encourage more appropriate student behavior and

**Table 21.1.** Teaching Plan for Hallway Behavior for Younger Students

Expected behavior: *Be responsible*
Common setting: *Hallways*

**Step 1: Explain**

| | |
|---|---|
| ❑ | Avoid disturbing others |
| ❑ | Avoid injury |
| ❑ | Save time |

**Step 2: Specify student behaviors**

| | |
|---|---|
| ❑ | Walk |
| ❑ | Keep hands, feet, and objects to self |
| ❑ | Be silent (no talking unless directed by the teacher) |
| ❑ | Stay on right side of hallway |
| ❑ | Keep in line |
| ❑ | Keep up with the group |

**Step 3: Practice**

| | |
|---|---|
| ❑ | Role play in the classroom |
| ❑ | Actually practice in the hallway |
| ❑ | Have regular practices (once or twice each term, when there are problems and as booster sessions before or after breaks) |
| ❑ | Provide frequent reminders |

**Step 4: Monitor**

| | |
|---|---|
| ❑ | Vary your position (front, back, and middle of line) |
| ❑ | Scan the whole line |
| ❑ | Interact with the students |
| ❑ | Reinforce, remind, and correct student behavior |

**Step 5: Review**

| | |
|---|---|
| ❑ | Give the students feedback (praise appropriate behavior and identify problems) |
| ❑ | Solicit student feedback: "How did we do on keeping in line today?" |
| ❑ | Deliver consequences as necessary |

**Table 21.2.** Teaching Plan for Older Students for Transition/Hallway Behavior

**Schoolwide behavior expectation:** *Be responsible*
Common setting: *Hallways (transitioning between classrooms)*
Specific behaviors: *Be on time for class and behave appropriately in the hallways*

**Remind:** Explain to the students that they need to be behaving appropriately in the hallways and get to class on time. Point out that it is okay to chat, but hanging out to chat is not acceptable (i.e., they need to keep moving). The expected behaviors are (a) keep the noise down, (b) use appropriate language, and (c) keep moving. Provide these reminders just before the end of the period when the students are about to exit the classroom. The expectations are also read out during the morning announcements on the address system.

**Supervise:** All staff are asked to position themselves near the doorway, or even a little out in the hallway, so that they can observe the students' behavior and so the students can see them. Use prompts to keep the students moving as needed and use this opportunity to greet the students as they come to class.

**Provide Feedback:** Conduct a brief discussion at the start of the period on how the students cooperated with the expectations (kept the noise down, used appropriate language, and kept moving). Acknowledge the students who were on time for class and cooperated with the three expectations. Provide some indicators regarding whether the class is doing better or worse each day.

discourage rule violations in settings involving large groups of students (e.g., recess, hallways, cafeteria) and during transition events. Elements of active supervision include (a) movement around the setting in close proximity to students, (b) visual scanning, and (c) high rates of interaction with students, with interactions comprised of prompts, feedback, praise, error correction, and encouragement. Each element is briefly described.

### *Movement and Proximity*

A direct relationship exists between teacher proximity and student behavior. Physical movement throughout the environment by the supervisor serves as a deterrent to inappropriate behavior and as an opportunity to observe student performance and provide relevant feedback (e.g., praise, correction, encouragement).

### *Visual Scanning*

Visually scanning the area provides opportunities to observe student performance, provide feedback, and intervene early when students are engaged in inappropriate behaviors. Visual scanning also aids in the early identification of students who may require redirection. At times, manipulation of the physical environment may be necessary to allow maximum visual scanning of student activity. For instance, entry to isolated areas of a playground may be restricted if such areas allow students to move out of visual contact.

### *High Rate of Interaction*

Maintaining a high rate of positive adult-to-student interactions is another important component of active supervision. The nature of these interactions is directly related to the quality of the environment and student performance. Behavior is functionally related to the environment and is more efficiently shaped by positive consequences than negative consequences. Casual, brief, intermittent, and specific verbal praise from adult supervisors circulating among students will maintain and strengthen appropriate student behaviors.

A final consideration in active supervision is to avoid distractions that draw attention away from student activity (e.g., conversations with other adults, taking phone calls, completing paperwork). Teachers and adult supervisors must model the behaviors they expect from their students. Consider a school assembly where teachers are lined up along the wall and talking to each other. Their behavior creates a situation in which (a) they have limited their ability and opportunities to actively supervise and provide positive reinforcement or corrections, and (b) they are modeling inappropriate behavior that is in violation of the expectations to which students will be held accountable.

*Precorrection* involves providing students with information on what is required of them *before* they have a chance to exhibit the behaviors in the target setting. In essence, precorrection procedures are antecedent manipulations designed to prevent the occurrence of predictable problems and facilitate correct responding (Colvin & Sugai, 1988). Precorrection procedures involve five basic steps:

1. Identify the context and the predictable problem behavior.
2. Specify the expected behaviors.
3. Modify the context to support the expected behavior (as discussed in the section that outlines physical features).
4. Provide behavior rehearsals of the expected behaviors and routines.
5. Prompt students on expected behavior before they enter and when they are in the setting. For example, the principal may provide reminders over the public address system of the expected behaviors of the students at lunch time in the cafeteria just before they go to the cafeteria. Or, teachers may conduct a brief discussion with their students on expectations and routines for the playground just before they leave the classroom for recess. A variety of precorrection strategies should be used to remind students of expected behaviors, such as announcements, discussions, posters, assembly presentations, and classroom role-playing. Precorrection activities should also be scheduled throughout the term or semester.

A checklist and action plan for adequate supervision is presented in Table 21.3.

**Table 21.3.** Supervision: Checklist and Action Plan

| Item | In Place | Action Plan (For Items Marked No) | Date Completed |
|---|---|---|---|
| 1. Ratio of supervisors to students is adequate. | Yes No | | ____/ ____/____ |
| 2. Supervisors use active supervision procedures: | | | |
| Moving around | Yes No | | ____/ ____/____ |
| Looking around | Yes No | | |
| Frequent interaction with the students | Yes No | | |
| Catching problems early | Yes No | | |
| 3. Students can be observed at all times (barriers to supervision are removed or minimized). | Yes No | | ____/ ____/____ |
| 3. Supervision is provided at all times: | | | |
| Supervisor is first to area | Yes No | | |
| Supervisor remains for the lunch period | Yes No | | ____/ ____/____ |
| Supervisor is last to leave | Yes No | | |
| 4. Supervisor provides constant feedback (reinforcement and correction) | Yes No | | ____/ ____/____ |
| 5. Precorrection: | | | ____/ |
| A variety of activities are used | Yes No | | |
| Activities are scheduled | Yes No | | ____/ ____ |
| Activities are conducted | Yes No | | |

The following review of studies demonstrates the efficiency and effectiveness of PBS strategies to teach universal expectations and implement proactive systems to supervise and monitor student behavior in nonclassroom settings. Across all of these examples, the interventions are designed to meet the unique characteristics and needs of the specific school and are based on a combination of the effective practices previously outlined (e.g., clearly defined rules and routines, active supervision, and precorrections and group contingencies). Nelson, Colvin, and Smith (1996) demonstrated the effects of a proactive instructional approach to improve behavior in common areas of an urban elementary school. First, staff developed instructional procedures to provide an explanation of the behavioral goals and a corresponding rationale for the students along with demonstration of the desired behavior. Second, students participated in guided practice with feedback. Third, precorrects and reminders were provided to prompt appropriate behavior. Results showed a clear improvement in social behavior and a reduction in office referrals. The results were maintained during and after the intervention across settings.

Many of the case studies in the literature have focused on improving the behavior and efficiency of transitions. The effects of precorrections and active supervision on the running, hitting, and yelling behavior of elementary school students entering the cafeteria for lunch and entering and exiting the building were examined by Colvin, Sugai, Good, and Lee (1997). Baseline data reflected a very low rate of precorrections and active supervision on the part of the staff. Supervisory staff were trained in active supervision, and prior to each transition the principal would prompt teachers to precorrect students on behavioral expectations. Increases in precorrects and active supervision were accompanied by concomitant, substantial reductions in student problem behavior. Results indicated that the more frequently staff interacted with students in the targeted transitions, the fewer the occurrences of problem behavior were.

Lewis & Garrison-Harrell (1999) examined the effectiveness of a system of PBS on the playground, cafeteria, and hallway transitions. Universal schoolwide expectations were established and taught to all students, and a reinforcement system was introduced to encourage compliance. Assessment of routines and physical structures resulted in adjustments to the organizational and structural characteristics of the areas (e.g., clearly marking the entrance and exit doors to cafeteria, closing off areas that could not be easily supervised, scheduling adult supervision for transitions). Interventions (i.e., precorrects, active supervision, group contingencies) were then put in place to extend the systems to specific settings. Their results are interesting in that they indicated that the teaching of behavioral expectations alone did not effectively reduce the frequency of problem behaviors in the cafeteria, on the playground, and during transitions. Significant reductions only occurred when precorrects, active supervision, and group contingencies were included in the intervention.

Lewis, Colvin, and Sugai (2000) reported similar results in a follow-up investigation that examined the effectiveness of social skill instruction, precorrects, and active supervision during recess. After teachers instructed students on playground rules and social skills, precorrections and active supervision were implemented. Again, low rates of problem behavior were reported. It is significant to note that a limited generalization effect of social skills training occurred across settings without the addition of precorrects and active supervision.

Finally, directly teaching playground-related behaviors and the use of a group contingency to reinforce skill mastery in an elementary school has also been demonstrated to be an effective approach (Lewis, Powers, Kelk, & Newcomer, 2002). Students received direct social skill instruction on behavior expectations and rules for the playground. Supervisors then reinforced students by giving them a cotton loop typically used for weaving potholders whenever they observed students engaging in appropriate playground behavior. Students would wear the loops on their wrists until they returned to their classroom, where they would give the loops to the classroom teacher. When a predetermined number of loops were collected, the class received a reinforcer (e.g., extra recess time, class party). Results indicated that the intervention reduced the frequency of problem behavior across three recess periods.

Even though hallway noise is not a serious behavior, it does erode the educational quality of a school and contributes to an unpleasant social environment. To address hallway noise during transitions, one middle school staff used similar PBS procedures: (a) Students were taught appropriate transition behaviors, (b) the environment was altered to clarify when the behaviors were expected, and (c) group contingencies were put in place to support the occurrence of the desired behaviors (Kartub, Taylor-Greene, March, & Horner, 2000). Training was provided to help students discriminate between "loud" and "quiet" behavior using student volunteers to model both excessive and appropriate levels of noise. In addition, hallway lights were dimmed, and a small blinking light was used during lunch transitions to indicate when the quiet behavior was expected. Students were taught the motto, "When you see the blinking light, lips stay tight." Decibel recordings indicated decreased variability and noise levels across grade levels and lunch transitions.

Staub (1990) addressed hallway disruption and noise levels in a middle school by pairing public posting and verbal praise and feedback. Posters were used to communicate to students the percentage of change in daily occurrence of disruptive hallway behavior, displaying the "best record to date." Trends in the data suggest that posting alone had a mild positive effect on the noise level and disruptive behavior, while pairing posting with the additional treatment variables of praise and feedback produced even more positive results.

Bus discipline continues to be a challenging context for schools to deal with. Twenty years ago, George and George (1987) observed, "While transportation service is an integral—indeed mandated—component of the overall educational process, it remains divorced from the rigors of programmatic scrutiny and evaluation" (p. 185). To date, there is still limited research to indicate best practice for behavior programs for bus transportation. Hirsch, Lewis-Palmer, Sugai, and Schnacker (2004) pointed to the need to examine bus referrals to identify patterns unique to a particular bus or school. In their review of two case studies, they described strategies for using patterns of bus discipline referral data to target factors associated with bus misbehavior on both district and single-school levels. They concluded that analysis of bus discipline referrals by average per month, grade level, repeat infraction, route, and driver could be used to (a) isolate variables related to high rates of misbehavior and (b) compare districtwide and single-school-bus discipline referral patterns to determine appropriate level for bus program implementation (i.e., single bus, schoolwide, or district level). Greene, Bailey, and Barber (1981) established an effective system to reduce noise and improve behavior on bus rides. A noise guard (e.g., meter to monitor noise) and speaker system were installed on the bus. When the noise level was at an acceptable level, music suggested by the students was played through the speakers. If noise exceeded an acceptable threshold, a light was activated, and the music stopped. The number of times the music was stopped was recorded daily. When the number of times the threshold was exceeded remained lower than the previous day, reinforcement was delivered through a raffle system. The procedure nearly eliminated outbursts of noise and generalized to a reduction of out-of-seat and disruptive behavior. A follow-up study resulted in noise reduction with only the lights and music.

These studies demonstrated proactive and effective ways to reduce problem behavior and encourage desired behavior in common areas without resorting to extensive punishers. A common theme throughout the studies was the use of clearly defined routines and expectations, simple instructional and reinforcement strategies, combined with precorrects and active supervision, resulting in substantial behavioral improvement. From a practical standpoint, these results have important implications for practice. First, schools were able to achieve substantial behavior improvement with minimal training and technical assistance. Second, they demonstrated efficient systems variables (i.e., active supervision and precorrections) to support effective generalization of social skills to the nonclassroom setting.

Creating contexts in which problem behavior is reduced through positive strategies as opposed to punishment can lead to corollary outcomes such as improvements in school climate, teacher confidence to address behavior, and a reallocation of resources. The next section addresses the steps and processes to facilitate implementation of nonclassroom systems of support.

## IMPLEMENTATION STEPS AND PROCESSES

As demonstrated by the review of studies, examples of PBS in specific settings continue to appear in the literature. Most of these examples share a common approach. First, leadership teams recognize that high rates of student problem behavior in a specific setting are an indication that the environment needs to change, not the students. Second, the teams used assessment (e.g., direct observation, office referrals, and focus groups) to identify the antecedent conditions that occasioned and encouraged the problem behavior. Third, the teams identified the desired replacement behavior and developed systems to teach, monitor, and reward appropriate behavior. Finally, interventions were monitored to ensure the effectiveness, practicality, and durability of procedures.

The design and implementation of systems of support in specific settings focuses on the integration of four key elements:

1. *Outcomes:* A clearly articulated description of the behaviors required to promote safe and effective nonclassroom environments that are endorsed by staff, parents, and students.
2. *Practices:* A set of evidence-based interventions and strategies used to teach, supervise, and monitor nonclassroom settings.
3. *Data:* Information used to identify the current status and need for change and to monitor effects of interventions and guide decisions.
4. Systems: The supports needed to implement and sustain systems of PBS in specific settings.

These elements become mechanisms of support when they are put into operation through a series of specific steps and processes to facilitate implementation in nonclassroom settings: (a) establish a leadership team, (b) assess current setting conditions, (c) assess of setting routines, (d) assess physical features, (e) identify desired behaviors, (f) specify measurable outcomes related to the context, (g) develop an effective plan based on evidence-based practices, (h) identify needed supports to implement the plan, (i) use data-based decision making, and (j) provide fidelity of implementation. Each of these activities and key organizational features are described next.

## Establish a Leadership Team

The PBS leadership team is responsible for guiding the implementation of schoolwide PBS, including nonclassroom systems of support. Effective teams are made up of representatives of the school administration, faculty, staff, and parents and meet regularly at an established time. The team takes primary responsibility for the development, evaluation, and maintenance of the plan and oversees the organization of resources needed to assess and support accurate and sustained implementation. To do this, members of the team should have effective communication and problem-solving skills. Effective teams also have systemic supports that promote regular attendance, participation, data-based decision making, and communication with the rest of the staff (Horner & Sugai, 2004)

## Assess Current Conditions

Data are used to pinpoint those systems in need of intervention. The PBS leadership team uses extant data such as office discipline referrals, disciplinary actions, and administrative measures to identify existing problem contexts and develop intervention priorities. Fundamental questions used to guide analysis and decision making when reviewing the data include

1. Where do the majority of rule violations occur?
2. What are the specific behavior problems?
3. What proportion of the student population violates the rules?
4. Are specific students responsible for the majority of the violations?
5. What time of day do the problems occur?

The team develops hypotheses about the problem context and chooses appropriate intervention features based on the evidence provided by the data. An example of discipline referrals based on location is presented in Fig. 21.2. In this example, the data indicate a disproportionate number of referrals from the cafeteria, playground, and classroom. To further pinpoint and direct intervention efforts, the PBS leadership team uses the data to identify specific behavior problems in these areas. Disaggregating the data as shown in Fig. 21.3 indicates that many referrals are for physical aggression, harassment, disruption, and disrespect. The team can break the data down even further to determine if the problem behaviors are demonstrated by many students or a relatively few students. If many students have been cited for inappropriate behavior in a specific setting, the team then has relevant information to narrow their focus on the characteristics of the setting that may set the occasion for problem behaviors.

Extant data are the most efficient source of information; however, referral data are not always available for all nonclassroom settings. In general, behavior incidents in nonclassroom settings tend to be underreported. To gain reliable information on a specific setting, alternative means of collecting data may be used. The simplest form of data collection for student behavior is to train some of the faculty, often members of a leadership team, to sample student behavior at each of the nonclassroom settings. Specific behaviors are counted for a set period

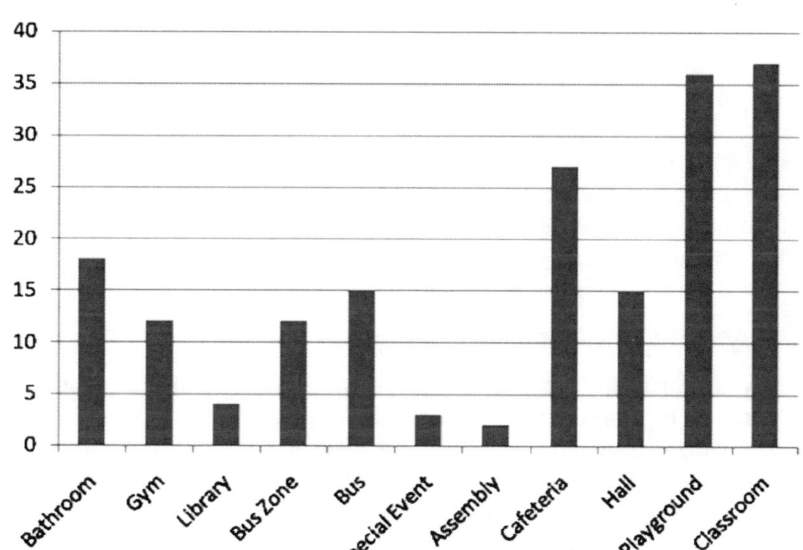


**Fig. 21.2.** Office discipline referrals (ODRs) by setting.

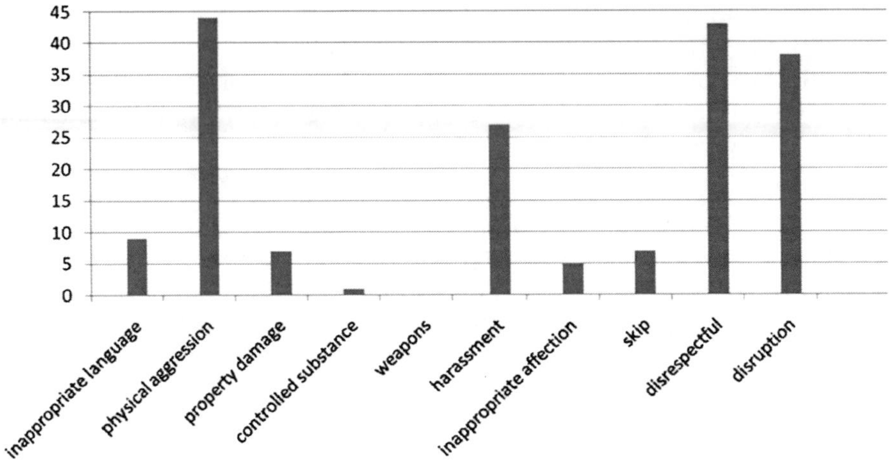


**Fig. 21.3.** Office discipline referrals (ODRs) by behavior.

of time in the main settings. These data are tracked over time to assess trends either in terms of improvement (increases in expected behavior) or deterioration (increases in problem behavior). Data should be constructed in report form for faculty to address and for decisions to be made as necessary.

Table 21.4 outlines possible data sources to assess specific settings when extant data are not available or sufficient.

## Assess Setting Routines

Common areas are assessed to determine (a) whether sufficient routines have been established, (b) if students have been taught the routines, and (c) if staff are aware of and consistently enforce the routines. Nelson and Colvin (1996) outlined a three-step process to evaluate and improve routines. First, identify existing and needed routines. Second, task analyze the routines to identify key student and staff behaviors needed to complete the routine successfully and minimize the opportunities for problem behavior. Third, develop strategies to teach, practice, and maintain the routines. A checklist for assessing setting routines is presented in Table 21.5.

## Assess Physical Features

Identify and modify problematic features with logistical and organizational changes if possible. Assessment can be quite informal and can easily be accomplished by posting two staff members in an area to observe transitions, focusing on congestion, obstructed views that hinder visual supervision, and ways that the physical attributes of the area contribute to the problems. Student focus groups and student observers can also serve as a resource for the purpose of assessing common areas. They are often witnesses to and have experienced many problems that do not

**Table 21.4.** Assessment Data Sources

| Data Source | Advantages | Disadvantages |
|---|---|---|
| **Extant Data:** Existing data, information, and observations that have been collected or that are available for use in the assessment and evaluation processes (e.g., discipline referrals) | The most cost-effective way to gather information is to analyze data that you already have. | Occurrence of behavior incidents are typically underreported for nonclassroom settings; therefore, discipline referral data may not reflect the nature of the specific setting. |
| **Focus Groups:** A focus group is typically 7–10 individuals (students, staff, parents) who are unfamiliar with each other and have experience with the specific setting. The interviewer creates a permissive and nurturing environment that encourages different perceptions and points of view. The interview is conducted several times with similar different participants to identify trends and patterns in perceptions. A standardized open-ended interview format asks all interviewees the same questions. In a closed, fixed-response format, interviewees must choose answers from among the same set of alternatives. | A good method to obtain data from children or from individuals who do not respond to a written format. Focus groups provide data more quickly and at lower cost than if individuals are interviewed separately. Groups can be assembled on shorter notice than for a more systematic survey and generally require less preparation and are comparatively easy to conduct. The interviewer can interact directly with respondents (allows clarification, follow-up questions, probing). | Groups that are not facilitated well can produce relatively chaotic data, making data analysis more difficult. Small numbers and convenience sampling limit the ability to generalize to larger populations. The moderator may knowingly or unknowingly bias results by providing cues about what types of responses are desirable. There may be uncertainty about the accuracy of results as they may be biased by the presence of a very dominant or opinionated member; more reserved members may be hesitant to talk. |
| **Survey:** Surveys (questionnaires) can be used to obtain information from students, staff, and parents with the benefit of a uniform question presentation. | Surveys are a very cost-effective way to gather data. Many questions can be asked about a given topic, giving considerable flexibility to the analysis. Standardized questions make measurement more precise by enforcing uniform definitions on the participants.<br>Data entry and tabulation for nearly all surveys can be easily completed with many computer software packages, or results can be hand tabulated. | Written questionnaires and surveys run the risk of low response rates. Respondents are not able to ask for clarifications. Participants returning surveys often represent extremes in responses, leading to skewed responses. |

(continued)

**Table 21.4.** (continued)

| Data Source | Advantages | Disadvantages |
|---|---|---|
| **Observation Sampling:** Sampling procedures are used to identify problem behaviors or to determine the degree to which behaviors occur in a setting by observing and recording the incidence of behaviors during intervals or at specific moments in time. Measures obtained from the "samples" are considered to be representative of the behaviors in the specific setting. | Sampling can provide an estimate of the rate of occurrence in a specific area. Sampling does not require continuous observation and therefore does not require the observers' undivided attention. | Much behavior can be missed with sampling procedures, particularly if the intervals are long. Sampling is not effective at measuring low-frequency or short-duration behaviors and provides only an estimate of the actual occurrence of the behavior. |
| **Full Direct Observation:** Direct observation within a specific setting, using either event or duration recording. Discrete behaviors (e.g., hands on, name calling, out of area) can be recorded and tallied, while continuous behaviors can be recorded by duration (e.g., how long it takes a group to line up). | Direct observation is easy to do and conduct with accuracy. Event recording provides a useful measurement for most behaviors. While conducting a direct observation, the observer may detect physical characteristics that set the stage for problem behaviors to occur. | Direct observation can be expensive in terms of time and resources. If behaviors occur at a high rate or the setting is physically large or has obstructed views, collecting data will be difficult. |

**Table 21.5.** Specific Setting Routine Checklist: Checklist for Determining the Adequacy of Existing Common Area Routines and Practices

| Yes | No | |
|---|---|---|
| ❑ | ❑ | 1. Are the behavioral expectations for each area of the school established? |
| ❑ | ❑ | ▪ There is a consensus among staff/community on behavioral expectations. |
| ❑ | ❑ | ▪ Behavioral expectations are stated objectively. |
| ❑ | ❑ | ▪ Behavioral expectations are reasonable and limited in number. |
| ❑ | ❑ | 2. Is there an implementation plan to ensure staff, students, and parents understand the behavioral expectations? |
| ❑ | ❑ | ▪ Behavioral expectations are written down. |
| ❑ | ❑ | ▪ Teaching plans for the behavioral expectations are developed. |
| ❑ | ❑ | ▪ 180-day implementation plan is established to ensure students understand and can perform the common area routines. |
| ❑ | ❑ | ▪ Staff understand their responsibility in ensuring students and parents understand their behavioral expectations. |
| ❑ | ❑ | 3. Is supervision adequate? |
| ❑ | ❑ | ▪ Supervisors are trained. |
| ❑ | ❑ | ▪ Ratio of supervisors to students is adequate to promote positive social behavior. |
| ❑ | ❑ | ▪ There are established patterns of supervision. |
| ❑ | ❑ | ▪ Natural supervision is utilized (e.g., natural flow of parents, staff, etc. is used to promote positive student behavior). |
| ❑ | ❑ | ▪ Students are reinforced for exhibiting appropriate behavior |
| ❑ | ❑ | 4. Are there effective reactive strategies in place to address minor problem behavior? |
| ❑ | ❑ | ▪ Reactive strategies are reasonable, decisive (limited warnings), and provide students an opportunity to try again. |
| ❑ | ❑ | ▪ Reactive strategies reduce opportunities for students to manipulate or engage staff. |
| ❑ | ❑ | ▪ Strategies are designed to reduce the need for communication and record keeping. |
| ❑ | ❑ | 5. Is a continuum of structures in place to address serious or challenging problem behavior? |
| ❑ | ❑ | ▪ Behaviors warranting office referral are delineated. |
| ❑ | ❑ | ▪ Efficient record keeping and communication system is established to monitor serious or challenging problem behavior. |
| ❑ | ❑ | ▪ There are progressive levels of discipline that are focused on increasing levels of support for the student and staff. |

necessarily occur when adults are observing in an area. The purpose is to identify unsafe objects, areas of student density, long wait lines, and poor traffic flow that can be eliminated with logistical modifications.

## Identify Desired Behaviors

Expected behaviors are identified that are in concert with schoolwide expectations and address the unique characteristics of the setting. For each school rule, the leadership team identifies specific examples for the targeted nonclassroom setting. The examples should indicate what the students are expected to do, be stated in positive observable terms, and be inherent in the setting-specific routines. For example, if the school expectation is to "Be respectful," the behavioral example for the hallway may be to walk quietly when classes are in session. If noise is an issue of concern for the cafeteria, the behavioral example of "Be respectful" in the cafeteria may be defined as talking quietly at the lunch table. As with the schoolwide expectations, the behavioral examples focus on the desired behavior and are positively stated.

### Specify a Measurable Outcome Related to the Context

To specify a measurable outcome, the team must be clear about the purpose and desired results of the intervention. Measuring outcomes is critical to assess student response to the intervention. Measurable outcomes can reflect (a) setting characteristics, (b) supervisor behavior, and (c) student behavior. Colvin et al. (1997) measured setting characteristics by counting the number of supervisory staff and students present during transitions. Adult behavior was observed and recorded to determine the extent to which staff was actively supervising. Student behavior was measured to determine the frequency of problem behaviors. Questions to consider when defining the measurable outcomes are (a) What is the goal we are trying to achieve (e.g., reduce noise, eliminate congestion, reduce fights)? (b) What behaviors do we expect to see? (c) How can change in behavior be measured? (e) What dimension of the behavior will be measured? (d) What is the target for performance? Measures must be objective, reliable, and sensitive to change in the target behavior and setting (Lane & Beebe-Frankenberger, 2004).

### Develop an Effective Plan Based on Evidence-Based Practices

An effective plan should incorporate logistical and organization arrangements and behavioral management strategies to address the management, systems, and features unique to the setting. The plan should provide detailed action steps that the faculty and staff will execute for implementation. Key features of the plan include

1. Modification of physical and environmental arrangements.
2. Instructional procedures to teach and practice common routines and behavioral expectations.
3. Supervision plans to facilitate consistent active supervision.
4. Procedures to acknowledge appropriate behavior.
5. Procedures to monitor and assess results of intervention.
6. A structured schedule for implementation.

The success of any plan depends on the precision and consistency with which it is implemented. It is important that roles and responsibilities for implementation be designated, and that the plan is communicated to all participants. All staff should be involved in teaching routines and skills within the setting using scripted lessons that provide clarifications of the critical rule, demonstrations by the teacher, role-playing with the students, practice, and review (Sugai & Lewis, 1996). Experience has demonstrated that consistency and fidelity of instruction improve when teachers are provided with clear lesson plans, a teaching script, and a schedule for instruction. Opportunities should be arranged for students to practice the routines within the setting and receive feedback on their performance. Appropriate behavior is acknowledged informally (verbal praise) and by structured reinforcement systems.

## Identify Needed Supports to Implement the Plan

Important systems features include comprehensive schoolwide implementation by all staff, direct instruction, and regular review, practice, and acknowledgment of skills and routines. The leadership team will need to determine which support structures are needed to promote and sustain implementation of setting routines. Considerations may include in-service presentations to familiarize staff with the new routines and teaching strategies, providing schedules for skill instruction and practice, and planning incentives to encourage students to practice the routines. Providing scripted lessons and a structured schedule for instruction can increase consistency and fidelity of instruction across all teachers. Staff may require training in active supervision strategies and effective use of precorrects, and staff schedules may need to be modified to allow for adequate supervision.

## Data-Based Decision Making

The most reliable and objective way to assess the effectiveness of plans for nonclassroom settings is to develop and use a data management system. This system typically involves three broad targets: (a) to assess fidelity of implementation in which measures are taken to determine if the faculty are implementing the plan as intended, (b) to assess student behavior in the various nonclassroom settings to determine if the plan is effective in reducing problem behavior and increasing appropriate behavior, and (c) to use the data to make decisions on whether additional training is needed for staff or whether modifications may need to be made to the plans. Interpreting data is the surest way for a school to determine the adequacy or effectiveness of their plan for developing expected behavior in nonclassroom settings. Once data have been collected and organized into a report form, it is up to a team or the faculty to analyze the data and make corresponding decisions. If the student behavioral data show increasing trends in expected behavior, then both the faculty and students need to be acknowledged for their efforts, and the decision would be to maintain the plan. If data indicate there are problems, then the plan needs to be examined and modifications made as appropriate. The checklist and action plan form in Table 21.6 could be used to operationalize the data collection system in a school.

## Fidelity of Implementation

Fidelity of implementation is a necessary component of evaluating intervention outcomes. Even plans based on evidence-based practices can fail to yield positive results if faculty do not follow the procedures of the plan

**Table 21.6.** Data Collection Checklist and Action Plan

| Item | In Place | Action Plan (For Items Marked No) | Date Completed |
|---|---|---|---|
| 1. A data collection system has been developed for nonclassroom settings. | Yes No | | ___/ ___/___ |
| 2. Administrators (or designees) conduct scheduled "walk-throughs" for all nonclassroom settings to assess fidelity of implementation. | Yes No | | ___/ ___/___ |
| 3. Administrators provide regular feedback to faculty on fidelity of implementation. | Yes No | | ___/ ___/___ |
| 4. Sample data collection forms are developed for student behavior in nonclassroom settings. | Yes No | | ___/ ___/___ |
| 5. Designated faculty members are trained in using forms and collecting student data. | Yes No | | ___/ ___/___ |
| 6. Data are recorded and arranged in report form for dissemination. | Yes No | | ___/ ___/___ |
| 7. Time is scheduled for faculty to review, address, and discuss data reports. | Yes No | | ___/ ___/___ |
| 8. Data are used to make decisions. | Yes No | | ___/ ___/___ |

or follow them inconsistently. It is important to implement the intervention as designed; therefore, implementation must be monitored to ensure accuracy. Without accurate and consistent implementation, it is impossible to draw valid conclusions regarding the effectiveness of the intervention. Once the plan has been developed and the faculty have been trained in the procedures, nonclassroom settings need to be monitored to determine if the procedures are implemented as intended. Various methods can be used to assess fidelity of implementation. Direct observation procedures can be used to assess if critical components of the procedures are in place. "Walk-throughs," typically conducted by principals and administrators, can be used as opportunities to assess fidelity of implementation and provide faculty feedback. Checklists that operationally define each critical component of the intervention are useful to guide observation and determine if critical components were present. Implementation efforts can be rated on a range from low integrity to high integrity using Likert-type scales. Finally, self-reporting such as self-assessment checklists can provide feedback on consistency of implementation and can serve as a prompt to staff to self-monitor their accuracy of implementation. If data on fidelity of implementation reveal that the faculty is following the plan, then their efforts should be publicly acknowledged. If there are problems with consistency of implementation, then more in-service might be scheduled or more reminders provided.

In summary, modification of the physical arrangements, clearly defined behavior expectations and routines, direct instruction, active supervision, precorrects, and procedures to acknowledge appropriate behavior are key

**Table 21.7.** Cafeteria Checklist and Action Plan: Organizational Structures: Checklist and Action Plan

| Item | In Place | Action Plan (For Items Marked No) | Date Completed |
|---|---|---|---|
| 1. Unsafe physical arrangements are eliminated or adjusted. | Yes No | | ___/ ___/___ |
| 2. Routine permits orderly flow: | Yes No | | ___/ ___/___ |
| Entry | Yes No | | |
| Food pickup | Yes No | | |
| Movement to table | Yes No | | |
| Cleanup | Yes No | | |
| Exit | Yes No | | |
| 3. Space occupied by students is maximized. | Yes No | | ___/ ___/___ |
| 3. Wait time is minimized. | Yes No | | ___/ ___/___ |
| 4. Congestion is absent or minimized. | Yes No | | ___/ ___/___ |

features of proactive nonclassroom systems. Effective plans, based on careful assessment and planning, can greatly influence the quality of the school environment and have an impact on both student and staff behavior. In addition, well-conceived plans are more readily embraced by the staff, therefore increasing fidelity of implementation. A checklist and action plan should be developed for each of the major nonclassroom settings. The basic approach is to list the organization factors, assess whether these factors have been addressed and implemented effectively, and develop an action plan based on the results of the assessment. A sample checklist and action plan for the cafeteria is presented in Table 21.7.

## CONCLUSION

Throughout this chapter and text, a clear emphasis has been made on identifying appropriate behaviors to replace problem behaviors, explicitly teaching appropriate behaviors, and providing specific feedback to acknowledge mastery. This instructional focus is especially relevant to nonclassroom settings given the long history of failing to identify expectations within various settings and the overreliance on minimal, often poorly trained, supervision. This chapter has carefully laid out the steps, building on the basic logic of essential features of schoolwide PBS. In addition to identifying which key behaviors students should master, based on current problem behaviors schools wish to impact, and explicitly teaching and practicing skills, two additional areas were addressed: assessing the physical characteristics of the setting and ensuring adequate supervision.

Three primary factors should be considered when examining the physical characteristics of the setting relative to the number of students within the setting. The first focuses on areas where the density of students is too great. Long lines in the cafeteria causing significant wait times or narrow hallways creating too much physical contact during transitions can all increase rates of problem behavior. The second focuses on areas that are too large to adequately supervise with limited adult presence. Playgrounds that are laid out in a manner that prevents easy visual scans to see all students, alcoves and extended hallways where students gather during lunch or passing time, or structures that prevent clear sight lines can also increase incidences of problem behavior. The final focus is on settings where adult supervision is typically lacking across the majority of the school day and includes settings such as restrooms or hallways during class time.

Each of these challenges requires a two-step process to achieve improved outcomes. First, which physical characteristics that may be contributing to problem behavior can be altered? Can student release for lunch be staggered to avoid long lines, can areas of the playground be restricted, can routines within the settings be altered to reduce density of students? Second, if the setting itself or routines within it cannot be altered, the issue becomes one of supervision. Simply stated, success in nonclassroom settings will take clear delineation of expectations, systemic teaching to master expectations, altering of routines, and most important, adequate adult presence.

A related emphasis running parallel to those practices schools should put in place to improve nonclassroom setting outcomes is on supports for the adults who are responsible for students within and across school settings. All adults within the school building should be fluent in routines, expectations, feedback strategies, and supervision assignments within and across each nonclassroom setting. Special attention should be paid to systemic support across nonclassroom practices in that schools often rely on instructional support personnel such as teaching assistants to provide supervision. Instructional support personnel are often not included within PBS team memberships, present at faculty meetings where issues are discussed, or invited to attend training related to nonclassroom processes. To reach similar outcomes that were shared in this chapter related to nonclassroom research, school teams should make a noted effort to ensure that school personnel responsible for supervision (a) understand and can state the nonclassroom expectations; (b) understand their supervision duties; (c) consistently implement nonclassroom rules, routines, and feedback; (d) understand who they should contact with questions and concerns; and (e) are contributing to the database to assist in decision making.

As emphasized throughout this chapter and demonstrated through the cited research (e.g., Colvin et al., 1997; Lewis et al., 2000, 2002; Lewis & Garrison-Harrell, 1999), schools can have an impact on nonclassroom settings through extensions of their schoolwide efforts. Using the basic problem-solving logic of schoolwide PBS, targeting practices based on data patterns and building in systemic supports to assist adult implementation, schools have can create safe and orderly learning environments across school settings. Essential to success are systemic planning and clear and consistent support to ensure adults are supported in their implementation efforts.

## ACKNOWLEDGMENT

Development of this chapter was supported in part by a grant from the Office of Special Education Programs, U.S. Department of Education (H326S030002). Opinions expressed here are those of the authors and do not necessarily reflect the position of the U.S. Department of Education, and such endorsements should not be inferred.

## REFERENCES

Colvin, G. (2007). *Seven steps for developing a proactive schoolwide discipline plan: A guide for principals and leadership teams.* Thousand Oaks, CA: Corwin Press.

Colvin, G., Kame'enui, E., & Sugai, G. (1993). Reconceptualizing behavior management and school-wide discipline in general education. *Education and Treatment of Children, 16,* 361–381.

Colvin, G., & Sugai, G (1988). Proactive strategies for managing social behavior problems: An instructional approach. *Intervention in School and Clinic, 28,* 143–150.

Colvin, G., Sugai, G., Good, R., & Lee, Y. (1997). Using active supervision and precorrection to improve transition behaviors in an elementary school. *School Psychology Quarterly, 12,* 344–355.

Cotton, K. (1995). *Effective schools research summary: 1995 update.* Portland, OR: Northwest Regional Educational Laboratory.

Crone, D. A., & Horner, R. H. (2003). *Building positive behavior support systems in schools: Functional behavioral assessment.* New York: Guilford Press.

George, M. P., & George, N. L. (1987). Transporting behaviorally disordered adolescents: A descriptive analysis. *Behavior Disorders, 3,* 185–192.

Greene, B. F., Bailey, J. S., & Barber, F. (1981). An analysis and reduction of disruptive behavior on school buses. *Journal of Applied Behavior Analysis, 14,* 177–192.

Hirsch, E. J., Lewis-Palmer, T., Sugai, G., & Schnacker, L. (2004). Using school discipline referral data in decision making: Two case studies. *Preventing School Failure, 48,* 4–9.

Horner, R., & Sugai, G. (2004). *School-wide positive behaviors support implementers' blueprint and self-assessment.* Eugene: University of Oregon, Center on Positive Behavioral Intervention and Support.

Kartub, D. T., Taylor-Greene, S., March, R. E., & Horner, R. H. (2000). Reducing hallway noise: A systems approach. *Journal of Positive Behavior Interventions, 2,* 179–182.

Lane, K. L. & Beebe-Frankenberger, M. (2004). School-based interventions: The tools you need to succeed. Boston, MA: Pearson.

Leedy, A., Bates, P., & Safran, S. (2004). Bridging the research-to-practice gap: Improving hallway behavior using positive behavior supports. *Behavioral Disorders, 29,* 130–139.

Lewis, T. J., Colvin, G., & Sugai, G. (2000). The effects of pre-correction and active supervision on the recess behavior of elementary students. *Education and Treatment of Children, 23,* 109–121.

Lewis, T. J., & Garrison-Harrell, L. (1999). Effective behavior support: Designing setting-specific interventions. *Effective School Practices, 17*(4), 38–46.

Lewis, T. J., & Sugai, G. (1999). Effective behavior support. Asystems approach to proactive schoolwide management. Focus on Exceptional Children, 31(6), 1.

Lewis, T. J., Powers, L. J., Kelk, M., & Newcomer, L. (2002). Reducing problem behaviors on the playground: An investigation of the application of schoolwide positive behavior supports. *Psychology in the Schools, 39,* 181–190.

Nelson, J. R., & Colvin, G. (1996). Designing supportive school environments. *Special Services in the Schools, 11,* 169–186.

Nelson, J. R., Colvin, G., & Smith, D. (1996). The effects of setting clear standards on students' social behavior in common areas of the school. *The Journal of At-Risk Issues, 3*(10), 10–19.

Nelson, J. R., Smith, D., & Colvin, G. (1995). The effects of a peer-mediated self evaluation procedure on the recess behavior of students with behavior problems. *Remedial and Special Education, 16*, 117–126.

Staub, R. (1990). The effects of public posted feedback on middle school students' disruptive hallway behavior. *Education and Treatment of Children, 13*, 249–252.

Sugai, G., & Lewis, T. J. (1996). Preferred and promising practices for social skills instruction. *Focus on Exceptional Children, 29*(4), 1–16.

Taylor-Greene, S., Brown, D., Nelson, L., Longton, J., Gassman, T., Cohen, J., et al. (1997). School-wide behavioral support: Starting the year off right. *Journal of Behavioral Education, 7*, 99–112.

Todd, A. W., Haugen, L., Anderson, K., & Spriggs, M. (2002). Teaching recess: Low-cost efforts producing effective results. *Journal of Positive Behavior Interventions, 4*, 46–52.

Todd, A. W., Horner, R. H., Sugai, G., & Colvin, G. (1999). Individualizing school-wide discipline for students with chronic problem behaviors: A team approach. *Effective School Practices, 17*, 72–82.

# 22

# Facilitating Academic Achievement Through Schoolwide Positive Behavior Support

**BOB ALGOZZINE and KATE ALGOZZINE**

Two pieces of federal legislation—the No Child Left Behind Act of 2001 (NCLB) and the Education Sciences Reform Act of 2002—put forth the idea that education should be an evidence-based field of practices for which verifiable information exists to support adoption and sustained use (cf. Fuchs & Deshler, 2007; Kratochwill &. Shernoff, 2004; Merrell & Buchanan, 2006; National Research Council, 2005). As a result, the search for and development and use of evidence-based practices has become the driving force in school improvement efforts across the country. Schoolwide positive behavior support (SW-PBS) is an evidence-based practice with broad applicability for improving academic and behavior outcomes in schools.

The purpose of this chapter is to present elements of SW-PBS that relate to academic achievement. We provide an overview of the key features of SW-PBS, including team and data-based decision making, implementation outcomes, and research addressing academic and behavior supports. We also summarize efforts to implement SW-PBS in a variety of educational settings and discuss implications of using SW-PBS to improve academic and behavior outcomes in schools.

**BOB ALGOZZINE** • University of North Carolina at Charlotte
**KATE ALGOZZINE** • University of North Carolina at Charlotte

## FOUNDATIONS OF SCHOOLWIDE POSITIVE BEHAVIOR SUPPORT

The *Implementers' Blueprint and Self-Assessment* (OSEP Center on Positive Behavioral Interventions and Supports, 2005) describes SW-PBS as "comprised of a broad range of systemic and individualized strategies for achieving important social and learning outcomes while preventing problem behavior with all students" (p. 11). It states that SW-PBS is not a specific "model" but rather an approach encompassing practices, interventions, and systems change strategies that are evidence based, including the following processes:

- Establishing a school-based collaborative team, including teachers, administrators, or special services personnel, parents, and other stakeholders (Colvin, 1991; Colvin, Sugai, & Kameenui, 1994; Lewis & Sugai, 1999).
- Defining schoolwide behavioral expectations and teaching them directly to students (Colvin, 1991; Colvin et al., 1994; Lewis & Sugai, 1999).
- Developing procedures for acknowledging appropriate behaviors and discouraging inappropriate behavior (Colvin, 1991; Colvin et al., 1994; Lewis & Sugai, 1999).
- Using data to analyze, describe, and prioritize issues particular to groups of students, specific school settings, or the entire school (OSEP Center on Positive Behavioral Interventions and Supports, 2005).
- Specifying measurable outcomes indicating improvement directly related to issues and context (OSEP Center on Positive Behavioral Interventions and Supports, 2005).
- Selecting evidence-based practices to achieve specified outcomes and providing supports to sustain the adoption and implementation of those practices (OSEP Center on Positive Behavioral Interventions and Supports, 2005).
- Monitoring the implementation of practices and progress toward outcomes (Colvin, 1991; Colvin et al., 1994; Lewis & Sugai, 1999).
- Modifying practices based on analysis of data (Colvin, 1991; Colvin et al., 1994; Lewis & Sugai, 1999).

### Importance of Team and Data-Based Decision Making

SW-PBS gives priority to team-based problem solving and action planning based on data. The schoolwide positive behavior support team (SW-PBST) is the crucial decision-making body that matches evidence-based practices to schoolwide, group, or individual student problems:

> One of the major activities of the SW-PBS leadership team is to develop an action plan that guides the systematic implementation of SW-PBS systems and practices. Activities and timelines are based on regular review of behavioral and academic student data and structured staff self-assessment information" (Sugai & Horner, 2006, p. 251).

Implementers of SW-PBS have gained insight from problem-solving research that has focused on helping school-based teams update and restructure so that they can make more effective, efficient, and thorough data-based decisions and improve their role as conduit from research to practice, bringing evidence-based practices to teachers, and ensuring implementation in the classroom to promote the achievement of all students. This problem-solving research is the result of federal legislation holding schools accountable for implementation and evaluation of research-based intervention prior to referring students for special education (Individuals With Disabilities Education Act [IDEA], 1997/1999; NCLB, 2001).

Similar to recent SW-PBS research, problem-solving studies are focusing on both behavior and academic outcomes. For instance, Bahr and Kovaleski (2006) described a school in rural southern Virginia that has implemented instructional support teams since 1999. This school has not only decreased special education referrals significantly, but also has achieved a proficiency rate of more than 90% on the Virginia Standards of Learning test and has reduced discipline referrals by two thirds.

The *Illinois PBIS Network Update* (2007) spotlights three districts receiving technical assistance and training provided by the Illinois PBIS (Positive Behavioral Interventions and Supports) Network and Illinois ASPIRE (Alliance for School-Based Problem-Solving and Intervention Resources in Education) for the purpose of integrating a blended approach to problem-solving and multitier interventions in their schools.

> Waukegan Unified District 60 combined three district teams into one leadership team that focuses on academic and social-emotional learning strategies that support school improvement goals. The goal is merged problem-solving teams and integrated training at the building level. Problem-solving teams in Indian Prairie Community Unit District 204 use outcomes and current data in reading, math, and behavior to guide them to interventions that support both the academic and the social-emotional aspect of the child. Waterloo Community Unit District 5 is working to integrate key program initiatives including PBIS, Project CHOICES, standards aligned classrooms, and flexible service delivery (Illinois State Technical Assistance Center [ISTAC], 2007, p. 6).

McIntosh, Horner, Chard, Boland, and Good (2006) addressed the need for one leadership team supporting an integrated approach to meeting the academic and behavioral needs of students. They pinpointed one of the most glaring needs in making this effort successful, that is, the retraining of school psychologists, who must be an integral part of these teams.

> Responsibilities that may be new to some school psychologists included (a) implementing schoolwide academic and behavioral systems designed to prevent school problems; (b) monitoring their fidelity of implementation and academic and behavioral outcomes; (c) detecting students who are not responding to the interventions; and (d) providing additional support to these students (McIntosh, Horner, et al., 2006, p. 288).

## Implementation Outcomes

Evidence from research on SW-PBS processes and practices addresses varied and important areas and outcomes related to school improvement, including but not limited to

- Effects of schoolwide changes on individual, group, or schoolwide behavior (Bohanon et al., 2006; E. G. Carr et al., 1999; Chapman & Hofweber, 2000; Colvin & Fernandez, 2000; Colvin, Sugai, Good, & Lee, 1997; Gottfredson, Gottfredson, & Hybl, 1993; Hawken & Horner, 2003; Kartub, Taylor-Greene, March, & Horner, 2000; Lassen, Steele, &Sailor, 2006; Lewis, Colvin, & Sugai, 2000; Lewis & Garrison-Harrell, 1999; Lewis, Powers, Kelk, & Newcomer, 2002; Lewis & Sugai, 1999; Lewis, Sugai, & Colvin, 1998; Lohrmann-O'Rourke et al., 2000 Luiselli, Putnam, & Handler, 2001; Luiselli, Putnam, Handler, & Feinberg, 2005; Luiselli, Putnam, & Sunderland, 2002; Marquis et al.,2000; McCurdy, Kunsch, & Reibstein, 2007; McCurdy, Mannella, & Eldridge, 2003; McIntosh, Chard, Boland, & Horner, 2006; Metzler, Biglan, Rusby, & Sprague, 2001; Nakasato, 2000; Nelson, 1996; Nelson, Colvin, & Smith, 1996; Nelson, Martella, & Marchand-Matella; Nersesian, Todd, Lehman, & Watson, 2000; Sadler, 2000; Scott, 2001; Sprague et al., 2001; S. D. Taylor-Greene et al., 1997; S. J. Taylor-Greene & Kartub, 2000; Todd, Haugen, Anderson, & Spriggs, 2002; Todd, Horner, Sugai, & Sprague, 1999; Turnbull et al., 2002; Warren et al., 2003)
- The use of office discipline referrals (ODRs) to make decisions about issues related to individual students, groups of students, or the school as a whole (Clonan, McDougal, Clark, & Davison, 2007; Colvin, Kameenui, & Sugai, 1993; Gottfredson et al., 1993; Nelson, Benner, Reid, Epstein, & Currin, 2002; Skiba, Peterson, & Williams, 1997; Sugai, Sprague, Horner, & Walker, 2000; S. D. Taylor-Greene et al., 1997; Warren et al., 2003; Wright & Dusek, 1998)
- The reliability or validity of SW-PBS resources and tools (e.g., Schoolwide Evaluation Tool [SET], Effective Behavioral Support [EBS] Self-Assessment Survey) (Hagan-Burke et al., 2005; Horner et al., 2004; Safran, 2006)
- Curricula for establishing a schoolwide positive behavior plan (Colvin et al., 1994; Nelson et al., 1996; S. D. Taylor-Greene et al. 1997)
- The role of school psychologists and behavior specialists in implementing schoolwide behavior support programs (March & Horner, 2002)
- Family involvement in functional assessment and PBS (Dunlap, Newton, Fox, Benito, & Vaughn, 2001)
- Application in the context of family-centered early intervention (Fox, Dunlap, & Cushing, 2002)

While SW-PBS addresses "important social and *learning* [italics added] outcomes" (OSEP Center on Positive Behavioral Interventions and Supports, 2005, p. 11), most reports of effectiveness have focused on the impact of implementation with fidelity on behavioral outcomes, such as reductions in ODRs and improvements in general school climate in areas like safety.

School improvement efforts guided by the NCLB have added renewed interest in not only the effect of SW-PBS on behavior, but also its effect on achievement. For example, NCLB has mandated that schools show improvements in the numbers of students who reach academic proficiency on an annual basis, toward an overall goal of 100% by 2014. The start of the Reading First initiative, the annual yearly progress-reporting requirements for schools, and the increases in statewide testing for accountability also helped establish the importance of bringing "evidence-based interventions into the schools" (Shapiro, 2006, p. 260). Demonstrating the extent to which SW-PBS has a significant impact on improving academic performance is not easy because multiple factors play a role in academic outcomes (Lassen et al., 2006). Research is limited in linking academic failure and behavior problems especially in the early grades. Evidence for this connection is found primarily in the literature on juvenile delinquency.

In a meta-analysis of academic and behavior research conducted over 10 years ago (Manguin & Loeber, 1996), three relationships were identified and shared by Scott, Nelson, and Liaupsin (2001, p. 312):

> First, poor academic performance is related to the onset, frequency, persistence, and seriousness of delinquent offending, while higher academic performance is associated with refraining or desisting from offending in both boys and girls. Second, cognitive deficits and attention problems are strongly associated with both poor academic performance and delinquency. Finally, interventions that improve academic performance are associated with a reduction in the prevalence of delinquency.

In a position paper addressing the relationship between academic achievement and social behavior, Algozzine, Putnam, and Horner (2007) argued that the causal link between achievement and behavior is not established by these consistent findings of comorbidity between school performance and delinquency in adolescents and young adults. Opinions related to cause are also available. For example, some researchers argued that because disruptive behavior results in lost instructional time for students, student academic achievement is influenced by student problem behavior (Luiselli et al., 2005; Morrison & D'Incau, 1997; Warren et al., 2006). Discussion by Lassen et al. (2006) related to ODRs is illustrative:

> The amount of instructional time a student loses for each ODR incurred has been estimated to be 45 min (Horner & Sugai, 2003). This time begins when a student leaves a classroom to meet with an administrator in the office and ends when the student is back in the classroom. Even using a more conservative estimate of 20 min per ODR, this middle school has recovered approximately 659 instructional hours (or eighty-two 8-hour days) per year since implementing school-wide PBS. Certainly, schools function much more effectively, academically and behaviorally, when students are in class. Additionally, since administrators must personally deal with each ODR within a school, ODRs can also be viewed as depleting administrator time. From this perspective, decreases in ODRs can translate into considerable time added to administrators' schedules that can then be used in other, more preventative and positive activities (i.e., training teachers, acknowledging student achievements). Thus, reducing ODRs in a school is likely to produce a number of positive effects and result in overall improved functioning and performance. (p. 709)

One of the problems with the hypothesis that increased time in the classroom (i.e., improved behavior) translates to achievement gains is that it is based on the belief that each student is experiencing quality instruction and learning in the classroom. If this condition has not been verified, researchers will continue to have a difficult time finding a causal relationship between decreased ODRs and increased academic gains. Interestingly, Scott et al. (2001) reported that:

> Students identified as having challenging behaviors or academic deficits in the classroom are more likely to experience negative or punitive interactions with their teachers, regardless of their behavior (Denny, Epstein, & Rose, 1992; Gunter, Jack, DePaepe, Reed, & Harrison, 1994; Shores, Jack, Gunter, Ellis, DeBriere, & Wehby, 1994). ... Carr, Taylor, and Robinson (1991) found that, among a group of students with disabilities, teachers provided less instruction and reduced demands for student who exhibited disruptive behaviors. (p. 313)

## Focus on Academic and Behavior Support

Recognizing the need to ensure quality instruction for all students in all school settings, some researchers have taken a different approach to addressing the achievement issue by integrating effective, research-based practices (i.e., evidence-based interventions, EBIs) into school settings where SW-PBS is being implemented with fidelity (Ervin, Schaughency, Matthews, Goodman, McGlinchey, & Matthews, 2006; George, White, & Schlaffer, 2007; McIntosh, Chard et al., 2006; D. N. Miller, George, & Fogt, 2005). The argument is that these practices will not be "add-ons" that tend to come and go but will last and result in powerful changes because of the way they will be implemented within the structure of a school implementing SW-PBS with fidelity (D. N. Miller et al., 2005). PBS teams will not only determine the "contextual fit" (Walker, Ramsey, & Gresham, 2004) of research-based practices (e.g., the school's capacity to support them), but also data from multiple sources will help determine needs for successful implementation as well as fidelity and outcomes of implementation. Informed decision making will lead to schools developing systems (e.g., increased professional development) for supporting effective, research-based practices. Horner, Sugai, and Vincent (2005) cited the benefits of implementing EBI in SW-PBS schools:

> When investments are made in both behavior support and effective instruction, improvements in academic performance are experienced. During 2003–03, 52 elementary schools in Illinois using SWPBS to criterion were compared with 69 schools that were just adopting SWPBS and were not at criterion. On average, 62.19% of third graders in schools using SWPBS met or exceeded the state reading standard. By comparison, an average of 46.6% of third graders in schools not using SW-PBS met the same standard. (p. 5)

An example of an approach to addressing both behavior and academics by implementing EBI into SW-PBS schools can be found in "Merging Research and Practice Agendas to Address Reading and Behavior School-Wide" (Ervin et al., 2006). The authors described their 4-year project as a "preventative, data-informed, problem-solving approach, with attention to skill-building systems development for sustained change, and efficient allocation and use of school resources" (p. 213). The project, funded by a grant from the Office of Special Education Programs (OSEP), partnered county school district consultants and university faculty with schools to (a) provide a comprehensive approach to reading and discipline problems, (b) use local data to inform service delivery systems, (c) be more efficient and effective, and (d) use EBI. Core project elements were guided by SW-PBS (Horner, Sugai, Todd, & Lewis-Palmer, 2005), schoolwide approaches to improving reading (e.g., Simmons et al., 2002), as well as Adelman and Taylor's (1997) model for replicating new approaches in schools. Ervin et al. made the following recommendations based on their work in the schools:

- Take into consideration that schools are unique, evolving systems that differ in their needs or readiness for innovations (e.g., the difference between two schools' comfort level in using particular assessments for goal setting and informing intervention in reading and the unique challenges that schools serving impoverished communities face).
- Address improvement of achievement and behavior by providing a systematic continuum of supports and interventions as well as an interactive and self-checking process to guide systems change and improvement.

They also pointed out the need for flexibility in bringing about academic and behavior change in schools (Ervin et al., 2006):

> In our project, schools had the common goals of providing a continuum of supports and interventions to address reading and behavior, but the practices adopted to achieve these goals and the outcomes obtained differed across schools. Information collected on systems variables, practices, and student outcomes helped guide the context-specific process of change at each school. (p. 218)

In addition, Ervin et al. (2006) indicated that for accurate decision making, program evaluation data should focus on outcome data at the level targeted for intervention (e.g., grade, classroom, individual) in addition to evidence at a schoolwide level. They emphasized that exposure to an innovation does not necessarily equate to implementation, and that schoolwide approaches to improving behavior and reading should be aligned with external support at the local, state, and national levels for lasting implementation.

The model for addressing student behavior and reading that Ervin et al. (2006) recommended is a grounded in a three-tier public health prevention continuum of support practices; that is, effective prevention efforts emerge from primary, secondary, and tertiary tiers of intervention. Primary-tier prevention involves all students and adults within the school and is implemented across all school and school-related settings. Secondary-tier strategies support students for whom the primary prevention is not enough. The tertiary tier involves more intensive supports. Additional learning opportunities and support from school staff are available for all students on an "as-needed" basis. Data inform decision making concerning the level of support needed by individual students, groups of students, or the school as a whole.

A study by McIntosh, Chard et al. (2006) provided descriptive data on the rates of ODRs and beginning reading skills for students in Grades K–3 for one school district that, like Ervin et al. (2006), implemented a three-tier prevention model for both reading and behavior support. Universal interventions were delivered to all students and were preventive and proactive. In reading, a core curriculum was implemented, while in behavior, for example, behaviorally defined expectations were taught directly to students and encouraged. If assessment indicated that a student needed additional support beyond what was provided in universal interventions, educators provided a continuum of services to supplement them. These interventions matched student needs and included targeted interventions or intensive, individual interventions. ODRs were used for screening and assessment for behavior support, and *Dynamic Indicators of Basic Early Literacy Skills, Sixth Edition* (DIBELS; Good & Kaminski, 2002) was adopted for reading. Both reading and behavior systems shared team-based implementation and data-based decision making.

EBI that have been implemented in SW-PBS schools as part of effectiveness studies include but are not limited to

- A greater emphasis on matching curriculum to students' instructional levels through the use of curriculum-based assessment and progress monitoring (Ervin et al., 2006; George et al., 2007; D. N. Miller et al., 2005)
- Modifying curriculum to promote desirable behavior by making it more stimulating and relevant (George et al., 2007; D. N. Miller et al., 2005)
- Increasing students' academic engaged time and active responding through direct instruction procedures (George et al., 2007; D. N. Miller et al., 2005)
- Training teachers to recognize that effective academic instruction and effective behavior management are reciprocally related (D. N. Miller et al., 2005)
- Providing teachers with intensive training in effective instructional techniques (George et al., 2007)

These practices are supported by school-based research and illustrate key aspects of SW-PBS implementations. In the next sections, we illustrate relationships with characteristics of high-performing schools and describe implications for addressing achievement as well as behavior in schools implementing SW-PBS.

## IMPLEMENTATION OF POSITIVE BEHAVIOR SUPPORT IN SCHOOLS

The Office of the Superintendent of Public Instruction (OSPI; 2007; Shannon & Bylsma, 2007) of the state of Washington published a literature review of 20 studies that identified nine characteristics of effective, high-performing schools and schools implementing SW-PBS:

- Clear and shared focus
- High standards and expectations for all students
- Effective school leadership
- High levels of collaboration and communication
- Curriculum, instruction, and assessments aligned with state standards
- Frequent monitoring of learning and teaching
- Focused professional development
- A supportive learning environment
- High levels of family and community involvement

To further investigate the relationship between student achievement and SW-PBS, we compared these characteristics to those found in schools implementing SW-PBS with fidelity or a combination of EBI and SW-PBS. Table 22.1 provides an illustration of how these characteristics are reflected in schools implementing SW-PBS.

In Table 22.2, we illustrate relationships between the characteristics of high-performing schools and key aspects of programs described in the five studies. In their original works, the researchers not only described key features of their programs but also reported schoolwide outcomes if the programs are implemented with fidelity. We briefly summarize their work to illustrate the systems of SW-PBS in schools.

## Focus on Behavior

The High Five Program (S. J. Taylor-Greene & Kartub, 2000) implemented in Fern Ridge Middle School, Elmira, OR since 1994 is grounded in PBS practices and represents an early attempt to determine the benefits of SW-PBS. The practice was engaged in response to a "negative and reactive" school culture resulting in more than 5,000 ODRs a year (S. J. Taylor-Greene & Kartub, p. 233). All students and staff at the school adhere to five expectations: Be respectful, be responsible, follow directions, keep hands and feet to self, and be there—be ready. Over 5 years of implementation, administrators observed a 47–68% reduction in ODRs.

George et al. (2007) summarized successful implementations of SWPBS in a day school (Centennial School of Lehigh University in Bethlehem, PA) providing special education services (cf. Fogt & Piripavel, 2002; George, 2000; D. N. Miller et al., 2005) and a public elementary school enrolling large numbers of children at risk for school failure in a high-crime urban area in Eastern Pennsylvania. The Centennial program

> produced substantial reductions in antisocial behavior as indicated in part by the virtual elimination of physical restraint (e.g., 122 episodes during the first 20 days of school as compared to no occurrences during the last 20 days of the school year) and the closing of the only two seclusionary time-out rooms at the school. Follow-up interviews with teachers at the end of the school year indicated a high degree of teacher satisfaction with the interventions and with the magnitude of positive student outcomes, resulting in a commitment from teachers and other school staff to continue the innovation the subsequent year. (George et al., pp. 42–43)

**Table 22.1.** Shared Characteristics of High-Performing and Schoolwide Positive Behavior Support (SW-PBS) Schools

| High-Performing Schools | SW-PBS Schools |
|---|---|
| 1. A clear and shared focus | SW-PBS schools focus on beliefs based on behavioral and biomedical research.<br>• Behavior is learned and can be taught.<br>• Behavior is lawful and predictable.<br>• Behavior occurrences are affected by environmental factors that interact with characteristics of the individual.<br>• Physiology factors interact with environmental variables, especially for students with behavioral, social, emotional, and mental health issues.<br>• Assessing and manipulating environmental factors can predictably affect occurrences of behavior.<br>• Active data-based decision making is important for continuous intervention, program, and system improvement (OSEP Center on PBIS, 2005). |
| 2. High standards and expectations for all students | SW-PBS schools have written, operationally defined student outcomes based on data. (OSEP Center on PBIS, 2005). |
| 3. Effective school leadership | "An administrator is involved and actively supports the initiative" (Clonan et al, 2007, p. 20).<br>Leadership provides ongoing support for innovative practices (Sugai & Horner, 2006).<br>A SW-PBS leadership team is at the core of the systems approach and is comprised of individuals who have policy and programmatic decision-making responsibilities across a range of behavior-related content areas (e.g., instruction and curriculum, safe and drug-free schools, special education, mental health, juvenile justice, title programs, special education, general education, families, mental health, administration (Sugai & Horner, 2006).<br>Effective team members are dedicated, credible, and leaders among their colleagues in part, because, for example, they are active in the teachers' union or knowledgeable veteran staff (Handler et al., 2007). |
| 4. High levels of collaboration and communication | "With administrative involvement, teams with representatives across grade levels and specialization areas meet on a regular basis to review data to develop, implement, and monitor [proactive] and intervention activities" (Clonan et al., 2007, p. 21).<br>Teams are responsible for creating policies related to PBS practices and systems, funding and resources to sustain implementation, professional development, and ongoing evaluation of implementation (Sugai & Horner, 2006).<br>"The [SW-PBS] team functions more effectively when team members are equipped with skills in effective communication and team building. Given that the work of the leadership team primarily involves the review of school information and the assessment of intervention effectiveness and need for modifications, this process requires effective problem solving. Team members who can effectively communicate their perspectives and allow for useful dialogue toward resolving identified problems help to contribute to a team-building process that leads to satisfied, unified, and effective teams. Pupil support personnel, such as school psychologists or counselors, are often helpful team members in this regard. These individuals may possess a high level of respect among staff, knowledge of PBS strategies and problem-solving skills, and skills in facilitating team process" (Handler et al., 2007, p. 30). |

| | |
|---|---|
| 5. Curriculum, instruction, and assessments aligned with state standards | Student outcomes are linked to annual school improvement objectives as well as local and state initiative priorities (OSEP Center on Positive Behavioral Interventions and Supports, 2005). |
| 6. Frequent monitoring of learning and teaching | "Ongoing monitoring allows for timely revision or intensification of school-wide, classroom, small group, and individual interventions" (Clonan et al., 2007, p. 21). |
| 7. Focused professional development | "Professional development that addresses these shared beliefs is ongoing. Not only does it revisit these beliefs but indicates to all administrators, teachers, and staff how these beliefs are operationally defined. Professional development introduces effective behaviors, strategies, and interventions derived from key beliefs and provides modeling and practice using them. School district support is provided in terms of functional policies, professional development opportunities, and options for data collection" (Clonan et al., 2007, p. 20). |
| 8. A supportive learning environment | Rewards are provided for following expectations that have been clearly defined and taught to all students (Clonan et al., 2007). |
| 9. High levels of parent and community involvement | The systems approach considers multiple points of support, among them collaborative intervention and support efforts for students and families that involve mental health, public health, juvenile justice, and other community agencies and resources (OSEP Center on Positive Behavioral Interventions and Supports, 2005). |

**Table 22.2.** Illustrations of PBS Focused on Improving Behavior

| Features and Effectiveness Critical Feature | School/Project/Report | |
|---|---|---|
| | S. J. Taylor-Greene & Kartub, 2000 | George et al., 2007<br>D. N. Miller et al., 2005 |
| 1. A clear and shared focus | • In Oregon, all public schools are required to develop and submit an annual school improvement plan (SIP), a plan that includes a series of prioritized goals focused on improved student performance. At Fern Ridge Middle School, improving student attendance, grades, and discipline is included in the first goal: student accountability. Additional aspects of the High Five Program are incorporated into the SIP, and it is supported with release time and resources as well as staff development. | • Model of schoolwide change was grounded on a series of agreements among administrators, teachers, assistants, ancillary staff including school psychologists and others to adhere to certain procedures within the school and classroom environments.<br>• Mission statement reflected shared school improvement goal: To create a place where students, staff, and parents want to be and where they can learn new skills that would benefit them now and in the future. |
| 2. High standards and expectations for all students | • All students and staff focus on the "High Fives": Be respectful, be responsible, follow directions, keep hands and feet to self, and be there—be ready.<br>• Improving student attendance, grades, and discipline is included in the first goal of the SIP: student accountability. | • Schools used brief slogans to focus attention expectations and school rules, including (a) be there be ready, (b) be respectful, (c) be responsible, (d) keep hands and feet to self (personal space), and (e) follow directions.<br>• The agreements reached among school staff during the planning and implementation of the schoolwide interventions were codified and written into the schools' policy and procedures manuals. The procedures that were developed prior to and during the schoolwide innovation supplied the basis for training newly recruited teachers to the schools. |
| 3. Effective school leadership | • The principal and assistant principal actively support the schoolwide effort; they agree with positive behavioral interventions and support (PBIS) principles, and they are adamant that financial support, grants, teacher release time, and staff development remain available to support the program. | • The administrators spearheaded the initial assessments, conducted the preliminary research, articulated the rationale for change, created the vision, rallied support among their respective staffs, and managed nearly every aspect of implementation, including the collection and use of schoolwide data. They listened, they problem solved, and they were visible when times were difficult. They modeled the changes for their staffs and made the innovations the top priorities in their respective schools. |

| | | |
|---|---|---|
| | • Administrators actively participate in the High Five fall training and the various reinforcement activities during the school year. They seek to hire professionals who will work within the framework of the established High Five Program.<br>• The superintendent and school board members approve general fund monies to help support the program at the building level. | |
| 4. High levels of collaboration and communication | • The school climate committee is composed of staff members and administrators, and this group is responsible for maintaining the High Five Program. These committee members meet at least twice a month to plan for all aspects of the schoolwide effort. They plan for fall training, collect and monitor outcome data, plan High Five booster and reinforcement activities, and facilitate ongoing communication with the entire school community. They are also responsible for the High Five budget.<br>• District administration (e.g., the superintendent and school board members) also support the PBIS program, dedicating the first two school days to High Five training. District administration has allowed teachers to travel and make professional presentations on the High Five Program. Also, they approve general fund monies to help support the program at the building level. | • The roles of the school psychologists were reconfigured and eventually transformed as the schoolwide innovations evolved and moved forward from traditional screening and assessments, discipline, and crisis intervention to providing antecedent interventions for problem prevention rather than reactive and routine applications of negative consequences after problems had occurred.<br>• With the advent of the schoolwide intervention, the school psychologist's role evolved into one of providing greater support to children who clearly required more assistance to succeed (i.e., those requiring selected/targeted and tertiary level). |
| 5. Curriculum, instruction, and assessments aligned with state standards | • The first 2 days of each school year the entire staff, administrators, and parent volunteers actively participate in training related to actively teaching students behavioral expectations.<br>• Because the school culture has been transformed, the more at-risk student population, around 35 to 50 students, is supported through what is referred to as the Behavioral Education Plan or BEP. | • School teams committed to incorporating intensive academic interventions as part of the schoolwide interventions. Teachers filled every moment of allocated time with relevant activities for boosting students' active engagement in instructional lessons. To support such efforts, new curriculum materials and equipment were purchased, teacher preparation periods were added to teachers' schedules, and "teaching teams" were formed to deliver instruction. |

(continued)

**Table 22.2.** (continued)

| Features and Effectiveness Critical Feature | School/Project/Report | |
|---|---|---|
| | S. J. Taylor-Greene & Kartub, 2000 | George et al., 2007<br>D. N. Miller et al., 2005 |
| | • Students are consistently rewarded for following the program; they earn coupons as part of a token economy and redeem them throughout the school year for products and entry into various activities. | • Teachers also were provided with intensive training in various evidence-based instructional techniques for enhancing the delivery of interesting and engaging lessons.<br>• Students in different grades were grouped for reading and math instruction based on their functioning levels. Teachers also received training in direct instruction to assist struggling readers. Acquisition of academic skills became the central mission at both schools. |
| 6. Frequent monitoring of teaching and learning | • Formative evaluation helps keep the program operating at optimum capacity. The school climate committee members, and in turn the entire staff, regularly review outcome data to make program decisions. Referral data (i.e., percentage of referrals by month, student, location, and time of day provide important information for program improvement. Trends in the data over time direct when booster activities are planned. Data help determine which students require support and structure beyond the regular High Five activities. Staff and student surveys are administered following the fall training and various booster activities. The results of these are used during the school climate committee meeting decision-making process. | • Agreements were reached on universal interventions for teachers to employ in their classrooms prior to sending children to the principal's office. Interventions consisted of a set of sequential steps that provided teachers with a structure to use for managing low-level misbehavior. These steps provided direct instruction in appropriate class behavior though oral reviews, modeling, and reinforcement of the classroom expectations and allowed students to receive multiple opportunities through reminders, prompts, and private warnings to regain their focus and remain in class.<br>• Rules were created and taught to students for different settings (e.g., cafeteria). Teachers and staff modeled the desired behaviors and provided opportunities for students to rehearse and practice them throughout the school.<br>• Greater emphasis was placed on curriculum-based assessment and progress monitoring. |

| | | |
|---|---|---|
| 7. Focused professional development | • The first two school days were dedicated to High Five training. Teachers traveled and made professional presentations about the program at other schools.<br>• Administrators actively participated in the fall training and various reinforcement activities during the school year. They tried to hire professionals who would work within the framework of the established positive behavior support program. | • The administrators signaled to the staffs the importance of the schoolwide innovation by allocating time for teachers to learn, practice, analyze, and modify new behaviors.<br>• School psychologists also provided professional development in areas such as applied behavior analysis, progress monitoring, functional behavior assessments, PBS plans, charting and graphing students' behavioral progress, and the use of data for making instructional decisions. |
| 8. A supportive learning environment | • All adults in the school operate from a positive team approach. Efforts are directed toward working with students—helping them to make appropriate choices and stay in school. Staff encourage students to be part of the solution rather than the problem, and they have learned the value of teaching and reinforcing students for appropriate behavior. Consequently, the school climate can now be described as proactive and positive. Teachers, parents, and students support the High Five Program.<br>• Students are consistently rewarded for following the High Fives. The program incorporates the use of a token economy—the High Five coupon. Coupons are redeemed throughout the school year for products and entry into various activities. High Five booster activities such as open gym, Be There–Be Ready classroom visits, raffles, and Gold Card night are but a few examples of the various reinforcement activities. | • Time for teachers to collaborate, to study data, and to make adjustments to their teaching repertoires was a critical resource in the successful implementation of the schoolwide model in these schools.<br>• Faculty meeting time was no longer primarily used for "housekeeping information" but instead was reserved for data presentations, discussions troubleshooting specific cases with implementation difficulties, and for updates regarding training on the schoolwide model.<br>• Adoption of a schoolwide system of behavior support in conjunction with other research-based practices of behavior management and support led to substantial reductions in incidents of antisocial behavior in the school and concomitant increases in students' prosocial behavior. This created a more positive and predictable school environment where all students felt valued. |
| 9. High levels of parent and community involvement | • Teachers, parents, and students support the High Five Program. | • Parent contact emphasizing students' positive school accomplishments was increased, a parent and student handbook was created in which policies and procedures could be clearly communicated, two parent nights per year were held, a parent advisory council was initiated, a newsletter for parents was created, and an honors program ceremony was developed.<br>• A bilingual individual was hired to serve as a community liaison across multiple environments. |

Similar outcomes were evident at Northwest:

> By the end of Year 1 of implementation, the system of PBS produced decreases in the frequencies of both disciplinary referrals and after-school detentions. Office referrals for the year decreased from 1,717 to 702 (i.e., 1,015 fewer than in the baseline year), and after-school detentions decreased from 845 to 85 (i.e., 760 fewer than in the baseline year). By the end of Year 2 of the school-wide innovation, office referrals were further reduced to 619, and the number of after-school detentions were reduced to 21. (George et al., pp. 43–44)

Favorable changes in attitudes and other positive outcomes (e.g., high levels of teacher satisfaction, rise in family attendance at first open house of the year) were also evident.

## Focus on Reading and Behavior

In Table 22.3, we link general features of high-performing schools to specific characteristics of SW-PBS. The projects defining this work are summarized next.

Ervin et al. (2006) described a program to enhance the capacity of personnel in four elementary schools to implement EBI and promote students' behavioral competence. A core project team was formed consisting of two school practitioners with doctoral degrees in psychology and three university trainers who were professional child psychologists with backgrounds in developmental, behavior, and learning disorders. Program activities incorporated features associated with successful implementation and capacity building: (a) working in collaboration with building teams to develop problem-solving strategies; (b) creating data systems for decision making and evaluation; (c) developing methods for sustained impact; and (d) providing staff with information, knowledge, skills, procedures, tools, incentives, and feedback to support implementation. State and federal funds facilitated resource allocation (i.e., time, space, funding, administrative support) to support project activities, including monies for on-site project facilitators.

Warren et al. (2006) described "the implementation and preliminary evaluation of school-wide PBS in an urban middle school located in a community characterized by poverty, crime, and limited social resources" (pp. 190–191). The intervention took place in an inner-city middle school (approximately 737 students, Grades 6–8) in a midwestern city (also see Warren et al., 2000, 2003). The student body included 41% of students from African American families, 35% from Hispanic families, and 18% from European American families. Approximately 80% of the student body received free lunch. In the year preceding the schoolwide intervention, 42% of the student body received at least five ODRs, and 81% received at least one. The researchers' contact with the school began in August of Year 1, although the schoolwide intervention did not begin until the beginning of the following school year. From August to December of Year 1, researchers participated in school activities, developed relationships with staff, and formed a better understanding of the procedures and needs of the school. In January and February of Year 1, two training sessions of an hour and a half each were provided on (a) the fundamentals of PBS, (b) the fundamentals of functional

**Table 22.3.** Illustrations of Positive Behavior Support (PBS) Focused on Improving Reading and Behavior

| Features and Effectiveness Critical Feature | School/Project/Report: Ervin et al., 2006 | School/Project/Report: Warren et al., 2006 |
|---|---|---|
| 1. A clear and shared focus | • Members of the core team outlined goals, desired outcomes, anticipated costs, incentives, activities, and nonnegotiable and adaptable aspects to administrators, teachers, and staff of interested schools.<br>• To be included, a school had to have a minimum staff vote of 80% agreeing to support implementation; principal commitment to the project and attendance at monthly meetings; agreement to designate a team to deal with action planning, data interpretation, and reporting; reading and behavior improvement included in top three school improvement goals; and agreement to ongoing data collection. | • Administrators and teachers began by developing and defining a short list of positively stated behavioral expectations for students at their school: (a) Be responsible, (b) be respectful, (c) be ready to learn, (d) be cooperative, and (e) be safe. |
| 2. High standards and expectations for all students | • Schools developed a behavior matrix to establish and define universal behavioral expectations (school rules).<br>• Using formative data, schools developed reading and behavior-focused action plans that attended to student needs at the universal, strategic, and intensive levels. Action plans functioned as school improvement plans for the following year and included measurable goals based on needs from assessments. | • Expectations were defined, directly taught, and rewarded. After the behavioral expectations were introduced to all students at the beginning of Year 2, teachers made use of the lesson plan outlines to teach each of the behavioral expectations to their classes. Part of this instruction included direct modeling and practice of the behavioral expectations in different settings. |
| 3. Effective school leadership | • The principal of each school that participated in this project promised commitment to it and agreed to attend monthly meetings along with principals from other participating schools.<br>• An on-site facilitator was assigned to schools to help with implementation.<br>• Site-specific action plans were developed. | • Researchers trained teachers and administrators to become self-sufficient in the application and evaluation of schoolwide PBS. As a result, researchers helped school personnel identify and train additional school personnel who could act as PBS "mentors" or facilitators once the researchers' involvement was phased out. |

(continued)

**Table 22.3.** (continueed)

| Features and Effectiveness Critical Feature | School/Project/Report | |
|---|---|---|
| | Ervin et al., 2006 | Warren et al., 2006 |
| 4. High levels of collaboration and communication | • Building teams worked in collaboration with core teams to develop localized problem-solving strategies.<br>• The core team worked together to formulate the project plan, goals, and objectives, linking with broader academic (e.g., forming a national advisory board of experts in systems change, assessment, reading, and behavior) and school (e.g., parents and general and special educators) networks in this process.<br>• Staff were provided with information, knowledge, skills, procedures, tools, incentives, and feedback to support implementation.<br>• To assist in developing support networks, core project and school team members participated in a state-funded conference on PBS.<br>• At each school, grade-level meetings were held to identify current reading practices and investigate additional resource needs. From these meetings, teachers requested assistance regarding instruction for struggling readers. In response, direct instruction curriculum materials were purchased for the schools and professional development was provided. | • At the onset of implementation, a 2-day training session on individual and schoolwide PBS was provided for a group of "key players" (administrators, teachers, and parents) who would be involved directly in the implementation of PBS in the school. This group consisted primarily of self-selected individuals who had expressed a desire to help the school succeed in its efforts to remove behavioral impediments to school learning.<br>• Researchers provided specialized training and assistance to individual teachers who requested special help with their classes. For example, one first-year teacher who struggled with the challenging behavior of one of her classes was helped to refine behavior management strategies in her classroom. Through supplementary instruction, role-playing, and practice sessions with students, she reported that her confidence as a teacher increased and problem behavior in her classroom was reduced.<br>• Ongoing consultations with individual teachers proved particularly important in enhancing and maintaining rapport with the school staff. |
| 5. Curriculum, instruction, and assessments aligned with state standards. | • Schools developed site-specific action plans based on local performance data and formative evaluation. | • Teachers and administrators developed outlines for lesson plans to teach five schoolwide behavior expectations to all students. Teachers and students also incorporated the five expectations into their own "codes of conduct" (classroom rules). For the first 5 weeks, they focused on one expectation per week during schoolwide morning announcements and within the individual classrooms. |

| | | |
|---|---|---|
| | • Staff focused on developing and implementing plans to teach and encourage students to follow school rules. Methods for conveying school rules included announcements, assemblies, PowerPoint presentations (School A), or videos (School B) that provided an overview of the school rules, their definitions, and clear examples of students following and not following the rules in different school contexts (e.g., classroom, hallway, bus).<br>• One school used grant money to adopt curriculum materials from Project Optimize for its first-grade students. | • A system was established for rewarding students who demonstrated these expectations. Teachers awarded students with "positive behavior referrals," tickets that noted the behavioral expectation demonstrated by the student. These tickets could be turned in during frequent drawings for special prizes. |
| 6. Frequent monitoring of teaching and learning. | • Schools expanded implementation activities to targeted and individual student behavioral support levels, informed by formative evaluation and action plans.<br>• Data systems were created and used for decision making and evaluation.<br>• Schools used SWIS, DIBELS, and SET to monitor both behavior and reading.<br>• Some schools piloted DIBELS to monitor progress of students at the intensive or strategic levels, while one school used it for all children. | • Teachers and administrators became self-sufficient in the application and evaluation of schoolwide PBS.<br>• Data were used by staff to plan and modify subsequent interventions. Researchers provided staff with technical assistance that taught them how to obtain and display relevant data from the discipline tracking system used by the school district. |
| 7. Focused professional development. | • Workshops on PBS were provided to each school as well as guidance in developing a behavior matrix to establish and define universal behavioral expectations (school rules). Schools received training in early literacy skills assessment, schoolwide information systems, and implementation fidelity measures.<br>• To build a capacity to serve students needing strategic or intensive behavioral support, schools conducted professional development on functional assessment. | • Lesson plans were shared with instructions on how the five behavioral expectations could be demonstrated in a variety of school settings (e.g., how students could "be responsible" in the classroom, cafeteria, and halls).<br>• An hour-and-a-half workshop was provided to the entire school on the schoolwide expectations and the methods/lesson plans that would be used to teach these expectations to students. |

(continued)

**Table 22.3.** (continued)

| Features and Effectiveness Critical Feature | School/Project/Report | |
|---|---|---|
| | Ervin et al., 2006 | Warren et al., 2006 |
| | • To assist in developing support networks, core project and school team members participated in a state-funded conference on PBS. Professional development was provided via regularly occurring events (e.g., staff meetings).<br>• At each school, grade-level meetings were held to identify current reading practices and investigate additional resource needs. From these meetings, teachers requested assistance regarding instruction for struggling readers. In response, direct instruction curriculum materials were purchased for the schools, and professional development was provided. | • Schoolwide behavior support efforts were supplemented by the researchers' continued involvement in training teachers in the use of PBS for individual students. These strategies included, when appropriate, altering the classroom environment, increasing choice making for students, making curricular adaptations, reinforcing positive behaviors, and teaching replacement skills. Continued staff training in how to use PBS approaches for individual students helped staff understand the similarities between individual and schoolwide PBS (e.g., providing supports that match the needs of the school or individual, examining outcomes and using data to design interventions, the value of school/family/community partnerships). |
| 8. A supportive learning environment | • Schools developed feedback and incentive systems (e.g., a raffle program for students caught following school rules).<br>• Students received vouchers to buy items from the school store.<br>• Special acknowledgment banners were distributed for classrooms caught following school rules. | • Researchers helped school personnel identify and train additional school personnel who could act as PBS mentors or facilitators once the researchers' involvement was phased out. |
| 9. High levels of parent and community involvement. | • A parent video presentation was created in English and in Spanish and shared at the parent open house and with new children and parents throughout the year.<br>• Schools made presentations to their school boards. | • The school formed partnerships with community agencies that could potentially provide funding and support for their continued PBS efforts.<br>• Researchers shared outcome data with teachers, administrators, and community members throughout the course of the program implementation. |

DIBELS, Dynamic Indicators of Basic Early Literacy Skills; SET, School-wide Evaluation Tool; SWIS, School-wide Information System.

behavioral assessment, (c) what the staff was currently doing with regard to behavior, and (d) the comparisons and contrasts of PBS with their current behavioral processes and policies (Warren et al., 2006, p. 191).

In another study, researchers examined the relationship of SW-PBS-induced reductions in ODRs to student academic achievement (Lassen et al., 2006). Data on ODRs, suspensions, standardized reading and math test scores, and treatment fidelity were gathered and analyzed in an urban, inner-city middle school in the Midwest over a 3-year period. Results revealed a consistent increase in student test scores from Year 1 to Year 3 of the study. There also was a decrease in the number of office referrals and suspensions. In addition, regression analysis suggested a significant relationship between student problem behavior and performance on standardized tests. The authors described the implementation of SW-PBS as follows:

> Contact with the target school, which was initiated in Year 1 (2000–2001) before the school year began, consisted of researchers gaining an understanding of the organization of the school and learning about the specific school culture. ... Consistent with the fundamental components of PBS, implementation focused on the following areas: (a) evidence-based practices (e.g., positive reinforcement, teaching social skills), (b) systems improvement (e.g., team-based action planning, data-based decision making), and (c) implementation support/facilitation (e.g., coaching, ongoing staff development). ... Teachers and administrators developed a list of six behavioral expectations for the school. The new "Steps to Success" were (a) Be Responsible, (b) Be Respectful, (c) Be Ready to Learn, (d) Be Cooperative, (e) Be Safe, and (f) Be Honest. These expectations were designed to establish a standard set of behavioral expectations for the entire school [and] ... a training session was held for a group of teachers and administrators who were to be instrumental in the direct application of the school-wide PBS system. During this training session the group devised plans for teaching the new student expectations and determining how this instruction could be generalized outside the classroom setting. ... During the third quarter of Year 1 another training session was held for the entire school staff. This instruction included the introduction of the new "Steps to Success" and difference methods for teaching the expectations to students across school settings. ... After initial training on the school expectations was completed "Steps to Success" posters were displayed in hallways, the cafeteria, the office, the gymnasium, and each classroom. Teachers then taught the expectations to the students, through direct instruction and role-playing. ... A reward system was developed to reinforce students for behaviors consistent with "Steps to Success." ... SWPBS efforts were maintained through regular training by the researchers at quarterly training sessions during inservice meetings with teachers and administrators. These training sessions focused on providing teachers with classroom management strategies and techniques to effectively deal with challenging student behavior. ... During Year 3, the school offered group-level support for students who had been identified by teachers and administrators as continuing to have serious behavior problems and not responding well to school-wide interventions. This intervention consisted of weekly group meetings with selected students to offer

more intensive instruction on appropriate behaviors that were consistent with school-wide behavioral expectations. (pp. 705–706)

## IMPLICATIONS FOR IMPROVING ACHIEVEMENT WITH BEHAVIOR OR BEHAVIOR WITH ACHIEVEMENT

Algozzine et al. (2007) reviewed research related to the relationship between academic achievement and social behavior. They found that most studies illustrated covariation or simple correlations, and that few researchers investigated or demonstrated functional relationships. Regardless, research on the effects of SW-PBS on academics and behavior provides a strong base for hypothesis testing and further research. For example, Luiselli et al. (2005) described the effects of whole-school behavior support on behavior problems and academic outcomes in an urban elementary school. They found decreases in office referrals and suspensions as well as improvements in reading and math skills but noted that because of the quasi-experimental nature of their study, the outcomes "were associated with, but could not be attributed unequivocally to, [the] intervention" (p. 195). Their discussion illustrates a common hypothesis-maintaining interest in the relationship between achievement and behavior: "By virtue of reducing discipline problems, teachers *can* [italics added] devote more time to instruction and other learning opportunities that maximize educational progress" (p. 196).

McIntosh, Chard, et al. (2006) provided descriptive data on the rates of ODRs and beginning reading skills for students in Grades K–3 in a school district implementing a prevention model for both reading and behavior support. They found that combined efforts to implement schoolwide reading and behavior interventions resulted in fewer students needing additional support and put forth a different view about the need and direction for continued study of achievement and behavior:

> Some researchers assert that implementation of school-wide behavioral programs may be associated with an increase in academic achievement, and we hypothesize that the implementation of a school-wide reading program has reduced the frequency of problem behavior occasioned by academic failure. In that way, *both programs may work symbiotically, with each program having beneficial effects on both sets of outcomes* [italics added]. (p. 153)

This perspective of academic and behavior linkage is consistent with early explanations for learning disabilities that focused on the concept of learned helplessness (Seligman, 1975) and attribution theory (Weiner, 1974) or the belief that one has little control or influence on achievement or academic outcomes. These conceptualizations also have value in explaining behavior problems. For example, "Seligman suggested that learned helplessness produces three deficits: (a) an undermining of one's motivation to respond; (b) a retardation of one's ability to learn that responding work; and (c) an emotional disturbance, usually depression or anxiety" (Sutherland & Singh, 2004, p. 171). Correlation does not prove causation. Changes in aggressive behavior and changes in achievement may be mediated by any number of other variables; children with achievement and behavior problems may be both architects and victims in the world of failure in school. Thinking this way has value in both assessment and intervention; when data point to explanations that support and extend how achievement and behavior are related, the road ahead is clear.

## Use Assessment Effectively

Schools use assessment information for many purposes, including screening, identification, placement, and progress and program evaluation (Salvia & Ysseldyke, 2006). Using this information is valuable in identifying "co-occurring" problems of students performing poorly in school. The history of special education is replete with efforts to improve the identification side of the diagnostic-prescriptive model as a basis for improving outcomes for children with disabilities. In the end, these efforts have been largely academic and unproductive. For example, since the inception of interest in children with "learning disabilities" (LDs), professionals have labored mightily and long to identify the "right" students (cf. Ysseldyke, Algozzine, & Thurlow, 2000). Over the years, the numbers identified grew at uncomfortable rates, and the latest iteration of new alternatives in the diagnostic process emerged at least in part as an attempt to stem the rising tide of disability evidence primarily by failure to learn to read:

> For decades, policymakers and academics have been frustrated by the LD construct. ... One prominent reason is economics. In a sense, LD became too successful for its own good—*if success may be defined by the number of children with the label* [italics added]. Shortly after LD was legitimized as a special-education category in the Education of All Handicapped Children Act of 1975, the proportion of children with LD in the general U.S. population skyrocketed from less than 2% in 1976–1977 to more than 6% in 1999–2000. This increase has proved expensive for school districts because, on average, it costs two to three times more to teach children with disabilities. (Fuchs & Fuchs, 2006, p. 93)

Arguing the merits or demerits of response to intervention (RTI) is beyond the focus of this chapter, but the continuing failure of efforts to "identify in order to teach" children begs for looking at the problem in a different way. Doing the same thing (e.g., identifying students needing assistance) differently (RTI vs. ability-achievement discrepancy vs. process disorders vs. teacher ratings) will likely produce marginal, if any, effects on outcomes for children. We are not saying that assessment is unimportant. We are saying that focusing assessment on an alternate purpose is necessary. Rather than searching for pathologies in children, the first course in using assessment effectively is determining the extent to which the fundamentals of effective instruction are evident and implemented with fidelity in the child's classroom and knowing the extent to which the child is participating and actively engaged. This means that direct and frequent monitoring of academic and behavior performance is essential to implementing effective instruction programs to skills related to them in elementary, middle, and high schools.

### Implement Effective Interventions With Fidelity

The body of knowledge on components of effective instruction is vast, and we know that intervening early, relentlessly, and appropriately produces important outcomes for children (cf. Algozzine, Ysseldyke, & Elliott, 2000; McIntosh, Chard, et al., 2006; McIntosh, Horner, et al., 2006; Torgesen, 2004; Ysseldyke & Algozzine, 2006). We also know that teachers do not consistently use evidence-based practices for a variety of reasons (Gersten, Chard, & Baker, 2000; Gersten, Vaughn, Deshler, & Schiller, 1997; Greenwood & Delquardri, 1993). We also know that teachers inadvertently may encourage rather than discourage behavior problems and ensure that high rates of problem behaviors persist, including, but not limited to, (a) failing to teach prosocial skills; (b) providing rich schedules of reinforcement for problem behaviors; (c) using reinforcement and punishment inconsistently; and (d) using weak punishers as consequences or weak rewards as reinforcers for other behaviors (cf. Patterson, 1976).

What is less known, especially in the lives of children experiencing significant academic and behavior failure in school, is the extent to which these "best practices" are being implemented with fidelity (i.e., as intended and consistent with guidelines and expectations), especially with children with the greatest needs. A study by Cochrane and Laux (2007) is revealing. When nationally certified school psychologists were surveyed regarding their beliefs about the importance of measuring treatment integrity in school-based interventions for children with academic and behavior concerns, they agreed emphatically that doing it was important, but "only 10.7% reported that they always measured it in one-to-one consultation and only 3.6% reported that they always measured it in group or team consultation" (p. 29). The potential effects are direct of a "belief-to-practice" gap such as this: The finest medicine in the world does not work if the patient does not receive it.

The body of knowledge on the effects of high-fidelity implementation of the components on effective instruction is not news. Good teaching works, and there are no boundaries on where it will occur and who will benefit from it. The body of knowledge on the value of SW-PBS is growing, and the parameters on when and whether it occurs with fidelity appear to be the only boundaries likely to affect its continued and increasing success. Sugai and Horner (2006) stated that one of the areas in which further research is needed is the nature of the relationship between SW-PBS implementation and student academic achievement within the three-tier continuum of behavior support. For that to happen, we must continue to be vigilant in monitoring the extent to which effective schoolwide academic *and* behavior instruction is implemented with fidelity in our schools.

## ACADEMIC ACHIEVEMENT AND BEHAVIOR SUPPORT

We have described and examined key features of SW-PBS, with a focus on illustrating the importance of team and data-based decision making, summarizing implementation outcomes, and reviewing research of projects focused on both academic and behavior supports. We draw the following conclusions from our work:

- SW-PBS shares characteristics with those identified in effective schools research and evidenced in high-performing schools.
- When implemented with fidelity, SW-PBS results in favorable behavior outcomes.
- Two types of studies link SW-PBS with important outcomes for students.
- The first indicates the number of hours of instruction gained by decreases in ODRs and makes a leap of faith that more time in the classroom will result in improved achievement.
- The other demonstrates that high-quality implementation of SW-PBS and evidence-based reading intervention results in improvements in behavior and reading.
- Evidence for improvements in academic achievement as a result of adding SW-PBS in an effective school is less clearly established in research.
- Continued research is needed to show that schools implementing SW-PBS with fidelity show improvements in academic and behavior outcomes.
- Continued study of simultaneous implementation of SW-PBS and evidence-based academic interventions is clearly warranted.

## REFERENCES

Adelman, H. S., & Taylor, L. (1997). Toward a scale-up model for replicating new approaches to schooling. *Journal of Educational and Psychological Consultation, 8*, 197–230.

Algozzine, B., Putnam, B., & Horner, R. (2007). *Which came first? The achievement or the behavior problem?* Charlotte, NC: University of North Carolina at Charlotte, Behavior and Reading Improvement Center.

Algozzine, B., Ysseldyke, J. E., & Elliott, J. (2000). *Strategies and tactics for effective instruction* (2nd ed.). Longmont, CO: Sopris West.

Bahr, M. W., & Kovaleski, J. F. (2006). The need for problem-solving teams: Introduction to the special issue. *Remedial and Special Education, 27*(1), 2–5.

Bohanon, H., Fenning, P., Carney, K. L., Minnis-Kim, M. J., Anderson-Harriss, S., Moroz, K. B., et al. (2006). Schoolwide application of positive behavior support in an urban high school: A case study. *Journal of Positive Behavior Interventions, 8*, 131–145.

Carr, E. G., Horner, R. H., Turnbull, A. P., Marquis, J. G., Magito McLaughlin, D., McAtee, M. L., et al. (1999). *Positive behavior support for people with developmental disabilities: A research synthesis*. Washington, DC: American Association on Mental Retardation.

Carr, E. J., Taylor, J. C., & Robinson, S. (1991). The effects of severe behavior problems in children on the teaching behavior of adults. *Journal of Applied Behavior Analysis, 24*, 523–535.

Chapman, D., & Hofweber, C. (2000). Effective behavior support in British Columbia. *Journal of Positive Behavior Interventions, 2*, 235–237.

Clonan, S. M., McDougal, J. L., Clark, K., & Davison, S. (2007). Use of office discipline referrals in school-wide decision-making: A practical example. *Psychology in the Schools, 44*, 19–27.

Cochrane, W. S., & Laux, J. M. (2007). Investigating school psychologist's perceptions of treatment integrity in school-based interventions for children with academic and behavior concerns. *Preventing School Failure, 51*, 29–34.

Colvin, G. (1991). *Procedures for establishing a proactive school-wide discipline plan.* Eugene: University of Oregon, College of Education.

Colvin, G., & Fernandez, E. (2000). Sustaining effective behavior support systems in an elementary school. *Journal of Positive Behavior Interventions, 2*, 251–253.

Colvin, G., Kameenui, E.J., & Sugai, G. (1993). School-wide and classroom management: Reconceptualizing the integration and management of students with behavior problems in general education. *Education and Treatment of Children, 16*, 361–381.

Colvin, G., Sugai, G., Good, R. H., & Lee, Y. (1997). Effect of active supervision and precorrection in transition behaviors of elementary students. *School Psychology Quarterly, 12*, 344–363.

Colvin, G., Sugai, G., & Kameenui, E. (1994). *Curriculum for establishing a proactive school-wide discipline plan. Project Prepare. Behavioral research and teaching.* Eugene: University of Oregon, College of Education.

Denny, R. K., Epstein, M., & Rose, E. (1992). Direct observation of adolescents with serious emotional disturbance and their nonhandicapped peers in mainstream vocational education classrooms. *Behavioral Disorders, 18*, 33–41.

Dunlap, G., Newton, J. S., Fox, L., Benito, N., & Vaughn, B. (2001). Family involvement in functional assessment and positive behavior support. *Focus on Autism and Other Developmental Disabilities, 16*, 215–221.

Ervin, A., Schaughency, E., Matthews, A., Goodman, S. D., McGlinchey, M. T., & Matthews, A. (2006). Merging research and practice agendas to address reading and behavior school-wide. *School Psychology Review, 35*, 198–223.

Fogt, J. B., & Piripavel, C. M. D. (2002). Positive school-wide interventions for eliminating physical restraint and exclusion. *Reclaiming Children and Youth, 10*, 227–232.

Fox, L., Dunlap, G., & Cushing, L. (2002). Early intervention, positive behavior support, and transition to school. *Journal of Emotional and Behavioral Disorders, 10*, 149–157

Fuchs, D., & Deshler, D. D. (2007). What we need to know about responsiveness to intervention (and shouldn't be afraid to ask). *Learning Disabilities Research and Practice, 22*, 129–136.

Fuchs, D., & Fuchs, L. (2006). Introduction to response to intervention: What, why, and how valid is it? *Reading Research Quarterly, 41*, 93–99.

George, M. P. (2000). Establishing and promoting disciplinary practices at the building level that ensure safe, effective, and nurturing school environments. In L. M. Bullock & R. A. Gable (Eds.), *Positive academic and behavioral supports: Creating safe, effective, and nurturing schools for all students* (pp. 11–15). Reston, VA: Council for Exceptional Children.

George, M. P., White, G. P., & Schlaffer, J. J. (2007). Implementing school-wide behavior change: Lessons from the field. *Psychology in the Schools, 44*, 41–51.

Gersten, R., Chard, D., & Baker, S. (2000). Factors influencing sustained use of research-based instructional practices. *Journal of Learning Disabilities, 33*, 445–457.

Gersten, R., Vaughn, S., Deshler, D., & Schiller, E. (1997). What we know about using research findings: Implications for improving special education practice. *Journal of Learning Disabilities, 30*, 466–476.

Good, R. H., & Kaminski, R. A. (Eds.). (2002). *Dynamic indicators of basic early literacy skills* (6th ed.). Eugene, OR: Institute for the Development of Education Achievement. Available at http://dibels.uoregon.edu

Gottfredson, D. C., Gottfredson, G. D., & Hybl, L. G. (1993). Managing adolescent behavior: A multiyear, multischool study. *American Educational Research Journal, 30*, 179–215.

Greenwood, C., & Delquardri, J. (1993). Current challenges to behavioral technology in the reform of schooling: Large-scale, high-quality implementation and sustained use of high quality instructional practices. *Education and Treatment of Children, 16*, 401–440.

Gunter, P. L., Jack, S. L., DePaepe, P., Reed, T. M., & Harrison, J. (1994). Effects of challenging behaviors of students with EBD on teacher instructional behavior. *Preventing School Failure, 38*, 35–39.

Hagan-Burke, S., Burke, M. D., Martin, E., Boon, R. T., Fore, C., III, & Kirkendoll, D. The internal consistency of the school-wide subscales of the Effective Behavioral Support Survey. *Education and Treatment of Children, 28*, 400–413.

Handler, M. W., Rey, J., Connell, J., Their, K., Feinberg, A., & Putnam, R. (2007). Practical considerations in creating school-wide positive behavior support in public schools. *Psychology in the Schools, 44*, 29–39.

Hawken, L. S., & Horner, R. H. (2003). Evaluation of a targeted group intervention within a school-wide system of behavior support. *Journal of Behavioral Education, 12*, 225–240.

Horner, R. H., & Sugai, G. (2003). School-wide positive behavior support: An alternative approach to discipline in schools (pp. 359–390). In L. Bambara & L. Kern (Eds.), *Positive behavior support*. New York: Guilford Press.

Horner, R. H., Sugai, G., Todd, A. W., & Lewis-Palmer, T. (2005). School-wide positive behavior support: An alternative approach to discipline in the schools. In L. M. Bambara & L. Kern (Eds.), *Individualized supports for students with problem behavior: Designing positive behavior plans* (pp. 359–390). New York: Guilford.

Horner, R., Sugai, G., & Vincent, C. (2005). School-wide positive behavior support: Investing in student success. *Impact, 18*(2), 4–5.

Horner, R. H., Todd, A. W., Lewis-Palmer, T., Irvin, L. K., Sugai, G., & Boland, J. B. (2004). The School-wide Evaluation Tool (SET): A research instrument for assessing school-wide positive behavior support. *Journal of Positive Behavior Interventions, 6*, 3–12.

Illinois Technical Assistance Center (ISTAC). (2007). A blended response to intervention (RtI) model: Behavior and academics addressed through Illinois PBIUS and Illinois ASPIRE integration. *Illinois PBIS Network Update, 11*(2), 1, 6.

Individuals With Disabilities Education Act. (1997) Amendments of 1997, 20 U.S.C.A § 1400 et. seq. (statute); CFR 300. (Regulations published in 1999)

Kartub, D. T., Taylor-Greene, S., March, R. E., & Horner, R. H. (2000). Reducing hallway noise: A systems approach. *Journal of Positive Behavior Interventions, 2*, 179–182.

Kratochwill, T. R., & Shernoff, E. S. (2004). Evidence-based practice: Promoting evidence-based interventions in school psychology. *School Psychology Review, 33*(1), 34–48.

Lassen, S. R., Steele, M. M., & Sailor, W. (2006). The relationship of school-wide positive behavior support to academic achievement in an urban middle school. *Psychology in the Schools, 43*, 701–712.

Lewis, T. J., Colvin, G., & Sugai, G. (2000). The effects of pre-correction and active supervision on the recess behavior of elementary school students. *Education and Treatment of Children, 23*, 109–121.

Lewis, T. J., & Garrison-Harrell, L. (1999). Effective behavior support: Designing setting specific interventions. *Effective School Practices, 17*, 38–46.

Lewis, T. J., Powers, L. J., Kelk, M. J., & Newcomer, L. L. (2002). Reducing problem behaviors on the playground: An investigation of the application of schoolwide positive behavior supports. *Psychology in the Schools, 39*, 181–190.

Lewis, T. J., & Sugai, G. (1999). Effective behavior support: A systems approach to proactive school management. *Focus on Exceptional Children, 31*(6), 24–47.

Lewis, T. J., Sugai, G., & Colvin, G. (1998). Reducing problem behavior through a school-wide system of effective behavioral support: Investigation of a school-wide social skills training program and contextual interventions. *School Psychology Review, 27*, 446–459.

Lohrmann-O'Rourke, S., Knoster, T., Sabatine, K., Smith, D., Horvath, B., & Llewellyn, G. (2000). School-wide application of PBS in the Bangor Area School District. *Journal of Positive Behavior Interventions, 2*, 238–240.

Luiselli, J. K., Putnam, R. F., & Handler, M. W. (2001). Improving discipline practices in public schools: Description of a whole-school and district-wide model of behavior analysis consultation. *The Behavior Analyst Today, 2*, 18–27.

Luiselli, J. K., Putnam, R. F., Handler, M. W., & Feinberg, A. B. (2005). Whole-school positive behaviour support: Effects on student discipline problems and academic performance. *Educational Psychology, 25*, 183–198.

Luiselli, J. K., Putnam, R. F., & Sunderland, M. (2002). Longitudinal evaluation of behavior support intervention in a public middle school. *Journal of Positive Behavior Interventions, 4*, 182–188.

Manguin, E., & Loeber, R. (1996). Academic performance and delinquency. In M. Tonry (Ed.), *Crime and justice: A review of research* (Vol. 20, pp. 145–264). Chicago: University of Chicago Press.

March, R. E., & Horner, R. H. (2002). Feasibility and contributions of functional behavioral assessment in schools. *Journal of Emotional and Behavioral Disorders, 10*, 158–170.

Marquis, J. G., Horner, R. H., Carr, E. G., Turnbull, A. P., Thompson, M., Behrens, G. A., et al. (2000). A meta-analysis of positive behavior support. In R. Gersten, E. P. Schiller, & S. Vaughn (Eds.), *Contemporary special education research: Syntheses of knowledge base on critical instructional issues* (pp. 137–178). Mahwah, NJ: Erlbaum.

McCurdy, B. L., Kunsch, C., & Reibstein, S. (2007). Secondary prevention in the urban school: Implementing the Behavior Education Program. *Preventing School Failure, 51*(3), 12–19.

McCurdy, B. L., Mannella, M. C., & Eldridge, N. (2003). Positive behavior support in urban schools: Can we prevent the escalation of antisocial behavior? *Journal of Positive Behavior Interventions, 5*, 158–170.

McIntosh, K., Chard, D. J., Boland, J. B., & Horner, R. H. (2006). Demonstration of combined efforts in school-wide academic and behavioral systems and incidence of reading and behavior challenges in early elementary grades. *Journal of Positive Behavior Interventions, 8*, 146–154.

McIntosh, K., Horner, R. H., Chard, D. J., Boland, J. B., & Good, R. H. (2006). The use of reading and behavior screening measures to predict non-response to school-wide positive behavior support: A longitudinal analysis. *School Psychology Review, 35*, 275–291.

Merrell, K. W., & Buchanan, R. (2006). Intervention selection in school-based practice: Using public- health models to enhance systems capacity of schools. *School Psychology Review, 35*, 167–180.

Metzler, S. W., Biglan, A., Rusby, J. C., & Sprague, J. R. (2001). Evaluation of a comprehensive behavior management program to improve school-wide positive behavior support. *Education and Treatment of Children, 24*, 448–479.

Miller, D. N., George, M. P., & Fogt, J. B. (2005). Establishing and sustaining research-based practices at Centennial School: A descriptive case study of systemic change. *Psychology in the Schools, 42*.

Morrison, G. M., & D'Incau, B. (1997). The web of zero-tolerance: Characteristics of students who are recommended for expulsion from school. *Education and Treatment of Children, 20*, 316–335.

Nakasato, J. (2000). Data-based decision making kin Hawaii's behavior support effort. *Journal of Positive Behavior Interventions, 2*, 247–251.

National Research Council. (2005). *Advancing scientific research in education*. Washington, DC: National Academies Press.

Nelson, J. R. (1996). Designing schools to meet the needs of students who exhibit disruptive behavior. *Journal of Emotional and Behavioral Disorders, 4*, 147–161.

Nelson, J. R., Benner, G., Reid, R., Epstein, M. H., & Currin, D. (2002). The convergent validity of office discipline referrals with the TRF. *Journal of Emotional and Behavioral Disorders, 10*, 181–189.

Nelson, J. R., Colvin, G., & Smith, D. J. (1996). The effects of setting clear standards on students' social behavior in common areas of the school. *The Journal of At-Risk Issues, 2*, 10–19.

Nelson, J. R., Martella, R C., & Marchand-Martella, N. E. (2002). Maximizing student learning: The effects of a comprehensive school-based program for preventing disruptive behaviors. *Journal of Emotional and Behavioral Disorders, 10*, 136–148.

Nersesian, M., Todd, A. W., Lehmann, J., & Watson, J. (2000). School-wide behavior support through district-level system change. *Journal of Positive Behavior Interventions, 2*, 244–247.

No Child Left Behind Act of 2001. (2002). Pub. L. 107-110, 115 Stat. 1425.

Office of the Superintendent of Public Instruction (OSPI). (2007). *Nine characteristics of high-performing schools: A research-based resource for schools and districts to assist with improving student learning.* Olympia, WA: Author. Retrieved August 18, 2007, from http://www.k12.wa.us/research/default.aspx

OSEP Center on Positive Behavioral Interventions and Supports. (2005). *School-wide positive behavior support: Implementers' blueprint and self-assessment.* Eugene, OR: Author.

Patterson, G. R. (1976). The aggressive child: Victim and architect of a coercive system. In E. J. Mash, L. A. Hamerlynck, & L. C. Handy (Eds.), *Behavior modification and families* (pp. 267–316). New York: Brunner/Mazel.

Sadler, C. (2000). Effective behavior support implementation at the district level: Tigard-Tualatin school district. *Journal of Positive Behavior Interventions, 2*, 241–243.

Safran, S. (2006). Using the Effective Behavior Supports Survey to guide development of schoolwide positive behavior support. *Journal of Positive Behavior Interventions, 8*, 3–9.

Salvia, J., & Ysseldyke, J. E. (2006). *Assessment.* Boston: Houghton-Mifflin.

Scott, T. (2001). A schoolwide example of positive behavioral support. *Journal of Positive Behavior Interventions, 3*, 88–94.

Scott, T. M., Nelson, C. M., & Liaupsin, C. J. (2001). Effective instruction: The forgotten component in preventing school violence. *Education and Treatment of Children, 24*, 309–322.

Seligman, M. E. (1975). *Helplessness: On depression, development, and death.* San Francisco: Freeman.

Shannon, G. S., & Bylsma, P. (2007). *The nine characteristics of high-performing schools: A research-based resource for schools and districts to assist with improving student learning* (2nd ed.). Olympia, WA: Office of the Superintendent of Public Instruction.

Shapiro, E. S. (2006). Are we solving the big problems? *School Psychology Review, 35*, 260–265.

Shores, R. E., Jack, S. L., Gunter, P. L., Ellis, D. N., DeBriere, T. J., & Wehby, J. H. (1994). Classroom interactions of children with behavior disorders. *Journal of Emotional and Behavioral Disorders, 1*, 27–39.

Simmons, D. C., Kame'enui, E. J., Good, R. H., Harn, B. A., Cole, C., & Braun, D. (2002). Building, implementing, and sustaining a beginning reading model: Lessons learned school by school. In M. R. Shinn, H. M. Walker, & G. Stoner (Eds.), *Interventions for academic and behavioral problems II: Preventive and remedial approaches* (pp. 537–570). Bethesda, MD: National Association of School Psychologists.

Skiba, R. J., Peterson, R. L., & Williams, T. (1997). Office referrals and suspensions: Disciplinary intervention in middle schools. *Education and Treatment of Children, 20*, 295–315.

Sprague, J., Walker, H., Golly, A., White, K., Myers, D. R., & Shannon, T. (2001). Translating research into effective practice: The effects of a universal staff and student intervention on indicators of discipline and school safety. *Education and Treatment of Children, 24*, 495–511.

Sugai, G., & Horner, R. H. (2006). A promising approach for expanding and sustaining school-wide positive behavior support. *School Psychology Review, 35*, 245–259.

Sugai, G., Sprague, J. R., Horner, R. H., & Walker, H. M. (2000a). Preventing school violence: The use of office discipline referrals to assess and monitor school-wide discipline interventions. Journal of Emotional and Behavioral Disorders, 8, 94–101. Sutherland, K. S., & Singh, N. N. (2004). Learned helplessness and students with emotional and behavioral disorders: Deprivation in the classroom. *Behavioral Disorders, 29*, 169–181.

Taylor-Greene, S. D., Nelson, L., Longton, J., Gassman, T., Cohen, J., Swartz, J., et al. (1997). School-wide behavioral support: Starting the year off right. *Journal of Behavioral Education, 7*, 99–112.

Taylor-Greene, S. J., & Kartub, D. T. (2000). Durable implementation of school-wide behavior support: The high five program. *Journal of Positive Behavior Interventions, 2*, 233–235.

Todd, A., Haugen, L., Anderson, K., & Spriggs, M. (2002). Teaching recess: Low-cost efforts producing effective results. *Journal of Positive Behavior Interventions, 4*, 46–52.

Todd, A. W., Horner, R. H., Sugai, G., & Sprague, J. R. (1999). Effective behavior support: Strengthening school-wide systems through a team-based approach. *Effective School Practices, 17*(4), 23–27.

Torgesen, J. (2004, Fall). Preventing reading failure—and its devastating downward spiral. *American Educator*. Retrieved December 25, 2006, from http://www.aft.org/pubs-reports/american_educator/issues/fall04/reading.htm

Turnbull, A., Edmonson, H., Griggs, P., Wickham, D., Sailor, W., Freeman, R., et al. (2002). A blueprint for schoolwide positive behavior support: Implementation of three components. *Exceptional Children, 68*, 377–402.

Walker, H. M., Ramsey, E., & Gresham, F. M. (2004). *Antisocial behavior in schools: Evidence-based practices*. Belmont, CA: Wadsworth/Thompson Learning.

Warren, J. S., Bohanon-Edmonson, H. M., Turnbull, A. P., Sailor, W., Wickham, D., Griggs, P., et al. (2006). School-wide positive behavior support: Addressing behavior problems that impede student learning. *Educational Psychology Review, 18*, 187–198.

Warren, J. S., Edmonson, H. M., Griggs, P., Lassen, S., McCart, A., Turnbull, A., et al. (2003). Urban applications of school-wide positive behavior support: Critical issues and lessons learned. *Journal of Positive Behavior Interventions, 5*, 80–91.

Warren, J. S., Edmonson, H. M., Sailor, W., Turnbull, A., Wickham, D., Griggs, P., et al. (2000, August). *Positive behavioral supports: Implementation and evaluation of a school-wide behavioral intervention*. Paper presented at the annual convention of the American Psychological Association, Washington, DC.

Weiner, B. (1974). *Achievement motivation and attribution theory*. Morristown, NJ: General Learning Press.

Wright, J. A., & Dusek, J. B. (1998). Research into practice: Compiling school base rates for disruptive behaviors form student disciplinary referral data. *School Psychology Review, 27*, 138–147.

Ysseldyke, J. E., & Algozzine, B. (2006). *A practical approach to special education for every teacher*. Thousand Oaks, CA: Corwin.

Ysseldyke, J. E., Algozzine, B., & Thurlow, M. L. (2000). *Critical issues in special education* (3rd ed.). Boston: Houghton-Mifflin.

# 23

# Using a Problem-Solving Model to Enhance Data-Based Decision Making in Schools

**STEPHEN J. NEWTON, ROBERT H. HORNER, ROBERT F. ALGOZZINE, ANNE W. TODD, and KATE M. ALGOZZINE**

Making decisions is a core activity in schools. Every school has faculty teams that meet regularly to make decisions concerning logistical, administrative, academic, and social issues. The thesis of this chapter is that team decisions will be more effective and efficient when they occur in the context of a formal problem-solving model with access to the right data, in the right format, at the right time.

We focus in this chapter on problem solving and data-based decision making related to behavior support in schools because that is where our experience has greatest depth. The principles and practices regarding problem solving and data-based decision making about behavior support, however, also extend to academic achievement and other areas of support. Themes emphasized throughout this chapter are that data-based decision making (a) occurs in the context of team meetings with a "structure" that sets the occasion for effectiveness; (b) is embedded in a formal problem-solving model with processes that ensure a meeting is logical, thorough, and efficient; and (c) is continuously informed by accurate and timely data.

**J. STEPHEN NEWTON** • University of Oregon
**ROBERT H. HORNER** • University of Oregon
**ROBERT F. ALGOZZINE** • University of North Carolina at Charlotte
**ANNE W. TOOD** • University of Oregon
**KATE M. ALGOZZINE** • University of North Carolina at Charlotte

Application of a problem-solving model can be particularly useful in schools implementing schoolwide positive behavior support (SW-PBS; e.g., Lewis & Sugai, 1999; Sugai & Horner, 2006). SW-PBS is a systems-level approach to establishing the social culture and behavior supports needed for improving the social behavior and academic achievement of students. SW-PBS is based on the three-tier prevention model that Walker and his colleagues (Walker et al., 1996; Walker & Shinn, 2002) adapted from community mental health (Larson, 1994; National Research Council & Institute of Medicine, 1999; Shonkoff & Phillips, 2000), emphasizing prevention of violent, disruptive, and other problem behavior as the most pragmatic and effective approach for improving school social culture.

SW-PBS involves three levels of prevention and intervention. *Primary* prevention and intervention is schoolwide and classroomwide in that it targets all children in all contexts, involves all adults, applies to all settings, and covers all times of the school day. Primary prevention emphasizes defining, teaching, and acknowledging appropriate behavior before students develop problem behaviors (Evertson & Emmer, 1982; R. G. Mayer, 1995; G. R. Mayer & Butterworth, 1979; Nelson, Martella, & Galand, 1998; Sprick, Sprick, & Garrison, 1992; Weissberg, Caplan, & Sivo, 1989). *Secondary* prevention and intervention focuses on specific groups of students who are at risk for social problem behavior and who may be responsive to group interventions rather than requiring individualized, intensive interventions (e.g., Crone, Horner, & Hawken, 2004; Davies & McLaughlin, 1989; Hawken & Horner, 2003; Lewis, Colvin, & Sugai, 2000; Nelson & Carr, 2000). *Tertiary* prevention and intervention is reserved for the 5–7% of students whose problem behaviors have not been responsive to primary- and secondary-level prevention and intervention and thus require functional behavioral assessment and individualized interventions (e.g., Carr et al., 1999; Crone & Horner, 2003; Martella, Nelson, & Marchand-Martella, 2003; O'Neill et al., 1997; Repp & Horner, 1999).

Within SW-PBS, a positive behavior support team is charged with holding regularly scheduled meetings at which team members make decisions about primary, secondary, and tertiary behavior supports. A major feature of the team process within SW-PBS is the collection and use of data to aid in decision making. Recognition that important decisions should be guided by a review of pertinent data helps explain the widespread use of the term *data-based decision making* (e.g., Hyatt & Howell, 2004; Poynton & Carey, 2006; Scott & Martinek, 2006) and its near-incantatory status in school reform efforts.

## DATA-BASED DECISION MAKING AND PBS TEAMS

The data-based decision making of PBS team members is referenced to core outcomes targeted by a school. Team members use data to guide their decisions about how to improve student performance in accordance with the targeted outcomes. Team members operate with maximal effectiveness when (a) core outcomes of the school are defined, (b) measures used to monitor the outcomes are formulated, and (c) standards for the identified measures are established and applied.

## Core Outcomes Defined

All schools are clear about the importance of student academic performance as a core outcome. Increasingly, schools are also recognizing student social competence as a basic outcome (Walker, Ramsey, & Gresham, 2004). If school faculty has defined social and academic competence as core outcomes, they will want access to data concerning social and academic outcomes to review on a regular basis (e.g., monthly, quarterly). These data will be particularly important for that subset of faculty members who serve as members of the PBS team and have the task of continually assessing and improving behavior support in the school.

## Measures for Outcomes Formulated

A major challenge for schools is the formulation of useful measures of targeted outcomes. Although school personnel may have little difficulty accessing academic and social data, these data may be in a format, or at a level of detail, that is not sufficiently helpful for identifying problems and making decisions. Measures at the level of whole-school outcomes can be particularly useful to PBS team members during an initial identification of discrepancies between actual and expected outcome levels. (Teachers will be examining measures of student outcomes on a daily or weekly basis to aid in decision making regarding their individual students, but the responsibility of PBS team members to make decisions about whole-school interventions requires that they begin by reviewing measures of whole-school outcomes.) For example, the identification of whole-school problems is aided by such measures as the percentage of students who are achieving reading level expectations or the average number of office discipline referrals per school day per month.

## Standards for Measures Established and Applied

The PBS team members operate most effectively if standards (criterion levels) for outcome measures are established either (a) formally and in advance or (b) informally and in the context of PBS team meetings. When standards for outcomes exist, team members will find it easy to identify a discrepancy between the current level and the expected/desired level (i.e., the standard) for an outcome. Such discrepancies constitute "problems" (e.g., Bransford & Stein, 1984), and team members will engage in decision making to determine whether the magnitude of the discrepancy is such that a solution is needed for addressing the discrepancy and, if so, which solution is likely to reduce or eliminate the discrepancy. For example, at the level of the individual student, we expect a problem to be defined and action to be prompted if any child is identified as falling below the established standards for academic or social performance. For example, we want all third graders to be reading at benchmark levels, and we want all children behaving appropriately.

At a broader level, an important issue is how to establish standards regarding whole-school outcome measures and how to interpret related whole-school data. For example, when considering office discipline referrals

(ODRs), faculty and PBS team members are encouraged to establish standards for outcome measures by reviewing (a) the level, trend, and variability of the school's referrals during the previous school year; (b) the level, trend, and variability of referrals of other schools of similar size and grade level (e.g., a national average); and (c) the social expectations of the school's community members, faculty, and students. Establishing and monitoring standards for social behavior require that the team has access to, at a minimum, data concerning ODR rates per school day per month over the course of a school year. When a PBS team reviews whole-school data and finds that a great number of students are failing to meet an established social behavior standard, this will serve as a prompt for the team to develop a structural (e.g., whole-school) intervention designed to solve the problem.

A set of core outcomes, measures, and standards establish an important backdrop for a PBS team meeting. However, even the combination of this background information with access to and review of related, pertinent data constitute necessary but insufficient conditions for engaging in the kind of decision making that ultimately results in students achieving targeted outcomes. To achieve such outcomes, data-based decision making should be embedded in a broader problem-solving model that has a defined structure, processes, and accomplishments (Gilbert, 1978). A brief overview of the elements of such a problem-solving model is provided here and is followed by an extended discussion—with examples—of how the model can be applied by PBS teams to address students' social behavior problems at the primary and secondary levels of prevention and intervention. We have chosen to focus on these levels for two reasons. First, the problem-solving processes associated with tertiary-level (individual-student) interventions (e.g., conducting a functional assessment or functional analysis, developing and implementing a behavior support plan, etc.) are well known and well documented (e.g., Crone & Horner, 2003; O'Neill et al., 1997); however, this is not the case for primary- and secondary-level prevention and interventions. Second, PBS teams often "hand off" the responsibility for tertiary-level problem solving to some other school team or to an individual (e.g., a school psychologist) but typically retain the responsibility for problem solving at the primary and secondary levels. We recognize, however, that whether to pass the responsibility of coordinating a student's support to another team is itself a decision that should be guided by data.

## OVERVIEW OF A PROBLEM-SOLVING MODEL FOR PBS TEAMS

The "structure" of a problem-solving model for PBS team meetings refers to the environmental supports (e.g., an agenda, data summaries, roles assumed by team members, action plan, or minutes from previous meetings) that aid a team as it engages in its problem-solving processes, including the process of making data-based decisions. Because the world has long been rife with meetings devoted to solving problems, it is not surprising that the structural components of a successful meeting have become largely generic. Regardless of whether a meeting concerns a business, industry, school, or social service, there are components that set the occasion for a successful meeting (e.g., Gilbert, 1978; Jorgensen, Scheier, & Fautsko, 1981; Tropman, 1996).

The "processes" of a problem-solving model for a PBS team meeting refer to the actual behaviors of team members as they act in concert to solve students' social and academic problems. Just as the structural components of a successful meeting have become generic, so have the processes identified in most problem-solving models. For example, Bransford and Stein (1984) provided an approach to problem solving that integrates research findings into a simple, easy-to-understand framework that they refer to as the "IDEAL" model. Each letter in the IDEAL acronym represents an important process (behavior) in a general approach to problem solving:

- I: Identify the problem (look for a difference between the present situation and the desired situation).
- D: Define the problem (be as precise as possible about the nature of the problem).
- E: Explore possible strategies for solving the problem (systematically analyze the problem to generate possible solutions; select an appropriate solution strategy).
- A: Act on the strategies (implement the selected solution strategy).
- L: Look back and evaluate the effects of your activities (determine whether the implemented strategy helped solve the problem).

Deno (1989, 2005) translated the IDEAL model into problem-solving processes specifically designed for school-based problem solvers:

- Problem identification: Measure student performance; decide whether a problem exists.
- Problem definition: Measure degree of discrepancy between desired student performance and actual student performance; decide whether problem is important enough to address.
- Design intervention plan: Generate alternative hypotheses and solutions regarding the problem; decide which hypothesis/solution appears to be best.
- Implement intervention: Initiate selected solution, measure fidelity of implementation, collect student performance data; decide whether solution is being implemented as intended and is beginning to reduce discrepancy.
- Problem solution: Use collected data to continue measuring possible discrepancy; decide whether the solution has solved the problem.

Note that the problem-solving processes are tied to measurement procedures and decision making, highlighting the pervasive role of data-based decision making within the problem-solving model. Deno advocated use of this model within curriculum-based measurement (CBM), an exemplar of a data-based approach to problem solving that is focused on the academic behavior of students (e.g., Alonzo, Ketterlin-Geller, & Tindal, 2007; Deno, 1985, 2005; Shinn, 1989).

When PBS team members engage in these problem-solving processes within a structured context, the meeting should produce valuable results. In Tom and Marilyn Gilbert's (1978, 1992) influential approach to performance engineering (which informs much of this chapter), they referred to such valuable results as "accomplishments." The Gilberts used the memorable, pithy phrase, "Behavior you take with you; accomplishments you leave behind" (Gilbert & Gilbert, 1992, p. 46) to describe the difference between behavior and accomplishment, emphasizing that accomplishments are the *products* of behavior. Because PBS team members are "knowledge workers" (Drucker, 1967), their accomplishments typically take the form of written products, such as action plans. A problem-solving model for PBS teams should include a clear definition of the team's expected accomplishments as well as feedback on the extent to which the team is achieving them. The remainder of this chapter provides details and examples of how a PBS team can develop and implement a problem-solving model that enhances data-based decisions concerning how best to solve social-behavior problems experienced by students. The model is generic and thus could be applied across an array of contexts and problems.

## THE STRUCTURE OF A PBS TEAM MEETING

Environmental supports provide the structure for a PBS team meeting and set the occasion for a successful meeting in which team members perform at a high level of competence. Gilbert (1978) persuasively argued that competence can be improved by (a) altering the person's repertoire of behavior through the provision of training, (b) changing the person's supporting environment, or (c) both. Gilbert's troubleshooting logic advises that changing the supporting environment is the logical beginning point because it demonstrates the most efficiency—in terms of both time and money—for engineering competent performance. The following environmental supports can set the occasion for a successful PBS team meeting:

- *Regular Meetings:* PBS teams should meet on a regular basis, preferably at least monthly, with the date, time, location, and duration of the meeting specified in advance. Meetings should begin and end at the specified time unless otherwise agreed to by team members.
- *The Right People:* The team should reflect a desirable range of representation. Team members should have the right "mix" of skills, decision-making authority, and school roles. The team should be stable, with individuals serving as team members for an agreed-on "term" (e.g., a school year).
- *Roles of Team Members:* Team members should establish a set of team roles (e.g., facilitator, minute taker, lead data analyst). Team members may fill these roles on a permanent or rotating basis.
- *Specification of Meeting Accomplishments:* The team should agree to a definition of a "successful" meeting. At a minimum, this will involve specifying the accomplishments of a team meeting, such as agreeing on the products of a meeting (e.g., team meeting minutes, an action plan) and the standards by which the products will be internally evaluated.
- *Advanced Preparation for Meeting:* To avoid scrambling at the last minute, several issues should be handled in advance of each meeting,

for example, (a) meeting room reserved; (b) agenda items solicited from team members; (c) agenda produced and distributed; (d) team member who will assume each role determined; (e) preliminary set of pertinent data summaries prepared and ready for discussion at meeting; (f) data summaries reviewed by at least one team member who is prepared to lead team through initial discussion (e.g., a lead data analyst); (g) laptop computer with access to online social behavior database reserved; (h) LCD projector reserved and set up to project data summaries (or data summaries distributed at, or prior to, meeting)

- *Team Member Notebooks:* Each PBS team member should have a notebook that he or she brings to each meeting. The notebook will contain dividers for pertinent current and historical documents, such as blank forms, completed meeting minutes and action plans, expected team accomplishments, data summaries.
- *Evaluation of Meeting:* During or at the close of a meeting, team members may choose to evaluate aspects of their efforts. Such an evaluation might include team members' impressions concerning the extent to which (a) meeting accomplishments were achieved, (b) decisions reached at previous meetings were implemented as intended, and (c) faithfully implemented decisions were followed by intended effects on student social behavior.

## THE PROCESSES OF A PBS TEAM MEETING

When the environmental supports for a PBS team meeting are in place, the team can engage in the problem-solving processes more efficiently and effectively. The problem-solving models of Bransford and Stein (1984) and Deno (1989, 2005) provide excellent starting points for creating a problem-solving model consisting of processes appropriate for a PBS team meeting. The model's broad processes involve (a) identifying problems, (b) developing and refining hypotheses, (c) discussing and selecting solutions, (d) developing and implementing action plans, and (e) evaluating and revising action plans. Figure 23.1 provides an overview of these processes and demonstrates that each process is dependent on the collection and use of pertinent data.

### Identify Problems

Identifying social behavior problems is the crucial first process in a problem-solving model for PBS teams. Problems that are identified early may be easier to address. As noted, a *problem* is simply a discrepancy between an actual condition and an expected or desired condition (e.g., Bransford & Stein, 1984), and *problem solving* refers to engaging in a series of actions designed to eliminate the discrepancy. If school personnel have defined a set of core outcomes, measures, and standards and have ready access to associated data, the ability of PBS team members to identify problems will be greatly enhanced.

Data accessed via the School-wide Information System (SWIS) (Irvin et al., 2006; Irvin, Tobin, Sprague, Sugai, & Vincent, 2004; May et al., 2003)

**Fig. 23.1.** Problem-solving model.

can be particularly helpful in identifying problems. SWIS is a three-part decision system that provides (a) an approach for defining and collecting information about ODRs; (b) a Web-based computer application for entering, organizing, managing, and producing reports on student ODRs; and (c) a formal process for using those data for decision making (May et al., 2003).

The SWIS report most commonly used for identifying whole-school problems is a report of ODRs per school day per month. For example, consider the Fig. 23.2 bar graph for the hypothetical Rose Elementary School. As the Rose Elementary PBS team members prepare for the start of a new school year, they examine data from the previous two school years to determine if a problem exists within their schoolwide behavior support systems. In reviewing these data—as well as anecdotal reports from teachers, families, and students—PBS team members compare the school's rate of ODRs against several data sources: (a) the level, trend, and variability of ODR rates from the school's previous year; (b) the level, trend, and variability of ODR rates across corresponding months of the previous two school years; and (c) the ODR rate of the school with the national average for ODR rates at elementary schools of comparative enrollment size. In using this problem identification process, team members note the following:

- For every month during the last school year (2004–2005), the rate of ODRs per school day exceeded the national average of other elementary schools of comparative enrollment size (1.70 ODRs per school day per month).
- The data show a minimal trend across months, but there are noticeable increases in the ODR level in December and March.
- For each month of the last school year (2004–2005), the level of ODRs per school day exceeded the level from the corresponding month during the prior school year (2003–2004)

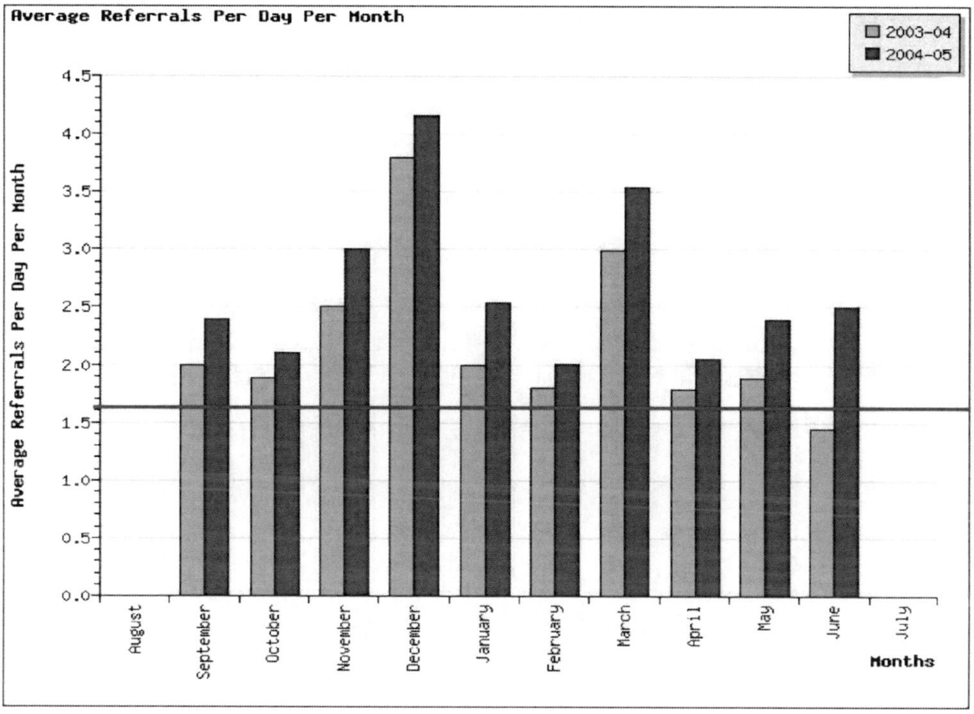


**Fig. 23.2.** Rose Elementary School average office discipline referrals (ODRs) per school day per month across successive school years, with national average.

- Teachers, families, and students themselves have reported in letters, faculty meetings, and meetings with administrators that student problem behavior is unacceptable and presents a barrier to effective instruction.

Taken together, these data are sufficient for members of the Rose Elementary PBS team to identify a problem regarding the school's approach to schoolwide behavior support. (Even if the Rose Elementary faculty has not formally established a whole-school outcome standard for student social behavior, the fact that PBS team members have access to data that can be used as informal, ad-hoc "standards" makes the process of identifying problems much less ambiguous for team members.)

Now consider the problem identification process for the hypothetical Clifford Sweet Middle School. The Clifford Sweet PBS team held one of its regular meetings in March to assess the month-to-month status of the schoolwide behavior support systems. In examining the data in the Fig. 23.3 bar graph, they noted the following:

- For every month of this school year (2004–2005), the rate of ODRs per school day exceeded the national average of other middle schools of comparative enrollment size (7.8 per school day per month).
- The level of ODRs per school day per month for this school year shows an increasing trend.

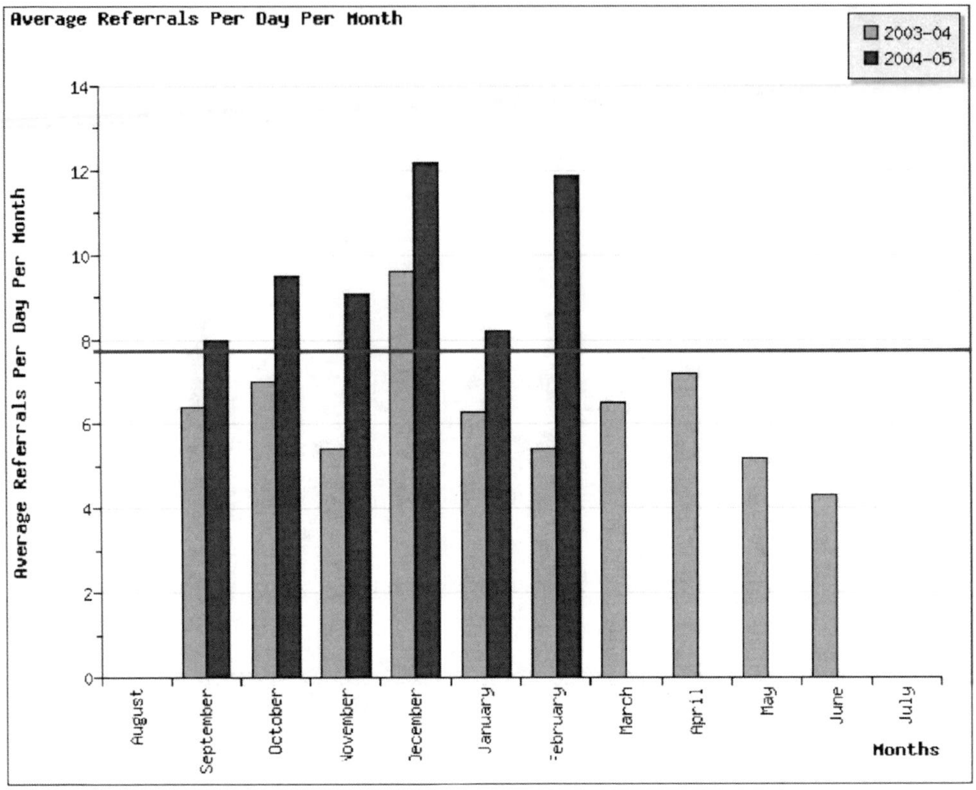


**Fig. 23.3.** Clifford Sweet Middle School average office discipline referrals (ODRs) per school day per month across successive school years, with national average.

- For each month of this school year (2004–2005), the level of ODRs per school day exceeds the level from the corresponding month of the previous school year (2003–2004).
- When asked, teachers indicated that they view problem behavior in Clifford Sweet as a major problem.

Taken together, these data are sufficient for the Clifford Sweet PBS team to identify a problem regarding the school's approach to schoolwide behavior support.

### *Defining and Clarifying Problems With Precision*

Using data to identify a problem is the first process in the problem-solving model. But, additional data are usually required to better understand the precise nature of the problem. For example, although team members' review of the ODRs per school day per month data at both Rose Elementary School and Clifford Sweet Middle School led to identification of problems, team members will require additional data to generate potential solutions that "fit" the precise nature of the problems. Specifically, team members must both define and clarify an identified problem with precision.

In general, *defining* a problem with precision involves obtaining an answer to a "what question"—namely, precisely *what* specific problem behaviors were involved in the ODRs? *Clarifying* the problem with precision requires obtaining answers to "who," "when," and "where" questions.

- Who are the students that produced ODRs (and how many did they produce)?
- When during the school day were the ODRs most often produced?
- Where were the ODRs most often produced?

The more precisely the identified problem is defined and clarified, the more likely it is that the team can develop an effective solution. Defining and clarifying the problem involves "drilling down" into additional, related data summaries that allow the team to move from general to specific information. This kind of troubleshooting algorithm (Gilbert, 1978) ensures that team members use their time efficiently—they review additional, fine-grained data only if and when a higher-level problem has been identified.

To extend our previous examples, consider the define-and-clarify process used by the PBS team at Rose Elementary School. After having identified that the number of ODRs per school day per month constitutes a problem, team members produced additional data reports from their computerized database management system (Figs. 23.4 through 23.7). By referring to these data, team members were able to define and clarify the nature of the identified problem:

- Forty-eight percent of the ODRs involved disruption and aggression/fighting (what) (Fig. 23.4).
- A large proportion of students produced ODRs (more than 55% of the enrolled students had at least one ODR) (Who) (Fig. 23.5).
- Seventy-one percent of the ODRs were produced between 9:45 and 10:00 a.m., 11:45 and 12:00p.m., and 2:00 and 2:15 p.m. (when) (Fig. 23.6),
- Thirty-four percent of the ODRs occurred on the playground (where) (Fig. 23.7).

These additional data led the team to an understanding that many students in the school were engaging in disruptive and aggressive behaviors on the playground during the recess time periods.

Consider now the experience of the Clifford Sweet Middle School PBS team. They too had decided that the number of ODRs per school day per month constituted a problem. They then decided to review additional related data (Figs. 23.8 through 23.11) that would allow them to define and clarify the identified problem. In doing so, they found that

- Of the ODRs, 301 (34%) involved disrespect (what) (Fig. 23.8).
- Twenty students contributed 10 or more ODRs (who) (Fig. 23.9).
- Of the ODRs, 25% were produced during three time periods (9:00–9:15 a.m., 11:00–11:15 a.m., and 2:00–2:15 p.m.) (when) (Fig. 23.10).
- A large proportion of the ODRs occurred in the classroom (where) (Fig. 23.11).

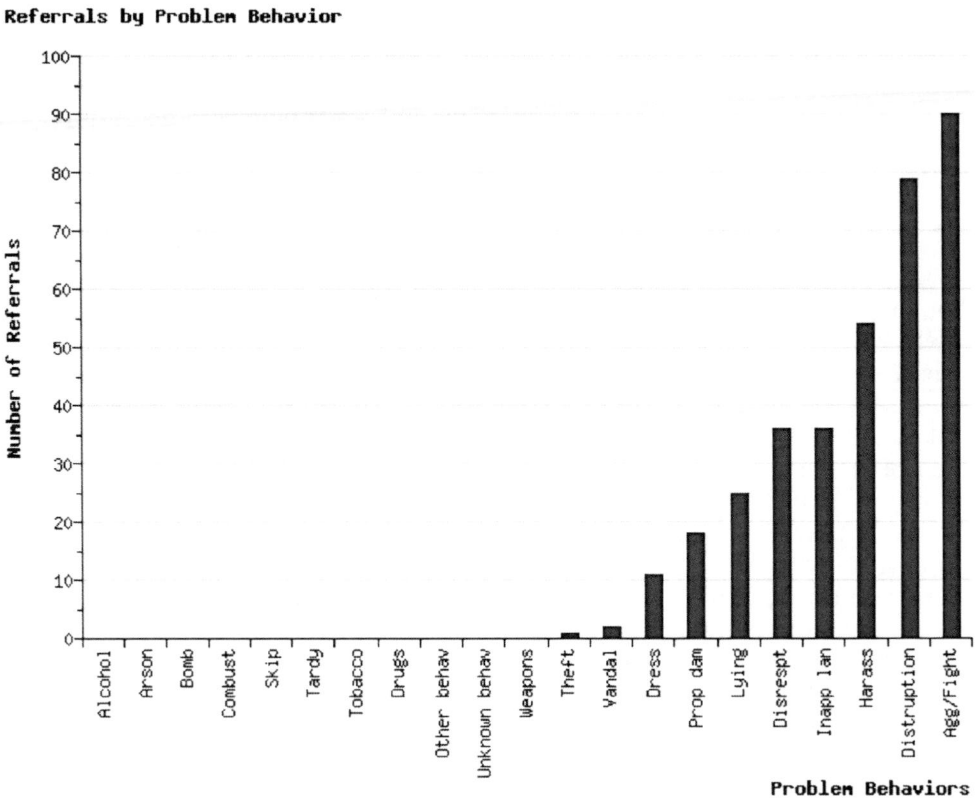


**Fig. 23.4.** Rose Elementary School office discipline referrals (ODRs) by type of problem behavior.

If the initial processes of identifying, defining, and clarifying a problem sound familiar to readers, it is no coincidence. Problem solving at the primary and secondary levels of prevention and intervention begins with what might be called functional assessment "writ large." While functional assessment and support plan development at the tertiary level of intervention are focused on a specific student, the problem-solving processes at the primary and secondary levels of prevention and intervention are focused on one or more *groups* of students (including the schoolwide group). Further parallels between approaches to solving individual-level and group-level social behavior problems will be apparent as we move through the additional processes of the problem-solving model.

## Develop and Refine Hypotheses

Although the problem-solving model (Fig. 23.1) indicates that identifying a problem is followed by developing and refining a hypothesis about the problem, PBS team members are, in practice, likely to begin developing and refining hypotheses from the moment they begin reviewing pertinent data. Gaining answers to the what, who, when, and where questions explored

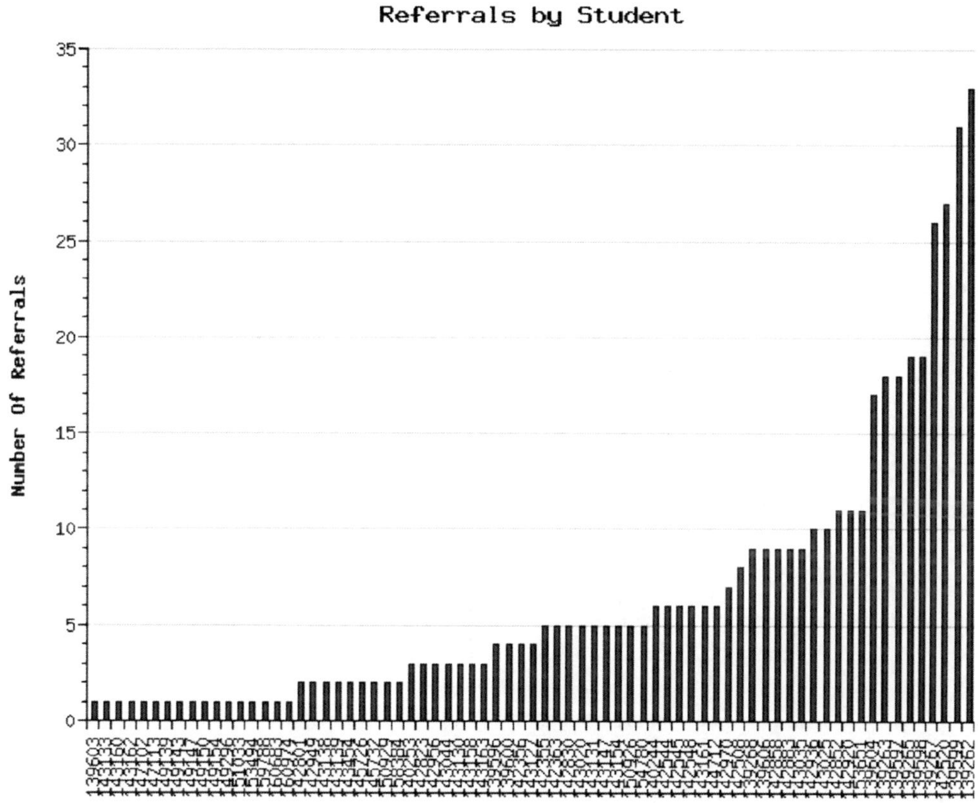


**Fig. 23.5.** Rose Elementary School office discipline referrals (ODRs) by student.

during the problem definition and clarification process will almost immediately guide PBS team members to begin asking why questions, such as

- Why do these particular types of problem behavior account for a large majority of ODRs?
- Why does this particular group of students account for a large majority of this particular type of problem behavior (and ODRs in general)?
- Why is this type of problem behavior (and ODRs in general) happening most often at this time of the school day?
- Why is this type of problem behavior (and ODRs in general) happening most often during these particular months of the school year?
- Why is this type of problem behavior (and ODRs in general) happening most often in this school location?

Thanks to the data analyzed during the problem clarification process, the collective knowledge and experience of the PBS team members, and their answers to the why questions, team members will often find it possible to write one or more hypothesis statements concerning the problem without obtaining any further data. Creating a hypothesis statement in writing is useful because it increases consistency among staff who must eventually

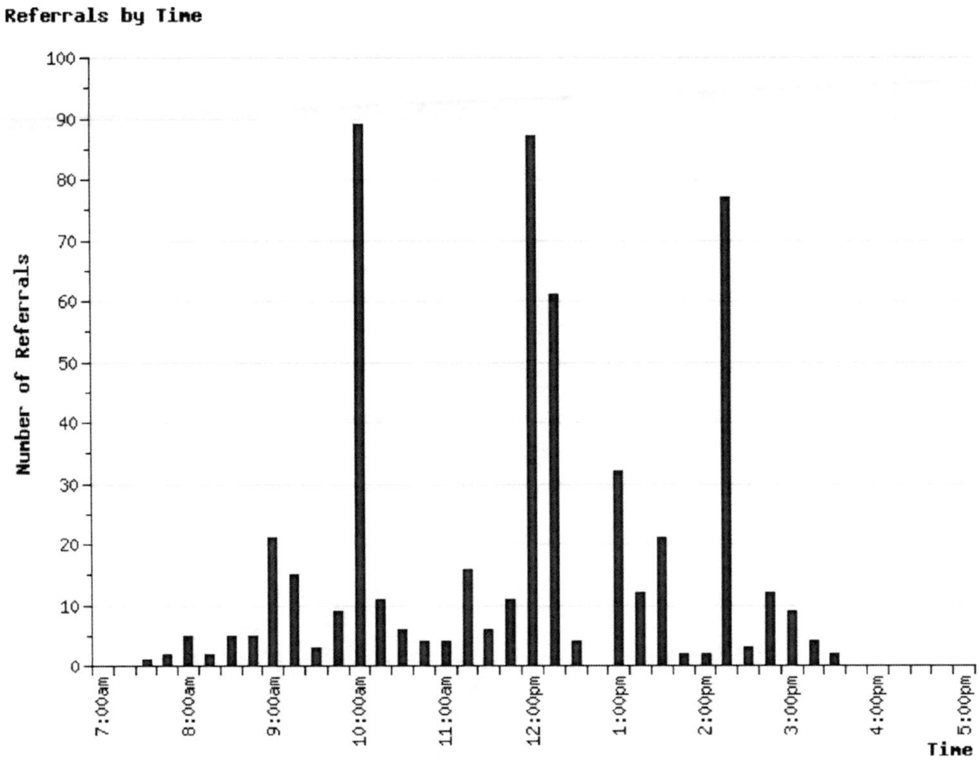


**Fig. 23.6.** Rose Elementary School office discipline referrals (ODRs) by time of day.

implement an intervention, and it provides the team with a "logic trail." For example, if a solution/intervention based on a hypothesis is ineffective, it may indicate that the hypothesis, and the logic surrounding it, is faulty. When team members are dealing with many problems, many hypotheses, and many potential solutions, it will to help to have a written record of the assumptions they have made, assumptions that are, after all, guiding their intervention efforts. This way, when a "solution" fails to produce desired results, team members can easily revisit the possibly faulty hypothesis statement and ask themselves which alternative hypothesis might better account for the continuing problem social behavior and which solution would best fit the revised hypothesis.

To continue with our example, the members of the Rose Elementary School PBS team needed a hypothesis that could explain the disruption and aggression/fighting that was occurring during recess on the playground. Prior to the problem definition and clarification process, team members had developed an initial hypothesis that "students were simply more likely to engage in problem behavior in less-structured contexts." But this hypothesis was neither adequately comprehensive nor supported by the data. There were, for example, a number of unstructured settings in which children were well behaved, and this hypothesis does not indicate which problem behaviors are emitted by whom and why problem behaviors

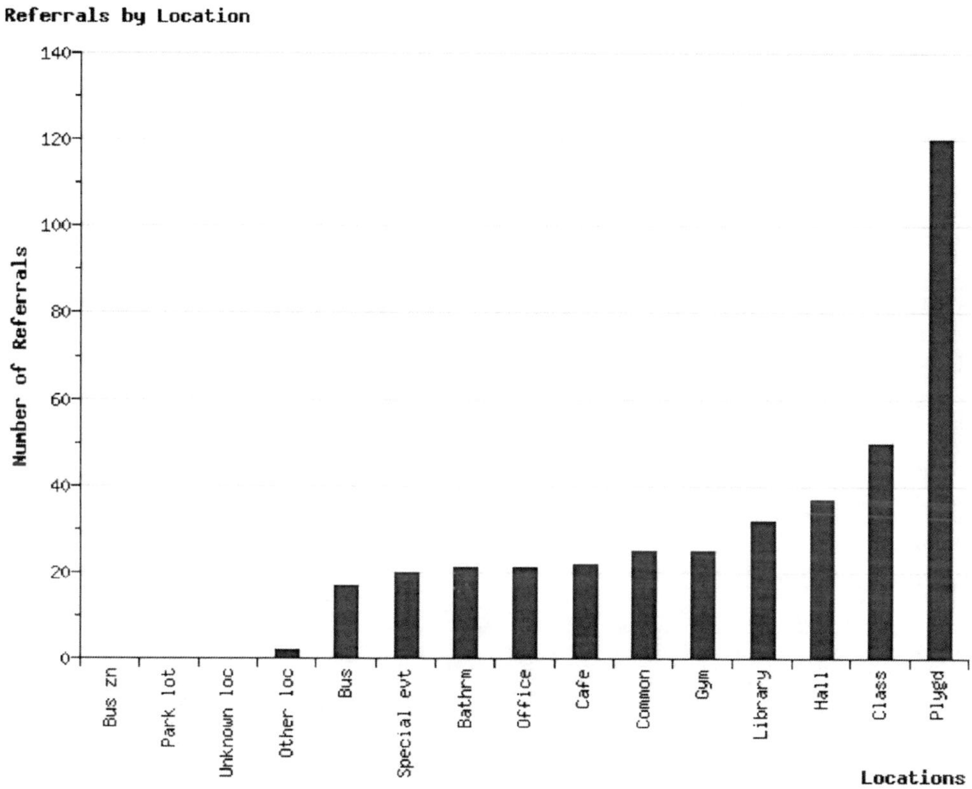


**Fig. 23.7.** Rose Elementary School office discipline referrals (ODRs) by location.

are being maintained (what reward is present). To refine the hypothesis, the team noted the following:

- Students had been taught behavioral expectations.
- None of the expectations were playground specific.
- Staff who supervised the playground during recess had not participated in the planning, teaching, or evaluation of the schoolwide behavioral expectations.

This led the team to write the following hypothesis statement:

A large proportion of students (no distinguishable individuals or groups) are engaging in disruption and aggression/fighting on the playground during recess because (a) we have not developed playground-specific expectations and taught them to students; (b) playground supervisors have not been included as participants in the planning, teaching, and evaluation of the school's behavioral expectations; and (c) disruption, aggression, and fighting is resulting in access to peer attention and ACCESS TO preferred recreation equipment.

The members of the Clifford Sweet Middle School PBS team followed a similar process to arrive at their final hypothesis. They needed a hypothesis that could explain why students were engaging in disruption and

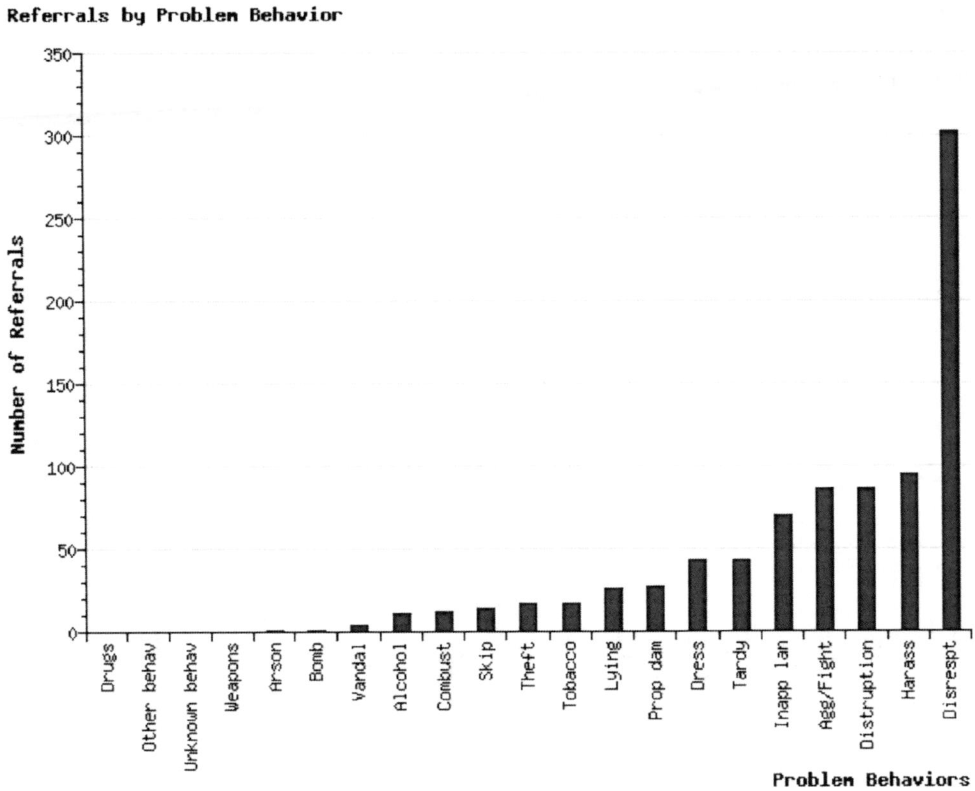


**Fig. 23.8.** Clifford Sweet Middle School office discipline referrals (ODRs) by type of problem behavior.

noncompliant behavior at very specific times of the school day. At first, they hypothesized that only a small number of students or a small number of teachers were contributing to the high level of these ODRs, but during the problem definition and clarification process they discovered that many students and many teachers were involved. Thanks to both the data obtained when "drilling down" into the problem and the combined knowledge and experience of the PBS team members, they discovered that

- ODRs were occurring during the last 15 min of the 90-min classroom block periods.
- During this 15-min period, students are often assigned independent seat work after having spent a long period of time in direct instruction.

This led team members to write the following hypothesis statement:

> A large proportion of students (no defined individuals or groups) are engaging in disruption and noncompliance during the last 15 min of 90-min classroom block periods because (a) the time involved follows a long instructional period without social contact; (b) they are often assigned independent seat work, which is often a low-preference activity; and (c) disruptive behavior is associated with peer attention or escape from the assigned task.

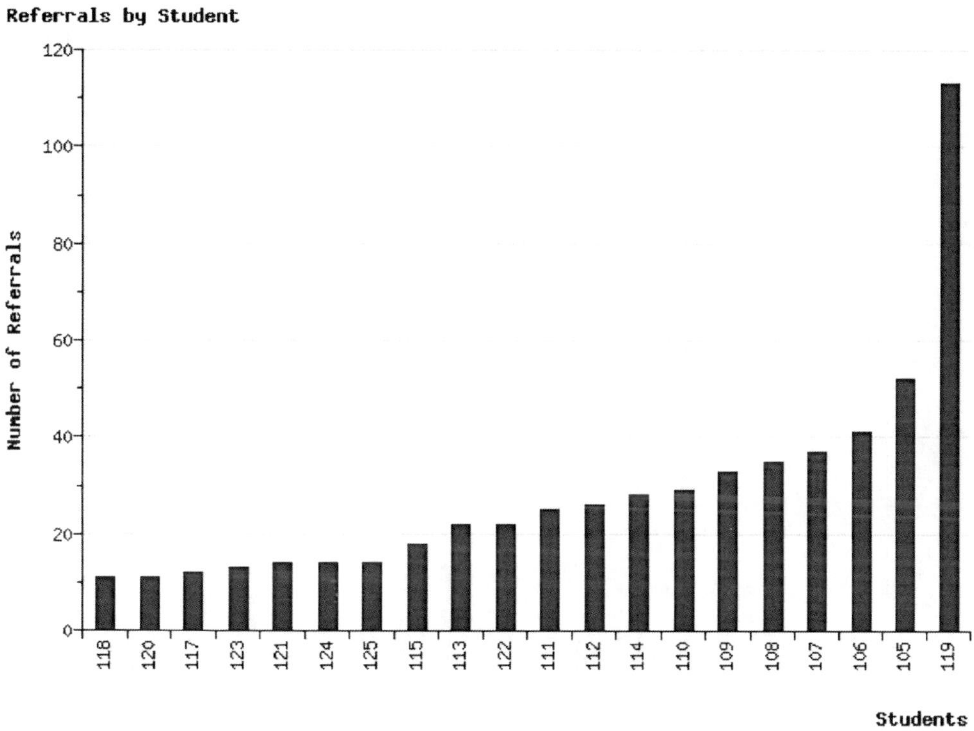


**Fig. 23.9.** Clifford Sweet Middle School students with 10 or more office discipline referrals (ODRs) (through February).

## *Inability to Generate a Hypothesis*

In some cases, team members may find either that they are unable to answer the why questions with sufficient precision to write a hypothesis statement, or that they lack confidence in, or consensus on, a tentative hypothesis statement they *have* written. When this is the case, team members may decide to gather additional data before generating possible solutions to the problem. These additional data may lie outside any existing data collection and summarization system (otherwise, the team could, under ideal circumstances, simply use a computer to access the online database and produce the desired data during the course of the meeting). If so, the team will create a plan for collection of these ad hoc data and for making sure that the data are available for review at a subsequent meeting.

The purpose of gathering these additional data is, of course, to enable the team to (a) write an initial hypothesis statement, (b) obtain confirming evidence for a written hypothesis statement that the team regards as merely tentative, or (c) obtain disconfirming evidence for a tentative hypothesis statement. In any event, until these additional data are reviewed by team members, the team will not be in a position to continue with the remaining processes of the problem-solving model for this *particular* identified problem. Rather, the team will simply return to the first process in the

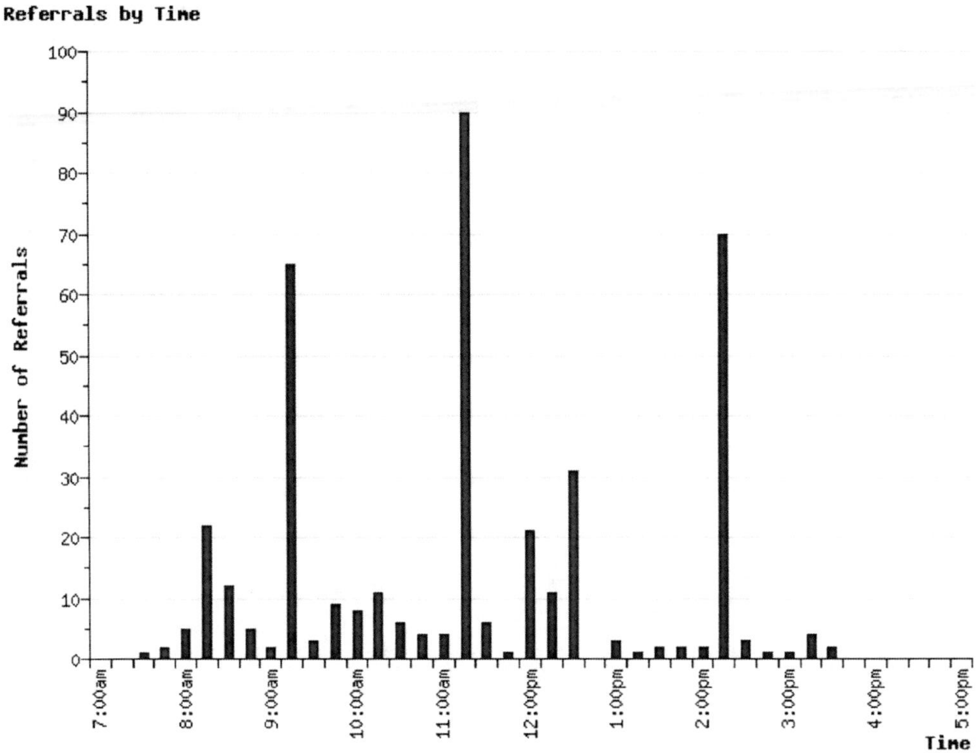


**Fig. 23.10.** Clifford Sweet Middle School office discipline referrals (ODRs) by time of day.

problem-solving model and begin reviewing additional, currently available data to identify any additional problems.

## Discuss and Select Solutions

If team members have written a hypothesis statement in which they have confidence, they are in a position to use the hypothesis statement to guide the development of possible solutions to the problem. Effective solutions typically combine team members' knowledge about the local context, the specific problem, and behavioral theory. With information about the what, who, when, and where of problem behaviors—and a hypothesis about why the problem behaviors are occurring—a team can make use of the following five broad solution strategies to generate, discuss, and select possible solutions that "fit" their hypothesis statement:

1. Prevent problem behavior situations: In many cases, the situation that sets the occasion for problem behavior can be prevented or avoided. For example, simply ensuring appropriate supervision on the playground reduces a key contextual variable that may lead to problem behavior.
2. Define and teach appropriate behavior: Ensure that appropriate behavior has been defined, taught, and rewarded before relying on negative consequences.

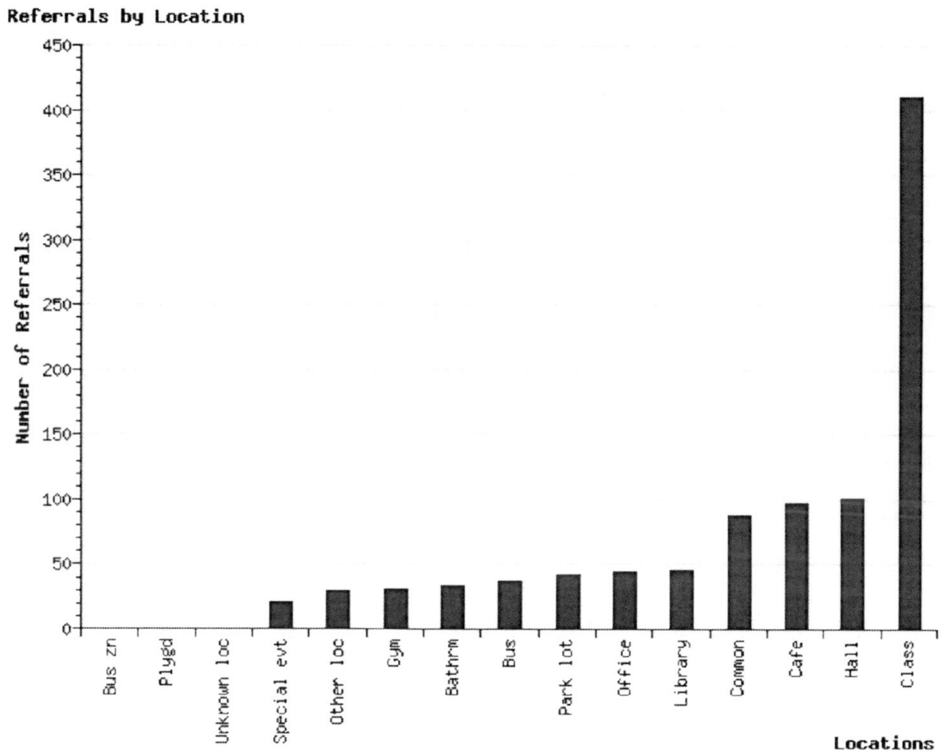


**Fig. 23.11.** Clifford Sweet Middle School office discipline referrals (ODRs) by location.

3. Reward appropriate behavior: School personnel must ensure that the recognition and rewards that students may be inadvertently receiving for inappropriate behavior are instead delivered contingent on appropriate behavior.
4. Reduce rewards for problem behavior: Problem behaviors will not continue to occur unless they result in obtaining positive outcomes or avoiding negative outcomes. Examine the natural context and determine how inadvertent rewarding of problem behaviors can be eliminated or minimized.
5. Deliver corrective consequences for problem behavior: A continuum of clear, consistent consequences for problem behavior should be specified and in effect.

The Rose Elementary PBS team members used their what, who, when, where, and why information to generate, discuss, and ultimately select specific solutions (interventions) derived from the five broad solution strategies (see Table 23.1). At Clifford Sweet (see Table 23.2), the staff employed the same broad solution strategies, but their specific solutions (interventions) were different. The Clifford Sweet team considered an array of options but made a careful effort to focus on the smallest changes that were likely to have the largest impact on the targeted student problem. In this case, the team's examination of their data, hypothesis, and existing behavior support efforts resulted in a set of relatively simple solutions.

**Table 23.1.** Rose Elementary School Playground Solutions (Interventions)

| Broad Solution Strategy | Specific Solution Selected by Team |
|---|---|
| Prevent problem behavior situations | Ensure supervisors are on playground and are engaged in active supervision (Lewis, Colvin, & Sugai, 2000) |
| Define and teach appropriate behavior | Teach schoolwide behavior expectations of being safe, respectful, and responsible; do teaching with students on playground where problem behaviors are most likely |
| Reward appropriate behavior | Create formal system for playground supervisors to recognize appropriate play on playground; teach to supervisors |
| Reduce rewards for problem behavior | Teach students to signal "stop" when they are treated disrespectfully; teach playground supervisors to ensure that aggression and disruption are not allowed to gain access to preferred activities or materials |
| Deliver corrective consequences for problem behavior | Review continuum of corrective consequences for problem behavior on playground with students and supervisors; make sure continuum is in effect |

**Table 23.2.** Clifford Sweet Middle School Disruption Solutions (Interventions)

| Broad Solution Strategy | Specific Solution Selected by Team |
|---|---|
| Prevent problem behavior situations | Eliminate tradition of using last 15 min of class for independent seat work; instead deliver independent seat work in *middle* of the block period; ensure that active instruction occurs during last 20 min of the period |
| Define and teach appropriate behavior | Already done |
| Reward appropriate behavior | Already in place |
| Reduce rewards for problem behavior | (Removing peer attention in this context is difficult; teachers must redirect attention quickly.) |
| Deliver corrective consequences for problem behavior | Continuum of corrective consequences already defined and in use |

As the preceding examples demonstrate, specific solutions to a problem can be based on data and a team's detailed knowledge of the school environment. However, when discussing and selecting solutions from a range of possible options that might fit the hypothesis, the team must also consider the extent to which a given solution exhibits, or can be modified to exhibit, "contextual fit" (Albin, Lucyshyn, Horner, & Flannery, 1996; Bailey et al., 1990; Benazzi, Horner, & Good, 2006). Contextual fit refers to the relationship between an intervention and the people who will be asked to implement it as well as the setting in which it will be implemented. The likelihood that relevant personnel (e.g., teachers) will implement a solution with fidelity may be dependent on whether they (a) believe that the problem identified by the PBS team is, in fact, a problem; (b) hold values that are consistent with the outcomes, measures, and standards representing the perceived need to reduce or eliminate the problem; (c) believe the solution can be embedded into the school's natural routines and structures; (d) possess the skills and resources needed to implement the solution with fidelity and to maintain implementation as necessary across time; and (e) see the proposed solution as having a high likelihood of succeeding at reducing the problem and achieving the standard.

## Develop and Implement Action Plan

Having used the hypothesis and the contextual fit logic to make a decision about which solutions to implement for the targeted problem, team members will next want to demonstrate accountability for implementation of their selected solution. This can be done by writing brief statements in an action plan that team members will be creating during the course of the meeting.

An action plan (see Table 23.A in the appendix for a sample) is simply a record of the problem-solving decisions reached at a meeting and the actions that must be completed to implement the decisions. To create a complete and useful record, each item (row) in an action plan is referenced to a specific problem and thus should contain concise descriptions of (a) the defined and clarified problem the solution has been designed to address (i.e., a problem statement); (b) the hypothesis generated by the team; (c) the selected solutions and tasks that must be undertaken to implement the solution; (d) the name of the PBS team member who will coordinate completion of a task; (e) the date by which a task will be completed; and (f) a goal, a timeline, and a decision rule concerning the effect that full implementation of the solution is expected to have on the targeted problem. Table 23.A shows a single item from an action plan created by the PBS team members at Rose Elementary School. The item is referenced to the problem of students engaging in disruptive and aggressive behaviors on the playground during recess. Note that the form also includes space for the team to record its "meeting minutes." Given that PBS team members will often find it necessary to discuss administrative/general information and issues, it is useful for the form to include space to address those matters.

In some cases, PBS team members may be responsible for coordinating the completion of tasks rather than completing the tasks themselves. If possible, team members *may* complete tasks, but more often they will have to confer with others (e.g., teachers) who are in a better position to undertake a task and then provide those people with any information and resources they may need. Prior to the next PBS team meeting, team members who have responsibility for coordinating tasks should have talked with those who are undertaking tasks and should be ready to provide an update on the extent to which the tasks are, in fact, being completed.

## Evaluate and Revise Action Plan

Members of the PBS team can use the goal, timeline, and decision rule section of the action plan to create an explicit goal for an individual item

# APPENDIX

**Table 23.A** Positive Behavior Support (PBS) Team: Meeting Minutes and Problem-Solving Action Plan

Today's date:____________________

Today's facilitator:____________________

Today's note taker:____________________

Team members (list and check if present):

☐________________ ☐________________

☐________________ ☐________________

☐________________ ☐________________

☐________________ ☐________________

☐________________ ☐________________

Date, time, location of next meeting:

____________________

Next meeting's facilitator:____________________

Next meeting's note taker:____________________

Today's agenda items (ask team members for items to add):

1.____________________ 7.____________________

2.____________________ 8.____________________

3.____________________ 9.____________________

4.____________________ 10.____________________

5.____________________ 11.____________________

6.____________________ 12.____________________

## Meeting Minutes: Administrative/General Information and Issues

☐ Minutes from last meeting reviewed ☐ Tasks from last meeting's minutes reviewed and updated as

| Information for Team or Issue for Team to Address | Decision/Task (If Applicable) | Who? | By When? |
|---|---|---|---|
| | | | |
| | | | |
| | | | |
| | | | |
| | | | |
| | | | |

| Information for Team or Issue for Team to Address | Decision/Task (If Applicable) | Who? | By When? |
|---|---|---|---|
| | | | |
| | | | |
| | | | |
| | | | |
| | | | |
| | | | |
| | | | |
| | | | |
| | | | |
| | | | |
| | | | |
| | | | |
| | | | |

**Problem-Solving Action Plan**

☐ Action plan from last meeting reviewed ☐ Tasks from last meeting's action plan reviewed and updated as necessary

| Problem Statement (Who, What, When, Where) | Hypothesis (why) | Solutions/Tasks | Who? | By When? | Goal, Timeline, & Decision Rule |
|---|---|---|---|---|---|
| Many students are engaging in disruptive and aggressive behaviors on playground during recess... | because (a) we have not developed playground-specific expectations and taught to students; (b) playground supervisors not included as participants in planning, teaching, evaluation of behavioral expectations; and (c) disruption, aggression, and fighting are resulting in access to peer attention and time<qu ref=3> with preferred equipment | Create system for playground supervisors to recognize appropriate play on playground; teach to supervisors | Jane | 09/15/05 | Reduce level of playground aggression and disruption office discipline referral |

(continued)

**Table 23.A** (continued)

| Problem Statement (Who, What, When, Where) | Hypothesis (why) | Solutions/Tasks | Who? | By When? | Goal, Timeline, & Decision Rule |
|---|---|---|---|---|---|
| | | Review continuum of corrective consequences for problem behavior on playground with students and supervisors; make sure continuum in effect | Jane | 09/19/05 | (ODRs) by at least 25% from June 2005 level by 11/30/05 |
| | | | | | Review November data at December PBS team meeting; revise hypothesis and/or solutions/tasks if goal not met |
| | | Teach playground supervisors to ensure aggression and disruption not allowed to result in access to preferred activities or materials | Sam | 09/20/05 | |
| | | Teach schoolwide behavior expectations (safe, respectful, responsible); do teaching on playground with students | Sam | 09/20/05 | |
| | | Teach students to signal "stop" when treated disrespectfully; do teaching on playground | Sam | 09/20/05 | |
| | | Ensure supervisors are on playground and engaged in active supervision | Sam | 09/21/05 | |
| | | Collect data to assess whether (a) solution is implemented with fidelity and (b) ODRs being reduced per our goal | Janice | 10/07/05 | |

in the action plan. This will allow team members to evaluate the success of the implemented solution and—if the solution is not succeeding—revise their hypothesis or specific solutions accordingly. If the school has already established formal standards for social behavior outcomes, the goal statement may include the school's standard. For example, the school may have already established formal standards regarding the expected level, trend, or variability of the school's ODRs (a) as compared against the previous school year's ODRs, (b) as measured across successive months of the current school year, (c) as compared against the national average for ODRs at other schools of similar enrollment size and grade level, or (d) based on explicit social expectations voiced by the community members, faculty, and students. If the school has *not* established formal standards, the PBS team members will establish their own informal, ad hoc standards by which to judge the success of the to-be-implemented solutions. This is the approach that was adopted by the Rose Elementary School PBS team (see Table 23.A).

Note that the action plan goal is accompanied by a timeline and a decision rule. The timeline indicates how much time the team is willing to allow a given solution to be implemented before considering a revision. A solution must be given some time to produce the desired effect. This can be a particularly important consideration when a solution targets all of a school's students: A solution is unlikely to produce a widespread effect until a majority of the students come in "contact" with the solution's contingencies.

Finally, note that the action plan's decision rule simply states that if the solution has not produced the desired effect (the goal) within the established timeline, the team will revise the hypothesis (which may be faulty) or the specific solutions that have been implemented. Of course, this will necessarily result in the team (a) establishing a revised goal, timeline, and decision rule for the revised solution; and (b) implementing the revised solution in an effort to solve the problem. Difficult problems may require several iterations of this cycle before the goal is achieved, providing valuable lessons in the inherent rigor of a true data-based decision-making approach to solving problems.

### *Implementation of Solutions With Fidelity*

Although the team's primary evaluation concern will be with whether an implemented solution is producing the desired effect, the team must also be concerned with whether the solution is being implemented with fidelity. The team has predicted that the solution will produce the desired effect, but the solution will have little chance to produce that effect if it is not implemented as the team intended. The easiest way for team members to determine whether a solution is implemented as intended is to use a portion of the team meeting to review the current action plans (e.g., any plans with in-process items developed at previous meetings) and to ask whether the item's solutions/tasks are being completed by the people to whom they have been assigned (the "whos") within the agreed-on time (the "by whens"). When a solution is not being implemented as intended, team members may need to provide additional support to the person charged with implementing the solution/task, assign the solution/task to another person, or revise the date by which the solution/task will be fully implemented.

Monitoring in-process action plan items requires that teams be highly organized and efficient. This is why it is important for each PBS team member to have a notebook that he or she brings to each meeting. If the notebook contains dividers for pertinent current and historical documents (including blank forms, completed action plans, and action plans with in-process items) there is an increased likelihood that team members will be able to monitor action plans. And, unless solutions/tasks change, it would be pointless and time consuming if each team meeting resulted in team members rerecording solutions/tasks that had already appeared on previous weeks' action plans. Thus, it is imperative that team members be able to refer to older, but still-in-process action plan items that were developed at previous meetings. In fact, if no new problems are identified at a team meeting, the bulk of the meeting might be devoted to monitoring those still-in-process action plan items.

### *Evaluating the Meeting Itself*

At the close of each meeting (or on some other periodic schedule), team members may also choose to conduct an informal "evaluation" of the team meeting itself. Teams may develop a short questionnaire or rating scale that members complete at the close of a meeting, or teams may simply reserve a few minutes to have an open-ended discussion about the virtues and shortcoming of the day's meeting and how the shortcomings could be eliminated in future meetings.

## DOCUMENTING ACCOMPLISHMENTS OF A TEAM MEETING

The accomplishments of a PBS team meeting are the products that team members "leave behind" when the meeting has concluded. The primary accomplishment of the meeting will be the meeting minutes/action plan, which provides a complete, useful record of the decisions reached at the meeting; the actions that must be completed to implement the decisions; and a method for evaluating success. Someone who did not attend the meeting but had access to the meeting's written agenda, printed data summaries, and meeting minutes/action plan would have a very good idea of what transpired at the meeting. If, following each meeting, team members file these products in their team member notebooks, they will have an excellent historical record of the team's accomplishments and the rationale surrounding their decisions.

## DEVELOPING A RESEARCH AGENDA

In this chapter, we have presented a problem-solving model designed to enhance the data-based decision making of school-based PBS team members. Of course, it is one thing to *declare* that a team's data-based decision making can be enhanced through use of the model and another thing to *demonstrate* that data-based decision making has been enhanced. Similarly, it is one thing to provide readers with the chapter's simple descriptions of the data and processes they may need to become competent problem solvers in the context of PBS team meetings and another thing to provide readers with systematic instruction in how to use the data and processes to best advantage. We believe that what is needed now is a research program that achieves the following:

- A complete description of the data and processes that PBS team members may need for their teams to become competent data-based decision makers in the context of their regular meetings (based on the problem-solving model presented in this chapter).
- "Packaging" of the problem-solving model's data samples and processes into a user-friendly manual for PBS team members, to be accompanied by systematic instruction designed to teach team members how to use the data and processes to best advantage.
- Concurrent research that demonstrates the extent to which the preceding "works," that is, the extent to which there is a functional relationship between the provision of instruction and improvements in the "quality" of a team's data-based decision making.

There are at least four ways in which the quality of a team's data-based decision making might demonstrate improvement via instruction of the type suggested. First, we would expect that teams would become more "thorough" in their data-based decision making by engaging in more of the problem-solving processes (identifying problems, developing and refining hypotheses, discussing and selecting solutions, etc.)—and would engage in those processes in a more systematic manner—than they did prior to instruction. Second, teams would become more "logical" in their data-based decision making. Following instruction, teams would develop hypotheses that were more logically related to the data and would develop solutions that were more logically related to the hypotheses. Third, teams would become more "efficient" in their meetings. For example, following instruction, teams would reach more decisions per minute and would perhaps demonstrate a decreasing trend in the average amount of time required to complete iterations of the problem-solving model's processes. Finally, when a team's efforts are thorough, logical, and efficient, their data-based decision making would become more "effective." That is, when the team uses the problem-solving model and implements its solutions with fidelity, we would expect decreases in the level and trend of problems that are superior to those achieved by the team prior to the instruction.

## CONCLUSIONS

In this chapter, we focused on the responsibility of school-based positive behavior support team members to make decisions and implement solutions designed to support students, with particular emphasis on supporting whole-school, social behavior outcomes. We argued that the data-based decision making of team members can be enhanced through use of (a) environmental supports that set the occasion for effective and efficient meetings and (b) data that inform each of the processes of a formal problem-solving model: identifying problems, developing and refining hypotheses, discussing and selecting solutions, developing and implementing action plans, and evaluating and revising action plans.

When the problem-solving model is employed within a school with a faculty who have already established social behavior outcomes, measures, and standards, PBS team members can identify problems by using data to discover discrepancies between students' current social behaviors and desired social behaviors, as defined by the school's standards. Once the team has identified a problem, its members can use the other processes of the model to create, implement, and monitor solutions designed to reduce or eliminate the discrepancies.

What we now require is a program of systematic research that will allow for a rigorous testing of the hypothesis that use of the proposed problem-solving model will result in (a) meetings that are more thorough, logical, and efficient and (b) solutions that are more effective in addressing the student social behavior problems.

## ACKNOWLEDGMENT

Preparation of this chapter was supported by grant R324A070226 from the Institute of Education Sciences, U.S. Department of Education. However, the opinions expressed herein are those of the authors, and no official endorsement should be inferred.

## REFERENCES

Albin, R. W., Lucyshyn, J. M., Horner, R. H., & Flannery, K. B. (1996). Contextual fit for behavior support plans: A model for "goodness-of-fit." In L. K. Koegel, R. L. Koegel, & G. Dunlap (Eds.), *Positive behavioral support: Including people with difficult behavior in the community* (pp. 81–98). Baltimore: Brookes.

Alonzo, J., Ketterlin-Geller, L. R., & Tindal, G. (2007). Curriculum-based measurement in reading and math: providing rigorous outcomes to support learning. In L. Florian (Ed.), *The SAGE handbook of special education* (pp. 307–318). Thousand Oaks, CA: Sage.

Bailey, D. B., Simeonsson, R. J., Winton, P. J., Huntington, G. S., Comfort, M., Isbell, P., et al. (1990). Family-focused intervention: A functional model for planning, implementing, and evaluating individualized family services in early intervention. *Journal of the Division of Early Childhood, 10*, 156–171.

Benazzi, L., Horner, R. H., & Good, R. H. (2006). Effects of behavior support team composition on the technical adequacy and contextual fit of behavior support plans. *The Journal of Special Education, 40*, 160–170.

Bransford, J. D., & Stein, B. S. (1984). *The IDEAL problem solver: A guide for improving thinking, learning, and creativity*. New York: Freeman.

Carr, E. G., Horner, R. H., Turnbull, A. P., Marquis, J. G., McLaughlin, D. M., McAtee, M. L., et al. (1999). *Positive behavior support for people with developmental disabilities: A research synthesis*. Washington, DC: American Association on Mental Retardation.

Crone, D. A., & Horner, R. H. (2003). *Building positive behavior support systems in schools: Functional behavioral assessment.* New York: Guilford.

Crone, D. A., Horner, R. H., & Hawken, L. S. (2004). *Responding to problem behavior in schools: The behavior education program.* New York: Guilford.

Davies, D. E., & McLaughlin, T. F. (1989). Effects of a daily report card on disruptive behaviour in primary students. *Journal of Special Education, 13*, 173–181.

Deno, S. L. (1985). Curriculum-based measurement: The emerging alternative. *Exceptional Children, 52*, 219–232.

Deno, S. L. (1989). Curriculum-based measurement and alternative special education services: A fundamental and direct relationship. In M. R. Shinn (Ed.), *Advanced applications of curriculum-based measurement* (pp. 1–17). New York: Guilford.

Deno, S. L. (2005). Problem-solving assessment. In R. Brown-Chidsey (Ed.), *Assessment for intervention: A problem-solving approach* (pp. 10–40). New York: Guilford.

Drucker, P. F. (1967). *The effective executive.* New York: Harper & Row.

Evertson, C. M., & Emmer, E. T. (1982). Preventive classroom management. In D. L. Duke (Ed.), *Helping teachers manage classrooms* (pp. 2–31). Alexandria, VA: Association for Supervision and Curriculum Development.

Gilbert, T. F. (1978). *Human competence: Engineering worthy performance.* New York: McGraw-Hill.

Gilbert, T. F., & Gilbert, M. B. (1992). Potential contributions of performance science to education. *Journal of Applied Behavior Analysis, 25*, 43–49.

Hawken, L. S., & Horner, R. H. (2003). Evaluation of a targeted group intervention within a schoolwide system of behavior support. *Journal of Behavioral Education, 12*, 225–240.

Hyatt, K. J., & Howell, K. W. (2004). Curriculum-based measurement of students with emotional and behavioral disorders: Assessment for data-based decision making. In R. B. Rutherford & M. M. Quinn (Eds.), *Handbook of research in emotional and behavioral disorders* (pp. 181–198). New York: Guilford.

Irvin, L. K., Horner, R. H., Ingram, K., Todd, A. W., Sugai, G., Sampson, N. K., et al. (2006). Using office discipline referral data for decision making about student behavior in elementary and middle schools: An empirical evaluation of validity. *Journal of Positive Behavior Interventions, 8*, 10–23.

Irvin, L. K., Tobin, T. J., Sprague, J. R., Sugai, G., & Vincent, C. G. (2004). Validity of office discipline referral measures as indices of school-wide behavioral status and effects of school-wide behavioral interventions. *Journal of Positive Behavior Interventions, 6*, 131–147.

Jorgensen, J. D., Scheier, I. H., & Fautsko, T. F. (1981). *Solving problems in meetings.* Chicago: Nelson-Hall.

Larson, J. (1994). Violence prevention in schools: A review of selected programs and procedures. *School Psychology Review, 23*, 151–164.

Lewis, T. J., Colvin, G., & Sugai, G. (2000). The effects of pre-correction and active supervision on the recess behavior of elementary students. *Education and Treatment of Children, 23*, 109–121.

Lewis, T. J., & Sugai, G. (1999). Effective behavior support: A systems approach to proactive school-wide management. *Focus on Exceptional Children, 31*(6), 1–24.

Martella R. C., Nelson, J. R., & Marchand-Martella, N. E. (2003). *Managing disruptive behaviors in the schools: A schoolwide, classroom, and individualized social learning approach.* Boston: Allyn and Bacon.

May, S., Ard, W., Jr., Todd, A. W., Horner, R. H., Glasgow, A., & Sugai, G. (2003). *Schoolwide information system.* Eugene: University of Oregon, Educational and Community Supports.

Mayer, G. R., & Butterworth, T. W. (1979). A preventive approach to school violence and vandalism: An experimental study. *Personnel and Guidance Journal, 57*, 436–441.

Mayer, R. G. (1995). Preventing antisocial behavior in the schools. *Journal of Applied Behavior Analysis, 28*, 467–478.

National Research Council and Institute of Medicine. (1999). *Risk and opportunities: Synthesis of studies on adolescence.* Washington, DC: National Academy Press.

Nelson, J. R., & Carr, B. A. (2000). *The Think Time strategy for schools.* Denver, CO: Sopris West.

Nelson, J. R., Martella, R., & Galand, B. (1998). The effects of teaching school expectations and establishing a consistent consequence on formal office disciplinary actions. *Journal of Emotional and Behavioral Disorders, 6*, 153–161.

O'Neill, R. E., Horner, R. H., Albin, R. W., Sprague, J. R., Storey, K., & Newton, J. S. (1997). *Functional assessment of problem behavior: A practical handbook* (2nd ed.). Pacific Grove, CA: Brookes/Cole.

Poynton, T. A., & Carey, J. C. (2006). An integrative model of data-based decision making for school counseling. *Professional School Counseling, 10*, 121–130.

Repp, A. C., & Horner, R. H. (Eds.). (1999). *Functional analysis of problem behavior: From effective assessment to effective support*. Belmont, CA: Wadsworth.

Scott, T. M., & Martinek, G. (2006). Coaching positive behavior support in school settings: Tactics and data-based decision making. *Journal of Positive Behavior Interventions, 8*, 165–173.

Shinn, M. R. (1989). *Curriculum-based measurement: Assessing special children*. New York: Guilford.

Shonkoff, J. P., & Phillips, D. A. (Eds.). (2000). *From neurons to neighborhoods: The science of early childhood development*. Washington, DC: National Academy Press.

Sprick, R., Sprick, M., & Garrison, M. (1992). *Foundations: Developing positive school-wide discipline policies*. Longmont, CO: Sopris West.

Sugai, G., & Horner, R. H. (2006). A promising approach for expanding and sustaining school-wide positive behavior support. *School Psychology Review 35*, 245–259.

Tropman, J. E. (1996). *Making meetings work: Achieving high quality group decisions*. Thousand Oaks, CA: Sage.

Walker, H. M., Horner, R. H., Sugai, G., Bullis, M, Sprague, J., Bricker, D., et al. (1996). Integrated approaches to preventing antisocial behavior patterns among school-age children and youth. *Journal of Emotional and Behavioral Disorders, 4*, 194–209.

Walker, H. M., Ramsey, E., & Gresham, F. (2004). *Antisocial behavior in school: Evidenced-based practices* (2nd ed.). Belmont, CA: Thomson/Wadsworth.

Walker, H. M., & Shinn, M.R. (2002). Structuring school-based interventions to achieve integrated primary, secondary, and tertiary prevention goals for safe and effective schools. In M. R. Shinn, H. M. Walker, & G. Stoner (Eds.), *Interventions for academic and behavior problems II: Preventive and remedial approaches* (pp. 1–26). Bethesda, MD: National Association of School Psychologists.

Weissberg, R. P., Caplan, M. Z., & Sivo, P. J. (1989). A new conceptual framework for establishing school-based social competence promotion programs. In L. A. Bond & B. E. Compas (Eds.), *Primary prevention and promotion in the schools* (pp. 255–296). Thousand Oaks, CA: Sage.

# 24

# Finding a Direction for High School Positive Behavior Support

**HANK BOHANON, PAMELA FENNING, CHRIS BORGMEIER, BRIGID FLANNERY, and JOANNE MALLOY**

The purpose of this chapter is to discuss the similarities and differences between high school applications of positive behavior support (PBS) and primary school settings. An increased focus on the organizational impact of size and departmental structure is discussed. Connections between academic, behavioral, social, and academic supports are highlighted.

High school support has been framed under many unique labels, and the current emphasis on restructuring secondary schools has received considerable programmatic and monetary attention (Gates Foundation, 2003). Researchers, practitioners, and policy makers have been struggling to find new ways to address the needs of larger, highly departmentalized schools. Distinguishing promising practices with limited data from well-documented evidenced-based supports appears to become problematic as students get older and move into high school environments.

An area of increasing interest is the connection between comprehensive high school reform and three-tier models of prevention. By providing a comprehensive continuum of support for students, staff, and families, researchers hypothesize that prevention and data-based decision making may provide greater efficacy than reactionary and compulsory punitive polices (Fenning & Bohanon, 2006). One such model of prevention is PBS

---

**HANK BOHANON** • Loyola University of Chicago
**PAMELA FENNING** • Loyola University of Chicago
**CHRIS BORGMEIER** • Portland State University
**BRIGID FLANNERY** • University of Oregon
**JOANNE MALLOY** • University of New Hampshire

(Carr et al., 2002). While evidence of PBS exists for elementary schools, efficacy data are limited for high schools (Bohanon et al., 2006; Bohanon, Eber, Flannery, & Fenning, 2007; Bohanon-Edmonson, Flannery, Eber, & Sugai, 2005). The purposes of this chapter are to (a) illustrate a rationale for PBS in secondary schools, (b) identify critical features of PBS as they are applied to typical school settings, (c) discuss possible adaptations of the basic model for secondary schools, (d) discuss preliminary findings for high school pilots, and (e) propose directions for future practice and research.

## RATIONALE FOR SCHOOLWIDE SUPPORTS

According to the Bill and Melinda Gates Foundation (2003), full participation in society, socially and economically, is dependent on providing effective education for all citizens. Unfortunately, the efficacy of educational interventions for students at an early age decreases over time without continued support (Joint Center for Poverty Research, 2000). While high schools offer a wide range of programs for students, nearly one third of eight graders will not graduate from high school, particularly students from minority backgrounds (Gates Foundation, 2003)

When students fail in school and as citizens, they do not simply leave behind a benign vacuum. A wake of events can be set in motion that can have a negative impact on society at large. Within the school, the level of violent behavior (National Center for Educational Statistics, 2003) and of the number of students dropping out of school can increase (Kortering & Braziel, 1999; Office of Vocational and Adult Education, 2004). Further, "low-performing high schools that produce most of the state's high school dropouts, are the same high schools attended by most of the adolescents who have contact with the juvenile justice system" (National Governor's Association, 2003, p. 16). Not surprisingly, these schools also produce most of the young adults who are unemployed (National Governor's Association, 2003).

Termed the "school-to-prison pipeline" (Wald & Losen, 2003), high school age students who are caught in the web of removal for discipline issues have a high probability of entering the prison system and a low probability of returning to school. Further evidence for this link are findings that high school discipline data mirror those of prisons in terms of overrepresentation of students of color, particularly African American males (Skiba, Michael, Nardo, & Peterson, 2000; Wald & Losen, 2003). High school PBS initiatives must address academic and behavioral components and student needs as part of the problem-solving process (Fenning, Theodos, Benner, Bohanon–Edmonson (2004).

Interdisciplinary, coordinated efforts may lead to just such an environment. As Glover (2005) found, coordinated schoolwide efforts may be related to an improvement in perceived positive interactions between secondary students and the school personnel who serve them. Unfortunately, evidence of wide adoption of these promising practices is sparse, leading to the premise that high schools have been considered the fundamental test of standards-based reform (National Governor's Association, 2003). Next, we consider unique features of high schools that should be considered in the implementation of any school reform effort.

## CRITICAL FEATURES OF HIGH SCHOOL ENVIRONMENTS

Schools differ widely from one another because the operational context influences the culture of that school. The school context is influenced by how staff members work together, how schools relate to their community, and how administration and districtwide policies support school efforts (Renihan & Renihan, 1995). While systematic secondary school reform can be problematic, components of effective environments for high schools that retain and engage their students are known. "Successful schools combine rigor, high expectations and a meaningful course of study with relationships, powerful, sustained involvement with caring adults who mentor, advise, and support students throughout their high school careers" (Bill and Melinda Gates Foundation, 2003, p. 5).

Although the basic principles of schoolwide PBS (SW-PBS) are the same at all grade levels, implementation at the high school level may differ because of the unique context of secondary schools (Bohanon et al., 2005, 2006, 2007). Age level is only one way that high schools differ from elementary and middle schools. Other particularly salient features make high schools, and thus the strategies used to improve them, very different from elementary schools and middle school environments (Bohanon et al., 2007): (a) size and organizational structure, (b) adolescent development, and (c) emphasis on academics. However, the PBS approach has the advantage of being able to unite the whole school in the context of multiple and diverse competing initiatives and unique strengths, issues, and concerns

### *Structure and Size of High Schools*

High schools have larger student bodies, offer more and longer classes, have larger campuses, and employ more and different staff members who are organized by subject area rather than by grade (Newman et al., 2000). The development and implementation of schoolwide systems requires careful consideration of their sheer size, complex departmental and administrative organizational structure comprised of multiple vice principals and department heads, and shift toward postsecondary and vocational career goals (Lee & Smith, 1994).

High schools are divided and subdivided into content-based departments, each having unique goals and expectations. Teachers use departments as their reference point for defining what they teach (e.g., subject, content), how they teach, and how they are perceived by others (Murphy et al., 2001; Siskin, 1994). This departmental alignment is so strong that teachers make statements aligning themselves more with departments than their school as a whole (Siskin, 1994). For example, teachers referenced their department more often with respect to improving or sustaining practices, accessing resources, making personnel decisions (e.g., hiring, assignments, evaluation), dispensing rewards, and channeling communication (Siskin, 1994).

Because high schools tend to be the feeder site for multiple middle schools, their enrollment numbers tend to be larger, which has an impact on implementation of innovations. Large student enrollments require larger buildings, more educators and support staff, greater organization planning and management (e.g., cafeteria, busing and transportation, maintenance, athletics, student clubs, security), and varied levels of personal attention. Each of these factors can affect the quality and quantity of interactions students have with each other and staff members and in turn the kinds of personal and instructional relationships that are established. Ultimately, expectations, norms, and standards of coordinated behavior and support can be highly variable across the high school culture and environment (Felner et al., 1993; Sato & McLauglin, 1992; Siskin, 1994). Thus, agreeing to and implementing a single set of expectations, establishing a uniform positive reinforcement system, implementing a single leadership team to coordinate a schoolwide implementation, and developing a culture of data-based decision making around school discipline information become much more difficult. In sum, bigger enrollments foster generally impersonal learning environments, which can impede the development of positive bonds between teachers and students (Felner et al., 1993).

It would appear that social support and connectedness for students at the high school level also are important to academic success. Schools need to create smaller more personal environments and work toward a sense of belonging (Murphy, Beck, et al., 2001). To reduce the flux and complexity that students confront, smaller schools, (McQuillan, 1998) or schools within schools (Felner et al., 1993), are being created. Thus, students experience a more consistent set of peers and mutual support (Felner et al., 1993; McQuillan, 1998). Discipline becomes less of a concern when teachers and students know each other (McQuillan, 1998; Meier, 1995; Raymid, 1995). Further, when students and teachers move within a smaller area, the school seems more manageable (Felner et al., 1993).

### *Student Age*

High school students expect to "have a say" in what goes on in their school and learn responsibility and self-control by being taught to make thoughtful decisions (Daniels, Bizar, & Zemelman, 2001; Kohn, 1993). Students need to be given a voice in policy decisions, school organization, discipline, academic areas, and activities (Murphy et al., 2001), In addition, schools need to look for ways to gain input from students, including students who usually remain unheard (Murphy et al., 2001). Academic achievement of students and teachers' satisfaction with their students' work increase when students have a voice and choice (Daniels et al., 2001).

High schools should be viewed as connected communities that will lead to an increased student role in decision making. At the high school level, students must participate in maintaining a positive climate and following guidelines built on mutual respect and individual responsibility (Gilchrist, 1989; Mackin, 1996; Murphy et al., 2001; Wilson & Corcoran, 1988).

### *Connection of Social and Academic Behavior.*

Academic expectations increase, and student academic performance often declines, on entry into high school (Isakson & Jarvis, 1999). The focus on "social promotion" is replaced by emphasis on earning credits for graduation. In addition, instructional expectation shifts from learning skills to applying and integrating academic skills (Bohanon-Edmonson, Flannery, Eber, Sugai; 2005), which is difficult for students who enter high school with deficits in areas such as reading and mathematics.

Obtaining high levels of academic achievement in today's high schools is not simple and will require melding both academic and social concerns (Byrk & Deabster, 1994; Jerald, 2006; Masten & Coatesworth, 1998). For example, academic problems are the strongest predictor of punitive school consequences, such as suspension and expulsion (Morrison & D'Incau, 1997, Morrison, Furlong, & Morrison, 1994). McKinney (1989) found a greater risk of dropout for students with deficits in both academics and social behavior than students with problems in only one area.

High school academic remediation or support is often offered in a way that delays entry into grade-level course work (Education Trust, 2005) and means not gaining credits at the same rate as their peers, not graduating with their peers, and eventually dropping out (Finn & Rock, 1997; Slavin, 1999). This lack of progression is most noticeable at ninth grade and has become known as the "ninth-grade bulge." Persistently low academic skills reduce student access to daily success and the development of close teacher-student relationships (Finn & Rock 1997; Slavin, 1999).

Without modification of academic curriculum or remediation of academic skills, students experience high rates of academic frustration and may respond with escape- or avoidance-maintained behavior (Bohanon et al.,). As concern for student safety and discipline increases, high schools tend to rely heavily on reactive, exclusionary responses (e.g., suspension, expulsion) to problem behavior. These practices are largely ineffective in changing student behavior but are successful in removing the student from important teaching and learning environments (Colvin, Kameenui, & Sugai, G. 1993; Farmer, 1996; Mayer, 1995; Noguera, 1995; Skiba & Peterson, 2003). Students who receive frequent exclusionary consequences ultimately are highly likely to leave school (i.e., drop out) (Skiba & Peterson, 1999). The act of dropping out of school is the culmination of "a long-term process" of disengagement, including frequent mobility (changing schools frequently), truancy (absenteeism), learning challenges, grade retention, and negative school experiences (Croninger & Lee, 2001; Lehr, Hansen, Sinclair, & Christenson, 2003). Rumberger (2001) added that student engagement (academic and social) and parental involvement are strong indicators of school success or failure.

## CONSIDERATIONS FOR ADAPTATION OF THE BASIC PBS MODEL FOR USE IN HIGH SCHOOLS

We focus next on how implementation of basic PBS features and principles can be adapted for the high school context. The similarities of PBS implementation between elementary and secondary schools are described.

## Elementary and High School Similarities

The PBS approach strives to create a consistent, predictable, and positive environment for all students, and SW-PBS is rooted in an understanding that we cannot expect student behavioral changes if we do not make environmental changes to support them. The following foundational principles of PBS are consistent across all levels of implementation (Sugai & Horner, 1999): (a) a systemic approach (levels of support), (b) team-based leadership, (c) research-based interventions, and (d) data-based decision making.

### *Systemic Approach*

In the field of education, in which the next trend is always right around the corner, PBS challenges schools to commit minimally for 3–5 years to work toward a consistent vision for implementing sustainable systemic change. Due to infrastructure complexity, high school implementation to a standard may take longer than in elementary and middle schools. High schools also may face a greater challenge in committing to a consistent, sustained schoolwide vision, which may require a more concerted effort to establish readiness, plan for communication, and all staff participation and feedback (Bohanon et al., 2006). The increased complexity of communication in high schools often requires that administrators actively lead through close participation, flexible scheduling for meetings, and encouragement of full staff involvement.

### *Team-Based Leadership*

Recognizing that schools are complex environments, team-based leadership is critical to strategically implementing systemic change, especially in high schools that are comprised of multiple organizational levels (e.g., all school, departments, programs). A credible leadership team that adequately represents all staff in the building is important to successfully guiding the development and implementation of PBS, fostering staff buy-in, and developing sustainable SW-PBS systems. PBS implementation seems to be more varied in high schools than elementary and middle schools. Typically, elementary and middle schools start by getting the schoolwide components fully in place in all settings and contexts of the school. In contrast, high schools may focus implementation in specific contexts of concern (e.g., behavior in hallways, cafeteria, or reducing tardies) to increase staff buy-in and participation. The team guides this adaptation and prioritization process and monitors staff readiness.

The leadership team must have the close support and participation of the building administration to foster staff buy-in. Administrative participation also is necessary in high schools because additional attention to scheduling and resources may be required to carry out systemic change efforts. Further, the distribution of responsibilities may take a more ad hoc committee-like structure. For instance, rather than have one person from the schoolwide team in charge of developing teaching tools, a teaching subcommittee may be formed. The teaching chair reports to the schoolwide coordinator. Distributed leadership may be a key element in the functioning of high school teams.

The implementation of PBS practice includes the direct teaching of expectations, acknowledging appropriate behavior, consistent consequences for mis-behavior strategies for redirection, function based supports and person centered planning. While these components are SIMILAR at the elementary level, it may be necessary to ensure the systems and data components (see below) are fully addressal prior to implementation at practice.

### *Data-Based Decision Making*

One of the most important aspects of responding to problem behavior is reviewing relevant data on a regular and frequent basis to determine individual student problem behavior and indicators of larger, systemic problem areas. For example, data review may reveal that many referrals are coming from a certain location, time of day, or grade level. Perhaps a disproportionate number of these referrals are coming from a specific student demographic (e.g., grade, those with nonattendance, low academic performers, at-risk group, social network)

The documentation of change in high schools appears to be more difficult. Although commonly available in high schools, office discipline referrals (ODRs) may not accurately reflect the school's disciplinary climate and social culture. High school ODR rates may be low because many problems are handled at the classroom level, and only "big" offenses (e.g., fighting, chronic nonattendance/tardies) are recorded. Many high schools explore other data sources to better assess the status of PBS (e.g., surveys, focus groups).

### *Considerations for Universal Systems*

The foundational interventions for universal systems of PBS implementation at the high school level are consistent with application at the elementary and middle school levels and include (a) creating consistent expectations, (b) teaching behavioral expectations and routines across settings, (c) increasing acknowledgment of positive student behavior, and (d) responding fairly and consistently to problem behavior with a focus on maximizing student instructional time.

To pique and maintain the attention of adolescent students and a potentially more resistant staff, high school teams may have to be more innovative in implementation. Increased participation in the development and implementation of each element of PBS is suggested as a way to improve buy-in for both students and staff. Many schools will include student participants on the school leadership team or even have a coexisting student leadership team with reciprocal faculty and student representatives. The challenge to effective high school implementation seems to be creatively negotiating the contextual challenges of high schools to deliver these same foundational interventions in genuine, contextually and developmentally appropriate ways.

Students and staff in high schools, and even in some middle schools, often will not respond well to the simple positively stated expectations or rules that are implemented in elementary schools (e.g., be safe, be responsible, be respectful). Many high schools use more sophisticated language in creating a more developmentally appropriate set of three to five guiding principles, values, or expectations. For example, one high school adopted the acronym "PRIDE" for more sophisticated behavioral constructs: perseverance, respect, integrity, diversity, and excellence. The team identified specific behavioral expectations for PRIDE across environments in the school and, like many high schools, increased the visibility of their catchy mantra by placing it on t-shirts and school athletic uniforms.

Teaching behavioral expectations is another element of SW-PBS that can seem much less daunting to a group of elementary students than to high school students. However, with additional time and creativity, beneficial outcomes are possible, especially if students are actively involved. At the high school level, for example, using multimedia options for teaching lessons and utilizing student and staff talents in the development of lesson plans can result in entertaining lessons on behavioral expectations and routines at the high school level. The use of older students as mentors during orientation for incoming ninth-grade students also can be a way to set the tone for students entering high school and to teach organizational skills and study skills that are important for student success in high school.

The acknowledgment of student positive behavior is another foundational intervention common to PBS implementation. Schools implementing PBS strive for a ratio of five positive for each negative interaction, that is, recognize student positive behavior five times for every time attention is given to negative student behavior. Some staff members routinely acknowledge student behavior at a five-to-one ratio, but Beaman and Wheldall (2000) found that these teachers are the exception in most schools. Staff members in many elementary and middle schools implementing schedule PBS commonly give tokens to students to symbolically acknowledge their positive behavior. These tangible acknowledgment systems function to provide important reminders to staff to regularly catch students doing the right thing.

Many high schools have successfully implemented high-frequency acknowledgement systems (e.g., "caught you doing the right thing" ticket) similar to those used in elementary and middle schools. High schools often use concrete acknowledgment systems (e.g., tickets) periodically throughout the year and combine them with other methods to achieve that five-to-one ratio throughout the year and group acknowledgment also are utilized for recognizing appropriate behaviour (e.g., class with the best "on-time-to-class" data, school store discounts, parking lot privileges, cafeteria discounts) (Flannery, Sugai, & Anderson, in press).

At the high school level, some staff members question why students should receive acknowledgment for "expected" behavior ("They should be doing it anyway," "That's not how the real world works," "Tangible rewards foster a dependence on external motivators"). When looking at the research, increasing evidence indicates that increasing the ratio of positive to negative interactions has many benefits for society. The five-to-one ratio not only applies to schools and classrooms, but also research suggests that this is a predictor of enduring marital relationships (Gottman, 1994) and productive business teams (Losada & Heaphy, 2004). Thus, high schools and the next generation may benefit from improving on their ratio of positive to negative interactions.

When responding to problem behavior, PBS aims to (a) provide a remedial or instructional response to student problem behavior and (b) use responses that maintain academic instructional time to the greatest extent possible. The ultimate evaluation of the success of responses to problem behavior is whether the behavior continues to occur. In the worst-case scenario, recurring use of detention, suspension, or other punitive or exclusionary discipline methods may be inadvertently acting to reinforce student problem behavior. Through the process of implementing SW-PBS, high schools must take a close look at how they respond to problem behavior, particularly their use of suspension, detention, and other punitive responses that may result in students missing instructional time (Fenning et al., in press).

Beyond schoolwide expectations and acknowledging student behavior, concerted efforts are being made in some high schools to create a welcoming environment for all students. Events targeting the strengths and interests of all students, particularly those students who are often marginalized in high schools, can be important in creating a positive, welcoming community. Schools are creating opportunities to showcase the talents and skills of students with interests beyond the typical school-based athletics, drama, and band. For example, one large school held a "Battle of the Bands," which provided a group of often marginalized "punk" students the chance to showcase their talents, receive recognition from their peers, and develop a relationship with the school principal. The same school has created leadership and support opportunities for students of different ethnicities and religious beliefs. In response to data revealing a disproportionate percentage of discipline referrals and students receiving failing grades across ethnicities, the school focused on ways to better support students from diverse backgrounds. Though not part of the foundational PBS interventions, such efforts to create a positive and welcoming environment for all students in high schools show significant promise.

### *Secondary-Level System*

The majority of students who do not respond to an effective universal system fall within the secondary level of prevention. The goal of secondary-level prevention is to most efficiently and effectively provide support to those students who will respond to "targeted" or "group" interventions and to refer those students who fail to respond to more intensive support. Targeted or group interventions are designed with the intention of being quickly accessible, low-cost interventions that can be used to support multiple students at one time. Our sense is that there will be an increased focus on academic supports for students in high schools supported at this level. Further, there will need to be efficient and effective ways to address the increased number of students who will require these supports in larger high school settings.

Since students who require secondary supports often have needs or deficits that are common to other students, there is an opportunity to offer interventions that are likely to be beneficial for multiple students. To address common needs or deficits of at-risk students, secondary prevention systems often include group interventions that (a) increase student motivation, (b) provide increased monitoring and supervision, (c) teach organizational skills and study skills, and (d) provide academic support. Schools are encouraged to develop a range of interventions that address each of these four areas. The following are examples of some commonly used research-supported, targeted interventions, not necessarily specific to high school level supports: the Behavior Education Program (Crone, Horner, & Hawken, 2004; also referred to as the Daily Point Card system, Fairchild, 1983; Schumaker, Hovell, & Sherman, 1977); social skills instruction (Brant & Christensen, 2002; Lane et al., 2003); mentoring programs (Sinclair, Christenson, Evelo, & Hurley, 1998); and academic support.

The overall model of support should look similar in high schools with a focus on creating a range of interventions to adequately support student need, particularly in the area of academic supports. As mentioned, little research has been conducted on secondary-level prevention systems in high schools, and identification of the most appropriate interventions or adapting the previously mentioned interventions to fit within a high school is necessary.

### *Tertiary-Level Systems*

As student needs become more complex, interventions must be increasingly individualized through the use of functional behavioral assessment and behavior support plans. Using functional behavioral assessment to inform intervention is the hallmark of individualized secondary- and tertiary-level support at the elementary and middle school levels. Other considerations for tertiary-level supports in high schools that are not present as frequently in lower grade levels are interventions focused on reduction of truancy, school dropout or substance use, as well as use of credit recovery options. Any of these concerns pose significant challenges to high school teams in providing student behavioral support. In high schools, many students who have been exposed to multiple risk factors may require interventions that include community services or mental health support (Kern & Manz, 2004). Identifying the personnel and resources in schools to support students with such intense behavioral support needs is a significant challenge in all settings. This issue can be exacerbated in high schools, where student problems are often even more complex and systems are (a) often less flexible to student programming and (b) more rigidly bound by strict graduation requirements. The latter factor unfortunately leaves many students with little hope of graduating, thereby increasing the likelihood of school dropout. Effective intensive-level services for youth who have significant challenges in multiple life domains requires a model of services that is driven by experiences and opportunities that foster self-determination, offering the youth chances to make choices, to plan, to problem solve, and to take action toward goals developed by the youth.

## OUTCOMES OF PBS IMPLEMENTATION

### *Schoolwide Applications*

It is only in very recent years that PBS components have been applied to high school settings. The data that are available show significant promise in improving the lives of high school youth. We have emerging high school examples at the schoolwide, secondary/classroom, and individual levels. For example, Bohanon et al. (2006) implemented PBS in an urban high school within the third largest public school district in the United States. The student body was racially and ethnically diverse, with an overwhelming majority of students qualifying for free and reduced lunch (89%) as well as a high percentage of students who were English language learners (ELLs) (21%). In the initial 2 years of the study, the external team collaborated with school personnel to conduct unstructured interviews about staff needs, to organize discipline referral data, and to form an internal PBS team. In Year 3, PBS components were implemented, including typical procedures for developing, teaching, and acknowledging expectations (using schoolwide celebrations and a ticket system). During this implementation year, there was a 20% reduction in ODRs. Further, a change in proportion of students at the primary level of support and a decrease in the proportion of students requiring more intensive support (those at the secondary and tertiary levels within the three-tier triangle) were found.

Fidelity of implementation, as measured by the School-wide Evaluation Tool (SET; Sugai, Lewis-Palmer, Todd, & Horner, 2001), indicated that, overall, this school reached 80% capacity of implementation. Two components (teaching and district-level support) fell below 80% capacity. This study was the first of its kind to adapt PBS to high school settings.

In New Hampshire, two statewide dropout prevention initiatives funded by the U. S. Department of Education, APEX I (Achievement in Dropout Prevention and Excellence) and APEX II, have engaged 10 of the state's lowest-performing high schools to implement all three levels of PBS. In addition to the SET, APEX is measuring behavioral and academic outcomes, including ODRs, suspensions, 10th-grade assessments, and dropout rates. The APEX schools implement PBS at all three tiers and are using schoolwide student data to identify patterns and trends and to design interventions. Most of the high schools have found that rates of behavior problems are much higher among ninth graders, and several schools have linked their PBS interventions to their ninth-grade programs or have created ninth-grade advisories as a result, an activity that is consistent with high school reform efforts.

### *Secondary-Level Applications*

In addition, high school examples are beginning to emerge at the classwide/secondary level. Moroz, Fenning, and Bohanon (in submission) applied

PBS principles to two classrooms that were having difficulties with tardy behavior and were located in the same school as that involved in the Bohanon et al. (2006) work. A high school's database was used to identify two classrooms in which a high frequency of tardies occurred, and the teachers wanted assistance. The direct teaching of expected behaviors using a lesson plan, the daily acknowledgment of students who were on time using the schoolwide ticket system, public posting of classwide tardies using a graph format, and weekly classroom goal setting were the components of the intervention. The results in both classrooms were that the proportion of students who fell within the primary level of support (measured by those with no or one tardy) increased following the intervention, while those at the secondary (those with two to five tardies) and tertiary (those with six or more tardies) levels of support decreased. Tracking of the intervention components using a treatment integrity checklist, as well as direct observations of implementation, indicated strong implementation fidelity.

### *Tertiary-Level Applications*

At the tertiary level or individual support level, much of the existing literature for secondary-aged students comes from the field of disability research. Students with emotional and behavioral disorders (EBDs) experience significantly negative high school transition and education outcomes, particularly when compared to students without disabilities or students in other disability groups. Students with EBDs show patterns of school disengagement, high rates of academic failure, high dropout rates, higher criminal justice involvement, and somewhat lower employment rates (Bullis & Cheney, 1999; Wagner, 1991; Wehman, 1996; Wagner, Kutash, Duchnowski, & Epstein, 2005). Studies also have shown that youth with EBDs have high rates of mental health utilization, are more likely to be poor, and are incarcerated at significantly higher rates than the general population (Alexander, Entwisle, & Horsey, 1997; Kortering & Braziel, 1999; Lee & Burkam, 1992; Wagner, 1992; Wagner, D'Amico, Marder, Newman, & Blackorby, 1992; Wagner et al., 2005). Researchers in the areas of special education and secondary transition for youth with EBDs indicate that interventions in the public high school that intentionally target the academic and social needs of students with EBDs are rare (Lane, Carter, Pierson, & Glaeser, 2006), but could have a substantial impact on the poor outcomes experienced by those youth (Carter, Lane, Pierson, & Glaeser, 2006; Kutash & Duchonowski, 1997; Wagner & Davis, 2006).

Key components that will increase the likelihood that those who require individualized support have been articulated. (Eber, Nelson, Miles, Stroul, 1997; Friedman 1986) In particular, Bryk and Thum (1989) found that high schools that emphasize academic pursuits, orderly environments, differentiated instruction, and smaller school size graduated more students. It would be logical, then, that PBS, with its emphasis on positive schoolwide interventions, early identification of at-risk students based on data, and intensive interventions for students with multiple and significant support needs would counterbalance some of the aforementioned stressors.

Students at risk, particularly those with emotional or behavioral challenges, come to school with certain significant and individualized support needs (Wagner, Marder, Blackorby, Cameto, Neuman, Levine & David-Mercers, 2003). These supports include the need for positive relationships, academic supports, and positive school-to-adult-life transition experiences. The intensive level of supports within a PBS context for high school students should include evidence-supported practices that promote self-determined skills and behaviors. Further, these interventions should enhance and create work experiences and other activities that relate to individually constructed postschool outcomes that build linkages to natural and paid supports (Lane & Carter, 2006; Wagner & Davis, 2006).

One such tertiary model, Rehabilitation and Empowerment for Natural Supports, Education, and Work (RENEW), is based on a collaboration between a nonprofit corporation and a university (Bullis & Cheney, 1999; M. Malloy & Cormier, 2004; Cheney, Malloy, Hagner, Cormier & Bernstein, 1998). This process focuses on the needs of adolescents at risk for connectedness to school-based and work-based experiences as part of a coherent, "results-oriented" orientation for transition from school to adult life. The RENEW model has in the early stages of demonstrated positive outcomes for youth with serious emotional and behavioral challenges and has more recently been used as the intensive intervention within the state's high school PBS dropout prevention model. The first high school that implemented RENEW as part of a three-tier PBIS model showed significant improvement in the functioning of youth with the most significant needs as assessed by the Child and Adolescent Functional Assessment Scale (Wells, Malloy, & Cormier, 2005).

### *Self-Determination and Person-Centered Planning*

Studies showed that when students with disabilities have the opportunities and support they need to become more "self-determined," they are far more likely to have better education and secondary transition outcomes and are more likely to persist in their education (Benz, Yovanoff, Doren, 1997; Carter et al., 2006; Eisenman, 2007; Wehmeyer & Palmer, 2003) While elements of self-determination can be found within all three tiers of support, much of the related research focuses on tertiary interventions. Self-determined motivation is a critical factor in student success, yet the research and interventions that target the development of self-determination skills and experiences among students who are at risk is lacking (Carter et al., 2006). Research is needed that demonstrates tools that build skills and knowledge associated with a person who is self-determined. These tools include experiences and knowledge that would lead to increased self-awareness, goal setting, problem solving, self-evaluation, and self-advocacy.

A critical tool for the creation of opportunities for self-determination is person-centered planning (Malloy, Cheney, Hagner, Cormter, Bernstein, 1998; Mount, 1992). There are various models for planning, including personal futures planning (Mount, 1989), MAPS (O'Brien & Forest, 1989), PATH (Pearpoint, O'Brien, & Forest, 1992), and various hybrid models (e. g.) person centered planning (Cotton, 2003). These supports can be implemented within both secondary (class-level planning) and tertiary supports. Although person-centered planning has been used primarily for planning around major life transitions with individuals with developmental disabilities, there has been some use with a broader population. It has been helpful in transition planning with a broad range of individuals with disabilities (Blackorby, 1996; Flannery et al., 2000). The use of a person-centered plan can be the focal point to drive the secondary transition planning and program (Hagner, Cheney, Malloy, 1999). For example, a young person can use the process to identify (a) what he or she wants to do, (b) personal strengths, (c) needs for support, and (d) goals after high school (such as college, employment, among others). The planning process can guide the young person toward those goals. No goal of the young person is, in and of itself, unrealistic.

The process, when conducted with fidelity, builds self-determination, unlike traditional service-planning processes, which are focused on agency needs, compliance (e.g., individualized educational plans), and treatment. The plan is often revisited and revised. The person-centered plan can be an assessment instrument. Further, the young person, with good facilitation, can use it to self-assess progress and adjust his or her actions as a result.

What can be most valuable in the person-centered planning process is the identification of the student's needs and natural resources. Often, youth who are at risk are disengaged and have "burned their bridges" to important social resources such as teachers, coaches, family members, peers, and adults in the community. The planning process identifies where the team needs to (a) make connections that do not exist, (b) reconnect with people who are important to achievement of the young person's goal, and (c) identify which "natural supports" exist to help with goal attainment. Unfortunately, there are limited data on the connection of these types of supports within the systematic implementation of PBS (Bohanon et al., 2007).

## DIRECTIONS FOR FUTURE PRACTICE AND RESEARCH

The application of PBS components at all levels (primary, secondary, and tertiary components) to high schools is in the early stages of development relative to examples at the elementary and middle school levels. We have illustrated some very promising examples that we hope will be expanded over the next several years. In this section, we describe practice adaptations from lessons learned in preliminary implementation in pilot high schools, followed by directions for future research.

There is clearly significant work to be done as we begin to understand applications of the three PBS tiers at the high school level. As emphasized throughout the chapter, delivering effective interventions that attend to the academic and behavioral needs of high school students is paramount. The current PBS triangle incorporates the design and delivery of academic supports as we move across tiers of intervention.

### *Consideration of Academic Issues.*

The consideration of student academic issues in a systemic fashion is a relatively new phenomenon in high schools. Fortunately, emerging response-to-treatment intervention (RTI) models are increasingly being developed (Brown-Chidsey & Steege, 2005). The RTI model takes a similar three-tier, problem-solving, and data-based approach that is the cornerstone of PBS, yet the focus is on the delivery of academic supports. Promising evidence exists that RTI models offer a systemwide approach to addressing student behavior through benchmarking, evidence-based practice, and early identification and remediation of student academic concerns. The use of curriculum-based measurement to drive and monitor interventions is a major tenet of this approach (Shapiro, 1996; Shinn, 1998).

Certainly, there are more examples of the application of RTI and problem-solving components of academic assessment and remediation in elementary and middle school environments. However, there are increasing high school applications of curriculum-based measurement as measures to monitor student progress in critical academic areas (Espin & Foegen, 1996). Large-scale research sites (e.g., the Research Institute on Progress Monitoring) funded by the U.S. Department of Education (USDOE) are increasingly providing examples of curriculum-based measurement probes that can be used at the high school level. These national projects have the potential to provide high school personnel with valuable information about the ways to develop and maintain schoolwide benchmarking and progress-monitoring data for high school students.

In addition, the systematic evaluation of universal design of learning (Rose & Meyer, 2006) and differentiated instruction (e.g., providing options with regard to presentation style and response formats) (Tomlinson, 1999) needs to happen at the high school level. Relatively minor modifications to academic curriculum can result in drastic changes in student behavior (Tomlinson). Setting up conditions in which the needs of all learning styles are met through visual and auditory presentation of material, structuring lessons using objectives, and having a clear vision regarding whether these objectives have been met are such adaptations that can result in significant changes in the classroom environment (Rose & Meyer).

Determining the efficacy of skill-based academic remediation programs at the high school level and decisions regarding when and where to use them is an important subsequent research activity. Further, process variables that are associated with problem-solving teams that incorporate PBS and academic RTI components in their decision making are needed. Large-scale evaluation of combined system change efforts that incorporate academic and behavioral supports for students at the high school level are desperately needed to inform practice.

Finally, the long-time work of Deschler and colleagues in their development of content enhancement series modules at the middle and high school levels (e.g., Deschler & Schumaker, 2005) is very important as we increasingly address the impact of academic issues on behavioral outcomes in secondary school settings. Such resources are powerful tools that can fuel our shift to addressing academic components as part of an overall schoolwide approach to addressing student needs.

Although research with students in the early grades has documented the relationship between behavior and academic problems (Fleming,

Harachi, Cortes, Abbott, & Catalano, 2004; Kellam, Ling, Merisca, Brown, & Ialongo, 1998; McIntosh, Horner, Chard, Boland, & Good, 2006; Morrison, Anthony, Storino, & Dillon, 2001), this same relationship in high school is just beginning to be explored (McIntosh, Flannery, Sugai, Braun, & Cochrane, in press; Morrison et al., 2001; Nelson, Benner, Lane, & Smith, 2004; Sinclair, Christenson, Thurlow, 2005) and requires further attention.

### *Research Examining High School Structural Variables*

As stated throughout the chapter, the very nature and structure of high schools make systematic PBS implementation a unique challenge. The sheer size of high schools (particularly in urban environments) means that when implementing any school reform effort, we may be dealing with over 1,500 students, over 150 staff, related service personnel (e.g., security, cafeteria workers), parents, and the larger community. Larger schools are predictive of negative outcomes, such as school dropout (Sugai et al., 2005), particularly for students with the most intensive needs (Stroul & Friedman, 1996). As a result, communicating and conducting professional development with such a large group is a challenge. Further complicating the size of schools is the departmentalized structure of schools, which often have centralized decision-making procedures (e.g., through department chairs) and are organized along content area (e.g., history) rather than by student academic and behavioral needs, which is more likely in elementary schools and, to a lesser extent, in middle school environments (Sugai et al., 2005).

Understanding the impact of these structural variables on the efficacy of PBS implementation at all levels is a much-needed future research activity. For example, in the Bohanon et al. study (2006), it took 2 years before systematic application of SW-PBS took place. In a second implementation school with similar student and teacher demographics (Hicks, 2008), it has taken considerably less time in initial implementation of PBS efforts. Through systematic replication of these efforts in multiple contexts (e.g., schools that range in size, location, teacher and student variables), we hopefully will begin to understand the conditions under which these structural variables have an impact on implementation at all levels and to what degree.

Further, there is much more to learn about the most efficient forms of professional development and how these efforts relate to PBS outcomes. It would be important to know how professional development should be adapted, based on (a) critical demographic variables in high schools that include the size of the school, the cultural background of the students, and the faculty in the setting; (b) whether students are meeting academic performance objectives, as articulated by meeting No Child Left Behind (NCLB) standards (2001); and (c) the existence of other initiatives in the building. Professional development models that involve the meaningful participation of school personnel (Knight, 2002) and that involve opportunity for direct practice, modeling, and feedback about specific skills seem to have the most promise (Noell et al., 2000) for sustaining large-scale efforts, such as PBS.

We are at a critical time in the development of PBS models that are effective in high schools. While there is limited research on effective universal interventions at the high school level, there is even less related to the implementation of PBS systems of secondary- and tertiary-level supports in high schools. But, the preliminary examples of schoolwide efforts (Bohanon et al., 2006), group/classroom supports (Moroz et al., in submission), and individualized tertiary supports (Cheney, Malloy, & Hagner, 1998) are very promising. We have our last chance to have an impact on the lives of individuals who will soon be adults and enter society. Challenges related to the nature of high schools (e.g., size, departmental structure, academic concerns) have been articulated (Bohanon-Edmonson, Flannery, Eber, Sugai, 2005). It is our hope that we can build on this work to greatly expand our knowledge base related to high school PBS and ultimately have an impact on the lives of those we serve.

## REFERENCES


Alexander, K. L., Entwisle, D. R., & Horsey, C. S. (1997). From first grade forward: Early foundations of high school dropout. *Sociology and Education, 70*, 87–107.

Benz, M., Yovanoff, P., & Doren, B. (1997). School-to-work components that predict post school success for children with and without disabilities. *Exceptional Children, 63*, 151–165.

Beaman, R., & Wheldall, K. (2000). Teachers' use of approval and disapproval in the classroom. *Educational Psychology, 20*(4), 431–446.

Blackorby, J. W. M. (1996). Longitudinal postschool outcomes of youth with disabilities: Findings from the National Longitudinal Transition Study. *Exceptional children 62*, 399–413.

Bohanon, H., Eber, L., Flannery, B., & Fenning, P. (2007). Identifying a roadmap of support for secondary students in school-wide positive behavior support applications. *International Journal of Special Education, 22*, 39–60.

Bohanon, H., Fenning, P. Carney, K., Minnis-Kim, M, Anderson-Harriss, S., Moroz, K., et al. (2006). School-wide applications of positive behavior support in an urban high school: A case study. *Journal of Positive Behavior Interventions, 8*, 131–145.

Bohanon-Edmonson, H., Flannery, B., Eber, L., & Sugai, G. (Eds.). (2005). *Positive behavior support in high schools*. Monograph from the 2004 Illinois High School Forum of Positive Behavioral Interventions and Supports. Retrieved July 30, 2007, from www.pbis.org/highschool.htm

Bohanon-Edmonson, H.& Flannery, B., Sugai, G., & Eber, L. (Eds) (2005). *School-wide PBS in High Schools Monograph.* Retrieved January 25, 2005, from http://www.pbis.org/highschool.htm.

Brown-Chidsey, R., & Steege, M. W. (2005). *Response to intervention: Principles and strategies for effective practice*. New York: Guilford Press:.

Bullis, M., & Cheney, D. (1999). Vocational and transition interventions for adolescents and young adults with emotional or behavioral disorders. *Focus on Exceptional Children 31*(7), 1–24.

Brant, R., & Christensen, M. (2002). *Improving student social skills through the use of cooperative learning, problem solving*. Unpublished master's thesis.

Bryk, A. S., & Thum, Y. M. (1989). The effects of high school organization on dropping out: An exploratory investigation. *American Education Research Journal 26*, 353–383.

Bryk, A. S., & Deabster, P. E. (1994). Measuring achievement gains in the Chicago public schools. *Education & Urban Society, 26*(3), 306–320.

Carr, E., Dunlap, G., Horner, R. H., Koegel, R. L., Turnbull, A. P., Sailor, W., et al. (2002). Positive behavior support: Evolution of an applied science. *Journal of Positive Behavior Interventions, 4*, 4–16.

Cheney, D., Malloy, J., Hagner, D., Cormier, G., & Bernstein, S. (1998). Finishing high school in many different ways: Project RENEW in Manchester, New Hampshire. *Effective School Practices, 17*(2), 43–52.

Cheney, D., Malloy, J., & Hager, D. (1998). Finishing high school in many different ways: Project RENEW in Manchester, New Hampshire. *Effective School Practices, 17*(2). 45–54.

Colvin, G., Kameenui, E. J., & Sugai, G. (1993). School-wide and classroom management: Reconceptualizing the integration and management of students with behavior problems in general education. *Education and Treatment of Children, 16*, 361–381.

Cotton, P. (2003). *Elements of design: Frameworks for facilitating person-centered planning.* Durham: University of New Hampshire, Institute on Disability.

Croninger, R. G., & Lee, V. E. (2001). Social capital and dropping out of high school: Benefits to at-risk students of teachers' support and guidance. *Teachers College Record, 103*, 548–581.

Daniels, H., Bizar, M., Zemelman, S. (2001). *Rethinking high school: Best practices in teaching, learning, and leadership.* Portsmouth: Heinemann, Reed Eleveir, Inc.

Deschler, D. D., & Schumaker, J. B. (2005). *High school students with disabilities: Strategies for accessing the curriculum.* New York: Corwin Press.

Eber, L., Nelson, C. M., & Miles, P. (1997). School-based wraparound planning: Integrating services for students with emotional and behavioral challenges. *Exceptional Children, 64*, 539–555.

Education Trust. (2005). *Gaining traction, gaining ground: How some high schools accelerate learning for struggling students.* Washington, DC: Author.

Eisenman, L. T. (2007). Self-determination interventions: Building a foundation for school completion. *Remedial and Special Education, 28*, 2–8.

Espin, C. A., & Foegen, A. (1996). Validity of general outcome measures for predicting secondary students' performance on content-area tasks. *Exceptional Children, 62*, 497–514.

Fairchild, T. N. (1983). The effects of a daily report card on an eighth grader exhibiting behavioral and motivational problems. *School Counselor, 31*(1), 83–86.

Farmer, C. D. (1996). Proactive alternatives to school suspension: Reclaiming children and youth. *Journal of Emotional and Behavioral Problems, 5*, 47–51.

Fenning, P., & Bohanon, H. (2006). School-wide discipline policies: An analysis of the discipline code of conduct. In C. M. Evertson & C. S. Weinstein (Eds.), *Handbook of classroom management: Research, practice and contemporary issues.* Mahway, NJ: Erlbaum.

Fenning, P., Golomb, S., Gordon, V., Kelly, M., Scheinfield, R., Morello, T., et al. (in press). Written discipline policies used by administrators: Do we have sufficient tools of the trade? *Journal of School Violence.*

Fenning, P., Theodos, J., Benner, C., & Bohanon-Edmonson, H. (2004). Integrating proactive discipline practices into codes of conduct. *Journal of School Violence, 3*, 45–61.

Finn, J. D., & Rock, D. A. (1997). Academic success among students at risk for school failure. *Journal of Applied Psychology, 82*(2), 221–234.

Gates Foundation (2003). *Annual Report 2003.* Retrieved September 2, 2008, from Bill and Melinda Gates Foundation Website: http://www.gatesfoundation.org/nr/public/media/annualreports/annualreport03/flash/Gates_AR-2003.html

Gilchrist, R. S. (1989). *Effective schools: Three case studies of excellence.* Bloomington: National Educational Service.

Glover, D. (2005). *The impact of a school-wide positive behavior support plan on high school student's perceptions of school climate and peer relationships.* Unpublished dissertation, Loyola University, Chicago. Pro Quest 3180952.

Gottman, J. M. (1994). *What Predicts Divorce? The Relationship Between Marital Processes and Marital Outcomes.* Hillsdale: Lawrence Erlbaum Associates, Inc.

Hagner, D., Cheney, D., & Malloy, J. (1999). Career-related outcomes of a model transition demonstration for young adults with emotional disturbance. *Rehabilitation Counseling Bulletin, 42*, 228–242.

Hicks, K., Bohanon, H., Fenning, P., Weber, S., Ramono, S., Stone, L., Akins, B., & Irvin, L. (2008). Case study of the implementation of positive behavior supports in an

urban high school, *International Conference for the Association of Positive Behavior Supports*, Chicago, IL. March 2008.
Kern, L., & Manz, P. (2004). A look at current validity issues of school-wide behavior support. *Behavioral Disorders, 30*(1), 47–59.
Knight, J. (2002). *Partnership learning field book*. Retrieved July 30, 2007, from www.instructionalcoach.org/ParternshipLearningFieldBook.pdf
Kohn, A. (1993). *Punished by rewards*. Boston: Houghton Mifflin
Kortering, L., & Braziel P. (1999). School dropout from the perspective of former students. *Remedial and Special Education, 20*(2), 61–70.
Kutash, K., & Duchonowski, A. (1997). Creating comprehensive and collaborative systems. *Journal of Emotional and Behavioral Disorders, 5*, 66–75.
Lane, K. L., Wehby, J., Menzies, H. M., Doukas, G. L., Munton, S. M., & Gregg, R. M. (2003). Social skills instruction for students at risk for antisocial behavior: The effects of small-group instruction. *Behavioral Disorders, 28*(3), 229–248.
Lee, V. E., & Smith, J. B. (1994). High school restructuring and student achievement: A new study finds strong links. *Issues in Restructuring Schools, 7*, 1-5, 16.
Lee, V. E., & Burkam, D. T. (2001). *Dropouts in America: How severe is the problem. What do we know about intervention and prevention?* Paper presented at the Dropouts in America: How Severe is the Problem? What Do We Know about Intervention and Prevention? Harvard Graduate School of Education, Cambridge, MA.
Lehr, C. A., Hansen, A., Sinclair, M., & Christenson, S. L. (2003). Moving beyond dropout towards school completion: An integrative view of the literature. *School Psychology Review, 32*, 342–364.
Losada, M., & Heaphy, E. (2004). The role of positivity and connectivity in the performance of business teams. *American Behavioral Scientist, 47*(6), 740–765.
Mackin, R. A. (1996). Hey Dr. Bob, can we talk?: Toward the creation of a personalized high school. *NASSP Bulletin, 80*(584), 9 pgs.
Masten, A. S., & Coatsworth, J. D. (1998). The development of competence in favorable and unfavorable environments: Lessons from research on successful children. *American Psychologist, 53*(2), 205–220.
Malloy, J. M., Cheney, D., Hagner, D., Cormier, G. M., & Bernstein, S. (1998). Personal futures planning for youth with EBD. *Reaching Today's Youth, 2*(4), 25–29.
Malloy, M., & Cormier, G. (2004). Project RENEW: Building the community's capacity to support youths' transition from school to adult life. In D. Cheney (Ed.), *Transition of secondary students with emotional or behavioral disorders: Current approaches for positive outcomes* (pp. 180–200). Arlington, VA: Council for Children With Behavioral Disorders.
Mayer, G. R. (1995). Preventing antisocial behavior in the schools. *Journal of Applied Behavioral Analysis*, 28(4), 467–478.
Meier, Deborah. 1995. The Power of Their Ideas. Boston: Beacon Press.
McQuillan, J. (1998). *Seven myths about literacy in the United States*. College Park: ERIC Clearinghouse on Assessment and Evaluation.
Moroz, K., Fenning, P., & Bohanon, H. (in submission). The effects of guided practice, publicly posted feedback, and acknowledgement on classroom tardies in an urban high school implementing school-wide positive behavioral interventions and supports. *Journal of Positive Behavior Interventions.*
Morrison, G. M., & D'Incau, B. (1997). The web of zero tolerance: Characteristics of students who are recommended for expulsion from school. *Education and Treatment of Children, 20*, 316–335.
Morrison, G. M., Furlong, M. J., & Morrison, R. L. (1994). School violence to school safety: Reframing the issue for school psychologists. *School Psychology Review, 23*, 236–256.
Mount, B. (1992). *Person-centered planning: Finding directions for change using personal futures planning*. New York: Graphic Futures.
Murphy, S. A., van der Laan, M. J., Robins, J. M., & Conduct Problems Prevention Research Group. (2001). Marginal mean models for dynamic regimes. *Journal of the American Statistical Association, 96*, 1410–1423.
National Center for Educational Statistics. (n.d.). *Violence and crime at school: Public school reports. In Indicators of school crime and safety, 2003* (section 7). Retrieved October 1, 2004, from http://nces.ed.gov/pubs2004/crime03/7.asp?nav=2

National Governor's Association. (2003). *Reaching new heights: A governor's' guide to turning around low-performing schools.* Retrieved October 1, 2004, from http://www.nga.org/cda/files/0803REACHING.PDF

No Child Left Behind Act (2001) (NCLB). Public Law 107–110.

Noell, G. H., Witt, J. C., Lafleur, L. H., Mortenson, B. P., Ranier, D. D., & LeVelle, J. (2000). Increasing intervention implementation in general education following consultation: A comparison of two follow-up strategies. *Journal of Applied Behavior Analysis, 33,* 271–284.

Noguera, P. A. (1995). Preventing and producing violence: A critical analysis of responses to school violence. *Harvard Educational Review,* Summer 1995, 189–212.

Newman, B. M., Myers, M. C., Newman, P. R., Lohman, B. J., & Smith, V. L. (2000).The transition to high school for academically promising, urban, low-income African American youth. *Adolescence, 35,* 45–66.

O'Brien, J., & Forrest, M. (1987). *Action for inclusion.* Toronto: Frontier College Press.

Office of Vocational and Adult Education (2004). *High school leadership summit issue papers.* Washington, D.C.: U.S. Department of Education, Washington, D. C. Retrieved April 15, 2005, from http://www.ed.gov/about/offices/list/ovae/pi/hsinit/papers/index.html

Pearpoint, J., O'Brien, J., & Forest, M. (1992). *PATH: A workbook for planning better futures.* Toronto: Inclusion Press.

Raywid, M.A. (1995). Alternative schools: The state of the art. *Educational Leadership,* 52(1), 26–31.

Renihan, F. I., & Renihan, P. J. (1995). Responsive high schools: Structuring success for the at-risk student. *The High School Journal, 79*(1): 1-13.

Rose, D. H., & Meyer, A. (Eds.). (2006). *A practical reader in universal design for learning.* Cambridge, MA: Harvard Education Press.

Rumberger, R. W. (2001). *Why students drop out of school and what can be done.* Santa Barbara, CA: University of California–Santa Barbara. Retrieved May 15, 2003, from http://www.civilrightsproject.harvard.edu/research/dropouts/rumberger.pdf

Sato, N., & McLaughlin, M. W. (1992). Context matters: Teaching in Japan and in the United States. *Phi Delta Kappan,* 73(5), 359–366.

Schumaker, J. B., Hovell, M. F., & Sherman, J. A. (1977). An analysis of daily report cards and parent-managed privileges in the improvement of adolescents' classroom performance. *Journal of Applied Behavioral Analysis,* 10(3), 449–464.

Shapiro, E. S. (1996). *Academic skills problems: Direct assessment and intervention* (2nd ed.). New York: Guilford Press.

Shinn, M. R. (Ed.). (1998). *Advanced applications of curriculum-based measurement.* New York: Guilford Press.

Sinclair, M. F., Christenson, S. L., Evelo, D. L., & Hurley, C. M. (1998). Dropout prevention for youth with disabilities : Efficacy of a sustained school engagement procedure. *Exceptional Children, 65* (1), 7-21.

Sinclair, M., Christenson, S. L., & Thurlow, M. L. (2005). Promoting school completion of urban secondary youth with emotional or behavioral disabilities. *Exceptional Children, 71,* 465–482.

Skiba, R. J., Michael, R. S., Nardo, A. C., & Peterson, R. (2000, June). *The color of discipline: Sources of racial and gender disproportionality in school punishment.* Retrieved August 20, 2006, from http://www.indiana.edu/~safeschl/cod.pdf/minor.html

Skiba, R., & Peterson, R. (1999). The dark side of zero tolerance: Can punishment lead to safe schools? *Phi Delta Kappan, 80,* 372–376, 381–382.

Skiba, R., & Peterson, R. (2003). Teaching the social curriculum: School discipline as instruction. *Preventing School Failure, 47*(2), 66–73.

Siskin, L. S. (1994). *Realms of knowledge: Academic departments in secondary schools.* Washington DC: Falmer Press.

Stroul, B. A., & Friedman, R. M. (1986). *A system of care for seriously emotionally disturbed children and youth.* Washington, DC: CASSP Technical Assistance Center, Georgetown University Child Development Center.

Sugai, G., & Horner, R. H. (1999). Discipline and behavioral support: Preferred processes and practices. *Effective School Practices, 17*(4), 10–22.

Sugai, G., Lewis-Palmer, T. L., Todd, A. W., & Horner, R. H. (2001). *School-wide Evaluation Tool (SET)*. Eugene, OR: Educational and Community Supports. Available at http://www.pbis.org

Sugai, G., Flannery, B., & Bohanon-Edmonson, H. (2005). *School-wide positive behavior support in high schools: What will it take?* Unpublished paper

Tomlinson, C. (1999). *The differentiated classroom: Responding to the needs of all Learners*. Alexandria, VA: ASCD.

Vandercook, T., York, J., & Forest, M. (1989). The McGill Action Planning System (MAPS). *Journal of the Association for Persons with Severe Handicaps, 14*, 205–215.

Wagner, M. (1991). *Dropouts with disabilities: What do we know? What can we do?* A report from the National Longitudinal Transition Study of Special Education studnets. Menlo Park, CA: SRI International.

Wagner, M., D'Amico, R., Marder, C., Newman, L., & Blackorby, J. (1992). *What happens next? Trends in postschool outcomes of youth with disabilities*. Menlo Park, CA, SRI International.

Wagner, M., & Davis, M. (2006). How are we preparing students with emotional disturbances for the transition to young adulthood?: Findings from the National Longitudinal Transition Study-2. *Journal of Emotional and Behavioral Disorders, 14*(2), 86–98.

Wagner, M. M., Kutash, K., Duchnowski, A. J., & Epstein, M. H. (2005). The Special Education Elementary Longitudinal Study and the National Longitudinal Transition Study: Study designs and implications for children and youth with emotional disturbance. *Journal of Emotional and Behavioral Disorders, 13*(1), 25–41.

Wagner, M., Marder, C., Blackorby, J., Cameto, R., Newman, L., Levine, P., & Davies-Mercier, E. (2003). *The achievements of youth with disabilities during secondary school: A report from the National Longitudinal Transition Study-2*. Menlo Park, CA: SRI International.

Wald, J., & Losen, D. J. (2003). Editors' notes. In J. Wald and D. J. Losen (Eds.), *New directions for youth development: Deconstructing the school-to-prison pipeline* (pp. 1–2). San Francisco: Jossey-Bass.

Wehmeyer, M. L., & Palmer, S. B. (2003) Adult outcomes for students with cognitive disabilities three years after high school: The impact of self-determination. *Education and Training in Developmental Disabilities, 38*, 131–144.

Wehman, P. (1996). *Life beyond the classroom: Transition strategies for young people with disabilities* (2nd. ed.). Baltimore: Brookes.

Wilson, B., & Corcoran, T. (1988). *Successful Secondary Schools: Visions of Excellence in American Public Education*. London: Falmer.

# 25

# Systems Change and the Complementary Roles of In-Service and Preservice Training in Schoolwide Positive Behavior Support

**RACHEL FREEMAN, SHARON LOHRMANN, LARRY K. IRVIN, DON KINCAID, VICTORIA VOSSLER, and JOLENEA FERRO**

Over the years, a growing number of states have adopted schoolwide positive behavior support (SW-PBS) as part of school improvement and reform efforts and, more recently, as part of the federally mandated State Performance Plan process. The essential features of the SW-PBS approach have been well described in previous chapters in this book and in the professional and academic literature (Crone, Horner, & Hawken, 2004; Horner, Sugai, Todd, & Lewis-Palmer, 2005; Liaupsin, Jolivette, & Scott, 2004; Taylor-Greene et al., 1997; Sugai et al., 2000; Todd, Horner, Sugai, & Colvin, 1999). Thus, this chapter focuses on the professional development (PD) needs related to sustainable SW-PBS implementation.

**RACHEL FREEMAN** • University of Fansas
**SHARON LOHRMANN** • University of Medicine & Dentistry of New Jersey
**LARRY K. IRVIN** • Lawrence, KS
**DON KINCAID** • University of South Florida
**VICTORIA VOSSLER** • Topeka Public School, Topeka, Kansas
**JOLENEA FERRO** • PBISAZ Project Coordinator

The experiences of states pioneering SW-PBS implementation have advanced our understanding of how to expand necessary PD services in ways that produce sustainable implementation (Muscott, Mann, Gately, Bell, & Muscott, 2004). Strategies for SW-PBS funding have varied significantly, and many SW-PBS projects have been funded initially to support small cohorts of model demonstration school sites. Success at these sites led to expansion designed to reach larger and larger cohorts of schools. These early projects experienced many SW-PBS training and technical assistance challenges as they expanded, which have informed our current approaches to PD.

To optimize effectiveness and usefulness, PD providers must understand the (a) foundational principles that define high-quality PD; (b) need to match PD based on the roles of the SW-PBS implementers and the contextual features (resources, skills, and values) of each school, district, state, or region; and (c) changing in-service and preservice training needs of school-based teams implementing SW-PBS.

The purpose of this chapter is to describe what has been learned about PD in the implementation of SW-PBS and the growing expansion of complementary preservice training systems. Specifically, we describe (a) current examples of statewide approaches of SW-PBS implementation that link preservice and in-service training efforts, (b) critical features of design and delivery of in-service training and technical assistance efforts at the statewide level, and (c) how statewide planning teams can use evaluation to build complementary in-service and preservice systems through statewide leadership teams.

## SW-PBS AND SYSTEMS CHANGE

Implementation of any type of new program is optimized when organizations create and provide (a) the infrastructure necessary for carefully coordinating training and mentoring, (b) frequent performance assessments of practitioners, (c) an approach for integrating regular process and outcome evaluations, (d) opportunities for communities and consumers to be fully involved in the selection and evaluation of programs and practices, and (e) support for state and federal funding, policies, and regulations (Fixen, Naoom, Blasé, Friedman, & Wallace, 2005). SW-PBS includes careful consideration for and planning about system changes that are necessary for effective implementation, especially contextual features that are unique to individual schools, districts, regions, and states. Similarly, as efforts to implement SW-PBS expand systematically across the state, PD capacity also must grow.

Although states design and implement PD for SW-PBS in a variety of ways, all SW-PBS projects seem to follow similar developmental implementation stages that have an impact on the kind of training and technical assistance that is needed and provided: (a) initial design and implementation, (b) expansion, and (c) sustainability.

### *Initial Design and Implementation*

During the initial stage of systems change, the focus is on establishing a preliminary infrastructure that will guide the emergence of model implementation sites and set the stage for later expansion. A number of key steps occur at this phase: (a) forming a state or district leadership team; (b) determining how to coordinate efforts across schools and districts; (c) establishing four to six or more training days for school teams with technical assistance support for schools throughout the year; (d) dedicating resources for establishing demonstration sites; (e) cultivating a cadre of skilled trainers; and (f) identifying coaches and creating a support network for internal district SW-PBS capacity. At this initial stage, the establishment of visible policies, political support, and "front-end" resources is a major focus.

### *Expansion*

The hard work of establishing an initial foundation is rewarded with the opportunity to begin systematic expansion efforts. The focus of the leadership team shifts from creating demonstration sites to building the capacity for training broader cohorts of implementation sites and expanding training opportunities across multiple SW-PBS roles (e.g., behavior specialists, coaches, administrators). Activities during this phase include adjusting training materials and delivery methods, replacing key trainers when turnover occurs, tracking maintenance within schools already implementing SW-PBS, and fine-tuning policies and procedures to support continued SW-PBS implementation.

### *Sustainability*

Sustainability planning occurs throughout initial implementation and expansion efforts. The ways in which initial PD systems are established will increase or decrease the likelihood that SW-PBS efforts expand effectively. However, once the foundation for SW-PBS implementation is established and plans for expansion are implemented, attention shifts to ensuring implementation fidelity. For example, as trained staff move on and new untrained professionals enter the system, fidelity of SW-PBS implementation may decrease. This sustainability challenge signals the need for capacity-building PD. Because most SW-PBS PD approaches rely on in-service training, state leadership teams should anticipate the need for ongoing PD by extending into preservice arenas. One strategy is to establish collaborations with institutions of higher education (IHEs), which infuse the system with newly certified professionals who have the skills and knowledge necessary to enter a system and implement with accuracy. Collaboration with IHEs ensures adequate numbers of behavior specialists, administrators, and other professionals with experience in SW-PBS implementation.

A second important consideration during the sustainability stage is finding a balance between SW-PBS implementation efforts and other high-priority initiatives. As new key initiatives emerge, statewide planning teams should consider ways in which SW-PBS can complement these priorities. For instance, a number of state teams address response to intervention (RTI) from both behavioral and academic perspectives using the concept of multitier systems of support (e.g., Michigan's Integrated Behavior and Learning Initiative, 2007; Florida's Response to Intervention and Positive Behavior Support Projects). Planning processes that assist districts and schools to implement multiple initiatives increase the likelihood that SW-PBS will be sustained over time and not dropped in favor of funding new programs.

Finally, leadership teams must avoid dependence on time-limited resources (e.g., grants, temporary budget reallocations) to sustain SW-PBS implementation. Shifts in funding streams require balancing and redistributing resources each year to maintain and expand implementation efforts. If SW-PBS is needed and a priority, efforts should be directed at funding PD for 3- to five-year cycles.

Given these challenges, a major focus of planning at the sustainability stage is interagency collaboration with IHEs and other service systems to ensure personnel across systems are adequately prepared to continue high-fidelity implementation. State leadership team responsibilities at this stage include, for example, (a) designing practicum opportunities at implementation sites for undergraduate and graduate students, (b) recommending changes in certification requirements, and (c) adjusting training materials and delivery methods to integrate multiple complementary priorities (e.g., Ohio's PBS Reading Initiative).

## INFUSING CAPACITY ACROSS SYSTEMS THROUGH COORDINATED AND COMPLEMENTARY PRESERVICE AND IN-SERVICE TRAINING

Optimal personnel preparation requires a complementary approach to both preservice and in-service training in SW-PBS. Furthermore both in-service and preservice systems should be nested within the larger cultural, organizational, and social systems change context at the state and local levels. Accomplishing such a coordinated effort requires an understanding of how various state approaches came into existence, the implication these approaches have for moving forward, and the challenges commonly encountered.

### *The Emergence of State Projects*

Many current statewide efforts for implementing SW-PBS have evolved from federal and state funding (e.g., Individuals with Disabilities Education Improvement Act IDEIA, safe and drug-free schools, state improvement grants), have relied on in-service PD approaches, and are most closely linked with special education systems. For example, New Jersey began developing cohorts of model implementation sites through the Office of Special Education Programs (OSEP) state improvement grant. As federal funding ended, ongoing and expanded implementation efforts continued through OSEP state funding. Like New Jersey, most state planning teams have tended to focus directly on the parameters set out by their existing funding streams, followed by efforts to sustain results by embedding training and technical assistance into state and district systems.

## *Key Roles of Leadership Teams*

As a result of the diverse methods of funding and the differing priorities that served as a catalyst for the emergence of the statewide approach, each state leadership team has unique characteristics and composition. To achieve the goal of sustainable systemic change, leadership teams must be certain that their membership is composed of individuals who represent their major constituencies and stakeholders. Statewide leadership and planning teams commonly include professionals representing key roles within the state Department of Education, including curriculum and instruction, counseling and special services, special education, safe and drug-free schools, RTI initiatives, and teacher certification. Other agencies often participating at statewide planning meetings include mental health, developmental disability, child welfare, and juvenile justice. Various local educational district representatives may also be involved in statewide team meetings, including administration, professionals responsible for SW-PBS coordination, or school administration. Experienced trainers or outside consultants often facilitate initial statewide team meetings to guide action planning. Professionals from IHEs are sometimes members of the leadership team based on who initiated the SW-PBS effort, how the leadership was formed, and where the content and practices knowledge was located. However, because most states began with an in-service approach, few examples currently exist of state leadership teams that have strong interconnected preservice training in SW-PBS across multiple IHEs.

State teams that have completed the initial implementation stage and are interested in expanding SW-PBS to create and support sustainability must begin planning processes that will have large-scale impact on educators and education-related professionals (e.g., those involved with specialized related services, therapists, and mental health clinicians) in training. Preservice training that is directly linked to the application of SW-PBS provides state teams with an important resource for preparing professionals in education to be effective trainers, administrators, team members, or behavior specialists. Preservice training allows educators a variety of supervised learning opportunities regarding application of important SW-PBS concepts before assuming responsibilities within a school. In-service training on SW-PBS and the process of change can be easier and more effective when educators are already familiar through preservice educational experiences with SW-PBS concepts, strategies, and tools. In addition, preservice exposure establishes a standard expectation for the use of SW-PBS, thereby reducing the "resistance" sometimes experienced in schools when something "new" is introduced.

## *Expansion to Disciplines Beyond Special Education*

A number of SW-PBS preservice training examples currently implemented nationally rely on links within IHEs' departments of special education. Many of these initial preservice training systems include SW-PBS curriculum primarily because a small number of professors or other university faculty in special education settings and university research centers have taken an active role in leading PBS and SW-PBS implementation efforts. For example, SW-PBS leaders at the University of Oregon in Eugene have designed exemplary preservice training in SW-PBS within already existing preservice course requirements for individuals seeking master's and doctoral-level degrees. Undergraduate classes are also available at the University of Oregon for preservice teachers interested in learning more about SW-PBS.

To a great extent, certification requirements of states do not include standards for PBS at the individual or schoolwide level, and preservice curriculum and practicum opportunities are not designed to expose the educator in training to PBS at a theoretical or practical level. As a result, many newly certified professionals needed preservice training prior to that primarily provided through in-service approaches.

A great need also exists to expand knowledge and awareness of SW-PBS beyond special education departments to other areas of training and certification, such as those for elementary and secondary educators, education leadership, school psychology, and social work. Preservice PD could be integrated into the educational experiences of elementary and secondary general education teachers as part of courses related to school reform efforts such as RTI initiatives or as a component of effective classroom management. Practicum assignments linked to schools implementing SW-PBS would assist elementary and secondary educators in training to more fully understand how the concepts learned in class are applied in real settings. Future administrators should be exposed to SW-PBS with an emphasis on the importance of district and school data systems, the roles of principals and superintendents in SW-PBS leadership, and how policies and procedures can be used as an important element in preventing problem behavior. School psychologist and social work preservice trainees must be prepared to assist teaching professionals how to lead or participate in secondary and tertiary prevention systems intended to support students who need more individualized academic or behavior supports. Preservice training in all of these professions could proactively teach roles and responsibilities of team members within SW-PBS implementation.

### *Reaching Outside Education*

The preservice training needs of professionals working with youth are not confined to the school building. Professionals who support children and families through state and county human service agencies and programs are collaborating with educators in a growing number of states, districts, and schools by participating in systems of care for students in need of individualized tertiary plans of support. Social workers, mental health professionals, juvenile justice authorities, and child welfare staff are all examples of professionals who are already participating in SW-PBS in-service training and who are beginning to be actively involved in SW-PBS implementation. Extending the reach of professional preparation programs to include trainees linked to education would further strengthen the network of capacity within a state.

### *Establishing Interagency Relationships*

The design for implementing SW-PBS systems varies depending on the unique resources, collaborating organizations (IHEs, mental health, state systems), and personnel skill sets that participating stakeholders bring to the statewide leadership planning team. Each state needs to build on its existing strengths and identify areas of PD training need. In some state teams, strong relationships exist between the Department of Education and IHE professionals in special education. The state team may begin building preservice PD within the Department of Special Education as a starting point for larger PD systems change efforts.

At the University of Kansas (Lawrence, KS), SW-PBS leaders are also involved in the implementation of a PD training system for professionals in mental health, developmental disability, and children and family services. By creating interagency agreements across the Department of Education and other state agencies, PD is now available through that non-education-based program for SW-PBS district trainers in Kansas who are learning how to facilitate individualized PBS plans for students with severe problem behavior.

The ways in which interagency resources and relationships evolve sets the stage for the extent to which in-service and preservice training systems complement one another. SW-PBS leaders who are part of an IHE often incorporate SW-PBS into existing preservice course curriculum. The state leadership planning team may build on this initial progress by forming partnerships with the leaders of IHE departments to explore other resources that may be available to connect in-service and preservice PD such as practicum sites linked to SW-PBS efforts or personnel preparation grants. The state may also invite professionals from other departments within the same IHE, such as psychology, education leadership, or schools of social work, to state training team meetings or schedule individualized meetings to introduce SW-PBS to department chairs.

Statewide planning in SW-PBS, by its nature, encourages inter- and intraagency collaboration. To be more effective, general and special education departments are becoming directly involved in decision making within state leadership teams. Interagency connections within social work, mental health, developmental disabilities, juvenile justice, and other services increase the ability of state teams to "braid" funding sources, connect training efforts, and increase communication. Some state leadership teams have actively recruited professionals from these other human service agencies. Such interagency connections are often formed when one or more people from different agencies make a commitment to explore the ways in which SW-PBS can improve outcomes for students by integrating or braiding services. For instance, in Illinois, SW-PBS was embedded within a program supporting students with significant emotional and behavioral needs using wraparound supports at a tertiary level (Freeman et al., 2006). The expansion toward a multitier system of support increased positive outcomes and assisted in creating host contexts in which interagency collaboration could thrive. The program, funded through the Illinois Department of Education, has continued to emphasize an interagency approach to SW-PBS implementation (Illinois State-wide Technical Assistance Center, 2007).

## *Overcoming Challenges*

In general, continuous change at the school, district, state, and national levels creates challenges in efforts to connect preservice and in-service training approaches. When multiple systems have many divergent policies, procedures, or certification requirements, communications, scheduling, decision making, and action planning become more complex for leadership teams. Political changes (e.g., from public election results) at any of these levels can have the same or even larger effects.

As state teams design complementary in-service and preservice personnel preparation systems, they should anticipate three specific challenges. First, a paucity of leaders who have experience in the area of applied behavior analysis or positive behavior support reduces both the establishment of a conceptual foundation and the PD capacity needed to support the implementation of SW-PBS practices. With only a surface-level understanding of SW-PBS or systems change approaches, training and implementation may become overly simplified, not contextualized to local norms and characteristics or excessively manualized. System-level capacity building requires investments in resources that support the establishment of highly trained professionals who can lead complex training systems involving both in-service and preservice education in SW-PBS.

Second, preservice training will be less effective without real-life examples and opportunities that illustrate SW-PBS implementation at the school and district levels. Thus, IHE requirements should include practicum experi ences that provide exposure to SW-PBS implementation, and these experiences should be located in sites that represent accurate SW-PBS implementation. To ensure that practicum experiences provide students with sufficient exposure, IHEs should give priority and dedicate resources to finding, recruiting, and cultivating sites that have rich and accurate examples of SW-PBS implementation. For instance, three case studies in this chapter describe university partnerships in which professionals in training at the master's and doctoral level can participate directly in SW-PBS implementation.

Third, IHEs involved in preservice training must stay apprised of the state's leadership team efforts to ensure that information is timely and accurate. In turn, state leadership team members must be sensitive to the needs of IHE faculty as they build practicum experiences, curriculum content, and course sequences.

In addition to IHE and state coordination, PD efforts should consider other training collaborators, for example, professionals in mental health, child welfare, and juvenile justice. Examples of these types of partnerships have occurred in states such as Maryland and Illinois, where mental health organizations and professionals are directly involved in SW-PBS implementation efforts. Although complementary systems of training and technical assistance may be challenging, a number of IHE settings are providing examples of successful training and educational experiences in SW-PBS.

## EXAMPLES OF STATEWIDE PLANNING

Thus far, PD for SW-PBS has been discussed in terms of systems change need at the local, regional, and state levels and provided a rationale for complementary in-service and preservice training systems. In this section, ongoing SW-PBS efforts in Oregon, Florida, and Arizona are described. To gather this information, we conducted structured phone interviews with one or two state leadership team members from each of the three states to determine their perspectives on how PD planning and implementation have been conducted in their state. These perspectives may include perceptions unique to the interviewee and may not reflect the details of the entire SW-PBS efforts within a state.

### Oregon Statewide Training and Technical Assistance

#### *Origins of SW-PBS*

SW-PBS has been implemented in districts and schools in Oregon since the early 1990s. In the early days of implementation, professionals from the University of Oregon took a lead role in providing technical assistance, primarily funded by various federal research grants. Schools were initially recruited by university researchers to become demonstration sites for SW-PBS. As the number of demonstration sites grew, districts began self-initiating requests for training. School districts in Oregon are divided into educational service districts (ESDs). To support the growing interest in SW-PBS, the researchers at the University of Oregon recruited ESD staff to become district trainers. Over time, implementation efforts in Oregon became increasingly coordinated, resulting in the formation of a state leadership team in 2005.

#### *State Leadership Team*

The state leadership team in Oregon is relatively new and evolving with a gradually increasing membership. Approximately 25 people meet monthly for 3 hours in a central location in Oregon. Leadership team members include SW-PBS trainers, University of Oregon and Portland State University representatives, a state coordinator, and independent consultants. The leadership team is currently reorganizing the state's SW-PBS training systems. Since 2005, the leadership team has focused most of their efforts on conference coordination. In addition, three subcommittees within the state leadership team address topic areas related to policy, conference planning, and evaluation. Each meeting includes time for each subcommittee to meet and then to report progress at the end of the meeting. The team has a grant from the Oregon Department of Education that is awarded to an ESD to fund a full-time state coordinator, a statewide trainer, and a secretarial position. The statewide team is considering application for nonprofit organization status to give them the ability to apply for grants and seek external funds. The state team is planning to increase interagency membership in their next team-planning process. A survey was sent to all team members asking for feedback about how to proceed with preservice training goals in the state's planning process.

### In-Service Training and Technical Assistance

The state leadership team in Oregon has designed a 3-day summer training event to support SW-PBS. Day 1 includes introductory training for new teams. Day 2 is organized into breakout sessions offering content addressing the SW-PBS continuum of behavior support (universal, targeted, intensive). On Day 3, school teams work independently on SW-PBS implementation with technical assistance support from coaches and state leadership team members. Coaching conferences are scheduled in January and August of each year. Additional follow-up training for school teams occurs throughout the year by ESD or district trainers, not by the state leadership team. This approach emphasizes the development of training and PD capacity within districts and ESDs so new school teams receive training by internal expertise and support from district coaches, facilitators, and coordinators. Approximately 400 schools are implementing SW-PBS in Oregon. The state team has future plans to conduct a trainer-of-trainers conference, which would provide updates and current research findings for the professionals providing district or ESD school team training and technical assistance across the state.

### Preservice Training and Technical Assistance

As one of the original preservice programs to offer training on PBS, the University of Oregon has a long and distinguished history in preparing education professionals to implement SW-PBS. Currently, the University of Oregon provides preservice course materials related to SW-PBS within the College of Education in the Department of Special Education and Clinical Sciences. This college includes the Departments of School Psychology, Special Education, and Early Intervention. A small number of professors are directly involved in SW-PBS, and several centers and institutes are associated with research and technical assistance in SW-PBS. The following courses include instruction and activities related to SW-PBS:

- Behavioral Assessment and Consultation I and II, focusing on functional behavioral assessment processes.
- SW-PBS, focusing on universal implementation.
- Advanced Applied Behavior Analysis.
- Behavior and Classroom Management.
- Advanced Behavior and Classroom Management.
- Doctoral-level seminars on the design of instruction for advanced learners.

Approximately three graduate students a year are involved in advanced practicum experiences in PBS, and on average six dissertations per year focus on behavior analysis research occurring within the context of SW-PBS. Most student research projects are single-subject designs, although some dissertations also involve group designs. In addition, many of these dissertations are focused on issues related to secondary and tertiary implementation.

## Florida Statewide Training and Technical Assistance

### *Origins of SW-PBS*

Florida's involvement in PBS grew out of research activities associated with the Rehabilitation Research and Training Center for Positive Behavior Support, a project funded for nearly 15 years by the National Institute on Disability and Rehabilitation Research (NIDRR). This project provided much of the research foundation for supporting individual students with severe problem behaviors that came to be known as PBS. In 1997, the state Department of Education contracted with the Florida Mental Health Institute (FMHI), a research and technical assistance center connected to the University of South Florida, to provide training and technical assistance at the tertiary or individual student level. The Florida Positive Behavior Support Project was provided with resources and significant latitude in expanding and modifying its PBS approach, such that it moved from a tertiary project to a training system focused on universal SW-PBS in 2001. The project has now integrated secondary and tertiary levels into the universal training system in response to the increase in number of school teams achieving high fidelity of implementation in primary prevention.

Project staff members are located in one IHE and are supported through the Individuals With Disabilities Education Improvement Act (IDEIA) flow-through funds by the Department of Education. Over half of the annual project budget of $1.3 million is distributed directly to districts to support training stipends, travel expenses, and evaluation activities. Some funds were used to develop an information system software and evaluation program for statewide, data-based decision making.

### *State Leadership Team*

Florida does not have a state leadership team. However, all district coordinators, state Department of Education professionals, and project staff meet one to two times each year. The project collaborates with juvenile justice state professionals, safe and healthy schools projects, a project supporting students with severe emotional disorders, and another state-funded program implementing RTI in education. Independent contractors are not involved in SW-PBS training and technical assistance through this statewide approach.

### *In-Service Training and Technical Assistance*

Training is provided by project staff at a designated district location if a district commits at least three schools for participation. Districts also must commit to an annual planning process if they wish to add new schools each year, and each school and district must complete and submit a readiness application to the project prior to the initiation of training.

Small districts with only a few schools may be asked to join training events hosted by a nearby district.

The SW-PBS content involves short presentations followed by team activities. Eighty to 100 schools are trained every year during 3- to 4-day training activities. Nearly 80% of district/school trainings occur in the summer. The project has added booster sessions on topics related to secondary and tertiary interventions and practices, administrator role, and SW-PBS implementation and sustainability. Coaches are required to participate in all team-based SW-PBS training activities and receive additional training before and after these activities. Coaches also meet at least once each month at the district level in meetings cofacilitated by project staff and the district coordinators.

The project includes district coordinators identified in each district and internal or external coaches required for each school. Each district decides how to structure the SW-PBS system through the district leadership team process. All district and school involvement is strictly voluntary. Schools are initially trained in universal implementation and are supported to develop their capacities at classroom, targeted/secondary, and tertiary/individual levels when they have implemented the universal level of SW-PBS with fidelity as measured by project evaluation activities. The project pays districts $800 per school per year for data submitted by each school at the end of the year and midyear. These funds are used by districts to implement SW-PBS. Thirty-six school districts and over 350 schools currently are involved in SW-PBS activities. Schools may become temporarily inactive due to, for example, staff turnover or failure to submit data.

### *Preservice Training and Technical Assistance*

An advanced behavioral interventions course that includes a SW-PBS emphasis within the School Psychology Department and a programwide PBS in early childhood settings within the Department of Special Education are the two main courses offered at the University of South Florida. Other courses with SW-PBS content are offered occasionally within the school psychology and special education departments. A new master's degree behavior analysis program is now available in the Division of Applied Research and Educational Support (DARES). All preservice PBS-related content complements SW-PBS in-service efforts.

The training in the behavior analysis program has an applied emphasis and includes guest lectures by PBS implementers, practicum and internship experiences in SW-PBS placements, and training materials from actual SW-PBS sites. A student can minor or receive a certificate within this program by completing 9–12 credit hours. Formal collaborations do not exist with other IHEs, although some university professionals in the state of Florida have requested curriculum, training tools, and information on SW-PBS. The project's web site experiences more than 1 million hits each year, with many IHE faculty using the free resources and materials in their undergraduate and graduate course work. SW-PBS training will soon be available via Web-based courses in addition to on-site courses that will result in a certificate program in SW-PBS at the master's degree level.

## Arizona Statewide Training and Technical Assistance

### *Origins of SW-PBS*

Arizona's SW-PBS efforts and funding were initiated through the state's Professional Development Department. A professional within the Office of Exceptional Education who is in charge of comprehensive PD has taken the lead role in securing contracted funding for the three universities. Faculty and PBS professionals from Arizona State University, Northern Arizona University, and the University of Arizona support the PBS effort. Funding comes from a variety of sources each year depending on the availability of resources.

The IHEs work collaboratively, but for efficiency have divided the state into north, central, and south regions based on university location. Training is provided in the central region of the state because of its location. Together, the universities support state-level conferences, technical assistance, and individualized training for coaches. Arizona has been implementing SW-PBS for more than 6 years. Initially, interested schools applied for a grant that supported training and technical assistance. However, a districtwide approach was adopted in 2005.

### *State Leadership Team*

In the last few years, the Arizona State leadership team has been formed to guide SW-PBS implementation. Meetings are focused on statewide policy issues related to public relations and marketing of PBS across the state, SW-PBS PD needs, and efforts to infuse PBS language, concepts, and resources into existing aspects of the public education system. The state leadership team also encourages interagency collaboration and connects to larger efforts to implement RTI strategies related to academics and social behavior. Because the team includes members from many different agencies, an outside facilitator led initial meetings to establish a common mission, vision, and set of goals.

The state leadership team includes representatives from a variety of agencies: (a) state Department of Education, (b) safe and drug-free schools, (c) RTI initiative, (d) teacher certification, (e) mental/behavioral health services, (f) principals and district special education coordinators, and (g) IHEs. The state team uses a subcommittee structure to manage task completion. For example, one subcommittee is currently exploring inclusion of PBS terminology in state teacher certification requirements and in IHE functions.

### *In-Service Training and Technical Assistance*

The implementation of in-service training and technical assistance coordination is mainly managed through the IHE meeting process across the three universities and includes coaches who are external to the school teams and support more than one school, district-level coordination, and district-level team meetings, where planning for in-service training and technical assistance is conducted. Training and technical assistance to schools and districts are provided through state funding for 2 years, with additional technical assistance available postfunding to ensure sustainability. Districts may apply for competitive grants through the Arizona Department of Special Education or pay for the training from other funding. Year 1 training includes three events scheduled throughout the year, starting with a 2-day training event in August. The content in Year 1 is focused on the universal intervention tier. Technical assistance is provided by university professionals and internal or mentor coaches between scheduled training events. In addition, coaches attend four 2-day training events designed to develop coaching skills, understand psychosocial issues, skills for working effectively with groups, and motivating participation. Coaches also attend a half-day training before each of the school-team events. In Year 1, district team members are trained with the schools to provide the background they need to coordinate action planning.

Year 2 training includes two 2-day trainings on secondary prevention for school teams and two 2-day trainings on roles and responsibilities for district teams. In Year 3, teams receive technical assistance support; regional meetings are scheduled with all of school teams in a region. Schools and districts that have been implementing more than 3 years are also invited to attend these regional meetings. The state leadership team sponsors an annual conference for new individuals who are interested in learning about SW-PBS and for veteran implementers who are seeking more advanced SW-PBS content. Their second conference was sponsored jointly by the SW-PBS leadership team and the coordinators of the RTI Project.

### *Preservice Training and Technical Assistance*

Departments of Special Education are involved at the University of Arizona and Arizona State University. At Northern Arizona University, PBS is supported through the Institute for Human Development, a university center on disabilities. Course information for all universities is available online. The University of Arizona and Northern Arizona University offer a three-course graduate-level sequence to train behavior support specialists for tertiary-level support and PBS planning. At the University of Arizona, the first course is also available, in a slightly modified form, to undergraduate students. Arizona State University and Northern Arizona University offer a general SW-PBS course. Each participating school district must have at least one person complete a three-course sequence at one of the universities and two additional people complete one of the eight university courses, providing a link between in-service and preservice training. The courses are slightly different at each of the three universities. Master's and doctoral-level students can include SW-PBS in their educational experiences and doctoral dissertations across all three universities. Approximately eight doctoral/master's students specialize in SW-PBS across the universities.

## IMPLICATIONS FOR DESIGNING SYSTEMS FOR IN-SERVICE PROFESSIONAL DEVELOPMENT

As illustrated in the three state examples, SW-PBS PD and technical assistance vary at the district and state levels depending on a variety of factors, for example, size of initial and ongoing implementation efforts, funding sources, types of resources available, state and local agencies involved, policies, individuals leading technical assistance efforts, and local and state policies and procedures. Although the design of statewide planning and technical assistance efforts varies because of individual strengths, limitations, and resources, some characteristics of in-service training are similar across the three states (and others) and based on research in in-service training.

### Features Common to SW-PBS In-Service Approaches

Throughout this chapter, we have described several principles influential in the design of an effective in-service PD approach for SW-PBS. First and most important, state leadership teams must design a capacity-building infrastructure to achieve accurate and sustainable implementation. Planned, coordinated, and systematic efforts are needed to infuse SW-PBS within local, regional, and state systems (Fixen et al., 2005). Second, the infrastructure itself must be responsive to the dynamic changes and challenges that emerge during implementation over time and across contexts. Training and technical assistance approaches must focus at both the macrolevel (e.g., training a network of skilled people who can support schools through implementation) and at the microlevel (i.e., training an individual school to implement).

Third, it is clear that no single "right" way exists to design PD for SW-PBS systems-level implementation. From anecdotal information, the design of PD systems appears to be affected, for example, by size of initial and ongoing implementation efforts, types of resources available, state and local agencies involved, individuals leading technical assistance efforts, and local and state policies and priorities. Although variation exists, a number of service delivery features are similar across different state approaches. Five common SW-PBS PD in-service features are as follows:

- Identifying a process to carefully screen and secure commitment of key personnel involved in PD training and implementation activities.
- Building a network of professionals who provide local expertise and follow-up support over time, contributing to a sustainable PD infrastructure at the school/district level.
- Designing PD strategies that are based on the SW-PBS systems established within the school/district.
- Distributing training opportunities over time.
- Providing PD using adult learning strategies and a curriculum that includes easy-to-access tools, materials, and processes.

### *In-Service Feature 1: Identify a Process to Carefully Screen and Secure Commitment of Key Personnel Involved in the Training and Implementation Activities*

Most state SW-PBS initiatives use a "self-initiating" approach in which schools volunteer (as opposed to being mandated) to participate in training. Current PD approaches in SW-PBS are often initiated only after a careful process of screening for level of interest, readiness, and school and district commitment. The application process is an opportunity for districts/schools to consider their unique combination of needs, the long-term outcomes desired, and how those needs/outcomes can be addressed through implementation of SW-PBS. In addition, the application process is an opportunity to obtain written commitments from district and school professionals before initiating training and implementation activities. Many state teams provide districts with a list of roles and responsibilities for district and school teams with a signature sign-off document indicating the district will be providing, for example, resources for ensuring data-based decision-making systems, attendance of district administration in planning meetings, staff for key positions (e.g., coordinator), and team meeting attendance (Florida's PBS Project, 2007, District Readiness Checklist; New Jersey's PBSIS Project 2007).

### *In-service Feature 2: Building a Network of Professionals Who Provide Local Expertise and Follow-up Support Over Time to Contribute to a Sustainable PD Infrastructure at the School/District Level*

For PD to be effective, training must be tied to systems change efforts that often require sustained energy, resource, and persistence. Too often, school personnel receive training in "one-shot workshop" formats that are conducted at an off-site location by an expert external to the schools. These workshops can be exciting and uplifting, but without ongoing support, research suggests that faculty members will often fail to implement what they have learned (National Commission on Teaching and America's Future, 1996; NEA Foundation, 1996; Smith, Parker, Taubman, & Lovaas, 1992). Knowledge obtained in these traditional PD formats does not enable school professionals to know operationally how and where to start the implementation process. Initial implementation can fail without a person (i.e., a coach) available to provide ongoing support and guidance. Also, environmental contingencies may make it difficult to implement new changes or to address peer "resistance" to change during implementation. Identifying and training key professionals who take a lead role within an organization to guide PD with peers has been demonstrated as both essential and effective in a number of different settings (Fredericks & Templeman, 1990; Jones, Fremouw, & Carples, 1977; Page, Iwata, & Reid, 1982; Reid et al., 2003; Smith et al., 1992). Furthermore, effective coaching and mentoring strategies have been reported as key components in educational in-service PD research (Fleming & Leo, 1999; Johnson & Pugach, 1991; Joyce & Showers,

1995; Knowledgeloom, 2000; Pugach & Johnson, 1995). SW-PBS in-service PD involves the identification of professionals who will lead PD at the district level, as well as coaches who are both internal (persons within the school) and external (persons within the district) who can provide support at the school team level.

Most state projects have some mechanism for offering schools follow-up support via coaching networks. For instance, in some states, SW-PBS trainers meet on a regular basis with district coordinators from each participating district. District coordinators in turn meet with all coaches on a monthly basis to problem solve and support implementation. Ongoing follow-up contacts may be provided by trainers or district coordinators in the form of on-site visits to school teams, phone calls, e-mails, or additional training.

To take SW-PBS PD to scale, state teams must focus on PD needs across different stages of various local capacity-building efforts. For example, more state trainers and district coordinators are needed to directly support districts implementing SW-PBS. External and internal coaching are needed to provide local peer-based leadership and to embed access to local behavioral expertise within each school's secondary- and tertiary-level planning. Although the ways in which states design PD may vary, capacity building is focused on establishing a network of professionals who can provide local support and thereby decrease reliance on individuals who provide external support.

Many state projects hold quarterly, semiannual, or annual events that provide opportunities for school teams to share data, progress, and ideas with other districts and school teams implementing SW-PBS. This lateral networking approach is another way to provide ongoing local support and increase sustainability over time (Fullan, 2005). Opportunities for teams to participate in supportive and collegial events with multiple districts and schools also allows individuals to celebrate, problem solve, and discuss issues related to PD and SW-PBS implementation. Building this type of collaborative climate among school staff helps to unite members of a widespread group work in their efforts to work together as they implement positive change collaboratively (Joyce & Showers, 1995; Lieberman, 1995; Pugach & Johnson, 1990,1995).

### *In-Service Feature 3: PD Strategies Are Based on the SW-PBS Infrastructure or System Established Within the School/District/State*

One of the major decisions that has an impact on the design of a PD in-service approach is the way in which schools are exposed to all three intervention tiers: primary, secondary, and tertiary. For example, in some states, the leadership team may choose an approach for SW-PBS implementation that involves three separate teams within a school: an overall schoolwide PBS planning team, a secondary support team, and a tertiary-level team. Other states have designed PD around schools with two teams within the school responsible for facilitating the implementation of SW-PBS: a planning team to focus on overall schoolwide PBS efforts and a behavior support team that leads and facilitates both secondary and tertiary support programs in the school. In this approach, individual team members lead in identifying and facilitating specific strategies that provide targeted interventions for groups of students and in coordinating tertiary intervention tier support for individual students. Other states add additional training to these SW-PBS PD approaches. For instance, individuals may be identified and trained within the school or district to become tertiary-level trainers responsible for assisting with more challenging individualized PBS plan development and implementation.

The ways in which schools structure their teams and make decisions guide PD efforts. In addition, setting timelines for introducing primary, secondary, and tertiary intervention tier curricula and selecting who receives training varies across districts and states. The Florida system provides secondary prevention training when the team can show data indicating primary prevention has had an impact on office discipline referrals and accurate implementation has been accomplished (Cohen, Kincaid, & Childs, in press). In New Jersey, school child study teams are trained in functional assessment at the same time the school leadership team is trained in primary prevention. During the second year, school personnel designated for prereferral interventions are trained in secondary prevention. To ensure a link across all three planning groups, at least one member of the universal team participates on all three teams.

Another in-service PD consideration is determining how many teams will be trained at one time. In some states, larger events are scheduled at the universal level with 20 to 30 school teams participating. In other states, the state team limits the number of schools participating in SW-PBS training events, creating a learning context with fewer individuals attending. Other training systems require that at least three school teams participate in universal school team training. In some cases, the size of training depends on the number of professionals who can provide technical assistance during breakout activities, on available training funds, or on the level of individualized support teams might need to learn more specialized knowledge and skills (e.g., secondary/tertiary prevention). Oregon, for example, schedules breakout sessions and strands around prevention level (i.e., universal, targeted, intensive) and provides separate, structured time for teams to work on action plans. Trainers are available to provide coaching and technical assistance.

### *In-service Feature 4: Distribute Training Opportunities Throughout the Year*

Another common feature across in-service approaches is that PD for school teams and coaches are distributed throughout the year. Comprehensive, longitudinal PD systems are better able to address the developmental pace of learning (Colvin, Kameenui, & Sugai, 1993) and provide opportunities for school staff to engage in collaborative dialogue, feedback, and reflection about their practices (Elmore & McLaughlin, 1988; Guskey, 1995). State leadership teams frequently plan for 4–6 days of PD for school teams and 2–3 days of training for coaches. These distributed training events are typically provided over a 3- to 5-year period. Coaches' training or meeting days are often scheduled before school team-training events so state trainers can provide coaches with information that will be used during breakout activities by their school teams. Like the Oregon example, many projects begin with an initial 2- to 5-day summer event at which multiple districts participate, so administrators do not have to plan for "release time" from classes, which is a benefit from both substitute time coverage and instructional time considerations. In Florida, training for districts is initiated at any time during the year depending on district readiness. Offering individualized training events for each district may make it easier for district administration since dates and times can be negotiated with trainers, and on-site training decreases travel reimbursement costs for individual school team members.

### *In-Service Feature 5: Provide PD Using Adult Learning Strategies and a Curriculum That Includes Easy-to-Access Tools, Materials, and Processes*

The design and delivery of the training curriculum that includes a valuable set of practices can be a rewarding experience for the state planning team. Peer-to-peer coaching and consensus building can, however, be challenging for teachers and school professionals. For instance, some coaches and school planning team members express discomfort and are not always sure how to structure positive collegial training events. Assisting school personnel to learn and apply new practices, particularly when those practices also require a philosophical shift in thinking, can be a demanding experience for trainers.

A key function of any PD system should be to unite staff within their school as they work together to implement positive change (Joyce & Showers, 1995). Training curriculum designed for adult learners that creates an atmosphere of group learning and community building can function to reduce the stress related to peer-to-peer coaching and supports. SW-PBS PD uses a trainer-of-trainers approach that helps ensure that school teams receive structured materials that are highly relevant to their application of SW-PBS. One of the most exciting aspects of many SW-PBS in-service training approaches is that whole teams come to the training events and have the opportunity to work together on meaningful planning activities.

To be effective, training delivery methods should emphasize instructional strategies tailored for adult learners. Small chunks of new content that are presented should be followed by action-planning activities related to each school to increase opportunities that result in a sense of progress. Varying content dissemination with activities that are more applied and aimed at resulting in direct outcomes for each school is naturally more reinforcing than straight didactive forms of information transfer. Part of school and district action planning should include the identification of in-service time, staff meetings, and other events scheduled throughout the school year that can be made available to school teams for building school-wide consensus, scheduling school planning meetings, and structuring in-service training events.

Materials presented to school teams during state training events can in turn be used by school teams to present information to their colleagues throughout the year. Including rich examples, templates, and adapted materials, particularly in electronic and online formats, greatly eases the development burden on school personnel. Many state leadership teams have created web sites that allow for easy access to these types of materials (e.g., Positive Behavioral Interventions and Supports Arizona, 2007; Delaware's Positive Behavior Support Project, 2007; Florida's PBS Project, 2007; Maryland's Positive Behavioral Interventions and Supports, 2007; New Jersey's PBSIS Project, 2007).

## PRESERVICE SW-PBS TRAINING TO COMPLEMENT STATEWIDE SW-PBS IN-SERVICE TRAINING AND TECHNICAL ASSISTANCE

Insufficient information precludes identifying "essential elements" of preservice SW-PBS, but the examples from Oregon, Florida, and Arizona do demonstrate some promising ways in which leadership teams are beginning to plan, develop, and implement complementary SW-PBS training. It is apparent from the examples that, to paraphrase and generalize slightly from several of Stephen Covey's (1989) key "habits" underlying "effectiveness", these statewide initiatives have a heuristic foundation. They demonstrate, in part, that Covey's rubric, for example, "Start With the End in Mind", "Do the Right Things," "Do Things Right," and "First Things First," can (and does) provide a practical and useful guide for systematic and effective systems change initiatives just as it can for effectiveness in our individual lives. We cite Covey's rubric regarding effectiveness both for this reason and because it may enhance understanding of the systems change process for readers who find simple (though by no means simplistic) aphorisms helpful as organizing devices to use with the many examples of systems change provided by the three states.

The examples from all three states demonstrate that they did indeed start with the end in mind by describing complementary preservice and in-service training as a guiding goal that is becoming more important as implementation proceeds. The state team in Oregon is doing first things first by initially conducting surveys to learn more about what team members believe should be goals for expanding preservice training. To do the right thing in Arizona, the state team, in coordination with state IHEs and state personnel knowledgeable about teacher certification, has explored strategies for including SW-PBS language in their state teacher certification requirements. This effort is a good example of how state leadership teams can investigate broader state policy issues related to SW-PBS.

Systems change efforts that focus on preservice policy changes may lead to changes in teacher certification policies that will in turn change how IHEs provide preservice training. Successful policy modifications resulting in changes in teacher certification requirements will in turn have an impact on the amount of time spent on preservice planning and development since IHEs will need more information and training in SW-PBS so that courses can be offered and curriculum developed linked directly to statewide implementation of SW-PBS.

Examples of both doing the right things and doing things right regarding preservice SW-PBS training are many and varied in the descriptions from the three states. All three states built in-service content and format on preservice courses that already existed as part of training in applied behavior analysis. Each of the state examples included university professionals who were cofacilitating or leading the in-service training and technical assistance efforts. In each case, state SW-PBS PD leaders began by expanding content and time dedicated to SW-PBS and adapting existing courses. Additional courses were added and graduate courses emphasized opportunities to obtain direct applied experience in SW-PBS through implementation efforts supported by in-service training. In Arizona, all three universities engage in ongoing discourse about courses offered. Although there is some variability in course content across the three IHEs, the universities meet on a regular basis and post university course information on the Arizona PBIS Web site, which shows the collaborative nature of preservice training system. In Oregon, the SW-PBS universal preservice training course is taught by individuals actively applying, facilitating, and supporting SW-PBS elements in school and other education-related settings. Florida has focused on increasing opportunities for teachers in preservice and in-service training contexts to access Web-based and on-site classes for graduate credits.

Without reference to specific states, to do the right thing regarding preservice SW-PBS training might include efforts to influence state standards, practices, and licensing board requirements in other fields of study such as social work and school psychology. And, to do things right, a state leadership team may choose to invite new IHE members from those other fields of study to the planning process or decide to create a series of events to broaden awareness and interest in SW-PBS among them. Systems change efforts to expand preservice training may include inviting professionals from various IHE departments to state team meetings. Some teams may seek to expand the availability of preservice training by inviting leaders from IHEs in areas where SW-PBS is being implemented to team meetings so that practicum experiences can be linked to statewide implementation efforts. Other state leadership team goals might do the right thing by broadening the base of IHE stakeholders and do things right with first things first by inviting departmental leaders to join the team and providing awareness-level presentations to groups in conferences or other formal settings to ensure school psychologists, social workers, those in general education, education leadership, and others are exposed to SW-PBS content.

State teams interested in going to scale with the implementation of SW-PBS across a large number of schools will need to spend time planning for an increase in the number of professionals who can provide technical assistance to districts and assist with the state's in-service training. At this time, graduates specializing in SW-PBS at the master's and doctoral levels are relatively few, even in states with larger in-service systems. As the numbers of districts and schools implementing SW-PBS grow, more opportunities become available for these students to participate in practicum experience, doctoral dissertations, and other research projects. Preservice experiences linked directly to applied in-service training contexts provide students with opportunities to learn more about SW-PBS and build important mentoring relationships. This type of experience would be valuable for administrators in education leadership courses, general and special education teachers, as well as professionals preparing to support students who may receive tertiary supports as behavior specialists, social workers, counselors, and school psychologists.

It is our opinion that both in-service and preservice training are necessary but insufficient alone to meet the needs of a growing statewide implementation process. Furthermore, the state leadership's team planning process is a perfect vehicle for building these complementary in-service and preservice systems in SW-PBS. Comprehensive planning that will allow teams to expand preservice training options will require an action-planning process that is based on collaborative identification of existing or (more likely) to-be-developed preservice training needs, goals, resources, design, content, implementation, and assessments of effectiveness.

The next section of this chapter describes how state teams interested in designing complementary in-service and preservice training systems can use evaluation strategies to assist action-planning activities.

## USING FORMATIVE EVALUATION STRATEGIES TO DESIGN COMPLEMENTARY, INTEGRATED PRESERVICE AND IN-SERVICE TRAINING FOR STATEWIDE SW-PBS

The SW-PBS Implementer's Blueprint and Self-Assessment (Sugai et al., 2005) emphasize that statewide, district, or school leadership teams can and should assume responsibilities for capacity building in three main areas: training, coaching, and evaluation. Evaluation capacity is referred to as "the system's ability to establish measurable outcomes, methods for evaluating progress toward these measurable outcomes, and modified or adapted action plans based on these evaluations" (p. 24). State leadership teams implementing SW-PBS establish evaluation systems that are data based and focus on essential SW-PBS implementation elements. A number of existing tools are available from the Office of Special Education Program's Technical Assistance Center on Positive Behavioral Interventions and Supports (www.pbis.org).

Evaluation capacity requires establishment of evaluative activities and measures for both formative and summative evaluation purposes. Formative evaluation strategies provide continuous information for program improvement, modification, and management (Patton, 1982). Contextual or settings features, resource allocation, and SW-PBS implementation are of primary interest. Summative evaluation focuses on the effects, results, and long-term outcomes of SW-PBS to assist leadership teams in making judgments about the basic value of the program. The Leadership Team Implementation and Self-Assessment Planning Tool (OSEP Blueprint,

Sugai et al., 2005) addresses categories of activities that are important for high-quality SW-PBS implementation (see Fig. 25.1). Each category includes one or more activity that must be accomplished. On a regular basis, activities (i.e., "Team is developed with representation from appropriate range of stakeholders.") are marked as "yes" (completed), "partial" (incomplete), or "no" (not started). Items marked as partial or no are discussed for possible action-planning activities. For instance, a team may decide to invite additional stakeholders to the state leadership team before considering that particular category of activities completed.

The themes identified in Fig. 25.1 can be used for problem solving at any stage within the state planning team process. For instance, as state teams move toward sustainability, they review "team representation" and determine whether new state team stakeholders need to be added, for example, a policy leader related to teacher certification or IHE professionals; as another example, the team may decide to identify 10 or more preservice practicum sites for IHEs.

Leadership teams should conduct periodic "audits" (formative or summative evaluative reviews) to document progress and to provide data for decision making related to preservice/in-service training, program implementation fidelity, future action planning, and so on. To develop periodic audits for formative evaluation, the state leadership team should identify and operationally define "indicators" (concise, measurable milestones) of program status and progress. Based on these indicators, simple measures should be identified or developed (e.g., Sugai et al., 2005, ratings of "yes," "partial," "no"). Information and data based on these indicators can be of enormous value for improvement of a program because they provide

| Leadership Team |
|---|
| Coordination |
| Funding |
| Visibility |
| Political Support |
| Training Capacity |
| Coaching Capacity |
| Demonstrations |
| Evaluation |

**Fig. 25.1.** Leadership team self-assessment and implementation tool: major categories.

information that is considered essential from the perspectives of those most directly involved in and responsible for the program.

Most, if not all, of the sections of this chapter have described at least an initial basis for identifying and operationally defining such indicators (e.g., see sections including Initial Design and Implementation, Expansion, Sustainability, Infusing Capacity Across Systems, Overcoming Challenges, Using Formative Evaluation Strategies to Design Complementary, and Integrated Preservice and In-Service Training for Statewide SW-PBS).

For example, the core elements previously identified as key components of preservice planning and training can serve also as progress indicators (see Fig. 25.2):

1) SW-PBS Preservice program components build on existing preservice courses and practica.
2) Preservice courses and practica allow students to get direct, applied SW-PBS experiences in the field.
3) Preservice SW-PBS educational experiences include easy access to web-based training materials and resources.
4) Preservice training exposes students to high quality inservice training and technical assistance.
5) Preservice SW-PBS training is offered across fields for a range of possible SW-PBS implementers.
6) SW-PBS-related training and types of content disseminated have expanded over time.
7) Preservice training is provided by faculty involved SW-PBS implementation.
8) IHE preservice training personnel co-facilitate and/or actively participate in SW-PBS inservice/technical assistance in the state.
9) State certification personnel participate in SW-PBS state leadership team and/or committee meetings and assist in policy development.
10) State leadership team members create goals for increasing the number of SW-PBS-trained and certified personnel who can provide SW-PBS training and technical assistance in the state.
11) The statewide leadership team has an action planning process in place for increasing collaboration with IHEs, state education agency (SEA), local education agency (LEA), juvenile justice (JJ), and other related profession al education staff.

**Fig. 25.2.** Eleven core elements of designing complementary preservice planning. IHE, institution of higher education.

In the instances where "core elements" or "key components" include multiple activities (e.g., especially Items 10 and 11), each of the multiple activities in an element/component would be the focus of a simple evaluation indicator.

## CONCLUSION

To the best of our knowledge, most state projects/initiatives began by first providing PD through in-service approaches (i.e., the training of existing school personnel). The emphasis on in-service (as opposed to preservice) has likely occurred because SW-PBS is a relatively new model. Building complementary preservice and in-service training systems in SW-PBS is a natural step for state leadership teams moving out of initial implementation into expansion and sustainability phases. To truly "go to scale," state teams must consider using the evaluation and planning processes already established to create new goals that include expanding the roles and responsibilities of state teams related to policy development, interagency collaboration, evaluation, and training. Processes, tools, and evaluation guidelines for state teams will be needed for state teams to begin systematically building complementary preservice and in-service systems.

Formative evaluation processes will allow state teams to continually adjust training and technical assistance efforts as the developmental implementation stages change across time. These evaluation processes should employ simple measures of program indicators that can be used for improvement purposes because they provide information that is considered essential from the perspective(s) of those most directly involved in and responsible for the program. Modification to some existing SW-PBS tools will be necessary for those state teams entering expansion and sustainability stages of implementation. One example of SW-PBS tools that could be adapted is the Leadership Team Implementation and Self-Assessment Planning Tool (OSEP Blueprint; Sugai et al., 2005), which addresses categories of activities that are important for high-quality SW-PBS implementation.

Networking opportunities that allow planning teams to learn more about how PD is being implemented in other states are essential due to the complexities of how state systems operate, the ways in which SW-PBS implementation evolves through various funding sources, and the diversity of professionals involved in key stakeholder roles. Web-based systems and national or regional conferences that establish networking opportunities for state teams could provide a key opportunity to share formative evaluation tools, learn about the evolution and expansion of state SW-PBS PD, and generalize new ideas that will allow for continued large-scale expansion of SW-PBS in the United States. This networking concept is a key feature of sustainability according to Fullan (2005) and has already made a great contribution to the SW-PBS field.

## REFERENCES


Cohen, R., Kincaid, D., & Childs, K. (2007). Measuring school-wide positive behavior support implementation: Development and validation of the Benchmarks of Quality (BoQ). *Journal of Positive Behavior Interventions*. 9, 203–213

Colvin, G., Kameenui, E. J., & Sugai, G. (1993). Reconceptualizing behavior management and school-wide discipline in general education. *Education and Treatment of Children, 16*, 361–381.

Covey, S. (1989). *The seven habits of highly successful people*. New York: Simon & Shuster.

Crone, D. A., Horner, R. H., & Hawken, L. S. (2004). *Responding to problem behavior in schools: The behavior education program*. New York: Guilford Press.

Delaware's Positive Behavior Support Project. (2007). Retrieved August 29, 2008 from http://www.udel.edu/cds/pbs/

Elmore, R. F., & McLaughlin, M. W. (1988). *Steady work: Policy, practice, and reform in American education* (R-3574-NIE/RC). Santa Monica, CA: Rand.

Fixen, D. L., Naoom, S. F., Blasé, K. A., Friedman, R. M., & Wallace, F. (2005). *Implementation research: A synthesis of the literature*. Tampa: University of South Florida.

Fleming, G., & Leo, T. (1999). *Principals and teachers: Continuous learners*. Retrieved January 12, 2008, from http://sedl.org/change/issues/issues72/welcome.html.

Florida's PBS Project. (2007). District readiness checklist. Retrieved August 29, 2008 from http://flpbs.fmhi.usf.edu/requestservices_training.asp

Fredericks, H. D., & Templeman, T. P. (1990). A generic in-service training model. In A. P. Kaiser & C. M. McWhorter (Eds.), *Preparing personnel to work with severe disabilities* (pp. 301–317). Baltimore: Brookes.

Freeman, R., Eber, L., Anderson, C., Irvin, L., Bounds, M., Dunlap, G., et al. (2006). Building inclusive school cultures using school-wide PBS: Designing effective individual support systems for students with significant disabilities. *Research and Practice for Persons With Severe Disabilities*, 1, 4–17.

Fullan, M. (2005). *Leadership and sustainability*. Thousand Oaks, CA: Corwin Press.

Guskey, T. (1995). Professional development in education: In search of the optimal mix. In T. R. Guskey & M. Huberman (Eds.), *Professional development in education* (pp. 113–131). New York: Teachers College Press.

Horner, R. H., Sugai, G., Todd, A., & Lewis-Palmer, T. (2005). Schoolwide positive behavior support. In L. M. Bambara & L. Kern (Eds.), *Individualized supports for students with problem behaviors* (pp. 359–390). New York: Guilford Press.

Illinois State-wide Technical Assistance Center. (2007). *Illinois positive behavioral interventions and support project, 2004–2005 progress report*. LaGrange Park, IL. Retrieved August 29, 2008 from http://www.pbisillinois.org

Johnson, L. J., & Pugach, M. C. (1991). Accommodating the needs of students with mild learning and behavior problems through peer collaboration. *Exceptional Children, 57*, 41–47.

Jones, F. H., Fremouw, W., & Carples, S. (1977). Pyramid training of elementary school teachers to use a classroom management skills package. *Journal of Applied Behavior Analysis, 10*, 239–253.

Joyce, B., & Showers, B. (1995). *Student achievement through staff development: Fundamentals of school renewal* (2nd ed.). White Plains, NY: Longman.

Knowledgeloom. (2000, February). *What works in teaching and learning*. Review of research. Retrieved February 16, 2000, from http://knowledgeloom.org

Liaupsin, C. J., Jolivette, K., & Scott, T. M. (2004). School-wide systems of support: Maximizing student success in schools. In R. B. Rutherford, M. M. Quinn, & R. Sathur (Eds.), *Handbook of research in emotional and behavioral disorders* (pp. 487–501). New York: Guilford Press.

Lieberman, A. (1995). *The work of restructuring schools: Building from the ground up*. New York: Teachers College Press.

Maryland's Positive Behavioral Interventions and Supports Web site. (2007). Retrieved August 29, 2008 from http://www.pbismaryland.org/

Michigan's Integrated Behavior and Learning Initiative. (2007). Retrieved July 23, 2007, from http://www.cenmi.org/miblsi/downloads/MiBLSi_Brochure.pdf

Muscott, H. S., Mann, T. B., Gately, S., Bell, K. E., & Muscott, A. J. (2004). Positive behavioral interventions and supports in New Hampshire: Preliminary results of a state-wide system for implementing schoolwide discipline practices. *Education and Treatment of Children, 27*, 453–475.

National Commission on Teaching and America's Future. (1996). *What matters most: Teaching for America's Future.* New York. Retrieved August 29, 2008 from http://www.netuf.org/documentwhatMattersMost.Pdf

NEA Foundation. (1996). *Teachers take charge of their learning: Transforming professional development for student success.* Washington, DC. Retrieved January 12, 2008, from http://www.neafoundation.org/

New Jersey's PBSIS Project. (2007). *New Jersey positive behavior support in schools.* Retrieved July 31, 2007, from http://www.njpbs.org/

Page, J. J., Iwata, B. A., & Reid, D. H. (1982). Pyramidal training: A large-scale application with institution staff. *Journal of Applied Behavior Analysis, 15*, 33–351.

Patton, M. Q. (1982). *Practical evaluation.* Newbury Park, CA: Sage.

Positive Behavioral Interventions and Supports Arizona. (2007). Retrieved July 31, 2007, from http://abi.ed.asu.edu/basics/basics.htm

Pugach, M. C., & Johnson, L. J. (1990). Meeting diverse needs through professional peer collaboration. In M. W. Stainback & S. Stainback (Eds.), *Support networks for inclusive schooling* (pp. 123–137). Baltimore: Brookes.

Pugach, M. C., & Johnson, L. J. (1995). Unlocking expertise among classroom teachers through structured dialogue: Extending research on peer collaboration. *Exceptional Children, 62*, 101–110.

Reid, D. H., Rotholz, D. A., Parsons, M. B., Morris, L., Braswell, B. A., Green, C. W., et al. (2003). Training human service supervisors in aspects of PBS: Evaluation of a statewide, performance-based program. *Journal of Positive Behavior Interventions, 5*, 35–46.

Smith, T., Parker, T., Taubman, M., & Lovaas, O. I. (1992). Transfer of staff training from workshops to group homes: A failure to generalize across settings. *Research in Developmental Disabilities, 13*, 57–71.

Sugai, G., Horner, R. H., Dunlap, G., Hieneman, M., Lewis, T. J., Nelson, C. M., et al. (2000). Applying positive behavioral support and functional behavioral assessment in schools. *Journal of Positive Behavioral Interventions, 2*, 131–143.

Sugai, G., Horner, R., Sailor, W., Dunlap, G., Eber, L., Lewis, T., et al. (2005). *School-wide positive behavior support: Implementers' blueprint and self-assessment.* Technical Assistance Center on Positive Behavioral Interventions and Supports. University of Deaoa; EUGENE, OR

Taylor-Greene, S., Brown, D., Nelson, L., Longton, J., Gassman, Cohen, J., et al. (1997). School-wide behavioral support: Starting the year off right. *Journal of Behavioral Education, 7*, 99–112.

Todd, A., Horner, R. H., Sugai, G., & Colvin, G. (1999). Individualizing school-wide discipline for students with chronic problem behaviors: A team approach. *Effective School Practices, 17*(4), 72–82.

# Section IV

## New Directions

# 26

# Sustaining Positive Behavior Support in a Context of Comprehensive School Reform

**WAYNE SAILOR, NIKKI WOLF, HOON CHOI, and BLAIR ROGER**

## CONSIDERATIONS IN IMPLEMENTING SCHOOLWIDE POSITIVE BEHAVIOR SUPPORT

Beginning about 1999, researchers at the University of Kansas Beach Center on Disability began studying schoolwide positive behavior support (SW-PBS) in urban schools, specifically the processes associated with and the effects of implementation (cf. Lassen, Steele, & Sailor, 2006; Sailor & Roger, 2006; Sailor, Zuna, Choi, Thomas, McCart & Roger, 2006; Turnbull et al., 2002; Utley & Sailor, 2002; Warren et al., 2003, 2006). Much of this work has been in association with an ongoing research partnership of the University of Kansas and USD 500, Kansas City, Kansas. The framework of research that forms the basis for this chapter also includes results from an ongoing program of research within the Ravenswood City School District, East Palo Alto, California (cf. Sailor & Roger, 2005; Sailor et al., 2006) and, most recently, a program of research in conjunction with the Recovery School District (RSD), New Orleans, Louisiana.

**WAYNE SAILOR** • University of Kansas
**NIKKI WOLF** • University of Kansas
**HOON CHOI** •
**BLAIR ROGER** • Oakland, CA

All three of these districts are located in urban, low-income, multicultural areas with high crime rates, unemployment, and urban blight. Each of these districts has struggled and continues to struggle with the federal No Child Left Behind (NCLB) Act requirements for demonstration of adequate yearly progress (AYP) each year based on grade level, annual, standardized state assessments. All of the schools that we have studied through this ongoing research agenda have experienced high rates of poverty among their children and families. All are schools with high percentages of free and reduced price lunch eligibility.

Our experience over nearly a decade of work in these urban schools has led us to conclude that there are three major considerations that must be addressed in bringing about a successful implementation of SW-PBS in urban core schools (and perhaps in any school). These considerations are (a) the problem of "siloization"; (b) the problem of *bifurcation* of professional practice; and (c) the problem of *sustainability* of effects of professional practice. In this chapter, we address each of these considerations, examine its implications, and then suggest a framework for school organization and service delivery that can be delivered through comprehensive school reform (CSR) that holds the potential, as yet untested with scientific criteria, for their resolution.

We begin with an in-depth examination of the three considerations. We then examine the recent history of and trends in school reform, with particular emphasis on urban core schools, and conclude with a close look at a particular schoolwide organizational and professional practice model that systematically addresses each consideration. Finally, we suggest some implications for future efforts to restructure low-performing, urban core schools that hold the potential for enabling the kids in those schools to demonstrate just how successfully they can learn.

## SILOIZATION: THE "NOT ONE MORE THING" PROBLEM

In Kansas, we have silos. Elegant prairie high-rises, they dot the landscape wherever there are railroad tracks. They stand alone and seem to represent bastions of fierce independence against the awesome forces of nature that regularly sweep the plains. For that reason, they make a good metaphor for America's public schools, as Michael Fullan (2001) and others have pointed out. Our national system of moving from public policy to operations favors siloization. Support and solutions are offered in a disjointed manner without consideration for how the "fix" fits into the current working of the schools. A problem is identified, say deteriorating literacy; hearings are held, the curriculum publishers' lobby becomes activated, statutory language emerges, funds are appropriated, and local operations begin as if the problem being addressed is totally unrelated to the myriad other problems facing urban schools. A silo of literacy enhancement ("Reading First") is built.

The implementation of SW-PBS has followed this pattern to a degree. Specific language added to the Individuals With Disabilities Education Improvement Act (IDEA, 2004) has resulted in large-scale efforts to move

SW-PBS into schools nationwide. The problem is that the addition of extra supports and services are viewed by many urban schools as yet another "add-on." Urban schools have lots of silos. There are safe and drug-free school programs, AIDS programs, literacy enhancement programs, English language learner programs, and on and on. When we began to extend professional development activities to Unified School District (USD 500) schools in the year 2000 on positive behavior support (PBS), one middle school principal expressed resistance to the idea saying, "Not one more thing!"

So, special challenge 1, to accomplish full implementation of SW-PBS in urban schools is to ensure that it is neither perceived as, nor likely to become, a silo. In a least-case scenario, it should be introduced into the culture of any school with clearly identified linkages with the existing curriculum, instructional framework, and existing silos at the school. In the best-case scenario, SW-PBS can be introduced into a school as a driver for developing processes to integrate programs and functions within the school. In other words, SW-PBS holds the potential to desiloize schools by offering a framework for problem solving, but as we argue in this chapter, the process may require embedding SW-PBS in a larger, CSR process.

## BIFURCATION: THE GENERAL EDUCATION/SPECIAL EDUCATION GREAT DIVIDE

Challenge 2 to implementing SW-PBS in urban schools is to keep the process together as a three-tier, response-to-intervention (RTI) logic system (cf. chapter 29, this volume) that is grounded in scientific research and characterized by reliable and valid systems of measurement. Accomplishing this task requires careful attention to strong forces that exist within urban schools that keep general education functions separate from special education functions. For SW-PBS to reach its potential of increasing instructional time for all students by reducing time out of class through office disciplinary referrals (ODRs), the process must function as an integrated, three-tier system across the entire professional community of the school (Fairbanks, Sugai, Guardino, & Lathrop, 2007; Sailor et al., 2006).

In an article presenting data that supports the need to embed SW-PBS in CSR (Sailor et al., 2006), one of the authors, Jeong Hoon Choi, provided an analysis of the problem of bifurcation by examining 185 published articles from the *Journal of Positive Behavior Interventions*, the primary outlet for data from research in positive behavior support, to examine the question of who is conducting what studies at each of the three tiers of SW-PBS. The hypothesis of special education–general education bifurcation would suggest findings that Tier 1 (primary interventions) would primarily be identified with general education, while Tiers 2 and 3 (secondary and tertiary supports) would primarily be identified with special education.

The results of the article review found that most of the Tier 1 published studies (29% of the 185 articles) appeared, on the basis of the descriptions in the articles, to have been entirely driven by general education, whereas "virtually all of the individual support reports for tier 3 support were associated with special education" (Sailor et al., 2006, p. 21). These individual support studies comprised 67% of the studies that made the cut for examination on the basis of having a controlled experimental or quasi-experimental design. Further, there were virtually no secondary-tier studies in the sample, hence the "great divide" between general education and special education.

We propose that SW-PBS, to be successful, must hang together as a unified, RTI-driven process that involves the entire professional community of the school. Again, CSR with SW-PBS at its heart holds, in our view, the greatest potential for the prevention of bifurcation (and potential siloization) of SW-PBS.

## SUSTAINABILITY: THE LESSONS FROM EDUCATIONAL ANTHROPOLOGY

Years ago, when the senior author was conducting research in San Francisco Bay area schools on the topic of inclusion of students with disabilities, a Cal-Berkeley professor, Dr. John Ogbu, an educational anthropologist, was publishing results of his investigations into the importance of school culture as a determinant of student academic performance (cf. Ogbu, 1982, 1985). More recently, David Fetterman, a medical anthropologist on the faculty in the School of Education at Stanford, has been publishing results of culture-building processes that can result in whole-organization adoption ("buy-in") of massive systems change processes (cf. Fetterman, Kaftarian, & Wandersman, 1995).

Schools today, we would argue, have largely lost the thread of systemic influence contributed by the science of anthropology. Instead, we as a nation have adopted a rational/technical model for school organization and its functions (i.e., Danforth & Rhodes, 1997; Danforth, Rhodes, & Smith, 1995; Sailor & Paul, 2004; Sailor & Skrtic, 1996; Skrtic, 1995; Skrtic & Sailor, 1996; Skrtic, Sailor, & Gee, 1996). This rational/technical model, with its emphasis on school accountability driven by high-stakes standardized assessment, has all but brought about a complete disregard for the critical importance of school culture and nurturance of professional communities (i.e., Burrello, Hoffman, & Murray, 2004; Darling-Hammond, 2004; O'Day, 2003).

The question of sustainability of scientifically verified innovation applied to urban schools is critical. Urban schools at times can seem like bullfrogs on a pond. The frogs hang out on a lily pad snapping up occasional insects and then leap to the next lily pad, presumably in hopes of more and better insects. In education, this process is often referred to as "the next big thing."

The senior author recently had the experience of visiting a number of urban school sites on the West Coast that had received extensive training and, in many cases, follow-up technical assistance on SW-PBS in the period from 2000 to 2002. What he found was disturbing. Many of the schools had "moved on," according to administrators, to other systems of school "discipline." In many cases, artifacts of SW-PBS remained, in the form of posted signs around the schools announcing the school's expectations of students' behavior (a typical Tier 1 intervention). When teachers and students were asked, neither group could provide reliable definitions and examples of the posted expectations. Many of the schools had reverted to more punitive practices. It became clear that SW-PBS had never become a sustainable part of the school culture. It had the status of the newest add-on, and the school had moved on to the next big thing.

In this chapter, we examine a process derived from anthropological science, called school-centered planning (SCP), which we believe holds potential for embedding SW-PBS, as an integral part of CSR, in the culture of the school and thus as an ongoing component of the community of professional practice at the school. The question of sustainability is, of course, an *empirical* one and, as Jimmy Buffet sings, "only time will tell."

## SCHOOL REFORM

School reform in America dates to Reconstruction and the post–Civil War era. Various "waves" of reform have swept the country from time to time (cf. Lawson & Sailor, 2000), but the present wave of reform can be traced to the early 1980s with the publication of *A Nation at Risk* (National Commission on Excellence in Education, 1983). This summary report of a massive Carnegie Foundation-funded project highlighted the increasingly dismal performance of American schoolchildren, particularly when compared with rising performances on the same measures of science, math, and literacy of children in those nations with whom the United States competes in the world markets. These findings found their way into Congressional debates and launched a series of reform efforts geared to finding reasons for school failure and probing potential solutions (Lawson & Sailor, 2000).

The dominant theme of American school reform efforts since 1980 has unquestionably been *accountability*. If children are failing to learn, who or what is responsible? Where should we place the blame? From 1980 to 1990, schools were deemed to be the culprit. The era of school report cards was launched, and results of state test scores began to be published in the local newspapers so families could see how "their" school fared compared to other schools. The theory was that if low-performing schools were sufficiently embarrassed through public exposure, they would self-correct and perform to a higher standard.

When school accountability failed to reverse the downward spiral, the focus shifted in the 1990s to teacher accountability (Miles & Darling-Hammond, 1998; O'Day, 2002). The theory shifted to a kind of "if the child has failed to learn, the teacher has failed to teach" notion. Teaching standards were developed and put into place, and the teachers' unions came under fire for "protectionist" tactics (Kirst, 1994). Interestingly, during this period, no particular movement surfaced in the Congress as a response to repeated calls for professionalizing the teaching workforce by tightening personnel preparation standards and elevating the status of teaching by substantially increasing teacher salaries to attract a high-quality workforce (Darling-Hammond, 2003; Miles & Darling-Hammond, 1998).

Finally, during this period, academicians (i.e., Adelman & Taylor, 2000; M. P. Gallagher, 1993; Lawson & Sailor, 2000; Schorr, 1992) and some politicians (Hillary Clinton, *It Takes a Village*, 1996) pointed out the fallacy in assuming that schools alone can deal with the consequences of poverty and other community social issues. Thus, the community school movement was launched (Blank & Cady, 2004; Blank et al., 2001; Kagan & Neville, 1993; Lawson & Sailor, 2000), and efforts were begun to link community supports and services to schools and to integrate within-school services (i.e., Fullan, 2001; Gardner, 1992). The community school movement gained some traction during the Clinton administration and under Goals, 2000 (20 U.S.C. § 5811), but with the advent of the Bush administration and passage of No Child Left Behind [NCLB; 20 U.S.C. § 7912 (2001)] (U.S. Congress, 2002; U.S. Department of Education, 2004), the emphasis firmly shifted to pupil performance, where it resides today.

Under NCLB, schools must pursue a rising bar of child performance at grade level on state-administered, standardized tests. Under terms of high-stakes assessment, schools that fail to make AYP suffer district- and state-assessed penalties as they come under "improvement." Families, in some states, are provided with vouchers that can be redeemed at private schools, thus further removing resources through child attrition from low-performing schools.

So we, as a nation, have come at the process of reforming schools through a kind of de facto cycle of blame. First, the schools were perceived to be the problem, then teachers, then communities, and finally the students themselves. O'Day (2002) concisely revealed this convoluted logic of the present student accountability emphasis in examining school reform processes in Chicago public schools. Professional communities of practice are held hostage, in a sense, to scarce resources that are nevertheless expected to produce positive pupil performance outcomes. In Chicago, as elsewhere, pupil achievement is subject to myriad influences, many of which are completely outside the reach of school professionals.

The senior author saw the dark side of pupil accountability while watching the Channel 5 evening news in Kansas City a few years ago. The Missouri State grade-level assessments were about to take place, and a reporter had gone to a local elementary school to interview teachers and students to assess their level of preparedness for these high-stake tests. During the interview a little girl, about 9 years old, broke down and began crying, saying that if she failed to do well, her whole school might be closed: an emotional moment—a child feels responsible for her school's potential failure.

The most ambitious effort at reforming underperforming, primarily urban schools emerged from the school restructuring research of the 1990s (Newmann, 1996) and gave rise to a large-scale U.S. Department of Education initiative known as the Comprehensive School Reform Demonstration Project (CSRDP), begun in 1998 (c.f., Borman, Hewes, Overman, & Brown, 2002). The Office of Educational Research and Improvement (OERI) noted that there were striking commonalities across several independent school reform efforts being reported by a small number of highly visible "developers." These efforts, which included Henry Levin's *Accelerated Schools* (1991); James Comer's *School Development Program* (1993, 1996); and Robert Slavin's *Success for All* (Slavin & Madden, 2000; Slavin, Madden, Dolan, & Wasik, 1993), were pulled together, with others, and offered as a menu to suffering urban school districts as a kind of "recipe" for success. Districts could choose which developer to work with and be awarded a large federal grant to support startup of the reform effort, which in each case was expected to move rapidly to scale within the district. In many cities, local philanthropy chipped in with matching resources so that these massive CSR efforts would be well funded.

While some of the more prominent CSR models were able to show at least some moderate gains in standardized test scores from year to year in math and literacy (c.f., Viadero, 2001), the process ran into trouble when efforts to replicate the models outside their developers' sphere of influence failed. The Success for All model, for example, began moving to scale in the huge Miami-Dade School District with 45 schools, but after poor gains, only 7 schools were still using the model after 2 years (Viadero, 2001).

When NCLB was authorized in 2001, the federal government moved the funds from the Comprehensive School Reform Demonstration Program (CSRDP), into the Comprehensive School Reform program; CSR was now officially regarded as an appropriate intervention for schools that struggled to meet the academic outcomes set by NCLB. Most recently, in fiscal year 2006, the evolution of CSR resulted in funding of the CSR Clearinghouse, which is responsible for evaluating CSR initiatives. There are no longer federal funds available for the Comprehensive School Reform Program.

The CSR Clearinghouse is charged with evaluation of CSR models and sharing information to help educators make informed decisions on reform models. The questions around how to measure success of public education and in turn how to have an impact on those measures have become some of the most critical social questions of our time. American Institutes for Research (AIR), quoting Borman et al. (2002) stated:

> Since the mid-1900s, approximately 6,000 schools, serving several millions of students, have used federal funds to adopt more than 500 distinct CSR models and approaches. So far, overall results of the CSR approach have demonstrated promise, with some models helping schools make significant student achievement gains. For example, a 2002 systematic analysis by Dr. Geoffrey Borman and his colleagues of the student achievement outcomes of 29 leading K–12 CSR models reported that (AIR, 2006, p. 3) "... the overall effects of CSR are statistically significant, meaningful, and appear to be greater than the effects of other interventions that have been designed to serve similar purposes and student and school populations". (Borman et al., 2002, p. 34)

A significant problem for the CSR program, however, surfaced following publication of the report by the Comprehensive School Reform Quality Center (CSRQ) of the AIR in November, 2005 (AIR, 2006). By definition "CSR models must be scientifically based. This means that a model or approach must demonstrate strong research evidence that it can improve students' academic achievement" (CSRQ, 2005). AIR examined 22 of the most widely used CSR models using the federal government's own standard for scientific research on "what works." They found that none of the 22 presented very strong evidence of effectiveness. Only two models, direct instruction, a behavioral approach grounded in the work of Siegfried Engelmann at the University of Oregon (Becker, & Carnine, 1980; Becker & Engelmann, 1976) and Slavins' Success for All (Slavin & Madden, 2000) achieved a "moderately strong" rating. On the positive side, many of the common elements of these packaged school improvement models have become standard practice in large numbers of American schools. Grade-level teams, smaller learning communities within large middle and high schools, and family outreach and partnership efforts have achieved widespread acceptance, to name but a few features.

Obviously, the major hallmark of a good CSR model is improvement in student achievement. In addition, the adoption of strategies and integration of practices into the existing school culture is imperative. CSR model components as suggested by the U.S. Department of Education include the following (CSRQ, 2005):

- Employs proven methods and strategies based on scientific research.
- Integrates a comprehensive design with aligned components.
- Provides ongoing, high-quality professional development for teachers and staff.
- Includes measurable goals and benchmarks for student achievement.
- Is supported within the school by teachers, administrators, and staff.
- Provides support for teachers, administrators, and staff.
- Provides for meaningful parent and community involvement in planning, implementing, and evaluating school improvement activities.
- Uses high-quality external technical support and assistance from an external partner with experience and expertise in schoolwide reform and improvement.
- Plans for the evaluation of the CSR model implementation and impact on annual student results.
- Identifies resources to support and sustain the school's comprehensive reform effort.
- Has been found to significantly improve the academic achievement of students or demonstrates strong evidence that it will improve the academic achievement of students.

Now, within the U.S. Department of Education, OERI has been replaced by the Institute for Education Science (IES), with a general education research center and special education research center as parts of its structure. Within IES, the burden of proof shifts to developers to demonstrate with large-scale, randomized trial, research designs with large effect sizes that their models can be moved to scale in areas removed from their research and development sites. While government grants are available to fund the CSR research, the money for development, training, and implementation is largely left to state and local resources, including private philanthropy.

## WHAT WENT WRONG: THE MISSING INGREDIENTS

In our view, all efforts to reform the educational process in America by focusing exclusively on general education processes within schools and their districts will be doomed, if not to fail, at least to be confined to only modest gains. As James Gallagher pointed out early in the CSR movement's history, "Education alone is a weak treatment" (p. 43,00) (1998). If the packaged school reform developers had perhaps paid closer attention to some of the more sporadic and isolated examples of the parallel, community schools movement (cf. Blank & Shah, 2003), some additional elements might have helped to make a difference in their school perfor-mance evaluations. Children must arrive at school ready to learn. If conditions in the home and community are such that children are placed at risk for school failure, then home and community cannot be ignored in the school reform process.

Secondly, there is the silo effect we discussed. There is more to a school than general education reading and math and their respective assessments. While general education is undeniably the "800 pound gorilla" in every school, there are a few other respectfully sized "apes" in the school as well, and these are often ignored by the CSR managers. These include, for example, Title I programs; English language learner (ELL) programs; and, most important, special education. None of the large CSR programs has paid any significant attention to special education. For school reform to be truly comprehensive, all school resources must be included in the mix.

The third missing ingredient, and the one most central to the topic of this book, is a focus on behavior. Just as a child must come to school ready to learn for the school to benefit from the child's standardized test score gains (i.e., O'Day, 2002), so must a child's behavior, if it impedes the learning process, be addressed in some systematic fashion (Sailor, 1996).

These three missing ingredients (the community school linkages, integration of services and educational supports within schools, and SW-PBS), addressed to remediation of behavior that impedes the learning process, should collectively be a part of the next series of conversations on meaningful school reform. The complex and critical issues having an impact on the education of our future citizens deserve and demand a comprehensive, solutions-focused approach.

One important step in this direction is reflected in the idea of a universal design for learning (UDL) (Center for Universal Design, 1997; Curry, 2003; Rose, Sethuraman, & Meo, 2000). UDL is an approach to educational systems change and curriculum development that is intended to ensure that students with a wide spectrum of learning problems, including those associated with disabilities, can gain access to and derive benefit from, the general curriculum. UDL provides a rubric for differentiated instruction focused on (a) multiple means of teaching (i.e., "multimodal"); (b) multiple means of expression (i.e., oral and written tests); and (c) multiple means of student engagement (i.e., maximum student motivation to tackle different material) (Curry, 2003).

Unlike CSR, which is directed to restructuring and realignment of all curricula, instruction, and assessment processes linked directly to state content standards (Elmore, 2004), newer school reform approaches must be comprehensive and become focused on systems that can facilitate (or inhibit) the results of CSR interventions (Fullan, 1999). Next efforts, in our view, need to consist of schoolwide applications of all available resources, with community resources linked to and integrated with school resources. Further, this "scaffold" of structural elements must include partnership arrangements between schools and the families of children who attend the school. Finally, a fully integrated and coordinated system of supports and services, including SW-PBS, needs to be implemented at the level of individual schools, each with its unique school culture, and reinforced by restructured processes at the district level to enhance academic and social outcomes for all students.

In our view, one of the most significant contributions to the failure of CSR models to "scale up" in remote (from the developer's research and development site) urban school districts is the failure to recognize that packaged school reform cannot be imposed on schools in top-down fashion as if each model were a "one-size-fits-all" template. Schools must "own" systems change processes, particularly when these processes are difficult and require a great deal of new learning on the part of administrators, professionals, staff, families, and students.

Schools need to figure out the models for themselves, engage in discourse communities (Skrtic, 1995) within the schools, rename the processes to fit into the culture of each school, and then come together as communities of practice (Burrello & Hoffman, 2001–2002) to begin to make the model work for them. Districts that tell schools, "now do this or suffer the consequences," will likely see gains only in that subset of schools with cultures that happen to resonate with the requirements of the particular CSR.

Special education is a major focus of the new schoolwide applications reform process because it is the single largest categorical program of supplementary supports and services and is, at the same time, the most isolated from the general education curriculum and assessment processes in traditionally structured schools and school districts (Lipsky & Gartner, 1997). A central question for new schoolwide application approaches is, Can special education and other discrete, categorical programs be fully integrated and woven into a UDL such that all students can derive measurable academic and social benefits from all available resources at the school site and from within the schools' community?

## POTENTIAL PATHWAY TO SUSTAINABLE REFORM

To frame this question around whole-school reform issues offers a potential pathway to the solution of some thorny problems. For one, it engages general educators in the task of identifying special education practices that offer benefits to students who are not identified for special education supports and services while at the same time supporting those identified (for special education) [IDEA, 20 U.S.C. § 1413(a)(4)(A)]. Practices arising from research and development within the field of special education, such as SW-PBS, can be applied at all three tiers of a schoolwide, data-based prevention system such as RTI (see chapter 29). General educators, through this process, come to value special educators for what they offer the total school (Carr et al., 2002; Sugai et al., 2000; Turnbull et al., 2002).

One critical element in integrating school resources for the benefit of all students in a schoolwide applications context is that of inclusive education. If special educators and special education resources are "locked up" in special classrooms, this integration mechanism cannot be actualized (Lawson & Sailor, 2000). An early question that needed to be addressed in this process was to satisfy special educators that students with disabilities could be successfully educated outside a need for self-contained educational placements.

Sailor (2002) provided a comprehensive review of the literature in response to a request from the President's Commission on Excellence in Special Education to address the question, What outcomes accrue to both special and general education students (separately or together) from inclusive education practices? To undertake the review, Sailor adopted as a standard for claiming scientific evidence the National Research Council publication, *Scientific Research in Education* (Shavelson & Towne, 2002). Studies claiming evidence of efficacy from inclusive practices were rejected unless the standards for investigative rigor suggested by Shavelson and Towne were met.

For students with high-incidence disabilities (i.e., learning disabilities and other mild intellectual disabilities), the President's Commission report findings mirrored those of Lenz and Deshler (2004), which concluded that, with the use by teaching and support personnel of a broad array of instructional strategies and techniques in a coordinated fashion, available scientific evidence revealed significant gains for students with disabilities as well as for students without disabilities when instruction was carried out in inclusive settings.

Evidence for academic and social outcomes for the inclusion of students with low-incidence disabilities (i.e., severe, multiple disabilities) was reviewed by Halvorsen and Sailor (1990), Hunt and Goetz (1997), McGregor and Vogelsberg (1998), and Sailor (2002). The sum of these reviews suggests caution in drawing inferences.[1] There have been too few comparative investigations between inclusive and separate programs for students with low-incidence disabilities to draw firm conclusions; however, a number of comparative studies (e.g., Fisher & Meyer, 2002; Foreman, Authur-Kelly, Pascoe, & King, 2004; Logan & Keefe, 1997; Peetsma, Vergeer, Roeleveld, & Karsten, 2001; Wehmeyer, Lattin, Lapp-Rincker, & Agran, 2003) have provided evidence that inclusive educational practices for students with significant disabilities are associated with increased developmental, social, and academic outcomes. Early concerns that inclusion would prove detrimental to general education students have not been substantiated through research. In fact, there has been some mounting evidence that innovations introduced into general education classrooms to accommodate students with a variety and range of disabilities directly benefit general education students (Lenz & Deshler, 2004; Luiselli, Putnam, Handler, & Feinberg 2005; Manset & Semmel, 1997).

The sum of evidence from controlled investigations as well as an analysis of current policy directions suggest that research directed to teaching and learning processes with students who require specialized supports and services should be organized within a universal design (Center for Universal Design, 1997; Curry, 2003; Rose et al., 2000) rubric with schoolwide applications of categorical supports from all sources, including special education (Ferguson, Kozleski, & Smith 2001; Sailor & Roger, 2005). Furthermore, structural reform policy affecting inner-city schools increasingly stresses efforts to bring schools, their families, and their community leaders together in a common reform agenda (Anyon, 2005; Lawson & Sailor, 2000; Sailor & Roger, 2005). Under schoolwide applications theory, *all* students are general education students, as called for under NCLB, and general education teachers collaborate and partner with support teachers to determine how and where the teaching/learning process will occur for all students, including those with individualized educational plans (IEPs).

## Urban Applications

Inner-city, urban schools are often affected by conditions of extreme poverty, sometimes resulting in a designation of "low-performing" school or a school under "improvement" for failing to meet the AYP required by NCLB. Such schools afford a fertile test ground for a comprehensive, integrated service/support system because in these schools just about all of the students can benefit from extra supports. Recent research indicated that positive academic as well as social outcomes can be realized for all students from integrated applications of special education practices in urban schools (Carr et al., 2002; Utley & Sailor, 2002). In the case of fully integrated applications of learning strategies designed for students with mild/moderate learning problems, such as those representative of the multicultural achievement gap in urban schools, evidence is accruing that NCLB-sanctioned accountability (i.e., "universal access") measures for all students reflect increases as a result (Lenz & Deshler, 2004). Where problems of social development, reflected in behavior problems leading to ODRs for general education students (and possible removal to categorical placement for special education students), are at issue, applications of SW-PBS have generated evidence that standardized test scores for general education students in low-performing schools can be turned around and enhanced as a result of an integrated application of special education practice (Cole, Waldron, & Majd, 2004; Lassen et al., 2006; Luiselli et al., 2005).

Thus far, we have examined three considerations or potential threats to efforts to scale up SW-PBS practices in America's schools: (a) the problem of silos and the difficulties associated with introducing something that might be perceived, particularly by teachers and administrators in urban schools, as an add-on; (b) the bifurcation problem, by which general education takes responsibility for Tier 1 of the RTI process, Primary Interventions of SW-PBS, and special education takes control of Tier 3, tertiary interventions, with neither attending much to secondary interventions;

and (c) the sustainability problem, viewed here as a problem of ensuring that SW-PBS becomes a part of the culture of the school and is identified as part of its community of practice.

We suggested that these problems might best be addressed by nesting their solutions within processes of CSR. We then undertook a critique of the school reform processes identified with the present wave of school reform (Lawson & Sailor, 2000) that began about 1983 and in particular examined some of the shortcomings of the CSRDP for accomplishing these aims (CSRQ, 2005). We then suggested that a new trend in school reform focused on schoolwide applications of fully integrated supports and services, including community school features, might provide a good pathway for advancing SW-PBS to scale across America's school districts. In the next section, we examine a particular example of this type of school reform, called the schoolwide applications model (SAM) (Sailor & Roger, 2005), and examine how the process addresses the three barriers to sustainability of SW-PBS.

## SAM: A FULLY INTEGRATED, COMMUNITY SCHOOL APPROACH TO SCHOOL REFORM

The SAM originated from an ongoing research partnership between researchers associated with the Lawrence Campus of the University of Kansas and USD 500, Kansas City, Kansas School District, beginning in the early 1990s and continuing today. In the period from about 1993 to 1998, research efforts were focused on inclusive educational practices and led, ultimately, to a decision to eliminate all categorical, special classes serving students with disabilities at White Church Elementary School. White Church became the district's first fully integrated educational support school in the 2000 academic year.

Perhaps more germane to the purposes of the present volume, the second major program of research undertaken through the partnership was the establishment of the first tier of the three-tier program of SW-PBS. Called the *universal support level* of SW-PBS, the process was begun in a number of USD 500 schools, of which White Church Elementary was one.

### White Church

White Church Elementary School has long been recognized as a neighborhood community school. The school was originally built in 1833 as a log structure and had 32 students, 27 of whom were Native American and 5 of whom were Caucasian. A wooden frame structure replaced the log school, and after the community members painted the school white, the Native Americans named the building White Church because it was used for church on Sunday, and the color was white. The name White Church has remained to this day.

During the 1800s, several changes to both the school structure and population occurred. In the 1840s, the school accepted only Caucasian children, and the Native Americans sold the land that had been "deeded" to them by the government. A school district was established, using the legal name of White Church, making it the first public school in Wyandotte County. In the late 1800s, the school accepted both Caucasian and African American students, with Caucasians taught on the first floor and African American students on the second floor.

This separation continued through the early to mid-1900s. White Church was completely segregated during this period, with the Caucasian students in three multiage classrooms, first through third grade, fourth and fifth grade, and seventh and eighth grades. The African American students were all in one room off the back of the school building. The African American and Caucasian students were not allowed to talk to each other, eat together, or go to recess together. School times and schedules for arrival, lunch, recess, and departure were arranged around separation. During this time, changes in the school building structure also occurred. In 1924, the current brick building was built and remains the same to this time. Today, White Church is best known as a racially diverse neighborhood school. The last few years have brought demographic changes in the surrounding community in terms of changing Section 8 housing, school population, parent involvement, and socioeconomic status.[2]

In 2004, the school population included 284 students, of whom 49.5% were African American, 16.5% were Caucasian, and 30.7% were from Hispanic backgrounds; 142 students (50%) received free or reduced lunch, and 37 students with IEPs (13%) received special education services in a fully inclusive educational environment. Eighty six percent of the White Church population was considered to be economically disadvantaged.

In the spring of 2005, the Wyandotte County community served by White Church Elementary was struck by a devastating tornado that ripped out large sections of the area's low-income neighborhoods. As a result, the demographics of White Church have undergone dramatic changes, with steadily increasing numbers of Latino students.

## SW-PBS at White Church

In partnership with University of Kansas researchers, White Church Elementary began a program of implementation and associated research on Tier 1 of SW-PBS in the 2000 academic year. The SW-PBS implementation began by working with a school improvement team (SIT). The SIT was a group the school's principal had pulled together to develop a plan to enhance student achievement. It was a decentralized, shared process that included people such as administrators, teachers, support staff, students, business leaders, and parents who sincerely cared about all students in that school and what they needed to learn to succeed. Because both SIT and SW-PBS were focused on a team-based approach and a data-based decision-making process, the two programs were able to be interrelated well.

To assess and evaluate the fidelity with which Tier 1 SW-PBS was being implemented at White Church, the Schoolwide Evaluation Tool (SET; Horner et al., 2004) was administered by the research team prior to the intervention (SW-PBS Tier 1 implementation) and once during each subsequent academic year, a process that continues at present. The SET was developed to assess the fidelity of SW-PBS Tier 1 applications over time and to evaluate critical features of the process through repeated-measures assessments. Thus, the tool can be used to check for sustainability of the total Tier 1 process over time; can be used to analyze patterns of change across the critical features; and can be used to assess the impact of Tier 1 SW-PBS on indicators of student academic and social achievement through regression analysis (Choi, 2006).

The survey has 28 questions and requires information to be obtained from a variety of sources, including a review of school artifacts (i.e., written school improvement plans, discipline procedures manual); direct observations of students and teachers; and interviews with school personnel, including students. The SET has seven subscales: (a) defining schoolwide behavioral expectations; (b) teaching the expectations to all students; (c) providing reinforcement for meeting expectations; (d) establishing a range of consequences for problem behavior that are followed consistently by school staff; (e) collecting data on problematic patterns of behavior and using the data to make decisions; (f) active support from school site administration for the total process; and (g) active support from district-level administration through relevant policy implementation, training opportunities, and opportunities to collect and use relevant data. Horner et al. (2004) reported appropriate psychometrics for the instrument, including internal consistency ($r = .96$); test-retest reliability (97.3%); interobserver agreement (99%); and construct validity ($r = 75$; $p < .01$).

Figure 26.1 presents SET scores at White Church (shown as averaged scores across all critical features for the 2001 through 2007 academic years). Horner et al. (2004) consider 80% to be full implementation of Tier

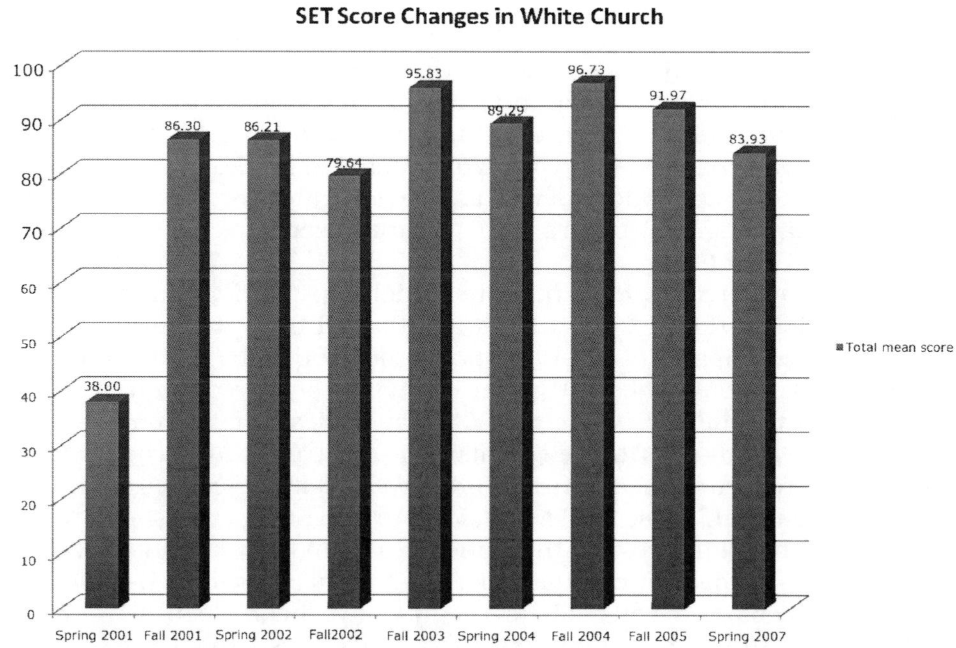


**Fig. 26.1.** School-wide Evaluation Tool (SET) score changes at White Church Elementary School in Kansas City, Kansas, through 2007.

1 SW-PBS. As the figure shows, White Church achieved their criterion after 1 year of training and technical assistance by the research team, but then slipped in the second semester of the second year (79.64%). This slippage, which raised concerns with the partnership team about the sustainability of the process, led to a decision to effect a change in procedure during the 2003 academic year, which became the third research endeavor of the partnership and ultimately led to the development of SAM. Meanwhile, the SW-PBS line of research continues at White Church with ongoing implementation of secondary and tertiary levels (Tiers 2 and 3) of support. The individual and secondary SET (Anderson et al., 2007) has been added to the SW-PBS fidelity of assessment process.

## School Culture and Data-Based Decision Making

The central thesis of this chapter is that enculturation of innovation is seriously compromised by the three issues we discussed at the outset: siloization, bifurcation, and sustainability. The question for the White Church partnership in the 2003 academic year became, How can we juggle all of these innovative practices at the same time without allowing any of the balls to drop? The answer that emerged through the ongoing discourse of the SIT/University of Kansas partnership at White Church led to a further restructuring of the school organizational processes.

With inclusive educational supports and integrated instruction begun and SW-PBS beginning to be operative at all three levels, many of the ingredients were in place at White Church to begin to produce significant academic as well as social progress on the part of students. What remained to be accomplished was a structure by which systematic data could be collected at proximal levels (high-frequency, near-term measures) as well as distal levels (annual grade-level, standardized assessments).

The third program of research through the partnership, which continues today, includes combining several special-purpose teams, such as the PBS team and the SIT into a single-site leadership team (SLT). This team, which was chaired by the principal, included grade-level team representation, general education as well as special education representatives, support therapists, and others and was representative of the school's community of practice.

The KU researchers took the site leadership team through the SCP process (Sailor & Roger, 2005) that was adapted from the empowerment evaluation participant evaluation model developed by Fetterman and Wandersman (2005). The SCP process, which occurred each semester during 2003 through 2005, required a day and a half to complete and enabled the SLT to prioritize elements of its restructuring process to set annual goals reflecting the priorities and to set specific objectives, with timelines, to accomplish those goals. In addition, the SCP process established a communicative link between the leadership team and the school staff, so everybody was made aware of the process and outcomes to be pursued.

This process and some of its results have been documented in a video produced in conjunction with Indiana University, called *Creating a Unified System* (www.forumoneducation.org). The video shows the gradual transformation of White Church Elementary into a culture of learning. All silos are gone; all teaching is collaborative, with general and special educators responsible for all tiers of SW-PBS; and the process has sustained to date despite several changes in site administrators, coaches, and teachers.

In our terms, the merging of these three lines of research and practice (inclusion, SW-PBS, and coordinated, data-based decision making around educational interventions) led to a process of enculturation in which the school assumed "ownership" of all of the processes, and buy-in was pretty much unanimous. Did this process of becoming a culture of learning make a difference for the students? Figure 26.2 presents the pattern of math and reading performance by White Church students as measured by state annual, standardized assessments (averaged across grades) for the years from 2000 (startup of SW-PBS) through 2005. These data, which include all special education students except those with severe disabilities, have made White Church a legend within the state.

In 2006, Kansas changed the test used for state assessments, so data points after 2005 cannot be considered continuous with data from the previous years. Performance levels on more recent state assessments, however, remain high, lending some support to the hypothesis of sustainability of school reform through systemic enculturation.

The restructuring processes at White Church became the prototype for a formulation, during the period from 2003 to 2006, of a CSR "package" called the schoolwide applications model or SAM (Sailor & Roger, 2005). Fifteen critical features were identified and formulated into a set of 15 measurable indicators that could be assessed in any school. In 2003, an instrument was created using a Likert-scaled set of 15 assessment items

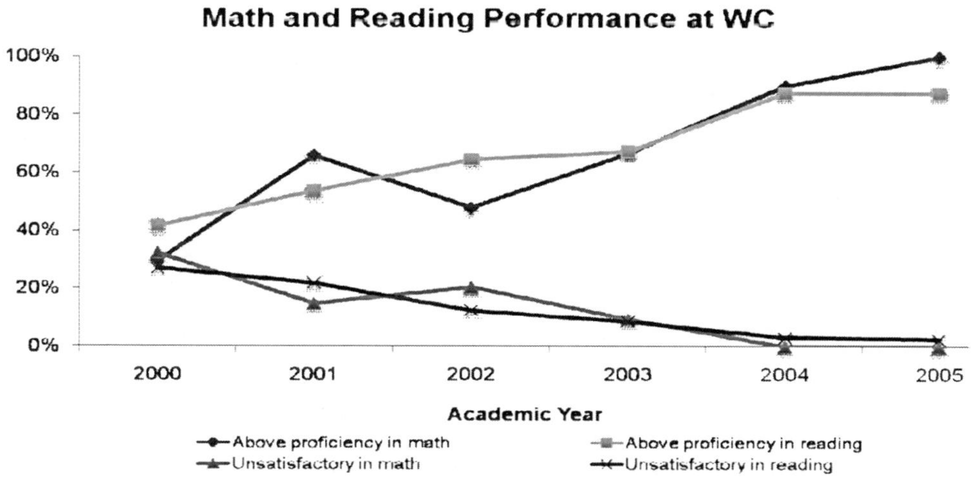


**Fig. 26.2.** Math and reading performance at White Church (WC) Elementary School in Kansas City, Kansas, 2000–2005.

and an accompanying manual to be used to train assessors. Called the Schoolwide Applications Model Analysis System (SAMAN; Sailor & Roger, 2003), the instrument is presently undergoing psychometric standardization across 19 schools in three districts within California, Kansas, and Louisiana. Preliminary results of interrater agreement using the SAMAN with two independent assessments yielded an average interrater agreement of 87% (Sailor, et al., 2006). If the psychometrics study continues to show scientific acceptability, the SAMAN can serve the function of providing a valid and reliable tool with which to estimate the fidelity of implementation of the SAM school reform process.

To conserve space in this chapter, we describe the SAM (Sailor & Roger, 2005) in terms of 6 guiding principles and 15 critical features, each of which can be measured for progress over time with SAMAN. Table 26.1 presents the conceptual framework of SAM.

## Principles 1 and 2

The first two principles are designed to encourage schools to avoid alternative placements such as private or public special schools for students who require extensive services and supports. Through SAM, schools

**Table 26.1.** Six Guiding Principles and Their Corresponding Critical Features

1. General education guides all instruction.
   CF1. All students are served at the school in which they would be served if they had no need for special services or supports.
   CF2. All students at school are considered general education students.
   CF3. General education teachers assume primary responsibility for all students at the school.
2. All school resources are configured to benefit all students.
   CF4. School is inclusive of all students for all school functions.
   CF5. School is organized to provide all specialized support, adaptations and accommodations to students in such a way as to maximize the number of students who will benefit.
   CF6. All students are taught in accordance with the general curriculum with accommodations, adaptation supports, and services as needed.
3. School proactively addresses social development and citizenship.
   CF7. The school has an active, schoolwide positive behavior support (SWPBS) program.
4. School is a democratically organized, data-driven, problem-solving system.
   CF8. The school is a data-driven, collaborative, decision-making, learning organization with all major functions guided by team processes.
   CF9. School effectively incorporates general education students in the instructional process.
   CF10. All personnel at the school participate in the teaching/learning process and are valued for their respective contributions to pupil academic and social outcomes.
   CF11. School personnel use a uniform, non-categorical lexicon to describe both personnel and teaching/learning functions.
   CF12. School has established a Site Leadership Team (SLT) empowered by the school and the district to implement SAM at the school.
5. School has open boundaries in relation to its families and its community.
   CF13. School has working partnership with families of students who attend the school.
   CF14. School has working partnership with its community business and service providers.
6. School enjoys district support for undertaking extensive systems change.
   CF15. SAM implementation at the school site is fully recognized and supported by the district.

welcome these students for the opportunity to generate additional funds for services and supports that can be configured to benefit a variety of students through integrated applications, consistent with IDEA (1997, 2004), encouraging "incidental benefits" [IDEA, 20 U.S.C. § 1413(a)(4)]. At SAM school sites, it is a policy to encourage parent participation and involvement, and parents are provided extensive information about the schoolwide model. In those rare cases when parents feel strongly that their child requires a separate, self-contained placement and the district concurs, the student may be referred to a school elsewhere that offers self-contained classes for students with disabilities

SAM does not utilize separate classes for students with disabilities or those who are ELLs at the school site; therefore, the challenge to the school is to focus on how such students are supported in the general education classroom, how they are supported in other environments, and how specialized therapies and services are to be provided. Utilization of space at the school, deployment of support personnel, and scheduling issues became significant in realizing these critical features. At SAM schools, very little attention is drawn to the existence of differences among some students and the need for special services and supports. Every effort is made to foster friendships and positive relationships among students with and without disabilities or language issues.

Under the SAM practice, general education teachers have primary responsibility for all students, consider themselves responsible for implementing IEPs, and seek consultation from or collaboration with special education professionals to educate students with disabilities. At SAM schools, the general education teacher is the chief agent of each child's educational program with support from others, including special educators, second language teachers, therapists, paraprofessionals, and others, as needed.

Rather than organizing services and special supports so that only identified students receive benefits, this schoolwide model organizes all categorical supports to benefit the most students possible (cf. Burrello et al., 2004). For urban, multicultural schools that are at risk for punitive consequences under NCLB, this feature allows nonidentified, low-perfor-ming students to receive "incidental" benefits from the integrated applications of special education services and supports, those available through Title I, ELL, vocational education, and so on. School administrators must pay careful attention to state requirements in the implementation of federal, categorical programs such as IDEA. For example, identified students with IEPs still need to be primary recipients of services and supports provided through special education. General education students can receive benefits from the provision of these supports in well-integrated circumstances.

## Principle 3

SW-PBS is an excellent example of a comprehensive intervention package originally developed to meet the specialized need for social development instruction for students in special education who have behavioral disabi-lities (Carr et al., 2002) that has demonstrated efficacy for all students, particularly those in schools challenged by urban blight and poverty (Utley & Sailor, 2002). SAM schools incorporate PBS as an excellent way to extend special education innovation to help meet the social development needs of all students; for example, PBS has generated recent evidence that schools with high rates of disciplinary referrals can cut those rates significantly over a 2-year period and can increase levels of standardized test scores in math and literacy (Luiselli et al., 2005; OSEP Center on Positive Behavioral Interventions and Supports, 2004).

## Principle 4

SAM schools are encouraged to incorporate additional software at the district level to enable school leadership teams to benefit from all available databases affecting the social and academic performance of their students. Through the SCP process, SAM schools use a variety of performance data fields, disaggregated at the district level, to make decisions about setting priorities concerning ongoing elements of school reform.

SAM schools recognize that all salaried personnel at a school can contribute to the teaching-learning process. A school custodian may have hidden talents for information technology training with students, or a speech therapist may be skilled in music appreciation. This enables all school personnel to be able to contribute to the primary mission of the school and not be completely constrained by bureaucratic role specification. Furthermore, SAM schools avoid on-site use of categorical descriptors (e.g., "learning disabilities," "inclusion," "special," "push in–pull out services," etc.). Two kinds of teachers are described in the noncategorical lexicon: classroom (i.e., general education) teachers and support (i.e., special education, ELL) teachers.

## Principle 5

An SLT is established at SAM sites that is representative of all school personnel, including parents, and has community representation. This team utilizes a distributed leadership rubric based on the work of Spillane, Halverson, and Diamond (Burrello, Lashley, & Beatty, 2001) to undertake an SCP process to evaluate data from school processes linked to student academic and social performance outcomes, to prioritize specific new schoolwide interventions to improve outcomes, and to advance the mission of the school through development of an action plan to fully implement SAM.

SAM schools also go beyond traditional parent-teacher associations (i.e., PTAs) to solicit active participation on the part of family members in the teaching/learning process, usually in home and community settings. Some SAM sites have set the establishment of a family resource center (Lawson & Sailor, 2000) at the site as a schoolwide priority. The creation of a "parent liaison" position is a related priority. SAM schools also reach beyond the "business partner" relationship that has characterized some school reform processes. Schools undertake a "community-mapping" process to understand and relate to their respective community constituencies.

The process includes nontraditional schools such as magnet schools; racial balance schools under busing arrangements; cross-district grade configuration schools; charter schools; and so on where the "community" of the school may not be easily geographically configured. The point is to engage the community in the life of the school and vice-versa, regardless of how community is defined.

## Principle 6

Finally, schoolwide models such as SAM that offer a significant departure from traditional educational management, finance, and communication processes will encounter difficulties early on in the absence of district support. Structural features at the district level are required for schools to enact the other critical features of SAM.

### Structural Elements of SAM

Two elements, SCP and an SLT, occur at the level of the school. Two additional elements are required at the level of the district, a district leadership team (DLT) and a district resource team (DRT).

The SLT, usually between 8 and 12 members, has the function of evaluating schoolwide progress data and setting priorities, goals, and objectives for each school term and networking with, as well as reporting to, the other teams and committees that make up school operations. The principal is usually a member of the SLT but not necessarily its chair. SLTs follow strict and efficient team procedures (agenda, rules for membership, rules for recognition to speak, minutes, etc.) so that precious school time is not wasted. SLTs meet at least biweekly and undergo full-day "retreats" at least twice per year (semester school calendars) prior to the onset of each new term. The SCP process is engaged during these retreats. Membership on SLTs is usually a mix of principal and teacher nominations with elections for 1-year (renewable) terms and invitations to specific parents and community members to solicit participation.

The SCP process, as discussed, is a variant of, and patterned after, empowerment evaluation (Fetterman, 2001). Using this process, a facilitator, supplied by the district or arranged through a university partnership, assists the SLT to begin with a vision for the school in undertaking the SAM. A set of goals is derived to realize the vision, and a set of specific objectives is delineated to be undertaken by various school/community personnel for the coming term. Measurement strategies are identified for each objective so that subsequent SCPs can proceed with priority and objective-setting discussions occurring on the basis of pupil performance data linked to specific measurable processes. Interim meetings are held by the SLT to review progress in the implementation of each SCP action plan for the term.

The DLT is composed of district personnel with a vested interest in SAM implementation. The DLT may have the superintendent as a member, but usually not in the role of chair of the team. DLTs are usually chaired by the assistant superintendent for curriculum and instruction because SAM processes are driven primarily by general education. Other members typically include the head of pupil support services, the special education director, the Title I director, and the director of ELL programs. The DLT usually meets three or four times per year to review SAM school site plans and consider requests for approval for policy and budgetary considerations arising from these plans and originating through the DRT.

The final structural component is the DRT. This team is usually made up of district-level staff who work closely with the schools such as regional special education personnel, grade-level specialists, a principal, a parent support coordinator, transportation officials, and the like. The function of the DRT is to consider each school site for the coming term and assist the DLT in recommending approval, disapproval, or further negotiation with the site over requested resources. If a SAM site, for example, requests two additional paraeducators to implement one or more objectives on the action plan (from the SCP process) for the coming term, the DRT will consider the request, balance the needs of the site against the collective needs of all district schools, and make recommendations to the DLT. Typically, DRTs with several SAM sites in the district will meet on a fairly frequent basis to assist the district to stay ahead of the curve of systems change.

Based in part on results from Ravenswood (Sailor, et al., 2006), SAM has now been extended to six schools in the Louisiana RSD in New Orleans. SAM is also being implemented at a second elementary school in Kansas City, Kansas, which was added in 2005 (Keetle, 2007).

It is our hypothesis that SW-PBS can be sustained as ongoing school practice once personnel have been trained and the process has been implemented to the 80% criterion of its fidelity instruments, the SET (Tier 1) and the new Individual Student Systems Evaluation Tool (ISSET) (Tiers 2 and 3). We further hypothesize that the probability of SW-PBS sustainability over time will increase when the processes are fully nested within a CSR package that has become enculturated within a school. That hypothesis cannot, however, be directly tested absent a full-blown, controlled experimental design.

Table 26.2 presents the operational definitions of the 15 critical features estimated by the SAMAN. Note that Critical Feature 7 is the extent to which the school is implementing SW-PBS, and Table 26.3 presents the critical features of SET.

Various conceptual frameworks for fully integrated, schoolwide models have been around for over a decade (e.g., Burrello et al., 2001; Sailor, 1991; Sailor et al., 1989), but only recently have operational models appeared that can be moved to the status of intervention and replication (Ferguson et al., 2001; Sailor & Roger, 2005). SAM is presently being implemented in various phases at scale (11 schools) in the Ravenswood City School District in East Palo Alto, California. Ravenswood and the California Department of Education, in response to a federal district court consent decree, secured the services of Dr. Wayne Sailor at KU, and later Blair Roger in California, to develop a fully integrated schoolwide model to go to scale in the district over a 3-year period beginning in 2003. The SAM system was developed and critiqued each step of its trajectory by groups of parents, people of color, people with disabilities, teachers, school staff, students, and administrators through the mechanism that has now been identified as the DLT.

**Table 26.2.** Critical Features of SAM Estimated by SAMAN.

| Feature | Assessment | Source |
|---|---|---|
| 1. School serves all students | • Extent to which special needs students are outsourced<br>• Outreach to families of special needs students | • Principal<br>• Coordinator for special needs students |
| 2. All students at school are considered general education students | • Integrated uses of all school space<br>• Grade level placement is only distinction groupings of students | • Map of space utilization at school<br>• Support teachers for special needs populations<br>• Sample of student schedules<br>• Sample of service specifications on IEPs |
| 3. General education teachers assume respon-sibility for all students at the school | • General ed teachers' perception of respon-sibility and "ownership" of all students | • General ed teachers<br>• Observations of Gen Ed classes |
| 4. School is inclusive of all students for all school functions | • All students participate in all school functions | • General ed teachers<br>• Observations of functions<br>• Sample of field trip schedules<br>• Classroom observations |
| 5. School is organized to provide all accommo-dations to students in such a way as to maximize the number of students who will benefit | • All students benefit from all specialized resources at school | • Specialized personnel (i.e., therapists)<br>• Observations of applications of specialized supports<br>• Review service specifications on sample of IEPs<br>• General Ed teachers |
| 6. All students are taught in accordance with the general curriculum | • All instruction geared to general curriculum | • IEP review<br>• Gen ed teachers<br>• Support teachers<br>• Classroom observations<br>• Review sample of student schedules |
| 7. The school has an active, schoolwide PBS program operating at all 3 levels | • Extent of Schoolwide Positive Behavior Support (PBS) Practices<br>• Extent of PBS Training in school<br>• Extent of ODR data tracking to reflect PBS outcomes | • PBS Coach<br>• ODR and other PBS Databases<br>• PBS support Plan Reviews<br>• Observations of PBS implementations at 3 levels |

(continued)

**Table 26.2.** (continued)

| Feature | Assessment | Source |
|---|---|---|
| 8. School is a data-driven, collective, decision-making, learning organization with all major functions guided by team processes. | • Extent of democratic decision making within school<br>• Collaboration<br>• Team processes for distributed leadership<br>• School Centered Planning process | • Team map at school of team structure<br>• Principal<br>• Teachers<br>• Staff<br>• Observations of team process<br>• Team meeting minutes-attendance |
| 9. School effectively utilizes general education students in the instruction of students in need of support in all instructional environments | • Peer Tutoring<br>• Peer assisted instruction<br>• Student directed instruction | • students<br>• general education teachers<br>• paraprofessionals<br>• Classroom observation<br>• Non-classroom observation<br>• Parents |
| 10. All personnel at the school participate in the teaching/learning process and are valued for their respective contributions to pupil academic and social outcomes. | • Extent to which all school staff are responsible for pupil progress in social and academic | • Principal<br>• Teachers<br>• Staff<br>• Non-classroom environment observations (i.e., cafeteria) |
| 11. School personnel use a uniform, non-categorical lexicon to describe both personnel and teaching/learning functions | • Non-categorical use of language to describe spaces, students and personnel functions<br>• Use of formal policy to guide language descriptors | • Teachers<br>• Administrators<br>• Staff<br>• Observations of meetings of school personnel<br>• Policy language reviews |
| 12. School has established a SLT empowered by the school and the District to implement SAM at the school | • Use of Site Leadership Team to implement SAM | • Principal<br>• SAM document review<br>• SAM Coordinator at school |
| 13. School has working partnership with families of students who attend the school | • Extent of school/family partnership<br>• Use of family resource center at site | • Families<br>• Principal<br>• Review of Family Resource Center documentation<br>• SAM Coordinator<br>• PTA members<br>• School site council members |

| | | |
|---|---|---|
| 14. School has working partnership with its community businesses and service providers | • Extent of school/community partnership<br>• Community participation on teams<br>• School hosts community/<br>• school events | • community service providers<br>• community business representatives<br>• Principal<br>• Document review of community partnership records |
| 15. SAM implementation at the school site is fully recognized and supported by the District | • Extent of District support<br>• District Leadership Team to respond to SAM issues at school site<br>• District plan to implement SAM in other schools<br>• District Resource Team to meet TA and training needs to implement SAM at school site | • Superintendent<br>• Principal<br>• SAM document review at District level<br>• Observations of District Leadership Team meetings<br>• Observations of District Resource Team meetings |

**Table 26.3.** Critical features of SET.

| Feature | Assessment | Source |
|---|---|---|
| A. Commitment | 1. Does the administrator attend training with team on function-based support? | • Administrator interview<br>• Other |
| | 2. Does the administrator regularly attend school TAT/BST meetings? | • Administrator interview<br>• Other |
| | 3. Do scores on the SET, TIC, BOQ or equivalent measure indicate that SWPBS is in place and is implemented with fidelity? | • SET, TIC, BOQ or equivalent measure.<br>• Other |
| | 4. Does the school-wide team monitor the number of students receiving targeted and/or intensive supports on at least a monthly basis? | • Behavior support team leader interview & school-wide team meeting minutes.<br>• Other |
| | 5. Can the administrator identify a person who is coordinating function-based support across all students in a school? | • Administrator interview<br>• Other |
| | 6. Is there a person in (or available to) the school who is trained to implement functional behavioral assessment, and behavior support intervention implementation? | • Administrator interview<br>• Other |
| B. Team Based Planning | 1. Is there a team that receives requests for behavioral assistance, develops behavior support plans, and monitors impact of support? | • Administrator interview.<br>• Other |
| | 2. Is there documentation (e.g., meeting minutes, schedule) that the behavior support team meets at least twice a month? | • Behavior support team meeting minutes.<br>• Other |
| | 3. Is there documentation that a predictable and standardized process is used to monitor student progress on a monthly basis? | • Behavior support team meeting minutes or monitoring/tracking form.<br>• Other |
| | 4. Do report that at least 50% of behavior support team members asked attend annual professional development training in targeted and intensive interventions? | • Behavior support team leader interview.<br>• Other |
| C. Student Identi-fication | 1. Does the behavior support team leader report that office discipline referral (ODR) patterns are regularly used to identify individual students who might benefit from a targeted or intensive intervention? | • Behavior support team leader interview.<br>• Permanent Product<br>• Other |

| | | |
|---|---|---|
| | 2. Does a behavior support team review student data to determine whether targeted or intensive interventions need to be developed or modified at least three times per year? | • Behavior support team leader interview |
| | 3. Does the ODR form have preliminary FBA information: (a) time, (b) location, (c) behavior, (d) administrative decision, (e) possible motivation, and (f) others involved? | • ODR form.<br>• Other |
| | 4. Do at least 80% of staff asked (at least 5) agree with the team leader on the process for requesting assistance? | • Behavior support team leader interview and staff interview.<br>• Other |
| | 5. Do team meeting minutes document that at least 4 of 5 of the most recent requests for assistance received support (meeting held or had an FBA conducted and intervention planned) within 10 school days of the request? | • Behavioral support team meeting minutes.<br>• Other |
| | 6. Does the intervention planning process (e.g., behavior support team meeting) result in information needed to complete a functional behavior assessment: (a) operational definition of problem behavior, (b) antecedents, (c) consequences/functions, (d) setting events, (e) prior interventions, and (f) other information (e.g., medical, academic)? | • Request for assistance form, team meeting minutes.<br>• Other |
| | 7. Does the TAT/BST leader describe a process for determining if a student begins a targeted or intensive intervention? | • Behavior support team leader interview.<br>• Other |
| D. Monitoring & Evaluation | 1. Does the behavior support team leader report that outcomes of students recei-ving targeted or intensive behavior support are monitored at least monthly via agreed upon data (e.g., teacher collected data, direct observations, teacher report, ODRs)? | • Behavior support team leader interview<br>• Other |
| | 2. Does the administrator report that the status of students referred for targeted and intensive support is reported at least quarterly to teachers who have students receiving interventions? | • Administrator interview.<br>• Other |
| | 3. Does the administrator report that the number of students receiving targeted or intensive interventions and their relative status (in aggregate form) is reported to faculty at least quarterly? | • Administrator interview.<br>• Other |
| | 4. Is there a documented process for notifying staff members involved with students needing targeted or intensive behavior support? | • Staff handbook and/or process description.<br>• Other |

(continued)

**Table 26.3.** (continued)

| Feature | Assessment | Source |
|---|---|---|
| | 5. Is there a documented process for notifying family members when a student needs targeted or intensive behavior support? | • Parent notification letter/form and/or process description.<br>• Other |
| E. Implementation | 1. Does the most commonly used targeted intervention include 80% of implementation features as defined on the Targeted Intervention Implementation Feature checklist? | • Targeted intervention feature checklist & written program description.<br>• Behavior support team leader interview |
| | 2. Are training and orientation procedures for the most commonly used targeted interventions documented for staff, volunteers, substitutes, students, families? | • Training & orientation materials.<br>• Behavior support team leader interview |
| | 3. Does the most commonly used targeted intervention have dedicated FTE allocated for managing, coordinating, and monitoring the intervention? | • Behavior support team leader interview & coordinator job description for most commonly used targeted interventions.<br>• Other |
| | 4. Does the behavior support team leader report that the most commonly used targeted intervention requires no more than 10 min. per day from any instructional/supervisory staff (other than people who coordinate, implement, or manage the program)? | • Behavior support team leader interview.<br>• Other |
| | 5. Can at least 80% of staff asked (out of at least 5) describe the general features of the most commonly used targeted intervention? | • Behavior support team leader interview & staff interviews.<br>• Other |
| F. Evaluation & Monitoring | 1. Does the behavior support team leader report that there is a scheduled process to modify targeted intervention plans based on student data? | • Behavior support team leader interview.<br>• Other |
| | 2. Does the team leader report that the team uses data to monitor intervention outcomes at least quarterly? | • Behavior support team leader interview.<br>• Other |
| | 3. Are there documented decision rules for monitoring, modifying, or discontinuing the targeted intervention for a student? | • Behavior support team leader interview.<br>• Other |
| | 4. Does the team gather data at least annually to evaluate fidelity of implementation of the most commonly used targeted intervention? | • Behavior support team leader interview.<br>• Other |

| | | |
|---|---|---|
| G. Assessment | 1. Do at least two and up to 5 sampled functional behavior assessments or behavior intervention plans (written within the past academic school year), include a description of student strengths and preferences and an operational definition of problem behavior? | • Direct observation data or graph, report from teacher, teacher-collected data, written FBA/BSP summary/plan.<br>• Other |
| | 2. Do at least two and up to 5 sampled functional behavior assessments or behavior intervention plans (written within the past academic school year), include a statement about the relation between events that precede (trigger) problem behavior and/or events that follow and maintain the behavior? | • Direct observation data or graph, report from teacher, teacher-collected data.<br>• Other |
| | 3. When a team meets to complete an FBA, does the team include individuals with knowledge about a) the student, b) the context, and c) behavior theory? | • Behavior support team leader interview. |
| H. Implementation | 1. Is there documented evidence that a student's behavior support plan includes an operational definition of problem behavior? | • Written BSP and/or team meeting minutes.<br>• Other |
| | 2. Is there an FBA associated with the BSP? | • Written process description.<br>• Other |
| | 3. Do at least 2 and up to 5 behavior support plans sampled, alter events identified in the FBA that precede (trigger) problem behavior and/or events that follow and maintain the behavior? | • Intensive Individualized Interventions Features Checklist. |

East Palo Alto, California, is an economically depressed area with a very culturally diverse population. Ravenswood is a "primary" district in California, so there are no high schools. Schools pass through three distinct phases in undergoing the SAM systems change process: initiation, implementation, and fluency/sustainability. These phases are defined by means of the 15 critical features' scale scores over two consecutive assessments using the SAMAN. Mean scale scores under 2.0 reflect progress in the phase of initiation; 2.0–2.5 the phase of implementation; and 2.5–3.0 (with no critical feature less than 2) reflect fluency/sustainability. Table 26.4 presents the measured status of each of Ravenswood's 1 schools on SAM progress by average SAMAN assessment score at the conclusion of the 2006–2007 year. Figure 26.3 presents summary data from repeated assessments of School A, a Cohort 1 school in Ravenswood.

On an annual basis, Ravenswood typically services about 4,500 students. In the 2005 school year, 94% of the students qualified for free and reduced lunch, making the district one of the most significantly impacted districts in California for risk factors arising from low socioeconomic conditions. Table 26.5 presents the demographics of each of the Cohort 1 schools in Ravenswood in 2005. As the table reflects, about three quarters of Ravenswood students are Latino, about 15% are African American, and the remainder are Pacific Islanders. There were no European American (Caucasian) students served in the district as of 2007.

The SAM process addresses the issue of desiloization by integrating all school resources such as special education and ELLs and using an RTI model to focus those resources on all students. The absence of special classes based on categorical eligibility determination enables collaborative teaching to occur. The site leadership team uses screening as well as proximal and distal outcome assessments, both academic and behavioral, to make decisions about interventions to be marshaled across the three tiers of the RTI model.

Bifurcation is addressed in SAM by ensuring that all three tiers of SW-PBS implementation are guided by school teams that are made up

**Table 26.4.** SAM progress data.

| | COHORT 1 Schools | | | COHORT 2 Schools | | | | COHORT 3 Schools | | | |
|---|---|---|---|---|---|---|---|---|---|---|---|
| | A | B | C | D | E | F | G | H | I | J | K |
| Time | K-8 | 4-8 | K-8 | K-3 | K-3 | Pre-K | K-8 | 6-8 | 4-8 | K-8 | K-8 |
| Jan.04 | 1.47 | 1.53 | 1.20 | 1.27 | | | | | | | |
| Apr.-May04 | 2.13 | 2.20 | 1.80 | 1.60 | | | | | | | |
| Nov.-Dec.04 | | | | 2.27 | | | 1.73 | | | | |
| Jan.-Feb.05 | 2.47 | 2.53 | 2.00 | | 1.33 | 1.13 | | | | | |
| May05 | | | | | 1.53 | 1.87 | | | | | |
| Nov.05-Jan.06 | 2.20 | 2.47 | 2.33 | 2.40 | 2.26 | 2.33 | 2.33 | 1.73 | 1.07 | 1.13 | 1.93 |
| Mar.06 | | | | | | | | | 2.00 | | |
| May-Jun.06 | 2.46 | 2.73 | 2.26 | 2.53 | 2.33 | 2.26 | 2.26 | | | | |
| Oct.-Dec.06 | 2.60 | 2.66 | 2.00 | | 2.40 | 2.33 | 2.53 | 2.53 | | 2.06 | 2.50 |
| Jan.07 | | | | 2.53 | | | | | 2.26 | | |
| May-Jun.07 | 2.46 | | 1.73 | | 2.20 | 2.20 | 2.20 | 2.46 | 2.13 | 2.06 | 2.30 |

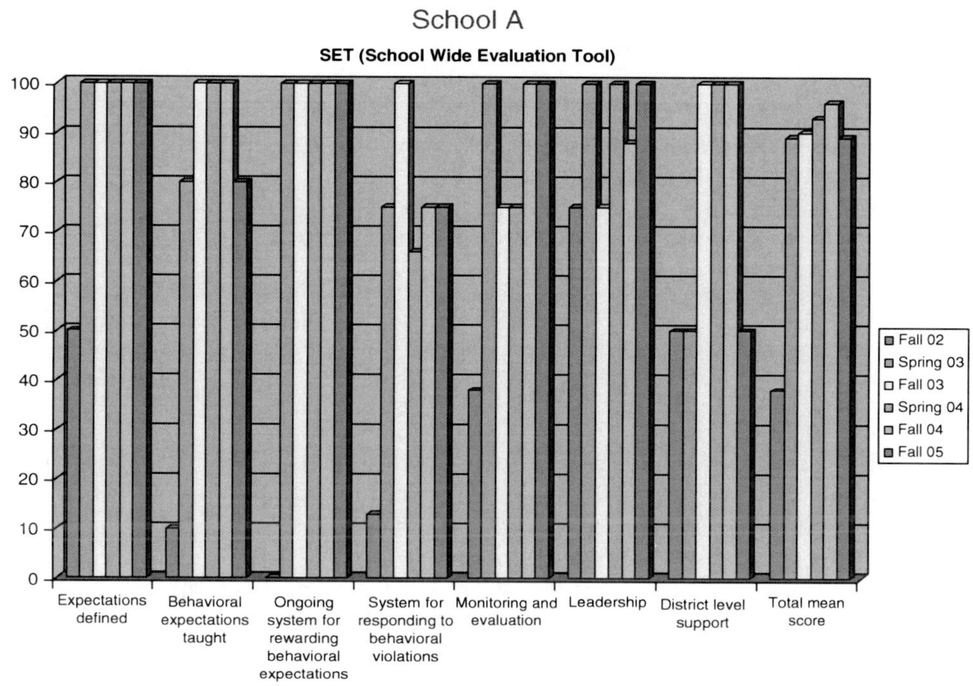


**Fig. 26.3.** Schoolwide Applications Model Analysis System (SAMAN) critical features progress for School A in the Ravenswood City School District, East Palo Alto, California.

**Table 26.5.** Demographics of Cohort 1 Schools in the Ravenswood City School District.

| School Type (Elem/Middle) | | # of Students ('04-'05) | Demographics |
|---|---|---|---|
| **School A** | Middle School<br>Grades 5-8 | 346 | 82% Latino<br>8% African American<br>7% Pacific Islander<br>3% Other (non-White) |
| **School B** | Middle School<br>Grades 5-8 | 514 | 80% Latino<br>7% African American<br>10% Pacific Islander<br>3% Other (non-White) |
| **School C** | Middle School<br>Grades 5-8 | 443 | 68% Latino<br>17% African American<br>10% Pacific Islander<br>3% Other (non-White) |
| **School D** | Elementary<br>Charter School<br>Grades K-3 | 456 | 85% Latino<br>10% African American<br>3% Pacific Islander<br>2% Other (non-White) |

of general educators as well as special educators and other school professionals. General educators under SAM undergo extensive professional development on tertiary interventions of SW-PBS, including wraparound, the most intensive form of support (see chapter 27). Conversely, special educators are fully involved in universal (primary) support addressed to all students in the school.

Finally, sustainability is addressed by focusing on enculturation by the school of the 15 critical features of the SAM CSR model. Ongoing professional development and technical assistance on SAM are provided to a school until the SAMAN fidelity estimation tool indicates that average scores across the 15 features achieve the sustainability range of 2.5–3.0 for at least two consecutive assessments. Future research will test the assumptive assessments. Further research will test the assumption that the present operational definition of sustainability actually achieves the goal of having SAM, including SW-PBS, become an ongoing "business-as-usual" aspect of school culture over time.

## CONCLUSION

In this chapter, we have posited the argument that SW-PBS at all three levels faces three challenges, at least in urban core schools, as it moves to become praxis at scale throughout America's public schools. These challenges are respectively described as *siloization*, the tendency to fragment programs and services in schools, with few bridging systems from one to another; *bifurcation*, the tendency to split SW-PBS into general education and special education functions, with general education assuming responsibility for the implementation of Level 1 (primary applications) and special education assuming responsibility primarily for Level 3 (tertiary applications); and *sustainability*, the tendency of schools to return to stasis over time following intensive training and short term, follow-up technical assistance. We suggested that one way to overcome these challenges might be found through the process of *enculturation*, or the manner in which a school embeds a systems change process into its own unique culture, assumes "ownership" of the process, and has the process become a part of business as usual at the school.

Finally, we presented a CSR model called the schoolwide applications model (SAM) that, we suggest, holds the potential to achieve enculturation of SW-PBS by embedding it as 1 of 15 critical features of the total process. Since SAM is driven by a school-based planning process, called school-centered planning, problem solving related to behavioral issues at all levels is nested within efforts to improve the overall teaching-learning process at the school.

## NOTES

1. A new comprehensive review of the evidence base for inclusive education is presently being conducted by a work group convened by the Office of Special Education Programs (OSEP) in conjunction with AIR. The senior author (Sailor) is a member of that work group. The findings of the work group will be compiled and disseminated by AIR in a forthcoming publication.
2. We thank Kerry Lida for her contributions to the background research on the history and demographics of White Church Elementary School.

## REFERENCES


Adelman, H. S., & Taylor, L. (2000). Promoting mental health in schools in the midst of school reform. *Journal of School Health*, 70(5), 171–178.

American Institutes for Research (AIR). (2006, November). *CSRQ Center report on elementary school comprehensive school reform models*. Retrieved July 2, 2007, from http://www.csrq.org

Anderson, C., Lewis-Palmer, T., Todd, A. W., Horner, R. H, Sugai, G., & Sampson N. K (2007). *Individual student systems evaluation tool* (Version 2.0). Eugene: University of Oregon, Educational and Community Supports.

Anyon, J. (2005). What "counts" as educational policy? Notes toward a new paradigm. *Harvard Educational Review*, 75, 65–88.

Becker, W. C., & Carnine, D. W. (1980). Direct instruction: An effective approach to educational intervention with the disadvantaged and low performers. In B. B. Lahey & A. E. Kazdin (Eds.), *Advances in clinical child psychology* (Vol. 3, pp. 429–473). New York: Plenum.

Becker, W. C., & Engelmann, S. (1976). *Analysis of achievement data on six cohorts of low-income children from 20 school districts in the University of Oregon Direct Instruction Follow Through Model.* Oregon University Eugene, O.R. (ERIC Document Reproduction Service No. ED 145922).

Blank, M. J., & Cady, D. (2004). System change through community schools: District leaders cite the benefits they are reaping through external partnering. *School Administrator*, 61, 26.

Blank, M. J., Hale, E. L., Housman, N., Kaufmann, B., Martinez, M., McCloud, B., et al. (2001). *School-community partnerships in support of student learning: Taking a second look at the governance of the 21st century community learning centers program.* Flint, MI: Mott (C.S.) Foundation.

Blank, M. J., & Shah, B. P. (2003). Community schools improve outcomes for students, families, schools, and communities. *State Education Standard*, 4(2), 36–40.

Borman, G. D., Hewes, G. M., Overman, L. T., & Brown, S. (2002). *Comprehensive school reform and student achievement.* Baltimore: Johns Hopkins University, Center for Research on the Education of Students Placed at Risk.

Burrello, L. C., & Hoffman, L. P. (2001–2002). *Annual reports on the conference on teaching and learning* (submitted to the Superintendents Advisory Board, Forum on Education). Bloomington: Indiana University.

Burrello, L. C., Hoffman, L., & Murray, L. (2004). *School leaders building capacity from within: Resolving competing agendas creatively.* Thousand Oaks, CA: Corwin Press.

Burrello, L. C., Lashley, C., & Beatty, E. E. (2001). *Educating all students together.* Thousand Oaks, CA: Corwin Press.

Carr, E. G., Dunlap, G., Horner, H. R., Koegel, R. L., Turnbull, A. P., Sailor, W., et al. (2002). Positive behavior support: Evolution of an applied science. *Journal of Positive Behavioral Interventions*, 4(1), 4–16.

Center for Universal Design. (1997). What is universal design? Raleigh, NC: Author. Retrieved December 2002 from http://www.design.ncsu.edu:8120/cud/univ_design/princ_overview.htm

Choi, J. (2006). *The relationship between school-wide positive behavior support status and school personnel perceptions of the behavior support system.* Paper presented at the comprehensive exam for doctoral degree of the University of Kansas School of Education, Lawrence.

Clinton, H. R. (1996). *It takes a village: And other lessons children teach us.* New York: Simon & Schuster.

Cole, C., Waldron, N., & Majd, M. (2004). Academic progress of students across inclusive and traditional settings. *Mental Retardation*, 42, 136–144.

Comer, J. P. (1993). James P. Comer, M.D., on the school development program: *Making a difference for children.* NC REST, New York, NY. (ERIC Document Reproduction Service No. ED358959)

Comer, J. P. (1996). *Rallying the whole village: The Comer process for reforming education.* New York: Teachers College Press.

Comprehensive School Reform Quality Center (CSRQ). (2005). *Moving forward: A guide for implementing comprehensive school reform and improvement strategies (training manual)*. Retrieved August 15, 2007, from http://www.csrq.org/documents/MovingForwardGuideFinal11-09-05.pdf

Curry, C. (2003). Universal design: Accessibility for all learners. *Educational Leadership*, 61(2), 55–60.

Danforth, S., & Rhodes, W. C. (1997). Deconstructing disability: A philosophy for inclusion. *Remedial and Special Education*, 18, 357–366.

Danforth, S., Rhodes, W., & Smith, T. (1995). Inventing the future: Postmodern challenges in educational reform. In J. L. Paul, H. Roselli, & D. Evans (Eds.), *Integrating school: Restructuring and special education reform* (pp. 214–236). Orlando, FL: Harcourt Brace Jovanovich.

Darling-Hammond, L. (2003). Keeping good teachers: Why it matters, what leaders can do. *Educational Leadership*, 60(8), 6–13.

Darling-Hammond, L. (2004). Standards, accountability, and school reform. Teachers College Record, 106, 1047–1085.

Elmore, R. F. (2004). The problem of stakes in performance-based accountability systems. In S. H. Fuhrman & R. F. Elmore (Eds.), *Redesigning accountability systems for education*. New York: Teachers College Press.

Fairbanks, S., Sugai, G., Guardino, D., & Lathrop, M. (2007). Response to intervention: An evaluation of a classroom system of behavior support for second grade students. *Exceptional Children*, 73, 288–310.

Ferguson, D. L., Kozleski, E. B., & Smith, A. (2001). *Transformed, inclusive schools: A framework to guide fundamental change in urban schools*. Denver: National Institute for Urban Improvement, Office of Special Education Programs.

Fetterman, D. M. (2001). The transformation of evaluation into a collaboration: A vision of evaluation in the 21st century. *American Journal of Evaluation*, 22, 381–385.

Fetterman, D. M., Kaftarian, S., & Wandersman, A. (1995). *Empowerment evaluation: Knowledge and tools for self-assessment and accountability*. Thousand Oaks, CA: Sage.

Fetterman, D. M., & Wandersman, A. (Eds.). (2005). *Empowerment evaluation principles in practice*. New York: Guilford.

Fisher, M., & Meyer, L. H. (2002). Development and social competence after two years for students enrolled in inclusive and self-contained educational programs. *Research and Practice for Persons With Severe Disabilities*, 27, 165–174.

Foreman, P., Arthur-Kelly, M., Pascoe, S., & King, B. S. (2004). Evaluating the educational experiences of students with profound and multiple disabilities in inclusive and segregated classroom settings: An Australian perspective. *Research and Practice for Persons With Severe Disabilities*, 29, 183–193.

Fullan, M. G. (1999). *Change forces*: The sequel. London: Falmer.

Fullan, M. (2001). *The new meaning of educational change* (3rd Ed.). New York: Teachers College Press.

Gallagher, J. J. (1998). Education, alone, is a weak treatment. *Education Week*, 17(72) pp. 43, 60.

Gallagher, M. P. (1993). *Proficiency testing and poverty: Looking within a large urban district*. Paper presented at the annual meeting of the American Educational Research Association, Atlanta, CA. April.

Gardner, S. L. (1992). Key issues in developing school-linked, integrated services. *Future of Children*, 2(1), 85–94.

Goals 2000: Educate America Act of 1994, P.L. 103-227, 20 U.S.C. § 5811 et seq.

Halvorsen, A. T., & W. Sailor (1990). Integration of students with severe and profound disabilities: A review of research. In R. Gaylord-Ross (Ed.), *Issues and research in special education* (Vol. 1). New York: Teachers College, *Columbia University*. (p. 110–172)

Horner, R. H., Todd, A. W., Lewis-Palmer, T., Irvin, L. K., Sugai, G., & Boland, J. B. (2004). The School-wide Evaluation Tool (SET): A research instrument for assessing school-wide positive behavior support. *Journal of Positive Behavior Interventions*, 6, 3–12.

Hunt, P., & Goetz, L. (1997). Research on inclusive educational programs, practices, and outcomes for students with severe disabilities. *Journal of Special Education*, 31(1), 3–29.

Individuals With Disabilities Education Act (IDEA) Amendments of 1997, P.L. 105-17, 20 U.S.C. § 1400 et seq.

Individuals With Disabilities Education Improvement Act (IDEA) of 2004, P.L. 108-446, 20 U.S.C. §§ 1400 et seq.

Kagan, S. L., & Neville, P. (1993). *Integrating services for children and families: Understanding the past to shape the future*. New Haven, CT: Yale University Press.

Keetle, S. (2007). *Implementing comprehensive school reform in an urban multicultural school: An embedded case study*. Unpublished doctoral dissertation, University of Kansas, Lawrence.

Kirst, M. W. (1994). The politics of nationalizing curricular content. *American Journal of Education*, 102, 383–393.

Lassen, S., Steele, M., & Sailor, W. (2006). The relationship of school-wide positive behavior support to academic achievement in an urban middle school. *Psychology in Schools* 43, 701–712.

Lawson, H. A., & Sailor, W. (2000). Integrating services, collaborating, and developing connections with schools. *Focus on Exceptional Children, 33*(2), 1–22.

Lenz, B. K., & Deshler, D. D. (2004). *Teaching content to all. Evidence-based inclusive practices in middle and secondary schools*. Boston: Pearson.

Levin, H. M. (1991). *Accelerating the progress of ALL students*. Rockefeller Institute Special Report, Number 31, The Nelson A. Rockofeller Institute of Government, Albany, N.Y.

Lipsky, D. K., & Gartner, A. (1997). *Inclusion and school reform: Transforming America's classrooms*. Baltimore: Brookes.

Logan, K. R., & Keefe, E. B. (1997). A comparison of instructional context, teacher behavior, and engaged behavior for students with severe disabilities in general education and self-contained elementary classrooms. *Journal of the Association for Persons With Severe Handicaps, 22*, 16–27.

Luiselli, J. K., Putnam, R. F., Handler, M. W., & Feinberg, A.B. (2005). Whole-school positive behavior support: Effects on student discipline problems and academic performance. *Educational Psychology, 25*, 183–198.

Manset, G., & Semmel, M. I. (1997). Are inclusive programs for students with mild disabilities effective? *Journal of Special Education, 31*, 155–180.

McGregor, G., & Vogelsberg, R. T. (1998). *Inclusive schooling practices: Pedagogical and research foundations. A synthesis of the literature that informs best practices about inclusive schooling*. Washington, DC: Special Education Programs (ED/OSERS).

Miles, K. H., & Darling-Hammond, L. (1998). Rethinking the allocation of teaching resources: some lessons from high-performing schools. *Educational Evaluation and Policy Analysis, 20*, 9–29.

National Commission on Excellence in Education. (1983). *A nation at risk: the imperative of educational reform*, Washington, DC: U.S. Government Printing Office.

Newmann, F. M. (1996). *Center on organization and restructuring of schools: Activities and accomplishments, 1990–1996*. Final report. Washington, DC: Office of Educational Research and Improvement (ED).

O'Day, J. A. (2002). Complexity, accountability, and school improvement. *Harvard Educational Review, 72*, 293–329.

O'Day, J. A. (2003). Partnership, accountability, and standards-based reform: Reflections on the Baltimore city-state partnership. *Journal of Education for Students Placed at Risk, 8*, 149–163.

Ogbu, J. (1982). Cultural discontinuities and schooling. *Anthropology and Education Quarterly, 13*, 290–307.

Ogbu, J. (1985). Research currents: Cultural-ecological influences on minority school learning. *Language Arts, 62*, 860–869.

OSEP Center on Positive Behavior Interventions and Supports. (2004). *School-wide positive behavior support implementer's blueprint and self-assessment*. Eugene: University of Oregon.

Peetsma, T., Vergeer, M., Roeleveld, J., & Karsten, S. (2001). Inclusion in education: comparing pupils' development in special and regular education. *Educational Review, 53*, 125–135.

Rose, D., Sethuraman, S., & Meo, G. J. (2000). Universal design for learning: Associate editor's column. *Journal of Special Education Technology, 15*(2), 56–60.

Sailor, W. (1991). Special education in the structured school. *Remedial and Special Education, 12*(6), 8–22.

Sailor, W. (1996). New structures and systems change for comprehensive positive behavioral support. In L. K. Koegel, R. L. Koegel, & G. Dunlap (Eds.), *Positive behavioral support* (pp. 163–206). Baltimore: Brookes.

Sailor, W. (2002). *Inclusion.* Testimony given before the President's Commission on Excellence in Special Education, Nashville, TN, April 18, 2002.

Sailor, W., Anderson, J., Halvorsen, A., Doering, K. F., Filler, J., & Goetz, L. (1989). *The comprehensive local school: Regular education for all students with disabilities.* Baltimore: Brookes.

Sailor, W., & Paul, J. (2004). Framing positive behavior support in the ongoing discourse concerning the politics of knowledge. *Journal of Positive Behavior Interventions, 6,* 37–49.

Sailor, W., & Roger, B. (2003). *SAMAN, an instrument for the analysis of critical features of the schoolwide applications model (SAM).* Unpublished research instrument.

Sailor, W., & Roger, B. (2005). Rethinking inclusion: Schoolwide applications. *Phi Delta Kappan, 86,* 503–509.

Sailor, W., & Roger, B. (2006). PBS in the urban core. *TASH Connections 32*(1/2), 23–24.

Sailor, W., & Skrtic, T. M. (1996). School/community partnerships and educational reform: Introduction to the topical issue. *Remedial and Special Education, 17,* 267–270, 283.

Sailor, W., Zuna, N., Choi, J., Thomas, J., McCart, A., & Roger, B. (2006). Anchoring schoolwide positive behavior support in structural school reform. *Research and Practice for Persons With Severe Disabilities, 31*(1), 18–30.

Schorr, L. B. (1992). Commentary: Reason to hope. *Teachers College Record,* 93, 710–716.

Shavelson, R. J., & Towne, L. (Eds.). (2002). *Scientific research in education.* Washington, DC: National Research Council, National Academy Press.

Skrtic, T. M. (1995). *Disability and democracy: Reconstructing (special) education for postmodernity. Special education series.* New York: Columbia University, Teachers College Press.

Skrtic, T. M., & Sailor, W. (1996). School-linked services integration: Crisis and opportunity in the transition to postmodern society. *Remedial and Special Education, 17,* 271–283.

Skrtic, T. M., Sailor, W., & Gee, K. (1996). Voice, collaboration, and inclusion: Democratic themes in educational and social reform initiatives. *Remedial and Special Education, 17,* 142–157.

Slavin, R. E., & Madden, N. A. (2000). Research on achievement outcomes of Success for All: A summary and response to critics. *Phi Delta Kappan, 82,* 38–40, 59–66.

Slavin, R. E., Madden, N. A., Dolan, L. J., & Wasik, B. A. (1993). *Success for all: Evaluations of national replications* (Report No. 43). Baltimore: Johns Hopkins University, Center for Research on Effective Schooling for Disadvantaged Students.

Sugai, G., Horner, R. H., Dunlap, G., Hieneman, M., Lewis, T., Nelson, C., et al. (2000). Applying positive behavioral support and functional behavior assessment in the schools. *Journal of Positive Behavior Interventions, 2,* 131–143.

Turnbull, A., Edmondson, H., Griggs, P., Wickham, D., Sailor, W., Beech, S., et al. (2002). A blueprint for the four components of a positive behavior support schoolwide model. *Exceptional Children, 66,* 377–402.

U.S. Congress. (2002). No Child Left Behind Act of 2001. P.L. 107-110. Retrieved August 6, 2007, from www.ed.gov/policy/elsec/leg/esea02/index.html

U.S. Department of Education. (2004). Amendments to the Individuals With Disabilities Education Act, P. L. No. 108-446, 118, Stat. 2647–2808. Washington, DC: Author.

Utley, C. A., & Sailor, W. (2002). Guest editorial: Positive behavior support and urban school improvement: A special section of the *Journal of Positive Behavior Interventions. Journal of Positive Behavior Interventions, 4,* 195.

Viadero, D. (2001). Whole-school projects show mixed results. *Education Week, 21,* 24–25.

Warren, J. S., Bohannon-Edmonson, H. M., Turnbull, A. P., Sailor, W., Wickham, D., Griggs, P., et al. (2006). School-wide positive behavior support: Addressing behavior problems that impede student learning. *Educational Psychology Review, 18*, 187–198.

Warren, J. S., Edmonson, H. M., Griggs, P., Lassen, S., McCart, A., Turnbull, A., et al. (2003). Urban applications of school-wide positive behavior support: Critical issues and lessons learned. *Journal of Positive Behavior Interventions 5*, 80–91.

Wehmeyer, M. L., Lattin, D. L., Lapp-Rincker, G., & Agran, M. (2003). Access to the general curriculum of middle school students with mental retardation: An observational study. *Remedial and Special Education, 24*, 262–272.

# 27

# Completing the Continuum of Schoolwide Positive Behavior Support: Wraparound as a Tertiary-Level Intervention

**LUCILLE EBER, KELLY HYDE, JENNIFER ROSE, KIMBERLI BREEN, DIANE MCDONALD, and HOLLY LEWANDOWSKI**

Positive behavior support (PBS) is based on the core belief that all children can learn and succeed, and that schools, in partnership with families and communities, are responsible to identify and arrange the physical, social, and educational conditions that ensure learning. However, many schools find this to be a daunting task (Brown & Michaels, 2006; Hawken & O'Neill, 2006), especially with regard to students who have complex emotional-behavioral needs. Special education, although intended to be a support system for these students, often functions as an

**LUCILLE EBER** • Illinois PBS Network
**KELLY HYDE** • Illinois PBS Network
**JENNIFER ROSE** • Illinois PBS Network
**KIMBERLI BREEN** • Illinois PBS Network
**DIANE MCDONALD** • Illinois PBS Network
**HOLLY LEWANDOWSKI** • Illinois PBS Network

exclusionary default, with limited social and academic success (National Center for Education Statistics, 2005; Wagner, Newman, Cameto, Levine, & Garza, 2006). Improving educational outcomes for all students requires significant changes in how schools respond to students with complex needs, including application of research-based behavioral practices, and integration of community/family supports with school-based services.

As described in previous chapters, application of PBS schoolwide is expected to improve schools' capacity to effectively educate the 1–15% of students with emotional-behavioral and related learning challenges. We propose that the family-centered wraparound process (Burns & Goldman, 1999) is an essential component of schoolwide positive behavior support (SW-PBS) if schools are to ensure success for students who require comprehensive mental health supports. The wraparound approach provides a structure for schools to establish proactive partnership with families and community supports, a necessary component for arranging successful environments around students with complex emotional-behavioral needs. Families (including the student) are positioned as key informants and decision makers in prioritizing desired outcomes and strength-based strategies. Embracing such person-/family-centered values and techniques, the wraparound process results in uniquely tailored interventions that are carefully implemented with families and teachers in lead roles, ensuring contextual fit (Albin, Lucyshyn, Horner, & Flannery, 1996; Crone & Horner, 2003) and therefore increasing likelihood of effectiveness across home, school, and community.

This chapter describes how the system and practice features of the wraparound process, traditionally used in mental health systems, have been integrated into the tertiary level of SW-PBS. This includes (a) definition and contextual foundation of wraparound; (b) links with SW-PBS; (c) integration of data-based decision making into the wraparound process; (d) system structures needed at the tertiary tier; and (e) implications for mental health collaborators. The ongoing development of process and outcome tools used by school-based practitioners applying the wraparound process with students with complex needs and their families within SW-PBS, including implementation results, is included. Interface with interagency system-of-care (SOC) approaches applied through mental health and the person-centered planning (PCP) process associated with PBS are also discussed.

## SETTING THE CONTEXT

### What Is Wraparound?

Wraparound is both a philosophy of care and a defined process for developing a plan of care for an individual youth and his or her family (Burns & Goldman, 1999). Wraparound supports students and their families by proactively organizing and blending natural supports, interagency services, PBS, and academic interventions as needed. Other life domain needs such as medical, safety, cultural, spiritual, social, and so on may be addressed by wraparound teams as well. Wraparound distinguishes itself from traditional service delivery in special education and mental health with its focus on connecting families, schools, and community partners in effective problem-solving relationships. Unique implementation features include (a) family and youth voice guide the design and actions of the team; (b) team composition and strategies reflect unique youth and family strengths and needs; (c) the team establishes the commitment and capacity to design and implement a comprehensive plan over time; and (d) the plan addresses outcomes across home, school, and community through one synchronized plan.

The wraparound process includes specific steps to establish ownership, and therefore investment, of people who spend the most time with the student (i.e., family, teacher). This creates an environment in which a range of interventions, including behavioral supports, are more likely to be executed with integrity. As such, the wraparound process includes systematic assessment of the needs of the adults who support the youth and can arrange supports for these adults on behalf of the youth (Eber, 2003). For example, a wraparound team may solicit involvement from the community to assist a family with accessing stable housing and other basic living supports as parents may be better able to focus on a home-based behavior change plan for their child if stress about being evicted from an apartment is alleviated. Other examples include teams facilitating transportation, recreation opportunities, and social supports. Teams can also tailor supports for teachers who may be challenged with meeting the unique needs of a student. For example, a plan to change problem behavior at school may be more likely to succeed if the teacher has a trusted colleague of choice who models the instruction of the replacement behavior or how to naturally deliver the reinforcement in the context of the classroom.

Differing from individualized educational plans (IEPs) and other typical school-based team processes, the wraparound process delineates specific roles for team members, including natural support persons (Eber, 2003), and detailed conditions for interventions, including specifying roles each person will play in specific circumstances. The role of a designated team facilitator is critical to ensure the process is adhered to and that the principles of the strength-based person-/family-centered approach are held fast. The wraparound facilitator, often a school social worker, counselor, or school psychologist, guides the team through the phases of wraparound (discussed in this chapter), ensuring a commitment to "remain at the table," despite challenges and setbacks, until the needs of the youth and family are met and can be sustained without the wraparound team.

Although on the surface wraparound can be seen as similar to the typical special education or mental health treatment planning process, it actually goes much further as it dedicates considerable effort on building constructive relationships and support networks among the youth and his or her family (Burchard, Bruns, & Burchard, 2002; Eber, 2005). This is accomplished by establishing a unique team with each student and the student's family that is invested in achieving agreed-on quality-of-life indicators. Key questions asked of youth and their families and teachers during team development (Phase I) of wraparound often include the following: "What would a good school day for you (or for your child) look like to you?" "What would life at home look or feel like if it was better?" "How would you define success for your child 5 years from now?" Following a response to intervention (RTI) model in which problem-solving methods become more refined for smaller numbers of students, these more intensive techniques for engagement and team development are needed to ensure that a cohesive wraparound team and plan are formed.

Wraparound is characterized by a deliberate and consistent focus on strengths and needs as defined by the youth and family (VanDenBerg, 1999). This requires significant effort and purposeful techniques by the team facilitator as team members may have defaulted into a problem-focused mode and predetermined ideas of "needs" that are often stated as services (i.e., "He needs an alternative placement," "She needs counseling," "She needs a one-on-one aide"). A key component in the wraparound process is the development of a rich and deep strength profile that identifies very explicit strengths across settings (e.g., home, school, community) and life domains (i.e., social, cultural, basic living skills, academics, etc.). Similar to quality-of-life indicators in the person-centered planning (PCP) process associated with PBS, we define *big needs* in wraparound as follows: (a) The needs are big enough that it will take a while to achieve, such as "James needs to feel respected at school." (b) There is more than one way to meet it; for example, "Hector needs to feel competent/able about learning" instead of "Hector will complete his assignments." (c) The need will motivate the family to want to participate on the team. For instance, Maria's mother needs to feel confident that Maria will get treated fairly at school. (d) If met, the need will improve quality of life for the youth or those engaged with the youth on a regular basis (e.g., the family, the teacher).

The wraparound process helps ensure the development of a cohesive team of family members, natural support providers, and professionals. Interventions designed and applied within the context of those closest to the student allow for ownership around success being enjoyed by students, families, teachers, and others involved in the day-to-day life of the youth. Therefore, the likelihood of interventions being applied effectively, monitored, and revised as needed to ensure sustainable outcomes across home, school, and community is greatly increased.

## The Need for Comprehensive and Collaborative Approaches

The historically dismal outcomes for youth struggling with emotional-behavioral challenges clearly indicate that not only schools, but also mental health, child welfare, and juvenile justice struggle to effectively meet their responsibilities for supporting them (Cauffman, Scholle, Mulvey, & Kelleher, 2005). The documented poor prognosis for youth with identified emotional and behavioral disorders (EBDs) is only part of the reality as these youth are historically underidentified and underserved. The U.S. Department of Health and Human Services (1999) asserted that approximately one in every five children between the ages of 9 and 17 has a diagnosable mental health or addictive disorder. The mental health literature reports prevalence rates of youth with diagnosable mental health conditions ranging from 13% (Costello, Mastillo, Erkanli, Keeler, & Angold, 2003) to 20% (Friedman, Katz-Levy, & Manderschied, 1996; Shaffer et al.,

1996), with less than half of these youth reported as actually engaged in treatment with mental health providers (Burns et al., 1995; Strein, Hoagwood, & Cohn, 2003). Most youth who do connect with mental health providers (70–80%) do so through schools, including contacts with school psychologists, social workers, and counselors (Rones & Hoagwood, 2000). However, the numbers of students identified with an EBD who receive special education services under the Individuals With Disabilities Education Act (IDEA) 2004 usually represent only about 1% of total school enrollment (National Center for Education Statistics, 2005). The different systems designated to serve these youth report a range of prevalence rates and define service delivery options with different criteria. Nonetheless, it is fair to say that alarmingly low numbers of youth who need such supports receive them, and those that do, fair poorly. The need for more effective systems that systematically provide comprehensive and collaborative interventions is evident.

For over 20 years, service providers, researchers, and advocates have been focusing on how to improve the outcomes for youth with complex emotional-behavioral challenges by building collaborative networks that coordinate the full range of services and supports needed by these youth and their families. Led primarily by mental health, youth-serving agencies and communities have struggled to develop more comprehensive and effective options. First proposed by Jane Knitzer in her seminal document *Unclaimed Children* (Knitzer, 1982), national, state, and local mental health and other agencies have focused on development of SOC approaches during the past 20 plus years. The concept of SOC has come to be understood as approaches that are strength based, culturally relevant, include a range of choices along a continuum, draw on natural settings and caretakers, and design unique interventions responsive to the preferences of the youth and family (Eber & Keenan, 2004; Hernandez & Hodges, 2003; Stroul & Friedman, 1986). Coordination of a variety of services across settings and providers in the community is a critical feature. Advocacy is a key component of the SOC concept since tailoring services to meet needs as defined by the family is, unfortunately, often inconsistent with traditional service delivery models in mental health, child welfare, juvenile justice, and education (Burchard et al., 2002).

## SW-PBS and Students With Complex Needs

Since approximately 1998, schoolwide applications of PBS have emerged with the intent to build capacity for schools to provide effective behavior supports to all students, including those with complex behavioral needs, through a comprehensive prevention-based approach. As described in this volume, SW-PBS applies the science of behavior schoolwide using systems change structures that include a representative leadership team, ongoing self-assessment of the fidelity of the process, and rigorous application of data-based decision making. Consistent with the public health model, SW-PBS is a systemic approach that focuses on large units of analysis (e.g., school buildings and classrooms) and incorporates a three-tier framework:

1. Universal prevention addresses the entire school population via evidence-based instructional practices, precorrection, and adjustment of the environment to foster prosocial behavior.
2. Secondary or selected prevention delivers higher-level, more specialized interventions to 10–15% of students whose lack of response to universal prevention places them at risk for problem behaviors.
3. Tertiary or indicated prevention delivers specific interventions to the 1–5% of students with the highest needs due to a highly disproportionate level of risk relative to protective factors.

Within such a comprehensive system of behavioral support in schools, students with complex social-emotional needs should fare well as they can access evidence-based behavioral practices across all settings in the schools. For example, it is logical to assume that a student with an attention deficit disorder who has trouble managing his or her behavior will benefit greatly from the ongoing instruction of prosocial behavior provided to all students in hallways, classrooms, and so on, including consistent prompts and recognition for adhering to the schoolwide expectations. This same student may also be part of a "check-in/check-out" system (secondary-level intervention) in which about 4–7% of students in the school systematically receive a higher rate of prompts and recognition for positive behavior as they check in with teachers and other designated staff systematically throughout the day. This same student may have a uniquely designed wraparound team that arranges and monitors other more individualized interventions, such as additional academic or behavioral supports, arrangement of socialization opportunities at school or in the community, and so on. Supports for the family may include linkages with community resources (i.e., mental health providers, family support groups) and may involve natural supports that may be suited to the cultural lifestyle preferences of the youth and family. For example, a mentor or "big brother" may be enlisted to support the youth's participation in a youth group at the family's church or on a Little League team.

As described in previous chapters, schoolwide application of research-based behavioral practices can and should result in earlier and more accurate identification of students who need higher levels of behavioral support. The logic is that effective individualized interventions would then be made available for the small number of students with this need for higher-level behavior support. However, there is limited research that verifies how students with emotional-behavioral and other severe disabilities actually benefit from SW-PBS (Safran & Oswald, 2003). But, there is emerging evidence that supports the logic that investment in SW-PBS increases the likelihood that effective, individualized interventions will be provided to these students. In fact, schools in Illinois that have reached full implementation of the universal level of SW-PBS as measured by the School-wide Evaluation Tool (SET; Sugai, Lewis-Palmer, Todd, & Horner, 2001) are twice as likely to implement individualized interventions (rated as effective) than schools that have not yet fully implemented SW-PBS structures (Illinois FY05 PBIS Annual Progress Report available at www.pbisillinois.org). This fiscal year (FY) 2005 finding is consistent with similar results in FY03 and FY04 (Illinois FY04 PBIS Annual Progress Report available at www.pbisillinois.org).

In spite of the logic and early indicators that suggest that implementation of SW-PBS will benefit students with the most complex emotional-behavioral needs, low-fidelity implementation of SW-PBS can set up risky conditions. For example, behavioral data collected in schools have been used as documentation to remove students to more restrictive settings rather than to guide proactive intervention. Poorly implemented or nonexistent behavior supports result in relatively high numbers of students with complex behavioral needs being educated in separate environments from their general education peers (Crimmins & Farrell, 2006; Freeman et al., 2006). Questions raised about the potential shortcomings of SW-PBS for students with significant emotional-behavioral challenges include: (a) Will school personnel focus on universal supports at the detriment of acquiring the complex skill sets needed to provide effective secondary- and tertiary-level support? (b) Will responses to problem behavior continue to overlook evidence-based practices in favor of traditional, punitive discipline strategies (Brown & Michaels, 2006; Crimmins & Farrell, 2006; Hawken & O'Neill, 2006)?

Recognizing and responding to these concerns, Carr (2006) offered several potential benefits of SW-PBS for students with the most complex needs:

1. The skills acquired by school personnel at the universal level can provide the context for learning the more complex skills needed to implement successively intensive levels of intervention.
2. Fewer office discipline referrals frees up staff time to concentrate on students with higher rates of behavior problems.
3. The expectations taught at the universal level may, in fact, reduce the number of triggers or setting events in the school environment for students with the most complex behavioral needs, leading to fewer discipline incidents for these students.
4. Implementing SW-PBS with integrity may generate multiple peer role models that may influence students to follow their lead (Carr, 2006).

These potential benefits of SW-PBS for students with EBD and other complex circumstances seem logical. However, the multifarious needs of some of these students call for an intervention process commensurate with their level of need, making the person-/family-centered wraparound process an essential element of SW-PBS.

## Tracing the Roots of Wraparound

The SOC principles proposed by Knitzer (1982) were formulated into a blueprint for change in the landmark document *A System of Care for Children and Youth With Severe Emotional Disturbances* (Stroul & Friedman, 1986). Wraparound, a philosophy of care as well as a defined planning process, emerged from grassroots efforts as practitioners sought to implement the SOC principles called for by Knitzer (1982) and more distinctly defined by Stroul and Friedman (1986). Wraparound became embraced by state and local communities as federal funds encouraged them to implement comprehensive systems of care as a strategy for reducing overreliance on costly, yet ineffective, restrictive placements that removed youth from their families/communities and often lacked adequate treatment (Kendziora,

Bruns, Osher, Pacchiano, & Mejia, 2001.) The logic is that a wraparound team, which includes natural support providers (extended family, friends, mentors), is more likely to be effective in designing a plan that will be embraced by the family and youth with realistic and practical strategies that address what the family feels are desired goals within usual settings, (home, neighborhood school, local community). In a preliminary study of the effectiveness of wraparound, Burns, Goldman, Faw, and Burchard (1999) documented 16 studies that were conducted in nine states (Alaska, Illinois, Vermont, Kentucky, Maryland, Wisconsin, Indiana, New York, and Florida). The studies explicitly identified as school-based programs (Clarke, Schaefer, Burchard, & Welkowitz, 1992; Eber, 1994; Eber & Osuch, 1995; Eber, Osuch, & Rolf, 1996; Kamradt, 1996; Rotto, Sokol, Matthew, & Russell 1998) produced results indicating that school-based wraparound can effectively retain children in their communities and home schools

The concept of wraparound has been operationalized in numerous forms (Bruns, Suter, Force, & Burchard, 2005; Burchard et al., 2002; Burns & Goldman, 1999; Miles, Bruns, Osher, Walker, & National Wraparound Initiative Advisory Group, 2006). In fact, the absence of an established theoretical framework has contributed to the lack of consistency regarding procedural guidelines for wraparound (J. S. Walker & Schutte, 2004). Arguably, the two theories that are most compatible with wraparound are ecological systems theory (Bronfenbrenner, 1979) and environmental ecology theory (Munger, 1998). Both theories stress the influence of various systems (e.g., schools, health care, etc.) on the level of functioning for children and their families. Two related theories reflect the family-centered (Allen & Petr, 1998), strengths-based approach (Saleebey, 2001) of wraparound. The consistent underlying philosophy of wraparound is a change from “expert-driven” models as it places the family, not a mental health agency or the school, in the leadership role within the team process. Furthermore, the wraparound process emphasizes that services are identified and designed based on the needs of the families and youth rather than what the system has available and is experienced with providing. The ultimate goal is success for the youth within the context of their families and their home schools. These characteristics are what make wraparound a unique, family and community-based process that is often experienced as antithetical to traditional mental health treatment planning or IEP procedures (Burchard et al., 2002). The spirit of wraparound and its elements were summarized by Burns and Goldman (1999) with 10 guiding principles:

1. Strength-based family leadership.
2. Team based.
3. Flexible funding/services.
4. Individualized.
5. Perseverance.
6. Outcome focused.
7. Community based.
8. Culturally competent.
9. Natural supports.
10. Collaborative.

Concurrent with the development of SOC approaches, the science of behavior was being applied through a new lens as PBS emerged as a method for applying individualized behavior plans through a PCP process (Agosta et al., 1999; Cheney, Malloy, & Hagner, 1998; O'Brien & O'Brien, 2000; Wehmeyer, Baker, Blumberg, & Harrison, 2004). Used primarily with persons with developmental disabilities and their families, PCP focuses first on improving quality of life (Risley, 1996) as defined by the family and youth (e.g., having friends, feeling accepted by others in their community, etc). If the PCP team addresses these quality-of-life indicators first, a variety of problem behaviors may be eliminated or significantly reduced (O'Neill et al., 1997). This may also provide information needed to conduct functional behavioral assessment for behaviors that persist after a team has begun to address quality-of-life outcomes (Kincaid & Fox, 2002). Replacing problem behaviors with prosocial behaviors through application of function-based behavioral interventions is a key component of PCP as well as wraparound as applied in schools implementing SW-PBS. Each student's wraparound team begins with a focus on improved quality-of-life indicators as defined by the family and youth and concurred with by school and other partners participating on the wraparound team.

One of the essential features of PCP, also key to wraparound, is the concept of self-determination. *Self-determination* has been defined as a right (Wehmeyer, 1999), a skill set (e.g., self-regulation, problem-solving ability), and a disposition (Palmer & Wehmeyer, 1998). The defining characteristic of self-determination is the ability of and opportunity for the individual to exercise his or her own choice, echoing the predominant wraparound theme of "family voice and choice." Self-determination has been successfully applied with secondary students with EBDs (Malloy, Cheney, & Comier, 1998) through personal futures planning, a theoretical framework that has roots in the field of developmental disabilities (Vandercook, York, & Forest, 1989).

## WRAPAROUND AS A TERTIARY PROCESS: SYSTEMS DATA AND PRACTICES DEFINED

### Wraparound Further Defined

Consistent with SOC principals, wraparound has evolved into a planning process that includes careful attention to developing a team that, by its membership, reflects the strengths, values, and spoken needs of the family. A uniquely constructed team, including natural support persons selected by the family and youth, develops, monitors, and continuously revises a plan focused on ensuring success, as defined by the family and youth, in their home, neighborhood school, and community settings. As with PCP, family and youth voice and ownership of the plan are emphasized to ensure interventions produce effective and timely outcomes for students, their families, and teachers. With an eye toward independence, natural support persons such as extended family, friends, a coach, a youth minister, or others with positive connections are sought for the teams. As teams problem solve how to effectively meet students' needs, they combine supports for natural activities (e.g., child care, mentoring, making friends) with more traditional interventions (e.g., function-based behavioral interventions, specialized reading instruction, medication, etc.).

Individuals who perform the function of team facilitation should ideally possess certain skill sets and dispositions, including the ability to translate the family's, youth's, and teachers' "stories" and experiences into strengths and needs data that can be used to guide the team. Other crucial facilitator skills include the ability to respectfully articulate the family's vision without judgment. This includes helping teams clarify the big needs that, if met, will improve the quality of life for the youth and family. Examples of big need statements to guide wraparound teams include the following: "Jose needs to feel respected by teachers"; "Tracy needs to feel accepted by other students and teachers." The identified facilitator also must have the ability to facilitate problem solving and decision making in a consensual manner. Potential wraparound facilitators, readily available in school systems, include personnel who already lead intervention planning and meetings for students with or at-risk of EBDs. Typical persons who are trained and coached to facilitate strength and needs-based wraparound meetings include school social workers, school psychologists, counselors, special education specialists, administrators, and the like (Eber, 2003).

## Implementing Wraparound

As the wraparound philosophy of care has evolved into a more in-depth planning process, defined steps and phases of wraparound implementation have emerged (Miles et al., 2006; J. S. Walker et al., 2004). The identified team facilitator initiates wraparound using individualized engagement strategies with the family and youth, teacher, and other potential team members. Assuming lower-level interventions (i.e., universal and secondary PBS, parent conferences, function-based behavioral intervention plans, etc.) have not resulted in enough positive change, families may be understandably cautious about engaging in yet another meeting about their child. Therefore, a wraparound team facilitator may need to approach a family carefully to ensure that the family does not feel judged or blamed. Families who have had a lot of contact with school but little success may need to be assured that they are not expected to change the problem behavior of their child at school. For example, facilitators may use a statement such as, "At school, we feel we are not being successful enough or positive enough with your child, so we are going to change our approach to make sure he is going to have success." This may be a different message than what the parent is used to hearing from school and can set the stage for a different type of process that is scaled up yet positive

Family trust, buy-in, and voice, requisite benchmarks of wraparound, must be established before the team can proceed to designing interventions or supports. During the initial conversations used to engage and develop the team, the family helps select team members, meeting location, and other team logistics (Eber, 2003). Then, initial meetings are held at which the team comes to consensus about the strengths of the youth and family and the big needs on which they will focus; only then does the team begin to develop strategies to ensure improved quality of life. Progress toward achieving the quality-of-life indicators are assessed continuously in subsequent meetings as strengths- and needs-based interventions are continuously implemented, monitored, and revised to ensure success across home, school, and community. The focus on natural supports (e.g., people, settings, and resources) ensures cultural and contextual fit (Albin et al., 1996) so that the capacity for the youth and family and teacher to function independently with less intense supports and services over time is possible. Next is a brief description of the phases of wraparound implementation with emphasis on how the team facilitator guides participants through the process:

### *Phase I: Engagement and Team Preparation*

During Phase I, the facilitator works closely with the family, student, and teacher to build trust and ownership of the process. The first step is for the facilitator to reach out to the family and arrange a time and place to have an "initial conversation" with them to hear their story and begin the process of building a relationship and a team. The family is encouraged to tell "their story" by articulating their perception of the strengths, needs, and experiences of their child and family. This initial contact should be a low-key conversational discourse with the goals of (a) developing a trusting relationship, (b) establishing an understanding of the process and what they can expect, and (c) seeking information about potential team members, strengths, and big needs. Facilitators should use open-ended questions (e.g., "Tell me about some of your concerns about Denise's progress") and active listening skills to track key information that will help determine priorities areas for support or intervention. It is helpful for the family to select the meeting location (e.g., local restaurant, a community building such as a church, etc.) as this can contribute to a sense of neutrality, allowing the family to relax and begin to trust the process. At first, this Phase I approach may seem awkward since traditionally most parent meetings take place on school grounds and are led by educators in an "expert" model. However, it is empowering for the family to be able to share their perspective freely in a meeting place of their own choice. Furthermore, careful listening to the family's story may be more effective in identifying the family and youth's big needs or elements at the root of the problem behaviors than using standard school-based approaches. For example, during a facilitator's initial meeting with Jacob's family, his older (fifth-grade) brother shared his knowledge of how Jacob's retention in second grade and subsequent separation from his friends made him feel lonely and contributed to his refusal to participate in classroom activities.

During the initial conversations with the family, the facilitator should assist the family to identify the natural supports or persons who are connected to the family by relationship (e.g., relatives, friends, a pastor) who may be able to participate in the wraparound process. The focus is on roles, not job titles. For example, Jacob's big brother, who was a fifth grader at the time of the initial conversation, was a support person for Jacob who helped make sure Jacob's "voice" was heard by the team. His brother, by being included in Phase I conversations, was able to provide data about Jacob's real big need (to feel accepted at school).

The facilitator, after securing permission from the family, should also have individual conversations with other potential team members (e.g., a teacher, a coach, a probation officer) to listen with an impartial ear to their perspective. When the facilitator has a dialogue with the family and other potential team members before the initial wrap meeting, the participants have an opportunity to provide their perceptions, including frustrations, which are validated by the facilitators' approach/techniques (i.e., nonjudgmental, reflective listening, etc.). When team members have a sense of confirmation regarding their experiences and emotions, they are more likely to make positive contributions once the wrap process begins. The facilitator's role is to translate the family's (and other team members') story, including what has or has not worked in the past, into data that can be used to ensure efficient and effective team meetings. Necessary information organized during Phase I includes potential team members, a comprehensive strength profile, a list of two to four big needs, and baseline data culled from the Wraparound Date Tools (discussed in another section of this chapter), which will serve as benchmarks for ongoing progress monitoring overtime.

### *Phase II: Initial Plan Development*

During Phase II, the facilitator moves from engagement and assessing strengths and needs with the family and other potential team members to guiding the team through the initial wraparound meetings. This shift into team meetings needs to occur as quickly as possible, typically within 2 weeks from the initial Phase I conversations. Baseline data reflecting youth, family, and teacher perception of strengths and needs are shared and used to guide team consensus on and commitment to quality-of-life indicators (the big needs). During Phase II, facilitators share the strengths and needs data with the team. Needs are prioritized, and action planning begins as the facilitator guides team members to brainstorm strategies to increase strengths and meet needs. As strategies are developed, tasks and roles for all team members are clarified. A safety plan for school or home is developed if team members feel this to be an imminent need. Facilitators should continue to gather and review the data across settings and from multiple perspectives (examples of wraparound data tools are discussed separately in this chapter) to assist the team in monitoring progress continuously. When the team is able to focus on meaningful data (e.g., data representing their perception of strengths and needs that they feel would improve quality of life), the tendency for team members to judge and blame one another or to resort to reactive, punitive strategies is significantly reduced.

Wraparound team facilitators must be adept advocates who can address team functioning or individual team member behavior that may circumvent the wrap process. For example, facilitators must be aware that some team members, used to the "expert approach" prevalent in special education, may attempt to influence the family to agree to an intervention the family is not invested in, typically referring to the recommended service as a need (e.g., "The family needs counseling"). For instance, if a team member is adamant about a student "needing a placement," the facilitator may ask the team member, "What outcome do you hope to achieve through this?" or "How is this suggestion relevant to the family's stated big needs we have agreed on to guide us?"

From the Field: Mary Ellen's Story

"Mary Ellen," a student who was described as "highly anxious" was of concern to the school due to inappropriate behaviors during passing periods in the hallways. The school provided Mary Ellen with an escort in the hallway as an intervention. However, the intervention was not successful as Mary Ellen's problem behavior in the hallway escalated, and she tried to run away from the escort. The school suspected that there might be a mental health issue driving Mary Ellen's behavior, so they recommended that the parents seek a psychiatric evaluation; they also indicated they wanted to begin testing for special education eligibility. The family, who had never been comfortable with the escort intervention, balked at the insinuation that Mary Ellen was possibly "emotionally disturbed," and a rift began to form between the school and her family. The SW-PBS coach suggested they switch to the wraparound approach, so a school psychologist trained in wraparound facilitation approached the family from a strengths-and-needs perspective. The strengths and needs data gathered during Phase I and shared with the team during Phase II helped the team determine that the escort intervention was unsuccessful because it was counterindicated to her real big need, which was to feel accepted and liked by peers and teachers. Although the family and the school were previously not aligned, the data indicated that both family and school had concerns about Mary Ellen not feeling accepted by her peers. The data were augmented by Mary Ellen's father, who expressed deep concern regarding his daughter's lack of friends and limited social contact with her peers outside school. Family data also indicated she did not have enough to do outside school, and although she actively sought adult recognition, they felt she did not have adequate decision-making abilities or judgment when approaching adults in the community. The family and the school both recognized that Mary Ellen needed to learn how to interact with peers and adults differently so she could feel accepted. Once the team reached consensus about big needs, an atmosphere of mutual trust began to develop. As the school switched from an expert model to seeking the family's perspective about strengths and needs, the family became more comfortable and shared that they had sought a medical evaluation from their family doctor. Mary Ellen was eventually diagnosed as a child with Asperger's, an autism spectrum disorder. By the time she was officially diagnosed, the wrap team had already developed strategies to increase contact with peers over the summer and teach her how to interact in the community safely.

Mary Ellen's story illustrates how using data during Phase I helps to build consensus about needs. This field example also speaks to the power of investing in family engagement and data-based decision (during Phase I) so wraparound facilitators can effectively guide teams to proactive strategies. During Phase II, the wraparound plan should be taking shape, and the team may expand to include representatives from the community, including resource agencies, if needed. The written plan of care, initiated during Phase II, should include (a) the agreed-on primary big need (often referred to as the mission statement for the team); (b) detailed strengths for enhancement; (c) specific initial strategies agreed on by the team; (d) persons involved and the timeline for interventions; and if needed, (5) a safety plan that clearly delineates responses for any anticipated challenging behaviors/situations.

### *Phase III: Ongoing Plan Implementation and Refinement*

During Phase III, data-based progress monitoring is used to review initial plans and revise interventions in response to ongoing efforts. The facilitator ensures a regular meeting schedule for the team and continuous data collection and review of results so that data informs the team when things are/not working, thus sustaining objectivity among team members.

From the Field: Roman's Story

"Roman," a sixth grader, had problems with anger control at school and home. The priority big need his mother identified for the team was "have good days at school." An individualized behavior support plan was designed for Roman that included a mentor who played basketball in the mornings before school, a time when anger outbursts were likely to occur. The school also helped Roman to improve his organization skills to help address his academic struggles, another source of frustration that also led to anger outbursts. Roman's ability to manage his anger eventually became a strength at school; however, his mother indicated (using the wraparound data tools) that anger outbursts continued at home. The initial wraparound plan included family counseling. However, Roman and his mother experienced ongoing transportation and related attendance issues. The school interpreted their behavior as a lack of commitment to the counseling process. However, during a wrap meeting, the mother stated that she did not feel that counseling was going to address the real source of Roman's problem: their disruptive, unsafe home environment. Roman lived with his mother, who was a single parent. Due to their limited financial means, they lived in an apartment with other people who were abusing drugs. Hence, their living environment was highly chaotic. Roman's mother believed that the anger that Roman demonstrated at home was a natural response to his frustration with his turbulent home environment. Furthermore, the mother believed that the most important need was for her to get a better job so that they could move. After hearing the mother's story, a local interagency area network was able to provide assistance for the family, including a mattress, money for a Little League uniform, and assistance in obtaining a job and locating a new apartment.

Roman's story highlights important Phase III activities, including (a) regular use of data as an assessment tool, (b) checking with the family to ensure that the plan is working, and (c) making adjustments to the wrap plan as indicated by feedback from team members. Roman's story also illustrates how investing in building a trusting relationship with the family over time increases the likelihood that the interventions can address environmental setting events that are often beyond the reach of school teams not using the family-centered wraparound approach. The significance of incorporating interventions across home, school, and community is also highlighted.

### *Phase IV: Transition From Wraparound*

The final phase of the wraparound process marks the formal point of transition when frequent/regular meetings are not needed. During this phase, accomplishments are reviewed and celebrated, and a transition plan is developed. The family may elect at this stage to share their experience with other families who are currently participating in the wraparound process.

## How Does Wraparound "Fit" Within a System of SW-PBS?

To date, the three-tier SW-PBS approach most commonly described in the literature defines the secondary tier as small-group interventions and tertiary tier as interventions tailored for individual students, typically through a person-centered functional behavioral assessment/behavior intervention plan (FBA/BIP) process (H. M. Walker et al., 1996). Consistent with the RTI model described in chapter 29, we propose that it is useful to broaden this framework and view the secondary and tertiary tiers of SW-PBS as a continuum of interventions that progress through a "scaling up" of supports with a broader range of delineated steps or stages. Fig. 27.1 depicts this secondary-to-tertiary continuum, moving from (a) small-group interventions, to (b) a small-group intervention with a unique feature for an individual student (i.e., a unique reinforcement schedule), to (c) an individualized function-based behavior support plan for a student (typically focused

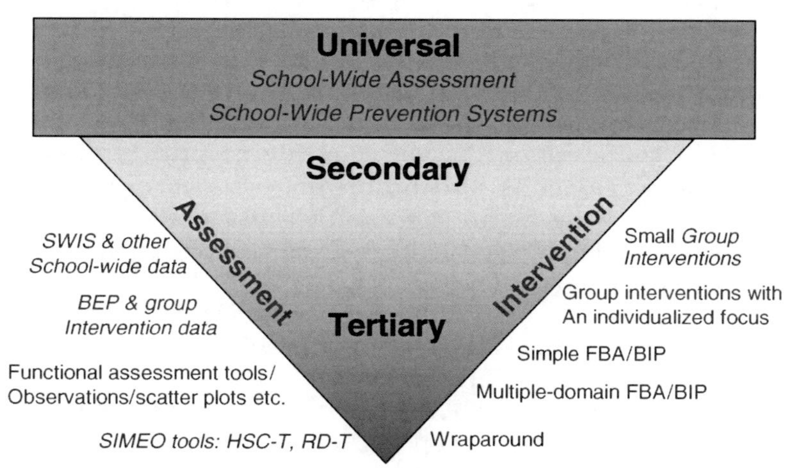


**Fig. 27.1.** Positive Behavior Interventions & Supports: A Response to Intervention (RtI) Model.

on one specific problem behavior), to (d) behavior support plans that cross settings (i.e., home and school), to (e) more complex and comprehensive (wraparound) plans that address multiple life domains (i.e., safety, basic needs, behavioral, emotional, medical cultural, etc) across home, school, and community.

Following the logic of the three-tier SW-PBS approach, the wraparound process is more complex than the lower-level school-based interventions that are effective with most students (e.g., schoolwide teaching of behavior, small-group instruction, simple behavioral intervention plan, etc.). Similar to the universal level of SW-PBS, establishing trust and buy-in are requisite benchmarks of wraparound. However, at this level, highly specialized techniques are needed to engage the youth and families for whom typical school-based interventions, including special education, have not been effective. The use of more detailed data gathered from conversations and tools involving key people (i.e., youth, family, teacher) represents another difference in the intervention approach needed at the very top of the SW-PBS continuum. Additional features needed in this scaled-up intervention process include the tailoring of team membership to incorporate family strengths. This is notably different from the universal and tertiary-level teams that generally consist of a fixed membership of school personnel.

The continuum of interventions along the secondary and tertiary tiers of SW-PBS are interdependent and reflect common elements. For example, a group check-in check-out system (secondary) is built directly from the schoolwide expectation taught to all students through universal strategies (primary), and both use data continuously to increase effects (Fairbanks, Sugai, Guardino, & Lathrop, 2007). However, the intensity of instruction and complexity of data increases as you scale up from schoolwide to smaller groups of students. Likewise, the wraparound process at the top of the tertiary tier possesses characteristics that are unique to this highest level of intervention. For example, the children and families involved at this level of intervention have typically experienced repeated negative interactions with school, necessitating the more precise engagement techniques previously described. At this level of intervention, it is vital (and sometimes difficult) to invest the time needed to generate trust between the family and the school. Some potential team members may need to be shifted from viewing the youth and family as dysfunctional or as primarily a youth and family with an accumulation of deficits and problems to a youth and family that possesses innate strengths and the ability, albeit with some supports, to chart their own life course (Scott & Eber, 2003). As the wraparound team is established, lower-level interventions (schoolwide instruction, small-group instruction, etc.) often begin to have an effect, thus effectively including the student with complex needs in the daily routines and instruction provided to all students.

Wraparound can be integrated into school-based planning for students with special needs, regardless of special education label or agency involvement. Bringing families, friends, and other natural support persons together with teachers, behavior specialists, and other professionals involved with the student and family can be done for students at the first indication of need (Scott & Eber, 2003). Per the SW-PBS model, these would include students whose needs are not met through universal and secondary interventions and are at risk of developing emotional-behavioral problems. As family or teacher needs and areas of concern are strategically linked to strengths in the student, themselves, and others around them, effective behavior, social, and instructional interventions are more likely to be implemented. Informal supports or access to community-based services may be part of early intervention plans as well.

Schools should generally follow the continuum of secondary/tertiary interventions depicted in Fig. 27.1 as this will allow for more efficient decision making, effective planning, and quicker access to interventions. However, helping a student address important big needs and improving quality of life may efficiently reduce or eliminate a range of problem behaviors (Freeman et al., 2006; O'Neill et al., 1997). Therefore, teams need to remain open minded about sometimes starting the process of wraparound before lower levels of support have been exhausted. Also, school teams may want to initiate wraparound before specific function-based behavioral interventions are designed if they recognize the adults involved are not well positioned to invest in behavioral supports due to quality-of-life issues, including high stress, frustration, anger, defensiveness, etc. The engagement and team development components of wraparound may be need to establish conditions conducive to an effective FBA/BIP. It should also be noted that a school may need to move to a higher level of support for a student if safety or an imminent restrictive placement becomes a concern. In other situations, the school may need to continue on to the wraparound level of intervention, even if lower-level interventions achieve some success. For example, a student's detentions may have been reduced, but other factors at home and in the community suggest the student is still at high risk for school failure.

## How Does Wraparound Support SW-PBS?

As suggested by Carr (2006), schools that establish effective universal systems for the 80–90% of students in their buildings seem to be better positioned to design and implement effective plans for students who require more comprehensive supports (Illinois FY05 PBIS Annual Progress Report available at www.pbisillinois.org). The wraparound approach is a critical part of the SW-PBS system as it offers a means for schools to succeed with the 1–2% of students whose needs have become so complex that starting with an FBA/BIP process for one selected problem behavior is not efficient, effective, or enough to improve quality-of-life issues for all those affected. These students may have a range of problem behaviors with different or multiple functions across different settings. Typically, the adults in the youth's life are not getting along very well as failed interventions, which may have been too weak in dosage or intensity, can foster frustration, anxiety, and possibly fear. Blame is not uncommon; the schools may be blaming the family, the family may be blaming the school, and both school and family may be blaming mental health or some other agency for not "fixing" the problems sufficiently. Schools need to be able to shift into a more complex process that matches the intensity of problems described.

This includes the capability to partner effectively with families and community partners in a systematic process that blends home, school, and community interventions through a comprehensive yet practical plan.

Competency with the family-centered wraparound approach can enhance function-based behavioral intervention plans, a critical component of the SW-PBS system. When school teams begin an FBA/BIP but do not experience success, they may become frustrated, often reverting to punitive approaches or highly restrictive placements that are often ineffective. A common example is when a school, in the course of a function-based behavioral intervention, identifies a setting event for the problem (i.e., environmental factors, biological/medical conditions) that they deem to be of primary concern and beyond their control. As illustrated by Sam's story, when schools are unable to effect setting events, they may feel powerless, and then it is easy for the school to become immobilized and reactive:

> From the Field: Sam's Story
>
> Working through the FBA process around disruptive classroom behavior, "Sam's" teacher and the school psychologist were resolute in their feeling that Sam has attention deficit-hyperactivity disorder (ADHD; possible setting event) and could benefit from medication. The family did not believe medication should be used. Rather than moving on to other steps on the behavioral pathway where they could intervene (i.e., the trigger or maintaining consequence), the team focused their energy trying to convince the parents to pursue medication. Sam's behavior escalated, and the school moved to punitive, restrictive responses and "blamed" the family for not medicating him. Switching to the wraparound approach, the family and teacher were guided through identification of strengths and needs. The family was able to identify the big need from their perspective as, "Sam needs to feel/experience success and be happy about being in school." This changed the course of the meetings from a power struggle about medication to brainstorming strategies (e.g., interventions) to ensure Sam had opportunities to experience success and be happy at school. Strategies to ensure his success were actually connected to a particular antecedent event linked to his problem behavior (seat work he did not feel competent doing) and the maintaining consequence (avoiding the work). Pairing him with students he felt liked and felt accepted by or wanted to be recognized by illustrates how strengths were used in the process.

As illustrated by Sam's story, the wraparound process can establish a milieu in which the development of proactive behavior supports can proceed with success. Behavioral interventions developed in the context of a strengths- and needs-based wraparound process have a higher likelihood of producing desired effects, often in part by addressing challenges related to setting events. In this manner, wraparound goes beyond FBA/BIP in that an effective wraparound plan actually increases the utility of an FBA process.

## How Does SW-PBS Support Wraparound?

Wraparound has been implemented successfully in school communities in which SW-PBS is not present (Clarke et al., 1992; Eber, 1994; Eber & Osuch, 1995; Eber et al., 1996; Kamradt, 1996; Rotto et al., 1998).

However, sustaining these practices over time in schools for the small percentage of students with this level of need is challenging. As stated, program evaluation data in Illinois suggest that schools that implement SW-PBS with measured fidelity at the universal level are more likely (than schools not yet reaching fidelity at the universal level of SW-PBS) to implement individualized interventions, including wraparound. This suggests that SW-PBS practices create environments in schools in which successful wraparound plans are more easily developed and implemented.

The benefits that SW-PBS offer to the highest level of support on the continuum (wraparound) include experience with a problem-solving approach and using data to guide decisions. Also, full implementation of SW-PBS at the universal level provides a solid base of lower-level interventions (e.g., primary and secondary) to build on and more effective and supportive environments in which to implement wraparound plans. Within a three-tier system of behavioral support, students who need tertiary-level supports also have access to and can benefit from universal and secondary supports. Each level of support in SW-PBS is "in addition to" the previous level. In other words, no student only needs wraparound as the wraparound plan, with its multiple life-domain and multiple-perspective focus, often makes the universal and secondary supports available in the school effective for the student.

In schools not using SW-PBS, there is often a huge gap between what they do for all students and what they do for these students with more intensive needs. Without intermediary levels of support provided by universal/secondary SW-PBS, these youth often go long periods of time without experiencing success and could appear to be in much greater need, or crisis, than they really are by the time the wraparound process is initiated. However, in schools implementing SW-PBS, teams can embed elements of wraparound (e.g., voice/choice, strength focus) within the context of ongoing secondary group interventions (Freeman et al., 2006) or tie individualized wraparound plans to the schoolwide system for acknowledgment or teaching of behavioral expectations. In this way, tertiary-level wraparound is truly a scaling up of existing PBS to a more comprehensive and individualized level of support.

Participating in the design of successful interventions for the most challenging youth can provide a sense of competency as well as relief for teachers as the wraparound team frequently acts as a support to the teacher. The emphasis on the cooperative planning and data-based decision making consistent with wraparound reduces the feelings of isolation and sense of failure that teachers may experience in the traditional child study model typically used in special education, which tends to focus more on eligibility and placement than ongoing monitoring and refinement of specific interventions.

Last, youth who need wraparound usually respond best in environments that are predictable (setting behavioral expectations), clear (direct teaching of behavioral expectations), with high levels of prompts (reteaching), strength based (acknowledgment systems), and safe (schoolwide discipline policies and practices). SW-PBS supports these youth by providing these components across all school settings and creates climates in which all youth in the building are supported and are therefore calmer and better behaved. Peers can help support or prompt one another because the expectations are positively stated and well understood.

Teacher and administrative time is not taken up by responding to multiple low-level problems throughout the building, giving the time necessary to provide the extra support to those students who need more comprehensive planning time.

A critical element of SW-PBS is ongoing use of data to make decisions (progress monitoring) within a problem-solving model. Prior to merging wraparound into SW-PBS, there has been limited, if any, structured progress monitoring with wraparound teams. Although problem-solving processes are often used by wraparound teams, tools for organizing strength-needs data across settings and for effectively monitoring progress have not been evident. Assessment, when used, has typically been after the fact or has relied on external evaluations using tools that have not been part of the decision-making process of the wraparound team. To integrate wraparound into the SW-PBS model, efficient tools are needed that benchmark strengths and needs across multiple life domains (social-emotional, academic, basic living/safety, medical, etc.), and from multiple perspectives (i.e., family/student, teacher, community representatives). Tools for use by wraparound teams within SW-PBS and an online system to allow tertiary-level implementers ready access to data in formats easy to use at team meetings with families and teachers are described in the following section.

## Integrating Data-Based Decision Making Into Wraparound

As described in previous chapters, proactive use of data to drive instructional decision making is a hallmark principle and practice of SW-PBS (Lewis-Palmer, Sugai, & Larson, 1999; Nakasato, 2000; Sugai & Horner, 1999). Participating schools not only gather, report, and use data related to student's social and academic behavior but are also encouraged to self-assess SW-PBS implementation fidelity (e.g., SET) and effectiveness of schoolwide practices (Horner et al., 2004). Tertiary-level SW-PBS practices, including wraparound, also require the use of data to facilitate positive change for students. Most critical for this purpose is the use of data by individual family and youth teams for purposes of making decisions about effective interventions. In turn, the systems surrounding the child and family teams can make changes that support and sustain effective practices as evidenced by positive student outcomes.

Traditionally, use of data by schools for the purpose of driving proactive change at the individual student level has been limited. Teachers, school social workers, and other school personnel are often not trained in the use of data for purposes of facilitating positive change. As stated, behavioral data have been typically used to label students and justify removing the student to more restrictive settings rather than to design proactive interventions.

With numerous responsibilities taking precedence, proactive student data collection, analysis, and use have not necessarily been high on the list of priorities for service providers working with students with complex challenges. Many individuals in direct service positions view data as useless, or "something someone else does" (Usher, 1995), and not necessarily a means to a justifiable end when the target is a high-risk student with complex needs. More important, school personnel have come to believe that even when student data could be of use, they are often stored in formats that are difficult to access, manipulate, and interpret (Wayman, 2005). Technology or computerized data storage systems often further impede the use of data by being too complicated and disengaged from the day-to-day, internal social structures of the school (Zhao & Frank, 2003). Lachat and Smith (2005) contended that successful data use by schools and school staff are related to several key factors, which include quality and accuracy of available data, staff access to data, the capacity for data disaggregation, the organization of data around a clear set of questions, and leadership structures that support schoolwide use of data.

Recognizing that effectiveness is predicated on the availability and use of data for decision making and change at all levels of wraparound implementation, it is essential for schools to have access to tools and technology that are efficient, simple, accessible, and user friendly (Wayman, 2005). Similar to data systems for universal SW-PBS, tools that can guide individualized teams through the four phases of the wraparound process are needed. The Illinois PBIS Network, with a history of SOC and wraparound implementation (Eber & Hyde, 2006; Eber & Nelson 1997; Eber, Palmer, & Pacchiano, 2003), has been developing tools and computerized technology that support and encourage the use of data with individual wraparound teams. Although these tools are in development and testing, we offer the following information as an example of how the need for data-based decision-making processes with wraparound within a system of SW-PBS can be addressed.

## Data-Based Decision-Making Tools for Wraparound

The Illinois wraparound data tools were originally designed via focus groups of wraparound implementers for the purpose of statewide evaluation of wraparound through interagency community-based local-area networks (LANs) from 2000 to 2002. The tools have been revised and used in schools implementing tertiary-level SW-PBS in Illinois on a pilot basis for 3 years (2004–2007). The tools were developed with the intent of providing youth and family teams with the data necessary for decision making and change on behalf of the youth with complex needs, while also serving as a mechanism for the collection of a data repository on students and families with tertiary-level needs. Under the guidance of the wraparound team facilitator, these data are collected and used by the team at 30- to 90-day intervals throughout the wraparound teaming process.

The wraparound tools were designed to generate multiple-perspective information relative to the students, including information regarding strengths, need, educational outcomes, placement risk, use of data at team meetings, and family satisfaction. The Home School Community Tool (HSC-T) is the primary tool used at all phases of the wraparound process. This tool is designed to assess strengths and needs of the student relative to functioning across five domains: health/safety, social, emotional, behavioral, and cultural. In addition to probing for data across multiple life domains, this tool includes ratings in three different settings (home, school, and community) and therefore facilitates information sharing from multiple perspectives as different members of the team (teacher, family, and student) are involved in data gathering. See Fig. 27.2 for sample items from the HSC-T. An additional tool used at all phases is the Educational Information Tool (EI-T), which provides teacher rating of classroom functioning in academic and social/emotional domains. Sample items rated by the teacher on a Likert scale (1 = Never, 4 = Always) include "passes quizzes and tests," "participates in classroom discussions/activities," "has friends," and "engages in appropriate classroom behavior with adults." Generating information from different informants provides an opportunity to present "situation- or setting-specific" data from team members and to present information on different areas of functioning (i.e., behavior, academics) observed by different team members (Richardson & Day, 2000). While there is much debate surrounding the validity of differing perspective data from multiple sources (De Los Reyes & Kazdin, 2005; Offord et al., 1996; Renck, 2005), it has been suggested (Achenbach, McConaughy, & Howell, 1987) that it is essential to preserve the contributions of different informants, even if their reports are not correlated. The wraparound process supports this theory, with the belief that the richness and uniqueness of differing viewpoints offers the team the opportunity to learn from strategies and techniques used by the different sources in different situations with a student with complex needs.

The initial strengths and needs data are collected (using the HSC-T and EI-T) through the initial conversations that take place in Phase I of the wraparound. This is accomplished by the wraparound facilitator, who enters the data in a user-friendly, immediately accessible, online database system known as SIMEO (Systematic Information Management of Educational Outcomes). This system provides immediate opportunity for single-student graphs to be developed and used by the team to guide decision making at wraparound team meetings. Team facilitators are trained and supported in how to integrate data collection during the engagement of team members (Phase I). Skill sets include entry and organization of data for use at team meetings. Coaching support focuses on how to use the data to engage team members, keep them at the table over time, and refine and monitor interventions continuously. Figure 27.3 provides an example of SIMEO data used to focus an emerging wraparound team on strengths and needs as described in Tim's story.

From the Field: Tim's Story

"Tim," a third grader, was often late for school and, when in class, was frequently disruptive and inattentive. The teacher reported that she was spending more and more of her time attempting to keep Tim on task and out of fights. After numerous attempts with secondary interventions, Tim was referred for tertiary-level support. When the team initially met, they were primarily focused on reactions to Tim's disruptive behavior and became overwhelmed by his increasingly aggressive classroom behavior; the discussion rapidly moved to referring Tim for special education testing. His teacher mentioned that he often arrived at school sleep deprived and hungry; his mother did not participate much in the

**Example of questions from Home, School, Community Tool**

**High Need** = student demonstrates significant and/or extreme challenge and need in this area of functioning, potentially leading to failure of the home, school, and/or community placement.

**Somewhat Need** = student demonstrates challenge and need in this area of functioning but not enough to warrant failure of home, school, and/or community placement.

**Somewhat Strength** = student demonstrates growth and maturation in this area of functioning, and at times still needs guidance and direction.

**High Strength** = student demonstrates above average or excellent growth and maturation in this area of functioning requiring no additional guidance or direction.

| Needs/Strengths | COMMUNITY | | | | HOME | | | | SCHOOL | | | |
|---|---|---|---|---|---|---|---|---|---|---|---|---|
| | need | | strength | | need | | strength | | need | | strength | |
| | high | some what | some what | high | high | some what | some what | high | high | some what | some what | high |
| | 1 | 2 | 3 | 4 | 1 | 2 | 3 | 4 | 1 | 2 | 3 | 4 |
| **Safety/Medical/Basic Needs** | | | | | | | | | | | | |
| 7) Has adequate/safe physical environment | | | | | | | | | | | | |
| **Social Relationships** | | | | | | | | | | | | |
| 8) Gets along with adults | | | | | | | | | | | | |
| **Emotional Functioning** | | | | | | | | | | | | |
| 9) Feels that he/she belongs | | | | | | | | | | | | |
| **Behavioral** | | | | | | | | | | | | |
| 10) Controls him/herself | | | | | | | | | | | | |

**Fig. 27.2.** Example of questions from Home, School, Community Tool.

discussion at the meetings. The SW-PBS coach recommended they move to wraparound, so a trained wraparound facilitator was identified (school social worker) who met with the family and listened to their concerns. The facilitator did the same with the teacher, thus gathering multiple-perspective data (using the HSC-T). When the wraparound team was convened (Phase II), the facilitator used the data to focus the team on listening to Tim's mother's concerns. Through data taken in the home school and community environment and anecdotal reports from his mother, the team soon realized that Tim's mother was asking for help on how to better prepare Tim for the school day. They designed interventions that included behavioral instruction for his mother to use at bedtime and mealtime at home. When they met 3 months later, the facilitator brought graphs to demonstrate that when Tim got adequate sleep and adequate nutrition at home, he was often less aggressive and more focused in class. Figure 27.3 displays Tim's home school and community functioning data for baseline and 3 months later.

The SIMEO system is an example of how tertiary-level teams can be provided with access to useful, simple, and secure individual as well as aggregate student data that provide an in-depth "picture" of their individual strengths and complex needs. This information assists schools in expanding the implementation of SW-PBS to those students with complicated mental health needs who have been traditionally beyond the capacity of schools to support. A 3-year pilot implementation of SIMEO (FY 2003 to FY 2006) that included 47 students over a 3-year period indicate how

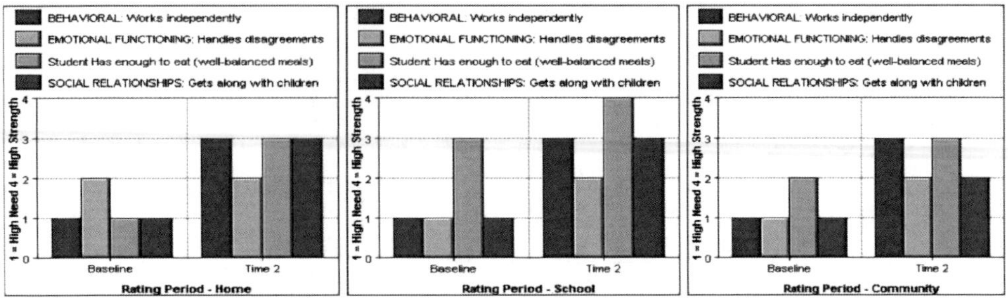


**Fig. 27.3.** Example of graph from Home, School, Community Tool.

ongoing monitoring of a range of variables, such as those documented through SIMEO tools, can be established. For example, evaluators noted that as students' need for behavioral interventions decreased, their teachers were more likely to identify/recognize their needs for academic assistance, suggesting that as their wraparound teams facilitated behavioral improvement, they became more aware of academic needs, suggesting earlier interventions targeted to academic progress may be more efficient in the future. Other reported findings include decreases in students at risk for more restrictive placement by achieving improved behavioral and emotional functioning at home and school, improvement in academic functioning, and decreases in high-risk behaviors (Eber & Hyde, 2006).

## Self-Assessment of the Integrity of the Wraparound Process

The measure of the fidelity or integrity of a "treatment model" is essential to the efficacy of the outcomes of any intervention, such as wraparound. As noted by Dobson and Cook (1980), if treatment strategies are not clearly specified and services and supports are delivered in a way that is inconsistent with program model objectives, the resulting outcomes will likely be useless or less meaningful (p. 270). Although outcomes have been both positive and significant as evidenced by the 3-year tracking of students within the SIMEO system (Eber & Hyde, 2006), the testing of fidelity of the wraparound model provided within SW-PBS is still in its infancy. Although fidelity of schoolwide behavioral supports has universally been measured using the SET (Horner et al., 2004), tools to measure efficacy and evidence to support the use of the wraparound approach has been limited, and the study of the adherence to wraparound principles has rarely been assessed (Ogles et al., 2006).

However, several attempts within the field of child and family services have been made to measure the fidelity of wraparound (Bruns, Burchard, Suter, Leverentz-Brady, & Force 2004; Epstein et al., 1998); findings from recent literature are starting to support a link between treatment fidelity and youth and family outcomes. In particular, Bruns and colleagues have been instrumental in continuing to refine the measurement of wraparound fidelity with the Wraparound Fidelity Index-4 (WIFI4) (Bruns et al., 2004).

This measure, however, provides only a post facto measure of fidelity as reported by the youth, caregiver, and team members and does not provide the opportunity for self-assessment of wraparound during the active team process.

In an effort to provide tertiary-level wraparound teams within SW-PBS with a tool that allows for continuous assessment of fidelity, the Illinois PBIS Network has been developing the Wraparound Integrity Tool (WIT). The WIT is designed to provide wraparound teams with the opportunity to self-assess relative to wraparound fidelity on a regular basis (at the start of the team process and every one to three team meetings thereafter) and therefore provide teams with the opportunity to use WIT findings to "self-correct," thereby ensuring a more stringent adherence to the wraparound principles. At present, the WIT is being piloted with families engaged in the wraparound process with the intent to continue to refine the tool administration process and develop procedures to ensure validity and reliability.

From the Field: Family Voice

"James's" mother has, historically, been reluctant to come to the school for meetings about James as the meetings have, from her perspective, felt like opportunities to tell her how "bad" James was and, in turn, how bad of a parent she was. She felt she was doing the best she could as a single mother with two young boys, working two jobs to make ends meet. The wraparound meetings, however, have been a different experience for her. Now, at the meetings with the school team they actually asked her about her past experiences with meetings and asked her what she thought worked or did not work. They seemed to want to do things differently. They cared about what she had to say, and she felt included in important decisions; it really seemed that her voice mattered. Everything was far from perfect, but this thing they called "wraparound" sure felt a lot better to her than the other meetings she attended on James's behalf before. Figure 27.4 illustrates James' mother's perception of the inclusion of her voice at team meetings prior to wraparound and since wraparound.

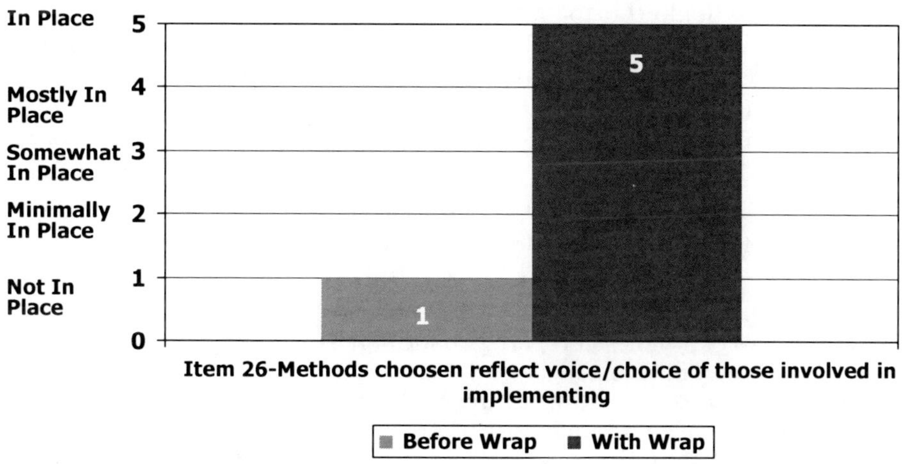


**Fig. 27.4.** Example of Question from Wraparound Integrity Tool.

## INTEGRATING WRAPAROUND INTO SW-PBS: CHALLENGES AND STRATEGIES

### System, Data, and Practice Challenges

Building tertiary-level capacity within a system of SW-PBS is hard work. One reason is that school personnel have not had adequate training and support with the skill sets needed to be effective with students who need comprehensive behavior supports, not only at school but also at home and in the community. Developing the skills for engaging families, students, and teachers who may be frustrated and experiencing stress requires systematic training and opportunities to practice over time. Staff development time and resources are not always allocated sufficiently to ensure the depth of skill development and ongoing support to teachers needed at this level. Without adequate training and support, decisions about behavior support are often reactive and punitive, without the comprehensive interventions needed to effect change. The referral and testing process for special education is often viewed as the "intervention" as that is what the school personnel know how to accomplish.

A related system challenge to tertiary-level implementation is that the time required to engage a team and systematically apply interventions is often not available. In other words, the current systems in schools do not allocate planning time commensurate with level of need for 1–2% of students. This results in inadequate data, weak interventions, or faulty implementation. Students are often removed to restrictive settings before the wraparound process can be implemented. Specialized personnel are not positioned to guide teams of parents and teachers through the team development process so that highly individualized interventions can be provided, monitored, and refined over time. Instead, they spend the bulk of their time assessing students for special education eligibility or attempting to provide interventions listed on IEPs that are often insufficient in intensity or dosage to effect change for a student. School psychologists, social workers, and counselors may feel "locked into" providing the interventions written on IEPs (or requested by other school personnel) even though these interventions may not have an adequate evidence base for the presenting problem. When these special services personnel participate in training for secondary and tertiary levels of SW-PBS, they often have to assess their job roles, and sometimes they feel powerless to change the practices that have deep roots in the cultures of their schools and districts.

From the Field: Changes in Job Functions?

"Vanessa," a school social worker, has 15 students on her "case load" at a middle school. All of their IEPs indicate the need for "social work 20 min a week." Vanessa reports frustration as the teachers expect the students' disruptive behavior in the classroom to change as a result of their social work time. Vanessa reports that 12 of the 15 students she sees weekly have had increases in problem behavior (i.e., detentions, suspensions), and 5 of them have been recommended for further testing to determine if "more restrictive placements are needed." She knows she needs to switch to higher-level interventions (i.e., the wraparound process) but is not sure how to go about making the change in her job function. While recognizing lack of effectiveness, she feels the "system" holds her responsible for delivering the IEP services.

## Strategies for Building Tertiary Capacity

Developing the practices needed for school personnel to effectively support students with complex behavior needs is a major undertaking. Establishing sustainable systems at the school and district levels for supporting these students successfully over time is an even greater challenge. The following strategies are offered to guide schools in developing tertiary-level systems commensurate with this 1–2% of students.

### *Position Personnel to Facilitate Wraparound*

Many school systems struggle with allocation of specialized personnel. Per the field example of Vanessa, specialized personnel are often positioned to conduct tests, suggest placements, and provide IEP-designated services, which often do not have the depth needed for effective interventions for students with complex behavioral needs. Team facilitation has been considered a critical job role for implementing wraparound since its inception through SOC (Burns & Goldman, 1999). Similarly, Scott and his colleagues (Scott, Nelson, & Zabala, 2003) suggested that, even with training and tools (i.e., FBA/BIP forms) in place, the FBA/BIP process implemented in schools may lack fidelity (and therefore effect) without ongoing training and technical assistance for key personnel on how to effectively *facilitate* the team through the process with integrity. Following the established wraparound model, each individual student's wraparound team is led by a facilitator who functions as the primary point person on the individual student/family team. Therefore, each school and district needs to have designated staff (typically counselors, social workers, psychologists, and other specialized staff with behavioral/clinical training) who are trained to function as wraparound team facilitators. These personnel are positioned within the school or district to engage, develop, and facilitate highly unique teams capable of using data to design supports and interventions that are realistic, practical, and likely to have the effect desired by those key team members (e.g., families, teachers). It may be necessary for school leaders to reallocate personnel from "testing and placing" to facilitating and coaching the wraparound team process.

### *Organize School and District-Based Leadership Teams to Address Tertiary System Components*

If effective practices for students with emotional-behavioral challenges are to become the norm, training practitioners in the skill sets of wraparound facilitation and effective behavioral interventions is necessary, but training alone is not sufficient. System leaders at both the building and district levels must engage in a problem-solving process focused on the processes and procedures that have an impact on how students with the most complex needs are supported. This is likely to involve identifying and changing some traditional (yet less-effective) practices that can become roadblocks to building effective tertiary levels of support. To accomplish this, school leaders need to consistently review the data on all their students, including those placed in special education and other specialized programs, to identify strategies that yield success for these students. In addition, leadership teams need to look closely at the roles of personnel working with these students and programs for possible modifications needed to ensure that more comprehensive approaches are implemented when needed. An important leadership team activity is to review data on specialized populations (e.g., special education and other specialized programs) to determine practices and job roles of staff that may need to be changed based on trends in their data. For example, in a middle school, high use of "escorts" in the hallways for students with problem behavior typically results in students escalating the problem behavior and ending up in restrictive settings. Or, certain populations (i.e., students with autism spectrum disorder or African American males) may be identified as receiving a disproportionate amount of punitive responses and restrictive placements. When trends such as these are recognized, strategies to change these trends must be identified. Examples include repositioning specialized staff to design individualized function-based behavior support plans or identifying wraparound facilitators to develop unique teams that ensure more effective interventions in a timelier manner.

### *Ensuring Access and Use of Systems for Data-Based Decision Making at the Tertiary Level*

As discussed, decisions regarding students with complex behavioral needs are often reactive, based on emotion and concerns about safety, and often are triggered by and based on single behavioral incidents. Early efforts at integrating data-based decision-making structures into systems that plan for and support these students in Illinois have driven home how important yet challenging this change in practice can be in schools. Wraparound teams need simple tools that quickly assess a broad range of strengths and needs across multiple settings and can be used on a frequent basis (every 30–90 days). The HSC-T is an example of such a tool, and it has been useful in identifying big needs as well as confirming data obtained through conversations. Other data that system leaders need quick access to includes special education referral rates, educational placement data, and trend data on restrictive placements such as alternative schools. Behavioral and mental health screeners, as part of the systematized early intervention process to identify youth and intervene early, are also needed. Stakeholders need access to a fully integrated evaluation system designed for easy access/use by local implementers (teacher, families, coaches, administrators, etc.) but also organized to provide aggregate information to inform and guide district, regional, and state infrastructures.

### *Integration With Mental Health*

We have explored the resulting problems for youth/families when the challenges discussed are not addressed, including students not receiving timely and effective early intervening services, interventions not having adequate dosage/complexity/fidelity for level of need, students identified for special education having limited rates of success (especially students who have emotional-behavioral components to their disability), and reactive system responses (i.e., punishment, exclusion) that lead to escalation of problems and high rates of restrictive placements. When youth and family needs are not met, school, district, and community needs also are not met. These are not just quality-of-life issues for those youth and families as these problems/challenges affect schools, districts, and communities. Schools alone cannot adequately address the full complement of needs. School districts and mental health and other community-based partners need to develop active partnerships with a shared vision, with a willingness to develop new roles to collectively address needs indicated by community as well as school data (Kutash, Duchnowski, & Lynn, 2006).

## FUTURE DIRECTIONS

Schools need to expedite efforts to build competency and capacity for supporting students with complex emotional and behavioral needs. This will require an uncompromising commitment to policy and research that prioritizes effective support for emotional/behavioral needs of students on an equal level to academic learning. This includes ensuring the use of (a) universal application of effective behavioral supports in schools, (b) mandated early screening and detection of students at risk for mental health problems, (c) systematic application of evidenced-based interventions that are (d) efficiently scaled up to ensure adequate dosage for prevention through comprehensive supports for students with complex needs. The wraparound process, with its focus on linking families, schools, and community partners on behalf of individual students should be an integral part of this prevention-based system. To ensure optimal outcomes, the critical features of SW-PBS, including data-based decision making, ongoing self-assessment of fidelity, and rigorous progress monitoring, need to become routine within the wraparound process.

## REFERENCES


Achenbach,T. M., McConaughy, S. H., & Howell, C.T. (1987). Child/adolescent behavioral and emotional problems: Implications of cross informant correlations for situation specificity. *Psychological Bulletin, 101*, 213–232.

Agosta, J., Bradley, V., Taub, S., Melda, K., Taylor, M., Kimmich, M., et al. (1999). *The Robert Wood Johnson Foundation Self-Determination Initiative: Year one impact assessment report.* Cambridge, MA: Human Services Research Institute.

Albin, R. W., Lucyshyn, J. M., Horner, R. H., & Flannery, K. B. (1996). Contextual fit for behavioral support plans, In L. K. Koegel, R. L. Koegel, & G. Dunlap (Eds.), *Positive behavioral support: Including people with difficult behavior in the community* (pp. 81–98). Baltimore: Brookes.

Allen, R. I., & Petr, C. G. (1998). Rethinking family-centered practice. *American Journal of Orthopsychiatry, 68*, 196–204.

Brofenbrenner, U. (1979). *The ecology of human development.* Cambridge, MA: Harvard University Press.

Brown, F., & Michaels, C. A. (2006). School-wide positive behavior support initiatives and students with severe disabilities: A time for reflection. *Research and Practice for Persons With Severe Disabilities, 31*, 57–61.

Bruns, E. J., Burchard, J. D., Suter, J. C., Leverentz-Brady, K., & Force, M. M. (2004). Assessing fidelity to a community based treatment for youth: The wraparound fidelity index. *Journal of Emotional and Behavioral Disorders, 12*, 79–89.

Bruns, E. J., Suter, J. C., Force, M. M., & Burchard, J. D. (2005). Adherence to wraparound principles and association with outcomes. *Journal of Child and Family Studies, 14*, 521–534.

Burchard, J. D., Bruns, E. J., & Burchard, S. N. (2002). The wraparound approach. In B. Burns & K. Hoagwood (Eds.), *Community treatment for youth: Evidence-based interventions for severe emotional and behavioral disorders.* New York: Oxford University Press.

Burns, B. J., Costello, E. J., Angold, A., Tweed, D., Stangl, D., Farmer, E. M. Z., et al. (1995). Children's mental health service use across service sectors. *Health Affairs, 14*, 147–159.

Burns, B. J., & Goldman, S. K. (Eds.). (1999). *Promising practices in wraparound for children with serious emotional disturbance and their families. Systems of Care: Promising Practices in Children's Mental Health, 1998 Series* (Vol. 4). Washington, DC: Center for Effective Collaboration and Practice, American Institutes for Research.

Burns, B. J., Goldman, S. K., Faw, L., & Burchard, J. D. (1999). The wraparound evidence base. In B. J. Burns & S. K. Goldman (Eds.), *Promising practices in wraparound for children with serious emotional disturbance and their families. Systems of care: Promising practices in children's mental health, 1998 series* (Vol. 4, pp. 95–118). Washington, DC: Center for Effective Collaboration and Practice, American Institutes for Research.

Carr, E. G. (2006). SWPBS: The greatest good for the greatest number, or the needs of the majority trump the needs of the minority? *Research and Practice for Persons With Severe Disabilities, 31*, 54–56.

Cauffman, E., Scholle, S. H., Mulvey, E., & Kelleher, K. J. (2005). Predicting first time involvement in the juvenile justice system among emotionally disturbed youth receiving mental health services. *Psychological Services, 2*, 28–38.

Cheney, D., Malloy, J., & Hagner, D. (1998). Finishing high school in many different ways: Project RENEW in Manchester, New Hampshire. *Effective School Practices, 17*, 45–54.

Clarke, R., Schaefer, M., Burchard, J., & Welkowitz, J. (1992). Wrapping community-based mental health services around children with a severe behavioral disorder: An evaluation of project wraparound. *Journal of Child and Family Studies, 1*, 241–61.

Costello, J. E., Mastillo, S., Erkanli, A., Keeler, G., & Angold, A. (2003). Prevalence and development of psychiatric disorders in childhood and adolescence. *Archives of General Psychiatry, 60*, 837–894.

Crimmins, D., & Farrell, A.F. (2006). Individualized behavioral supports at 15 years: It's still lonely at the top. *Research and Practice for Persons With Severe Disabilities, 31*, 31–45.

Crone, D. A., & Horner, R. H. (2003). *Building positive behavior support systems in schools: Functional behavioral assessment.* New York: Guilford Press.

De Los Reyes, A., & Kazdin, A. E. (2005). Informant discrepancies in the assessment of childhood psychopathology: A critical review, theoretical framework, and recommendations for further study. *Psychological Bulletin, 131*, 483–509.

Dobson, D., & Cook, T. J. (1980). Avoiding type III error in program evaluation: Results from a field experiment. *Evaluation and Program Planning, 3*, 269–276.

Eber, L. (1994). The wraparound approach. *Illinois School Research and Development Journal, 30*, 17–21.

Eber, L. (2003). *The art and science of wraparound: Completing the continuum of schoolwide behavioral support.* Bloomington, IN: Forum on Education at Indiana University.

Eber, L. (2005). Wraparound: Description and case example. In G. Sugai & R. Horner (Eds.), *Encyclopedia of behavior modification and cognitive behavior therapy: Educational applications* (pp. 1601–1605). Thousand Oaks, CA: Sage.

Eber, L., & Hyde, K. (2006). *Integrating data-based decision into the wraparound process within a system of school-wide positive behavior supports (PBS)*. Summary of conference proceedings for the 18th Annual Research Conference for Children's Mental Health, Tampa, FL, March.

Eber, L., & Keenan, S. (2004). Collaboration with other agencies: Wraparound and systems of care for children and youths with emotional and behavioral disorders. In R. B. Rutherford, M. M. Quinn, and S. R. Mathur (Eds.), *Handbook of research in emotional and behavioral disorders* (pp. 502–516). New York: Guilford Press.

Eber, L., & Nelson, C. M. (1997). School-based wraparound planning: Integrating services for students with emotional and behavioral needs. *American Journal of Orthopsychiatry, 67*, 385–396.

Eber, L., & Osuch, R. (1995). Bringing the wraparound approach to school: A model for inclusion. In C. Liberton, K. Kutash, & R. Friedman (Eds.), *The seventh annual research conference proceedings. A system of care for children's mental health: Expanding the research base* (pp. 143–151). Tampa, FL: University of South Florida, Florida Mental Health Institute, Research and Training Center for Children's Mental Health.

Eber, L., Osuch, R., & Rolf, K. (1996). School-based wraparound: How implementation and evaluation can lead to system change. In C. Liberton, K. Kutash, & R. Friedman (Eds.), *The eighth annual research conference proceedings. A system of care for children's mental health: Expanding the research base* (pp. 143–147). Tampa, FL: University of South Florida, Florida Mental Health Institute, Research and Training Center for Children's Mental Health.

Eber, L., Palmer, T., & Pacchiano, D. (2003). *School-wide positive behavior systems: Improving school environments for all students including those with EBD*. Summary of conference proceedings for the 14th Annual Research Conference for Children's Mental Health, Tampa, FL, March.

Epstein, M. H., Jayanthi, M., McKelvey, J., Frankenberry, E., Hardy, R., & Dennis, K. (1998). Reliability of the Wraparound Observation Form: An instrument to measure the wraparound process. *Journal of Child and Family Studies, 7*, 161–170.

Fairbanks, S., Sugai, G., Guardino, D., & Lathrop, M. (2007). Response to intervention: Examining classroom behavior support in second grade. *Exceptional Children, 73*, 288–310.

Freeman, R., Eber, L., Anderson, C., Irvin, L., Horner, R., Bounds, M., et al. (2006). Building inclusive school cultures using school-wide positive behavior support: Designing effective individual support systems for students with significant disabilities. *Research and Practice for Persons With Severe Disabilities, 31*, 4–17.

Friedman, R. M., Katz-Levy, J. W., & Manderschied, R. W. (1996) Prevalence of serious emotional disturbance in children and adolescents. In R. W. Manderschied & M. A. Sonnenschein (Eds.), *Mental health, United States 1996*. Rockville, MD: Center for Mental Health Sciences, 71–89.

Hawken, L. S., & O'Neill, R. E. (2006). Including students with severe disabilities in all levels of school-wide positive behavior support. *Research and Practice for Persons with Severe Disabilities, 31*, 46–53.

Hernandez, M., & Hodges, S. (2003). Building upon the theory of change for systems for care, *Journal of Emotional and Behavioral Disorders, 11*, 19–26.

Horner, R. H., Todd, A. W., Lewis-Palmer, T., Irvin, L. K., Sugai, G., & Boland, J. B. (2004). The School-wide Evaluation Tool (SET): A research instrument for assessing school-wide positive behavior support, *Journal of Positive Behavior Interventions, 6*, 3–12.

Milwaukee, Wisconsin, Kamradt, B., October (1996). *The 25 kid project: How Milwaukee utilized a pilot project to achieve buy-in among stakeholders in changing the system of care for children with severe emotional problems*. Paper presented to the Washington Business Group on Health.

Kendziora, K., Bruns, E., Osher, D., Pacchiano, D., & Mejia, B.(2001). *Systems of care promising practices in children's mental health, 2001 series* (Vol. 1). Washington, DC: American Institute for Research, Center for Effective Collaboration and Practice.

Kincaid, D., & Fox, L. (2002). Person-centered planning and positive behavior support. In S. Holburn & P. Vietze (Eds.), *Person-centered planning: Research, practice, and future directions* (pp. 29–49). Baltimore: Brookes.

Knitzer, J. (1982). *Unclaimed children: The failure of public responsibility to children and adolescents in need of mental health services.* Washington, DC: Children's Defense Fund.

Kutash, K., Duchnowski, A. J., & Lynn, N. (2006). *School-based mental health: An empirical guide for decision-makers.* Tampa, FL: University of South Florida, Louis de la Parte Florida Mental Health Institute, Department of Child and Family Studies, Research and Training Center for Children's Mental Health.

Lachat, M. A., & Smith, S. (2005). Practices that support data use in urban high schools. *Journal of Education for Students Placed At-Risk, 10,* 333–349.

Lewis-Palmer, T., Sugai, G., & Larson, S. (1999). Using data to guide decisions about program implementation and effectiveness. *Effective School Practices, 17,* 47–53.

Malloy, J. M., Cheney, D., & Cormier, G. M. (1998). Interagency collaboration and the transition to adulthood for students with emotional or behavioral disabilities. *Education and Treatment of Children, 21,* 303–321.

Miles, P., Bruns, E. J., Osher, T. W., Walker, J. S., & National Wraparound Initiative Advisory Group. (2006). *The wraparound process user's guide: A handbook for families.* Portland, OR: National Wraparound Initiative, Research and Training Center on Family Support and Children's Mental Health, Portland State University.

Munger, R. L. (1998). *The ecology of troubled children.* Cambridge, MA: Brookline Press.

Nakasato, J. (2000). Data-based decision making in Hawaii's behavior support effort. *Journal of Positive Behavior Interventions, 2,* 247–251.

National Center for Education Statistics (2006). Digest of education statistics. Retrieved June 20, 2007, from http://nces.ed.gov/

O'Brien, C. L., & O'Brien, J. (2000) The origins of person-centered planning: A community of practice perspective. In S. Holburn & P. M. Vietze (Eds.), *Person-centered planning: Research, practice, and future directions* (pp. 3–27). Baltimore: Brookes.

Ogles, B. M., Carlston, D., Hatfield, D., Melendez, G., Dowell, K., & Fields, S. A. (2006). The role of fidelity and feedback in the wraparound approach. *Journal of Child and Family Studies, 15,* 114–128.

Offord, D. R., Boyle, M. H., Racine, Y., Szatmari, P., Fleming, J. E., Sanford, M., et al. (1996). Integrating assessment data from multiple informants. *Journal of the American Academy of Child and Adolescent Psychiatry, 35,* 1078–1086.

O'Neill, R. E., Horner, R. H., Albin, R. W, Sprague, J. R., Storey, K., & Newton, J. S. (1997). *Functional assessment and program development for problem behavior: A practical handbook* (2nd ed.). Pacific Grove, CA: Brookes.

Palmer, S. B., & Wehmeyer, M. L. (1998). Students' expectations of the future: Hopelessness as a barrier to self-determination. *Mental Retardation, 36,* 128–136.

Renck, K. (2005). Cross informant ratings of behavior of children and adolescents: The "gold standard." *Journal of Child and Family Studies, 14,* 457–468.

Richardson, G. A., & Day, N. L. (2000). Epidemiologic considerations. In M. Hersen & R. T. Ammermans (Eds.), *Advanced abnormal child psychology* (2nd ed.). Mahwah, NJ: Erlbaum, pp. 33-46.

Risley, T. (1996). Get a life! Positive behavioral intervention for challenging behavior through life arrangement and life coaching. In L. K. Koegel, R. L. Koegel, & G. Dunlap (Eds.), *Positive behavior support: Including people with difficult behavior in the community.* Baltimore: Brookes, pp. 425-437.

Rones, M., & Hoagwood, K. (2000). School-based mental health services: A research review. *Clinical Child and Family Psychology Review, 3,* 223–241.

Safran, S. P., & Oswald, K. (2003). Positive behavior supports: Can schools reshape disciplinary practices? *Exceptional Children, 69,* 361–373.

Saleebey, D. (2001). *The strengths perspective in social work practice* (2nd ed.). New York: Longman.

Scott, T., & Eber, L. (2003). Functional assessment and wraparound as systemic school processes: Primary, secondary, and tertiary systems examples. *Journal of Positive Behavior Supports, 5,* 131–143.

Scott, T., Nelson, C. M., & Zabala, J. (2003). Functional behavior assessment training in public schools: Facilitating systemic change. *Journal of Positive Behavior Interventions, 5,* 216–224.

Shaffer, D., Fisher, P., Dulcan, M. K., Davies, M., Piacentini, J., Schwab-Stone, M. E., et al. (1996). The NIMH Diagnostic Interview Schedule for Children version 2.3 (DISC-2.3): Description, acceptability, prevalence rates, and performance in the MECA study. *Journal of the American Academy of Child and Adolescent Psychiatry, 35*, 865–877.

Strein, W., Hoagwood, K., & Cohn, A. (2003). School psychology: A public health perspective I. Prevention, populations, and systems change. *Journal of School Psychology, 41*, 23–38.

Stroul, B. A., & Friedman, R. M. (1986). *A system of care for children and youth with severe emotional disturbances* (Rev. ed). Washington, DC: Georgetown University Child Development Center, CASSP Technical Assistance Center.

Sugai, G., & Horner, R. H. (1999). Discipline and behavioral support: Preferred processes and practices. *Effective School Practices, 17*, 10–22.

Sugai, G., Lewis-Palmer, T., Todd, A. W., & Horner, R. H. (2001). *School-wide Evaluation Tool* (Version 2.0). Eugene: University of Oregon, Educational and Community Supports.

U.S. Department of Health and Human Services. (1999). *Mental health: A report of the surgeon general—executive summary.* Rockville, MD: U.S. Department of Health and Human Services, Substance Abuse and Mental Health Services Administration, Center for Mental Health Services, National Institutes of Health, National Institute of Mental Health.

Usher, C. L. (1995). Improving evaluability through self-evaluation. *Evaluation Practice, 16*, 59–68.

VanDenBerg, J. (1999). History of the wraparound process. In B. J. Burns and S. K. Goldman (Eds.), *Promising practices in wraparound for children with serious emotional disturbance and their families* (Vol. 4, pp. 19–26). Washington, DC: Center for Effective Collaboration and Practice, American Institute for Research.

Vandercook, T., York, J., & Forest, M. (1989) The McGill Action Planning System (MAPS): A strategy for building the vision. *Journal of the Association for Persons with Severe Handicaps, 14*, 205–215.

Wagner, M., Newman, L., Cameto, R., Levine, P., & Garza, N. (2006). *An overview of findings from wave 2 of the National Longitudinal Transition Study-2 (NLTS2)* (NCSER 2006–3004). Menlo Park, CA: SRI International.

Walker, H. M., Horner, R. H., Sugai, G., Bullis, M., Sprague, J. R., Bricker, D., et al. (1996). Integrated approaches to preventing antisocial behavior patterns among school-age children and youth. *Journal of Emotional and Behavioral Disorders, 4*, 194–209.

Walker, J. S., Bruns, E. J., VanDenBerg, J. D., Rast, J., Osher, T. W., et al., & National Wraparound Initiative Advisory Group. (2004). *Phases and activities of the wraparound process.* Portland, OR: National Wraparound Initiative, Research and Training Center on Family Support and Children's Mental Health, Portland State University.

Walker, J. S., & Schutte, K. M. (2004). Practice and process in wraparound teamwork. *Journal of Emotional and Behavioral Disorders, 12*, 182–192.

Wayman, J. C. (2005). Using teachers in data-driven decision making: Using computer data systems to support teacher inquiry and reflection. *Journal of Education for Students Placed At-Risk, 10*, 295–308.

Wehmeyer, M. L. (1999). A functional model of self-determination: Describing development and implementing instruction. *Focus on Autism and Other Developmental Disabilities, 14*, 53–61.

Wehmeyer, M. L., Baker, D. J., Blumberg, R., & Harrison, R. (2004). Self-determination and student involvement: Innovative practices. *Journal of Positive Behavior Supports, 6*, 29–35.

Zhao, Y., & Frank, K. A. (2003). Factors affecting technology uses in schools: An ecological perspective. *American Educational Research, 40*, 807–840.

# 28

# Implementing Function-Based Support Within Schoolwide Positive Behavior Support

**CYNTHIA M. ANDERSON and TERRANCE M. SCOTT**

Educators face increasing challenges in educating today's youth. Schools must cope with myriad challenges, including budget cuts, increased student enrollment, and an increasing range of student skill levels. In addition, discipline problems are a growing concern for educators. Although the relatively rare instances of school violence and other extreme behaviors are highlighted nationally when they occur, less-severe problems such as defiance, noncompliance, bullying, and disruptive behavior are far more common and result in significant disruption of the learning environment. To illustrate, 70% of middle and high school teachers reported that disruptive behavior was a serious problem in their schools, and 85% of new teachers reported feeling unprepared to manage discipline problems (Public Agenda, 2004). Equally disturbing, the vast majority of teachers said that, while their school's plan for responding to serious problems (e.g., weapons violations) was appropriate, the schools did not have effective approaches for preventing and responding to the occurrence of less-severe but far more prevalent discipline problems such as noncompliance, disrespect, and tardiness.

In attempting to respond to discipline problems in schools, educators historically have relied on a variety of reactive approaches, including detention, suspension, and expulsion—strategies that have not proven effective (Skiba & Raush, 2006; Skiba, Ritter, Simmons, Peterson, & Miller, 2006; Sulzer-Azaroff & Mayer, 1994). Research increasingly suggests that

**CYNTHIA M. ANDERSON** • University of Oregon
**TERRANCE M. SCOTT** • University of Louisville

effective strategies for reducing discipline problems are proactive and systematic and use multicomponent, evidence-based strategies. Importantly, there exist a fairly large number of interventions that meet these criteria—what has been missing is a system for implementing and sustaining evidence-based interventions in schools. Intensive positive behavior support (IPBS) is a team-based, data-driven framework for helping schools meet the needs of students exhibiting behavioral challenges. The IPBS model is implemented within the context of schoolwide positive behavior support (SWPBS), described in some depth in chapter 14. In this chapter, we begin with a brief review of SWPBS as this serves as the foundation for IPBS. We next describe the IPBS framework illustrating how IPBS uses a nested model of support such that students are supported by school teams, which are in turn supported by district-provided resources.

## SCHOOLWIDE POSITIVE BEHAVIOR SUPPORT: THE UNIVERSAL LEVEL

If schools are to provide an effective and safe environment for students, they require access to comprehensive interventions supported by empirical data. As reviewed in chapter 14, SWPBS) is a three-tier model designed to assist schools in implementing and sustaining comprehensive, evidence-based interventions by increasing the school's capacity to facilitate and maintain systems change. In other words, SWPBS involves changing the behavior of adults (i.e., teachers, administrators, staff) to affect the behavior of students. The three tiers of SWPBS (depicted in Fig. 28.1) are primary or universal systems that focus on the entire school, targeted interventions or targeted systems that focus on students who do

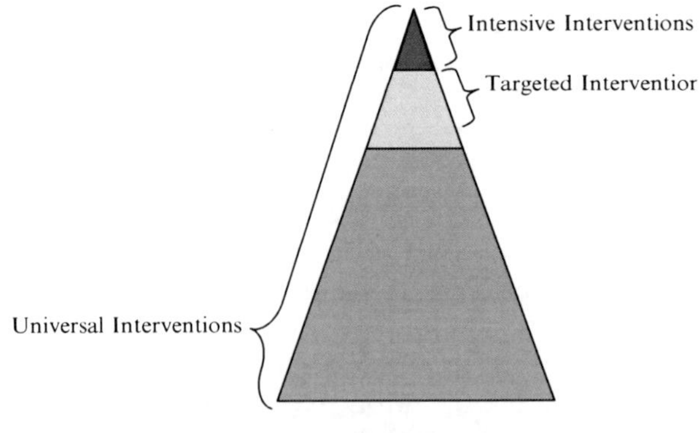


**Fig. 28.1.** Continuum of interventions in schoolwide positive behavior support (SWPBS). The universal intervention is in place for all students and will meet the needs of about 80% of students in a school. Targeted interventions are designed for students at risk for more challenging behavior, and intensive interventions meet the needs of the 1–5% of students in a school who require individualized supports. Intensive positive behavior support (IPBS) focuses on targeted and intensive interventions.

not respond to schoolwide systems, and intensive interventions that focus on students for whom no schoolwide or small-group interventions have been successful.

Universal interventions are designed for all students and are implemented across settings. The goal of universal interventions is to encourage prosocial behavior and decrease the likelihood that problem behavior will develop. Two important foci of universal interventions are (a) preventing the occurrence of problem behavior by encouraging prosocial behavior through the use of proactive, evidence-based strategies, and (b) evaluating data frequently to guide decision making.

In SWPBS, universal interventions are developed and implementation is planned by a team of individuals who are representative of the school. Thus, an elementary school team might consist of an administrator, grade-level representative, a special educator, a parent, and a staff member. In high school, instead of grade-level representation, the emphasis might be on representing various academic departments, such as the history department and the science department. At the universal level, schools develop schoolwide expectations that describe broad goals for students (e.g., be responsible, be a good citizen) and then use the expectations to develop clear rules for specific settings. Rules specify the behaviors to be exhibited; for example, being responsible in the hallway might mean walking on the right side, whereas in the cafeteria it is defined as cleaning up after yourself. Rather than assume that students (and faculty) know the rules and know what is appropriate in a given setting, a key part of the universal level of SWPBS is explicitly teaching the expectations and the rules in specific settings. Rules are taught when school begins and then retaught several times throughout the year.

In addition to developing and teaching expectations and rules, schools implement a system for acknowledging prosocial behavior, usually through the use of tangible (e.g., colored pencils, stickers, parking space for a week in high schools) and intangible (e.g., lunch with the principal, extra library time, help with announcements, participating in "jeans day") acknowledgments that can be earned via a cumulative point system (technically known as a *token economy*). Using such a system, teachers and staff would provide students with coupons (e.g., Bronco Bucks) for following rules. For example, if a teacher sees a student helping a peer pick up books that were dropped, the teacher might give the student a reward coupon for "being responsible." Students save coupons and trade them at prespecified times for school rewards.

Schools also work to ensure that a system exists for responding to problem behavior in an effective manner. This often involves a continuum of consequences for "minor" infractions such as talking out of turn, gum chewing, or yelling and "major" problems such as fighting and weapons violations.

After schools begin SWPBS, data are analyzed frequently—at least monthly—using a variety of data sources, such as patterns of office discipline referrals (ODRs), student and staff surveys, and direct observations to modify the program as needed and to evaluate effects. For example, patterns of ODRs could be assessed to identify the most common locations and times of day for office referrals, students who receive frequent referrals, and staff who frequently generate referrals. Any of this information could be used to fine-tune the schoolwide intervention. For example, if an increasing number of referrals are generated in the cafeteria during seventh-grade lunch, the schoolwide team would work to identify the reason for the increase—perhaps lunch staff are not using the acknowledgment system or perhaps rules have not been taught in some time—and then implement an intervention to address the problem (e.g., helping staff use the acknowledgment system, reteaching rules). If specific students are receiving frequent referrals, the team would work to ensure that these students received an intervention to increase prosocial behavior and decrease problem behavior. Finally, if a specific teacher was generating a great deal of referrals, the team might meet with the teacher to determine what, if any, additional supports were needed. For example, a teacher might need additional assistance with classroom management.

To summarize, the universal component of SWPBS consists of developing and explicitly teaching prosocial behavior, acknowledging students for exhibiting appropriate behavior, instituting a continuum of consequences for inappropriate behavior, and using data to guide decision making. (For more detailed information on SWPBS, including an implementation guide, see Colvin, 2007, or C. M. Anderson & Kincaid, 2005). Schools implementing only the universal level of SWPBS with fidelity can expect approximately 80% of their students to be successful; the remaining 20% will require additional supports (Horner, Sugai, Todd, & Lewis-Palmer, 2005). IPBS provides the framework within which schools develop, implement, and evaluate interventions for these students.

## INTENSIVE POSITIVE BEHAVIOR SUPPORT: AN OVERVIEW

Intensive positive behavior support is a framework for supporting students with behavior challenges. The goals of IPBS are to (a) provide support for students exhibiting behavior problems, (b) organize intervention development and implementation, (c) provide a system for useful yet efficient ongoing data collection to guide decision making within schools, and (d) ensure school teams have the resources and skills needed to implement IPBS with fidelity and in a manner that can be sustained over time. In IPBS, students are supported by school teams that receive ongoing assistance from the district. We next describe implementation of IPBS within a school and conclude by discussing the critical role of school districts in initiating and sustaining IPBS.

### IPBS in a School

In a school implementing IPBS, a team is formed to provide support to students who have not responded to universal interventions. The school IPBS team is responsible for (a) identifying students who might benefit from support, (b) ensuring that appropriate interventions are implemented, and (c) monitoring outcomes over time.

### *IPBS Team Membership*

In most schools, the IPBS team consists of three to five individuals with the following skills and functions: (a) allocation of resources, (b) coordination of targeted interventions, (c) skills in function-based support, and (d) familiarity with regular and special education in the school. First, at least one team member should have the capacity to allocate resources in a school for training or supporting students in different ways; this person typically is an administrator. Next, a team member is identified to coordinate targeted interventions; this is discussed in depth in the interventions section. Similarly, one member is appointed the coordinator of function-based supports. This person must be familiar with and able to implement a functional behavior assessment (FBA) and lead a team in development of a behavior support plan. This process is described in detail in the interventions section. Finally, both regular and special education should be represented on the team so that IPBS is not viewed as exclusive to only general education or special education students.

### *Identifying Students Who May Benefit From Intervention*

A crucial role the IPBS team fulfills in a school is ensuring that students who are not responding to universal interventions receive support. Schools use a variety of strategies to identify students who may benefit from more support, including a request-for-assistance process, monitoring ODRs, and conducting periodic formative evaluations. In IPBS, efforts are made to ensure that a streamlined process is used consistently, and that multiple methods are in place to reach students with varying levels of need.

One way that students needing more assistance can be identified is by instituting a formal request-for-assistance process. Such a process ensures that teachers and staff have a means to document that a problem exists and to access a formalized mechanism for receiving assistance from the school to solve the problem. Beyond providing basic identifying information (e.g., student's name and grade, the name of the referring teacher, and the date of the request), a request-for-assistance form should allow the teacher to provide information about the problem. First, the form should include space for *describing the problem.* Rather than just asking the teacher to explain the problem and leaving a blank space to fill in, the form might instead contain a checklist of common concerns (e.g., disruptive, talking out of turn, out of seat, hitting others, using inappropriate language, verbal defiance, not following instructions) and then a blank space that the teacher can use to identify behaviors not listed. Checklists take less time to complete and leave less room for interpretation (for example, "insubordinate" likely means very different things to different individuals, whereas "talking out of turn" provides a clearer picture of the problem). Once the problem is identified, space should be allotted for *specifying when the problem occurs.* This might be accomplished most easily by providing a table within which teachers can identify the time of day and routines a student engages in (e.g., biology, physical education, English, recess). Next, using a rating scale, teachers could indicate how often the problem happens in that routine—from almost never to almost always. Teachers also should have space to indicate whether a student's *academic skills* might have an impact on their behavior and provide a place to give their best guess of *why the behavior is occurring*. A checklist of possible functions (described in detail in the interventions section) might be useful at this point to help teachers isolate possible contributing factors. For example, teachers could be asked to indicate whether they think the behavior is occurring to get attention (and whose attention—the teacher's, other students'), to avoid attention from others, to avoid completing specific tasks or activities, or to gain access to specific tasks or activities. Finally, teachers should describe *what they have tried thus far* and how successful any intervention attempts have been. Collectively, this information is useful for the IPBS team in determining what interventions might be implemented initially; for example, if the teacher reports that a student frequently is disruptive when asked to read aloud but also that the student is getting poor grades on reading tests, then an initial intervention might focus on small-group reading instruction because it is likely that a skill deficit makes reading aloud aversive, and addressing the skill deficit may result in the problem simply disappearing. After developing a request-for-assistance form, the IPBS team should define the process for responding to requests. One or more individuals should be identified to receive requests and to make initial determinations about the intervention to be implemented (process described in depth in a separate section). In addition, the team should determine how referring teachers will be informed of steps to be taken (e.g., beginning a targeted intervention, initiating an FBA); this should occur within 3 days of receipt of the request for assistance.

Request-for-assistance forms are useful for identifying students for whom teachers have concerns. Sometimes, however, a student may be struggling but may not come to the attention of a teacher. This could occur, for example, if a student exhibits relatively minor behaviors across a variety of settings; thus, any one teacher may not necessarily view the situation as problematic, but across settings a problem clearly exists. For such students, it is possible that the problem may grow worse over time, and because a goal of IPBS is to intervene early whenever possible, it is important to reach students who are exhibiting only mild behavioral challenges in addition to those students with significant need. To make it more likely that such students receive assistance, school teams implementing IPBS evaluate patterns of ODRs at least monthly. This initial screening often is done by the SWPBS team in a school. Teams identify students who receive more than some predetermined number of referrals in a given time period, for example, three referrals in a month or six in a year. For students who receive more than the predetermined number of office referrals, the following should be addressed: (a) what behaviors are occurring and in which settings; (b) whether the student currently is receiving an intervention and whether the intervention is having an effect; and (c) whether a new intervention or a modification of the previous intervention is needed. If a student already is receiving an intervention, then the IPBS team is monitoring that student's progress and modifying the intervention as needed. If a student is continuing to receive frequent office referrals even after an intervention has been in place for several weeks, this would suggest that the intervention should be modified. Alternatively, if a student is not receiving any intervention, the IPBS team becomes responsible for meeting with the student's teachers to gather more information and identify an appropriate intervention to support the student in becoming more successful in school.

Although most students needing assistance likely will be identified via the request-for-assistance process and frequent reviews of ODRs, some students needing intervention may not be identified in these ways. For example, students emitting a low level of problem behavior not sufficient for office referrals, but across multiple settings, or students who exhibit behaviors that are often labeled as anxiety or depression, may not come to the attention of adults as their behavior challenges do not disrupt the situation or the learning of others. For these students, periodic formative evaluation might be useful. This practice is becoming increasingly common for academics (e.g., schoolwide screening for foundational reading skills), and we apply the same logic to social behavior. When using schoolwide screening, teams first determine the type of screen to be used and next identify the frequency and timing of screening. Finally, they determine how data will be used to guide decision making. Teams can consider both published screening tools with established psychometric properties, such as one or more gates of the Systematic Screening for Behavior Disorders (SSBD; Walker & Severson, 1992), or they might develop their own form. When choosing a screening tool, teams look for a measure that (a) provides information about students emitting a variety of potentially problematic behaviors, including both disruptive behaviors and behaviors often labeled as "internalizing," such as withdrawn behavior; (b) can be completed by teachers in an efficient manner (i.e., takes less than 5 min to complete); and (c) provides a rubric for identifying students who need immediate intervention, should be monitored but might not require intervention, and do not need intervention. Once a screening measure is chosen, teams determine how often they will conduct screenings and when screenings will occur; a reasonable schedule might be three times per year, in the late fall, early spring, and late spring. The goal of the last screen is to determine whether there are some students who would benefit from an intervention started immediately—even though school is almost out—and then continued into the next academic year or students who simply need to be monitored when school starts again in the fall.

### *Implementing Interventions*

The range of behavior problems presented by students varies widely from very intense, serious behaviors such as frequent fights, self-injury, or suicidal behavior to mildly disruptive problems such as talking out of turn or failing to complete homework. To respond to problems effectively but also in as efficient a manner as possible, schools need a continuum of evidence-based interventions such that less-intensive interventions are readily available as are more comprehensive interventions that require more effort to implement. Schools using IPBS develop a continuum of intervention options to (a) allocate resources appropriately and (b) better meet the needs of all students. The intervention continuum frequently used in IPBS is depicted in Fig. 28.1. As is shown in Fig. 28.1, the majority of students in a school (approximately 80%) will benefit from a universal intervention (i.e., SWPBS) that is in place across settings for all students. For students who are not successful with this level of support, targeted interventions are implemented. Only about 15% of students in a school will require this level of support. Finally, intensive supports are in place for the 1–5% of students who require individualized supports to be successful.

### *Targeted Interventions*

IPBS encompasses both targeted and intensive interventions. For students who require more support beyond a universal intervention such as SWPBS, the first level of intervention implemented is often a targeted intervention such as Check-In Check-Out (CICO; Crone, Horner, & Hawken, 2003). Targeted interventions are designed to be implemented in a similar manner across students; thus, they often are referred to as group interventions. A large number of interventions exist that are akin to targeted interventions in that they are implemented similarly across students; examples include social skills groups, lunch buddies (students have lunch with preidentified members of the faculty or eat with a specific peer), and the like. What separates targeted interventions from these other interventions is that targeted interventions (a) are implemented only for students for whom data suggest the intervention will be effective and (b) data are collected and analyzed to monitor outcomes. When a school chooses to invest in targeted interventions, the SWPBS team picks one to three targeted interventions that have been shown to be effective for problems that commonly occur in their school. If, for example, many students in a school are mildly disruptive during classes, an appropriate intervention might be CICO (described next). Although it may be tempting to implement many interventions, school staff will struggle to use data to identify students likely to benefit and to monitor outcomes if more than about three interventions are implemented, at least initially. In fact, school teams would be wise to begin with one intervention and to add additional interventions only after they are able to systematically implement the initial intervention with fidelity for at least 2 years. After choosing the targeted interventions, the school team gathers all needed resources and trains teachers and staff in the intervention. In addition, they determine how data will be used to (a) identify students who might benefit from the intervention and (b) evaluate student progress once the intervention is implemented. Commonly used evidence-based targeted interventions include CICO or Behavior Education Program (Crone et al., 2003) and Check and Connect (A. R. Anderson, Christenson, Sinclair, & Lehr, 2004). In many schools, implementing IPBS, CICO is chosen as the targeted intervention implemented first for students who are not succeeding under universal interventions.

CICO is an intervention for students exhibiting inappropriate behavior (e.g., off task, talking out of turn, out of seat) across multiple classes. It is implemented across the entire day by all teachers interacting with the student. Briefly, when students arrive at school each day, they check in with the targeted interventions coordinator, who goes over expectations for the day and gives students their daily point card. As students go throughout the day, they give the point card to their teachers. At scheduled intervals (e.g., three times per day), the student approaches his or her teacher and gets feedback on the extent to which expectations have been met thus far. The teacher rates the student's behavior on identified expectations (e.g., be prepared, be respectful) on a scale of 1 ("struggled today") to 3 ("great job") and provides a brief verbal explanation of the rating. At the end of the day, students check out with the coordinator, who summarizes points, provides encouragement (e.g., "Fantastic job today," or "Looks like you had some trouble today, but I bet you can do better tomorrow") and gives each student a home report that students take home and have signed. Students can trade points periodically for a variety of tangible and nontangible rewards. Preliminary research suggests that CICO is effective for reducing problem behavior, increasing academic skills, and enhancing prosocial skills (Filter et al., 2007; Hawken, 2006; Hawken & Horner, 2003; Todd, Kauffman, Meyer, & Filter et al 2007, Horner, in press), and that it can be adapted easily to meet the needs of a variety of students, including students whose problem behavior is maintained by peer attention or by task avoidance (March & Horner, 2002). Because it is easily adaptable and requires few resources and little time to implement, CICO is a good choice for targeted interventions for many schools.

Regardless of the targeted intervention chosen, data should be used to determine whether the intervention is likely to be effective; someone with a basic understanding of function-based support (e.g., the targeted interventions coordinator) should make this determination based on available data. If ODRs were used to identify a student, then the source of the referrals might be used to determine the intervention. For example, if problems occur only in one class (e.g., during history), then a schoolwide targeted intervention such as CICO would not be appropriate. If a request for assistance was the source of information, the request-for-assistance form should provide basic information about the student's behavior and possible motivations; this information can be used to determine whether a targeted intervention is appropriate.

### *Individualized Functional Behavior Assessment and Behavior Support Planning*

For students who do not respond to the targeted intervention or who need an individualized intervention, an FBA is conducted. The goal of any FBA is to develop hypotheses about why a problem behavior is occurring instead of more appropriate, prosocial behavior. For example, an FBA could be used to determine why a seventh grader writes swear words and draws inappropriate pictures on class assignments instead of completing the work appropriately. In the continuum used in IPBS, there are three levels of function-based support and FBA: efficient, formal, and expert driven (see Fig. 28.2). Although the different levels of FBA and resulting support plans differ in intensity, all share common features.

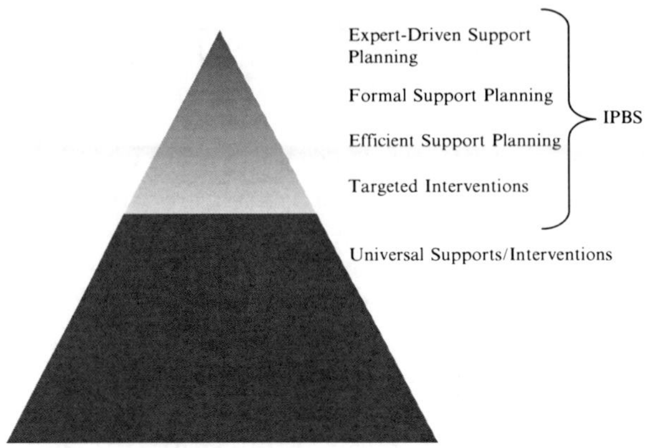


**Fig. 28.2.** Continuum of interventions in intensive positive behavior support (IPBS). School-wide positive behavior support (SWPBS) is the universal intervention in place for all students. IPBS focuses on secondary interventions and includes as well three progressively more intensive levels of functional behavior assessment and behavior support plans.

*Key Features of a Functional Behavior Assessment and Behavior Support Plans.* As described in some depth in chapter 19, all types of FBA share a common purpose—identifying why a problem behavior is occurring—and thus share key features. First, all methods of FBA provide an operational definition of the problem. An *operational definition* of behavior specifies what it is that a person does or says that is problematic; the focus is on observable events rather than constructs. For example, rather then targeting "conduct problems," an operational definition labels what specifically occurs. This is important because different people might consider such constructs to be very different things. One person might consider behaviors such as hitting others, pushing, shoving, name calling, and destroying objects to be conduct problems, whereas another person might focus on behaviors such as eye rolling or sighing when asked to do something. The issue here is not that any one individual is correct or incorrect about what is a conduct problem, but rather that, instead of leaving the behaviors of concern up for conjecture, it is more efficient to come to agreement on precisely what it is that the student does—or does not do—that is of concern.

Once the problem is defined, the next step in any FBA is to assess the context in which the behavior occurs. This involves first determining events that often precede the problem behavior—settings or specific activities that make it very likely that the behavior will occur. The goal here is to look for patterns evident over time, not simply one-time occurrences. When considering events that often proceed the behavior (called *antecedents*), it is useful to first identify routines during which the problem is most likely to occur. Common routines during school hours include different academic situations, such as group work or independent work, unstructured situations with a high student-to-teacher ratio (e.g., cafeteria during lunch), and times when the student is relatively alone (e.g., in the hallway with a bathroom pass). Once routines are identified, the task becomes identifying specific events that seem to trigger or set off the problem behavior. Examples of these events include (but certainly are not limited to) requests to complete specific tasks such as math worksheets, a favorite teacher interacting with another student, or having to wait in line to engage in a preferred activity. Once antecedents are identified, the focus shifts to what typically happens after the problem behavior. As with antecedents, the focus is on what actually is observed, not what we think might be occurring inside the person. For example, it would not be useful to speculate that, when asked to do math assignments (the antecedent), a student wanders around the room (the problem behavior) because he or she is bored—speculation about unobservable events does not help us identify possible interventions—in this case, we still need to ask why the student is bored. Possible reasons might be that the work is too difficult or too easy, or that the student's best friend is sitting across the room. When identifying consequences using an FBA, the focus is on what a person might be getting or avoiding when the behavior occurs. For example, wandering around the room could be maintained by teacher attention or by peer attention—perhaps others talk to the student. Alternatively, by wandering around the room the student might successfully be avoiding working on the math problems.

When antecedents and consequences have been identified for the problem behavior, the information is compiled into a hypothesis statement. As is depicted here, a hypothesis statement describes events that trigger a problem behavior and the consequences for the behavior. In addition, the hypothesis statement identifies the likely function of the behavior. The function is what reinforces the behavior and is a general description of what the student gets or avoids. Consider the case of a third-grade student, Carolina. Although Carolina does very well in math class—she earns As and high Bs on all tests—she often wanders around the room instead of doing work. An FBA was conducted (methods of conducting an FBA are described next), and the following hypothesis statement was generated:

> When asked to complete math worksheets, Carolina wanders around the room because when she does so, Ms. Lisa directs her back to her seat and works with her on the math problems. Thus, Carolina's wandering is maintained by teacher attention.

In this hypothesis statement, both the triggers (requests to complete math worksheets) and consequences (attention from Ms. Lisa) are identified. In addition, the function of the behavior is labeled—obtaining adult attention. Because events going on in the environment are identified, the hypothesis statement can be used to develop an intervention to decrease wandering around the room and increase academic work.

Regardless of the type of FBA completed, the hypothesis statement is used to develop an intervention or behavior support plan. Interventions based on an FBA typically are multicomponent and include one or more of the following types of strategies: antecedent interventions, skill-building strategies, and consequence manipulations.

Antecedent interventions are designed to prevent the problem from occurring in the first place; they involve altering those events that often trigger the problem. Continuing with the example of Carolina, if wandering often occurs after Carolina has been working for about 5 min on a math worksheet, her teacher might go to her after about 1–2 min and interact with her for a few minutes. Because Carolina's wandering is maintained by teacher attention, she no longer will need to wander around the room—she already has the attention.

Skill-building strategies are an important part of most behavior support plans. Here, the focus is on identifying a more appropriate behavior that will take the place of the problem behavior. A substantive body of research now demonstrates that changing consequences—as described next—such that problem behavior no longer pays off while alternative, more acceptable behaviors are rewarded is an effective intervention approach (e.g., Durand, 1999; Durand & Carr, 1985, 1992; Kurtz et al., 2003; Peterson et al., 2005; Wacker et al., 2005). When identifying appropriate behavior, a useful strategy was delineated by O'Neill et al (1997): identifying an "alternative behavior" and, if needed, a "replacement behavior." The alternative behavior is what the student should be doing, in Carolina's case, working quietly on her math worksheets. For some students, this is all that is needed, and the focus of the intervention is on using antecedent and consequence manipulations to increase this behavior. In many cases, however, it is unlikely that the student will simply begin to exhibit the alternative behavior; when this is the case, a replacement behavior is identified. The replacement behavior is like "baby steps" toward the alternative behavior; it is a response that is more acceptable than the problem behavior but not what we ultimately want the student to do. Replacement behaviors are necessary when a student does not currently have the skills to exhibit the alternative response or when the problem behavior occurs with high frequency or intensity, and it may not be possible to completely eliminate the payoff or reinforcement for that behavior. In Carolina's case, given that she only works for a few minutes, it may be unreasonable to expect her simply to begin working quietly for the entire 35-min class period (the alternative behavior). Thus, a replacement behavior might be raising her hand to ask her teacher to come over. Although not ideal, we want her to work quietly for the class period; hand raising certainly is more acceptable than wandering around the room. Over time, Carolina can be expected to work for longer periods before teacher attention is delivered. For example, when she raises her hand, her teacher could say, "I will be there when you have finished two problems on your own" (gradually increasing the expectation for independent work).

Consequence manipulations are the third intervention component often used in behavior support plans. The goal is to minimize the payoff for problem behavior and maximize the reward for exhibiting the alternative or replacement behavior. The first step is to make sure that appropriate behavior is acknowledged. One easy way to do this is to provide the consequence that maintains problem behavior—for Carolina, teacher attention. Thus, when Carolina raises her hand or works quietly, her teacher frequently provides attention. Sometimes, it is not feasible to provide the same consequence for appropriate behavior. For example, if a student's running down the hallway is maintained by attention from other adults and from peers, it might be difficult to provide this attention consistently and in such magnitude (running down the hallway banging doors probably evokes a high-intensity response from adults). In such cases, it is important to work with the student to identify other items or activities the student might earn. For example, the student might earn weekly lunches with a favorite adult or access to other preferred activities, such as an extra 10 min in the library. Although providing reinforcement for engaging in appropriate behavior is important, it is equally important to minimize the likelihood that problem behavior will be reinforced. The goal here is to make it less likely the behavior will pay off. Sometimes, it is possible simply to arrange the environment such that the rewarding consequence no longer is forthcoming. For example, if a student often whines to get teacher attention, whining could simply be ignored. Most often, however, this is not feasible as either the student will try other inappropriate behavior or the rewarding consequence simply cannot be removed. In the case of Carolina, for example, if her teacher ignored wandering around the room, it might stop eventually, but in the meantime Carolina would be disrupting others who are trying to work and would not be working herself. It also is possible that Carolina would begin to exhibit behavior that was more difficult to ignore, such as humming to herself or banging objects while walking around the room—all in an attempt to gain teacher attention. In such cases, a better alternative is to minimize the consequence—such that what follows problem behavior is less rewarding than what follows appropriate behavior. Using this guideline, Carolina's teacher spends longer amounts of time with Carolina when she has been working quietly or when she raises her hand. In contrast, should Carolina wander around the room, her teacher simply says, "Carolina, please return to your seat" and avoids further engagement.

*Levels of Functional Behavior Assessment in IPBS* A variety of types of FBA exist, ranging from indirect methods that are relatively quick to conduct, to experimental methods that require extensive time and expertise. In IPBS, the type of FBA (and the complexity of the resulting support plan) is matched to the severity of the problem. Levels of FBA and support planning include efficient, formal, and comprehensive (see Fig. 28.2).

The first level of function-based support is called efficient behavior support planning. At this level, someone who has some expertise in FBA and building support plans (i.e., has taken course work in function-based supports and has conducted a number of FBAs and support plans with supervision) and is a member of the IPBS team meets with the student's teachers and completes a functional assessment interview such as the Functional Assessment Checklist for Teachers and Staff (FACTS; March et al., 2000). At this level of support planning, the interview should be able to be completed in no more than 30 min. The interview is used to operationally define the behavior and to gather information about events that reliably precede and follow the behavior (antecedents and consequences). Using this information, they develop a hypothesis statement identifying the problem behavior and events that precede and follow the behavior. Once a hypothesis statement is developed, the person who conducted the FBA interview schedules a time to observe the student. The observation should occur during a time the hypothesized antecedent or trigger (e.g., requests to read out loud) is very likely to occur. During the observation, which typically is 10 to 15 min in length, the observer records any instances of the problem behavior and records as well events that precede the problem and follow the problem behavior. The goal of the observation is to gather enough information to confirm or disconfirm the hypothesis statement.

After completion of the functional assessment interview and brief observation, a student support team meeting is scheduled with the person who conducted the FBA, the student's teachers, other key individuals such as the speech therapist (if the student has a speech deficit) or the instructional specialist (if the student is struggling academically), and the administrator who participates in the IPBS team meetings to develop a behavior support plan. As a group, the team considers the hypothesis statement and then develops an intervention consisting of one or more of the intervention components described—antecedent manipulation, skill building, and consequence manipulation.

If schools are to sustain implementation of function-based support over time, they need to build capacity such that at least three individuals in a school have the knowledge, skills, and resources to conduct efficient behavior support planning. The rationale for this is two-fold. First if an individual with this level of expertise accepts a position elsewhere, the school is not suddenly unable to complete behavior support planning. Second, if multiple individuals are available with this capacity, then implementation can occur in a more timely manner—the process will not be dependent on one individual finding time to complete the assessment; instead, the IPBS team can identify a person who is available for any given student. In most schools, one individual has time allotted to complete the majority of FBAs; the additional individuals provide support on an as-needed basis.

If a student is not making adequate progress after development of an initial behavior support plan, then the second level, formal behavior support planning (see Fig. 28.2), is conducted. At this point, someone with more advanced expertise assists in conducting the FBA. Typically, staff within a school do not have this level of expertise; instead, the person who conducts the FBA works in the district, for example, as a school psychologist. It is important, however, that the person is familiar with the school and has time allocated to providing this service. At this level, the FBA consists not only of the interview and brief observation used in efficient support planning but also of multiple, systematic direct observations. The goal of direct observations is to gather more information by observing when the behavior does and does not occur. To conduct direct observations, an FBA interview is completed (as during efficient behavior support planning). Next, a series of observations is scheduled during those times when problem behavior often occurs, for example, during math class. Observations occur for predetermined amounts of time (e.g., 20 min), and several observations are scheduled. The observer records any instances of problem behavior as well as what specifically preceded and followed the behavior (i.e., antecedents and consequences). Sometimes, the observer may structure the situation to make it more or less likely that the problem behavior occurs, for example, by asking a teacher to present or withdraw the trigger. Continuing with the example of Carolina, the observer might ask her teacher to assign math worksheets and to ask the class to work on them quietly for 15 min while the teacher works at her desk. Then, the observer might ask the teacher to make the same assignment but to provide frequent attention to Carolina. If problem behavior happens most often when Carolina is working independently but only rarely when her teacher is interacting with her, this would be further evidence that problem behavior is maintained by teacher attention. In this process, observations are conducted until the observer has a clear idea about the function of the behavior—what events trigger the problem behavior and what maintains it. After completion of the interview and direct observations (formal FBA), the person who conducted the FBA meets with the support team (teachers, involved specialists, administrator) to develop an intervention. In some cases, new information gleaned from observations might result in only a slight modification of the existing intervention. In other cases, an entirely new intervention might be developed.

The final level of FBA and behavior support planning is comprehensive behavior support planning (see Fig. 28.2). As described in the next section on IPBS in the district, school districts invest in one or more individuals skilled at all levels of FBA and at developing comprehensive behavior support plans. The number of individuals hired in the district depends on the size of the district, but typically at least one person is available for every 10–12 schools. Comprehensive support planning requires the involvement of this district-level individual and involves first conducting a comprehensive FBA that builds on other, previously completed methods of FBA (interviews, observations) and includes other, more systematic methods as well. For example, experimental methods of FBA might be used (e.g., Carr, Sidener, Sidener, & Cummings, 2005; Conroy, Asmus, Sellers, & Ladwig, 2005; English & Anderson, 2006; Wilder, Chen, Atwell, Pritchard, & Weinstein, 2006) in which hypothesized antecedent and consequent stimuli are manipulated repeatedly and in a systematic manner. Alternatively, a structural functional analysis might be conducted (e.g., English & Anderson; Stichter & Conroy, 2005) in which only hypothesized antecedents are altered. At this level, other types of assessment might be included as well. For example, person-centered planning (Flannery et al., 2000; Holburn & Vietz, 2002; Smull & Harrison, 1991) might be used to assist family members, the student, and school staff to better understand one another and to identify common goals. During comprehensive support planning, community agencies often are involved as support typically is needed, not only in the school, but also in the student's home and community. For example, if a student is seeing a therapist in the community, that person might be invited to participate to better align school-based interventions with the goals of therapy.

*Continuum of Interventions: A Caveat.* Schools implementing IPBS build a continuum of interventions to better meet the needs of all students while matching resources to the severity of the problem. Thus, most students needing additional support do not receive comprehensive support planning but rather begin a targeted intervention. This is because targeted interventions—while not requiring intensive resources—should meet the needs of most students who require additional supports. Importantly, not all students will be successful on a targeted intervention, and indeed a small percentage of those students will require comprehensive support planning in which time-extensive assessments are needed and community partners are involved actively in support planning and implementation.

Although the continuum of interventions indicates a progression from targeted interventions to comprehensive support planning, it is not the case that all students progress from one level to the next. There may be some students whose behavior is so severe that a team may decide to go straight from universal intervention to the top level of expert-driven function-based support. This might occur, for example, if a student suddenly begins to engage in suicidal behavior or if a student engages in high rates of self-injury or aggression. As described next, all students on a targeted or function-based intervention are followed by the school IPBS team, which meets twice per month. Thus, if an intervention is not resulting in improvements in the student's behavior, the data will be reviewed, and modifications will be implemented within a maximum of 2 weeks.

### *Monitoring Interventions Over Time*

Although developing and implementing interventions is an important responsibility, it is not enough simply to identify students who may benefit and then put an intervention into place. Equally important is monitoring effects of the intervention over time and making modifications as needed. To this end, when an intervention is developed, the team (the IPBS team for targeted interventions and the team that completed the FBA and behavior support plan for intensive support) develops data-based decision-making rules. First, the team identifies progress goals for determining whether an intervention is successful. The team might begin by determining the goal for intervention and a time frame for reaching that goal. For example, the team might target a 95% reduction in absenteeism (relative to the frequency of absenteeism in the month prior to intervention) and state that the intervention will be considered a success if this goal is reached within 16 weeks. Next, the team identifies "intermittent goals," targets to be reached prior to the end date; the rationale is to provide markers to evaluate the likelihood of intervention success. For example, the team might determine that, within 3 weeks absenteeism will be reduced by 15–20%.

The team also must determine what action will be taken based on data. Decisions to be reached include when an intervention decision should be revisited (e.g., if an intermittent goal is not reached) and when an intervention should be removed completely or have components of the intervention removed. Although some interventions may be left in place indefinitely, in most cases interventions require extended effort on the part of one or more adults or the student, and thus the team may develop criteria for removing the intervention and specify how the intervention will be removed: Will the intervention be discontinued all at once, or will components be removed sequentially? Some interventions require an intensive effort early on; in such cases, teams will set a criterion for fading the intervention. For example, intervention for a student who presents very disruptive behavior when asked to complete tasks orally might initially consist of simply providing reinforcement if the student remains in his or her seat during class without making any requests. Of course, this is not likely to result in significant learning, so once the student has achieved an intermittent goal (e.g., remained in class for the entire period for 7 days), the team might alter the intervention such that when the student enters the room the teacher tells the student that he or she will be asked to answer a question and what the question will be (and the answer if necessary). If the student continues to meet intermittent goals, the intervention might be further modified; for example, the teacher might tell the student that a question will be asked, but not what the question is. This fading continues over time—based entirely on student progress.

*Use of Data for Ongoing Progress Monitoring.* As described, data are used to identify students who may benefit from additional support through such mechanisms as requests for assistance, patterns of ODRs, and periodic schoolwide screening. Once a student is receiving an intervention, the IPBS team monitors student progress at team meetings, which typically occur twice per month.

The type of data monitored for students varies depending on the level and intensity of the intervention. For students on a targeted intervention such as CICO, the primary data source might be the proportion of points earned in a given day. For students receiving function-based support, teachers could provide a daily or weekly summary of the student's behavior, or an IPBS team member might conduct periodic direct observations. Regardless of the data source, collected data should be objective and quantifiable. Thus, instead of providing a written description of the student's progress, the teacher might complete a daily rating scale with numbers on the scale linked to descriptions relevant to the student. For example, a 1–5 scale for one student might have 1 equivalent to "never occurred" and 5 equivalent to "occurred five or more times," whereas the 1–5 scale for another student goes from 1, "occurred one to three times" to 5, "occurred 50 times or more." Such scales provide more useful information than do verbal descriptions alone because ratings can be graphed and progress monitored over time. At the IPBS meeting, the people responsible for coordinating interventions—the targeted interventions coordinator and the function-based support coordinator—provide a brief report summarizing the progress of all students receiving intervention and then focus the discussion on students who are not meeting predetermined goals. For example, the function-based support coordinator might tell the team, "There are four students receiving function-based support. Three students met their goals this month, but I am concerned about Jared." The coordinator might then show Jared's data to the group, and state the problem, and possibly offer a solution. If the team cannot come to a solution within a couple of minutes, the team develops a plan (e.g., the coordinator will schedule a second efficient FBA meeting with the teacher to review the competing behavior pathway and behavior support plan and to identify why the intervention is not succeeding). For such a system to be successful, it is critical that the coordinators summarize data for all students prior to the meeting and bring the summary with them to the IPBS meeting—this allows the team to focus on students in need of further assistance rather than spending excessive time discussing students who are doing well.

*Monitoring Effects of IPBS Across the School.* Because IPBS is embedded within SWPBS and implemented across a school, it is important that schools measure outcomes not only for specific students receiving an intervention but also across the school. Specific outcomes to be measured are determined by the school leadership team and are related to the goals of the IPBS system within the school. First, as most schools monitor office referral patterns, data could be examined to see if an overall reduction in the number of students receiving repeated office referrals is noted after implementation of the IPBS system. Schools also might evaluate whether the number of students referred to special education due to behavior concerns is affected by implementation of IPBS; one would hope that such a system would result in fewer referrals to restrictive placements as students are more likely to be identified before problems become severe and evidence-based interventions are implemented with greater regularity. Schools might measure as well the capacity to implement targeted and intensive interventions within the school: How many individuals have needed skills and are readily available to assist? Capacity to implement targeted and intensive interventions also could be evaluated. For example, schools could compare the number of students receiving targeted interventions prior to implementation of IPBS to the number of students currently receiving targeted interventions. Schools also might evaluate the quality of their FBAs and behavior support plans; What proportion of FBAs now contains key features of good assessments? Finally, schools might conduct global assessments of satisfaction (social validity)—the extent to which teachers, students, and parents view the IPBS system as important within the school.

## IPBS in the District

One important lesson learned in implementation of SWPBS is that implementation is unlikely to be sustained over time if there is not active involvement and support from the district (Sugai & Horner, 2001; Sugai, Horner, & McIntosh, in press). IPBS requires that (a) districts provide ongoing support to schools that are implementing IPBS, (b) districts establish and maintain the link between IPBS and SWPBS across the district, and (c) outcomes are monitored districtwide.

### *Ongoing Support for Schools Implementing IPBS*

Schools implementing IPBS will require support from the district not only to begin implementation but also to sustain implementation over time. District support entails allocation of resources within schools as well as allocation of resources at the district administration level.

*Support in a School.* Within a school, resources must be allocated such that the school is able to hire and maintain positions for at least three individuals who can conduct efficient behavior support planning. The expertise to conduct an efficient FBA and build the resulting behavior support plan cannot be acquired by attending one or more workshops on FBA; what is required is one or more graduate-level courses on FBA that include opportunities for "hands-on" practice. In our experience, individuals must be familiar with the conceptual underpinnings of FBA and support plan development (e.g., basic principles of behavior analysis such as an understanding of how events in the environment can evoke and maintain behavior) and also fluent with using efficient as well as more complex formal and comprehensive methods of FBA. In addition, skills in translating information from an FBA into a behavior support plan must be developed—both from that conceptual understanding as well as through supervised experience doing so in schools. As noted, although schools should invest in at least three positions with time allocated to conducting efficient FBAs and leading behavior support plan development, in most schools so doing will not be the full-time job of these three individuals, and they will not conduct equal amounts of efficient support planning; more often, one person has the time allocation to conduct the majority of efficient FBAs and behavior support plans, and the other individuals fill in only occasionally as needed. Districts must work with schools to ensure that time is allotted not only for completion of the FBA and for building a behavior support plan, but also for implementing and sustaining the IPBS process. This will involve protected time for regular IPBS meetings (usually every other week) and time for key staff to prepare for meetings, which will include updating graphs regularly and summarizing information for team meetings. Time will be needed as well for training of staff in interventions.

*District Support.* Beyond ensuring that schools have resources internally (staff with expertise and time available to implement IPBS), IPBS requires an investment districtwide. This investment includes (a) providing a coordinator who can conduct comprehensive FBAs and build behavior support plans, (b) ensuring that schools have access to people who can conduct formal FBAs, and (c) providing ongoing training to school teams.

First, districts need to invest in one or more—depending on the size of the district—positions filled by someone who is responsible for conducting comprehensive behavior support planning and guiding ongoing training and technical assistance for school IPBS teams. District coordinators need to have advanced skills in FBA and behavior support planning—this typically involves at least a master's degree but often a doctoral degree with a concentration in applied behavior analysis and behavior support planning. Beyond the skills needed for conducting a variety of methods of FBAs, this person must have expertise in leading teams in the development of comprehensive behavior support plans and must be skilled in working with families and linking schools and community agencies. Often, it is useful for the district coordinator to have proficiency in working with students with significant needs, including students diagnosed with autism spectrum disorders, students diagnosed with mental health needs or developmental disabilities, such as depression, attention deficit-hyperactivity disorder, anxiety disorders, and mental retardation. Finally, district coordinators must be facile in the field of education; they must understand educational policy and laws and must be familiar with how the district in which they are employed functions.

Between efficient FBA, which school staff conduct, and comprehensive FBA, conducted by a district-level specialist, lies formal FBA. As described in some depth, formal FBAs include indirect assessment as well as fairly structured observations—the time and level of expertise involved, most often, are beyond the capacity of any one school. School districts implementing IPBS have defined completing formal FBAs, and working with teams to build the resulting support plans, as a role played by school professionals. Often, this responsibility is met by school psychologists or school counselors. The title of the individuals meeting this need is not important and differs from district to district; what is important is that the district has defined completion of formal FBA as a role to be fulfilled across all schools and has invested in hiring individuals with those skills and ensuring that all schools can access this support in a timely manner.

District support involves not only conducting formal and comprehensive FBAs but also investing in periodic retraining (particularly as team membership changes over time) and ongoing training and technical assistance. A good model for a school district might be to hold monthly IPBS district meetings that are attended by one or more representatives from each school IPBS team. At these meetings, about 40% of the time could be spent on technical assistance and team problem solving. For example, a team member might ask for advice regarding the behavior of a student on CICO, but someone who does not require comprehensive behavior support planning. The remainder of the meeting—and the majority of the time—should be spent on providing ongoing training. Topics to be covered should be determined by the district coordinator and IPBS school teams but could include strategies for conducting formative schoolwide evaluations, fading CICO, involving parents, and working with students who are on the autism spectrum.

### *Maintaining the Link With Schoolwide Positive Behavior Support*

The IPBS framework is designed to be implemented within the context of SWPBS. It is important that the link between IPBS and SWPBS be sustained over time; this is an important role of the school district. If the link is not explicit between the two, then it is likely that students who require additional support will be viewed as not part of the SWPBS system. This could result in some teachers (e.g., special educators) feeling that the school is not invested in them or their students. In addition, if the two are not linked closely, then data will not be used as efficiently for decision making. For example, school IPBS teams might not access office referral data as a means for determining students who might benefit from additional support. Finally, ensuring SWPBS and IPBS are linked closely will make it easier to provide a continuum of interventions to meet the needs of all students.

Maintaining the link between SWPBS and IPBS requires active planning. First, the district IPBS coordinators should attend district SWPBS meetings. At these meetings, the IPBS coordinator will be able to learn about new initiatives or interventions that might affect IPBS and will be able to share data, as discussed next, from IPBS across the district. In many school districts, training for new staff as well as "booster" training for returning staff are coordinated through the SWPBS team, and thus the IPBS coordinator will work with this team to schedule training in IPBS as well as in schoolwide supports. In addition, at least one person in each school should attend both SWPBS and IPBS meetings to facilitate information sharing. Finally, districtwide in-services should periodically highlight the link between SWPBS and IPBS and provide an opportunity for school members to ask questions and provide input about how IPBS fits within the SWPBS model.

### *Monitoring Outcomes Across the District*

If IPBS is to be maintained over time, outcomes across schools implementing IPBS must be examined. Further, these data must be shared with key stakeholders, including parents, community members, the board of education, and the district positive behavior support team. One obvious source of data to be examined is ODR patterns within and across schools. In addition, the proportion of students referred out of district due to behavioral concerns should be assessed regularly, as should the frequency with which students who have been placed outside of the district are able to successfully transition back into their home schools. Districts might also assess their capacity to provide support within the district: How often must they rely on outside assistance to conduct assessments and develop interventions? Social validity could be evaluated via surveys of administrators, teachers, staff, and parents. In addition, districts might calculate litigation brought against the district by parents or other consumers: Does implementation of a comprehensive system result in any reductions in due process hearings? Districtwide cost/benefit evaluations could be conducted by examining as well the cost of district- and schoolwide training and the number of individuals needed to coordinate IPBS across the district and within individual schools. These costs could be weighed against the benefits—tangible and intangible—of the system.

## SUMMARY AND CONCLUSIONS

Successful schools prepare students to succeed in our society. This involves imparting both academic and social skills. Because students present with an array of skill sets and abilities, schools must provide a continuum of supports to help students succeed. Such a continuum will be necessary for academic as well as social behavioral interventions. In the current chapter, a system for meeting the social behavioral needs of students within a school was presented, IPBS. IPBS, which is implemented within the framework of SWPBS, is a model for helping school districts and schools develop systems to support evidence-based practices.

IPBS builds off years of research documenting that effective interventions for students exhibiting challenging behavior must be function based—matched to the reasons why challenging behavior is occurring. Function-based interventions thus involve altering events outside the person, things that happen before a problem occurs (to make it less likely that challenging behavior will occur) and things that occur after behavior (to make it less likely that challenging behavior will occur again and more likely that prosocial behavior occurs). A vast body of research supports the use of function-based supports for relatively minor problems such as off-task behavior as well as for very intensive problem behavior such as self-injury and aggression. IPBS builds on this research by providing a framework within which interventions can be implemented in an effective and sustainable manner. To this end, IPBS consists of systems within schools that are supported by district systems. Within schools, a team-based approach is used for data-based decision making that includes identifying students who will benefit from additional support, determining which interventions are likely to be successful, and evaluating outcomes. School teams implement a continuum of interventions to match the intensity of the assessment and intervention to the severity of a student's difficulties and to better meet the needs of all students. School districts ensure schools have the capacity to support all students by providing expertise in function-based supports (within and across schools) and by providing opportunities for ongoing training. In addition, districts provide schools with systems for efficient and effective use of data to guide decision making.

## REFERENCES


Anderson, A. R., Christenson, S. L., Sinclair, M. F., & Lehr, C. A. (2004). Check and Connect: The importance of relationships for promoting engagement with school. *Journal of School Psychology, 42*, 95–113.

Anderson, C. M., & Kincaid, D. (2005). Applying behavior analysis to school violence and discipline problems: Schoolwide positive behavior support. *Behavior Analyst, 28*, 49–63.

Carr, J. E., Sidener, T. M., Sidener, D. W., & Cummings, A. R. (2005). Functional analysis and habit-reversal treatment of tics. *Behavioral Interventions, 20*, 185–202.

Colvin, G. (2007). *Seven steps for developing a proactive schoolwide discipline plan.* Thousand Oaks, CA: Corwin Press.

Conroy, M. A., Asmus, J. M., Sellers, J. A., & Ladwig, C. N. (2005). The use of an antecedent-based intervention to decrease stereotypic behavior in a general education classroom: A case study. *Focus on Autism and Other Developmental Disabilities ,20*, 223–230.

Crone, D. A., Horner, R. H., & Hawken, L. S. (2003). *Responding to problem behavior in schools: The Behavior Education Program.* New York: Guilford.

Durand, V. M. (1999). Functional communication training using assistive devices: Recruiting natural communities of reinforcement. *Journal of Applied Behavior Analysis, 32*, 247–267.

Durand, V. M., & Carr, E. G. (1985). Self-injurious behavior: Motivating conditions and guidelines for treatment. *School Psychology Review, 14*, 171–176.

Durand, V. M., & Carr, E. G. (1992). An analysis of maintenance following functional communication training. *Journal of Applied Behavior Analysis, 25*, 777–794.

English, C. L., & Anderson, C. M. (2006). Evaluation of the treatment utility of the analog functional analysis and the structured descriptive assessment. *Journal of Positive Behavior Interventions, 8*, 212–229.

Filter, K., Benedict, E., McKenna, M., Horner, R. H., Todd, A., & Watson, J. (in press). Check In/Check Out: A post-hoc evaluation of an efficient, secondary-level targeted intervention for reducing problem behaviors in schools. *Education and Treatment of Children.*

Filter, K. J.; McKenna, M. K.; Benedict, E. A.; Horner, R. H.; Todd, A.W.; Watson, J. (2007). Check In/Check Out: A post-hoc Evaluation of an efficient, secondary-level targeted intervention for reducing problem behaviors in schools. *Education and Treatment of Children*, 30, 69–94.

Flannery, K. B., Newton, S., Horner, R. H., Slovic, R., Blumberg, R., & Ard, W. I. (2000). The impact of person centered planning on the content and organization of individual supports. *Career Development of Exceptional Individuals, 23*, 123–137.

Hawken, L. S. (2006). School psychologists as leaders in the implementation of a targeted intervention: The Behavior Education Program (BEP). *School Psychology Quarterly, 21*, 91–111.

Hawken, L. S., & Horner, R. H. (2003). Evaluation of a targeted intervention within a schoolwide system of behavior support. *Journal of Behavioral Education, 12*, 225–240.

Holburn, S., & Vietz, P. M. (Eds.). (2002). *Person-centered planning: Research, practice, and future directions.* Baltimore: Brookes.

Horner, R., Sugai, G., Todd, A., & Lewis-Palmer, T. (2005). Schoolwide positive behavior support. In L. M. Bambara & L. Kern (Eds.), *Individualized supports for students with problem behaviors: designing positive behavior plans* (pp. 359–390). New York: Guilford Press.

Kurtz, P. F., Chin, M. D., Huete, J. M., Tarbox, R. S. F., O'Connor, J. T., Paclawskyj, T. R., et al. (2003). Functional analysis and treatment of self-injurious behavior in young children: A summary of 30 cases. *Journal of Applied Behavior Analysis, 36*, 205–219.

March, R. E. & Horner, R. H. (2002). Feasibility of contributions of functional behavioral assessment in schools. *Journal of Emotional and Behavioral Disorders, 10*, 158–171.

March, R. E., Horner, R. H., Lewis-Palmer, T., Brown, Crone, D., Todd, A., et al. (2000). *Functional Assessment Checklist for Teachers and Staff (FACTS).* Eugene, OR: Author.

O'Neill, R. E., Horner, R. H., Albin, R. W., Sprague, J. R., Storey, K., & Newton, J. S. (1997). *Functional assessment and program development for problem behavior : A practical handbook* (2nd ed.). Pacific Grove, CA: Brooks/Cole.

Peterson, S. M., Caniglia, C., Royster, A. J., Macfarlane, E., Plowman, K., Baird, S. J., et al. (2005). Blending functional communication training and choice making to improve task engagement and decrease problem behavior. *Educational Psychology, 25*, 257–274.

Public Agenda. (2004). *Teaching interrupted: Do discipline policies in today's public schools foster the common good?* Retrieved from http://www.publicagenda.org

Skiba, R., & Raush, M. K. (2006). School disciplinary systems: Alternatives to suspension and expulsion. In G. G. Bear & K. M. Minke (Eds.), *Children's needs III: Development, prevention, and intervention.* Bethesda, MD: National Association of School Psychologists, pp 631–650.

Skiba, R., Ritter, S., Simmons, A., Peterson, R. L., & Miller, C. (2006). The safe and responsive schools project: A school reform model for implementing best practices in violence prevention. In S. R. Jimerson & M. Furlong (Eds.), *Handbook of school violence and school safety: From research to practice.* Bethesda, MD: National Association of School Psychologists.

Smull, M., & Harrison, S. (1991). *Supporting people with severe reputations in the community—A handbook for trainers.* Baltimore: Department of Pediatrics.

Stichter, J. P., & Conroy, M. A. (2005). Using structural analysis in natural settings: A responsive functional assessment strategy. *Journal of Behavioral Education, 14*, 19–34.

Sugai, G., & Horner, R. H. (2001). Features of effective behavior support at the district level. *Beyond Behavior, 11*, 16–10.

Sugai, G., Horner, R. H., & McIntosh, K. (in press). Best practices in developing a broad scale system of school-wide positive behavior support. In A. Thomas & J. Grimes (Eds.), *Best practices in school psychology* (5th ed.).

Sulzer-Azaroff, B., & Mayer, G. R. (1994). *Achieving educational excellence: Behavior analysis for achieving classroom and schoolwide behavior change*. San Marcos, CA: Western Image.

Todd, A., Kauffman, A., Meyer, G., & Horner, R. (in press). Evaluation of a targeted group intervention in elementary students: The Check In Check Out program. *Journal of Positive Behavior Interventions*.

Wacker, D. P., Berg, W. K., Harding, J. W., Barretto, A., Rankin, B., & Ganzer, J. (2005). Treatment effectiveness, stimulus generalization, and acceptability to parents of functional communication training. *Educational Psychology, 25*, 233–256.

Walker, H. M., & Severson, H. H. (1992). *Systematic Screen for Behavior Disorders* (2nd ed.). Longmont, Co: Sopris West.

Wilder, D. A., Chen, L., Atwell, J., Pritchard, J., & Weinstein, P. (2006). Brief functional analysis and treatment of tantrums associated with transitions in preschool children. *Journal of Applied Behavior Analysis, 39*, 103–107.

# 29

# Response to Intervention and Positive Behavior Support

**WAYNE SAILOR, JENNIFER DOOLITTLE, RENÉE BRADLEY, and LOU DANIELSON**

Special education in the United States emerged as an extension of the medical model that experienced explosive growth in the decades of the fifties and sixties (cf. Sailor & Guess, 1980). The construct of *disability* (or "handicap" as it was largely described in that period) placed the locus of educational impairment squarely on the individual. Failure to progress educationally or developmentally along expected age norms was considered the result of a quasi-disease state. This was during the testing movement, when the fields of psychiatry and psychology were growing rapidly. Thus, when a pattern of deficit in educational progress was determined, the student would be referred for diagnostic testing. Analysis of test results would then determine a likely category of disability, and a prescription would result, often in the form of referral to special education, usually to a special class formed to address the needs of students in that category.

More recently, a different logic model has begun to emerge for providing services and supports to students who fail to progress as expected in the general curriculum, one that stands in contrast to the extant medical model and challenges it as having the potential to be a better service model. *Response to intervention* (RTI) is the prevalent term for this logic model, and as of this writing, it is gaining rapid momentum across all aspects of preschool through 12-grade education in America.

**WAYNE SAILOR** • University of Kansas
**JENNIFER DOOLITTLE** • US Office of Special Education Programs
**RENÉE BRADLEY** • US Office of Special Education Programs
**LOU DANIELSON** • US Office of Special Education Programs

In this chapter, we trace the origins of RTI as a community mental health prevention model and examine its emergence into service eligibility determination in special education. We consider some current definitions of RTI and focus on the alignment of RTI and positive behavior support (PBS) as two sides of the same coin (or "pyramid," in this case, as we shall describe): academics and behavior. We examine the emerging model with particular attention to its linkages with PBS research. We describe emerging policy frameworks that are helping to drive the RTI agenda and consider some of the cultural issues in its application. Finally, we examine emerging personnel preparation requirements concerning implementation of RTI and briefly examine current trends in RTI research and practice in education.

## HISTORY OF RESPONSE TO INTERVENTION

First, through describing an exemplar student going through the two different procedures for identification, we consider the contrast evident in the two logic models. Susie is a first grader who is falling behind her classmates in reading. Her teacher notices that she regularly gets stuck on the early passages and seems to be getting increasingly frustrated. Furthermore, her teacher notes that Susie has been scribbling on and otherwise defacing her reader, in some cases tearing out pages. Individual attention does not seem to be resulting in improvement, and the teacher finds herself calling on Susie less and less frequently to avoid slowing the progress of the other students. Finally, Susie is referred to the school psychologist for psychological and psychoeducational testing to see if there is a disability present that would explain Susie's lack of progress. On the basis of the psychologists' interpretation of IQ test data and other test results, Susie is diagnosed as having a learning disability (LD) and is assigned, through the individual educational plan (IEP) process, to a "resource room," a special class for students with LD.

Now, consider an RTI logic model applied to Susie's case that exemplifies just one possible model of RTI implementation. In the fall, Susie would be screened with all of the other students. If Susie falls below a certain criterion, she will begin receiving extra services beyond the general curriculum/regular class instruction that she will continue to receive. This extra assistance will likely be provided in a small-group setting, with other students who have similar academic needs as determined by the screening and teacher report. Susie's progress will be monitored, perhaps once a week, with a curriculum-based measure (CBM), and if she is not progressing as quickly or as greatly as has been set as a benchmark/criterion after a reasonable amount of time, a specialized team will examine her progress-monitoring results, screening results, and teacher observations and will make recommendations for intensive and/or individualized instruction to be delivered for a specified intensity, duration, and frequency. If Susie does not meet the criterion set for her at that point, the 60-day timeline begins for special education evaluation.

First, we notice that emphasis is placed on identifying and describing Susie's specific problem rather than on quickly arriving at a disability diagnosis. The emphasis shifts to identification of a specific learning disability (SLD) by matching a particular intervention to address the deficit on the basis of scientific evidence for procedural efficacy. As much attention will be paid to the instructional process as to Susie's particular characteristics. Once a reasonable hypothesis was advanced to explain Susie's deficit in reading, a specific set of interventions was applied, and frequent progress-monitoring efforts occurred to determine if the deficit was being resolved. The interventions were managed entirely on the basis of results from progress monitoring.

RTI, in this example, does not present a challenge to the concept of SLD. There is an impressive body of evidence for the existence of disorders of learning and cognition that are intrinsic to the individual and that interact negatively under the conditions imposed by the teaching/learning process (Caffrey & Fuchs, 2007; McDermott, Goldberg, Watkins, Stanley, & Glutting, 2006; Sideridis, Morgan, Botsas, Padeliadu, & Fuchs, 2006). RTI does, however, put the spotlight on specific measured performance under conditions of learning rather than on the individual as a member of a quasi-medical disability category.

A similar base of evidentiary knowledge concerning children who experience emotional or behavioral disorders (emotional disturbance [ED]: in the special education categorical framework) is not yet available to efficiently and effectively identify and intervene with students before problem behaviors take root as life-persistent disabilities (Feil, Severson, & Walker, 1998; Walker et al., 1990). In fact, fewer than one in four students with significant emotional and behavioral disorders that impede their academic achievement are receiving minimally adequate treatment (U.S. Surgeon General, 2001). An argument may be made that children with emotional or behavioral disorders (EBDs), similar to those who experience LD, would benefit from an RTI model, a model that will link the early identification of such students to specific interventions.

RTI is rooted in three major beliefs that resulted from a 1982 National Research Council study by Heller, Holtzman, and Messick. Heller and colleagues proposed three criteria that need to be met before a student's special education classification can be deemed valid: (a) mainstream education that is generally effective; (b) special education that improves student outcomes; and (c) valid use of assessments for identification (Fuchs, Fuchs, & Compton, 2004). In other words, students must be receiving adequate base instruction in general education classes to determine that their problems stem from a disability and not from inadequate instruction. Further, if the services students receive in special education do not have significantly improved outcomes for student achievement, the determination that the student is eligible for services is meaningless (Heller et al., 1982). Last, if the measurement tools used to determine qualification for special education are assessing something other than the students' actual performance (e.g., tests that have linguistic, cultural, or disability bias), the special education classification itself is worth little.

Simeonsson (1994), in reviewing the literature on risk prevention and resilience factors that may shield some children from the adverse effects of dysfunctional community circumstances, reported a publication by Caplan and Grunebaum (1967) that called for a community health risk prevention model for children. Caplan and Grunebaum's model was grounded in three tiers: primary, secondary, and tertiary. This three-tier conception of risk prevention became prevalent in the literature of school psychology and is reflected at present in the writings of Adelman and Taylor (1996, 2006) in application to academic deficits in school and in the writings of George Sugai and Rob Horner (2002) in application to behavioral deficits that function to impede the learning process.

This three-tier RTI model is described in detail in the section that follows, but for now consider that Tier 1 (primary prevention) is characterized by application of evidence-based curricula and instructional practices applied to all students (classroom, grade level, or school). Furthermore, all students are screened during the earliest possible grade levels, using reliable and valid screening tools that are minimally time consuming and invasive, to determine risk probabilities in all students. Frequent progress monitoring then occurs with all students, with particular attention paid to those students for whom specific deficits in one or more content areas or in social/behavioral development may occur on the basis of screening evidence.

Students who begin to exhibit clear deficits in Tier 1 may advance to a Tier 2 (secondary-) level prevention status. In this tier, specific analyses are applied to isolate probable sources of deficits (academic or behavioral), and targeted interventions are applied, usually to small groups of students with similar needs. Continued failure to respond to Tier 2 efforts as determined from progress monitoring may result in a decision to advance to the third tier of prevention (tertiary). Tier 3 interventions are often highly individualized, with services and supports being provided through federal, categorical resources such as special education, Title I, English language learners, and the like. Students whose measured deficits are pervasive across all academic areas or whose behavioral manifestations are extreme may be determined to require Tier 3 interventions early on.

The origins of the RTI logic model in education can be traced to an early article by Stanley Deno (Deno & Mirkin, 1977), who was engaged during this period in the development of CBMs (Deno, 1985). CBMs have now become a principal source of progress-monitoring data for RTI applications in the schools (National Association of State Directors of Special Education [NASDSE], 2006). At about the same time, CBMs were being developed, J. R. Bergan published a behavioral consultation model that evolved into an RTI system for addressing emerging behavior problems that placed children at risk for school failure (Bergan & Kratochwill, 1990; NASDSE, 2006).

Bergan's conceptualization has emerged as an overarching RTI framework with application to behavior and to academics when the school is the focus. Deno and his colleagues in special education, meanwhile, moved to the development of specific sets of decision rules to guide multitier interventions for identified skill deficits (i.e., Fuchs, Deno, & Mirkin, 1984; Ysseldyke, 2005; Ysseldyke et al., 1983). NASDSE summarized the RTI logic model stemming from Bergan and Kratochwill (1990) as a "problem-solving" system and the Deno model as a "standard protocol" model, focused primarily on reading interventions (e.g., Reschly, Tilly, & Grimes, 1998; S. Vaughn & Linan-Thompson, 2003). NASDSE recently compared these emergent RTI models as "largely parallel problem-solving and standard protocol treatments described in the current literature (e.g., Reschly, Tilly, & Grimes, 1998; S. Vaughn & Linan-Thompson, 2003)" (NASDSE, 2006, p. 7). As pointed out in the NASDSE article, the sequence of operational steps in the two models are very nearly identical (p. 8). For the purposes of this writing, the conceptual distinction between problem-solving RTI and standard protocol RTI is not expanded. What is important to know is that standard protocol RTI can be viewed as a particular application of the broader-based concept of problem-solving RTI, in this case focused on eligibility determination for services under the LD category specified in the Individuals With Disability Education Improvement Act of 2004 (IDEIA, 2004).

In addition to these contributions, the contributions of the LD eligibility determination research group to the knowledge base on RTI has been enormous. Using rigorous scientific methods, Doug and Lynn Fuchs, Don Compton, Dan Reschly, and others, many at Vanderbilt University, have developed a strong foundation for RTI school-based practices and have opened the door for expansion of the approach to those with EBDs and other children who are likely to benefit from a systematic prevention model to guide their services and support (see particularly McMasters, Fuchs, Fuchs, & Compton, 2005; Fuchs, Compton, et al., 2005; Reschly, 2005).

The overarching stimulus for this burst of scientific activity in special education over the last decade unquestionably arose from the focus placed by the Bush administration on accountability in educational innovation. The IDEIA definition of LD prior to 2004 required a discrepancy between ability (measured by an IQ test) and achievement (measured by a norm-referenced achievement test) that most children with LD do not display until they are well into elementary school, thus implying a wait-to-fail approach to identification and preventing students from receiving early intervention services (Ortiz & Yates, 2002). The National Longitudinal Transition Study II (NLTS2) data demonstrate that on average students with LD were first identified at age 6.5 and began receiving services 1.5 years later (Blackorby et al., 2003). Considering that 7–25% of preschool-aged children demonstrate significant problem behavior (Webster-Stratton, 1997) and that 50% of these children will continue to have significant problems (Campbell, 1995), the number of years that many students go without services appears even more wasteful.

The Bush administration position on service eligibility under IDEIA began to be articulated in earnest with the publication of the Fordham Foundation Progressive Policy Institute position paper on LD (Lyon et al., 2001). This essentially threw down the gauntlet on the use of intelligence testing and psychoeducational evaluation to establish eligibility for services under the LD provisions of IDEIA. This controversial publication was followed with a series of hearings by the President's Commission on Excellence in Special Education and subsequent publication of the findings of the commission (2002).

The next turning point for the LD eligibility determination issue came in the form of the U.S. Office of Special Education Programs (OSEP) LD Initiative, which gathered current research and encouraged multiple stakeholders to work together to solve systemic problems. The multiyear process of the initiative was intended to bring researchers, members of professional organizations, advocacy groups, and parents to a consensus regarding the identification and classification of children with LD (Bradley & Danielson, 2004). The initiative ensured that diverse stakeholders had a voice in the creation of goals for the field of LD and that they achieved a consensus in developing the questions that would help the field to progress.

The LD Initiative, subsequent to various roundtables, symposiums, conferences, and the production of "state-of-the-field" papers, concluded that RTI models are a viable method to identify and support students who have SLDs. RTI is based on the primary concept that quality instruction must be in place for *all* before it can be said that *some* have a disability. In the RTI model, a student who does not respond to instruction that is evidence based and has been effective with the majority of students of that age receives increasingly more intensive and individualized support. Special education is viewed as an option only when evidence-based interventions are not working in the general education environment, not as the first means of supporting a student when he or she is not achieving on par with his or her peers. RTI is a method of prevention and intervention combined. Most students will benefit from evidence-based instruction and will not need more intensive treatment; however, in the RTI continuum of academic supports, intensive treatment is available for those children who need it.

### *Screening for Education and Supports*

Screening for early identification, a requirement of RTI, is presently used infrequently in schools for both LDs and EBDs (Conroy & Brown, 2004). When screening for EBD does occur, it is generally highly subjective and is completed only by the teacher, usually in the form of a questionnaire, checklist, or rating scale (Merrell, 2001). Screening and later identification are made problematic by the federal definition of ED, which is the only definition in IDEIA that applies to students with emotional or behavioral disorders. Stakeholders have long complained that the definition of LD is subjective, is not based on findings from the field, and does not lead to appropriate identification or to appropriate interventions. Similarly, the federal definition of ED has gained the ire of many EBD stakeholders due to its ambiguous and contradictory language within the definition. The definition was not amended in the 2004 Individuals With Disabilities Education Improvement Act; thus, it remains:

> (i) The term means a condition exhibiting one or more of the following characteristics over a long period of time and to a marked degree that adversely affects a child's educational performance: (A) An inability to learn that cannot be explained by intellectual, sensory, or health factors; (B) An inability to build or maintain satisfactory interpersonal relationships with peers and teachers; (C) Inappropriate types of behavior or feelings under normal circumstances; (D) A general pervasive mood of unhappiness or depression; (E) A tendency to develop physical symptoms or fears associated with personal or school problems.

(ii) The term includes schizophrenia. The term does not apply to children who are socially maladjusted, unless it is determined that they have an emotional disturbance. (Individuals with Disabilities Education Improvement Act, 1998, p. II-46)

This definition has been described as ambiguous, contradictory, and difficult to operationalize (Forness & Kavale, 2000). The vague terms used in the definition cannot easily be used for measurement purposes, as in "long period of time" and "marked degree." One of the main complaints regarding the definition of ED is that its statement concerning social maladjustment is illogical. It would seem that a student with "interpersonal relationship problems" might also be considered to be socially maladjusted. With a definition that people feel to be subjective and contradictory, it is not surprising that educators and school psychologists have difficulty adjoining the definition to specific screening and identification measures, which in turn makes the delivery of appropriate services to the appropriate students more difficult.

## DEFINITIONS AND APPLICATIONS OF RESPONSE TO INTERVENTION

Brown-Chidsey and Steege (2005), in providing an introduction to RTI for general educators stated: "Essentially RtI is an objective examination of the cause-effect relationship(s) between academic or behavioral *intervention* and the student's *response* to the intervention." (p. 2). And, "In essence, RtI integrates high quality teaching and assessment methods in a systematic way so that students who are not successful when presented with one set of instructional methods can be given the chance to succeed with the use of other practices" (p. 3).

The primary goal of using an RTI model is to catch students early, before they have a chance to fail. The most popular representation of RTI is the three-tier model we briefly described (e.g., S. Vaughn, 2003), which layers instruction over time in response to students' increasing needs. Tier 1 is the instruction available to all students and is sufficient for most students to achieve grade-level standards *if* (a) a research-based core curriculum is used, (b) students are tested for achievement as compared to specific benchmarks (i.e., progress monitoring) at least three times a year and, preferably, more frequently to determine instructional needs, and (c) ongoing professional development is provided for the classroom educators. If Tier 1 is not sufficient (as demonstrated by unmet benchmarks and other validation that a problem exists), students will receive Tier 2 interventions in the form of supplemental small-group instruction that enhances and supports the Tier 1 instruction. A student who is still not meeting grade-level expectations will receive Tier 3 intervention in the form of intensive and strategic supplemental instruction.

The logic of using three tiers has resulted from research and discussion over many years, but in current practice is somewhat arbitrary. Gradations of intensity and types of intervention and support can exist within the tiers. It is likely that RTI applications as they gain momentum across general and special education will approximate a continuum of intensity rather than a precise three-tier model of delivery as presently framed. Lucille Eber and her colleagues, for example, use a multitier approach to adjust support intensity in operationalizing the identification of students moving from Tier 2 supports to Tier 3 supports (see chapter 27, this volume).

Bradley, Danielson, and Doolittle (2007), in summarizing the 1997 OSEP Learning Disabilities Initiative and its subsequent impact provided the following operational definition of RTI:

> RtI has been conceptualized as a multitier prevention model that has at least three tiers. The first tier, referred to as primary intervention, consists of high-quality, research-based instruction in the general education setting, universal screening to identify at-risk students, and progress monitoring to detect those students who might not be responding to this primary intervention as expected. Within this multitier framework, decisions regarding movement from one level to the next are based on the quality of student responses to research-based interventions. Subsequent levels differ in intensity (i.e., duration, frequency, and time) of the research-based interventions being delivered, the size of the student groupings, and the skill level of the service provider. These secondary interventions typically are 8 to 12 weeks in duration. Findings from the National Research Center on Learning Disabilities (NRCLD) indicate that the length of time needed for the second tier can vary, but generally it should not exceed 8 weeks. Eight weeks is an adequate amount of time to realize the response or lack of response of a student to a well-matched evidence-based intervention. (Cortiella, 2006)

The final—or tertiary—level consists of individualized and intensive interventions and services, which might or might not be similar to traditional special education services. In most models, the lack of appropriate response to the more intensive and more individualized research-based instruction at this tertiary tier results in referral for a full and individual evaluation under IDEIA.

Of interest in this definition is the suggestion of deferral of full evaluation for special education pending results of tertiary-level interventions. While flexibility remains in the special education referral process, the OSEP definition should have the net effect of reducing referrals for special education for students on the basis of suspicion of disability in the absence of academic performance monitoring under a series of increasingly intense levels of support and teaching interventions with the aim of addressing the specific performance problem difficulty.

NASDSE (2006) summarized six areas of ongoing research that have enhanced the emergence of RTI in practice since 1985: (a) scientifically based curricula and instruction; (b) other related multitier models; (c) progress monitoring and formative evaluation; (d) analysis and remediation of academic achievement problems; (e) functional behavioral assessment (FBA); and (f) standard treatment protocol interventions. First, the emergence of scientifically based curricula and instruction has provided grounding for the data-based decision processes underlying RTI. Recent innovations in curriculum and instruction related to RTI include the emergence of early screening measures (i.e., Davis, Lindo, & Compton, 2007); assessment protocols to identify young at-risk readers (i.e., Fuchs et al., 2007); innovations in providing Tier 2 interventions in reading (S. Vaughn & Roberts, 2007); and recent developments in the emergence of Tier 3 applications to academic problems (i.e., Stecker, 2007).

The second area of RTI-supportive intervention identified by NASDSE is the emergence of other related multitier models. These include school-based mental health (i.e., Adelman & Taylor, 2006) and PBS (i.e., Sugai, Horner, & Gresham, 2002).

The third area is the growing evidence-based framework of progress monitoring and formative evaluation. The growing number of psychometrically validated CBMs, for example, lends extensive support for determination of need, progress monitoring, and application of decision rules regarding intervention (NASDSE, 2006). These include, for example, Dynamic Indicators of Basic Early Literary Skills (DIBELS) and AIMSweb. Currently, OSEP's National Center on Student Progress Monitoring (NCSPM) provides technical assistance to a broad audience on the topics of CBMs and choosing progress-monitoring tools. For an extensive summary of published CBMs currently in use, see the work of Brown-Chidsey and Steege (2005, particularly chapter 7).

Fourth, NASDSE cites some of the recent innovations in the analysis and remediation of academic achievement problems. Foremost among considerations in adopting published interventions is the issue of treatment fidelity (i.e., Sanetti & Kratochwill, 2005), a reliable and valid estimate of the consistency and integrity of the intervention with different populations and under varying conditions.

The fifth and sixth emergent areas of support for RTI identified by NASDSE are FBA (see particularly chapters 13 and 18, this volume) for applications of RTI to behavioral problems that may impede a student's ability to respond to the teaching-learning process (i.e., Chandler & Dahlquist, 2002) and the emergence of standard treatment protocol interventions. These protocols are designed for small-group interventions with children who have been determined to need additional support to progress at grade level in a particular curricular area. These interventions may, for example, include content strategy enhancements (i.e., Lenz & Deshler, 2004). For summaries of research on standard protocols, NASDSE (2006) directs readers to the work of Fuchs et al. (2004); Torgesen et al. (2001); Speece, Pericola-Case, and Eddy-Molloy (2003); S. Vaughn, Linan-Thompson, and Hickman (2003); and Vellutino et al. (1996).

Finally, a comprehensive review of the rapidly emerging evidence base for RTI practices in special education applications are available through the continuing (as of this writing) special sections on responsiveness to intervention that began with a special issue dedicated to RTI of the *Journal of Learning Disabilities* (2006) (Vol. 39, no. 2), followed by another informative special issue on RTI published by *Teaching Exceptional Children* (2007).

## RESPONSE TO INTERVENTION AND POSITIVE BEHAVIOR SUPPORT

As we mentioned at the outset, PBS is exactly the same logical model as RTI for academics, only it is applied to behavior rather than academics. Just as in RTI for academics, PBS begins with universal screening, which in this case is for risk of the emergence of internalizing or externalizing behavior that may impede learning. Systemic instruction and reinforcement for meeting school behavioral expectations occurs in the first tier. Frequent assessment of students determined to be at risk follows a data-based decision-making logic in which a team of professionals empowered to make decisions regarding school resources may make a decision to use a secondary-tier intervention for a smaller group of students. Examples of secondary-tier interventions include classroom management procedures and interventions on playgrounds, hallways, cafeteria, school bus, and other nonclassroom areas. Identification of functions of risk behavior through FBA may begin in Tier 2 and proceed to the full development of a behavior intervention plan (BIP) at the level of Tier 3. Because these sets of procedures under RTI for academics and PBS follow an identical logic model, conceptually and practically integrating the two processes as shown in Fig. 29.1 is more efficient and logical. Conceptualized as a split pyramid, academic screening, monitoring, and interventions at all three tiers are shown on the left side with corresponding behavioral processes on the right. Although expected percentages of engagement of each of the three tiers can vary from school to school, it is reasonable to expect about 80–85% of students in a "typical" school to respond to high-quality teaching methods (both RTI and PBS) at Level 1; about 10–15% of students to require Level 2 interventions; and about 5–10% of students to require Level 3, or tertiary, interventions.

### *Universal Screening*

On the behavioral side, teacher referral is generally the first step in the screening process, although some schools are using other measures to ensure adequate screening. Common screening tools include the School Social Behavior Scale (SSBS; Merrell, 1993), the Social Skills Rating System (Gresham & Elliott, 1990), and the Revised Behavior Problem Checklist (Quay & Peterson, 1987). The SSBS is a behavior-rating instrument for teachers and other school personnel and is used to evaluate the social and antisocial behavior of children in Grades K through 12. The Revised Behavior Problem Checklist is another teacher-rating scale that has been widely used with school-aged children. In addition to these tools, Systematic Screening for Behavior Disorders (SSBD; Walker et al., 1990) provides a psychometrically sound assessment for possible emotional and behavioral problems.

The SSBD is a prime candidate for a schoolwide screening tool because it takes approximately 1 hr to complete the primary screening for all students in the class (Walker & Severson, 1992). SSBD is a multigated screening device performed twice a year. At the first gate, the teacher selects 10

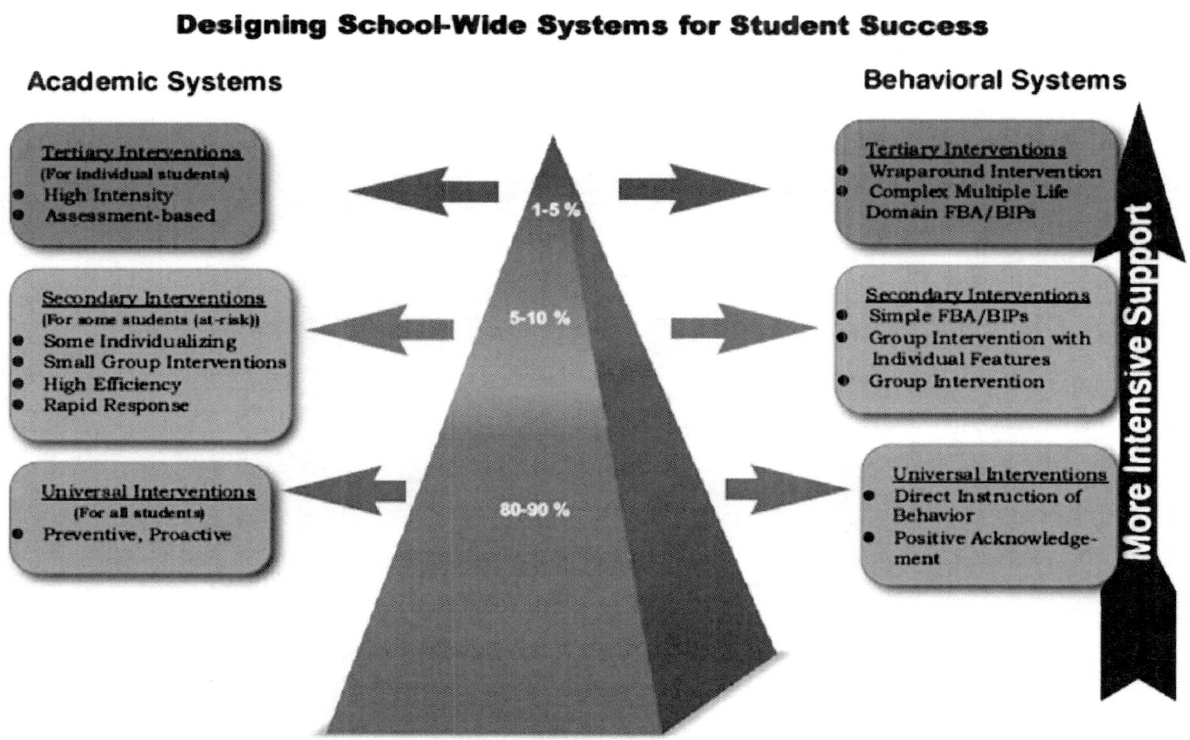


**Fig. 29.1.** The integrated response-to-intervention (RTI) and positive behavior support (PBS) logic models. BIP, behavior intervention plan; FBA, functional behavioral assessment.

students who are demonstrating externalizing problem behaviors and 10 students who are demonstrating internalizing behaviors. At the second gate, the teacher completes a behavior-rating scale on each of the three highest-ranked students in the externalizing and internalizing areas. At the third gate, school professionals directly observe the students to assess their level of adjustment at school. The multiple-gating procedure ensures that teachers do not spend unnecessary time screening children who are not truly at risk. Although the second and third gates are more time consuming, they serve as a means of cross-validation. The third gate involves a trained school professional, such as a school psychologist, in direct observation of the designated students in the classroom and interacting with peers outside the classroom. Ultimately, the involvement of a school psychologist may help to decrease subjectivity that may be the result of a single teacher's assessment.

Whatever measurement tool is chosen for universal screening, it must be short and effective whether it is used for behavior or academic content areas. DIBELS, for example, is one example of a universal screening tool for reading (University of Oregon Center on Teaching and Learning, 2007; Good & Kaminski, 2002). DIBELS is a valid and reliable set of 10 brief measures (approximately 2-min assessments) designed to monitor progress and identify children in the early stages of reading problems. DIBELS evaluates a set of early literacy skills directly related to and facilitative of later reading competence. These indicators have revolutionized early and universal screening for risk of reading problems because they have allowed teachers to briefly and effectively assess students for reading progress (Elliott, Lee, & Tollefson, 2001). The brevity and effectiveness of DIBELS still needs to be mirrored by behavior-screening and progress-monitoring tools.

The PBS model can use screening and progress-monitoring assessment results to help provide a continuum of supports—from the schoolwide universal supports in Tier 1, to the secondary level of supports in Tier 2, such as the Check-In Check-Out program, and then finally to Tier 3 supports at the tertiary level of intervention, which are individualized to the student's needs. An integrated RTI/PBS model follows IDEIA's guidance by providing PBS for individual students who have serious behavioral needs that are impeding their learning or the learning of those around them and emphasizing the use of the FBA to create secondary- and tertiary-level interventions.

To ensure that preventive interventions are available to all students when those interventions will be most successful, elementary schools work with local preschool programs to encourage the use of universal screening of students before they enter kindergarten, knowing that early identification is the best hope for successfully treating students at risk for behavior problems. In addition, students at the elementary school are assessed during the second month of every year. In the case of a student who transfers into the school, has not previously been screened, and for whom the teacher has a reason to believe that this student may have or be at risk of having a behavior disorder, the student may be referred to the school study team or the teacher may screen the student singly.

As stated, the SSBD is an appropriate assessment tool for universal screening beginning in the first grade, while the Early Screening Project (ESP) (the early childhood version of the SSBD) may be used for students in preschool and kindergarten. In keeping with best practice and IDEIA regulations, multiple assessments, such as direct observation, records reviews, interviews, and standardized behavior rating scales, should be used to validate screening results.

Teachers, school psychologists, and principals all need to receive the necessary training to conduct the screening assessment. An initial training is necessary for each educator using the assessment; in deciding on the level of behavioral supports, a student who does not pass through the first two gates of the SSBD, thereby not meeting the criteria for needing behavioral support, remains in the primary level of schoolwide PBS (SW-PBS), Tier 1 universal support. The student who does meet the criteria for needing behavioral support will be evaluated for the secondary level of SW-PBS, Tier 2 group intervention. If at the time of screening the student's behavior is dangerous to himself or others, the student will automatically receive intensive, individualized services at the tertiary, or Tier 3, level of intervention, in essence "skipping" the secondary level because severe need has been demonstrated. Further, if the student is receiving Tier 2 interventions and is not experiencing success at this level of intervention, the student will be moved to the tertiary level of intervention.

### *Criteria for Movement Between Tiers*

In the multitier PBS model just described, decisions made regarding student movement from one level of prevention to another are based on defined criteria for each mode of assessment. For example, in one version of the Check-In Check-Out group intervention (cf., Fairbanks, Sugai, Guardino, & Lathrop, in press), the student brings a report card to each teacher, to a supervising educator, and to his parent. An appropriate criterion to determine that a student in the Check-In Check-Out program is receiving the right level of services might be a certain percentage of positive reports. Criteria at the secondary level could work in three different ways: First, a student who demonstrates success for a specified amount of time may be returned to the less-intensive level of support, Tier 1; second, a student who demonstrates some success but not to the previously described criterion may remain in the Tier 2 intervention; third, a student who is not demonstrating the expected level of success for an intervention period may be moved to the tertiary level of supports. Tier 2 supports are based on an FBA and a BIP. A critical point is that movement from one level of intervention to the next is fluid, meaning that a student may move from one tier to another based on prespecified, established, criteria of demonstrated progress and maintenance.

### *Interventions Matched to Students Needs*

A critical component of RTI for behavior or academics is that assessment be linked to intervention. In an RTI model, assessment is continuous across the multiple levels of prevention. The assessment of the student's RTI provides valuable information to the practitioner about what is working about needed modifications to the intervention and may demonstrate a need for new interventions. Prior to assessment of the intervention, the screening will inform educators of a student's possible educational needs in the area of behavior. In addition, direct observation of the student both inside and outside the classroom is important so that academic engaged time and peer social behavior can be observed. Directly observing a student during academic periods and when interacting with other students will lead to hypotheses about the student's needs and should also evoke intervention options.

At the secondary level of prevention, an accurate FBA will ensure that a student is receiving an intervention that is appropriate for the function that maintains the student's behavior—in other words, the purpose of the behavior (Crone, Horner, & Hawken, 2004). More specifically, if the purpose of a student's behavior is to help the student escape from something unwanted in the environment, applying a group intervention that relies heavily on attention may be ineffective and could actually be harmful to the student's progress (Crone & Horner, 2003). The tertiary level of support is, by definition, individualized; therefore, an FBA will assist educators in determining the type of intervention that would best meet the student's needs. Further, IDEIA (2004) strongly recommends that schools use FBA procedures to develop support strategies for students with disabilities whose behavior interferes with their learning or the learning of others. Even though the law only requires an FBA for any student who is at risk for expulsion, alternate school placement, or more than 10 days of suspension (615[k][1][B]), a behavior support plan based on an FBA is more likely to be effective than a behavior plan that is not based on an FBA. The results of the FBA will assist the behavior support team to create appropriate goals and objectives for the student, leading to more efficient resolution of reduction of problem behaviors.

### *Continuous Monitoring of Interventions*

Progress monitoring ensures that either the student is progressing in the curriculum or the curriculum is modified in intensity to fit the student's needs. DIBELS, for example, takes a benchmark approach toward assessing students' skills. The Test of Oral Reading Fluency (TORF) is another example of a brief but informative benchmark assessment in reading. This measure is very brief but provides the teacher with important information that will inform academic instruction. Just as brief benchmark assessments inform reading instruction, they could inform behavioral instruction. Educators need a very brief instrument that they can use at set times throughout the year to take a measure of students' social-behavioral fluency. Assessments of social-behavioral skills that are used multiple times during the year and help behavior support teams to plan their instruction would be optimal. Assessments that meet these criteria include direct observation of pertinent behaviors; alternatively, standardized behavior rating scales provided at regular intervals could be used.

Just as a strong curriculum is the foundation for RTI in academics, social-behavioral instruction must be occurring in the school for a benchmark measure, such as those described, to be useful because students should have adequate opportunity to learn the skills they are expected to demonstrate (National Center for Culturally Responsive Education Systems [NCCRESt], 2005). Instruction should be provided that has proven to be effective for students who have similar behavioral needs. If effective instruction is not in place, educators will not have the capacity to determine the deficits in need of remediation because they may be the result of poor or absent interventions. A critical feature of the SW-PBS program is instruction of behavioral expectations. Students in schools implementing a schoolwide model of PBS and RTI have opportunities to become fluent with their new behavioral skills and to generalize the use of these skills. In these schools, instruction of behavioral expectations is provided by all staff across all settings in the school.

Many of the students served by the secondary and tertiary tiers of SW-PBS have difficulty acquiring social skills that lead to social competence, thus creating serious barriers to success both inside and outside the school (Smith & Gilles, 2003). Social skills instruction can be effective, but programming social skills instruction so that generalization and maintenance occur is very difficult and has not been broadly perfected (Gresham, Sugai, & Horner, 2001). The behavioral concepts that are used in PBS to increase generalization, such as using strategies to provide students with multiple opportunities to practice skills in novel environments, may be applied to social skills instruction.

Evidence supports the claim that early identification and academic intervention for learning problems together can reduce disruptive classroom behavior (Osher, Dwyer, & Jackson, 2003). If students know the behavioral expectations and are reinforced for meeting the expectations, they will be better prepared for academic instruction. Nelson, Martella, and March-and-Martella (2002) found that students attending schools with schoolwide behavior support not only had significant decreases in ODRs, but also demonstrated significant gains in most academic areas. Kellam, Rebok, Ialongo, and Mayer (1994) found that in a sample of schools those implementing a schoolwide behavioral component along with the reading curriculum demonstrated more academic gains along with behavior gains than did schools that were only implementing the reading curriculum. Other studies have made similar findings: Effective behavioral systems integrated with effective instruction are associated with improved academic achievement (Horner et al., 2004). If the true goal is to improve students' academic skills, we will also need to give students a solid education in social-behavioral skills, therefore for as effective behavioral *and* academic instruction is necessary to support students (Wehby, Lane, & Falk, 2003).

### *Active and Continuous Roles for Parents and Caregivers and the Community*

Successful programs involve parents from the very beginning of implementation and rely on parent involvement for success. Schools that implement SW-PBS often involve parents and the rest of the community in teaching students the behavioral expectations. In certain communities, the three behavioral expectations that are found on signs all over the school campus can also be found on the walls of local fast food restaurants. SW-PBS indirectly benefits families by supporting students so that they may be more successfully included in schools, but a call for more research is needed regarding how families may be more successfully included in the PBS system has been made (B. J. Vaughn, White, Johnston, & Dunlap, 2005).

## RESPONSE TO INTERVENTION AND PUBLIC POLICY

As Brown-Chidsey and Steege (2005) pointed out, RTI as public policy has its origins in community public health and population-based decision making (cf., Sandomierski, Kincaid, & Algozzine, 2007). When entire school districts screen all young children for academic or behavioral risk factors with an eye to prevention, then population-based educational policy is in full swing (Brown-Chidsey & Steege, 2005; Coyne, Kame'enui, Simmons, & Harn, 2004).

While No Child Left Behind (NCLB) 2001 does not contain statutory language directed specifically to RTI, it can be argued that the impetus for the emergence of an RTI logic is reflected in the emphasis on "evidence-based" practices. This emphasis is particularly strong in the sections on Early Reading First and Reading First (www.ed.gov/nclb/methods/reading/readingfirst.HTML).

NCLB is arguably the most significant piece of education policy affecting students today; however, NCLB's emphasis on academic achievement virtually ignores the importance of social behavior and the link between behavior and achievement in improving outcomes (Children's Behavioral Alliance, 2003; Sailor, Stowe, Turnbull, & Kleinhammer-Tramill, 2007).

The real shift to RTI in policy originated with this statement in the Individuals With Disabilities Education Improvement Act (IDEIA, 2004):

> Notwithstanding section 607(b), when determining whether a child has a specific learning disability as defined in section 602, a local educational agency shall not be required to take into consideration whether a child has a severe discrepancy between achievement and intellectual ability. ... In determining whether a child has a specific learning disability, a local educational agency may use a process that determines if the child responds to a scientific, research-based intervention as part of the evaluation procedures. [H.R. 1350, 2004, Section 614(b)(6)(A & B)]

This section of IDEIA does not mandate the use of RTI, but it does provide an opening for the use of RTI when previously a significant discrepancy between intelligence and achievement was thought to be the only allowable means for determining eligibility for SLD. IDEIA also does not abolish use of the significant discrepancy formula. Local educational agencies are given more control in determining the methods they will use (McCook, 2006).

> OSEP's Project Forum held a multistakeholder forum to determine the current needs in the field to support scale-up and sustainability of RTI. Project Forum published a specific set of policy recommendations. The first set of recommendations was published in 2004 and focused on early intervention services. These included (a) embed RTI language into NCLB reauthorization; (b) provide comprehensive training; (c) focus on implementation of high-quality instruction at the classroom level; (d) encourage research, synthesis, and the development of implementation tools; (e) develop a national coordinating body to support implementation of RTI; (f) develop a common understanding to encourage interdisciplinary collaboration; (g) develop state and local implementation infrastructures; (h) develop and implement a marketing strategy; (i) develop guidelines to help local education agencies (LEAs) capitalize on EIS provisions; and (j) align RTI implementation with state plans under both NCLB and IDEIA (pp. 6–7).

EIS in the quote above refers to Early intervention services. NASDSE provided further RTI policy recommendations in 2006. They stated that state education agencies (SEAs) should support a system within the context of NCLB in which a multitier model of differentiated intervention is implemented for organizing and implementing educational support within *general, remedial,* and special education on a *school and schoolwide* basis (italics ours). They also put forward the recommendation that SEAs should provide leadership that supports the use of RTI for eligibility determinations for students with learning disabilities and possibly for *students with other disabilities* (italics ours), especially high-incidence disabilities. Finally, NASDSE recommended that SEAs support RTI data-based decision making within special education.

These policy recommendations seem to reflect the beginning of a sea change in the way schools and their districts make decisions about allocating resources to students who require extra support to successfully engage in the general curriculum. First, reading researchers began to question the eligibility determination process involved in SLDs (Bradley, Danielson, & Hallahan, 2002; Lyon et al., 2001). Then, NCLB includes strong statutory and regulatory language on accountability in educational interventions. The field of special education responded with RTI recommendations that culminated in NASDSE suggesting new RTI language to be included in further versions of NCLB.

As mentioned, what is missing in the present thrust to advance new policy language in federal and state statutes are specific recommendations that focus RTI on both academics and behavior (Fig. 29.1). Since SW-PBS is a form of RTI and has a solid base of scientific evidence for its fidelity and efficacy, it calls for a broader RTI logic approach that fully integrates academic and behavioral functions and interventions. Sailor et al. (2007) sought to advance this agenda by presenting the case for adding one or more new standards related to behavior to standards-based education with resultant, measurable indicators. These new behavior standards would further operationalize SW-PBS as a three-tier prevention model for the nation's schools and position the effort to fully align with school-based RTI.

We conclude this section on RTI and public policy with a cautionary note from the Commission for Special Education Research of the Institute for Education Sciences (IES) (Kame'enui, 2007).

> Because RTI is ripe in the current discourse and practice of the profession, the implementation of RTI at the child, classroom, school, and district levels will be decidedly varied in form, process, and technical substance. Additionally and not surprisingly, although RTI holds significant promise for the practice of special education, it is seriously underdetermined empirically, particularly the use of interventions that are yoked to the use of "technically sound instruments" as required by the federal law. Although it would be easy to view RTI as singular in its focus on interventions and a child's responses to those interventions, what the law makes transparent is that RTI is essentially and instrumentally an assessment and instructional process that is dynamic, recursive, and based on rigorous scientific research. (p. 7)

In this discourse, Kame'enui describes RTI as a framework and process that will allow educators to make evidence-based decisions that may greatly benefit all students. In the next section, we describe cultural considerations that must be taken into account so that all students will truly benefit from instruction.

## PERSONNEL PREPARATION AND CULTURAL CONSIDERATIONS IN RESPONSE TO INTERVENTION

Because RTI involves repeated assessments of child responsiveness to instruction, and particularly because it includes screening for risk assessment at early ages, practitioners must pay particular attention to cultural considerations in application. By *cultural*, we mean all special considerations applying to one's national identity, language groups, ethnicity, religion, and even regional norms of educational practices within the United States. Language makes a difference in how culture and diversity are seen. Cultural expectations of Latino families around school practices differ from those of African Americans and whites. A Latino child whose language spoken in the home is exclusively Spanish cannot be expected to respond to instruction in English, for example, in the same way that characterizes a Latino child whose family uses English in the home.

Brown-Chidsey and Steege (2005) pointed out, "Knowledge about racial inequality in U.S. schools is important for those who implement RtI policies, because many of the students most in need of effective teaching and tier 2 interventions are students from racial minorities" (p. 103). Helms (1992) raised the important issue of why we as a nation avoid the issue of cultural equivalence in moving to accountability systems through standardized testing, often with high-stakes outcomes. Helms cited evidence that students of all racial backgrounds have the potential for school success but respond differently to test protocols. Studies cited by Brown-Chidsey and Steege (2005) have contributed evidence for the need to build cultural considerations into assessments of academic achievement so that students' achievement can be measured in an equitable way (Carter, Helms, & Juby, 2004; Chall, 2000; Tatum, 1997).

Even the cultures of professional practice within schools can become an important consideration within RTI applications. Educators will need to see all students as "their students" if an RTI process is to be successful. As Hardcastle and Justice (2006) described:

> Over the years, education has become divided. General education and special education typically operate within two separate worlds. A unique aspect of RTI is its focus on bringing these two systems together. According to Bill Tollestrup, director of special education at Elk Grove (Calif.) Unified School District, RTI is a general education process that can be supported by special education and facilitated by administrative leadership. RTI reminds us that special education was not designed to be a "place," but instead was intended as a support to general education to help address the needs of students experiencing difficulties. (p. 8)

We use the term *personnel preparation* here to refer to preservice training for teachers. *Staff development* refers to in-service training for non-professionally certified personnel such as paraprofessionals and security personnel; *professional development* to in-service training with professionally certified personnel such as teachers, speech therapists, and psychologists; and *parent training* to efforts to extend specialized knowledge on RTI practices and procedures to family members.

Hardcastle and Justice (2006) listed eight key areas that will need to be addressed in creating a culture of RTI practice in a school: (a) RTI and student achievement; (b) research-based instruction and interventions; (c) the problem-solving method; (d) guided intervention practice; (e) progress monitoring and computer-based intervention elements of technology; (f) data-based decision making; (g) RTI versus discrepancy model; (h) RTI and assessments. Families cannot be forgotten when determining how best to implement RTI. In fact, the NRCLD (2007) lists parent involvement as one of the key components of RTI. The National Joint Committee on Learning Disabilities (NJCLD, 2005) reminded the field that parent involvement must be a well-thought-out aspect of the RTI process. The NJCLD has asked the following questions that have implications for parent training: How will families be included in state and local planning and in all phases of an RTI process? How will parents be informed of their referral rights? The NJCLD concluded that a true partnership will depend on the commitment of families and education professionals.

In introducing this chapter, we described differences between a medical model of disability and an RTI model. RTI for academics and PBS both emphasize instruction and other environmental inputs that make it more likely that a behavior will or will not occur, whereas the medical model of disability views the student as being the origin of difficulties in his or her academic or social behaviors. In the PBS/RTI model, adult behavior is changed to change student behavior, while in the medical model the student's behavior is the main focus. Both parents and classroom teachers can be expected to react initially to the strong environmental influence embedded in RTI logic, particularly as these apply to the identification of function-based antecedent conditions to development and maintenance of behaviors that impede learning. A parent who has come to view his or her child's behavioral manifestations as due to the child's disability, and therefore not something that can be remediated pedagogically, may require time and repeated exposure to RTI and PBS strategies to address behavior problems and, perhaps, particularly to come to recognize and address his or her own contributions to reinforcement of the child's problem behavior. The same can be said of teachers, particularly general education teachers who have received no personnel preparation in PBS or RTI.

Brown-Chidsey and Steege (2005) outlined an RTI training plan that includes a number of key features in professional training, including scheduling of RTI trainings; teacher learning outcomes from RTI professional development efforts; and specific indicators of teachers' mastering of RTI methods (see chapter 11, pp. 139–162). The training protocol outlined by Brown-Chidsey and Steege for general educators who are learning about RTI is also reflected in the NASDSE (2006) introduction to RTI for special education administrators (chapter 8, pp. 39–42). Taken together, these two resources, one for general educators and one for special education administrators, provide a strong initial framework for identifying training considerations for each of the identified personnel categories for whom training issues are rapidly becoming paramount.

In our view, the next generation of RTI personnel preparation and development frameworks will need to focus on the fully integrated RTI/PBS reflected at the outset of this chapter in Fig. 29.1. As Sailor et al. (2007) pointed out, the possibility of bifurcation of practice looms large in applications of SW-PBS, with general education assuming responsibility for Tier 1 applications and special educators for Tier 3 applications, with little attention directed to Tier 2. The promise of an RTI/PBS system lies in its application as a fully integrated logic model focusing all school resources on the academic and social-behavioral requirements of all students and using evidence-based interventions and scientifically validated assessments at each step of the way.

## THE FUTURE OF RESPONSE TO INTERVENTION

With this chapter, we have attempted to describe RTI in terms of its history and origins in public health prevention, and its emergence in special education research, policy, and practice, as an alternative to IQ discrepancy evaluation for the purpose of determining if an LD exists. We considered current applications of RTI, particularly in scientifically guided special education practices, and we examined current policy consideration in educationally related statutes and regulations that pertain to RTI. Finally, we examined some of the cultural issues that need to be considered in applying RTI, and we focused on some of the emerging personnel training frameworks that will move the field ahead on these practices.

RTI, at present, certainly looks like "the next big thing." It can be viewed as having the potential to bring about a sea change in the way the children of the United States are educated. Or, it can be viewed as a potential "runaway train" (Sandomierski et al., 2007). Kame'enui (2007) raised the concern that RTI as praxis is only as good as its grounding in careful science, in assessing students (i.e., screening for prevention and progress monitoring), and in intervening at each of the three tiers for both. There is an obvious danger that widespread rush to full implementation and incorporation into state policy frameworks will move RTI away from its careful grounding in scientific research. Personnel preparation and professional development, in addition to supportive policy, hold the best promise for keeping RTI/PBS successfully operational as a major innovation in pedagogy.

## REFERENCES


Adelman, H. S., & Taylor, L. (1996). *Policies and practices for addressing barriers to student learning and current status and new directions* (SMHS Policy Report). Los Angeles: UCLA Center for Mental Health in Schools, Department of Psychology.

Adelman, H. S., & Taylor, L. (2006). *The school leader's guide to student learning supports: New directions for addressing barriers to learning.* Thousands Oaks, CA: Corwin Press.

Bergan, J. R., & Kratochwill, T. R. (1990). *Behavioral consultation and therapy.* New York: Plenum.

Blackorby, J., Wagner, M., Cameto, R., Davies, E., Levine, P., Newman, L., et al. (with Chorost, M., Garza, N., & Guzman, A.). (2003). *Engagement, academics, social development, and independence: The achievements of elementary and middle school students with disabilities.* Review draft. Menlo Park, CA: SRI International.

Bradley, R., & Danielson, L. (2004). The Office of Special Education Program's LD Initiative: A context for inquiry and consensus. *Learning Disability Quarterly, 27*, 186–188.

Bradley, R., Danielson, L., & Doolittle, J. (2007). Responsiveness to intervention: 1997 to 2007. *Teaching Exceptional Children, 39*(5), 8–12.

Bradley, R., Danielson, L., & Hallahan, D. P. (Eds.). (2002). *Identification of learning disabilities: Research to practice.* Mahwah, NJ: Erlbaum.

Brown-Chidsey, R., & Steege, M. W. (2005). *Response to intervention principles and strategies for effective practice.* New York: Guilford Press.

Caffrey, E., & Fuchs, D. (2007). Differences in performance between students with learning disabilities and mild mental retardation: Implications for categorical instruction. *Learning Disabilities Research and Practice, 22*, 119–128.

Campbell, S. H. (1995). Behavior problems in preschool children: A review of recent research. *Journal of Child Psychology and Psychiatry and Allied Disciplines, 36*, 113–149.

Caplan, G., & Grunebaum, H. (1967). Perspectives on primary prevention. *Archives of General Psychiatry, 17*, 331–346.

Carter, R. T., Helms, J. E., & Juby, H. L. (2004). The relationship between racism and racial identity for white Americans: A profile analysis. *Journal of Multicultural Counseling and Development, 32*, 2–18.

Chall, J. S. (2000). *The academic achievement challenge: What really works in the classroom?* New York: Guilford Press.

Chandler, L. K., & Dahlquist, C. M. (2002). *Functional assessment: Strategies to prevent and remediate challenging behavior in school settings.* Upper Saddle River, NJ: Merrill Prentice Hall.

Children's Behavioral Alliance. (2003). *In the best interests of all: A position paper of the Children's Behavioral Alliance.* Retrieved December 11, 2004, from http://www.chadd.org/pdfs/inthebestinterestsofall.pdf

Conroy, M. A., & Brown, W. H. (2004). Early identification, prevention, and early intervention with young children at risk for emotional or behavioral disorders: Issues, trends, and a call for action. *Behavioral Disorders, 29*, 224–236.

Cortiella, C. (2006). A parent's guide to response-to-intervention [Web site]. Retrieved January 12, 2007, from http://www/ncld.org/images/stories/downloads/parent_center/rti_final.pdf

Coyne, M. D., Kame'enui, E. J., Simmons, D. C., & Harn, B. A. (2004). Beginning reading intervention as inoculation or insulin: First-grade reading performance of strong responders to kindergarten intervention. *Journal of Learning Disabilities, 37*, 9–105.

Crone, D. A., & Horner, R.H. (2003). *Building positive behavior support systems in schools*. New York: Guilford Press.

Crone, D. A., Horner, R. H., & Hawken, L. S. (2004). *Responding to problem behavior in schools: The behavior education program*. New York: Guilford Press.

Davis, G. N., Lindo, E. J., & Compton, D. L. (2007). Children at risk for reading failure. Constructing an early screening measure. *Teaching Exceptional Children, 39*(5), 32–37.

Deno, S. L. (1985). Curriculum-based measurement: The emerging alternative. *Exceptional Children, 52*, 219–232.

Deno, S. L., & Mirkin, P. K. (1977). *Data-based program modification: A manual*. Minneapolis, MN: Leadership Training Institute for Special Education.

Elliott, J., Lee, S. W., & Tollefson, N. (2001). A reliability and validity study of the Dynamic Indicators of Basic Early Literacy Skills—modified. *School Psychology Review, 30*, 33–49.

Fairbanks, S., Sugai, G., Guardino, D., & Lathrop, M. (2007). Response to intervention: Examining Classroom behaviour support in second grade. *Exceptional Children, 73*, 288–310.

Feil, E. G., Severson, H. H., & Walker, H. M. (1998). Screening for emotional and behavioral delays: The Early Screening Project. *Journal of Early Interventions, 21*, 252–266.

Forness, S. R., & Kavale, K. A. (2000). Emotional or behavioral disorders: Background and current status of the E/BD terminology and definition. *Behavioral Disorders, 25*, 264–270.

Fuchs, L. S., Compton, D. L., Fuchs, D., Paulsen, K., Bryant, J., & Hamlett, C. L. (2005). Responsiveness to Intervention: Preventing and identifying mathematics disability. *Teaching Exceptional Children, 37*(4), 60–63.

Fuchs, L. S., Deno, S. L., & Mirkin, P. K. (1984). The effects of frequent curriculum-based measurement and evaluation on pedagogy, student achievement, and student awareness of learning. *American Educational Research Journal, 21*, 449–460.

Fuchs, L. S., Fuchs, D., & Compton, D. L. (2004). Monitoring early reading development in first grade: Word identification fluency versus nonsense word fluency. *Exceptional Children, 71*, 7–21.

Fuchs, D., Fuchs, L. S., Compton, D. L., Bouton, B., Caffrey, E., & Hill, L. (2007). Dynamic assessment as responsiveness to intervention. A scripted protocol to identify young at-risk readers. *Teaching Exceptional Children, 39*(5), 58–63.

Good, R. H., & Kaminski, R. A. (Eds.). (2002). *Dynamic indicators of basic early literacy skills* (6th ed.). Eugene, OR: Institute of the Development of Education Achievement. Available at http://dibel.uoregon.edu

Gresham, F., & Elliott, S. (1990). *The social skills rating system*. Circle Pines, MN: American Guidance Service.

Gresham, F. M., Sugai, G., & Horner, R. H. (2001). Social competence of students with high-incidence disabilities: Conceptual and methodological issues in interpreting outcomes of social skills training. *Exceptional Children, 67*, 311–344.

Hardcastle, B., & Justice, K. (2006). *RTI and the classroom teacher. A guide for fostering teacher buy-in and supporting the intervention process*. Horsham, PA: LRM.

Heller, K. A., Holtzman, W. H., & Messick, S. (Eds.). (1982). *Placing children in special education: Equity through valid educational practices. Final report*. Washington, DC: National Academy Press.

Helms, J. E. (1992). Why is there no study of cultural equivalence in standardized cognitive ability testing? *American Psychologist, 47*, 1083–1102.

Horner, R. H., Todd, A. W., Lewis-Palmer, T., Irvin, L. K., Sugai, G., & Boland, J. B. (2004). The School-wide Evaluation Tool (SET): A research instrument for assessing school-wide positive behavior support. *Journal of Positive Behavior Interventions, 6*, 3–12.

Individuals With Disabilities Education Improvement Act (IDEIA) of 1998, P.L. 105-17, 20 U.S.C. § 1400 et seq.

Individuals With Disabilities Education Improvement Act (IDEIA) of 2004, P.L. 108-446, 20 U.S.C. §§ 1400 et seq.

Kame'enui, E. J. (2007). Responsiveness to intervention. *Teaching Exceptional Children, 39*(5), 6–7.

Lenz, B. K., & Deshler, D. D. (2004). *Teaching content to all. Evidence-based inclusive practices in middle and secondary schools.* Boston: Pearson.

Lyon, G. R., Fletcher, J. M., Shaywitz, S. E., Shaywitz, B. A., Torgesen, J. K., Wood, F., et al. (2001). Rethinking learning disabilities. In C. E. Finn Jr., A. J. Rotherham, & C. R. Hokanson Jr. (Eds.), *Rethinking special education for a new century* (pp. 259–287). Washington, DC: Fordham Foundation.

McCook, J. E. (2006). *The RTI guide: Developing and implementing a model in your schools.* Horsham, PA: LRP.

McDermott, P. A., Goldberg, M. M., Watkins, M. W., Stanley, J. L., & Glutting, J. J. (2006). A nationwide epidemiologic modeling study of LD: Risk, protection, and unintended impact. *Journal of Learning Disabilities, 39*, 230–251.

McMasters, K. L., Fuchs, D., Fuchs, L. S., & Compton, D. L. (2005). Responding to non-responders: An experimental field trial of identification and intervention methods. *Exceptional Children, 71*, 445–463.

Merrell, K. W. (1993). *School social behavior scales.* Brandon, VT: Clinical Psychology.

Merrell, K. W. (2001). Assessment of children's social skills: Recent developments, best practices, and new directions. *Exceptionality, 9*(1/2), 3–18,

National Association of State Directors of Special Education (NASDSE). (2006). *Response to intervention policy consideration and implementation.* Alexandria, VA: Author.

National Center for Culturally Responsive Education Systems. (2005). *Cultural considerations and challenges in response-to-intervention models* (NCCRESt position statement). Retrived June 23, 2007, from http://www.ncrest.org/publications/position_statements.html

National Joint Committee on Learning Disabilities. (2005). *Responsiveness to intervention and learning disabilities.* Retrieved June 23, 2007, from www.ldonline.org/njcld

National Research Center on Learning Disabilities. (2007). Responsiveness to intervention school-based practices. Retrieved June 15, 2007, from www.nrcld.org/rti_practices/indelc.html

Nelson, J. R., Martella, R., & Marchand-Martella, N. (2002). Maximizing student learning: The effects of a comprehensive school-based program for preventing problem behaviors. *Journal of Emotional and Behavioral Disorders, 10*, 136–148.

Office of the Surgeon General. (2001). *Youth violence: A report of the surgeon general.* Washington, DC: Department of Health and Human Services.

Ortiz, A., & Yates, J. (2002). Considerations in the assessment of English language learners referred to special education. In A. Artiles & A. Ortiz (Eds.), *English language learners with special education needs: Identification, assessment and instruction* (pp. 65–86). McHenry, IL: Center for Applied Linguistics and Delta Systems.

Osher, D., Dwyer, K., & Jackson, S. (2003). *Safe, supportive, and successful schools: Step by step.* Longmont, CO: Sopris West.

President's Commission on Excellence in Special Education. (2002). *A new era: Revitalizing special education for children and their families.* Washington, DC: Author.

Quay, H. C., & Peterson, D. R. (1987). *Manual for the revised behavior problem checklist.* Coral Gables, FL: Author.

Reschly, D. (2005). Learning disabilities: Primary intervention, secondary intervention, and then what? *Journal of Learning Disabilities, 28*, 510–515.

Reschly, D. J., Tilly, W. D., III, Grimes, J. P. (1998). *Functional and noncategorical identification and intervention in special education.* Des Moines: Iowa Department of Education.

Sailor, W., & Guess, D. (1980). *Severly Handicapped Students. An Instructional Design.* Boston: Houghton Mifflin Co.

Sailor, W., Stowe, M. J., Turnbull, R., III, & Kleinhammer-Tramill, P. J. (2007). A case for adding a social-behavioral standard to standards-based education with schoolwide positive behavior support as its basis. *Remedial and Special Education, 28*, 366–376.

Sandomierski, T., Kincaid, D., & Algozzine, B. (2007). Response to intervention and positive behavior support: Brothers from different mothers or sisters with different misters? *PBIS Newsletter* 4(2). Retrieved October 5, 2007, from www.pbis.org/new/New/Newsletters/Newsletter4-2.aspx

Sanetti, L. H., & Kratochwill, T. R. (2005). Treatment integrity assessment within a problem-solving model. In R. Brown-Chidsey (Ed.), *Assessment for intervention: A problem-solving approach* (pp. 304–325). New York: Guilford Press.

Sideridis, G., Morgan, P. L., Botsas, G., Padeliadu, S., & Fuchs, D. (2006). Predicting LD on the basis of motivation, metacognition, and psychopathology: An ROC analysis. *Journal of Learning Disabilities, 39*(3), 215–229.

Simeonsson, R. J. (1994). *Risk, resilience, and prevention: Promoting the well-being of all children.* Baltimore: Brookes.

Smith, S. W., & Gilles, D. L. (2003). Using key instructional elements to systematically promote social skills generalization for students with challenging behavior. *Intervention in School and Clinic, 39*, 30–38.

Speece, D. L., Case-Pericola, L., & Eddy-Molloy, D. (2003). Responsiveness to general education instruction as the first gate to learning disabilities identification. *Learning Disabilities Research and Practice, 18*, 147–156.

Stecker, P. M. (2007). Tertiary intervention. Using progress monitoring with intensive services. *Teaching Exceptional Children, 39*(5), 50–57.

Sugai, G., & Horner, R. H. (2002). Introduction to the special series on positive behavior support in schools. *Journal of Emotional and Behavioral Disorders, 10*(3), 130–136.

Sugai, G., Horner, R. H., & Gresham, F. M. (2002). Behaviorally effective school environments. In M. Shinn, H. Walker, & G. Stoner (Eds.), *Interventions for academic and behavior problems II* (pp. 315–350). Bethesda, MD: National Association of School Psychologists.

Tatum, B. D. (1997). *Why are all the black kids sitting together in the cafeteria? And other conversations about race: A psychologist explains the development of racial identity* (rev. ed). New York: Basic Books.

Torgesen, J. K., Alexander, A. W., Wagner, R. K., Rashotte, C. A., Voeller, K. S., & Conroy, T. (2001). Intensive remedial instruction for children with reading disabilities: Immediate and long-term outcomes from two instructional approaches. *Journal of Learning Disabilities, 34*, 33–58, 78.

Vaughn, B. J., White, R., Johnston, S., & Dunlap, G. (2005). Positive behavior support as a family-centered endeavor. *Journal of Positive Behavior Interventions, 7*, 55–58.

Vaughn, S. (2003). *How many tiers are needed for response to intervention to achieve acceptable prevention outcomes?* Paper presented at the National Research Center on Learning Disabilities Response to Intervention Symposium, Kansas City, MO. December 4, 2003

Vaughn, S., & Linan-Thompson, S. (2003). Group size and time allotted to intervention: Effects for students with reading difficulties. In B. Foorman (Ed.), *Preventing and remediating reading difficulties: Bringing science to scale* (pp. 275–298). Parkton, MD: York Press.

Vaughn, S., Linan-Thompson, S., & Hickman, P. (2003). Response to instruction as a means of identifying students with reading/learning disabilities. *Exceptional Children, 69*, 391–409.

Vaughn, S., & Roberts, G. (2007). Secondary interventions in reading. Providing additional instruction for students at risk. *Teaching Exceptional Children 39*(5), 40–46.

Vellutino, F. R., Scanlon, D. M., Sipay, E. R., Small, S. G., Pratt, A., Chen, R., et al. (1996). Cognitive profiles of difficult-to-remediate and readily remediated poor readers: Early intervention as a vehicle for distinguishing between cognitive and experiential deficits as basic causes of specific reading disability. *Journal of Educational Psychology, 88*, 601–638.

Walker, H. M., & Severson, H. H. (1992). *Systematic Screening for Behavior Disorders (SSBD)* (2nd ed.). Eugene, OR: Oregon Research Institute.

Walker, H. M., Severson, H. H., Todis, B. J., Black-Pedego, A. E., Williams, G. J., Haring, N. G., et al. (1990). Systematic Screening for Behavior Disorders (SSBD): Further validation, replication, and normative data. *Remedial and Special Education, 11*(2), 32–46.

Webster-Stratton, C. (1997). From parent training to community building. *Families in Society, 78*(2), 156–171.

Wehby, J. H., Lane, K. L., & Falk, K. B. (2003). Academic instruction for students with emotional and behavioral disorders. *Journal of Emotional and Behavioral Disorders, 11*, 194–197.

Ysseldyke, J. (2005). Assessment and decision making for students with learning disabilities: What if this is as good as it gets? *Learning Disability Quarterly 28*, 125–128.

Ysseldyke, J., Thurlow, M., Graden, J., Wesson, C., Algozzine, B., & Deno, S. (1983). Generalizations from five years of research on assessment and decision making: The University of Minnesota Institute. *Exceptional Education Quarterly, 4*, 75–93.

# Index

# Erratum

Handbook of Positive Behavior Support
Sailor, W.; Dunlap, G.; Sugai, G.; Horner, R. (Eds.)
ISBN 978-0-387-09631-5, DOI: 10.1007/978-0-387-09632-2
Springer Science + Business Media LLC 2009

---

The chapter entitled "Toward an Ecological Unit of Analysis in Behavioral Assessment and Intervention With Families of Children With Developmental Disabilities," pages 73–106, DOI: 10.1007/978-0-387-09632-2_4 was authored by: Joseph M. Lucyshyn, Lauren Binnendyk, Brenda Fossett, Christy Cheremshynski, Sharon Lohrmann, Lauren Elkinson and Lynn Miller.

The Publisher regrets that by mistake the name of Joseph M. Lucyshyn, Corresponding Author of the Chapter, appeared only in the Volume's Contributors section and is missing on the Chapter Opening Page.

---

The chapter entitled "Using a Problem-Solving Model to Enhance Data-Based Decision Making in Schools," pages 551–580, DOI: 10.1007/978-0-387-09632-2_23:

The Publisher regrets that by mistake on the Chapter Opening Page name of the author J. Stephen Newton incorrectly appears as Stephen J. Newton.